BATTLES AND LEADERS OF THE CIVIL WAR

VOLUME FOUR

ON THE CONFEDERATE LINE OF BATTLE "WITH FATE AGAINST THEM."

FROM THE PAINTING BY GILBERT GAUL.

BATTLES AND LEADERS OF THE CIVIL WAR

VOLUME IV

BEING FOR THE MOST PART CONTRIBUTIONS
BY UNION AND CONFEDERATE OFFICERS.
BASED UPON "THE CENTURY WAR SERIES."
EDITED BY ROBERT UNDERWOOD JOHNSON
AND CLARENCE CLOUGH BUEL, OF THE EDI-
TORIAL STAFF OF "THE CENTURY MAGAZINE."

CASTLE

Castle Books ®

A division of Book Sales, Inc.
276 Fifth Ave., Suite 206
New York, NY 10001

Manufactured in the United States
of America

ISBN 0-89009-572-8

ISBN 978-0-89009-572-0

The **CASTLE** trademark is registered in
the U.S. Patent and Trademark Office.

CONTENTS OF VOLUME FOUR.

CHARLESTON.

⨍ In order to save much repetition, particular credit is here given to the Massachusetts Commandery of the Loyal Legion, to Colonel Arnold A. Rand, General Albert Ordway, and Charles B. Hall for the use of photographs and drawings. War-time photographers, whose work is of the greatest historical value and has been freely drawn upon in the preparation of the illustrations, are M. B. Brady, Alexander Gardner, and Captain A. J. Russell in the North; and D. H. Anderson of Richmond, Va., and George S. Cook of Charleston, S. C.— the latter, since the war, having succeeded to the ownership of the Anderson negatives.

PAGE

ATLANTA.

UP AND DOWN THE SHENANDOAH.

PETERSBURG.

THE CONFEDERATE CRUISERS.

ARTISTS.

BACHER, OTTO H.	GOATER, WALTER H.	MEEKER, EDWIN J.	SMITH, XANTHUS
BURNS, M. J.	GRIBAYEDOFF, V.	OGDEN, HENRY A.	TABER, WALTON
CHAMPNEY, J. WELLS	HALM, GEORGE R.	PENNELL, JOSEPH	TAYLOR, JAMES E.
DAVIDSON, J. O.	HAWLEY, HUGHSON	REDWOOD, ALLEN C.	TREGO, W. T.
DAVIS, THEO. R.	HENRY, EDWARD L.	REED, C. W.	TURNER, A. M.
EATON, WYATT	HOGAN, THOMAS	RUNGE, J. F.	VANDERHOOF, C. A.
ELDER, J. A.	HOKE, M. H.	SCHELL, FRANK H.	WAUD, A. R.
FENN, HARRY	HOMER, WINSLOW	SHEPPARD, W. L.	WILL, AUGUST
FORBES, EDWIN	KEMBLE, E. W.	SITTS, FRED. E.	WOODWARD, J. D.
GAUL, GILBERT			

DRAUGHTSMEN.

COURT, E. E.	HOTCHKISS, JED.	NOETZEL, GREGOR	WELLS, JACOB

ENGRAVERS.

AITKEN, PETER	DAVIS, JOHN P.	KRUELL, G.	SYLVESTER, H. E.
ANDREWS, JOHN	ENGBERG, J.	MORSE, WILLIAM H.	TIETZE, R. G.
ATWOOD, K. C.	ERTZ, EDWARD	MULLER, R. A.	TYNAN, JAMES
BARTLE, GEORGE P.	EVANS, J. W.	NAYLOR, JESSIE A.	UNDERHILL, M. J.
BUTLER, T. A.	FAY, GASTON	NAYLOR, OLIVIA	VARLEY, ROBERT
CLEMENT, E.	HEINEMANN, E.	NICHOLS, DAVID	VELTEN, H.
CLOSSON, W. B.	HELD, E. C.	OWENS, MARY L.	WELLINGTON, F. H.
COLLINS, R. C.	IRWIN, ALLEN	POWELL, C. A.	WINHAM, E. A.
COUGHLAN, J. A.	JOHNSON, T.	REED, C. H.	WITTE, W. B.
CULLEN, CHARLES	JONES, M.	SCHUSSLER, T.	WOLF, HENRY
DANA, W. J.	JUNGLING, J. F.	SCHWARTZBURGER, C.	WRIGHT, CHAUNCEY
DAVIDSON, H.	KLASEN, W.	SPIEGLE, CHARLES	

EDITORS' NOTE.

In addition to the acknowledgments made in the preface to Volume I. (to which the reader is referred) the Editors are under obligations to Professor James Russell Soley, U. S. N., for expert aid of an editorial character relating to naval operations; to Colonel Richard B. Irwin, and George L. Kilmer, a veteran of the Army of the Potomac, for historical research and careful and unstinted work upon the proofs, and for other daily assistance since the second volume was begun; to Mr. Allen Thorndike Rice, Editor of the "North American Review," and to the Editors of the Philadelphia "Press" and "Times," for permission to use articles from those sources; and to Mr. W. M. Griswold for the preparation of the index. Credit should have been given to the Philadelphia "Press" for the letter from General Meade to Colonel Benedict, page 413 of Vol. III., and for the article by Captain William E. Miller, on page 397 of the same volume. The editing of the work in book form was begun in April, 1887. Volume I. was finished in November, 1887; Volume II. in April, 1888; Volume III. in August, 1888, and Volume IV. in January, 1889.

CORRECTIONS IN VOLUME IV.

Page 60, 5th line from the top. For "Colonel John S. Chatfield," read "Colonel John L. Chatfield."

Page 89, 7th line. For "A. H. Terry's division," read "H. D. Terry's division."

Page 91, 4th line from the last. For "conscription system," read "draft system."

Page 187, second column, 3d line from top. For "Brigadier-General James H. Martindale," read "Brigadier-General John H. Martindale."

Page 247, second note. That portion beginning with "A force of cavalry," to the end of the note, should read: "A mounted column, numbering about 7000 effectives, and commanded by General W. Sooy Smith, set out from Memphis on the 11th under instructions to drive the Confederate cavalry in northern Mississippi southward, and sweep down the Mobile and Ohio railroad from the north toward Meridian. This column failed to reach Meridian [see p. 416], and on the 20th Sherman abandoned the expedition, and put his troops in motion toward central Mississippi, whence they were transferred, later, to Vicksburg and Memphis."

Page 257, second column of note, 9th line. For "an army of 65,000," read "an army of 60,000."

Page 277, under title. For "By W. P. C. Breckinridge," read "By W. C. P. Breckinridge."

Page 335, first column, 39th line. For "seventy-five days," read "forty-five days."

Page 342, add as foot-note to third paragraph: "General Wheeler reported the breaking up of the raiding party under General McCook, and the capture of some 950 of his men, two pieces of artillery, and 1200 horses. General Iverson reported the surrender of Stoneman with 500 men, and the subsequent capture of some of his command who were flying toward Eatonton."

Page 401, first column, 9th line from the last. For "Mr. Henry Pearce," read "Mr. Joseph Pearce." Second column, 24th line. For "Naval Constructor, Thomas Porter," read "Sidney D. Porter, a naval architect."

Page 536, first column, 32d and 33d line. For "bring back his brigade," read "bring up the reserve infantry."

Page 579, second article, second column. For "small field redoubt mounting 6 guns," read "strong field redoubt mounting 4 rifled guns."

Page 659, first column, third line from the last. Captain James Parker writes: "I did not waive my rank. My language to Breese when he showed me Admiral Porter's letter was, 'I have nothing left to do, except to go into the fight at the head of my men, trusting that you will make the situation as little disagreeable as possible.'"

Page 747. The account of the preparation of the Farewell Address of General Lee to his army, is taken from a letter written by Lieutenant-Colonel Charles Marshall, of General Lee's staff, to General Bradley T. Johnson, dated September 27th, 1887.

ADDITIONAL CORRECTIONS IN VOLUME III.

Page 317, second column, 26th line from the last. For "Shaler's and Canda's," read "Shaler's and Candy's."

Page 327, 3d line. For "Generals J. B. Anderson and G. T. Robertson," read "Generals G. T. Anderson and J. B. Robertson."

Page 336, 13th line from bottom (also page 437, first column, 14th line from bottom). For "Colonel W. G. de Saussure," read "Colonel W. D. de Saussure."

Page 569, 4th line from the last. For "on the 9th," read "on the 8th."

Page 599, roster, second column. For "25th Conn., Lieut.-Col. Mason C. Wild," read "25th Conn., Lieut.-Col. Mason C. Weld."

Page 620, 9th line from last. For "Colonel Bradley of the 52d Illinois," read "Colonel Bradley of the 51st Illinois."

Page 635, third note. For "November 26th," read "November 27th."

Page 729, second column, 9th line. For "82d Indiana," read "83d Indiana."

Page 730, second column. For "Maj.-Gen. Ambrose P. Stewart," read "Maj.-Gen. Alexander P. Stewart."

ADDITIONAL CORRECTIONS IN VOLUME II.

Page 152, 6th line. For "(My command was the 2d, 10th, and 9th New York, and the 9th Massachusetts,)" read "(My command was the 2d, 7th, and 10th New York, and the 29th Massachusetts.)"

Page 270, 2d line from bottom. For "Captain John Wilkes," read "Captain Charles Wilkes."

Page 404, the last line of text. For "10,000," read "6000."

Page 459, first column, 5th line from the bottom. For "J. L. Archer and E. C. Thomas," read "J. J. Archer and E. L. Thomas."

ADDITIONAL CORRECTIONS IN VOLUME I.

Page 317, 8th line from the bottom. For "Major Mezaros," read "Major Meszaros."

Page 393, 6th line from bottom. For "Colonel John H. Trigg," read "Colonel Robert C. Trigg."

Page 420, 2d line from bottom. For "Colonel John A. Thayer," read "Colonel John M. Thayer."

Page 637, 7th line from the bottom. For "the 8th Georgia," read "the 3d Georgia."

Page 677, 19th line. For "C. A. Boutelle," read "C. O. Boutelle."

ON THE UNION PICKET LINE—RELIEVING PICKETS.

THE DEFENSE OF CHARLESTON.|

BY G. T. BEAUREGARD, GENERAL, C. S. A.

A TELEGRAM from General Cooper, dated Richmond, September 10th, 1862, reached me on that day in Mobile, ⚓ and contained the information that, by special orders issued August 29th, I had been assigned to the command of the Department of South Carolina and Georgia, with headquarters at Charleston. The next day I left for my new scene of action, where I arrived on the 15th of September, relieving General J. C. Pemberton.

The work before me was serious; all the more so that it had to be executed without loss of time. Rumors and threats were afloat, filling the columns of the Northern journals, to the effect that preparations were being made for such a land and naval attack upon the city of Charleston as would prove irresistible. This, at the North, was deemed all the more easy of accomplishment because the harbor and inner defenses were believed to be insufficient to withstand a well-directed and prolonged assault; and for the further reason that there existed several avenues of approach, by any of which, it was thought, the ulterior object aimed at could be attained.

That there was ample cause for apprehension on our part became apparent to me upon my first conference with General Pemberton, in which I learned that by his orders a complete abandonment had been made, not only of the

| Condensed from the "North American Review" for May, 1886. See also articles in Vol. I., pp. 40–83, on the operations in Charleston harbor in 1861.— EDITORS.

⚓ It was to Bladon Springs, 75 miles north of Mobile, that, on the 17th of June, 1862, General Beauregard had gone from Tupelo for his health, on a certificate of his physicians, leaving General Bragg in temporary command of the Western Department and of the army which had been withdrawn from Corinth before Halleck. Beauregard having reported this action to the War Department, Bragg's assignment was made permanent by Mr. Davis on the 20th of June. On the 25th of August General Beauregard officially reported "for duty in the field."— EDITORS.

system of coast defense devised by me as early as April, 1861, but also of the one said to have been projected by General R. E. Lee while in command of the same department from December, 1861, to March, 1862. For these had been substituted another and an interior system, rendering our lines vulnerable at various points, and necessitating more labor and a greater armament than we could command. The inspection made by me a few days later confirmed that opinion; for the works in and around Charleston, most of which had been badly located, were not in a state of completion, nor was their armament by any means adequate to the dimensions of some of them.

The defenses of the harbor existing at that time consisted of: 1. Fort Sumter, with an armament of 79 guns of diverse caliber, from 32-pounders to 8-inch Columbiads, and seven 10-inch mortars, and manned by 350 effectives of the First South Carolina Artillery (regulars). 2. Fort Moultrie, with 38 guns, ranging from 24-pounders to 8-inch Columbiads, and having a garrison of 300 effectives belonging to the First South Carolina Infantry (regulars). These works were in very good condition, though repairs were then in progress in the former. 3. Battery Beauregard, across Sullivan's Island, the location of which I had selected in the spring of 1861, in advance of Fort Moultrie, with a view to protect the approach from the east. It was armed with five guns. 4. Four sand batteries, *en barbette*, erected at the west end of Sullivan's Island, and bearing on the floating boom then in process of construction across the Fort Sumter channel. These batteries were not completed, and had at the time only four guns, two of them being 10-inch Columbiads. No magazines had been constructed for them. 5. The "Neck" battery, on Morris Island, afterward called Battery Wagner, an open work erected to defend the approach to Fort Sumter. It was intended for eleven guns, and was not entirely finished, even as originally designed. 6. A small work (Fort Ripley) equidistant from Castle Pinckney and Fort Johnson, not yet armed, but planned for four heavy guns *en barbette* [only two put in.—EDITORS]. 7. Castle Pinckney, armed with nine 24-pounders and one 24-pounder rifled, a work of no value for the defense of the city. 8. Fort Johnson, near the north-east end of James Island, with one rifled 32-pounder, likewise of very little importance.

Some batteries had also been arranged and begun for the defense of the city proper, but no heavy guns had been procured for them, and none were disposable. The floating boom was incomplete, and was destined to remain so. I never looked upon it as a serious barrier to the enemy's fleet. The defensive line on James Island from the Wappoo to Secessionville consisted of "a system of forts, redoubts, redans, and *crémaillères*," very injudiciously located, except Fort Pemberton on the Stono and some few of the redoubts. There were also two batteries on the Ashley River, for its protection and that of the entrance of Dill's Creek and the Wappoo. One of them had no guns; the other, at Lawton's, was armed with four 32-pounders, but could be of little use. The works at Secessionville, which were poorly devised and poorly executed, were still unfinished. Their armament was two 8-inch naval guns, one 18-pounder howitzer, six 32-pounders, one 32-pounder rifle, two 24-pounder rifles, and two 10-inch mortars.

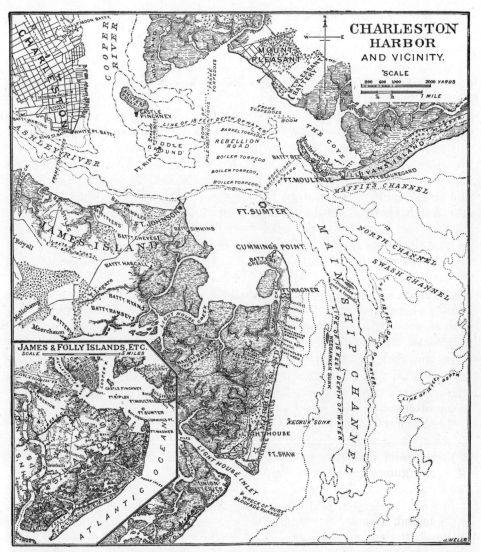

There were four batteries on Sullivan's Island between Battery Beauregard and Fort Marshall, the latter being at the eastern extremity of the island, just outside the limits of the map. Between Battery Bee and Moultrie was Battery Marion, and another work, called Battery Rutledge, was close to Fort Moultrie on the east. Secessionville, near the center of James Island, will be found on the map of James and Folly islands. When Cumming's Point was evacuated by the Confederates, Battery Gregg was named Putnam, after Colonel Haldimand S. Putnam, and a work east of Battery Gregg, and facing the main channel, was called Battery Chatfield, after Colonel John L. Chatfield; both lost their lives in the assault on Battery Wagner.

The line of defenses constructed on the Neck to protect the city from a land attack on the north side, was made up of a continuous "bastion line," which was not suitable to the site where it had been located.

The total number of troops of all arms in South Carolina at that time was: infantry, 6564; artillery in position, 1787; field artillery, 1379; cavalry, 2817,—total, 12,547. Adding the number of troops then in the State of Georgia, 7189, the aggregate force in the whole department amounted on the 24th of September, 1862, to 19,736 men. Before being relieved, General

Pemberton, at my request, gave an estimate of the minimum force requisite, in his opinion, for the department, namely, 43,650 men of all arms, which I adopted as the basis of my future calculations.

On the 30th of September, and again on the 2d of October, I urgently called on the War Department for an increase of heavy ordnance for the works intended to command the anchorage in the Charleston harbor and the entrance into the Ashley and Cooper rivers. I asked for twenty 10-inch Columbiads, five banded rifled 42-pounders, and five banded 32-pounders; or "fifteen of the first quality, ten of the second, and five or more of the third." The Secretary of War, Mr. Randolph, had used every endeavor to assist me in my efforts to be ready for the impending attack of the enemy; but he had just at this time, unfortunately, tendered his resignation, and had been succeeded in office by Mr. Seddon. From that moment my demands on the War Department seemed to meet with much less favor, and I had to rely, in a great measure, on the scant resources of my command to accomplish the work necessary for the safety of the city of Charleston. The State authorities, and in fact the whole people of South Carolina, were equally anxious with myself for the rapid completion of my preparations, and afforded me every assistance in their power, though I was never able to procure the necessary amount of slave-labor required for work on the fortifications. By great exertion, and with no assistance from the Government, was executed under my orders the rifling and banding of guns otherwise too inferior for the proper armament of our works. This was done at the rate of one gun in two and a half days, whereas it had required thirty-five days to remodel each gun under the supervision of the War Department.

My anxiety was all the greater since the enemy, before making his final attack upon Charleston, and with a view, no doubt, to distract attention from it, had been for some time past preparing a descent along the Southern Atlantic coast, though he afterward appeared to have altered his original purpose and to be directing his course toward Cape Lookout, on the coast of North Carolina. With the inadequate force under me, my only hope was to endeavor to frustrate any demonstration that might be attempted within the limits of my own extensive command; and yet the War Department, through the new Secretary of War, was at that very time, and against repeated protests on my part, depleting it of troops to reënforce other points.

The approaches to Charleston were five in number: 1. The enemy could land a large force to the northward, at or in the close vicinity of Bull's Bay, and from thence, marching across the country, could take possession of Mount Pleasant and all the north shore of the inner harbor. 2. A large force of the enemy could also land to the southward, destroy the Charleston and Savannah railroad, and invest Charleston in the rear. These two avenues of approach, however, were not likely to be adopted by the enemy, as the strength of his land force would not have justified such an attempt, unaided by his iron-clads and gun-boats. The coöperation of the Federal fleet was possible for any one of the other three modes of approach, namely: James Island, Sullivan's Island, and Morris Island. 3. Of these, the approach by

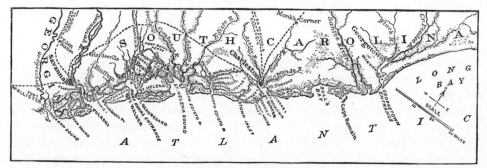

MAP OF THE SOUTH CAROLINA COAST.

James Island was unquestionably the one to be most apprehended. The Confederate troops stationed there were insufficient in number and had to defend "a long, defective, and irregular line of works." The enemy, after overpowering them, could have constructed batteries which would have controlled the inner harbor, taken in rear our outer lines of defenses, and opened fire directly against Charleston itself, thus forcing an almost immediate surrender. 4. By Sullivan's Island the approach was also a very important one. In taking it, Fort Sumter might have been silenced and the inner harbor thrown open to the enemy's iron-clad fleet. 5. The approach by Morris Island was, as afterward proved, the least dangerous to us. It involved none of the contingencies threatened by the other modes of attack. It had always been my opinion, however, that the enemy would elect to make his approach by that route, for the reason that, being already in possession of Folly Island, which was in close proximity to Morris Island, he would thereby enjoy certain facilities for the movements of his troops, while close at hand lay the harbor of Edisto, convenient as a shelter for his fleet. The seizure of Morris Island would also be a great encouragement to the North.

The preparations of the North were upon a scale of such magnitude—with engines of war "*such as the hand of man had never yet put afloat*"—that they had consumed more time than was at first anticipated. Thus an opportunity was afforded me to perfect our means of resistance.

Weeks and months went by, during which I succeeded in nearly doubling the strength of Sumter, of Moultrie, and of all the defensive works of the harbor, including Battery Wagner, which was thus almost entirely rebuilt. I also established along the coast of South Carolina, Georgia, and Florida a continuous line of signal (flag) stations, by means of which constant information was furnished department headquarters of the exact movement and of the least change that took place in the Federal fleet. I multiplied the laying out of torpedoes in all navigable streams liable to be ascended by Federal gunboats and other craft, and gave close attention to the rope obstructions dividing the outer and inner harbors. I likewise used my best endeavors, and importuned the War and Navy Departments, to have constructed a few "torpedo-rams," on the model by Captain F. D. Lee, with which it was my firm conviction more injury could be inflicted upon the Federal fleet than could be hoped for from all such gun-boats as the Government was then having built for the protection of Charleston harbor. That this appreciation was not exaggerated has been shown by many results accomplished at a subsequent date by torpedo-boats in our own war and in naval encounters between foreign nations, notably during the late Franco-Chinese war. ↓

There were two Confederate gun-boats (iron-clad rams) at that time in Charleston, the *Palmetto State* and the *Chicora*. Lieutenant-Commander John Rutledge, C. S. N., commanded the first, and Captain John R. Tucker, C. S. N.,

CASTLE PINCKNEY, CHARLESTON HARBOR.

commanded the second. Besides these there were three small harbor steamers, to be used as tenders for them. The *Palmetto State* and the *Chicora* were, unfortunately, of too heavy a draught to be of much practical use in the defense of the harbor. They were also lacking in motive power, consequently in speed; and their guns, on account of the smallness of the port-holes, could not be sufficiently elevated, and were of but very short range. Ably officered and manned as they were known to be, they proved of real service only once during the whole siege of Charleston.

While our work of armament and of general preparation was progressing on all points of the department, it occurred to me that our two gunboats, inferior as they were in many respects, could, nevertheless, by a bold night attack on the wooden fleet of the enemy, cause considerable damage and compel it to leave its anchorage outside the bar; and the time to do it, I suggested, was before the threatened arrival of the Federal monitors.↓ Commodore Ingraham\ agreed with me, and immediately ordered the attack. It took place on the early morning of January 31st.☆ The *Palmetto State*, on board of which, for the occasion, was Commodore Ingraham himself, steamed out directly toward the Federal fleet, followed by the *Chicora*, and fell upon and fired into the steamer *Mercedita* before the latter had fully realized the peril she was in. Disabled and reported to be

↓It is but simple justice to add that from the first experiments made, in April, 1861, against Fort Sumter with an iron-clad floating battery and an iron-clad land battery, the respective inventions of Captain John Randolph Hamilton, formerly of the U. S. N., and of Mr. C. H. Stevens, afterward brigadier-general in the Confederate army, and both from South Carolina, is attributable also the revolution in naval architecture and armaments by which iron-clad war vessels have entirely superseded the now almost obsolete wooden men-of-war.— G. T. B.

↓ The blockading-fleet off Charleston consisted, at this time, of the *Powhatan, Canandaigua, Housatonic, Unadilla, Mercedita, Keystone State, Memphis,* *Stettin, Ottawa, Flag, Quaker City,* and *Augusta*. The *Powhatan, Canandaigua,* and *Housatonic* were the strongest vessels in the fleet.— EDITORS.

\Commodore Duncan N. Ingraham, formerly of the United States Navy. He was at one time Chief of the Bureau of Ordnance and Hydrography in the Navy Department, and was popularly known for his successful interference while in command of the *St. Louis*, in the harbor of Smyrna, resulting in the release from a Turkish prison of Martin Kószta, a Hungarian refugee who had declared his intention of becoming a citizen of the United States.— EDITORS.

☆ The *Powhatan* and *Canandaigua* were absent at the time, coaling, at Port Royal.— EDITORS.

sinking, the *Mercedita* immediately surrendered. The *Palmetto State* left her and went in pursuit of two other Federal steamers, but was soon distanced. The *Chicora*, meanwhile, set fire to a schooner-rigged propeller, engaged and crippled the *Quaker City*, and ran into and fired the *Keystone State*, which then and there struck her flag. | The other vessels composing the blockading squadron, seeing the fate of their consorts and fearing the same one for themselves, hurriedly steamed out to sea and entirely disappeared. The outer harbor remained in the full possession of the two Confederate rams. Not a Federal sail was visible, even with spy-glasses, for over twenty-four hours. It is, therefore, strictly correct to state that the blockade of the port of Charleston had been raised, for the time being, as was certified to by Commodore Ingraham, by the foreign consuls then in Charleston, and by myself. ⚓

It is evident that had the seaworthy qualities of the two Confederate gun-boats been greater, and could we have given them the coöperation of the torpedo-rams I had anxiously endeavored to have constructed, the blockade of Charleston would not have been at that time, and for months afterward, an impediment to our free and open intercourse with the outer world. And it is simple history to add that, even as it was, through private enterprise which should have tempted our Government to a bolder course, lines of blockade-running steamers entered and left the port of Charleston at regular, stated intervals, up to nearly the very close of the war. Almost at the moment of this naval attack on the Federal fleet occurred another incident of note in the operations around Charleston.

General Pemberton had caused to be removed from Cole's Island eleven guns of heavy caliber which served to guard the entrance of the Stono River. This barrier removed, the Federal gun-boats had free ingress to the river, and as often as they chose to do so plied with impunity as near to Fort Pemberton as safety allowed, harassing our camps on James and John's islands, by the fire of their long-range rifled guns. The *Isaac Smith*, carrying nine heavy guns, was one of these. Desirous of putting a stop to such incursions, I called the commander of the First Military District [General R. S. Ripley] to a conference at department headquarters, and instructed him at once to organize an expedition and have masked batteries erected at designated points on the banks of the Stono, near where the Federal gun-boat habitually passed and occasionally remained overnight. The instructions were to allow her to steam by unmolested as far as she chose to go, then to open fire and cut off her retreat. The expedition was intrusted to Lieutenant-Colonel Joseph A. Yates, First South Carolina Artillery (regulars), and was most successfully conducted. On the evening of January 30th the *Isaac*

| Commander Le Roy, of the *Keystone State*, reported officially that the colors of his vessel were run up, after being lowered, and her guns resumed firing, because the *Chicora* did not respect the signal.—EDITORS.

⚓ This view of the affair is strenuously disputed. A statement, signed on the 10th of February, 1863, by the commanders of the *Housatonic*, *Flag*, *Quaker City*, *Augusta*, *Memphis*, and *Stettin*, and forwarded to the Secretary of the Navy by Rear-Admiral Du Pont, sets forth that only the *Keystone State* and *Mercedita* were seriously damaged; that no vessels were greatly injured by fire, and that none of the fleet abandoned the blockading line, except on duty; they also state that the Confederate rams retreated to the cover of the forts.—EDITORS.

Smith came up the Stono, and leisurely anchored just above our masked batteries. Fire was now opened upon her. She endeavored to make her escape, returning our fire as she passed, but was so roughly handled, and at such close range, that she dropped anchor and surrendered. Her armament consisted of one 30-pounder Parrott and eight 8-inch heavy Columbiads. Her crew was of 11 officers and 108 men. Upon examination the damage she had sustained was found to be slight. She was thoroughly repaired and, under the name of the *Stono*, became a guard-boat in the Charleston harbor, with Captain H. J. Hartstene, C. S. N., as commander.

As a corollary to this engagement

INTERIOR OF FORT PUTNAM, FORMERLY THE CONFEDERATE BATTERY GREGG, CUMMING'S POINT, S. C. FROM A PHOTOGRAPH.

SOUTH-EAST ANGLE OF THE CONFEDERATE FORT MARSHALL, ON THE EASTERN END OF SULLIVAN'S ISLAND. FROM A PHOTOGRAPH.

on the morning of February 1st another Federal iron-clad, afterward ascertained to be the single-turreted monitor *Montauk*, appeared before Fort McAllister, at Genesis Point, in the Georgia district, and, accompanied by three gun-boats and a mortar-boat, approached to within a short distance of the work, and opened a heavy fire upon it. The action was very brisk on both sides. The parapet of the fort was breached, and both guns and gunners were fully exposed. Nevertheless, after a four-hours' combat the monitor slowly retired, evidently in a damaged condition. The importance of the success of this engagement lay in the demonstrated fact that iron-clads were not as formidable as they were supposed to be against land-batteries. As yet, their final test of invulnerability had not been fully ascertained. Reflecting upon the result of that encounter, I wrote to Brigadier-General Ripley, February 8th, 1863, minute instructions, ⇃ because,

⇃ "But I consider also that the attack on Sumter, whenever it takes place, will probably be made at long range with their heaviest guns and mortars. This being admitted, they will necessarily attack it where it is weakest,—*i. e.*, the gorge, south-east angle, and east face,—taking their position close along the eastern shore of Morris Island, after silencing Wagner. By adopting this plan their steamers, gun-boats, etc., would be, moreover, farther removed from the batteries of Sullivan's Island.

though he was an able artillery officer, I knew that he possessed but scant knowledge, and no experience, of military engineering. My best and almost only assistant for planning the construction of batteries and making the selection of the sites on which they were to be erected was Major D. B. Harris, the chief engineer of the department, on whom I placed the utmost reliance, and who always thoroughly understood and entered into my views. It is an error to state, as I am informed one or two writers have done, even in South Carolina, that the erection of batteries along the shores of the inner harbor, and in the city of Charleston itself, was due to what has been termed the untiring zeal, forethought, and engineering ability of General Ripley. My letters of instruction and my official orders to General Ripley, from his arrival in my department up to the time of my leaving it in April, 1864, conclusively show that those batteries were all planned and located by me, and that I passed upon all questions relative not only to their armament, but even to the caliber of the guns that were to be placed in them.

My fear was that an attack upon Sumter might be attempted at night. One or two monitors, I thought, during a dark night could approach the fort within easy range, and open fire upon its weakest face with almost certain impunity. Sumter, even at night, could be sufficiently seen by the monitors to be seriously damaged by their fire; whereas the monitors, being very low in the water, could only be visible from the fort by the flash of their guns. To guard against such an attempt of the enemy, on the 1st of March I wrote to Commodore Ingraham:

"I must therefore request that the Confederate steamer *Stono* should take her position as a guard-boat, in advance of the forts as far as practicable, to-night, and thereafter every night for the present."

I also caused a train of cars to be held in readiness at the Pocotaligo Station, to bring such reënforcements as might be drawn from the military district [lying between the Ashepoo and Savannah rivers] commanded by General W. S. Walker.

On the 28th of February the enemy attacked Fort McAllister with an

"The enemy may also establish land rifled and mortar batteries on the sand-hills along the sea-shore of Morris Island, at the distance of from one to two miles from Sumter. He might possibly send one or more monitors during the night to take a position in the small channel north of Cumming's Point, within close range, to batter down the gorge of Sumter and endeavor to blow up the magazines.

"That mode of attack, being the one most to be apprehended, should be guarded against as well as our limited means will permit—first, by transferring as many heavy rifled guns as can be spared from the other faces of the fort to the gorge, angle, and face already referred to; and the Brooke's rifled gun now on its way here from Richmond must likewise be put there, substituting in its place at Fort Johnson the ten-inch gun now expected from that city, so locating it as to fire toward Morris Island when required; secondly, a strong field-work should be thrown up as soon as sufficient labor can be procured on Cumming's Point, open in the gorge toward Fort Sumter — to act, besides, as a kind of traverse to this work from the fire of the batteries located by the enemy along the sea-shore of Morris Island. The Cumming's Point battery should be armed with the heaviest and longest-ranged guns we may be able to obtain for that purpose.

"The introduction of heavy rifled guns and iron-clad steamers in the attack of masonry forts has greatly changed the condition of the problem applicable to Fort Sumter when it was built, and we must now use the few and imperfect means at our command to increase its defensive features as far as practicable. The chief engineers of this department and of the State will be ordered to report to you at once, to confer with you, so as to carry out the views expressed by me in this letter."

iron-clad, three gun-boats, and a mortar-boat, and also, on the 3d of March, with three monitors. He was evidently trying his hand before his final venture against Fort Sumter. But the result must sorely have disappointed him; for notwithstanding the vigor of these two engagements — the first lasting more than two hours, the second at least seven — the Confederate battery was found, after inspection, to have sustained no material damage.

On the 5th of April the enemy's force had materially increased in the Stono and the North Edisto. His iron-clads, including the frigate *New Ironsides* and eight monitors, had crossed the outer bar and cast anchor in the main channel. No doubt could be had of their intention.

COLONEL D. B. HARRIS, C. S. A.
FROM A PHOTOGRAPH.

Two days later,— on the 7th,— a date ever memorable in the annals of the late war, the signal for the attack on Fort Sumter, so long anticipated and so long delayed, was finally given.

First steamed up, in line, one following the other, the *Weehawken*, the *Passaic*, the *Montauk*, and the *Patapsco*, four single-turreted monitors. The *New Ironsides*, the flag-ship of the fleet, came next. Then came the *Catskill*, the *Nantucket*, the *Nahant*, three other single-turreted monitors. The double-turreted *Keokuk* was the eighth, and closed the line. Experienced and gallant officers commanded them all. Rear-Admiral Du Pont was on board the flag-ship. Other Federal steamers stood outside the bar, but evidently with no intent to take part in the action. They were the *Canandaigua*, the *Housatonic*, the *Unadilla*, the *Wissahickon*, and the *Huron*. The armament of all the iron-clads that were to take part in the engagement consisted of 33 guns "of the heaviest caliber ever used in war" up to that time, to wit, 15 and 11 inch Dahlgren guns and 8-inch rifled pieces.

To oppose this formidable array of new, and it was thought invulnerable, floating batteries, prepared at such heavy cost and with every anticipation of success by the Federal Government, we had on our side: 1. Fort Sumter, under Colonel Alfred Rhett, with a garrison of seven companies of the 1st South Carolina Artillery (regulars); the guns it brought into action on that day being two 7-inch Brookes, two 9-inch Dahlgrens, four 10-inch Columbiads, four 8-inch navy guns, four 8-inch Columbiads, six banded and rifled 42-pounders, eight smooth-bore 32-pounders, and three 10-inch sea-coast mortars,—in all, thirty-three guns and mortars. 2. Fort Moultrie, under Colonel William Butler, with five companies of the 1st South Carolina Infantry (regulars); the guns engaged being nine 8-inch Columbiads, five banded and rifled 32-pounders, five smooth-bore 32-pounders, and two 10-inch mortars,— in all, twenty-one guns and mortars. 3. Battery Bee, on Sullivan's Island, under

Lieutenant-Colonel J. C. Simkins, with three companies of the 1st South Carolina Infantry (regulars) and six guns: five 10-inch and one 8-inch Columbiads. 4. Battery Beauregard, under Captain Julius A. Sitgreaves, with two companies of regulars—one from Sumter and one from Moultrie—and three guns: an 8-inch Columbiad and two 32-pounders, rifled. 5. Battery Wagner, under Major C. K. Huger, with two companies of regulars from Sumter. There four guns were used: one 32-pounder, rifled; one 24-pounder, rifled; and two smooth-bore 32-pounders. 6. Cumming's Point Battery, under Lieutenant Henry R. Lesesne, with a detachment of regulars from Fort Sumter. Two guns were engaged: one 10-inch Columbiad and one 8-inch Dahlgren. The number of guns actually engaged on our side against the iron-clad fleet, on the 7th of April, was therefore 69, of which five were mortars.

Two companies of infantry had been placed on Sullivan's and Morris islands, to guard against a land attack. Commodore Ingraham had also been cautioned to hold the gun-boats *Palmetto State* and *Chicora* in readiness to assist our batteries in case of need; but they were not needed.

The approach of the monitors was slow and cautious. They dreaded the rope obstructions which were known to be connected with heavily charged torpedoes. ♭ But the report afterward circulated,—to which Mr. Seward gave the weight of his official name,—that the "rope obstructions in the channel fouled the screws of the iron-clads," was entirely erroneous. Not one of the iron-clads ever approached nearer than 600 yards to any of these obstructions, with the exception of the *Keokuk*, which dropped in to about 300 yards of them before being able to get under way again.

The first shot was fired at 3 o'clock P. M. It came from Fort Moultrie, and was aimed at the *Weehawken*. No heed was taken of it. ❧ The turreted iron-clad kept on her way until within fourteen hundred yards of Fort Sumter, when she paused a moment and opened fire on it. Fully two minutes elapsed, and then Sumter replied, firing by battery. The other monitors now steamed up, taking their respective positions, but with apparent hesitation and as far out of range as possible. The action had become general, Sumter being the central point of the attack. An occasional shot was sent at Moultrie, an occasional one at Batteries Bee and Beauregard.

The spectacle of this singular combat between the fort and what appeared to be nine floating iron turrets—for the hulls of the monitors were almost wholly submerged—was, indeed, an impressive one, not to be easily forgotten.

After a lapse of about three-quarters of an hour, Admiral Du Pont's flag-ship, the *New Ironsides*, advanced to within some seventeen hundred yards of Sumter, evidently with a view to breach its walls. But the concentrated fire from our batteries forced her to withdraw hurriedly out of range, as the *Passaic* had already done, in an apparently crippled condition. The fire of Sumter was so accurate that two other monitors were compelled

♭ In commenting on this passage Major John Johnson says in a letter to the editors: "After the most thorough study of all the evidence, I am convinced that there were no torpedoes in connection with those rope obstructions until a later date."

❧ Captain Percival Drayton, of the *Passaic*, second in line, reported that the opening shots came from Fort Moultrie and the batteries on Sullivan's Island, and that his vessel replied to them in passing " and pushed on for Sumter."—EDITORS.

to retire. At 4 o'clock P. M. the *Keokuk* advanced to within nine hundred yards of Sumter, but with no better success than her consorts. She soon withdrew, badly worsted. The whole attacking squadron now slowly withdrew from an engagement which had lasted not more than two hours and twenty-five minutes, but which had been, for the enemy, a most disastrous defeat. ☆ [See also papers to follow.]

In the communication sent by me to the War Department, dated May 24th, with regard to the attack of April 7th, I made the following statement:

"The action lasted two hours and twenty-five minutes, but the chief damage is reported by the enemy to have been done in thirty minutes. The *Keokuk* did not come nearer than nine hundred yards of Fort Sumter; she was destroyed. The *New Ironsides* could not stand the fire at the range of a mile; four of her consorts (monitors) were disabled at the distance of not less than thirteen hundred yards. They had only reached the gorge of the harbor—never within it—and were baffled and driven back before reaching our lines of torpedoes and obstructions, which had been constructed as an ultimate defensive resort as far as they could be provided. The heaviest batteries had not been employed. Therefore it may be accepted, as shown, that these vaunted monitor batteries, though formidable engines of war, after all are not invulnerable nor invincible, and may be destroyed or defeated by heavy ordnance properly placed and skillfully handled. In reality they have not materially altered the military relations of forts and ships. On this occasion the monitors operated under the most favorable circumstances. The day was calm, and the water, consequently, was as stable as that of a river; their guns were fired with deliberation, doubtless by trained artillerists. According to the enemy's statements, the fleet fired 151 shots. . . . Not more than thirty-four shots ⎰ took effect on the walls of Fort Sumter. . . . Fort Moultrie and our other batteries were not touched in a way to be considered, while in return they threw 1399 shots. At the same time Sumter discharged 810 shots; making the total number of shots fired 2209, of which the enemy reports that 520 struck the different vessels; a most satisfactory accuracy when the smallness of the target is considered."

The repulse had not been looked upon as a thing possible by the North, and when the news reached that section it engendered a heavy gloom of disappointment and discouragement—a feeling not unlike that which had prevailed there after the Confederate victory at Manassas on July 21st, 1861. It was clear to me, however, that the enemy, whose land forces had not coöperated in this naval attack, would not rest upon his defeat, but would soon make another effort, with renewed vigor, and on a larger scale. I was therefore

☆ The following are extracts from reports of officers in command or on duty that day.

Colonel Rhett said:

"The enemy's fire was mostly ricochet and not very accurate; most of their shot passed over the fort, and several to the right and left. The greater portion of their shots were from 1300 to 1400 yards distant, which appeared to be the extent of their effective range. Some shots were from a greater distance, and did not reach the fort at all."

General Ripley said:

"The action was purely of artillery,—forts and batteries against the iron-clad vessels of the enemy,—other means of defense, obstructions and torpedoes, not having come into play.

"Fort Sumter was the principal object of the attack, and to that garrison . . . special credit is due for sustaining the shock, and, with their powerful armament, contributing principally to the repulse."

Major Echols, of the Corps of Engineers, in his report to Major Harris, Chief Engineer of the department, used this language:

"She [the *Keokuk*] sank off the south end of Morris Island at half-past eight o'clock the following morning (April 8). Her smoke-stack and turrets are now visible at low water. From her wreck floated ashore a book, a spy-glass, and pieces of furniture bespattered with blood, and small fragments of iron sticking in them. . . . The total number [of shots] fired by the enemy [was] about 110 [in fact, 151 to 154.—G. T. B.], which were principally directed at Sumter. Her walls show the effect of fifty-five missiles—shot, shells, and fragments. . . . The casualties are slight. At Sumter five men were wounded by fragments of masonry and wood. . . . At Moultrie one man was killed by the falling of the flag-staff when shot away. At Battery Wagner an ammunition chest . . . exploded from the blast of the gun, killing three men, mortally wounding one, slightly wounding Lieutenant Steedman, in charge of the gun, and three men."   G. T. B.

⎰ Major Echols's report puts the number at *fifty-five*, which it is conceded is the correct one.—G. T. B.

very much concerned when, scarcely a week afterward, the War Department compelled me to send Cooke's and Clingman's commands back to North Carolina, and, early in May, two other brigades [S. R. Gist's and W. H. T. Walker's], numbering five thousand men, with two batteries of light artillery, to reënforce General Joseph E. Johnston at Jackson, Mississippi. The fact is that, on the 10th of May, Mr. Seddon, the Secretary of War, had even directed that still another force of five thousand men should be withdrawn from my department to be sent to Vicksburg to the assistance of General Pemberton. But my protest against so exhaustive a drain upon my command was fortunately heeded, and I was allowed to retain the reduced force I then had under me, amounting on the 1st of June, for the whole State of South Carolina, to not more than ten thousand men. With these, it was evident, I could not protect every vulnerable point at the same time; and thereafter, whenever the occasion arose, I had to withdraw troops from one quarter of the department to reënforce another.

The fact that a new commander of high engineering repute, General Gillmore, had been sent to supersede General Hunter ⚓ confirmed me in the opinion that we would not have to wait long before another and more serious attack was made. A further reason for such a belief was the presence at that time of six Federal regiments on Folly Island, under Brigadier-General Israel Vogdes, an officer of merit, perfectly familiar with Charleston and the surrounding country, having been stationed at Fort Moultrie before the war.

On the 7th of July four monitors were seen off the Charleston bar. The fleet had not otherwise increased up to that day. During the night of the 8th the noise, apparently made by extensive chopping with axes, was distinctly heard from the extreme southern end of Morris Island. The sand-hills, so numerous on Little Folly Island, afforded much facility to the enemy for keeping us in the dark as to his ulterior designs, although nothing indicated any effort on his part at concealment. ↓

⚓ General Hunter was transferred from the Department of Kansas to the command of the Department of the South on the 31st of March, 1862, relieving Brigadier-General Thomas W. Sherman, and was himself relieved by General Quincy A. Gillmore on the 12th of June, 1863. Among the chief events of General Hunter's administration were the capture of Fort Pulaski, April 11th, 1862 (see General Gillmore's description of these operations, Vol. II., p. 1); the declaration of freedom (April 12th, 1862) to slaves in Fort Pulaski and on Cockspur Island, Ga.; a similar declaration (May 9th) to slaves in Georgia, Florida, and South Carolina, which was annulled, ten days later by President Lincoln; and the enlistment of the first colored troops, called the 1st South Carolina regiment.—EDITORS.

↓ The following is an extract from my official report to the War Department upon this important event in the siege of Charleston:

"At 5 o'clock on the morning of the 10th of July the enemy's attack commenced by a heavy fire on our position from a great number of light guns, apparently placed during the preceding forty-eight hours in the works lately thrown up on Little Folly Island. Three monitors about the same time crossed the bar and brought their formidable armaments to bear on the left flank of our position, while several barges with howitzers, in Lighthouse Inlet, flanked our right. For two hours the enemy kept up the fire from these three different points, our batteries replying vigorously.

"The barges of the enemy, filled with troops, having been seen in Lighthouse Inlet in the direction of Black Island, and Oyster Point being the nearest and most accessible spot for debarkation from them, it was justly considered the one most necessary to protect, and therefore the infantry, consisting of the 21st South Carolina Volunteers, about 350 effective men, were stationed by Colonel R. F. Graham, the immediate commander of the island, on the peninsula leading to that point.

"In this position the infantry were unavoidably exposed to the fire of the boat howitzers, but sheltered by the nature of the ground from that of the guns on Little Folly Island.

"About 7 o'clock the enemy advanced on Oyster Point in a flotilla of boats containing between two and three thousand men, a considerable portion of whom endeavored to effect and hold a landing, in which they were opposed by the infantry until about 8 o'clock, when another force of two or three regiments made good a landing in front of our batteries on the south end of Morris Island proper. These formed in line of battle on the beach, and advanced directly upon our works, throwing

It is not true that this attack was a surprise. The commander of Morris Island and all the troops on it knew that the enemy was preparing to make one from Little Folly. I knew it as well. The real cause of the Federal success on the 10th of July was the insufficiency of our infantry force on Morris Island, let alone the fact that I could not, for want of necessary labor, complete the battery already referred to, and which was of no service whatever to us on that occasion.♭ Nor should it be forgotten that the enemy, in order to divert our attention from the main object he had in view, was not only landing troops at the southern end of Morris Island, but was also seriously threatening James Island, and had made a strong demonstration against it by the Stono River. It is clear to me that, but for my determination not to weaken my force there for the support of Morris Island, this demonstration would have been converted into a real attack, the results of which might have been far more disastrous; for, as I have already stated, James Island was the avenue of approach I dreaded the most to see selected, and which on that account I feared the enemy would select. It was, in reality, the gateway to the avenue which would have almost assuredly led into the heart of Charleston. The enemy had preferred breaking in through the window, and I certainly had no cause to regret it. He was held in check there, and never got in until we finally opened the gate ourselves toward the end of the war.

On the evening of July 10th detachments from various Georgia regiments which I had called for began to arrive. I pressed the War Department for Clingman's brigade. Part of it came on the 12th. The day before, at early dawn, the enemy assaulted Battery Wagner, but was repulsed with great loss to him. Two Federal officers and some 95 men were killed within pistol-range of our works. We captured six officers and about 113 men. Most of them were wounded. Three monitors and three wooden gun-boats assisted the Federal land forces on that occasion. Battery Wagner was again shelled on the 12th by part of the fleet, while the

out on each flank numerous skirmishers, who very soon succeeded in flanking and taking the batteries in reverse. After an obstinate resistance our artillery had to abandon their pieces,—three 8-inch navy shell guns, two 8-inch sea-coast howitzers, one rifled 24-pounder, one 30-pounder Parrott, one 12-pounder Whitworth, three 10-inch sea-coast mortars,—eleven in all, and fall back.

"Two companies of the 7th South Carolina Battalion, which arrived about this time, were ordered to the support of the batteries; but they could not make head against the overwhelming numbers of the enemy.

"This success of the enemy threatened to cut off our infantry engaged at Oyster Point from their line of retreat; and, consequently, about 9 o'clock Colonel Graham gave the order to fall back to Battery Wagner, which was accomplished under a severe flanking fire from the monitors. The enemy thus gained possession of the south end of Morris Island by rapidly throwing a large number of troops across the inlet, which it was impossible for the available infantry on the spot, about four hundred effective men, to resist. It was not the erection of works on Little Folly Island that caused the abandonment of our position; it was clearly the want on our side of infantry support, and the enemy's superior weight and number of guns, and the heavy supporting brigade of infantry that swept away our feeble, stinted means of resistance." G. T. B.

♭ The following table shows what force I could dispose of, at the time, in and around Charleston, that is to say, in all the First Military District of South Carolina. I had:

1.—On James Island—
Infantry	1184	
Heavy and light artillery	1569	
Cavalry	153	
		2906

2.—On Morris Island—
Infantry	612	
Heavy and light artillery	289	
Cavalry	26	
		927

3.—On Sullivan's Island—
Infantry	204	
Heavy and light artillery	726	
Cavalry	228	
		1158

4.—In Charleston proper—
Infantry	462	
Heavy and light artillery	235	
Cavalry	153	850

Total................................ 5841

G. T. B.

THE "WEEHAWKEN."

EFFECT OF BLAKELY SHOT FROM FORT SUMTER ON THE
PLATING AND THE SMOKE-STACK OF THE MONITOR
"WEEHAWKEN." FROM PHOTOGRAPHS.

land forces were engaged in putting up works near the middle of Morris Island. They were very much disturbed by the accurate firing of Fort Sumter and of Battery Gregg.

On the arrival of the remainder of Clingman's brigade and of other troops called from the Second and Third Military Districts of my department, I was about to issue an order for an attempt in force to expel the enemy from Morris Island. But the configuration of that island, its proximity to the Federal monitors, and the fact, no less important, that fully four thousand men would have been required for that purpose, convinced me that no step of that kind could then have been successful. Our limited means of transportation was also a great drawback to us. Upon further reflection I came to the conclusion that we could do more toward checking the progress of the enemy by erecting new batteries on James Island, and by strengthening others already in position there and elsewhere. I issued orders to that effect, and they were vigorously carried out. Battery Simkins, in advance of Fort Johnson, on Shell Point, was one of these new batteries. It was armed with one 10-inch Columbiad, one 6.40 Brooke, and three 10-inch mortars; and guns were taken from Sumter to increase the armament of Moultrie.

The damages in Battery Wagner were soon repaired, and the fire of the monitors and gun-boats was regularly answered. Three guns, instead of two, were mounted at the Shell Point Battery; and I also caused gun-batteries of 10-inch Columbiads to be substituted for the mortar-batteries at Fort Johnson. I ordered the forces on Morris Island to be reduced to a number strictly sufficient to hold our works there; and, the enemy's pickets along the Stono having been increased at that time, I instructed General Johnson Hagood to advance at once on the position occupied by the Federals, and thus ascertain what was their real intent as to James Island. This was done with General

Hagood's usual promptitude of action, and on the 16th the Federal forces were driven to the shelter of their gun-boats, our troops occupying the ground they had lost on that occasion. My order to Major Harris, Chief Engineer, was, nevertheless, "to increase the batteries on James Island bearing on Morris Island by at least twenty guns on siege-carriages, so as to envelop the enemy with a 'circle of fire' whenever he might gain possession of the north-east end of Morris Island; all works to be pushed on day and night." On the 18th the Federal troops crowded the south end of Morris Island and took position behind their breastworks. It was clear that another attempt was about to be made against Wagner, and it was made with no less vigor than obstinacy. The *New Ironsides*, five monitors, and a large wooden frigate joined in the bombardment. The firing of the enemy was more rapid on that occasion than it had ever been before. General W. B. Taliaferro, of Virginia, the gallant and efficient officer in command of Battery Wagner at the time, estimated "that nine hundred shot and shell were thrown in and against the battery during the eleven hours that the bombardment lasted." Wagner answered but slowly to this terrible onslaught. Not so, however, with Sumter and Gregg, which fired with even more rapidity than the enemy, and, as ever, did splendid work. After dusk on the same evening the Federal fleet was seen to retire, and the land forces advanced to attack Wagner. They displayed great determination. A portion of them succeeded in crossing the ditch and actually gained a foot-hold on the southern salient of the battery. General Hagood, with Colonel G. P. Harrison's 32d Georgia, arrived opportunely at that hour, in obedience to my orders, and was of great assistance in precipitating the flight of the enemy, though it had fairly begun before his arrival. My report says:

"The assault was terribly disastrous to the enemy. His loss in killed, wounded, and prisoners must have been 3000, as 800 bodies were interred in front of Battery Wagner on the following morning. . . . Our own loss during the bombardment and assault was 174, killed and wounded."

' From that time up to the evacuation of Morris Island the enemy scarcely allowed a day to pass without heavily firing upon our works—sometimes with his land forces alone, at other times with these and his fleet combined. He was also busily engaged on his batteries and trenches, while, on our side, we were straining every nerve to repair the damages done to our works and to strengthen the weakened walls of Sumter, whose disarmament was carefully carried on at night, in view of the disastrous effects of the enemy's heavy guns, from stationary batteries, which would eventually render it untenable as an artillery post. That such a result was inevitable no one could possibly doubt, and that the whole of Morris Island would sooner or later fall into the hands of the enemy, was no less evident. But, so long as the batteries in process of construction on the mainland were unfinished, I had resolved to hold Wagner and Gregg to the last extremity. Every movement of the enemy was in the meantime watched with the utmost vigilance, while the accurate firing of Sumter, Gregg, and Wagner continued seriously to interfere with the working parties engaged on his lines of gradual approaches.

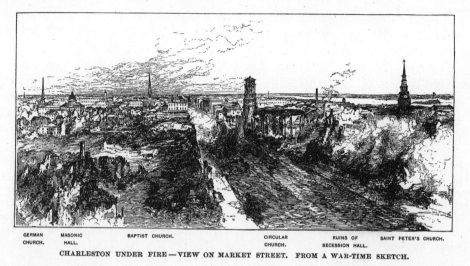

GERMAN   MASONIC   BAPTIST CHURCH.   CIRCULAR   RUINS OF   SAINT PETER'S CHURCH.
CHURCH. HALL.   CHURCH.   SECESSION HALL.

CHARLESTON UNDER FIRE — VIEW ON MARKET STREET. FROM A WAR-TIME SKETCH.

Among the most memorable incidents of this period of the siege was the seven days' bombardment of Fort Sumter, which commenced on the 17th of August and lasted up to the 23d. It appeared to be, on the part of the Federals, a desperate and final attempt to force the surrender of the fort, and thus effect the reduction of Morris Island, and even of the city of Charleston. This was evidenced by the peremptory demand which I received from General Gillmore on the 21st for the "immediate evacuation of Morris Island and Fort Sumter," followed by the threat that if, within "four hours" after the delivery of his letter into the hands of the commander of Battery Wagner, no reply was had, he would "open fire on the city of Charleston from batteries already established within easy range of the heart of the city." This communication reached me after the time specified. [See p. 66.]

I protested against the bombardment of a city filled with old men, women, and children before giving the customary notice of three or four days in which to allow them to escape from danger. From a work which was called the "Swamp Angel," because of the spot where it had been erected, the enemy, with an 8-inch Parrott rifle-gun, and before receiving my answer, did open fire upon "the heart" of the city. I have reason to believe, however, that the energy of my protest, which in due time reached the headquarters of the Federal commander, forced him to recede somewhat from the position he had at first taken, for he ultimately ordered the firing upon the city to be suspended for the space of two days. When resumed it was not continued long; the "Swamp Angel" gun, after 36 rounds, very fortunately burst, and none other was mounted in that locality to take its place. The result of the seven days' bombardment of Sumter was to convert that historic fort into a confused mass of crumbling débris, but without altogether impairing its capacity of resistance. The greatest danger threatening the garrison just then, and one no doubt counted upon by the enemy, was the probability of the explosion by shot and shell of its powder magazine, which was, indeed, momentarily apprehended by the gallant men within the work.

In the meanwhile, General Gillmore's working parties, ever on the increase, were gradually but surely extending their trenches and mining operations nearer and nearer to Battery Wagner. On the 26th our rifle-pits in front of the work were assailed by an overpowering force and taken, and on the 1st of September the fire on Sumter was so intense as to effect its virtual destruction. The following extract from the Engineer's report, forwarded at that time to the War Department, will give an idea of the condition of the work:

" Toward noon the effect of the fire was to carry away at one fall four rampart arches on north-east front, with *terre-plein* platforms and guns, thus leaving on this front only one arch and a half, which are adjacent to the east spiral stair. Some of the lower casemate piers of same front have been seriously damaged, rendering unsafe the service of two guns hitherto available in that quarter. On the exterior, the chief injury done is to be noticed at south-east *pan-coupé* and two next upper casemates on east front. From these localities the scarp wall has fallen away completely and left the arches exposed, as well as the sand filling half down to the floor of the second tier."

The next day six monitors, together with the *Ironsides*, opened fire on the fort, using the heaviest projectiles, namely, 8-inch Parrotts, rifle-shells, and 11 and 15 inch smooth-bore shot and shell. Sumter remained silent. It had not one single gun in working order with which to reply. The following is an extract from my report to the War Department:

" The north-east and north-west *terre-pleins* had fallen in, and the western wall had a crack entirely through from parapet to berme. The greater portion of the southern wall was down, the upper east magazine penetrated, and lower east magazine wall cracked ; the eastern wall itself nearly shot away, and large portions down ; ramparts gone, and nearly every casemate breached. The casemates on the eastern face were still filled with sand, and gave some protection to the garrison from shells. Not a single gun remained in barbette, and but a single smooth-bore 32-pounder in the west face that could be fired as the morning and evening gun."

While Sumter had thus been made a mass of crumbling ruins, the enemy, except at short intervals, spared no effort to effect the demolition of Wagner also. In spite of the ability and determination of the several commanders — Taliaferro, Hagood, A. H. Colquitt, Clingman, R. F. Graham, Harrison, and L. M. Keitt — who, in turn, were placed there; in spite of the almost superhuman energy and pluck of its garrison and working parties to repair, at night, the damage done during the day, it became evident, on the 5th of September, that any further attempt to retain possession of it would result in the useless loss of the garrisons of both Wagner and Gregg. The enemy's sap had reached the moat of the former work. The heavy Parrott shells used against its parapets had breached them and knocked away the bomb-proofs. It had become impossible to repair the damages done.

Colonel Rhett and his artillery command of regulars had already been transferred to the batteries forming the inner defenses, which were now almost entirely completed, and mostly armed with the very guns of Sumter. Major Stephen Elliott, with an infantry force taken from various regiments in and around the city, had been put there to hold the ruins of the fort against any storming parties of the enemy, and to give the morning and evening salute to the Confederate flag, still floating to the breeze. Major

THE FIRST BREACH IN FORT SUMTER.   FROM A PHOTOGRAPH.

Major John Johnson writes to the editors that the photograph was taken on September 8th, 1863, during a heavy engagement between the iron-clad fleet and the forts on Sullivan's Island, including Fort Moultrie. Sumter had been silenced for a week prior to that date. The picture shows the full height of the wall of the parapet, the first breach, and the fallen casemates of the north-western wall of Fort Sumter.

Elliott had been selected by me with care for that post of honor and danger. He proved himself worthy of the confidence placed in him; as did, later on, Captain John C. Mitchel, who relieved him on the 4th of May, 1864, and lost his life while in command there on the 20th of July, 1864; he was succeeded by another brave officer, Captain T. A. Huguenin, who was fortunate enough to escape uninjured and only left the fort at its final evacuation on the 17th of February, 1865. Another gallant officer, Major John Johnson, of the Confederate States Engineers, was of much assistance in the defense of the ruins, and remained therein while they were held by us.

The instructions for the evacuation of Batteries Wagner and Gregg had been prepared by me with much deliberation and thought. The withdrawal of the troops began as previously agreed upon, and was conducted in silence, with great coolness and precision. My orders were carried out almost to the letter. Owing to some defect in the fuses, however, the powder magazines of neither Wagner nor Gregg were exploded, although they had been lit, with all due precaution, by able officers. The wounded and sick had been first removed; then the companies were marched by detachments to the boats prepared to receive them, and embarked under the supervision of the

"THE BATTERY," CHARLESTON.   FROM A SKETCH MADE IN 1873.

naval officers in command. Two companies remained in Battery Wagner, as a rear-guard, until all the others were embarked, when they also were withdrawn. Our loss was slight both in men and materials, and the Federal victory was barren. ⸜

I have dwelt somewhat at length upon the details of the gradual destruction of Fort Sumter for the reason that, apart from the high interest of the recital, the matchless spirit and discipline displayed by its commander and garrison reacted upon all the commands in my department, and aroused a feeling of pride and emulation among the troops defending Charleston, which resulted in the greatest heroism. And it is history to say that the defense of Sumter and Wagner are feats of war unsurpassed in ancient or modern times.

I now propose, before closing, to review a few passages of General Gillmore's book, published just after the war, and, as appears on its title-page, "by authority." Most of its errors have already been refuted in my "Morris Island Report," which is given, *in extenso*, in the second volume of the "Military Operations of General Beauregard" (Harper & Brothers: pp. 102 *et seq.*) It only remains, therefore, to comment briefly upon certain misapprehensions and false conclusions of the author. ☆

General Gillmore was considered during the war the first engineer officer in the Federal service. Such is his standing up to this day. He had evidently been sent in command of the Department of the South, to effect what General Hunter had failed to do, to wit, the capture of Charleston.

⸜ In General Gillmore's dispatch to Admiral Dahlgren, dated September 7th, 5:10 A. M., he said: "The whole island is ours, but the enemy have escaped us."—G. T. B.

☆ See paper by General Gillmore, written in 1887, to follow.—EDITORS.

General Gillmore's book is valuable in many respects. It furnishes new and important information to the student of military history. Its tabular statements are generally accurate; the plates, drawings, and carefully prepared maps annexed to it are interesting and instructive. The description he gives of the city of Charleston, and of the fortifications in and around its harbor, is exact. But the inference to be drawn from the paragraph numbered nineteen in the book [p. 11] is exceptionable. It reads as follows:

" The strength of the James Island works was tested by a bold but unsuccessful assault upon them by our forces under Brigadier-General [H. W.] Benham on the 16th of June, 1862."

I deem it necessary to place the facts of this attack in their proper light, because that is the reason assigned by Gillmore for not having attacked by James Island in July, 1863, when he attempted the Morris Island route.

The truth of the matter is, that the point attacked by Generals Benham and I. I. Stevens near Secessionville┃ was the strongest one of the whole line, which was then unfinished and was designed to be some five miles in length.

The two Federal commanders might have overcome the obstacles in their front had they proceeded farther up the Stono. Even as it was, the fight at Secessionville was lost, in great measure, by lack of tenacity on the part of Generals Benham and Stevens. Their troops outnumbered ours more than two to one, and fought with considerable dash. Some of them, in the impetus of the assault, went even inside one of the salients of the work. It was saved by the skin of our teeth. General Benham's attack was, therefore, hardly a " test " of the possibility or impossibility of carrying the James Island works. The failure in June, 1862, was no good reason for not making the attempt over again in July, 1863 — 1. Because that point of the attack was the strongest instead of the weakest of the line, other parts of it, further west, being but feebly guarded and poorly armed. 2. Because the forces under me in July, 1863, were much less than those under General Pemberton in June, 1862. 3. Because in July, 1863, I had only 1184 infantry on the whole of James Island; whereas, in order to guard the defensive lines properly, I should have had a force of at least 8000 men there. General Gillmore says, p. 12:

" A land attack upon Charleston was not even discussed at any of the interviews to which I was invited, and was certainly never contemplated by me."

His reasons for not having contemplated such a movement are shown in paragraph 27 of his book, where he asserts, in substance, that beyond the capture of Morris Island and the demolition of Fort Sumter he never intended, with an army of only 11,000 men, and with so many difficulties in his way, to undertake any operations against the land defenses of Charleston, knowing as he did how superior my forces were to his own, and what facili-

┃ The assault at Secessionville was made by Stevens's division of about 3500 men, supported by General H. G. Wright's division, numbering 3100. Wright's troops were not seriously engaged. The aggregate Union loss was 683, of whom 529 belonged to Stevens's division. According to the report of General David Hunter, who commanded the department, the attack was made by General Benham in violation of his instructions.

The Confederate force engaged was commanded by General N. G. Evans, and sustained a loss of about 200.—EDITORS.

ties I had "for concentrating troops by railroad." "The capture of Charleston" was, after all,— and General Gillmore admits it,—"the ultimate object in view." The possession of Morris Island and the demolition of Sumter by the Federal land and naval forces were mere incidents in the drama. These did not cause the fall of the much hated and much coveted rebel city;

GENERAL QUINCY A. GILLMORE.
FROM A PHOTOGRAPH.

and General Gillmore, "though he had overcome difficulties almost unknown in modern sieges,"[†] did not achieve "the ultimate object in view."

The fact is that on or about the 10th of July, 1863, the Confederate forces available for the defense of the exterior lines of Charleston did not exceed 6500 men, distributed to the best advantage for the protection of James, Sullivan's, and Morris islands, and of the city proper; whereas General Gillmore had at that time, according to his own estimate, 11,000 men, whom he might have easily concentrated against any special point. Supposing that point to have been the James Island lines, the weak Confederate force there stationed: 1184 infantry, would have had to withstand an overwhelming assault. Transportation was altogether inadequate, and all effort made to reënforce any of the above-named localities would have necessarily uncovered some other points equally liable to attack.

General Gillmore exaggerates "the formidable strength of 'Fort' Wagner," as he persistently calls it, and explains how "its position, trace, armament, and interior arrangements" compelled him to change the plan of operations first adopted against it. He says, p. 43 of his book:

"It had an excellent command and a bold relief. . . . It was constructed of compact sand, upon which the heaviest projectiles produce but little effect, and in which damages could be easily and speedily repaired. It was known to contain a secure and capacious bomb-proof shelter for its entire garrison, and to be armed with between fifteen and twenty guns of various calibers, nearly all bearing upon and completely covering the only approach to it, which was over a shallow and shifting beach, of scarcely half a company front in width in many places, subject to frequent overflow by the tides, and swept by the guns of not only Fort Wagner itself, but of Battery Gregg, Fort Sumter, and several heavily armed batteries on James Island."

"Battery" Wagner, as it should be called, for it never was a "fort," had successfully repulsed two assaults by overpowering numbers, and with such bloody results as to deter the enemy from again attempting the same mode of attack. It withstood and baffled the combined efforts of the Federal naval and land forces during fifty-eight consecutive days. Indisputably General Gillmore's success on Morris Island was tardy and barren of the fruit expected and sought.

Battery Wagner was originally an ordinary field-battery, erected, as

[†] General Halleck's report of November 15th, 1863.

already stated, by General Pemberton to prevent a near approach from the south end of Morris Island. It was pierced for eleven guns, only three of which were heavy pieces. These were two 10-inch Columbiads and one 32-pounder rifled, which was of but slight service, for it burst after firing a few rounds and was never replaced. The other guns were 32-pounder carronades and 12-pounder mortars, placed on the "curtain" of the battery, facing the approach from the south. Most of these had been disabled by the terrible fire opened upon them. The remaining ones were field-pieces and two 8 and 10 inch mortars, the latter being used as "coehorns" against the enemy's trenches. The work was strengthened and improved, its plan gradually modified; traverses and merlons, and bomb-proofs capable of sheltering some 750 men (not 1600, as General Gillmore says, p. 74 of his book), were added to it by my orders, partly before the attack, partly after, and while the enemy was still making his advance. By the addition of a light parapet which I had caused to be thrown across its gorge, Wagner had thus become a closed battery, protected from a surprise on the rear. But it never was a "formidable work"; and, in fact, it fought the enemy from the 10th of July, 1863, to the 6th of September of the same year, with men, artillery, and with sand.

The defense of Battery Wagner, with the great difficulty of access to it and the paucity of our resources, while those of the enemy were almost unlimited, will bear a favorable comparison with any modern siege on record. The last bombardment of Wagner began on the morning of the 5th of September, and lasted 42 hours, during which were thrown by the Federal land-batteries alone 1663 rifle projectiles and 1553 mortar-shells. The total number of projectiles thrown by the land-batteries against Fort Sumter up to September 7th was 6451, and against Battery Wagner, from July 26th to September 7th, 9875, making in all 16,326. And yet only Wagner was taken. Sumter, though a mass of ruins, remained ours to the last, and Charleston was evacuated by the Confederate troops near the close of the war, namely, on the 17th of February, 1865, and then only to furnish additional men to the army in the field.

THE CONFEDERATE DEFENSE OF FORT SUMTER.

BY MAJOR JOHN JOHNSON, C. S. ENGINEERS.

MY first recollections of Fort Sumter date back to my boyhood, about 1844, when the walls had not yet been begun, and the structure was only a few feet above high-water mark. Captain A. H. Bowman, of the Corps of Engineers of the United States Army, was in charge of works in Charleston harbor, and it was my fortune to visit the fort very frequently in his company.

A year and three months of my life were afterward spent in the fort, as engineer-in-charge, during the arduous and protracted defense by the Confederate forces in the years 1863 and 1864.

In the beginning of 1863 the fort was garrisoned by the greater part of the 1st South Carolina regiment of artillery, enlisted as regulars, and commanded by Colonel Alfred Rhett, Lieut.-Colonel Joseph A. Yates, and Major Ormsby Blanding. The drill, discipline, and efficiency of the garrison were maintained at the height of excellence. A spirit of emulation existed between this garrison and that of Fort Moultrie, on the opposite side of the channel, consisting of the 1st South Carolina Infantry (regulars), commanded by Colonel William Butler. The people of the State and city were proud of the two regiments; and the Charlestonians thought of no greater pleasure for their visitors than to give them an afternoon trip down the harbor to see the dress-parade and hear the band play at Fort Sumter. The fine record of this garrison, beginning with the 7th of April, 1863, when Rear-

CAPTAIN THOMAS A. HUGUENIN IN THE HEADQUARTERS-ROOM, FORT SUMTER, DECEMBER 7, 1864.
FROM A WAR-TIME SKETCH.

Admiral Du Pont's attack with nine iron-clad vessels was repulsed, continued until September of the same year, when the fort, silenced by Major-General Gillmore's breaching batteries, had no further use for artillerists, and was thenceforth defended mostly by infantry. One or two companies of artillerists would serve their turns of duty, but the new garrison was made up of detachments from infantry regiments of Georgia, North Carolina, and South Carolina, relieving one another every fortnight.

The walls of the fort rose, on all its five sides, to a height of forty feet above high-water in the harbor; but they varied in material and thickness. The materials used were the best Carolina gray brick, laid with mortar, a concrete of pounded oyster-shells and cement, and another and harder sort of concrete known as *béton*, and used only for the embrasures.

The scarp wall was five feet in thickness, but as it was backed by the piers and arches of the casemates, "the walls of Fort Sumter," as they are popularly called, varied from five to ten feet in thickness.

The damage done to Fort Sumter by Du Pont's naval attack was severe in a few places. [See p. 19.] The combined effect of two shells, 11-inch and 15-inch, respectively, striking near together on the outer eastern wall, or sea-front, was to make a complete breach on the interior of the upper casemates, and to show a crater six feet in height and eight feet in width, on the exterior of the wall. In another place the parapet was loosened for twenty-five feet of its length, some of the bricks falling out and exposing the gun-carriage behind it.

The magazines of the fort naturally gave the defenders special concern. There were four, situated at the extremities of the gorge, nearest to Morris Island, and in pairs, one over the other. The stone-work built for their protection externally had been carried up only to the tops of the lower magazines. All were used in the naval fight of April 7th, for they were not then so imperiled by a naval fire as later when the eastern wall became reduced in height, and the monitors could look into the arches of the western casemates. Before Gillmore's guns opened, on the 17th of August, his operations on Morris Island caused the upper magazines to be abandoned and partly filled with sand to protect the lower ones. Only the eastern magazine then became endangered by his fire, and that so gradually as to allow ample time for the removal of its contents. It was my duty to examine and report the condition of these magazines almost hourly, and I well remember how, by the aid of a little bull's-eye lantern hanging from my finger, and casting fantastic shadows on the piled-up kegs of cannon powder, I would enter the chamber, apply my ear close to the surface of the massive wall, and await the coming of the next rifle-shell, to hear how much more it shook the fort than the last, and to estimate its gain of penetration. Then, at night, when the firing slackened, I would take a rod and tape-line and inspect the damage from the outside. The time came at length when it appeared prudent to remove the 11,000 pounds of powder from the eastern lower magazine, but it was never breached, and was even used as a store-room to the last.

The western magazine was less exposed to the direct fire from Morris Island; and on only two occasions was it in any great danger from the fleet. The fort had been nearly silenced by the land-batteries, when there occurred two night attacks on the part of the iron-clad squadron, and shells were thrown over the sea-wall into the vicinity of the only remaining magazine. One shell, well aimed, was stopped by sand-bags in the gallery opening on the parade; one exploded near the closed copper doors of the outer chamber; another sent its smoke down the ventilator, and one set fire to some combustibles in the adjacent room used for charging shells. After that night of the 1st and 2d of September, the magazine was emptied of all but small-arms ammunition, the last of some 70,000 pounds of cannon-powder being removed from the fort under fire without accident.

But on the morning of the 11th of December, 1863, this small-arms magazine was blown up with disastrous effects. There had been quite a lull in the bombardment, and no firing on the fort for several days. The cause of the explosion was never discovered. A lower casemate on the western or city front, near the south-western angle, where the magazine lay, was occupied by Lieutenant Colonel Stephen Elliott (who had succeeded Colonel Rhett in command) and myself. As duty required night to be turned into day, we had not long turned day into night, but were fast asleep, when we were aroused by the noise of a great explosion, the dull sound of heavy falling masses, and the rush of sulphurous smoke into our quarters. I jumped out of bed and made for the embrasure, closed in wintry weather with a heavy oaken shutter. The casemates were so dark in winter mornings as to require lighting; and now every light had been extinguished by the explosion. We were well-nigh suffocated, but, quickly raising and propping up the heavy shutter, jumped out through the opening upon the rocky foundation of the fort, all awash with a high tide that chilled our bare feet. On reaching the new sally-port, on the city front, near the north-western angle, we found the smoke decreasing, but as no entrance into the magazine through those casemates could yet be effected, we were obliged to work our way around the outside of the fort nearly half of its entire circuit, and enter by another embrasure on the front opposite Sullivan's Island. Hastening into the parade of the fort, we found that the shelling had been resumed by the enemy as soon as they perceived the explosion; and, in crossing the parade diagonally to the point where the magazine-gallery had its entrance, the commander was slightly wounded on the head. Entering the narrow gallery, that grew darker as we penetrated into it, we met scorched men jostling us as they hurried to the light and the air. Nearing the magazine, before we were aware of it we trod in the darkness on the dead bodies of others tumbled together in the narrow gang-way. When the last body had been removed, and the passage once more was regained, it was seen that a fire was burning fiercely

in the outer chamber of the magazine, used for provisions. Here Captain Edward D. Frost, then serving as post-commissary, must have been engaged at the moment of the explosion, issuing rations. He was instantly killed, and others with him; their bodies were never recovered.

The gathering smoke and flames soon drove us back again to the parade. Efforts were made to confine the flames to the magazine, by erecting some barricades; but no good came of it; and the only success that I remember at this juncture was achieved by the telegraph operator, Mr. W. R. Cathcart, who gathered up his wires, rescued his apparatus, and remounted it within another quarter of the fort. The fire, now beyond all control, spread rapidly upward, by the stairway, into the soldiers' quarters of the upper casemates, and swept destructively through the lower ones. Many were scorched in their bunks, and some were cut off from the stairway and had to be rescued through an opening in the wall, by a long ladder. By this accident 11 men were killed and 41 injured.

For several nights, everything—provisions, water, even the reliefs of fresh troops—had to be brought in by ladders from the wharf to the upper casemates; then it was necessary, after this level was gained, to ascend yet higher, to the top of the massive embankment of sand and débris that closed and protected these high-arched casemates from the fire of the fleet and batteries. Thence, from the crown of those arches, and through a small opening, men, boxes, and barrels had to be brought by ladder, down fully thirty feet to the interior of the fort. It was weeks before the burnt quarters could be reoccupied.

The use of the calcium light was resorted to by Major-General Gillmore in his siege of Fort Wagner, and again from Cumming's Point. Considering the distance, three-quarters of a mile, the illuminating power at Fort Sumter was very great. The first night the light was displayed, in the winter of 1863, I read by it the largest type of a newspaper. Our sentinels on the wall were dazzled and annoyed by it. The darkness of the night and of the waters around the fort was seemingly increased tenfold by the contrast. The appearance of this light, thrown upon the battered walls and arches of Fort Sumter, was always striking and beautiful.

In the days of Fort Sumter's prime, a conspicuous object was the great flag-staff in the northern angle. Rising to a height of 80 or 100 feet above the harbor, it received the bolts and shells of Gillmore's first bombardment, until, splintered to a stump, it ceased to be used, and a smaller flag was displayed on the walls. Before that, the large garrison flag had been cut away seven times, and replaced by climbing. This I saw done repeatedly by Private John Drury, and once by Sergeant Schaffer, both of the 1st South Carolina Artillery. Afterward, when the flag was flown from the south-eastern angle, and again from the center of the gorge-wall, I witnessed feats of replacing it under fire.

---

‡ November 27th, 1863, the shot-marker at the lookout on the western extremity of the gorge, Private James Tupper, Jr., of the Charleston Battalion, seeing

the flag shot away, walked, exposed the whole length of the crest, to the point where he was met by three others of the same command, C. B. Foster, W. C. Buck-

It is a great mistake to suppose that Fort Sumter owed its protection mainly to the accumulation of its own débris. The bursting of a single large shell on the exterior slopes would often be attended with the absolute loss to the fort of a ton's weight of material. The waste of material from the combined effects of battering missiles, bursting shells, scattering winds, and boisterous waves was simply enormous. The excavation of the parade, carried down four or five feet, at first furnished the material needed for the precautionary filling of passages and casemates. But it soon became necessary to supply the fort almost nightly with large quantities of sand in bags, ready to be placed wherever it was needed. And whenever this source failed, resort was had to scraping up sand and gathering débris from the water's edge on the exterior.

To keep the fort from going to pieces under its terrible bombardments was not the only concern of its defenders. They had nightly to take every precaution against attack by small boats landing columns on the two fronts most exposed to assault. This mode of attack, tried by Rear-Admiral Dahlgren on the night of September 8th, 1863, failed in twenty minutes, with loss of life and the capture of 10 officers and 92 men. [See p. 50.] Afterward, when the walls were battered down much lower, and the task of climbing the exterior slopes was made much easier, it became necessary to anchor a boom of heavy logs off the exposed slopes, to spread wire entanglements near the base of them, and to place a bristling array of *fraises* — sharpened wooden pikes, set in frames, all along the crest. These obstructions had to be removed in daytime, or they would have been destroyed. The exposure of the men assigned to this duty was very great; they were always personally directed by Lieutenant John H. Houston, of the Engineer troops. It was while engaged inspecting these obstructions that Captain Frank Huger Harleston, of the 1st Artillery, was mortally wounded on the night of November 24th, 1863.

A complete system of interior defense was perfected as early as December, 1863, consisting of barricades and blindages of sand-bags or logs as the case required, loop-holed for infantry and pierced for howitzer fire, searching every part of the interior of the fort. The garrison, in event of being driven to take refuge in the casemates and bomb-proofs, could thus protect itself, while all the Confederate batteries around the harbor could be signaled to open on the fort.

The successor of Lieutenant-Colonel Elliott in command of the fort was Captain John C. Mitchel, of the old garrison, viz., the 1st South Carolina Artillery. Few young Confederate officers impressed me more favorably. He was a born soldier, a man of nerve, finely tempered as steel, with habits of order, quick perception, and decision, and he had been earnestly recommended for promotion. A little after noon on the 20th of July, 1864, he took with him up to the highest point in the fort, the south-western angle, his favorite telescope, which he was using to observe the enemy's works on Morris Island, when he was mortally wounded.

When demolished by land-batteries of unprecedented range, the fort endured for more than eighteen months their almost constant fire, and for a hundred days and nights their utmost power, until it could with truth be said that it at last tired out, and in this way silenced, the great guns that once had silenced it. ⚓ From having been a desolate ruin, a shapeless pile of shattered walls and casemates, showing here and there the guns disabled and half-buried in splintered wrecks of carriages, its mounds of rubbish fairly reeking with the smoke and smell of powder, Fort Sumter under fire was transformed within a year into a powerful earth-work, impregnable to assault, and even supporting the other works at the entrance of Charleston harbor with six guns of the heaviest caliber.

Thus it was not until February, 1865, a few months only before the war came to an end, that General Sherman's march through the interior of South Carolina obliged the withdrawal of Confederate garrisons and troops from Charleston and its vicinity. I had been sent elsewhere on duty, and was glad to be spared the leave-taking that fell to others. On the night of the 17th of February, 1865, the commander, Captain Thomas A. Huguenin, silently and without interruption effected the complete evacuation. He has often told me of the particulars, and I have involuntarily accompanied him in thought and feeling as, for the last time, he went the rounds of the deserted fort. The ordered casemates with their massive guns were there, but in the stillness of that hour his own footfall alone gave an echo from the arches overhead. The labyrinthine galleries, as he traversed them, were lighted for a moment by his lantern; he passed out from the shadows to step aboard the little boat awaiting him at the wharf, and the four years' defense of Fort Sumter was at an end.

---

heister, and A. J. Bluett, who had clambered up by the ladders. But his comrades were ready, and with their assistance he managed to display the flag in about twelve minutes. They were all exposed to great danger. One shell struck the flag-staff out of their hands.

January 29th, 1864, the flag was shot away at the same locality, and replaced by Privates Shafer and Banks, assisted by Corporal Brassingham, all of Lucas's Battalion of Artillery, and greatly aided by the acting adjutant of the post, H. Bentivoglio Middleton of the Signal Corps.

Later in the same year, the flag of the post was moved to the center of the gorge-wall, at a point on the crest, accessible by a short ladder from the top of the bomb-proof quarters. The practice with two 30-pounder Parrott rifles, at Cumming's Point, distant three-quarters of

a mile, was so fine that more than three shots were seldom required for cutting down the staff; sometimes a single shot sufficed. June 20th, 1864, the flag was reported shot away. The larger part of the staff remained fast in the crest of the gorge, while the splintered spar, bearing the flag, was thrown inwardly to the ground. But some slight delay arising in the planting, Lieutenant Charles H. Claibourne, of the 1st South Carolina Infantry (regulars), mounted the wall with the colors, and in full view of the enemy, and under a rapid fire, lashed the two parts of the staff together with the halyard ropes, assisted by two brave, spirited men of the Engineer Department, Sergeant Nicholas F. Devereux and Corporal B. Brannon.—J. J.

⚓ Fifty-one heavy rifle cannon were expended on Morris Island by the Union batteries.—J. J.

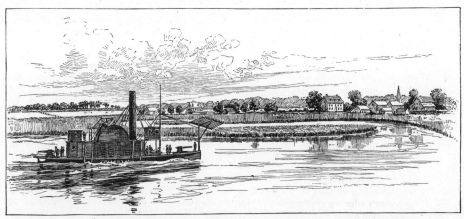

THE UNION TUG "PLATO" (WITH TORPEDO RAKE AT THE BOW) IN THE STONO RIVER, NEAR CHARLESTON. FROM A WAR-TIME SKETCH.

MINOR OPERATIONS OF THE SOUTH ATLANTIC SQUADRON UNDER DU PONT.

BY PROFESSOR JAMES RUSSELL SOLEY, U. S. N.

DURING the six months immediately following the battle of Port Royal [see Vol. I., p. 671] Du Pont was principally engaged in reconnoitering and gaining possession of the network of interior waterways which extends along the coast of South Carolina, Georgia, and Florida, from Bull's Bay to Fernandina. Detachments of vessels under Commander Drayton visited the inlets to the northward, including St. Helena Sound and the North and South Edisto, while other detachments, under Commanders John and C. R. P. Rodgers, examined the southerly waters, especially those about Tybee Roads and Wassaw and Ossabaw sounds. Nearly all the fortifications in these waters, with the exception of Fort Pulaski on the Savannah River, were found abandoned. The coast blockade was thus partially converted into an occupation. In March an expedition on a large scale proceeded farther south, to attack Fernandina and the neighboring posts; but before it reached the spot the greater part of the troops garrisoned there had been withdrawn, under an order of February 23d, issued by General R. E. Lee, at that time in command of the district. The expedition therefore met with little opposition, and occupied all important points in the neighborhood of Cumberland Sound and the St. Mary's River, including Fernandina and Fort Clinch, St. Mary's, and Cumberland Island. Subsidiary expeditions were sent out from this new base, and St. Augustine and Jacksonville to the south, and Brunswick and St. Simon's Island to the north, also came into the possession of the Union forces.

The remainder of the year 1862, after the fall of Fort Pulaski [see Vol. II., p. 1], was passed by Du Pont's squadron in maintaining the blockade and in strengthening the extended line of maritime occupation, which now reached from Georgetown, in South Carolina, to Mosquito Inlet, in Florida. Small encounters were frequent, and important captures of blockade-runners were made from time to time, but nothing occurred in the nature of a sustained offensive movement. A boat reconnoissance in April from the *Penguin* and *Henry Andrew*, at Mosquito Inlet, resulted in the capture of the party and the death of Budd and Mather, the commanding officers of the two ships. A small flotilla occupied the St. John's River, and was constantly engaged in conflicts with guerrillas on the banks of the stream and its tributaries. In one of these encounters Lieutenant John G. Sproston, of the *Seneca*, an officer of high reputation for gallantry, was killed. The yacht *America*, the famous winner of the Queen's Cup, was found sunk in one of the neighboring creeks and was recovered. In the North and South Edisto Lieutenant Rhind was actively occupied, and on April 29th, in the *E. B. Hale*, he captured and destroyed a battery. On the 13th of May the Confederate army steamer *Planter* was brought out of Charleston Harbor, in broad daylight, by the colored pilot Robert Smalls, and delivered to the blockading squadron. A week later, the *Albatross* and *Norwich*, under Commander Prentiss, steamed up to Georgetown, S. C., and, finding the works deserted, passed along the city wharves. No attack was made on the vessels; but Prentiss did not land, as he had no force of troops to hold the city. Toward the end of the same month Commander Drayton, in consequence of information given by the pilot Smalls, ascended the Stono River with a force of gun-boats, occasionally engaging the enemy.

In September, 1862, the Confederates in Florida attempted to regain possession of the St. John's River, and for this purpose constructed a fort at St. John's Bluff, arming it with heavy rifles. Commander Steedman, of the *Paul Jones*, then in command in the St. John's, supported by a force of troops under General John M. Brannan,[attacked and captured the battery on the 5th of October. The expedition then made a demonstration two hundred

[Later a division commander in the Army of the Cumberland, to which he was transferred in April, 1863.— EDITORS.

miles up the river. Later in the year a combined expedition, also under Steedman and Brannan, made an unsuccessful attempt to destroy the bridge over the Pocotaligo River in South Carolina.

The first month of the year 1863 witnessed two serious disasters in the South Atlantic squadron. Toward the close of the month the force in Stono Inlet was composed of the *Commodore McDonough*, Lieutenant-Commander George Bacon, and the *Isaac Smith*, Acting-Lieutenant F. S. Conover. On the afternoon of the 30th Bacon sent the *Smith* up the Stono River to Legareville on a reconnoissance. Notwithstanding the vigilance of the lookouts, the *Smith* passed, without observing them, three batteries which the enemy had planted under a thick cover of trees at a bend in the river. The *Smith* was lying at anchor six hundred yards above the highest battery when it suddenly opened fire. The gun-boat replied, and Conover, seeing that he was caught in a trap, attempted to run down past the batteries, but upon reaching a point at the center of the enemy's concentrated fire, his vessel received a shot in the steam-chimney which disabled the engine. As there was neither wind nor tide to help him, Conover surrendered, after losing 8 killed and 17 wounded. The impossibility of bringing off the wounded prevented him from destroying the vessel. Upon hearing the firing, Bacon moved up the river in the *Commodore McDonough* to assist his consort, but when he arrived she had already surrendered, and he was compelled to withdraw to avoid a similar fate.

On the following day, the 31st, a second disaster overtook the squadron. Before daybreak on this date the force blockading Charleston was attacked by two Confederate iron-clad rams, the *Palmetto State* and *Chicora*, commanded by Flag-Officer D. N. Ingraham. The blockading vessels included the sloop-of-war *Housatonic*, the gun-boats *Unadilla* and *Ottawa*, and seven altered merchant vessels, of which the principal ones were the *Mercedita*, *Augusta*, *Keystone State*, *Memphis*, and *Quaker City*, none of which was fitted to engage a ship-of-war, even an unarmored one. The night was dark and thick, the blockading line was strung out over several miles, with long intervals between the vessels, and the arrangements for signaling were imperfect.

The first attack was made on the *Mercedita* by the *Palmetto State*. Approaching under cover of the darkness, the assailant was not observed until she was close aboard, and the guns could not be depressed sufficiently to reach her. At the moment of being hailed she fired her heavy rifle, and the shell passed through the *Mercedita's* condenser and steam-drum, exploding on the opposite side of the vessel. Stellwagen, the commander, finding his ship disabled, surrendered, and in response to a demand from the ram the first lieutenant, Abbott, was sent in a boat to her and gave a parole for the officers and crew.

The *Palmetto State* now joined the *Chicora*, which had already attacked the *Keystone State*, Commander Le Roy. The latter vessel, having been set on fire by the explosion of a shell in her hold,

withdrew to extinguish the flames, but, returning presently, renewed the contest, looking for an opportunity to ram one of the Confederates. Her fire produced no impression on the rams, but, after a short struggle, she received a shot in both steam-drums which filled the ship forward with steam and rendered the engine useless. At the same time the ship was filling rapidly from the shot-holes already opened in her side, and Le Roy hauled down his flag and prepared to abandon her. No notice being taken of the surrender, Le Roy presently hoisted his colors again, and gradually withdrew from the scene of action.

Of the other ships, the *Memphis*, *Quaker City*, and *Augusta* took but slight part in the engagement, and the two latter only toward the end. In close action they would have run the risk of being disabled in the same manner as their consorts. The *Housatonic*, the largest vessel present, was at the other end of the blockading line, and, under the supposition that the firing was caused by blockade-runners, was not aware until daybreak of the necessity for her presence. By this time the rams had discontinued their attack and were returning to Charleston. The *Housatonic* exchanged shots with them at long range, but without inflicting material injury. A proclamation was issued on the same afternoon by General Beauregard and Flag-Officer Ingraham to the effect that the blockade was raised, and that the rams had sunk, dispersed, or driven off or out of sight the blockading fleet. Counter-statements were made by the captains of the squadron, showing that there had been no cessation of the blockade.

The attack of the rams disclosed the necessity of a more powerful squadron on the Charleston blockade, and the Navy Department had already taken steps to this end, having also in contemplation an active offensive movement against Charleston. ✠ The great broadside iron-clad *New Ironsides* had already arrived at Port Royal, and during January and February several monitors joined the station. The original *Monitor*, sent down for the same purpose at the close of December, had foundered off Hatteras, as already related. [See Vol. I., p. 745.] The *Montauk* and *Passaic* had reached their destination safely, and they were followed by the *Patapsco*, *Nahant*, *Weehawken*, *Catskill*, and *Nantucket*, and by the experimental iron-clad *Keokuk*.

In view of the contemplated movement, Du Pont desired to give the monitors a preliminary trial, and for this purpose the *Montauk*, Commander John L. Worden, was sent to attack Fort McAllister, on the Great Ogeechee River. A line of obstructions had been placed in the river opposite the fort. The first attack was made January 27th, 1863. The enemy's range-marks having been removed by a party in boats, under Lieutenant-Commander Davis, the *Montauk* steamed up to a position 150 yards below the obstructions and came to anchor, her attendant gun-boats, the *Seneca*, *Wissahickon*, *Dawn*, and *Williams*, anchoring a mile astern of her. The bombardment continued for four hours, until all the *Montauk's* shells had been expended. Lying thus close under the fire of the fort, the

✠ The history of the projected attack on Charleston is given by Admiral C. R. P. Rodgers in a following article.

THE MONITOR "MONTAUK" DESTROYING THE CONFEDERATE PRIVATEER "NASHVILLE," NEAR FORT
MᶜALLISTER, OGEECHEE RIVER, GEORGIA, FEBRUARY 28, 1863.

monitor was repeatedly hit, and nearly all the enemy's shot that did not hit came within a few feet of her. She was entirely uninjured. On the other hand, it was not apparent that any serious damage had been done to the fort, though its fire gradually slackened. The attack was renewed on the 1st of February, but at a greater distance, owing to the state of the tide. The monitor's shells appeared to do good execution in tearing up the parapets, but the Confederates, by constantly moving their guns, thwarted Worden's attempts to disable them. The *Montauk* was struck by heavy projectiles forty-six times, but still remained uninjured.

At the time of these attacks, the Confederate steamer *Nashville*, which had already done considerable service as a cruiser and as a blockade-runner, was lying in the Ogeechee waiting for an opportunity to run out. The prospect of her escaping and attacking the commerce of the United States gave the Government no little uneasiness. She had been sighted from time to time at her anchorage above the obstructions, but these protected her from capture, and upon the approach of the *Montauk* she always fled out of range. Her movements were closely watched, however, and late on the 27th of February Worden discovered that she had run aground a short distance above the barrier. Waiting until the next morning (28th), in order that he might have daylight for the work, Worden steamed up as close to the barrier as he thought it safe to go. From this point,

directly under a hot fire from the fort, to which he made no reply, he attacked the *Nashville*. Only her upper works were visible across the intervening neck of land. Obtaining the range accurately, Worden opened upon her with his two guns, the 11-inch and the 15-inch, and the exploding shells soon set her on fire. After a short time a fog shut out the Confederate vessel from view, but the *Montauk* continued firing at intervals, according to the elevation and direction that had been already ascertained. When the fog lifted, the *Nashville* was discovered to be in flames, and just an hour after the beginning of the engagement her destruction was completed by the explosion of her magazine. The artillerymen in the fort did not fire with their usual accuracy, for the *Montauk* was struck only five times. In descending the river subsequently, she ran upon and exploded a torpedo which blew a hole in her bottom, and she was beached in the mud. Some days later, she was repaired and her efficiency was completely restored.

On the 30th of March a more protracted attack was made on the fort by the monitors *Passaic*, *Patapsco*, and *Nahant*, under Commander Drayton. The bombardment lasted eight hours, but, as Drayton said in his report, "no injury was done which a good night's work would not repair."

After Drayton's bombardment, all attempts on Fort McAllister were abandoned, and the efforts of the squadron were directed wholly to the attack on Charleston.

The only event of importance during the remainder of Du Pont's command was the capture of the Confederate iron-clad *Atlanta*. This vessel, formerly known as the *Fingal*, an English blockade-runner, had been converted at Savannah into an armored ram of the *Merrimac* type, armed with six heavy Brooke rifles and a spar-torpedo, and placed under the command of Commander William A. Webb. She was met on the 17th of June, in Wassaw Sound, by the monitors *Weehawken*, Captain John Rodgers, and *Nahant*, Commander John Downes. The *Weehawken* engaged her, firing five shots, of which four struck the *Atlanta*. The injury inflicted by these was enough to show that a protracted action would end in the demolition of the Confederate vessel, and she accordingly surrendered. She was towed to Port Royal, where the damages received were readily repaired.

THE EARLY MONITORS.

BY CAPTAIN JOHN ERICSSON.

IMPREGNABILITY, proved by capability to keep out Confederate shot, being demanded by President Lincoln and promised by the constructor of the monitor fleet which was built during the early part of 1862, it will be proper to inquire how far the performance accorded with the anticipation. Admiral Dahlgren, the distinguished naval artillerist, commanding the blockading fleet at Charleston,

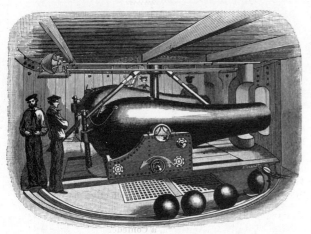

INTERIOR VIEW OF THE TURRET OF A SEA-GOING MONITOR.

The compact form of the gun-carriages, the simplicity of the massive port-stoppers, and the enormous size of the spherical projectiles (15-inch diameter) were surprises to naval experts.—J. E.

reported to the Navy Department that from July 18th to September 8th, 1863, a period of 52 days, the monitors *Weehawken, Patapsco, Montauk, Nahant, Catskill*, and *Passaic* engaged Forts Sumter, Moultrie, Wagner, Gregg, and the batteries on Morris and Sullivan's islands, on an average ten times each, the *Montauk* going before the muzzles of the enemy's guns fifteen times during the stated period, while the *Patapsco* was engaged thirteen times and the *Weehawken* twelve times. The number of hits received by the six vessels mentioned amounted to 629; yet not a single penetration of side armor, turret, or pilot-house took place. Admiral Dahlgren observes that the *Montauk* was struck 154 times during the engagements referred to, "almost entirely," he states, "by 10-inch shot." Considering that the hull of the *Montauk* was nearly submerged, and hence presented a very small tar-

get, the recorded number of hits marked splendid practice on the part of the Confederate gunners. The report of the experienced commander concludes thus: "What vessels have ever been subjected to such a test?" It merits special notice that the same monitors which Admiral Dahlgren found to possess such remarkable power of endurance had led the unsuccessful attack at Charleston three months before,—a circumstance which shows that difficulties presented themselves during that attack which had not been foreseen, or the magnitude of which had not been properly estimated. The following facts rebut the allegation that injudicious advice to certain officers induced the Navy Department to adopt hazardous expedients in connection with the attack on Charleston. A letter from the Assistant-Secretary of the Navy to me in reference to the contemplated attack, written before the news of its failure had been received, contained the following sentence:

"Though everybody is despondent about Charleston, and even the President thinks we shall be defeated, I must say that I have never had a shadow of a doubt as to our success, and this confidence arises from careful study of your marvelous vessels."

To this letter I sent the following reply the next day:

"I confess that I cannot share in your confidence relative to the capture of Charleston. I am so much in the habit of estimating force and resistance that I cannot feel sanguine of success. If you succeed, it will not be a mechanical consequence of your 'marvelous vessels,' but because you are marvelously fortunate. The most I dare hope is, that the contest will end without the loss of that prestige which your iron-clads have conferred on the nation abroad. A single shot may sink a ship, while a hundred rounds cannot silence a fort, as you have proved on the Ogeechee. The immutable laws of force and resistance do not favor your enterprise. Chance, therefore, can alone save you."

The discomfiture of the "marvelous" vessels before Charleston, however, did not impair their fitness to fight other battles. It will be recollected that the *Weehawken*, commanded by the late Admiral John Rodgers, defeated and captured the Confederate ram *Atlanta*, in Wassaw Sound, June 17th, 1863, ten weeks *after* the battle of Charleston, consequently *previous* to the engagements in

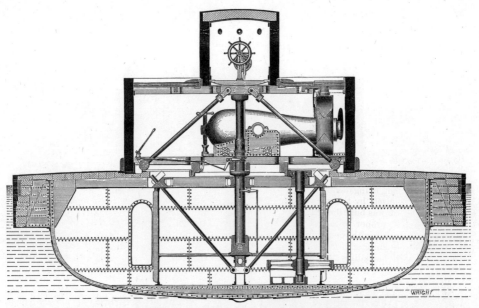

SECTION OF THE HULL OF A SEA-GOING MONITOR.

The cut represents a transverse section through the center-line of the turret and pilot-house of the *Montauk* and other sea-going vessels of the monitor type. For an account, of the original *Monitor*, see Vol. I., p. 730.

which this monitor participated, as reported by Admiral Dahlgren. The splendid victory in Wassaw Sound did not attract much attention in the United States, while in the European maritime countries it was looked upon as an event of the highest importance, since it established the fact, practically, that armor-plating of the same thickness as that of *La Gloire* and the *Warrior* could be readily pierced, even when placed at an inclination of only twenty-nine degrees to the horizon. Moreover, the shot from the *Weehawken* struck at an angle of fifty degrees to the line of keel, thereby generating a compound angle, causing the line of the shot to approach the face of the armor-plate within twenty-two degrees. The great amount of iron and wood dislodged by the 15-inch spherical shot entering the citadel, protected by 4-inch armor-plating and 18-inch wood backing, was shown by the fact that forty men on the *Atlanta's* gun-deck were prostrated by the concussion, fifteen being wounded, principally by splinters, a circumstance readily explained, since penetration at an angle of twenty-two degrees means that, independent of deflection, the shot must pass through nearly five feet of obstruction,—namely, eleven inches of iron and four feet of wood. Rodgers's victory in Wassaw Sound, therefore, proved that the 4½-inch vertical plating of the magnificent *Warrior* of nine thousand tons—the pride of the British Admiralty—would be but slight protection against the 15-inch monitor guns.

The destruction of the Confederate privateer *Nashville* by the *Montauk*, February 28th, 1863, also calls for a brief notice. The expedient by which this well-appointed privateer was destroyed, just on the eve of commencing a series of depreda-

tions in imitation of the *Alabama*, must be regarded as a feat which has no parallel in naval annals. The commander of the *Montauk*, now Rear-Admiral Worden, having received stringent orders to prevent the *Nashville* from going to sea, devised a plan for destroying the privateer (then occupying a safe position beyond the torpedo obstruction on the Ogeechee River), by means of the 15-inch shells which formed part of his equipment; but in order to get near enough for effective shelling, he was compelled to take up a position under the guns of Fort McAllister, then commanded by Captain G. W. Anderson, a Confederate officer of distinguished ability. Obviously, the success of the daring plan of not returning the concentrated flanking fire from the fort while shelling the privateer depended on the power of endurance of the *Montauk*, then for the first time subjected to such a crucial test. The result proved that Worden had not over-estimated the resisting power of his vessel. The fifth shell had scarcely reached its destination when signs of serious damage on board the privateer were observed; a few additional shells being dispatched, a volume of black smoke was seen rising above the doomed *Nashville*. The shelling was continued for a short time, with the result that the entire hull of the intended depredator was enveloped in flames. The magazine ultimately exploded with terrific violence, tearing part of the structure into fragments. The gunners in the fort had in the meantime continued to practice against the *Montauk*; but no serious damage having been inflicted, the anchor was raised and the victor dropped down the river, cheered by the crews of the blockading fleet.

THE MONITOR "MONTAUK" BEACHED FOR REPAIRS.

DU PONT'S ATTACK AT CHARLESTON.

BY C. R. P. RODGERS, REAR-ADMIRAL, U. S. N.,—DURING THE ATTACK CHIEF-OF-STAFF.

AS Boston was regarded as the cradle of American liberty, where the infancy of the Union was nurtured, so Charleston, in later days, came to be considered the nursery of disunion. Therefore, during our civil war, no city in the South was so obnoxious to Union men as Charleston. Richmond was the objective point of our armies, as its capture was expected to end the war, but it excited little sentiment and little antipathy. It was to South Carolina, and especially to Charleston, that the strong feeling of dislike was directed, and the desire was general to punish that city by all the rigors of war.

Charleston too, in spite of an energetic blockade, conducted with great hardihood and patience, was one of the two chief points through which munitions of war and other supplies from Europe found entrance to the Confederate States. Naturally, then, the Government of the Union looked longingly for its capture, to give fresh hope and much-needed encouragement to the North, and to strike a heavy blow at the rebellion.

The most dramatic conflict between the *Monitor* and the *Merrimac*, with its incidents and consequences, gave to the Navy Department the hope that its turret vessels might do what unarmored ships could not attempt. Mr. Fox, the Assistant Secretary of the Navy, a skillful and well-tried naval officer, a man of much ability and energy, pushed the new monitors forward with his whole power, having formed the highest opinion of their irresistible force and invulnerability. The first monitor had done so much, had saved such great interests in a moment of supreme peril, that Mr. Fox's strong imagination led him to hopes that were not destined to be fully realized. To carry them into execution he now addressed himself with his usual vigor; the preparation of the armored ships for the attack on Charleston was hastened, their commanders were selected by Mr. Fox himself, who knew the navy well, and he chose the best commanding officers in it who were available for the great work he had so much at heart. Percival Drayton, John Rodgers, Worden, Ammen, George Rodgers, Fairfax, Downes, and Rhind were chosen for the turret ships, and Commodore Thomas Turner for the *Ironsides*. It would have been difficult to find in the navy men of higher reputation for skill and courage, of better nerve, or more fully possessing the confidence of the service. As fast as their ships were ready, they were hurried to Port Royal, where they found in command Rear-Admiral Du Pont, who, by his skillful capture of Port Royal and his vigorous repossession of the coast of South Carolina, Georgia, and Florida, had won the thanks of Congress and the complete confidence of the Navy Department. He had not only its confidence, but also to an extraordinary degree that of the commanding officers under him. Few commanders-in-chief have had the good fortune to inspire the same admiration, affection, and trust that the officers who came in contact with Admiral Du Pont felt for him.

The *Montauk*, Captain John L. Worden, was the first monitor to arrive, and as months would pass before all the others could be expected, Admiral Du Pont, on the 1st of February, 1863, sent that officer in the *Montauk*, supported by the gun-boats *Wissahickon*, Lieutenant-Commander John Lee Davis; the *Seneca*, Lieutenant-Commander William Gibson; and the *Dawn*, Lieutenant-Commander John S. Barnes, to try her powers against the earth-works of Fort McAllister, on the Ogeechee River, behind which the Confederate steamer *Nashville* was waiting for an opportunity to sail, on a cruise of pillage and destruction, against our ships of commerce upon the high seas.

On the 28th of February, 1863, Captain Worden was so fortunate as to find the *Nashville*, aground, near Fort McAllister, and to approach within twelve hundred yards of her. He was able to set her on fire and destroy her with his shells, while he patiently endured the fire of the batteries, giving his whole attention to the cruiser. The so-called *Alabama* claims were much diminished by this episode of Worden's, characterized by his usual skill and judgment. The *Montauk*, in retiring from the fort, was injured by a torpedo and compelled to run upon a bank to repair damages, her pumps keeping her afloat with difficulty. The injury was at once repaired, temporarily, and more permanently upon her return to Port Royal.

Still desirous to measure the iron-clads against forts on obstructed channels, Admiral Du Pont sent Captain Drayton with the *Passaic*, accompanied by the *Patapsco*, Commander Ammen, and the *Nahant*, Commander Downes, to try the batteries of these three monitors against Fort McAllister; with them were three gun-boats and three mortar-schooners. The result of this attack by the monitors, conducted by one of his ablest officers, led Admiral Du Pont to say to the Navy Department that "whatever degree of impenetrability they might have, there was no corresponding quality of destructiveness as against forts."

The two operations left the admiral impressed with the great value of the resisting power of the monitors, but revealed some of their points of weakness, and satisfied him that their power had been overrated by the Navy Department, and that he should need as many of them as the department could give him to take Charleston. He fully appreciated the great desire of the Government to repossess that city, and he addressed himself earnestly and loyally to carry out his Government's wish. He expressed no doubts even to his most confidential officers, and did his best with the means supplied. The Assistant Secretary had written to him repeatedly that such vessels could steam into Charleston harbor and come out unharmed, that even the original monitor could do so; to use his own words, "can go all over the harbor and return with impunity. She is absolutely impregnable." His sanguine temperament had led him to imaginations that were not destined to be fulfilled; for even after Admiral Du Pont's brave and ambitious successor, Admiral Dahlgren, the foremost gunnery officer of the navy, had secured a greater number of monitors, and after the army had taken Battery Wagner by regular approaches, had captured all the batteries on Morris Island, and had reduced Fort Sumter to a heap of ruins, no monitor ever ventured to pass into the harbor and attempt to take Charleston by the purely naval attack which Admiral Du Pont had declared impracticable.

It had always been the opinion of Admiral Du Pont that the attack on Charleston should be a combined effort by the army and the navy, and when he visited Washington, in the fall of 1862, he stated to the Navy Department

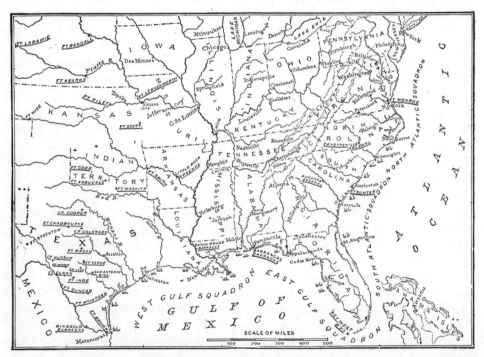

MAP OF THE BLOCKADE OF CONFEDERATE PORTS.

that at least twenty-five thousand troops should attack from James Island, while the fleet attacked the harbor. No such force could be spared.

Assistant Secretary Fox, the executive officer of the Navy Department, patriotic, fertile of resource, full of zeal, resolute, and always able, rendered great service to the Union in creating so rapidly the new navy that did such good work in crushing the great rebellion; for this the country owes him a lasting debt. He now did his best to strengthen Admiral Du Pont's squadron, and in March, 1863, the *Catskill*, the last available iron-clad, reached Port Royal. The others had been somewhat strengthened and improved by the light of the Ogeechee experience, and the naval force was ready for the attack. The monitors assembled at North Edisto, and on the 6th of April crossed the Charleston bar and anchored off Morris Island; for after crossing, the weather had become so hazy that the pilots could not see the landmarks to direct their course, and the attack was necessarily deferred until the following day.

REAR-ADMIRAL C. R. P. RODGERS.
FROM A PHOTOGRAPH.

On the 7th at noon the signal was made to weigh anchor; it was the earliest hour at which the pilots would consent to move, owing to the state of the tide. The movement was still further delayed by the *Weehawken*, whose chain became entangled with one of the grapnels of the cumbrous torpedo raft devised by Mr. Ericsson, and it was a quarter-past one when the iron-clads left their anchorage, in the following order: the *Weehawken*, Captain John Rodgers; the *Passaic*, Captain Percival Drayton; the *Montauk*, Captain John L. Worden; *Patapsco*, Commander Daniel Ammen; *New Ironsides*, Commodore Thomas Turner; *Catskill*, Commander George W. Rodgers; *Nantucket*, Commander Donald M. Fairfax; *Nahant*, Commander John Downes; and *Keokuk*, Commander Alexander Rhind. The admiral had arranged to lead in the *Ironsides*, but, much against his will, after earnest persuasion from his captains, consented to occupy the center. As the fleet slowly passed near the beach of Morris Island, no shot was fired from ship or shore; Battery Wagner was also silent as it was passed; but as the leading monitor came within range of Fort Moultrie the Confederate and Palmetto flags were hoisted on the batteries, and a salute of thirteen guns was fired.

It was 3 o'clock when the first shot was fired from Moultrie and returned by the *Weehawken*. Then Sumter and Batteries Bee and Beauregard, Cumming's Point, and Wagner opened fire, and the action became general. The *Ironsides*, flat-bottomed and with greater draught than the monitors, found herself within one foot of the bottom, and under the influence of the current steered so badly that it became necessary to drop an anchor to bring her head to tide. The anchor was quickly raised, and she was again under way, but the delay threw the line into some unavoidable confusion, and two of the following monitors came in harmless collision with the flag-ship. They were directed to go on, disregarding the order of sailing, and the *Ironsides* quickly followed them; but when it was fifteen hundred yards or less from Sumter, the same difficulty in steering occurred, and the anchor was again dropped to prevent stranding and to bring the ship's head in the right direction. As the *Ironsides* swung to the tide into deeper water, she came directly over a huge torpedo, made from an old boiler, filled with gunpowder, and connected with Battery Wagner by an electric wire; but, fortunately for those on board, the electrician at Battery Wagner, to his great disgust, could not send the electric spark to the powder. The officers of the *Ironsides* were unaware of their danger until a letter from Mr. Cheves, the electrician in charge, to an officer on board the *Atlanta*, and captured in that vessel, revealed the fact, stating that had he himself been allowed to place the Yankee flag-ship, he could not have put her more precisely over his great torpedo. [See map, p. 3.]

In his order for the day, Admiral Du Pont had planned to deliver his first attack upon the north-west face of Sumter, passing inside the gorge of the harbor for that purpose, and lingering before the fort until he should have reduced it, or at least silenced its fire. The *Weehawken*, the leading monitor, pressing forward with this view, came to the floating obstructions between Sumter and Moultrie, and the probability of her screw being entangled and the vessel held immovable under a fire more deadly than any ship had ever before encountered led her commander to turn from the obstructions and begin the attack short of the place designated in the plan of battle. As he turned, a torpedo exploded under him, giving a shock but no serious injury to the monitor. In the whole navy there was no cooler, more gallant, more judicious man than John Rodgers. It was he who had fought the *Galena* so desperately under the fire at Drewry's Bluff, and continued the action until his ammunition was exhausted, his ship riddled, and his loss of men very severe. [See Vol. II., p. 270.] It was he to whom Secretary Welles wrote, June 25th, 1863:

" To your heroic daring and persistent moral courage, beyond that of any other individual, is the country indebted for the development, under trying and varied circumstances on the ocean, under enormous batteries on land, and in successful rencontre with a formidable floating antagonist, of the capabilities and qualities of attack and resistance of the monitor class of vessels and their heavy armament."

No officer in the navy was better qualified to command its confidence when he decided not to attempt to force the obstructions. He was followed by Percival Drayton, Farragut's trusted and well-tried chief-of-staff, by John Worden, of monitor fame, and by that grim, true-hearted, fighting man, Daniel Ammen. These, all turning short of the obstructions, threw the vessels following into some confusion, and caused the *Ironsides* to lose her steerage-way and to anchor as already mentioned.

While the anchor was being lifted to move forward, Admiral Du Pont turned to his chief-of-staff and asked the time. Upon being told that it was nearly 5 o'clock he quietly said, "Make signal to the ships to drop out of fire; it is too late to fight this battle to-night; we will renew it early in the morning." At that time he had not the slightest thought of abandoning the attack; no such idea had occurred to him or to any of his staff who were with him. He had chosen the north-west face of Sumter as his point of attack, because after careful study he found it the point where his ships would be least exposed to the enemy's fire from the surrounding batteries. The north-east face was struck, as was afterward learned, fifteen times, the attacking vessels never having reached the position chosen by the admiral; the east pan-coupé five times, the east face thirty-one times. Very few shots were aimed at Moultrie. Admiral Du Pont did not wish the *Ironsides* to fire until very close to Sumter, and her fire was accordingly withheld; but after he had made the signal to retire for the night, he was asked to permit the men to try their guns, and with his habitual consideration for the feelings and wishes of those under his command, he allowed them to fire one broadside, eight guns, at Moultrie. This caused the enemy to open a heavy fire on the flag-ship, and as it was coincident with her retirement, it was supposed at Fort Moultrie to have injured her and caused her withdrawal.

The day on which this engagement took place was very beautiful; there was little wind and the sea was smooth. When the Confederate guns of 10-inch, 9-inch, 8-inch Columbiads and 7-inch Brooke rifles, with many other rifled and smooth-bore guns, were turned upon the iron-clads, the sight was one that no one who witnessed it will ever forget; sublime, infernal, it seemed as if the fires of hell were turned upon the Union fleet. The air seemed full of heavy shot, and as they flew they could be seen as plainly as a base-ball in one of our games. On board the *Ironsides*, the sense of security the iron walls gave those within them was wonderful—a feeling akin to that which one experiences in a heavy storm when the wind and hail beat harmlessly against the windows of a well-protected house. This, however, was not equally felt in the monitors; for in their turrets the nuts that secured their laminated plates flew wildly, to the injury and discomfiture of the men at the guns, while the solid plates of the *Ironsides* gave no such trouble; and although she was reported to have been struck ninety-five times, she was uninjured except by the loss of a port shutter and the piercing of her unarmored ends. In fact the *Ironsides* may be considered to have taken no active part in the attack, for she fired no shot except as she passed out of action, although she fairly tested her endurance.

As the *Ironsides* lifted her anchor to drop down to the anchorage for the night, the admiral meaning to close with the enemy and force his way into the harbor the next morning, the other vessels, retiring from closer action in obedience to his signal, came near, some of them within hail. The first was the *Keokuk* [see p. 11], riddled like a colander, the most severely mauled ship one ever saw, and on her deck the daring and able Rhind, than whom no braver man ever commanded a ship, and who came limping forward, wounded,

"NEW IRONSIDES."   "KEOKUK."

BOMBARDMENT OF FORT SUMTER AND ADJACENT FORTS BY THE UNION FLEET, APRIL 7, 1863.
The monitors engaged were the *Weehawken, Passaic, Montauk, Catskill, Nahant, Patapsco,* and *Nantucket.*

to tell in a few emphatic words that his ship was disabled. Then followed two or three of the monitors, their captains telling the story of disabled guns or crippled turrets. The others reported by signal. Orders were at once given to the mechanics of the squadron to work all night in repairing damages, and after dark the commanding officers, having made their ships secure, came on board the flag-ship to report in person. They assembled in the large cabin of the *Ironsides* and sat at the table where the admiral had already taken his seat. Each captain then told the story of his ship, its action and its condition, and when they had done, Admiral Du Pont went to his state-room and, having already given his orders to his staff, he was seen no more that night.

The approaching darkness, and the difficulties presented by the outer obstructions in the channel, had decided Admiral Du Pont to defer the attempt to reach the city or pass inside Sumter until the following morning should give him a long day for such serious work. Before the morning came, he had learned the crippled condition of his iron-clad ships, and had become convinced that the force given him could not accomplish the end desired. His effort, therefore, on the evening of the 7th of April, may be looked upon as a reconnoissance in force, showing that the plan he had formed for the capture of Charleston was impracticable.

During the war there had been instances of similar reconnoissances by land, where deference to the public clamor for action at any cost had produced hopeless but very bloody and disastrous battles; and perhaps the public mind had been more sympathetically thrilled by them and better satisfied than if those in command had been guided by wiser and more prudent conclusions, and had spared the lives of their men, hopelessly hurled against insurmountable barriers. Admiral Du Pont never showed greater courage or patriotism than when he saved his ships and men, and sacrificed himself to the clamor and disappointment evoked by his defeat.

In the brief engagement of the 7th of April, the *Keokuk*, the iron-clad that was nearest to Sumter, was struck ninety times; nineteen shots pierced her armor at or below the water-line; both her turrets were pierced in many places; the forward gun was disabled early in the contest, and the vessel was with great difficulty kept afloat until the next morning, when she fell over on her side and sank at the lower anchorage. No ship was ever more gallantly fought or better handled. The *Weehawken* was struck fifty-three times; her deck was pierced so that the water ran through it; her side armor was in one place so shattered by repeated blows that it only remained in splintered fragments which could be picked off by hand, and at one time the turret revolved with difficulty, owing to heavy blows. The *Passaic* was struck thirty-five times. Early in the action, shot striking the turret disabled the 11-inch gun, rendering it useless for the remainder of the engagement. Soon after, the turret was found to be jammed, and for a time immovable, but this injury was so far repaired that it could be revolved, although for a time irregularly. In his report, Captain Drayton says, " A little after, a very heavy rifle-shot struck the upper edge of the turret, broke all its eleven plates, and then, glancing upward, took the pilot-house, yet with such force as to make an indentation of two and a half inches, extending nearly the whole length of the shot. The blow was so severe as to considerably mash in the pilot-house, bend it over, open the plates, squeeze out the top, so that on one side it was lifted up three inches above the top on which it rested, exposing the inside of the pilot-house and rendering it likely that the next shot would take off the top itself entirely."

The *Montauk* was struck fourteen times but was not materially injured. The *Patapsco*, the fourth vessel in the line, was struck forty-seven times, and her 150-pounder rifle was disabled at its fifth discharge and could not be used again during the action, and that monitor was able to fire only five shots from each of its two heavy guns. The *Catskill* was struck twenty times, but was in no point disabled. The *Nantucket* was struck fifty-one times, and its 15-inch gun was disabled after its third discharge, by shots received on its port-stopper and turret, driving in the plating, and rendering the gun useless for the rest of the day. The turret was jammed for a time, so that it would not turn; the deck was much cut, and the side plates so much injured in one part that, in the opinion of the reporting officer, another blow in that quarter would have knocked them off. The *Nahant* was struck thirty-six times and was badly mauled. The turret was jammed by the blows of heavy shot so that it was disabled and could no more be revolved during the day. A piece of iron weighing seventy-eight pounds was broken from the pilot-house and thrown across it, deranging the steering gear, killing the quartermaster at the helm, striking down the pilot, and leaving the commander alone in the pilot-house. The vessel was entirely disabled and was compelled to drop out of action, as were the *Passaic* and *Keokuk* also, before the signal to retire

REAR-ADMIRAL D. M. FAIRFAX. FROM A PHOTOGRAPH.

was made. These statements are taken from the official reports of the commanders of the vessels engaged, which give much more elaborate and striking statements of the injuries received; they are significant of what would have happened in a prolonged conflict.

The Confederate officers, in preparing for the defense, had moored buoys at proper places to give them accurate ranges, and as the Union ships came in line with these buoys, the forts fired by batteries with perfect precision and tremendous effect. Each ship was only about forty-five minutes under the heavy fire, and they encountered only the outer line of defense, but their battered armor, their crippled turrets, and their disabled guns proved the power of the forts and the coolness and skill of the Southern gunners.

At daylight, when the chief-of-staff went on deck, he found the admiral already there, who said to him, with his usual straightforward frankness, " I have given careful thought during the night to all the bearings of this matter, and have come to a positive determination from which I shall not swerve. I ask no one's opinion, for it could not change mine. I have decided not to renew the attack. During the few minutes we were under the heaviest fire of the batteries we engaged, half of our turret-ships were in part or wholly disabled. We have only encountered the outer line of defense, and if we force our way into the harbor we have not men to occupy any forts we may take, and we can have no communication with our force outside except by running the gauntlet. In the end we shall retire, leaving some of our iron-clads in the hands of the enemy, to be refitted and turned against our blockade with deplorable effect. We have met with a sad repulse; I shall not turn it into a great disaster."

Grieved as was his listener by the thought of losing a success which had been looked forward to with great hope, he was compelled to admit that the reasoning and the conclusion were sound and wise. And so it was announced to the fleet and to the army that the attack would not be renewed. The monitor *Patapsco* was sent at once to Port Royal to make that place secure, and the other monitors were ordered to be ready to sail as soon as the *Ironsides* could cross the bar.

As the morning passed the captains of the iron-clads came on board the flag-ship in a body to pay their respects to the admiral. He asked for no expression of their opinion, but they took occasion to assert it frankly and fully, and all concurred in the belief that it would be useless and unwise to renew the attack with the existing force. This unasked opinion was, of course, gratifying to Admiral Du Pont. It came from men of recognized judgment and experience, and they never flinched from it in later days when they might have won favor in high places had they wavered in their disinterested allegiance to their old leader. The iron-clad captains stood like a wall of iron about Admiral Du Pont's reputation, and there was no joint to be pierced in their armor.

While still at anchor inside the bar, and near Morris Island, Admiral Du Pont received the following order, brought with all speed by Colonel John Hay, the President's private secretary, and delivered on the 8th of April, the day after the battle:

"(Confidential.)   Navy Department, April 2d, 1863.

"Sir: The exigencies of the public service are so pressing in the Gulf that the Department directs you to send all the iron-clads that are in a fit condition to move, after your present attack upon Charleston, directly to New Orleans, reserving to yourself only two. Very respect-fully,   Gideon Welles."

There came also at the same time this informal letter from the Assistant Secretary of the Navy:

"Navy Department, April 2d, 1863.

"Dear Admiral: Matters are at a standstill on the Mississippi River, and the President was with difficulty restrained from sending off Hunter and all the iron-clads directly to New Orleans, the opening of the Mississippi being considered the principal object to be attained. It is, however, arranged, as you will see by to-day's order, that you are to send all the iron-clads that survive the attack upon Charleston immediately to New Orleans, reserving for your squad-ron only two. We must abandon all other operations on the coast, where iron-clads are neces-sary, to a future time. We cannot clear the Mississippi River without the iron-clads, and as all the supplies come down the Red River, that stretch of the river must be in our possession. This plan has been agreed upon after mature consideration and seems to be imperative.

"With my sincere prayers in your behalf, my dear Admiral, I remain, sincerely, yours,

"G. V. Fox.

"Rear-Admiral S. F. Du Pont, Commanding South Atlantic Blockading Squadron, Port Royal."

These communications made it still more necessary to get the monitors ready for service with the least possible delay, and on the 11th, there being a sufficient depth of water, the *Ironsides* and the monitors crossed the bar: the former resuming her station on the blockade, the latter returning to the workshops at Port Royal. Late at night on the 8th of April, after Admiral Du Pont had received the letters just quoted, General Hunter sent his chief-of-staff and his chief-of-engineers to propose to the admiral that the army should land on Morris Island and occupy it, supported by the naval force. Admiral Du Pont showed these officers the order he had received from the Navy Department, and declined the proposition they brought him. After leaving the admiral's cabin, these distinguished staff-officers sought the naval chief-of-staff and wished him to urge their proposal. He again showed them the order from the Navy Department directing the transfer of the iron-clads to the Mississippi, and asked them if any right-minded officer in his position, in the face of such an order, could urge his chief to do what they proposed. The chief-of-engineers, Colonel Duane, replying, frankly admitted he could not.

THE MONITOR "WEEHAWKEN" CAPTURING THE CONFEDERATE IRON-CLAD RAM "ATLANTA" (FORMERLY
THE BLOCKADE-RUNNER "FINGAL"), WASSAW SOUND, GEORGIA, JUNE 17, 1863.

Before leaving Port Royal, General Hunter had constantly insisted that with his force he could do nothing until the navy should put him in possession of Morris Island by the capture of its batteries. At that time [Spring, 1863] it was known that thirty thousand or more troops were at Charleston and its immediate neighborhood. These, by interior lines covered by strong defenses, were in easy communication with Morris Island. The island itself had at its north end the Cumming's Point battery, and it was completely crossed from sea to marsh by Battery Wagner, that strong work which the army attempted to carry by assault in July, and from which it was repulsed with great slaughter.

The inland side of Morris Island is in some measure protected from a naval fire by sand dunes and ridges forming in places a natural parapet; and when General Hunter, on the 8th of April, proposed to occupy that island, the Confederate troops, in force three times greater than his, passing to the island by their well-protected interior lines, might have overwhelmed the Union troops by their superior numbers, and have captured them, or driven them to their ships. In July, when General Gillmore, who on the 12th of June had succeeded General Hunter, executed his very skillful and well-arranged movement upon Morris Island, the thirty thousand troops who were present in April, and had witnessed Admiral Du Pont's attack and stood ready to oppose it, had been withdrawn from Charleston to distant fields of service. [See p. 13.] In fact, so small a force was left for its occupation as to create the gravest apprehension in the minds of its defenders, who were very anxious lest a night landing should be made at Sullivan's Island, for the defense of whose long line only about six hundred Confederate troops could be made available.

Upon the failure to carry Battery Wagner by assault, General Gillmore besieged it until it was at last taken by regular approaches, the enemy evacuating it and the whole island on the 7th of September, when our engineers had pushed their trenches up to its ditch. During all the operations against Wagner, Admiral Dahlgren [succeeded Du Pont, July 6th, 1863] gave the army his most vigorous support by the fire of his monitors and the *Ironsides*. On the 17th of August, in one of the many engagements with this fort, Commander George W. Rodgers, Admiral Dahlgren's chief-of-staff, was killed, while temporarily commanding the *Catskill*, the same monitor he had commanded under Admiral Du Pont in the action of the 7th of April. He had taken his ship very close to the enemy, resolved that no one should be closer than he, when a heavy shot struck the pilot-house and, breaking through its armor, instantly killed him and Paymaster Woodbury, who was standing by his side. Commander Rodgers was an officer of great courage and rare skill in his profession, a man of very pure and devout character.

Cumming's Point and Battery Wagner having been occupied by General Gillmore, that skillful officer turned his increased fire upon Sumter; the fleet battered it with heavy guns, and the fort became in appearance a heap of ruins. Its artillery fire ceased, but its garrison held the ruins with tenacious grasp; the attempt to occupy it by our forces was repulsed with heavy loss, and it remained in the possession of the rebels until General Sherman's march to the sea and through the Carolinas in February, 1865, placed him in the rear of Charleston and compelled the evacuation of that city and its defenses. This was nearly two years after Admiral Du Pont had declared it could not be taken by a purely naval attack, and had declined General Hunter's proposal to make Morris Island his base of operations. Admiral Du Pont believed that the troops should attack from James Island with at least double the force General Hunter could put in the field. Events proved the wisdom of this belief, but it brought the admiral professional mortification and great wrong. History abounds in examples of the anger and bitterness with which, under popular governments, ministries have been ready to sacrifice commanders who have not strengthened their administration by success in war. The great President was superior to such littleness; so much cannot be said for his Navy Department. Admiral Du Pont's failure to take Charleston with the means allotted for its capture occurred before General Grant's magnificent strategy and persistence had defeated the rebel armies in the field and taken Vicksburg, and before Meade and Hancock with the Army of the Potomac had broken the back of the rebellion at Gettysburg. It was of immense importance that some great feat of arms by land or by sea should cheer the supporters of the Union, strengthen our Government, and discourage the friends of our dismemberment on the other side of the ocean. Iron-clads and fast cruisers were being built in England and France for the so-called Confederate States, the French Emperor was seeking opportunity to declare against us, and the ruling class in England was too ready to join hands with him. The "plain people" of that country were steadfastly our friends, a fact we should never forget. The Navy Department had formed extravagant ideas of the power and invulnerability of what Mr. Fox called "these marvelous vessels," ideas not fully shared, while they were in their tentative and undeveloped state, by their great designer, as may be seen in his paper on the monitor class of vessels in "The Century" magazine for December, 1885. [See p. 31.]

On the 31st of January the Secretary of the Navy had sent the following hedging letter to Admiral Du Pont, a letter contradictory in its terms, but declaring that the necessity for the capture of Charleston had become imperative, and that the department would share the responsibility with commanders who made the attempt:

REAR-ADMIRAL DANIEL AMMEN.   FROM A PHOTOGRAPH.

"SIR: Your confidential dispatch, No. 36, dated the 14th instant, has been received.

"The department does not desire to urge an attack upon Charleston with inadequate means; and if, after careful examination, you deem the number of iron-clads insufficient to render the capture of that port reasonably certain, it must be abandoned. The department is not acquainted with the harbor obstructions constructed by the rebels, and therefore cannot advise with you in regard to those obstacles. If they are not considered sufficient to prevent your entrance, it is not believed possible for the rebels to prevent your success with all other means combined. The five iron-clads sent you are all the department has completed on the Atlantic coast, with the exception of one retained at Newport News to watch the iron-clad *Richmond*. ☆ No others are likely to be finished and sent to sea within the next six weeks. A large number of our best wooden vessels, necessary for the blockade, but not for the attack, are unfortunately required in the West Indies to pursue the *Florida* and *Alabama*. This withdrawal of blockading vessels renders the capture of Charleston and Mobile imperative, and the department will share the responsibility imposed upon the commanders who make the attempt. Inclosed is a copy of a memorandum furnished by the Secretary of War.   Very respectfully, GIDEON WELLES, Secretary of the Navy.

"REAR-ADMIRAL S. F. DU PONT, commanding South Atlantic Blockading Squadron, Port Royal, S. C."

It was impossible for an admiral to decline the responsibility which the Secretary offered to share, or to consider discretionary what the Secretary told him was imposed, or to abandon what the Secretary told him was imperative. On the 26th of March Assistant Secretary Fox wrote to Admiral Du Pont: "General Halleck told the President that you had serious doubts as to the capture of Charleston. In our department, where we know best your character and the skill and judgment you bring to bear upon the great undertaking, there does not exist a doubt of your complete success." Fox had always favored a purely naval attack, with the army looking on, as at Port Royal.

☆ The *Richmond* was built in 1862 with means raised by subscription, and was the first fully armored ship put afloat on James River by the Confederates. She remained in the James River Squadron to the end of the war.— EDITORS.

The attack was delivered as the Navy Department wished. That it was earnestly and loyally delivered, those accomplished and well-tried fighting men who commanded the iron-clads have established by their testimony. That Admiral Du Pont was right in his decision not to renew the attack, the events of the next two years conclusively proved. No ship of the navy entered the harbor of Charleston, even after Sumter was in ruins, its fire silenced, and the batteries of Morris Island in our possession. The harbor was a *cul-de-sac*, a circle of fire not to be passed. It was not the same problem so magnificently solved by the great sea king, Farragut. He passed the guns of his enemies, and having passed, his fleet was in a place of safety, whence he compelled surrender.

Admiral Dahlgren, an officer of great personal intrepidity, long our chief of ordnance, goaded by newspaper attacks, chafed under his inability to do what had been expected from him; but his judgment concurred with that of his predecessor, and he recognized the fact that his force could not take Charleston. The councils of war that he called on the 22d of October, 1863, and on the 12th of May, 1864, advised against the attempt, and it was never made. Since his death, we learn from his biography, written by his most trusted confidante, his very clever and devoted wife, that he addressed a long letter to the Navy Department, justifying his course and vindicating the navy from the unfair attacks made against it. The biographer goes on to say:

" But the Navy Department seems to have lacked, at the time, the moral courage to assume fearlessly the full responsibility of its action which this publication would have involved, and the letter was read and returned to Admiral Dahlgren. We hold the manuscript in our possession, thus indorsed by the admiral, ' Withdrawn November 8th, 1865, the department objecting to the introduction of Du Pont and the opinion of the officers, and to those parts where it is assumed, or seems to be so, that the department did not send vessels enough.—J. A. D.' The department was too inimical and revengeful to Du Pont to be just or to be willing to have him relieved in any measure, through any act of theirs, of any possible effect of their continuous displeasure."

The journal kept by Admiral Dahlgren during his service before Charleston, recording from day to day the difficulties he encountered month after month, against which he struggled manfully but hopelessly, is the perfect vindication of Admiral Du Pont's sound judgment and wise discretion.

The story of the first attack upon Charleston is finished. Grieved by his unsuccessful effort to take that city, Admiral Du Pont was deeply pained by the attitude of the Navy Department toward him. Swift stories of harsh comment, perhaps exaggerated, were brought to him from Washington, wounding him to the quick, as did also the significant silence of the Secretary in relation to his reports. A correspondence followed that at last became acrimonious. He did not ask to be relieved from his command, but in one of his letters to the Navy Department, in speaking of an implied censure, he said, "I have the honor to request that the department will not hesitate to relieve me by any officer who, in its opinion, is more able to execute the service in which I have had the misfortune to fail—the capture of Charleston." Anxious to throw the blame upon any shoulders but its own, the brave veteran was deprived of his command by the Navy Department.

REAR-ADMIRAL J. A. DAHLGREN.   FROM A PHOTOGRAPH.

It was the old story, but a very sad one. Admiral Du Pont took with him to his retirement the respect and sympathy of those who had been with him in his active service. In the words applied to another commander-in-chief, by the historian, General Sir William Napier, they "had served long enough under his command to know why the soldiers of the tenth legion were attached to Cæsar."

Arriving at Port Royal, Admiral Du Pont hurried forward the repairs of the monitors with the view of sending them to the Gulf, as directed by the Secretary of the Navy. On the 16th, however, came orders to renew the menace against Charleston, but his monitors were not repaired, nor could the *Ironsides* cross the bar until the next spring-tides. Meanwhile, the dispatches reciting the details of the battle of the 7th of April had, on their way north, crossed the orders from the Government, and after they were received with their development of weakness in the attacking force, the obstructions in the channel, and the strength of the defenses to be overcome, the order for continuing to menace Charleston was not reiterated, nor was the proposal of the admiral to make the next demonstration from Edisto, instead of Morris Island, rejected, approved, or made the subject of the Department's letters. The plan of sending the monitors to the Gulf was abandoned, and the Navy Department sent a large body of workmen to strengthen the monitors, work that was estimated to require twelve weeks' labor. General Gillmore, General Hunter's successor, began his preparations to occupy Morris Island, and while they were in progress Admiral Du Pont received notice that Admiral Foote had been appointed to succeed him. This distinguished officer died on the 26th of June, and Admiral Dahlgren, who was to have been Foote's second in command, was appointed commander-in-chief. It is curious to observe in Admiral Dahlgren's biography how little he approved the scheme of attacking Charleston by Morris Island, and how inadequate he thought the force assigned for this important undertaking. One notes also how sanguine of success he found the high functionaries of the Navy Department.

Awaiting the arrival of his successor, Admiral Du Pont would not commit him to a plan that did not commend itself to his own judgment. He had always thought Charleston could not be taken from Morris Island, but, with the loyal fidelity that had always characterized him, he put his whole force in preparation to move at a day's notice if his successor should so elect. The ammunition and coal vessels were made ready, the repairs on the monitors were held in readiness to be ended at a day's notice, preparatory orders were sent to the force off Charleston, and had Admiral Dahlgren so desired, the fleet could have moved to the attack the moment his arrangements with General Gillmore were completed.

The new and the old admirals exchanged cordial greetings; they were old friends, and the good feeling between them was not disturbed. Both had the same object at heart, the suppression of the rebellion and the restoration of the Union. Admiral Dahlgren assumed command on the 6th of July, and Admiral Du Pont left forever the active service of the navy. When, somewhat later, he was offered the command of the Pacific Squadron, far from the seat of war, he repelled with indignation the proposal that he should be employed anywhere but in the face of the enemy.

Those who did him great wrong have passed away, but his statue in imperishable bronze stands to-day in one of the most conspicuous quarters of the capital of the Republic, a quarter called by his name, to show how highly the country valued his services.

THE BOAT ATTACK ON SUMTER.

BY THOMAS H. STEVENS, REAR-ADMIRAL, U. S. N.

By July 10th, 1863, a combined movement of the United States land and naval forces in the neighborhood of Charleston had given them a footing on the south end of Morris Island, and active preparations followed for the reduction of Batteries Wagner and Gregg. The results of the movement referred to, and the establishment of batteries, gave General Gillmore's command a position about half a mile from Wagner. For two months operations were conducted against the enemy, and during this period one or two unsuccessful sorties ‡ were made from Wagner. On July 18th the second of two assaults was made against that fort, which resulted in a loss to us of from six to seven hundred men out of four regiments.⚓ Of this affair Rear-Admiral Dahlgren says in his "Memoirs":

"About sunset an aide brought a note from General Gillmore on half a blank leaf, written in pencil, saying that he had ordered an assault; and by the waning light we could see the masses coming along the beach, but the darkness shut them in ere they reached the fort. Presently came the flashes of light and the sharp rattle from muskets and cannon. There could be no help from us, *for it was dark and we might kill friend as well as foe.*

All we could do was to look on and await an issue not in our control. The contest went on for an hour and a half, and then died away. It was over; but who had won?"

This and other statements in the "Memoirs" show the lack of mutual support between the two commanders. Without such support failure was inevitable. Had the time for the assault been fixed so that the navy could have supported the movement,— as, later, at Fort Fisher, when the fire of the ships was directed by signal,— it is fair to presume that the effect of our supporting fire would have been most demoralizing, and might have been enough so to have produced a different result.

From this time until the abandonment of Wagner and Gregg, hardly a day passed without urgent appeals for the assistance of the fleet from the commanding general, who was at times apprehensive of a sortie from the fort. Now aid was asked to intercept probable reënforcing expeditions of the enemy, and again the vessels were called on to interpose for the protection of the forces engaged in the trenches and approaches to Wagner. To all of these appeals the navy responded promptly and zealously, and under the protection of our

‡ In the "Military Operations of General Beauregard" mention is made of a reconnoissance in small force on the night of July 14th-15th.— EDITORS.

⚓ Ten regiments participated in the attack. The

four suffering the greatest losses were the 54th Massachusetts (colored), 272; the 48th New York, 242; the 7th New Hampshire, 216; and the 100th New York, 175 = 905. The total Union loss was 1515.— EDITORS.

guns work on the trenches went on steadily until September 6th, when they were pushed up to the ditch of Wagner. All that day we cannonaded the fort, preparing the way for an assault to be made the next day at 9 A. M. Wagner was soon silenced, and thereafter the men worked in broad daylight without molestation, whereas, before that time, as Admiral Dahlgren states, "a man could not show a finger."

About daylight on the 7th a message was received by the admiral from army headquarters, stating that the enemy had evacuated Wagner and Gregg, and that Morris Island was in our possession. The news spread quickly, and afloat and ashore speculation was rife as to what the next move would be and how the great advantage gained would be improved. "On to Charleston!" was the prevailing sentiment.

General Gillmore, anticipating an attempt of the enemy to recover a footing on Morris Island, requested the admiral to send a monitor up as near as practicable to Battery Gregg to frustrate any attempt in this direction, and the present Rear-Admiral E. R. Colhoun with the *Weehawken* was finally selected for the duty. In carrying out these orders the monitor grounded badly within easy range of the Confederate batteries on Sullivan's Island. About 5 o'clock all the other iron-clads came up to engage the batteries on Sullivan's Island, while an examination was being made of the obstructions across the channel-way, two hundred yards above Sumter, as the admiral was desirous of learning if there was a passage on either side of them, and also, what was the condition of Sumter's channel-face. For this duty my command, the *Patapsco*, was designated, with the *Lehigh* as a support. We had to run some fifteen hundred yards of batteries on Sullivan's Island before Sumter could be reached. Realizing the insignificant power of two monitors against the force of the enemy's batteries, and the fact that the more quickly the duty was performed the fewer were the chances of disaster, I determined not to jeopardize the *Lehigh's* safety as well as the *Patapsco's*, and orders were given to get up a good head of steam, to load the guns with grape and canister, and to turn the turrets fore and aft in a line with the keel, the guns pointing forward. Waiting until the iron-clads were hotly engaged with the enemy, the order "four bells and a jingle" (full speed ahead) was given, and, not waiting for her consort, the *Patapsco* dashed forward. When the enemy perceived the object of this movement, many of their batteries opened on us heavily, but it was not until we had reached a point about 150 yards from Sumter and the like distance from the obstructions, that we encountered the terrific converging fire from Fort Moultrie, Batteries Bee and Beauregard, and the batteries still farther up the bay. To make an examination of Sumter and the obstructions occupied 25 or 30 minutes, during which time we were struck 25 times by the heaviest projectiles of the enemy, and suffered serious damage. We fired several rounds of grape and canister at buoys supporting the obstructions, supposed to be of rope and extending from shallow water at a point two hundred yards above Sumter, in a north-

easterly direction, to the shoals on the Sullivan's Island side. We did not see a man on Sumter nor any sign of a gun on the channel-face, which seemed to be intact. Having accomplished the object of our mission, the bow of the *Patapsco* was turned seaward to run the gauntlet again and report to Admiral Dahlgren the result of our examination. The iron-clads were still heavily engaged when we came up to the *Ironsides*, to which vessel the admiral had gone at the beginning of the engagement; I found him in the gangway, looking ill and anxious, but evidently much relieved at the *Patapsco's* safe return. Many officers of the vessel and the fleet shared in this feeling. When it is remembered that, since the first attack on Sumter by Du Pont, no demonstration had been made, except in full force and under cover of the night, that the enemy had exact range to cover with their guns the approach to the obstructions, and that while making the examination we were enduring the converging fire of the enemy's heaviest batteries, only about eight hundred yards distant, our escape from more serious results seems remarkable.

As soon as my report was made the iron-clads withdrew from action and took up their usual anchorage for the night.

The morning of the next day (September 8th) found the *Weehawken* still aground and the enemy pounding away at her. About 10 A. M. signal was made from the flag-ship, "Iron-clads assist *Weehawken*." Slipping the moorings of the *Patapsco* we hastened to the relief, but before we had gathered headway a shot from the grounded monitor landed in Moultrie and exploded a magazine; this elicited loud cheers from sailors and soldiers, and the admiral signaled, "Well done, *Weehawken*." Colhoun was defending his vessel vigorously and valiantly when, by 11 A. M., the iron-clads moved into position and opened a strong fire on the Sullivan's Island batteries. Colhoun was then left in peace and afforded an opportunity to arrange for the liberation of his vessel from her extremely perilous position. About 4 P. M. she floated. About 1:30 P. M., as we were heaving up the *Patapsco's* anchor, in obedience to the signal, "Withdraw from action," our engine was disabled from the effect of our own fire. I hailed the *Nahant* and directed Lieutenant Cornwell, her commanding officer, to drop down to our assistance and take us in tow. This order was given through our surgeon, Dr. Wheeler, who, at great personal risk, went forward and passed it along. Cornwell was prompt and efficient in obeying the order, under a heavy fire, and he soon had us within easy hail of the present Vice-Admiral Rowan's vessel, the *Ironsides*, which had taken up her anchorage beyond the range of the enemy's guns. As we approached, Rowan made a welcome signal for me to come on board his ship to dine, as usual. His views and mine in regard to the situation, and our ideas as to future operations, were in perfect harmony. He had had a large professional experience, and I never saw his equanimity or judgment disturbed under the most trying circumstances; while the intelligent handling and fighting of his ship showed conclusively that a master of his art was in command. In the incomparable Belknap—the present commodore—he had an executive always ready to do his will, and in the best possible way.

We had just lighted our pipes on the *Ironsides* for an after-dinner chat when Flag-Lieutenant S. W. Preston was announced, with orders for the commander of the *Patapsco* to report on board the flag-ship. On our way to the vessel Preston informed me that it was the intention of the admiral to attack Sumter that night in boats, and added: "You are selected to command." This information was corroborated by the admiral. My judgment opposed the movement on the grounds that we were without reliable knowledge of the internal or external condition of the fort, and of the practicability of scaling the walls, for which no provision had been made; that sufficient time had not been allowed for the proper organization of a force for service of so desperate a character; that the enemy had been fully notified that some demonstration was to be made by the gathering of boats around the flag-ship, in open daylight; that they would naturally conclude Sumter to be the objective point and would defend it to the last extremity; and, finally, that if a lodgment were by any possibility effected on the fort, and the fort taken, we could not hold it so long as the obstructions remained in the channel. For the enemy's iron-clads and batteries above and around Sumter, being unmolested and beyond our reach, would sever our communications and starve our people out. I made these representations and asked permission to decline the command. To this no direct response was given, but, in the course of conversation, the admiral said: "You have only to go and take possession. You will find nothing but a corporal's guard to oppose you."

Going down to the wardroom, my decision was briefly made known in reply to the interrogations of friends. Within half an hour Preston joined us; he had evidently been conversing with the admiral, for he was thoroughly informed on the situation and used his best efforts to alter my determination, urging among other reasons that the army was organizing for an independent demonstration to be led by General T. G. Stevenson, an officer of tried valor and established reputation for whom we all had a great personal liking. As Stevenson was the ranking officer, General Gillmore contended that the expedition should combine under his leadership. The admiral would not consent to this, on the ground that it was a boat expedition and purely naval in its character. After giving me this information, Preston added: "If you do not go, the naval demonstration will fall through and the army will reap all the glory."

My convictions of the impracticability of the assault were unshaken, but my reasons could not be made known without injurious results. I was in a quandary and saw no way out of it, but personal appeals from such men as Lieutenants B. H. Porter, Preston, and Moreau Forrest, with other considerations, finally had their effect, and I reluctantly consented to go.

By the time the watchword for the night had been arranged it was half-past ten o'clock. As we were taking leave of our friends, the present Rear-Admiral Rhind suggested to me that one division of boats should be sent around Sumter as a feint, while the remainder should wait within easy distance of the fort for the order to advance. This suggestion was adopted, and Lieutenant (now Captain) Francis J. Higginson was selected for the command of the party. His demonstration, among other things, was to develop the extent of the enemy's defensive preparations.

The admiral's barge was placed at my disposal, and Lieutenant Forrest, an officer of rare judgment, intelligence, and merit, was appointed as my aide. Final instructions were given to the officers commanding divisions to make the best of their way to the fort when the divisions were formed and the order was given to advance. Instructions of a general character were given to Lieutenant Higginson, and a tug having been brought into service, its commander was directed to lie by the *Patapsco* on leaving the flag-ship. The barge was to stop alongside the former vessel for Dr. Wheeler, as we had no medical officer with us.

We finally shoved off, and after the necessary short delay by the *Patapsco* while the surgeon was making his preparations, were towed by the tug toward the picket monitors *Montauk* and *Lehigh*, which I instructed to move up to our support, as the admiral, at my request, had authorized me to do. We moved slowly on our way to the fort. It was a calm, clear, starlight night. The only sound was the steady thumping of the tug's propeller, and nothing was seen ahead but the grim, half-defined outline of the fort. When the master of the tug reported that he could go no farther, the boats were cast off, the divisions were formed, and Higginson, an officer of courage and judgment, was directed to carry out the instructions previously given him. He accordingly moved off to do so, and most of the division commanders dashed off also, under the impression that his movement was a general one, and that the order to advance had been given. Efforts to recall them were made, but in vain. Nothing remained to do but to give the order for the remaining boats to make the best of their way to the fort. Through this misapprehension all the good effects of Higginson's demonstration were lost. On our way to the fort in the barge, fairly flying under the strokes of the oarsmen, we observed a large number of boats lying on their oars; we hailed them and directed them to pull in, but as no sign of a movement was made by them, then,—or, indeed, during the whole affair,—we concluded that it was the army force awaiting the result of our demonstration. As we neared Sumter we were hailed loudly by the enemy, but no answer was returned. Simultaneously a rocket was sent up from the fort, and almost as it exploded the air was filled with hissing, shrieking missiles from the James and Sullivan's Island batteries, which seemed alive with fire, while an iron-clad was pouring grape and canister into the boats and sweeping the approaches to the gorge. The parapets and crown of Sumter were

THE BOAT ATTACK ON FORT SUMTER.

filled with men pouring a murderous fire down on our defenseless party, and heavy missiles and hand-grenades helped on the work of destruction. Before this fire had fully developed, two boats from the *Powhatan* and others had effected a landing. As was subsequently learned, their crews and officers were driven to shelter and taken prisoners. All these things were evidences of the enemy's foreknowledge of our purpose and complete preparation to frustrate it. The "corporal's guard" that we were to have encountered proved to exceed our own numbers. Under these conditions but one expedient was left—to effect an early withdrawal. The order to retire was accordingly given through Lieutenant Forrest, and was several times repeated.

Admiral Dahlgren, who was watching the operations from a boat in the distance, says in his journal, "Moultrie fired like a devil, the shells breaking around me and screaming in chorus." What must have been the impression in the midst of the cyclone, where the air was blazing with bursting shells, and the ear was deafened with the roar of cannon, the rattle of musketry, the whistling of grape, and the explosion of hand-grenades!

Withdrawing in the barge from the vortex of the fire, we remained near the fort to afford assistance to any disabled comrades, and about 4 o'clock, as day broke, we pulled to the flag-ship to report the results of the assault and determine the extent of our loss. We found this amounted to 124 killed, wounded, and missing, out of 400 men. Among the killed was Lieutenant C. H. Bradford

of the Marines. Lieutenant E. P. Williams, Executive of the *Powhatan*, a brave and dashing officer, and Lieutenants B. H. Porter and S. W. Preston were taken prisoners. They were all exchanged, and Porter and Preston were killed in the second attack on Fort Fisher. Preston, Porter, and Forrest — the last of whom died of yellow fever in the West Indies — were close friends, and alike in those qualities that adorn humanity and make heroes of men. Lieutenant F. W. Bunce and Dr. Wheeler, both of the *Patapsco*, in this affair sustained the high reputation they had already earned on every occasion when the *Patapsco* had been engaged on perilous service. Conspicuous, also, were the services of Daniel Leech, Acting Paymaster of the *Patapsco*, who at the same time performed the duties of signal officer. There was material in the command, both in officers and men, that would have insured success, had this been within the range of human endeavor. Five thousand men could not have captured the fort that night.

After the war General Beauregard wrote me two letters on the subject of the attack, in which he says, in effect: "After the fall of Wagner and Gregg, acting under the belief that our forces were thereby demoralized, the enemy would doubtless make a demonstration against Sumter. Our impression to this effect was strengthened by the number of armed boats seen to be gathering around the flag-ship, from vessels inside and outside, during September 8th. We were, moreover, able to read all the signals made that day.⚓ Sumter was

⚓ On the 13th of April, 1863, Beauregard announced to the War Department that he had obtained a key to the signals, but suspected deception. Major John Johnson writes to the editors that advantage was taken of the signals in preparing to resist the assault on Wagner, July 18th, and the boat attacks on Cumming's Point and

Fort Sumter, in September. On the other hand, General W. B. Taliaferro, who commanded on Morris Island at the time of the attack on Battery Wagner referred to by Major Johnson, states in the "Philadelphia Times," November 11th, 1882, that the Union signals were not interpreted on that occasion.— EDITORS.

accordingly reënforced,[b] and, when attacked, contained 450 men. One of our iron-clads was ordered to take up a position to sweep the approaches to the gorge with canister and grape. The guns in the shore batteries were loaded and trained upon the approaches to the fort, and the men were ordered to stand by their guns, lock-strings in hand. At the given signal of a rocket from the fort, all the batteries were to open." And farther: "If our guns had not opened so soon and fired so rapidly, we would have captured or destroyed your whole command." This is true.

[b] Major John Johnson says of this statement: "Sumter was not reënforced; but on the night of September 4th-5th, Rhett's enfeebled garrison had been

In the "Memoirs" of Admiral Dahlgren I find, under the date of November 20th, 1863, the following: "Last night the army undertook to feel the force in Sumter, and sent two hundred men in boats for that purpose. About thirty yards from the fort a dog barked and aroused the garrison, which fired, wounding two of our men. The rumor was, the night before, that an attack was to be made, and I ordered the monitors on picket to cover our men. A few shots were fired by the fort and then there was quiet." I think this was the last demonstration of the kind attempted.

relieved by Major Elliott and the Charleston Battalion of infantry, 320 strong. No troops after that date were sent to the fort before the boat attack on September 8th."

SOUTH ATLANTIC BLOCKADING SQUADRON. (January–July, 1863.)

Rear-Admiral S. F. Du Pont, commanding. Commander C. R. P. Rodgers, Chief-of-Staff.

SCREW-FRIGATE.—*Wabash*, Com. T. G. Corbin, 1 150-p'der Parrott, 1 10-inch, 1 30-p'der Parrott, 42 9-inch.

SCREW-SLOOPS.—*Pawnee*, Com. G. B. Balch, 8 9-inch, 1 100-pounder Parrott, 1 50-pounder Dahlgren; *Canandaigua*, Capt. J. F. Green, 2 11-inch pivot, 1 150-pounder Parrott pivot, 3 20-pounder Parrotts, 2 12-pounder rifle howitzers, 2 12-pounder S. B. howitzers; *Housatonic*, Capt. W. R. Taylor, 1 11-inch, 1 100-pounder Parrott, 3 30-pounder Parrotts, 4 32-pounders, 1 12-pounder S. B. howitzer, 1 12-pounder rifle howitzer; *Mohawk*, Com. A. K. Hughes, 6 32-p'ders, 1 24-p'der S. B., 1 12-p'der howitzer.

SIDE-WHEEL STEAMER.—*Powhatan*, Capt. S. W. Godon, Capt. Charles Steedman, 7 9-inch, 1 100-pounder Parrott pivot, 1 12-inch pivot.

GUN-BOATS.—*Wissahickon*, Lieut.-Com. J. L. Davis, 1 150-pounder Parrott pivot, 1 20-pounder Parrott pivot, 2 24-pounder S. B. howitzers, 1 12-pounder rifle howitzer; *Seneca*, Lieut.-Com. William Gibson, 1 11-inch pivot, 1 20-pounder Parrott pivot, 2 24-pounder S. B. howitzers; *Unadilla*, Lieut.-Com. S. P. Quackenbush, 1 11-inch pivot, 1 20-pounder Parrott pivot, 4 24-pounder S. B. howitzers, 1 12-pounder S. B. howitzer; *Marblehead*, Lieut.-Com. R. W. Scott, 1 11-inch pivot, 1 20-pounder Parrott pivot, 2 24-pounder S. B. howitzers; *Ottawa*, Lieut.-Com. W. D. Whiting, 1 11-inch, 1 20-pounder Parrott, 2 24-pounder howitzers; *Water Witch*, Lieut.-Com. A. Pendergrast; *Huron*, Lieut.-Com. G. A. Stevens, 1 11-inch pivot, 1 20-pounder Parrott rifle, 2 24-pounder S. B. howitzers.

DOUBLE-ENDERS.—*Sebago*, Com. J. C. Beaumont, 1 100-pounder Parrott pivot, 5 9-inch, 2 24-pounder S. B. howitzers; *Cimarron*, Com. A. G. Drake, 1 100-pounder Parrott, 1 9-inch, 2 9-inch pivot, 4 24-pounder S. B. howitzers; *Conemaugh*, Com. Reed Werden, 1 100-pounder Parrott pivot, 4 9-inch, 2 24-pounder S. B. howitzers, 1 11-inch pivot; *Paul Jones*, Com. Charles Steedman; Com. A. C. Rhind; Lieut.-Com. E. P. Williams, 1 100-pounder Parrott pivot, 1 11-inch pivot, 4 9-inch, 1 12-pounder S. B. light.

PURCHASED STEAMERS.—*South Carolina*, Com. J. J. Almy, 1 30-pounder Parrott, 1 24-pounder S. B. howitzer, 4 8-inch, 2 32-pounders; *Dawn*, Act. Lieut. John S. Barnes, Act. Master James Brown, 2 32-pounders, 1 100-pounder Parrott, 1 20-pounder Parrott, 1 12-pounder howitzer; *Mercedita*, Com. H. S. Stellwagen; *Quaker City*, Com. J. M. Frailey; *Commodore McDonough*, Lieut.-Com. George Bacon, 1 9-inch pivot, 1 100-pounder Parrott, 2 50-pounder Dahlgren rifles, 2 24-pounder S. B. howitzers; *Potomska*, Act. V.-Lieut. William Budd, 5 guns; *E. B. Hale*, Act. Lieut. E. Brodhead, 4 32-pounders, 1 30-pounder Parrott pivot; *Lodona*, Com. E. R. Colhoun, 1 100-pounder Parrott pivot, 1 30-pounder Parrott pivot, 1 9-inch, 4 24-pounder S. B. howitzers; *Norwich*, Com. J. M. Duncan, 4 8-inch, 1 30-pounder Parrott, 1 12-pounder rifle howitzer; *Wamsutta*, Act. V.-Lieut. J. W. Kittredge, 4 32-pounders, 1 20-pounder Parrott, 1 12-pounder rifle howitzer; *Keystone State*, Com. W. E. Le Roy, 6 8-inch, 2 32-pounders, 1 50-pounder Dahlgren, 2 30-pounder Parrotts, 2 12-pounder

rifle howitzers; *Madgie*, Act. Master F. B. Meriam, 1 30-pounder Parrott pivot, 1 20-pounder Parrott pivot, 2 24-pounder S. B. howitzers, 1 12-pounder S. B. howitzer; *Isaac Smith*, Act. Lieut. F. S. Conover; *James Adger*, Com. T. H. Patterson, 1 9-inch, 6 32-pounders, 1 20-pounder Parrott, 1 12-pounder S. B. howitzer; *Augusta*, Com. E. G. Parrott, 6 8-inch, 1 100-pounder Parrott rifle, 2 30-pounder Parrott rifles, 1 12-pounder rifle howitzer; *Flag*, Com. J. H. Strong, 4 8-inch, 1 10-inch pivot, 2 30-pounder Parrotts; *Flambeau*, Lieut.-Com. J. H. Upshur, 1 30-pounder Parrott pivot, 1 20-pounder Parrott pivot, 2 12-pounder heavy howitzers; *Stettin*, Act. Master C. J. Van Alstine, 1 30-pounder Parrott pivot, 4 24-pounder S. B. howitzers; *Uncas*, Act. Master William Watson, 4 32-pounders, 1 20-pounder Parrott; *Memphis*, Lieut.-Com. P. G. Watmough, Act. Master C. A. Curtis, 4 24-pounder S. B. howitzers, 1 30-pounder Parrott rifle, 2 12-pounder rifle howitzers.

MONITORS.— (1 15-inch, 1 11-inch, each.) *Patapsco*, Com. D. Ammen; *Passaic*, Captain P. Drayton; *Nahant*, Com. John Downes; *Montauk*, Com. John L. Worden, Com. D. M. Fairfax; *Nantucket*, Com D. M. Fairfax, Lieut.-Com. L. H. Newman, Com. J. C. Beaumont; *Weehawken*, Captain John Rodgers; *Catskill*, Com. George W. Rodgers.

OTHER IRON-CLADS.—*Keokuk*, Com. A. C. Rhind, 2 11-inch S. B.; *New Ironsides*, Com. T. Turner, 14 11-inch, 2 150-pounder Parrotts, 2 50-pounder Dahlgrens.

SAILING VESSELS (Barks).—*Kingfisher*, Act. Master J. C. Dutch, 4 8-inch; *Braziliera*, Act. Master W. T. Gillespie, 6 32-pounders; *Restless*, Act. Master W. R. Browne; *Midnight*, Act. Master N. Kirby, 1 20-pounder Parrott pivot, 6 32-pounders; *Fernandina*, Act. Master E. Moses, 6 32-pounders, 1 20-pounder Parrott pivot, 1 24-pounder S. B. howitzer.

MORTAR-SCHOONERS.— *C. P. Williams*, Act. Master, S. N. Freeman, 2 32-pounders, 1 20-pounder Parrott rifle, 1 13-inch mortar; *Para*, Act. Master E. G. Furber, Act. Master Edward Ryan, 2 32-pounders, 1 13-inch mortar; *Norfolk Packet*, Act. Ensign George W. Wood, 2 32-pounders, 1 13-inch mortar, 1 12-pounder rifle howitzer.

STORESHIPS.— *Vermont*, Com. William Reynolds, 10 8-inch, 8 32-p'ders; *Valparaiso*, Act. Master A. S. Gardner.

TUGS, TENDERS, AND DISPATCH BOATS.— *O. M. Pettit*, Act. Ensign T. E. Baldwin, 1 20-pounder Parrott, 1 30-pounder Parrott; *Rescue*, Act. Ensign C. A. Blanchard, 1 20-pounder Parrott, 1 12-pounder rifle howitzer; *Hope*, Act. Master J. E. Rockwell, 1 20-pounder Parrott pivot; *Daffodil*, Act. Master E. M. Baldwin, 1 20-pounder Parrott rifle, 1 20-pounder Dahlgren rifle; *Dandelion*, Act. Ensign William Barrymore, 2 guns; *Columbine*, Act. Master J. S. Dennis, Act. Ensign E. Daly, 2 20-pounder Parrotts; *G. W. Blunt*, Act. Master J. R. Beers, 1 12-pounder rifle howitzer, 1 12-pounder S. B. howitzer; *America*, Act. Master J. Baker; *Oleander*, Act. Master J. S. Dennis, 2 30-pounder Parrott pivots.

THIRTY-POUNDER PARROTT RIFLES IN BATTERY HAYS, ON THE UNION LINE, FACING BATTERY WAGNER.

THE ARMY BEFORE CHARLESTON IN 1863.

BY QUINCY A. GILLMORE, BREVET MAJOR-GENERAL, U. S. A.

CHARLESTON HARBOR somewhat resembles the harbor of New York in general outline, and is about half its size. The city itself, occupying the lower end of a narrow peninsula between two navigable rivers, is distant about seven miles from a bar which obstructs the entrance from the sea, stretching bow-shaped from Sullivan's Island on the north side to Morris Island on the south side of this approach. These islands and others adjacent to them are separated from the main-land by soft alluvial marshes that range in width from one to three miles, and in depth from about fifteen to eighteen feet, and are cut up by numerous creeks and deep bayous, and are submerged by all tides higher than an ordinary flood. The width of the throat of the harbor between Sullivan's and Morris islands is 2700 yards, which is practically narrowed to about one mile by a shoal that makes out from the south side, on the northern edge of which stands Fort Sumter.

The position in its general features seemed to invite an assault by water, and to present a peculiarly attractive field for naval heroism and prowess; while its approaches by land from the sea islands which we occupied were practically closed by impassable swamps to any but a greatly superior force. The defenses which had been constructed by the United States for the harbor and city of Charleston were designed to resist a naval attack only. They comprised: (1) Fort Sumter, a strong brick work, as strength was reckoned in those days, mounting two tiers of guns in casemates and one tier *en barbette*. It stands on the southern edge of the channel, distant three and one-third miles from the nearest point of the city. It was planned for 135 guns, but never received its full armament. The embrasures or ports of the second tier, not having been finished when the war began, were bricked up by

Major Anderson's command early in 1861, and were left in that condition until destroyed by our fire from Morris Island. When this fort fell into the enemy's hands, April 14th, 1861, it contained seventy-eight pieces of serviceable ordnance, all smooth-bores, ranging from 24-pounders to 10-inch Columbiads. (2) Fort Moultrie, a brick work located on Sullivan's Island about one mile from Fort Sumter, mounting one tier of guns *en barbette*. Before the outbreak of the war its armament consisted of fifty-two pieces, of which the heaviest were 10 and 8 inch Columbiads and the lightest a battery of field-guns. (3) Castle Pinckney, an old brick fort one mile east of the city on Shutes Folly Island. Its armament at the beginning of the war comprised twenty-eight pieces of rather small calibers.

At the outbreak of the war the Confederates began to add largely to the strength of the existing defenses by constructing strong and well-armed earth-works at the upper and lower ends, as well as at intermediate points, of both Sullivan's and Morris islands; by reënforcing the walls of Fort Sumter adjacent to the magazine; by increasing the armament of that work and of Fort Moultrie with heavier calibers, including large rifles; by rebuilding and rearming old Fort Johnson, on James Island, on the south side of the inner harbor west of Fort Sumter; by constructing several batteries on the shell beach south-east of Fort Johnson; by mounting some heavy rifles, including 13-inch Blakely guns, upon the lower water-front of the city; by building a new battery at Mount Pleasant, and by the construction of iron-clad rams.

Ample preparations against a land attack were also made. On James Island strong works were built to close the approach from Stono River. Stono inlet and harbor were occupied by an inclosed fort on Cole's Island, which held under control all the anchorage ground and landing-place inside the Stono bar. This advanced position was abandoned by the enemy prior to the naval attack on Fort Sumter, giving us the possession of Folly Island and the lower Stono and inlet. The upper Stono was held by a heavily armed earth-work called Fort Pemberton, and the water approach to Charleston by Wappoo Cut, west of James Island Creek, was defended by powerful earth-works, while strong batteries on the eastern shore of James Island swept all the practicable water routes from Morris and Folly islands. North-east of the city a line of intrenchments reaching from Copahee Sound to Wandoo River guarded the land approaches from Bull's Bay. Suitable works were also built on the peninsula in the rear of the city, covering the roads from the interior. Indeed, no avenue of attack, by land or water, was left without ample means of protection. General R. S. Ripley, who had immediate command of the defense, recently stated that he had under his control 385 pieces of artillery of all calibers, including field-batteries, and an ample force of skilled men to serve them. When the position was evacuated by the Confederates, February 18th, 1865, 246 guns were left behind in the several works.

The James Island defenses were especially strong. They had repulsed a bold and spirited assault upon them from the Stono River side, made by forces under General H. W. Benham, on the 16th of June, 1862, and had been greatly strengthened since that time.

A gallant and well-directed attack upon Fort Sumter on April 7th, 1863, by a squadron composed of nine iron-clad vessels, under command of Rear-Admiral Du Pont, had signally failed, after a sharp engagement lasting about one hour. [See p. 32.] The squadron carried 15-inch and 11-inch shell guns and 150-pounder Parrott rifles. Five of the iron-clads were reported by their respective commanders to be wholly or partly disabled in their power of inflicting injury by their guns. They had been under the concentrated fire of some of the most destructive guns of that period for nearly one hour, although they did not advance far enough to draw the fire of some of the heaviest pieces in Fort Sumter. The thin-armored *Keokuk* was so seriously injured that she sank the following morning off Morris Island, and her armament fell into the hands of the enemy. The fleet received the fire from the Sullivan's Island, the Morris Island, and the Mount Pleasant batteries, as well as from Fort Sumter, and during the attack divided its own fire between Fort Wagner, Fort Sumter, and Fort Moultrie. After this repulse Admiral Du Pont expressed the opinion that Charleston could not be taken by a purely naval attack, and some of his subordinate commanders held similar views. At Washington it was deemed of so much importance to present an actively aggressive front in this quarter in aid of projected operations elsewhere that orders were issued by the President himself to hold the position inside of Charleston bar, and to prevent the erection of new batteries and new defenses on Morris Island, and if such batteries had been begun by the enemy to "drive him out." A keen sense of disappointment pervaded the Navy Department at the repulse of April 7th, finding expression, among the higher officials, in a determination to retrieve the fortunes of that day, and reinstate the iron-clads in the confidence of the country at the earliest possible moment. The gallantry of the attack, the skill with which the fleet had been handled, the terrific fire to which it had been exposed, and the prudence that prompted its recall before a simple repulse could be converted into overwhelming disaster were measurably lost sight of in the chagrin of defeat. The disheartening fact was that the iron-clads had conspicuously failed in the very work for which they had been supposed to be peculiarly fit, and the country had nothing whatever to take their place.

Late in May I was called to Washington, ‖ and was informed at the consultations which followed that it was the intention to make another attack with the iron-clads, provided Fort Sumter, which was regarded as the most formidable obstacle and the key of the position, could be eliminated from the conflict, so that the fleet could pass up on the south side of the channel, leaving Fort Moultrie and the other Sullivan's Island works nearly a mile to the right. The army was therefore asked if it could coöperate to the extent of destroying the offensive power of Fort Sumter. I expressed the opinion that Fort Sumter could be reduced and its offensive power entirely destroyed with

‖ General Gillmore was on leave of absence at this time. From September 18th, 1862, to April, 1863, he had held important commands in Kentucky and West Virginia.—EDITORS.

rifle guns, planted on Morris Island, and that beyond the capture of that island and the demolition of the fort, the available land forces, numbering scarcely eleven thousand men of all arms, could not take the initiative in any operation against Charleston that would involve their leaving the sea islands, upon which the enemy derived no advantage from his superior strength or from the railroad facilities under his control for concentrating troops and bringing reënforcements from the interior on short notice. It was finally decided that the army should undertake the capture of Morris Island and the reduction of Fort Sumter, unless it should become necessary, before preparations for the attack were completed, to detach some of the troops for the purpose of reënforcing General Grant or General Banks, then operating on the Mississippi; and it was announced with emphasis that no additional troops would be sent to South Carolina. The capture of the city by a land attack was not, in any sense, the object of these operations. No project of that nature was discussed or even mentioned at the conference.

The following general plan of campaign was agreed upon, comprising four distinct steps, and the army was to take the lead in executing the first, second, and third. First, to make a descent upon and obtain possession of the south end of Morris Island, then held by the enemy with infantry and artillery; second, to lay siege to and reduce Battery Wagner, a strong and well-armed earth-work, located near the north end of Morris Island, about 2600 yards from Fort Sumter; with Battery Wagner the works at Cumming's Point, the extreme north end of the island, would also fall; third, from the position thus secured on Morris Island to destroy Fort Sumter with breaching batteries of rifle guns, and afterward by a heavy artillery fire coöperate with the fleet when it should be ready to move in; fourth, the fleet to enter, remove the channel obstructions if any should be encountered, run by the batteries on James and Sullivan's islands, and reach the city. For the special purpose of this contemplated attack Rear-Admiral Andrew H. Foote, an officer of tried bravery and cool and mature judgment, was assigned to the command of the South Atlantic blockading squadron, comprising the naval forces available for operations against Charleston; but he was not permitted to enter upon this new field of labor, his sudden and untimely death leaving the command with Rear-Admiral John A. Dahlgren. [See p. 46.]

Charleston was located in the Military Department of the South, comprising the narrow strip of sea-coast held by the Union forces in South Carolina, Georgia, and Florida. Upon relieving General David Hunter and assuming command of this department in June, I found our troops actually occupying eleven positions on this stretch of coast, while a small blockading squadron held a variable and more or less imperfect control of the principal inlets. In the neighborhood of Charleston we held all the coast line south of Morris Island, while all the other islands around the harbor, and to the northward, were either controlled or occupied by the enemy. It was found, after abolishing some of these detached posts and reducing the force at others, that the aggregate means for carrying on the contemplated operations against Charleston comprised only about 10,000 effective volunteer infantry, 600 engineer

THE NIGHT ASSAULT ON BATTERY WAGNER, JULY 18, 1863.

troops, and 350 artillerists.   The ordnance on hand, deemed more or less
suitable for our purpose, consisted of 200-pounder, 100-pounder, and 30-
pounder Parrott rifles, and some 13-inch, 10-inch, and 8-inch mortars.   The
projectiles for the 200-pounders, however, weighed only 150 pounds, and
those for the 100-pounders only 80 pounds.   With this feeble array of
guns—feeble because largely wanting in the strength required for throwing,
with a breaching velocity, even the light projectiles provided for them—the
great work of the siege was begun.   During the operations fifty-one of these
Parrott rifles were expended by bursting, most of them prematurely.

    Meanwhile between the middle of June and the 6th of July preparations
for the descent upon Morris Island went quietly forward.   It was deemed
necessary that this attack should be a surprise in order to insure suc-

cess.   On the extreme northern end of Folly Island forty-seven field and siege guns and mortars were quietly placed in position, screened by thick undergrowth from the view of the enemy on the opposite side of Light-House inlet. They were intended to operate against his batteries there, protect the column of boats in its advance across the stream, or cover its retreat in case of repulse.   The entrance to Stono inlet was lighted up at night, and all transports bringing troops were ordered to enter after dark and leave before morning.   All appearance of preparations for offensive operations was carefully suppressed, while upon General Israel Vogdes's defensive works on the south end of Folly Island a semblance of activity was conspicuously displayed.   Brigadier-General A. H. Terry's division, about 4000 effective, and Brigadier-General George C. Strong's brigade, numbering about 2500, were quietly added to the Folly Island command under cover of darkness.

The project for securing a lodgment on Morris Island comprised, as one of its features, a demonstration in force on James Island by way of Stono River, over the same ground where Brigadier-General Benham had met with repulse the year before.   The object in the present case was to prevent the sending of reënforcements to the enemy on Morris Island from that quarter, and possibly to draw a portion of the Morris Island garrison in that direction. Everything being in readiness, the character of the assault about to be ordered, the risk involved therein, and the magnitude of the interests at stake became for the moment subjects of grave consideration.   For if this assault failed, the promise to demolish Fort Sumter failed also, carrying in its train the failure of the naval project to capture Charleston and inflict punishment in the place where the rebellion had its birth, and the further failure to destroy this great blockade-running thoroughfare, and to restore confidence in the efficiency of the iron-clads, upon which special stress had been laid.   The storming of a position strongly held by both artillery and infantry, is always an operation attended with imminent peril in its execution, and great uncertainty as to results.   The best troops can seldom be made to advance under the fire of even a few well-served pieces of artillery supported by the fire of small-arms.   No lesson of our great civil war was learned at greater cost than this.   But the hazard of such an undertaking, great as it is under ordinary circumstances where the aggressive force operates on firm ground, becomes greatly and painfully intensified when the assaulting column has to approach in small boats from a distant point, exposed to full view and constant fire, to disembark and form upon an open beach in the presence of an enemy covered by parapets, and finally to advance to the attack against the combined fire of artillery and small-arms.   Yet this was the work we had set out to do, and it was believed we had the men to do it.

The demonstration up the Stono River was begun in the afternoon of July 8th, by Brigadier-General Terry, who landed on James Island with about 3800 men.   The effect as subsequently ascertained was to draw a portion of the enemy's forces from our front on Morris Island.⚓

On the evening of July 9th a small brigade was silently embarked in row-

⚓ It is understood that General Beauregard denies this.—Q. A. G.   But see p. 14.—EDITORS.

boats in Folly River behind Folly Island. It was commanded by Brigadier-General George C. Strong, who had received orders to carry the south end of Morris Island by storm. By break of day the leading boats had reached Light-house inlet, where the column was halted under cover of marsh grass to await orders. The point where the landing was to be made was still nearly

COLONEL ROBERT G. SHAW, 54TH MASSACHUSETTS (COLORED) VOLUNTEERS — KILLED IN THE ASSAULT ON BATTERY WAGNER. FROM A PHOTOGRAPH.

a mile distant, and this stretch of river had to be passed in full view under fire. All our Folly Island batteries opened before sunrise, and soon after this four iron-clad monitors, led by Rear-Admiral Dahlgren, steamed up abreast of Morris Island and took part in the action. After the cannonade had lasted nearly two hours General Strong was signaled to push forward and make the attack. This was promptly and gallantly done under a hot fire. The men did not hesitate or waver for a moment. All the enemy's batteries on the south end of the island, containing eleven pieces of artillery, were captured in succession, and by 9 o'clock we occupied three-fourths of the island, with our skirmishers within musket-range of Battery Wagner. Thus was the first

step in the plan of joint operation successfully taken. The intense heat, which prostrated many of the men, forced a suspension of operations for the day.

Two unsuccessful attempts were made to carry Battery Wagner by assault. In the first, which took place at daybreak on the morning of July 11th, the parapet of the work was reached, but the supports recoiled under the heavy fire of grape and canister that met them, and the advantage gained could not be held. This repulse demonstrated the remarkable strength of the work and the necessity of establishing counter-batteries against it, which, with the coöperation of the fleet, might dismount the principal guns and either drive the enemy from it or open the way to a successful assault. After the first assault Battery Wagner was inclosed [see p. 23]; it reached entirely across the island from water to water; it mounted some heavy guns for channel defense, and several siege-guns that swept the narrow beach over which we would have to approach from the south; and a large bomb-proof shelter afforded the garrison absolute protection when the fire became so hot that they could not stand to their guns or man the parapet. ↓ To us the place presented the appearance of a succession of low, irregular sand-hills like the rest of the island. Battery Gregg, on the north end of the island at Cumming's Point, was known to be armed with guns bearing on the channel. Of one important

↓ Major John Johnson writes to the editors that the "heavy guns for channel defense" consisted of two 10-inch Columbiads; also, that absolute protection was afforded to about 600 men, little more than half the garrison.

topographical change we were entirely ignorant. We did not know that the island at its narrowest point between us and Battery Wagner, and quite near to the latter, had been worn away by the encroachments of the sea to about one-third the width shown on our latest charts, and so much reduced in height that during spring-tides or heavy weather the waves swept entirely over it to the marsh in rear. Against us the fort presented an armed front about 800 feet in length reaching entirely across the island, while our advance must be made over a strip of low shifting sand only about 80 feet wide, and two feet above the range of ordinary tides.

Between the 16th and 18th of July, as preliminary to a second attempt to get possession of Battery Wagner by assault, 41 pieces of artillery, comprising light rifles and siege-mortars, were put in position on an oblique line across the island at distances from the fort ranging from 1300 to 1900 yards. The rifles were intended principally to dismount the enemy's guns. Early in the afternoon of the 18th all these batteries opened fire, and the navy closed in on the fort and took an active and efficient part in the engagement. In a short time the work became absolutely silent on the faces looking toward us, and practically so on the sea front, from which at the beginning of the action a severe fire had been delivered against the fleet. The work was silenced for the time at least, but whether this was due to the injury inflicted on its armament, or to the inability of the men to stand to their pieces, or to these two causes combined, we had no means of knowing.

An assault was ordered. The time of evening twilight was selected for the storming party to advance, in order that it might not be distinctly seen from the James Island batteries on our extreme left, and from Fort Sumter and Sullivan's Island in our distant front. Brigadier-General Truman Seymour organized and commanded the assaulting column, composed of Brigadier-General G. C. Strong's brigade supported by the brigade of Colonel Haldimand S. Putnam. As the column left the line of our batteries and began its advance along the narrow strip of beach, a rapid fire was opened upon it from Fort Sumter and from the works on James Island and on Sullivan's Island. When it reached a point so near to Battery Wagner that the fire from our own guns and those of the navy had to be suspended from fear of destroying our own men, a compact and deadly sheet of musketry fire was instantly poured upon the advancing column by the garrison, which had suddenly issued forth from the security of the bomb-proof shelter. Although the troops went gallantly forward and gained the south-east bastion of the work and held it for more than two hours, the advantages which local knowledge and the deepening darkness gave the enemy forced a withdrawal. The repulse was complete, and our loss severe, especially in officers of rank. The gallant Strong, who had been the first man to land on Morris Island a few days before, actually leading his entire command in that descent and in the daring assault that followed, was fatally wounded. As he was being conveyed to the rear I stopped the ambulance for a moment to ask if he was badly hurt. He recognized my voice, and replied, "No, General, I think not; only a severe flesh-wound in the hip." He was taken to Beaufort that night and placed in hospital under excellent attendance. But he was seized with a yearning desire to go home, and, without my knowledge, took the first steamer for the North. Being the senior officer on board, the excitement of the trip, aggravated by the chase and capture of a blockade-runner, brought on lock-jaw, of which he died shortly after reaching New York. Colonel John S. Chatfield was mortally wounded; Colonel Haldimand S. Putnam and Colonel Robert G. Shaw were killed; and Brigadier-General Truman Seymour and several regimental commanders were wounded.

It may be said that in making this assault the traditions and maxims of the engineer and his reverence for the spade and shovel as weapons of war were placed in abeyance. Although no dissenting voice was raised among the subordinate commanders called into council, it may be doubted by some whether a step so grave in character and so uncertain in results was the unquestionable outcome of existing military necessity. Perhaps only an engineer would doubt this. At all events its full justification was assumed to rest on the presumption that Fort Sumter must be destroyed by guns placed as near to it as to the site of Battery Wagner, and that every hour's delay in capturing that work permitted the enemy to strengthen his interior defenses, and thus render the entrance of our fleet more difficult.

To meet the contingency brought on by the failure it was determined to change slightly the prearranged order of operations by attempting the demolition of Fort Sumter with our heavy rifles, at a distance of two miles and upward, by firing over Battery Wagner and its garrison from ground already in our possession. It was urged adversely to this plan that there existed no precedent for it. This was true, the nearest approach to it being the reduction of Fort Pulaski ♭ the year before by breaching at the distance of one mile and more. [See Vol. II., p. 9.] But the fact that we could throw heavier metal and do heavier work now than we could then, promised success, and the placing of guns in position against Fort Sumter was promptly begun. For this purpose 16 Parrott rifles and two Whitworth rifles were placed in batteries at distances from Fort Sumter ranging from 3428 to 4290 yards. The slow, tedious, and hazardous labor of moving into position and mounting these heavy guns and their carriages could be performed during the night-time only, under a constant and galling fire from the front and one flank. There was great danger that guns and carriages, as well as the appliances for putting them in position, would be destroyed. As contemporary with these operations, arrangements had been perfected for pressing the siege of Battery Wagner, and the work was fairly under way. And here the limitations of the books had to be irreverently set aside. Instead of our being able to envelop any portion of the work, we were practically enveloped by it. It presented to us an armed front of four times the average width of the low beach over which we had to force our way, and as we neared the work this ratio reached as high as ten to'one. It was now known, from the latest infor-

---

♭ At that siege the engineer and his devices had full sway. So perfect, indeed, were the arrangements for the safety of the troops, that only one of our men was struck during the eight weeks of preparation and the two days' engagement, and he lost his life through disregard of instructions.—Q. A. G.

mation, to contain a rather heavy armament, of which at least a dozen pieces could be trained upon our narrow, shifting line of approach—in many places scarcely half a company front in width, subject to frequent overflow by the waves and tides, and swept not only by the guns of Wagner itself, but also by those of Cumming's Point and Fort Sumter and several batteries on James Island. Indeed, the ground over which our men had to force their way, under such meager cover as could be made by sinking trenches to the water-level, and gaining the requisite height with sand and other material brought by hand from the rear, was seen by the enemy's batteries in front, flank, and reverse. Having its communications open with Charleston and the interior, the armament and garrison of Fort Sumter could always be maintained at the maximum state of efficiency. The first parallel was established, July 19th, on the line occupied the day before by our batteries against Battery Wagner, and the second parallel on the night of the 23d by the flying sap, about six hundred yards in advance of the first. Eleven of the breaching guns against Fort Sumter were located in these two parallels, and the other seven to the left and rear of the first parallel. Those in the second parallel were perilously near to Battery Wagner, the most advanced piece being only 820 yards distant from the guns of that work. One of the batteries was efficiently commanded by Commander Foxhall A. Parker, U. S. N. On the night of August 9th the position selected for the third parallel was reached by the flying sap, 330 yards in advance of the right of the second parallel. It was deemed inexpedient to push the approaches beyond this point until after the breaching batteries should open on Fort Sumter.

From this time forward the fire from the enemy's guns in our front and on our extreme left was severe and almost uninterrupted. So incessant had it become that many officers and men, especially those who did not carry their sense of responsibility very lightly, could not sleep at night if from any cause the cannonade was suspended. For a while the advance of our trenches was entirely stopped by it, and it became a question of the gravest doubt in some quarters whether any farther progress was possible, and, what was of infinitely greater importance, whether we could complete the erection of any of the breaching batteries, or serve them when erected. It is a pleasure to be able to state without qualification that the officers and men were fully equal to the extraordinary demands made upon them. Not a murmur of discontent was heard on the island. Finally some of the breaching batteries opened fire on the 17th of August, and by the 19th all were in successful operation. The result was soon clearly foreshadowed. Nothing, indeed, but the destruction of our guns, either by the enemy's shot or through their own inherent weakness, would long delay it. About 450 projectiles struck the fort daily, every one of which inflicted an incurable wound. Large masses of the brick walls and parapets were rapidly loosened and thrown down. The bulk of our fire was directed against the gorge and south-east face, which presented themselves diagonally to us. They were soon pierced through and through, and cut down on top to the casemate arches. The shot that went over them took the north and north-west faces in reverse.

The condition of the work, as it appeared to us after six days' bombardment, is thus described by General J. W. Turner, chief of artillery:

" The fire upon the gorge had by the morning of the 23d succeeded in destroying every gun upon its parapet, and as far as could be observed had disabled or dismounted all the guns upon the parapet of the two faces looking toward the city which it had taken in reverse. The parapet and rampart of the gorge were for nearly the entire length of the face completely demolished, and in places everything was swept off down to the arches, the débris forming an accessible ramp to the top of the ruins.

" The demolition of the fort at the close of this day's firing (August 23d) was complete so far as its offensive powers were considered. Every gun upon the parapet was either dismounted or seriously damaged. The parapet could be seen in many places both on the sea and channel faces completely torn away from the *terre-plein*. The place, in fine, was a ruin, and effectually disabled for any immediate defense of the harbor of Charleston. Having accomplished the end proposed, orders were accordingly issued on the evening of the 23d for the firing to cease, having been continuously sustained for seven days. There had been thrown 5009 projectiles, of which about one-half had struck the fort."

Colonel Alfred Rhett, C. S. A., commanding Fort Sumter, reports, August 24th, "One 11-inch Dahlgren, east face, the only gun serviceable"; and on September 1st, "We have not a gun *en barbette* that can be fired; only one gun and casemate."

General Stephen Elliott, C. S. A., writes as follows:

" When I assumed command of Fort Sumter on the 4th of September, 1863, there were no guns in position except one 32-pounder in one of the north-west casemates. This gun was merely used for firing at sunset, and was not intended for any other purpose. Early in October I mounted in the north-east casemates two 10-inch Columbiads and one 7-inch rifle. In January one 8-inch and two 7-inch rifles were mounted in the north-west casemates."

The seven days' service of the breaching batteries, ending August 23d, left Fort Sumter in the condition of a mere infantry outpost, without the power to fire a gun heavier than a musket, alike incapable of annoying our approaches to Battery Wagner, or of inflicting injury upon the fleet. In this condition it remained for about six weeks. A desultory fire was kept up to prevent repairs, and on the 30th of August another severe cannonade was opened and continued for two days at the request of the admiral commanding, who contemplated entering the inner harbor on the 31st. Some time before this the enemy began to remove the armament of Fort Sumter by night, and many of its guns were soon mounted in other parts of the harbor.

During the progress of the operations thus briefly outlined, the navy had most cordially coöperated whenever and wherever their aid could best be rendered. The service of the monitors was notably efficient in subduing the fire of Battery Wagner, which at times not only seriously retarded the labors of the sappers, but threatened the destruction of some of the most advanced of the breaching guns. While the breaching of Fort Sumter was still in progress, active work was resumed on the approaches to Battery Wagner by pushing the full sap from the left of the third parallel. Meanwhile the spring-tides had come with easterly winds, flooding the trenches to the depth of two feet and washing down the parapets. The progress of the sap was hotly contested with both artillery and sharp-shooters. The latter had taken possession of a ridge about 240 yards in advance of the main work, where they had placed themselves under such cover that they could not be dislodged by our fire or the flank fire of the fleet, while that from their own guns in rear passed harmlessly over their heads. An attempt to capture this ridge having failed, a fourth parallel was established on the night of August 21st, about five hundred yards in advance of the third. From this point the ridge was carried [by the 24th Massachusetts] at the point of the bayonet on the 26th, under the direction of Brigadier-General Terry, and the fifth parallel was established thereon. The resistance to our advance now assumed a most obstinate and determined character, being evidently under skillful and intelligent direction, while the firing from the James Island batteries became more steady and accurate.

Over the narrow strip of shallow shifting beach between us and the fort, the flying sap was pushed forward from the right of the fifth parallel. An ingenious system of subsurface torpedo mines, to be exploded by the tread of persons walking over them, was soon encountered, and we learned from prisoners that they were planted thickly over all the ground in our front. But the mines were a defense to us as well as to the besieged garrison, as they brought a sense of security from sorties which the enemy's broader development and converging fire would otherwise have enabled him to make with nearly every condition in his favor. The sappers soon reached a point only one hundred yards from the ditch of the work. Beyond this our progress became exceedingly slow and uncertain. Our daily losses were on the increase. The concentric fire from Battery Wagner alone almost enveloped the head of our sap, while the flank fire from the James Island batteries increased in power and accuracy every hour. To push the work forward by day was found to be impossible, while a brilliant harvest-moon, which seemed to shine with more splendor than ever before, rendered an advance at night almost equally hazardous. Matters seemed to be at a stand-still. A sense of gloom and despondency began to pervade the command, under the impression that all the expedients of the engineer had been exhausted.

In this emergency it was determined, as well to hasten the final result as to revive the flagging spirits of the men, to carry on simultaneously against Battery Wagner two distinct kinds of attack: First, to silence the work by an overpowering bombardment with siege and Coehorn mortars, so that our sappers would have only the James Island batteries to annoy them; and, second, to breach the bomb-proof shelter with our heavy rifles, and thus force a surrender. During the day-time the *New Ironsides*, Captain S. C. Rowan, was to coöperate with her eight-gun broadsides. These operations were actively begun at break of day on the 5th of September.

Seventeen siege and Coehorn mortars dropped their shells unceasingly into the work over the heads of our sappers; ten light siege-rifles covered and swept the approach to the work from the rear; fourteen heavy Parrotts thundered away at the great bomb-proof shelter; while, during the daylight, the *New Ironsides*, with the most admirable regularity and precision, kept an almost continuous stream of 11-inch shells rolling over the water against the sloping parapet of Battery Wagner, whence, deflected upward with a low remaining velocity, they dropped vertically, exploding in and over the work, mercilessly searching every part of it except the subterranean shelters. The calcium lights turned night into day, throwing our own works into obscurity and bringing the minute details of the fort into sharp relief.] For forty-two consecutive hours this work went on, presenting a spectacle of remarkable magnificence and splendor. As a pyrotechnic achievement alone, the exhibition at night was brilliant and attractive, while the dazzling light thrown from our advanced trenches, the deafening roar of our guns, and the answering peals from James Island added sublimity and grandeur to the scene. The imagination was beguiled and taken captive, and all the cruel realities of war were for a time forgotten in the unwonted excitement of this novel spectacle.

The garrison soon sought safety in the bomb-proof shelter, and the fort showed but little sign of life. Occasional shots were delivered at the *New Ironsides*, and a few sharp-shooters from time to time opened a harmless fire upon the head of the trenches. But the engineers rapidly pushed forward their work. They suffered principally from the James Island batteries, which night and day maintained a most annoying fire upon our mortar-batteries and the head of the sap, following the latter in its progress toward the fort until it reached a point so near that friends and foes were alike exposed to the perils of the cannonade. It then ceased entirely, and our men pushed forward the trenches with entire immunity from serious danger. Their sense of security was so sudden and complete, and their position so novel and exciting, with the entire garrison, once so defiant, now helplessly at bay only a few feet distant, that the reliefs of sappers off duty mounted the parapet of the trenches, or wandered forward into the ditch of the work to take a survey of the surroundings. A formidable line of frise work, consisting of pointed stakes alternating with boarding-pikes or lances, was removed from the ditch of the sea front. Early on the night of September 6th our sap was pushed forward entirely beyond the south front of the work, and between the sea front and the water, crowning the crest of the counterscarp at the north or farthest end of that front, and completely masking all the guns of the work. An order was issued to carry the place the next morning by assault on the north front at the time of low tide when the width of beach would be the greatest, and the troops could promptly pass beyond the work to the point of attack. On the north side the work was closed by an ordinary infantry parapet. During the night the fort was evacuated with such celerity that only two boat-loads of men were captured. The north end of the island was at once occupied by our forces. Eighteen pieces of ordnance were found in Battery Wagner, and seven in Battery Gregg on Cumming's Point, most of them being comparatively large, as calibers were estimated in those days.

Battery Wagner was found to be a work of greater defensive strength than the most exaggerated statements of prisoners and deserters had led us to expect. Its bomb-proof shelter, affording a safe retreat to its entire garrison, remained practically intact after perhaps the severest cannonade to which any earth-work had ever been subject. Its covering, composed of sea-shore sand,

] The calcium light was so strong that the garrison was prevented from making repairs.—EDITORS.

had been struck by sixty-one net tons of metal, thrown with a breaching charge at comparatively short ranges, and yet the injury inflicted could easily have been repaired in eight or ten hours.

These operations left the whole of Morris Island in our possession, and Fort Sumter in ruins and destitute of guns. A powerful armament was mounted on the north end of the island, to coöperate with the monitors when they should move in, and to prevent the remounting of guns on Fort Sumter. Early on the morning following the capture of Battery Wagner, the admiral, under a flag of truce, demanded the surrender of Fort Sumter. It was refused. On the night of the 8th a naval assault was made on the work about midnight, and repulsed with considerable loss.

A prominent historian of the war states, on the alleged authority of the naval commander, that army coöperation was expected in this assault in compliance with previous arrangement. As this statement is entirely destitute of truth, the admiral could not have made it, and must have been misunderstood in what he did say. Although I had ordered an assault for the same evening by two small regiments, before the admiral's intentions were known to me, he was told, in response to a request for information on that point, that the boats with the storming party could not leave their rendezvous in the small creek behind Morris Island until midnight, on account of low tide; and yet at 10 P. M. the naval column left the fleet, advanced quickly to the attack, and by midnight had been repulsed.\ No assistance from the land forces was expected or desired. In point of fact, it was declined. Each party was organized without any expectation of aid from the other, and no reference to any expected coöperation from the army was made by the admiral, or by any of his subordinate commanders in their official reports of the assault. ☆

General Elliott [Confederate] reports in his journal, November 20th, that "at 3 o'clock a detachment of the enemy's barges, variously estimated at from four to nine in number, approached within three hundred yards of the fort and opened fire with musketry. Most of the troops got into position very rapidly, but in spite of all instructions commenced a random fire into the air on the part of many, at the distant boats on the part of others." And the General adds afterward that "no rockets were sent up because positive attacks were not made." From this Colonel Alfred Roman, in his "Military Operations of General Beauregard," makes the statement that "another boat attack was made by General Gillmore's forces against Fort Sumter resulting in utter failure, as had been the case with the former attempt"; and another writer, going still further, asserts that the admiral ordered his pickets to cover the assaulting party—in sharp contrast with the behavior of the commanding general at the time of the naval repulse on September 9th. This may enliven what would otherwise have been dull reading, perhaps, but nevertheless it is pure fiction. No such attack was ordered, attempted, or even contemplated by

---

\ The attack seems to have been made soon after midnight. The Confederates place it between 1 and 2 A. M.—EDITORS.

☆ See papers accompanying report of Secretary of the Navy, 1863; and also official correspondence in "Engineer and Artillery Operations against the Defenses of Charleston Harbor in 1863."—Q. A. G.

THE MARSH BATTERY AFTER THE EXPLOSION OF THE "SWAMP ANGEL." FROM A PHOTOGRAPH.

the land forces after the naval repulse in September.　General Elliott's statement that "positive attacks were not made" is strictly true, of course, because no semblance of an attack was made.　The boat party seen was doubtless the regular patrol, larger probably than usual, according to the duty required of them that particular night.　There existed no military reason at that time for risking an assault.　The fort was destitute of cannon, could take no part in a defense against a fleet, and as an infantry outpost could be of no value to us if captured.　It was heroically held by the enemy in a spirit of commendable pride and audacity, and had been made very strong against capture by assault. An attacking column, even if it should gain possession of the parade of the work, could not reach the garrison in their subterranean galleries, protected by heavy loop-holed doors, and, moreover, would be at the mercy of the enemy's guns on Sullivan's Island and those on the east front of James Island.　The controlling conditions differed essentially, now, from those which obtained when the surrender of the place was demanded by the admiral early in September. At that time the capture of the parade carried with it that of the work.

While Fort Sumter was rapidly crumbling under our first cannonade the evacuation of that work and of Morris Island was demanded, the condition of refusal being that fire would be opened on the city of Charleston.　Existing circumstances furnished a full justification for this step.　Charleston had been besieged for seven weeks, was occupied by the enemy's troops and batteries, gun-boats had been built and were then building along its water front, and the avenue of escape for non-combatants was open and undisputed.　The demand being refused [see p. 17], the marsh battery, containing one 8-inch Parrott rifle, previously referred to as the "Swamp Angel," opened fire on the night of August 21st.　The gun burst on the second night at the thirty-sixth round. Some of the projectiles reached a distance of about five and three-quarter miles.　Firing on the city was subsequently resumed from Cumming's Point.

Fort Sumter was subjected to another severe cannonade of some days' duration,┃ beginning October 26th, directed mainly against the south-east face, on a report from deserters, afterward found to be untrue, that the garrison was remounting guns thereon. In a short time that face was more completely a ruin than the gorge wall. Throughout the length of both those faces the débris formed a practicable ramp from the water to the summit of the breach.

This ended all aggressive operations against the defenses of Charleston, ⚓ although a desultory fire was maintained against Fort Sumter during the months of November and December to prevent the remounting of guns, pending the completion of the naval preparations for passing into the inner harbor. It was not entirely suspended until the idea of removing the channel obstructions and running the James and Sullivan's islands batteries appeared to be indefinitely postponed. No official notification of this abandonment of plan was made by the naval authorities. On October 20th I was verbally informed by the admiral that he would probably await the arrival of more monitors, which were expected in a few days; and as early as September 29th a couple of weeks was thought to be needed to complete the repairs to the monitors before operating against the channel obstructions.

In point of fact there were no formidable obstructions in Charleston harbor. The popular ideas with regard to them which pervaded the public mind, and even influenced and directed official action in some quarters, were erroneous in a most notable degree. The belief entertained at the time by many practical men, whose official relations required them to form opinions on the subject, that they were either flimsy counterfeits or in large degree mythical, has been fully confirmed. Brigadier-General Ripley, C. S. A., and other officers of the Confederate service, whose positions enabled them to speak from positive knowledge, have furnished some interesting information on this subject. From their statements, some of which are written, it appears to have been the constant and studied practice of the Confederate commanders to spread exaggerated and incorrect reports concerning this special means of defense. To such extent and with such skill was this ruse made use of that, with few exceptions, neither the inhabitants of the city nor the troops defending it possessed any knowledge of the channel obstructions. Such a semblance of necessary and systematic labor in their construction, management, and repair was kept up, and such an affectation of secrecy concerning their character and of confidence in their efficiency was assumed in order to keep all knowledge of the huge fiction from us, that the blockade-runners themselves, although making frequent and regular trips, were kept in the profoundest ignorance of the harmless character of the dangers they were told to avoid. The credulous commander of a foreign man-of-war who in 1863 was permitted to go up to the city in a small boat, returned to his ship outside the bar filled with the most extravagant admiration for the extensive scheme which he believed to be in constant readiness for conducting a defense by submarine mines; and, although he had really seen nothing except a few harmless barrels floating on

┃ The bombardment continued forty days and nights without intermission.— EDITORS.

⚓ The author doubtless refers to operations conducted by himself, for the third great bombardment of Fort Sumter took place after his assignment to another field in the spring of 1864.— EDITORS.

the water, reported the entire channel to be literally filled with fixed and floating obstructions and subaqueous mines and torpedoes. When the harbor and its defenses came into our possession on the 18th of February, 1865, and the novel spectacle was presented of a large fleet, comprising gun-boats, army and navy transports, a coast-survey steamer, dispatch boats, tugs, sutlers' and traders' vessels, passing up to the city and dispersing themselves at pleasure over the harbor without encountering any of those hidden objects of terror whose existence in formidable shape no one, except civilians on shore, had ever shown any disposition to doubt, the question naturally arose whether at any previous time during the war the various channel obstructions, mines, and torpedoes had in reality been in a more efficient condition than we found them at that time. Among the troops, down to the lowest private, the belief was expressed with a freedom which the Union soldier claimed to be his inalienable right that the practice of running the blockade at night, which was constantly and most successfully carried on at Charleston throughout the years 1863–64, proved the existence of a wide and practicable channel up to the city; and steamers bearing flags of truce had not unfrequently come down to the outer harbor and returned to the city during the day-time, and the route they took was well known. Efforts made soon after the close of the war to obtain full and exact information concerning the obstructions, from officers of the Confederate service who put them down and had them in charge, met with a cheerful response. From the concurrent testimony, written and oral, thus procured, it appears that there were no channel obstructions or torpedoes in 1863 and 1864 that would be expected to prevent or even seriously retard the passage of a fleet up to Charleston city and above it, or likely to afford any effective protection in the event of an actual attack; that the main channel next Fort Sumter was never obstructed by torpedoes or otherwise until the winter of 1864–65, a few months before the close of the war, and that at no time was the condition of this auxiliary means of channel defense any better, or its efficiency any more to be relied on to stop or delay the entrance of a hostile fleet, than at the time the city and its defenses were evacuated in February, 1865.

General Beauregard, in correcting what he calls errors in the preliminary official dispatch sent from the field, takes exception to the statement therein made that Battery Wagner was a most formidable kind of work, and claims that it was " an ordinary field-work, with thick parapet and ditches of little depth." To this it may be said that within certain limits, embracing all works of the Battery Wagner type and many others, the elements of defensive strength are determined more by the environment and approaches than by the dimensions, trace, and relief of the work itself. No one should concede the soundness of this principle more freely than an engineer of General Beauregard's attainments and varied experience. Measured by this, the only appropriate standard, Battery Wagner was beyond question a work of the most formidable kind, while if it had stood upon a site practically approachable on all sides, or on two sides, it would not be classed as such. In point of fact, it presented a case of the defense of a narrow causeway swept by both an enfilading and a cross-fire of artillery and small-arms. All things considered, it should be regarded as a very formidable work.

With regard to the character of the Confederate defense, Colonel Alfred Roman ["The Military Operations of General Beauregard"] aptly says: "It is a matter of history to-day that the defense of Fort Sumter and that of Battery Wagner are looked upon as two of the most desperate and glorious achievements of the war. They stand unsurpassed in ancient or modern times." Without altogether adopting the superlative tone of this statement, it may be conceded that the defense of Fort Sumter in 1863, when the garrison burrowed in the ruins of the work as it rapidly crumbled over their heads, was a notable one. The claim has been made, by those who like to indulge in comparisons, that this defense stands in sharp contrast to the apparently feeble effort to provision and hold the place in 1861.

Many of the popular fallacies of the day with regard to harbor defenses are based upon just such operations as those developed in the conflict before Charleston, and formerly in the "Battle of the Earth-works" on the Crimea. The defensive strength of Battery Wagner throughout the siege, and the alleged strength of Fort Sumter after it had been battered into a shapeless mass of ruins, are mistakenly cited as evidence that earth-works are better than forts of brick or stone, and are quite sufficient to meet any expected naval attack. Of torpedoes it has been claimed that if a very imperfect system, existing largely in the imagination only, succeeded in keeping a powerful fleet at bay for half a year, it would be entirely safe to depend on a well-equipped torpedo defense for the protection of our important harbors; and many professional men, mostly of naval tendencies, drawing a comparison between the thin-plated and weakly armed iron-clads of 1863 and the powerful men-of-war of more recent type, look upon an armored navy as the only safe means of sea-coast protection.

These points will bear a brief discussion. It will doubtless not be denied that the requirements of a good defense are determined by the character and magnitude of the attack. If an enemy brings heavy guns against us, we must of course protect our own guns from heavy shot, or they will be destroyed. If his vessels are incased in thick armor, we must use heavy projectiles against it, or our defense is worthless; for where a crushing blow from a large gun is needed, no possible accumulation of smaller guns will suffice. Cumulative force implies unity of mass and impact. A thousand pounds of grape-shot, even if fired at short range in one volley, can be stopped by a 1-inch steel plate; but the same weight, sent as a single ball, will shatter the best 12-inch armor. We must, therefore, have heavy guns, and they must be so mounted as to be measurably safe from the enemy's fire. If to these conditions we add one more, that the guns shall have time to do their work,—that is, that the hostile fleet cannot run past them at full speed, but will be arrested by torpedoes,—we have the whole theory and practice of harbor defense by fortifications and their auxiliary submarine mines.

It is an error to suppose that a defense by torpedoes, however perfect in itself, can stand alone. To be of any practical use, the torpedoes must be protected from removal by the enemy, the only efficient protection yet devised being shore-batteries of heavy guns. Otherwise they are a harmless and therefore a worthless obstruction. Fortifications and channel torpedoes mutually supplement and support each other. If the torpedoes be omitted, an armored fleet can run by the forts without stopping, and probably without suffering serious injury. If the forts be omitted, the enemy would stop and remove the torpedoes at his leisure, and then pass on. Our own great civil war, and other wars of more recent date, bear ample testimony to the fact that torpedoes exposed to unmolested hostile approach afford no defense to a channel, and cause but a trifling delay to the passage of the fleet.

It is unquestionably true that casemated forts built of stone or brick after the old types do not fulfill the requirements of a good defense against an armor-plated navy. The walls which should protect both guns and gunners are too thin to sustain the shock of heavy projectiles, and in most cases would be pierced through and through by a single shot from a heavy rifle. The obvious and commonly adopted remedy for this weakness is to strengthen the walls with metal shields or armor plating, rather than discard all protection by resorting to open batteries or earth-works, in which both guns and gunners are in full view of the enemy. It might be impossible to serve guns so exposed, even for a brief period, against armored or iron-clad ships showering grape and canister from large calibers, and leaden bullets from machine-guns

BREVET BRIGADIER-GENERAL E. W. SERRELL (SEE P. 72).
FROM A PHOTOGRAPH.

and sharp-shooters. The protection of the men at their·guns is beyond question a consideration of the highest moment; it is indeed an essential consideration. Even in our casemated works special precautions are taken to prevent the entrance of missiles. In those last built the embrasures were supplied with iron shutters to stop grape, canister, and rifle bullets, so that the men might not be driven from their guns. The lessons of all modern wars, so far from justifying a dependence on open batteries for channel defense, all point the other way. At Port Royal our fleet of wooden vessels drove the enemy precipitately from their guns on both sides of the harbor; and in the operations before Charleston it was no uncommon exploit for the *New Iron-sides* alone to silence the fire of Battery Wagner. From the very beginning of the war, "running a battery" became almost an every-day affair, the most important question being whether the channel itself was free from obstructions. A proper defense, therefore, requires that the shore-batteries should be armed with heavy guns, that the guns should be protected from the enemy's fire, and that the auxiliary defense by torpedoes should be of such magnitude that no fleet could attempt to run the gauntlet through them without imminent risk of destruction. A defense of this potential character is calculated quite as much to prevent an attack as to defeat it. It is a most powerful conservator of international quiet and good-will. Indeed, the chief office of permanent fortifications is to avert war. They are the guardians, rather than the champions, of the public good and of the prosperity of the people.

A confusion of ideas seems to prevail with regard to the appropriate work of a navy in a scheme of national defense, frequently taking form in the assertion that an iron-clad navy alone—a navy of cruisers as distinguished from non-seagoing batteries, rams, and the like—will furnish a sure defense. This sentiment, although both attractive and popular, finds no practical existence among naval powers. A home fleet, if as powerful as the enemy's, would be expected to make, and no doubt would make, a good defense. But in that case, at the very best our chances of victory would be only equal to those of the enemy, while the risks taken and the consequences to ensue from failure would be largely unequal. Where interests of great magnitude are at stake, ordinary prudence would suggest that as little as possible be left to the caprice of chance. A trustworthy defense of this character, therefore, implies a harbor fleet a little more powerful than the enemy's. It implies, further, that such a fleet must be provided for each locality to be protected. Not knowing where the enemy will strike, we must be prepared for him with a fleet at all important points. But no antagonist, especially if he be on the defensive, can wisely place his main reliance upon a weapon which can be as readily procured and as skillfully used by his adversary as by himself. Destructive energy of the same denomination is neutralized when placed in opposing hands. Fleet arrayed against fleet leaves too much to risk and accident, with our stake on the issue immeasurably greater than the enemy's. These maxims unmistakably point to the necessity of depending mainly upon those agencies, exclusively our own, which cannot be neutralized or duplicated by our antagonist, and will therefore always keep him at disadvantage, to wit: permanent shore-batteries and their accessory channel torpedoes. Auxiliary rams, torpedo-boats, submarine guns, and other forms of naval power may in great measure be counterbalanced by others of like character from beyond the seas. Indeed, all naval power possessing sea-going qualities may be neutralized entirely. Our main reliance, after all, must be upon shore-batteries and channel torpedoes, and the combined strength of these must be as great as if no floating auxiliary aid were employed. Otherwise, when these auxiliaries fail, no adequate defense would remain, and the position would be lost.

THE MARSH BATTERY ARMED WITH MORTARS, AFTER THE EXPLOSION OF THE " SWAMP ANGEL."

THE "SWAMP ANGEL" IN POSITION. FROM A SKETCH MADE AT THE TIME.

THE "SWAMP ANGEL."

BY WILLIAM S. STRYKER, BREVET LIEUTENANT-COLONEL, U. S. V., A. D. C. TO GENERAL GILLMORE.

THE Confederate attack on Fort Sumter marked the beginning, and the second and third bombardments by the Union guns the middle period of the civil war. Morris Island and Folly Island, two low sand-reefs, constitute the southerly bounds of the outer harbor of the city of Charleston. Morris Island, which is nearly four miles long, contains about four hundred acres of sand dunes and salt marshes; the portion of the island lying toward James Island being formed almost entirely of very soft morasses, and traversed by deep bayous and crooked creeks in every direction.

The Union troops under Major-General Quincy A. Gillmore, the Tenth Army Corps, in the early morning of July 10th, 1863, crossed Light-house Inlet from Folly Island and captured a large portion of Morris Island. [See p. 58.] The Confederate forces still held Cumming's Point Battery and Battery Wagner on that part of Morris Island nearest to Fort Sumter and to Charleston. On the 13th day of July, 1863, General Gillmore directed Lieutenant Peter S. Michie, United States Corps of Engineers,—now Colonel Michie, a professor in the Military Academy at West Point,—to make an examination of the marshes on the left of our position toward Charleston and ascertain if it were possible to construct a battery from which to fire into that city. In compliance with this order he spent some time in the examination of the swamp district of Morris Island, and then reported the result of his investigations to the commanding general. On the morning of July 16th General Gillmore, while at breakfast, told Colonel Edward W. Serrell, Volunteer Engineers,—now General Serrell, the distinguished civil engineer of New York City,—of the great desirability of securing a position from which fire could be opened upon the city of Charleston, and directed him to inquire into

the matter. As soon as breakfast was finished, Colonel Serrell and Lieutenant Nathan M. Edwards, of his own command, started across the marsh, carrying a fourteen-foot plank between them. When the mud would not bear them they sat on the plank and pushed it forward between their legs. When, again, the soil appeared stiffer, they carried the plank until they reached the soft mud once more. And so the first examination was made in open view of three Confederate forts and twelve batteries, and on a day of most intense heat. However, a spot was found where the mud seemed of slight depth and where the city of Charleston could be distinctly seen. A position was selected by Colonel Serrell, as he says in his official report, "at a point bearing from the south-westerly end of the hard ground a course by magnetic compass north 40° west, to a point from which the bearing to Fort Sumter is north 12° east, and to the old beacon-light south 86° east." This place was about 7900 yards from Charleston. In the evening Colonel Serrell reported to General Gillmore that he believed a battery could be constructed at a place which he indicated on the map, and suggested that it be made of sand-bags with a platform of grillage. He thought a gun weighing not over 10,000 pounds could be placed on skids having a bearing of 100 square feet and taken across the marsh, in the same manner in which Bonaparte took his field-pieces over the Alps on the snow. He estimated that 2300 men could carry, in one night, filled sand-bags sufficient in number to make the battery; that 60 soldiers could carry the platform; that 450 men could put the gun into the battery, and 35 men could carry the magazine.

For several days after the report was prepared careful examinations were made by Colonel Serrell, and various experiments tried under his direction to ascertain the bearing qualities of the marsh. Many soundings were made at various points with a thirty-foot iron rod, and the mud was found in places to be twenty feet deep, the rod being pushed down to that depth with ease. The swamp was covered with wild grass; but this grass had no sustaining power whatever, and it was quite easy for men on a plank to start waves of mud across the surface of the marsh. A platform was constructed, and piles of sand-bags, regularly laid, were mounted on it. It was found that the platform held 600 pounds to the square foot, uniformly distributed, but at 900 pounds to the foot the platform sank at one corner, and the sand-bags slid off and vanished in the mud. A story was current in the department at the time that a requisition had been sent to Colonel Serrell by some one, more of a wit than an officer, in which a detail was called for of "twenty men eighteen feet long to do duty in fifteen feet of mud."

On the morning of the 2d of August a general plan for the construction of the marsh battery was submitted by Colonel Serrell to General Gillmore. It received his immediate approval, and preparations were begun for cutting the timber and building a trestle-work roadway across the marsh. This road, some two and a half miles long, was made during the following week, and then the difficult construction of the marsh battery was commenced under the direct fire of Batteries Haskell, Cheves, and Simkins and the other smaller Confederate works on James Island. A very large party of soldiers was detailed to make and fill sand-bags. A mock battery was built under Colonel Serrell's orders to the left of the proposed marsh battery by Lieutenants Edwards and Charles V. Hartman, of the Volunteer Engineers, for the purpose of drawing the Confederate fire from our working parties.

This plan was successful. The foundation for the real battery was commenced under the direction of Colonel Serrell by placing two large platforms on the surface of the marsh. Sheet piling was driven to surround the gun-platform. The piling to be pressed down into the mud, pointed at one end, was fastened crosswise to a long pole by a rope. The shorter end of this pole having been attached to one of the platforms loaded with sand-bags, a party of men on the other platform, pulling on the long end of the pole, pushed the piling down the twenty feet to the sand substratum. In this way much of it was done, but it was found most convenient to work about fifteen soldiers at each end, and by the weight of thirty men push the pile down. When this foundation of piling had all been pressed down into place surrounding what was to be the gun-deck, a grillage of pine logs was bolted securely together surrounding three sides of it. On this construction of cross-beams 13,000 sand-bags weighing over 800 tons were placed, having been carried from the camp of the Volunteer Engineers

across the trestle work, and a parapet with epaulement was built upon it.

On the 12th day of August a careful picketing of all the streams and inlets thereabout was made by boats armed with naval howitzers, so that the soldiers at work in the marsh should not be surprised, and on the 17th an 8-inch 200-pounder Parrott rifle gun was successfully transported over the marsh and mounted in the battery.⎰ It was immediately christened the "Swamp Angel" by the soldiers in the camp.

On the morning of August 21st General Gillmore sent a communication to General Beauregard, who was in command of the Confederate troops in the military district of Charleston, with the demand for the immediate evacuation of Morris Island and Fort Sumter, and stating that unless this was done the city itself would be shelled from "batteries already established within easy and effective range of the heart of the city." No attention was paid to this notice, and that night General Gillmore ordered Lieutenant Charles Sellmer, 11th Regiment Maine Volunteers, who had been a sergeant of artillery in the old army before the war, and is now a captain in the 3d Regiment United States Artillery, to take a detachment of his command to the battery and sight the gun just to the left of the steeple of St. Michael's Church in Charleston. Colonel Serrell, assisted by Lieutenant Edwards, had laid the line of fire in the afternoon. They were kept in the battery for over three hours under a tremendous fire from the enemy while putting in range stakes to fire by in the night, as no part of the city could then be seen. The gun was given an elevation of 31° 30′, Colonel Serrell having had the top carriage altered to enable this to be done; and it was charged, by special instructions, with twenty pounds of powder, being four pounds greater than the ordinary service charge.

At half-past one on the morning of August 22d the first shell with percussion-fuse was fired from the "Swamp Angel." The noise made by bells and whistles in the middle of the night told the Union soldiers that the shell had fallen into the city. Sixteen shells were fired that early morning hour. Twelve of the shells fired were of Mr. R. P. Parrott's own construction at the West Point foundry, and filled with a fluid composition, and the other four shells were filled with "Short's Solidified Greek Fire." General Beauregard wrote General Gillmore on the morning of August 22d, saying, "Your firing a number of the most destructive missiles ever used in war into the midst of a city taken unawares and filled with sleeping women and children will give you a bad eminence in history." The general replied, and on August 23d twenty more shells, filled with "Greek fire," were fired from the gun in the marsh. Six of these shells exploded in the gun, doubtless shortening the life of the piece to some extent. On the thirty-sixth discharge of the "Swamp Angel," the breech of the gun just behind the vent blew out of its jacket and the gun was thrown forward on the

⎰ This gun never was used in breaching the walls of Fort Sumter, and the great 300-pounder rifle gun which did such execution on that fort never fired into Charleston.— EDITORS.

parapet. The gun as it appeared on the parapet seemed to the Confederates as if in position for firing, and a large amount of ammunition was needlessly expended upon it.

From the hour of 1 o'clock on the afternoon of August 21st, when Lieutenant Sellmer's detachment started for the battery, thirteen guns and mortars, among which were two 10-inch Colum-

THE "SWAMP ANGEL" MOUNTED AS A MONUMENT, IN TRENTON, NEW JERSEY.

biads and two 10-inch sea-coast mortars, were trying to prevent the manning of the gun, and, after it had commenced firing, to silence it. But they did little damage to the battery and none to the men. The mortar shells, with long-time fuses, did not explode until they had stuck in the mud, and the

shells from the Columbiads burst in front of the parapet and did no damage.

No other guns were mounted in the marsh battery until September 7th, when Battery Wagner surrendered to the Union troops. ⸯ Then two 10-inch sea-coast mortars were placed there to draw off the fire of the batteries on James Island.

Colonel Serrell says that the distinctive features of the marsh battery as a work of engineering were "that the gun-platform was placed upon a gun-deck resting upon vertical sheet piling, outside and around which there was a grillage of logs. If the gun and the other weights upon the gun-deck were heavy enough to tend to sink in the mud, the weight upon the grillage, in the form of sand in bags, which formed the parapet and epaulement of the battery, by being increased, counterpoised the gun-deck. It was simply a force meeting another force of a like amount in an opposite direction." The English journal, "Engineering," in its review of the operations of the Federal and Confederate armies at the close of the war, speaks of the construction of this battery as one of the most important engineering works done by either army. It was a successful piece of difficult engineering, and a practical method of inflicting damage on a city nearly five miles distant, regardless of its army, its cannon, and its great fortifications, which were within close sight and easy range.

The "Swamp Angel" was purchased after the war with some condemned metal and sent to Trenton, New Jersey, to be melted, but, having been identified, was set up on a granite monument in that city on the corner of Perry and Clinton streets.

ⸯ After the capture of Batteries Wagner and Gregg, guns were mounted on the latter fortification. General Gillmore, in his exhaustive work on "Engineer and Artillery Operations against the Defenses of Charleston

in 1863" (New York, Van Nostrand, 1865), gives the record of one 30-pounder Parrott that sent 4253 shells toward the city of Charleston, many of them reaching it, others falling short.—W. S. S.

THE OPPOSING LAND FORCES AT CHARLESTON, S. C.

The composition, losses, and strength of each army as here stated give the gist of all the data obtainable in the Official Records. K stands for killed; w for wounded; m w for mortally wounded; m for captured or missing; c for captured.

Union: Maj.-Gen. Quincy A. Gillmore, commanding Department of the South.
Confederate: General G. T. Beauregard, commanding Department of South Carolina, Georgia, and Florida. ⸯ

Battery Wagner, July 18th.

UNION.

FIRST DIVISION, Brig.-Gen. Truman Seymour (w).
First Brigade, Brig.-Gen. George C. Strong (m w): 6th Conn., Col. John L. Chatfield (m w), Capt. John N. Tracy; 9th Me., Col. Sabine Emery (w); 54th Mass. (colored). Col. Robert G. Shaw (k), Capt. Luis F. Emilio; 3d N. H., Col. John H. Jackson (w); 48th N. Y., Col. William B. Barton (w); 76th Pa., Capt. John S. Littell. *Second Brigade*, Col. Haldimand S. Putnam (k): 7th N. H., Lieut.-Col. Joseph C. Abbott; 100th N. Y., Col.

George B. Dandy; 62d Ohio, Col. Francis B. Pond; 67th Ohio, Col. Alvin C. Voris. *Artillery*, Lieut.-Col. Richard W. Jackson and Capt. Loomis L. Langdon (in charge of siege-batteries): C, 3d R. I., Capt. Charles R. Brayton; E, 3d U. S., Lieut. John R. Myrick.

Total Union loss: killed, 246; wounded, 880; captured or missing, 389 = 1515. The strength of the assaulting column (exclusive of Stevenson's brigade, held in reserve) is estimated at 5000.

CONFEDERATE.

Garrison, Brig.-Gen. William B. Taliaferro: 32d Ga., Col. George P. Harrison, Jr.; 31st N. C., Lieut.-Col. C. W. Knight; 51st N. C., Col. Hector McKethan; Charleston (S. C.) Battalion, Lieut.-Col. P. C. Gaillard (w); 7th S. C. Battalion, Maj. J. H. Rion. *Artillery*, Lieut.-Col. J. C. Simkins (k): 63d Ga. (2 co's), Capts. J. T. Buckner

and W. J. Dixon; 1st S. C. (2 co's), Capts. W. T. Tatom (k) and Warren Adams; S. C. Battery, Capt. W. L. De Pass.

Total Confederate loss: killed and wounded, 174.

Total force guarding fortifications around Charleston, about 8500.

Total engaged at Battery Wagner, about 1000.

ⸯ That part of Florida east of the Apalachicola River was added to General Beauregard's command October 7th, 1862.

Siege Operations, August–September, 1863.

UNION.— MORRIS ISLAND, Brig.-Gen. Alfred H. Terry. *First Brigade*, Col. Henry R. Guss : 9th Me., Lieut.-Col. Z. H. Robinson ; 3d N. H., Capt. James F. Randlett ; 4th N. H., Lieut.-Col. Louis Bell ; 97th Pa., Maj. Galusha Pennypacker. *Second Brigade*, Col. Joshua B. Howell : 39th Ill., Col. Thomas O. Osborn ; 62d Ohio, Col. F. B. Pond ; 67th Ohio, Maj. Lewis Butler ; 85th Pa., Maj. Edward Campbell. *Third Brigade*, Brig.-Gen. Thomas G. Stevenson : 7th Conn., Col. Joseph R. Hawley ; 10th Conn., Maj. Edwin S. Greeley ; 24th Mass., Col. Francis A. Osborn ; 7th N. H., Lieut.-Col. J. C. Abbott ; 100th N. Y., Col. G. B. Dandy. *Fourth Brigade*, Col. James Montgomery : 54th Mass. (colored), Col. M. S. Littlefield ; 2d S. C. (colored), Lieut.-Col. W. W. Marple ; 3d U. S. C. T., Col. B. C. Tilghman. *Fifth Brigade*, Col. W. W. H. Davis : 47th N. Y., Maj. C. R. McDonald ; Independent Battalion N. Y., Capt. M. Schmitt ; 52d Pa., Lieut.-Col. H. M. Hoyt ; 104th Pa., Maj. E. L. Rogers. *Artillery*, Lieut.-Col. R. W. Jackson and Capt. L. L. Langdon : B, 3d R. I., Capt. Albert E. Green ; C, 3d R. I., Capt. Charles R. Brayton ; D, 3d R. I., Capt. Richard G. Shaw ; H, 3d R. I., Capt. Augustus W. Colwell ; I, 3d R. I., Capt. Charles G. Strahan ; M, 3d R. I., Capt. Joseph J. Comstock, Jr. ; B, 1st U. S., Lieut. Guy V. Henry ; C, 1st U. S. (detachment), Lieut. James E. Wilson ; E, 3d U. S., Lieut. John R. Myrick ; B, 3d N. Y., Capt. James E. Ashcroft ; F, 3d N. Y., Lieut. Paul Birchmeyer. *Miscellaneous :* Detachment 11th Me., Lieut. Charles Sellmer ; Detachment I, 1st Mass. Cav., Lieut. Charles V. Holt ; 1st N. Y. Engineers, Col. Edward W. Serrell.

NORTH END OF FOLLY ISLAND, Brig.-Gen. Israel Vogdes. *African Brigade*, Brig.-Gen. Edward A. Wild : 55th Mass., Col. Norwood P. Hallowell ; 1st N. C., Col. James C. Beecher ; 2d N. C. (detachment), Col. Alonzo G. Draper ; 3d N. C. (detachment), Capt. John Wilder. *Foster's Brigade*, Brig.-Gen. R. S. Foster : 13th Ind., Col. Cyrus J. Dobbs ; 112th N. Y., Col. Jeremiah C. Drake ; 169th N. Y., Col. Clarence Buell. *Alford's Brigade*, Col. Samuel M. Alford : 3d N. Y., Lieut.-Col. E. G. Floyd ; 89th N. Y., Col. Harrison S. Fairchild ; 103d N. Y., Col. William Heine ; 117th N. Y., Col. Alvin White. *Artillery :* 1st Conn., Capt. A. P. Rockwell.

SOUTH END OF FOLLY ISLAND, Brig.-Gen. Geo. H. Gordon. *First Brigade*, Brig.-Gen. A. Schimmelfennig : 41st N. Y., Lieut.-Col. Detleo von Einsiedel ; 54th N. Y., Capt. Clemens Knipschild ; 127th N. Y., Lieut.-Col. Stewart L. Woodford ; 142d N. Y., Col. N. Martin Curtis ; 107th Ohio, Capt. William Smith ; 74th Pa., Capt. Henry Krauseneck. *Second Brigade*, Brig.-Gen. Adelbert Ames : 17th Conn., Col. W. H. Noble ; 40th Mass., Lieut.-Col. Joseph A. Dalton ; 144th N. Y., Col. David E. Gregory ; 157th N. Y., Maj. James C. Carmichael ; 25th Ohio, Capt. Nathaniel Haughton ; 75th Ohio, Col. A. L. Harris.

Recapitulation of Union losses, July 10th–Sept. 7th :

	Killed.	Wounded.	Captured or Missing.	Total.
Morris Island, July 10	15	91		106
Battery Wagner, July 11	49	123	167	339
Battery Wagner, July 18	246	880	389	1515
Siege operations, July 18–Sept. 7	71	278	9	358
Total on Morris Island	381	1372	565	2318

The effective strength of the land forces employed in the direct operations against Charleston, ranged from 11,000 to 16,000.

The loss from Sept. 8th to Dec. 31st, 1863, was 14 killed and 42 wounded = 56.

☆ The troops and commanders employed in the defense of Morris Island were relieved from time to time. The commanders were Brig.-Gen. W. B. Taliaferro, Brig.-Gen. John-

CONFEDERATE.— FIRST MILITARY DISTRICT, ☆ Brig. Gen. R. S. Ripley. *First Subdivision*, Brig.-Gen. William B. Taliaferro : 6th Ga., Col. John T. Lofton ; 19th Ga., Col. A. J. Hutchins ; 32d Ga., Col. George P. Harrison, Jr. ; 54th Ga., Col. C. H. Way ; 31st N. C., Col. John V. Jordon ; 21st S. C., Col. R. F. Graham ; 25th S. C., Col. C. H. Simonton ; Marion (S. C.) Art'y, Capt. E. L. Parker ; Chatham (Ga.) Art'y, Capt. John F. Wheaton ; Palmetto (S. C.) Battalion Art'y, Lieut.-Col. E. B. White ; S. C. Batt'y, Capt. J. T. Kanapaux ; A, 1st S. C. Art'y, Capt. F. D. Blake ; Ga. and S. C. Siege Train, Maj. Edward Manigault ; 2d S. C. Art'y, Col. A. D. Frederick ; S. C. Art'y, Capt. John R. Mathewes ; Gist Guard (S. C.) Art'y, Capt. C. E. Chichester ; 5th S. C. Cav. (4 co's), Col. John Dunovant ; Lucas's (S. C.) Battalion, Maj. J. J. Lucas ; 23d Ga., Maj. M. R. Ballenger ; 27th Ga., Maj. James Gardner ; 28th Ga., Capt. W. P. Crawford ; 1st, 12th, and 18th Ga. Battalions, Col. C. H. Olmstead ; C, F, and I, 1st S. C. Art'y, Lieut.-Col. J. A. Yates ; Savannah River Batteries, Capt. W. W. Billop ; 11th S. C., Col. F. H. Gantt. *Second Subdivision*, Brig.-Gen. Thomas L. Clingman : 7th S. C. Battalion, Lieut.-Col. P. H. Nelson ; 8th N. C., Col. H. M. Shaw ; 51st N. C., Col. H. McKethan ; 61st N. C., Col. J. D. Radcliffe ; 20th S. C., Col. L. M. Keitt ; German Art'y, Capt. F. W. Wagener ; Inglis (S. C.) Art'y, Capt. W. E. Charles ; 1st S. C., Col. William Butler ; S. C. Cav., Capt. A. D. Sparks ; E, 5th S. C. Cav., Capt. L. A. Whilden ; H and K, 1st S. C. Art'y, Capts. H. R. Lesesne and A. S. Gaillard. *Third Subdivision* (Morris Island), Brig.-Gen. A. H. Colquitt : [The troops of this command were drawn from other subdivisions and appear in the commands to which they properly belonged.] *Fourth Subdivision* (Fort Sumter), Col. Alfred Rhett, Maj. Stephen Elliott, Jr. : B, D, and E, 1st S. C. Art'y ; B, 27th Ga. ; F, 28th Ga. Castle Pinckney and Fort Ripley : G, 1st S. C. Art'y, Capt. W. H. Peronneau. [Subsequent to the fall of Morris Island other troops were detailed, in turn, to garrison Fort Sumter.] *Fifth Subdivision*, Brig.-Gen. W. G. DeSaussure : 1st S. C. (Mil.), Col. Ed. Magrath ; 1st S. C. Art'y (Mil.), Col. J. A. Wagener ; 18th S. C. (Mil.), Col. J. E. Carew ; Battalion State Cadets, Maj. J. B. White ; D and H, 5th S. C. Cav., Lieut.-Col. R. J. Jeffords ; K, 4th S. C. Cav., Capt. R. H. Colcock ; S. C. Battery, Capt. W. E. Earle ; Charleston Battalion, Maj. Julius A. Blake. *Evans's Brigade*, ⚓ Brig.-Gen. N. G. Evans : 17th S. C., Col. F. W. McMaster ; 18th S. C., Col. W. H. Wallace ; 22d S. C., Col. S. D. Goodlett ; 23d S. C., Col. H. L. Benbow ; 26th S. C., Col. A. D. Smith ; Holcombe Legion, Lieut.-Col. W. J. Crawley. *Anderson's Brigade*, ⚓ Brig.-Gen. G. T. Anderson : 7th Ga., Col. W. W. White ; 8th Ga., Col. John R. Towers ; 9th Ga., Col. B. Beck ; 11th Ga., Col. F. H. Little ; 59th Ga., Col. Jack Brown. *Wise's Brigade*, ⚓ Brig.-Gen. Henry A. Wise : 26th Va., Col. P. R. Page ; 4th Va. Heavy Art'y, Col. J. T. Goode ; 46th Va., Col. R. T. W. Duke ; 59th Va., Col. W. B. Tabb.

General Beauregard, in his official report, says : " The total loss in killed and wounded on Morris Island from July 10th to Sept. 7th was only 641 men ; and deducting the killed and wounded due to the landing on July 11th and 18th, the killed and wounded by the terrible bombardment, which lasted almost uninterruptedly, night and day, during fifty-eight days, only amounted to 296 men, many of whom were only slightly wounded. It is still more remarkable that during the same period of time, when the enemy fired 6202 shots and shells at Fort Sumter, varying in weight from 30 to 300 pounds, only three men were killed and 49 wounded."

The entire loss in the defenses of Charleston from July 10th to September 7th was 157 killed, 674 wounded, and 159 captured or missing = 990. (See " Official Records," Vol. XXVIII., Part I., p. 409.)

It is estimated that the force defending the immediate approaches to Charleston ranged from 6500 to 18,000.

son Hagood, Brig.-Gen. A. H. Colquitt, Col. R. F. Graham, Col. George P. Harrison, Jr., and Col. L. M. Keitt.

⚓ Joined after capture of Morris Island by Union forces.

THE BATTLE OF OLUSTEE, OR OCEAN POND, FLORIDA.

BY SAMUEL JONES, MAJOR-GENERAL, C. S. A.

THE fourth year of the war was also the year for the election of a President of the United States, and it would have been strange if an event of so much importance had not in some measure shaped the conduct of the campaigns of that year. If any one of the Southern States could be brought so effectually under the control of the Union army as to give plausible pretext to any considerable portion of the inhabitants, white and black, to form a quasi State government recognizing the authority of the United States, it would not only be received as an earnest of the success of the Union arms, but the State could be represented in the approaching convention for the nomination of a candidate for President, and take part in the election to follow.

Florida appeared to offer better prospect of success in such an undertaking than any other Southern State. Its great extent of coast and its intersection by a broad and deep river, navigable by vessels of war, exposed a great part of the State to the control of the Union forces whenever it should be thought desirable to occupy it. The exigencies of the Confederate service had in a great measure stripped Florida of troops. If a column of Union troops could penetrate the country westward from Jacksonville, occupy a point in the interior, and break up communication between east, middle, and west Florida by the destruction of the railroad and bridges about the Suwanee River, the Southern Confederacy would not only be deprived of a large quantity of the food drawn from east and south Florida, but a *point d'appui* would be established for any of the inhabitants who might be disposed to attempt the organization of a State acknowledging allegiance to the United States.

President Lincoln's views on the subject are expressed in the following letter:

"EXECUTIVE MANSION, WASHINGTON,
January 13th, 1864.

"MAJOR-GENERAL GILLMORE:

"I understand an effort is being made by some worthy gentlemen to reconstruct a loyal State government in Florida. Florida is in your department, and it is not unlikely that you may be there in person. I have given Mr. Hay a commission of major, and sent him to you with some blank-books and other blanks to aid in the reconstruction. He will explain as to the manner of using the blanks, and also my general views on the subject. It is desirable for all to coöperate; but if irreconcilable differences of opinion shall arise, you are master. I wish the thing done in the most speedy way possible, so that when done it will be within the range of the late proclamation on the subject. The detail labor of course will have to be done by others; but I shall be greatly obliged if you will give it such general supervision as you can find convenient with your more strictly military duties. Yours very truly,

"A. LINCOLN."

Under these instructions General Gillmore, on the 5th of February, ordered General Truman Seymour to proceed with a division of troops from Hilton Head to Jacksonville, Florida. Admiral Dahlgren, who seems to have been always ready to coöperate with the land forces, sailed with the expedition with a squadron of five gun-boats, and

was in readiness, if needed, to cover the landing. No opposition was met with, however, and on the 7th General Seymour's force of about seven thousand men landed at Jacksonville.

The objects of the expedition as reported by General Gillmore to the general-in-chief (who did not approve it) were: *First.* To procure an outlet for cotton, lumber, timber, etc. *Second.* To cut off one source of the enemy's commissary stores. *Third.* To obtain recruits for the negro regiments. *Fourth.* "To inaugurate measures for the speedy restoration of Florida to her allegiance," etc.

It was known that the few Confederate troops in east Florida were widely scattered, and no opposition was anticipated until reënforcements could arrive. Celerity of movement was therefore important. General Seymour promptly marched inland,—Colonel McCormick, commanding a picket at McGirt's Creek, retiring,— captured five field-pieces which the Confederates could not move for want of horses, and reached Baldwin, twenty miles from Jacksonville, February 9th, where he was joined by General Gillmore. Colonel Guy V. Henry, commanding a small brigade of cavalry and mounted infantry, marched westward and encountered a picket of about 150 men at the crossing of the south fork of the St. Mary's River, which, with the loss of twenty-five of his men, killed and wounded, and without loss to the Confederates, he dislodged, and proceeded to within three miles of Lake City, when he was recalled, and on the 11th joined the main body, which had reached Barber's plantation on the south fork of the St. Mary's. Here the command was delayed for the lack of transportation. The railroad had been relied on for transportation, but there was only one engine on the road, and that in such wretched condition that it could not be used within several days, if at all.

From Baldwin General Gillmore returned to Jacksonville, and on the 13th to Hilton Head, whence he issued a proclamation announcing his occupancy of Florida, calling on the people to take the oath of allegiance to the Union, assuring them that the State had been recovered from rebel rule, and would not again be abandoned, the United States being able to protect all loyal citizens.

There seems to have been some vacillation in the execution of the expedition. General Seymour, on whom the execution of General Gillmore's plans devolved, wholly disapproved it. The movement on Lake City he regarded as in opposition to sound strategy, and inadvisable, and he had discovered that what had been said of the desire of Florida to come back into the Union was a delusion. "Do not," he writes to Gillmore, "fritter away your infantry in the interior," but at once withdraw the whole force back to Jacksonville and Palatka, points which could be easily held and would serve as rendezvous for such Floridians (if any) as should desire to form a new State government under the Union flag. To this Gillmore replied telling him not to risk a repulse by an advance on Lake City; if he met serious opposition he should concentrate at

Sanderson's on the St. Mary's. But how was he to advance at all without risking a repulse, seeing that there was an enemy in his path? Nor could he remain at Sanderson's with entire safety, for Seymour reported that Sanderson's could not be fortified to advantage or the troops supplied there. Gillmore then directed him to concentrate without delay at Baldwin, but that point offered scarcely more advantages of strength than Sanderson's, and was, besides, twenty miles from his supplies at Jacksonville, and he had but little transportation.

Whilst General Gillmore was at his headquarters at Hilton Head and the army in the interior of Florida was beyond the reach of telegraphic communication, much of necessity was left to the discretion of General Seymour. Having obtained reliable information that the strength of the enemy in his front did not exceed his own, the excellent character of his own troops, as he reports to his chief, forbade any doubt as to the propriety of a conflict on equal terms. Accordingly he resolved to carry out the general plan on which he supposed the occupation and control of east Florida had been based, by marching at once to the Suwanee River and destroying the bridges and railroad, thus breaking up communication between east and west Florida. On the receipt of Seymour's letter communicating his determination, Gillmore promptly returned a sharp and emphatic disapproval; but it was too late.

On the landing of Seymour's expedition at Jacksonville, Brigadier-General Joseph Finegan, the Confederate commander of east Florida, immediately telegraphed to Savannah and Charleston for reënforcements, and by February 10th had collected at Lake City 490 infantry, 110 cavalry, and two field-pieces of his own widely scattered force. That night he placed the men in position two and a half miles east of that town, and reënforcements were sent to him from Charleston and Savannah. Demonstrations were made by the Union commanders at these points, but they failed to prevent the departure of reënforcements for Florida.

By the 13th a Confederate force of about 4600 infantry, 600 cavalry, and three field-batteries (12 guns) was concentrated near Lake City. This force was organized into two brigades; the first, A. H. Colquitt's, made up of the 6th, 19th, 23d, 27th, and 28th Georgia regiments, the 6th Florida, and the Chatham battery of Georgia artillery. The second brigade was composed of the 32d and 64th Georgia Volunteers, 1st Regiment Georgia Regulars, 1st Florida Battalion, Bonaud's Battalion of Infantry, and Guerard's Light Battery. Colonel George P. Harrison, Jr., of the 32d Georgia, commanded the brigade. The cavalry was commanded by Colonel Caraway Smith, and the Florida light artillery was unattached and in reserve. The whole force numbered about 5400 men at Ocean Pond on the Olustee, 13 miles east of Lake City.

The country along the railroad from the Suwanee River eastward is low and flat, without streams to delay the march of an army, and covered with open pine forests unobstructed by undergrowth. The only natural features which could serve any purposes of defense were the lakes and ponds scattered over the country. The position at Ocean Pond offered these advantages. From the 13th to the 20th some defensive works were begun, but little progress was made toward completing them, on a line extending from Ocean Pond on the left, a sheet of water of about four miles in length by from two to two and a half miles in width, to another pond about two miles long, on the right and to the south of the railroad. A short distance in front of the left was another pond, and in front of the right a bay or jungle, passable only within two hundred yards to the right or south of the railroad. The position possessed strength provided the enemy would attack it directly in front, but could be readily turned.

Early on the morning of February 20th, Seymour marched westward from his camp on the south fork of the St. Mary's River, to engage the enemy near Olustee, about eighteen miles distant. The country over which he marched was open and level, presenting no strategic points, and the ground was firm, offering no difficulty to the march of troops of any amount. Colonel Henry was in advance with his small brigade of cavalry and Elder's Horse Artillery (Battery B, First U. S. Artillery). Though there was no lack of general officers in General Gillmore's command, on this expedition the three infantry brigades were commanded by colonels. Colonel (afterward General and United States Senator) J. R. Hawley led in three parallel columns, marching by flank, the center one on the road, the other two dressing on it. Colonels W. B. Barton's and James Montgomery's brigades followed in the same order of march. Captain John Hamilton's Light Battery "E," 3d United States Artillery, and Captain L. L. Langdon's "M," 1st United States Artillery, and a section of Rhode Island Artillery, under Lieutenant Metcalf, followed. One regiment, the 55th Massachusetts, was left in camp, which, with other regiments detached, reduced the force engaged to about 5500 men, with 16 field-pieces.

General Finegan had thrown forward Colonel Smith's cavalry, supported by the 64th and two companies of the 32d Georgia regiments, to skirmish with the advancing enemy and endeavor to draw them on to attack in the selected position. Apprehending, however, that the Union commander would be too cautious to attack a relatively strong position which could be so easily turned, he ordered forward General Colquitt with three of his regiments and a section of Gamble's artillery to assume command of all the troops in front. About two miles east of Olustee Colquitt found the enemy, who had driven in the pickets, advancing rapidly.

The colonel of the 64th Georgia, a new regiment, never before in action, supposing that only

Hawley's brigade was composed of the 7th Conn., Capt. B. H. Skinner; 7th New Hampshire, Col. J. C. Abbott; and 8th U. S. Colored Troops, Col. Charles W. Fribley — Barton's brigade of the 47th N. Y., Col. Henry Moore; 48th N. Y., Major W. B. Coan; and 115th N. Y., Col. Simeon Sammon — Montgomery's brigade of the 54th Mass., Col. E. N. Hallowell; 55th Mass. (not engaged), Col. N. P. Hallowell; and 1st N. C., Lieut.-Col. W. N. Reed.

mounted troops were advancing against him, had formed square to resist cavalry. Colquitt arrived just in time to save the square from being ripped open by the enemy's artillery. He threw forward skirmishers and quickly formed line of battle under a brisk fire, the 19th Georgia on the right, the 28th on the left, with the section of Gamble's battery in the center. The 64th and the two companies of the 32d Georgia were formed on the left of the 28th. The 6th Georgia was thrown still farther to the left to check any movement by that flank; the cavalry was divided and thrown to the two flanks. In this order the line advanced, the enemy yielding slightly but stubbornly contesting the ground. Finding the enemy in force in his front, Colquitt called for reënforcements, but General Finegan had anticipated him and Colonel Harrison was at hand with his brigade. The 6th Florida Battalion was put in line on the right of the 19th Georgia, and the 23d on the left of the 64th Georgia. Colonel Harrison with his own regiments, the 32d Georgia and 1st Georgia Regulars, took position between the 23d and 64th Georgia, and by Colquitt's order assumed direction of affairs on the left of the line. Instead, therefore, of attacking the Confederates in a selected position strengthened by field-works as the Union officers supposed, the battle was joined about 3 o'clock P. M. on level ground covered with open pine forest, offering no advantage of position to either.

General Seymour's plan was to concentrate his artillery in the center, strongly supported on both flanks by the first brigade, and while the two brigades in rear were hastening into position, to overwhelm his enemy by a rapid fire of his superior artillery, and then charge. Hamilton's and Langdon's batteries were hurried forward to join Elder's, which had been in advance with the cavalry. The 7th Connecticut, which so gallantly had led the first assault on Battery Wagner, July 11th, 1863, had first felt and driven back the advanced Confederates, and in turn had itself yielded ground, was withdrawn to unmask the line; the 7th New Hampshire moved forward into line on the right and the 8th United States Colored Troops on the left of the batteries. The fire of the latter was exceedingly effective. The section of Gamble's battery was soon put *hors de combat*. It was replaced by the Chatham Artillery of Savannah, which, under Captain John F. Wheaton, was drawn from the right to the center under a galling fire. The whole Confederate force on the field moved forward and the action became general along the whole line. The 7th New Hampshire, a veteran regiment armed with superior rifles, broke and fled in confusion; not, however, until it had suffered severely in killed and wounded. The most strenuous efforts of its colonel, Abbott, and of Colonel Hawley, aided by staff-officers, could not stem its flight and reform it. The 8th United States

(colored) on the left experienced the same fate. Its colonel, Fribley (white), had fallen mortally wounded; other commissioned officers and many of the rank and file had fallen, when it too fled and did not appear again as a regiment on the field. Barton's brigade replaced the 7th New Hampshire and Montgomery's the 8th United States Colored Troops, but the flight of those regiments had greatly exposed the artillery. Though it continued its fire with admirable effect, the men and horses were falling fast, and some of these, becoming unmanageable, dashed and locked their carriages against the trees, until so many of the men and horses were killed and wounded that five guns were abandoned to the advancing Confederates. ⚓

By that time the Confederates had exhausted their ammunition, and there was none near at hand. The regiments were halted, the few men who had ammunition returning a slow fire to the very brisk fire from the other side, while staff-officers, couriers, and orderlies were riding at utmost speed between the line and an ammunition-car on the railroad some distance in the rear, bringing up cartridges in haversacks, pockets, caps, in anything into which they could be crammed, and distributing them along the line. To hold a line under a heavy fire which it cannot return is a severe trial to the steadiness of the best troops. During this trying pause Lieutenant Hugh H. Colquitt of the general's staff was a conspicuous object to the troops in both lines as he galloped in front of the Confederates, waving a battle-flag and exhorting the men to stand fast, not to lie down or shelter themselves behind the pine-trees, lest the enemy should suppose the line had broken and melted away, and assuring them that their cartridge-boxes would soon be replenished.↓ The men were equal to the emergency and stood fast until they were supplied with ammunition. In the meantime the 27th Georgia Regiment, Bonaud's Battalion, the 1st Florida Battalion, and a section of Guerard's Battery arrived from the intrenched lines in the rear. They were put in position near and a little in advance of the center, to hold the enemy in check until the other commands could be supplied with ammunition. By direction of General Colquitt, Colonel Harrison had formed the 6th and 32d Georgia regiments on the extreme left, thus securing an effective cross-fire on Seymour's right. A general advance along the whole Confederate line followed, and the Union line yielded ground, first reluctantly and sullenly, then with some precipitation which presently became a confused flight. When the Union line gave way, the Confederates sprang forward with a yell and pursued the enemy several miles and until night closed in on the scene and stopped pursuit.

During the engagement Colonel Smith's cavalry had guarded the flanks, Lieutenant-Colonel A. H. McCormick, 2d Florida Cavalry, on the right, and Colonel Duncan L. Clinch, 4th Georgia Cavalry, on

⚓ The old regular soldiers of the artillery seem to have borne themselves with conspicuous gallantry. Captain Langdon speaks of a driver, whose name surely deserved to be recorded, who, with his life-blood streaming from a mortal wound, struggled to extricate his

team and carry off the gun until he fell dead in the resolute but vain attempt.—S. J.

↓ Senator Hawley told me that he was impressed with the daring gallantry of the young aide-de-camp, and subsequently learned his name from Senator Colquitt.—S. J.

the left. Early in the action Colonel Clinch was so severely wounded as to necessitate his removal from the field, and was succeeded by Captain N. A. Brown. When the Union line finally gave way and the flight commenced, the cavalry was ordered to pursue and seize every opportunity to strike the retreating enemy. But from some excess of caution, or other unexplained cause, the pursuit was not vigorous, and thus the full fruits of a dearly won victory on a well-contested field were not gathered. The retreat was covered by Colonel Henry's cavalry and the 7th Connecticut Volunteers, which halted for a time at the St. Mary's and Baldwin, but the main body of the shattered army continued its flight until it gained the shelter of the gun-boats at Jacksonville. As so often happened during the war, the victors were ignorant of the full extent of the victory, which, on this occasion, was so complete that a vigorous pursuit could scarcely have failed at least to double the already heavy Union loss.

General Seymour, who throughout the day had shown his usual coolness and gallantry, attributed his disaster to the "great numerical superiority of the Confederates," an opinion which doubtless he held with sincerity at the time, but which was soon found to be entirely erroneous, the numbers engaged being nearly equal. General Gillmore and his staff sharply criticised the whole affair, and even charged Seymour with disobedience of orders, but did not give the specifications. In the Union camps in the Department of the South the affair was characterized as a second Dade's massacre, or Braddock's defeat. It was, however, a fair fight in an open field. The tenacity with which the Union troops contested the field is shown by the losses on both sides. Theirs was about one-third of their

number engaged, and 120 horses killed. It was especially heavy in officers : Colonel Fribley was mortally wounded and died on the field, Lieutenant-Colonel Reed was mortally, and the major of his regiment, Boyle, severely wounded, as were Colonels Moore of the 47th, Sammon of the 115th New York, and the chief of artillery, Captain Hamilton. Captain Vandervere of the 115th New York was killed. General Seymour commended the good conduct of all the troops engaged except the 7th New Hampshire and 8th United States Colored Troops. The former's misconduct he attributed to the presence in the ranks of a number of inferior conscripts and substitutes. It lost in the engagement 209, and the 8th United States Colored Troops 310, officers and men. In addition to five or six field-pieces, the Confederates captured 1600 rifles and muskets, a flag, and a quantity of ammunition.

The Confederate loss was 940 killed and wounded. The 32d Georgia had suffered most severely, losing 164 officers and men. Among the killed or mortally wounded were Lieutenant-Colonel James Barrow and Lieutenant P. A. Waller, 64th Georgia ; Captain H. A. Cannon, commanding the 1st Georgia Regulars ; Adjutant William H. Johnson, 19th Georgia ; Lieutenant W. H. Combs, 6th Georgia ; Lieutenant Thomas J. Hill, 6th Florida ; and Lieutenant W. W. Holland, 28th Georgia. Lieutenant R. T. Dancey, 32d Georgia, on Colonel Harrison's staff, was killed by the side of his chief early in the action.

This expedition to Olustee, the only one of any magnitude which General Gillmore had undertaken beyond the range of the gun-boats, terminated his campaign in the Department of the South. [See papers on Drewry's Bluff, to follow.]

COMMENTS ON GENERAL JONES'S PAPER, BY JOSEPH R. HAWLEY, BREVET MAJOR-GENERAL, U. S. V.

I HAVE read General Jones's paper upon the battle of Olustee with much interest. It is clearly his sincere endeavor to write an impartial statement of the facts ; it is amusing to see how widely he varies from the exaggerated reports of Generals Beauregard and Finegan.

He fairly presents the differences between Generals Gillmore and Seymour. At Baldwin, a night or two before the battle, General Seymour called together six or eight of his officers for consultation. Some were cautious, others were outspoken, but it was decidedly the general opinion that it would be impossible to hold permanently a position out toward the center of the State, having for its line of communication a rickety railroad with one engine running fifty or sixty miles back to the base at Jacksonville. It would take more than our whole little army simply to hold the line against the force that would certainly soon be collected against us. The Confederates could have ruined us by letting us march one more day without interruption and then sitting down on the railroad between us and home with their rapidly increasing force. Most of us thought it would be sufficient to attempt to make the St. John's River our main

western line, but Seymour thought it his duty to go on. He was, and is, a brave and honorable patriot and soldier.

General Jones shows that the Confederates had chosen a strong position. They had their line of battle fully formed to meet us. My old regiment, the 7th Connecticut Infantry, about 330 strong, armed with Spencer carbines, led the advance guard, commanded by Colonel Henry, and composed of the mounted 40th Massachusetts Infantry (a small regiment), Captain Samuel S. Elder's regular battery, and a detachment of the 1st Massachusetts Cavalry. Between 2 and 3 P. M. they met and drove back the enemy's cavalry, and soon found the main line, striking up a vigorous combat. Our troops were stretched along the road in the order General Jones describes. When the artillery opened, General Seymour told me the enemy had but a section of artillery "up there" and that it could be captured. Under his orders I put the 8th United States Colored Troops, Colonel Fribley, in line and sent them up the road and led the 7th New Hampshire to the right, moving around to strike the enemy's left flank. Our artillery began to work fast. My little regiment of three hundred, deployed as skirmishers in rather close order, went straight into the face of General Colquitt's brigade in full line waiting for us. Suddenly the 7th New Hampshire, moving in column of companies, saw the solid gray line about 250 yards ahead. A heavy fire was opened on us. Colonel Abbott misunderstood my order of deployment; I undertook to correct the error, and the regiment broke. Here General Jones is in error; they re-formed and did excellent service on our right flank, and later rejoined the 7th Connecticut in the center. They lost in all 209; there were never braver men. In the meantime Colonel Fribley's black men met the enemy at short range. They had reported to me only two or three days before; I was afterward told that they had never had a day's practice in loading and firing. Old troops, finding themselves so greatly overmatched, would have run a little and re-formed — with or without orders. The black men stood to be killed or wounded — losing more than 300 out of 550. General Jones is again in error; they fell back and reorganized. Colonel Fribley's monument shows where he fell.

The 7th Connecticut assembled on their colors in response to their bugle-call, and I placed them in the center of the field opposite to my friend General Colquitt, and they were supplied with ammunition. Several times they checked the enemy with their seven-shooters, and they did not stir from their position until they received a second order from General Seymour to fall back. The 54th Massachusetts (colored) after a time came and stood on their left. The next brigade, under Colonel Barton, of the 48th New York, came up and deployed. But the whole Confederate force of five thousand was there. Barton's brigade suffered frightfully. Montgomery's two regiments, both colored, were heavily punished.

Omitting further details of the battle, which lasted over three hours, shortly after sunset General Seymour ordered us to fall back to a new line. We did so, and several regiments successively gave three cheers. This was the occasion of the report to the Confederate commander that we had formed a new line. Their cavalry so reported, and, though six hundred strong, never fired a shot at us, nor came within our sight. Behind us was a small body of water — an acre, it may be — beside which were gathered a large number of our wounded, under the care of surgeons. All who could walk or be put into wagons were started off, and several surgeons ordered to stay with the remainder.

Our whole column was put in motion deliberately. Seymour took my regiment from me again, to serve as infantry skirmishers in the rear-guard with Henry's mounted men. The 54th Massachusetts was sent to report to me, and with three regiments, moving by the flank, in parallel lines my brigade marched eastward, with our comrades.

General Jones says the Union forces "yielded ground first reluctantly and sullenly, then with some precipitation, which presently became a confused flight. When the Union line gave way, the Confederates sprang forward with a yell and pursued the enemy several miles, and until night closed in on the scene and stopped pursuit."

This must have been borrowed from some of the wild reports made by the enemy immediately after the battle. Our last formation in line of battle (just referred to) was a few hundred yards in rear of the center of the field. It was fast growing dark in the pine woods. Not a yell nor a shot pursued us that long night. When my command reached Baldwin on the 21st, we picked up some of our equipments, left there two or three days before, destroyed some stores, loaded up the cars and moved on to McGirt's Creek. Crossing on the narrow road through the swamp, we formed line on the eastern bank, put out pickets, and took a good sleep. Colonel Henry and his mounted men and the 7th Connecticut stopped at Baldwin over the night of the 21st.

General Finegan's report of the 23d (three days after the battle) says: "I occupy Barber's place this morning and my cavalry are in the vicinity of Baldwin." He says, also, "I left Ocean Pond [the battle-field] yesterday" — that is to say, two days after the fight.

The reports of Generals Colquitt, Finegan, Gardner, and others give reasons for the feeble pursuit — "fatigue, absence of rations, disadvantages of pursuit in the dark," etc. It is stated that the order to pursue was withdrawn "in consequence of a report from the advanced cavalry picket that the enemy had halted for the night and taken a position (subsequently ascertained to be incorrect)." General Colquitt says he sent "repeated orders to Colonel Smith of the cavalry to continue the pursuit, but only two companies on the left, and those but for a short distance, followed the enemy." Smith was relieved from his command, and he requested a court of inquiry. Finegan was relieved by Gardner. General Beauregard, reporting to Richmond, March 25th, says "the fruits of the victory were comparatively insignificant," laying the blame on the cavalry commander, through "whose lack of energy and capacity for the service no serious attempt was made to pursue with his command, while the exhaustion of the infantry . . . and our want of subsistence supplies and ammunition made an immediate pursuit by them impracticable."

It was a fair, square, stand-up fight in pine woods, just there not very thick, and having little undergrowth, save about an occasional swampy hole. There was probably a difference of less than five hundred in the numbers engaged. The Confederates knew the ground and were formed for battle. We rushed in, not waiting for the proper full formation, and were fought in detail. The enemy had the great advantage, with modern weapons, of being on the defensive and ready. There was absolutely no pursuit of the defeated party until the next day. The Confederate loss was 940; the Union loss 1861. This left the former with say 4500; the latter with about 3700, or in about that proportion. It was one of the side-shows of the great war, but the loss on the Union side was proportionately about three times as great as at Buena Vista. I suppose it did help to whittle away the great rebellion.

FROM GETTYSBURG TO THE COMING OF GRANT.

BY MARTIN T. McMAHON, BREVET MAJOR-GENERAL, U. S. V.

THE chief events of this chapter in the history of the Army of the Potomac were the pursuit of Lee to Virginia, the affair of the Vermont brigade at Beaver Creek, in Maryland, the cavalry engagements at Hagerstown and Williamsport, the action at Bristoe Station, the taking of the Rappahannock redoubts, the movement to Mine Run, and the Kilpatrick-Dahlgren raid to Richmond.

After the battle of Gettysburg two corps of the army, the First and the Sixth, under Major-General John Sedgwick, pressed Lee's retreating forces to the pass at Fairfield. [See maps, Vol. III., pp. 381 and 382.] A strong rear-guard held the pursuit in check, compelling frequent formations of the leading brigades in line of battle. Every house and barn along our route of march was filled with wounded Confederates. Lee passed through the mountains in the night of July 5th. One brigade, General T. H. Neill's, was detailed by General Sedgwick to follow and observe the enemy's movements, and the rest of the corps rejoined the main body of the army in the neighborhood of Emmitsburg, crossed the Catoctin range at Hamburg, and came upon the enemy at Beaver Creek July 10th, 1863. At this point it seemed that Lee intended to make a decided stand. His position was a strong one, and apparently was held by a sufficient number of troops. The Vermont brigade, under Colonel L. A. Grant, was ordered to the front as skirmishers and deployed in a piece of woods covering a front of about half a mile. The rest of the command was massed in readiness, and a general engagement was confidently expected. The enemy advanced in line of battle upon the woods where the Vermonters with one battery, somewhat in the rear of their skirmish-line, were posted. In general, a skirmish-line, upon being confronted by the advance of a line of battle, is expected to retire. The Vermonters, however, did not so understand it, and, each one holding his position, they delivered such a steady and telling fire that the enemy's line was twice repulsed. The history of war furnishes few instances such as this, yet the Vermonters did not seem to think that they had accomplished anything out of the usual line of duty.

The enemy, moving from Beaver Creek, took position on the 12th in the neighborhood of Funkstown and fortified heavily. His line ran in general to the right from Funkstown, forming the arc of a circle, the right resting near the field of Antietam. The country was familiar to many of us, who had served in the South Mountain and Antietam campaign. A council of war was called that night at General Meade's headquarters, and the question was discussed whether an attack should be ventured on the following morning upon Lee's intrenched position. Our right covered Hagerstown without occupying the city. Our general line extended to the left, following the direction of the enemy's position. General Sedgwick proposed at the council to take the Sixth and Eleventh corps from our right and, moving by night through and beyond Hagerstown, to occupy by daylight a position upon the enemy's flank and rear, and by a determined attack cut him off from the Potomac while the rest of the army moved directly on his front. This proposition, it appears, was negatived in the council. [See Vol. III., p. 382.] The next day was passed in observation and in preparations for an attack. In the night-time (July 13th) Lee's army withdrew, and, falling rapidly back, crossed the Potomac in safety. Longstreet's corps moved up the valley, crossed the Blue Ridge by way of Chester Gap, and proceeded to Culpeper Court House,

FORT RAMSEY, UPTON'S HILL, VIRGINIA, SHOWING MRS. FORNEY'S HOUSE AND SIGNAL OBSERVATORY, 1863.

VIEW OF ALDIE GAP, VIRGINIA.

where it arrived on the 24th. Hill's corps followed closely by the same route. Ewell, delayed by a fruitless pursuit of General Kelley's force west of Martinsburg, found the Gap obstructed by Meade, crossed the mountains farther up at Thornton's Gap, and joined the other corps in the vicinity of Culpeper.

Kilpatrick's cavalry, which had been sent by way of the Monterey pass, destroyed some of the enemy's trains but had accomplished little in the way of interrupting the passage of the river. The pontoons were again brought into use, and once more the Army of the Potomac entered upon "the sacred soil." The men were in excellent spirits and condition, and as they marched over the bridges of boats at Harper's Ferry and Berlin the men broke out into the refrain, "Carry me back to old Virginny." Meade advanced to Warrenton and the Rappahannock, where he took position confronting Lee. Before the season for operations had finally closed, Meade had pushed his advance to and beyond the Rapidan, the enemy giving up Culpeper Court House, which Meade occupied as headquarters September 13th. ⎰

On the 7th of October the enemy's signal-flags, which were read by our signal-officers on Pony Mountain as ours no doubt were read by the enemy, communicated intelligence which indicated that General Lee was making a formidable movement. This proved to be a movement to his left with the evident purpose of turning our right flank. For reasons never fully explained nor understood, the whole Army of the Potomac, which had marched all the way from Gettysburg for the purpose of engaging Lee, was ordered to retreat. It fell back in good order, certainly, but without apparent occasion. After passing the Rappahannock, General Meade ordered a halt and directed

⎰ It was on the 25th of September, on receipt of the news of Rosecrans's defeat at Chickamauga, that the Government withdrew the Eleventh Corps (Howard's) and the Twelfth (Slocum's) from the Army of the Potomac for service in Tennessee under Hooker. The transfer of these troops was a notable achievement of the Quartermaster-General's Department.— EDITORS.

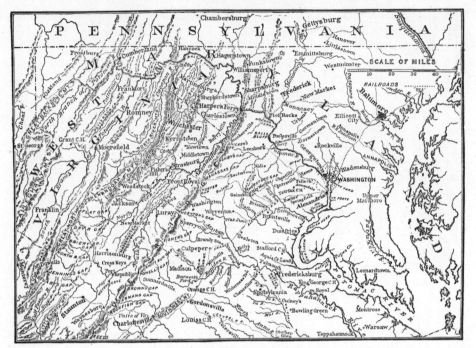

MAP OF NORTHERN VIRGINIA.

General Sedgwick to recross in the direction of Brandy Station and give battle. The movement was executed; but General Lee was not found in the position indicated, being actually engaged in crossing the Rappahannock some miles above, at the Sulphur Springs. General Sedgwick desired and proposed to move in that direction and attack him while crossing. General Meade did not approve of the suggestion and the retreat continued. On the 14th Warren was attacked at Bristoe Station and won a brilliant victory.⚓ The situation at that time was singularly precarious. All the transportation of the army was massed in fields off the road, and a breaking of our line at any point would have inflicted incalculable damage. A panic among teamsters is a thing greatly to be dreaded in an army.

When we reached the vicinity of Centreville the army was halted and took position to await attack. Lee had followed closely, destroying the railroad as he advanced. After a brief reconnoissance he started in his turn to retreat to the Rapidan. Meade pursued, pressing him closely and rebuilding

⚓ The Confederate troops engaged at Bristoe were the divisions of Heth and Anderson of A. P. Hill's corps. On the Union side the action was sustained by the divisions of Hays and Webb. The main attack was made by Heth's division and fell upon the first and third brigades of Webb's division and the third brigade of Hays's. Colonel James E. Mallon, commanding a brigade under Webb, was among the killed. The following order shows the importance of the action:

"HEADQUARTERS, ARMY OF THE POTOMAC, Oct. 15, 1863.
"The Major-General commanding announces to the army that the rear-guard, consisting of the Second Corps, was attacked yesterday while marching by the flank. The enemy, after a spirited contest, was repulsed, losing a battery of five guns, two colors, and 450 prisoners.

"The skill and promptitude of Major-General Warren, and the gallantry and bearing of the officers and soldiers of the Second Corps, are entitled to high commendation.

"By command of Major-General Meade.
"S. WILLIAMS, Asst. Adjt.-General."

The Union loss was 50 killed, 335 wounded, and 161 captured or missing = 546. The Confederate loss was 136 killed, 797 wounded, and 445 captured or missing = 1378.— EDITORS.

the railroad as rapidly as he marched. At Gainesville, or Buckland Mills, on October 19th, there was an affair with the cavalry advance in which both Custer and Kilpatrick distinguished themselves, each in his own way. Custer with one brigade became engaged with part of Fitzhugh Lee's command, which retired before him after crossing the stream at Gainesville. The rest of Lee's command had been drawn off to the left for the purpose of attacking in the rear in case Kilpatrick afforded the opportunity, which he promptly did. With his second brigade he moved forward in support of Custer, who needed no support, however, and the enemy's cavalry came in upon Kilpatrick's rear and scattered him. Kilpatrick believed and reported that he had been routed by infantry. General Custer and the evidence were to the contrary, however; those who came in upon the rear were dismounted cavalry. Some sensation was created throughout the army by this repulse of the cavalry and by the reports of General Kilpatrick, and an order was issued by General Meade, evidently in anticipation of a general engagement the next day. One division of infantry sent over the stream at nightfall, however, developed the fact that all of Lee's army except Stuart's cavalry had already recrossed the Rappahannock. The next day Warrenton was occupied and the Army of the Potomac halted for some time in the vicinity of the river.

On the 7th day of November there was a general movement. The Fifth and Sixth corps under Sedgwick were directed to the redoubts of the Rappahannock near the site of the old railroad bridge, which had been destroyed. The rest of the army, under General French, was to force the passage at Kelly's Ford, some distance below. Sedgwick's orders were to "push the enemy across the river before dark, if possible." The redoubts of the Rappa-

ON THE ROAD TO WARRENTON.

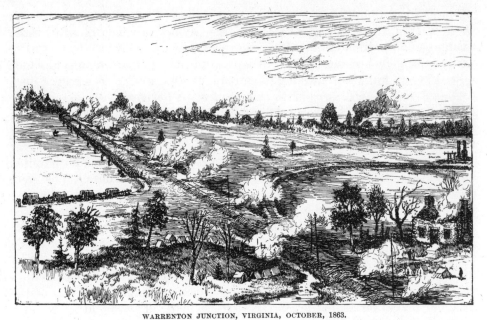

WARRENTON JUNCTION, VIRGINIA, OCTOBER, 1863.

The smoke shown in the picture was caused by burning buildings and piles of railway ties fired by the Confederates when they abandoned this region. [See p. 84.]   The troops on the left are
Birney's division, Third Union Corps.

hannock were two formidable works, both on the left of the railroad, and connected by a curtain or chain of rifle-pits; a further line of rifle-pits ran left from the left redoubt some distance along the river. Two brigades of General Early's corps held the works. The Sixth Corps went into position about midday to our right of the railroad and opened fire from its batteries. The Fifth Corps occupied the river-front below the line of the railroad. The batteries made but little impression. Daylight was fast disappearing. General Sedgwick asked the writer for the order of the day; he read it through, and, riding slowly forward, joined General Wright, commanding the Sixth Corps. "Wright," he said, "what do you think are the chances of an assault with infantry on that position?" General Wright replied, somewhat inconsequently, "Just as you say, General." "What does Russell think about it?" asked Sedgwick. Russell's division was in line of battle upon the rough and somewhat stony slope leading up to the works, one brigade, Colonel Upton's, being deployed as skirmishers. "Here comes Russell; he can speak for himself," answered Wright. As Russell joined the group, Sedgwick asked, "Russell, do you think you can carry those works with your division?" Russell replied very quietly, "I think I can, sir." "Go ahead and do it."

In less than five minutes Russell's line was seen advancing at trail-arms, picking up the skirmish-line as it was reached, and moving forward until lost in the smoke and the darkness. The enemy's fire was steady, destructive, and continuous, and was accompanied by derisive yells. The 6th Maine and the 5th Wisconsin, moving directly upon the redoubts, broke over the parapet. A sergeant of the 6th Maine, who was the first man inside the works, finding himself surrounded called out that he surrendered, but instantly seeing men of his command tumbling over the parapet, he yelled, "I take it back," and made a dash for the colors, which he secured. He was mentioned in orders the next day. Upton's men had swarmed over the rifle-pits and rapidly advanced to the head of the pontoon-bridges, thereby cutting off the enemy's retreat. This affair was singularly brilliant. More than 1600 prisoners, eight colors, all the guns, 2000 stand of small-arms, and the pontoon-bridges were captured.⧧ Colonels D. B. Penn and A. C. Godwin, commanding the two brigades of Hays's Confederate division, shared the fate of their men. They breakfasted with me on the following morning, and were both very complimentary to our troops in speaking of the engagement. One of them described it as the most brilliant feat of arms he had yet seen, and said, with some mixture of humor and pathos, that less than half an hour before our attack he made reply to a question from General Lee, who had ridden over to the works with General Early, that he wanted no more men, and that he could hold the position against the whole Yankee army. The position captured was commanded, and in some sense supported, by works on the farther side of the river, but the capture of the redoubts was so quick and complete that the enemy's guns on the right bank were of no service to him. They could indeed have swept the interior of the redoubts, which were open in the direction of the river, but it would have been very destructive to the garrison. ⧪

⧧ The loss of the Union Army was 83 killed, 330 wounded, and 6 missing = 419. The Confederate loss (as reported by General Lee) was 6 killed, 39 wounded, and 1629 captured or missing = 1674. But General Lee says, "Some reported as missing were probably killed or wounded and left in the hands of the enemy."—EDITORS.

⧪ The brilliant affair of the Rappahannock redoubts was very gratifying to the commanding general, and the captured flags, eight in number, were ordered to be formally presented at headquarters by General David A. Russell, escorted by one company of each of the regiments engaged, the column under the command of Colonel Emory Upton. It was an interesting occasion. The flags of all the regiments represented were carried in the same group with the captured colors, preceded by the band of the New Jersey brigade. General Meade ordered General Russell to Washington, accompanied by the sergeant of the 6th Maine (Otis O. Roberts, of Company H), to present the flags formally to the Government. In the armies of civilized nations such a mission, when intrusted to such an officer, bearing the trophies of a victory won by his skill and courage, particularly when suffering from a painful wound received in the

ARMY FORGE, BRANDY STATION. FROM A PHOTOGRAPH.

CAMP OF THE MILITARY TELEGRAPH CORPS, BRANDY STATION, VA.

At Kelly's Ford, on the same day, a slight success was achieved, and the Army of the Potomac on the next day effected the passage of the Rappahannock. Headquarters were established at Brandy Station and pickets thrown out over forty miles of territory.

There was a period of inaction, of fun and festivity, until the 26th of November, when the army crossed the Rapidan at Germanna and other fords and moved in the direction of Mine Run. The season was not favorable. The weather was bitterly cold and the roads were difficult. General French with the Third Corps, crossing the Rapidan at Germanna Ford, became engaged with the enemy on the 27th at Payne's Farm. He advanced through heavy undergrowth and an almost impassable tangle and was sharply resisted by the enemy — Edward Johnson's division and Gordon's brigade. French's advance was checked. Part of the Sixth Corps was hurried forward to French's support but took no part in the action. Night coming on, a further attempt to advance was deemed unadvisable. Meanwhile, and several miles to the left, on broader and better roads, the other corps of the army had passed the Rapidan and had moved out to the position of Mine Run. This little stream runs northward into the Rapidan through a valley bordered on both sides by gradual slopes more or less wooded, with here and there a farm-house. The enemy occupied the crest of the western slope. Our position was naturally on the eastern ridge. During the night Sedgwick was ordered to withdraw his own corps and French's and join the main body of the army, connecting with Warren's right at Locust Grove. This movement was completed by

action where the trophies were won, results, as a matter of military etiquette, in his promotion. Russell was also offered a leave of absence after the presentation of the flags, although he insisted that his wound was so slight as not to require care or treatment. He returned in three days. His experience was interesting if unsatisfactory. Upon arriving in Washington he addressed the Secretary of War, informing him of his mission and asking at what time it would be agreeable to him to receive the flags. After waiting the entire day and receiving no answer he called in person at the War Department, sent in his name, and was promptly informed that the Secretary was busy and could not see him. He thereupon sent the flags to the

War Department and rejoined his command by the next train, but his wound proving more serious than he was willing to acknowledge, he was subsequently sent to the hospital. Having remained there more than the sixty days' limit, it required the combined influence of Generals Wright, Sedgwick, and Meade to prevent his being mustered out under an arbitrary rule then in force. General Russell was subsequently killed in battle at the Opequon, in the Shenandoah Valley. He was one of the bravest and most beloved of officers. — M. T. M.

At Kelly's Ford the Union loss was 6 killed and 36 wounded, and that of the Confederates 5 killed, 59 wounded, and 295 captured or missing. — EDITORS.

daylight on the morning of the 28th of November. An angry skirmish-fire continued all day, and upon our part reconnoissances were made in various directions.

On the evening of the 28th a council of war was called, and at this council it was decided that a flank movement to the left under the command of General Warren, who had proposed and advocated it, should be attempted. The troops assigned to this duty under Warren were his own corps, A. H. Terry's division of the Sixth, and 300 cavalry, reënforced later by the divisions of Prince and Carr of the Third Corps. It was generally understood that Warren's movement as a flank operation was to have been upon a much wider scale than it subsequently proved to be. It was thought that he was to make a circuit of perhaps several days' march, cutting Lee off from all communication, and coming in not so much upon his immediate flank as upon his line of communication and his rear, while Meade with the rest of the army moved upon his actual front.

Warren's command marched in the night-time. During the next day, November 29th, Sedgwick, holding our right, discovered that the enemy's left flank was unprotected by earth-works, slashings, or abatis, and reported to General Meade that a movement during the night of a strong body of troops, massing them before morning upon the enemy's left, might by a

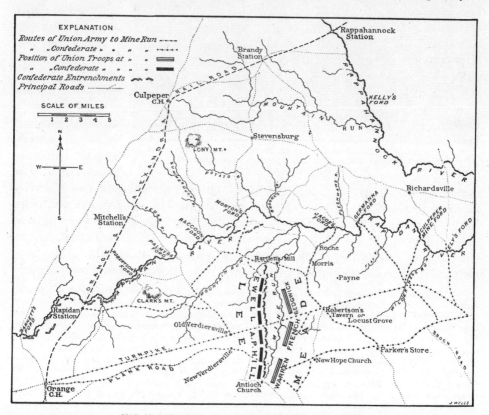

MAP OF THE FIELD OF OPERATIONS OF NOVEMBER, 1863.

sudden attack at daylight reach his flank and rear and double him up on Warren, who was expected to come in on his extreme right. After some delay and further examination of the position this movement was ordered, and two corps, the Fifth and the Sixth, under Sedgwick, proceeded during the night to the position indicated, and were massed in the woods without having attracted the attention of the enemy. Meade's orders were to open with artillery at 7, and at

1. "THE SHEBANG," QUARTERS OF THE UNITED STATES SANITARY COMMISSION. †
2. GENERAL POST-OFFICE, ARMY OF POTOMAC, DECEMBER, 1863,
AT BRANDY STATION. ⚓

8 to attack along the line with infantry. These orders were also sent to Warren.

Warren's movement had been made upon a more circumscribed line than was understood in the council which had approved it. It was, moreover, anticipated or discovered by the enemy, who diligently and heavily fortified to resist it. Upon reaching the position he sought, Warren, with the good instincts of a soldier, recognized that an attack upon a position so defended would be foolish and disastrous, and so reported to General Meade.

In the meantime Sedgwick opened fire with all his batteries at the hour indicated. The enemy replied with spirit, but in such a manner as to confirm

† The object of the Sanitary Commission was to alleviate the hardships of soldier life, to afford physical comfort to the sick and wounded, and supply such of the well as were needy with suitable underclothing, etc. The funds of the commission were raised by means of sanitary fairs in the principal cities, and by voluntary subscription. The report of the treasurer shows that from June 27th, 1861, to July 1st, 1865, the receipts were $4,813,750.64, and the disbursements $4,530,774.95.—Editors.

⚓ In the Army of the Potomac each regiment had a post-boy, who carried the letters of his command to brigade headquarters. There the mails of the different regiments were placed in one pouch and sent up to division headquarters, and thence to corps headquarters, where mail agents received them and delivered them, at the principal depot of the army, to the agent from general headquarters. The cases for the letters were made of rough boards, which on a march were packed away in the bottom of an army wagon, one wagon being sufficient to carry the whole establishment, including the tent and its furniture.—Editors.

the view that his line at this point was not strongly held. Our infantry as yet were concealed in the woods, the two corps massed in column of brigades, and held like hounds in the leash. There was much rivalry between these two corps, and between the divisions and the brigades of each, and they sent committees inviting each other to a reunion in the enemy's works, each one promising to be there first to receive the others.

The fire of the batteries prevented anything looking to the reënforcement of the enemy's position, which was in our left front. Our right, when deployed, would have overlapped them. Suddenly over the wires came a message from General Meade, "Suspend the attack until further orders." We stopped firing. The enemy did likewise, gun for gun. Meade had heard from Warren that his movement had failed. Sedgwick, Sykes, and Wright believed, however, that their movement on the right, if it had not been suspended, would have been completely successful. A few minutes later another dispatch directed Sedgwick to report at the headquarters of the commanding general. I accompanied him. We found General Meade evidently greatly disappointed and angry at the failure of Warren's movement. He had sent for Sedgwick to take command at headquarters while he rode to join Warren, who could only be reached by a long and somewhat difficult route. He returned later in the day in the worst possible humor and ordered the withdrawal of the troops of the Fifth and Sixth corps to the position held by them the day before, closer to the center of the line. That night he asked Sedgwick by telegraph as to the chances of success of an attack in his immediate front, or of an attack upon that part of the enemy's lines which had been threatened by him in the morning. Sedgwick replied that the line threatened by him in the morning had been so heavily intrenched and fortified after the suspension of his fire that he deemed it now the least available point of assault, and that the chance of carrying the position then in his front, moving across the open valley and up the other slope against well-constructed lines of rifle-pits, was not encouraging.

In this movement the men suffered greatly from the rain, which froze as it fell; they were without shelter, and had had long marches and severely trying ones; yet they were in excellent spirits and physically in good condition; but the heart was taken out of everybody when on the 1st of December the order came to retire across the Rapidan and resume the camps from which we had started out so gayly a week before.↓ The troops burrowed in the earth and built their little shelters, and the officers and men devoted themselves to unlimited festivity, balls, horse-races, cock-fights, greased pigs and poles, and other games such as only soldiers can devise.

At this time the abuses of the conscription system were made manifest to the men at the front by the character of a large part of the recruits who were sent through that agency. The professional bounty-jumper and the kidnapped emigrant and street boy, who were "put through" the enlistment

↓ During this campaign the Union army lost 173 killed, 1099 wounded, and 381 captured or missing = 1653; and the Confederates 98 killed, 610 wounded, and 104 captured or missing = 812.— EDITORS.

MAJOR-GENERAL JOHN SEDGWICK, KILLED AT SPOTSYLVANIA IN THE WILDERNESS CAMPAIGN,
MAY 9, 1864.

offices in New York and elsewhere, came in large numbers, the professionals with the intention of deserting at the earliest opportunity and repeating the profitable experiment of enlisting for large bounties. Their favorite time for leaving was during their first tour of picket duty, and it was found necessary to throw a cordon of cavalry outside our own picket lines. A gallows and a shooting-ground were provided in each corps, and scarcely a Friday passed during the winter while the army lay on Hazel River and in the vicinity of Brandy Station that some of these deserters did not suffer the death penalty. During the winter the army grew again into superb condition, and awaited with high spirits the opening of the spring campaign.

On the 23d of March a reorganization of the Army of the Potomac took place, when its five corps were consolidated into three. The First Corps was transferred to the Fifth; two divisions of the Third were incorporated with the Second, but permitted to retain their distinctive flag and badge; the other division of the Third Corps was transferred to the Sixth, but directed to abandon its own flag and badge and assume that of the Greek cross. The corps commanders retained were—of the Second, General W. S. Hancock; of the Fifth, General G. K. Warren; of the Sixth, General John Sedgwick. The First and Third corps thus passed out of existence.

The only other event of note, before the arrival of General Grant, was the Kilpatrick-Dahlgren raid upon Richmond. It was authorized directly from Washington, and was not the suggestion of General Meade, nor did it have his approval; however, he set about carrying it into effect with all proper spirit and energy. The movement depended largely for its success upon its secrecy, and, therefore, when Colonel Dahlgren arrived from Washington before the preparations were completed, and asked to be permitted to accompany Kilpatrick, Meade was annoyed to learn that the expedition was currently discussed in the capital. The plan was for Kilpatrick to move generally from our left, passing the right flank of Lee's army, and to proceed to Richmond by as direct routes as possible, while, as diversions, and to cover his movement, Custer, with 2000 cavalry, was to make a raid beyond Gordonsville, and the Sixth Corps and Birney's division of the Third were to move in support of Custer to Madison Court House on Robinson's River. No effort was made to conceal this movement, as it was intended to convey the impression to the enemy that a formidable attempt was to be made upon his left flank. Upon the arrival of Sedgwick and Birney at Robinson's River at nightfall of the 27th of February, Custer went by with his command, with instructions to proceed toward Charlottesville, and, if possible, to destroy the railway bridge near that place.

While his command was passing, Custer inquired of Sedgwick as to the relative importance of his movement as compared with that of Kilpatrick, and asked whether in the council at which the movement was discussed it was stated or understood that the bridge-head near Charlottesville was fortified and defended with infantry; also whether it was known that Rosser with 5000 Confederate cavalry was in the valley through which Custer might be obliged to return after doing his work, and that, moreover, probably the road by which he advanced would be occupied in his rear by Stuart and the main body of the cavalry of Lee's army. Sedgwick assured him that all these points had been discussed and considered. Custer thought a moment and said, " Well, then, I may have to do one of two things : either strike boldly across Lee's rear and try to reach Kilpatrick, or else start with all the men I can keep together and try to join Sherman in the south-west." Upon reaching the neighborhood of Charlottesville he found, as he expected, that the bridge-head was heavily held by infantry and artillery, and retraced his march. Stuart meantime had placed his troops across the road by which Custer had advanced, and was awaiting him. Through the treachery of a guide the head of Custer's column was turned off to the right for the purpose, it was believed, of bringing it in upon the main body of Lee's infantry, where its capture would be certain. Custer discovered the attempt in time and retraced his steps to the main road which he had left. Stuart meantime had learned of the departure of Custer from the direct route, and at once moved his command to intercept him. This cleared the way for Custer and enabled him to return within the lines of the Sixth Corps, with only an affair with a rear-guard. His movement had certainly had the desired effect as a diversion. While these operations were taking place Kilpatrick had advanced in the direction of Richmond and had divided his forces, sending a portion under Dahlgren to strike the James River above Richmond, retaining the main body under his own command until he was satisfied that the experiment was not feasible. He made his way down the Peninsula in the direction of Butler's command, and was subsequently transferred by boat to rejoin the Army of the Potomac, or more properly the horse-hospital camp, near Washington. Aside from our losses in men, and among them the gallant and heroic Dahlgren, the result of this movement was to disable for the time being 3000 or 4000 of the very flower of our cavalry.

FUGITIVE NEGROES AT THE RAPIDAN.   FROM A PHOTOGRAPH.

KILPATRICK'S AND DAHLGREN'S RAID TO RICHMOND.

BY GEORGE E. POND.

ON the night of Sunday, the 28th of February, 1864, General Judson Kilpatrick, leaving Stevensburg with four thousand cavalry and a battery of horse artillery, crossed the Rapidan at Ely's Ford, surprised and captured the enemy's picket there, and marched rapidly by Spotsylvania Court House toward Richmond.

His object was to move past the enemy's right flank, enter the Confederate capital, and release the Union captives in its military prisons. This bold project had grown out of President Lincoln's desire to have his amnesty proclamation circulated within the Confederate lines; and General Kilpatrick, with whom Mr. Lincoln directly conferred, had reported to General Meade, on this officer's application, a plan which included the release of the Richmond prisoners and a raid upon the enemy's communications and supplies. His force was to be chosen from the cavalry corps, mostly from his own — the Third — division; and Colonel Ulric Dahlgren, separating from him near Spotsylvania, with five hundred picked men, was to cross the James, enter Richmond on the south side, after liberating the Belle Isle prisoners, and unite with Kilpatrick's main force entering the city from the north at 10 A. M. of Tuesday, March 1st. General Meade aided the enterprise with simultaneous demonstrations of the Sixth Corps and of Birney's division of the Third against Lee's left, and of Custer's cavalry division toward Charlottesville.

Reaching Spotsylvania Court House at early dawn of February 29th, Kilpatrick moved south through Chilesburg to the Virginia Central Railroad, which he struck during the day at Beaver Dam Station. The telegraph operator was seized, the wires were cut, the track was destroyed, and the station buildings were burned. Detachments were also sent to destroy bridges and track on the Fredericksburg Railroad, and during the raid the amnesty proclamation was distributed. At nightfall the main body moved forward and crossed the South Anna at Ground Squirrel Bridge. Early on Tuesday, March 1st, the column was again in motion, and by 10 o'clock faced the northern lines of Richmond, on the Brook pike, five miles from the city. Its arrival was wholly unexpected; still a telegraphic dispatch that Union cavalry were raiding south of the Rapidan having reached Richmond the day before, General Elzey had that morning, as a precaution, sent out troops to the west of the city under General G. W. C. Lee, and to the north under Colonel Stevens, those sent to the Brook road consisting of five hundred men and six guns. Kilpatrick's advance quickly drove back the pickets of this last force and their supports, and thus found itself close up to the inner lines of the Richmond defenses. Some skirmishing with artillery firing went on for several hours, Kilpatrick meanwhile awaiting signs of the approach of Dahlgren.

The latter officer, on separating from the main body below Spotsylvania, moving south-westerly, had, before noon of the 29th, struck and broken the Virginia Central Railroad a little east of Frederick's Hall Station, capturing a detachment of Maryland artillerymen and also about a dozen commissioned officers, who were holding a court-martial. At Frederick's Hall Station were eighty or more pieces of Lee's reserve artillery, and the news that it was exposed to attack created some excitement in Richmond; but Colonel Dahlgren's information and purposes determined him not to risk an attack on the artillery camp. At night he crossed the South Anna, and early the next morning reached the James River canal, about eight miles east of Goochland. There he directed Captain J. F. B. Mitchell to take the detachment of one hundred men of the 2d New York, and, proceeding down the canal, to destroy locks and burn mills, grain, and boats, and then to send the ambulances and prisoners to General Kilpatrick at Hungary Station. Meanwhile Dahlgren himself was to cross the river at a ford which a negro guide had promised to indicate. Captain Mitchell destroyed six grist-mills, a saw-mill, six canal-boats loaded with grain, the barn of Secretary Seddon, and the coal-works at Manikin's Bend, with a neighboring lock. But Colonel Dahlgren did not find the expected fording place, and proceeded instead on the north side of the river. About eight miles from Richmond he was overtaken by Captain Mitchell, at 3:30 P. M. A picket of Custis Lee's city battalion had there been captured, and during a halt the men had coffee and the horses were fed on captured corn. Guns supposed to be Kilpatrick's were heard, and Dahlgren, moving forward, about five miles from the city encountered sharp musketry. The resistance grew heavier, darkness came on, and the firing attributed to Kilpatrick ceased. In fact, the latter officer, ignorant how small a force he really had in his front, wondering what had become of Dahlgren, and seeing what he took to be reënforcements for the enemy, had now abandoned the attempt to enter the city, and had fallen back several miles to camp at Atlee's Station. Dahlgren, on his part, feeling it to be hopeless at that hour and with his small force to advance, gave the order to withdraw. The attempt to release the Union prisoners had failed. Extrication from this position was the next step. Bradley T. Johnson's cavalry had followed Kilpatrick down from Beaver Dam, and, uniting with Wade Hampton's, now sharply attacked him late at night at Atlee's Station. The following day his rear-guard was harassed somewhat as he moved down the peninsula. According to the original plan he proceeded to Williamsburg, within the lines then occupied by the troops of General B. F. Butler. Dahlgren was less fortunate. Putting Captain Mitchell in charge of the rear-guard on Tuesday night, he, with Major Cooke, had gone forward with the advance. In the darkness the column became scattered, and Captain Mitchell found himself in charge of the main portion, about three hundred strong, Dahlgren having moved with the remainder in a direction unknown to him. By great exertions and with sharp skirmishing, Captain Mitchell broke his way through the enemy, and joined Kilpatrick the next day, the 2d, at Tunstall's Station, near White House. Meanwhile Dahlgren had crossed the Pamunkey at Hanovertown and the Mattapony at Aylett's; but late on Wednesday night, March 2d, he fell into an ambush near Walkerton, formed by Captain Fox with home guards of King and Queen County, furloughed men, and Magruder's squadron, and by Lieutenant Pollard with a company of the 9th Virginia. Dahlgren, at the head of his men, fell dead, pierced with a bullet. The greater part of his command was captured.

On the second morning after Colonel Dahlgren's death, Lieutenant Pollard carried to General Fitzhugh Lee, in Richmond, some papers which he said had been taken from Dahlgren's body, together with the artificial leg which the young officer wore in place of a limb amputated a short time before. The documents were published in the Richmond newspapers, and afterward in the newspapers at the North. One of them, signed Ulric Dahlgren, purporting to be an address to his men, contained this passage: "We hope to release the prisoners from Belle Isle first, and having seen them fairly started, we will cross the James River into Richmond, destroying the bridges after us, and exhorting the released prisoners to destroy and burn the hateful city; and do not allow the rebel leader, Davis, and his traitorous crew to escape." The second document, a paper of instructions not signed, declared that "once in the city it must be destroyed, and Jeff Davis and cabinet killed. Pioneers will go along with combustible material." On observing these publications, General Meade at once, on the 14th of March, directed an inquiry to be made into their authenticity. On the 16th, General Kilpatrick, having carefully ex-

amined officers and men who accompanied Colonel Dahlgren, and having received a written account from Captain Mitchell, reported to General Meade that the unanimous testimony was that Colonel Dahlgren "published no address whatever to his command, nor did he give any instructions"; but he added that Colonel Dahlgren had submitted to him an address which he had accordingly indorsed in red ink "approved" over his official signature. This address, he said, conformed to the one published in the Richmond newspapers, "save so far as it speaks of 'exhorting the prisoners to destroy and burn the hateful city and kill the traitor Davis and his cabinet.' All this is false, and published only as an excuse for the barbarous treatment of the remains of a brave soldier." A fortnight later, General R. E. Lee sent to General Meade photographic copies of the two documents, with a letter making the extracts already quoted with their context, and requesting to know whether these alleged designs and instructions of Colonel Dahlgren were authorized by the United States Government, or by his superior officer, or were now approved by them. This letter being referred to General Kilpatrick, he replied substantially as in his previous report, adding, however, that the photographic papers "do not contain the indorsement referred to as having been placed by me on Colonel Dahlgren's papers. Colonel Dahlgren received no orders from me to pillage, burn, or kill, nor were any such instructions given me by my superiors." This letter was inclosed by General Meade to General Lee with the statement that "neither the United States Government, myself, nor General Kilpatrick authorized, sanctioned, or approved the burning of the city of Richmond and the killing of Mr. Davis and his cabinet, nor any other act not required by military necessity and in accordance with the usages of war."

CAMP OF THE 18TH PENNSYLVANIA CAVALRY, KILPATRICK'S DIVISION, ON THE UNION LEFT, BETWEEN THE RAPPAHANNOCK AND THE RAPIDAN (FEBRUARY OR MARCH, 1864). FROM A PHOTOGRAPH.

HEADQUARTERS OF THE ARMY OF THE POTOMAC AT BRANDY STATION. FROM A PHOTOGRAPH.

PREPARING FOR THE CAMPAIGNS OF '64.[

BY ULYSSES S. GRANT, GENERAL, U. S. A.

HEADQUARTERS FLAG, ARMY OF
THE POTOMAC.

General Meade adopted solferino as the color of his headquarters flag, and a golden eagle in a silver wreath as the emblem, the latter having been in use as a badge for headquarters aides. It was a showy standard, and A. R. Waud, the war artist, remembers that General Grant, when he first saw it unfurled, as they broke camp for the Wilderness campaign, exclaimed: "What's this! — Is Imperial Cæsar anywhere about here?"— EDITORS.

MY commission as lieutenant-general was given to me on the 9th of March, 1864. On the following day I visited General Meade, commanding the Army of the Potomac, at his headquarters, Brandy Station, north of the Rapidan. I had known General Meade slightly in the Mexican war, but had not met him since until this visit. I was a stranger to most of the Army of the Potomac; I might say to all except the officers of the regular army who had served in the Mexican war. There had been some changes ordered in the organization of that army before my promotion. One was the consolidation of five corps into three, thus throwing some officers of rank out of important commands. Meade evidently thought that I might want to make still one more change not yet ordered. He said to me that I might want an officer who had served with me in the West, mentioning Sherman especially, to take his place; if so, he begged me not to hesitate about making the change. He urged that the work before us was of such vast importance to the whole nation that the feeling or wishes of no one person should stand in the way of selecting the right men for all positions. For himself, he would serve to the best of his ability wherever placed. I assured him that I had no thought of substituting any one for him. As to Sherman, he could not be spared from the West.

This incident gave me even a more favorable opinion of Meade than did his great victory at Gettysburg the July before. It is men who wait to be selected, and not those who seek, from whom we may always expect the most efficient service.

Meade's position afterward proved embarrassing to me if not to him. For nearly a year previous to my taking command of all the armies he had been at the head of the Army of the Potomac, commanding an army independently. All other general officers occupying similar positions were independent in their commands so far as any one present with them was concerned. I tried to make General Meade's position as nearly as possible what it would have been if I had been in Washington or

BEALTON STATION, ORANGE AND
ALEXANDRIA RAILWAY.
FROM A WAR-TIME SKETCH.

any other place away from his command. I therefore gave all orders for the movements of the Army of the Potomac to Meade to have them executed. To avoid the necessity of having to give orders direct, I established my

BRANDY STATION, ORANGE AND ALEXANDRIA RAILWAY.
FROM A WAR-TIME SKETCH.

headquarters near his, unless there were reasons for locating them elsewhere. This sometimes happened, and I had on occasions to give orders direct to the troops affected.

On the 11th of March I returned to Washington, and on the day after orders were published by the War Department placing me in command of all the armies. I had left Washington the night before to return to my old command in the West and to meet Sherman, whom I had telegraphed to join me in Nashville.

Sherman assumed command of the Military Division of the Mississippi on the 18th of March, and we left Nashville together for Cincinnati. I had Sherman accompany me that far on my way back to Washington, so that we could talk over the matters about which I wanted to see him, without losing any more time from my new command than was necessary. The first point which I wished to discuss particularly was about the coöperation of his command with mine when the spring campaign should commence. There were also other and minor points,—minor as compared with the great importance of the question to be decided by sanguinary war,—the restoration to duty of officers who had been relieved from important commands, namely, McClellan, Burnside, and Frémont in the East, and Buell, McCook, Negley, and Crittenden in the West.

Some time in the winter of 1863–64 I had been invited by the general-in-chief to give my views of the campaign I thought advisable for the command under me — now Sherman's. General J. E. Johnston was defending Atlanta and the interior of Georgia with an army, the largest part of which was stationed at Dalton, about 38 miles south of Chattanooga. Dalton is at the junction of the railroad from Cleveland with the one from Chattanooga to Atlanta.

There could have been no difference of opinion as to the first duty of the armies of the Military Division of the Mississippi. Johnston's army was the first objective, and that important railroad center, Atlanta, the second. At the time I wrote General Halleck giving my views of the approaching campaign, and at the time I met General Sherman, it was expected that General Banks would be through with the campaign upon which he had been ordered ⚓ before my appointment to the command of all the armies, and would be ready to coöperate with the armies east of the Mississippi; his part in the programme being to move upon Mobile by land, while the navy would close the harbor and assist to the best of its ability. The plan, therefore, was for Sherman to attack Johnston and destroy his army if possible, to capture Atlanta and hold it, and with his troops and those of Banks to hold a line through to Mobile, or at least to hold Atlanta and command the railroad running east and west, and the troops from one or other of the armies to hold important points on the southern road, the only east-and-west road that would be left in the possession of the enemy. This would cut the Confederacy in two again, as our gaining possession of the Mississippi River had done before. Banks was not ready in time for the part assigned to him, and circumstances that could not be foreseen determined the campaign which was afterward made, the success and grandeur of which has resounded throughout all lands.

In regard to restoring to duty officers who had been relieved from important commands, I left Sherman to look after those who had been removed in the West, while I looked out for the rest. I directed, however, that he should make no assignment until I could speak to the Secretary of War about the matter. I shortly after recommended to the Secretary the assignment of General Buell to duty. I received the assurance that duty would be offered to him, and afterward the Secretary told me that he had offered Buell an assignment and that the latter declined it, saying that it would be a degradation to accept the assignment offered. I understood afterward that he refused to serve under either Sherman or Canby because he had ranked them both. Both were graduated before him, and ranked him in the old army. Sherman ranked him as brigadier-general. All of them ranked me in the old army, and Sherman and Buell did as brigadiers. The worst excuse a soldier can make for declining service is that he once ranked the commander he is ordered to report to.

⚓ The Red River campaign. See papers to follow.— EDITORS.

GENERAL MEADE'S HEADQUARTERS AT CULPEPER. FROM A WAR-TIME SKETCH.

On the 23d of March I was back in Washington, and on the 26th took up my headquarters at Culpeper Court House, a few miles south of the headquarters of the Army of the Potomac.

Although hailing from Illinois myself, the State of the President, I never met Mr. Lincoln until called to the capital to receive my commission as lieutenant-general. I knew him, however, very well and favorably from the accounts given by officers under me at the West who had known him all their lives. I had also read the remarkable series of debates between Lincoln and Douglas a few years before, when they were rival candidates for the United States Senate. I was then a resident of Missouri, and by no means a "Lincoln man" in that contest; but I recognized then his great ability.

In my first interview with Mr. Lincoln alone he stated to me that he had never professed to be a military man or to know how campaigns should be conducted, and never wanted to interfere in them; but that procrastination on the part of commanders, and the pressure from the people at the North and from Congress, *which was always with him*, forced him into issuing his series of "Military Orders"—No. 1, No. 2, No. 3, etc. He did not know that they were not all wrong, and did know that some of them were. All he wanted, or had ever wanted, was some one who would take the responsibility and act, and call on him for all the assistance needed; he would pledge himself to use all the power of the Government in rendering such assistance. Assuring him that I would do the best I could with the means at hand, and avoid as far as possible annoying him or the War Department, our first interview ended.

The Secretary of War I had met once before only, but felt that I knew him better. While I had been commanding in west Tennessee we had held conversations over the wires at night. He and Halleck both cautioned me against giving the President my plans of campaign, saying that he was so kind-hearted, so averse to refusing anything asked of him, that some friend would be sure to get from him all he knew. I should have said that in our interview the President told me that he did not want to know what I proposed to do. But he submitted a plan of campaign of his own which he wanted me to hear and then dispose of as I pleased. He brought out a map of Virginia, on which he had evidently marked every position occupied by the Federal and Confederate armies up to that time. He pointed out on the map two streams which empty into the Potomac, and suggested that the army might be moved on boats and landed between the mouths of these streams. We would then have the Potomac to bring supplies, and the tributaries would protect our flanks while we moved out. I listened respectfully, but did not suggest that the same streams would protect Lee's flanks while he was shutting us up. I did not communicate my plans to the President or to the Secretary or to General Halleck.

On the 26th of March, with my headquarters at Culpeper, the work of preparing for an early campaign commenced.

When I assumed command of all the armies the situation was about this: The Mississippi was guarded from St. Louis to its mouth; the line of the Arkansas was held, thus giving us all the North-west north of that river. A few points in Louisiana, not remote from the river, were held by the Federal troops, as was also the mouth of the Rio Grande. East of the Mississippi we held substantially all north of the Memphis and Charleston railroad as far east as Chattanooga, thence along the line of the Tennessee and Holston rivers, taking in nearly all of the State of Tennessee. West Virginia was in our hands, and also that part of old Virginia north of the Rapidan and east of the Blue Ridge. On the sea-coast we had Fort Monroe and Norfolk in Virginia; Plymouth, Washington, and New Berne in North Carolina; Beaufort, Folly and Morris islands, Hilton Head, and Port Royal, in South Carolina, and Fort Pulaski in Georgia; Fernandina, St. Augustine, Key West, and Pensacola in Florida. The remainder of the Southern territory, an empire in extent, was still in the hands of the enemy.

Sherman, who had succeeded me in the command of the Military Division of the Mississippi, commanded all the troops in the territory west of the Alleghanies and north of Natchez, with a large movable force about Chattanooga. His command was subdivided into four departments, but the commanders all reported to Sherman, and were subject to his orders. This arrangement, however, insured the better protection of all lines of communication through the acquired territory, for the reason that these different department commanders could act promptly in case of a sudden or unexpected raid within their respective jurisdictions, without waiting the orders of the division commander.

In the east the opposing forces stood in substantially the same relations toward each other as three years before, or when the war began; they were both between the Federal and Confederate capitals. It is true footholds had been secured by us on the sea-coast, in Virginia and North Carolina, but beyond that no substantial advantage had been gained by either side. Battles had been fought of as great severity as had ever been known in war, over ground from the James River and the Chickahominy, near Richmond, to Gettysburg and Chambersburg, in Pennsylvania, with indecisive results, sometimes favorable to the National army, sometimes to the Confederate army, but in every instance, I believe, claimed as victories for the South by the Southern press if not by the Southern generals. The Northern press, as a whole, did not discourage their claims; a portion of it always magnified rebel success and belittled ours, while another portion, most sincerely earnest in their desire for the preservation of the Union and the overwhelming success of the Federal arms, would nevertheless generally express dissatisfaction with whatever victories were gained because they were not more complete.

MAJOR-GENERAL GEORGE G. MEADE.
FROM A PHOTOGRAPH.

That portion of the Army of the Potomac not engaged in guarding lines of communication was on the northern bank of the Rapidan. The Army of Northern Virginia, confronting it on the opposite bank of the same river, was strongly intrenched and was commanded by the acknowledged ablest general in the Confederate army. The country back to the James River is cut up with many streams, generally narrow, deep, and difficult to cross except where bridged. The region is heavily timbered, and the roads are narrow and very bad after the least rain. Such an enemy was not, of course, unprepared with adequate fortifications at convenient intervals all the way back to Richmond, so that, when driven from one fortified position, they would always have another farther to the rear to fall back into. To provision an army, campaigning against so formidable a foe through such a country, from wagons alone, seemed almost impossible. System and discipline were both essential to its accomplishment.

The Union armies were now divided into nineteen departments, though four of them in the West had been concentrated into a single military division. The Army of the Potomac was a separate command, and had no territorial limits. There were thus seventeen distinct commanders. Before this time these various armies had acted separately and independently of each other, giving the enemy an opportunity, often, of depleting one command, not pressed, to reënforce another more actively engaged. I determined to stop this. To this end I regarded the Army of the Potomac as the center, and all west to Memphis, along the line described as our position at the time, and north of it, the right wing; the Army of the James, under General Butler, ♭ as the left wing, and all the troops south as a force in rear of the enemy.   Some of these last were occupying positions from which they could not render service proportionate to their numerical strength. All such were depleted to the minimum necessary to hold their positions as a guard against blockade-runners; when they could not do this, their positions were abandoned altogether.   In this way ten thousand men were added to the Army of the James from South Carolina alone, with General Gillmore in command.⸜ It was not contemplated that Gillmore should leave his department; but as most of his troops were taken, presumably for active service, he asked to accompany them, and was permitted to do so.   Officers and soldiers on furlough, of whom there were many thousands, were ordered to their proper commands; concentration was the order of the day, and the problem was to accomplish it in time to advance at the earliest moment the roads would permit.

As a reënforcement to the Army of the Potomac, or to act in support of it, the Ninth Army Corps, over twenty thousand strong, under General Burnside, had been rendezvoused at Annapolis, Maryland.☆ This was an admirable position for such a reënforcement. The corps could be brought at the last moment as a reënforcement to the Army of the Potomac, or it could be thrown on the sea-coast, south of Norfolk, to operate against Richmond from that direction.   In fact, up to the last moment Burnside and the War Department both thought the Ninth Corps was intended for such an expedition.

My general plan now was to concentrate all the force possible against the Confederate armies in the field.   There were but two such, as we have seen, east of the Mississippi River and facing north: the Army of Northern Virginia, General Robert E. Lee commanding, was on the south bank of the Rapidan, confronting the Army of the Potomac; the second, under General Joseph E. Johnston, ↓ was at Dalton, Georgia, opposed to Sherman, who was still at Chattanooga. Besides these main armies, the Confederates had to guard the Shenandoah Valley — a great storehouse to feed their armies from — and their line of communications from Richmond to Tennessee. Forrest, a brave and intrepid cavalry general, was in the West, with a large force, making a larger command necessary to hold what we had gained in middle and west Tennessee.   We could not abandon any territory north of the line held by the enemy, because it would lay the Northern States open to invasion.   But

♭ From December 17th, 1862, when he was superseded in command of the Gulf Department by General Banks, General Butler was not in active service until November 11th, 1863, when he assumed command of the Department of Virginia and North Carolina (the Army of the James).— EDITORS.

⸜ These troops, the Tenth Corps, left the Department of the South during the month of April for rendezvous at Gloucester Point, Virginia.— EDITORS.

☆ General Burnside had been relieved of the command of the Department of the Ohio on the 12th of December, by General J. G. Foster, and on the 7th of January, 1864, had been assigned to the command of the Ninth Corps. This corps left Knoxville, Tennessee, March 17th–23d, and was reorganized at Annapolis for the spring campaign, and received an addition to its strength of five cavalry and twelve infantry regiments and five batteries of artillery.— EDITORS.

↓ General Johnston was relieved of the command of the Department of Tennessee by General Bragg, July 23d, 1863, and continued in command of the Department of Mississippi and East Louisiana. On December 27th, 1863, he assumed command of the Army of Tennessee, superseding Bragg.— EDITORS.

as the Army of the Potomac was the principal garrison for the protection of Washington, even while it was moving on to Lee, so all the forces to the West, and the Army of the James, guarded their special trusts when advancing from them as well as when remaining at them — better, indeed, for they forced the enemy to guard his own lines and resources, at a greater distance from ours and with a greater force, since small expeditions could not so well be sent out to destroy a bridge or tear up a few miles of railroad track, burn a storehouse, or inflict other little annoyances. Accordingly I arranged for a simultaneous movement all along the line.

Sherman was to move from Chattanooga, Johnston's army and Atlanta being his objective points. General George Crook, commanding in West Virginia, ⚓ was to move from the mouth of the Gauley River with a cavalry force and some artillery, the Virginia and Tennessee railroad to be his objective. Either the enemy would have to keep a large force to protect their communications or see them destroyed, and a large amount of forage and provisions, which they so much needed, would fall into our hands. Sigel, ↓ who was in command in the valley of Virginia, was to advance up the valley, covering the North from an invasion through that channel as well while advancing by remaining near Harper's Ferry. Every mile he advanced also gave us possession of stores on which Lee relied. Butler was to advance by the James River, having Richmond and Petersburg as his objective. Before the advance commenced I visited Butler at Fort Monroe. This was the first time I had ever met him. Before giving him any order as to the part he was to play in the approaching campaign I invited his views. They were very much such as I intended to direct, and as I did direct, in writing, before leaving.

General W. F. Smith, who had been promoted to the rank of major-general shortly after the battle of Chattanooga on my recommendation, had not yet been confirmed. I found a decided prejudice against his confirmation by a majority of the Senate, but I insisted that his services had been such that he should be rewarded. My wishes were now reluctantly complied with, and I assigned him to the command of one of the corps under General Butler. I was not long in finding out that the objections to Smith's promotion were well founded. ♭

⚓ General Crook was transferred from the command of a cavalry division in the Army of the Cumberland and assumed command of an infantry division in the Department of West Virginia, February 15th, 1864.—EDITORS.

↓ General Sigel succeeded General Benjamin F. Kelley in command of the Department of West Virginia on the 10th of March, 1864. After the second battle of Bull Run Sigel had been in command of the Eleventh Corps, the Reserve Grand Division of the Army of the Potomac, and the Lehigh District in Pennsylvania.—EDITORS.

♭ After the appearance of General Grant's paper in "The Century" magazine for February, 1886, General William F. Smith made the following reply, which was printed in that magazine for May, 1886:

"General Grant makes this general charge without assigning a reason for it or attempting to justify it by citing any instance in which I had failed in any duty I had been called upon to perform. This gives me the right to call General Grant himself as a witness in my own behalf, and to assert that the reasons which moved him to say that 'the objections to my confirmation were well founded' were of a personal, and not of a public nature.

"The battle of Chattanooga ended on the 25th of November, 1863 — my name was not sent to the Senate till the 15th of March, 1864. On the 18th it was returned to the President, with the request that the date of rank should conform to the date of nomination.

"On the 23d of the same month it was again sent to the Senate, and my nomination was confirmed on the same day. It was therefore nearly four months after the battle when my name was sent to the Senate for promotion, and in three days thereafter the Senate asked the President to make the date of rank conform to the date of nomination; and on the same day that my name was returned to the Senate my nomination was confirmed. The question of my confirmation therefore was

FROM A PHOTOGRAPH.

BREVET MAJOR-GENERAL M. C. MEIGS, QUARTERMASTER-GENERAL.
U. S. A. FROM A PHOTOGRAPH.

In one of my early interviews with the President I expressed my dissatisfaction with the little that had been accomplished by the cavalry so far in the war, and the belief that it was capable of accomplishing much more than it had done if under a thorough leader. I said I wanted the very best man in the army for that command. Halleck was present and spoke up, saying: "How would Sheridan do?" I replied: "The very man I want."

The President said I could have anybody I wanted. Sheridan was telegraphed for that day, and on his arrival was assigned to the command of the cavalry corps with the Army of the Potomac. This relieved General Alfred Pleasonton. It was not a reflection on that officer, however, for as far as I knew he had been as efficient as any other cavalry commander.

Banks in the Department of the Gulf was ordered to assemble all his troops at New Orleans in time to join in the general move, Mobile to be his objective.

At this time I was not entirely decided as to whether I should move the Army of the Potomac by the right flank of the enemy or by his left. Each

settled on the 18th of March, when the request was made to have the date of rank conform to the date of nomination, and during this time and up to the time of my confirmation General Grant was not in the city of Washington.

"He left Washington on the night of the 11th of March for Nashville and did not return till some time during the 23d—the day on which the President returned my name to the Senate and upon which final action was taken. Shortly thereafter I was informed by a senator that my name had passed the Senate without having been referred to the Military Committee, which he stated to be a 'high compliment and one seldom paid by the Senate.' As to the fact whether this confirmation was made without a reference to the Military Committee, the records of the Senate will show.

"But much more important to me is the fact that this sweeping denunciation was not founded upon any failure on my part to perform the duty I owed to the country, then in its struggle for existence, and that no one knew this better than the general who was in command of its armies. On the 12th of November, 1863, General Grant had addressed the Secretary of War as follows:

"'I would respectfully recommend that Brigadier-General William F. Smith be placed first on the list for promotion to the rank of major-general. He is possessed of one of the clearest military heads in the army—is very practical and industrious—no man in the service is better qualified than he for our largest commands.'

"On July 1st, 1864, General Grant, from City Point,

Virginia, addressed a letter to General Halleck, chief-of-staff, from which the following extracts are taken:

"'Mr. Dana, Assistant Secretary of War, has just returned. He informs me that he called attention to the necessity of sending General Butler to another field of duty. . . . I have feared that it might become necessary to separate him and General Smith. The latter is really one of the most efficient officers in the service, readiest in expedients, and most skillful in the management of troops in action. I would dislike removing him from his present command unless it was to increase it, but, as I say, I may have to do it if General Butler remains. . . . I would feel strengthened with Smith, Franklin, or J. J. Reynolds commanding the right wing of this army. . . .'

"So that on the 1st of July, 1864, General Grant thought he would be strengthened with General Smith commanding the right wing of that army. On the strength of that letter I was placed in command of the troops in the field belonging to the Army of the James, and General Butler was ordered back to administrative duty at Fort Monroe.

"Being much out of health at this time, I had asked for a short leave of absence, to which this answer was returned:

"'HEADQUARTERS, CITY POINT, July 2d, 1864.

"'TO MAJOR-GENERAL WILLIAM F. SMITH: Your application for leave of absence has just come to me. Unless it is absolutely necessary that you should leave at this time, I would much prefer not having you go. It will not be necessary for you to expose yourself in the hot sun, and if it should

plan presented advantages. If by his right — my left — the Potomac, Chesapeake Bay, and tributaries would furnish us an easy line over which to bring all supplies to within easy hauling distance of every position the army could occupy from the Rapidan to the James River. But Lee, if he chose, could detach, or move his whole army north on a line rather interior to the one I would have to take in following. A movement by his left — our right — would obviate this; but all that was done would have to be done with the supplies and ammunition we started with. All idea of adopting this latter plan was abandoned when the limited quantity of supplies possible to take with us was considered. The country over which we would have to pass was so exhausted of all food or forage that we would be obliged to carry everything with us.

While these preparations were going on the enemy was not entirely idle. In the West, Forrest made a raid in west Tennessee up to the northern border, capturing the garrison of four or five hundred men at Union City, and followed it up by an attack on Paducah, Kentucky, on the banks of the Ohio. While he was able to enter the city, he failed to capture the forts or any part of the garrison. On the first intelligence of Forrest's raid I telegraphed Sherman to send all his cavalry against him, and not to let him get out of the trap he had put himself into. Sherman had anticipated me by sending troops against him before he got my order. Forrest, however, fell back rapidly, and attacked the troops at Fort Pillow, a station for the protection of the navigation of the Mississippi River. The garrison consisted of a regiment of colored infantry and a detachment of Tennessee cavalry. These troops fought bravely, but were overpowered. I will leave Forrest in his dispatches to tell what he did with them.

"The river was dyed," he says, "with the blood of the slaughtered for two hundred yards. The approximate loss was upward of five hundred killed; but few of the officers escaped. My loss was about twenty killed. It is

become necessary I can temporarily attach General Humphreys to your command.

"'U. S. GRANT.'

"As my health did not improve I repeated my request for leave, and on the 9th of July I received the following from General Grant at City Point:

"'General Ord can be assigned to the command of your corps during your absence if you think it advisable.'

"I left my command on that day, and City Point on the following day, and it is manifest General Grant up to that moment had not changed the opinion he had expressed in recommending my promotion. I returned to the army on the 19th of July, to find myself relieved from my command. During this absence of ten days, nothing connected with my military duties could have occurred to impair the confidence in me expressed in General Grant's communication of the 9th.

"I sought an explanation from him on the day of my return, and he was as reticent in assigning any cause for his action then as he was twenty-one years after, when, in preparing a contribution to the history of the war, he again passed sentence upon me without assigning a reason of any kind for his condemnation. I am to-day as ignorant of the causes for his action as I was then. That they were purely personal, and had not the remotest connection with my conduct as a soldier, I submit is proved by his own testimony, and it is upon this question alone that I care to defend myself."

In "The Century" magazine for September, 1886, Captain Joel B. Erhardt contributed the following extract from a letter that had never been made public:

"COLLEGE POINT, L. I., July 30th, 1864.
"HON. S. FOOT.

"DEAR SENATOR: I am extremely anxious that my friends in my native State [Vermont] should not think that the reason of General Grant relieving me from duty was brought about by any misconduct of mine, and therefore I write to put you in possession of such facts in the case as I am aware of, and think will throw light upon the subject. . . .

"On my return from a short leave of absence, on the 19th of July, General Grant sent for me to report to him, and then told me that he 'could not relieve General Butler,' and that as I had so severely criticised General Meade, he had determined to relieve me from the command of the Eighteenth Corps, and order me to New York City to await orders. The next morning the general gave some other reasons, such as an article in the 'Tribune' reflecting on General Hancock, which I had nothing in the world to do with, and two letters which I had written, before the campaign began, to two of General Grant's most devoted friends, urging upon them to try and prevent him from making the campaign he had just made. . . . Very truly yours,

"WILLIAM F. SMITH, Major-General."
EDITORS.

hoped that these facts will demonstrate to the Northern people that negro soldiers cannot cope with Southerners." Subsequently Forrest made a report in which he left out the part which shocks humanity to read.

At the East, also, the rebels were busy. I had said to Halleck that Plymouth and Washington, North Carolina, were unnecessary to us, that it would be better to have the garrisons engaged there added to Butler's command. If success should attend our arms, both places, and others, would fall into our hands naturally. These places had been occupied by Federal troops before I took command of the armies, and I knew that the executive would be reluctant to abandon them, and therefore explained my views; but before my views were carried out, the rebels captured the garrison at Plymouth. \ I then ordered the abandonment of Washington, but directed the holding of New Berne at all hazards. This was essential, because New Berne was a port into which blockade-runners could enter.

General Banks had gone on an expedition up the Red River long before my promotion to general command. I had opposed the movement strenuously, but acquiesced because it was the order of my superior at the time. ☆ By direction of Halleck I had reënforced Banks with a corps of about ten thousand men from Sherman's command. This reënforcement was wanted back badly before the forward movement commenced. But Banks had got so far that it seemed best that he should take Shreveport, on the Red River, and turn over the line of that river to Steele, who commanded in Arkansas, to hold instead of the line of the Arkansas. Orders were given accordingly, and with the expectation that the campaign would be ended in time for Banks to return A. J. Smith's command to where it belonged, ⌡ and get back to New Orleans himself in time to execute his part in the general plan. But the expedition was a failure. Banks did not get back in time to take part in the programme as laid down; nor was Smith returned until long after the movements of May, 1864, had been begun. The services of forty thousand veteran troops over and above the number required to hold all that was necessary in the Department of the Gulf were thus paralyzed. It is but just to Banks, however, to say that his expedition was ordered from Washington, and he was in no way responsible except for the conduct of it. I make no criticism on this point. He opposed the expedition.

By the 27th of April spring had so far advanced as to justify me in fixing a day for the great move. On that day Burnside left Annapolis to occupy Meade's position between Bull Run and the Rappahannock. Meade was notified and directed to bring his troops forward to his advance; on the following

---

⌐ The engagement at Plymouth extended from the 17th to the 20th of April, 1864. The garrison consisted of four regiments of infantry, with detachments of artillery and cavalry, under command of General H. W. Wessells. The principal reliance was the navy, which, however, was neutralized by the Confederate ram *Albemarle.* [See papers on the *Albemarle,* to follow.] After repulsing five charges General Wessells surrendered, with about 1500 men, to General R. F. Hoke. —EDITORS.

☆ General Halleck's instructions for this movement were promulgated during January and February, 1864.— EDITORS.

⌡ The 10,000 troops under General A. J. Smith that had been thus detached belonged to the 16th and 17th corps (Sherman's army), at the time (March, 1864,) in the Mississippi Valley. Portions of these corps subsequently joined Sherman and Thomas. See also papers on the Red River Campaign, to follow.—EDITORS.

FROM A PHOTOGRAPH.

day Butler was notified of my intended advance on the 4th of May, and he
was directed to move, the night of the same day, and get as far up the James
River as possible by daylight, and push on from there to accomplish the
task given him. He was also notified that reënforcements were being collected in Washington, which would be forwarded to him should the enemy
fall back into the trenches at Richmond. The same day Sherman was
directed to get his forces up ready to advance on the 5th. Sigel, at Winchester, was notified to move in conjunction with the others.

The criticism has been made by writers on the campaign from the Rapidan
to the James River that all the loss of life could have been obviated by moving the army there on transports. Richmond was fortified and intrenched so
perfectly that one man inside to defend was more than equal to five outside
besieging or assaulting. To get possession of Lee's army was the first great
object. With the capture of his army Richmond would necessarily follow.
It was better to fight him outside of his stronghold than in it. If the Army
of the Potomac had been moved bodily to the James River by water, Lee
could have moved a part of his forces back to Richmond, called Beauregard
from the South to reënforce it, and with the remainder moved on to Washington. Then, too, I ordered a move simultaneous with that of the Army of
the Potomac up the James River, by a formidable army already collected at
the mouth of the river.

While my headquarters were at Culpeper, from the 26th of March to the
4th of May, I generally visited Washington once a week to confer with the
Secretary of War and the President. On the last occasion, a few days before
moving, a circumstance occurred which came near postponing my part in
the campaign altogether. Colonel John S. Mosby had for a long time been
commanding a partisan corps, or regiment, which operated in the rear of
the Army of the Potomac. On my return to the field on this occasion, as the
train approached Warrenton Junction, a heavy cloud of dust was seen to the
east of the road, as if made by a body of cavalry on a charge. Arriving at
the junction, the train was stopped and inquiries were made as to the cause
of the dust. There was but one man at the station, and he informed us that
Mosby had crossed a few minutes before at full speed in pursuit of Federal
cavalry. Had he seen our train coming, no doubt he would have let his prisoners escape to capture the train. I was on a special train, if I remember
correctly, without any guard. Since the close of the war I have come to
know Colonel Mosby personally, and somewhat intimately. He is a different
man entirely from what I had supposed. He is slender, not tall, wiry, and
looks as if he could endure any amount of physical exercise. He is able, and
thoroughly honest and truthful. There were probably but few men in the
South who could have commanded successfully a separate detachment, in the
rear of an opposing army and so near the border of hostilities, as long as he
did without losing his entire command.

On this same visit to Washington I had my last interview with the President before reaching the James River. He had, of course, become acquainted
with the fact that a general movement had been ordered all along the line,

FROM A PHOTOGRAPH.

111

and seemed to think it a new feature in war. I explained to him that it was necessary to have a great number of troops to guard and to hold the territory we had captured, and to prevent incursions into the Northern States. These troops could perform this service just as well by advancing as by remaining still; and by advancing they would compel the enemy to keep detachments to hold them back or else lay his own territory open to invasion. "Oh! yes, I see that," he said. "As we say out West, If a man can't skin he must hold a leg while somebody else does."

The following correspondence closed the first chapter of my personal acquaintance with President Lincoln:

"EXECUTIVE MANSION, WASHINGTON, April 30, 1864.

"LIEUTENANT-GENERAL GRANT: Not expecting to see you again before the Spring campaign opens, I wish to express in this way my entire satisfaction with what you have done up to this time, so far as I understand it. The particulars of your plans I neither know or seek to know. You are vigilant and self-reliant; and, pleased with this, I wish not to obtrude any constraints or restraints upon you. While I am very anxious that any great disaster, or the capture of our men in great numbers, shall be avoided, I know these points are less likely to escape your attention than they would be mine. If there is anything wanting which is within my power to give, do not fail to let me know it. And now with a brave army, and a just cause, may God sustain you.   Yours very truly,

"A. LINCOLN."

"HEADQUARTERS, ARMIES OF THE UNITED STATES,
CULPEPER COURT HOUSE, VIRGINIA, May 1, 1864.

"THE PRESIDENT: Your very kind letter of yesterday is just received. The confidence you express for the future and satisfaction for the past in my military administration is acknowledged with pride. It shall be my earnest endeavor that you and the country shall not be disappointed. From my first entrance into the volunteer service of the country to the present day, I have never had cause of complaint — have never expressed or implied a complaint against the Administration or the Secretary of War, for throwing any embarrassment in the way of my vigorously prosecuting what appeared to be my duty. And since the promotion which placed me in command of all the armies, and in view of the great responsibility and the importance of success, I have been astonished at the readiness with which everything asked for has been yielded, without even an explanation being asked. Should my success be less than I desire and expect, the least I can say is, the fault is not with you.   Very truly, your obedient servant,

"U. S. GRANT, Lieutenant-General."

The armies were now all ready to move for the accomplishment of a single object. They were acting as a unit so far as such a thing was possible over such a vast field. Lee, with the capital of the Confederacy, was the main end to which all were working. Johnston, with Atlanta, was an important obstacle in the way of our accomplishing the result aimed at, and was therefore almost an independent objective. It was of less importance only because the capture of Johnston and his army would not produce so immediate and decisive a result in closing the rebellion as would the possession of Richmond, Lee and his army. All other troops were employed exclusively in support of these two movements. This was the plan; and I will now endeavor to give, as concisely as I can, the method of its execution, outlining first the operations of minor detached but coöperative columns.

As stated before, Banks failed to accomplish what he had been sent to do on the Red River, and eliminated the use of 40,000 veterans whose coöperation

Executive Mansion
Washington, April 30. 1864

Lieutenant General Grant.

Not expecting to see you again before the Spring campaign opens, I wish to express, in this way, my entire satisfaction with what you have done up to this time, so far as I understand it. The particulars of your plans I neither know, or seek to know. You are vigilant and self-reliant; and, pleased with this, I wish not to obtrude any constraints or restraints upon you. While I am very anxious that any great disaster, or the capture of our men in great numbers, shall be avoided, I know these points are less likely to escape your attention than they would be mine— If there is anything wanting which is within my power to give, do not fail, to let me know it. And now with a brave Army, and a just cause, may God sustain you.

Yours very truly
A. Lincoln.

LINCOLN'S GOD-SPEED TO GRANT. (FAC-SIMILE OF THE ORIGINAL, SLIGHTLY REDUCED IN SCALE.)

[This remarkable letter was received by General Grant on the 1st of May, three days before the Wilderness campaign began. He was always careless about his papers, and private or semi-official ones were often thrust into his pockets, where they remained for months. In some such way Mr. Lincoln's letter was mislaid. General Grant had forgotten its existence, until in 1866 I came across it in my researches for my history of his campaigns. He was so pleased at the discovery, or recovery, that he gave me the original letter at the time. It is my intention eventually to present it either to the Government or to the family of General Grant.

ADAM BADEAU.

NEW YORK, November 10, 1885.]

in the grand campaign had been expected—10,000 with Sherman and 30,000 against Mobile.

Sigel's record is almost equally brief. He moved out, it is true, according to programme; but just when I was hoping to hear of good work being done in the Valley I received instead the following announcement from Halleck: "Sigel is in full retreat on Strasburg. He will do nothing but run; never did anything else." The enemy had intercepted him about New Market and handled him roughly, capturing 6 guns and some 900 men out of 6000.⚓

The plan had been for an advance of Sigel's forces in columns. Though the one under his immediate command failed ingloriously, the other proved more fortunate. Under Crook and Averell, his western column advanced from the Gauley in West Virginia at the appointed time, and with more happy results. They reached the Virginia and Tennessee railroad at Dublin, and destroyed a depot of supplies besides tearing up several miles of road and burning the bridge over New River. Having accomplished this, they recrossed the Alleghanies to Meadow Bluffs, and there awaited further orders.

Butler embarked at Fort Monroe with all his command, except the cavalry and some artillery which moved up the south bank of the James River. His steamers moved first up Chesapeake Bay and York River as if threatening the rear of Lee's army. At midnight they turned back, and by daylight Butler was far up the James River. He seized City Point and Bermuda Hundred early in the day, without loss, and no doubt very much to the surprise of the enemy.

This was the accomplishment of the first step contemplated in my instructions to Butler. He was to act from here, looking to Richmond as his objective point. I had given him to understand that I should aim to fight Lee between the Rapidan and Richmond if he would stand; but should Lee fall back into Richmond, I would follow up and make a junction of the armies of the Potomac and the James on the James River. He was directed to secure a footing as far up the south side of the river as he could at as early a date as possible.

By the 6th of May Butler was in position and had begun intrenching, and on the 7th he sent out his cavalry from Suffolk to cut the Weldon railroad. He also sent out detachments to destroy the railroads between Petersburg and Richmond, but no great success attended these latter efforts. He made no great effort to establish himself on that road, and neglected to attack Petersburg, which was almost defenseless. About the 11th he advanced slowly until he reached the works at Drewry's Bluff, about half-way between Bermuda Hundred and Richmond. In the meantime Beauregard ‡ had been gathering reënforcements. On the 16th he attacked Butler with great vigor, and with such success as to limit very materially the further usefulness of the Army of the James as a distinct factor in the campaign. I afterward ordered a portion of it ♭ to join the Army of the Potomac, leaving a sufficient

---

⚓ See papers to follow.—EDITORS.

‡ On the 20th of April, 1864, General Beauregard was relieved of the command at Charleston, and on the 23d he assumed command of the

Department of North Carolina, which on May 14th was extended to cover all of Virginia south of the James, including Drewry's Bluff.— EDITORS.

♭ Smith's 18th Corps and two divisions of the 10th.

force with Butler to man his works, hold securely the footing he had already gained, and maintain a threatening front toward the rear of the Confederate capital.

The position which General Butler had chosen between the two rivers,⸓ the James and Appomattox, was one of great natural strength, and where a large area of ground might be thoroughly inclosed by means of a single intrenched line, and that a very short one in comparison with the extent of territory which it thoroughly protected. His right was protected by the James River, his left by the Appomattox, and his rear by their junction—the two streams uniting near by. The bend of the two streams shortened the line that had been chosen for intrenchment, while it increased the area which the line inclosed.

Previous to ordering any troops from Butler I sent my chief engineer, General Barnard, from the Army of the Potomac to that of the James, to inspect Butler's position and ascertain whether I could again safely make an order for General Butler's movement in coöperation with mine, now that I was getting so near Richmond; or, if I could not, whether his position was strong enough to justify me in withdrawing some of his troops and having them brought round by water to White House to join me and reënforce the Army of the Potomac. General Barnard reported the position very strong for defensive purposes, and that I could do the latter with great

MAJOR-GENERAL A. A. HUMPHREYS,
CHIEF-OF-STAFF, ARMY OF THE POTOMAC.
FROM A PHOTOGRAPH.

security; but that General Butler could not move from where he was, in coöperation, to produce any effect. He said that the general occupied a place between the James and Appomattox rivers which was of great strength, and where with an inferior force he could hold it for an indefinite length of time against a superior; but that he could do nothing offensively. I then asked him why Butler could not move out from his lines and push across the Richmond and Petersburg railroad to the rear and on the south side of Richmond. He replied that it was impracticable because the enemy had substantially the same line across the neck of land that General Butler had. He then took out his pencil and drew a sketch of the locality, remarking that the position was like a bottle, and that Butler's line of intrenchments across the neck represented the cork; that the enemy had built an equally strong line immediately in front of him across the neck; and it was, therefore, as if Butler was in a bottle. He was perfectly safe against an attack; but, as Barnard expressed it, the

⸓ See map of Bermuda Hundred and papers, to follow.— EDITORS.

enemy had corked the bottle, and with a small force could hold the cork in its place. This struck me as being very expressive of his position, particularly when I saw the hasty sketch which General Barnard had drawn; and in making my subsequent report I used that expression without adding quotation marks, never thinking that anything had been said that would attract attention, as this did, very much to the annoyance, no doubt, of General Butler, and I know very much to my own. I found afterward that this was mentioned in the notes of General Badeau's book, which, when they were shown to me, I asked to have stricken out; yet it was retained there, though against my wishes. ☆

I make this statement here because, although I have often made it before, it has never been in my power until now to place it where it will correct history; and I desire to rectify all injustice that I may have done to individuals, particularly to officers who were gallantly serving their country during the trying period of the war for the preservation of the Union. General Butler certainly gave his very earnest support to the war; and he gave his own best efforts personally toward the suppression of the rebellion.

The further operations of the Army of the James can best be treated of in connection with those of the Army of the Potomac, the two being so intimately associated and connected as to be substantially one body in which the individuality of the supporting wing is merged. I will briefly mention Sheridan's first raid upon Lee's communications which, though an incident of the operations on the main line and not specifically marked out in the original plan, attained in its brilliant execution and results all the proportions of an independent campaign.

On the 8th of May, just after the battle of the Wilderness, and when we were moving on Spotsylvania, I directed Sheridan, verbally, to cut loose from the Army of the Potomac, pass around the left of Lee's army and attack his cavalry; to cut the two roads—one running west through Gordonsville, Charlottesville, and Lynchburg, the other to Richmond; and, when compelled to do so for want of forage and rations, to move on to the James River and draw these from Butler's supplies. This move took him past the entire rear of Lee's army. These orders were also given in writing through Meade.

The object of this move was threefold: 1. If successfully executed—and it was—he would annoy the enemy by cutting his lines of supplies and telegraphic communications, and destroy or get for his own use supplies in store in the rear and coming up; 2. He would draw the enemy's cavalry after him, and thus better protect our flanks, rear, and trains than by remaining with the army; 3. His absence would save the trains drawing his forage and other supplies from Fredericksburg, which had now become our base. He started at daylight the next morning, and accomplished more

☆ The words used in General Grant's report, dated July 22d, 1865, are these:

"His [Butler's] army, therefore, though in a position of great security, was as completely shut off from further operations directly before Richmond as if it had been in a bottle strongly corked. . . . The army sent to operate against Richmond having hermetically sealed itself up at Bermuda Hundred, the enemy was enabled to bring the most if not all of the reënforcements brought from the South by Beauregard against the Army of the Potomac." EDITORS.

than was expected. It was sixteen days before he got back to the Army of the Potomac. |

Sheridan in this memorable raid passed entirely around Lee's army; encountered his cavalry in four engagements and defeated them in all; recaptured four hundred Union prisoners and killed and captured many of the enemy; destroyed and used many supplies and munitions of war; destroyed miles of railroad and telegraph, and freed us from annoyance by the cavalry for more than two weeks.

I fixed the day for Sherman to start when the season should be far enough advanced, it was hoped, for the roads to be in a condition for the troops to march. General Sherman at once set himself to work preparing for the task which was assigned him to accomplish in the spring campaign.

The campaign to Atlanta was managed with the most consummate skill, the enemy being flanked out of one position after another all the way there. It is true this was not accomplished without a good deal of fighting, some of it very hard fighting, rising to the dignity of very important battles; neither were positions gained in a single day. On the contrary, weeks were spent at some; and about Atlanta more than a month was consumed.

Soon after midnight, May 3d–4th, the Army of the Potomac moved out from its position north of the Rapidan, to start upon that memorable campaign destined to result in the capture of the Confederate capital and the army defending it.

| From "Personal Memoirs of U. S. Grant" (New York: C. L. Webster & Co.) we take this account of the raid:

"The course Sheridan took was directly to Richmond. Before night Stuart, commanding the Confederate cavalry, came on to the rear of his command. But the advance kept on, crossed the North Anna, and at Beaver Dam, a station on the Virginia Central Railroad, recaptured four hundred Union prisoners on their way to Richmond, destroyed the road, and used and destroyed a large amount of subsistence and medical stores.

"Stuart, seeing that our cavalry was pushing toward Richmond, abandoned the pursuit on the morning of the 10th, and by a detour and an exhausting march, interposed between Sheridan and Richmond at Yellow Tavern, only about six miles north of the city. Sheridan destroyed the railroad and more supplies at Ashland, and on the 11th arrived in Stuart's front. A severe engagement ensued, in which the losses were heavy on both sides, but the rebels were beaten, their leader mortally wounded, and some guns and many prisoners were captured.

"Sheridan passed through the outer defenses of Richmond, and could, no doubt, have passed through the inner ones; but, having no supports near, he could not have remained. After caring for his wounded, he struck for the James River below the city, to communicate with Butler, and to rest his men and horses as well as to get food and forage for them.

"He moved first between the Chickahominy and the James, but in the morning (the 12th) he was stopped by batteries at Mechanicsville. He then turned to cross to the north side of the Chickahominy by Meadow Bridge. He found this barred, and the defeated Confederate cav-

alry, reorganized, occupying the opposite side. The panic created by his first entrance within the outer works of Richmond having subsided, troops were sent out to attack his rear.

"He was now in a perilous position; one from which but few generals could have extricated themselves. The defenses of Richmond, manned, were to the right, the Chickahominy was to the left, with no bridge remaining, and the opposite bank guarded; to the rear was a force from Richmond. This force was attacked and beaten by Wilson's and Gregg's divisions, while Sheridan turned to the left with the remaining division and hastily built a bridge over the Chickahominy under the fire of the enemy, forced a crossing and soon dispersed the Confederates he found there. The enemy was held back from the stream by the fire of the troops not engaged in bridge-building.

"On the 13th Sheridan was at Bottom's Bridge, over the Chickahominy. On the 14th he crossed this stream, and on that day went into camp on the James River at Haxall's Landing. He at once put himself into communication with General Butler, who directed all the supplies he wanted to be furnished.

"Sheridan had left the Army of the Potomac at Spotsylvania, but did not know where either this or Lee's army was now. Great caution therefore had to be exercised in getting back. On the 17th, after resting his command for three days, he started on his return. He moved by the way of White House. The bridge over the Pamunkey had been burned by the enemy, but a new one was speedily improvised, and the cavalry crossed over it. On the 22d he was at Aylett's on the Mattapony, where he learned the position of the two armies. On the 24th he joined us on the march from North Anna to Cold Harbor, in the vicinity of Chesterfield."

WATERING HORSES IN THE RAPIDAN.

FROM THE WILDERNESS TO COLD HARBOR.

BY E. M. LAW, MAJOR-GENERAL, C. S. A.

ON the 2d of May, 1864, a group of officers stood at the Confederate signal station on Clark's Mountain, Virginia, south of the Rapidan, and examined closely through their field-glasses the position of the Federal army then lying north of the river in Culpeper county. The central figure of the group was the commander of the Army of Northern Virginia, who had requested his corps and division commanders to meet him there. Though some demonstrations had been made in the direction of the upper fords, General Lee expressed the opinion that the Federal army would cross the river at Germanna or Ely's. Thirty-six hours later General Meade's army, General Grant, now commander-in-chief, being with it, commenced its march to the crossings indicated by General Lee.

The Army of the Potomac, which had now commenced its march toward Richmond, was more powerful in numbers than at any previous period of the war. It consisted of three corps: the Second (Hancock's), the Fifth (Warren's), and the Sixth (Sedgwick's); but the Ninth (Burnside's) acted with Meade throughout the campaign. Meade's army was thoroughly equipped, and provided with every appliance of modern warfare. On the other hand, the Army of Northern Virginia had gained little in numbers during the winter just passed, and had never been so scantily supplied with food and clothing. The equipment as to arms was well enough for men who knew how to use them, but commissary and quartermasters' supplies were lamentably deficient. A new pair of shoes or an overcoat was a luxury, and full rations would have astonished the stomachs of Lee's ragged Confederates. But they took their privations cheerfully, and complaints were seldom heard. I recall an instance of one hardy fellow whose trousers were literally "worn to a frazzle" and would no longer adhere to his legs even by dint of the most persistent patching. Unable to buy, beg, or borrow another pair, he wore instead a pair of thin cotton drawers. By nursing these carefully he managed to get through the winter. Before the campaign opened in the spring a small lot of clothing was received, and he was the first man of his regiment to be supplied.

I have often heard expressions of surprise that these ragged, barefooted, half-starved men would fight at all. But the very fact that they remained with their colors through such privations and hardships was sufficient to prove that they would be dangerous foes to encounter upon the line of battle. The *morale* of the army at this time was excellent, and it moved forward confidently to the grim death-grapple in the wilderness of Spotsylvania with its old enemy, the Army of the Potomac.

General Lee's headquarters were two miles north-east of Orange Court House; of his three corps, Longstreet's was at Gordonsville, Ewell's was on and near the Rapidan, above Mine Run, and Hill's on his left, higher up the stream. When the Federal army was known to be in motion, General Lee prepared to move upon its flank with his whole force as soon as his opponent should clear the river and begin the march southward. The route selected by General Grant led entirely around the right of Lee's position on the river above. Grant's passage of the Rapidan was unopposed, and he struck boldly out on the direct road to Richmond. Two roads lead from Orange Court House down the Rapidan toward Fredericksburg. They follow the general direction of the river, and are almost parallel to each other, the "Old turnpike" nearest the river, and the "Plank road" a short distance

UNION TROOPS CROSSING THE RAPIDAN AT GERMANNA FORD, MAY 4, 1864.
FROM A SKETCH MADE AT THE TIME.

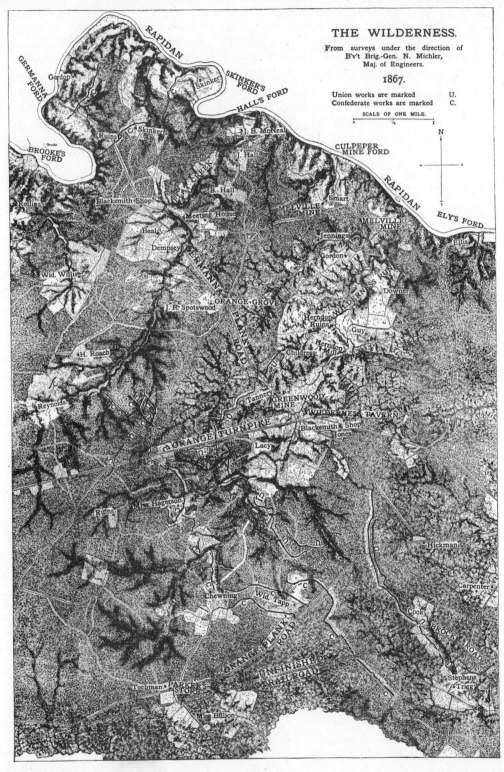

THE WILDERNESS.

From surveys under the direction of
B'v't Brig.-Gen. N. Michler,
Maj. of Engineers.

1867.

Union works are marked   U.
Confederate works are marked   C.

SCALE OF ONE MILE.

south of it. The route of the Federal army lay directly across these two roads, along the western borders of the famous Wilderness.

About noon on the 4th of May, Ewell's corps was put in motion on and toward the Orange turnpike, while A. P. Hill, with two divisions, moved parallel with him on the Orange Plank road. The two divisions of Longstreet's corps encamped near Gordonsville were ordered to move rapidly across the country and follow Hill on the Plank road. Ewell's corps was the first to find itself in the presence of the enemy. As it advanced along the turnpike on the morning of the 5th, the Federal column was seen crossing it from the direction of Germanna Ford. Ewell promptly formed line of battle across the turnpike, and communicated his position to General Lee, who was on the Plank road with Hill. Ewell was instructed to regulate his movements by the head of Hill's column, whose progress he could tell by the firing in its front, and not to bring on a general engagement until Longstreet should come up. The position of Ewell's troops, so near the flank of the Federal line of march, was anything but favorable to a preservation of the peace, and a collision soon occurred which opened the campaign in earnest.

General Warren, whose corps was passing when Ewell came up, halted, and turning to the right made a vigorous attack upon Edward Johnson's division, posted across the turnpike. J. M. Jones's brigade, which held the road, was driven back in confusion.⏐ Steuart's brigade was pushed forward to take its place. Rodes's division was thrown in on Johnson's right, south of the road, and the line, thus reëstablished, moved forward, reversed the tide of battle, and rolled back the Federal attack. The fighting was severe and bloody while it lasted. At some points the lines were in such close proximity in the thick woods which covered the battle-field that when the Federal troops gave way several hundred of them, unable to retreat without exposure to almost certain death, surrendered themselves as prisoners.

Ewell's entire corps was now up—Johnson's division holding the turnpike, Rodes's division on the right of it, and Early's in reserve. So far Ewell had been engaged only with Warren's corps, but Sedgwick's soon came up from the river and joined Warren on his right. Early's division was sent to meet it. The battle extended in that direction, with steady and determined attacks upon Early's front, until nightfall. The Confederates still clung to their hold on the Federal flank against every effort to dislodge them.

When Warren's corps encountered the head of Ewell's column on the 5th of May, General Meade is reported to have said: "They have left a division to fool us here, while they concentrate and prepare a position on the North Anna." If the stubborn resistance to Warren's attack⏐ did not at once

⏐ Major Jed. Hotchkiss, Topographical Engineer of the Confederate Second Corps, who witnessed this movement and mapped it at the time, writes to the editors:

"The attack was made by Jones, *not* by Warren. Early in the day Jones drove the Federal flanking videttes back very near Wilderness Run; then, having developed the Federal march, Jones fell back about two miles, and took position where the Flat Run road, from the Germanna road, intersects the old turnpike, but keeping his skirmishers engaged. It was not until *afternoon* that Warren turned his right and drove him back about one-quarter mile; Battle's brigade of Rodes's division, which was in support, then moved forward, but was confused by Jones's retreating men and also forced back; then Gordon's brigade, of Early's division, which had been formed facing south-east, its left on the turnpike, advanced and drove back the Federal advance and reëstablished the line as first held by Jones."

convince him of his mistake, the firing that announced the approach of Hill's corps along the Plank road, very soon afterward, must have opened his eyes to the bold strategy of the Confederate commander. General Lee had deliberately chosen this as his battle-ground. He knew this tangled wilderness well, and appreciated fully the advantages such a field afforded for concealing his great inferiority of force and for neutralizing the superior strength of his antagonist. General Grant's bold movement across the lower fords into the Wilderness, in the execution of his plan to swing past the Confederate army and place himself between it and Richmond, offered the expected opportunity of striking a blow upon his flank while his troops were stretched out on the line of march. The wish for such an opportunity was doubtless in a measure "father to the thought" expressed by General Lee three days before, at the signal station on Clark's Mountain.

Soon after Ewell became engaged on the Old turnpike, A. P. Hill's advance struck the Federal outposts on the Plank road at Parker's store, on the outskirts of the Wilderness. These were driven in and followed up to their line of battle, which was so posted as to cover the junction of the Plank

road with the Stevensburg and Brock roads, on which the Federal army was moving toward Spotsylvania. The fight began between Getty's division of the Sixth Corps and Heth's division, which was leading A. P. Hill's column. Hancock's corps, which was already on the march for Spotsylvania by way of Chancellorsville, was at once recalled, and at 4 o'clock in the afternoon was ordered to drive Hill "out of the Wilderness." Cadmus Wilcox's division went to Heth's support, and Poague's battalion of artillery took position in a little clearing on the north side of the Plank road, in rear of the Confederate infantry. But there was little use for artillery on such a field. After the battle was fairly joined in the thickets in front, its fire might do as much damage to friend as to foe; so it was silent.

It was a desperate struggle between the infantry of the two armies, on a field whose physical aspects were as grim and forbidding as the struggle itself. It was a battle of brigades and regiments rather than of corps and divisions. Officers could not see the whole length of their commands, and could tell whether the troops on their right and left were driving or being driven only by the sound of the firing. It was a fight at close quarters too, for as night came on, in those tangled thickets of stunted pine, sweet-gum, scrub-oak, and cedar, the approach of the opposing lines could be discerned only by the noise of their passage through the underbrush or the flashing of their guns. The usually silent Wilderness had suddenly become alive

CONFEDERATE LINE WAITING ORDERS IN THE WILDERNESS.

with the angry flashing and heavy roar of the musketry, mingled with the yells of the combatants as they swayed to and fro in the gloomy thickets. Among the killed were General Alexander Hays, of Hancock's corps, and General J. M. Jones, of Ewell's.

When the battle closed at 8 o'clock, General Lee sent an order to Longstreet to make a night march, so as to arrive upon the field at daylight the next morning. The latter moved at 1 A. M. of the 6th, but it was already daylight when he reached the Plank road at Parker's store, three miles in rear of Hill's battle-field.↓ During the night the movements of troops and preparations for battle could be heard on the Federal line, in front of Heth's and Wilcox's divisions, which had so far sustained themselves against every attack by six divisions under General Hancock. But Heth's and Wilcox's men were thoroughly worn out. Their lines were ragged and irregular, with wide intervals, and in some places fronting in different directions. In the expectation that they would be relieved during the night, no effort was made to rearrange and strengthen them to meet the storm that was brewing.

As soon as it was light enough to see what little could be seen in that dark forest, Hancock's troops swept forward to the attack. The blow fell with greatest force upon Wilcox's troops south of the Orange Plank road. They made what front they could and renewed the fight, until, the attacking column overlapping the right wing, it gave way, and the whole line "rolled up" from the right and retired in disorder along the Plank road as far as the position of Poague's artillery, which now opened upon the attacking force.

↓ The right of Ewell's corps formed a junction with the left of A. P. Hill's at a point about half-way between Parker's store and the Orange turnpike on the afternoon of the 5th. — EDITORS.

The Federals pressed their advantage and were soon abreast of the artillery on the opposite side, their bullets flying across the road among the guns where General Lee himself stood. For a while matters looked very serious for the Confederates. General Lee, after sending a messenger to hasten the march of Longstreet's troops and another to prepare the trains for a movement to the rear, was assisting in rallying the disordered troops and directing the fire of the artillery, when the head of Longstreet's corps appeared in double column, swinging down the Orange Plank road at a trot. In perfect order, ranks well closed, and no stragglers, those splendid troops came on, regardless of the confusion on every side, pushing their steady way onward like "a river in the sea" of confused and troubled human waves around them. Kershaw's division took the right of the road, and, coming into line under a heavy fire, moved obliquely to the right (south) to meet the Federal left, which had "swung round" in that direction. The Federals were checked in their sweeping advance and thrown back upon their front line of breastworks, where they made a stubborn stand. But Kershaw, urged on by Longstreet, charged with his whole command, swept his front, and captured the works.

Nearly at the same moment Field's division took the left of the road, with Gregg's brigade in front, Benning's behind it, Law's next, and Jenkins's following. As the Texans in the front line swept past the batteries where General Lee was standing, they gave a rousing cheer for "Marse Robert," who spurred his horse forward and followed them in the charge. When the men became aware that he was "going in" with them, they called loudly to him to go back. "We won't go on unless you go back," was the general cry. One of the men dropped to the rear, and taking the bridle turned the general's horse around, while General Gregg came up and urged him to do as the

CAPTURE OF A PART OF THE BURNING UNION BREASTWORKS ON THE BROCK ROAD ON THE
AFTERNOON OF MAY 6. FROM A SKETCH MADE AT THE TIME.

men wished. At that moment a member of his staff (Colonel Venable) directed his attention to General Longstreet, whom he had been looking for, and who was sitting on his horse near the Orange Plank road. With evident disappointment General Lee turned off and joined General Longstreet.

The ground over which Field's troops were advancing was open for a short distance, and fringed on its farther edge with scattered pines, beyond which began the Wilderness. The Federals [Webb's brigade of Hancock's corps] were advancing through the pines with apparently resistless force, when Gregg's eight hundred Texans, regardless of numbers, flanks, or supports, dashed directly upon them. There was a terrific crash, mingled with wild yells, which settled down into a steady roar of musketry. In less than ten minutes one-half of that devoted eight hundred were lying upon the field dead or wounded; but they had delivered a stagger- ing blow and broken the force of the Federal advance. Benning's and Law's brigades came promptly to their support, and the whole swept forward together. The tide was flow- ing the other way. It ebbed and flowed many times that day, strewing the Wilderness with human wrecks. Law's brigade captured a line of log breastworks in its front, but had held

BRIGADIER-GENERAL MICAH JENKINS, C. S. A., KILLED MAY 6, 1864. FROM A TINTYPE.

them only a few moments when their former owners [Webb's brigade] came back to claim them. The Federals were driven back to a second line several hundred yards beyond, which was also taken. This advanced position was attacked in front and on the right from across the Orange Plank road, and Law's Alabamians "advanced backward" without standing on the order of their going, until they reached the first line of logs, now in their rear. As their friends in blue still insisted on claiming their property and were advancing to take it, they were met by a counter-charge and again driven beyond the second line. This was held against a determined attack, in which the Federal General Wadsworth was shot from his horse as he rode up close to the right of the line on the Plank road. The position again becoming untenable by reason of the movements of Federal troops on their right, Law's men retired a second time to the works they had first captured. And so, for more than two hours, the storm of battle swept to and fro, in some places passing several times over the same ground, and settling down at length almost where it had begun the day before.

About 10 o'clock it was ascertained that the Federal left flank rested only a short distance south of the Orange Plank road, which offered a favorable opportunity for a turning movement in that quarter. General Longstreet at once moved Mahone's, Wofford's, Anderson's, and Davis's brigades, the whole under General Mahone, around this end of the Federal line. Forming at right angles to it, they attacked in flank and rear, while a general advance was made in front. So far the fight had been one of anvil and hammer. But this first display of tactics at once changed the face of the field. The Federal left wing was rolled up in confusion toward the Plank road and then back upon the Brock road.

This partial victory had been a comparatively easy one. The signs of demoralization and even panic among the troops of Hancock's left wing, who had been hurled back by Mahone's flank attack, were too plain to be mistaken by the Confederates, who believed that Chancellorsville was about to be repeated. General Longstreet rode forward and prepared to press his advantage. Jenkins's fresh brigade was moved forward on the Plank road to renew the attack, supported by Kershaw's division, while the flanking column was to come into position on its right. The latter were now in line south of the road and almost parallel to it. Longstreet and Kershaw rode with General Jenkins at the head of his brigade as it pressed forward, when suddenly the quiet that had reigned for some moments was broken by a few scattering shots on the north of the road, which were answered by a volley from Mahone's line on the south side. The firing in their front, and the appearance of troops on the road whom they failed to recognize as friends through the intervening timber, had drawn a single volley, which lost to them all the fruits of the splendid work they had just done. General Jenkins was killed and Longstreet seriously wounded by our own men. The troops who were following them faced quickly toward the firing and were about to return it; but when General Kershaw called out, "They are friends!" every musket was lowered, and the men dropped upon the ground to avoid the fire.

The head of the attack had fallen, and for a time the movements of the Confederates were paralyzed. Lee came forward and directed the dispositions for a new attack, but the change of commanders after the fall of Longstreet, and the resumption of the thread of operations, occasioned a delay of several hours, and then the tide had turned, and we received only hard knocks instead of victory. When at 4 o'clock an attack was made upon the Federal line along the Brock road, it was found strongly fortified and stubbornly defended. The log breastworks had taken fire during the battle, and at one point separated the combatants by a wall of fire and smoke which neither could pass. Part of Field's division captured the works in their front, but were forced to relinquish them for want of support. Meanwhile Burnside's corps, which had reënforced Hancock during the day, made a vigorous attack on the north of the Orange Plank road. Law's (Alabama) and Perry's (Florida) brigades were being forced back, when, Heth's division coming to their assistance, they assumed the offensive, driving Burnside's troops beyond the extensive line of breastworks constructed previous to their advance.

The battles fought by Ewell on the Old turnpike and by A. P. Hill on the Plank road, on the 5th of May, were entirely distinct, no connected line existing between them. Connection was established with Ewell's right by Wilcox's division, after it had been relieved by Longstreet's troops on the morning of the 6th. While the battle was in progress on the Orange Plank road, on the 6th, an unsuccessful attempt was made to turn Ewell's left next the river,

BREASTWORKS OF HANCOCK'S CORPS ON THE BROCK ROAD—MORNING OF MAY 7.
FROM A SKETCH MADE AT THE TIME.

and heavy assaults were made upon the line of Early's division. So persistent were these attacks on the front of Pegram's brigade, that other troops were brought up to its support, but the men rejected the offer of assistance.

Late in the day General Ewell ordered a movement against the Federal right wing, similar to that by which Longstreet had "doubled up" Hancock's left in the morning. Two brigades, under General John B. Gordon, moved out of their works at sunset, and lapping the right of Sedgwick's corps [the Sixth] made a sudden and determined attack upon it. ♭ Taken by surprise, the Federals were driven from a large portion of their works with the loss of six hundred prisoners,—among them Generals Seymour and Shaler. Night closed the contest, and with it the battle of the Wilderness.

When Lee's army appeared on the flank of the Federal line of march on the 5th of May, General Grant had at once faced his adversary and endeavored to push him out of the way. Grant's strongest efforts had been directed to forcing back the Confederate advance on the Orange Plank road, which, if successful, would have enabled him to complete his plan of "swinging past" that army and placing himself between it and Richmond. On the other hand, Lee's principal effort had been to strike the head of Grant's

♭ In this movement General Early was in command, and all of his division shared in the attack except Johnston's brigade, which was to the west of Flat Run. The Confederate brigades confronting Sedgwick on the east of the run were Gordon's, Pegram's, and Hays's. Gordon, on the left, began the movement against Sedgwick's right, and Hays and Pegram followed up the attack. According to

General A. A. Humphreys ("The Virginia Campaign of 1864 and 1865." New York: Charles Scribner's Sons), "General Early drew back his brigades and formed a new line in front of his old. During the night an entirely new line was taken up by the Sixth Corps, its front and right thrown back—a change which the right of the Fifth Corps conformed to."—EDITORS.

column a crushing blow where it crossed the Plank road, in order to force it from its route and throw it in confusion back into the Wilderness. Both attempts had failed. What advantages had been gained by the two days' fighting remained with the Confederates. They held a position nearer the Federal line of march than when the battle began, and had inflicted losses incomparably heavier than they had themselves sustained. Both sides were now strongly intrenched, and neither could well afford to attack. And so the 7th of May was spent in skirmishing, each waiting to see what the other would do. That night the race for Spotsylvania began. General Lee had been informed by "Jeb" Stuart of the movement of the Federal trains south-ward during the afternoon. After dark the noise of moving columns along the Brock road could be heard, and it was at once responded to by a similar movement on the part of Lee. The armies moved in parallel columns sep-arated only by a short interval. Longstreet's corps (now commanded by R. H. Anderson) marched all night and arrived at Spotsylvania at 8 o'clock on the morning of the 8th, where the ball was already in motion. Stuart had thrown his cavalry across the Brock road to check the Federal advance, and as the Federal cavalry had failed to dislodge him, Warren's corps had been pushed forward to clear the way. Kershaw's, Humphreys's, and Law's brigades were at once sent to Stuart's assistance. The head of Warren's column was forced back and immediately commenced intrenching. Spot-sylvania Court House was found occupied by Federal cavalry and artillery, which retired without a fight. The Confederates had won the race.

The troops on both sides were now rapidly arriving. Sedgwick's corps joined Warren's, and in the afternoon was thrown heavily against Anderson's right wing, which, assisted by the timely arrival of Ewell's corps, repulsed the attack with great slaughter. Hill's corps (now under command of Gen-eral Early) did not arrive until the next morning, May 9th. General Lee's line now covered Spotsylvania Court House, with its left (Longstreet's corps) resting on the Po River, a small stream which flows on the south-west; Ewell's corps in the center, north of the Court House, and Hill's on the right, crossing the Fredericksburg road. These positions were generally maintained during the battles that followed, though brigades and divisions were often detached from their proper commands and sent to other parts of the field to meet pressing emergencies.

No engagement of importance took place on the 9th, which was spent in intrenching the lines and preparing places of refuge from the impending storm. But the 10th was "a field-day." Early in the morning it was found that Hancock's corps had crossed the Po above the point where the Confed-erate left rested, had reached the Shady Grove road, and was threatening our rear, as well as the trains which were in that direction on the Old Court House road leading to Louisa Court House. General Early was ordered from the right with Mahone's and Heth's divisions, and, moving rapidly to the threatened quarter, attacked Hancock's rear division as it was about to recross the Po — driving it, with severe loss, through the burning woods in its rear, back across the river.

Meanwhile General Grant was not idle elsewhere. He had commenced his efforts to break through the lines confronting him. The first assault was made upon Field's division of Longstreet's corps and met with a complete and bloody repulse. Again at 3 o'clock in the afternoon, the blue columns pressed forward to the attack, and were sent back torn and bleeding, leaving the ground covered with their dead and wounded. Anticipating a renewal of the assaults, many of our men went out in front of their breastworks, and, gathering up the muskets and cartridge-boxes of the dead and wounded, brought them in and distributed them along the line. If they did not have repeating-rifles, they had a very good substitute—several loaded ones to each man. They had no reserves, and knew that if they could not sufficiently reduce the number of their assailants to equalize matters somewhat before they reached the works, these might become untenable against such heavy and determined attacks.

A lull of several hours succeeded the failure of the second attack, but it was only a breathing spell preparatory to the culminating effort of the day. Near sunset our skirmishers were driven in and the heavy, dark lines of attack came into view, one after another, first in quick time, then in a trot, and then with a rush toward the works. The front lines dissolved before the pitiless storm that met them, but those in the rear pressed forward, and over their dead and dying comrades reached that portion of the works held by the Texas brigade. These gallant fellows, now reduced to a mere handful by their losses in the Wilderness, stood manfully to their work. Their line was bent backward by the pressure, but they continued the fight in rear of the works with bayonets and clubbed muskets. Fortunately for them, Anderson's brigade had cleared its own front, and a portion of it turned upon the flank of their assailants, who were driven out, leaving many dead and wounded inside the works.

While this attack was in progress on Field's line, another, quite as determined, was made farther to the right, in front of Rodes's division of Ewell's corps. Doles's brigade was broken and swept out of its works with the loss of three hundred prisoners. But as the attacking force poured through the gap thus made, Daniel's brigade on one side and Steuart's on the other drew back from their lines and fell upon its flanks, while Battle's and Johnston's brigades were hurried up from the left and thrown across its front. Assailed on three sides at once, the Federals were forced back to the works, and over them, whereupon they broke in disorderly retreat to their own lines.

The next day was rainy and disagreeable, and no serious fighting took place. There were movements, however, along the Federal lines during the day that indicated a withdrawal from the front of Longstreet's corps. Late in the afternoon, under the impression that General Grant had actually begun another flanking movement, General Lee ordered that all the artillery on the left and center that was "difficult of access" should be withdrawn from the lines, and that everything should be in readiness to move during the night if necessary. Under this order, General Long, Ewell's chief of artillery, removed all but two batteries from the line of General Edward

McCOOL'S IN 1884.

McCOOL'S FARM-HOUSE, WITHIN THE "BLOODY ANGLE," SPOTSYLVANIA. FROM A WAR-TIME PHOTOGRAPH.

Johnson's division, for the reason given, that they were "difficult of access." Johnson's division held an elevated point somewhat advanced from the general line, and known as "the salient" [or "Bloody Angle"; see map], the breastworks there making a considerable angle, with its point toward the enemy. This point had been held because it was a good position for artillery, and if occupied by the enemy would command portions of our line. Such projections on a defensive line are always dangerous if held by infantry alone, as an attack upon the point of the angle can only be met by a diverging fire; or if attacked on either face, the troops holding the other face, unless protected by traverses or by works in rear (as were some of the Confederates), are more exposed than those on the side attacked. But with sufficient artillery, so posted as to sweep the sides of the angle, such a position may be very strong. To provide against contingencies, a second line had been laid off and partly constructed a short distance in rear, so as to cut off this salient.

After the artillery had been withdrawn on the night of the 11th, General Johnson discovered that the enemy was concentrating in his front, and, convinced that he would be attacked in the morning, requested the immediate return of the artillery that had been taken away. The men in the trenches were kept on the alert all night and were ready for the attack, when at dawn on the morning of the 12th a dense column emerged from the pines half a mile in the front of the salient and rushed to the attack. They came on, to use General Johnson's words, "in great disorder, with a narrow front, but extending back as far as I could see." Page's battalion of artillery, which had been ordered back to the trenches at 4 o'clock in the morning, was

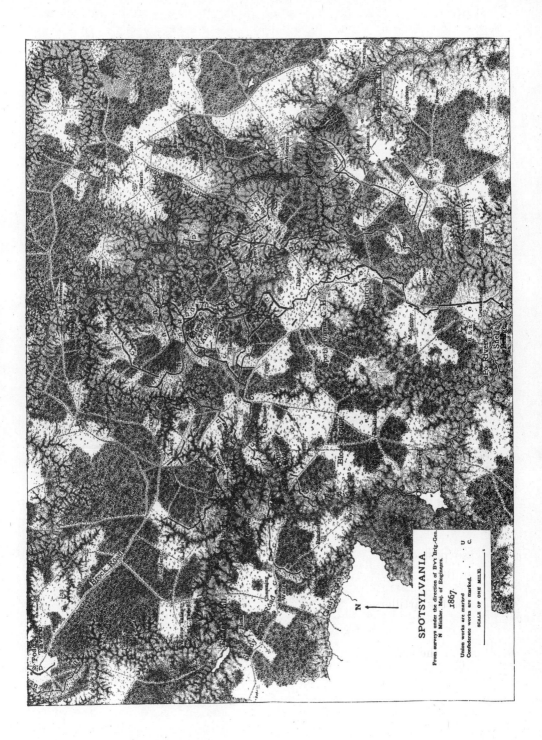

SPOTSYLVANIA.

From surveys under the direction of Bv't Brig.-Gen.
N Michler. Maj. of Engineers.

1867.

Union works are marked . . . . U
Confederate works are marked. . . C.

SCALE OF ONE MILE

just arriving and was not in position to fire upon the attacking column, which offered so fair a mark for artillery. The guns came only in time to be captured. The infantry in the salient fought as long as fighting was of any use; but deprived of the assistance of the artillery, which constituted the chief strength of the position, they could do little to check the onward rush of the Federal column, which soon overran the salient, capturing General Johnson himself, 20 pieces of artillery, and 2800 men—almost his entire division. The whole thing happened so quickly that the extent of the disaster could not be realized at once. Hancock's troops, who made the assault, had recovered their formation, and, extending their lines across the works on both sides of the salient, had resumed their

SPOTSYLVANIA COURT HOUSE.

SPOTSYLVANIA TAVERN, NEAR THE COURT HOUSE.
BOTH FROM WAR-TIME PHOTOGRAPHS.

advance, when Lane's brigade of Hill's corps, which was immediately on the right of the captured works, rapidly drew back to the unfinished line in rear, and poured a galling fire upon Hancock's left wing, which checked its advance and threw it back with severe loss. General Gordon, whose division (Early's) was in reserve and under orders to support any part of the line about the salient, hastened to throw it in front of the advancing Federal column. As the division was about to charge, General Lee rode up and joined General Gordon, evidently intending to go forward with him. Gordon remonstrated, and the men, seeing his intention, cried out, " General Lee to the rear!" which was taken up all along the line. One of the men respectfully but firmly took hold of the general's bridle and led his horse to the rear, and the charge went on. The two moving lines met in the rear of the captured works, and after a fierce struggle in the woods the Federals were forced back to the base of the salient. But Gordon's division did not cover their whole front. On the left of the salient, where Rodes's division had connected with Johnson's, the attack was still pressed with great determination. General Rodes drew out Ramseur's brigade from the left of his line (a portion of Kershaw's division taking its place), and sent it to relieve the pressure on his right and restore the line between himself and Gordon. Ramseur swept the trenches the whole length of his brigade, but did not fill the gap, and his right was exposed to a terrible fire from the works still held by the enemy. Three brigades from Hill's corps were ordered up. Perrin's, which was the first to arrive, rushed forward through a fearful fire and recovered a part of the line on Gordon's left. General Perrin fell dead from his horse just as he reached the works. General Daniel had been killed, and Ramseur painfully wounded, though remaining in the trenches with his men. Rodes's right being still hard pressed, Harris's (Mississippi) and McGowan's (South Carolina) brigades were ordered forward and rushed through the blinding storm into the works on Ramseur's right. The Federals still held the greater part of the salient, and though the Confederates were unable to drive them out, the Federals could get no farther. Hancock's corps, which had made the attack, had been reënforced by Russell's and Wheaton's divisions of the Sixth Corps and one-half of Warren's corps, as the battle progressed. Artillery had been brought up on both sides, the Confederates using every piece that could be made available upon the salient. Before 10 o'clock General Lee had put in every man that could be spared for the restoration of his broken center. It then became a matter of endurance with the men themselves.

VIEWS OF CONFEDERATE INTRENCH-
MENTS AT SPOTSYLVANIA.
FROM WAR-TIME PHOTOGRAPHS.

All day long and until far into the night the battle raged with unceasing fury, in the space covered by the salient and the adjacent works. Every attempt to advance on either side was met and repelled from the other. The hostile battle-flags waved over different portions of the same works, while the men fought like fiends for their possession. [See "Hand-to-Hand Fighting at Spotsylvania," to follow.]

During the day diversions were made on both sides, to relieve the pressure in the center. An attack upon Anderson's (Longstreet's) corps by Wright's

Sixth Corps (Sedgwick having been killed on the 9th) was severely repulsed, while, on the other side of the salient, General Early, who was moving with a part of Hill's corps to strike the flank of the Federal force engaged there, met and defeated Burnside's corps, which was advancing at the same time to attack Early's works.

WHILE the battle was raging at the salient, a portion of Gordon's division was busily engaged in constructing in rear of the old line of intrenchments a new and shorter one, to which Ewell's corps retired before daylight on the 13th. Never was respite more welcome than the five days of comparative rest that followed the terrible battle of the 12th to our wearied men, who had been marching and fighting almost without intermission since the 4th of May. Their comfort was materially enhanced, too, by the supply of coffee, sugar, and other luxuries to which they had long been strangers, obtained from the haversacks of the Federal dead. It was astonishing into what close places a hungry Confederate would go to get something to eat. Men would sometimes go out under a severe fire, in the hope of finding a full haversack. It may seem a small matter to the readers of war history; but to the *makers* of it who were in the trenches, or on the march, or engaged in battle night and day for weeks without intermission, the supply of the one article of coffee, furnished by the Army of the Potomac to the Army of Northern Virginia, was *not* a small matter, but did as much as any other material agency to sustain the spirits and bodily energies of the men, in a campaign that taxed both to their utmost limit. Old haversacks gave place to better ones, and tin cups now dangled from the accouterments of the Confederates, who at every rest on the march or interval of quiet on the lines could be seen gathered around small fires, preparing the coveted beverage.

In the interval from the 12th to the 18th our army was gradually moving east to meet corresponding movements on the other side. Longstreet's corps was shifted from the left to the extreme right, beyond the Fredericksburg road. Ewell's corps still held the works in rear of the famous salient, when on the morning of the 18th a last effort was made to force the lines of Spotsylvania at the only point where previous efforts had met with even partial success. This was destined to a more signal failure than any of the others. Under the fire of thirty pieces of artillery, which swept all the approaches to Ewell's line, the attacking force ⸴ was broken and driven back in disorder before it came well within reach of the muskets of the infantry. After the failure of this attack, the "sidling" movement, as the men expressed it, again began, and on the afternoon of the 19th Ewell's corps was thrown round the Federal left wing to ascertain the extent of this movement. After a severe engagement, which lasted until night, Ewell withdrew, having lost about nine hundred men in the action. This seemed a heavy price to pay for information that might have been otherwise obtained, but the enemy had suffered more severely, and General Grant was delayed in his turning movement for twenty-four hours. He however got the start in the race for the

⸴ The attacking column consisted of the Second and Sixth corps, the Second Corps leading.— EDITORS.

North Anna; Hancock's corps, leading off on the night of the 20th, was followed rapidly by the remainder of his army.

On the morning of the 21st Ewell's corps moved from the left to the right of our line, and later on the same day it was pushed southward on the Telegraph road, closely followed by Longstreet's corps.☆ A. P. Hill brought up the rear that night, after a sharp "brush" with the Sixth Corps, which was in the act of retiring from its lines. Lee had the inside track this time, as the Telegraph road on which he moved was the direct route, while Grant had to swing round on the arc of a circle of which this was the chord. About noon on the 22d the head of our column reached the North Anna, and that night Lee's army lay on the south side of the river. We had won the second heat and secured a good night's rest besides, when the Federal army appeared on the other side in the forenoon of the 23d.

Warren's corps crossed the river that afternoon without opposition at Jericho Ford, four miles above the Chesterfield bridge on the Telegraph road; but as it moved out from the river it met Cadmus Wilcox's division of Hill's corps, and a severe but indecisive engagement ensued, the confronting lines intrenching as usual. Meanwhile a small earth-work, that had been built the year before, covering the approaches to the bridge on the Telegraph road and now held by a small detachment from Kershaw's division, was attacked and carried by troops of Hancock's corps, the Confederates retiring across the river with the loss of a few prisoners.

It did not seem to be General Lee's purpose to offer any serious resistance to Grant's passage of the river at the points selected. His lines had been

CONFEDERATE TRENCHES AT CHESTERFIELD BRIDGE ON THE NORTH ANNA, HALF A MILE ABOVE THE RAIL-ROAD BRIDGE. [SEE MAP, NEXT PAGE.] FROM A WAR-TIME PHOTOGRAPH.

retired from it at both these points, but touched it at Ox Ford, a point intermediate between them. Hancock's corps, having secured the Chesterfield bridge, crossed over on the morning of the 24th, and, extending down the river, moved out until it came upon Longstreet's and Ewell's corps in position and ready for battle. The Sixth Corps (General Wright) crossed at Jericho Mill and joined Warren. The two wings of Grant's army were safely across the river, but there was no connection between them. Lee had only thrown back his flanks and let them in on either side, while he held the river between; and when General Grant attempted to throw his center, under Burnside, across between the ford and the bridge, it was very severely handled and failed to get a foothold on the south side. A detachment from

☆ Swinton and others state that Longstreet moved on the night of the 20th, followed by Ewell. This is an error.—E. M. L.

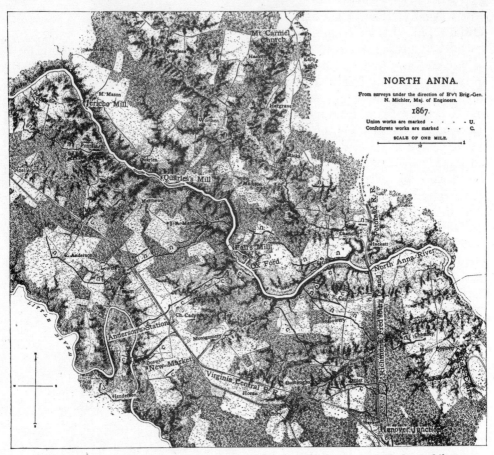

NORTH ANNA.

From surveys under the direction of B'v't Brig.-Gen.
N. Michler, Maj. of Engineers.

1867.

Union works are marked · · · · U.
Confederate works are marked · · C.

SCALE OF ONE MILE.

Ox Ford is otherwise known as Anderson Bridge and Ford.   Anderson's Station is Verdon, and the
Ch. Cady house is J. Anderson's.

Warren's corps was sent down on the south side to help Burnside across, ⎰ but
was attacked by Mahone's division, and driven back with heavy loss, narrowly escaping capture.   General Grant found himself in what may be called
a military dilemma.   He had cut his army in two by running it upon the
point of a wedge.   He could not break the point, which rested upon the river,
and the attempt to force it out of place by striking on its sides must of necessity be made without much concert of action between the two wings of his
army, neither of which could reënforce the other without crossing the river
twice; while his opponent could readily transfer his troops, as needed, from
one wing to the other, across the narrow space between them.

The next two days were consumed by General Grant in fruitless attempts
to find a vulnerable point in our lines.   The skirmishers were very active,
often forcing their way close up to our works.   The line of my brigade
crossed the Richmond and Fredericksburg railroad.   It was an exposed point,
and the men stationed there, after building their log breastwork, leant their

⎰ Crittenden's division of Burnside's corps forded the river on the 24th at Quarles's Mill, between Ox
Ford and Jericho Mill, and connected with Warren's left.   Potter's division of this corps was with
Hancock, leaving only one division, O. B. Willcox's, at Ox Ford.— EDITORS.

muskets against it and moved out on one side, to avoid the constant fire that was directed upon it. As I was passing that point on one occasion, the men called to me, "Stoop!" At the same moment I received a more forcible admonition from the whiz of a minie-ball close to my head. Turning quickly, I caught a glimpse of something blue disappearing behind a pile of earth that had been thrown out from the railroad cut some distance in front. Taking one of the muskets leaning against the works I waited for the reappearance of my friend in blue, who had taken such an unfair advantage of me. He soon appeared, rising cautiously behind his earth-work, and we both fired at the same moment, neither shot taking effect. This time my friend didn't "hedge," but commenced reloading rapidly, thinking, I suppose, that I would have to do the same. But he was mistaken; for, taking up another musket, I fired at once, with a result at which both of us were equally surprised, he probably at my being able to load so quickly, and I at hitting the mark. He was found there, wounded, when my skirmishers were pushed forward.

On the morning of May 27th General Grant's army had disappeared from our front. During the night it had "folded its tents like the Arab and as quietly stolen away," on its fourth turning movement since the opening of the campaign. The Army of the Potomac was already on its march for the Pamunkey River at Hanovertown, where the leading corps crossed on the morning of the 27th. Lee moved at once to head off his adversary, whose advance column was now eight miles nearer Richmond than he was. In the

JERICHO MILLS — UNION ENGINEER CORPS AT WORK. FROM A WAR-TIME PHOTOGRAPH.

afternoon of the 28th, after one of the severest cavalry engagements of the war, in which Hampton and Fitz Lee opposed the advance of Sheridan at Hawes's Shop, the infantry of both armies came up and again confronted each other along the Totopotomoy. Here the Confederate position was found too strong to be attacked in front with any prospect of success, and again the "sidling" movements began — this time toward Cold Harbor.

Sheridan's cavalry had taken possession of Cold Harbor on the 31st, and had been promptly followed up by two corps of infantry.⚓ Longstreet's and a part of Hill's corps, with Hoke's and Breckinridge's divisions,↓ were thrown across their front. The fighting began on the Cold Harbor line, late in the afternoon of the 1st of June, by a heavy attack upon the divisions of Hoke and Kershaw. Clingman's brigade on Hoke's left gave way, and Wofford's on Kershaw's right, being turned, was also forced back; but the further progress of the attack was checked and the line partly restored before night. By the morning of the 2d of June the opposing lines had settled down close to each other, and everything promised a repetition of the scenes at Spotsylvania.

Three corps of Grant's army (General W. F. Smith's Eighteenth Corps having arrived from Drewry's Bluff) now confronted the Confederate right wing at Cold Harbor, while the other two looked after Early's (Ewell's) corps near Bethesda Church. In the afternoon of June 2d, General Early, perceiving a movement that indicated a withdrawal of the Federal force in his front, attacked Burnside's corps while it was in motion, striking also the flank of Warren's corps, and capturing several hundred prisoners. This was accomplished with small loss, and had the effect of preventing the coöperation of these two corps in the attack at Cold Harbor the next day.

Early in the morning of the 2d I was ordered to move with my own and Anderson's brigades, of Field's division, "to reënforce the line on the right," exercising my own discretion as to the point where assistance was most needed. After putting the troops in motion I rode along the line, making a personal inspection as I went. Pickett's division, the first on our right, held a strong position along the skirt of a wood, with open fields in front, and needed no strengthening. The left of Kershaw's division, which was the next in order, was equally strong; but on calling at General Kershaw's quarters I was informed of the particulars of the attack upon his own and Hoke's divisions the evening before, and requested by him to place my troops as a support to his right wing, which had been thrown back by the attack. On examining the line I found it bent sharply back at almost a right angle, the point of which rested upon a body of heavy woods. The works were in open ground and were ill-adapted to resist an attack. The right face of the angle ran along a slope, with a small marshy stream behind and higher ground in front. The works had evidently been built just where the troops found themselves at the close of the fight the previous evening.

⚓ The Sixth and Eighteenth corps reached Cold Harbor on the 1st of June.—EDITORS.

↓ Breckinridge came from the Valley and joined Lee's army at the North Anna [Hanover Junction] with about 2700 men. Hoke had just arrived from Petersburg. Pickett's division, which had been serving in the Department of North Carolina, had also joined its corps at the North Anna.— E. M. L.

THE PENNSYLVANIA RESERVES RESISTING A CONFEDERATE ATTACK NEAR THE BETHESDA
CHURCH, JUNE 2. FROM A SKETCH MADE AT THE TIME.

Convinced that under such assaults as we had sustained at Spotsylvania our line would be broken at that point, I proposed to cut off the angle by building a new line across its base, which would throw the marshy ground in our front and give us a clear sweep across it with our fire from the slope on the other side. This would not only strengthen but shorten the line considerably, and I proposed to General Kershaw to build and occupy it with my two brigades that night.

Meanwhile the enemy was evidently concentrating in the woods in front, and every indication pointed to an early attack. Nothing could be done upon the contemplated line during the day, and we waited anxiously the coming of night. The day passed without an attack. I was as well satisfied that it would come at dawn the next morning as if I had seen General Meade's order directing it. That no mistake should be made in the location of the works, I procured a hatchet, and accompanied by two members of my staff, each with an armful of stakes, went out after dark, located the line, and drove every stake upon it. The troops were formed on it at once, and before morning the works were finished. Artillery was placed at both ends of the new line, abreast of the infantry. General Kershaw then withdrew that portion of his division which occupied the salient, the men having leveled the works as far as possible before leaving them.

Our troops were under arms and waiting, when with the misty light of early morning the scattering fire of our pickets, who now occupied the abandoned works in the angle, announced the beginning of the attack. As the assaulting column swept over the old works a loud cheer was given, and it rushed on into the marshy ground in the angle. Its front covered little more than the line of my own brigade of less than a thousand men; but line followed line until the space inclosed by the old salient became a mass of writhing humanity, upon which our artillery and musketry played with cruel effect. I had taken position on the slope in rear of the line and was carefully noting the firing of the men, which soon became so heavy that I feared they

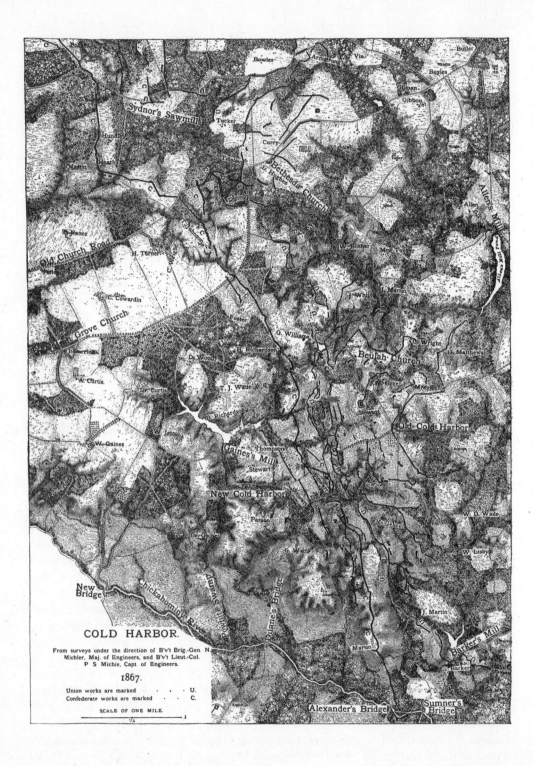

COLD HARBOR.

From surveys under the direction of B'v't Brig.-Gen. N.
Michler, Maj. of Engineers, and B'v't Lieut.-Col.
P S Michie, Capt of Engineers.

1867.

Union works are marked · · · U.
Confederate works are marked · · · C.

SCALE OF ONE MILE.

would exhaust the cartridges in their boxes before the attack ceased. Sending an order for a supply of ammunition to be brought into the lines, I went down to the trenches to regulate the firing. On my way I met a man, belonging to the 15th Alabama regiment of my brigade, running to the rear through the storm of bullets that swept the hill. He had left his hat behind in his retreat, was crying like a big baby, and was the bloodiest man I ever saw. "Oh, General," he blubbered out, "I am dead! I am killed! Look at this!" showing his wound. He was a broad, fat-faced fellow, and a minie-ball had passed through his cheek and the fleshy part of his neck, letting a large amount of blood. Finding it was only a flesh-wound, I told him to go on; he was not hurt. He looked at me doubtfully for a second as if questioning my veracity or my

THE TAVERN AT NEW COLD HARBOR, HANOVER COUNTY, VIRGINIA, AS IT APPEARED IN 1864, NOT LONG AFTER GENERAL GRANT'S CHANGE OF POSITION.

surgical knowledge, I don't know which; then, as if satisfied with my diagnosis, he broke into a broad laugh, and, the tears still running down his cheeks, trotted off, the happiest man I saw that day.

On reaching the trenches, I found the men in fine spirits, laughing and talking as they fired. There, too, I could see more plainly the terrible havoc made in the ranks of the assaulting column. I had seen the dreadful carnage in front of Marye's Hill at Fredericksburg, and on the "old railroad cut" which Jackson's men held at the Second Manassas; but I had seen nothing to exceed this. It was not war; it was murder. When the fight ended, more than a thousand men lay in front of our works either killed or too badly wounded to leave the field.♭ Among them were some who were not hurt, but remained among the dead and wounded rather than take the chances of going back under that merciless fire. Most of these came in and surrendered during the day, but were fired on in some instances by their own men (who still held a position close in our front) to prevent them from doing so. The loss in my command was fifteen or twenty, most of them wounded about the head and shoulders, myself among the number. Our artillery was handled superbly during the action. Major Hamilton, chief of artillery of Kershaw's division, not only coöperated with energy in strengthening our line on the night of June 2d, but directed the fire of his guns with great skill during the attack on the 3d, reaching not only the front of the attacking force, but its flanks also, as well as those of the supporting troops.

While we were busy with the Eighteenth Corps on the center of the general line, the sounds of battle could be heard both on the right and left, and we

♭From the close range of the artillery and musketry, there must have been a much greater proportion of these than usual. I estimated the whole loss of the Eighteenth Corps, which made the attack, at between 4000 and 5000.— E. M. L. [The "Official Records" show that the losses of that corps at Cold Harbor aggregated 3019.— EDITORS.]

knew from long use what that meant. It was a general advance of Grant's whole army. Early's corps below Bethesda Church was attacked without success. On our right, where the line extended toward the Chickahominy, it was broken at one point, but at once restored by Finegan's (Florida) brigade, with heavy loss to Hancock's troops who were attacking there. The result of the action in the center, which has been described, presents a fair picture of the result along the entire line — a grand advance, a desperate struggle, a bloody and crushing repulse. Before 8 o'clock A. M. on the 3d of June the battle of Cold Harbor was over, and with it Grant's "overland campaign" against Richmond.

When General Grant was appointed to the command of the Union armies and established his headquarters with the Army of the Potomac, we of the Army of Northern Virginia knew very little about his character and capacity as a commander. Even "old army" officers, who were supposed to know all about any one who had ever been in the army before the war, seemed to know as little as anybody else. The opinion was pretty freely expressed, however, that his Western laurels would wither in the climate of Virginia. His name was associated with Shiloh, where it was believed that he had

been outgeneraled and badly beaten by Albert Sidney Johnston, and saved by Buell. The capture of Vicksburg and the battle of Chattanooga, which gave him a brilliant reputation at the North, were believed by the Confederates to be due more to the weakness of the forces opposed to him and the bad generalship of their commanders than to any great ability on his part.

EXTREME RIGHT OF THE CONFEDERATE LINE, COLD HARBOR.
FROM A WAR-TIME PHOTOGRAPH.

That he was bold and aggressive, we all knew, but we believed that it was the boldness and aggressiveness that arise from the consciousness of strength, as he had generally managed to fight his battles with the advantage of largely superior numbers. That this policy of force would be pursued when he took command in Virginia, we had no doubt; but we were not prepared for the unparalleled stubbornness and tenacity with which he persisted in his attacks under the fearful losses which his army sustained at the Wilderness and at Spotsylvania. General Grant's method of conducting the campaign was frequently discussed among the Confederates, and the universal verdict was that he was no strategist and that he relied almost entirely upon the brute force of numbers for success. Such a policy is not characteristic of a high order of generalship, and seldom wins unless the odds are overwhelmingly on the side of the assailant. It failed in this instance, as shown by the result at Cold Harbor, which necessitated an entire change in the plan of campaign. What a part at least of his own men thought about General Grant's methods was shown by the fact that many of the prisoners taken during the campaign complained bitterly of the "useless butchery" to which they were subjected, some going so far as to prophesy the destruction of their army. "He fights!" was the pithy reply of President Lincoln to a deputation of influential politicians who urged his removal from the command of the army. These two words embody perfectly the Confederate idea of General Grant at that time. If, as the mediæval chroniclers tell us, Charles Martel (the Hammer) gained that title by a seven days' continuous battle with the Saracens at Tours, General Grant certainly entitled himself to a like distinction by his thirty days' campaign from the Wilderness to Cold Harbor.

General Lee held so completely the admiration and confidence of his men that his conduct of a campaign was rarely criticised. Few points present themselves in his campaign from the Wilderness to Cold Harbor upon which criticism can lay hold, when all the circumstances are considered. His plan of striking the flank of Grant's army as it passed through the Wilderness is above criticism. Fault can be found only with its execution. The two divisions of Longstreet at Gordonsville, and Anderson's division of Hill's corps left on the Upper Rapidan, were too widely separated from the rest of the army, and, as the event proved, should have been in supporting distance of A. P. Hill on the Orange Plank road on the afternoon of the 5th of May. That Lee did not strike Grant a damaging blow when he had him at such disadvantage on the North Anna may seem strange to those who had witnessed his bold aggressiveness at the Wilderness and on other fields. He was ill and confined to his tent at the time; but, as showing his purpose had he been able to keep the saddle, he was heard to say, as he lay prostrated by sickness, "We must strike them a blow; we must never let them pass us again."⸮ Whatever General Lee did, his men thought it the best that could be done under the circumstances. Their feeling toward him is well illustrated by the remark of a "ragged rebel" who took off his hat to the general as he was passing and received a like courteous salute in return: "God bless Marse Robert! I wish he was emperor of this country and I was his carriage-driver."

The results of the "overland campaign" against Richmond, in 1864, cannot be gauged simply by the fact that Grant's army found itself within a few miles of the Confederate capital when it ended. It might have gotten there in a much shorter time and without any fighting at all. Indeed, one Federal army under General Butler was already there, threatening Richmond, which was considered by the Confederates much more secure after the arrival of the armies of Lee and Grant than it had been before. Nor can these results be measured only by the losses of the opposing armies on the battle-field, except as they affected the *morale* of armies themselves; for their losses were about proportional to their relative strength. So far as the Confederates were concerned, it would be idle to deny that they (as well as General Lee

⸮ Statement of Colonel Venable of General Lee's staff.—E. M. L.

himself) were disappointed at the result of their efforts in the Wilderness on the 5th and 6th of May, and that General Grant's constant "hammering" with his largely superior force had, to a certain extent, a depressing effect upon both officers and men. "It's no use killing these fellows; a half-dozen take the place of every one we kill," was a common remark in our army. We knew that our resources of men were exhausted, and that the vastly greater resources of the Federal Government, if brought fully to bear, even in this costly kind of warfare, must wear us out in the end. The question with us (and one often asked at the time) was, "How long will the people of the North, and the army itself, stand it?" We heard much about the demoralization of Grant's army, and of the mutterings of discontent at home with the conduct of the campaign, and we verily believed that their patience would soon come to an end.

So far as the fighting qualities of our men were concerned, they were little if at all impaired by the terrible strain that had been put upon them. Had General Lee so ordered, they would have attacked the Federal army, after the battle of Cold Harbor, with the same courage, though perhaps more quiet, that they had displayed on entering the campaign thirty days before. The Army of Northern Virginia was so well seasoned and tempered that, like the famous Toledo blade, it could be bent back and doubled upon itself, and then spring again into perfect shape.

It may justly be said of both armies that in this terrible thirty days' struggle their courage and endurance was superb. Both met "foemen worthy of their steel," and battles were fought such as could only have occurred between men of kindred race, and nowhere else than in America.

A RABBIT IN A CONFEDERATE CAMP.

SECOND DAY OF THE BATTLE OF THE WILDERNESS, MAY 6, 1864 — VIEW TOWARD PARKER'S STORE, FROM THE LACY HOUSE, THE HEADQUARTERS OF GRANT, MEADE, AND WARREN. FROM A SKETCH MADE AT THE TIME.

GENERAL GRANT ON THE WILDERNESS CAMPAIGN.

EXTRACT FROM HIS REPORT AS LIEUTENANT-GENERAL, DATED JULY 22D, 1865.

GENERAL GRANT WHITTLING DURING THE BATTLE OF THE WILDERNESS. FROM A SKETCH MADE AT THE TIME.

THE movement of the Army of the Potomac commenced early on the morning of the 4th of May, under the immediate direction and orders of Major-General Meade, pursuant to instructions. Before night, the whole army was across the Rapidan (the Fifth and Sixth corps crossing at Germanna Ford, and the Second Corps at Ely's Ford, the cavalry, under Major-General Sheridan, moving in advance), with the greater part of its trains, numbering about four thousand wagons, meeting with but slight opposition. The average distance traveled by the troops that day was about twelve miles. This I regarded as a great success, and it removed from my mind the most serious apprehensions I had entertained: that of crossing the river in the face of an active, large, well-appointed, and ably commanded army, and how so large a train was to be carried through a hostile country and protected. Early on the 5th the advance corps (the Fifth, Major-General G. K. Warren commanding) met and engaged the enemy outside his intrenchments near Mine Run. The battle raged furiously all day, the whole army being brought into the fight as fast as the corps could be got upon the field, which, considering the density of the forest and narrowness of the roads, was done with commendable promptness.

General Burnside, with the Ninth Corps, was, at the time the Army of the Potomac moved, left with the bulk of his corps at the crossing of the Rappahannock River and Alexandria Railroad, holding the road back to Bull Run, with instructions not to move until he received notice that a crossing of the Rapidan was secured, but to move promptly as soon as such notice was received. This crossing he was apprised of on the afternoon of the 4th. By 6 o'clock of the morning of the 6th he was leading his corps into action near the Wilderness Tavern, some of his troops having marched a distance of over thirty miles, crossing both the Rappahannock and Rapidan rivers. Considering that a large proportion, probably two-thirds of his command, was composed of new troops, unaccustomed to marches and carrying the accouterments of a soldier, this was a remarkable march.

The battle of the Wilderness was renewed by us at 5 o'clock on the morning of the 6th, and continued with unabated fury until darkness set in, each army holding substantially the same position that they had on the evening of the 5th. After dark, the enemy made a feeble attempt to turn our right flank, capturing several hundred prisoners and creating considerable confusion. But the promptness of General Sedgwick, who was personally present and commanded that part of our line, soon re-formed it and restored order. On the morning of the 7th reconnoissances showed that the enemy had fallen behind his intrenched lines, with pickets to the front, covering a part of the battle-field. From this it was evident to my mind that the two days' fighting had satisfied him of his inability to further maintain the contest in

TODD'S TAVERN IN WAR-TIME. FROM A PHOTOGRAPH.

being in possession of the main roads, was enabled to reach the North Anna in advance of us, and took position behind it. The Fifth Corps reached the North Anna on the afternoon of the 23d, closely followed by the Sixth Corps. The Second and Ninth corps got up about the same time, the Second holding the railroad bridge, and the Ninth lying between that and Jericho Ford. General Warren effected a crossing

the open field, notwithstanding his advantage of position, and that he would wait an attack behind his works. I therefore determined to push on and put my whole force between him and Richmond; and orders were at once issued for a movement by his right flank. On the night of the 7th the march was commenced toward Spotsylvania Court House, the Fifth Corps moving on the most direct road. But the enemy, having become apprised of our movement and having the shorter line, was enabled to reach there first. On the 8th General Warren met a force of the enemy, which had been sent out to oppose and delay his advance to gain time to fortify the line taken up at Spotsylvania. This force was steadily driven back on the main force, within the recently constructed works, after considerable fighting, resulting in severe loss to both sides. On the morning of the 9th General Sheridan started on a raid against the enemy's lines of communication with Richmond. The 9th, 10th, and 11th were spent in manœuvring and fighting, without decisive results. Among the killed on the 9th was that able and distinguished soldier Major-General John Sedgwick, commanding the Sixth Army Corps. Major-General H. G. Wright succeeded him in command. Early on the morning of the 12th a general attack was made on the enemy in position. The Second Corps, Major-General Hancock commanding, carried a salient of his line, capturing most of [Edward] Johnson's division of Ewell's corps and twenty pieces of artillery. But the resistance was so obstinate that the advantage gained did not prove decisive. The 13th, 14th, 15th, 16th, 17th, and 18th were consumed in manœuvring and awaiting the arrival of reënforcements from Washington. Deeming it impracticable to make any further attack upon the enemy at Spotsylvania Court House, orders were issued on the 18th with a view to a movement to the North Anna, to commence at 12 o'clock on the night of the 19th. Late in the afternoon of the 19th, Ewell's corps came out of its works on our extreme right flank; but the attack was promptly repulsed with heavy loss. This delayed the movement to the North Anna until the night of the 21st, when it was commenced. But the enemy, again having the shorter line and

the same afternoon, and got a position without much opposition. Soon after getting into position he was violently attacked, but repulsed the enemy with great slaughter. On the 25th General Sheridan rejoined the Army of the Potomac from the raid on which he started from Spotsylvania, having destroyed the depots at Beaver Dam and Ashland stations, four trains of cars, large supplies of rations, and many miles of railroad-track; recaptured about four hundred of our men on their way to Richmond as prisoners of war; met and defeated the enemy's cavalry at Yellow Tavern; carried the first line of works around Richmond (but finding the second line too strong to be carried by assault), recrossed to the north bank of the Chickahominy at Meadow Bridge under heavy fire, and moved by a detour to Haxall's Landing, on the James River, where he communicated with General Butler. This raid had the effect of drawing off the whole of the enemy's cavalry force, making it comparatively easy to guard our trains.

General Butler moved his main force up the James River, in pursuance of instructions, on the 4th of May, General Gillmore having joined him with the Tenth Corps. At the same time he sent a force of 1800 cavalry, by way of West Point, to form a junction with him wherever he might get a foothold, and a force of 3000 cavalry, under General Kautz, from Suffolk, to operate against the road south of Petersburg and Richmond. On the 5th he occupied, without opposition, both City Point and Bermuda Hundred, his movement being a complete surprise. On the 6th he was in position with his main army, and commenced intrenching. On the 7th he made a reconnoissance against the Petersburg and Richmond Railroad, destroying a portion of it after some fighting. On the 9th he telegraphed as follows:

"HEADQUARTERS, NEAR BERMUDA LANDING,
May 9th, 1864.

"Hon. E. M. STANTON, Secretary of War:
"Our operations may be summed up in a few words. With 1700 cavalry we have advanced up the Peninsula, forced the Chickahominy, and have safely brought them to their present position. These were colored cavalry, and are now holding our advance pickets toward Richmond.

"General Kautz, with three thousand cavalry from Suffolk, on the same day with our movement up the James River, forced the Black Water, burned the railroad bridge at Stony Creek, below Petersburg, cutting into Beauregard's force at tnat point.

"We have landed here, intrenched ourselves, destroyed many miles of railroad, and got a position which, with proper supplies, we can hold out against the whole of Lee's army. I have ordered up the supplies.

"Beauregard, with a large portion of his force, was left south by the cutting of the railroads by Kautz. That portion which reached Petersburg under Hill I have whipped to-day, killing and wounding many, and taking many prisoners, after a severe and well-contested fight.

"General Grant will not be troubled with any further reënforcements to Lee from Beauregard's force.

"BENJ. F. BUTLER, Major-General."

On the evening of the 13th and morning of the 14th he carried a portion of the enemy's first line of defenses at Drewry's Bluff, or Fort Darling, with small loss. The time thus consumed from the 6th lost to us the benefit of the surprise and capture of Richmond and Petersburg, enabling, as it did, Beauregard to collect his loose forces in North and South Carolina, and bring them to the defense of those places. On the 16th, the enemy attacked General Butler in his position in front of Drewry's Bluff. He was forced back, or drew back, into his intrenchments between the forks of the James and Appomattox rivers, the enemy intrenching strongly in his front, thus covering his railroads, the city, and all that was valuable to him. His army, therefore, though in a position of great security, was as completely shut off from further operations directly against Richmond as if it had been in a bottle strongly corked. It required but a comparatively small force of the enemy to hold it there.

On the 12th General Kautz, with his cavalry, was started on a raid against the Danville Railroad, which he struck at Coalfield, Powhatan, and Chula stations, destroying them, the railroad track, two freight trains, and one locomotive, together with large quantities of commissary and other stores; thence, crossing to the South Side Road, struck it at Wilson's, Wellsville, and Black's and White's stations, destroying the road and station-houses; thence he proceeded to City Point, which he reached on the 18th.

On the 19th of April, and prior to the movement of General Butler, the enemy, with a land force under General Hoke and an iron-clad ram, attacked Plymouth, N. C., commanded by General H. W. Wessells, and our gun-boats there; and, after severe fighting, the place was carried by assault, and the entire garrison and armament captured. The gun-boat *Smithfield* was sunk, and the *Miami* disabled.

The army sent to operate against Richmond having hermetically sealed itself up at Bermuda Hundred, the enemy was enabled to bring the most, if not all, the reënforcements brought from the South by Beauregard against the Army of the Potomac. In addition to this reënforcement, a very considerable one, probably not less than fifteen thousand men, was obtained by call-

ing in the scattered troops under Breckinridge from the western part of Virginia.

The position of Bermuda Hundred was as easy to defend as it was difficult to operate from against the enemy. I determined, therefore, to bring from it all available forces, leaving enough only to secure what had been gained; and accordingly, on the 22d, I directed that they be sent forward, under command of Major-General W. F. Smith, to join the Army of the Potomac.

On the 24th of May the Ninth Army Corps, commanded by Major-General A. E. Burnside, was assigned to the Army of the Potomac, and from this time forward constituted a portion of Major-General Meade's command.

Finding the enemy's position on the North Anna stronger than either of his previous ones, I withdrew on the night of the 26th to the north bank of the North Anna, and moved via Hanover Town to turn the enemy's position by his right.

Generals Torbert's and Merritt's divisions of cavalry, under Sheridan, and the Sixth Corps led the advance; crossed the Pamunkey River at Hanover Town, after considerable fighting, and on the 28th the two divisions of cavalry had a severe but successful engagement with the enemy at Hawes's Shop. On the 29th and 30th we advanced, with heavy skirmishing, to the Hanover Court House and Cold Harbor road, and developed the enemy's position north of the Chickahominy. Late on the evening of the last day the enemy came out and attacked our left, but was repulsed with very considerable loss. An attack was immediately ordered by General Meade, along his whole line, which resulted in driving the enemy from a part of his intrenched skirmish line.

On the 31st General Wilson's division of cavalry destroyed the railroad bridges over the South Anna River, after defeating the enemy's cavalry. General Sheridan, on the same day, reached Cold Harbor, and held it until relieved by the Sixth Corps and General Smith's com-

THE WILDERNESS TAVERN. FROM A PHOTOGRAPH TAKEN IN 1884.

BRASS COEHORNS IN USE AT COLD HARBOR. FROM A WAR-TIME SKETCH.

mand, which had just arrived, via White House, from General Butler's army.

On the first day of June an attack was made at 5 P. M. by the Sixth Corps and the troops under General Smith, the other corps being held in readiness to advance on the receipt of orders. This resulted in our carrying and holding the enemy's first line of works in front of the right of the Sixth Corps, and in front of General Smith. During the attack the enemy made repeated assaults on each of the corps not engaged in the main attack, but was repulsed with heavy loss in every instance. That night he made several assaults to regain what he had lost in the day, but failed. The 2d was spent in getting troops into position for an attack on the 3d. On the 3d of June we again assaulted the enemy's work, in the hope of driving him from his position. In this attempt our loss was heavy, while that of the enemy, I have reason to believe, was comparatively light. It was the only general attack made from the Rapidan to the James which did not inflict upon the enemy losses to compensate for our own losses. I would not be understood as saying that all previous attacks resulted in victories to our arms, or accomplished as much as I had hoped from them; but they inflicted upon the enemy severe losses, which tended, in the end, to the complete overthrow of the rebellion.

From the proximity of the enemy to his defenses around Richmond, it was impossible by any flank movement to interpose between him and the city. I was still in a condition either to move by his left flank, and invest Richmond from the north side, or continue my move by his right flank to the south side of the James. While the former might have been better as a covering for Washington, yet a full survey of all the ground satisfied me that it would be impracticable to hold a line north and east of Richmond that would protect the Fredericksburg Railroad, a long, vulnerable line, which would exhaust much of our strength to guard, and

that would have to be protected to supply the army, and would leave open to the enemy all his lines of communication on the south side of the James. My idea, from the start, had been to beat Lee's army north of Richmond, if possible; then, after destroying his lines of communication north of the James River, to transfer the army to the south side, and besiege Lee in Richmond, or follow him south if he should retreat. After the battle of the Wilderness, it was evident that the enemy deemed it of the first importance to run no risks with the army he then had. He acted purely on the defensive, behind breastworks, or feebly on the offensive immediately in front of them, and where, in case of repulse, he could easily retire behind them. Without a greater sacrifice of life than I was willing to make, all could not be accomplished that I had designed north of Richmond. I therefore determined to continue to hold substantially the ground we then occupied, taking advantage of any favorable circumstances that might present themselves, until the cavalry could be sent to Charlottesville and Gordonsville to effectually break up the railroad connection between Richmond and the Shenandoah Valley and Lynchburg; and when the cavalry got well off, to move the army to the south side of the James River, by the enemy's right flank, where I felt I could cut off all his sources of supply, except by the canal.

On the 7th, two divisions of cavalry, under General Sheridan, got off on the expedition against the Virginia Central Railroad, with instructions to Hunter, whom I hoped he would meet near Charlottesville, to join his forces to Sheridan's, and after the work laid out for them was thoroughly done, to join the Army of the Potomac by the route laid down in Sheridan's instructions.

On the 10th of June General Butler sent a force of infantry under General Gillmore, and of cavalry under General Kautz, to capture Petersburg, if possible, and destroy the railroad and common bridges across the Appomattox. The cavalry carried the works on the south side, and penetrated well in toward the town, but were forced to retire. General Gillmore, finding the works which he approached very strong, and deeming an assault impracticable, returned to Bermuda Hundred without attempting one.

Attaching great importance to the possession of Petersburg I sent back to Bermuda Hundred and City Point General Smith's command by water via the White House, to reach there in advance of the Army of the Potomac. This was for the express purpose of securing Petersburg before the enemy, becoming aware of our intention, could reënforce the place.

The movement from Cold Harbor commenced after dark on the evening of the 12th. One division of cavalry, under General Wilson, and the Fifth Corps crossed the Chickahominy at Long Bridge, and moved out to White Oak Swamp, to cover the crossings of the other corps. The advance corps reached James River, at Wilcox's Landing and Charles City Court House, on the night of the 13th.

During three long years the armies of the Potomac and Northern Virginia had been confronting each other. In that time they had fought more desperate battles than it probably ever before fell to the lot of two armies to fight, without materially changing the vantage-ground of either. The Southern press and people, with more shrewd-

ness than was displayed in the North, finding that they had failed to capture Washington and march on to New York, as they had boasted they would do, assumed that they only defended their capital and Southern territory. Hence, Antietam, Gettysburg, and all the other battles that had been fought were by them set down as failures on our part and victories for them. Their army believed this. It produced a *morale* which could only be overcome by desperate and continuous hard fighting. The battles of the Wilderness, Spotsylvania, North Anna, and Cold Harbor, bloody and terrible as they were on our side, were even more damaging to the enemy, and so crippled him as to make him wary ever after of taking the offensive. His losses in men were probably not so great, owing to the fact that we were, save in the Wilderness, almost invariably the attacking party; and when he did attack, it was in the open field. The details of these battles, which for endurance and bravery on the part of the soldiery have rarely been surpassed, are given in the report of Major-General Meade and the subordinate reports accompanying it.

During the campaign of forty-three days, from the Rapidan to the James River, the army had to be supplied from an ever-shifting base, by wagons, over narrow roads, through a densely wooded country, with a lack of wharves at each new base from which to conveniently discharge vessels. Too much credit cannot therefore be awarded to the quartermaster and commissary departments for the

MANSION AND GROUNDS ON MARYE'S HILL.

This sketch is from a photograph taken during the Wilderness campaign when the mansion and grounds were filled with Union wounded. The portico faces Fredericksburg, and a few paces in front of it the hill drops abruptly to the sunken Telegraph road and stone wall.

GENERAL GRANT AND STAFF AT BETHESDA CHURCH, NORTH OF COLD HARBOR.   FROM A WAR-TIME PHOTOGRAPH.

General Grant is sitting with his back to the smaller tree.

zeal and efficiency displayed by them. Under the general supervision of the chief quartermaster, Brigadier-General R. Ingalls, the trains were made to occupy all the available roads between the army and our water-base, and but little difficulty was experienced in protecting them.

The movement in the Kanawha and Shenandoah valleys, under General Sigel, commenced on the 1st of May. General Crook, who had the immediate command of the Kanawha expedition, divided his forces into two columns, giving one, composed of cavalry, to General Averell. They crossed the mountains by separate routes. Averell struck the Tennessee and Virginia Railroad, near Wytheville, on the 10th, and, proceeding to New River and Christiansburg, destroyed the road, several important bridges and depots, including New River

Bridge, forming a junction with Crook at Union on the 15th. General Sigel moved up the Shenandoah Valley, met the enemy at New Market on the 15th, and, after a severe engagement, was defeated with heavy loss, and retired behind Cedar Creek. Not regarding the operations of General Sigel as satisfactory, I asked his removal from command, and Major-General Hunter was appointed to supersede him. His instructions were embraced in the following dispatches to Major-General H. W. Halleck, chief-of-staff of the army:

"NEAR SPOTSYLVANIA COURT HOUSE, VA.,
May 20th, 1864.

"The enemy are evidently relying for supplies greatly on such as are brought over the branch road running through Staunton. On the whole, therefore, I think it would be better for General Hunter to move in that direction; reach Staunton and Gordonsville or Charlottesville, if he does not meet too much opposition. If he can hold at bay a force equal to his own, he will be doing good service. . . .

"U. S. GRANT, Lieutenant-General.
"MAJOR-GENERAL H. W. HALLECK."

"JERICHO FORD, VA.,
May 25th, 1864.

"If Hunter can possibly get to Charlottesville and Lynchburg, he should do so, living on the country. The railroads and canal should be destroyed beyond possibility of repairs for weeks. Completing this, he could find his way back to his original base, or from about Gordonsville join this army.

"U. S. GRANT, Lieutenant-General.
"MAJOR-GENERAL H. W. HALLECK."

General Hunter immediately took up the offensive, and, moving up the Shenandoah Valley, met the enemy on the 5th of June at Piedmont, and, after a battle of ten hours, routed and defeated him, capturing on the field of battle 1500 men, three pieces of artillery, and 300 stand of small-arms. On the 8th of the same month he formed a junction with Crook and Averell at Staunton, from which place he moved direct on Lynchburg, via Lexington, which place [Lynchburg] he reached and invested on the 16th day of June. Up to this time he was very successful; and but for the difficulty of taking with him sufficient ordnance stores over so long a march, through a hostile country, he would, no doubt, have captured that, to the enemy important, point. The destruction of the enemy's supplies and manufactories was very great. To meet this movement under General Hunter, General Lee sent a force, perhaps equal to a corps, a part of which reached Lynchburg a short time before Hunter. After some skirmishing on the 17th and 18th, General Hunter, owing to a want of ammunition to give battle, retired from before the place. Unfortunately, this want of ammunition left him no choice of route for his return but by way of Kanawha. This lost to us the use of his troops for several weeks from the defense of the North.

Had General Hunter moved by way of Charlottesville, instead of Lexington, as his instructions contemplated, he would have been in a position to have covered the Shenandoah Valley against the enemy, should the force he met have seemed to endanger it. If it did not, he would have been within easy distance of the James River canal, on the main line of communication between Lynchburg and the force sent for its defense. I have never taken exception to the operations of General Hunter, and am not now disposed to find fault with him, for I have no doubt he acted within what he conceived to be the spirit of his instructions and the interests of the service. The promptitude of his movements and his gallantry should entitle him to the commendation of his country.

To return to the Army of the Potomac: The Second Corps commenced crossing the James River on the morning of the 14th by ferry-boats at Wilcox's Landing. The laying of the pontoon-bridge was completed about midnight of the 14th, and the crossing of the balance of the army was rapidly pushed forward by both bridge and ferry.

After the crossing had commenced, I proceeded by steamer to Bermuda Hundred to give the necessary orders for the immediate capture of Petersburg.

The instructions to General Butler were verbal, and were for him to send General Smith immediately, that night, with all the troops he could give him without sacrificing the position he then held. I told him that I would return at once to the Army of the Potomac, hasten its crossing, and throw it forward to Petersburg by divisions as rapidly as it could be done; that we could reënforce our armies more rapidly there than the enemy could bring troops against us. General Smith got off as directed, and confronted the enemy's pickets near Petersburg before daylight next morning, but, for some reason that I have never been able to satisfactorily understand, did not get ready to assault his main lines until near sundown. Then, with a part of his command only, he made the assault, and carried the lines north-east of Petersburg from the Appomattox River, for a distance of over two and a half miles, capturing fifteen pieces of artillery and three hundred prisoners. This was about 7 P. M. Between the line thus captured and Petersburg there were no other works, and there was no evidence that the enemy had reënforced Petersburg with a single brigade from any source. The night was clear — the moon shining brightly — and favorable to further operations. General Hancock, with two divisions of the Second Corps, reached General Smith just after dark, and offered the service of these troops as he (Smith) might wish, waiving rank to the named commander, who he naturally supposed knew best the position of affairs, and what to do with the troops. But instead of taking these troops and pushing at once into Petersburg, he requested General Hancock to relieve a part of his line in the captured works, which was done before midnight.

By the time I arrived the next morning the enemy was in force. An attack was ordered to be made at 6 o'clock that evening by the troops under Smith and the Second and Ninth corps. It required until that time for the Ninth Corps to get up and into position. The attack was made as ordered, and the fighting continued with but little intermission until 6 o'clock the next morning, and resulted in our carrying the advance and some of the main works of the enemy to the right (our left) of those previously captured by General Smith, several pieces of artillery, and over four hundred prisoners.

The Fifth Corps having got up, the attacks were renewed and persisted in with great vigor on the 17th and 18th, but only resulted in forcing the enemy into an interior line, from which he could not be dislodged. The advantages of position gained by us were very great. The army then proceeded to envelop Petersburg toward the South Side Railroad, as far as possible without attacking fortifications.

UP-HILL WORK.

THROUGH THE WILDERNESS.

BY ALEXANDER S. WEBB, BREVET MAJOR-GENERAL, U. S. A.

IN '61, '62, and '63, the Army of the Potomac, under McClellan, Hooker, and Meade, had by constant attrition worn down Lee's command until, in the minds of many officers and men who were actively engaged in the front, there was confidence that Lee would not hold out against our army another year.

On April 9th, 1864, General Grant instructed General Meade that Lee's army would be his objective. Meade had with him, according to his report of April 30th, 95,952 enlisted men, 3486 officers, and 274 guns. Hancock's corps contained 26,676 men; Warren's, 24,125 men; Sedgwick's, 22,584 men;⎰ while Sheridan controlled 12,525 in the cavalry. To guard all the trains there was a special detail of 1200 men. General Grant had also attached the Ninth Corps (an independent command) to the army operating under his eye. The total force under General Grant, including Burnside, was 4409 officers and 114,360 enlisted men. For the artillery he had 9945 enlisted men and 285 officers; in the cavalry, 11,839 enlisted men and 585 officers; in the provost guards and engineers, 120 officers and 3274 enlisted men. His 118,000 men, properly disposed for battle, would have covered a front of 21 miles, two ranks deep, with one-third of them held in reserve; while Lee, with his 62,000 men similarly disposed, would cover only 12 miles. Grant had a train which he states in his "Memoirs" would have reached from the Rapidan to Richmond, or sixty-five miles.

⎰ These three corps had been increased by the consolidation with them of the First and Third corps (see p. 93). Besides causing great dissatisfaction throughout the army, this consolidation, in my opinion, was the indirect cause of much of the confusion in the execution of orders, and in the handling of troops during the battles of the Wilderness.—A. S. W.

Of Lee's army, Longstreet's corps (two divisions) numbered about 10,000; Ewell's corps about 17,000. A. P. Hill went into the Wilderness with about 22,000 men for duty in the ranks; "Jeb" Stuart's cavalry numbered about 8000, and the artillery about 4800. Lee's total strength, as estimated by General Humphreys, was 61,953 men, and the number of field-guns 224.

General Grant's aggregate over Lee was therefore 94 guns and 56,819 enlisted men; but then Lee had, at the outset, his position in the Wilderness, and Grant did not know at that time, as did General Meade and General Hooker, to what advantage Lee could turn the Wilderness, with its woods, ravines, plank roads, and dirt roads.

The Army of the Potomac began to cross the Rapidan at midnight of May 3d, after due preparation on the part of Sheridan's cavalry to cover our front. A canvas and a wooden pontoon bridge were laid at at Ely's Ford,

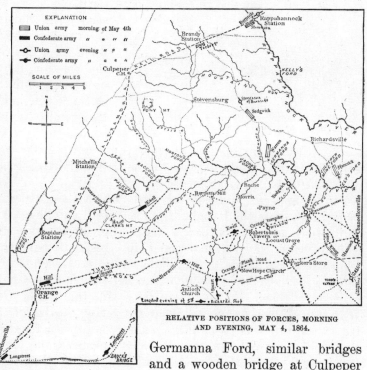

RELATIVE POSITIONS OF FORCES, MORNING AND EVENING, MAY 4, 1864.

Germanna Ford, similar bridges and a wooden bridge at Culpeper Mine Ford. These three fords cover about seven miles of the Rapidan River, which in general flows south-east.

Hancock, preceded by Gregg's cavalry, crossed at Ely's Ford and moved to Chancellorsville, which placed him on the left, or south-east, side of the Wilderness battle-field. Warren, with Wilson's cavalry in front (and followed by Sedgwick), crossed at Germanna Ford and followed the Germanna Plank road, due south-east, to Wilderness Tavern. Sedgwick encamped for the night three miles south of the ford. The sixty-five miles of trains were until 2 P. M. of May 5th in passing over Culpeper Mine Ford and Germanna Ford. General Humphreys, who was Meade's chief-of-staff at the time, states that the halt of the infantry on the 4th at Chancellorsville and the Wilderness was caused by the difficulty in moving the trains across the Rapidan.

General Law, who commanded a brigade under Longstreet, states that on the 2d of May General Lee, in the presence of a number of his officers, expressed the opinion that the Union army would cross the river at Germanna or Ely's Ford. [See p. 118.] General Lee's headquarters were at Orange Court House; Longstreet, with his corps, was distant at Gordonsville; Ewell was near at hand on the Rapidan, above Mine Run; and A. P. Hill was on his left, higher up the stream; and it seems that Lee intended to move with his whole force against Grant's right flank as soon as Grant was far enough advanced into the Wilderness on the road to Richmond.

As for the Wilderness, it was uneven, with woods, thickets, and ravines right and left. Tangled thickets of pine, scrub-oak, and cedar prevented our

TODD'S TAVERN. FROM A SKETCH MADE IN 1884.

seeing the enemy, and prevented any one in command of a large force from determining accurately the position of the troops he was ordering to and fro. The appalling rattle of the musketry, the yells of the enemy, and the cheers of our own men were constantly in our ears. At times, our lines while firing could not see the array of the enemy, not fifty yards distant. After the battle was fairly begun, both sides were protected by log or earth breastworks.

For an understanding of the roads which shaped the movements in the Wilderness, cross the Rapidan from the north and imagine yourself standing on the Germanna Plank road, where the Brock road intersects it, a little south of Wilderness Tavern, and facing due west. In general, the Union right wing (Sedgwick) held the Germanna road, and the left wing (Hancock) the Brock road, while the center (Warren) stretched across the obtuse angle formed by them. At the Lacy house, in this angle, Grant, Meade, and Warren established their headquarters during the day of the 5th. If, standing at the intersection of these roads, you stretch forward your arms, the right will correspond with the Orange turnpike, the left with the Orange Plank road. Down the Orange turnpike, on May 5th, Lee sent Ewell against Warren, while two divisions of A. P. Hill advanced by the Orange Plank road to check Hancock. Nearly a day later, Longstreet reached the field on the same road as Hill. The engagements fought on May 5th by Ewell on the Orange turnpike, and by A. P. Hill on the Orange Plank road, must be regarded as entirely distinct battles.

Warren received orders from Meade at 7:15 in the morning to attack Ewell with his whole force. General Sedgwick, with Wright's division and Neill's brigade of Getty's division, was ordered to move out, west of the Germanna Plank road, connecting with the Fifth Corps, which was disposed across the turnpike in advance of Wilderness Tavern. At this time also, General Hancock, at Chancellorsville, was warned by General Meade that the enemy had been met on the turnpike, and he was directed to halt at Todd's tavern until further orders. Meantime, Crawford's division of Warren's corps, between the turnpike and plank road, in advancing, found Wilson's cavalry skirmishing with what he supposed to be the enemy's cavalry. At 8 A. M., under

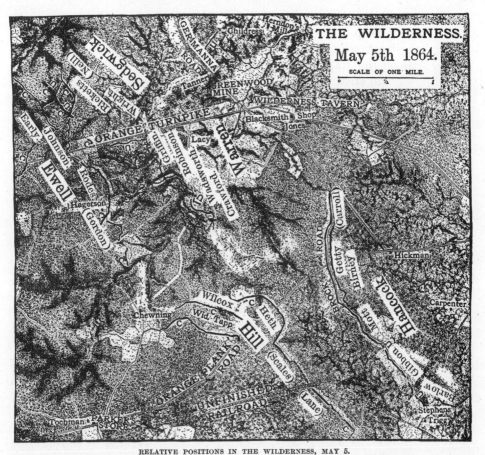

RELATIVE POSITIONS IN THE WILDERNESS, MAY 5.

For the most part the troops are indicated by divisions, and when a name designates
a brigade it is inclosed in parentheses.— EDITORS.

orders, Crawford halted, and, hearing that our cavalry, at Parker's store,
almost directly south of him, was in need of support, he sent out skirmishers
to assist them. Those skirmishers struck Hill's corps, moving down the
Orange Plank road toward the Brock road. Thus at 8 A. M. General Grant
and General Meade had developed the presence of Hill on their left and
Ewell on their right. Getty's division of Sedgwick had reached Wilderness
Tavern; and when it was learned that Hill was coming down the Orange
Plank road, Getty was directed to move out toward him, by way of the Brock
road, and drive Hill back, if possible, behind Parker's store.

On our right Johnson's division of Ewell was driven back along the Orange
turnpike in confusion by General Griffin of Warren's corps. Ricketts and
Wright of Sedgwick were delayed in reaching their position on the right of
Warren, and for lack of such support Griffin's right brigade under Ayres
was forced back and two guns were abandoned. Wadsworth, with his division
of Warren's corps, supplemented by Dennison's brigade of Robinson's division, of the same corps, had started forward in a westerly direction, until he
found himself with his left toward the enemy. McCandless's brigade of Craw-

THROWING UP BREASTWORKS IN THE WILDERNESS. FROM A SKETCH MADE AT THE TIME.

ford's division (also of Warren's corps) had endeavored to obtain a position on the left of Wadsworth, but lost its bearings in the entangled woods so that its left came in contact with Ewell's right, and it, as well as Wadsworth's left, was driven in by Daniel's and Gordon's brigades, forming the right of Ewell. Thus Crawford was left with his left flank in the air, and he of necessity was drawn in about 2 o'clock and posted about a mile south-west from the Lacy house, facing toward his first position at Chewning's house. Wadsworth finally took position on the left of Crawford, facing toward the south and west, with his back toward the Lacy house. Griffin, on Crawford's right, reached to the Orange turnpike. Wright's division of Sedgwick formed on the right of Griffin, with the left of Upton's brigade resting on the pike; then came the brigades of Penrose and Russell, then Neill's brigade of Getty's division. Soon after getting into position Neill and Russell were attacked by Johnson, who was repulsed. Still farther to the right, toward the Germanna Plank road, Seymour, of Ricketts's division, came up and took position. The entire Union front line was now intrenched.

At this time on the center and right Warren and Sedgwick were securely blocked by Ewell's single corps. On the left of the line the situation was this: At 11 A. M. Hancock, whose advance had passed Todd's tavern, received a dispatch stating that the enemy was coming down the Orange Plank road in full force, and he was directed to move his corps up to the Brock road, due north. He was further informed that Getty had been sent to drive the enemy back, and must be supported immediately; that on the turnpike Griffin had been pushed back somewhat, and that he (Hancock) must push out on the Plank road and connect his right with Warren's left.

Hancock promptly started his column, and met General Getty at the junction of the Plank and Germanna roads. Getty's division was then in line of battle, along the Brock road, with Grant's brigade on the left of the Plank road, and Wheaton's and Eustis's brigades on the right of the road which the troops were intrenching. This was at 2 P. M. of the 5th. Getty informed Hancock that there were two divisions of A. P. Hill out in his front, and Hancock directed the finishing of the works that had been begun, before any advance should be made. Hancock placed Birney's division on the left of Getty, in two lines of battle along the Brock road, and Mott's and Gibbon's divisions on Birney's left; Barlow's division held the extreme left and formed an angle on the Brock road overlooking the bed of an unfinished railroad. Most of the artillery of Hancock's corps was posted with Barlow's division.| Frank's brigade of Barlow's division was stationed partly across the Brock road, near the junction of the Brock road and a cross-road leading to the Catharpin road. All of Hancock's corps were directed to throw up breastworks of logs and earth, the intrenched line beginning at Getty's left and extending to Barlow's left, where it was refused to cover the flank. The second line, of the Second Corps, also threw up earth-works, and a third intrenched line was formed behind Birney and Mott nearest the Plank road.

At 4:30 P. M. Getty started to the attack, and marched but four hundred yards when he struck Heth's division of Hill's corps, and found the enemy in force, his right having been reënforced by Wilcox's division. Hancock threw forward Birney and Mott on the left of Getty, and put a section of Ricketts's old battery on the Plank road. General Hancock says in his report: "The fight here became very fierce at once, the lines of battle were exceedingly close, the musketry continuous and deadly along the entire line." Carroll's and Owen's brigades of Gibbon's division were sent in to support Getty, upon the Plank road. Colonel Carroll, an excellent fighting man, was wounded, but remained on the field. More to the left, Brooke and Smyth, of Barlow's division, attacked the right of Hill, and forced it back. About 4 o'clock, also, Wadsworth, who had been sent from his position near the Lacy house to strike across the country toward the Plank road, halted for the night in line of battle, facing nearly south between Tapp's house and the Brock road.| This ended the operations of May 5th, leaving the Army of the Potomac in close contact with Ewell and Hill.

| According to General Francis A. Walker's account, in the "History of the Second Army Corps," Dow's 6th Maine Battery was placed in the second line on Mott's left, and a section of Ricketts's "F," 1st Pennsylvania Artillery was posted with the troops of General Getty.— EDITORS.

Colonel Theodore Lyman informs me that on a visit he made to the battle-field of the Wilderness after the war, in going over the ground where on May 6th, the next day, the 20th Massachusetts, of my brigade, lost a third of its numbers, he found the line occupied by the enemy to be just behind the crest of a slight elevation, where they had placed a row of logs, by which they were effectually screened from the bullets and the sight of our troops; for in front of and around them was a dense forest of saplings, the 20th Massachusetts and other of our troops were in the thicket, not more than twenty or thirty yards distant. Their presence was made known by their advance through the brush, and their return fire, aimed as they supposed at the enemy, had cut off the saplings four and five feet above the ground, as regularly as if they had been cut by a machine. Many of the broken tree-tops were still hanging when Colonel Lyman visited the ground.— A. S. W.

| Humphreys, to show how bewildering was the dense forest growth, says, "Many men from both armies, looking for water during the night, found themselves within the opposite lines."— A. S. W.

During the night of the 5th orders were given for a general attack by Sedgwick, Warren, and Hancock at 5 o'clock the next morning.

Burnside, who, with his corps, had been holding the line of the Orange and Alexandria railroad back to Bull Run, set his corps in motion the afternoon of the 4th and made a forced march to the field. The leading division, under Stevenson, moving from Brandy Station, crossed at Germanna Ford the night of the 5th, was held in reserve at Wilderness Tavern, and joined Hancock on the Brock road at 8 A. M. of the 6th. Potter and Willcox, coming from Bealton and Rappahannock Station, reached the field about daylight, and were ordered to fill the gap between Warren and Hancock and join in the general attack.⟩ Ferrero's colored division, after a forced march of forty miles, was held in the rear to guard the trains.

Longstreet's arrival on the field was known and reported by General Hancock to General Meade at 7 A. M. on the 6th; indeed, it was found that Longstreet was present when, at 5 o'clock, my brigade (of Gibbon's division) was ordered to relieve General Getty. When I advanced I immediately became engaged with Field's division, consisting of Gregg's, Benning's, Law's, and Jenkins's brigades, on the north side of the Orange Plank road.

Just before 5 o'clock the right of the line under Sedgwick was attacked by the Confederates, and gradually the firing extended along the whole front. Wadsworth's division fought its way across Hancock's front to the Plank road, and advanced along that road. Hancock pushed forward Birney with his own and Mott's divisions, Gibbon's division supporting, on the left of the Plank road, and soon drove his opponents from their rifle-pits, and for the time being appeared to have won a victory. His left, however, under Barlow, had not advanced. From information derived from prisoners and from the cavalry operating in the vicinity of Todd's tavern, it was believed at this time that Longstreet was working around the left to attack the line along the Brock road. Instead of attacking there, Longstreet moved to the support of Hill, and just as the Confederates gave way before Birney's assault, Longstreet's leading division, under General C. W. Field, reached Birney's battle-ground and engaged my line.

Thus at 8 o'clock Hancock was battling against both Hill and Longstreet. General Gibbon had command on the left. Hancock himself was looking out for the Plank road.

Warren's Fifth Corps, in front of Ewell, had obeyed the orders of General Grant, in making frequent and persistent attacks throughout the morning, without success. The same may be said of Wright, of Sedgwick's Sixth Corps, who was attacking Ewell's left; but Ewell was too strongly intrenched to be driven back from his line by the combined Fifth and Sixth corps.

General Burnside, with the divisions of Willcox and Potter, attempted to relieve Hancock by passing up between the turnpike and the Plank road to

---

⟩ General Humphreys remarks in his account as follows: "For, so far as could be ascertained, the gap between Hill and Ewell was not yet closed, neither was that between Hancock and Warren." As I held the right of Hancock on May 6th until 1 o'clock, I can state that it was never closed on the part of the Union troops. My aide, Colonel W. T. Simms, was badly wounded, on my right, while seeking to form a junction with the Ninth Corps or with Crawford of the Fifth Corps.—A. S. W.

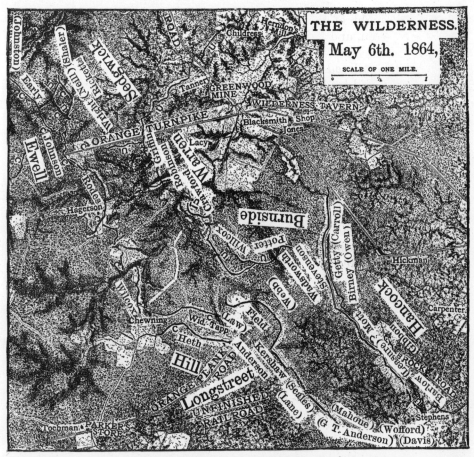

RELATIVE POSITIONS IN THE WILDERNESS, MAY 6.

For the most part the troops are indicated by divisions, and when a name indicates a brigade it is inclosed in parentheses. It should be noted that Griffin's line, before connecting with Wright, extended a short distance parallel with the Orange turnpike. Wadsworth, early in the morning, advanced south from near the Lacy house to the Orange Plank road, and formed across that road as indicated. Leasure's brigade, of Stevenson's division, coming into the line in Gibbon's first position, advanced north across Hancock's front to the Plank road. On the morning of the second day Webb, of Gibbon, fought on, and north of, the Plank road, while his other two brigades, Owen and Carroll, were supporting Getty on, and north of, the Plank road. Gibbon had general charge of Hancock's left, and Birney of Hancock's right.— EDITORS.

Chewning's farm, connecting his right with Warren and joining the right of Hancock, now held by my brigade.\ Burnside's other division, under Stevenson, moved up the Plank road in our support, and I placed four of his regiments, taken from the head of his column, on my right, then pressed to the rear and changed my whole line, which had been driven back to the Plank road, forward to its original line, holding Field's division in check with the twelve regiments now under my command. Now, at this very moment, General Wadsworth (who had assumed command over me because he stated that Stevenson ranked me, and he must take us both in his command) had given to me the most astonishing and bewildering order,— which was to leave

\ The right of the column under Willcox advanced beyond the Lacy house to Wilderness Run, and found the enemy well posted on high ground, behind the swamps along the creek. An attack here was deemed impracticable, and Willcox was moved to the left toward the Tapp house in support of Potter, who had gone in near the Plank road.— EDITORS.

BRIGADIER-GENERAL JAMES S. WADSWORTH, MORTALLY WOUNDED
MAY 6, 1864. DIED MAY 8. FROM A PHOTOGRAPH.

the twelve regiments under my command at his (Wadsworth's) disposal, and to go to the left, find four regiments, and stop the retreat of those troops of the left of our line who were flying to the Brock road. ☆ When I rode off to obey this unfortunate order, General Wadsworth, in order to stop the enemy's attack upon Birney upon his left, went to the 20th Massachusetts of my brigade and ordered that regiment to leave its log-works and charge the enemy's line, a strong breastwork on the west side of a ravine on Wadsworth's front.

General Wadsworth was told that the regiment could not safely be moved, that I had changed my front on that regiment and held the line by means of it. Wadsworth answered that the men were afraid, leaped his horse over the logs and led them in the charge himself. He was mortally wounded, ǀ and my line was broken by Field, and swept

☆ Of this incident, Col. C. H. Banes, in his "History of the Philadelphia Brigade" (Owen's), says:

"Webb's First Brigade of the Second Division was moved from its position on the Brock road, and quickly advanced on either side of the Plank road. By 8 o'clock the fighting had become continuous along the entire front of the Second Corps, and was raging at some points with great fury. . . . Toward 9 o'clock there was an almost entire cessation, followed soon after by furious assaults that expended their force before anything definite was accomplished, and these were followed in turn by desultory firing. . . . A few moments before 12 o'clock, General Wadsworth, whose division had pushed its way during the morning until it connected with [Webb], . . . rode through the woods to the Plank road, and began to ascertain the location of the corps with a view to concerted action. While General Wadsworth was on the edge of the road, near the line of battle, and engaged in making these observations, and before his command was really assured of its position, there occurred one of the strangest scenes of army experience. Without any apparent cause that could be seen from the position of the brigade, the troops on our left began to give way, and commenced falling back toward the Brock road. Those pressing past the left flank of the Second Division did not seem to be demoralized in manner, nor did they present the appearance of soldiers moving under orders, but rather of a throng of armed men who were returning dissatisfied from a muster. Occasionally some fellow, terror-stricken, would rush past as if his life depended on speed, but by far the larger number acted with the utmost deliberation in their movements. In vain were efforts put forth to stop this retrograde movement; the men were alike indifferent to commands or entreaties. . . . The division of Wadsworth, being on the right of the Plank road, was the last to feel this influence; but, in spite of the most gallant efforts of its commander, it soon joined with the other troops in moving to the rear, leaving the brave Wadsworth mortally wounded."

A. S. W.

ǀ General Wadsworth and myself had been discussing why I did not have certain men carried off the field who had been shot in the head. I told him that from my observation I had never considered it worth while to carry a man off the field if, wounded in the head, he slowly lost his vertical position and was incapable of making a movement of his head from the ground. I considered such cases as past cure. When I was shot in the head in the works at Spotsylvania Court House on the morning of the 12th, at the Bloody Angle, the bullet passed through the corner of my eye and came out behind my ear. While falling from the horse to the ground I recalled my conversation with General Wadsworth; when I struck the ground I made an effort to raise my head, and when I found I could do so I made up my mind I was not going to die of that wound, and then I fainted.—A. S. W.

off as by a whirlwind. Birney's line, as a consequence, was broken to pieces, and back to the Brock road went the troops. This attack was directed by Lee in person. [See also p. 124.] When I came back from endeavoring to carry out the order that Wadsworth had given me, I found the 19th Maine, under Colonel Selden Connor, on the Plank road. Another regiment also staid with me to hold the Plank road and to deceive the Confederates, by fighting as though they had a continuous line. Colonel Connor was shot in the leg after a long skirmish; I offered him my horse, but his wounds being such as to render him unable to mount, he had to be carried to the log-works. His regiment staid there until I gave the order to break like partridges through the woods for the Brock road.

Burnside had finally become engaged far out on our right front; Potter's division came upon the enemy intrenched on the west side of a little ravine extending from Ewell's right. General Burnside says that after considerable fighting he connected his left with Hancock's right and intrenched.

Hancock was out of ammunition, and had to replenish the best way he could from the rear. At 3:45 P. M. the enemy advanced in force against him to within a hundred yards of his log-works on the left of the Plank road. The attack was of course the heaviest here. Anderson's division came forward and took possession of our line of intrenchments, but Carroll's brigade was at hand and drove them out at a double-quick.

Now let us return to our right, and stand where General Meade and General Grant were, at the Lacy house. The battle was finished over on the left so far as Hancock and Burnside were concerned. Grant had been thoroughly

DISTRIBUTING AMMUNITION UNDER FIRE TO WARREN'S FIFTH CORPS, MAY 6.
FROM A SKETCH MADE AT THE TIME.

THE BURNING WOODS, MAY 6—RESCUING THE WOUNDED. FROM A SKETCH MADE AT THE TIME.

defeated in his attempt to walk past General Lee on the way to Rich-mond. Shaler's brigade of Wright's division of Sedgwick's corps had been guarding the wagon-trains, but was now needed for the fight and had returned to the Sixth Corps lines. It was placed on the extreme right on the Germanna Plank road, due north from where General Grant was stand-ing. Shaler's brigade was close up to the enemy, as indeed was our whole line. Shaler was busy building breastworks, when it was struck in the flank, rolled up in confusion, and General Seymour and General Shaler and some hundreds of his men were taken prisoners. But the brigade was not destroyed. A part of it stood, and, darkness helping them, the assailants were prevented from destroying Wright's division. Wright kept his men in order. [See p. 127.]

This is in fact the end of the battle of the Wilderness, so far as relates to the infantry. Our cavalry was drawn in from Todd's tavern and the Brock road. The enemy's cavalry followed them. They were all intrenched, and General Grant decided that night that he would continue the movement to the left, as it was impossible to attack a position held by the enemy in such force in a tangled forest. To add to the horrors of war, we had the woods on fire all around us, and Humphreys estimates that about two hundred of our men were burned to death. The best possible proof that this was an accidental battle can be found in the movements of the troops. There was no intention to attack Lee in the Wilderness.

The 6th of May was the last day of the battle of the Wilderness. Ewell had most effectually stopped the forward movement of the right wing of Meade's army, and Hill and Longstreet defeated our left under Hancock. The fact is that the whole of the left was disorganized. From Hancock down through Birney and Gibbon, each general commanded something not strictly in his command. Hancock had "the left," Gibbon "the left" of Hancock; Birney had his own and Mott's divisions, and Wadsworth had Webb and Stevenson. The troops of these division commanders were without proper leaders.

We had seen the mixed Second and Ninth corps driven in, in detail, on our left. We knew that the Fifth and Sixth corps were blocked, and we felt deeply the mortification consequent upon our being driven back to the Brock road. From personal contact with the regiments who did the hardest fighting, I declare that the individual men had no longer that confidence in their commanders which had been their best and strongest trait during the past year. We are told by General Badeau in his history that at the very time our men were being tossed about on the Plank road "General Grant lay under the trees awaiting Burnside's advance, and revolving the idea of a movement still farther to the Union left, thrusting his whole force between Lee and Richmond."

We did move toward Spotsylvania. Warren's Fifth Corps was directed to withdraw from the Wilderness after dark on the 7th of May, and to move by the left behind Hancock on the Brock road, with Sedgwick (the Sixth Corps) following him, and to proceed toward the court house. [See map,

VIEW FROM NEAR THE WILDERNESS TAVERN, LOOKING TOWARD THE BATTLE-FIELD—2 P. M., MAY 7.
FROM A SKETCH MADE AT THE TIME.

OUT OF THE WILDERNESS, SUNDAY MORNING, MAY 8—THE MARCH TO SPOTSYLVANIA.
FROM A SKETCH MADE AT THE TIME.

p. 167.] This was attempted, but Warren found that he was required with his corps to help Sheridan's cavalry, which was detained by J. E. B. Stuart at Todd's tavern, or near that point. Warren gave the required assistance, driving out of his way Stuart, who was assisted by infantry.

At 8:30 P. M. Warren moved by the Brock road to the left of the Second Corps, and Sedgwick moved by the pike and Germanna Plank road to Chancellorsville, thence by the Piney Branch Church road to the intersection of that road with the Brock road. At this point Sedgwick was ordered to leave a division, with another at Piney Branch Church, and a third midway between these two. Burnside started to follow Sedgwick, but early on the morning of the 8th he was ordered to halt at Aldrich's, where the Piney Church road leaves the main Fredericksburg Plank road, to guard the trains. Ferrero's division of this corps was now detached for this service.

Warren was delayed by the blocking of the Brock road by the mounted troops of the provost guard, and this delay gave Longstreet's men, under R. H. Anderson, the opportunity to reach Spotsylvania in advance of Warren. When Warren reached Todd's tavern at 3 A. M., he found Merritt's cavalry engaging the Confederates. Hancock had waited for the whole army to pass, and reached the tavern at 9 o'clock on the 8th.✠ At 11 A. M., says General Humphreys, "Hancock sent his leading brigade under Miles to make a reconnoissance down the Catharpin road toward Corbin's Bridge, about two miles distant." Miles had his own brigade, one battery, and one brigade

✠ My notes show that we of the Second Corps obeyed orders implicitly. We waited to cover the movements of the rest of the army, and then took our place at 4 P. M. of the 8th of May on the Brock road, about one mile south-east of Todd's tavern.—A. S. W.

of Gregg's cavalry. He found Hampton's cavalry, and held them at bay until 5:30 P. M. While returning, Miles was attacked by Mahone's infantry, and was compelled to call up reënforcements. At 1:30 P. M. Hancock sent Gibbon east ten miles to support Warren and Sedgwick.

About 8 A. M. on the 8th Warren's leading division, under General John C. Robinson, deployed into the clearing north of Spotsylvania Court House, and was fired upon by Confederates upon Spotsylvania Ridge. General Robinson was severely wounded in the first fire. Griffin's division advanced on the right of Robinson's; but the line, being unable to sustain itself, soon fell back until it was succored by the divisions of Crawford and Wadsworth, which now reached the front. A line was taken up east of the Brock road, near Alsop's. Sedgwick came up about noon, and the Fifth Corps, supported by Sedgwick, were at 1 P. M. directed to storm the Confederate position on Spotsylvania Ridge. Sedgwick moved south to join Warren's left; but it was late in the day when Crawford's division of the Fifth and one of Wright's brigades under Penrose assaulted what proved to be Rodes's division of Ewell's corps in position and intrenched.

On the morning of the 9th Burnside's corps moved across from the Plank road to the Fredericksburg road at the crossing of the Ny River. This brought him east of the court house one and a half miles. He pushed over the river one division under O. B. Willcox. Stevenson's division came up at noon. Potter's division remained a mile in rear on the Fredericksburg road. Willcox fought a brigade of R. H. Anderson and some dismounted cavalry. Hancock moved east to the right of Warren, and intrenched overlooking the Po. On the morning of the 9th Sheridan started on a raid around Lee's army.↓

In front of Hancock the Po River ran from west to east, then it turned due south opposite Warren's right. The Confederate left rested for a time on this south bend, and the bridge over it at the crossing of the Shady Grove Church road was fortified by Longstreet. While the several corps were adjusting their lines on the 9th, General Sedgwick, our most esteemed general, was killed by a sharp-shooter, and Horatio G. Wright took command of the Sixth Corps.

General Burnside had reported to General Grant on the 9th that he had met the enemy on the east of Spotsylvania Court House, and he had added to his report that he judged, from the indications in his front, that Lee was about to move north toward Fredericksburg. It was therefore determined that Hancock should make a reconnoissance toward Lee's left, crossing the east and west bend of the Po River, moving south as far as the Shady Grove road, turning the enemy's left; then to move east, and cross the Po River again by the Block House road bridge. Hancock crossed three of his divisions (Mott was with Wright) at different points at 6 o'clock in the morning, forcing the crossing, and meeting a very stubborn resistance in front of Barlow, who was on his left, and but little in front of Gibbon, who was on his right. He now laid three pontoon-bridges over the river, it being fifty feet wide and not fordable, and then pushed due south toward the Block House bridge, but reached that point too late that night to attempt a crossing.

↓ See note, p. 117, and article to follow.— EDITORS.

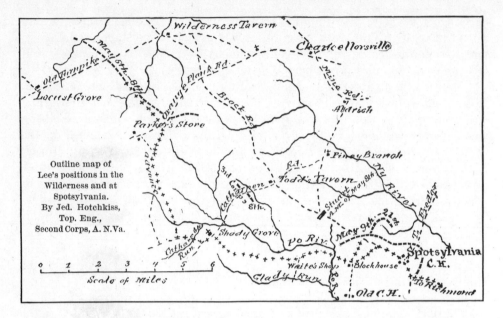

Outline map of Lee's positions in the Wilderness and at Spotsylvania. By Jed. Hotchkiss, Top. Eng., Second Corps, A. N. Va.

During this night orders were issued from Meade for the operations of the next day: Hancock was to endeavor to find the position of the enemy's left, to force him from the position of his (Hancock's) front. The Sixth Corps was ordered to feel the intrenchments near the center. Mott's division of Hancock's corps, still kept north of the Po River with Wright, and on the left of the Sixth Corps, was to prepare to join Burnside, who with his corps (the Ninth) was to attack Early from the east on the morning of the 10th.

But at dawn on the 10th an examination of the Block House bridge, made by Hancock, showed that the enemy was strongly intrenched on the east side of the Po at that point. However, Brooke's brigade of Barlow's division was sent down the Po River to a point half a mile below the bridge. Brooke discovered the enemy in strong force holding intrenchments extending nearly half a mile below the bridge, their left resting on the Po River.

But other arrangements had been made for the movement of the army, and Meade now ordered Hancock back. Meade was directed to arrange for the assault at 5 o'clock, under General Hancock's command, in the afternoon on the front of Warren and Wright.

Birney, while withdrawing, was attacked; Hancock, who had started ahead with Gibbon to prepare for the attack, recrossed to the south bank of the Po and joined Barlow. Barlow was half a mile south of his bridges. His left, composed of Miles's and Smyth's brigades, was along the Shady Grove road, facing south, their left rested at the bridge. Brooke's and Brown's brigades were in front, or south of the Shady Grove road. North-east, and to their rear one and a half miles, Field's guns were planted in intrenchments, sweeping the ground behind them and covering the pontoon-bridge over the Po. Hancock drew back Brooke and Brown to the right and to the rear; and then Miles and Smyth retired to the crest south of the pontoon-bridges.

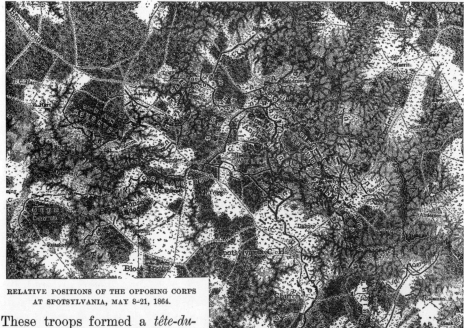

RELATIVE POSITIONS OF THE OPPOSING CORPS
AT SPOTSYLVANIA, MAY 8-21, 1864.

These troops formed a *tête-du-pont* facing south. Heth's division, of Hill's corps, attacked the two right brigades with vigor, but was twice repulsed. The Union loss was very heavy.

Hancock, finding the enemy repulsed and the woods on fire in the rear of his line, crossed to the north side of the Po River. One gun, the first ever lost by the Second Corps, was jammed between two trees in the midst of this fire, and was abandoned by Birney's men. Many of our wounded perished in the flames.

Of this battle on our right, General Hancock said, "The enemy regarded this as a considerable victory. Had not Barlow's division received imperative orders to withdraw, Heth's division would have had no cause for congratulation."

Meanwhile, Warren had determined to make the attack, and at 3:45 he did so, directing it personally and leading in full uniform. ♭

The assaulting column was composed of Crawford's division, Cutler's division (formerly Wadsworth's), and Webb's and Carroll's brigades of the Second Corps. The official diary of Longstreet's corps says that "some of the enemy succeeded in gaining the works, but were killed in them." We were driven back, however, with heavy loss, including Brigadier-General James C. Rice, of Cutler's division, killed.

♭ Warren had made reconnoissances in force, with division front, twice. He knew his ground, as he always did. — A. S. W.

General Hancock returned to us at half-past five, and we were ordered to make another attack at 7 P. M. with Birney's and Gibbon's divisions and part

BRIGADIER-GENERAL JOHN M. JONES, C. S. A.

of the Fifth Corps. We made the assault, but we were driven back a second time. Our men were demoralized by fruitless work. Over on our left, in the Sixth Corps, General Wright had found what he deemed to be a vulnerable place in the Confederate line. It was on the right of Rodes's rebel division and on the west face of the salient. Colonel Emory Upton was selected to lead this attack. Upton's brigade was of the First Division, Sixth Corps. He had four regiments of Neill's brigade attached to his command; and General Mott, commanding a division of the Second Corps, had been ordered by General Wright to assault the works in his front at 5 o'clock to assist and support Upton's left.

Upton formed in four lines. The Sixth Corps batteries played upon the left of the enemy's salient, enfilading it, and, as they ceased firing, Upton charged. Rushing to the parapet with a wild "Hurrah," heedless of the terrible front and flank fire he received, his men poured over the enemy's works; captured many prisoners, after a hand-to-hand fight; and, pressing forward, took the second line of rebel intrenchments with its battery.

Mott, who was on Upton's left, did not support him. The enemy being reënforced, Upton was ordered to retire, but he carried back with him several stand of colors and 1200 prisoners.\ On the left Burnside made an attack in conjunction with those on the right. He pushed close to the enemy, on the Fredericksburg road, and intrenched. General T. G. Stevenson, commanding one of his divisions, was killed in making this assault.

MAJOR-GENERAL JOHN C. ROBINSON, WOUNDED
AT SPOTSYLVANIA.   FROM A PHOTOGRAPH.

On the 10th of May the Second, Fifth, and Sixth corps lost 4100 men killed and wounded. Not many were missing. The Confederates lost probably two

\ For gallant conduct displayed during the assaults on the 10th, Colonels Upton and Carroll
were made brigadier-generals.— A. S. W.

thousand men. On the 11th ☆ dispositions were made for the grand assault the next day on the "Bloody Angle."

Of that assault I have little to write. Grant had his back to the north, and enwrapped the V-shaped salient occupied by Lee. During the night three divisions of the Second Corps were to move to the left behind the Sixth and Fifth, and join the Ninth Corps in an assault at 4 A. M. on the 12th. Warren and Wright were to hold their corps in readiness to take part. We moved to the attack at 4:35 A. M. on the 12th, and captured Johnson and four thousand men from Ewell; also twenty pieces of artillery. At this time I was shot in the head and went to the rear. Another will tell of the incidents of our bloody but fruitless assault.

☆ It was at this time that General Grant sent his famous "all summer" dispatch, in these words:

"HEADQUARTERS, ARMIES OF THE U. S., NEAR SPOTSYLVANIA COURT HOUSE, May 11th, 1864, 8:30 A. M.

"MAJOR-GENERAL HALLECK, Chief-of-Staff of the Army.

"GENERAL: We have now ended the sixth day of very heavy fighting. The result to this time is much in our favor. But our losses have been heavy, as well as those of the enemy. We have lost to this time eleven general officers killed, wounded, or missing, and probably twenty thousand men. I think the loss of the enemy must be greater, we having taken over four thousand prisoners in battle, whilst he has taken but few, except stragglers. I am now sending back to Belle Plain all my wagons for a fresh supply of provisions and ammunition, and propose to fight it out on this line if it takes all summer.

"The arrival of reënforcements here will be very encouraging to the men, and I hope they will be sent as fast as possible, and in as great numbers. My object in having them sent to Belle Plain was to use them as an escort to our supply train. If it is more convenient to send them out by train to march from the railroad to Belle Plain or Fredericksburg, send them so.

"I am satisfied the enemy are very shaky, and are only kept up to the mark by the greatest exertions on the part of their officers, and by keeping them intrenched in every position they take.

"Up to this time there is no indication of any portion of Lee's army being detached for the defense of Richmond.

"Very respectfully your obedient servant,

"U. S. GRANT, Lieutenant-General."

GENERAL BURNSIDE'S HEADQUARTERS, MAY 22D, AT BETHEL CHURCH, NEAR MILFORD, ON THE MATTAPONY RIVER. FROM A WAR-TIME PHOTOGRAPH.

STRUGGLING FOR THE WORKS AT THE "BLOODY ANGLE."

HAND-TO-HAND FIGHTING AT SPOTSYLVANIA.

BY G. NORTON GALLOWAY.

GENERAL HANCOCK'S surprise and capture of the larger portion of Edward Johnson's division, and the capture of the salient "at Spotsylvania Court House on the 12th of May, 1864, accomplished with the Second Corps," have been regarded as one of the most brilliant feats of that brilliant soldier's career; but without the substantial assistance of General Wright, grand old John Sedgwick's worthy successor, and the Sixth Corps, a defeat as bitter as his victory was sweet would have been recorded against the hero of that day.

The storm which had set in early in the afternoon of the 11th of May continued with great severity, and but little rest was obtained during the night. Soon after dark, however, a remarkable change in the weather took place, and it became raw and disagreeable; the men gathered in small groups about half-drowned fires, with their tents stretched about their shoulders, while some hastily pitched the canvas on the ground, and sought shelter beneath the rumpled and dripping folds. Others rolled themselves up, and lay close to the simmering logs, eager to catch a few moments' sleep; many crouched about, without any shelter whatever, presenting a pitiable sight.

Throughout the day some skirmishing and sharpshooting had occurred, but this had been of a spasmodic character, and had elicited no concern. About dusk the Sixth Corps moved to a position on the right and rear of the army. The stormy night was favorable to Hancock's movement, and

about 10 o'clock he put his troops in motion, marching to a point on the left of the Sixth Corps' former position in the neighborhood of the Brown house, massing his troops in that vicinity. [See map, p. 167.]

General Grant's orders to Hancock were to assault at daylight on the 12th in coöperation with Burnside on his left, while Wright and Warren were held in readiness to assault on his right. The Confederate army was composed of three corps — Longstreet (now R. H. Anderson) on their left, Ewell in the center, and A. P. Hill (now under Early) on the right. The point to be assaulted was a salient of field-works on the Confederate center, afterward called the "Bloody Angle." It was held by General Edward Johnson's division. Here the Confederate line broke off at an angle of ninety degrees, the right parallel, about the length of a small brigade, being occupied by General George H. Steuart's regiments.‖ This point was a part or continuation of the line of works charged and carried by General Upton on May 10th, and was considered to be the key to Lee's position.

Just as the day was breaking, Barlow's and Birney's divisions of Hancock's corps pressed forward upon the unsuspecting foe, and leaping the breastworks after a hand-to-hand conflict with the bewildered enemy, in which guns were used as clubs, possessed themselves of the intrenchments. Over three thousand prisoners were taken, including General Johnson and General Steuart. Twenty

‖ Steuart occupied only part of the right parallel; Jones, Stafford, and Hays were on his left, and Lane was on his right in that parallel.— EDITORS.

Confederate cannon became the permanent trophies of the day, twelve of them belonging to Page and eight to Cutshaw.

Upon reaching the second line of Lee's works, held by Wilcox's division, who by this time had become apprised of the disaster to their comrades, Hancock met with stern resistance, as Lee in the meantime had been hurrying troops to Ewell from Hill on the right and Anderson on the left, and these were sprung upon our victorious lines with such an impetus as to drive them hastily back toward the left of the salient. ⚓

As soon as the news of Hancock's good and ill success reached army headquarters, the Sixth Corps — Upton's brigade being in advance — was ordered to move with all possible haste to his support. At a brisk pace we crossed a line of intrenchments a short distance in our front, and, passing through a strip of timber, at once began to realize our nearness to the foe. It was now about 6 o'clock, and the enemy, reënforced, were making desperate efforts to regain what they had lost. Our forces were hastily retiring at this point before the concentrated attack of the enemy, and these with our wounded lined the road. We pressed forward and soon cleared the woods and reached an insidious fen, covered with dense marsh grass, where we lay down for a few moments awaiting orders. I cannot imagine how any of us survived the sharp fire that swept over us at this point — a fire so keen that it split the blades of grass all about us, the minies moaning in a furious concert as they picked out victims by the score.

The rain was still falling in torrents and held the country about in obscurity. The command was soon given to my regiment, the 95th Pennsylvania Volunteers, Captain Macfarlain commanding, — it being the advance of Upton's brigade, — to "rise up," whereupon with hurrahs we went forward, cheered on by Colonel Upton, who had led us safe through the Wilderness. It was not long before we reached an angle of works constructed with great skill. Immediately in our front an abatis had been arranged consisting of limbs and branches interwoven into one another, forming footlocks of the most dangerous character. But there the works were, and over some of us went,

many never to return. At this moment Lee's strong line of battle, hastily selected for the work of retrieving ill fortune, appeared through the rain, mist, and smoke. We received their bolts, losing nearly one hundred of our gallant 95th. Colonel Upton saw at once that this point must be held at all hazards; for if Lee should recover the angle, he would be enabled to sweep back our lines right and left, and the fruits of the morning's victory would be lost. The order was at once given us to lie down and commence firing; the left of our regiment rested against the works, while the right, slightly refused, rested upon an elevation in front. And now began a desperate and pertinacious struggle.

Under cover of the smoke-laden rain the enemy was pushing large bodies of troops forward, determined at all hazards to regain the lost ground. Could we hold on until the remainder of our brigade should come to our assistance? Regardless of the heavy volleys of the enemy that were thinning our ranks, we stuck to the position and returned the fire until the 5th Maine and the 121st New York of our brigade came to our support, while the 96th Pennsylvania went in on our right; thus reënforced, we redoubled our exertions. The smoke, which was dense at first, was intensified by each discharge of artillery to such an extent that the accuracy of our aim became very uncertain, but nevertheless we kept up the fire in the supposed direction of the enemy. Meanwhile they were crawling forward under cover of the smoke, until, reaching a certain point, and raising their usual yell, they charged gallantly up to the very muzzles of our pieces and reoccupied the Angle.

Upon reaching the breastwork, the Confederates for a few moments had the advantage of us, and made good use of their rifles. Our men went down by the score; all the artillery horses were down; the gallant Upton was the only mounted officer in sight. Hat in hand, he bravely cheered his men, and begged them to "hold this point." All of his staff had been either killed, wounded, or dismounted.

At this moment, and while the open ground in rear of the Confederate works was choked with troops, a section of Battery C, 5th United States Artillery, under Lieutenant Richard Metcalf, ↓

⚓ Of the Union troops on the left of Hancock, General Grant ("Personal Memoirs," p. 231) says:

"Burnside on the left had advanced up east of the salient to the very parapet of the enemy. Potter, commanding one of his divisions, got over, but was not able to remain there. . . . Burnside accomplished but little on our left of a positive nature, but negatively a great deal. He kept Lee from reënforcing his center from that quarter." **EDITORS.**

↓ This is, I believe, the only instance in the history of the war of a battery charging on breastworks. It was commanded by Lieutenant James Gilliss, and was attached to the Second Corps. Sergeant William E. Lines, one of only two survivors of the section that went in on that day, and who commanded the right gun, has given the writer the following facts relative to the matter:

"After the capture of the Confederate works, we were put in position just under the hill near the small pine-trees so much spoken of. We fired a few rounds of solid shot. Of course we could not see the Confederate line, but we elevated our guns so as to clear our own infantry. While we were

waiting, a staff-officer with a Sixth Corps badge rode up to Lieutenant Gilliss, and I could see they had some argument or dispute, for the officer soon went away. Directly another officer rode up to Gilliss, and the same sort of colloquy took place, the officer evidently wanting Gilliss to do something that the latter would not do. This officer rode away. In a very short time General Wright, who then commanded the Sixth Corps, rode up to Gilliss, and had a moment's conversation with him. Lieutenant Metcalf then came over to the first section, and gave the command, 'Limber the guns,' 'drivers mount,' 'cannoneers mount,' 'caissons rear,' and away we went, up the hill, past our infantry, and into position. The staff-officer who led us was shot before we got into position. I have often thought it was owing to that fact that we got so close to the enemy's works. We were a considerable distance in front of our infantry, and of course artillery could not live long under such a fire as the enemy were putting through there. Our men went down in short order. The left gun fired nine rounds. I fired fourteen with mine, and was assisted in the last four rounds by an officer of a Vermont regiment, and by another from the 95th Pennsylvania, both of whom were shot. The effect of our canister

UPTON'S BRIGADE AT THE "BLOODY ANGLE." AFTER DRAWINGS BY A PARTICIPANT.

was brought into action and increased the carnage by opening at short range with double charges of canister. This staggered the apparently exultant enemy. In the maze of the moment these guns were run up by hand close to the famous Angle, and fired again and again, and they were only abandoned when all the drivers and cannoneers had fallen. The battle was now at white heat.

The rain continued to fall, and clouds of smoke hung over the scene. Like leeches we stuck to the work, determined by our fire to keep the enemy from rising up. Captain John D. Fish, of Upton's staff, who had until this time performed valuable service in conveying ammunition to the gunners, fell, pierced by a bullet. This brave officer seemed to court death as he rode back and forth between the caissons and cannoneers with stands of canister under his "gum" coat. "Give it to them, boys! I'll bring you the canister," said he ; and as he turned to cheer the gunners, he fell from his horse, mortally wounded. In a few moments the two brass pieces of the 5th Artillery, cut and hacked by the bullets of both antagonists, lay unworked with their muzzles projecting over the enemy's works, and their wheels half sunk in the mud. Between the lines and near at hand lay the horses of these guns, completely riddled. The dead and wounded were torn to pieces by the canister as it swept the ground where they had fallen. The mud was half-way to our knees, and by our constant movement the fallen were almost buried at our feet. We now backed off from the breastwork a few yards, abandoning for a while the two 12-pounders, but still keeping up a fusillade. We soon closed up our shattered ranks and the brigade settled down again to its task. Our fire was now directed at the top of the breastworks, and woe be to the head or hand that appeared above it. In the meantime the New Jersey brigade, Colonel W. H. Penrose, went into action on our

upon the Confederates was terrible : they were evidently trying to strengthen their first line from the second when we opened on them, and you can imagine the execution at that distance. When Lieutenant Metcalf and myself could no longer serve the guns, we withdrew. Our section went into action with twenty-three men and one officer — Lieutenant Metcalf. The only ones who came out sound were the lieutenant and myself. Every horse was killed, seven of the men were killed outright, sixteen wounded ; the gun-carriages were so cut with bullets as to be of no further service.
. . . Twenty-seven balls passed through the lid of the limber-chest while Number Six was getting out ammunition, and he was wounded in the face and neck by the fragments of wood and lead. The sponge-bucket on my gun had thirty-

nine holes in it, being perforated like a sieve. The force of the balls can be imagined when I say that the bucket was made of one-eighth-inch iron. One curious circumstance on the morning we captured the works [May 12th] was, that musketry shots seemed to make such a slight noise ; instead of the sharp *bing* of the shot, it was a dull *thud*. This may have been an important aid to our success, as the [first] firing of the enemy's skirmishers did not alarm their men in the breastworks."

G. N. G.

It is also claimed that a section of Brown's Rhode Island battery was run up to the breastworks in a similar manner.— EDITORS.

right, and the Third Brigade, General Eustis's, was hard at work. The Vermont brigade, under Colonel Lewis A. Grant, which had been sent to Barlow's assistance, was now at the Angle, and General Wheaton's brigade was deep in the struggle. The Second and Third Divisions of the Sixth Corps were also ready to take part. It will thus be seen that we had no lack of men for the defense or capture of this position, whichever it may be termed.

The great difficulty was in the narrow limits of the Angle, around which we were fighting, which precluded the possibility of getting more than a limited number into action at once. At one time our ranks were crowded in some parts four deep by reënforcements. Major Henry P. Truefitt, commanding the 119th Pennsylvania, was killed, and Captain Charles P. Warner, who succeeded him, was shot dead. Later in the day Major William Ellis, of the 49th New York, who had excited our admiration, was shot through the arm and body with a ramrod during one of the several attempts to get the men to cross the works and drive off the enemy. Our losses were frightful. What remained of many different regiments that had come to our support had concentrated at this point, and had planted their tattered colors upon a slight rise of ground close to the Angle, where they staid during the latter part of the day.

To keep up the supply of ammunition pack mules were brought into use, each animal carrying three thousand rounds. The boxes were dropped close behind the troops engaged, where they were quickly opened by the officers or file-closers, who served the ammunition to the men. The writer fired four hundred rounds of ammunition, and many others as many or more. In this manner a continuous and rapid fire was maintained, to which for a while the enemy replied with vigor.

Finding that we were not to be driven back, the Confederates began to use more discretion, exposing themselves but little, using the loop-holes in their works to fire through, and at times placing the muzzles of their rifles on the top logs, seizing the trigger and small of the stock, and elevating the breech with one hand sufficiently to reach us. During the day a section of Cowan's battery took position behind us, sending shell after shell close over our heads, to explode inside the Confederate works. In like manner Coehorn mortars eight hundred yards in our rear sent their shells with admirable precision gracefully curving over us. Sometimes the enemy's fire would slacken, and the moments would become so monotonous that something had to be done to stir them up. Then some resolute fellow would seize a fence-rail or piece of abatis, and, creeping close to the breastworks, thrust it over among the enemy, and then drop on the ground to avoid the volley that was sure to follow. A daring lieutenant in one of our left companies leaped upon the breastworks, took a rifle that was

handed to him, and discharged it among the foe. In like manner he discharged another, and was in the act of firing a third shot when his cap flew up in the air, and his body pitched headlong among the enemy.

On several occasions squads of disheartened Confederates raised pieces of shelter-tents above the works as a flag of truce; upon our slacking fire and calling to them to come in, they would immediately jump the breastworks and surrender. One party of twenty or thirty thus signified their willingness to submit; but owing to the fact that their comrades occasionally took advantage of the

BREVET MAJOR-GENERAL EMORY UPTON, U. S. A.
FROM A PHOTOGRAPH.

cessation to get a volley into us, it was some time before we concluded to give them a chance. With leveled pieces we called to them to come in. Springing upon the breastworks in a body, they stood for an instant panic-stricken at the terrible array before them; that momentary delay was the signal for their destruction. While we, with our fingers pressing the trigger, shouted to them to jump, their troops, massed in the rear, poured a volley into them, killing or wounding all but a few, who dropped with the rest and crawled in under our pieces, while we instantly began firing.

The battle, which during the morning raged with more or less violence on the right and left of this position, gradually slackened, and attention was concentrated upon the Angle. So continuous and heavy was our fire that the head logs of the breastworks were cut and torn until they resembled hickory brooms. Several large oak-trees, which grew just in the rear of the works, were completely gnawed off by our converging fire, and about 3 o'clock in the day fell among the enemy with a loud crash. ⫶

⫶ The stump of one of these trees is preserved in Washington. In his official report, Brigadier-General Samuel McGowan, who commanded a brigade in Wilcox's Confederate division, says: "To give some idea of the intensity of the fire, an oak-tree twenty-two inches

in diameter, which stood just in rear of the right of the brigade, was cut down by the constant scaling of musket-balls, and fell about 12 o'clock Thursday night, injuring by its fall several soldiers in the 1st South Carolina regiment."— EDITORS.

UNION HOSPITAL AT ALSOP'S FARM-HOUSE, NEAR THE BROCK ROAD. FROM A WAR-TIME PHOTOGRAPH.

Toward dusk preparations were made to relieve us. By this time we were nearly exhausted, and had fired three to four hundred rounds of ammunition per man. Our lips were incrusted with powder from "biting cartridge." Our shoulders and hands were coated with mud that had adhered to the butts of our rifles. ⸸

The troops of the Second Corps, who were to relieve us, now moved up, took our position, and opened fire as we fell back a short distance to rearrange our shattered ranks and get something to eat, which we were sadly in need of. When darkness came on we dropped from exhaustion.

About midnight, after twenty hours of constant fighting, Lee withdrew from the contest at this point, leaving the Angle in our possession. Thus closed the battle of the 12th of May.

On the 13th, early in the day, volunteers were called for to bury the dead. The writer volunteered to assist, and with the detail moved to the works near the Angle, in front of which we buried a number of bodies near where they fell. We were exposed to the fire of sharp shooters, and it was still raining. We cut the name, company, and regiment of each of the dead on the lids of ammunition-boxes which we picked up near by. The inscriptions were but feebly executed, for they were done with a pocket-knife. This work ended, we went close up where we had fought on Thursday and viewed the "Bloody Angle."

A momentary gleam of sunshine through the gloom of the sky seemed to add a new horror to the scene. Hundreds of Confederates, dead or dying, lay piled over one another in those pits. The fallen lay three or four feet deep in some places, and, with but few exceptions, they were shot in and about the head. Arms, accouterments, ammunition, cannon, shot and shell, and broken foliage were strewn about. With much labor a detail of Union soldiers buried the dead by simply turning the captured breastworks upon them. Thus had these unfortunate victims unwittingly dug their own graves. ☆ The trenches were nearly full of muddy water. It was the most horrible sight I had ever witnessed.

The enemy's defenses at this point were elaborately constructed of heavy timber, banked with earth to the height of about four feet; above this was placed what is known as a head log, raised just high enough to enable a musket to be inserted between it and the lower work. Pointed pine and pin-oak formed an abatis, in front of which was a deep ditch. Shelves ran along the inside ledges of these works (a series of square pits) and along their flank traverses which extended to the rear; upon these shelves large quantities of "buck and ball" and "minie" cartridges were piled ready for use, and the guns of the dead and wounded were still pointing through the apertures, just as the men had fallen from them.

⸸ Our pieces at times would become choked with burnt powder, and would receive the cartridge but half way. This fact, however, did not interfere with their discharge.— G. N. G.

☆ The Confederate General McGowan officially says: "The trenches on the right in the 'Bloody Angle' ran with blood and had to be cleared of the dead bodies more than once."— EDITORS.

THE DEATH OF GENERAL JOHN SEDGWICK.

BY MARTIN T. MCMAHON, BREVET MAJOR-GENERAL, U. S. V.; CHIEF-OF-STAFF, SIXTH CORPS.

ON May 8th, 1864, the Sixth Corps made a rapid march to the support of Warren, near Spotsylvania Court House. We arrived there about 5 P. M., and passed the rest of the day in getting into position on Warren's left. After nightfall General Sedgwick rode back into an open field near General Warren's headquarters and, with his staff, lay down on the grass and slept until daylight. Shortly after daylight he moved out upon his line of battle. We had no tents or breakfast during that night or morning. The general made some necessary changes in the line and gave a few unimportant orders, and sat down with me upon a hard-tack box, with his back resting against a tree. The men, one hundred feet in front, were just finishing a line of rifle-pits, which ran to the right of a section of artillery that occupied an angle in our line. The 1st New Jersey brigade was in advance of this line.

After this brigade, by Sedgwick's direction, had been withdrawn through a little opening to the left of the pieces of artillery, the general, who had watched the operation, resumed his seat on the hard-tack box and commenced talking about members of his staff in very complimentary terms. He was an inveterate tease, and I at once suspected that he had some joke on the staff which he was leading up to. He was interrupted in his comments by observing that the troops, who during this time had been filing from the left into the rifle-pits, had come to a halt and were lying down, while the left of the line partly overlapped the position of the section of artillery. He stopped abruptly and said, "That is wrong. Those troops must be moved farther to the right; I don't wish them to overlap that battery." I started out to execute the order, and he rose at the same moment, and we sauntered out slowly to the gun on the right. About an hour before, I had remarked to the general, pointing to the two pieces in a half-jesting manner, which he well understood, "General, do you see that section of artillery? Well, you are not to go near it to-day." He answered good-naturedly, "McMahon, I would like to know who commands this corps, you or I?" I said, playfully, "Well, General, sometimes I am in doubt myself"; but added, "Seriously, General, I beg of you not to go to that angle; every officer who has shown himself there has been hit, both yesterday and to-day." He answered quietly, "Well, I don't know that there is any reason for my going there." When afterward we walked out to the position indicated, this conversation had entirely escaped the memory of both.

I gave the necessary order to move the troops to the right, and as they rose to execute the movement the enemy opened a sprinkling fire, partly from sharp-shooters. As the bullets whistled by, some of the men dodged. The general said laughingly, "What! what! men, dodging this way for single bullets! What will you do when they open fire along the whole line? I am ashamed of you. They couldn't hit an elephant at this distance." A few seconds after, a man who had been separated from his regiment passed directly in front of the general, and at the same moment a sharp-shooter's bullet passed with a long shrill whistle very close, and the soldier, who was then just in front of the general, dodged to the ground. The general touched him gently with his foot, and said, "Why, my man, I am ashamed of you, dodging that way," and repeated the remark, "They couldn't hit an elephant at this distance." The man rose and saluted, and said good-naturedly, "General, I dodged a shell once, and if I hadn't, it would have taken my head off. I believe in dodging." The general laughed and replied, "All right, my man; go to your place."

For a third time the same shrill whistle, closing with a dull, heavy stroke, interrupted our talk, when, as I was about to resume, the general's face turned slowly to me, the blood spurting from his left cheek under the eye in a steady stream. He fell in my direction; I was so close to him that my effort to support him failed, and I fell with him.

Colonel Charles H. Tompkins, chief of the artillery, standing a few feet away, heard my exclamation as the general fell, and, turning, shouted to his brigade-surgeon, Dr. Ohlenschlager. Major Charles A. Whittier, Major T. W. Hyde, and Lieutenant-Colonel Kent, who had been grouped near by, surrounded the general as he lay. A smile remained upon his lips but he did not speak. The doctor poured water from a canteen over the general's face. The blood still poured upward in a little fountain. The men in the long line of rifle-pits, retaining their places from force of discipline, were all kneeling with heads raised and faces turned toward the scene; for the news had already passed along the line.

I was recalled to a sense of duty by General Ricketts, next in command, who had arrived on the spot, and informed me, as chief-of-staff, that he declined to assume command of the corps, inasmuch as he knew that it was General Sedgwick's desire, if anything should happen to him, that General Horatio G. Wright, of the Third Division, should succeed him. General Ricketts, therefore, suggested that I communicate at once with General Meade, in order that the necessary order should be issued. When I found General Meade he had already heard the sad intelligence, and had issued the order placing General Wright in command. Returning I met the ambulance bringing the dead general's body, followed by his sorrowing staff. The body was taken back to General Meade's headquarters, and not into any house. A bower was built for it of evergreens, where, upon a rustic bier, it lay until nightfall, mourned over by officers and soldiers. The interment was at Cornwall Hollow, Connecticut.

⌡ Condensed from a letter to General J. W. Latta, President of the Sedgwick Memorial Association.

CENTER OF THE UNION POSITION AT SPOTSYLVANIA ON THE MORNING OF MAY 10, 1864. FROM A SKETCH MADE AT THE TIME.

McALLISTER'S BRIGADE AT THE BLOODY ANGLE.

BY ROBERT McALLISTER, BREVET MAJOR-GENERAL, U. S. V.

THE writer of the article on "Hand-to-hand Fighting at Spotsylvania" gives all the honor of holding the "salient" on May 12th, 1864, to the Sixth Corps. It was the Second Corps that made the grand charge of May 12th, and my brigade ‡ of that corps, the First Brigade of the Fourth Division, helped to defend the "Bloody Angle" from the first to the last of the fearful struggle. The brigade which I commanded during all these operations was composed of the 1st and 16th Massachusetts, the 5th, 6th, 7th, 8th, and 11th New Jersey, and the 26th and 115th Pennsylvania. In the great charge at dawn it was in the second line. At first we moved slowly up through the woods. When the first line reached the open field at the top of the hill, in sight of the enemy's works, the men rolled out a tremendous cheer which was taken up by the second line. Our boys started on a run. The first line parted in my front, *leaving a long open space,* and up to and partly into this space went my brigade, striking the enemy's works at the salient. At this place the Confederates had a field-battery of eight or ten guns. I ordered some of my men to draw back these guns on our side of the works, and with the remainder of the brigade pushed on toward the enemy. But we soon discovered another line of works, and large reënforcements coming to the aid of the enemy. I ordered "about face," and retreated to the first line and completed the hauling off of eight guns, two of which we manned; we had not gunners to man all. By the time we got the guns on our side of the works and my line formed, the enemy came in force determined to dislodge us, and succeeded in carrying the works on my right up to the salient. Encouraged by their success thus far, with traverses in their recaptured works behind which their sharpshooters could be protected while taking deadly aim at us, the enemy kept the offensive, and our position became very critical. Besides all this the Confederates here were more or less protected by fire from their second line of works. Many officers

without men and men without officers who had been driven from our line on the right came to our assistance and fought nobly, many of these from the Sixth Corps, and all were inspired by the one serious thought that we must hold this point or lose all we had gained that morning. It was a life or death contest. Their massed columns pushed forward to the "Bloody Angle." The stars and stripes and the stars and bars nearly touched each other across these works. Here were displayed on both sides of the breastworks more acts of individual bravery and heroism than I had yet seen in the war during three years of hard service. The gray and blue coats with rifles in hand would spring on top of the breastworks, take deadly aim and fire, then fall dead in the trenches below. This I saw again and again. More troops came to our aid and took a hand in the fight.

A new line of troops from different commands was formed at an obtuse angle from this fighting line to stay the progress of the enemy on our right; but no sooner was it formed than it was swept away by the enemy's deadly fire. The 16th Massachusetts, one of my regiments here on the left of my brigade, lost heavily, and its brave commander, Waldo Merriam, was killed. Here, also, Thomas W. Eayre, Assistant Adjutant-General of General Mott's staff, was killed.

It was in our immediate front that the large tree was cut down by rifle-balls, the stump of which was exhibited at the Centennial Exposition at Philadelphia. As night closed about us, the moment we would slacken fire the enemy would close in upon us, so determined were they to carry this point. Had they succeeded in driving us from it, all we had gained that morning would have been lost. Not till about 3 o'clock on the morning of the 13th did the battle cease. A dead and dying mass of humanity was lying in the Confederate trenches, while on our side the ground was covered with the dead.

Never during the war did braver men meet each other in battle than here.

‡ On the 13th came an order for consolidation, by which this brigade became the Third Brigade, Third Division, Second Corps, under which name it continued to the end of the war.— R. McA.

GENERAL EDWARDS'S BRIGADE AT THE BLOODY ANGLE.

BY JAMES L. BOWEN, HISTORIAN OF THE 37TH MASSACHUSETTS REGIMENT.

IN the article entitled "Hand-to-hand Fighting at Spotsylvania," the author, while generally accurate and graphic, omits any reference to that brigade of the Sixth Corps (Colonel Oliver Edwards's Fourth Brigade, Second Division) which was first engaged there, which was holding the key to the position when his own (Upton's) brigade came upon the field, and which fought longer than any other brigade of the Sixth Corps engaged. On that day the brigade had present for duty three small regiments, the 10th and 37th Massachusetts and the 2d Rhode Island. When the First and Second Divisions of the Sixth Corps, which had been massed the previous evening, were summoned to the support of Hancock, whose Second Corps had penetrated the Confederate lines, General Wright, who had just assumed command of the Sixth Corps, directed that the first brigade under arms and ready to move should lead the way. Edwards's brigade was first in line and led the march of the corps. It moved to the vicinity of the Landrum House, passing the Confederate generals and some of the prisoners who had been captured by Hancock, and, reaching the edge of the woods facing the scene of action, came into line of battle facing by the rear rank, and advanced toward the captured works with the 10th Massachusetts on the right, the 2d Rhode Island in the center, and the 37th Massachusetts on the left.

The situation at this time was simply this : The force of the Second Corps' attack had of itself broken up the organization of that command; the mass of men had been withdrawn to the outer face of the Confederate works and re-formed as well as possible under the circumstances. By the time this was accomplished the Confederates were prepared to undertake the recapture of the works they had lost. Then it was that Edwards's brigade moved forward and occupied the outer face of the intrenchments, relieving some troops already there and connecting with the Excelsior Brigade. As it came into position, it covered the nose or apex of the angle with the Rhode Island regiment, the 10th Massachusetts extending along the right face.

The brigade was scarcely in position when the Confederates advanced to the attack, the ground being extremely favorable for their purpose. On their side of the works it was wooded, and, in addition, scarcely forty yards to the rear of the fortifications was a hollow or ravine which formed a natural siege approach. In that ravine, almost within pistol-shot of the Union lines, they were enabled to form columns of assault entirely screened from view, and the resulting attack had the appearance of lines of battle suddenly springing from the bosom of the earth. Three times in rapid succession their columns formed and rushed upon the angle, and as often did Edwards and his 900 men repel them. To the right of Edwards's position, however, the defense was not so successful; the Union troops were driven back from the intrenchments, and the enemy, crossing the works and taking position in a piece of woods, gave an enfilading fire on Edwards's right, so severe and well directed that it threw the 10th Massachusetts into confusion. It was at this time that Upton's brigade came upon the field and, in the words of that officer himself, encountered so severe a fire that it was unable to occupy the intrenchments, but resting its left on them, near Edwards's right, lay down and opened fire.

As soon as the development of the Union line to the right relieved the flank fire somewhat, the 10th Massachusetts was returned to its place in the works, and throughout the remainder of that day the brigade held its position with a fire so deadly and well directed that no hostile lines of battle could live to cross the few yards between the works and the ravine spoken of. Once, indeed, by the use of a white flag the Confederates came near accomplishing by stratagem what they had failed to do by force of arms. This emblem of peace being displayed in front of the Fourth Brigade, an officer ranking Edwards, but himself ranked by General Eustis, who was present, unjustifiably ordered the Fourth Brigade to cease firing. Instantly the purpose of the movement was shown by the dash of the Confederate line of battle for the coveted works. Fortunately, however, Edwards and his command were on the alert, and repulsed the attack, but not until the hostile colors were for a moment planted on the works,—the only instance during the day in which anything like a line of battle was enabled to advance so far at that point.

Near night the brigade was relieved, but the 37th Massachusetts was almost immediately ordered back to hold the works, which had been vacated by a regiment of the Second Corps that was out of ammunition. The guns of the 37th also were empty, but they pushed their bayonets under the head log, and held the works until a fresh supply of ammunition could be procured, when the firing was resumed and continued until 3 o'clock on the morning of the 13th.

This regiment was in action continually for more than twenty hours, during which time it fired over four hundred rounds per man. At one time its guns became so foul that they could no longer be used, many of them bursting in the hands of the men. As it was impossible to relieve the line, a regiment from the Second Corps exchanged guns with the 37th, enabling the latter to continue its fire. It was in front of the right wing of this regiment and almost directly in the rear of the apex that the oak-tree, twenty-one inches in diameter, was cut down by bullets and fell within the Confederate lines. I believe every regiment that fought anywhere in that part of the field claims to have shot down this particular tree; but in truth no single organization is entitled to all the credit. The tree fell during the night, near midnight in fact, and hours after the firing had virtually ceased on all parts of the line save at this vital point.

GENERAL GRANT RECONNOITERING THE CONFEDERATE POSITION AT SPOTSYLVANIA COURT HOUSE.
FROM A SKETCH MADE AT THE TIME.

Mr. Reed, the artist, belonged to Bigelow's 9th Massachusetts battery, which, with a battery of the 5th Regular Artillery, was holding the Fredericksburg road (see map, p. 167) at the place where General Grant made his observation. The troops seen in the background are the 9th Massachusetts Volunteers, who at the time were crossing the road from the left toward the right of the line.— EDITORS.

BEATING THE LONG ROLL.

THE OPPOSING FORCES AT THE BEGINNING OF GRANT'S CAMPAIGN AGAINST RICHMOND.

For much of the information contained in this list and in similar lists to follow, the editors are indebted (in advance of the publication of the "Official Records") to Brigadier-General Richard C. Drum, Adjutant-General of the Army. During the movement to Cold Harbor some consolidations of brigades and divisions were made, organizations mustered out, and reënforcements received. For the composition of the army, June 1st, see pp. 184-87. The impossibility of obtaining complete data relative to the casualties among officers in this campaign makes it necessary to omit such information.— EDITORS.

THE UNION ARMY — Lieutenant-General, Ulysses S. Grant.

Escort: B, F and K, 5th U. S. Cav., Capt. Julius W. Mason.

ARMY OF THE POTOMAC, Maj.-Gen. George G. Meade.

Provost Guard, Brig.-Gen. Marsena R. Patrick: C and D, 1st Mass. Cav., Capt. Edward A. Flint; 80th N. Y. Inf. (20th Militia), Col. Theodore B. Gates; 3d Pa. Cav., Maj. James W. Walsh; 68th Pa. Inf., Lieut.-Col. Robert E. Winslow; 114th Pa. Inf., Col. Charles H. T. Collis.

Volunteer Engineer Brigade, ⚓ Brig.-Gen. Henry W. Benham: 15th N. Y. Engineers, Maj. William A. Ketchum; 50th N. Y. Engineers, Lieut.-Col. Ira Spaulding. *Battalion U. S. Engineers,* Capt. George H. Mendell. *Guards and Orderlies:* Oneida (N. Y.) Cav., Capt. Daniel P. Mann.

SECOND ARMY CORPS, Maj.-Gen. Winfield S. Hancock.

Escort: M, 1st Vt. Cav., Capt. John H. Hazelton.

FIRST DIVISION, Brig.-Gen. Francis C. Barlow.

First Brigade, Col. Nelson A. Miles: 26th Mich., Maj. Lemuel Saviers; 61st N. Y., Lieut.-Col. K. O. Broady; 81st Pa., Col. H. Boyd McKeen; 140th Pa., Col. John Fraser; 183d Pa., Col. George P. McLean. *Second Brigade*, Col. Thomas A. Smyth: 28th Mass., Lieut.-Col. Geo. W. Cartwright; 63d N. Y., Maj. Thomas Touhy; 69th N. Y., Capt. Richard Moroney; 88th N. Y., Capt. Denis F. Burke; 116th Pa., Lieut.-Col. Richard C. Dale. *Third Brigade*, Col. Paul Frank: 39th N. Y., Col. Augus-

tus Funk; 52d N. Y. (detachment 7th N. Y. attached), Maj. Henry M. Karples; 57th N. Y., Lieut.-Col. Alford B. Chapman; 111th N. Y., Capt. Aaron P. Seeley; 125th N. Y., Lieut.-Col. Aaron B. Myer; 126th N. Y., Capt. Winfield Scott. *Fourth Brigade*, Col. John R. Brooke: 2d Del., Col. William P. Baily; 64th N. Y., Maj. Leman W. Bradley; 66th N. Y., Lieut.-Col. John S. Hammell; 53d Pa., Lieut.-Col. Richards McMichael; 145th Pa., Col. Hiram L. Brown; 148th Pa., Col. James A. Beaver.

SECOND DIVISION, Brig.-Gen. John Gibbon.

Provost Guard: 2d Co. Minn. Sharp-shooters, Capt. Mahlon Black.

First Brigade, Brig.-Gen. Alex. S. Webb: 19th Me., Col. Selden Connor; 1st Co. Andrew (Mass.) Sharpshooters, Lieut. Samuel G. Gilbreth; 15th Mass., Maj. I. Harris Hooper; 19th Mass., Maj. Edmund Rice; 20th Mass., Maj. Henry L. Abbott; 7th Mich., Maj. Sylvanus W. Curtis; 42d N. Y., Maj. Patrick J. Downing; 59th N. Y., Capt. William McFadden; 82d N. Y. (2d Militia), Col. Henry W. Hudson. *Second Brigade*, Brig.-Gen. Joshua T. Owen: 152d N. Y., Lieut.-Col. George W. Thompson; 69th Pa., Maj. William Davis; 71st Pa., Lieut.-Col. Charles Kochersperger; 72d Pa., Col. De Witt C. Baxter; 106th Pa., Capt. Robert H. Ford. *Third Brigade*, Col. Samuel S. Carroll: 14th Conn., Col. Theodore G. Ellis; 1st Del., Lieut.-Col. Daniel Woodall; 14th Ind., Col. John Coons; 12th N. J., Lieut.-Col. Thomas H. Davis; 10th N. Y. (Battalion), Capt. George M. Dewey;

⚓ With the exception of eleven companies of the 50th N. Y. under Lieut.-Col. Spaulding, this command, with its commander, was at the Engineer Depot, Washington, D. C.

179

108th N. Y., Col. Charles J. Powers; 4th Ohio, Lieut.-Col. Leonard W. Carpenter; 8th Ohio, Lieut.-Col. Franklin Sawyer; 7th W. Va., Lieut.-Col. J. H. Lockwood.

THIRD DIVISION, Maj.-Gen. David B. Birney.

First Brigade, Brig.-Gen. J. H. H. Ward: 20th Ind., Col. W. C. L. Taylor; 3d Me., Col. Moses B. Lakeman; 40th N. Y., Col. Thomas W. Egan; 86th N. Y., Lieut.-Col. Jacob H. Lansing; 124th N. Y., Col. Francis M. Cummins; 99th Pa., Lieut.-Col. Edwin R. Biles; 110th Pa., Lieut.-Col. Isaac Rogers; 141st Pa., Lieut.-Col. Guy H. Watkins; 2d U. S. Sharp-shooters, Lieut.-Col. Homer R. Stoughton. *Second Brigade*, Brig.-Gen. Alexander Hays: 4th Me., Col. Elijah Walker; 17th Me., Col. George W. West; 3d Mich., Col. Byron R. Pierce; 5th Mich., Lieut.-Col. John Pulford; 93d N. Y., Maj. Samuel McConihe; 57th Pa., Col. Peter Sides; 63d Pa., Lieut.-Col. John A. Danks; 105th Pa., Col. Calvin A. Craig; 1st U. S. Sharp-shooters, Maj. Charles P. Mattocks.

FOURTH DIVISION, Brig.-Gen. Gershom Mott.

First Brigade, Col. Robert McAllister: 1st Mass., Col. N. B. McLaughlen; 16th Mass., Lieut.-Col. Waldo Merriam; 5th N. J., Col. William J. Sewell; 6th N. J., Lieut.-Col. Stephen R. Gilkyson; 7th N. J., Maj. Frederick Cooper; 8th N. J., Col. John Ramsey; 11th N. J., Lieut.-Col. John Schoonover; 26th Pa., Maj. Samuel G. Moffett; 115th Pa., Maj. William A. Reilly. *Second Brigade*, Col. William R. Brewster: 11th Mass., Col. William Blaisdell; 70th N. Y., Capt. William H. Hugo; 71st N. Y., Lieut.-Col. Thomas Rafferty; 72d N. Y., Lieut.-Col. John Leonard; 73d N. Y., Lieut.-Col. Michael W. Burns; 74th N. Y., Lieut.-Col. Thomas Holt; 120th N. Y., Capt. Abram L. Lockwood; 84th Pa., Lieut.-Col. Milton Opp.

ARTILLERY BRIGADE, Col. John C. Tidball: 6th Me., Capt. Edwin B. Dow; 10th Mass., Capt. J. Henry Sleeper; 1st N. H., Capt. Fred. M. Edgell; G, 1st N. Y., Capt. Nelson Ames; 4th N. Y. Heavy (Third Battalion), Lieut.-Col. Thomas R. Allcock; F, 1st Pa., Capt. R. Bruce Ricketts; A, 1st R. I., Capt. William A. Arnold; B, 1st R. I., Capt. T. Fred Brown; K, 4th U. S., Lieut. John W. Roder; C and I, 5th U. S., Lieut. James Gilliss.

FIFTH ARMY CORPS, Maj.-Gen. Gouverneur K. Warren.

Provost Guard: 12th N. Y., Battalion, Maj. Henry W. Rider.

FIRST DIVISION, Brig.-Gen. Charles Griffin.

First Brigade, Brig.-Gen. Romeyn B. Ayres: 140th N. Y., Col. George Ryan; 146th N. Y., Col. David T. Jenkins; 91st Pa., Lieut.-Col. Joseph H. Sinex; 155th Pa., Lieut.-Col. Alfred L. Pearson; B, C, F, H, I, and K, 2d U. S., Capt. James W. Long; B, C, D, E, F, and G, 1st Battalion 11th U. S., Capt. Francis M. Cooley; A, B, C, D, and G, 1st Battalion, and A, C, D, F, and H, 2d Battalion 12th U. S., Maj. Luther B. Bruen; 1st Battalion 14th U. S., Capt. E. McK. Hudson; A, C, D, G, and H, 1st Battalion, and A, B, and C, 2d Battalion 17th U. S., Capt. James F. Grimes. *Second Brigade*, Col. Jacob B. Sweitzer: 9th Mass., Col. Patrick R. Guiney; 22d Mass. (2d Co. Mass. S. S. attached), Col. William S. Tilton; 32d Mass., Col. George L. Prescott; 4th Mich., Lieut.-Col. George W. Lumbard; 62d Pa., Lieut.-Col. James C. Hull. *Third Brigade*, Brig.-Gen. Joseph J. Bartlett: 20th Me., Maj. Ellis Spear; 18th Mass., Col. Joseph Hayes; 1st Mich., Lieut.-Col. William A. Throop; 16th Mich., Maj. Robert T. Elliott; 44th N. Y., Lieut.-Col. Freeman Conner; 83d Pa., Col. O. S. Woodward; 118th Pa., Col. James Gwyn.

SECOND DIVISION, Brig.-Gen. John C. Robinson.

First Brigade, Col. Samuel H. Leonard: 16th Me., Col. Charles W. Tilden; 13th Mass., Capt. Charles H. Hovey; 39th Mass., Col. Phineas S. Davis; 104th N. Y., Col. Gilbert G. Prey. *Second Brigade*, Brig.-Gen. Henry Baxter: 12th Mass., Col. James L. Bates; 83d N. Y. (9th Militia), Col. Joseph A. Moesch; 97th N. Y., Col. Charles Wheelock; 11th Pa., Col. Richard Coulter; 88th Pa., Capt. George B. Rhoads; 90th Pa., Col. Peter Lyle. *Third Brigade*, Col. Andrew W. Denison: 1st Md., Maj. Benj. H. Schley; 4th Md., Col. Richard N. Bowerman; 7th Md., Col. Charles E. Phelps; 8th Md., Lieut.-Col. John G. Johannes.

THIRD DIVISION (Pennsylvania Reserves), Brig.-Gen. Samuel W. Crawford.

First Brigade, Col. William McCandless: 1st Pa., Col. William C. Talley; 2d Pa., Lieut.-Col. Patrick McDonough; 6th Pa., Col. Wellington H. Ent; 7th Pa., Maj. LeGrand B. Speece; 11th Pa., Col. Samuel M. Jackson; 13th Pa. (1st Rifles), Maj. W. R. Hartshorn. *Third Brigade*, Col. Joseph W. Fisher: 5th Pa., Lieut.-Col. George Dare; 8th Pa., Col. Silas M. Baily; 10th Pa., Lieut.-Col. Ira Ayer, Jr.; 12th Pa., Lieut.-Col. Richard Gustin.

FOURTH DIVISION, Brig.-Gen. James S. Wadsworth.

First Brigade, Brig.-Gen. Lysander Cutler: 7th Ind., Col. Ira G. Grover; 19th Ind., Col. Samuel J. Williams; 24th Mich., Col. Henry A. Morrow; 1st N. Y. Battalion Sharp-shooters, Capt. Volney J. Shipman; 2d Wis., Lieut.-Col. John Mansfield; 6th Wis., Col. Edward S. Bragg; 7th Wis., Col. William W. Robinson. *Second Brigade*, Brig.-Gen. James C. Rice: 76th N. Y., Lieut.-Col. John E. Cook: 84th N. Y. (14th Militia), Col. Edward B. Fowler; 95th N. Y., Col. Edward Pye; 147th N. Y., Col. Francis C. Miller; 56th Pa., Col. J. Wm. Hofmann. *Third Brigade*, Col. Roy Stone: 121st Pa., Capt. Samuel T. Lloyd; 142d Pa., Maj. Horatio N. Warren; 143d Pa., Col. Edmund L. Dana; 149th Pa., Lieut.-Col. John Irvin; 150th Pa., Capt. George W. Jones.

ARTILLERY BRIGADE, Col. Charles S. Wainwright: 3d Mass., Capt. Augustus P. Martin; 5th Mass., Capt. Charles A. Phillips; D, 1st N. Y., Capt. George B. Winslow; E and L, 1st N. Y., Lieut. George Breck; H, 1st N. Y., Capt. Charles E. Mink; 2d Battalion 4th N. Y. Heavy, Maj. William Arthur; B, 1st Pa., Capt. James H. Cooper; B, 4th U. S., Lieut. James Stewart; D, 5th U. S., Lieut. B. F. Rittenhouse.

SIXTH ARMY CORPS, Maj.-Gen. John Sedgwick.

Escort: A, 8th Pa. Cav., Capt. Charles E. Fellows.

FIRST DIVISION, Brig.-Gen. Horatio G. Wright.

First Brigade, Col. Henry W. Brown: 1st N. J., Lieut.-Col. William Henry, Jr.; 2d N. J., Lieut.-Col. Charles Wiebecke; 3d N. J., Capt. Samuel T. Du Bois; 4th N. J., Lieut.-Col. Charles Ewing; 10th N. J., Col. Henry O. Ryerson; 15th N. J., Col. William H. Penrose. *Second Brigade*, Col. Emory Upton: 5th Me., Col. Clark S. Edwards; 121st N. Y., Lieut.-Col. Egbert Olcott; 95th Pa., Lieut.-Col. Edward Carroll; 96th Pa., Lieut.-Col. William H. Lessig. *Third Brigade*, Brig.-Gen. David A. Russell: 6th Me., Maj. George Fuller; 49th Pa., Col. Thomas M. Hulings; 119th Pa., Maj. Henry P. Truefitt, Jr.; 5th Wis., Lieut.-Col. Theodore B. Catlin. *Fourth Brigade*, Brig.-Gen. Alexander Shaler: 65th N. Y., Col. Joseph E. Hamblin; 67th N. Y., Col. Nelson Cross; 122d N. Y., Lieut.-Col. Augustus W. Dwight; 82d Pa. (detachment).

SECOND DIVISION, Brig.-Gen. George W. Getty.

First Brigade, Brig.-Gen. Frank Wheaton: 62d N. Y., Col. David J. Nevin; 93d Pa., Lieut.-Col. John S. Long; 98th Pa., Col. John F. Ballier; 102d Pa., Col. John W. Patterson; 139th Pa., Lieut.-Col. William H. Moody. *Second Brigade*, Col. Lewis A. Grant: 2d Vt., Col. Newton Stone; 3d Vt., Col. Thomas O. Seaver; 4th Vt., Col. George P. Foster; 5th Vt., Lieut.-Col. John R. Lewis; 6th Vt., Col. Elisha L. Barney. *Third Brigade*, Brig.-Gen. Thomas H. Neill: 7th Me., Col. Edwin C. Mason; 43d N. Y., Lieut.-Col. John Wilson; 49th N. Y., Col. Daniel D. Bidwell; 77th N. Y., Maj. Nathan S. Babcock; 61st Pa., Col. George F. Smith. *Fourth Brigade*, Brig.-Gen. Henry L. Eustis: 7th Mass., Col. Thomas D. Johns; 10th Mass., Lieut.-Col. Joseph B. Parsons; 37th Mass., Col. Oliver Edwards; 2d R. I., Lieut.-Col. S. B. M. Read.

THIRD DIVISION, Brig.-Gen. James B. Ricketts.

First Brigade, Brig.-Gen. William H. Morris: 14th N. J., Lieut.-Col. Caldwell K. Hall; 106th N. Y., Lieut.-Col. Charles Townsend; 151st N. Y., Lieut.-Col. Thomas M. Fay; 87th Pa., Col. John W. Schall; 10th Vt., Lieut.-Col. William W. Henry. *Second Brigade*, Brig.-Gen. Truman Seymour: 6th Md., Col. John W. Horn; 110th Ohio, Col. J. Warren Keifer; 122d Ohio, Col. William H. Ball; 126th Ohio, Col. Benj. F. Smith; 67th Pa. (detachment), Capt. George W. Guss; 138th Pa., Col. Matthew R. McClennan.

ARTILLERY BRIGADE, Col. Charles H. Tompkins: 4th Me., Lieut. Melville C. Kimball; 1st Mass., Capt.

William H. McCartney; 1st N. Y., Capt. Andrew Cowan; 3d N. Y., Capt. William A. Harn; 4th N. Y. Heavy (First Battalion), Maj. Thomas D. Sears; C, 1st R. I., Capt. Richard Waterman; E, 1st R. I., Capt. William B. Rhodes; G, 1st R. I., Capt. George W. Adams; M, 5th U. S., Capt. James McKnight.

NINTH ARMY CORPS,↓ Major-General Ambrose E. Burnside.

Provost Guard : 8th U. S., Capt. Milton Cogswell.

FIRST DIVISION, Brig.-Gen. Thomas G. Stevenson.

First Brigade, Col. Sumner Carruth: 35th Mass., Maj. Nathaniel Wales; 56th Mass., Col. Charles E. Griswold; 57th Mass., Col. William F. Bartlett; 59th Mass., Col. J. Parker Gould; 4th U. S., Capt. Charles H. Brightly; 10th U. S., Maj. Samuel B. Hayman. *Second Brigade*, Col. Daniel Leasure: 3d Md., Col. Joseph M. Sudsburg; 21st Mass., Lieut.-Col. George P. Hawkes; 100th Pa., Lieut.-Col. Matthew M. Dawson. *Artillery :* 2d Me., Capt. Albert F. Thomas; 14th Mass., Capt. J. W. B. Wright.

SECOND DIVISION, Brig.-Gen. Robert B. Potter.

First Brigade, Col. Zenas R. Bliss: 36th Mass., Maj. William F. Draper; 58th Mass., Lieut.-Col. John C. Whiton; 51st N. Y., Col. Charles W. Le Gendre; 45th Pa., Col. John I. Curtin; 48th Pa., Lieut.-Col. Henry Pleasants; 7th R. I., Capt. Theodore Winn. *Second Brigade*, Col. Simon G. Griffin: 31st Me., Lieut.-Col. Thomas Hight; 32d Me., Maj. Arthur Deering; 6th N. H., Lieut.-Col. Henry H. Pearson; 9th N. H., Lieut.-Col. John W. Babbitt; 11th N. H., Col. Walter Harriman; 17th Vt., Lieut.-Col. Charles Cummings. *Artillery :* 11th Mass., Capt. Edward J. Jones; 19th N. Y., Capt. Edward W. Rogers.

THIRD DIVISION, Brig.-Gen. Orlando B. Willcox.

First Brigade, Col. John F. Hartranft: 2d Mich., Col. William Humphrey; 8th Mich., Col. Frank Graves; 17th Mich., Col. Constant Luce; 27th Mich. (1st and 2d Co's Mich. Sharp-shooters attached), Maj. Samuel Moody; 109th U. S., Col. Benjamin F. Tracy; 51st Pa., Lieut.-Col. Edwin Schall. *Second Brigade*, Col. Benjamin C. Christ: 1st Mich. Sharp-shooters, Col. Charles V. De Land; 20th Mich., Lieut.-Col. Byron M. Cutcheon; 79th N. Y., Col. David Morrison; 60th Ohio (9th and 10th Co's Ohio Sharp-shooters attached), Lieut.-Col. James N. McElroy; 50th Pa., Lieut.-Col. Edward Overton, Jr. *Artillery :* 7th Me., Capt. Adelbert B. Twitchell; 34th N. Y., Capt. Jacob Roemer.

FOURTH DIVISION,♭ Brig.-Gen. Edward Ferrero.

First Brigade, Col. Joshua K. Sigfried: 27th U. S., Lieut.-Col. Charles J. Wright; 30th U. S., Col. Delavan Bates; 39th U. S., Col. Ozora P. Stearns; 43d U. S., Lieut.-Col. H. Seymour Hall. *Second Brigade*, Col. Henry G. Thomas: 30th Conn. (detachment), Capt. Charles Robinson; 19th U. S., Lieut. Joseph Perkins; 23d U. S., Lieut.-Col. Cleveland J. Campbell. *Artillery :* D, Pa., Capt. George W. Durell; 3d Vt., Capt. Romeo H. Start.

CAVALRY: 3d N. Y., Col. Andrew J. Morrison; 22d N. Y., Col. Samuel J. Crooks; 2d Ohio, Lieut.-Col. George A. Purington; 13th Pa., Maj. Michael Kerwin.

RESERVE ARTILLERY, Capt. John Edwards, Jr.: 27th N. Y., Capt. John B. Eaton; D, 1st R. I., Capt. William W. Buckley; H, 1st R. I., Capt. Crawford Allen, Jr.; E, 2d U. S., Lieut. James S. Dudley; G, 3d U. S., Lieut. Edmund Pendleton; L and M, 3d U. S., Lieut. Erskine Gittings.

PROVISIONAL BRIGADE, Col. Elisha G. Marshall: 24th N. Y. Cav. (dismounted), Col. William C. Raulston; 14th N. Y. Heavy Art'y, Lieut.-Col. Clarence H. Corning; 2d Pa. Prov. Heavy Art'y, Col. Thomas Wilhelm.

CAVALRY CORPS, Maj.-Gen. Philip H. Sheridan.

Escort : 6th U. S., Capt. Ira W. Claflin.

FIRST DIVISION, Brig.-Gen. A. T. A. Torbert.

First Brigade, Brig.-Gen. George A. Custer: 1st Mich., Lieut.-Col. Peter Stagg; 5th Mich., Col. Russell A. Alger; 6th Mich., Maj. James H. Kidd; 7th Mich., Maj. Henry W. Granger. *Second Brigade*, Col. Thomas C. Devin: 4th N. Y. (guarding trains), Lieut.-Col. William R. Parnell; 6th N. Y., Lieut.-Col. William H. Crocker;

9th N. Y., Col. William Sackett; 17th Pa., Lieut.-Col. James Q. Anderson. *Reserve Brigade*, Brig.-Gen. Wesley Merritt: 19th N. Y. (1st Dragoons), Col. Alfred Gibbs; 6th Pa., Maj. James Starr; 1st U. S., Capt. Nelson B. Sweitzer; 2d U. S., Capt. T. F. Rodenbough; 5th U. S., Capt. Abraham K. Arnold.

SECOND DIVISION, Brig.-Gen. David McM. Gregg.

First Brigade, Brig.-Gen. Henry E. Davies. Jr.: 1st Mass., Maj. Lucius M. Sargent; 1st N. J., Lieut.-Col. John W. Kester; 6th Ohio, Col. William Stedman; 1st Pa., Col. John P. Taylor. *Second Brigade*, Col. J. Irvin Gregg: 1st Me., Col. Charles H. Smith; 10th N. Y., Maj. M. Henry Avery; 2d Pa., Lieut.-Col. Joseph P. Brinton; 4th Pa., Lieut.-Col. George H. Covode; 8th Pa., Lieut.-Col. Samuel Wilson; 16th Pa., Lieut.-Col. John K. Robison.

THIRD DIVISION, Brig.-Gen. James H. Wilson.

Escort : 8th Ill. (detachment), Lieut. William W. Long. *First Brigade*, Col. Timothy M. Bryan, Jr., Col. John B. McIntosh: 1st Conn., Maj. Erastus Blakeslee; 2d.N. Y., Col. Otto Harhaus; 5th N. Y., Lieut.-Col. John Hammond; 18th Pa., Lieut.-Col. William P. Brinton. *Second Brigade*, Col. George H. Chapman: 3d Ind., Maj. William Patton; 8th N. Y., Lieut.-Col. William H. Benjamin; 1st Vt., Lieut.-Col. Addison W. Preston.

ARTILLERY, Brig.-Gen. Henry J. Hunt.

Artillery Reserve, Col. Henry S. Burton.

First Brigade, Col. J. Howard Kitching: 6th N. Y. Heavy, Lieut.-Col. Edmund R. Travis; 15th N. Y. Heavy, Col. Louis Schirmer. *Second Brigade*, Maj. John A. Tompkins: 5th Me., Capt. Greenleaf T. Stevens; 1st N. J., Capt. William Hexamer; 2d N. J., Capt. A. Judson Clark; 5th N. Y., Capt. Elijah D. Taft; 12th N. Y., Capt. George F. McKnight; B, 1st N. Y., Capt. Albert S. Sheldon. *Third Brigade*, Maj. Robert H. Fitzhugh: 9th Mass., Capt. John Bigelow; 15th N. Y., Capt. Patrick Hart; C, 1st N. Y., Lieut. William H. Phillips; 11th N. Y., Capt. John E. Burton; H, 1st Ohio, Lieut. William A. Ewing; E, 5th U. S., Lieut. John R. Brinckle.

HORSE ARTILLERY.

First Brigade, ⸗ Capt. James M. Robertson: 6th N. Y., Capt. Joseph W. Martin; B and L, 2d U. S., Lieut. Edward Heaton; D, 2d U. S., Lieut. Edward B. Williston; M, 2d U. S., Lieut. A. C. M. Pennington; A, 4th U. S., Lieut. Rufus King, Jr.; C and E, 4th U. S., Lieut. Charles L. Fitzhugh. *Second Brigade*, Capt. Dunbar R. Ransom: E and G, 1st U. S., Lieut. Frank S. French; H and I, Capt. Alanson M. Randol; K, 1st U. S., Lieut. John Egan; A, 2d U. S., Lieut. Robert Clarke; G, 2d U. S., Lieut. William N. Dennison; C, F and K, 3d U. S., Lieut. James R. Kelly.

ARMY OF THE JAMES, Maj.-Gen. Benj. F. Butler.

TENTH ARMY CORPS, Maj.-Gen. Quincy A. Gillmore.

FIRST DIVISION, Brig.-Gen. Alfred H. Terry.

First Brigade, Col. Joshua B. Howell: 39th Ill., Col. Thomas O. Osborn; 62d Ohio, Col. Francis B. Pond; 67th Ohio, Col. Alvin C. Voris; 85th Pa., Lieut.-Col. Edward Campbell; *Second Brigade*, Col. Joseph R. Hawley: 6th Conn., Lieut.-Col. Lorenzo Meeker; 7th Conn., Lieut.-Col. Daniel C. Rodman; 3d N. H., Lieut.-Col. Josiah I. Plimpton; 7th N. H., Col. Joseph C. Abbott. *Third Brigade*, Col. Harris M. Plaisted: 10th Conn., Col. John L. Otis; 11th Me., Lieut.-Col. Winslow P. Spofford; 24th Mass., Col. Francis A. Osborn; 100th N. Y., Col. George B. Dandy. *Artillery :* 1st Conn., Capt. Alfred P. Rockwell; 5th N. J., Capt. Zenas C. Warren; M, 1st U. S., Capt. Loomis L. Langdon.

SECOND DIVISION, Brig.-Gen. John W. Turner.

First Brigade, Col. Samuel M. Alford : 40th Mass., Col. Guy V. Henry; 3d N. Y., Lieut.-Col. Eldridge G. Floyd; 89th N. Y., Lieut.-Col. Theophilus L. England; 117th N. Y., Col. Alvin White; 142d N. Y., Col. N. Martin Curtis. *Second Brigade*, Col. William B. Barton : 47th N. Y., Lieut.-Col. Christopher R. McDonald; 48th N. Y., Lieut.-

↓ This corps participated in the Wilderness and Spotsylvania campaigns, under the direct orders of Lieut.-Gen. U. S. Grant, until May 24th, 1864, when it was assigned to the Army of the Potomac.

♭ All the infantry were colored troops.   ⸗ Detached with Cavalry Corps.

Col. Dudley W. Strickland; 115th N. Y., Maj. Ezra L. Walrath; 76th Pa., Col. John C. Campbell. *Artillery:* 4th N. J., Capt. George T. Woodbury; B, 1st U. S., Capt. Samuel S. Elder; D, 1st U. S., Lieut. John S. Gibbs.

THIRD DIVISION, Brig.-Gen. Adelbert Ames.

First Brigade, Col. Richard White: 8th Me., Lieut.-Col. Henry Boynton; 4th N. H., Col. Louis Bell; 55th Pa., Lieut.-Col. Frank T. Bennett; 97th Pa., Col. Henry R. Guss. *Second Brigade,* Col. Jeremiah C. Drake: 13th Ind., Col. Cyrus J. Dobbs; 9th Me., Col. Sabine Emery; 112th N. Y., Lieut.-Col. Elial F. Carpenter; 169th N. Y., Col. John McConihe. *Artillery:* 33d N. Y., Capt. Alger M. Wheeler; C, 3d R. I., Capt. Martin S. James; E, 3d U. S., Lieut. Joseph P. Sanger.

UNATTACHED TROOPS: 1st N. Y. Engineers (8 co's), Col. Edward W. Serrell; 4th Mass. Cav. (First Battalion), Capt. Lucius Richmond.

EIGHTEENTH ARMY CORPS, Maj.-Gen. William F. Smith.

FIRST DIVISION, Brig.-Gen. William T. H. Brooks.

First Brigade, Brig.-Gen. Gilman Marston: 81st N. Y., Col. Jacob J. De Forest; 96th N. Y., Col. Edgar M. Cullen; 98th N. Y., Col. Frederick F. Wead; 139th N. Y., Col. Samuel H. Roberts. *Second Brigade,* Brig.-Gen. Hiram Burnham: 8th Conn., Col. John E. Ward; 10th N. H., Lieut.-Col. John Coughlin; 13th N. H., Col. Aaron F. Stevens; 118th N. Y., Col. Oliver Keese, Jr. *Third Brigade,* Col. Horace T. Sanders: 92d N. Y., Lieut.-Col. Hiram Anderson, Jr.; 58th Pa., Lieut.-Col. Montgomery Martin; 188th Pa., Lieut.-Col. George K. Bowen; 19th Wis., Lieut.-Col. Rollin M. Strong. *Artillery Brigade,* Maj. Theodore H. Schenck: 4th Wis., Capt. George B. Easterly; L, 4th U. S., Lieut. John S. Hunt; A, 5th U. S., Lieut. Charles P. Muhlenberg.

SECOND DIVISION, Brig.-Gen. Godfrey Weitzel.

First Brigade, Brig.-Gen. Charles A. Heckman: 23d Mass., Col. Andrew Elwell; 25th Mass., Maj. Cornelius G. Atwood; 27th Mass., Col. Horace C. Lee; 9th N. J., Col. Abram Zabriskie. *Second Brigade,* Col. Griffin A. Stedman: 11th Conn., Lieut.-Col. Wm. C. Moegling; 2d N. H., Col. Edward L. Bailey; 12th N. H., Maj. John F. Langley; 148th N. Y., Col. George M. Guion. *Artillery Brigade,* Capt. Frederick M. Follett: 7th N. Y., Capt. Peter C. Regan; E, 3d N. Y., Capt. George E. Ashby; F, 1st R. I., Capt. James Belger; D, 4th U. S., Lieut. James Thompson.

THIRD DIVISION, ☆ Brig.-Gen. Edward W. Hinks.

First Brigade, Brig.-Gen. Edward A. Wild: 1st U. S., Col. John H. Holman; 10th U. S., Lieut.-Col. Edward

H. Powell; 22d U. S., Col. Joseph B. Kiddoo; 37th U. S., Lieut.-Col. Abiel G. Chamberlain. *Second Brigade,* Col. Samuel A. Duncan: 4th U. S., Lieut.-Col. Geo. Rogers; 5th U. S., Col. James W. Conine; 6th U. S., Col. John W. Ames. *Artillery:* K, 3d N. Y., Capt. James R. Angel; M, 3d N. Y., Capt. John H. Howell; B, 2d U. S. (colored), Capt. Francis C. Choate.

UNATTACHED TROOPS: 1st N. Y. Mounted Rifles, Col. Benjamin F. Onderdonk.

CAVALRY DIVISION, Brig.-Gen. August V. Kautz.

First Brigade, Col. Simon H. Mix: 1st D. C., Lieut.-Col. Everton J. Conger; 3d N. Y., Lieut.-Col. George W. Lewis. *Second Brigade,* Col. Samuel P. Spear: 5th Pa., Lieut.-Col. Christopher Kleinz; 11th Pa., Lieut.-Col. George Stetzel. *Artillery:* 8th N. Y. (section), Lieut. Peter Morton.

UNATTACHED TROOPS: 1st U. S. Colored Cav., Maj. Harvey W. Brown; 2d U. S. Colored Cav., Col. George W. Cole; 13th Co. Mass. Heavy Art'y (pontoniers), Capt. John Pickering, Jr.

The effective strength of the Union army in the Wilderness is estimated at 118,000 of all arms.

The losses of this army (including those sustained by the reënforcements received at Spotsylvania and Smith's corps at Cold Harbor), from May 5th to June 15th, were as follows:

BATTLES, ETC.	Killed.	Wounded.	Captured or Missing.	Total.
The Wilderness....................	2246	12,037	3383	17,666
Spotsylvania	2725	13,416	2258	18,399
North Anna and Totopotomoy....	591	2,734	661	3,986
Cold Harbor and Bethesda Church	1844	9,077	1816	12,737
Sheridan's first expedition.........	64	337	224	625
Sheridan's second expedition......	150	741	625	1516
Grand total from the Wilderness to the James	7620	38,342	8967	54,929

During the same period Butler's army on the James River line numbered at its maximum about 36,000 effectives. Its losses amounted to 634 killed, 3903 wounded, and 1678 captured or missing = 6215, exclusive of the casualties sustained by W. F. Smith's command at Cold Harbor, which amounted to 448 killed, 2365 wounded, and 206 captured or missing = 3019, and which are included in the above table.

THE CONFEDERATE ARMY.

ARMY OF NORTHERN VIRGINIA — General Robert E. Lee.

FIRST ARMY CORPS, Lieut.-Gen. James Longstreet.

KERSHAW'S DIVISION, Brig.-Gen. Joseph B. Kershaw.

Kershaw's Brigade, Col. John W. Henagan: 2d S. C., Lieut.-Col. F. Gaillard; 3d S. C., Col. James D. Nance; 7th S. C., Capt. James Mitchell; 8th S. C., Lieut.-Col. E. T. Stackhouse; 15th S. C., Col. John B. Davis; 3d S. C. Battalion, Capt. B. M. Whitener. *Humphreys's Brigade,* Brig.-Gen. Benjamin G. Humphreys: 13th Miss., Maj. G. L. Donald; 17th Miss., ——; ⌡ 18th Miss., Capt. W. H. Lewis; 21st Miss., Col. D. N. Moody. *Wofford's Brigade,* Brig.-Gen. William T. Wofford: 16th Ga., ——; 18th Ga., ——; 24th Ga., ——; Cobb's Ga. Legion, ——; Phillips Ga. Legion, ——; 3d Ga. Battalion Sharp-shooters, ——. *Bryan's Brigade,* Brig.-Gen. Goode Bryan: 10th Ga., Col. Willis C. Holt; 50th Ga., Col. P. McGlashan; 51st Ga., Col. E. Ball; 53d Ga., Col. James P. Simms.

FIELD'S DIVISION, Maj.-Gen. Charles W. Field.

Jenkins's Brigade, Brig.-Gen. Micah Jenkins: 1st S. C., Col. James R. Hagood; 2d S. C. (Rifles), Col. R. E. Bowen; 5th S. C., Col. A. Coward; 6th S. C., Col. John

Bratton; Palmetto (S. C.) Sharp-shooters, Col. Joseph Walker. *Anderson's Brigade,* Brig.-Gen. George T. Anderson: 7th Ga., ——; 8th Ga., ——; 9th Ga., ——; 11th Ga., ——; 59th Ga., Lieut.-Col. B. H. Gee. *Law's Brigade,* Brig.-Gen. E. McIver Law: 4th Ala., Col. P. D. Bowles; 15th Ala., ——; 44th Ala., Col. W. F. Perry; 47th Ala., ——; 48th Ala., Lieut.-Col. W. M. Hardwick. *Gregg's Brigade,* Brig.-Gen. John Gregg: 3d Ark., Col. Van H. Manning; 1st Tex., ——; 4th Tex., Col. J. P. Bane; 5th Tex., Lieut.-Col. K. Bryan; *Benning's Brigade,* Brig.-Gen. Henry L. Benning: 2d Ga., ——; 15th Ga., Col. D. M. DuBose; 17th Ga., ——20th Ga., ——.

ARTILLERY, Brig.-Gen. E. Porter Alexander.

Huger's Battalion, Lieut.-Col. Frank Huger: Fickling's (Va.) Batt'y; Moody's (La.) Batt'y; Parker's (Va.) Batt'y; J. D. Smith's (Va.) Batt'y; Taylor's (Va.) Batt'y; Woolfolk's (Va.) Batt'y. *Haskell's Battalion,* Maj. John C. Haskell: Flanner's (N. C.) Batt'y; Garden's (S. C.) Batt'y; Lamkin's (Va.) Batt'y; Ramsay's (N. C.) Batt'y. *Cabell's Battalion,* Col. Henry C. Cabell: Callaway's

---

☆ All the infantry were colored troops.

⌡ Name not to be found in the "Official Records."

(Ga.) Batt'y; Carlton's (Ga.) Batt'y; McCarthy's (Va.) Batt'y; Manly's (N. C.) Batt'y.

SECOND ARMY CORPS, Lieut.-Gen. Richard S. Ewell.

EARLY'S DIVISION, Maj.-Gen. Jubal A. Early.

Hays's Brigade, Brig.-Gen. Harry T. Hays: 5th La., Lieut.-Col. Bruce Menger; 6th La., Maj. William H. Manning; 7th La., Maj. J. M. Wilson; 8th La., ——; 9th La., ——. *Pegram's Brigade,* Brig.-Gen. John Pegram: 13th Va., Col. James B. Terrill; 31st Va., Col. John S. Hoffman; 49th Va., Col. J. C. Gibson; 52d Va., ——; 58th Va., ——. *Gordon's Brigade,* Brig.-Gen. John B. Gordon: 13th Ga., ——; 26th Ga., Col. E. N. Atkinson; 31st Ga., Col. C. A. Evans; 38th Ga., ——; 60th Ga., Lieut.-Col. Thomas J. Berry; 61st Ga., ——.

JOHNSON'S DIVISION, Maj.-Gen. Edward Johnson.

Stonewall Brigade, Brig.-Gen. James A. Walker: 2d Va., Capt. C. H. Stewart; 4th Va., Col. William Terry; 5th Va., ——; 27th Va., Lieut.-Col. Charles L. Haynes; 33d Va., ——. *Steuart's Brigade,* Brig.-Gen. George H. Steuart: 1st N. C., Col. H. A. Brown; 3d N. C., Col. S. D. Thruston; 10th Va., ——; 23d Va., ——; 37th Va., ——. *Jones's Brigade,* Brig.-Gen. John M. Jones: 21st Va., ——; 25th Va., Col. J. C. Higginbotham; 42d Va., ——; 44th Va., ——; 48th Va., ——; 50th Va., ——. *Stafford's Brigade,* Brig.-Gen. Leroy A. Stafford: 1st La., ——; 2d La., Col. J. M. Williams; 10th La., ——; 14th La., ——; 15th La., ——.

RODES'S DIVISION, Maj.-Gen. Robert E. Rodes.

Daniel's Brigade, Brig.-Gen. Junius Daniel: 32d N. C., ——; 43d N. C., ——; 45th N. C., ——; 53d N. C., ——; 2d N. C. Batt'n, ——. *Ramseur's Brigade,* Brig.-Gen. Stephen D. Ramseur: 2d N. C., Col. W. R. Cox; 4th N. C., Col. Bryan Grimes; 14th N. C., Col. R. T. Bennett; 30th N. C., Col. F. M. Parker. *Doles's Brigade,* Brig.-Gen. George Doles: 4th Ga., ——; 12th Ga., Col. Edward Willis; 44th Ga., Col. W. H. Peebles. *Battle's Brigade,* Brig.-Gen. Cullen A. Battle: 3d Ala., Col. Charles Forsyth; 5th Ala., ——; 6th Ala., ——; 12th Ala., ——; 26th Ala., ——. *Johnston's Brigade,* Brig.-Gen. Robert D. Johnston: 5th N. C., Col. T. M. Garrett; 12th N. C., Col. H. E. Coleman; 20th N. C., Col. Thomas F. Toon; 23d N. C., ——.

ARTILLERY, Brig.-Gen. Armistead L. Long.

Hardaway's Battalion,⸙ Lieut.-Col. R. A. Hardaway: Dance's (Va.) Batt'y; Graham's (Va.) Batt'y; C. B. Griffin's (Va.) Batt'y; Jones's (Va.) Batt'y; B. H. Smith's (Va.) Batt'y. *Nelson's Battalion,*⸙ Lieut.-Col. William Nelson: Kirkpatrick's (Va.) Batt'y; Massie's (Va.) Batt'y; Milledge's (Va.) Batt'y. *Braxton's Battalion,* Lieut.-Col. Carter M. Braxton: Carpenter's (Va.) Batt'y; Cooper's (Va) Batt'y; Hardwicke's (Va.) Batt'y. *Cutshaw's Battalion,*⚓ Maj. W. E. Cutshaw: Carrington's (Va.) Batt'y; A. W. Garber's (Va.) Batt'y; Tanner's (Va.) Batt'y. *Page's Battalion,*⚓ Maj. R. C. M. Page: W. P. Carter's (Va.) Batt'y; Fry's (Va.) Batt'y; Page's (Va.) Batt'y; Reese's (Ala.) Batt'y.

THIRD ARMY CORPS, Lieut.-Gen. Ambrose P. Hill.

ANDERSON'S DIVISION, Maj.-Gen. Richard H. Anderson.

Perrin's Brigade, Brig.-Gen. Abner Perrin: 8th Ala., ——; 9th Ala., ——; 10th Ala., ——; 11th Ala., ——; 14th Ala., ——. *Mahone's Brigade,* Brig.-Gen. William Mahone: 6th Va., Lieut.-Col. H. W. Williamson; 12th Va., Col. D. A. Weisiger; 16th Va., Lieut.-Col. R. O. Whitehead; 41st Va., ——; 61st Va., Col. V. D. Groner. *Harris's Brigade,* Brig.-Gen. Nathaniel H. Harris: 12th Miss., ——; 16th Miss., Col. S. E. Baker; 19th Miss., Col. T. J. Hardin; 48th Miss., ——. *Wright's Brigade,* Brig.-Gen. Ambrose R. Wright: 3d Ga., ——; 22d Ga., ——; 48th Ga., ——; 2d Ga. Batt'n, Maj. C. J. Moffett. *Perry's Brigade,* Brig.-Gen. E. A. Perry: 2d Fla., ——; 5th Fla., ——; 8th Fla., ——.

HETH'S DIVISION, Maj.-Gen. Henry Heth.

Davis's Brigade, Brig.-Gen. Joseph R. Davis: 2d Miss., ——; 11th Miss., ——; 42d Miss., ——; 55th N. C., ——. *Cooke's Brigade,* Brig.-Gen. John R. Cooke: 15th N. C., ——; 27th N. C., ——; 46th N. C., ——; 48th N. C., ——. *Kirkland's Brigade,* Brig.-Gen. William W. Kirkland: 11th N. C., ——; 26th N. C., ——; 44th N. C., ——; 47th N. C., ——; 52d N. C., ——. *Walker's Brigade,* Brig.-Gen. Henry H. Walker: 40th Va., ——; 47th Va., Col. R. M. Mayo; 55th Va., Col. W. S. Christian; 22d Va., Batt'n, ——. *Archer's Brigade,* Brig.-Gen. James J. Archer: 13th Ala., ——; 1st Tenn. (Prov. Army), Maj. F. G. Buchanan; 7th Tenn., Lieut.-Col. S. G. Shepard; 14th Tenn., Col. William McComb.

WILCOX'S DIVISION, Maj.-Gen. Cadmus M. Wilcox.

Lane's Brigade, Brig.-Gen. James H. Lane: 7th N. C., Lieut.-Col. W. Lee Davidson; 18th N. C., Col. John D. Barry; 28th N. C., ——; 33d N. C., Lieut.-Col. R. V. Cowan; 37th N. C., Col. William M. Barbour. *Scales's Brigade,* Brig.-Gen. Alfred M. Scales: 13th N. C., Col. J. H. Hyman; 16th N. C., Col. W. A. Stowe; 22d N. C., ——; 34th N. C., Col. W. L. J. Lowrance; 38th N. C., Lieut.-Col. John Ashford. *McGowan's Brigade,* Brig.-Gen. Samuel McGowan: 1st S. C. (Prov. Army), Lieut.-Col. W. P. Shooter; 12th S. C., Col. John L. Miller; 13th S. C., Col. B. T. Brockman; 14th S. C., Col. Joseph N. Brown; 1st S. C. (Orr's) Rifles, Lieut.-Col. G. McD. Miller. *Thomas's Brigade,* Brig.-Gen. Edward L. Thomas: 14th Ga., ——; 35th Ga., ——; 45th Ga., ——; 49th Ga., Lieut.-Col. J. T. Jordan.

ARTILLERY, Col. R. Lindsay Walker.

Poague's Battalion, Lieut.-Col. William T. Poague: Richards's (Miss.) Batt'y; Utterback's (Va.) Batt'y; Williams's (N. C.) Batt'y; Wyatt's (Va.) Batt'y. *McIntosh's Battalion,* Lieut.-Col. D. G. McIntosh: Clutter's (Va.) Batt'y; Donald's (Va.) Batt'y; Hurt's (Ala.) Batt'y; Price's (Va.) Batt'y. *Pegram's Battalion,* Lieut.-Col. W. J. Pegram: Brander's (Va.) Batt'y; Cayce's (Va.) Batt'y; Ellett's (Va.) Batt'y; Marye's (Va.) Batt'y; Zimmerman's (S. C.), Batt'y. *Cutts's Battalion,* Col. A. S. Cutts: Patterson's (Ga.) Batt'y; Ross's (Ga.) Batt'y; Wingfield's (Ga.) Batt'y. *Richardson's Battalion,* Lieut.-Col. Charles Richardson: Grandy's (Va.) Batt'y; Landry's (La.) Batt'y; Moore's (Va.) Batt'y; Penick's (Va.) Batt'y.

CAVALRY CORPS, Maj. Gen. James E. B. Stuart.

HAMPTON'S DIVISION, Maj.-Gen. Wade Hampton.

Young's Brigade, Brig.-Gen. P. M. B. Young: 7th Ga., Col. W. P. White; Cobb's (Ga.) Legion, Col. G. J. Wright; Phillips (Ga.) Legion, ——; 20th Ga. Battalion, Lieut.-Col. John M. Millen; Jeff Davis (Miss.) Legion, ——. *Rosser's Brigade,* Brig.-Gen. Thomas L. Rosser: 7th Va., Col. R. H. Dulany; 11th Va., ——; 12th Va., Lieut.-Col. Thomas B. Massie; 35th Va. Battalion, ——. *Butler's Brigade,* Brig.-Gen. M. C. Butler: 4th S. C., Col. B. H. Rutledge; 5th S. C., Col. John Dunovant; 6th S, C., Col. Hugh K. Aiken.

FITZ. LEE'S DIVISION, Maj.-Gen. Fitzhugh Lee.

Lomax's Brigade, Brig.-Gen. Lunsford L. Lomax: 5th Va., Col. Henry C. Pate; 6th Va., ——; 15th Va., ——. *Wickham's Brigade,* Brig.-Gen. Williams C. Wickham: 1st Va., ——; 2d Va., Col. Thomas T. Munford; 3d Va., Col. Thomas H. Owen; 4th Va., ——.

W. H. F. LEE'S DIVISION, Maj.-Gen. W. H. F. Lee.

Chambliss's Brigade, Brig.-Gen. John R. Chambliss, Jr.: 9th Va., ——; 10th Va., ——; 13th Va., ——. *Gordon's Brigade,* Brig.-Gen. James B. Gordon: 1st N. C., ——; 2d N. C., Col. C. M. Andrews: 5th N. C., Col. S. B. Evans.

HORSE ARTILLERY, Maj. R. P. Chew.

Breathed's Battalion, Maj. James Breathed: Hart's (S. C.) Batt'y; Johnston's (Va.) Batt'y; McGregor's (Va.) Batt'y; Shoemaker's (Va.) Batt'y; Thomson's (Va.) Batt'y.

RICHMOND AND PETERSBURG LINES, Gen. G. T. Beauregard. ↓

RANSOM'S DIVISION, Maj.-Gen. Robert Ransom, Jr.

Gracie's Brigade, Brig.-Gen. Archibald Gracie, Jr.: 41st Ala., ——; 43d Ala., ——; 59th Ala., ——; 60th Ala., ——. *Kemper's Brigade,* Col. William R. Terry: 1st Va., Maj. George F. Norton; 3d Va., ——;

⸙ Under the direction of Colonel J. T. Brown.   ⚓ Under the direction of Colonel Thomas H. Carter.
↓ Major-General George E. Pickett commanded at Petersburg.

7th Va., Capt. W. O. Fry; 11th Va., ——; 24th Va., ——. *Barton's Brigade,* Brig.-Gen. Seth M. Barton: 9th Va., Col. James J. Phillips; 14th Va., Col. William White; 38th Va., Lieut.-Col. J. R. Cabell; 53d Va., Col. William R. Aylett; 57th Va., Col. C. R. Fontaine. *Hoke's (old) Brigade,* Lieut.-Col. William G. Lewis: 6th N. C., ——; 21st N. C., ——; 54th N. C., ——; 57th N. C., ——; 1st N. C. Batt'n, ——. *Artillery Battalion,* Lieut.-Col. C. E. Lightfoot: Va. Batt'y, Capt. J. D. Hankins; Va. Batt'y, Capt. J. H. Rives; Va. Batt'y, Capt. T. R. Thornton.

HOKE'S DIVISION, Maj.-Gen. Robert F. Hoke.

Corse's Brigade, Brig.-Gen. Montgomery D. Corse: 15th Va., Lieut.-Col. E. M. Morrison; 17th Va., Lieut.-Col. Arthur Herbert; 18th Va., Lieut.-Col. George C. Cabell; 29th Va., ——; 30th Va., Col. A. T. Harrison. *Clingman's Brigade,* Brig.-Gen. Thomas L. Clingman: 8th N. C., ——; 31st N. C., ——; 51st N. C., ——; 61st N. C., ——. *Johnson's Brigade,* Brig.-Gen. Bushrod R. Johnson, Col. John S. Fulton: 17th and 23d Tenn., Col. R. H. Keeble; 25th and 44th Tenn., Col. John S. Fulton, Lieut.-Col. J. L. McEwen, Jr.; 63d Tenn., Col. A. Fulkerson. *Hagood's Brigade,* Brig.-Gen. Johnson Hagood: 11th S. C., Col. F. H. Gantt; 21st S. C., Col. Robert F. Graham; 25th S. C., Lieut.-Col. John G. Pressley; 27th S. C., Col. P. C. Gaillard; 7th S. C. Batt'n, Maj. J. H. Rion. *Unattached:* 51st N. C., Col. Hector McKethan. *Artillery Battalion,* Lieut.-Col. B. F. Eshleman: Martin's (Va.) Batt'y; Owen's (La.) Batt'y; Payne's Batt'y.

COLQUITT'S DIVISION, Brig.-Gen. Alfred H. Colquitt.

Colquitt's Brigade: 6th Ga., Col. John T. Lofton; 19th Ga., ——; 23d Ga., Col. M. R. Ballenger; 27th Ga., Lieut.-Col. James Gardner; 28th Ga., ——. *Ransom's Brigade.*⟩ *Artillery Battalion,*⟩ Maj. W. M. Owen. *Cavalry:* 3d N. C., Col. John A. Baker; 7th S. C., Col. W. P. Shingler.

WHITING'S DIVISION, Maj.-Gen. W. H. C. Whiting.

Wise's Brigade, Brig.-Gen. Henry A. Wise: 26th Va., Col. P. R. Page; 34th Va., ——; 46th Va., ——; 59th Va., Col. William B. Tabb. *Martin's Brigade,* Brig.-Gen. James G. Martin: 17th N. C., ——; 42d N. C., ——; 66th N. C., ——. *Cavalry,* Brig.-Gen. James Dearing: 7th Confederate, Col. V. H. Taliaferro; 8th Ga., Col. Joel R. Griffin; 4th N. C., Col. Dennis D. Ferrebee; 65th N. C., Col. G. N. Folk. *Thirty-eighth Battalion Va. Artillery,* Maj. J. P. W. Read: Blount's, Caskie's, Macon's, and Marshall's batteries.

MISCELLANEOUS: *Elliott's Brigade,* Col. Stephen Elliott, Jr.: 61st N. C., ——; Holcombe (S. C.) Legion, ——. *Hunton's Brigade,* Brig.-Gen. Eppa Hunton: 8th Va., Capt. H. C. Bowie; 19th Va., Capt. J. G. Woodson; 25th Va. (Battalion), Lieut.-Col. W. M. Elliott; 32d Va., Col. E. B. Montague; 56th Va., Capt. John Richardson; 42d Va. Cav. Batt'n, Lieut.-Col. W. T. Robins. *Maryland Line,* Col. Bradley T. Johnson: 2d Md. Inf., Capt. J. P. Crane; 1st Md. Cav., Lieut.-Col. Ridgely Brown; 1st Md. Batt'y, Capt. W. F. Dement; 2d Md. Batt'y, Capt. W. H. Griffin; 4th Md. Batt'y, ——. *Engineers:* D, 1st Reg't, Capt. H. C. Derrick.

RICHMOND DEFENSES, Col. W. H. Stevens.

First Division, Inner Line, Lieut.-Col. J. W. Atkinson: 10th Va. H. A. Batt'n, Maj. J. O. Hensley; 19th Va. H. A. Batt'n, Maj. N. R. Cary. *Second Division, Inner Line,* Lieut.-Col. Jas. Howard: 18th Va. H. A. Batt'n, Maj. M. B. Hardin; 20th Va. H. A. Batt'n, Maj. J. E. Robertson. *Unattached:* La. Guard Art'y, Capt. C. A. Green.

CHAFFIN'S BLUFF, Lieut.-Col. J. M. Maury.

Goochland (Va.) Art'y, Capt. Jonathan Talley; James City (Va.) Art'y, Capt. L. W. Richardson; Lunenburg (Va.) Art'y, Capt. C. T. Allen; Pamunkey (Va.) Art'y, Capt. A. J. Jones.

DREWRY'S BLUFF, Maj. F. W. Smith.

Johnston (Va.) Art'y, Capt. Branch J. Epes; Neblett (Va.) Art'y, Capt. W. G. Coleman; Southside (Va.) Art'y, Capt. J. W. Drewry; United (Va.) Art'y, Capt. Thomas Kevill.

CHAFFIN'S FARM, Maj. A. W. Stark.

Matthews's (Va.) Art'y, Capt. A. D. Armistead; McComas's (Va.) Art'y, Capt. D. A. French.

ARTILLERY, Col. H. P. Jones.

Moseley's Battalion, Lieut.-Col. E. F. Moseley: Cumming's (N. C.) Batt'y; Miller's (N. C.) Batt'y; Slaten's (Ga.) Batt'y; Young's (Va.) Batt'y. *Coit's Battalion,* Maj. J. C. Coit: Bradford's (Miss.) Batt'y; Kelly's (S. C.) Batt'y; Pegram's (Va.) Batt'y; Wright's (Va.) Batt'y. *Unassigned:* Sturdivant's (Va.) Batt'y.

Lee's effective force at the commencement of the campaign was not less than 61,000, and Beauregard's command about Richmond and Petersburg, including the troops sent from North Carolina and South Carolina up to May 15th, approximated 30,000.

The losses of these armies are only partially reported. In the Wilderness Ewell's corps lost 1250 killed and wounded; McGowan's brigade (Wilcox's division), 481 killed, wounded, and missing; Lane's brigade (Wilcox's division), 272 killed and wounded, and 143 missing; Kershaw's brigade (under Henagan), 57 killed, 239 wounded, and 26 missing; Bryan's brigade (Kershaw's division), 31 killed and 102 wounded; Mahone's brigade, 20 killed, 126 wounded, and 7 missing; Gordon's brigade, 50 killed, wounded, and missing.

The reported casualties at Spotsylvania are as follows: Ewell's corps (May 10th), 650, and (May 19th), 900; Edward Johnson's division (May 12th), over 2000; and McGowan's brigade (May 12th), 86 killed, 248 wounded, and 117 missing.

The following summary, aggregating 3507, exhibits the losses of Beauregard's forces on the south side of the James from May 6th to June 2d, so far as reported:

COMMAND.	DATE.		Killed.	Wounded.	Captured or missing.	Total.
Ransom's, Hoke's, and Colquitt's divisions.	May	16	355	1941	210	2506
Barton's brigade.....	May	10	36	179	34	249
Hagood's brigade	May	6–9	54	253	37	344
B. Johnson's brigade.	May	7–9	2	10	....	12
Martin's brigade.....	May	20	13	92	8	113
Wise's brigade........	May	16–20	18	162	....	180
Wise's brigade........	June	2	9	49	....	58
Fifty-ninth Virginia..	May	8	3	22	20	45

⟩ Composition not indicated.

THE OPPOSING FORCES AT COLD HARBOR.

June 1st, 1864.

THE UNION ARMY, Lieutenant-General U. S. Grant.

ARMY OF THE POTOMAC, Major-General George G. Meade.

Provost Guard, Brig.-Gen. Marsena R. Patrick: C and D, 1st Mass. Cav., Capt. Charles F. Adams, Jr.; 80th N. Y. (20th Militia), Col. Theodore B. Gates; 3d Pa. Cav., Lieut.-Col. Edward S. Jones; 68th Pa., Lieut.-Col. Robert E. Winslow; 114th Pa., Col. Charles H. T. Collis. *Volunteer Engineer Brigade*, Brig.-Gen. Henry W. Benham: 50th N. Y., Lieut.-Col. Ira Spaulding. *Battalion U. S. Engineers*, Capt. George H. Mendell. *Guards and Orderlies*, Oneida (N. Y.) Cav., Capt. Daniel P. Mann.

SECOND ARMY CORPS, Maj.-Gen. Winfield S. Hancock.

Escort: M, 1st Vt. Cav., Capt. John H. Hazelton.

FIRST DIVISION, Brig.-Gen. Francis C. Barlow.

First Brigade, Col. Nelson A. Miles: 26th Mich., Capt. James A. Lothian; 2d N. Y. Art'y, Col. Joseph N. G. Whistler; 61st N. Y., Lieut.-Col. K. Oscar Broady; 81st Pa., Capt. Lawrence Mercer; 140th Pa., Capt. Samuel Campbell; 183d Pa., Capt. John McCullough. *Second Brigade*, Col. Richard Byrnes: 28th Mass., Capt. James Fleming; 63d N. Y., Capt. John R. Gleason; 69th N. Y., Maj. John Garrett; 88th N. Y., Capt. Denis F. Burke; 116th Pa., Col. St. Clair A. Mulholland, Capt. Richard Moroney. *Third Brigade*, Col. Clinton D. MacDougall: 39th N. Y., Maj. Joseph Hyde; 52d N. Y. (detachment 7th N. Y. attached), Capt. Henry P. Ritzius; 111th N. Y., Capt. Lewis W. Husk; 125th N. Y., Col. Levin Crandell; 126th N. Y., Lieut.-Col. William H. Baird. *Fourth Brigade*, Col. John R. Brooke: 2d Del., Maj. Peter McCullough; 7th N. Y. Art'y, Maj. Joseph M. Murphy; 64th N. Y., Capt. William Glenny; 66th N. Y., Col. Orlando H. Morris; 53d Pa., Capt. Henry S. Dimm; 145th Pa., Maj. Charles M. Lynch; 148th Pa., Col. James A. Beaver.

SECOND DIVISION, Brig.-Gen. John Gibbon.

Provost Guard: 2d Co. Minn. Sharp-shooters, Capt. Mahlon Black.

First Brigade, Col. Henry B. McKeen: 19th Me., Capt. Joseph W. Spaulding; 15th Mass., Maj. I. Harris Hooper; 19th Mass., Capt. Morcena Dunn; 20th Mass., Capt. Henry L. Patten; 1st Co. Mass. Sharp-shooters, Lieut. Samuel G. Gilbreth; 7th Mich., Maj. Sylvanus W. Curtis; 42d N. Y., Lieut. John Maguire; 59th N. Y., Lieut.-Col. Horace P. Rugg; 82d N. Y. (battalion), Lieut. Thomas Huggins; 184th Pa., Maj. Charles Kleckner; 36th Wis., Col. Frank A. Haskell. *Second Brigade*, Brig.-Gen. Joshua T. Owen: 152d N. Y., Capt. William S. Burt; 69th Pa., Maj. William Davis; 71st Pa., Lieut.-Col. Charles Kochersperger; 72d Pa., Lieut.-Col. Henry A. Cook; 106th Pa., Capt. John B. Breitenbach. *Third Brigade*, Col. Thomas A. Smyth: 14th Conn., Col. Theodore G. Ellis; 1st Del., Maj. William F. Smith; 14th Ind., Lieut.-Col. Elijah H. C. Cavins; 12th N. J., Capt. James McComb; 10th N. Y. (battalion), Maj. George F. Hopper; 108th N. Y., Capt. William H. Andrews; 4th Ohio, Lieut.-Col. Leonard W. Carpenter; 8th Ohio, Maj. Albert H. Winslow; 7th W. Va. (battalion), Capt. Isaac B. Fisher. *Fourth Brigade*, Brig.-Gen. Robert O. Tyler: 8th N. Y. Art'y, Col. Peter A. Porter; 155th N. Y., Capt. Michael Doran; 164th N. Y., Col. James P. McMahon; 170th N. Y., Capt. James P. McIvor; 182d N. Y. (69th N. Y., N. G. A.), Lieut.-Col. Thomas M. Reid.

THIRD DIVISION, Maj.-Gen. David B. Birney.

First Brigade, Col. Thomas W. Egan: 20th Ind., Col. William C. L. Taylor; 3d Me., Col. Moses B. Lakeman; 40th N. Y., Lieut.-Col. Augustus J. Warner; 86th N. Y., Maj. Michael B. Stafford; 124th N. Y., Capt. Henry S. Murray; 99th Pa., Maj. John W. Moore; 101st Pa., Lieut.-Col. Enoch E. Lewis; 141st Pa., Col. Henry J. Madill; 2d U. S. Sharp-shooters, Maj. Edward T. Rowell. *Second Brigade*, Col. Thomas R. Tannatt: 4th Me., Capt. Arthur

Libby; 17th Me., Lieut.-Col. Charles B. Merrill; 1st Mass. Art'y, Maj. Nathaniel Shatswell; 3d Mich., Col. Byron R. Pierce; 5th Mich., Lieut.-Col. Moses B. Houghton; 93d N. Y., Lieut.-Col. Benjamin C. Butler; 57th Pa., Capt. Alanson H. Nelson; 63d Pa., Capt. Isaac Morehead; 105th Pa., Maj. Levi B. Duff; 1st U. S. Sharpshooters, Capt. John Wilson. *Third Brigade*, Brig.-Gen. Gershom Mott: 1st Me. Art'y, Col. Daniel Chaplin; 16th Mass., Maj. Samuel W. Richardson; 5th N. J., Capt. Henry H. Woolsey; 6th N. J., Capt. Joseph Hays; 7th N. J., Maj. Frederick Cooper; 8th N. J., Maj. Virgil M. Healy; 11th N. J., Col. Robert McAllister; 115th Pa., Lieut.-Col. John P. Dunne. *Fourth Brigade*, Col. William R. Brewster: 11th Mass., Lieut.-Col. Porter D. Tripp; 70th N. Y., Capt. William H. Hugo; 71st N. Y., Lieut.-Col. Thomas Rafferty; 73d N. Y., Lieut.-Col. Michael W. Burns; 74th N. Y., Col. Thomas Holt; 120th N. Y. (3 co's 72d N. Y. attached), Lieut.-Col. John R. Tappen; 84th Pa., Capt. John R. Ross.

ARTILLERY BRIGADE, Col. John C. Tidball: 6th Me., Capt. Edwin B. Dow; 10th Mass., Capt. J. Henry Sleeper; 1st N. H., Capt. Frederick M. Edgell; 2d N. J., Capt. A. Judson Clark; G, 1st N. Y., Capt. Nelson Ames; 4th N. Y. Heavy, Lieut.-Col. Thomas R. Allcock; 11th N. Y., Capt. John E. Burton; 12th N. Y., Capt. George F. McKnight; F, 1st Pa., Capt. R. Bruce Ricketts; A, 1st R. I., Capt. William A. Arnold; B, 1st R. I., Capt. T. Fred Brown; K, 4th U. S., Lieut. John W. Roder; C and I, 5th U. S., Lieut. William B. Beck.

FIFTH ARMY CORPS, Maj.-Gen. Gouverneur K. Warren.

Provost Guard: 12th N. Y. (battalion), Maj. Henry W. Rider.

FIRST DIVISION, Brig.-Gen. Charles Griffin.

First Brigade, Brig.-Gen. Romeyn B. Ayres: 140th N. Y., Lieut.-Col. Elwell S. Otis; 146th N. Y., Maj. James Grindlay; 91st Pa., Maj. John D. Lentz; 155th Pa., Maj. John Ewing; 2d U. S. (6 co's), Lieut. George H. McLaughlin; 11th U. S. (6 co's) Capt. Francis M. Cooley; 12th U. S. (10 co's), Capt. Frederick Winthrop; 14th U. S. (First Battalion), Capt. David B. McKibbin; 17th U. S. (8 co's), Capt. Walter B. Pease. *Second Brigade*, Col. Jacob B. Sweitzer: 9th Mass., Lieut.-Col. Patrick T. Hanley; 22d Mass. (2d Co. Sharp-shooters attached), Col. William S. Tilton; 32d Mass., Col. George L. Prescott; 4th Mich., Capt. David D. Marshall; 62d Pa., Capt. William P. Maclay. *Third Brigade*, Brig.-Gen. Joseph J. Bartlett: 20th Me., Maj. Ellis Spear; 18th Mass., Maj. Thomas Weston; 29th Mass., Col. Ebenezer W. Peirce; 1st Mich., Lieut.-Col. William A. Throop; 16th Mich. (Brady's Co. Sharp-shooters attached), Capt. George H. Swan; 44th N. Y., Capt. Campbell Allen; 83d Pa., Lieut.-Col. De Witt C. McCoy; 118th Pa., Lieut.-Col. Charles P. Herring.

SECOND DIVISION, Brig.-Gen. Henry H. Lockwood.

First Brigade, Col. Peter Lyle: 16th Me., Col. Charles W. Tilden; 13th Mass., Col. Samuel H. Leonard; 39th Mass., Col. Phineas S. Davis; 94th N. Y., Lieut.-Col. Samuel A. Moffett; 104th N. Y., Col. Gilbert G. Prey; 90th Pa., Capt. William P. Davis; 107th Pa., Col. Thomas F. McCoy. *Second Brigade*, Col. James L. Bates: 12th Mass., Maj. Benj. F. Cook; 83d N. Y. (9th Militia), Lieut.-Col. William Chalmers; 97th N. Y., Capt. Delos E. Hall; 11th Pa., Capt. Benjamin F. Haines; 88th Pa., Capt. George B. Rhoads. *Third Brigade*, Col. Nathan T. Dushane: 1st Md., Lieut.-Col. John W. Wilson; 4th Md., Col. Richard N. Bowerman; 7th Md., Maj. Edward M. Mobley; 8th Md., Lieut.-Col. John G. Johannes; Purnell (Md.) Legion, Col. Sam'l A. Graham.

THIRD DIVISION, Brig.-Gen. Samuel W. Crawford (assigned to Second Division, June 2).

Veteran Reserve Brigade, Maj. William R. Hartshorne: 190th Pa., —— ; 191st Pa.,——. *Independent Brigade*, Col. J. Howard Kitching: 6th N. Y. Art'y, Maj. Absalom Crookston; 15th N. Y. Art'y (First and Third Battalions), Col. Louis Schirmer.

FOURTH DIVISION, Brig.-Gen. Lysander Cutler.

Provost Guard: 2d Wis., Capt. George H. Otis.

First Brigade, Col. William W. Robinson: 7th Ind., Lieut.-Col. William C. Banta; 19th Ind., Maj. John M. Lindley; 24th Mich., Lieut.-Col. William W. Wight; 1st Battalion N. Y. Sharp-shooters, Capt. Alfred Parry; 6th Wis., Lieut.-Col. Rufus R. Dawes; 7th Wis., Lieut.-Col. Mark Finnicum. *Second Brigade*, Col. J. William Hofmann: 3d Del., Lieut.-Col. William B. Dorrell; 46th N. Y., Lieut.-Col. George W. Travers; 76th N. Y., Capt. James I. Goddard; 95th N. Y., Maj. Robert W. Baird; 147th N. Y., Lieut.-Col. George Harney; 56th Pa., Maj. John T. Jack. *Third Brigade*, Col. Edward S. Bragg: 121st Pa., Capt. Samuel T. Lloyd; 142d Pa., Maj. Horatio N. Warren; 143d Pa., Maj. James Glenn; 149th Pa., Lieut.-Col. John Irvin; 150th Pa., Maj. George W. Jones.

ARTILLERY BRIGADE, Col. Charles S. Wainwright: 3d Mass., Lieut. Aaron F. Walcott; 5th Mass., Capt. Charles A. Phillips; 9th Mass., Capt. John Bigelow; B, 1st N. Y., Capt. Albert S. Sheldon; C, 1st N. Y., Capt. Almont Barnes; D, 1st N. Y., Lieut. Lester I. Richardson; E and L, 1st N. Y., Lieut. George Breck; H, 1st N. Y., Capt. Charles E. Mink; 15th N. Y., Capt. Patrick Hart; B, 1st Pa., Capt. James H. Cooper; B, 4th U. S., Lieut. James Stewart; D, 5th U. S., Lieut. Benjamin F. Rittenhouse.

SIXTH ARMY CORPS, Maj.-Gen. Horatio G. Wright.

Escort: A, 8th Pa. Cav., Capt. Charles E. Fellows.

FIRST DIVISION, Brig.-Gen. David A. Russell.

First Brigade, Col. William H. Penrose: 1st N. J., Lieut.-Col. William Henry, Jr.; 2d N. J., Col. Samuel L. Buck; 3d N. J., Col. Henry W. Brown; 4th N. J., Capt. Samuel M. Gaul; 10th N. J., Lieut.-Col. Charles H. Tay; 15th N. J., Lieut.-Col. Edward L. Campbell. *Second Brigade*, Col. Emory Upton: 2d Conn. Art'y, Col. Elisha S. Kellogg; 5th Me., Col. Clark S. Edwards; 121st N. Y., Maj. Henry M. Galpin; 95th Pa., Capt. John G. C. Macfarlan; 96th Pa., Lieut.-Col. William H. Lessig. *Third Brigade*, Brig.-Gen. Henry L. Eustis: 6th Me., Capt. Theodore Lincoln, Jr.; 49th Pa., Maj. Baynton J. Hickman; 119th Pa., Lieut.-Col. Gideon Clark; 5th Wis., Lieut.-Col. Theodore B. Catlin. *Fourth Brigade*, Col. Nelson Cross: 65th N. Y., Col. Joseph B. Hamblin; 67th N. Y., Lieut.-Col. Henry L. Van Ness; 122d N. Y., Lieut.-Col. Augustus W. Dwight; 23d Pa., Col. John F. Glenn; 82d Pa., Col. Isaac C. Bassett.

SECOND DIVISION, Brig.-Gen. Thomas H. Neill.

First Brigade, Brig.-Gen. Frank Wheaton: 62d N. Y., Col. David J. Nevin; 93d Pa., Lieut.-Col. John S. Long; 98th Pa., Col. John F. Ballier; 102d Pa., Lieut.-Col. William McIlwaine; 139th Pa., Lieut.-Col. William H. Moody. *Second Brigade*, Brig.-Gen. Lewis A. Grant: 2d Vt., Maj. Amasa S. Tracy; 3d Vt., Col. Thomas O. Seaver; 4th Vt., Lieut.-Col. Stephen M. Pingree; 5th Vt., Col. John R. Lewis; 6th Vt., Lieut.-Col. Oscar A. Hale; 11th Vt. (1st Heavy Art'y), Col. James M. Warner. *Third Brigade*, Col. Daniel D. Bidwell: 7th Me., Capt. John W. Channing; 43d N. Y., Lieut.-Col. James D. Visscher; 49th N. Y., Lieut.-Col. George W. Johnson; 77th N. Y., Lieut.-Col. Winsor B. French; 61st Pa., Capt. Lewis Redenbach. *Fourth Brigade*, Col. Oliver Edwards: 7th Mass., Col. Thomas D. Johns; 10th Mass., Lieut.-Col. Joseph B. Parsons; 37th Mass., Lieut.-Col. George L. Montague; 2d R. I., Maj. Henry C. Jenckes.

THIRD DIVISION, Brig.-Gen. James B. Ricketts.

First Brigade, Col. William S. Truex: 14th N. J., Lieut.-Col. Caldwell K. Hall; 106th N. Y., Lieut.-Col. Charles Townsend; 151st N. Y., Col. William Emerson; 87th Pa., Col. John W. Schall; 10th Vt., Col. William W. Henry. *Second Brigade*, Col. Benjamin F. Smith: 6th Md., Col. John W. Horn; 9th N. Y. Art'y (First and Third Battalions), Lieut.-Col. Edward P. Taft; 110th Ohio, Lieut.-Col. Otho H. Binkley; 122d Ohio, Col. William H. Ball; 126th Ohio, Lieut.-Col. Aaron W. Ebright;

67th Pa., Col. John F. Staunton; 138th Pa., Col. Matthew R. McClennan.

ARTILLERY BRIGADE, Col. Charles H. Tompkins: 4th Me., Lieut. Charles W. White; 5th Me., Capt. Greenleaf T. Stevens; 1st Mass., Capt. William H. McCartney; 1st N. J., Capt. William Hexamer; 1st N. Y., Capt. Andrew Cowan; 3d N. Y., Capt. William A. Harn; 2d Battalion 9th N. Y. Heavy, Maj. James W. Snyder; H, 1st Ohio, Capt. Stephen W. Dorsey; C, 1st R. I., Capt. Richard Waterman; E, 1st R. I., Capt. William B. Rhodes; G, 1st R. I., Capt. George W. Adams; E, 5th U. S., Lieut. John R. Brinckle; M, 5th U. S., Capt. James McKnight.

NINTH ARMY CORPS, Maj.-Gen. Ambrose E. Burnside.

Provost Guard: 8th U. S., Capt. Milton Cogswell.

FIRST DIVISION, Maj.-Gen. Thomas L. Crittenden.

First Brigade, Brig.-Gen. James H. Ledlie: 56th Mass., Col. Stephen M. Weld, Jr.; 57th Mass., Col. William F. Bartlett; 59th Mass., Lieut.-Col. John Hodges, Jr.; 4th U. S., Capt. Avery B. Cain; 10th U. S., Lieut. Jesse A. P. Hampson. *Second Brigade*, Col. Joseph M. Sudsburg: 3d Md., Lieut.-Col. Gilbert P. Robinson; 21st Mass., Lieut.-Col. George P. Hawkes; 100th Pa., Lieut.-Col. Matthew M. Dawson. *Provisional Brigade*, Col. Elisha G. Marshall: 2d N. Y. Mounted Rifles (dismounted), Col. John Fisk; 14th N. Y. Art'y, Maj. William H. Reynolds; 24th N. Y. Cav. (dismounted), Col. William C. Raulston; 2d Pa., Provisional Art'y, Col. Thomas Wilhelm. *Acting Engineers:* 35th Mass., Capt. Edward G. Park. *Artillery:* 3d Me., Capt. Albert F. Thomas; 14th Mass., Capt. Joseph W. B. Wright.

SECOND DIVISION, Brig.-Gen. Robert B. Potter.

First Brigade, Col. John I. Curtin: 36th Mass., Lieut.-Col. Arthur A. Goodell; 58th Mass., Lieut.-Col. John C. Whiton; 45th Pa., Lieut.-Col. Francis M. Hills; 48th Pa., Lieut.-Col. Henry Pleasants; 7th R. I., Capt. Percy Daniels. *Second Brigade*, Col. Simon G. Griffin: 2d Md., —— ; 31st Me., Col. Thomas Hight; 32d Me., Lieut.-Col. John M. Brown; 6th N. H., Maj. Phin. P. Bixby; 9th N. H., Capt. Andrew J. Hough; 11th N. H., Capt. Hollis O. Dudley; 17th Vt., Lieut.-Col. Charles Cummings. *Acting Engineers:* 51st N. Y., Capt. George W. Whitman. *Artillery*, Capt. Edward W. Rogers: 11th Mass., Capt. Edward J. Jones; 19th N. Y., Capt. Edward W. Rogers.

THIRD DIVISION, Brig.-Gen. Orlando B. Willcox.

First Brigade, Col. John F. Hartranft: 2d Mich., Col. William Humphrey; 8th Mich., Lieut.-Col. Ralph Ely; 27th Mich. (1st and 2d Co's Sharp-shooters attached), Col. Dorus M. Fox: 109th N. Y., Lieut.-Col. Isaac S. Catlin; 51st Pa., Lieut.-Col. Edwin Schall. *Second Brigade*, Col. Benjamin C. Christ: 1st Mich. Sharpshooters, Capt. Levant C. Rhines; 20th Mich., Col. Byron M. Cutcheon; 60th Ohio (9th and 10th Co's Sharpshooters attached), Lieut.-Col. James N. McElroy; 50th Pa., Lieut.-Col. Edward Overton, Jr. *Acting Engineers:* 17th Mich., Col. Constant Luce. *Artillery:* 7th Me., Capt. Adelbert B. Twitchell; 34th N. Y., Capt. Jacob Roemer.

FOURTH DIVISION, Brig.-Gen. Edward Ferrero.

First Brigade, Col. Joshua K. Sigfried: 27th U. S. C. T., Col. Charles J. Wright; 30th U. S. C. T., Col. Delavan Bates; 39th U. S. C. T., Col. Ozora P. Stearns; 43d U. S. C. T., Lieut.-Col. H. Seymour Hall. *Second Brigade*, Col. Henry G. Thomas: 19th U. S. C. T., Lieut.-Col. Joseph G. Perkins; 23d U. S. C. T., Lieut.-Col. Cleaveland J. Campbell; 31st U. S. C. T., Maj. Theo. H. Rockwood. *Artillery:* D, Pa., Capt. George W. Durell; 3d Vt., Capt. Romeo H. Start.

RESERVE ARTILLERY, Capt. John Edwards, Jr.: 27th N. Y., Capt. John B. Eaton; D, 1st R. I., Capt. William W. Buckley; H, 1st R. I., Capt. Crawford Allen, Jr.; E, 2d U. S., Lieut. Samuel B. McIntire.

CAVALRY CORPS, Maj.-Gen. Philip H. Sheridan.

Escort: 6th U. S., Capt. Ira W. Claflin.

FIRST DIVISION, Brig.-Gen. Alfred T. A. Torbert.

First Brigade, Brig.-Gen. George A. Custer: 1st Mich., Lieut.-Col. Peter Stagg; 5th Mich., Col. Russell A. Alger; 6th Mich., Maj. James H. Kidd; 7th Mich., Maj. Alexander Walker. *Second Brigade*, Col. Thomas C. Devin: 4th N. Y., Lieut.-Col. William R. Parnell; 6th N. Y.,

Lieut.-Col. William H. Crocker; 9th N. Y., Lieut.-Col. George S. Nichols; 17th Pa., Lieut.-Col. James Q. Anderson. *Reserve Brigade*, Brig.-Gen. Wesley Merritt: 19th N. Y. (1st Dragoons), Col. Alfred Gibbs; 6th Pa., Maj. William P. C. Treichel; 1st U. S., Capt. Nelson B. Sweitzer; 2d U. S., Capt. Theophilus F. Rodenbough; 5th U. S., } Capt. Abraham K. Arnold.
SECOND DIVISION, Brig.-Gen. David McM. Gregg.
First Brigade, Brig.-Gen. Henry E. Davies, Jr.: 1st Mass., Lieut.-Col. Samuel E. Chamberlain; 1st N. J., Lieut.-Col. John W. Kester; 10th N. Y., Maj. M. Henry Avery; 6th Ohio, Col. William Stedman; 1st Pa., Col. John P. Taylor. *Second Brigade*, Col. J. Irvin Gregg: 1st Me., Col. Charles H. Smith; 2d Pa., Lieut.-Col. Joseph P. Brinton; 4th Pa., Lieut.-Col. George H. Covode; 8th Pa., Col. Pennock Huey; 13th Pa., Maj. Michael Kerwin; 16th Pa., Lieut.-Col. John K. Robison.
THIRD DIVISION, Brig.-Gen. James H. Wilson.
Escort: 8th Ill. (detachment), Lieut. William W. Long.
First Brigade, Col. John B. McIntosh: 1st Conn., Maj. George O. Marcy; 3d N. J., Col. Andrew J. Morrison; 2d N. Y., Col. Otto Harhaus; 5th N. Y., Lieut.-Col. John Hammond; 2d Ohio, Lieut.-Col. George A. Purington; 18th Pa., Maj. John W. Phillips. *Second Brigade*, Col. George H. Chapman: 3d Ind., Maj. William Patton; 8th N. Y., Maj. Edmund M. Pope; 1st Vt., Maj. William Wells.
FIRST BRIGADE, HORSE ARTILLERY, Capt. James M. Robertson: 6th N. Y., Capt. Joseph W. Martin; B and L, 2d U. S., Lieut. Edward Heaton; D, 2d U. S., Lieut. Edward B. Williston; M, 2d U. S., Lieut. Carle A. Woodruff; A, 4th U. S., Lieut. Rufus King, Jr.; C and E, 4th U. S., Lieut. Charles L. Fitzhugh.
ARTILLERY, ⚔ Brig.-Gen. Henry J. Hunt.
Second Brigade, Horse Artillery, Capt. Dunbar R. Ransom: E and G, 1st U. S., Lieut. Frank S. French; H and I, 1st U. S., Capt. Alanson M. Randol; K, 1st U. S., Lieut. John Egan; A, 2d U. S., Lieut. Robert Clarke; G, 2d U. S., Lieut. W. Neil Dennison; C, F, and K, 3d U. S., Lieut. George F. Barstow. *Artillery Park*, Lieut.-Col. Freeman McGilvery: 15th N. Y. (Second Battalion), Maj. Julius Dieckmann.
EIGHTEENTH ARMY CORPS, ↓ Maj.-Gen. William F. Smith.
FIRST DIVISION, Brig.-Gen. William T. H. Brooks.
First Brigade, Brig.-Gen. Gilman Marston: 81st N. Y., Col. Jacob J. DeForest; 96th N. Y., Col. Edgar M. Cullen; 98th N. Y., Col. Fred F. Wead; 139th N. Y., Lieut.-Col. Edgar Perry. *Second Brigade*, Brig.-Gen. Hiram Burnham: 8th Conn., Capt. Charles M. Coit; 10th N. H., Lieut.-Col. John Coughlin; 13th N. H., Col. Aaron F. Stevens; 118th N. Y., Capt. Levi S. Dominy. *Third Brigade*, Col. Guy V. Henry: 21st Conn., Lieut.-Col. Thomas F. Burpee; 40th Mass., Lieut.-Col. George E. Marshall; 92d N. Y., Lieut.-Col. Hiram Anderson, Jr.; 58th Pa.,

Lieut.-Col. Montgomery Martin; 188th Pa., Lieut.-Col. George K. Bowen.
SECOND DIVISION, Brig.-Gen. James H. Martindale.
First Brigade, Brig.-Gen. George J. Stannard: 23d Mass., Col. Andrew Elwell; 25th Mass., Capt. Francis E. Goodwin; 27th Mass., Maj. William A. Walker; 9th N. J., Capt. Augustus Thompson; 89th N. Y., Col. H. S. Fairchild; 55th Pa., Capt. George H. Hill. *Second Brigade*, Col. Griffin A. Stedman: 11th Conn., Lieut.-Col. William C. Moegling; 8th Me., Maj. William M. McArthur; 2d N. H., Col. Edward L. Bailey; 12th N. H., Maj. John F. Langley; 148th N. Y., Col. George M. Guion.
THIRD DIVISION, Brig.-Gen. Charles Devens, Jr.
First Brigade, Col. William B. Barton: 47th N. Y., Lieut.-Col. C. R. Macdonald; 48th N. Y., Lieut.-Col. D. W. Strickland; 115th N. Y., Maj. Ezra L. Walrath; 76th Pa., Col. John C. Campbell. *Second Brigade*, Col. Jeremiah C. Drake: 13th Ind., Col. Cyrus J. Dobbs; 9th Me., Capt. Robert J. Gray; 112th N. Y., Capt. J. S. Mathews; 169th N. Y., Col. John McConihe. *Third Brigade*, Brig.-Gen. Adelbert Ames: 4th N. H., Col. Louis Bell; 3d N. Y., Col. Samuel M. Alford; 117th N. Y., Col. Alvin White; 142d N. Y., Col. N. Martin Curtis; 97th Pa., Col. Henry R. Guss.
ARTILLERY BRIGADE, Capt. Samuel S. Elder: B, 1st U. S., Capt. S. S. Elder; L, 4th U. S., Lieut. Henry B. Beecher; A, 5th U. S., Lieut. James E. Wilson.
On the 1st of June the Army of the Potomac, at and about Cold Harbor, numbered 103,875 "present for duty," and General W. F. Smith brought from the Army of the James about 10,000, exclusive of 2500 left to guard the landing at White House. The losses of the Union army from June 1st to 12th were as follows:

COMMAND.	Killed.	Wounded.	Captured or Missing.	Total.
Engineers	......	3	......	3
Second Army Corps	494	2442	574	3,510
Fifth Army Corps	149	749	442	1,340
Sixth Army Corps	483	2064	168	2,715
Ninth Army Corps	219	1126	356	1,701
Eighteenth Army Corps	448	2365	206	3,019
Cavalry Corps	51	328	70	449
Aggregate	1844	9077	1816	12,737

{ Co's B, F, and K, under Capt. Julius W. Mason, detailed as escort to Lieut.-Gen. U. S. Grant.
⚔ See also batteries with divisions and corps.
↓ Temporarily attached to the Army of the Potomac from the Army of the James.

THE CONFEDERATE ARMY, General Robert E. Lee.

The organization of the Army of Northern Virginia at Cold Harbor was substantially the same as at the Wilderness (see p. 183), with the exception of some transfers and consolidations of brigades (notably those of Ed. Johnson's division, which had been badly shattered at Spotsylvania) and the accession of Hoke's old brigade and the divisions of Pickett, Breckinridge, and Hoke. Insufficient data, however, prevent the preparation of a full list of the troops and commanders. For the same reason the editors have also found it impossible to give the strength of the army. It is nowhere authoritatively stated. Upon this subject Colonel Walter H. Taylor ("Four Years with General Lee," p. 136) remarks: "The only reënforcements received by General Lee were as

follows: Near Hanover Junction he was joined by a small force under General Breckinridge, . . . 2200 strong, and Pickett's division of Longstreet's corps, which had been on detached duty in North Carolina. Hoke's brigade of Early's division, 1200 strong, which had been on detached duty at the Junction, here also rejoined its division; and at Cold Harbor General Lee received the division of General Hoke, also just from North Carolina — the two divisions (Pickett's and Hoke's) numbering 11,000 men. The aggregate of these reënforcements (14,400 men), added to General Lee's original strength [which Colonel Taylor estimates at 64,000], would give 78,400 as the aggregate of all troops engaged under him from the Wilderness to Cold Harbor."

UNHORSED TROOPERS RETIRING FROM SHERIDAN'S RAID.

SHERIDAN'S RICHMOND RAID.

BY THEO. F. RODENBOUGH, BREVET BRIGADIER-GENERAL, U. S. A.

THE Army of the Potomac had been hibernating on the left bank of the Rapidan River, when as the season for active operations was about to open (April, 1864) there arrived a lieutenant-general commanding and a chief of cavalry. The one was not unknown to fame; the other was almost an entire stranger to his new command.

During the first two years of the war the Union cavalry lacked the paternal care essential to its proper development. Its first father was General Hooker, who organized a multitude of detachments into a compact army corps of 12,000 horsemen; transforming that which had been a by-word and a reproach into a force that, by its achievements in war, was ultimately to effect a radical change in the armament and use of mounted troops by the great military powers.

The winter of 1863–64 brought little rest to the cavalry. While the artillery and infantry were comfortably quartered, the cavalry was "hutted" three miles in front of the infantry picket lines, and a part was distributed as escorts and orderlies at infantry headquarters. Although the infantry maintained a picket line of its own, where it was useless, the cavalry was compelled to keep up a chain of videttes sixty miles in length, besides the necessary patrol duty and reconnoissances. Upon his arrival, Grant seems to have noted this maladministration and to have taken steps to correct it. For a chief of his cavalry, he told the President, he "wanted the very best man in the army," and few will deny that he got that man.

I remember Sheridan's arrival at the headquarters of the Cavalry Corps. We all thought a commander might have been selected from home material. One or two things that he did, however, met with warm approval. He set about reforming the abuses above referred to. On one occasion he was about to send a staff-officer to demand the immediate return to the corps of a small regiment which had been acting as "body-guard" for an infantry general. The officer, desiring for certain reasons to secure a modification of the order, sounded General Sheridan, who simply turned to him and in a low but distinct tone said: "Give my compliments to General X. and say that I have been placed in command of the cavalry of this army, and by —— I want it *all.*"

The 15,000 "paper strength" of the corps was sifted to 12,424 effectives. There were three divisions, subdivided into seven brigades. General A. T. A. Torbert was assigned to command the First Division, with General G. A. Custer, Colonel T. C. Devin, and General Wesley Merritt as brigade commanders; General D. McM. Gregg to the Second Division, with General H. E. Davies and Colonel J. Irvin Gregg to brigades; General J. H. Wilson to the Third Division, with Colonels J. B. McIntosh and G. H. Chapman to brigades. To each division were attached two batteries of horse artillery, with the same number as a reserve.

Sheridan's lieutenants were well chosen. Torbert had already distinguished himself as an infantry commander; Gregg had come from the regular cavalry and possessed the confidence of the whole corps for good judgment and coolness; Wilson, promoted from the corps of engineers, was very quick and impetuous; Merritt was a pupil of the Cooke-Buford school, with cavalry virtues well proportioned, and to him was given the Reserve Brigade of regulars — the Old Guard. Custer was the meteoric *sabreur;* McIntosh, the last of a fighting race; Devin, the "Old War Horse"; Davies, polished, genial, gallant; Chapman, the student-like; Irvin Gregg, the steadfast. There were, besides, Graham, Williston, Butler, Fitzhugh, Du Pont, Pennington, Clark, Randolph, Brewerton, Randol, Dennison, Martin, all tried men of the horse artillery.

The campaign was opened May 3d–4th, 1864,

with the crossing of the Rapidan River by the army in two columns: one (Hancock's corps), preceded by Gregg's cavalry division, at Ely's Ford; the other (Warren and Sedgwick), led by Wilson, at Germanna Ford. The enemy's pickets were brushed away, the pontoons laid down, and the troops and immense trains were moved to the south side, apparently before Lee had realized the fact. On the second day Warren was attacked and Wilson found himself, for the time, separated from our infantry and confronted near Todd's tavern by a strong force of cavalry under Hampton, which engaged Wilson vigorously and after some fighting began to press him back. The opportune reënforcement of two regiments from Gregg turned the tables, and the enemy was driven beyond Corbin's Bridge. From the start Lee's cavalry was aggressive, and by its ceaseless activity in that densely wooded region reminded one of a swarm of bees suddenly disturbed by strange footsteps. On the 7th a more determined effort was made by Stuart to get on the left and rear of Meade, tempted by the rich prize of four thousand wagons. Torbert and Gregg were pitted against Hampton and Fitz Lee. The fight lasted from 4 P. M. until after dark, the field remaining in possession of the Union force; it was renewed early on the 8th, and after an obstinate struggle, in which the losses were heavy on both sides,—especially in officers,—the Confederates gave it up and retired sullenly. This was a cavalry affair, although in sight of the infantry of both armies. The curious blending of tragic and commonplace elements in war was illustrated during the hottest of the fight on the second day. It was raging about a small farm-house apparently deserted; shells were bursting in the yard, especially around the old-fashioned "pole" well, bullets were pattering on the shingles, dead and wounded men and horses made the place a slaughter-house. As Captain Leoser, 2d United States Cavalry, was advancing his skirmishers near the house, the cellar door was slowly lifted and a harsh-featured woman poked her head out, looked at the well and then at the captain, and threw an empty bucket at him with the curt remark, "Yank, I reckon you kin tote me a pail o' water," and promptly disappeared.

General Grant states in his "Memoirs" that on the 8th of May he gave Sheridan verbal orders to start on an independent expedition toward Richmond.‖ But he does not mention an incident that may have precipitated that movement. It happened that on the 8th of May Grant, Meade, and Sheridan were together at army headquarters. Meade seemed somewhat anxious about his trains, and said something to which Sheridan took exception. Meade instantly remarked, "No, I don't mean that," and put his hand, in friendly fashion, on Sheridan's shoulder. The cavalry general moved aside impatiently and replied with spirit, "If I am permitted to cut loose from this army I'll draw Stuart after me, and whip him, too." This was the principal object of the Richmond raid; the damage to the enemy was only incidental.

MAJOR-GENERAL GEORGE A. CUSTER.
FROM A PHOTOGRAPH.

A few hours were spent in preparation. The command was stripped of all impedimenta, such as unserviceable animals, wagons, and tents. The necessary ammunition train, two ambulances to a division, a few pack-mules for baggage, three days' rations and a half-day's forage carried on the saddle, comprised the outfit. Torbert being disabled, Merritt assumed command of his division, and Gibbs of the Reserve Brigade. On the 9th of May, 1864, at 6 A. M., this magnificent body of 10,000 horsemen moved out on the Telegraph Road leading from Fredericksburg to Richmond. According to a Southern authority it took four hours at a brisk pace to pass a given point; to those who viewed it from behind barred windows and doors it was like the rush of a mighty torrent.

The column as it stood, "fours" well closed up, was thirteen miles long. It had been moving at a walk for two hours before the enemy caught up, and Wickham's brigade began to harass Sheridan's rear. It made no difference in the progress of the Union column, although numerous little brushes occurred. In one of these the 1st North Carolina Cavalry charged our rear-guard, consisting of the 6th Ohio Cavalry and a section of the 6th New York Battery. In the mêlée a Confederate officer cut his way through the column to the rear piece; placing his hand on the gun he exclaimed, "This is my piece." "Not by a d——d sight," replied a cannoneer, as with a well-planted blow of his fist he knocked the would-be captor off his horse and took him prisoner.

Passing through Chilesburg late in the afternoon, the leading brigade of Merritt's division (Custer's) took the trot and charged into Beaver Dam Station, on the Virginia Central Railroad, at an opportune moment. Two trains of cars carrying wounded

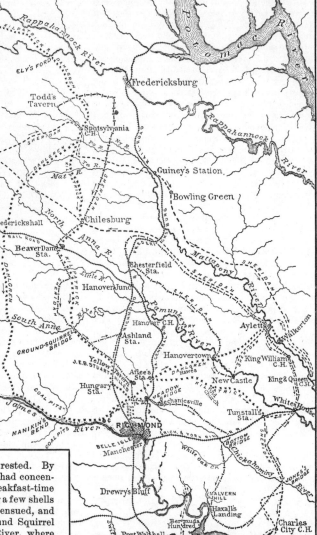

and prisoners from Spotsylvania were about to start for Richmond. In a moment 378 Union captives rent the air with their cheers; the guard accompanying the trains escaped, leaving their arms behind, together with a large quantity of small-arms from the battle-field. After reserving certain articles, the torch was applied to the trains and buildings, with 1,500,000 rations and medical stores for Lee's army. The railroad track and telegraph were destroyed for some distance, the work being continued throughout the night while the main body rested. By the morning of the 10th Stuart had concentrated a large force, and about breakfast-time he announced the fact by sending a few shells into Gregg's camp. A skirmish ensued, and the march was resumed to Ground Squirrel bridge over the South Anna River, where all bivouacked. Even during the night the enemy buzzed about us, evidently trying to wear us out. On the 11th, at 3 A. M., Davies moved to Ashland and, not without a severe encounter with Munford's Virginia cavalry, destroyed culverts, trestle-bridges, and six miles of track, besides a warehouse and a number of cars, losing thirty men.

At 5 A. M. the main column moved on to Glen Allen Station, where Stuart's skirmishers were encountered and pressed back to within two miles of Yellow Tavern. Here a determined stand was made for the right of way to the Confederate capital, distant only six miles. Devin was first engaged, and soon the entire First Division went in. Several mounted charges were made, and two guns

THE KILPATRICK-DAHLGREN RAID   FEB. 28
MARCH 2 } 1864 ×××××

SHERIDAN'S RICHMOND RAID   MAY 9
" 25 } 1864 —·—·—·—

SHERIDAN'S TREVILIAN RAID   JUNE 7
" 27 } 1864 - - - - -

BATTLES ⊕   SCALE   5   10   15 MILES

J. WELLS

NOTE.— For an account of the Kilpatrick-Dahlgren Raid, see p. 95; and of the Trevilian Raid, see p. 233.

and a number of prisoners were taken. A dispatch from Stuart to Bragg asking for reënforcements was intercepted, disclosing the enemy's weakness. Under the circumstances the Confederates are entitled to the greatest credit for the pertinacity and pluck displayed. Finally Wilson with part of his division was put in on Merritt's left, and the line, advancing, broke the enemy's grip and the fight was won. At this moment Stuart received his death-wound by a pistol-shot in the abdomen. Deep in the hearts of all true cavalrymen, North and South, will ever burn a sentiment of admiration mingled with regret for this knightly soldier and generous man. Sheridan had succeeded in his purpose, but he had found a foeman worthy of his steel.

If defeated at this point the enemy was not annihilated. Richmond was awakening to its peril; and, aware of the weakness of the garrison, the Confederate authorities felt very uneasy. As when the Germans approached Paris or when Early menaced Washington, a general call to arms was made. But Nature seemed rather favorable to defensive operations. For three days it had rained more or less, and a little rain in the region of the Chickahominy is known to go a great way toward making a mortar-bed of the roads and meadows. About midnight the column moved forward in the order: Wilson, Merritt, Gregg. Captain Field, 4th United States Artillery (then serving with Fitzhugh's battery), writes of the experience of Wilson's command:

"We marched all night, virtually. The halts were frequent and exasperating. It was so dark that we could only follow the cavalry by putting a bugler on a white horse directly in rear of the regiment in front of us, with orders to move on as soon as they did. Finally, whether the bugler fell asleep waiting or we fell asleep while watching the white horse, it happened that we found a gap of unknown dimensions in front of us and started at a trot to close it. I know of nothing which creates such an appalling sense of loneliness as the fact of being left behind in an enemy's country at night. It was a swampy region: the hoofs and the wheels made little or no sound. Once the deep blackness was pierced by a jet of vivid flame, and a sharp explosion on the road showed that we had sprung one of the torpedoes which had been to some extent planted there. While in doubt as to the road, we came upon a man wrapped in a blue overcoat standing near a gate, who told us that General Sheridan had left him to show us the way. Of course we followed his directions and entered the gate. It was evident that we were very near the city, as we could see the lights and hear the dogs barking. The road became less plainly marked and seemed to lead into extensive pleasure grounds, and finally we brought up on the edge of a large fish-pond. At that moment half a dozen flashes came from what seemed to be an embankment, and we found that we were in a regular trap and immediately under the fire of one of the outworks of the city. The guide who had given us the direction was either a deserter or a rebel in our uniform, and had deliberately misled us. He received the reward of his treachery, for Colonel McIntosh, who had from the first suspected him, kept him near him, and when their guns opened blew out his brains with a pistol."

About this time General Sheridan and staff, riding in rear of Wilson's division, hearing the firing, became convinced that the head of the column had passed the point where he had intended to turn in the direction of Mechanicsville. He sent off several of his staff to strike the road, which seemed

as easily found as the proverbial needle in a haystack. But Captain F. C. Newhall *did* find the needle, and Merritt was sent down to Meadow Bridge to cover a crossing. In the meanwhile, as day broke, part of Wilson's command, including Fitzhugh's battery, found itself within the outer line of fortifications and threatened from all sides. South of them lay Richmond and its garrison; on the east a struggle for the bridge was going on between Merritt and an unknown force; while in a northerly direction, in rear of the main column, Gregg was standing off a force under Gordon. It was the tightest place in which the corps ever found itself. Fitzhugh had just ordered his caissons to go down as near the bridge as he could get, as our only avenue of escape appeared to be in that direction, when upon the scene came the sturdy presence of Sheridan. He hailed Fitzhugh, "Hullo, Charley! What are you doing with your caissons?" Fitzhugh explained that if hard pressed he wanted them out of the way. With a hearty laugh Sheridan replied, "Pushed *hard!* Why, what do you suppose we have in front of us? A lot of department clerks from Richmond, who have been forced into the ranks. I could capture Richmond, if I wanted, but I can't hold it; and the prisoners tell me that every house in the suburbs is loopholed, and the streets barricaded. It isn't worth the men it would cost; but I'll stay here all day to show these fellows how much I care for them, and go when I get ready. Send for your caissons and take it easy." As Captain Field says, "It was a little thing, but here was the spirit that burned so high at Winchester."

The enemy had torn up the bridge, and were in some force on the opposite bank. Merritt dismounted all but three regiments, and Custer charged his men over the railroad bridge to cover the reconstruction, driving the enemy back some distance. As soon as the flooring was down the mounted force under Colonel Gibbs crossed. Gregg and Wilson covered the crossing of the ammunition and ambulance trains, and after a brisk affair with a brigade of infantry and cavalry under General Gordon, followed Merritt, to their common satisfaction. A small but enterprising Virginia newsboy had managed to slip into our lines with the morning papers, full of the alleged barbarities of the vandal horde. He seemed utterly indifferent to the horrors of war, crossed the bridge with the cavalry, and found his first Yankee customer in Lieutenant Whitehead, who eagerly exchanged a quarter for a Richmond "Inquirer," which he sent to General Sheridan.

As soon as the head of our column turned toward the James it lost interest as an objective for the enemy. They were glad to watch us at a respectful distance, now that their beloved capital was once more safe. By way of Bottom's Bridge the corps moved to Malvern Hill and Haxall's, where much-needed supplies were procured from Butler's army; many of us exchanged our mud-stained garments for blue flannel shirts from the gun-boats lying in the James, and for the nonce became horse-marines. On the 21st Sheridan, continuing his march to rejoin Grant, crossed the Pamunkey near White House, on the ruins

HENRY E. DAVIES, JR. D. McM. GREGG. PHILIP H. SHERIDAN. WESLEY MERRITT. A. T. A. TORBERT. JAMES H. WILSON.

SHERIDAN AND SOME OF HIS GENERALS. FAC-SIMILE OF A PHOTOGRAPH TAKEN IN 1864.

of the railroad bridge, after six hours' work at repairing it, two regiments at a time working as pioneers. The only incident of the crossing was the fall of a pack-mule from the bridge, from a height of thirty feet. The mule turned a somersault, struck an abutment, disappeared under water, came up and swam ashore without disturbing his pack. On the 23d the corps encamped at Aylett's, and at 5 P. M. I was sent with my regiment, 2d United States Cavalry, accompanied by Captains Wadsworth and Goddard of the staff, to open communication with the army, the sound of whose guns had been heard early in the day. After a forty-mile night march we had the good fortune to find General Grant near Chesterfield Station, where on the 25th the Cavalry Corps also reported, having fully performed its allotted task. It had deprived Lee's army, for the time, of its "eyes and ears," damaged his communications, destroyed an immense quantity of supplies, killed the leader of his cavalry, saved to our Govern-

ment the subsistence of ten thousand horses and men for three weeks, perfected the *morale* of the Cavalry Corps, and produced a moral effect of incalculable value to the Union cause. Sheridan's casualties on the raid were 625 men killed or wounded, and 300 horses.

The Cavalry Corps returned in time to take part in an important flanking movement by the army, which in the meantime had fought the battle of Spotsylvania and had moved by the left to the North Anna River. On the 26th of May the army was posted on the north bank of that stream, with our left resting near Chesterfield bridge. [See map, p. 136.] Our infantry was now cautiously transferred from the right by the rear around the left of the line south of the river, crossing by Hanover Ferry. Sheridan, with Gregg's and Torbert's divisions, was to precede the infantry on the left, while Wilson's division threatened the enemy's left at Little River. On the 27th Torbert crossed at Hanover Ferry after some resistance by the enemy's cavalry, and pushed on to Hanover Town, where he bivouacked, having captured sixty prisoners. Having secured the desired position, Grant directed Sheridan to regain the touch with Lee's main army. To this end Gregg was sent in the direction of Hanover Court House, but was opposed at Hawes's Shop by the enemy's dismounted cavalry (including a brigade of South Carolina troops with long-range rifles) in an intrenched position. General Gregg writes:

"In the shortest possible time both of my brigades were hotly engaged. Every available man was put into the fight, which had lasted some hours. Neither party would yield an inch. Through a staff-officer of General Sheridan I sent him word as to how we stood, and stated that with some additional force I could destroy the equilibrium and go forward. Soon General Custer reported with his brigade. This he dismounted and formed on a road leading to the front and through the center of my line. In column of platoons, with band playing, he advanced. As arranged, when the head of his column reached my line all went forward with a tremendous yell, and the contest was of short duration. We went right over the rebels, who resisted with courage and desperation unsurpassed. Our success cost the Second Division 256 men and officers, killed and wounded. This fight has always been regarded by the Second Division as one of its severest."

General Grant adds:

"But our troops had to bury the dead, and found that more Confederate than Union soldiers had been killed."

A number of prisoners were taken by Gregg. On the 29th of May a reconnoissance in force was ordered to locate the enemy's line. We could easily find his cavalry,—too easily sometimes,—but the main Army of Northern Virginia seemed to have hidden itself, and Grant's infantry moved cautiously to the left and front. Sheridan was charged with the protection of our left while the general movement lasted. On the 30th Hancock and Warren discovered the enemy in position. Torbert was attacked by the Confederate cavalry near Old Church, at 2 P. M., and fought until 5 P. M., when he succeeded in pressing the enemy toward Cold Harbor. Wilson had been sent to the right to cut the Virginia Central, and occupied Hanover Court House after a sharp skirmish with Young's cavalry. On the 31st Torbert saddled up at 2 A. M.; he moved toward Old Cold Harbor at 5 A. M., found the enemy's cavalry in position, and drove them three miles upon their infantry. Retiring leisurely in search of a suitable camping-ground, Sheridan was directed by Grant to return to Cold Harbor and "hold it at all hazards." So at 10 P. M., weary and disgusted, having been on duty for eighteen hours, we moved back and reoccupied the old rifle-pits — at least, part of the force did. The remainder were massed in rear, lying down in front of their jaded horses, bridle-rein on arm, and graciously permitted to doze. At 5 A. M., as things remained quiet in front, coffee was prepared and served to the men as they stood to horse. Officers' packs appeared in an adjoining field, and the mess-cooks managed to broil a bone, butter a hoe-cake, and boil more coffee, and although the command remained massed the surroundings seemed more peaceful. My fourth cup of coffee was in hand when a few shots were heard in front, causing a

general pricking up of ears. Soon skirmishers' compliments began to come our way and drop among the packs. Our line in the rifle-pits was at once reënforced. An amusing scene met the eye where the pack-mules had been standing: the ground was covered with the débris of officers' light baggage and mess-kits, mules were braying and kicking, and drivers were yelling, when, suddenly, jackasses, mules, and contrabands made for the rear, encountering on the way the corps commander and staff, who only by turning into a convenient farm-yard escaped the deluge.

The center of the line was occupied by the Reserve Brigade (Merritt's): six hundred dismounted men of the 1st and 2d United States, 6th Pennsylvania, and 1st New York Dragoons, armed with Sharps breech-loading carbines—excepting the 1st New York, which had Spencer magazine carbines (seven-shooters). The brigade was posted on the crest of a ravine, with timber in front and rear, excepting opposite the regiment on the left where there was a clearing, and on the right which rested on a swamp. The enemy kept up a desultory fire until 8 A. M., when a compact mass of infantry, marching steadily and silently, company front, was reported moving through the timber upon our position. This timber consisted of large trees with but little undergrowth. Our men were not aware of the character of the force about to attack us. But the *morale* of the corps was so good and their confidence in Sheridan so great that when the order "to hold at all hazards" was repeated they never dreamed of leaving the spot. Foreseeing a great expenditure of ammunition, some of the cavalrymen piled even their pistol-cartridges by their sides where they would be handy. On came the gray-coated foe, armed with Austrian muskets with sword-bayonets. These, flashing through the trees, caught the eye of a little Irish corporal of the 2d Cavalry, who exclaimed in astonishment, "Howly Mother! here they come wid sabers on fut!"

For a moment the skirmishers redoubled their fire, the enemy took the double-quick, and as they charged us the rebel yell rang through the forest. Then a sheet of flame came from the cavalry line, and for three or four minutes the din was deafening. The repeating carbines raked the flank of the hostile column while the Sharps single-loaders kept up a steady rattle. The whole thing was over in less than five minutes; the enemy, surprised, stunned, and demoralized, withdrew more quickly than they came, leaving their dead and wounded. We did not attempt to follow, but sent out parties to bring in the badly wounded, who were menaced with a new danger as the woods were now on fire. From prisoners we found that the attack was made by part of Kershaw's division (reported to be 1500 strong), and that they had advanced confidently, being told that "there was nothing in their front but cavalry." The tremendous racket we made hastened the approach of the Sixth Corps on its way to relieve us. To them we cheerfully gave place, having taken the initiative in what was destined to be, before the sun went down, the bloody and historic battle of Cold Harbor.

THE DEATH OF GENERAL J. E. B. STUART. ↓

BY A PRIVATE OF THE SIXTH VIRGINIA CAVALRY, C. S. A.

MAJOR-GENERAL FITZHUGH LEE, C. S. A.
FROM A PHOTOGRAPH.

O N the morning of the fight at Yellow Tavern, May 12th, 1864, I was acting as one of Stuart's couriers. At the beginning of it I was stationed in front of the tavern, under one of a row of trees that lined the way close by. To my left, about four hundred yards off, the enemy could be easily seen emerging from a piece of woods and forming for battle. A short distance to my right I saw an irregular line of Confederates. Pretty soon from the enemy came lively volleys whistling through the trees and starting the dust in the road. In a few minutes I saw two horsemen approach from the Confederate side. As they drew near I recognized General Stuart and Colonel Walter Hullion. They halted near by in the road, and Stuart, taking out his field-glass, deliberately watched the manœuvres of the enemy, though balls were whizzing past him. Presently, regardless of the increasing fire, which was now accompanied with shouts, Stuart put his glass

away, and taking out paper and pencil wrote an order. Handing it to Colonel Hullion, he told him to take it to General Lomax. That officer replied by pointing to me and suggesting that I should carry it. Stuart assented, and I rode off in search of General Lomax. The firing continued to increase, and many squadrons were in sight. The enemy, awake to their superior numbers, seemed about to make a general advance, while our men were availing themselves of the character of the ground to repel their attack. After going a few rods to the rear, my horse, excited by the firing, suddenly stopped and refused to budge. After several vain attempts with the spur and the flat side of my sword to start him, I at last struck him with all my strength right between the ears. This "downed" him, but he soon rose and ran off at the top of his speed. I soon came to where General Lomax was, and coming into collision with his horse gained his immediate attention. After reading the note he told me to go back and tell General Stuart that the order had been delivered. In a few moments I rejoined Stuart. He was sitting on his horse close behind a line of dismounted men, who were firing at the advancing Federals. The disparity of numbers between the opposing forces was very great, to judge from appearances. Our men seemed aware of their inferior strength, but were not dismayed. The enemy confidently pressed forward with exultant shouts, delivering tremendous volleys. The Confederates returned their fire with yells of defiance. Stuart, with pistol in hand, shot over the heads of the troops, while with words of cheer he encouraged them. He kept saying: "Steady, men, steady. Give it to them." Presently he reeled in his saddle. His head was bowed and his hat fell off. He turned and said as I drew nearer: "Go and tell General Lee and Dr. Fontaine to come here." I wheeled at once and went as fast as I could to do his bidding. Coming to the part of the line where General Lomax was, I told him Stuart was hurt and that he wanted General Fitz Lee. He pointed to the left and told me to hurry. Soon I found General Lee, and delivered the message. He was riding a light gray, if I remember, and instantly upon receipt of the news went like an arrow down the line. When I returned, Stuart had been taken from his horse and was being carried by his men off the field. I saw him put in an ambulance and I followed it close behind. He lay without speaking as it went along, but kept shaking his head with an expression of the deepest disappointment. He died the next day, May 12th.

↓ Reprinted from the "Southern Bivouac" for September, 1884.

LOOKING FOR A FRIEND.

THE DEFENSE OF DREWRY'S BLUFF.[*]

BY G. T. BEAUREGARD, GENERAL, C. S. A.

ON the 23d of April, 1864, at Weldon, N. C., I assumed command of the Department of North Carolina and Southern Virginia. It included "Virginia, south of the James and Appomattox, and all that portion of North Carolina east of the mountains."[†]

The War Department was closely engaged at that time with certain operations against Plymouth and New Berne, from which great results were expected at Richmond, but about which the enemy was not much concerned, as the main object of his campaign could in no wise be affected or seriously disturbed by such a diversion. I did not consider this move judicious on the part of the Government, because, irrespective of other considerations, it occasioned an untimely division of some of the most available troops in my new command, rendering their immediate concentration at any threatened point very difficult, if not impossible. The destination of General Burnside's corps was not, as yet, well defined. The opinion was entertained by many that it would march upon Richmond via Petersburg. Others thought its aim was Weldon. On either hypothesis we should have been prepared to meet the assault in time, and, clearly, we were not.

[*] Taken by permission from the "North American Review" for March, 1887, and condensed.

[†] General Beauregard was succeeded in command of the Department of South Carolina, Georgia, and Florida (April 19th, 1864) by Major-General Samuel Jones.— EDITORS.

As a matter of fact, when the Ninth Corps, under General Burnside, came from east Tennessee, it simply went to increase the strength of the Army of the Potomac. But the forces under General Butler, with the addition of the corps commanded by General Gillmore and by General Smith, amounted to about thirty thousand men,⧸ and were evidently being prepared for a determined advance upon Petersburg. Thus was the projected coöperation of Meade's and Butler's armies to be inaugurated. This gave the clew of the situation to the immediate advisers of President Davis. They realized, at last, the uselessness of the Plymouth and New Berne expedition; and orders came, one hurriedly following the other, instructing me to withdraw General Hoke and his forces from the outworks of New Berne, which they had already taken, and to rush them on to protect Richmond. "There is not an hour to lose," said Mr. Davis in one of his telegrams to me [May 4th]. "Had the expedition not started, I would say it should not go." ⧹

Other troops were also being ordered from other directions, and notably from South Carolina, to assist in the defense of the Confederate capital: first, Hagood's brigade; next, Wise's; and soon afterward, Colquitt's. So great was the anxiety of the Administration at this juncture that Hagood's brigade, which General Pickett, then in command of Petersburg, desired to halt on its passage through that city, was ordered to be pushed on to Richmond without an instant's delay.⧹ I succeeded, however, in having that order rescinded, and General Hagood was thus enabled to baffle General Butler's forces, May 6th and 7th, in their assault upon the Richmond railroad above Petersburg. General Bushrod Johnson, who had hurried from Drewry's Bluff to take part in this action, was of material assistance, although, from the position he occupied with his troops, his services were less conspicuous. Petersburg would inevitably have fallen into the hands of the enemy had not General Hagood been halted there at that most opportune hour. The Federal loss was computed at about one thousand men. Ours was quite insignificant. General Hagood and his command became the heroes of the day, and were justly looked upon as the saviors of Petersburg on that occasion.

The enemy, after this repulse, appeared to have relinquished all idea of striking another immediate blow at Petersburg, and seemed now to be aiming more directly at Richmond. I was pressingly urged to leave Weldon and repair to Petersburg, where all my available forces were being concentrated, with a view to coöperate with General Ransom for the defense of the capital. But, rapid as were the movements of our troops, withdrawn from North Carolina and other points, their celerity failed to satisfy or reassure the War Department, whose trepidation grew hourly more intense, and whose orders, telegrams, and suggestions became as harassing as they were numerous.

The incursion of the enemy's cavalry at Jarratt's, and the burning of Stony

---

⧸ General William F. Smith estimates the force at forty thousand. [See p. 207.] On the basis of the "Official Records" it would appear to have been about 36,000.—EDITORS.

⧹ Telegram from Mr. Davis to General Beauregard, May 4th, 1864.—G. T. B.

⧹ Telegram from General Bragg to General Beauregard, May 5th, 1864.—G. T. B.

Creek bridge, prevented me from reaching Petersburg before the 10th of May. Hoke also arrived on that day, and was placed by me at the head of our advancing column, consisting of six brigades of infantry and eight batteries of artillery, and began an immediate march toward Drewry's Bluff, with orders to form there, or thereabout, as early a junction as practicable with Ransom's forces.

As other troops were still coming in from Weldon and elsewhere, whose organization and assignment to duty I thought best to supervise personally, I concluded not to follow on with the forces under Hoke, but to await the arrival of Whiting, then on his way from Wilmington. He had been ordered to Petersburg to take charge of the troops in that city and its vicinity, and to relieve Pickett, who had reported himself ill, and was unable, for the time being, to perform any duty in the field. Drewry's Bluff was in imminent peril; so were the avenues leading from it to Richmond. Whiting reached Petersburg on the 13th. After explaining to him what my intentions were, and what I expected him to do, should I assume command at Drewry's Bluff, and give the enemy battle there, I left for the front, taking with me some twelve hundred men of Colquitt's brigade and Baker's regiment of cavalry.

The road was beset with difficulties; and it was by mere chance that I succeeded in passing safely between the enemy's extreme left and the river. Our exterior lines had already been attacked and partially carried by some of Butler's forces. It was 3 o'clock in the morning when I arrived at Drewry's Bluff. Without a moment's delay, I held a consultation with Colonel D. B. Harris and Colonel W. H. Stevens. The former was my chief engineer, a tried and most efficient officer, who served on my staff from the first Manassas up to the time of his death, which took place on the 10th of October, 1864; the latter was also an able engineer on duty in and around Richmond. They acquainted me with the exact state of affairs in our immediate front, and described the encounter of the previous evening between part of Butler's forces and ours. The outlook was not encouraging, although the damage incurred might have been more serious, and even General Butler, I thought, could have done better under the circumstances. Colonel Stevens had also given me, that morning, a succinct account of the last engagements between General Lee and General Grant, up to the 12th, and of the relative position of their two armies. Nor, in enumerating the strength then available for the protection of Richmond, had he omitted to mention a reserve force of some five thousand men stationed in and near the capital, and acting, at that time, as a separate command. I was thus made conversant with many a fact which greatly assisted me in forming a more correct opinion of the situation before us. Colonel Stevens had likewise furnished me with a topographical map of that portion of Virginia covered by the Confederate forces. Upon carefully examining it I saw that, as General Lee's army and my forces were on nearly a right line passing through Richmond, with General Grant's army on the left, and Butler's on the right, we still held the interior lines; and that it was possible, by prompt and decisive action, and a combined movement on our part, first, to attack and defeat Butler, and next, to turn our entire forces against Grant. I hurriedly formed a plan to that effect, and sent Colonel

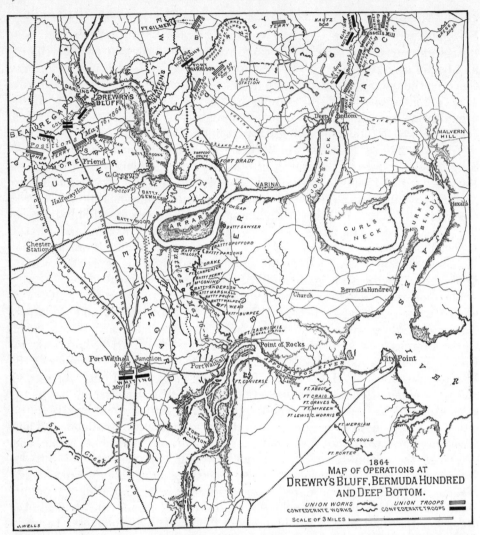

1864
MAP OF OPERATIONS AT
DREWRY'S BLUFF, BERMUDA HUNDRED
AND DEEP BOTTOM.

| UNION WORKS | | UNION TROOPS | |
| CONFEDERATE WORKS | | CONFEDERATE TROOPS | |

SCALE OF 3 MILES

J. WELLS.

Stevens to Richmond for the purpose of submitting it to Mr. Davis, and of asking his consent to carry it out. Mr. Davis could not be seen; but Colonel Stevens saw General Bragg [then Chief-of-staff, C. S. A.], who thought the plan a good one, and came at once to Drewry's Bluff to confer with me.

I proposed that General Lee, who was said to be, at that time, near Guiney's Station, should at once move back to the defensive lines of the Chickahominy, or even to the intermediate lines of Richmond; that a force of 10,000 men be detached from his army and sent to me without the loss of an hour, if possible; that the 5000 men kept near Richmond, under Major-General Ransom, be also ordered to report promptly to me. I stated that these forces, added to mine, would give me an effective of some 25,000 ☆ men, with whom, on the very next day, or as soon thereafter as practicable, I would attack Butler's right flank, with almost the certainty of separating him from his base at

☆ Including the forces at Petersburg, we estimate General Beauregard's strength at 30,000.— EDITORS.

Bermuda Hundred, and thus obtaining an easy victory over him. I proposed also, as an essential feature to the entire success of my plan, that, while this movement should be in progress, General Whiting, with all his available forces at Petersburg, amounting to about four thousand men, should march from Port Walthall Junction and fall upon Butler's right rear, forcing him to the very banks of James River, somewhat abreast of Drewry's Bluff, and by this manœuvre insure his unconditional surrender. And I proposed, furthermore, that with my own forces, added to those temporarily taken from the Army of Northern Virginia and the environs of Richmond, I should cross the James after disposing of Butler, and by a concerted movement strike General Grant on his left flank, while General Lee should attack him in front.

General Bragg, who certainly knew where and at what distance from Drewry's Bluff General Lee's army was at that moment, gave his unreserved approval to the plan thus submitted to him. He never said, nor did he intimate in any way, that the reënforcements I desired from the Army of Northern Virginia would not be able to reach Drewry's Bluff in time. He simply stated that, while concurring with me as to the feasibility of the movement, he could not command its execution without first consulting the President, and he hurried back to Richmond for the purpose of seeing him and of urging a favorable decision of the measure.

Mr. Davis arrived in person between 8 and 9 o'clock that morning. He listened to me with grave attention, and I did all in my power to convince him, not only of the advisability of my plan, but of its absolute necessity at that juncture. The substance of his reply was, that he could not be reconciled to the idea of ordering the Army of Virginia to fall back before the Army of the Potomac; that such a manœuvre would destroy the prestige of those heroic troops and create a feeling of distrust among the people which no after-event could mitigate or redeem. I remarked to him that, however painful the fact might be, it was evident the Army of Virginia, though still a barrier to the Army of the Potomac, and resolutely facing it wherever it moved, was none the less forcibly losing ground before it, and that the latter was gradually and surely approaching its objective point—Richmond. That in my opinion it would be better for General Lee to take a voluntary step rearward through motives of strategy, and with a view to foil the designs of his adversary, as I proposed he should do, than to maintain the passive defensive, and merely to follow the movements of the enemy, without making any possible headway against him. I added that the confidence of the people, far from being impaired by the carrying out of such a plan, would, on the contrary, be enhanced by it, as its plain result would be concentration, not retreat; and that concentration was, for us at this crisis, the surest—if not the only— assurance of victory. But I argued in vain. Mr. Davis adhered to his former determination, and would only agree to send me the five thousand men under Ransom. They joined my forces on the evening of the 15th.

In the meantime my command had been extended (May 14th) so as to include Drewry's Bluff and its defenses. I was also expected to protect Richmond, and to meet any sudden move against the city on the north side.

MAJOR-GENERAL R. F. HOKE, C. S. A.
FROM A PHOTOGRAPH.

But Mr. Davis had also objected to the coöperation of General Whiting, which formed a salient feature of my plan, because, as alleged in his book, "of the hazard during a battle of attempting to make a junction of troops moving from opposite sides of the enemy."⏐ I reluctantly yielded to the "*distinct objection*" of the President and Commander-in-Chief of our armies, and, at his request, changed General Whiting's order of march from Petersburg. But, when realizing that Ransom's forces would only join me on the evening of the 15th, and that the enemy was already erecting batteries and rifle-pits about Drewry's Bluff, I saw how important it was to attack Butler the very next morning; and, in pursuance of my original plan, after informing the President of the fact, on the 15th, at 10:45 A. M., I sent a telegram to General Whiting directing him to march to Port Walthall and join in the attack.⚓ To avoid all possible misconstruction of the real import of the telegram, I intrusted it to General (then Colonel) T. M. Logan, of the "Hampton Legion," temporarily on duty with me as one of my staff. I also gave him, for General Whiting, a rough copy of my order of battle for the next day.⏐

My object was to separate Butler from his base and capture his whole army, if possible. The active coöperation of Whiting was, I thought, indispensable to attain such an end.

I organized my forces into three divisions, under Hoke, Ransom, and Colquitt, and called these officers to my headquarters to explain to them the part I expected each and all to play in the impending attack. General Ransom was ordered to attack the Federal right flank at daybreak, to drive back the skirmishers in his front, and, following almost simultaneously with his entire

---

⏐ "Rise and Fall of the Confederate Government," Vol. II., p. 512.—G. T. B.

⚓ The text of the orders is as follows:

"I shall attack enemy to-morrow at daylight by river road, to cut him off from his Bermuda base. You will take up your position to-night on Swift Creek, with Wise's, Martin's, Dearing's, and two regiments of Colquitt's brigade, with about twenty pieces under Colonel Jones. At daybreak you will march to Port Walthall Junction; and when you hear an engagement in your front you will advance boldly and rapidly, by the shortest road, in direction of heaviest firing, to attack enemy in rear or flank. You will protect your advance and flanks with Dearing's cavalry, taking neces-

sary precautions to distinguish friends from foes. Please communicate this to General Hill. This revokes all former orders of movements.

"P. S.—I have just received a telegram from General Bragg, informing me that he has sent you orders to join me at this place; you need not do so, but follow to the letter the above instructions."—G. T. B.

⏐He delivered these papers during the night of May 15th, as he testifies in a letter to me bearing on this point, where he adds that "General Whiting read the dispatches, expressed himself as understanding them entirely, and gave orders for the advance of his entire force by daylight the next morning."—G. T. B.

force, to pivot at the proper time, and strike the enemy's flank and rear. His formation was to be in two distinct lines, supported by artillery and by Colonel Dunovant's regiment of cavalry.

General Hoke, who occupied the trenches on the right of Ransom, was also to engage the enemy at daybreak with a strong line of skirmishers, and, upon causing him to fall back or waver, was to push on the whole of his command and clear his entire front with rapidity and vigor. His orders were, likewise, to form in two lines, at an interval of four hundred yards, and abreast of the trenches, but in such a way as not to impede any of his after-movements. The use to be made of the artillery attached to his division and of Boykin's regiment of cavalry was left to his own judgment.

General Colquitt's command constituted the reserve. It was composed of the only troops which I personally knew, and which had already served under me. They were ordered to form rearward of General Hoke's forces, with the center of each brigade resting on the turnpike. Their first line was to be some five hundred yards distant from Hoke's second line. The artillery attached to that division was to follow along the turnpike about three hundred yards in rear of the last brigade.

General Whiting, with Wise's, Martin's, and Dearing's commands, with two regiments of Colquitt's brigade and twenty pieces of artillery under Colonel H. P. Jones, was to move from Petersburg, along the Petersburg and Richmond turnpike, and to strike the enemy's flank and rear.

The substance of the above, thus orally given to the three division commanders then with me at Drewry's Bluff, was also contained in a written circular delivered to each of them,—as it had been previously outlined to General Whiting,—so that none could be taken by surprise, no matter what movements might be executed the next day on the different parts of the field.

General Ransom began his advance at a quarter to 5 o'clock A. M. [of the 16th of May], but was much retarded by a dense fog of several hours' duration. He had with him Gracie's brigade, Kemper's under Colonel Terry, Barton's under Colonel Fry, and Hoke's old brigade commanded by Colonel Lewis.

At 6 o'clock A. M. he had carried the enemy's breastworks in his front, taking, it was claimed,—but this was afterward seriously contested,—several stand of colors and some five hundred prisoners. His troops had behaved with acknowledged gallantry, Gracie's and Kemper's commands having been mostly engaged, and the former having turned the enemy's right flank. But, for the purpose, it is alleged, of reëstablishing his line and procuring a fresh supply of ammunition, Ransom now came to a halt, and, reporting "his loss heavy and his troops scattered by the fog," called for immediate assistance. At 6:30 Colquitt's brigade, except the two regiments with Whiting, went to reënforce Ransom, with orders to resume its former position as soon as its services should no longer be needed. Just at that time General Ransom, upon being informed, as he alleged, that the enemy was driving Hoke's left, sent forward the right regiment of Lewis's brigade, which effectually checked the Federal advance until the reserve brigade came up and drove it back from our left center to the turnpike, over and beyond our works. General Ransom was wrong in believing Hoke's left in danger. His error lay in the fact that one of Hagood's advanced regiments, having unexpectedly come across the enemy, had been ordered back so as to give Ransom time to bring around his own left, in conformity with the order of battle already explained.

The relative confusion and lull which followed these ill-timed evolutions necessitated a slight change in the original movement, in order, as stated in my report, "to relieve Hoke, on whose front the enemy had been allowed to mass his forces by the inaction of the left." Ransom was ordered to change the front of his right brigade and support it by another, *en échelon;* then to push forward a third brigade toward Proctor's Creek and to keep a fourth one in reserve. This was to be temporary only, and the plan, as originally adopted, was to be executed as soon as we had taken possession of the river and of Proctor's Creek crossing. But the reserve brigade was already engaged with the enemy, and Ransom's own forces were advanced toward the firing of the center. He could not, therefore, carry out the order given to him, and he sent back Barton's instead of Colquitt's brigade; reporting, meanwhile, the necessity of straightening the lines he had stormed, and expressing the belief that the safety of his command would be compromised by a farther advance. Here ended the services of General Ransom and of his infantry on that day; for upon receiving the disappointing and unexpected report of the alleged situation in his front, I had ordered him to halt where he then was until further arrangements should be made to relieve him. His cavalry, however, and his artillery also, continued to do their full share of the work before them. The cavalry, under Dunovant, being dismounted, was deployed as skirmishers against a force occupying the ridge of Gregory's woods, the only hostile force — as afterward ascertained — which threatened the left of our line at that time. The right was seriously engaged; and there, early in the morning, Hoke had pushed on his skirmishers and freely used his artillery. The fog was an impediment for him, as it had been for Ransom, but he had none the less handled his command with that resolution and judgment for which he was conspicuous.

I now quote from my official report of the battle:

"Hagood and [Bushrod] Johnson were thrown forward with a section of Eshleman's Washington Artillery, and found a heavy force of the enemy, with six or eight pieces of artillery, occupying the salient of the outer line of works on the turnpike and his own defensive lines.

"Our artillery engaged at very short range, disabling some of the enemy's guns and blowing up two limbers. Another section of the same command opened from the right of the turnpike. They both held their positions, though with heavy loss, until their ammunition was spent, when they were relieved by an equal number of pieces from the reserve artillery, under Major Owen.

"Hagood, with great vigor and dash, drove the enemy from the outer lines in his front, capturing a number of prisoners, and, in conjunction ⱶ with Johnson, five pieces of artillery — three 20-pounder Parrotts and two fine Napoleons. He then took position in the works, his left regiment being thrown forward by Hoke to connect with Ransom's right. In advancing, his regiment encountered the enemy behind a second line of works in the woods, with abatis, interlaced with

ⱶ It was afterward claimed — and General Hoke confirmed the claim — that Hagood's brigade alone, with the assistance of no other command, captured these five pieces of artillery, the only ones taken by our troops from the enemy on that day.— G. T. B.

wire. Attack at that point not being contemplated, it was ordered back to the line of battle, but not before its intrepid advance had brought on it considerable loss. . . .

"Johnson, meanwhile, had been heavily engaged. The line of the enemy bent around his right flank, subjecting his brigade, for a time, to fire in flank and front. With admirable firmness he repulsed frequent assaults of the enemy, moving in masses against his right and rear. Leader, officers, and men alike displayed their fitness for the trial to which they were subjected. . . . The brigade, holding its ground nobly, lost more than a fourth of its entire number."

I hurried two regiments of the reserve to its support, but they were not properly posted by the officer leading them, and afforded but little assistance. Two regiments of Clingman's brigade were likewise sent by General Hoke to reënforce Johnson's left. They also failed to accomplish the object for which they were pressed forward. Seeing this, I now ordered Hoke to relieve his right center with his right; and Clingman's remaining regiments and [M. D.] Corse's whole brigade being used by him for that purpose, the enemy was soon forced to give way before them. A gap intervening between the troops on the left of Clingman and his own command led him to fall back to prevent a flank movement, thus isolating Corse, who, believing his right flank seriously menaced, retreated almost simultaneously, but not as far back as he was when first ordered to move forward. These two commands participated but little in the succeeding events of the day, though both were afterward marched again to the front, and gave evidence of their readiness to perform any duty that might be required of them. The enemy, however, did not occupy the ground from which Corse and Clingman had compelled him to retire, but held his own, none the less, with much stubbornness in Hagood's and Johnson's front; and, though giving way to Johnson's right, succeeded in securing a good position abreast of Proctor's Creek, near the turnpike, and also at the Charles Friend house. But General Johnson, with the timely assistance of the Washington Artillery, finally drove back the opposing forces from his right flank, and was thus enabled to clear his entire front. One of the pieces captured was now used against the enemy, who gave way beyond the Proctor Creek ridge, leaving but a skirmish line to keep up the appearance of a continuous contest. I took advantage of this somewhat unexpected lull in the movements of the enemy, first, to inquire into the whereabouts of General Whiting, the sound of whose guns was said to have been heard at 1:45 P. M., but who had given no further sign of an early junction with our forces; and second, to reorganize our lines, in order to present a more united front, were the enemy to show a desire to resume the offensive. No news came of Whiting. The only portion of his force which communicated with me on the 16th was a detachment of Dearing's command, acting as an escort to General T. M. Logan, one of the bearers of my instructions to General Whiting the day before, who had come, with the utmost celerity and through great danger, to inform me "that I need not rely on any advance being made that day by General Whiting." From him I also learned that Dearing, impatient at his commander's tardiness to obey my orders, and desirous of accelerating General Logan's return to me, had encountered the enemy's pickets near Chester, and had gallantly driven them in, forcing them back as far as the Half-way House and capturing a large number of stragglers; that there was great demoralization among the Federal troops; that nothing would have prevented Whiting from capturing the entire force of General Butler, had he followed my instructions.

I ordered the original formation of our lines to be resumed, and General Hoke was directed to send two regiments along the "Court House Road" to flank the enemy at that point, if possible, and erect enfilading batteries west of the railroad. A heavy storm of rain now came on, which very much retarded the movement. The enemy had opened a telling fire upon us just at that moment, but it took us very little time to silence it. Darkness prevented a farther advance that evening. Butler's intrenched camp was too near, and too many obstacles might have been met with to justify any unguarded move on my part. I therefore halted the troops for the night, and sent word to General Whiting that I expected his coöperation, early the next morning, at the railroad, on the right of our line.

We had defeated Butler and forced him to take refuge within his fortified lines. The communications south and west of Richmond were restored. We had achieved the main object for which our forces had encountered the enemy. But, though unable, for the present, to do us any harm,— though hemmed in, or "bottled up," as was said of him at that time,—he was none the less there, scarcely beyond cannon-shot of us; not much weakened in number, for during the progress of the fight we had only taken some 1400 prisoners, five pieces of artillery, and five stand of colors. We could and should have done more. We could and should have captured Butler's entire army.

Incomplete, however, as was the result of the Confederate victory at Drewry's Bluff, it had thwarted and annulled the main object of Butler's presence at Bermuda Hundred, and his expected coöperation, later on, with General Grant.

General Whiting joined me on the 17th near midday. He was thoroughly downcast. No word was spoken by him, and no attempt was made to throw off the responsibility of his failure to unite his forces to mine the day previous. He admitted the error of which he had been guilty, and expressed most heartfelt regret. At his own request he was relieved from duty in the field, and returned to the command of his department. His after-conduct during the closing scenes of the war, and his heroic conduct at Fort Fisher, contributed largely to reinstate him in the good opinion of his comrades-in-arms and of the entire South.

The forces just arrived from Petersburg had scarcely been put in position, when, by order of the War Department, and against my protest, the whole of Ransom's division was withdrawn from Drewry's Bluff and marched back to Richmond. I was then pursuing the enemy, and still driving him nearer and nearer to his base. Fortunately for us, his rout of the 16th had been such as to preclude, on his part, all thought of any determined resistance. He was clearly demoralized, if not destroyed, and his main object seemed to be to reach a secure position and shield himself from all further pursuit. He was successful in that, if in no other feature of his plan. General Grant, who fully understood Butler's actual position with respect to mine, took immediate advantage of the fact, and caused Smith's entire corps, numbering some sixteen thousand men, to be transferred from the Army of the James to the Army of the Potomac. Butler winced under the order, but obeyed. This reduced his force at Bermuda Hundred to about thirteen thousand. To oppose it I could command not more than twelve thousand men. The difference was insignificant; but it must be remembered that the Federal commander possessed many an advantage which I had not, and that, notwithstanding his defeat and the drain made upon him, he could, and eventually did, continue to threaten General Lee's communications with his main sources of supply through Richmond and Petersburg, thereby constantly endangering both of these cities. For that reason I considered it unwise to send reënforcements to the Army of Northern Virginia, as the War Department was already pressing me to do. Nor could I, later on, accept the proposition of General Lee to leave a sufficient guard for the purpose of watching Butler's movements, and with the rest of my command move to the north side of the James, to lead the right wing of his army.

But the War Department, in its great anxiety to increase the strength of the Army of Northern Virginia, readily yielded to the applications of its distinguished commander, and I was finally left with a portion only of Bushrod Johnson's division, say 3200 men, and Wise's brigade, 2200 more, including the local militia, making in all some 5400 men, with whom I was expected to protect, not only the Bermuda Hundred line, but also the city of Petersburg, and, to a certain extent, even Richmond itself. Nor should I omit to mention here that fully one-third of that force had to be kept unremittingly on picket duty.

CONFEDERATE ROLL-CALL.

BUTLER'S ATTACK ON DREWRY'S BLUFF.

BY WM. FARRAR SMITH, BREVET MAJOR-GENERAL, U. S. A.

A FIFTEEN-INCH GUN. FROM A PHOTOGRAPH.

ON the 31st of March, 1864, General Grant left Washington on a steamer to go and make the acquaintance of General B. F. Butler, then in command at Fort Monroe, and to determine for himself by personal observation if General Butler should be left in command of the force that was to operate from the Yorktown Peninsula in connection with the contemplated overland movement against Richmond. General Grant arrived at Fort Monroe on the morning of April 1st, went at once with General Butler to Norfolk, and satisfied himself during the day that it was proper to leave the command of the department in the hands of General Butler. Just as General Grant was about to leave Fort Monroe to return to Washington, about sunset of the evening of the 1st of April, a violent gale sprang up and detained his vessel at the wharf during that night and the next day. On the morning of the 2d General Grant went ashore, and General Butler then developed his idea of a campaign by making a landing in the "bottle" formed at Bermuda Hundred by the James and Appomattox rivers, and by operating from that position on the enemy in rear of Richmond.⎦ The plan was at once adopted. General Grant returned to Washington, leaving a letter of instructions dated Fort Monroe, April 2d, in which he said:

" When you are notified to move, take City Point with as much force as possible. Fortify, or rather intrench, at once and concentrate all your troops for the field *there* as rapidly as you can. From City Point directions cannot be given at this time for your further movements. The fact that has been already stated — that is, that Richmond is to be your objective point, and that there is to be coöperation between your force and the Army of the Potomac — must be your guide. This indicates the necessity of your holding close to the south bank of the James River as you advance. Then should the enemy be forced into his intrenchments in Richmond the Army of the Potomac would follow, and by means of transports the two armies would become a unit."

Had the order directing that City Point should be taken "with as much force as possible" been construed to mean the whole force under General Butler,

⎧On April 1st Butler disclosed to me his plan of landing at Bermuda Hundred. Having only reported to him two or three hours before, I did not like to say anything against the movement, or about my opinion that the first move should be for Petersburg. On April 2d, when General Grant came ashore, Butler got out his maps and sent for me. Not liking to oppose the campaign in Butler's presence, I did not go, but thought Grant would have some talk with me about it. He did not, but sat down and wrote Butler's instructions, which Butler understood as indorsing his plan entirely, and so I thought and still think from the text of them. After that of course I said nothing. After the movement, and our first move on Petersburg from Bermuda Hundred, Gillmore and I united in a letter to General Butler, telling him that Petersburg must be taken from the other side, and that he ought to bridge the Appomattox at the Point of Rocks so that we could cross there and get at Petersburg from the east. Butler declined, and said he was not going to build a bridge for West Point men to retreat over. After that we offered no advice.— W. F. S.

the campaign would have been entirely changed for the better, and any movement toward Richmond must have been by way of Petersburg, which was a vital strategic point, while the sequel will show that the position at Bermuda Hundred, though excellent for defensive purposes, was not properly situated for offensive action. Butler moved on the 5th of May in accordance with his own plan, with the Tenth and Eighteenth corps and the cavalry of the department, numbering in all about forty thousand men, landed at Bermuda Hundred, leaving a small force at City Point, and marched to the neck of land between the James and the Appomattox rivers. General Butler in his plan of campaign was tempted by the short line between the rivers, and, taking into account only the ease with which this line

MAJOR-GENERAL JOHN A. DIX. FROM A PHOTOGRAPH.

General Dix took command at Fort Monroe on June 2, 1862, and was relieved by General John G. Foster, July 18, 1863, and sent to succeed General Wool at New York City, where the draft riots had been in progress. General Foster was relieved at Fort Monroe by General Butler, November 11, 1863.

could be defended, forgot certain elements of great importance in an offensive campaign.

The James River will never again present such a scene as that of the 5th of May, 1864. An army of forty thousand men was afloat on its waters, convoyed by various vessels of the navy, then under command of Admiral Lee. It was a motley array of vessels. Coasters and river steamers, ferry-boats and tugs, screw and side-wheel steamers, sloops, schooners, barges, and canal-boats raced or crawled up the stream toward the designated landing. General Butler, to make his own command a perfect unit, had improvised for his own purposes a volunteer navy under the command of General C. K. Graham, an ex-navy officer, who, scorning the slow and steady progress of the admiral's squadron, took the lead, followed by the fastest transports in what seemed to be some grand national pageant. Fortunately no torpedoes or masked batteries checked General Butler's commodore, and by sunset a brigade had been landed at Bermuda Hundred above the mouth of the Appomattox River, and by 9 o'clock of the morning of the 6th

of May the Tenth and Eighteenth corps were in position on the line from
Walthall's Landing on the Appomattox across to the James, and the work of
intrenching called for by General Grant's letter of April 2d was begun, but
not in the specified place. The line taken up was about three and a half
miles in length. Richmond was on the right and Petersburg on the left. The
distance between the two cities was by the turnpike about twenty-one miles.
From the center of the lines to the turnpike was about two miles, and from
there to Petersburg about seven miles, with two unfordable streams, Swift
Creek and the Appomattox, intervening. Richmond, the objective of the
army, was covered by the works at Drewry's Bluff, a little over four miles
from our lines, and by the James River. Practically, the position taken up
was between two fortresses with wet ditches. In this campaign, whichever
way the Army of the James moved, it was weakened by two paralyzed forces,
one holding the line of intrenchments, and one necessarily posted to cover the
rear from the works in that direction. The colored troops, Hinks's division
of infantry, nominally attached to the Eighteenth Corps, and some cavalry
were left at City Point—for what purpose, unless to keep the letter of the
order of April 2d, it is hard to understand. In the movements of the campaign they might as well have been back in Fort Monroe. Though they
were wanting in drill, discipline, and actual service in the field, they had
many excellent officers and a division commander who united to great bravery much experience and the ability to take advantage of it.

On the 9th of May the two corps were ordered out in the direction of Petersburg. The enemy were easily driven back to Swift Creek, a distance of four
and a half miles, and the railroad and turnpike bridges were reached. The
stream was very narrow and with steep banks, and no crossing was possible
except by a bridge. Both bridges were guarded by artillery and infantry.
The railroad bridge, being only covered with "ties," was impassable in the
face of opposition, even by infantry. After several hours spent in ineffectual efforts to find a crossing place which offered a fair prospect of forcing a
passage, General Gillmore, commanding the Tenth Corps, and myself met for
consultation, and united in a letter advising General Butler that if Petersburg was to be taken, the proper way was to throw a bridge across the Appomattox behind our lines and, crossing there, to assault the works at Petersburg
from the east. General Butler's written answer disapproved of the suggestion; his spoken criticism was of such a character as to check voluntary
advice during the remainder of the campaign. [See p. 206.] The army
remained that night in its position on Swift Creek. On the 10th rumors
were current of a large force coming from Richmond, and under General
Butler's orders the troops fell back to the shelter of the intrenchments.

On the night of the 11th of May instructions were received from General
Butler for a movement at daybreak of the 12th in the direction of Richmond. The two white divisions of the Eighteenth Corps, with the exception
of the force necessary to leave in the lines, reënforced by a division of the
Tenth Corps, were to move out on the turnpike. General Gillmore, with the
remainder of his command, was to hold the road from Petersburg. As soon

as the Eighteenth Corps had passed Chester Station on the railroad, General Kautz was to move with his cavalry on the Danville road, destroying as much as possible of it. The colored division under General Hinks was to move up from City Point to Point of Rocks on the right bank of the Appomattox. The movement began shortly after daylight on the 12th, and General Weitzel in the advance on the turnpike began skirmishing shortly after leaving our lines, and steadily advanced until Red House or Red Water Creek was reached, when two pieces of artillery opened fire on him. These were driven away, and the creek was crossed and the line formed beyond it. Finding that the whole front of General Weitzel was covered by the enemy's skirmishers, his command was thrown to the right of the turnpike and six regiments of the reserve division were deployed on the left. This line was pressed forward, but the advance was slow, for on the left were a dense thicket and marshy ground extending from Red House in the direction of Proctor's Creek. As the entire line did not outflank the enemy's skirmishers there (but late in the day) General Gillmore with three brigades came up and took position on the left and the troops bivouacked in the rain. During the night another brigade was thrown to the left in order to give General Gillmore sufficient force to make a flank movement around the head of Proctor's Creek.

BREVET MAJOR-GENERAL JOSEPH R. HAWLEY.
FROM A PHOTOGRAPH.

Early on the morning of the 13th a brigade of General Brooks's division pushed forward and seized a hill beyond Cattle Run, overlooking the enemy's position on the left bank of Proctor's Creek. This cleared the country and allowed our line to press forward and re-form beyond Proctor's Creek at the Halfway House. In front was a line of woods. Pushing the line forward, the skirmishers found themselves on the outer edge of the woods in front of the heavy works at Drewry's Bluff. Strong profiles, with an outside ditch extending for over a mile, were in sight. Numerous embrasures were filled with artillery, and the ground had been cleared for a space of from 300 to 700 yards, which was entirely swept by the artillery in the works. A close reconnoissance by myself led me to report to General Butler that if the line were held in force by the enemy, it could not be carried by assault; that my troops were formed for an attack, and that I awaited orders to that effect.

Shortly after this news was received that General Gillmore had turned the enemy's outer works and held their extreme right. I was ordered to remain in my position. At daylight on the 14th skirmishers were ordered forward, and those of General Turner on my left soon occupied the enemy's works in their front. The right of General Brooks and all of the front of General Weitzel's command could make no impression upon the enemy's skirmishers. General Brooks's left occupied a portion of the line of works which Turner's command had entered. General Weitzel's advance through the woods had discovered a bastion salient on an eminence completely commanding Weitzel's position. The works on the enemy's left fell back to the James River and Drewry's Bluff, and on the right extended on the north-west beyond any point we could see. The prong or arm of the work which General Gillmore had turned, and which Turner and Brooks had entered, was like the spoke of a wheel, and started from the bastion salient before mentioned. A heavy fire of artillery was opened on Weitzel's lines from this salient, which he soon after checked by sharp-shooters. The day was spent in reconnoissances, and an assault ordered by General Butler was abandoned for the want of disposable troops to form a column.

On the morning of the 15th my position gave cause for anxiety. On my right, extending to the river and up to Drewry's Bluff, was an open, undulating country more than a mile in width, and offering every facility for the movement of a heavy column on our right and rear. This was covered by 150 mounted men of the colored cavalry. My troops were all in one thin line without reserves. I succeeded in getting two additional regiments to cover a road on my right and rear.

During the afternoon of the 15th I went with Generals Weitzel and Heckman to a farm-house about one hundred yards to the right and front of Heckman's command, forming Weitzel's right. This house [Willis's?] was situated on a knoll opposite the flank of the bastion before mentioned, and commanded a good view of the country between us and the James River. This farm-house I ordered to be heavily occupied by the reserves of the pickets. On reporting my weak and exposed condition to General Butler, I was informed that three regiments were at the Half-way House which could be used as a reserve. During the day I had instructed Generals Brooks and Weitzel to gather telegraph wire from the turnpike road and stretch it among the stumps in their front.✠ I left the farm-house after midnight, and returned to my headquarters a short time before daylight. All was quiet at that time and the moon was shining bright. Shortly after, I was aroused by a heavy musketry and artillery fire on my right. [See p. 201.] On going out I found a fog so dense that a horseman was not visible fifteen yards away. I established my headquarters on the turnpike as the only place where I could be found in the fog, communicated with Generals Brooks and Weitzel, sent a request to General Butler to order Gillmore to make an attack in his front, and ordered two of the reserve regiments at the Half-way House to march to the assistance of my right. I also sent orders for the artillery on the front to be withdrawn, as

✠ In 1883 General Butler claimed the credit for the use of the wire, and intimated that in Heckman's case his order with reference to it was not carried out. The fact is, there was not wire enough to go round. Brooks and one brigade of Weitzel were so near the enemy that I was fearful they might be run over. Heckman was not in such danger of a sudden rush, and so the wire was used in the direct front in contact with the enemy.—W. F. S.

the fog was so dense that it was of no use and was in danger of capture. The order did not reach some of the guns most exposed until it was too late, as the bearer of the message was killed. It must be understood that the guns had to be removed by hand, as they were too close to the enemy to keep horses in the vicinity. The two reserve regiments, the 112th New York and the 9th Maine, arrived on the right in time to check a force of the enemy that was moving on our rear. While this was going on the enemy made furious assaults on the brigades of Wistar and Burnham in my front. It was impossible to get any information from personal observation; fortunately the dense fog also hindered any intelli-gent movement of the enemy. General Weitzel soon reported to me a move-ment of the enemy still farther on his right, and as such a movement directly threatened our communications, my ar-tillery,—which had been withdrawn and which was without supports,—my am-munition train, and our lines at Bermuda Hundred, which had been left but feebly defended, I immediately ordered a re-tirement of the whole line, sending word to the right division of the Tenth Corps to conform to the movement in order to keep up the connection between the two corps. While this movement was going on [about 9 A. M.] the fog lifted and en-abled me to watch out for my right; and having rallied those troops of Heckman's brigade that had not been captured, I

MAJOR-GENERAL GODFREY WEITZEL.
FROM A PHOTOGRAPH.

ordered an advance which, however, by some mistake in the information he received, was not begun by General Weitzel. At this time I learned that the connection with the Tenth Corps had been broken, and then gave up the idea of an advance to recover my lines.

I then moved my entire line to the right to cover the turnpike and country road parallel to it, and again advanced for the purpose of recov-ering some of my wounded. The advance was maintained until a line of battle was met in the woods and the enemy was developed on both flanks. In obedience to the orders of General Butler, I then began to retire across Proctor's Creek to return to the intrenchments. The Tenth Corps, which had not been ordered to make a diversion in the early morning, was at that time across the turnpike in rear of Proctor's Creek to cover the crossing of the Eighteenth Corps. Without further molestation, both corps reëntered the historic bottle, which was at once carefully corked by a Confederate earth-work.

Of the details of the fight sustained by the Eighteenth Corps on the 16th a few may be given. Brooks and Weitzel report that not a man was driven from their lines in front; that the enemy in falling over the telegraph wire were slaughtered like partridges. General Weitzel says, May 22d, 1864:

" The four regiments of Heckman's brigade were crushed by the attack, but there was no surprise on account of the fog, as the whole line was in line of battle and prepared for the shock, having several times received warning from the farm-house. The other seven regiments of my line did not move until, after they had twice repulsed the enemy with terrible slaughter,— he being piled in heaps over the telegraph wire,— they were ordered to fall back."

In his report of May 29th General Weitzel adds:

" Have just received full files of Richmond papers from 16th to 28th. The force that attacked my division was six brigades of infantry, one unattached regiment of infantry, and three batteries of artillery, all under Major-General Ransom. His entire loss was near three thousand by official lists. They have about five hundred of my own men prisoners. General Heckman, who was captured in the fight, sends word that Gillmore could easily have gone in. They speak of the wire as a devilish contrivance which none but a Yankee could devise."

Ransom's division was demoralized by their repulse. Butler, on May 27th, 1864, says: "The number of Beauregard's wounded is 3040, which is considerably more than ours. We lost about 4500 in the two corps, of whom 1478 were missing." The Eighteenth Corps at Drewry's Bluff was composed of three and a half brigades stretched out in one thin line, with a mile of unguarded open country on its right. Against this force Beauregard brought seven brigades. It is the old story of masses thrown against a weak point. It is true that on this occasion the logical result did not follow, but the movement was skillfully planned, was as well carried out as circumstances would allow, and was a partial success. Beauregard's original plan contemplated the aid of a division from Petersburg. What changes that might have made in the result had it come on the field opportunely it is not pleasant to contemplate.

Had the instructions of April 2d of General Grant been strictly carried out, and had Petersburg been promptly attacked on the 6th of May, it would doubtless have fallen, and the Southern lines of communication would have been at the mercy of General Butler. He could then have waited patiently to be attacked, and the plum he so longed for might have dropped into his mouth. At any rate Lee could not have remained north of Richmond. Between a good plan of campaign and a faulty one, in this case, was only the width of a river, and the taking of the wrong bank of the Appomattox for a line of operations brought the campaign to a most lame and impotent conclusion in twelve days, including the day of leaving Fort Monroe.

On the 13th of May General Sheridan with his cavalry corps arrived at the James River opposite Bermuda Hundred. On the 14th he came to my headquarters and went with me to visit my lines. I pointed out to him my exposed right flank, and gave him a history of the campaign made by the Army of the James to that date, expressed my anxiety as to the future, and requested him on his return to the headquarters of General Grant to say to him for me that, in my opinion, the interests of the country would be best forwarded by withdrawing General Butler's army within its strong lines — leaving with him sufficient force to defend himself, and sending the remainder of the command to reënforce the Army of the Potomac.

FORDING THE MATTAPONY.

COLD HARBOR.

BY MARTIN T. McMAHON, BREVET MAJOR-GENERAL, U. S. V.

IN the opinion of a majority of its survivors, the battle of Cold Harbor never should have been fought. There was no military reason to justify it. It was the dreary, dismal, bloody, ineffective close of the Lieutenant-General's first campaign with the Army of the Potomac, and corresponded in all its essential features with what had preceded it. The wide and winding path through the tangled Wilderness and the pines of Spotsylvania, which that army had cut from the Rapidan to the Chickahominy, had been strewn with the bodies of thousands of brave men, the majority of them wearing the Union blue. No great or substantial success had been achieved at any point. The fighting in the Wilderness had told heavily against us, as it must necessarily against an assaulting army in such a country. A gleam of victory had come when the selected column of the Sixth Corps, under Russell and Upton, carried the works near Spotsylvania on the 10th of May.⎰ Failure elsewhere and conflicting orders had led to the abandonment of the works and the guns, and about one thousand prisoners remained as the sole fruits of the success. On the 12th, at the Bloody Angle, Hancock had inspired the army with new hope, taking there also four thousand prisoners by a brilliant dash, but the slaughter that followed in holding the works all day had saddened his success. Gloom and discouragement had taken hold of the army also, because of the death three days before of Sedgwick, an officer who would have been worth to that army many thousand men. Many other leaders had fallen whose names were familiar to the rank and file, but the Sixth Corps, although commanded by Sedgwick's most trusted lieutenant, General H. G. Wright, an able and gallant

⎰ Upton was promoted the next day by telegraph to be brigadier-general — an honor he had more than once deserved.—M. T. McM.

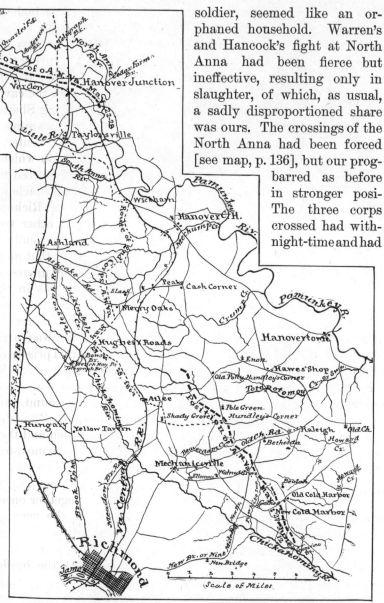

soldier, seemed like an orphaned household. Warren's and Hancock's fight at North Anna had been fierce but ineffective, resulting only in slaughter, of which, as usual, a sadly disproportioned share was ours. The crossings of the North Anna had been forced [see map, p. 136], but our progress had been barred as before by the enemy in stronger position than ever. The three corps which had crossed had withdrawn in the night-time and had commenced a movement toward the Pamunkey, a river formed by the junction of the North Anna and the South Anna. The passage of that river had been completed on May 28, and then, after three days of marching, interspersed with the usual amount of fighting, the army found itself again confronted by Lee's main

Confederate positions at the North Anna and at Cold Harbor, with the route of march of Ewell's corps to the latter place. By Jed. Hotchkiss, Top. Eng., Second Corps, A. N. V.

line on the Totopotomoy. The operations which followed were known as the battle of Cold Harbor.

On the afternoon of May 31st Sheridan, who was on the left flank of the army, carried, with his cavalry, a position near the old well and cross-roads known as Old Cold Harbor, and, with his men dismounted behind rough breastworks, held it against Fitzhugh Lee until night. To this point, during the night, marched the vanguard of the Army of the Potomac, the

Sixth Corps, under Wright, over roads that were many inches deep in dust. The night was sultry and oppressive. Many of our horses and mules were dying of thirst, yet they had to be forced through streams without halting to drink. Frequent messengers from Sheridan came during the night, urging the importance of rapid movement. About 9 the next day (June 1st) the head of the column reached Sheridan's position, and the cavalry was withdrawn. The enemy, who had been seriously threatening Sheridan, withdrew from our immediate front to within their lines and awaited us, occupying a strong outer line of intrenchments in front of our center, somewhat in advance of their main position, which included that on which the battle of Gaines's Mill had been fought two years before. It covered the approaches to the Chickahominy, which was the last formidable obstacle we had to meet before standing in front of the permanent works of Richmond. A large detachment, composed of the Eighteenth Corps and other troops from the Army of the James, under General W. F. Smith, had disembarked at White House on the Pamunkey, and was expected to connect that morning with the Sixth Corps at Cold Harbor. A mistake in orders caused an unnecessary march and long delay. In the afternoon, however, Smith was in position on the right of the Sixth Corps. Late in the afternoon both corps assaulted. The attack was made vigorously, and with no reserves. The outer line in front of the right of the Sixth and the left of the Eighteenth was carried brilliantly, and the enemy was forced back, leaving several hundred prisoners in our hands. On the left, where Russell advanced, our losses were severe. The men went forward under a terrible fire from front and flank, until they were ordered to lie down under such shelter as was afforded by the ground and the enemy's impenetrable slashing, to which they had advanced. Russell was wounded, but remained upon the field all day. This left the well and the old tavern at Cold Harbor in our rear, and brought us in front of the most formidable position yet held by the enemy. In front of him was a wooded country, interspersed with clearings here and there, sparsely populated, and full of swamps. Before daylight the Army of the Potomac stood together once more almost within sight of the spires of Richmond, and on the very ground where, under McClellan, they had defended the passage of the river they were now endeavoring to force.

On the 2d of June our confronting line, on which the burden of the day must necessarily fall, consisted of Hancock on the left, Wright in the center, and Smith on the right. Warren and Burnside were still farther to the right, their lines refused, or drawn back, in the neighborhood of Bethesda Church, but not confronting the enemy. The character of the country was such that at no point could the general direction of the various corps be seen for any considerable distance.

The enemy's general line, although refused at certain points and with salients elsewhere, because of the character of the country, was that of an arc of a circle, the concave side toward us, overlapping on both flanks the three corps intending to attack. The line of advance of Wright's command holding the center was therefore perpendicular to that of the enemy.

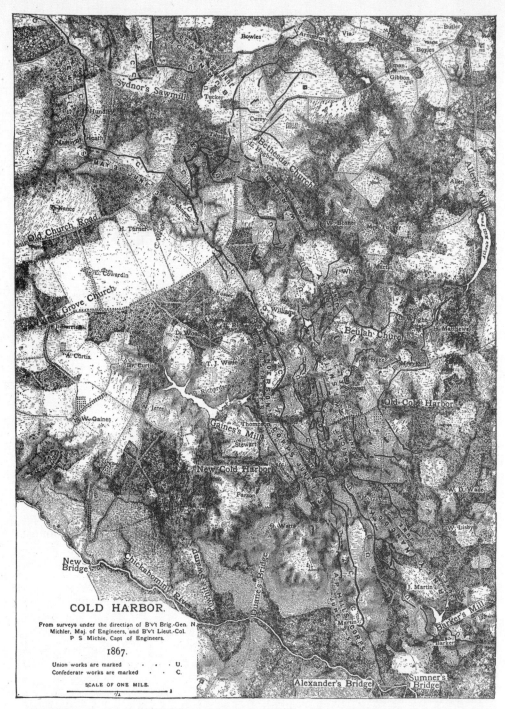

COLD HARBOR.

From surveys under the direction of B'v't Brig.-Gen. N.
Michler, Maj. of Engineers, and B'v't Lieut.-Col.
P S Michie, Capt of Engineers.

1867.

Union works are marked · · U.
Confederate works are marked · · C.

SCALE OF ONE MILE.

On the forenoon of June 1st Wright occupied an in-trenched line close to Old Cold Harbor. At that time Hoke's division formed the Confederate right, near New Cold Harbor, and Anderson's corps (Longstreet's) extended the line to a point opposite Beulah Church. During the afternoon W. F. Smith's corps arrived on the right of Wright, extending the Union line to Beulah Church. At 6 o'clock Smith and Wright drove the enemy through the woods along the road to New Cold Harbor and intrenched a new line. Warren was north of Smith. On June 2d Hancock formed on the left of Wright. Hill's corps and Breckinridge's division took position opposite, extending the Confederate line to the Chickahominy. Burnside, May 30th to June 1st, occupied lines facing south and west, above Sydnor's sawmill; June 2d he withdrew to Warren's right. Ewell's position throughout was on the Confederate left.

Hancock's line, connecting with Wright's left, extended obliquely to the left and rear. A movement upon his part to the front must necessarily take him off obliquely from the line of advance of the center. The same was true of Smith's command upon the right. What resulted from this formation the 3d of June developed. No reconnoissance had been made other than the bloody one of the evening before. Every one felt that this was to be the final struggle. No further flanking marches were possible. Richmond was dead in front. No further wheeling of corps from right to left by the rear; no further dusty marches possible on that line, even "if it took all summer." The general attack was fixed for the afternoon of the 2d, and all preparations had been made, when the order was countermanded and the attack postponed until half-past four the following morning. Promptly at the hour named on the 3d of June the men moved from the slight cover of the rifle-pits, thrown up during the night, with steady, determined advance, and there rang out suddenly on the summer air such a crash of artillery and musketry as is seldom heard in war. No great portion of the advance could be seen from any particular point, but those of the three corps that passed through the clearings were feeling the fire terribly. Not much return was made at first from our infantry, although the fire of our batteries was incessant. The time of actual advance was not over eight minutes. In that little period more men fell bleeding as they advanced than in any other like period of time throughout the war. A strange and terrible feature of this battle was that as the three gallant corps moved on, each was enfiladed while receiving the full force of the enemy's direct fire in front. The enemy's shell and shot were plunging through Hancock's battalions from his right. From the left a similarly destructive fire was poured in upon Smith, and from both flanks on the Sixth Corps in the center. At some points the slashings and obstructions in the enemy's front were reached. Barlow, of Hancock's corps, drove the enemy from an advanced position, but was himself driven out by the fire of their second line. R. O. Tyler's brigade (the Corcoran Legion) of the same corps swept over an advance work, capturing several hundred prisoners. One officer alone, the colonel of the 164th New York [James P. McMahon.— EDITORS.], seizing the colors of his regiment from the dying color-bearer as he fell, succeeded in reaching the parapet of the enemy's main works, where he planted his colors and fell dead near the ditch, bleeding from many wounds. Seven other colonels of Hancock's command died within those few minutes. No troops could stand against such a fire, and the order to lie down was given all along the line. At points where no shelter was afforded, the men were withdrawn to such cover as could be found, and the battle of Cold Harbor, as to its result at least, was over. Each corps commander reported and complained to General Meade that the other corps commanders, right or left, as the case might be, failed to protect him from enfilading fire by silencing batteries in their respective fronts: Smith, that he could go no farther until Wright advanced upon his left; Hancock, that it was useless for him to attempt a further advance until Wright advanced upon his right; Wright, that it was impossible for him to move until Smith and Hancock advanced to his support on the right and left to shield him from the enemy's enfilade. These dispatches necessarily caused mystification at headquarters; so much so that copies of Hancock's and Smith's dispatches were sent to Wright and copies of his to each of the others. The explanation was simple enough, although it was not known until reconnoissance had been made. The three corps had moved upon diverging lines, each directly facing the enemy in its immediate front, and the farther each had advanced the more its flank had become exposed.

Further telegraphic correspondence followed, and at last came a circular order to the corps commanders, understood to be from Lieutenant-General Grant. It directed, in substance, that the three corps should advance and attack with their entire forces the enemy's position in their respective fronts, without reference to the movements of other troops either upon their right or left. Unity of action, so necessary to success, could certainly not be expected from such an order. The attack was made here and there by the advance of troops that had retired for shelter, and by merely opening fire from troops that had already reached obstacles which they could not surpass; and the corps commanders duly reported that the attack had been made and had failed. A third time the order was given for a general assault along the whole line. It came to the corps head-

MAJOR-GENERAL FRANCIS C. BARLOW. FROM A PHOTOGRAPH.

quarters, was transmitted to the division headquarters, and to the brigades and the regiments without comment. To move that army farther, except by regular approaches, was a simple and absolute impossibility, known to be such by every officer and man of the three corps engaged. The order was obeyed by simply renewing the fire from the men as they lay in position. Shortly after midday came the order to suspend for the present all further operations, and directing corps commanders to intrench, "including their advance positions," and directing also that reconnoissances be made, "with a view to moving against the enemy's works by regular approaches."

The field in front of us, after the repulse of the main attack, was indeed a sad sight. I remember at one point a mute and pathetic evidence of sterling valor. The 2d Connecticut Heavy Artillery, a new regiment eighteen hundred strong, had joined us but a few days before the battle. Its uniform was bright and fresh; therefore its dead were easily distinguished where they lay. They marked in a dotted line an obtuse angle, covering a wide front, with its apex toward the enemy, and there upon his face, still in death, with his head to the works, lay the colonel, the brave and genial Colonel Elisha S. Kellogg.⚓

When night came on, the groans and moaning of the wounded, all our own, who were lying between the lines, were heartrending. Some were brought in by volunteers from our intrenchments, but many remained for three days uncared for beneath the hot summer suns and the unrefreshing dews of the sultry summer nights. The men in the works grew impatient, yet it was against orders and was almost certain death to go beyond our earthworks. An impression prevails in the popular

COLD HARBOR, JUNE 3—BOMB-PROOFS ON THE LINE OF THE SECOND CORPS. FROM A SKETCH MADE AT THE TIME.

mind, and with some reason perhaps, that a commander who sends a flag of truce asking permission to bury his dead and bring in his wounded has lost the field of battle. Hence the reluctance upon our part to ask a flag of truce. In effect it was done at last on the evening of the third day after the battle, when, for the most part, the wounded needed no further care and our dead had to be buried almost where they fell.

The work of intrenching could only be done at night. The fire of sharp-shooters was incessant, and no man upon all that line could stand erect and live an instant. This condition of things continued for twelve days and nights: Sharp-shooters' fire from both sides went on all day; all night the zig-zags and parallels nearer to the enemy's works were being constructed. In none of its marches by day or night did that army suffer more than during those twelve days. Rations and ammunition were brought forward from parallel to parallel through the zigzag trenches, and in some instances where regiments whose term of service had expired were ordered home, they had to leave the field crawling on hands and knees through the trenches to the rear. At 9 o'clock every night the enemy opened fire with artillery and musketry along his whole line. This was undoubtedly done under the suspicion that the Army of the Potomac had seen the hopelessness of the task before it and would withdraw in the night-time for another movement by the flank, and, if engaged in such a movement, would be thrown into confusion by this threat of a night attack. However, no advance was made by the enemy.

Another strange order came about this time. It opened with a preamble

⚓ Killed on June 1st, the day on which his regiment suffered great loss.—EDITORS.

that inasmuch as the enemy had without provocation repeatedly opened fire during the night upon our lines, therefore, at midnight of that day, the corps commanders were directed to open fire from all their batteries generally upon the enemy's position and continue it until daylight. This was coupled with the proviso that if in the opinion of a corps commander the fire would provoke a return from the enemy which would inflict severe damage upon his troops, then he was exempted from the operation of the order. The commanders of the three corps holding the front communicated with one another by telegraph with this result: Smith was satisfied that the fire which he would provoke would inflict upon him disproportionate damage. Hancock for the same reason did not intend to open fire unless the fire provoked by the other corps reached his lines. Wright adopted the same rule of action. Twelve o'clock came, and the summer night continued undisturbed.

Thus things went on until the 15th of June. Preparations had been made in the meantime for the abandonment of the position and the withdrawal of the army to another line of operations. Yet the summer had scarcely begun. The army was withdrawn successfully and skillfully, and, crossing to the south bank of the James, entered upon the new campaign before Petersburg, which culminated nearly a year thereafter in the capture of Richmond.

Cold Harbor was a discouraging fight in every particular. The men could not help recalling and discussing certain facts. Two years before, this same army had been placed much nearer Richmond with comparatively little loss. During Grant's advance from the Rapidan he had the advantage, of which he freely availed himself, of ordering troops to his assistance, not begging for them as McClellan did in vain. He depleted the defenses of Washington at his pleasure, and of new troops more than the number of men with which he commenced the campaign joined him before its termination at Appomattox. The line of the peninsula and the advance to Cold Harbor and the Chickahominy had been McClellan's second plan. His first had been a movement from Urbana [see Vol. II., p. 163], with the possibility in view of crossing to the south side of the James and compelling the evacuation of Richmond and its defenses. This plan had been overruled in Washington, and that of the peninsula, also suggested by McClellan, had been approved as a compromise. But the plan of an overland march to Richmond, while protected navigable waters within our control led to the very door, was fully tried between the 3d of May and the 15th of June and had failed. Whether the failure was due to faults inherent in the plan, or the belief upon the part of the Lieutenant-General that the Army of the Potomac had never been fought to its utmost in previous campaigns, or to the system, new to that army, of fighting battles by watch and wire, it is useless to inquire and difficult to determine.

"Cold Harbor," said General Grant, "is, I think, the only battle I ever fought that I would not fight over again under the circumstances" ("Around the World with General Grant," by John Russell Young, Vol. II., ch. XXXIV., p. 304); and again, in his "Memoirs," p. 276, Vol. II., "I have always regretted that the last assault at Cold Harbor was ever made."

A BOMB-SHELL IN AN ARTILLERY CAMP-FIRE — AN INCIDENT OF COLD HARBOR. FROM A SKETCH MADE AT THE TIME.

THE EIGHTEENTH CORPS AT COLD HARBOR.

BY WILLIAM FARRAR SMITH, BREVET MAJOR-GENERAL, U. S. A.

ON the 27th of May an order came from Washington to me near Bermuda Hundred to concentrate sixteen thousand men under my command ready for removal by water to a point opposite White House on the Pamunkey, there to protect a corps of bridge-builders. On the 28th I received the following order:

"HEADQUARTERS, IN THE FIELD, May 28th, 1864.

"MAJOR-GENERAL SMITH, Commanding Eighteenth Corps:

"The transportation for your column having arrived, although not in my judgment sufficient, yet in consequence of imperative orders from General Grant your column will move to his assistance. You will use the utmost expedition in embarking and getting on. If you desire any cavalry to accompany you, please designate what regiments or battalions. I grieve much that this weakness of the Army of the Potomac has called the troops away just as we were taking the offensive, and that the attack on Petersburg which was agreed on to take place to-morrow morning must be abandoned; but it is so ordered, and, however against our wishes and judgment, we must obey. I propose to give you every facility in going off. You will have to use great caution in going up the Pamunkey and in getting into White House. The torpedoes on the water or a well-arranged surprise on land would bring your expedition to grief, as you will not have the advantage in going away which we had coming. Your destination will be exactly known by the rebels the moment you start. Indeed, they have already predicted it in their newspapers. . . .

"BENJAMIN F. BUTLER, Major-General Commanding."

In half an hour after the receipt of this order my troops were moving to Bermuda Hundred and City Point for embarkation.

Learning at Fort Monroe by a telegram on the 29th that the Army of the Potomac had crossed the Pamunkey, I determined to land the troops directly at White House, and the debarkation began there on the morning of the 30th and proceeded as rapidly as the limited wharf facilities would admit.

The landing was covered by Captain Babcock of the U. S. Navy, in command of an old New York ferry-boat on which were mounted some bow and stern guns. The whirligig of time had brought me back to the Army of the Potomac, and that army to its campaigning grounds of 1862, it having in the interim traced a path resembling that reputed to have been made by the Israelites in the wilderness.

During the night of the 30th and the morning of the 31st I received three copies of an order dated Hanovertown, 1 P. M., May 28th, and signed by General Rawlins, chief-of-staff, directing me to leave a garrison at White House and move with the remainder of the command to New Castle, on the south side of the Pamunkey River. As none of the wagons or reserve ammunition had as yet arrived, and as some of the troops were still behind, I at once sent a confidential aide (Major P. C. F. West) to ask if the necessities were such as to make it incumbent on me to move as I then stood with reference to men, transportation, and supplies, or if I should wait until I could take with me the necessary transportation for the supplies. Fearing that there might be some urgent reason for the appearance at New Castle of such a force as I could gather, and in such condition as I could move it, I decided not to await an answer to my letter but to move at once. Leaving General Adelbert Ames with 2500 men at White House, I marched at 3:30 P. M. with about 10,000 infantry and artillery, but without wagons to carry supplies or ammunition. During the march I received the following autograph letter from General Grant:

" HEADQUARTERS, ARMIES OF THE UNITED STATES, NEAR HAWES'S SHOP, VA.,
May 30th, 1864, 7 : 30 P. M.

" MAJOR-GENERAL W. F. SMITH, Commanding Eighteenth Army Corps.

" GENERAL : Triplicated orders have been sent to you to march up the south bank of the Pamunkey to New Castle, there to await further orders. I send with this a brigade of cavalry to accompany you on the march.

" As yet no further directions can be given you than is contained in your orders. The movements of the enemy this evening on our left, down the Mechanicsville road, would indicate the possibility of a design on his part to get between you and the Army of the Potomac. They will be so closely watched that nothing would suit me better than such a move. Sheridan is on our left flank with two divisions of cavalry, with directions to watch as far out as he can go on the Mechanicsville and Cold Harbor roads. This, with the care you can give your left flank with the cavalry you have and the brigade sent to you, and a knowledge of the fact that any movement of the enemy toward you cannot fail to be noticed and followed up from here, will make your advance secure. The position of the Army of the Potomac this evening is as follows : The left of the Fifth Corps is on the Shady Grove road, extending to the Mechanicsville road and about three miles south of the Totopotomoy. The Ninth Corps is to the right of the Fifth ; then comes the Second and Sixth, forming a line being on the road from Hanover Court House to Cold Harbor and about six miles south of the Court House.

" U. S. GRANT, Lieut.-General."

At about 10 o'clock that night the command encamped at Bassett's, near Old Church, and about three miles from New Castle. The troops were not inured to long marches and suffered greatly from the heat. From Bassett's an aide was sent to inform General Grant of the position occupied by the Eighteenth Corps and to ask for further orders.

At daylight on June 1st I received from the headquarters of General Grant an order to proceed at once to New Castle ferry, and there place the command between the Fifth and Sixth Corps. From the urgency of the order I deemed minutes to be of importance, and the troops marched without breakfast. On reaching the ferry I found myself in a broad valley surrounded by hills within artillery range, but could find nothing of the Fifth or Sixth corps. I at once drew back to occupy the hills behind me, and send Captain Francis U. Farquhar of the Engineers to General Grant to say that there must have been some mistake in my order, and asking that it be rectified. Uncertain as to the position of the enemy, I began the construction of a bridge across the Pamunkey River, and while so engaged a staff-officer arrived from General Grant to say that there had been a mistake in my order, and that it should have read Cold Harbor instead of New Castle ferry.

The command was therefore marched back to Old Church and thence to Cold Harbor. The day was intensely hot, the dust stifling, and the progress slow, as the head of the column was behind the trains of the Sixth Corps. The ranks were consequently much thinned by the falling out of exhausted men. While we were on the march I received my first order from Meade, directing me to follow the Sixth Corps and form on its right at Cold Harbor. There I was to hold the line from Bethesda Church to Cold Harbor and join with the Sixth Corps in an attack. The distance between the two points was over three miles, and my force of less than ten thousand men would not have filled the space. As I could not fulfill both requirements of the order, I decided to join in the attack, and at once began the formation of the lines of battle.

A hasty reconnoissance of the ground showed that the enemy were posted in a wood in front, which was to be reached by crossing a wide open field. On the right two broad roads, leading from Mechanicsville and Shady Grove, united on an open plain which dominated the ground over which the attack was to be made. That point required a division to hold it, leaving only two divisions, numbering about six thousand men, for the assault. While preparations were being made for the attack, a note was sent to General Meade to inform him that, having moved from White House before the arrival of transportation or supplies, I had no ammunition except that in the cartridge-boxes, and asking that a supply might be sent to me as a reserve.

About the same time General Wright, commanding the Sixth Corps, sent to say that the enemy were turning his left flank, and asking for reënforcements. Though entirely without support on my right, I sent two regiments from the right division.

The attack was begun about 4:30 P. M. by the advance of the divisions of Generals Brooks and Devens. Under a severe fire they crossed the open field, and, entering the wood, made their way through slashings and interlaced tree-tops, and carried the rifle-pits, capturing about 250 prisoners. The brigade on the extreme right of the assaulting line, under the young and gallant Colonel Guy V. Henry, carried the rifle-pits in the front, but found the position commanded by an earth-work on the right flank against which no fire could be brought to bear, and the brigade fell back into the edge of the clearing. Beyond the woods, in another open field, was a second line of works, from which the troops received so heavy a fire that they fell back under

VIEW OF UNION BREASTWORKS ON THE COLD HARBOR LINE, JUNE 1.
FROM A SKETCH MADE AT THE TIME.

cover, and held the line of the captured rifle-pits. The advance of the line and the necessity for holding the roads on the right had increased the length of our front so that the greater part of it was held by one line of battle, and the two divisions which had been engaged had nearly exhausted their ammunition. At 10:30 P. M. I addressed a note to General Humphreys, chief-of-staff of the Army of the Potomac, in which I wrote:

" I have had the honor to report my necessities and requirements for ammunition, and, having now given the present condition of my situation, must leave it for the commanding general to determine how long I can hold this line if vigorously attacked."

About 12:30 A. M. of the 2d I received the following order :

"10:05 P. M., June 1st. You will make your dispositions to attack to-morrow morning on General Wright's right, and in conjunction with that officer's attack. This attack should be made with your whole force and as vigorously as possible.
"GEO. G. MEADE, Major-General."

To that I returned the following reply :

" Your order for an attack is received. I have endeavored to represent to you my condition. In the present condition of my line an attack by me would be simply preposterous — not only that, but an attack on the part of the enemy of any vigor would probably carry my lines more than half their length. I have called on General Wright for about 100,000 rounds of ammunition, and have asked it to-night. Deserters report enemy massing on my right for an attack in the morning."

About 2:30 A. M. I received an order postponing the contemplated attack until 5 P. M.

At 7 A. M. I received from General Wright sufficient ammunition to fill up the cartridge-boxes, which relieved a most pressing want; and during the morning a division of the Sixth Corps took the place of General Devens's division in the lines, enabling me to shorten my front so that it could be held. A division was also ordered to take post on my right, but it failed to appear.

The day was spent in strengthening the position and making ready for the next conflict. In the afternoon the following circular order was received:

"2:30 P. M., June 2d. Circular: The attack ordered for 5 P. M. this day is postponed to 4:30 A. M. to-morrow. Corps commanders will employ the interim in making examinations of the ground on their front and perfecting the arrangements for the assault.

"GEO. G. MEADE, Major-General Commanding."

Such an order of battle as was developed in that circular—an attack along the whole line—is denounced by the standard writers on the art of war, and belongs to the first period in history after man had ceased to fight in unorganized masses. Giving up the few advantages belonging to the assailants, it increases largely the chances of successful defense, and would never be adopted by a trained general, except perhaps under certain peculiar conditions, where also the attacking force had an overwhelming superiority in numbers. Aghast at the reception of such an order, which proved conclusively the utter absence of any military plan, I sent a note to General Wright, commanding the corps on my left, asking him to let me know what was to be his plan of attack, that I might conform to it, and thus have two corps acting in unison. General Wright replied that he was "going to pitch in." This left to me only the attack in front contemplated in the circular.

The position held by the Eighteenth Corps may be briefly given: A gap of nearly two miles between its right and the left of the Fifth Corps under Warren made it necessary to throw back the right flank of the corps to hold the open plain and roads and to prevent that flank from being turned. This necessity put the division on the right quite out of the battle, except in the use of its artillery at rather long range. In front of the center was a line of Confederate earth-works like a curtain, with a flanking arrangement at either end—that on the right being somewhat exposed to the fire of the artillery of my right division, that on the left being opposed to the left of the Eighteenth and right of the Sixth Corps. Near the center was a small stream with marshy sides running toward the enemy's lines. On its right was a bluff a few feet in height affording to the troops moving down the stream partial shelter from a cross-fire from the right.

The plan adopted gave to Devens, with his division, the duty of keeping the right flank secure. Martindale's division was to move down the stream to the assault, while the division of Brooks maintained our connection with the Sixth Corps on the left.

At precisely 4:30 on the morning of the 3d of June Martindale's command moved down the stream, out of the woods, and against the earth-works. The first line reached the foot of the works but fell back, under the heavy front and cross fire, to the edge of the woods, but within short musket range of the line they had gallantly attempted to carry.

Soon after the repulse of the first assault I made a personal inspection of General Martindale's front, and found that before again assaulting the works it would be necessary to form a line of battle faced to the right, to keep down in some measure the flank fire from the right on the assaulting column;

and also that to advance farther before the Sixth Corps advanced was to subject my troops to a heavy flank fire from the left. General Martindale was ordered to keep his column as well covered as possible, and only to advance when he saw an advance by General Brooks on his left. I then went to inspect the front of General Brooks and directed him to form a column for an assault, thinking then to inform General Wright that I would make with him a combined assault, and thus break up the cross-fire from the left. While General Brooks was forming his column, so heavy a fire from the right came in on his troops that I at once ordered him not to move, but to keep his men sheltered till the cross-fire slackened. Going back to the right to ascertain the cause of the firing, I found that Martindale had anticipated matters, and that under his orders Stannard's brigade had made three assaults, having been repulsed in all with severe loss.

I then made the following report to General Meade:

"General Martindale got into so hot a place that he was forced to assault the works without the assistance of the column of General Brooks. The assault was made three times, and each time repulsed. While I was on the front of General Brooks, the enfilading fire of the enemy was so heavy as to force me to give the order to General Brooks not to attempt to advance his column until the fire was slackened. This fire being entirely on my right, I have had nothing but artillery fire to use against it, and have therefore been unable to silence it. My troops are very much cut up, and I have no hopes of being able to carry the works in my front unless a movement of the Sixth Corps, on my left, may relieve at least one of my flanks from this galling fire."

In answer I received the following from the chief-of-staff of the Army of the Potomac, dated June 3d, 8 A. M.:

"General Wright has been ordered to assault and to continue his attack without reference to your advance, and the commanding general directs that your assault be continued without reference to General Wright's. General Wright has, but a very short time before the receipt of your communication through Major West, reported that he was waiting your advance to enable him to assault."

My right was held by General Devens, and his troops could not be spared for an assault. Of General Martindale's two brigades, Stannard's had been thoroughly used up, and Stedman, in addition to having been repulsed, was holding the line between Martindale and Devens, and also endeavoring to keep down the cross-fire from the right. Two of Brooks's brigades had suffered severely in the first advance and through holding their position under the terrible cross-fire. This left but one brigade of fresh troops, under General Burnham. I had had but about ten thousand men with me on the 1st of June, on my arrival, and had already lost heavily in killed and wounded.

On sending to the headquarters of the Army of the Potomac for artillery ammunition some strictures were made upon what was deemed my extravagant use of it, and I addressed a note to General Meade from which I make the following extract:

"I have nothing to cover the entire open space on my right but my artillery, and I have tried to keep down both the enemy's artillery and infantry fire which enfilades my front by artillery fire. I have a regiment so far advanced that I cannot withdraw it without serious loss, and the enemy are trying to get a battery in position to enfilade this regiment. It has become, therefore, somewhat of a question as to the expenditure of ammunition or *muscle*. All the artillery firing has been strictly under my orders, and has not exceeded the amount I have deemed necessary to cover my men. I regret exceedingly that the absence of my own ammunition should have forced me to make the requisition. Of its propriety the general commanding must himself be the judge."

To that General Meade replied, telling me to call for all the ammunition I required and additional batteries if they could be used, and adding:

"I am sorry to hear that General Martindale is unable to assault. I have just heard from Warren, who is forcing the enemy back on his right. I have directed him to push forward his left in order to relieve the attack you are able to make."

I then wrote and asked for two batteries of rifle guns, and stated:

"My last four regiments that I have got for an assault are now forming for an attack, but I dare not order it till I see more hope of success to be gained by General Warren's attack or otherwise."

Later in the day I received a verbal order from General Meade to make another assault, and that order I refused to obey.

I had carefully examined the entire front of my line, and was convinced that no assault could succeed that did not embrace a portion of the works in "front of my right," where I was powerless to make an attack.

An assault under such conditions I looked on as involving a wanton waste of life. An hour or more after I had declined to obey the order Colonel Comstock, an engineer officer of General Grant's staff, and to-day a distinguished officer of the Corps of Engineers, came to me and said that he had been ordered by General Grant to go over my lines. This visit was but the natural consequence of my act, and I at once directed Captain Farquhar, of the Engineers, who was on my staff, to accompany Colonel Comstock. After a reasonable lapse of time Captain Farquhar came back and, smiling, said, "Comstock was thoroughly satisfied and has gone back to report to General Grant." What Colonel Comstock reported I never knew, but I heard nothing more from headquarters on the subject. Some of the troops of other corps must have been more advantageously situated for making an attack than the Eighteenth Corps, but no success seemed to have attended the efforts made on any part of the line, for the next order I received was dated 1:30 P. M., and read:

"Orders. For the present all further offensive operations will be suspended. Corps commanders will at once intrench the positions they now hold, including their advance positions, and will cause reconnoissances to be made with a view to moving against the enemy's works by regular approaches."

My troops were put under cover as rapidly as possible and the front line was strengthened. The last order of the day was as follows, and dated 6:30 P. M.:

"Circular to Corps Commanders. The commanding general directs you to report the condition of affairs in your front and what it is practicable to do to-morrow."

In obedience to it I made this report:

"In reference to the condition of affairs in my front, I would respectfully state that I now hold and have held all that I have gained, and am now intrenching myself as rapidly as possible. In reference to what it may be practicable to do to-morrow on my front, I can only say that what I failed to do to-day, viz., to carry the enemy's works on my front by columns of assault on the most practicable point (on my front), I would hardly dare to recommend as practicable to-morrow with my diminished force. General Ames's column is reported quite near here, which will a little more than make good my loss of to-day."⸗

There was very little straggling during the battle,—far less than I had usually observed. Shortly after the attack began in the morning there came out from the fray a fine-looking sergeant in the new and untarnished uniform of a "Heavy Artillery Regiment" which had joined the army the day before. As he passed I asked him where he was going. Touching his hat in the most approved military manner, he said, "General, I am going back to the hill to rally."

MAJOR-GENERAL HORATIO G. WRIGHT.
FROM A PHOTOGRAPH.

The stragglers did not always succeed in reaching a place of safety, for four or five of them had hidden in a dense thicket in the ravine down which Martindale had moved. A series of most unearthly screams near headquarters occasioned the sending of a staff-officer to ascertain the cause. He reported that a shell which had passed over the column of assault had exploded in this thicket and had horribly mangled all the skulkers.

At the close of the battle the front of General Martindale was less than two hundred yards from the enemy's line, and in the open space between were many dead and wounded. For three days no cessation of hostilities was asked for, and common rumor gave as a reason that there was fear of a refusal, as there were no dead or wounded of the enemy between the lines to be cared for. Some of our wounded were brought in by men who risked their lives in the act, and some were rescued by digging trenches to them. The groans of such as could not be reached grew fainter and fainter until they ceased.

On the morning of June 5th General Meade came to my headquarters to say that he was going to fill the gap on my right, and during his visit I asked him how he came to give such an order for battle as that of the 2d. He replied that he had worked out every plan for every move from the crossing of the Rapidan onward, that the papers were full of the doings of *Grant's* army, and that he was tired of it, and was determined to let General Grant plan his own battles. I have no knowledge of the facts, but have always supposed that General Grant's order was to attack the enemy at 4:30 A. M. of the 3d, leaving the details to his subordinate.

⸗ During the evening some regiments rejoined which had been detained at the Pamunkey by want of transportation, and that night General Ames came up with 2500 men, having been relieved by other troops from duty at White House.—W. F. S.

On the 9th of July following, I had a conversation with General Grant about the campaign, in which I expressed the opinion that the battle of Cold Harbor was fought in contravention of military principles, with which, after some discussion, he seemingly agreed, saying that he had never said anything about it, because it could do no good. On the 19th of the same month he referred to the former discussion, saying that he had come to the conclusion that I had intended to whip him over Meade's shoulders, and that he thought " it was a very good battle anyhow."

In his report dated July 22d, 1865, General Grant devotes to the subject only the following sentences: " On the 3d of June we again assaulted the enemy's works in the hope of driving him from his position. In this attempt our loss was heavy, while that of the enemy I have reason to believe was comparatively light."

There is a branch of the art of war which can be executed with such precision as fairly to entitle it to be classed as a science. I refer to logistics, so far as that term relates to the moving of armies and the placing of troops at the proper time in the immediate vicinity of a chosen battle-field. Complete ignorance of this subject or culpable neglect ruled the logistics that brought the Army of the Potomac to the battle-field of Cold Harbor in 1864. The Union arms were robbed of the advantages of the position, and of the success gained by General Sheridan on the 31st of May, by a failure to concentrate the army against the right flank of the enemy early on the morning of the 1st of June. From the failure there resulted a concentration that left four exposed flanks ⚓ in close proximity to the enemy, caused a delay of many hours in the attack of the 1st of June, made that attack fruitless in results, and gave to us the murderous order of parallel advance to battle of June 3d.

In conclusion, let us review the logistics of Cold Harbor. On the 30th of May, the line held by the Army of the Potomac ran along the road from Hanover Court House to Cold Harbor, beginning at a point about six miles south of the Court House, where the right of the Sixth Corps rested. To the left came the Second, Ninth, and Fifth corps in the order named, the left of the latter corps being near Bethesda Church. On that day at White House, fifteen miles to the left, the Eighteenth Army Corps was debarking. On the 31st Sheridan, with two divisions of cavalry, had engaged and driven the enemy from their rifle-pits at Cold Harbor. The force he encountered consisted of infantry and dismounted cavalry, which proved that he was on Lee's flank when Lee had as yet but little infantry. Sheridan, thinking it unsafe to attempt to hold the place with his isolated command, retired from the town, but was met by an order to hold Cold Harbor at all hazards. Returning, he reoccupied the works, and strengthening them held his position until relieved by the Sixth Corps, about 10 o'clock the next morning.

On the 31st the determination was reached to concentrate at Cold Harbor, and that afternoon the Sixth Corps moved under orders for Cold Harbor, about fifteen miles distant; the Second Corps was ordered to march and take position on the left of the Sixth Corps, having about the same distance to

⚓ The wide gap between the Eighteenth and the Fifth corps made two additional flanks.—W. F. S.

move. The Eighteenth Corps, at White House, about thirteen miles from Cold Harbor, moved on the 31st, at 3:30 P. M., for New Castle, fifteen miles up the Pamunkey, and thence, on the 1st of June, about twelve miles to Cold Harbor, taking place on the right of the Sixth Corps, and thus crossing both the lines of march of the Sixth and Second corps. It arrived in time to join in an attack at 4:30 P. M. of the 1st. The Fifth Corps did not move at all, remaining in its position two miles to the right of the Eighteenth Corps. This gap threw one division of the Eighteenth Corps practically out of action on both the days of battle.

When the concentration near Cold Harbor was determined upon, had the Eighteenth Corps been ordered to join Sheridan it would have reached him on the night of the 31st, with about the same length of march it did make, and would have been fresh for battle early on the morning of the 1st. The Sixth Corps, moving to take position on the right of the Eighteenth, would have had a shorter march than it made, and should have been in position at an early hour of the same morning. The Second Corps, with a very short march, would have filled the gap between the Sixth and Fifth corps, and would also have been in position for an early battle. The Ninth Corps could have marched to a proper place as a reserve. The army would then have presented a continuous line and an oblique order of battle, with the right wing thrown back or refused.

In speaking of a concentration much better than the one which was made by the Army of the Potomac, Jomini says: " The logistics were contemptible."

NOTES ON COLD HARBOR.

BY GEORGE CARY EGGLESTON, SERGEANT-MAJOR, LAMKIN'S VIRGINIA BATTERY.

I ALWAYS think of our arrival at Cold Harbor as marking a new phase of the war. By the time that we reached that position we had pretty well got over our surprise and disappointment at the conduct of General Grant. I put the matter in that way, because, as I remember, surprise and disappointment were the prevailing emotions in the ranks of the Army of Northern Virginia when we discovered, after the contest in the Wilderness, that General Grant was not going to retire behind the river and permit General Lee to carry on a campaign against Washington in the usual way, but was moving to the Spotsylvania position instead. We had been accustomed to a programme which began with a Federal advance, culminated in one great battle, and ended in the retirement of the Union army, the substitution of a new Federal commander for the one beaten, and the institution of a more or less offensive campaign on our part. This was the usual order of events, and this was what we confidently expected when General Grant crossed into the Wilderness. But here was a new Federal general, fresh from the West, and so ill-informed as to the military customs in our part of the country that when the battle of the Wilderness was over, instead of re-

tiring to the north bank of the river and awaiting the development of Lee's plans, he had the temerity to move by his left flank to a new position, there to try conclusions with us again. We were greatly disappointed with General Grant, and full of curiosity to know how long it was going to take him to perceive the impropriety of his course.

But by the time that we reached Cold Harbor we had begun to understand what our new adversary meant, and there, for the first time, I think, the men in the ranks of the Army of Northern Virginia realized that the era of experimental campaigns against us was over; that Grant was not going to retreat; that he was not to be removed from command because he had failed to break Lee's resistance ; and that the policy of pounding had begun, and would continue until our strength should be utterly worn away, unless by some decisive blow to the army in our front, or some brilliant movement in diversion,—such as Early's invasion of Maryland a little later was intended to be,—we should succeed in changing the character of the contest. We began to understand that Grant had taken hold of the problem of destroying the Confederate strength in the only way that the strength of such an army, so commanded, could be destroyed, and that he intended to continue the plodding work till the task should be accomplished, wasting very little time or strength in efforts to make a brilliant display of generalship in a contest of strategic wits with Lee. We at last began to understand what Grant had meant by his expression of a determination to "fight it out on this line if it takes all summer."

Our state of mind, however, was curiously illustrative of the character of the contest, and of the people who participated in it on the part of the South. The Southern folk were always debaters, loving logic and taking off their hats to a syllogism. They had never been able to understand how any reasonable mind could doubt the right of secession, or fail to see the unlawfulness and iniquity of coercion, and they were in a chronic state of surprised incredulity, as the war began, that the North could indeed be about to wage a war that was manifestly forbidden by unimpeachable logic. In the same way at Cold Harbor we were all disposed to waste a good deal of intellectual energy in demonstrating to each other the absurd and unreasonable character of General Grant's procedure. We could show that he must have lost already in that campaign more men than Lee's entire force, and ought, logically, to acknowledge defeat and retire; that having begun the contest with an overwhelming advantage in point of numbers, he ought to be ashamed to ask for reënforcements; and that while by continuing the process of suffering great losses in order to inflict much smaller losses on us, he could ultimately wear us out, it was inconceivable that any general should consent to win in that unfair way. In like manner we were prepared to prove the wicked imbecility of his plan of campaign, a plan that could only end by placing him in a position below Richmond and Petersburg, which he might just as well reach by an advance from Fort Monroe, without the tremendous slaughter of the Wilderness, Spotsylvania, etc.

In view of General Grant's stolid indifference to considerations of this character, however, there was nothing for us to do but fight the matter out. We had no fear of the ultimate result, however plainly our own perception of facts pointed to the inevitable destruction of our power of resistance. We had absolute faith in Lee's ability to meet and repel any assault that might be made, and to devise some means of destroying Grant. There was, therefore, no fear in the Confederate ranks of anything that General Grant might do; but there was an appalling and well-founded fear of starvation, which indeed some of us were already suffering. From the beginning of that campaign our food supply had been barely sufficient to maintain life, and on the march from Spotsylvania to Cold Harbor it would have been a gross exaggeration to describe it in that way. In my own battery three hard biscuits and one very meager slice of fat pork were issued to each man on our arrival, and that was the first food that any of us had seen since our departure from Spotsylvania, two days before. The next supply did not come till two days later, and it consisted of a single cracker per man, with no meat at all.

We practiced a very rigid economy with this food, of course. We ate the pork raw, partly because there was no convenient means of cooking it, but more because cooking would have involved some waste. We hoarded what we had, allowing ourselves only a nibble at any one time, and that only when the pangs of hunger became unbearable.

But what is the use of writing about the pangs of hunger? The words are utterly meaningless to persons who have never known actual starvation, and cannot be made otherwise than meaningless. Hunger to starving men is wholly unrelated to the desire for food as that is commonly understood and felt. It is a great agony of the whole body and of the soul as well. It is unimaginable, all-pervading pain inflicted when the strength to endure pain is utterly gone. It is a great despairing cry of a wasting body — a cry of flesh and blood, marrow, nerves, bones, and faculties for strength with which to exist and to endure existence. It is a horror which, once suffered, leaves an impression that is never erased from the memory, and to this day the old agony of that campaign comes back upon me at the mere thought of any living creature's lacking the food it desires, even though its hunger be only the ordinary craving and the denial be necessary for the creature's health.

When we reached Cold Harbor the command to which I belonged had been marching almost continuously day and night for more than fifty hours without food, and for the first time we knew what actual starvation was. It was during that march that I heard a man wish himself a woman, — the only case of the kind I ever heard of, — and he uttered the wish half in grim jest and made haste to qualify it by adding, "or a baby."

Yet we recovered our cheerfulness at once after taking the first nibble at the crackers issued to us there, and made a jest of the scantiness of the supply. One tall, lean mountaineer, Jim Thomas by name, who received a slight wound every time he was under fire and was never sufficiently hurt to quit duty, was standing upon a bank of earth, slowly munching a bit of his last cracker and watching the effect of some artillery fire which was in progress at the time, when a bullet carried away his cap and cut a strip of hair from his head, leaving the scalp for a space as bald as if it had been shaved with a razor. He sat down at once to nurse a sharp headache, and then discovered that the cracker he had held in his hand was gone, leaving a mere fragment in his grasp. At first he was in doubt whether he might not have eaten it unconsciously, but he quickly discovered that it had been knocked out of his hand and crushed to bits by a bullet, whereupon as he sat there in an exposed place, where the fire was unobstructed, he lamented his loss in soliloquy. "If I had eaten that cracker half an hour ago, it would have been safe," he said. "I should have had none left for next time, but I have none left as it is. That shows how foolish it is to save anything. Whew! how my head aches! I wish it was from over-eating, but even the doctor couldn't lay it to that just now. The next time I stand up to watch the firing, I'll put my cracker — if I have any — in a safe place down by the breastwork, where it won't get wounded, poor thing! By the way, here's a little piece left, and that'll get shot while I sit here talking." And with that he jumped down into the ditch, carefully placed the mouthful of hard-tack at the foot of the works, and resumed his interested observation of the artillery duel.

Trifling of that kind was constant among the men throughout that terrible campaign from the Wilderness to Petersburg, and while it yielded nothing worth recording as wit or humor, it has always seemed to me the most remarkable and most significant fact in the history of the time. It revealed a capacity for cheerful endurance which alone made the campaign possible on the Confederate side. With mercenary troops or regulars the resistance that Lee was able to offer to Grant's tremendous pressure would have been impossible in such circumstances. The starvation and the excessive marching would have destroyed the *morale* of troops held together only by discipline. No historical criticism of our civil war can be otherwise than misleading if it omits to give a prominent place, as a factor, to the character of the volunteers on both sides, who, in acquiring the steadiness and order of regulars, never lost their personal interest in the contest or their personal pride of manhood as a sustaining force under trying conditions. If either side had lacked this element of personal heroism on the part of its men it would have been driven from the field long before the spring of 1865. It seems to me, the most important duty of those who now furnish the materials out of which the ultimate history of our war will be constructed is to emphasize this aspect of the matter, and in every possible way to illustrate the part which the high personal character of the volunteers in the ranks played in determining the events of the contest. For that reason I like to record one incident which I had an opportunity to observe at Cold Harbor.

Immediately opposite the position occupied by the battery to which I belonged, and about six or eight hundred yards distant across an open field, lay a Federal battery, whose commander was manifestly a man deeply in earnest for other and higher reasons than those that govern the professional soldier: a man who fought well because he fought in what he felt to be his own cause and quarrel. His guns and ours were engaged almost continuously in an artillery duel, so that I became specially interested in him, particularly as the extreme precision of his fire indicated thoroughness and conscientiousness of work for months before the campaign began. One day — whether before or after the great assault I cannot now remember — that part of our line which lay immediately to the left of the position occupied by the battery to which I belonged was thrown forward to force the opposing Federal line back. It was the only large movement in the way of a charge over perfectly open ground that I ever had a chance to observe with an unobstructed view, and merely as a spectator. When we, with a few well-aimed shells, had fired a barn that stood between the lines, and

driven a multitude of sharp-shooters out of it, the troops to our left leaped over their works and with a cheer moved rapidly across the field. The resistance made to their advance was not very determined, — probably the Federal line at that point had been weakened by concentration elsewhere, — and after a brief struggle our men crossed the slight Federal earth-works and pressed their adversaries back into the woods and beyond my view. It was a beautiful operation to look at, and one the like of which a soldier rarely has an opportunity to see so well; but my attention was specially drawn to the situation of the artillery commander, to whom I have referred as posted immediately in our front. His position was the pivot, the point where the Federal line was broken to a new angle, when that part of it which lay upon his right hand was pressed back while that on his left remained stationary. He fought like a Turk or a tiger. He directed the greater part of his rapid fire upon the advancing line of Confederates, but turned a gun every few moments upon our battery, apparently by way of letting us know that he was not unmindful of our attentions, even when he was so busily engaged elsewhere. The bending back of the line on his right presently subjected him to a murderous fire upon the flank and rear, a fire against which he had no protection whatever, while we continued a furious bombardment from the front. His position was plainly an untenable one, and, so far as I could discover with a strong glass, he was for a time without infantry support. But he held his ground and continued to fight in spite of all, firing at one time as from two faces of an acute triangle. His determination was superb, and the coolness of his gunners and cannoneers was worthy of the unbounded admiration which we, their enemies, felt for them. Their firing increased in rapidity as their difficulties multiplied, but it showed no sign of becoming wild or hurried. Every shot went straight to the object against which it was directed; every fuse was accurately timed, and every shell burst where it was intended to burst. I remember that in the very heat of the contest there came into my mind Bulwer's superb description of Warwick's last struggle, in which he says that around the king-maker's person there "centered a little *war*," and I applied the phrase to the heroic fellow who was so superbly fighting against hopeless odds immediately in front of me. Several of his guns were dismounted, and his dead horses were strewn in rear. The loss among his men was appalling, but he fought on as coolly as before, and with our glasses we could see him calmly sitting on his large gray horse directing the work of his gunners and patiently awaiting the coming of the infantry support, without which he could not withdraw his guns. It came at last, and the batteries retired to the new line.

When the battalion was gone and the brief action over, the wreck that was left behind bore sufficient witness of the fearfulness of the fire so coolly endured. The large gray horse lay dead upon the ground; but we preferred to believe that his brave rider was still alive to receive the promotion which he had unquestionably won.

SHERIDAN'S TREVILIAN RAID.

BY THEO. F. RODENBOUGH, BREVET BRIGADIER-GENERAL, U. S. A.

WHILE Torbert and Gregg had been engaged near Cold Harbor, Wilson had been operating on our right flank. He fought at Mechump's Creek on May 31st, 1864; Ashland, June 1st; and Hawes's Shop and Totopotomoy Creek, June 2d. The fight at Ashland was brought on by McIntosh, in a successful dash at the railroad bridges over the South Anna. The permanent injury of Lee's lines of supply was an important element in Grant's purposes. To this end, on the 26th of May, Hunter was directed to move down the Shenandoah Valley to Lynchburg, cut the canal, and return over the Lynchburg branch of the Virginia Central to Charlottesville, where it was expected he would meet Sheridan.

That officer was again to "cut loose" from the army, and, after tearing up the Virginia Central near Gordonsville, to coöperate with Hunter, if practicable. In obedience to instructions Sheridan, with the divisions of Torbert and Gregg, numbering, exclusive of non-combatants, about eight thousand men, started (June 7th) from New Castle on the Pamunkey, crossed that river on pontoons, moved rapidly via Aylett's, Polecat Station, Chilesburg, New Market, Mt. Pleasant, Young's Bridge, crossed the South Anna at Becker's Store, and bivouacked on the evening of the 10th at Buck Childs's, three miles from Trevilian Station. On the march, whenever the column passed near the railroad it was cut in several places. The weather was hot, and the roads heavy with dust, causing the weaker horses to drop out; in all cases where this occurred the disabled animals were shot by the rear-guard. As on the Richmond raid, transportation and supplies had been reduced to a minimum, the entire train, including ammunition wagons and ambulances, not exceeding 125 vehicles. Two days' short forage, carried on the saddle, three days' rations, and one hundred rounds of ammunition were carried by each trooper. While moving along the north side of the river, Sheridan heard that the infantry of Breckinridge was *en route* to Gordonsville, and that the cavalry of Hampton and Fitz Lee were in pursuit of Sheridan's column, and straining every nerve to reach the objective point first.

Sheridan's intention was to cut the main line of the Virginia Central at Trevilian Station, and the Lynchburg branch at Charlottesville. At dawn of the 11th of June shots were interchanged by the pickets near Trevilian. Custer was sent with his brigade by a wood-road to the left to strike the Louisa Court House road, and move up to the first-named station from the east, while the remainder of Torbert's division approached that point from the north-east. The bulk of Sheridan's command, preceded by the Reserve Brigade (Merritt's), passed through our picket line, and as the leading regiment, 2d United States Cavalry, took the trot it encountered a patrol, or advance-guard, of the enemy. This was driven back, and several prisoners taken, who stated that they belonged to the brigade of General M. C. Butler, of Hampton's cavalry. The Reserve Brigade advanced a quarter of a mile farther, when it found the enemy in force, dismounted, in a piece of timber, which extended across the road for some distance. Our cavalry was partly dismounted, and the entire First Division became engaged. Merritt reported that "the enemy was driven through a thick, tangled brushwood for over two miles to Trevilian Station; but not without serious loss to ourselves, though we inflicted heavy punishment on the adversary in killed, wounded, and prisoners. Among his wounded was General Rosser; a colonel commanding brigade was killed,— his body, together with most of the enemy's killed and wounded, falling into our hands. Few less than two hundred prisoners were taken by the brigade. The enemy's retreat finally became a rout; led horses, mounted men, and artillery all fled together in the wildest confusion. Williston, with his battery, did excellent practice with his guns, planting shells in the midst of the confused mass of the enemy. Trevilian Station was thus gained. In this retreat part of the enemy went toward Gordonsville, whilst fragments were driven off on the road to Louisa Court House. In their headlong career these latter came in contact with the First Brigade, which, being engaged toward its rear by the advance of Fitzhugh Lee's division, coming from Louisa Court House, was compelled to abandon some captures it had made from the led horses and trains of the force that was engaging the rest of the division.

General Custer's operations are described by Colonel A. C. M. Pennington, then commanding Horse Battery "M," 2d United States Artillery:

"We moved out about 6:30 A. M., the battery following the leading regiment. As the command struck the road we discovered the impedimenta of a cavalry column, pack-mules, ambulances, wagons, etc., all of which we captured and sent to our rear a short distance. The enemy, which turned out to be Hampton's division going toward Gordonsville ahead of us, halted and began to form. I was ordered to bring two guns forward to a position selected by General Custer; found Custer at a high board-fence, which separated him from the station (Trevilian). He told me to bring one gun on the road and bring the other to where he stood with his staff, mounted. I took up the gun and placed it in position, pointing at the board-fence, from which we were to knock the boards to enable us to enfilade a battery of the enemy. Number one at the gun had his axe uplifted in the act of striking, when we discovered a line of dismounted rebel cavalry getting over a rail-fence, about a hundred yards on our right. Custer ordered every one 'to get out of there,'— and we lost no time."

In the meanwhile part of Hampton's force attacked Custer, killing some of the men and horses of the battery before it could gallop into a more favorable position and open on the enemy. Colonel Alger, 5th Michigan Cavalry, got in between Hampton's dismounted men and their led horses,

See "Sheridan's Richmond Raid," p. 188, of which this article is a continuation, for a map giving Sheridan's route in the Trevilian raid.— EDITORS.

capturing about 350 men and horses. Custer sent his captures to his rear,—that is, toward Louisa Court House,— where also were parked his wagons and the caissons of Pennington's battery. It was supposed that Hampton's entire force was then in front. It appears, however, that Fitz Lee, who should have been closed up on Hampton, was late in getting out that morning, and Custer, without knowing it, struck the road between them. When Lee attempted to close up he espied a wagon-train, caissons, etc. (Custer's), and obligingly took them under his protection. The spoil included all of Custer's captures (except two hundred prisoners), his headquarters wagon, and his colored cook, "Eliza," who usually occupied an antique ruin of a family carriage on the march, and was called by the soldiers "the Queen of Sheba." In one of the fluctuations of the fight that day "the Queen" escaped, and came into camp with her employer's valise, which she had managed to secure.

While moving upon the rear of the First Brigade, Fitz Lee's men also espied one of Pennington's guns in a tempting spot; they drove away its slight support and captured the piece, but the limber and most of the artillerymen escaped. Upon reporting this loss, Pennington said he thought the enemy intended to keep it. "I'll be d——d if they do," responded his irate chief; and collecting some thirty men, Custer led them in person where the gun was being hauled off by hand. Failing in his first attempt, he dismounted every other man of a lot of horse-holders near, and, aided by several mounted staff-officers, charged and recovered the gun.

The First Brigade of Gregg's Division guarded the corps train and the rear; the Second Brigade (Irvin Gregg's) was put in on the left of Torbert, and by vigorously attacking Fitz Lee enabled Custer to retire in good order and rejoin the First Division.

Torbert tried to communicate with Custer several times, without success until after noon, when Captain Dana, assistant adjutant-general, managed to reach the isolated brigade, which he found in a tight place; it formed a hollow triangle pressed on all sides, but was banging away cheerfully. At one time Custer's color-bearer was killed, and to prevent the capture of the flag the brigade commander tore it from the staff and thrust it in his bosom. Finally about 5 P. M. the brigade was extricated and took position to Merritt's left rear. Fitz Lee now faced the Union left flank, his line being perpendicular to Merritt's. The two parts of the Union line formed a right angle; the Reserve Brigade occupying the right of the line to the vertex of the angle, the Second Brigade on its left occupying part of the other line with the Second Division, and the First (Custer's) Brigade formed en échelon to the left rear. On the night of the 11th the enemy retired toward Gordonsville.

The morning of the 12th was spent in a thorough destruction of the railroad for five miles, from Louisa Court House to a point one mile west of Trevilian. At 3 P. M. Torbert advanced toward Gordonsville to find the most direct route by which to return. He found the enemy strongly in-

trenched across his path. The Confederate line faced to the east, Fitz Lee being on the right, perpendicular to the railroad. Merritt says:

"The Reserve Brigade was ordered to attack the enemy's left, and it was intended that the First Brigade should coöperate on our left, while the Second Brigade was held in reserve. The Reserve Brigade went in on an open field to its right and attacked the enemy's left flank vigorously. It was slow work, however, and as the enemy was not pressed on the left, he concentrated his force on the brigade, and by larger numbers and fresh troops gave the command as much as it could attend to. . . . In thus advancing, the right of the brigade was so swung around as to be exposed to the enemy's attack on its wing. This he was not slow to take advantage of, when a squadron of the 2d Cavalry, my only remaining mounted support to the battery, was thrown in to meet the attack. Coming up on the right of the 6th Pennsylvania, which up to that time had been the extreme right regiment in line, they charged gallantly, and, though few in numbers, by the impetuosity of their onslaught drove the enemy back and protected the right until relieved by two regiments of the Second Brigade. After these two regiments got in position this squadron (2d United States Cavalry) was withdrawn to again act as support to the battery, which was ordered to advance, a good position having been gained on the right. Right gallantly did the battery come up in the midst of a heavy musketry fire, we being at that time so close to the enemy that their shells all flew far over us. Planting three guns of the battery in this position, where it dealt the enemy heavy blows, Lieutenant Williston moved one of the brass 12-pounders on to the skirmish-line; in fact, the line was moved to the front to allow him to get an eligible position, where he remained with his gun in the face of the strengthened enemy (who advanced to its very muzzle) dealing death and destruction in their ranks with double loads of canister. It was now dark, and I was directed to retire the brigade, . . . the enemy not advancing."

The 10th New York, of Davies's brigade, also distinguished itself in the assault; the remainder of Gregg's division continued the destruction of the railroad. General Hampton says:

"At 3:30 P. M. (12th) a heavy attack was made on my left, where Butler's brigade was posted. Being repulsed, the enemy made a succession of determined assaults, which were all handsomely repulsed. In the meantime General Lee had, by my direction, reënforced my left with Wickham's brigade, while he took Lomax's across to the Gordonsville road so as to strike the enemy on his right flank. This movement was successful, and the enemy, who had been heavily punished in front, when attacked on his flank fell back in confusion. I immediately gave orders to follow him up, but it was daylight before these orders could be carried out, the fight not having ended until 10 P. M."

Hampton reports a loss in his own division of 59 killed, 258 wounded, and 295 missing; aggregating 612. Fitzhugh Lee's losses are not given.

General Sheridan reported this day's fight as

"by far the most brilliant one of the present campaign. The enemy's loss was very heavy. My loss in killed and wounded will be about 575. Of this number 490 were wounded. I brought off in my ambulances 377 — all that could be transported. The remainder were, with a number of the rebel wounded that fell into my hands, left behind. Surgeons and attendants were detailed and remained in charge of them. I captured and have now with me 370 prisoners of war, including 20 commissioned officers. My loss in captured will not exceed 150."

From prisoners Sheridan learned that Hunter, instead of coming toward Charlottesville, was near Lexington, moving upon Lynchburg; that Ewell's corps was on its way to Lynchburg; and that

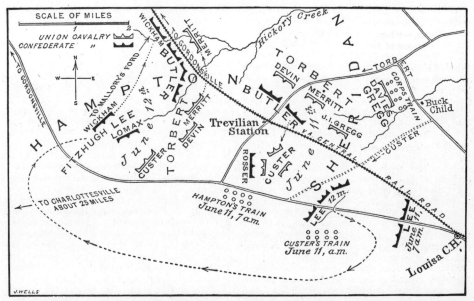

MAP OF THE BATTLE OF TREVILIAN STATION. FOR SHERIDAN'S ROUTE DURING THE RAID, SEE MAP, P. 190.

Breckinridge was at Gordonsville. ♱ He concluded, therefore, to return. During the night of the 12th the command moved back, recrossed the North Anna at Carpenter's Ford, unsaddled the horses and turned them out to graze; the poor animals had been without food for two days. The enemy came in sight but once during the entire march to West Point on the York River, from which place the wounded were sent by transport to Washington. Nothing could exceed the tender care bestowed upon the wounded, and the humane treatment of the prisoners by the commanding general and his staff. Every kind of conveyance was utilized to transport the disabled: ordinary army wagons, ancient family carriages, buggies, and gigs, in all stages of decrepitude, were appropriated for ambulance purposes. General Sheridan placed his own headquarters spring-wagon at the disposal of the medical director, Surgeon Pease, who is gratefully remembered by hundreds who came under his treatment at this time. When it was suggested that the prisoners be paroled on the spot, Sheridan replied, "In that case it might be hard to convince people that we have captured any." In order to keep them up with the column, a portion of the command was from time to time dismounted, and the prisoners permitted to ride, so that they came in as fresh as their captors. A large number of negro refugees attached themselves to the column and added to the difficulties of the subsistence department.

General Humphreys, an able and, in this case, impartial critic, says (after quoting the reports of Sheridan and Hampton):

"It is apparent from these accounts that General Hampton was defeated and driven several miles from the position he had determined to hold against Sheri-

dan's further advance. The conclusion of Sheridan, on the night of the 12th, was evidently sound; the movement of Hunter had rendered it impracticable to carry out his orders in the presence of Hampton."

On the 18th of June Sheridan learned that supplies awaited him at White House; which depot he was ordered to break up, transferring its contents to the new base. On the 19th the column crossed the Mattapony at Dunkirk, and on the 20th its commander learned that White House was threatened by the enemy. It was guarded by a small detachment, made up of invalids, dismounted cavalry, and colored infantry, commanded by General Getty, who was *en route* to join his permanent command. Sheridan moved leisurely to the spot, found the enemy on the bluffs overlooking the depot, and drove them away. Having made all preparations on the 24th, Sheridan took up the line of march for Petersburg, with his valuable charge of nine hundred wagons. The enemy, foiled at White House, were in an ugly mood. On this day Torbert was in front; Gregg was on the flank, where he was marching parallel with the train when he was attacked, at St. Mary's Church, by Hampton's entire corps. After the column had started Sheridan was compelled by circumstances to change the orders for the march. A courier was dispatched to Gregg but never reached him, and, largely outnumbered, Gregg was left to fight alone. He was severely handled, but lost no guns. Gregg states to the writer, "In this engagement the light batteries, commanded respectively by Randol and Dennison, did the most effective work, unsurpassed by that on any other field." Sheridan reports, "This very creditable engagement saved the train, which should never have been left for the cavalry to escort."

♱ This information was false. It is now known that Breckinridge had moved on Lynchburg.—T. F. R.

At daylight on the 29th, having seen the train safely over the James at Wilcox Landing, the Cavalry Corps crossed and went into camp at Windmill Point. Here a little rest was anticipated, but hardly had they unsaddled when Sheridan was ordered to move to the relief of Wilson, who, returning from a raid on the enemy's railroads, south of the James, was confronted by an overwhelming force. At midnight the divisions of Torbert and Gregg reached Prince George Court House, to learn that Wilson had returned within our lines.

Wilson's small division had been engaged in the varied and thankless duties of an infantry auxiliary until June 20th, when his command was swelled to 5000 effective men by the addition of Kautz's division (of Butler's army) of four regiments.

On the 22d Wilson started under orders from Meade to cut the Weldon and Southside roads, and to continue the work of destruction "until driven from it by such attacks of the enemy as you can no longer resist." This was carried out to the letter. He moved rapidly, preceded by Kautz's division, from Prince George Court House to the Weldon road, at Reams's Station; thence (via Dinwiddie Court House) to a point on the Southside road, fourteen miles from Petersburg. Here W. H. F. Lee failed to detain the leading division, but did interrupt the march of Wilson with his own division, under McIntosh. Pushing on, with the loss of seventy-five men, Wilson further destroyed the Southside road. At Burksville, on the 26th, Kautz inflicted great damage. Wilson found the bridge over the Staunton River in the enemy's possession and impassable. He then turned eastward, and moved on Stony Creek Station on the Weldon road. Here he had a sharp fight, and learned from prisoners that, in addition to a small infantry garrison, Hampton, just returned from Trevilian, was in his front. Wilson withdrew his train in the night, and headed for Reams's, where he had good reason to think he would find Meade's infantry. On the way he was severely handled. Upon reaching Reams's, Kautz, with Wilson's advance, found it in the possession of the enemy's infantry, and by the time Wilson came up he was virtually surrounded. Here he destroyed his wagons and caissons, and in an attempt to retire via Double Bridges on the Nottoway River was obliged to abandon all his artillery, and a general stampede ensued. Kautz returned with a fragment of the command by one route; Wilson, with the remnant that could be rallied, by another, and after meeting with many difficulties rejoined the Cavalry Corps at Lighthouse Point, July 2d. Wilson had been absent 10 days, had marched 300 miles, and had destroyed 60 miles of railroad and much valuable rolling-stock. He had lost nearly 1000 men and 16 guns. It is stated that General Grant declared, however, "the damage inflicted on the enemy more than compensated for any that had been received."

At an inspection of Wilson's command, soon after its return, the Corps Inspector was struck by the variety of costume worn. Some of the men were literally in rags from too intimate acquaintance with bush and brier. But they were in good spirits. One fine-looking specimen of the American volunteer, whose arms and brasses were very bright, paraded in a pair of trousers barely covering his knees and barefooted. "Have you no shoes or stockings?" demanded the astonished inspecting officer. "No, sir!" replied the man, with a grin; "not this side of Ohio."

The corps remained at Lighthouse Point for the next twenty days, recuperating after more than sixty days of continuous marching and fighting.

The final operations of the cavalry, prior to Sheridan's transfer to the Shenandoah, were not the least of its brilliant services.

In connection with the firing of the Burnside Mine, upon which so much depended, Grant arranged a coöperative demonstration by a force under Hancock, to consist of the Second Corps and two divisions of the Cavalry Corps. This force crossed the Appomattox at Point of Rocks on the night of July 26th; the bridge being covered with hay to muffle the sound. Before morning the James had been crossed at Deep Bottom, and some infantry at the bridge driven away. The cavalry moved toward New Market and Charles City; Torbert's division, headed by the 2d United States Cavalry, driving in the enemy's pickets on the New Market road. The Second Corps reconnoitered the enemy's works in the direction of Chaffin's Bluff. This combined advance developed a large force of the enemy's infantry in Sheridan's front, which extended from New Market to Malvern Hill — Gregg being on the right of the line with Kautz's brigade in his rear. The cavalry line had hardly been formed when the enemy advanced to the attack and pressed our skirmish-line back over the crest of the ridge, along which the dismounted men lay. Lieutenant W. H. Harrison, of the Reserve Brigade, says in "Everglade to Cañon with the Second Dragoons":

"The enemy's first volley passes over our heads. So closely are we pressed that we fear, unless reënforced speedily, we shall lose our led horses. With a cheer that makes our hearts bound, the 1st New York, 1st United States, and 6th Pennsylvania, on the run, dismounted, form themselves on our shattered line. A few volleys from our carbines make the line of rebel infantry waver, and in an instant the cry is heard along our entire line, "Charge!" "Charge!" We rush forward, firing as we advance, the enemy's colors fall, and the North Carolina brigade breaks in complete rout, leaving three stand of colors, all their killed and wounded, and many prisoners in our hands."

Two hundred and fifty prisoners were taken at this time. This counter-attack was made by the First and Second divisions simultaneously. The affair is called the battle of Darbytown.

The enemy, deceived by the extended front of Hancock's force, at once sent a large part of the Petersburg garrison to succor Richmond. The illusion was kept up until the next day, when preparations were made for withdrawal. On the 30th this was effected. On August 1st Sheridan was ordered with two divisions to the Shenandoah.

From May 5th to August 1st, 1864, the casualties in the Cavalry Corps are estimated at 5500 men, and the expenditure in horses, from all causes, about 1500. Our captures exceeded 2000 men and 500 horses, besides many guns and colors.

THE CAVALRY FIGHT AT TREVILIAN STATION.

BY M. C. BUTLER, MAJOR-GENERAL, C. S. A.

IN June, 1864, the armies of Northern Virginia and of the Potomac were confronting each other in front of Richmond. Grant, in command of the latter, had ventured to move upon the capital of the Confederacy and take it from the line of the Rapidan and Rappahannock, and every step of his march had been contested by General Lee, in command of the Army of Northern Virginia, until he finally turned the head of Grant's column toward the James River and compelled him to adopt a new line of attack. In the progress of these movements, while the splendid infantry and artillery of these two armies were struggling for the mastery around the Confederate capital, Hunter was moving up the valley at the head of a strong force toward Lynchburg to strike at the rear of Richmond. On the 5th of June Grant detached two divisions of his cavalry under Sheridan toward Gordonsville to destroy the railroad communications between Richmond and Gordonsville and Lynchburg, and possibly to form a junction with Hunter.

My brigade consisted of the 4th, 5th, and 6th South Carolina Cavalry, then recently transferred from the sea-coast of South Carolina, where they had seen little active service in the field; and this, with Young's and Rosser's brigades, constituted Hampton's division. On the evening of the 8th of June we were encamped not far from Atlee's Station, on the then Virginia Central Railroad. I received orders late in the day from division headquarters to have my command in readiness the next morning "for extended mounted service." On the morning of the 9th of June we marched up the turnpike toward Beaver Dam Station, and on the following day, the 10th, we passed Louisa Court House, and bivouacked not far from Trevilian Station. Rosser's and Young's brigades, the latter under command of Colonel Wright of the Cobb Legion (General Young being absent, wounded), were in advance of my brigade, and camped higher up the road toward Gordonsville. Besides his own division Hampton had Fitzhugh Lee's, consisting of Wickham's and Lomax's brigades, and this division was in our rear, toward Louisa Court House.

On the night of the 10th my orders were to be prepared the next morning at daylight for action. Accordingly at the dawn of day we were mounted and drawn up in column of regiments, prepared with the usual supply of ammunition, etc., for immediate action. It may be well to state just here that my brigade, about 1300 strong, was armed with long-range Enfield rifles, and was, in fact, mounted infantry, but for our sabers.

General Rosser rode down to my bivouac about sunrise and inquired if I was informed of what we were to do, to which I replied that I knew nothing except the orders above recited, to be prepared for action at daylight, and that I was awaiting instructions. Whereupon he proposed that we ride to General Hampton's headquarters at Netherland's house, about half a mile below Trevilian, and, if

possible, ascertain his plans. General Hampton informed us he expected to form a junction with General Fitzhugh Lee at Clayton's Store, where he would engage Sheridan. Rosser returned to his command, and General Hampton and I rode from Netherland's toward Clayton's Store, on a road that I was picketing, for the purpose of reconnoissance.

We had advanced but a short distance from the railroad when we were met by Captain Mulligan's squadron, of the 4th South Carolina, which had been on picket, retiring before the enemy, by whom he had just been driven in. General Hampton then ordered me to bring up my brigade and attack at once, telling me that he was expecting to hear Fitzhugh Lee's guns on my right on his way up by another road from Louisa Court House. I sent in Captain Snowden's squadron of the 4th South Carolina to charge whatever he met, and develop the force in front of us. It was soon ascertained that a heavy column of Sheridan's command was moving on us, and I thereupon dismounted squadron after squadron until my entire command was on foot, except Captain John C. Calhoun's squadron of the 4th South Carolina regiment, and we were soon driving the enemy before us in the very thick woods. I heard firing on my right and expected every moment to form a junction with Fitzhugh Lee. General Hampton also informed me, when I moved in from the railroad, that he would hold Young's brigade in readiness to reënforce my line as the exigency might require. Consequently I went ahead until the enemy had doubled on my left flank, when I sent to the rear for Young's brigade. On the arrival of the head of Colonel Wright's column, dismounted, I directed him to Colonel Rutledge, whose regiment, the 4th South Carolina, was on the left, and paid little attention to my right, where Colonel Aiken was stationed with the 6th South Carolina, as I supposed it was protected by Lee's division. Colonel Wright had some difficulty in the thick undergrowth in finding his position on Rutledge's left, the enemy meantime pounding us with all his might. While we were thus struggling with a superior force in my front, and the stubborn fight had been kept up at close quarters for several hours, I received information from the rear that Custer, with a mounted column, had moved by an open road to my right, around my right flank, and had captured some of my ambulances, whereupon I received orders from General Hampton to withdraw and mount my command. This was easier said than done, for Sheridan was pressing me in front and gradually outflanking my line. I slowly withdrew by mounting one regiment at a time on such horses as we could reach, and fell back to a point not far from the railroad. On reaching a position where the doctors had established a field infirmary under a large oak-tree, I found some ambulances parked and the wounded being cared for. Meantime Rosser had thundered down the Gordonsville road, charged and scattered Custer's forces, and, together with

MAJOR-GENERAL THOMAS L. ROSSER, C. S. A.
FROM A PHOTOGRAPH.

a charge by Captain Calhoun's squadron, recaptured what he had taken, and besides got possession of Custer's headquarters ambulances and a number of his horses and men. While I was massing my command near this field infirmary I received orders from division headquarters to take the Phillips Legion of Young's brigade and charge the crossing of the railroad. This I did, and drove a part of Custer's brigade in confusion into a field beyond. About the time I had reached the railroad I was recalled to the point from which we had started, and on reaching it discovered a compact line of battle of blue-coats advancing, dismounted. I must mention at this point an act of gallantry and dash I have never seen surpassed. Lieutenant Long, of the 6th South Carolina, had a small mounted detachment acting as a provost guard; I directed him to charge the advancing enemy and check them, while I ordered the removal of the ambulances and led horses. He promptly obeyed, and of course had many of his saddles emptied, but he accomplished the purpose I had in view.

I formed a new line on the crest of a hill running at right angles with the position I had occupied early in the day, and formed a junction with Rosser, and kept up the contest until nightfall.

My command camped that night at Green Spring Valley, two or three miles away, with light rations for the men, and nothing for our distressed and worn-out animals but bearded wheat. General Rosser was severely wounded in the leg late in the afternoon, while we were driving the enemy before us, and had to retire from the field, the command of his brigade devolving upon Colonel Richard H. Dulany, of the 7th Virginia. This day's operations

ended disastrously to our arms. I venture to believe that I am not claiming too much for the gallant troops under my immediate command when I say that they bore the brunt of the fight, and but for their stubborn and invincible courage must have been annihilated. In making this claim I do not wish to be understood as disparaging others, for I am confining this narrative to my own command.

The next morning, the 12th of June, General Hampton placed me in command of his division. The command of my brigade devolved upon Colonel Rutledge. Colonel Aiken had been severely wounded in the engagement of the day before. Early in the forenoon I posted the division on the railroad near Denny's house, about a mile above Trevilian Station; Rutledge on the left, Young's, still commanded by Colonel Wright, in the center, and Rosser's on the right. The line formed an obtuse angle on the railroad embankment, and extended off to the right with an open field in front, and to the left along the embankment. Beginning at the railroad, I had thrown up temporary breastworks of fence-rails and such materials as were available. The 6th South Carolina occupied the angle, with the 5th and 4th South Carolina regiments to its left along the embankment, and Young's and Rosser's brigades filling up the space to the right, with two batteries of horse artillery of four guns each — Hart's and Thomson's — stationed at convenient points on the line.

In this position I awaited Sheridan's attack, having kept scouts well to the front to watch his movements. Between 1 and 2 o'clock P. M. I was advised of his advance, and was prepared to receive him. He drove in my skirmishers, and moved promptly upon that portion of his line occupied by Rutledge with my brigade. This attack was repulsed without much effort. The second attack was made with more vigor, and was directed sharply upon the angle above described, where the 6th South Carolina was stationed. This, too, was repulsed; and between then and dark five distinct and determined assaults were made upon us, making seven in all. I had placed two brass howitzers of Thomson's battery just in the rear of our line, not far to the right of the angle, in the open field. As there was no protection to the men who served the guns, they were picked off and shot by Sheridan's sharp-shooters as fast as they could take their positions. I consequently directed Major Chew, commanding the artillery battalion, to have the survivors withdrawn to a place of safety, and had to rely upon Hart's and Thomson's guns stationed farther to the right. The attacking forces would spread out, and at times open fire along our entire front, but whoever was in command of the attacking column, with the eye of a good soldier, selected this angle for his most determined assaults. On the eve of every attack we could hear in the woods preparations for the onslaught, the sounding of bugles, words of command, etc.

Between sunset and dark, when the dusk of the evening was still further shrouded by the smoke of the battle, and after six assaults had been repulsed, we heard the usual preparation for another, and, as I concluded, the last desperate effort. Now that the dusky atmosphere would in a measure protect the cannoneers from the sharp-shooters, I directed Major Chew to reman the two howitzers and double-shot them with canister, as I believed the enemy would emerge from the woods a little more than a stone's-throw in our front, cross the fence (which they had not previously done), and rush for our line. They did just as I had anticipated, and came charging out of the woods in the open field and into the railroad cut immediately in our front. Before the canister and still steady fire of our carbines and rifles the enemy fell back for the last time before the deadly aim of our troops.

At one time during the progress of the fight, one or two of Sheridan's guns—as we were informed, of Pennington's battery—got in a position to enfilade my line along the railroad embankment and were playing havoc with my men. I called Captain Hart's attention to it, and directed him to concentrate the fire of the six guns to our right, and endeavor to silence Pennington's enfilading fire. This was done with great promptness and efficacy, and the enemy's guns were silenced. At another time, Sheridan's sharp-shooters effected a lodgment in the houses just across the railroad in our immediate front, and kept up a destructive fire upon us from their sheltered position. I directed the guns to be turned upon them, and in a short time they set fire to the house where the greatest number of the enemy's sharp-shooters had assembled, and it was consumed by fire. Sheridan must have begun his retreat soon after his last charge, about dark. Pursuit by my command was out of the question. We had been engaged in this bloody encounter from its beginning without food or rest for either men or horses, in the broiling sun of a hot June day, and recuperation was absolutely necessary. As it was, I was not relieved and did not withdraw from my lines until 2 o'clock on the morning of the 13th, and in the meantime had to care for the wounded and bury the dead.

Sheridan's forces consisted of two divisions, the First commanded by General A. T. A. Torbert, and the Second by General D. McM. Gregg. The First Division was composed of the Reserve Brigade, 1st, 2d, and 5th U. S. Cavalry (Regulars), 6th Pennsylvania Cavalry, 1st New York Dragoons, commanded by Brigadier-General Wesley Merritt, the First Brigade consisting of the 1st, 5th, 6th, and 7th Michigan Cavalry, commanded by Brigadier-General G. A. Custer; the Second Brigade, 4th, 6th, and 9th New York Cavalry and 17th Pennsylvania Cavalry, commanded by Colonel T. C. Devin. The Second Division, commanded by General David McM. Gregg, was composed of two brigades, the First, commanded by General H. E. Davies, consisted of the 1st Massachusetts, 1st New Jersey, 10th New York, and 1st Pennsylvania. The Second Brigade was commanded by Colonel J. Irvin Gregg, and consisted of the 2d Pennsylvania, 4th Pennsylvania, 8th Pennsylvania, 13th Pennsylvania, and 16th Pennsylvania, making twenty-two regiments in the two divisions.

Sheridan had four batteries of horse artillery, Batteries H and I, 1st United States (Regulars), Battery D, 2d United States, and Battery M, 2d United States. The returns of May 31st, 1864, show 450 officers and 9889 men "present for duty" in the First and Second divisions, making a total of 10,337 officers and men.‡

Hampton's command consisted of, as I have stated, Butler's brigade, the 4th, 5th, and 6th South Carolina; Rosser's brigade, 7th, 11th, and 12th Virginia, and White's battalion of two companies; Young's brigade, Cobb's Legion, ten companies; Phillips Legion, six companies; Jeff Davis Legion, four companies; 7th Georgia Cavalry, ten companies, and Millen's Georgia battalion, four companies. Fitzhugh Lee's division was composed of Wickham's brigade, the 1st, 2d, 3d, and 4th Virginia; Lomax's brigade, the 5th, 6th, and 15th Virginia, making for the two divisions, thirteen regiments and three battalions. The horse artillery, with Hampton at Trevilian, were three batteries, Hart's South Carolina, Thomson's Virginia, and one other Virginia battery. The strength of Hampton's forces cannot be given accurately, but is estimated at about 5000 all told.

‡ Sheridan estimated his effective force in that fight at 8000.—EDITORS.

WAITING FOR HIS BREAKFAST. FROM A WAR-TIME SKETCH.

GENERAL LEE IN THE WILDERNESS CAMPAIGN.

BY CHARLES S. VENABLE, LIEUTENANT-COLONEL, C. S. A., OF GENERAL LEE'S STAFF.

UNIFORM OF THE MARYLAND
GUARD, C. S. A.

DURING the winter of 1863–64 General Lee's headquarters were near Orange Court House. They were marked by the same bare simplicity and absence of military form and display which always characterized them. Three or four tents of ordinary size, situated on the steep hillside, made the winter home of himself and his personal staff. It was without sentinels or guards. He used during the winter every exertion for filling up the thin ranks of his army and for obtaining the necessary supplies for his men. There were times in which the situation seemed to be critical in regard to the commissariat. The supplies of meat were brought mainly from the States south of Virginia, and on some days the Army of Northern Virginia had not more than twenty-four hours' rations ahead. On one occasion the general received by mail an anonymous communication from a private soldier containing a very small slice of salt pork, carefully packed between two oak chips, and accompanied by a letter saying that this was the daily ration of meat, and that the writer having found it impossible to live on it had been, though he was a gentleman, reduced by the cravings of hunger to the necessity of stealing. The incident gave the commanding general great pain and anxiety, and led to some strong interviews and correspondence with the Commissary Department. During the winter General Lee neglected no interest of his soldiers. He consulted with their chaplains and attended their meetings, in which plans for the promotion of special religious services among the men were discussed and adopted.

While he was accessible at all times, and rarely had even one orderly before his tent, General Lee had certain wishes which his aides-de-camp knew well they must conform to. They did not allow any friend of soldiers condemned by court-martial (when once the decree of the court had been confirmed by him) to reach his tent for personal appeal, asking reprieve or remission of sentence. He said that with the great responsibilities resting on him he could not bear the pain and distress of such applications, and to grant them when the judge advocate-general had attested the fairness and justice of the court's decision would be a serious injury to the proper discipline of the army. Written complaints of officers as to injustice done them in regard to promotion he would sometimes turn over to an aide-de-camp, with the old-fashioned phrase, "'Suage him, Colonel, 'suage him"; meaning thereby that a kind letter should be written in reply. But he disliked exceedingly that

such disappointed men should be allowed to reach his tent and make complaints in person. On one occasion during the winter an officer came with a grievance and would not be satisfied without an interview with the commanding general. He went to the general's tent and remained some time. Immediately upon his departure General Lee came to the adjutant's tent with flushed face, and said warmly, "Why did you permit that man to come to my tent and make me show my temper?" The views which prevail with many as to the gentle temper of the great soldier, derived from observing him in domestic and social life, in fondling of children, or in kind expostulation with erring youths, are not altogether correct. No man could see the flush come over that grand forehead and the temple veins swell on occasions of great trial of patience and doubt that Lee had the high, strong temper of a Washington, and habitually under the same strong control. Cruelty he hated. In that same early spring of 1864 I saw him stop when in full gallop to the front (on report of a demonstration of the enemy against his lines) to denounce scathingly and threaten with condign punishment a soldier who was brutally beating an artillery horse.

The quiet camp-life at Orange had been broken in upon for a brief season in November by Meade's Mine-Run campaign. In this General Lee, finding that Meade failed to attack the Confederate lines, made arrangements on the night of December 1st to bring on a general battle on the next morning by throwing two divisions against the Federal left, held by Warren's corps, which had been found by a close cavalry reconnoissance to present a fair occasion for successful attack. He had hoped to deal a severe blow to Meade's army, and felt very keenly his failure to carry out his designs. When he discovered that Meade had withdrawn, he exclaimed in the presence of his generals, "I am too old to command this army; we should never have permitted these people to get away." Some who were standing by felt that in his heart he was sighing for that great "right arm" which he threw around Hooker at Chancellorsville. Both armies returned quietly to winter quarters and rested until May 4th, when Lee marched out in the early morning to meet the Federal army which had moved under its new commander, at midnight on the 3d, to turn his right flank. He took with him Ewell's corps (less two brigades which had been detached for duty elsewhere during the winter) and two divisions of Hill's corps —with artillery and cavalry —leaving Longstreet with two divisions at Gordonsville (Pickett's being absent below Richmond), Longstreet's third division and Anderson's division of Hill's corps, on the Rapidan heights, to follow him on the next day.

On the morning of the 5th General Lee, though generally reticent at table on military affairs, spoke very cheerfully of the situation, having learned that Grant was crossing at Germanna Ford and moving into the Wilderness. He expressed his pleasure that the Federal general had not profited by General Hooker's Wilderness experiences, and that he seemed inclined to throw away to some extent the immense advantage which his great superiority in numbers in every arm of the service gave him. On the 5th Ewell marched on the old turnpike, and Hill on the Plank road, and the cavalry on a road still farther to the right into the Wilderness. Lee rode with Hill at the head of his column. He was at the front in the skirmish at Parker's Store and moved with the advance to the field on the edge of the forest which became the scene of the great conflict on the Plank road. Riding on in advance of the troops, the party, consisting of Generals Lee, Hill, and Stuart and their staff-officers, dismounted and sat under the shade of the trees, when a party of the enemy's skirmishers deployed from a grove of old-field pines on the left, thus revealing the close proximity of Grant's forces, and the ease of concealing movements in the Wilderness.

Hill's troops were soon up and in line, and then began on the Plank road a fierce struggle, nearly simultaneously with that of Ewell's forces on the old turnpike. Thus was inaugurated a contest of many battles, in which the almost daily deadly firing did not cease for eleven long months.

Heth's and Wilcox's divisions, under Lee's eye, maintained themselves well against the heavy assault of the Federal forces which greatly outnumbered them; Ewell's corps did good work on the old turnpike in its contest with Warren's corps, and Rosser's cavalry on the right had driven Wilson back. Lee slept on the field not far from his line of battle, sending orders to Longstreet to make a night march and reach the front by daybreak on the 6th.

On that morning serious disaster seemed imminent. Longstreet did not arrive in time to reënforce Lee's line of battle in the position it held at the close of the engagement of the preceding evening. Hancock's well-planned attack on our right forced the two Confederate divisions from their position, and it seemed at one moment that they would sweep the field. Lee gave orders to get his wagon trains ready for a movement in retreat, and sent an aide to quicken the march of Longstreet's two divisions. These came soon, a little after sunrise, at double-quick, in parallel columns, down the Plank road. Lee was in the midst of Hill's sullenly retreating troops, aiding in rallying them, and restoring confidence and order, when Longstreet's men came gallantly in and reformed the line of battle under his eye. Lee's presence at the front aroused his men to great enthusiasm. He was a superb figure as he sat on his spirited gray with the light of battle on his face. His presence was an inspiration. The retreating columns turned their faces bravely to the front once more, and the fresh divisions went forward under his eye with splendid spirit. It was on this occasion that the men of the Texas brigade (always favorites of the general), discovering that he was riding with them into the charge, shouted to him that they would not go on unless he went back. The battle line was restored early in the morning. Soon afterward, Anderson's division, which had been left on the Rapidan heights, arrived on the ground; and a successful assault, which carried everything before it, was made on Grant's left. The Federal troops were driven back, with heavy loss, to their intrenchments on the Brock road. Longstreet's wounding, and the necessary delay in the change of commanders, caused loss of time in attacking them in this position. An attack made in the afternoon failed, after some partial successes, to gain possession of the Federal breastworks. The rumor which

MAJOR-GENERAL G. W. C. LEE, C. S. A.
FROM A PHOTOGRAPH.

General Grant mentions in his "Memoirs," and to which he seems to have given credence, that "Lee's men were in confusion after this attack, and that his efforts failed to restore order," was without foundation in fact. On the same afternoon, of the 6th, a successful flank assault was made by Gordon, with three brigades of Ewell's corps, the results of which were not so great as hoped for, because night put a stop to his further successful rolling up of Sedgwick's line.

The Wilderness fighting closed with the night of the 6th of May.

Lee's grand tactics in these two days of battle had been a superb exhibition of military genius and skill in executing his plan of throwing his little army boldly against his opponent, where his great inferiority in numbers would place him at the least disadvantage; where manœuvring of large

R. H. Anderson was taken from Hill's corps to command Longstreet's, and Mahone assumed command of Anderson's division.—EDITORS.

bodies was most difficult, and where superiority in cavalry and artillery counted almost for nothing.

The failure to push rapidly the successful movement in which Longstreet was wounded was a serious disappointment to General Lee. I believe his daring spirit conceived the signal defeat of Grant's army, and the driving it back across the Rapidan, as a possibility within his immediate grasp. One thing remarkable in the position of the

MAJOR-GENERAL STEPHEN D. RAMSEUR, C. S. A.
FROM A PHOTOGRAPH.

Confederate lines in these engagements is worthy of note, namely, the large gap between Ewell's right and Longstreet and Hill's left. I had occasion, on being sent with orders to General Ewell on the 6th, to ride across this lonesome interval of half a mile or more, and to meet or see no one, except two Federal soldiers, who had found it easier to desert to the front than to the rear.

The quiet on the 7th told Lee that Grant would move on around his left. When Grant did move, the Confederate general, with that firm reliance upon the steadfast courage of his men in fighting against odds which had never failed him, and in the consequent ability of a small body of his troops to hold superior forces in check until he could come to their support, sent Anderson with Longstreet's two divisions to support Stuart's cavalry in holding Spotsylvania Court House until he could come up with the rest of his army. This mutual confidence between the general and his men was a striking feature of the campaign, and, indeed, a prime necessity for any possibility of success. General Grant sent troops to occupy Spotsylvania Court House, but retained Hancock's corps to guard against the contingency of another attack from Lee in the Wilderness. Lee had evidently won the respect of his foes when, with his smaller force, reduced by two days' hard fighting, he could employ one part of his infantry to aid in checking the movement of the Army of the Potomac on Spotsylvania Court House, and at the

same time threaten its rear in the Wilderness. Meanwhile General Grant was sending to Washington for reënforcements.

Lee sent an aide-de-camp with Anderson under orders to keep him constantly advised, and, following with the main body of his army, took up his position on the Spotsylvania lines in the afternoon of the 8th. And Grant again found himself in a position which required hard fighting and in which he could not use to great advantage his superiority in numbers and equipment.

The Spotsylvania campaign of twelve days was marked by almost daily combats. It was General Lee's habit in those days of physical and mental trial to retire about 10 or 11 at night, to rise at 3 A. M., breakfast by candle-light, and return to the front, spending the entire day on the lines. The 9th of May was spent by both armies mainly in strengthening their positions by throwing up intrenchments. The day was marked, however, by the death of General Sedgwick, who was killed by a Confederate sharp-shooter. He was much liked and respected by his old West Point comrades in the Confederate army, and his death was a real sorrow to them. Early on the morning of the 10th Hancock's corps made an effort to pass around Lee's left wing and gain a position on his flank and rear. This was repulsed by Early, commanding Hill's corps (Hill being ill). Almost simultaneously came fierce assaults on Lee's left wing, which were repulsed with terrible slaughter. These were renewed again in the afternoon with the same result. The heaviest assault was made at 5 o'clock by Hancock and Warren, and again repulsed; again reorganized and hurled at Lee's lines only to meet with a still more bloody reception. In one of these attacks a small portion of the Confederate line was taken, but held for a short time only by the assailants. It was pitiful to see and hear the bravest of these brave men who had got up nearest to the Confederate lines as they lay the next day groaning with the pangs of thirst and pains of death, when to relieve them was impossible, on account of the active sharp-shooting of the Federal riflemen. One fair-haired New York youth lay thus twenty-four hours near the Confederate intrenchments before he was relieved from his sufferings by death, every effort to bring him in having been rendered unavailing by the sharp fire which his would-be rescuers met at the hands of his comrades, ignorant of their kind intentions. About the same hour at which these last assaults were made, there was a heavy attack by the Sixth Corps on Ewell's front, near Lee's headquarters for the day, about 200 yards in rear of Doles's brigade, which captured and held a portion of the lines for a short time. This attack was repulsed and the line recaptured by Gordon, the men and officers, as in the Wilderness, again beseeching Lee to go to the rear, and shouting their promises to retake the line if he would only go back.

The 11th of May was a comparatively quiet day, as there were no regular assaults on the Confederate lines. But on that day the gallant J. E. B. Stuart met his death in an engagement with

Sheridan, whom he had followed up from Spotsylvania and boldly attacked with greatly inferior numbers near Richmond. Stuart's loss was greatly mourned by General Lee,↓ who prized him highly both as a skillful soldier of splendid courage and energy, and a hearty, joyous, loving friend.

On the 12th, before dawn, came Hancock's famous assault on a weak salient in Ewell's front—the sole appreciable success in attack of all the hard fighting by the Federal troops since they crossed the Rapidan. The threatening attitude of Hancock's attacking column, as indicated by the noise of the preparations going on in front of the salient during the night, had not been communicated to General Lee. The announcement of the disaster was the first news which came to him of this movement of the enemy. He galloped forward in the darkness of the morning and learned the extent of it from those engaged in rallying the remnants of Edward Johnson's division and in making arrangements to check Hancock. The occasion aroused all the combative energies of his soldier nature, and he rode forward with his columns toward the captured angle. His generals expostulated with him, and his men cried him back shouting their promises to retake the lines. The advance of Hancock's troops, after his successful assault, was checked by the brigades of Hill's corps, under Early, which held the lines on the right of the salient, and by Ewell's troops on the left of it.

A line of battle was formed making the base of the triangle of the salient, and the work on the retrenchment (which had been begun the day before as a new line to remedy this weak point in the lines) was pushed rapidly forward. During the day General Lee sent three brigades and a number of batteries of artillery to reënforce Rodes's division, on which fell the main task of holding the enemy in check and recovering, if practicable, the salient and the eighteen pieces of Confederate artillery which lay silent between the opposing lines (having arrived too late in the morning for effective use against Hancock's assault). In that narrow space of the salient captured before dawn raged the fiercest battle of the war. Lee's position during the day was near Early's lines, where he observed, from time to time, the movements of the Federal troops in aid of Hancock's attack, and counter-movements of Early's troops. He was with the artillery when it broke Burnside's assault. Lee was present dictating notes and orders in the midst of his guns. At one time he rode at the head of Harris's Mississippi brigade, which by his orders I was guiding down in column to the assistance of Rodes. The men marched steadily on until they noticed that Lee at their head was riding across a space swept by the artillery fire of the enemy. Then were renewed the same protesting shouts of "Go back, General Lee," and the same promises to do their duty. The firing in the battle of the salient did not cease until far into the night. Hancock had been compelled to retire behind the lines which

he had captured, holding them as breastworks for the protection of his troops. The Confederate front at the close covered four of the eighteen pieces of artillery. Lee's retrenchment in rear of our battle-line (which rendered the salient a useless capture) had been completed. The wearied and worn Confederate battalions were withdrawn to this line late at night, but the four recovered guns, after being dragged off, were left hopelessly stuck in a swamp outside of the new lines, and became Hancock's trophies after all. General Grant did not leave Hancock unaided in this fight, having sent the Sixth and Fifth corps to his support. He expected much from Burnside also, but Early's counter-movements in part prevented the realization of these hopes. I have gone into some detail in this brief sketch of the battle of the salient, because, as perhaps the fiercest struggle of the war, it is illustrative of the valor of the troops on both sides.

On the 18th an attack was made on Early's left and easily repulsed, though some of the assailants reached the breastworks. On the 19th Ewell was sent to the north side of the Ny to threaten Grant's communications. He met some Federal reënforcements, and, being without artillery (finding the ground impracticable for it), he regained his position on the south side of that stream with some loss. Hampton's cavalry brigade and battery of horse artillery proved of great assistance in his withdrawal from his hazardous position.

The battles of Spotsylvania Court House closed with the 19th of May. It gives a clearer idea of the nature of this tremendous contest to group by

MAJOR-GENERAL EDWARD JOHNSON, C. S. A.
FROM A PHOTOGRAPH.

days and count its various combats from the beginning of the campaign: On May 5th, three; on May 6th, four; on May 8th, two; on May 10th, five; on May 12th, repeated assaults during twenty

↓ The news of Stuart's fall reached General Lee on the 12th.—C. S. V.

hours in salient and two combats on another part of the line; May 18th, one; May 19th, one. It is no wonder that on these fields the Confederate ordnance officers gathered more than 120,000 pounds of lead, which was recast in bullets and did work again before the campaign of 1864 was closed.

Lee, discovering that Grant had set out on the 20th of May on his flanking movement southward, immediately marched so as to throw his army between the Federal forces and Richmond. He crossed the North Anna on the 21st. General Grant arrived on the 23d. Lee would gladly have compelled battle in his position there. He was anxious now to strike a telling blow, as he was

BRIGADIER-GENERAL GEORGE H. STEUART, C. S. A.
FROM A PHOTOGRAPH.

convinced that General Grant's men were dispirited by the bloody repulses of their repeated attacks on our lines. Lee had drawn Pickett and Breckinridge to him. But in the midst of the operations on the North Anna he succumbed to sickness, against which he had struggled for some days. As he lay in his tent he would say, in his impatience, "We must strike them!" "We must never let them pass us again!" "We must strike them!" He had reports brought to him constantly from the field. But Lee ill in his tent was not Lee at the front. He was much disappointed in not securing larger results from the attack which prevented the junction of Hancock's and Warren's columns after they had crossed the North Anna.

On May 26th Grant withdrew his army from its rather critical position on the south side of the North Anna, and moved again to the east, down the Pamunkey, which he crossed on the 28th, to find Lee confronting him on the Totopotomoy. Grant had received reënforcements from Washington, and had drawn Smith's corps from Butler in Ber-

muda Hundred. This corps reached him at Cold Harbor on June 1st. On the 30th the Confederate forces were in line of battle, with the left at Atlee's Station confronting the Federal army. General Lee was still sick, and occupied a house at night for the first time during the campaign. As one of his trusted lieutenants has well said: "In fact, nothing but his own determined will kept him in the field; and it was then rendered more evident than ever that he was the head and front, the very life and soul of his army." Grant declined general battle and drew eastward; and after several lesser combats, with no serious results, the two armies confronted one another on the 3d of June at Cold Harbor. In these days Lee had drawn to himself Hoke's division from Beauregard, and had been reënforced by Finegan's Florida brigade and Keitt's South Carolina regiment.

The days from May 30th to June 2d were anxious ones for General Lee. For while General Grant had easy and safe communication with Petersburg and Bermuda Hundred, and commanded all the Federal troops north and south of Richmond, he commanded only the Army of Northern Virginia and was compelled to communicate his "suggestions" to General Beauregard through General Bragg and the War Department at Richmond. This marred greatly the unity, secrecy, and celerity of action so absolutely essential to success. That he considered this separation of commands, and the consequent circuitous mode of communication with its uncertain results, a very grave matter is plain from the telegrams which he sent at this time. General Beauregard had telegraphed from Chester (half-way between Richmond and Petersburg), on May 30th, 5:15 P. M., as follows:

"War Department must determine when and what troops to order from here. I send to General Bragg all information I obtain relative to movement of enemy's troops in front."

This called forth the following telegrams: ♭

"ATLEE'S, 7½ P. M., 30th May, 1864.
"GENERAL G. T. BEAUREGARD, Hancock's House:
"If you cannot determine what troops you can spare, the Department cannot. The result of your delay will be disaster. Butler's troops will be with Grant to-morrow.   R. E. LEE."

"ATLEE'S, 7½ P. M., 30th May, 1864.
"HIS EXCELLENCY JEFFERSON DAVIS, Richmond:
"General Beauregard says the Department must determine what troops to send from him. He gives it all necessary information. The result of this delay will be disaster. Butler's troops (Smith's Corps) will be with Grant to-morrow. Hoke's division at least should be with me by light to-morrow.   R. E. LEE."

INDORSEMENT.

"OPERATOR: Read last sentence 'by light to-morrow.'"   "C. S. V.,
"A. A. G."

The battle of the 3d of June was a general assault by Grant along a front nearly six miles in length, and a complete and bloody repulse at all points, except at one weak salient on Breckinridge's line, which the brave assailants occupied

Atlee's 7½ P. M. 30 May '64

Genl G T Beauregard
Hancocks House —

If you cannot determine what troops be you can spare the Dept cannot — The result will be disaster of your delay will be disaster — Butlers troops will be with Grant tomorrow

2 7/340 Chf

R E Lee

A CALL FOR REËNFORCEMENTS.

for a short time only to be beaten back in a bloody hand-to-hand conflict on the works. The Federal losses were naturally, under the circumstances, very large, and those of the Confederates very small. The dead and dying lay in front of the Confederate lines in triangles, of which the apexes were the bravest men who came nearest to the breastworks under the withering, deadly fire. The battle lasted little more than one brief hour, beginning between 5 and 6 A. M. The Federal troops spent the remainder of the day in strengthening their own lines in which they rested quietly. Lee's troops were in high spirits. General Early, on the 6th and 7th of June, made two efforts to attack Grant's forces on his right flank and rear, but found him thoroughly protected with intrenchments. On the 12th General Hampton met Sheridan at Trevilian and turned him back from his march to the James River and Lynchburg. General Grant lay in his lines until the night of June 12th.

On that night he moved rapidly across the peninsula. The overland campaign north of the James was at an end.

Except in the temporary driving back of Lee's right on the morning of May 6th before the arrival of Longstreet's divisions, the brief occupation of Rodes's front on May 10th, Hancock's morning assault on May 12th, and a few minor events, the campaign had been one series of severe and bloody repulses of Federal attacks. The campaign on the Confederate side was an illustration of Lee's genius, skill, and boldness, and as well of the steadiness, courage, and constancy of his greatly outnumbered forces, and of their sublime faith in their great commander.

After the battle of Cold Harbor, Lee felt strong enough to send Breckinridge toward the valley to meet Hunter's expedition, and on the 13th to detach Early with the Second Corps, now numbering some eight thousand muskets and twenty-four pieces of artillery, to join Breckinridge; he also restored Hoke's division to Beauregard.

When Grant set out for the James, Lee threw a corps of observation between him and Richmond. Grant moved his troops rapidly in order to capture Petersburg by a *coup de main*. Smith's corps was in front of the advanced lines of Petersburg on the morning of the 15th. The first brigade of Hoke's division reached Beauregard on the evening of the 15th. On the night of the 15th Lee tented on the south side of the James, near Drewry's Bluff. On the 16th and 17th, his troops coming up, he superintended personally the recapture of Beauregard's Bermuda Hundred line, which he found to be held very feebly by the forces of General Butler, who had taken possession of them on the withdrawal of Bushrod Johnson's division by Beauregard to Petersburg on the 16th. On the 17th a very pretty thing occurred, in these lines, of which I was an eye-witness, and which evinced the high spirit of Lee's men, especially of a division which had been with him throughout the campaign, namely, Field's division of Longstreet's corps. After the left of Beauregard's evacuated line had been taken up, there remained a portion the approach to which was more formidable. The order had been issued to General Anderson commanding the corps to retake this portion of the lines by a joint assault of Pickett's and Field's divisions. Soon afterward the engineers, upon a careful reconnoissance, decided that a good line could be occupied without the loss of life which might result from this recapture. The order to attack was therefore withdrawn by General Lee. This rescinding order reached Field but did not reach Pickett. Pickett's division began its assault under the first order. The men of Field's division, hearing the firing and seeing Pickett's men engaged, leaped from their trenches,—first the men, then the officers and flag-bearers,—rushed forward and were soon in the formidable trenches, which were found to be held by a very small force. On the 15th, 16th, and 17th battle raged along the lines of intrenchments and forts east of Petersburg, between Grant's forces and Beauregard's troops, who made a splendid defense against enormous odds. About dark on the 17th grave disaster to the Confederates seemed imminent, when Gracie's brigade of Alabamians, just returned from Chaffin's Bluff on the north side of the James, gallantly leaped over the works and drove the assailants back, capturing a thousand or more prisoners. Hoke, too, on his part of the lines, had easily repulsed Smith's assaults. This battle raged until near midnight. Meantime Beauregard's engineers were preparing an interior line, to which his wearied troops fell back during the night. A renewal of the attack on the lines held by the Confederate troops on the night of the 17th had been ordered by Grant along his whole front for an early hour on the 18th. But the withdrawal of the Confederates to interior lines necessarily caused delay, and, when the attack was made at noon, Lee and two of his divisions, Kershaw's and Field's, had reached the Petersburg lines. The attack made no impression on the lines, which were held until the evacuation on April 2d, 1865.

To some military critics General Lee seemed not to have taken in the full force of Beauregard's urgent telegrams in those critical days of June. But it must be remembered how easy it was for General Grant to make a forced march on Richmond from the north side of the James, accompanied by a strong feint on the Petersburg lines. Then, too, any strategist will see that Petersburg, cut off from Richmond by an enemy holding the railroad between the two cities (or holding an intrenched line so near it as to make its use hazardous), would not have been a very desirable possession. The fact is, that the defense of Richmond against an enemy so superior in numbers to the defending army, and in possession of the James River to City Point as a great water-way to its base of supplies, was surrounded with immense difficulties. And, in fact, in sending back Hoke's division to Beauregard, and in approving that general's withdrawing of Bushrod Johnson's division from the Bermuda Hundred line to Petersburg, Lee thereby sent him more reënforcements by far than he sent to Rodes on the 12th of May at Spotsylvania, when that general was holding the base of the salient against Hancock and Wright and Warren. Besides this, Lee had already detached Breckinridge's division and Early's corps to meet Hunter at Lynchburg. And, after all, the result showed that Lee's reliance on his men to hold in check attacking forces greatly superior in numbers did not fail him in this instance; that he was bold to audacity was a characteristic of his military genius.

The campaign of 1864 now became the siege of Petersburg. On the night of June 18th Hunter retreated rapidly from before Lynchburg toward western Virginia, and Early, after a brief pursuit, marched into Maryland, and on July 11th his advance was before the outer defenses of Washington.

BELLE PLAIN, POTOMAC CREEK, A UNION BASE OF SUPPLIES. FROM A PHOTOGRAPH TAKEN IN 1864.

A SHELL AT HEADQUARTERS.

THE GRAND STRATEGY OF THE LAST YEAR OF THE WAR.

BY WILLIAM T. SHERMAN, GENERAL, U. S. A.

ON the 4th day of March, 1864, General U. S. Grant was summoned to Washington from Nashville to receive his commission of lieutenant-general, the highest rank then known in the United States, and the same that was conferred on Washington in 1798. He reached the capital on the 7th, had an interview for the first time with Mr. Lincoln, and on the 9th received his commission at the hands of the President, who made a short address, to which Grant made a suitable reply. He was informed that it was desirable that he should come east to command all the armies of the United States, and give his personal supervision to the Army of the Potomac. On the 10th he visited General Meade at Brandy Station, and saw many of his leading officers, but he returned to Washington the next day and went on to Nashville, to which place he had summoned me, then absent on my Meridian expedition. ⚓ On the 18th of March he turned over to me the command of the Western armies, and started back for Washington, I accompanying him as far as Cincinnati. Amidst constant interruptions of a business and social nature, we reached the satisfactory conclusion that, as soon as the season would permit, all the armies of the Union would assume the "bold offensive" by "concentric lines" on the common enemy, and would finish up the job in a single campaign if possible. The main "objectives" were Lee's army behind the Rapidan in Virginia, and Joseph E. Johnston's army at Dalton, Georgia.

⚓ Re-arranged from "The Grand Strategy of the War of the Rebellion," by General Sherman, printed in "The Century" magazine for February, 1888, and from a letter by General Sherman to the editor, printed in that periodical for July, 1887. The figures in the text are from Phisterer's "Statistical Record." (Charles Scribner's Sons.)

⚓ On February 3d, 1864, General Sherman started from Vicksburg with two columns of infantry under Generals McPherson and Hurlbut, and marched to Meridian, Mississippi, to break up the Mobile and Ohio and the Jackson and Selma railroads. His force was about 20,000 strong. A force of cavalry, 10,000 strong, under General W. Sooy Smith, set out from Memphis on the 11th, intending to coöperate by driving Forrest's cavalry from northern Mississippi, but Smith was headed off by Forrest and defeated in an engagement at West Point, Mississippi, on the 21st. After destroying the railroads on the route, General Sherman abandoned the enterprise, and on February 20th put his troops in motion toward central Mississippi, whence they were transferred, later, to Vicksburg and Memphis.—EDITORS.

On reaching Washington, Grant studied with great care all the minutiæ of the organization, strength, qualities, and resources of each of the many armies into which the Union forces had resolved themselves by reason of preceding events, and in due time with wonderful precision laid out the work which each one should undertake. His written instructions to me at Nashville were embraced in the two letters of April 4th and April 19th, 1864, both in his own handwriting, which I still possess, and which, in my judgment, are as complete as any of those of the Duke of Wellington contained in the twelve volumes of his published letters and correspondence.

With the month of May came the season for *action*, and by the 4th all his armies were in motion. The army of Butler at Fort Monroe was his left, Meade's army the center, and mine at Chattanooga his right. Butler was to move against Richmond on the south of James River, Meade straight against Lee, intrenched behind the Rapidan, and I to attack Joe Johnston and push him to and beyond Atlanta. This was as far as human foresight could penetrate. Though Meade commanded the Army of the Potomac, Grant virtually controlled it, and on the 4th of May, 1864, he crossed the Rapidan, and at noon of the 5th attacked Lee. He knew that a certain amount of fighting, " killing," had to be done to accomplish his end, and also to pay the penalty of former failures. In the " wilderness " there was no room for grand strategy, or even minor tactics; but the fighting was desperate, the losses to the Union army being, according to Phisterer, 18,387,↓ to the Confederate loss of 11,400—the difference due to Lee's intrenchments and the blind nature of the country in which the battle was fought. On the night of May 7th both parties paused, appalled by the fearful slaughter; but Grant commanded, " Forward by the left flank." That was, in my judgment, the supreme moment of his life; undismayed, with a full comprehension of the importance of the work in which he was engaged, feeling as keen a sympathy for his dead and wounded as any one, and without stopping to count his numbers, he gave his orders calmly, specifically, and absolutely—" Forward to Spotsylvania." But his watchful and skillful antagonist detected his purpose, and, having the inner or shorter line, threw his army across Grant's path, and promptly fortified it. These field intrenchments are peculiar to America, though I am convinced they were employed by the Romans in Gaul in the days of Cæsar. Troops, halting for the night or for battle, faced the enemy; moved forward to ground with a good outlook to the front; stacked arms; gathered logs, stumps, fence-rails, anything which would stop a bullet; piled these to their front, and, digging a ditch behind, threw the dirt forward, and made a parapet which covered their persons as perfectly as a granite wall.

When Grant reached Spotsylvania, May 8th, he found his antagonist in his front thus intrenched. He was delayed there till the 20th, during which time there was incessant fighting, because he was compelled to attack his enemy behind these improvised intrenchments. His losses, according to Phisterer, were 12,564, ◖ while the Confederates lost 9000. Nevertheless, his renewed

---

↓ Later official compilation, 17,666.—EDITORS.   ◖ Later official compilation, 18,399.—EDITORS.

order, " Forward by the left flank," compelled Lee to retreat to the defenses of Richmond.

Grant's " Memoirs " enable us to follow him day by day across the various rivers which lay between him and Richmond, and in the bloody assaults at Cold Harbor, where his losses are reported 14,931 ╲ to 1700 by his opponent. Yet ever onward by the left flank, he crossed James River and penned Lee and his Army of Northern Virginia within the intrenchments of Richmond and Petersburg for ten long months on the pure defensive, to remain almost passive observers of local events, while Grant's other armies were absolutely annihilating the Southern Confederacy.

While Grant was fighting desperately from the Rapidan to the James, there were two other armies within the same " zone of operations "— that " of the James " under General Butler, who was expected to march up on the south and invest Petersburg and even Richmond; and that of Sigel at Winchester, who was expected to march up the Valley of Virginia, pick up his detachments from the Kanawha (Crook and Averell), and threaten Lynchburg, a place of vital importance to Lee in Richmond. Butler failed to accomplish what was expected of him; and Sigel failed at the very start, and was replaced by Hunter, who marched up the valley, made junction with Crook and Averell at Staunton, and pushed on with commendable vigor to Lynchburg, which he invested on the 16th of June.

Lee, who had by this time been driven into Richmond with a force large enough to hold his lines of intrenchment and a surplus for expeditions, detached General Jubal A. Early with the equivalent of a corps to drive Hunter away from Lynchburg. Hunter, far from his base, with inadequate supplies of food and ammunition, retreated by the Kanawha to the Ohio River, his nearest base, thereby exposing the Valley of Virginia; whereupon Early, an educated soldier, promptly resolved to take advantage of the occasion, marched rapidly down this valley northward to Winchester, crossed the Potomac to Hagerstown, and thence boldly marched on Washington, defended at that time only by militia and armed clerks. Grant, fully alive to the danger, dispatched to Washington, from his army investing Petersburg, two divisions of the Sixth Corps, and also the Nineteenth Corps just arriving from New Orleans. These troops arrived at the very nick of time,— met Early's army in the suburbs of Washington, and drove it back to the Valley of Virginia.

This most skillful movement of Early demonstrated to General Grant the importance of the Valley of Virginia, not only as a base of supplies for Lee's army in Richmond, but as the most direct, the shortest, and the easiest route for a " diversion " into the Union territory north of the Potomac. He therefore cast around for a suitable commander for this field of operations, and settled upon Major-General Philip H. Sheridan, whom he had brought from the West to command the cavalry corps of the Army of the Potomac.

Sheridan promptly went to his new sphere of operations, quickly ascertained its strength and resources, and resolved to attack Early in the position which he had chosen in and about Winchester, Va. He delivered his attack across

╲ Later official compilation, 12,737.— EDITORS.

broken ground on the 19th of September, beat his antagonist in fair, open battle, sending him "whirling up the valley," inflicting a loss of 5500 men to his own of 4873, and followed him up to Cedar Creek and Fisher's Hill. Early recomposed his army and fell upon the Union army on the 19th of October, at Cedar Creek, gaining a temporary advantage during General Sheridan's absence; but on his opportune return his army resumed the offensive, defeated Early, captured nearly all his artillery, and drove him completely out of his field of operations, eliminating that army from the subsequent problem of the war. Sheridan's losses were 5995 to Early's 4200; but these losses are no just measure of the results of that victory, which made it impossible to use the Valley of Virginia as a Confederate base of supplies and as an easy route for raids within the Union lines. General Sheridan then committed its protection to detachments, and with his main force rejoined General Grant, who still held Lee's army inside his intrenchments at Richmond and Petersburg.

I now turn with a feeling of extreme delicacy to the conduct of that other campaign from Chattanooga to Atlanta, Savannah, and Raleigh, which with liberal discretion was committed to me by General Grant in his minute instructions of April 4th and April 19th, 1864. To all military students these letters must be familiar, because they have been published again and again, and there never was and never can be raised a question of rivalry or claim between us as to the relative merits of the manner in which we played our respective parts. We were as brothers — I the older man in years, he the higher in rank. We both believed in our heart of hearts that the success of the Union cause was not only necessary to the then generation of Americans, but to all future generations. We both professed to be gentlemen and professional soldiers, educated in the science of war by our generous Government for the very occasion which had arisen. Neither of us by nature was a combative man; but with honest hearts and a clear purpose to do what man could we embarked on that campaign, which I believe, in its strategy, in its logistics, in its grand and minor tactics, has added new luster to the old science of war. Both of us had at our front generals to whom in early life we had been taught to look up, — educated and experienced soldiers like ourselves, not likely to make any mistakes, and each of whom had as strong an army as could be collected from the mass of the Southern people, — of the same blood as ourselves, brave, confident, and well equipped; in addition to which they had the most decided advantage of operating in their own difficult country of mountain, forest, ravine, and river, affording admirable opportunities for defense, besides the other equally important advantage that we had to invade the country of our unqualified enemy and expose our long lines of supply to the guerrillas of an "exasperated people." Again, as we advanced we had to leave guards to bridges, stations, and intermediate depots, diminishing the fighting force, while our enemy gained strength by picking up his detachments as he fell back, and had railroads to bring supplies and reënforcements from his rear. I instance these facts to offset the common assertion that we of the North won the war by brute force, and not by courage and skill.

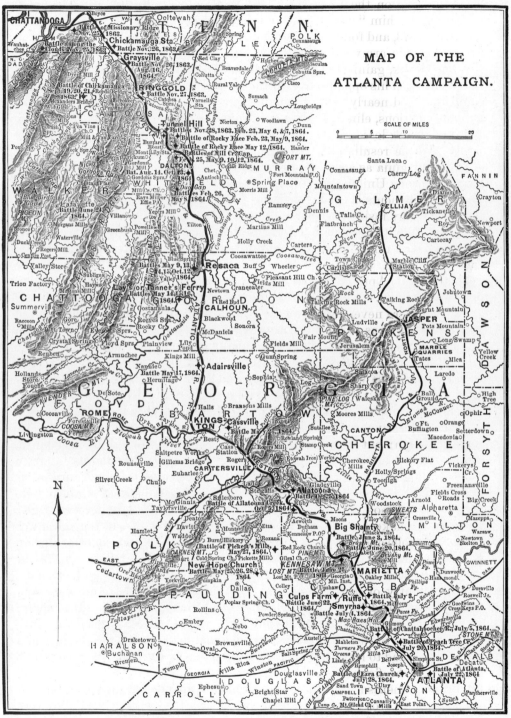

MAP OF THE
ATLANTA CAMPAIGN.

SCALE OF MILES

FROM "THE MOUNTAIN CAMPAIGNS IN GEORGIA; OR, WAR SCENES ON THE W. & A." PUBLISHED BY THE WESTERN & ATLANTIC R. R. CO.

On the historic 4th day of May, 1864, the Confederate army at my front lay at Dalton, Georgia, composed, according to the best authority, of about 45,000 men [see also p. 281], commanded by Joseph E. Johnston, who was equal in all the elements of generalship to Lee, and who was under instructions from the war powers in Richmond to assume the offensive northward as far as Nashville. But he soon discovered that he would have to conduct a defensive campaign. Coincident with the movement of the Army of the Potomac, as announced by telegraph, I advanced from our base at Chattanooga with the Army of the Ohio, 13,559 men; the Army of the Cumberland, 60,773, and the Army of the Tennessee, 24,465,— grand total, 98,797 men and 254 guns.

I had no purpose to attack Johnston's position at Dalton in front, but marched from Chattanooga to feign at his front and to make a lodgment in Resaca, eighteen miles to his rear, on " his line of communication and supply." The movement was partly, not wholly, successful; but it compelled Johnston to let go Dalton and fight us at Resaca, where, May 13th–16th, our loss was 2747 and his 2800. I fought offensively and he defensively, aided by earth parapets. He then fell back to Calhoun, Adairsville, and Cassville, where he halted for the battle of the campaign ; but, for reasons given in his memoirs, he continued his retreat behind the next spur of mountains to Allatoona.

Pausing for a few days to repair the railroad without attempting Allatoona, of which I had personal knowledge acquired in 1844, I resolved to push on toward Atlanta by way of Dallas; Johnston quickly detected this, and forced me to fight him, May 25th–28th, at New Hope Church, four miles north of Dallas, with losses of 3000 to the Confederates and 2400 to us. The country was almost in a state of nature—with few or no roads, nothing that a European could understand ; yet the bullet killed its victim there as surely as at Sevastopol.

Johnston had meantime picked up his detachments, and had received reënforcements from his rear which raised his aggregate strength to 62,000 men, and warranted him in claiming that he was purposely drawing us far from our base, and that when the right moment should come he would turn on us and destroy us. We were equally confident, and not the least alarmed. He then fell back to his position at Marietta, with Brush Mountain on his right, Kenesaw his center, and Lost Mountain his left. His line of ten miles was too long for his numbers, and he soon let go his flanks and concentrated on Kenesaw. We closed down in battle array, repaired the railroad up to our very camps, and then prepared for the contest. Not a day, not an hour, not a minute was there a cessation of fire. Our skirmishers were in absolute contact, the lines of battle and the batteries but little in rear of the skirmishers ; and thus matters continued until June 27th, when I ordered a general assault, with the full coöperation of my great lieutenants, Thomas, McPherson, and Schofield, as good and true men as ever lived or died for their country's cause; but we failed, losing 3000 men, to the Confederate loss of 630. Still, the result was that within three days Johnston abandoned the strongest possible position and was in full retreat for the Chattahoochee River. We were on his heels; skirmished with his rear at Smyrna Church on the 4th day of July, and saw him fairly across the Chattahoochee on the 10th, covered and protected by the best line of field intrenchments I have ever seen, prepared long in advance. No officer or soldier who ever served under me will question the generalship of Joseph E. Johnston. His retreats were timely, in good order, and he left nothing behind. We had advanced into the enemy's country 120 miles, with a single-track railroad, which had to bring clothing, food, ammunition, everything requisite for 100,000 men and 23,000 animals. The city of Atlanta, the gate city opening the interior of the important State of Georgia, was in sight; its protecting army was shaken but not defeated, and onward we had to go,— illustrating the principle that " an army once on the offensive must maintain the offensive."

We feigned to the right, but crossed the Chattahoochee by the left, and soon confronted our enemy behind his first line of intrenchments at Peach Tree Creek, prepared in advance for this very occasion. At this critical moment the Confederate Government rendered us most valuable service. Being dissatisfied with the Fabian policy of General Johnston, it relieved him, and General Hood was substituted to command the Confederate army [July 18th]. Hood was known to us to be a "fighter," a graduate of West Point of the class of 1853, No. 44, of which class two of my army commanders, McPherson and Schofield, were No. 1 and No. 7. The character of a leader is a large factor in the game of war, and I confess I was pleased at this change, of which I had early notice. I knew that I had an army superior in numbers and *morale* to that of my antagonist; but being so far from my base, and operating in a country devoid of food and forage, I was dependent for supplies on a poorly constructed railroad back to Louisville, five hundred miles. I was willing to meet the enemy in the open country, but not behind well-constructed parapets.

Promptly, as expected, General Hood sallied from his Peach Tree line on the 20th of July, about midday, striking the Twentieth Corps (Hooker), which had just crossed Peach Tree Creek by improvised bridges. The troops became commingled and fought hand to hand desperately for about four hours, when the Confederates were driven back within their lines, leaving behind their dead and wounded. These amounted to 4796 men, to our loss of 1710. We followed up, and Hood fell back to the main lines of the city of Atlanta. We closed in, when again Hood, holding these lines with about one-half his force, with the other half made a wide circuit by night, under cover of the woods, and on the 22d of July enveloped our left flank " in air," a movement that led to the hardest battle of the campaign. He encountered the Army of the Tennessee,—skilled veterans who were always ready to fight, were not alarmed by flank or rear attacks, and met their assailants with heroic valor. The battle raged from noon to night, when the Confederates, baffled and defeated, fell back within the intrenchments of Atlanta. Their losses are reported 8499 to ours of 3641; but among our dead was McPherson, the commander of the Army of the Tennessee. While this battle was in progress, Schofield at the center and Thomas on the right made efforts to break through the intrenchments at their fronts, but found them too strong to assault.

The Army of the Tennessee was then shifted, under its new commander (Howard), from the extreme left to the extreme right, to reach, if possible, the railroad by which Hood drew his supplies, when, on the 28th of July, he repeated his tactics of the 22d, sustaining an overwhelming defeat, losing 4632 men to our 700. These three sallies convinced him that his predecessor, General Johnston, had not erred in standing on the defensive. Thereafter the Confederate army in Atlanta clung to its parapets. I never intended to assault these, but gradually worked to the right to reach and destroy his line of supplies, because soldiers, like other mortals, must have food. Our extension to the right brought on numerous conflicts, but nothing worthy of note, till about the end of August I resolved to leave one corps to protect our communications to the rear, and move with the other five to a point (Jonesboro') on the railroad twenty-six miles below Atlanta, *not* fortified. This movement was perfectly strategic, was successful, and resulted in our occupation of Atlanta, on the 2d of September, 1864. The result had a large effect on the whole country at the time, for solid and political reasons. I claim no special merit to myself, save that I believe I followed the teachings of the best masters of the "science of war" of which I had knowledge; and, better still, I had pleased Mr. Lincoln, who wanted "success" very much. But I had not accomplished all, for Hood's army, the chief "objective," had escaped.

Then began the real trouble. We were in possession of Atlanta, and Hood remained at Lovejoy's Station, thirty miles south-east, on the Savannah railroad, with an army of about 40,000 veterans inured to war, and with a fair amount of wagons to carry his supplies, independent of the railroads. On the 21st of September he shifted his position to Palmetto Station, twenty-five miles south-west of Atlanta, on the Montgomery and Selma railroad, where he began systematic preparations for an aggressive campaign against our communications to compel us to abandon our conquests. Here he was visited by Mr. Davis, who promised all possible coöperation and assistance in the proposed campaign; and here also Mr. Davis made his famous speech, which was duly reported to me in Atlanta, assuring his army that they would make my retreat more disastrous than was that of Napoleon from Moscow. Forewarned, I took immediate measures to thwart his plans. One division was sent back to Rome, another to Chattanooga; the guards along our railroad were reënforced and warned of the coming blow. General Thomas was sent back to the headquarters of his department at Nashville, Schofield to his at Knoxville, while I remained in Atlanta to await Hood's "initiative." This followed soon. Hood, sending his cavalry ahead, crossed the Chattahoochee River at Campbelltown with his main army on the 1st of October, and moved to Dallas, detaching a strong force against the railroad above Marietta which destroyed it for fifteen miles, and then sent French's division to capture Allatoona. I followed Hood, reaching Kenesaw Mountain in time to see in the distance the attack on Allatoona, which was handsomely repulsed by Corse. Hood then moved westward, avoiding Rome, and by a circuit reached Resaca, which he summoned to surrender, but did not wait to attack. He continued thence the destruction of the railroad for about twenty miles to the tunnel, including Dalton, whose garrison he captured. I followed up to Resaca, then turned west to intercept his retreat down the Valley of Chattooga [see map, p. 249]; but by rapid marching he escaped to Gadsden, on the Coosa, I halting at Gaylesville, whence to observe his further movements. Hood, after a short pause, crossed the mountains to Decatur, on the Tennessee River, which point, as it was defended by a good division of troops, he avoided, and finally halted opposite Florence, Alabama, on the Tennessee. [See map, Vol. III., p. 6.] Divining the object of his movement against our communications, which had been thus far rapid and skillful, I detached by rail General Schofield and two of my six corps to Nashville, all the reënforcements that Thomas deemed necessary to enable him to defend Tennessee, and began my systematic preparations for resuming the offensive against Georgia. Repairing the broken railroads, we collected in Atlanta the necessary food and transportation for 60,000 men, sent to the rear all impediments, called in all detachments, and ordered them to march for Atlanta, where by November 4th were assembled four infantry corps, one cavalry division, and 65 field-guns, aggregating 60,598 men. Hood remained at Florence, preparing to invade Tennessee and Kentucky, or to follow me. We were prepared for either alternative.

According to the great Napoleon, the fundamental maxim for successful war is to "converge a superior force on the critical point at the critical time." In 1864 the main "objectives" were Lee's and Johnston's armies, and the critical point was thought to be Richmond or Atlanta, whichever should be longer held. Had General Grant overwhelmed and scattered Lee's army and occupied Richmond he would have come to Atlanta; but as I happened to occupy Atlanta first, and had driven Hood off to a divergent line of operations far to the west, it was good strategy to leave him to a subordinate force, and with my main army to join Grant at Richmond. The most practicable route to Richmond was nearly a thousand miles in distance, too long for a single march; hence the necessity to reach the sea-coast for a new base. Savannah, distant three hundred miles, was the nearest point, and this distance we accomplished from November 12th to December 21st, 1864. ☆ According to the Duke of Wellington, an army moves upon its belly, not upon its legs; and no army dependent on wagons can operate more than a hundred miles from its base, because the teams going and returning consume the contents of their wagons, leaving little or nothing for the maintenance of the men and animals at the front, who are fully employed in fighting; hence the necessity to "forage liberally on the country," a measure which fed our men and animals chiefly on the very supplies which had been gathered near the railroads by the enemy for the maintenance of his own armies. "The March to the Sea" was in strategy only a shift of base for ulterior and highly important purposes.

Many an orator in his safe office at the North had proclaimed his purpose to cleave his way to the sea. Every expedition which crossed the Ohio River in the early part of the war headed for the sea; but things were not ripe till the Western army had fought, and toiled, and labored down to Atlanta. Not

☆ The army reached the vicinity of Savannah, December 10th, but did not get possession of the city until the 21st.—EDITORS.

GENERAL WILLIAM T. SHERMAN AT ATLANTA. FROM A PHOTOGRAPH.

till then did a "March to the Sea" become practicable and possible of grand results. Alone I never measured it as now my eulogists do, but coupled with Thomas's acts about Nashville, and those about Richmond directed in person by General Grant, the "March to the Sea," with its necessary corollary, the march northward to Raleigh, became vastly important, if not actually conclusive of the war. Mr. Lincoln was the wisest man of our day, and more truly and kindly gave voice to my secret thoughts and feeling when he wrote me at Savannah from Washington under date of December 26th, 1864:

"When you were about leaving Atlanta for the Atlantic coast I was anxious, if not fearful; but feeling that you were the better judge, and remembering 'nothing risked, nothing gained,' I did not interfere. Now the undertaking being a success, the honor is all yours; for I believe none of us went further than to acquiesce; and taking the work of General Thomas into account, as it should be taken, it is indeed a great success. Not only does it afford the obvious and immediate military advantages, but in showing to the world that your army could be divided, putting the stronger part to an important new service, and yet leaving enough to vanquish the old opposing force of the whole, Hood's army, it brings those who sat in darkness to see a great light. But what next? I suppose it will be safer if I leave General Grant and yourself to decide."

So highly do I prize this testimonial that I preserve Mr. Lincoln's letter, every word in his own handwriting, unto this day; and if I know myself, I believe on receiving it I experienced more satisfaction in giving to his over-burdened and weary soul one gleam of satisfaction and happiness, than of selfish pride in an achievement which has given me among men a larger measure of fame than any single act of my life.   There is an old maxim of war, that a general should not divide his forces in the presence of an enter-prising enemy, and I confess that I felt more anxious for General Thomas's success than my own, because had I left him with an insufficient force it would have been adjudged ungenerous and unmilitary in me; but the result, and Mr. Lincoln's judgment *after* the event, demonstrated that my division of force was liberal, leaving to Thomas "enough to vanquish the old oppos-ing force of the whole, Hood's army," and retaining for myself enough to march to the sea, and thence north to Raleigh, in communication with the old Army of the Potomac which had so long and heroically fought for Richmond, every officer and soldier of which felt and saw the dawn of peace in the near approach of their comrades of the West, who, having finished their task, had come so far to lend them a helping hand if needed.   I honestly believe that the grand march of the Western army from Atlanta to Savannah, and from Savan-nah to Raleigh, was an important factor in the final result, the overwhelming victory at Appomattox, and the glorious triumph of the Union cause.⎱

Meantime Hood, whom I had left at and near Florence, 317 miles to my rear, having completely reorganized and resupplied his army, advanced against Thomas at Nashville, who had also made every preparation.   Hood first encountered Schofield at Franklin, November 30th, 1864, attacked him boldly behind his intrenchments, and sustained a positive check, losing 6252 of his best men, including Generals Cleburne and Adams, who were

⎱ One single fact about the "March to the Sea," unknown to me, revealed by General Grant in his "Memoirs," Vol. II., p. 376 :

"I was in favor of Sherman's plan from the time it was first submitted to me. My chief-of-staff, however, was very bitterly opposed to it, and as I learned subse-quently, finding that he could not move me, he appealed to the authorities at Washington to stop it."

I had been acquainted with General John A. Rawlins, General Grant's "chief-of-staff," from the beginning of the war. He was always most loyal and devoted to his chief, an enthusiastic patriot, and of real ability. He was a neighbor of General Grant in Galena at the breaking out of the war, a lawyer in good practice, an intense thinker, and a man of vehement expression; a soldier by force of circumstances rather than of education or practice, yet of infinite use to his chief throughout the war and up to the hour of his death as Secre-tary of War, in 1869. General Rawlins was en-thusiastically devoted to his friends in the West-ern army, with which he had been associated from Cairo to Vicksburg and Chattanooga, and doubt-less, like many others at the time (October, 1864) feared that I was about to lead his com-rades in a "wild-goose chase," not fully compre-hending the objects aimed at, or that I on the spot had better means of accurate knowledge than he in the distance. He did not possess the magnifi-cent equipoise of General Grant, nor the confidence in my military sagacity which his chief did, and I am not at all surprised to learn that he went to Washington from City Point to obtain an order from the President or Secretary of War to compel me, with an army of 65,000 of the best soldiers which America had ever produced, to remain idle when an opportunity was offered such as never occurs twice to any man on earth. General Raw-lins was right according to the light he possessed, and I remember well my feeling of uneasiness that something of the kind *might* happen, and how free and glorious I felt when the magic telegraph was cut, which prevented the possibility of orders of any kind from the rear coming to delay or hinder us from fulfilling what I knew was compara-tively easy of execution and was sure to be a long stride toward the goal we were all aiming at—victory and peace from Virginia to Texas. He was one of the many referred to by Mr. Lincoln who sat in darkness, but after the event saw a great light. He never revealed to me the doubts he had had.—W. T. S.

RATION-DAY AT CHATTANOOGA IN 1864. FROM A WAR-TIME SKETCH.

killed on the very parapets, to Schofield's loss of 2326. Nevertheless he pushed on to Nashville, which he invested. Thomas, one of the grand characters of our civil war, nothing dismayed by danger in front or rear, made all his preparations with cool and calm deliberation; and on the 15th of December sallied from his intrenchments, attacked Hood in his chosen and intrenched position, and on the next day, December 16th, actually annihilated his army, eliminating it thenceforward from the problem of the war. Hood's losses were 15,000 men to Thomas's 3057.

Therefore at the end of the year 1864 the conflict at the West was concluded, leaving nothing to be considered in the grand game of war but Lee's army, held by Grant in Richmond, and the Confederate detachments at Mobile and along the sea-board north of Savannah. Of course Charleston, ever arrogant, felt secure; but it was regarded by us as a "dead cock in the pit," and fell of itself when its inland communications were cut. In January Fort Fisher was captured by a detachment from the Army of the Potomac, aided by Admiral Porter's fleet, and Wilmington was occupied by Schofield, who had been brought by Grant from Nashville to Washington and sent down the Atlantic coast to prepare for Sherman's coming to Goldsboro', North Carolina,—all "converging" on Richmond.

Preparatory to the next move, General Howard was sent from Savannah to secure Pocotaligo, in South Carolina, as a point of departure for the north, and General Slocum to Sister's Ferry, on the Savannah River, to secure a safe lodgment on the north bank for the same purpose. In due time — in February, 1865 — these detachments, operating by concentric lines, met on the South Carolina road at Midway and Blackville, swept northward through Orangeburg and Columbia to Winnsboro', where the direction was changed to Fayetteville and Goldsboro', a distance of 420 miles through a difficult and hostile country, making junction with Schofield at a safe base with two good railroads back to the sea-coast, of which we held absolute dominion. The resistance of Hampton, Butler, Beauregard, and even Joe Johnston was regarded as trivial. Our "objective" was Lee's army at Richmond. When I reached Goldsboro', made junction with Schofield, and moved forward to Raleigh, I was willing to encounter the entire Confederate army; but the Confederate armies—Lee's in Richmond and Johnston's in my front—held interior lines, and could choose the initiative. Few military critics who have treated of the civil war in America have ever comprehended the importance of the movement of my army northward from Savannah to Goldsboro', or of the transfer of Schofield from Nashville to coöperate with me in North Carolina. This march was like the thrust of a sword toward the heart of the human body; each mile of advance swept aside all opposition, consumed the very food on which Lee's army depended for life, and demonstrated a power in the National Government which was irresistible.

Therefore, in March, 1865, but one more move was left to Lee on the chessboard of war: to abandon Richmond; make junction with Johnston in North Carolina; fall on me and destroy me if possible—a fate I did not apprehend; then turn on Grant, sure to be in close pursuit, and defeat him. But no! Lee clung to his intrenchments for political reasons, and waited for the inevitable. At last, on the 1st day of April, General Sheridan, by his vehement and most successful attack on the Confederate lines at the "Five Forks" near Dinwiddie Court House, compelled Lee to begin his last race for life. He then attempted to reach Danville, to make junction with Johnston, but Grant in his rapid pursuit constantly interposed, and finally headed him off at Appomattox, and compelled the surrender of the Army of Northern Virginia, which for four years had baffled the skill and courage of the Army of the Potomac and the power of our National Government. This substantially ended the war, leaving only the formal proceedings of accepting the surrender of Johnston in North Carolina and of the subordinate armies at the South-west.

THE "CALICO HOUSE," GENERAL SHERMAN'S FIRST HEADQUARTERS IN ATLANTA—AFTERWARD THE OFFICE OF HIS ENGINEERS; ALSO FOR SEVERAL MONTHS A HOSPITAL. FROM A PHOTOGRAPH.

OPPOSING SHERMAN'S ADVANCE TO ATLANTA.

BY JOSEPH E. JOHNSTON, GENERAL, C. S. A.

BUZZARD-ROOST GAP. FROM A WAR-TIME SKETCH.

PRESIDENT DAVIS transferred me from the Department of Mississippi to the command of the Army of Tennessee by a telegram received December 18th, 1863, in the camp of Ross's brigade of cavalry near Bolton. I assumed that command at Dalton on the 27th, and received there, on the 1st of January, a letter from the President dated December 23d, purporting to be "instructions."

In it he, in Richmond, informed me of the encouraging condition of the army, which "induced him to hope that I would soon be able to commence active operations against the enemy,"— the men being "tolerably" well clothed, with a large reserve of small-arms, the morning reports exhibiting an effective total that exceeded in number "that actually engaged on the Confederate side in any battle of the war." Yet this army itself had lost in the recent campaign at least 25,000 men in action, while 17,000 had been transferred from it in Longstreet's corps, and the two brigades (Quarles's and Baldwin's) that had been sent to Mississippi; so that it was then weaker by 40,000 men than it had been when "engaged on the Confederate side" in the battle of Chickamauga, in the September preceding.

In the inspections, which were made as soon as practicable, the appearance of the army was very far from being "matter of much congratulation." Instead of a reserve of muskets there was a deficiency of six thousand and as great a one of blankets, while the number of bare feet was painful to see. The artillery horses were too feeble to draw the guns in fields, or on a march, and the mules were in similar condition; while the supplies of forage were then very irregular, and did not include hay. In consequence of this, it was necessary to send all of these animals not needed for camp service to the valley of the Etowah, where long forage could be found, to restore their health and strength.

The last return of the army was of December 20th, and exhibited an effective total of less than 36,000, of whom 6000 were without arms and as many without shoes. The President impressed upon me the importance of recovering Tennessee with an army in such numbers and condition. On pages 548–9, Vol. II. of his work, "The Rise and Fall of the Confederate Government," he dwells upon his successful efforts to increase its numbers and means adequately. After the strange assertions and suggestions of December 23d, he did not resume the subject of military operations until, in a letter of February 27th to him through his staff-officer General Bragg, I pointed out the necessity of great preparations to take the offensive, such as large additions to the number of troops, an ample supply of field transportation, subsistence stores, and forage, a bridge equipage, and fresh artillery horses. This letter was acknowledged on the 4th of March, but not really replied to until the 12th, when General Bragg [see note, Vol. III., p. 711] wrote a plan of campaign which was delivered to me on the 18th by his secretary, Colonel Sale. It prescribed my invasion of Tennessee with an army of 75,000 men, including Longstreet's corps, then near Morristown, Tennessee. When necessary supplies and transportation were collected at Dalton, the additional troops, except Longstreet's, would be sent there; and this army and Longstreet's corps would march to meet at Kingston, on the Tennessee River, and thence into the valley of Duck River.

Being invited to give my views, I suggested that the enemy could defeat the plan, either by attacking one of our two bodies of troops on the march, with their united forces, or by advancing against Dalton before our forces there should be equipped for the field; for it was certain that they would be able to take the field before we could be ready. I proposed, therefore, that the additional troops should be sent to Dalton in time to give us the means to beat the Federal army there, and then pursue it into Tennessee, which would be a more favorable mode of invasion than the other.

General Bragg replied that my answer did not indicate acceptance of the plan proposed, and that troops could be drawn from other points only to advance. As the idea of advancing had been accepted by me, it was evidently his strategy that was the ultimatum.

I telegraphed again (and also sent a confidential officer to say) that I was anxious to take the offensive with adequate means, and to represent to the President the actual disparity of forces, but without result. The above is the substance of all said, written, or done on the subject of Mr. Davis's pages 548–9, before the armies were actually in contact, with odds of ten to four against us.

The instruction, discipline, and spirit of the army were much improved between the 1st of January and the end of April, and its numbers were increased. The efforts for the latter object brought back to the ranks about five thousand of the men who had left them in the rout of Missionary Ridge. On the morning report of April 30th the totals were: 37,652 infantry, 2812 artillery with 112 guns, and 2392 cavalry. This is the report as corrected by Major Kinloch Falconer, assistant adjutant-general, from official records in his office. ǀ Sherman had assembled at that time an army of 98,797 men and 254 guns; but before the armies actually met, three divisions of cavalry under Generals Stoneman, Garrard, and McCook added 10,000 or 12,000 men to the number. The object prescribed to him by General Grant was "to move against Johnston's army, to break it up, and to get into the interior of the enemy's country as far as he could, inflicting all the damage possible on their war resources."

The occupation of Dalton by General Bragg had been accidental. He had encamped there for a night in his retreat from Missionary Ridge, and had

ǀ See another estimate, p. 281.— EDITORS.

remained because it was ascertained next morning that the pursuit had ceased. Dalton is in a valley so broad as to give ample room for the deployment of the largest American army. Rocky-face, which bounds it on the the west, terminates as an obstacle three miles north of the railroad gap, and the distance from Chattanooga to Dalton around the north end exceeds that through the railroad gap less than a mile; and a general with a large army, coming from Chattanooga to attack an inferior one near Dalton, would follow that route and find in the broad valley a very favorable field.

Mr. Davis descants on the advantages I had in mountains, ravines, and streams, and General Sherman claims that those features of the country were equal to the numerical difference between our forces. I would gladly have given all the mountains, ravines, rivers, and woods of Georgia for such a supply of artillery ammunition, proportionally, as he had. Thinking as he did, it is strange that he did not give himself a decided superiority of actual strength, by drawing troops from his three departments of the Cumberland, the Tennessee, and the Ohio, where, according to Secretary Stanton's report of 1865, he had 139,000 men, fit for duty. The country in which the two armies operated is not rugged; there is nothing in its character that gave advantage to the Confederates. Between Dalton and Atlanta the only mountain in sight of the railroad is Rocky-face, which aided the Federals. The small military value of mountains is indicated by the fact that in the Federal attack on June 27th our troops on Kenesaw suffered more than those on the plain.

During the previous winter Major-General Gilmer, chief engineer, had wisely made an admirable base for our army by intrenching Atlanta.

As a road leads from Chattanooga through Snake Creek Gap to the railroad bridge at Resaca, a light intrenchment to cover 3000 or 4000 men was made there; and to make quick communication between that point and Dalton, two rough country roads were so improved as to serve that purpose. ⚓

On the 1st of May I reported to the Administration that the enemy was about to advance, suggesting the transfer of at least a part of General Polk's troops to my command. Then the cavalry with convalescent horses was ordered to the front,— Martin's division to observe the Oostenaula from Resaca to Rome, and Kelly's little brigade to join the cavalry on the Cleveland road.

On the 4th the Federal army, including the troops from Knoxville, was at Ringgold. Next day it skirmished until dark with our advanced guard of cavalry. This was repeated on the 6th. On the 7th it moved forward, driving our cavalry from Tunnel Hill, and taking a position in the afternoon in front of the railroad gap, and parallel to Rocky-face — the right a mile south of the gap, and the left near the Cleveland road.

Until that day I had regarded a battle in the broad valley in which Dalton stands as inevitable. The greatly superior strength of the Federal army made the chances of battle altogether in its favor. It had also places of refuge in case of defeat, in the intrenched pass of Ringgold and in the fortress of Chattanooga; while we, if beaten, had none nearer than Atlanta,

⚓ For maps of the campaign see p. 251 and the paper by General Howard, to follow.— EDITORS.

100 miles off, with three rivers intervening. General Sherman's course indicating no intention of giving battle east of Rocky-face, we prepared to fight on either side of the ridge. For that object A. P. Stewart's division was placed in the gap, Cheatham's on the crest of the hill, extending a mile north of Stewart's, and Bate's also on the crest of the hill, and extending a mile south of the gap. Stevenson's was formed across the valley east of the ridge, his left meeting Cheatham's right; Hindman in line with Stevenson and on his right; Cleburne behind Mill Creek and in front of Dalton. Walker's division was in reserve.

Cantey with his division arrived at Resaca that evening (7th) and was charged with the defense of the place. During the day our cavalry was driven from the ground west of Rocky-face through the gap. Grigsby's brigade was placed near Dug Gap,—the remainder in front of our right. About 4 o'clock P. M. of the 8th, Geary's division of Hooker's corps attacked two regiments of Reynolds's Arkansas brigade who were guarding Dug Gap, and who were soon joined by Grigsby's brigade on foot. The increased sound of musketry indicated so sharp a conflict that Lieutenant-General Hardee was requested to send Granbury's Texan brigade to the help of our people, and to take command there himself. These accessions soon decided the contest, and the enemy was driven down the hill. A sharp engagement was occurring at the same time on the crest of the mountain, where our right and center joined, between Pettus's brigade holding that point and troops of the Fourth Corps attacking it. The assailants were repulsed, however. The vigor of this attack suggested the addition of Brown's brigade to Pettus's.

On the 9th a much larger force assailed the troops at the angle, and with great determination, but the Federal troops were defeated with a loss proportionate to their courage. Assaults as vigorous and resolute were made at the same time on Stewart and on Bate, and were handsomely repulsed. The Confederates, who fought under cover, had but trifling losses in these combats, but the Federal troops, fully exposed, must have lost heavily—the more because American soldiers are not to be driven back without severe losses. General Wheeler had a very handsome affair of cavalry near Varnell's Station, the same day, in which he captured 100 prisoners, including a colonel, three captains, five lieutenants, and a standard. General Sherman regarded these actions as amounting to a battle.

Information had been received of the arrival of the Army of the Tennessee in Snake Creek Gap, on the 8th. At night on the 9th General Cantey reported that he had been engaged with those troops until dark. Lieutenant-General Hood was dispatched to Resaca with three divisions immediately. The next morning he reported the enemy retiring, and was recalled, with orders to leave two divisions midway between the two places. Spirited fighting was renewed in and near the gap as well as on the northern front. The most vigorous of them was made late in the day, on Bate's division, and repulsed. At night information was received from our scouts near the south end of Rocky-face, that the Army of the Tennessee was intrenching in Snake Creek Gap, and next morning reports were received which indicated a general

THE BATTLE OF RESACA, GEORGIA, MAY 14, 1864. FROM "THE MOUNTAIN CAMPAIGNS IN GEORGIA," ETC. PUBLISHED BY THE WESTERN & ATLANTIC R. R. CO.

movement of the Federal army to its right, and one report that General McPherson's troops were moving from Snake Creek Gap toward Resaca. General Polk, who had just reached that place with Loring's division, was charged with its defense.

General Wheeler was directed to move next morning with all the available cavalry around the north end of Rocky-face, to learn if a general movement of the enemy was in progress. He was to be supported by Hindman's division. In this reconnoissance General Stoneman's division of cavalry was encountered and driven back. The information gained confirmed the reports of the day before.

About 10 o'clock A. M. of the 13th the Confederate army moved from Dalton and reached Resaca just as the Federal troops approaching from Snake Creek Gap were encountering Loring's division a mile from the station. Their approach was delayed long enough by Loring's opposition to give me time to select the ground to be occupied by our troops. And while they were taking this ground the Federal army was forming in front of them. The left of Polk's corps occupied the west face of the intrenchment of Resaca. Hardee's corps, also facing to the west, formed the center. Hood's, its left division facing to the west and the two others to the north-west, was on the right, and, crossing the railroad, reached the Connasauga. The enemy skirmished briskly with the left half of our line all the afternoon.

On the 14th spirited fighting was maintained by the enemy on the whole front, a very vigorous attack being made on Hindman's division of Hood's corps, which was handsomely repulsed. In the meantime General Wheeler was directed to ascertain the position and formation of the Federal left. His report indicating that these were not unfavorable to an attack, Lieutenant-General Hood was directed to make one with Stewart's and Stevenson's divisions, strengthened by four brigades from the center and left. He was instructed to make a half change of front to the left to drive the enemy from the railroad, the object of the operation being to prevent them from using it. The attack was extremely well conducted and executed, and before dark (it was begun at 6 P. M.) the enemy was driven from his ground. This encouraged me to hope for a more important success; so General Hood was directed to renew the fight next morning. His troops were greatly elated by this announcement, made to them that evening.

On riding from the right to the left after nightfall, I was informed that the extreme left of our line of skirmishers, forty or fifty men, had been driven from their ground,—an elevation near the river,—and received a report from Major-General Martin that Federal troops were crossing the Oostenaula near Lay's Ferry on a pontoon-bridge — two divisions having already crossed. In consequence of this, Walker's division was sent to Lay's Ferry immediately, and the order to General Hood was revoked; also, Lieutenant-Colonel S. W. Presstman, chief engineer, was directed to lay a pontoon-bridge a mile above the railroad, and to have the necessary roadway made.

Sharp fighting commenced early on the 15th, and continued until night, with so much vigor that many of the assailants pressed up to our intrenchments. All these attacks were repelled, however. In General Sherman's language, the sounds of musketry and cannon rose all day to the dignity of a battle.

Soon after noon intelligence was received from Major-General Walker, that the report that the enemy had crossed the Oostenaula was untrue. Lieutenant-General Hood was therefore again ordered to assail the enemy with the troops he had commanded the day before. When he was about to move forward, positive intelligence was received from General Walker that the Federal right was actually crossing the Oostenaula. This made it necessary to abandon the thought of fighting north of the river, and the orders to Lieutenant-General Hood were countermanded, but the order from corps headquarters was not sent to Stewart promptly, and consequently he made the attack unsustained, and suffered before being recalled.

The occupation of Resaca being exceedingly hazardous, I determined to abandon the place. So the army was ordered to cross the Oostenaula about midnight,—Hardee's and Polk's corps by the railroad and trestle bridges, and Hood's by that above, on the pontoons.

General Sherman claims to have surprised us by McPherson's appearance in Snake Creek Gap on the 9th, forgetting that we discovered his march on the 8th. He blames McPherson for not seizing the place. That officer tried the works and found them too strong to be seized. General Sherman says that if McPherson had placed his whole force astride the railroad, he could have there easily withstood the attack of all Johnston's army. Had he done so, "all Johnston's army" would have been upon him at the dawn of the next day, the cannon giving General Sherman intelligence of the movement of that army. About twice his force in front and three thousand men in his immediate rear would have overwhelmed him, making a most auspicious beginning of the campaign for the Confederates.

General Sherman has a very exaggerated idea of our field-works. They were slighter than his own, because we had most inadequate supplies of intrenching tools. Two events at Resaca were greatly magnified to him. He says that toward evening on the 15th [14th] McPherson "moved his whole line of battle forward till he had gained a ridge overlooking the town" [there was no town.—J. E. J.], and that several attempts to drive him away were repulsed with bloody loss. The fact is, near night of the 14th, forty or fifty skirmishers in front of our extreme left were driven from the slight elevation they occupied, ⚓ but no attempt was made to retake it. Sherman also says that "Hooker's corps had also some handsome fighting on the left, . . . capturing a 4-gun intrenched battery." . . . From our view in the morning

⚓ In his published "Narrative" General Johnston says:

"On riding from the right to the left, after nightfall, I learned that Lieutenant-General Polk's advanced troops had been driven from a hill in front of his left, which commanded our bridges at short range."

And General J. D. Cox, in his volume "Atlanta" (Charles Scribner's Sons), says:

"Between 5 and 6 o'clock Logan [of McPherson] or-dered forward the brigades of Generals Giles A. Smith and C. R. Woods, supported by Veatch's division from Dodge's corps. The height held by Polk was carried, and the position intrenched under a galling artillery and musketry fire from the enemy's principal lines. During the evening Polk made a vigorous effort to re-take the position, but was repulsed, McPherson send-ing forward Lightburn's brigade to the support of the troops already engaged. The hill thus carried com-manded the railroad and wagon bridges crossing the Oostenaula." [See also p. 282.]   EDITORS.

of the 15th, Major-General Stevenson advanced four guns some eighty yards and began to intrench them. General Hood had their fire opened at once. A ravine leading from the Federal line within easy musket-range enabled the Federal troops to drive away the gunners; but their attempt to take off the guns was frustrated by the Confederate musketry. So the pieces remained in place, and fell into the possession of Hooker's corps on the 16th, after we abandoned the position.

The Confederate army was compelled to abandon its position in front of Dalton by General Sherman's flank movement through Snake Creek Gap, and was forced from the second position by the movement toward Calhoun. Each of these movements would have made the destruction of the Confederate army inevitable in case of defeat. In the first case the flank march was protected completely by Rocky-face Ridge; in the second, as completely by the Oostenaula. A numerical superiority of more than two to one made those manœuvres free from risk. General Sherman thinks that the impracticable nature of the country, which made the passage of the troops across the valley almost impossible, saved the Confederate army. The Confederate army remained in its position near Dalton until May 13th, because I knew the time that would be required for the march of 100,000 men through the long defile between their right flank near Mill Creek Gap and the outlet of Snake Creek Gap; and the shortness of the time in which 43,000 men could march by two good roads direct from Dalton to Resaca; and the further fact that our post at Resaca could hold out a longer time than our march to that point would require.

Mr. Davis and General Sherman exhibit a strange ignorance of the country between Dalton and Atlanta. Mr. Davis describes mountain ridges offering positions neither to be taken nor turned, and a natural fortress eighteen miles in extent, forgetting, apparently, that a fortress is strong only when it has a garrison strong enough for its extent; and both forget that, except Rocky-face, no mountain is visible from the road between Dalton and Atlanta. That country is intersected by numerous practicable roads, and is not more rugged than that near Baltimore and Washington, or Atlanta and Macon. When the armies confronted each other the advantages of ground were equal and unimportant, both parties depending for protection on earth-works, not on ridges and ravines.

In leaving Resaca I hoped to find a favorable position near Calhoun, but there was none; and the army, after resting 18 or 20 hours near that place, early in the morning of the 17th moved on seven or eight miles to Adairsville, where we were joined by the cavalry of General Polk's command, a division of 3700 men under General W. H. Jackson. Our map represented the valley in which the railroad lies as narrow enough for our army formed across it to occupy the heights on each side with its flanks, and therefore I intended to await the enemy's attack there; but the breadth of the valley far exceeded the front of our army in order of battle. So another plan was devised. Two roads lead southward from Adairsville,— one directly through Cassville; the other follows the railroad through Kingston, turns to the left there, and rejoins the other at Cassville. The interval between them is widest opposite Kingston, where it is about seven miles by the farm roads. In the expectation that a part of the Federal army would follow each road, it was arranged that Polk's corps should engage the column on the direct road when it should arrive opposite Kingston,— Hood's, in position for the purpose, falling upon its left flank during the deployment. Next morning, when our cavalry on that road reported the right Federal column near Kingston, General Hood was instructed to move to and follow northwardly a country road a mile east of that from Adairsville, to be in position to fall upon the flank of the Federal column when it should be engaged with Polk. An order announcing that we were about to give battle was read to each regiment, and heard with exultation. After going some three miles, General Hood marched back about two, and formed his corps facing to our right and rear. Being asked for an explanation, he replied that an aide-de-camp had told him that the Federal army was approaching on that road. Our whole army knew that to be impossible. It had been viewing the enemy in the opposite direction every day for two weeks. General Hood did not report his extraordinary disobedience—as he must have done had he believed the story upon which he professed to have acted. The time lost frustrated the design, for success depended on timing the attack properly.

Mr. Davis conceals the facts to impute this failure to me, thus: "The battle, for causes which were the subject of dispute, did not take place. . . . Instead of his attacking the divided columns of the enemy, the united Federal columns were preparing to attack him." There was no dispute as to facts.

An attack, except under very unfavorable circumstances, being impossible, the troops were formed in an excellent position along the ridge immediately south of Cassville, an elevated and open valley in front, and a deep one in rear of it. Its length was equal to the front of Hood's and Polk's and half of Hardee's corps. They were placed in that order from right to left.

As I rode along the line while the troops were forming, General Shoup, chief of artillery, pointed out to me a space of 150 or 200 yards, which he thought might be enfiladed by artillery on a hill a half mile beyond Hood's right and in front of the prolongation of our line, if the enemy should clear away the thick wood that covered it and establish batteries. He was desired to point out to the officer who might command there some narrow ravines very near, in which his men could be sheltered from such artillery fire, and to remind him that while artillery was playing upon his position no attack would be made upon it by infantry. The enemy got into position soon after our troops were formed and skirmished until dark, using their field-pieces freely. During the evening Lieutenant-Generals Polk and Hood, the latter being spokesman, asserted that a part of the line of each would be so enfiladed next morning by the Federal batteries established on the hill above mentioned, that they would be unable to hold their ground an hour; and therefore urged me to abandon the position at once. They expressed the conviction that early the next morning batteries would open upon them from a hill *then thickly covered with wood and out of range of brass field-*

pieces. The matter was discussed perhaps an hour, in which time I became apprehensive that as the commanders of two-thirds of the army thought the position untenable, the opinion would be adopted by their troops, which would make it so. Therefore I yielded. Lieutenant-General Hardee, whose ground was the least strong, was full of confidence. Mr. Davis says ("Rise and Fall," Vol. II., p. 533) that General Hood asserts, in his report and in a book, that the two corps were on ground commanded and enfiladed by the enemy's batteries. On the contrary, they were on a hill, and the enemy were in a valley where their batteries were completely commanded by ours.

The army abandoned the ground before daybreak and crossed the Etowah after noon, and encamped near the railroad. Wheeler's cavalry was placed in observation above, and Jackson's below our main body.

No movement of the enemy was discovered until the 22d, when General Jackson reported their army moving toward Stilesboro', as if to cross the Etowah near that place; they crossed on the 23d. On the 24th Hardee's and Polk's corps encamped on the road from Stilesboro' to Atlanta, south-east of Dallas, and Hood's four miles from New Hope Church, on the road from Alla-toona. On the 25th the Federal army was a little east of Dallas, and Hood's corps was placed with its center at New Hope Church, Polk's on his left, and Hardee's prolonging the line to the Atlanta road, which was held by its left. A little before 6 o'clock in the afternoon Stewart's division in front of New Hope Church was fiercely attacked by Hooker's corps, and the action contin-ued two hours without lull or pause, when the assailants fell back. The can-ister shot of the sixteen Confederate field-pieces and the musketry of five thousand infantry at short range must have inflicted heavy loss upon Gen-eral Hooker's corps, as is proved by the name "Hell Hole," which, General Sherman says, was given the place by the Federal soldiers. Next day the Federal troops worked so vigorously, extending their intrenchments toward the railroad, that they skirmished very little. The Confederates labored stren-uously to keep abreast of their work, but in vain, owing to greatly inferior numbers and an insignificant supply of intrenching tools. On the 27th, how-ever, the fighting rose above the grade of skirmishing, especially in the after-noon, when at half-past 5 o'clock the Fourth Corps (Howard) and a division of the Fourteenth (Palmer) attempted to turn our right, but the movement, after being impeded by the cavalry, was met by two regiments of our right division (Cleburne's), and the two brigades of his second line brought up on the right of the first. The Federal formation was so deep that its front did not equal that of our two brigades; consequently those troops were greatly exposed to our musketry—all but the leading troops being on a hillside facing us. They advanced until their first line was within 25 or 30 paces of ours, and fell back only after at least 700 men had fallen dead in their places. When the leading Federal troops paused in their advance, a color-bearer came on and planted his colors eight or ten feet in front of his regiment, but was killed in the act. A soldier who sprang forward to hold up or bear off the colors was shot dead as he seized the staff. Two others who followed successively fell like him, but the fourth bore back the noble emblem. Some time after nightfall the Confederates captured above two hundred prisoners in the hollow before them.

General Sherman does not refer to this combat in his " Memoirs," although he dwells with some exultation upon a very small affair of the next day at Dallas, in which the Confederates lost about three hundred killed and wounded, and in which he must have lost more than ten times as many.

In the afternoon of the 28th Lieutenant-General Hood was instructed to draw his corps to the rear of our line in the early part of the night, march around our right flank, and form it facing the left flank of the Federal line and obliquely to it, and attack at dawn — Hardee and Polk to join in the battle successively as the success on the right of each might enable him to do so. We waited next morning for the signal — the sound of Hood's musketry — from the appointed time until 10 o'clock, when a message from that officer was brought by an aide-de-camp to the effect that he had found R. W. Johnson's division intrenching on the left of the Federal line and almost at right angles to it, and asked for instructions. The message proved that there could be no surprise, which was necessary to success, and that the enemy's intrenchments would be completed before we could attack. The corps was therefore recalled. It was ascertained afterward that after marching eight or ten hours Hood's corps was then at least six miles from the Federal left, which was little more than a musket-shot from his starting-point.

The extension of the Federal intrenchments toward the railroad was continued industriously to cut us off from it or to cover their own approach to it. We tried to keep pace with them, but the labor did not prevent the desultory fighting, which was kept up while daylight lasted. In this the great inequality of force compelled us to employ dismounted cavalry. On the 4th or 5th of June the Federal army reached the railroad between Ackworth and Allatoona. The Confederate forces then moved to a position carefully marked out by Colonel Presstman, its left on Lost Mountain, and its right, of cavalry, beyond the railroad and somewhat covered by Noonday Creek, a line much too long for our strength.

On the 8th the Federal army seemed to be near Ackworth, and our position was contracted to cover the roads leading thence to Atlanta. This brought the left of Hardee's corps to Gilgal Church, Polk's right near the Marietta and Ackworth road and Hood's corps massed beyond that road. Pine Mountain, a detached hill, was held by a division. On the 11th of June the left of the Federal army was on the high ground beyond Noonday Creek, its center a third of a mile in front of Pine Mountain and its right beyond the Burnt Hickory and Marietta road.

In the morning of the 14th General Hardee and I rode to the summit of Pine Mountain to decide if the outpost there should be maintained. General Polk accompanied us. After we had concluded our examination and the abandonment of the hill that night had been decided upon, a few shots were fired at us from a battery of Parrott guns a quarter of a mile in our front; the third of these passed through General Polk's chest, from left to right, killing him instantly. This event produced deep sorrow in the army, in every battle of which he had been distinguished. Major-General W. W. Loring succeeded to the command of the corps.

A division of Georgia militia under Major-General G. W. Smith, transferred to the Confederate service by Governor Brown, was charged with the defense of the bridges and ferries of the Chattahoochee, for the safety of Atlanta. On the 16th Hardee's corps was placed on the high ground east of Mud Creek, facing to the west. The right of the Federal army made a corresponding change of front by which it faced to the east. It was opposed in this manœuvre by Jackson's cavalry as well as 2500 men can resist 30,000. The angle where Hardee's right joined Loring's left was soon found to be a very weak point, and on the 17th another position was chosen, including the crest of Kenesaw, which Colonel Presstman prepared for occupation by the 19th, when it was assumed by the army. In this position two divisions of Loring's corps occupied the crest of Kenesaw from end to end, the other division being on its right, and Hood's corps on the right of it, Hardee's extending from Loring's left across the Lost Mountain and Marietta road. The enemy approached as usual, under cover of successive lines of intrenchments. In these

CONFEDERATES DRAGGING GUNS UP KENESAW MOUNTAIN. FROM THE "VALENTINE," PUBLISHED BY THE WESTERN & ATLANTIC R. R. CO.

positions of the two armies there were sharp and incessant partial engagements until the 3d of July. On the 21st of June the extension of the Federal line to the south which had been protected by the swollen condition of Noses Creek, compelled the transfer of Hood's corps to our left, Wheeler's troops occupying the ground it had left. On the 22d General Hood reported that Hindman's and Stevenson's divisions of his corps, having been attacked, had driven back the Federal troops and had taken a line of breastworks, from which they had been driven by the artillery of the enemy's main position.

Subsequent detailed accounts of this affair prove that after the capture of the advanced line of breastworks General Hood directed his two divisions against the enemy's main line. The slow operation of a change of front under the fire of the artillery of this main line subjected the Confederates to a loss of one thousand men — whereupon the attempt was abandoned, either by the general's orders or by the discretion of the troops.

On the 24th Hardee's skirmishers were attacked in their rifle-pits by a Federal line of battle, and on the 25th a similar assault was made upon those of Stevenson's division. Both were repulsed, with heavy proportionate losses to the assailants.

In the morning of the 27th, after a cannonade by all its artillery, the Federal army assailed the Confederate position, especially the center and right — the Army of the Cumberland advancing against the first, and that of the Tennessee against the other. Although suffering losses out of all proportion to those they inflicted, the Federal troops pressed up to the Confederate intrenchments in many places, maintaining the unequal conflict for two hours and a half, with the persevering courage of American soldiers. At 11:30 A. M. the attack had failed. In General Sherman's words:

GENERAL SHERMAN AND GENERAL THOMAS DURING THE ASSAULT AT KENESAW MOUNTAIN, JUNE 27, 1864. FROM A SKETCH MADE AT THE TIME.

General Sherman is the slenderer figure, on the right. He and General Thomas were standing by the "signal tree" from which ran telegraphic wires to the front, by means of which reports were received and orders transmitted during the battle.

" About 9 o'clock A. M. of the day appointed [June the 27th], the troops moved to the assault, and all along our lines for ten miles a furious fire of artillery and musketry was kept up. At all points the enemy met us with determined courage and in great force. . . . By 11:30 the assault was over, and had failed. We had not broken the line at either point, but our assaulting columns held their ground within a few yards of the rebel trenches and there covered themselves with parapet. McPherson lost about 500 men and several valuable officers, and Thomas lost nearly 2000 men." ↓

↓ In his " Memoirs " Sherman says, in continuation of the quotation made by Johnston :

" This was the hardest fight of the campaign up to that date, and it is well described by Johnston in his 'Narrative [pp. 342, 343], where he admits his loss in killed and wounded as : Hood's corps (not reported) ; Hardee's corps, 286 ; Loring's (Polk's), 522, — total, 808. This, no doubt, is a true and fair statement ; but, as usual, Johnston over-estimates our loss, putting it at 6000, whereas our entire loss was about 2500 killed and wounded." EDITORS.

Such statements of losses are incredible. The Northern troops fought very bravely, as usual. Many fell against our parapets, some were killed in our trenches. Most of this battle of two hours and a half was at very short range. It is not to be believed that Southern veterans struck but 3 per cent. of Thomas's troops in mass at short range, or 1⅔ per cent. of McPherson's — and, if possible, still less so that Northern soldiers, inured to battle, should have been defeated by losses so trifling as never to have discouraged the meanest soldiers on record. I have seen American soldiers (Northern men) win a field with losses ten times greater proportionally. But, argument apart, there is a witness against the estimates of Northern losses in this campaign, in the 10,126 graves in the Military Cemetery at Marietta, of soldiers killed south of the Etowah. ♭ Moreover, the Federal dead nearest to Hardee's line lay there two days, during which they were frequently counted — at least 1000 ; and as there were seven lines within some 300 yards, exposed two hours and a half to the musketry of two divisions and the canister-shot of 32 field-pieces, there must have been many uncounted dead ; the counted would alone indicate a loss of at least 6000.

As to the " assaulting columns holding their ground within a few yards of the rebel trenches and there covering themselves with parapet," it was utterly impossible. There would have been much more exposure in that than in mounting and crossing the little rebel " parapet " ; but at one point, seventy-five yards in front of Cheatham's line, a party of Federal soldiers, finding themselves sheltered from his missiles by the form of the ground, made a " parapet " there which became connected with the main work. ⸮

As the extension of the Federal intrenched line to their right had brought *it* nearer to Atlanta than was our left, and had made our position otherwise very dangerous, two new positions for the army were chosen, one nine or ten miles south of Marietta, and the other on the high ground near the Chattahoochee. Colonel Presstman was desired to prepare the first for occupation, and Brigadier-General Shoup, commander of the artillery, was instructed to strengthen the other with a line of redoubts devised by himself.

The troops took the first position in the morning of the 3d, and as General Sherman was strengthening his right greatly, they were transferred to the second in the morning of the 5th. The cavalry of our left had been supported in the previous few days by a division of State troops commanded by Major-General G. W. Smith.

As General Sherman says, " it was really a continuous battle lasting

---

♭ Many of the burials at Marietta were of soldiers who died of disease before and after the battle of Kenesaw Mountain, and the following extract from the report, in 1874, of Colonel Oscar A. Mack, Inspector of National Cemeteries, shows that Marietta Cemetery includes dead from widely separated fields, and of other dates :

"The interments [Marietta Cemetery] are as follows : White Union soldiers and sailors (known, 6906 ; unknown, 2974),— total, 9880 ; colored Union soldiers (known, 158 ; unknown, 67),— total, 225 ; citizens, etc., 21 ;— total interments, 10,126.

"The bodies were removed from the National Cemetery at Montgomery, Ala. (which was discontinued), and from Rome, Dalton, Atlanta, and from many other places in Georgia. Several burials have been made, since my last inspection, from the garrison at Atlanta."
EDITORS.

⸮ Surgeon Joseph A. Stillwell, 22d Indiana Volunteers, writes to the editors that the point referred to was in front of General Daniel McCook's brigade, and was *seventy-five feet* from the enemy, and commanded by half a mile of the Confederate works.

from June 10th to July 3d." The army occupied positions about Marietta twenty-six days, in which the want of artillery ammunition was especially felt; in all those days we were exposed to an almost incessant fire of artillery as well as musketry — the former being the more harassing, because it could not be returned; for our supply of artillery ammunition was so small that we were compelled to reserve it for battles and serious assaults.

In the new position each corps had two pontoon-bridges laid. Above the railroad bridge the Chattahoochee had numerous good fords. General Sherman, therefore, directed his troops to that part of the river, ten or fifteen miles above our camp. On the 8th of July two of his corps had crossed the Chattahoochee and intrenched themselves. Therefore the Confederate army also crossed the river on the 9th.

About the middle of June Captain Grant of the engineers was instructed to strengthen the fortifications of Atlanta materially, on the side toward Peach Tree Creek, by the addition of redoubts and by converting barbette into embrasure batteries. I also obtained a promise of seven sea-coast rifles from General D. H. Maury [at Mobile], to be mounted on that front. Colonel Presstman was instructed to join Captain Grant with his subordinates, in this work of strengthening the defenses of Atlanta, especially between the Augusta and Marietta roads, as the enemy was approaching that side. For the same reason a position on the high ground looking down into the valley of Peach Tree Creek was selected for the army, from which it might engage the enemy if he should expose himself in the passage of the stream. The position of each division was marked and pointed out to its staff-officers.

On the 17th we learned that the whole Federal army had crossed the Chattahoochee; and late in the evening, while Colonel Presstman was receiving from me instructions for the next day, I received the following telegram of that date:

" Lieutenant-General J. B. Hood has been commissioned to the temporary rank of general under the late law of Congress. I am directed by the Secretary of War to inform you that, as you have failed to arrest the advance of the enemy to the vicinity of Atlanta, and express no confidence that you can defeat or repel him, you are hereby relieved from the command of the Army and Department of Tennessee, which you will immediately turn over to General Hood.
" S. Cooper, Adjutant and Inspector-General."

Orders transferring the command of the army ʔ to General Hood were written and published immediately, and next morning I replied to the telegram of the Secretary of War:

" Your dispatch of yesterday received and obeyed — command of the Army and Department of Tennessee has been transferred to General Hood. As to the alleged cause of my removal, I assert that Sherman's army is much stronger, compared with that of Tennessee, than Grant's compared with that of Northern Virginia. Yet the enemy has been compelled to advance much

ʔ I have two reports of the strength of the army besides that of April 30th, already given: 1. Of July 1st, 39,746 infantry, 3855 artillery, and 10,484 cavalry, — total, 54,085. 2. Of July 10th, 36,901 infantry, 3755 artillery, and 10,270 cavalry, — total, 50,926. — J. E. J.

GENERAL JOHN B. HOOD, C. S. A. FROM A PHOTOGRAPH.

more slowly to the vicinity of Atlanta than to that of Richmond and Petersburg, and penetrated much deeper into Virginia than into Georgia. Confident language by a military commander is not usually regarded as evidence of competence."

General Hood came to my quarters early in the morning of the 18th, and remained there until nightfall. Intelligence was soon received that the Federal army was marching toward Atlanta, and at his urgent request I gave all necessary orders during the day. The most important one placed the troops in the position already chosen, which covered the roads by which the enemy was approaching. After transferring the command to General Hood, I described to him the course of action I had arranged in my mind. If the enemy should give us a good opportunity in the passage of Peach Tree Creek, I expected to attack him. If successful, we should obtain important results, for the enemy's retreat would be on two sides of a triangle and our march on one. If we should not succeed, our intrenchments would give us a safe refuge, where we could hold back the enemy until the promised State troops should join us; then, placing them on the nearest defenses of the place (where there were, or ought to be, seven sea-coast rifles, sent us from Mobile by General Maury), I would attack the Federals in flank with the three Confederate corps. If we were successful, they would be driven against the Chattahoochee below the railroad, where there are no fords, or away from their supplies, as we might fall on their left or right flank. If unsuccessful, we could take refuge in Atlanta, which we could hold indefinitely; for it was too strong to be taken by assault, and too extensive to be invested. This would win the campaign, the object of which the country supposed Atlanta to be.

At Dalton, the great numerical superiority of the enemy made the chances of battle much against us, and even if beaten they had a safe refuge behind the fortified pass of Ringgold and in the fortress of Chattanooga. Our refuge, in case of defeat, was in Atlanta, 100 miles off, with three rivers intervening. Therefore victory for us could not have been decisive, while defeat would have been utterly disastrous. Between Dalton and the Chattahoochee we could have given battle only by attacking the enemy intrenched, or so near intrenchments that the only result of success to us would have been his falling back into them, while defeat would have been our ruin.

In the course pursued our troops, always fighting under cover, had very trifling losses compared with those they inflicted, so that the enemy's numerical superiority was reduced daily and rapidly; and we could reasonably have expected to cope with them on equal ground by the time the Chattahoochee was passed. Defeat on the south side of that river would have been their destruction. We, if beaten, had a place of refuge in Atlanta — too strong to be assaulted, and too extensive to be invested. I had also hopes that by the breaking of the railroad in its rear the Federal army might be compelled to attack us in a position of our own choosing, or forced into a retreat easily converted into a rout. After we crossed the Etowah, five detachments of cavalry were successively sent with instructions to destroy as much as they could of the railroad between Chattanooga and the Etowah. All failed, because they were too weak. Captain James B. Harvey, an officer of great courage and sagacity, was detached on this service on the 11th of June and remained near the railroad several weeks, frequently interrupting, but not strong enough to prevent, its use. Early in the campaign the impressions of the strength of the cavalry in Mississippi and east Louisiana given me by Lieutenant-General Polk, just from the command of that department, gave me reason to hope that an adequate force commanded by the most competent officer in America for such service (General N. B. Forrest) could be sent from it for the purpose of breaking the railroad in Sherman's rear. I therefore made the suggestion direct to the President, June 13th and July 16th, and through General Bragg on the 3d, 12th, 16th, and 26th of June. I did so in the confidence that this cavalry would serve the Confederacy far better by insuring the defeat of a great invasion than by repelling a mere raid.

In his telegram of the 17th Mr. Davis gave his reasons for removing me, but in Vol. II., pp. 556 to 561, of the "Rise and Fall" he gives many others, most of which depend on misrepresentations of the strength of the positions I occupied. They were not stronger than General Lee's; indeed, my course was as like his as the dissimilarity of the two Federal commanders permitted. As his had increased his great fame, it is not probable that the people, who admired his course, condemned another similar one. As to Georgia, the State most interested, its two most influential citizens, Governor Joseph E. Brown and General Howell Cobb, remonstrated against my removal.

The assertions in Mr. B. H. Hill's letter [of October 12th, 1878] quoted by Mr. Davis ["R. and F.," Vol. II., p. 557] do not agree with those in his oration delivered in Atlanta in 1875. Mr. Hill said in the oration: "I know that he (Mr. Davis) consulted General Lee fully, earnestly, and anxiously before this perhaps unfortunate removal." That assertion is contradicted by one whose testimony is above question—for in Southern estimation he has no superior as gentleman, soldier, and civilian—General Hampton. General Lee had a conversation with him on the subject, of which he wrote to me:

"On that occasion he expressed great regret that you had been removed, and said that he had done all in his power to prevent it. The Secretary of War had recently been at his head-quarters near Petersburg to consult as to this matter, and General Lee assured me that he had urged Mr. Seddon not to remove you from command, and had said to him that if you could not command the army we had no one who could. He was earnest in expressing not only his regret at your removal, but his entire confidence in yourself."

Everything seen about Atlanta proved that it was to be defended. We had been strengthening it a month, and had made it, under the circumstances, impregnable. We had defended Marietta, which had not a tenth of its strength, twenty-six days. General Sherman appreciated its strength, for he made no attack, although he was before it about six weeks.

I was a party to no such conversations as those given by Mr. Hill. No soldier above idiocy could express the opinions he ascribes to me.

Mr. Davis condemned me for not fighting. General Sherman's testimony and that of the Military Cemetery at Marietta refute the charge. I assert that had one of the other lieutenant-generals of the army (Hardee or Stewart) succeeded me, Atlanta would have been held by the Army of Tennessee.

THE OPENING OF THE ATLANTA CAMPAIGN.

BY W. P. C. BRECKINRIDGE, COLONEL, C. S. A.

IN his paper "Opposing Sherman's Advance to Atlanta," General Joseph E. Johnston—*clarum et venerabile nomen*—writes [see p. 263]:

"Cantey with his division arrived at Resaca that evening (7th), and was charged with the defense of the place. During the day our cavalry was driven from the ground west of Rocky-face through the gap. Grigsby's brigade was placed near Dug Gap,—the remainder in front of our right. About 4 o'clock P. M. of the 8th, Geary's division of Hooker's corps attacked two regiments of Reynolds's Arkansas brigade who were guarding Dug Gap, and who were soon joined by Grigsby's brigade on foot. The increased sound of musketry indicated so sharp a conflict that Lieutenant-General Hardee was requested to send Granbury's Texan brigade to the help of our

people, and to take command there himself. These accessions soon decided the contest, and the enemy was driven down the hill. . . .

"Information had been received of the arrival of the Army of the Tennessee in Snake Creek Gap on the 8th. At night on the 9th General Cantey reported that he had been engaged with those troops until dark. Lieutenant-General Hood was dispatched to Resaca with three divisions immediately."

It so happened that the brigade of Kentucky cavalry was present at Dug Gap and Snake Creek Gap, and that the regiment I commanded—the 9th Kentucky Cavalry—was in front at both places; and it may not be improper to put on record an account of those affairs, and thereby correct the unintentional mistakes in the meager statements given above.

The winter having ended, and all possible preparations having been made, the operations known as the Dalton-Atlanta campaign opened on May 5th, 1864, by the advance of General Thomas on Tunnel Hill, and on May 7th the withdrawal of our forces within Mill Creek Gap marked the beginning of the long retreat. Including the corps of General Polk, then under orders to join him, General Johnston had under his command, available for strategic purposes, between 65,000 and 70,000 men of all arms. It was a superb army of veterans, with implicit confidence in its general, and capable of great achievements. Deficient to a certain extent in supplies, it had enough for any possible movement its commander might order. Being a Confederate army, it necessarily was inferior to the army before it in numbers, equipment, and supplies. This was generally the case. It was necessarily so. With a white population of 5,000,000 to over 20,000,000; with no market, no ships, no factories, no credit; against a people commanding the sea, rich in all resources, and with all the world to buy from,—it was the fate of the Southern armies to confront armies larger, better equipped, and admirably supplied. Unless we could by activity, audacity, aggressiveness, and skill overcome these advantages it was a mere matter of time as to the certain result. It was therefore the first requisite of a Confederate general that he should be willing to meet his antagonist on these unequal terms, and on such terms make fight. He must of necessity take great risks and assume grave responsibilities. While these differences between the two armies that confronted each other in the mountains of North Georgia existed, they were no greater than usually existed, and for which every Confederate general must be presumed to have prepared. I repeat, ours was a superb army. While it had met defeat, and knew what retreat meant, it had fought battles which were and are among the bloodiest in all the annals of war; and it felt that under Johnston it could parallel Chickamauga and renew the glories of Shiloh.

The army lay behind an impassable ridge, through which, on its left flank, were only two accessible gaps,—Dug Gap, less than four miles south-west from Dalton, on the main road from Dalton to Lafayette, and perhaps six miles from Mill Creek Gap; and Snake Creek Gap, some eighteen miles south from Mill Creek Gap. [See map, p. 251.] With these gaps fortified, the left flank and rear of that army were absolutely safe; for while the Rocky-face and Chattooga ridges protected our flank, through these gaps we had access to attack the flank of the enemy if he attempted to make a march so far to the left and rear as to threaten our communication south of the Oostenaula or Coosa. These gaps were capable of easy and impregnable fortification. Dug Gap was a mere road cut out of the mountain-side and really needed no breastworks, for the natural palisades and contour of the mountain rendered easy its defense by resolute men. Snake Creek Gap was a gorge apparently cut through the mountains

by the creek that ran through it. It was a narrow defile between Milk Mountain and Horn Mountain, which are merely a prolongation of Chattooga Mountains, and capable of impregnable defense. These gaps were well known to both armies. Through them ran public roads, and soldiers of both armies had marched through both. Late in February Dug Gap had been seized by an Indiana regiment and held until Cleburne retook it. As early as February General Thomas, knowing that at that time Snake Creek Gap was unguarded, proposed a campaign, the plan being to attract General Johnston's attention by a demonstration on Buzzard Roost, and to throw the main body of the army through Snake Creek Gap, and cut his communications between Dalton and the Oostenaula.

Neither of these gaps was fortified, and on May 5th, when the campaign opened, Dug Gap was guarded by a small command of Arkansas troops under Colonel Williamson, numbering perhaps 250, while Snake Creek Gap was left wholly unprotected. At Resaca, where the railroad crosses the Oostenaula, Canty's brigade was held on the evening of the 7th of May, on its way from Rome to Dalton.

General Sherman had in hand for attack nearly 100,000 men and 254 guns, divided into three armies—the Army of the Cumberland, commanded by General Thomas, numbering 60,773; the Army of the Tennessee, General McPherson, 24,465; the Army of the Ohio, General Schofield, 13,559. It was a superb army, admirably equipped, abundantly supplied, excellently led. It was veteran, and had known victory. It had pushed its antagonist out of Kentucky with the surrender of Donelson; had captured Tennessee; captured Vicksburg; repossessed the Mississippi River; driven its foe over Missionary Ridge in flight. It knew how to fight, and was willing to fight.

On May 7th our cavalry was driven through Mill Creek Gap. On that night, after we had gone into camp, Colonel Grigsby, who commanded the Kentucky cavalry brigade, was ordered to send a regiment to the front of Dug Gap, to guard the approaches to it. In obedience to that order the 9th Kentucky Cavalry passed over Rocky-face Ridge, and near midnight bivouacked on Mill Creek, about a mile from, and in front of, Dug Gap. Heavy picket lines were thrown out on all the roads leading down the valley. There were several of these roads, and scouts were sent out to ascertain the movements of the enemy. By daylight it was discovered that very large bodies of troops were moving down the valley on all the roads leading to the south. General McPherson had marched from Chattanooga to Rossville, thence west of Chickamauga Mountain to Shipp's Gap and to Villanow, where the road forks—one branch leading down the east foot of Taylor's Ridge, the other leading across toward Rocky-face; this road again forks—one branch leading through Dug Gap, the other down the valley to Snake Creek Gap. Until McPherson reached Villanow it was only a conjecture as to his course, and until the head of his column turned toward Snake Creek Gap his destination was uncertain. His march was concealed by Hooker's corps of the Army of the Cumberland, which corps, forming Thomas's right, marching from Ringgold via Nickajack Gap and Trickum, hid the flank movement of McPherson. The plan was for Hooker to seize Dug Gap and push forward sufficiently to protect the flank of McPherson, and strike the flank of Johnston if he turned on McPherson; while McPherson, marching through Snake Creek Gap to Resaca, should not only destroy but hold the only railroad tributary to Johnston. The possession of Dug Gap by Hooker not only would render Dalton untenable, but would make a retreat from Dalton by the line of the railroad extremely hazardous, and completely protect McPherson from attack on his left flank. With Hooker descending from Rocky-face on our left flank and rear, McPherson holding Resaca, Thomas, with the corps of Howard and Palmer, pushing to Dalton, and Schofield to his left, our army would have been in a perilous situation.

The march of Hooker and McPherson was discovered early on the morning of May 8th by the scouts of the 9th Kentucky Cavalry, and timely information was given that at least an attack on Dug Gap was certain, and that the columns on the march were very heavy and their movements were guarded by forces too large to be either resisted or developed by the detachments sent out by the 9th Kentucky. On this information the remainder of Grigsby's brigade was ordered to Dug Gap, and reached there none too soon. All possible delay to the march of Hooker's corps was made, but about 2 P. M. Geary's division of that corps drove the 9th Kentucky across the creek and slowly up the mountain-side, until the regiment fell back in its proper position in the gap, where it found the brigade drawn in mere skirmish-line along the edge of the mountain-side. As one-fourth of cavalry soldiers are detailed to hold the horses, I presume that we had about 800 of our brigade in the fight and 250 Arkansas troops; and this handful of men held that gap until nightfall, repelling every assault. After nightfall Granbury's Texas brigade relieved us, but the assault was over. Hooker had failed in his part of the mission. That flank of our army was safe.

The importance of holding that gap was so manifest that Generals Hardee and Cleburne, with their staffs, galloped to the scene to encourage us by their presence and to aid Colonel Grigsby by their suggestions; and though the fight was made under their eye, that command needed no encouragement, and its officers and men knew that they were holding one of the doors to Dalton.

I hold in my hand the official report of General Geary, by whom that attack was made, and on the whole it is a fair and soldierly report. But he is mistaken in his belief that we had two lines of intrenchments, or that we were ever driven from our first position. Our loss was very small — in killed and wounded not a score. He reports that he made that attack with two brigades of infantry and two batteries, being an aggregate of perhaps 4500 men, or about four to one, besides the batteries. Assault after assault was made from 3 o'clock until after dark, and each assault was repulsed with loss. At first, in a mere spirit of exuberant fun, some of the men rolled stones down the mountain-side; but when the effect was noticed they were directed to use these means as part of our defense; great stones were rolled down on the supporting lines on the mountain-sides or at its foot; and as these bowlders would go leaping, crashing, breaking off limbs, crushing down saplings, we fancied we could see the effect of the unexpected missiles. It also proved a valuable resource to us, for without them our ammunition would have given out; indeed it was about exhausted when the attack ceased.

General Geary reports an aggregate loss of 357 officers and men, of whom some 50 were the adventurous advance, who actually reached the crest, only to be made prisoners. After dark our brigade, being relieved by the Texas brigade of Granbury, was ordered to the foot of the mountain to feed and to obtain ammunition.

While this attack had been going on, McPherson had steadily marched toward Snake Creek Gap, to protect which no steps had been taken. Undoubtedly if a cavalry force had been started to Snake Creek Gap at the moment Grigsby was ordered to Dug Gap, it would have reached there before McPherson, and held it during the night of the 8th, during which time infantry support could have reached there. I do not wish to be understood as offering any criticism on these facts; I am merely stating the facts as I believe them to be. Why these gaps were left unguarded, why a prompt effort was not made to hold Snake Creek Gap, I neither pretend to know nor venture to guess; nor do I offer any criticism. That they were not guarded, and that this gave Sherman the easy means of causing the evacuation of Dalton and the retreat to Resaca, is undoubtedly true. That we could have held Dalton or made an attack on Sherman if these gaps had been held is a problem over which military men may differ. Whatever may have been the reason or cause, the fact is that the provision made to hold Snake Creek Gap was an order to Grigsby during the night of the 8th to move his brigade to its mouth. The 9th Kentucky had been on duty continuously for over twenty-four hours; the whole brigade for over twelve hours, and under fire all the afternoon. But with cheerful alacrity the command began its march as soon as it could feed, after being relieved by Granbury — possibly about 10 o'clock. The night was dark, the road rough and unfamiliar, and it was difficult to find guides. But just at dawn we came in sight of the eastern mouth of the gap, and, contrary to our information, found it in possession of the enemy. Colonel Grigsby had been informed that a company of Georgia troops was on picket on the road to the gap, and at or near its eastern outlet. We had not seen that company, and Colonel Grigsby naturally concluded that the troops we saw a few hundred yards before us were those. The usual confusion of an all-night march and the halt of the head of the column had jammed the different organizations somewhat together in a narrow lane. The advanced vidette reported the troops to be Federals. Colonel Grigsby, still sup-

PART OF THE CONFEDERATE INTRENCHMENTS AT RESACA. FROM A PHOTOGRAPH.

posing them to be Georgians, ordered a small scout to the front. In these few minutes the enemy, having discovered us and being concealed by the character of the ground and the forest, had formed line of battle, while our column had become more confused by many of the men dismounting to rest. Between us and the foot of the mountain was a fallow cotton-field, on the near edge of which was a row of deserted cabins. The road ran along this field a few hundred yards with a gradual descent until it passed through a fringe of willows and underbrush, beyond which there were other open fields, and then on both sides of these open fields were also thick woods.

Suddenly a long skirmish-line broke from the woods, ran to the fringe of willows, and directly through toward the row of cabins, keeping up a brisk fire as they ran. Behind the skirmish-line was developed a line of infantry. For a moment the fire staggered the head of the column, and the order to fall back and form could not be executed. The 9th Kentucky was in front, and very quickly its front companies were dismounted and a dash made for the cabins. Fortunately our men reached them first and drove the Federal skirmishers back. This gave breathing time, of which immediate and brilliant advantage was taken by Major J. Q. Chenowith, who led a portion of the 1st Kentucky, on horseback, on a détour to the right through the woods until he reached the fringe of willows, when at full run he charged the skirmish-line on the left, and the dismounted men of the 9th Kentucky charged on foot through the open field. The audacity of this sudden and unexpected dash caused the skirmish-line to run at breakneck speed, and the line of infantry to halt and to await reënforcements. This gave ample time to form the brigade for its day's work of retreating fight.

The immediate result of this was a delay to the Federal column of several hours, increased caution on the part of McPherson in his march during the day, and prompt information of his movement to our army headquarters.

The force under McPherson was so large that our small brigade of cavalry could not force it to develop its line. All that was possible was to cause the march to be as slow as that of a skirmish-line. This was done. It was late in the afternoon when McPherson drove us into the works before Resaca, which were defended only by Canty's brigade and ours. It was a gloomy prospect. We knew that McPherson had a force of from 15,000 to 20,000, and that there was no possibility of our receiving any reënforcements that afternoon or night. One serious attack by McPherson, and Resaca must have been captured.

Fortunately McPherson knew that Hooker had failed in his attempt to seize Dug Gap, and that consequently the road from Dalton was free to any Confederate column moving on him. The intrenchments at Resaca were formidable, and when McPherson felt the lines, the response was resolute and spirited. As Hardee came to reënforce us at Dug Gap, so here Hood joined us. He and part of his staff came to share our fate. Calmly we waited for the inevitable assault. We did not doubt that it would be made. McPherson was young, ambitious, and able. In our ranks he was accounted the equal, perhaps the superior, of Sherman. Here was an opportunity that Sherman might well say "does not occur twice in a single life"; and not for a moment did we doubt that such a soldier, with such an army, would seize such an opportunity.

I recall the scene, as a group stood on a knoll and watched the skirmishers advance. As the puffs of smoke arose in the distance, as the sharpshooters paid compliments to this group, General Hood rode up, and after a few moments' gaze turned the head of his horse and rode a few feet, and by motion called Colonel Grigsby to him; in another moment Grigsby called me, and General Hood said in a cheery yet grave tone, "We must hold until night."

Just at dusk the enemy began to fall back, and to our surprise the retrograde movement ended near to the point at which we had commenced our fight in the morning.

THE CONFEDERATE STRENGTH IN THE ATLANTA CAMPAIGN.

BY E. C. DAWES, LATE MAJOR, 53D OHIO REGIMENT.

IN the foregoing paper [see p. 260] General Joseph E. Johnston asserts that on the 30th of April, 1864, the strength of the Confederate army was "37,652 infantry, 2812 artillery with 112 guns, and 2392 cavalry,"—in all, 42,856. But the return of that army for April 30th, 1864, on file in the War Department, signed by General Johnston and attested by his adjutant-general, shows its "present for duty" almost 53,000:

Infantry	41,279
Cavalry	8,436
Artillery, 144 pieces	3,277
	52,992

The difference between these figures and those given by General Johnston from the same return is, that in his paper he gives the footings of the column of "effective total." This, in all Confederate returns, includes only sergeants, corporals, and private soldiers "for duty, equipped." That the cavalry had an effective total of but 2392 with 8436 officers and men for duty is accounted for by the fact that a large number of horses were grazing in the rear because of the scarcity of forage at Dalton. They were brought to the front and the men became effective when Sherman's army began to advance. General Johnston's statement that his artillery comprised but 112 pieces is a manifest error, for the return plainly says 35 companies, 144 pieces.

The battle of Resaca was fought on the 13th, 14th, and 15th of May. Prior to that time the Confederate army was reënforced by General Mercer's brigade of four Georgia regiments, which had been on garrison duty on the Atlantic coast. A foot-note to the return of April 30th records that one of these regiments, the 63d Georgia, joined the army "since the report was made out," and that its effective total was 814. All of these regiments had full ranks; 2800 is a low estimate of their line-of-battle strength. Cantey's division, ⸸ two brigades of infantry and two batteries, 5300 for duty, came from Mobile about the 7th of May and was stationed at Resaca. Loring's division, three infantry brigades and two batteries, from General S. D. Lee's command, with 5145 for duty and a detachment of 550 from French's division, reached Resaca May 10th, 11th, and 12th. Meantime a regiment of the Georgia State line, estimated as six hundred strong, had been added to Hood's corps.

At Resaca General Johnston had at least 67,000 men for battle and 168 pieces of artillery. General Sherman had at most 104,000: ⸸ the odds against General Johnston when "the armies were actually in contact" were as 100 to 64, instead of "10 to 4," as stated in his article.

On the night of May 16th the Confederate army evacuated Resaca. On the following day, at Adairsville, it was reënforced by General W. H. Jackson's cavalry command, 4477 for duty, which was increased to 5120 by June 10th. On the 19th of May, at Cassville, the division of General French joined the army with 4174 effectives, exclusive of the detachment that was at Resaca. Another Georgia State line regiment, estimated as 600, was added to Hood's corps, and Quarles's brigade, 2200 strong, came on the 26th of May at New Hope Church. A comparison of the return of April 30th with that of June 10th shows an increase to the fighting strength of the army of 3399 from the return of men "absent with leave" in the corps of Hood, Hardee, Wheeler, and in the artillery. The return of May 20th is missing, but that of June 10th shows an increase since May 20th of 649 "returned from desertion" and 799 "joined by enlistment."

General Johnston has to account, between April 30th and June 10th, for at least the following men available for battle:

Present for duty at Dalton	April 30th	52,992
Mercer's brigade	May 2d	2,800
Cantey's division	May 7th	5,300
Loring's division ...May 10th, 11th, and 12th		5,145
French's detachment	May 12th	550
French's division	May 19th	4,174
Jackson's cavalry	May 17th	4,477
Jackson's cavalry increase before June 10th		643
Quarles's brigade	May 26th	2,200
Two regiments Georgia State line		1,200
Furloughed men returned		3,399
Recruits		799
Returned deserters		649
		84,328

All these figures are official except for Mercer's brigade and the two regiments of the Georgia

⸸ For Cantey's strength, see General D. H. Maury's return April 22d, 1864. For Loring's strength, see General S. D. Lee's return May 10th, 1864. For French's detachment, see General French's report of "effective when joined."—E. C. D.

⸸ For the strength of Sherman's army at Resaca, add 5200 for cavalry joined between May 1st and 12th to his strength, May 1st, of 98,797.—E. C. D.

State line.↓ The return of General Johnston's army June 10th is the first on file in the War Department that includes all these reënforcements. It shows "present for duty":

	Officers.	Men.
Infantry	5049	47,554
Cavalry	1232	12,372
Artillery, 187 pieces	257	4,414
	6538	64,340
Or in round numbers		71,000

The difference of over 13,000 is accounted for by losses in battle, desertion, and increase in absent sick. The incomplete return of Medical Director Foard shows killed and wounded, May 7th to 20th, inclusive, 3384. The return of June 10th shows 1551 killed and died since May 20th, indicating fully 6000 wounded. The same return shows 569 deserters. The 1542 prisoners captured from Hood and Hardee, shown by increase of absent without leave in their corps, account for the remainder, without examining the returns of Polk's corps and the cavalry.

General Johnston's army reached its maximum strength on the New Hope Church line, where he must have had 75,000 for battle when the armies faced each other May 27th. General Sherman's army ♭ there numbered, of all arms, for duty, 93,-600 men, and several brigades of this force were employed in guarding trains and watching roads in all directions, for Sherman's army had no rear. Odds of less than five to four against him is "the great inequality of force" which General Johnston complains compelled him "to employ dismounted cavalry" in holding this line.

In a foot-note [p. 274] General Johnston says:

"I have two reports of the strength of the army besides that of April 30th, already given: 1. Of July 1st, 39,746 infantry, 3855 artillery, and 10,484 cavalry,— total, 54,085. 2. Of July 10th, 36,901 infantry, 3755 artillery, and 10,270 cavalry,— total, 50,926."

The return of July 1st shows "present for duty," all arms, officers and men, 64,578, instead of 54,085. (As in case of the return of April 30th, General Johnston gives only the "effective total.") The loss since June 10th is accounted for by 1114 dead, 711 deserters, 1042 increase in absent without leave (prisoners), and 3693 in increase of absent sick and wounded. None of the returns of this army, either under Johnston or Hood, makes any account of the Georgia militia, a division of which under G. W. Smith joined the army about June 20th near Kenesaw, making its available force on that line nearly 70,000 men. [G. W. Smith, p. 334, says the militia were 2000, which would reduce Major Dawes's total to about 67,000.—EDITORS.] The return of July 10th gives the present for

↓ For the strength of Jackson's cavalry division, see General S. D. Lee's return May 10th, and the return of General Johnston's army June 10th, 1864. For the strength of General French's division, see his return of "effectives when joined." For the strength of Quarles's brigade, see "Johnston's Narrative," p. 575.

♭ For Sherman's strength on the New Hope line, see his return May 31st, and deduct Blair's Seventeenth Corps, which did not join the army until June 8th.

duty 60,032, instead of 50,926, the loss since July 1st being 1377 deserters, 526 dead, two regiments sent to Savannah, and prisoners and wounded. This with the Georgia militia (increased to about 9000 [G. W. Smith says 5000.—EDITORS] when the army reached Atlanta) represents the force turned over to Hood, July 18th, viz.:

Infantry	42,571
Cavalry	13,318
Artillery, 187 pieces	4,143
Militia (probably)	5,000
	65,032

General Johnston asserts that the only affair worth mentioning on his left at Resaca was near the night of May 14th, when "forty or fifty skirmishers in front of our extreme left were driven from the slight elevation they occupied, but no attempt was made to retake it." In his official report, made in October, 1864, he says that at 9 o'clock at night of May 14th he "learned that Lieutenant-General Polk's troops had lost a position commanding our bridges." Comment upon the generalship that would leave a position commanding the line of retreat of an army in charge of forty or fifty skirmishers within gunshot of a powerful enemy is unnecessary, for it was not done. The position was held by a line of men. It was carried on the evening of May 14th by a gallant charge of two brigades of the Fifteenth Corps of the Union army. Reënforced by another brigade, they held it against the repeated and desperate efforts of Polk's men to retake it. The battle lasted far into the night. General John A. Logan, in his official report of it, says that when at 10 o'clock at night "the last body of the enemy retired broken and disheartened from the field, . . . it was evident to the meanest comprehension among the rebels that the men who double-quicked across to their hills that afternoon had come to stay." General Logan also says that by the capture of this position "the railroad bridge and the town were held entirely at our mercy."

The Fifteenth Corps lost 628 killed and wounded at Resaca. The troops in its front, Loring's and Cantey's divisions and Vaughan's brigade, according to their incomplete official reports, lost 698. Much the greater part of this loss must have been on the evening of May 14th, for there was no other line-of-battle engagement on this part of the field.

General Johnston characterizes the battle of May 28th at Dallas as "a very small affair," in which the Confederates lost about three hundred men and the Union troops "must have lost more than ten times as many." This was an assault made upon troops of the Fifteenth Corps by two brigades of Bate's Confederate division and Armstrong's brigade of Jackson's cavalry dismounted, supported by Smith's brigade of Bate's division and Ferguson's and Ross's brigades of Jackson's cavalry. Lewis's Kentucky brigade attacked the front of Osterhaus's division without success. Bullock's Florida brigade charged along the Marietta road and was driven back, with heavy loss, by the fire of the 53d Ohio regiment. Armstrong assailed the position held by Walcutt's brigade across the Villa Rica road and met a bloody repulse. General Bate officially reported the loss in his division as 450. General Walcutt in his official report says that "244 dead and wounded rebels were found in my front," and many were doubtless removed. The Confederate loss in this "very small affair" was, therefore, over seven hundred. The loss of the Fifteenth Corps was 379, or about one-half the Confederate loss, instead of "more than ten times as many."

General Johnston assumes that General Sherman used his entire army in the assault of Kenesaw Mountain, when, in fact, he employed less than 15,000 men. The remainder of the army was not engaged, except in the continuous battle of the skirmish-lines. The assaulting column of the Army of the Cumberland, directed against Hardee's corps, was composed of five brigades about nine thousand strong. The formation was such that each brigade presented a front of but two companies. The leading regiments lost very heavily; those in the rear suffered few casualties. General Thomas reported the entire loss as 1580. The attack of the Army of the Tennessee was made upon the Confederate intrenchments held by French's division and a part of Walker's, by three brigades of the Fifteenth Corps, numbering 5500 men. Their formation was in two lines; their total loss 603, three-fourths of this falling on the regiments in the first line.

General Johnston expresses the belief that Northern soldiers could not be repulsed with casualties so small as reported at Kenesaw. In this he, unwittingly perhaps, compliments Sherman's army at the expense of his own. On the 22d of June, five days before the battle of Kenesaw, he tells us that the divisions of Stevenson and Hindman were repulsed, in an assault on the Union line, with a loss of one thousand men. These divisions, June 10th, numbered over eleven thousand for duty. Their loss, therefore, was but nine per cent., while that of the troops of the Army of the Cumberland engaged at Kenesaw was 17 per cent.; of the Army of the Tennessee, 11 per cent. In both cases the loss sustained was sufficient to demonstrate the futility of further effort. In neither case was it a fair test of the staying qualities of the troops, who on many fields had shown their willingness to shed any amount of blood necessary when there was reasonable hope of success.

CINCINNATI, September 8th, 1887.

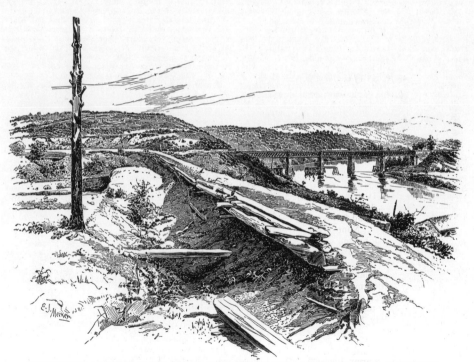

CONFEDERATE DEFENSES AT THE BRIDGE OVER THE ETOWAH. FROM A WAR-TIME PHOTOGRAPH.

THE OPPOSING FORCES IN THE ATLANTA CAMPAIGN.

May 3d–September 8th, 1864.

THE UNION ARMY.

Major-General William T. Sherman.

Headquarters Guard: 7th Co. Ohio Sharp-shooters,[1] Lieut. William McCrory.

Artillery:[2] Brig.-Gen. William F. Barry (chief-of-artillery).

ARMY OF THE CUMBERLAND, Maj.-Gen. George H. Thomas.

Escort, I, 1st Ohio Cav., Lieut. Henry C. Reppert.

Artillery:[2] Brig.-Gen. John M. Brannan (chief-of-artillery).

FOURTH ARMY CORPS, Maj.-Gen. Oliver O. Howard, Maj.-Gen. David S. Stanley.

FIRST DIVISION, Maj.-Gen. David S. Stanley, Brig.-Gen. William Grose, Brig.-Gen. Nathan Kimball.

First Brigade, Brig.-Gen. Charles Cruft, Col. Isaac M. Kirby: 21st Ill.,[3] Maj. James E. Calloway, Capt. William H. Jamison; 38th Ill.,[3] Lieut.-Col. William T. Chapman; 31st Ind., Col. John T. Smith; 81st Ind., Lieut.-Col. William C. Wheeler; 1st Ky.,[4] Col. David A. Enyart; 2d Ky.,[4] Lieut.-Col. John R. Hurd; 90th Ohio, Col. Samuel N. Yeoman; 101st Ohio, Col. Isaac M. Kirby, Lieut.-Col. Bedan B. McDonald. *Second Brigade,* Brig.-Gen. Walter C. Whitaker, Col. Jacob E. Taylor: 96th Ill., Col. Thomas E. Champion, Maj. George Hicks; 115th Ill., Col. Jesse H. Moore; 35th Ind., Maj. John P. Dufficy, Capt. James A. Gavisk, Lieut.-Col. A. G. Tassin; 84th Ind.,[5] Lieut.-Col. Andrew J. Neff, Capt. John C. Taylor, Capt. Martin B. Miller; 21st Ky., Col. Samuel W. Price, Lieut.-Col. James C. Evans; 40th Ohio, Col. Jacob E. Taylor, Capt. Chas. G. Matchett, Capt. Milton Kemper; 51st Ohio, Lieut.-Col. C. H. Wood, Col. Richard W. McClain; 99th Ohio,[6] Lieut.-Col. John E. Cummins, Capt. Jas. A. Bope, Lieut.-Col. J. E. Cummins. *Third Brigade,* Col. Wm. Grose, Col. P. Sidney Post, Brig.-Gen. Wm. Grose, Col. John E. Bennett: 59th Ill,,[7] Col. P. Sidney Post, Lieut.-Col. Clayton Hale, Col. P. Sidney Post, Capt. Samuel West; 75th Ill., Col. John E. Bennett, Lieut.-Col. William M. Kilgour; 80th Ill., Lieut.-Col. William M. Kilgour, Maj. James M. Stookey; 84th Ill., Col. Louis H. Waters; 9th Ind., Col. Isaac C. B. Suman; 30th Ind., Lieut.-Col. Orrin D. Hurd, Capt. William Dawson, Lieut.-Col. Orrin D. Hurd; 36th Ind., Lieut.-Col. O. H. P. Carey; 77th Pa., Capt. Joseph J. Lawson, Col. Thomas E. Rose. *Artillery,*[8] Capt. Peter Simonson, Capt. Samuel M. McDowell, Capt. Theodore S. Thomasson: 5th Ind., Lieut. Alfred Morrison; B, Pa., Capt. Samuel M. McDowell, Lieut. Jacob Ziegler.

SECOND DIVISION, Brig.-Gen. John Newton.

First Brigade, Col. Francis T. Sherman, Brig.-Gen. Nathan Kimball, Col. Emerson Opdycke: 36th Ill., Col. Silas Miller, Capt. James B. McNeal, Lieut.-Col. Porter C. Olson; 44th Ill., Col. Wallace W. Barrett, Lieut.-Col. John Russell, Maj. Luther M. Sabin, Lieut.-Col. John Russell; 73d Ill., Maj. Thomas W. Motherspaw; 74th Ill., Col. Jason Marsh, Lieut.-Col. John B. Kerr, Capt. Thomas J. Bryan; 88th Ill., Lieut.-Col. George W. Chandler, Lieut.-Col. George W. Smith; 28th Ky.,[9] Lieut.-Col. J. Rowan

Boone, Maj. George W. Barth; 2d Mo.,[10] Lieut.-Col. Arnold Beck, Col. Bernard Laiboldt; 15th Mo., Col. Joseph Conrad; 24th Wis., Lieut.-Col. Theodore S. West, Maj. Arthur MacArthur, Jr. *Second Brigade,* Brig.-Gen. George D. Wagner, Col. John W. Blake, Brig.-Gen. George D. Wagner: 100th Ill., Maj. Charles M. Hammond, Col. Frederick A. Bartleson, Maj. Charles M. Hammond; 40th Ind., Col. John W. Blake, Lieut.-Col. Henry Leaming; 57th Ind., Lieut.-Col. George W. Lennard, Lieut.-Col. Willis Blanch; 26th Ohio, Lieut.-Col. William H. Squires, Maj. Norris T. Peatman, Capt. Lewis D. Adair, Lieut.-Col. William H. Squires, Maj. Norris T. Peatman; 97th Ohio, Lieut.-Col. Milton Barnes, Col. John Q. Lane. *Third Brigade,* Brig.-Gen. Charles G. Harker, Brig.-Gen. Luther P. Bradley: 22d Ill.,[11] Lieut.-Col. Francis Swanwick; 27th Ill.,[11] Lieut.-Col. William A. Schmitt; 42d Ill., Lieut.-Col. Edgar D. Swain, Capt. Jared W. Richards, Maj. Frederick A. Atwater; 51st Ill., Col. Luther P. Bradley, Capt. Theodore F. Brown, Col. Luther P. Bradley, Capt. Albert M. Tilton; 79th Ill., Col. Allen Buckner, Lieut.-Col. Henry E. Rives, Maj. Terrence Clark, Capt. Oliver O. Bagley, Lieut.-Col. Terrence Clark; 3d Ky., Col. Henry C. Dunlap, Capt. John W. Tuttle, Col. Henry C. Dunlap; 64th Ohio, Col. Alexander McIlvain, Lieut.-Col. Robert C. Brown, Maj. Samuel L. Coulter, Lieut.-Col. Robert C. Brown; 65th Ohio, Lieut.-Col. Horatio N. Whitbeck, Capt. Charles O. Tannehill, Maj. Orlow Smith; 125th Ohio, Col. Emerson Opdycke, Lieut.-Col. David H. Moore. *Artillery,*[12] Capt. Charles C. Aleshire, Capt. Wilbur F. Goodspeed: M, 1st Ill., Capt. George W. Spencer; A, 1st Ohio, Capt. Wilbur F. Goodspeed, Lieut. Charles W. Scovill.

THIRD DIVISION, Brig.-Gen. Thomas J. Wood, Col. P. Sidney Post, Brig.-Gen. Thomas J. Wood.

First Brigade, Brig.-Gen. August Willich, Col. William H. Gibson, Col. Richard H. Nodine, Col. William H. Gibson, Col. Charles T. Hotchkiss: 25th Ill.,[13] Col. Richard H. Nodine; 38th Ill.,[14] Lieut.-Col. William P. Chandler; 89th Ill., Col. Charles T. Hotchkiss, Lieut.-Col. William D. Williams, Col. Charles T. Hotchkiss, Lieut.-Col. William D. Williams; 32d Ind.,[14] Col. Frank Erdelmeyer; 8th Kan.,[15] Col. John A. Martin, Lieut.-Col. James M. Graham; 15th Ohio, Col. William Wallace, Lieut.-Col. Frank Askew, Col. William Wallace, Col. Frank Askew; 49th Ohio, Col. William H. Gibson, Lieut.-Col. Samuel F. Gray; 15th Wis., Maj. George Wilson, Lieut.-Col. Ole C. Johnson. *Second Brigade,* Brig.-Gen. William B. Hazen, Col. Oliver H. Payne, Col. P. Sidney Post: 6th Ind.,[16] Lieut.-Col. Calvin D. Campbell; 5th Ky.,[17] Col. William W. Berry; 6th Ky.,[17] Maj. Richard T. Whitaker, Capt. Isaac N. Johnston; 23d Ky.,[18] Lieut.-Col. James C. Foy, Maj. George W. Northup; 1st Ohio,[19] Maj. Joab A. Stafford; 6th Ohio,[20] Col. Nicholas L. Anderson; 41st Ohio, Lieut.-Col. Robert L. Kimberly; 71st Ohio,[21] Col. Henry K. McConnell; 93d Ohio, Lieut.-Col. Daniel Bowman; 124th Ohio, Col. Oliver H. Payne, Lieut.-Col.

---

[1] Relieved two co's 10th Ohio Inf. May 20th.

[2] See batteries attached to divisions and corps.

[3] Non-veterans attached to 101st Ohio till June 4th and 9th, respectively, when regiments rejoined on veteran furlough.

[4] Ordered home for muster-out May 29th and June 3d, respectively.

[5] Transferred to Third Brigade August 16th.

[6] Transferred to Twenty-third Corps June 22d.

[7] Transferred to Second Brigade August 16th, and to Second Brigade, Third Division, August 19th.

[8] See also artillery brigade of corps.

[9] Transferred to Second Brigade May 28th.

[10] Remained at Dalton from May 14th.

[11] Relieved for muster-out June 10th and August 25th, respectively.

[12] See also artillery brigade of corps.

[13] Joined June 6th and relieved for muster-out August 1st.

[14] Relieved for muster-out August 25th and August 2d, respectively.

[15] Joined from veteran furlough June 28th.

[16] Relieved for muster-out August 22d.

[17] Transferred to Fourth Division, Twentieth Corps, July 25th and August 9th, respectively.

[18] Transferred to Second Brigade, First Division, August 19th.

[19] Ordered to Chattanooga July 25th.

[20] At Cleveland, Kingston, and Resaca; relieved for muster out June 6th.

[21] Joined August 31st.

James Pickands, Col. Oliver H. Payne. *Third Brigade,* Brig.-Gen. Samuel Beatty, Col. Frederick Knefler: 79th Ind., Col. Frederick Knefler, Lieut.-Col. Samuel P. Oyler, Maj. George W. Parker, Capt. John G. Dunbar, Capt. Eli F. Ritter; 86th Ind., Col. George F. Dick; 9th Ky., Lieut.-Col. Chesley D. Bailey, Col. George H. Cram; 17th Ky., Col. Alexander M. Stout; 13th Ohio, Col. Dwight Jarvis, Jr., Maj. Joseph P. Snider; 19th Ohio, Col. Charles F. Manderson, Lieut.-Col. Henry G. Stratton; 59th Ohio, Lieut.-Col. Granville A. Frambes, Capt. Charles A. Sheafe, Capt. John L. Watson, Capt. Robert H. Higgins. *Artillery,* Capt. Cullen Bradley: Ill. Battery, Capt. Lyman Bridges,[1] Lieut. Morris D. Temple, Lieut. Lyman A. White; 6th Ohio, Lieut. Oliver H. P. Ayres, Lieut. Lorenzo D. Immell, Lieut. Oliver H. P. Ayres, Lieut. Lorenzo D. Immell.

ARTILLERY BRIGADE (organized July 26th), Maj. Thomas W. Osborn, Capt. Lyman Bridges: M, 1st Ill., Capt. George W. Spencer; Bridges's Ill., Lieut. Lyman A. White; 5th Ind., Capt. Alfred Morrison, Lieut. George H. Briggs; A, 1st Ohio, Capt. Wilbur F. Goodspeed; M, 1st Ohio, Capt. Frederick Schultz; 6th Ohio, Lieut. Lorenzo D. Immell, Capt. Cullen Bradley; B, Pa., Capt. Jacob Ziegler.

FOURTEENTH ARMY CORPS, Maj.-Gen. John M. Palmer, Brig.-Gen. Richard W. Johnson, Brig.-Gen. Jefferson C. Davis.

FIRST DIVISION, Brig.-Gen. R. W. Johnson, Brig.-Gen. John H. King, Brig.-Gen. William P. Carlin.

Provost Guard: D, 1st Batt'n 16th U. S., Capt. C. F. Trowbridge.

First Brigade, Brig.-Gen. William P. Carlin, Col. Anson G. McCook, Col. Marion C. Taylor, Brig.-Gen. William P. Carlin, Col. Marion C. Taylor: 104th Ill., Lieut.-Col. Douglas Hapeman; 42d Ind., Lieut.-Col. W. T. B. McIntire, Capt. James H. Masters, Capt. Gideon R. Kellams, Lieut.-Col. W. T. B. McIntire; 88th Ind., Lieut.-Col. Cyrus E. Briant; 15th Ky., Col. Marion C. Taylor, Lieut.-Col. William G. Halpin; 2d Ohio,[2] Col. Anson G. McCook, Capt. James F. Sarratt; 33d Ohio, Lieut.-Col. James H. M. Montgomery, Capt. T. A. Minshall; 94th Ohio, Lieut.-Col. Rue P. Hutchins; 10th Wis.,[3] Capt. Jacob W. Roby; 21st Wis., Lieut.-Col. Harrison C. Hobart, Maj. Michael H. Fitch. *Second Brigade,* Brig.-Gen. John H. King, Col. William L. Stoughton, Brig.-Gen. John H. King, Col. William L. Stoughton, Col. Marshall F. Moore, Brig.-Gen. John H. King, Maj. John R. Edie: 11th Mich.,[4] Col. William L. Stoughton, Capt. Patrick H. Keegan, Col. William L. Stoughton, Capt. Patrick H. Keegan, Lieut.-Col. Melvin Mudge, Capt. P. H. Keegan; 69th Ohio,[5] Col. Marshall F. Moore, Lieut.-Col. Joseph H. Brigham, Capt. Lewis E. Hicks; 15th U. S. (9 co's 1st and 3d Batt'ns), Maj. Albert Tracy, Capt. Albert B. Dod, Capt. James Curtis, Capt. Horace Jewett; 15th U. S. (6 co's 2d Batt'n), Maj. John R. Edie, Capt. William S. McManus; 16th U. S. (4 co's 1st Batt'n), Capt. Alexander H. Stanton, Capt. Ebenezer Gay; 16th U. S. (4 co's 2d Batt'n), Capt. Robert P. Barry; 18th U. S. (8 co's 1st and 3d Batt'ns), Capt. George W. Smith, Capt. Lyman M. Kellogg, Capt. Robert B. Hull; 18th U. S. (2d Batt'n), Capt. William J. Fetterman; 19th U. S. (1st Batt'n and A, 2d Batt'n), Capt. James Mooney, Capt. Lewis Wilson, Capt. Egbert Phelps, Capt. James Mooney. *Third Brigade,* Col. Benjamin F. Scribner, Col. Josiah Given, Col. Marshall F. Moore: 37th Ind., Lieut.-Col. William D. Ward, Maj. Thomas V. Kimble, Lieut.-Col. William D. Ward; 38th Ind., Lieut.-Col. Daniel F. Griffin; 21st Ohio, Col. James M. Neibling, Lieut.-Col. Arnold Mc-

Mahan; 74th Ohio, Col. Josiah Given, Maj. Joseph Fisher, Col. Josiah Given; 78th Pa., Col. William Sirwell; 79th Pa.,[6] Col. Henry A. Hambright, Maj. Michael H. Locher, Capt. John S. McBride, Maj. Michael H. Locher; 1st Wis., Lieut.-Col. George B. Bingham. *Artillery,*[7] Capt. Lucius H. Drury: C, 1st Ill., Capt. Mark H. Prescott; I, 1st Ohio, Capt. Hubert Dilger.

SECOND DIVISION, Brig.-Gen. Jefferson C. Davis, Brig.-Gen. James D. Morgan, Brig.-Gen. Jefferson C. Davis.

First Brigade, Brig.-Gen. James D. Morgan, Col. Robert F. Smith, Brig.-Gen. J. D. Morgan, Col. Charles M. Lum: 10th Ill.,[8] Col. John Tillson; 16th Ill., Col. Robert F. Smith, Lieut.-Col. James B. Cahill, Col. R. F. Smith, Lieut.-Col. J. B. Cahill, Col. R. F. Smith, Lieut.-Col. J. B. Cahill; 60th Ill., Col. William B. Anderson; 10th Mich.,[9] Col. Charles M. Lum, Maj. Henry S. Burnett, Capt. William H. Dunphy; 14th Mich.,[10] Col. Henry R. Mizner; 17th N. Y.,[10] Col. W. T. C. Grower, Maj. Joel O. Martin. *Second Brigade,* Col. John G. Mitchell: 34th Ill., Lieut.-Col. Oscar Van Tassell; 78th Ill., Col. Carter Van Vleck, Lieut.-Col. Maris R. Vernon; 98th Ohio, Lieut.-Col. John S. Pearce, Capt. John A. Norris, Capt. David E. Roatch, Lieut.-Col. John S. Pearce; 108th Ohio,[11] Lieut.-Col. Joseph Good, Col. George T. Limberg, Lieut.-Col. Joseph Good; 113th Ohio, Lieut.-Col. Darius B. Warner, Maj. Lyne S. Sullivant, Capt. Toland Jones; 121st Ohio, Col. Henry B. Banning. *Third Brigade,* Col. Daniel McCook, Col. Oscar F. Harmon, Col. Caleb J. Dilworth, Lieut.-Col. James W. Langley: 85th Ill., Col. C. J. Dilworth, Maj. Robert G. Rider, Capt. James R. Griffith; 86th Ill., Lieut.-Col. Allen L. Fahnestock, Maj. Joseph F. Thomas, Lieut.-Col. A. L. Fahnestock; 110th Ill.,[12] Col. E. Hibbard Topping; 125th Ill., Col. O. F. Harmon, Maj. John B. Lee, Lieut.-Col. J. W. Langley, Capt. George W. Cook; 22d Ind., Lieut.-Col. William M. Wiles, Capt. William H. Taggart, Capt. William H. Snodgrass, Maj. Thomas Shea, Capt. W. H. Taggart, Capt. W. H. Snodgrass; 52d Ohio, Lieut.-Col. Charles W. Clancy, Maj. James T. Holmes, Capt. Samuel Rothacker, Maj. J. T. Holmes. *Artillery,*[13] Capt. Charles M. Barrett: I, 2d Ill., Lieut. Alonzo W. Coe; 5th Wis. (detachment 2d Minn. attached), Capt. George Q. Gardner.

THIRD DIVISION, Brig.-Gen. Absalom Baird.

First Brigade, Brig.-Gen. John B. Turchin, Col. Moses B. Walker: 19th Ill.,[14] Lieut.-Col. Alexander W. Raffen; 24th Ill.,[14] Capt. August Mauff; 82d Ind., Col. Morton C. Hunter; 23d Mo.,[15] Col. William P. Robinson; 11th Ohio,[14] Lieut.-Col. Ogden Street; 17th Ohio, Col. Durbin Ward; 31st Ohio, Col. M. B. Walker, Lieut.-Col. Frederick W. Lister; 89th Ohio, Maj. John H. Jolly, Col. Caleb H. Carlton; 92d Ohio, Col. Benjamin D. Fearing. *Second Brigade,* Col. Ferdinand Van Derveer, Col. Newell Gleason: 75th Ind., Lieut.-Col. William O'Brien, Maj. Cyrus J. McCole; 87th Ind., Col. N. Gleason, Lieut.-Col. Edwin P. Hammond; 101st Ind., Lieut.-Col. Thomas Doan; 2d Minn., Col. James George, Lieut.-Col. Judson W. Bishop; 9th Ohio,[16] Col. Gustave Kammerling; 35th Ohio,[16] Maj. Joseph L. Budd; 105th Ohio, Lieut.-Col. George T. Perkins. *Third Brigade,* Col. George P. Este: 10th Ind.,[17] Lieut.-Col. Marsh B. Taylor; 74th Ind., Lieut.-Col. Myron Baker, Maj. Thomas Morgan; 10th Ky., Col. William H. Hays; 18th Ky.,[18] Lieut.-Col. Hubbard K. Milward; 14th Ohio, Maj. John W. Wilson, Capt. George W. Kirk; 38th Ohio, Col. William A. Choate. *Artillery,*[19] Capt. George Estep: 7th Ind., Capt. Otho H. Morgan; 19th Ind., Lieut. William P. Stackhouse.

ARTILLERY BRIGADE,[20] Maj. Charles Houghtaling: C,

---

[1] Chief of corps artillery from May 23d.

[2] Ordered to Chattanooga July 27th.

[3] Ordered to Marietta July 28th.

[4] Ordered to Chattanooga August 25th.

[5] Joined from veteran furlough and assigned to Third Brigade July 15th.

[6] Joined from veteran furlough May 9th.

[7] See also artillery brigade of corps.

[8] Transferred to Fourth Division, Sixteenth Army Corps, August 20th.

[9] Joined from veteran furlough May 15th.

[10] Joined June 4th and August 21st, respectively.

[11] Employed mainly in guarding trains.

[12] Guarding trains till July 20th.

[13] See also artillery brigade of the corps.

[14] Relieved for muster-out June 9th, June 28th, and June 10th, respectively.

[15] Joined July 10th.

[16] Relieved for muster-out May 22d and August 3d, respectively.

[17] Part of time detached at Marietta.

[18] Detached at Ringgold.

[19] See also artillery brigade of corps.   [battalions.

[20] Organized July 24th; reorganized August 27th into three

1st Ill., Capt. Mark H. Prescott; I, 2d Ill., Capt. Charles M. Barrett; 7th Ind., Capt. Otho H. Morgan; 19th Ind., Lieut. W. P. Stackhouse; 20th Ind.,[1] Capt. Milton A. Osborne; I, 1st Ohio,[2] Capt. Hubert Dilger; 5th Wis., Capt. George Q. Gardner, Lieut. Joseph McKnight.

TWENTIETH ARMY CORPS, Maj.-Gen. Joseph Hooker, Brig.-Gen. Alpheus S. Williams, Maj.-Gen. Henry W. Slocum.

Escort: K, 15th Ill. Cav., Capt. William Duncan.

FIRST DIVISION, Brig.-Gen. Alpheus S. Williams, Brig.-Gen. Joseph F. Knipe, Brig.-Gen. A. S. Williams.

First Brigade, Brig.-Gen. J. F. Knipe, Col. Warren W. Packer, Brig.-Gen. J. F. Knipe: 5th Conn., Col. W. W. Packer, Lieut.-Col. Henry W. Daboll, Maj. William S. Cogswell, Col. W. W. Packer; 3d Md. (detachment), Lieut. David Gove, Lieut. Donald Reid, Lieut. David Gove; 123d N. Y., Col. Archibald L. McDougall, Lieut.-Col. James C. Rogers; 141st N. Y., Col. William K. Logie, Lieut.-Col. Andrew J. McNett, Capt. Elisha G. Baldwin, Capt. Andrew J. Compton; 46th Pa., Col. James L. Selfridge. Second Brigade, Brig.-Gen. Thomas H. Ruger: 27th Ind., Col. Silas H. Colgrove, Lieut.-Col. John R. Fesler; 2d Mass., Col. William Cogswell, Lieut.-Col. Charles F. Morse, Col. William Cogswell; 13th N. J., Col. Ezra A. Carman; 107th N. Y., Col. Nirom M. Crane; 150th N. Y., Col. John H. Ketcham; 3d Wis., Col. William Hawley. Third Brigade, Col. James S. Robinson, Col. Horace Boughton: 82d Ill., Lieut.-Col. Edward S. Salomon; 101st Ill., Lieut.-Col. John B. La Sage; 45th N. Y.,[3] Col. Adolphus Dobke; 143d N. Y., Col. Horace Boughton, Lieut.-Col. Hezekiah Watkins, Maj. John Higgins; 61st Ohio, Col. Stephen J. McGroarty, Capt. John Garrett; 82d Ohio, Lieut.-Col. David Thomson; 31st Wis.,[4] Col. Francis H. West. Artillery,[5] Capt. John D. Woodbury: I, 1st N. Y., Lieut. Charles E. Winegar; M, 1st N. Y., Capt. J. D. Woodbury.

SECOND DIVISION, Brig.-Gen. John W. Geary.

First Brigade, Col. Charles Candy, Col. Ario Pardee, Jr.: 5th Ohio, Col. John H. Patrick, Lieut.-Col. Robert L. Kilpatrick, Maj. Henry E. Symmes, Capt. Robert Kirkup; 7th Ohio,[6] Lieut.-Col. Samuel McClelland; 29th Ohio, Col. William T. Fitch, Capt. Myron T. Wright, Capt. Wilbur F. Stevens; 66th Ohio, Lieut.-Col. Eugene Powell, Capt. Thomas McConnell; 28th Pa., Lieut.-Col. John Flynn; 147th Pa., Col. Ario Pardee, Jr., Lieut.-Col. Craig. Second Brigade, Col. Adolphus Buschbeck, Col. John T. Lockman, Col. Patrick H. Jones, Col. George W. Mindil: 33d N. J., Col. George W. Mindil, Lieut.-Col. Enos Fourat, Capt. Thomas O'Connor; 119th N. Y., Col. J. T. Lockman, Capt. Charles H. Odell, Capt. Chester H. Southworth, Col. J. T. Lockman; 134th N. Y., Lieut.-Col. Allen H. Jackson, Capt. Clinton C. Brown; 154th N. Y., Col. P. H. Jones, Lieut.-Col. Daniel B. Allen, Maj. Lewis D. Warner, Lieut.-Col. Daniel B. Allen, Maj. L. D. Warner; 27th Pa.,[7] Lieut.-Col. August Riedt; 73d Pa., Maj. Charles C. Cresson; 109th Pa., Capt. Frederick I. Gimber, Capt. Walter G. Dunn, Capt. Hugh Alexander, Capt. William Geary. Third Brigade, Col. David Ireland, Col. William Rickards, Jr., Col. George A. Cobham, Jr., Col. David Ireland: 60th N. Y., Col. Abel Godard, Capt. Thomas Elliott, Col. Abel Godard, Capt. Thomas Elliott; 78th N. Y.,[8] Lieut.-Col. Harvey S. Chatfield, Col. Herbert von Hammerstein; 102d N. Y., Col. James C. Lane, Maj. Lewis R. Stegman, Capt. Barent Van Buren, Col. Herbert von Hammerstein; 137th N. Y., Lieut.-Col. Koert S. Van Voorhis; 149th N. Y., Lieut.-Col. Charles B. Randall, Col. Henry A. Barnum; 29th Pa., Col. William Rickards, Jr., Maj. Jesse R. Millison, Lieut.-Col. Thomas M. Walker, Capt. John H. Goldsmith, Capt. Benjamin F. Zarracher, Lieut.-Col. Samuel M. Zulich; 111th Pa., Col. George A. Cobham, Jr., Lieut.-Col. Thomas M. Walker, Col. G. A. Cobham, Jr., Lieut.-Col. T. M. Walker. Artillery, Capt. William

Wheeler, Capt. Charles C. Aleshire: 13th N. Y., Capt. William Wheeler, Lieut. Henry Bundy; E, Pa., Capt. James D. McGill, Lieut. Thomas S. Sloan.

THIRD DIVISION, Maj.-Gen. Daniel Butterfield, Brig.-Gen. William T. Ward.

First Brigade, Brig.-Gen. William T. Ward, Col. Benjamin Harrison, Brig.-Gen. William T. Ward, Col. Benjamin Harrison: 102d Ill., Col. Franklin C. Smith, Lieut.-Col. James M. Mannon, Col. F. C. Smith; 105th Ill., Col. Daniel Dustin, Lieut.-Col. Everell F. Dutton, Col. Daniel Dustin; 129th Ill., Col. Henry Case; 70th Ind., Col. Benjamin Harrison, Lieut.-Col. Samuel Merrill; 79th Ohio, Col. Henry G. Kennett, Lieut.-Col. Azariah W. Doan, Capt. Samuel A. West. Second Brigade, Col. Samuel Ross, Col. John Coburn: 20th Conn.,[9] Lieut.-Col. Philo B. Buckingham, Col. Samuel Ross, Lieut.-Col. P. B. Buckingham; 33d Ind., Maj. Levin T. Miller, Capt. Edward T. McCrea, Maj. L. T. Miller; 85th Ind., Col. John P. Baird, Lieut.-Col. Alexander B. Crane, Capt. Jefferson E. Brandt; 19th Mich., Col. Henry C. Gilbert, Maj. Eli A. Griffin, Capt. John J. Baker, Capt. David Anderson; 22d Wis., Col. William L. Utley, Lieut.-Col. Edward Bloodgood. Third Brigade, Col. James Wood, Jr.: 33d Mass., Lieut.-Col. Godfrey Rider, Jr.; 136th N. Y., Lieut.-Col. Lester B. Faulkner, Maj. Henry L. Arnold; 55th Ohio, Col. Charles B. Gambee, Capt. Charles P. Wickham, Lieut.-Col. Edwin H. Powers; 73d Ohio, Maj. Samuel H. Hurst; 26th Wis., Lieut.-Col. Frederick C. Winkler. Artillery, Capt. Marco B. Gary: I, 1st Mich., Capt. Luther R. Smith; C, 1st Ohio, Lieut. Jerome B. Stephens.

ARTILLERY BRIGADE (organized July 27th), Maj. John A. Reynolds.

I, 1st Mich., Capt. Luther R. Smith; I, 1st N. Y., Capt. Charles E. Winegar; M, 1st N. Y., Capt. John D. Woodbury; 13th N. Y., Capt. Henry Bundy; C, 1st Ohio, Lieut. Jerome B. Stephens, Capt. Marco B. Gary; E, Pa., Lieut. Thomas S. Sloan.

UNATTACHED TROOPS.

Reserve Brigade, Col. Joseph W. Burke, Col. Heber Le Favour: 10th Ohio,[10] Col. Joseph W. Burke; 9th Mich., Lieut.-Col. William Wilkinson; 22d Mich.,[11] Lieut.-Col. Henry S. Dean. Pontoniers,[12] Col. George P. Buell: 58th Ind., Lieut.-Col. Joseph Moore; Pontoon Battalion,[13] Capt. Patrick O'Connell. Siege Artillery: 11th Ind. Battery, Capt. Arnold Sutermeister. Ammunition Train Guard: 1st Batt'n Ohio Sharp-shooters, Capt. Gershom M. Barker.

CAVALRY CORPS, Brig.-Gen. Washington L. Elliott.

Escort: D, 4th Ohio, Capt. Philip H. Warner.

FIRST DIVISION, Brig.-Gen. Edward M. McCook.

First Brigade, Col. Joseph B. Dorr, Col. John T. Croxton, Col. J. B. Dorr, Lieut.-Col. James P. Brownlow, Brig.-Gen. John T. Croxton: 8th Iowa, Lieut.-Col. Horatio G. Barner, Col. J. B. Dorr, Maj. Richard Root, Maj. John H. Isett, Maj. Richard Root; 4th Ky.[14] (mounted inf'y), Col. J. T. Croxton, Lieut.-Col. Robert M. Kelly, Capt. James H. West, Lieut. Granville C. West, Capt. James I. Hudnall; 2d Mich.,[15] Maj. Leonidas S. Scranton, Lieut.-Col. Benjamin Smith; 1st Tenn., Lieut.-Col. James P. Brownlow. Second Brigade, Col. Oscar H. La Grange, Lieut.-Col. James S. Stewart, Lieut.-Col. Horace P. Lamson, Lieut.-Col. William H. Torrey, Lieut.-Col. H. P. Lamson: 2d Ind., Lieut.-Col. J. S. Stewart, Maj. David A. Briggs; 4th Ind., Lieut.-Col. H. P. Lamson, Maj. George H. Purdy, Capt. Albert J. Morley; 1st Wis., Maj. Nathan Paine, Capt. Henry Harnden, Capt. Lewis M. B. Smith, Lieut.-Col. William H. Torrey, Maj. Nathan Paine, Capt. L. M. B. Smith. Artillery: 18th Ind., Lieut. William B. Rippetoe, Capt. Moses M. Beck.

SECOND DIVISION, Brig.-Gen. Kenner Garrard.

First Brigade, Col. Robert H. G. Minty: 4th Mich., Lieut.-Col. Josiah B. Park, Maj. Frank W. Mix, Capt.

---

[1] Assigned August 14th.   [2] Relieved August 14th.
[3] Ordered to Nashville July 6th.   [4] Joined July 21st.
[5] Major John A. Reynolds, chief of corps artillery; see, also, artillery brigade of the corps.
[6] Relieved for muster-out June 11th.
[7] Relieved for muster-out May 23d.
[8] Consolidated with 102d New York July 12th.

[9] Transferred to Third Brigade May 29th.
[10] Relieved for muster-out May 27th.   [11] Joined May 31st.
[12] To June 17th Colonel Buell commanded the "Pioneer Brigade."
[13] Ordered to Chattanooga June 17th.
[14] Assigned June 30th.
[15] Ordered to Franklin, Tenn., June 29th.

L. Briggs Eldridge; 7th Pa., Col. William B. Sipes, Maj. James F. Andress, Maj. William H. Jennings; 4th U. S., Capt. James B. McIntyre. *Second Brigade,*[1] Col. Eli Long, Col. Beroth B. Eggleston: 1st Ohio, Col. Beroth B. Eggleston, Lieut.-Col. Thomas J. Patten; 3d Ohio, Col. Charles B. Seidel; 4th Ohio, Lieut.-Col. Oliver P. Robie. *Third Brigade* (mounted inf'y), Col. John T. Wilder, Col. Abram O. Miller: 98th Ill., Lieut.-Col. Edward Kitchell; 123d Ill., Lieut.-Col. Jonathan Biggs; 17th Ind., Lieut.-Col. Henry Jordan, Maj. Jacob J. Vail; 72d Ind., Col. Abram O. Miller, Maj. Henry M. Carr, Capt. Adam Pinkerton, Lieut.-Col. Samuel C. Kirkpatrick. *Artillery*: Chicago (Ill.) Board of Trade Battery, Lieut. George I. Robinson.

THIRD DIVISION, Brig.-Gen. Judson Kilpatrick, Col. Eli H. Murray, Col. William W. Lowe, Brig.-Gen. Judson Kilpatrick.

First Brigade, Lieut.-Col. Robert Klein, Lieut.-Col. Matthewson T. Patrick: 3d Ind. (4 co's), Maj. Alfred Gaddis, Lieut.-Col. Robert Klein; 5th Iowa,[3] Maj. Harlon Baird, Maj. J. Morris Young. *Second Brigade,*[2] Col. Charles C. Smith, Maj. Thomas W. Sanderson, Lieut.-Col. Fielder A. Jones: 8th Ind.,[3] Lieut.-Col. Fielder A. Jones, Maj. Thomas Herring; 2d Ky.,[3] Maj. William H. Eifort, Maj. Owen Star; 10th Ohio, Maj. Thomas W. Sanderson, Maj. William Thayer, Lieut.-Col. Thomas W. Sanderson. *Third Brigade,* Col. Eli H. Murray, Col. Smith D. Atkins, Col. Eli H. Murray: 92d Ill. (mounted inf'y), Col. Smith D. Atkins, Capt. Mathew Van Buskirk, Col. S. D. Atkins, Maj. Albert Woodcock, Col. S. D. Atkins; 3d Ky., Maj. Lewis Wolfley, Lieut.-Col. Robert H. King; 5th Ky., Col. Oliver L. Baldwin, Maj. Christopher T. Cheek, Col. O. L. Baldwin. *Artillery*: 10th Wis., Capt. Yates V. Beebe.

ARMY OF THE TENNESSEE, Maj.-Gen. James B. McPherson, Maj.-Gen. John A. Logan, Maj.-Gen. Oliver O. Howard.

Escort: 4th Co. Ohio Cav., Capt. John S. Foster, Capt. John L. King; B, 1st Ohio Cav., Capt. George F. Conn.

FIFTEENTH ARMY CORPS, Maj. John A. Logan, Brig.-Gen. Morgan L. Smith, Maj.-Gen. John A. Logan.

FIRST DIVISION, Brig.-Gen. Peter J. Osterhaus, Brig.-Gen. Charles R. Woods, Brig.-Gen. P. J. Osterhaus.

Third Brigade, Brig.-Gen. Charles R. Woods, Col. Milo Smith, Brig.-Gen. C. R. Woods, Col. Milo Smith: 26th Iowa, Col. Milo Smith, Lieut.-Col. Thomas G. Ferreby, Col. Milo Smith, Lieut.-Col. T. G. Ferreby; 30th Iowa, Lieut.-Col. Aurelius Roberts; 27th Mo., Col. Thomas Curly, Maj. Dennis O'Connor, Col. Thomas Curly; 76th Ohio, Col. William B. Woods. *Second Brigade,* Col. James A. Williamson: 4th Iowa, Lieut.-Col. Samuel D. Nichols, Capt. Randolph Sry; 9th Iowa, Col. David Carskaddon, Maj. George Granger; 25th Iowa, Col. George A. Stone; 31st Iowa, Col. William Smyth. *Third Brigade,* Col. Hugo Wangelin: 3d Mo., Col. Theodore Meumann; 12th Mo., Lieut.-Col. Jacob Kaercher, Maj. F. T. Ledergerber; 17th Mo., Maj. Francis Romer; 29th Mo., Lieut.-Col. Joseph S. Gage, Maj. Philip H. Murphy, Col. J. S. Gage; 31st Mo., Lieut.-Col. Samuel P. Simpson, Maj. Frederick Jaensch, Lieut.-Col. S. P. Simpson; 32d Mo., Capt. Charles C. Bland, Maj. Abraham J. Seay. *Artillery,*[4] Maj. Clemens Landgraeber: F, 2d Mo., Capt. Louis Voelkner, Lieut. Lewis A. Winn; 4th Ohio, Capt. Geo. Froehlich, Lieut. Lewis Zimmerer.

SECOND DIVISION, Brig.-Gen. Morgan L. Smith, Brig.-Gen. J. A. J. Lightburn, Brig.-Gen. M. L. Smith, Brig.-Gen. J. A. J. Lightburn, Brig.-Gen. William B. Hazen.

First Brigade, Brig.-Gen. Giles A. Smith, Col. James

S. Martin, Col. Theodore Jones: 55th Ill.,[5] Lieut.-Col. Theodore C. Chandler, Capt. Jacob M. Augustin, Capt. Francis H. Shaw, Capt. Cyrus M. Browne; 111th Ill.,[6] Col. James S. Martin, Maj. William M. Mabry, Col. J. S. Martin; 116th Ill., Lieut.-Col. Anderson Froman, Capt. Thomas White, Capt. John S. Windsor; 127th Ill., Lieut.-Col. Frank S. Curtiss, Capt. Alexander C. Little, Lieut.-Col. F. S. Curtiss, Capt. Charles Schryver; 6th Mo., Lieut.-Col. Delos Van Deusen; 8th Mo.,[7] Lieut.-Col. David C. Coleman, Capt. Hugh Neill, Capt. John W. White; 57th Ohio, Col. Americus V. Rice, Lieut.-Col. Samuel R. Mott. *Second Brigade,* Brig.-Gen. J. A. J. Lightburn, Col. Wells S. Jones, Brig.-Gen. J. A. J. Lightburn, Col. Wells S. Jones, Brig.-Gen. J. A. J. Lightburn, Col. Wells S. Jones: 83d Ind., Col. Benjamin J. Spooner, Capt. George H. Scott, Capt. Ben. North; 30th Ohio,[8] Col. Theodore Jones; 37th Ohio,[9] Lieut.-Col. Louis von Blessingh, Maj. Charles Hipp, Capt. Carl Moritz; 47th Ohio, Col. Augustus C. Parry, Lieut.- Col. John Wallace, Maj. Thomas T. Taylor; 53d Ohio,[10] Col. Wells S. Jones, Lieut.-Col. Robert A. Fulton, Col. W. S. Jones; 54th Ohio, Lieut.-Col. Robert Williams, Jr., Maj. Israel T. Moore. *Artillery,* Capt. Francis De Gress: A, 1st Ill., Capt. Peter P. Wood, Lieut. George McCagg, Jr., Lieut. Samuel S. Smyth, Lieut. George Echte; B, 1st Ill. (consolidated with Battery A, July 12th), Capt. Israel P. Rumsey; H, 1st Ill., Capt. Francis De Gress.

FOURTH DIVISION,[11] Brig.-Gen. William Harrow.

First Brigade, Col. Reuben Williams, Col. John M. Oliver: 26th Ill.,[12] Lieut.-Col. Robert A. Gillmore; 90th Ill., Lieut.-Col. Owen Stuart, Capt. Daniel O'Connor; 12th Ind., Lieut.-Col. James Goodnow, Col. Reuben Williams; 100th Ill.,[12] Lieut.-Col. Albert Heath. *Second Brigade,* Brig.-Gen. Charles C. Walcutt: 40th Ill.,[13] Lieut.-Col. Rigdon S. Barnhill, Maj. Hiram W. Hall, Capt. Michael Galvin, Capt. William Steward; 103d Ill., Maj. Asias Willison, Col. Willard A. Dickerman, Lieut.-Col. George W. Wright, Capt. Franklin C. Post; 97th Ind., Col. Robert F. Catterson, Lieut.-Col. Aden G. Cavins; 6th Iowa, Lieut.-Col. Alex. J. Miller, Maj. Thomas J. Ennis, Capt. William H. Clune, Lieut.-Col. A. J. Miller; 46th Ohio, Maj. Henry H. Giesy, Capt. Joshua W. Heath, Col. Isaac N. Alexander. *Third Brigade,*[14] Col. John M. Oliver: 48th Ill., Col. Lucien Greathouse, Maj. Edward Adams; 99th Ind., Col. Alex. Fowler, Lieut.-Col. John M. Berkey, Capt. Josiah Farrar, Lieut.-Col. J. M. Berkey; 15th Mich., Lieut.-Col. Austin E. Jaquith, Lieut.-Col. Fred. S. Hutchinson; 70th Ohio, Lieut.-Col. De Witt C. Loudon, Maj. William B. Brown, Capt. Louis Love, Capt. Henry L. Philips. *Artillery,* Capt. Henry H. Griffiths, Maj. John T. Cheney, Capt. H. H. Griffiths, Capt. Josiah H. Burton: F, 1st Ill., Capt. Josiah H. Burton, Lieut. Jefferson F. Whaley, Lieut. George P. Cuningham; 1st Iowa, Lieut. William H. Gay, Capt. H. H. Griffiths, Lieut. W. H. Gay.

SIXTEENTH ARMY CORPS (Left Wing), Maj.-Gen. Grenville M. Dodge, Brig.-Gen. Thomas E. G. Ransom.

General Headquarters: 1st Ala. Cav., Lieut.-Col. G. L. Godfrey, Col. George E. Spencer; A, 52d Ill. (detailed Aug. 8th), Capt. George E. Young.

SECOND DIVISION, Brig.-Gen. Thomas W. Sweeny, Brig.-Gen. Elliott W. Rice, Brig.-Gen. John M. Corse.

First Brigade, Brig.-Gen. Elliott W. Rice: 52d Ill., Lieut.-Col. Edwin A. Bowen; 66th Ind., Lieut.-Col. Roger Martin, Maj. Thomas G. Morrison, Capt. Alfred Morris; 2d Iowa, Col. James B. Weaver, Lieut.-Col. Noel B. Howard, Maj. Mathew G. Hamill, Capt. John A. Duckworth; 7th Iowa, Lieut.-Col. James C. Parrott, Maj. James W. McMullin, Lieut.-Col. J. C. Parrott, Maj.

---

[1] Operating in Northern Alabama to June 6th.

[2] Colonel Thomas J. Harrison, the commander of this brigade, was captured July 30th, while in command of a provisional division composed of the 8th Ind., 2d Ky., 5th Iowa, 9th Ohio, and 4th Tenn., and one section Battery E, 1st Mich. Art'y.

[3] In the field from July 27th.

[4] Chiefs of corps artillery: Major C. J. Stolbrand, Major Allen C. Waterhouse, Major Thomas D. Maurice.

[5] Joined from veteran furlough June 16th.

[6] Transferred to Second Brigade August 4th.

[7] Four companies relieved for muster-out June 16th, and five companies June 25th, Company K remaining.

[8] Joined from veteran furlough May 22d, and transferred to First Brigade August 4th.

[9] Joined from veteran furlough May 10th.

[10] Transferred from Third Brigade, Fourth Div., May 12th.

[11] The Third Division was stationed at Cartersville and other points in the rear of the army.

[12] Transferred to Second Brigade August 4th.

[13] Joined June 3d.   [Brigade.

[14] Discontinued August 4th, and troops transferred to First

J. W. McMullin, Capt. Samuel Mahon. *Second Brigade,* Col. Patrick E. Burke, Lieut.-Col. Robert N. Adams, Col. August Mersy, Lieut.-Col. Jesse J. Phillips, Col. Robert N. Adams: 9th Ill. (mounted), Lieut.-Col. Jesse J. Phillips, Maj. John H. Kuhn, Capt. Samuel T. Hughes; 12th Ill., Maj. James R. Hugunin, Lieut.-Col. Henry Van Sellar; 66th Ill., Maj. Andrew K. Campbell, Capt. William S. Boyd; 81st Ohio, Lieut.-Col. Robt. N. Adams, Maj. Frank Evans, Lieut.-Col. R. N. Adams, Capt. Noah Stoker, Capt. William C. Henry. *Third Brigade* (at Rome from May 22d), Col. Moses M. Bane, Brig.-Gen. William Vandever, Col. H. J. B. Cummings, Col. Richard Rowett: 7th Ill. (joined July 9th), Col. Richard Rowett, Lieut.-Col. Hector Perrin; 50th Ill., Maj. William Hanna; 57th Ill., Lieut.-Col. Frederick J. Hurlbut; 39th Iowa, Col. H. J. B. Cummings, Lieut.-Col. James Redfield, Col. H. J. B. Cummings, Maj. Joseph M. Griffiths, Lieut.-Col. James Redfield. *Artillery,*[1] Capt. Frederick Welker: B, 1st Mich. (at Rome from May 22d), Capt. A. F. R. Arndt; H, 1st Mo., Lieut. Andrew T. Blodgett.

FOURTH DIVISION, Brig.-Gen. James C. Veatch, Brig.-Gen. John W. Fuller, Brig.-Gen. Thomas E. G. Ransom, Brig.-Gen. J. W. Fuller.

First Brigade, Brig.-Gen. John W. Fuller, Col. John Morrill, Lieut.-Col. Henry T. McDowell, Brig.-Gen. J. W. Fuller, Lieut.-Col. H. T. McDowell: 64th Ill., Col. John Morrill, Lieut.-Col. M. W. Manning; 18th Mo., Lieut.-Col. Charles S. Sheldon, Maj. William H. Minter; 27th Ohio, Lieut.-Col. Mendal Churchill; 39th Ohio, Col. Edward F. Noyes, Lieut.-Col. H. T. McDowell, Maj. John S. Jenkins, Lieut.-Col. H. T. McDowell, Maj. John S. Jenkins. *Second Brigade,* Brig.-Gen. John W. Sprague: 35th N. J., Capt. Charles A. Angel, Col. John J. Cladek, Lieut.-Col. William A. Henry; 43d Ohio, Col. Wager Swayne; 63d Ohio, Lieut.-Col. Charles E. Brown, Maj. John W. Fouts; 25th Wis., Col. Milton Montgomery, Lieut.-Col. Jeremiah M. Rusk. *Third Brigade* (joined army from Decatur Aug. 7th), Col. William T. C. Grower, Col. John Tillson: 10th Ill. (assigned Aug. 20th), Capt. George C. Lusk; 25th Ind., Lieut.-Col. John Rheinlander, Capt. James S. Wright; 17th N. Y. (transferred to Second Division, Fourteenth Corps, Aug. 20th), Maj. Joel O. Martin; 32d Wis., Lieut.-Col. Charles H. De Groat. *Artillery,* Capt. Jerome B. Burrows, Capt. George Robinson: C, 1st Mich., Capt. George Robinson, Lieut. Henry Shier; 14th Ohio, Capt. J. B. Burrows, Lieut. Seth M. Laird, Lieut. George Hurlbut; F, 2d U. S., Lieut. Albert M. Murray, Lieut. Joseph C. Breckinridge, Lieut. Lemuel Smith, Lieut. Rezin G. Howell.

SEVENTEENTH ARMY CORPS (joined the army in Georgia June 8th), Maj.-Gen. Frank P. Blair, Jr.

Escort: M, 1st Ohio Cav. (relieved June 18th), Lieut. Charles H. Shultz; G, 9th Ill., Mounted Inf. (relieved July 24th), Capt. Isaac Clements; G, 11th Ill. Cav. (assigned Aug. 11th from escort of Fourth Division), Capt. Stephen S. Tripp.

THIRD DIVISION, Brig.-Gen. Mortimer D. Leggett, Brig.-Gen. Charles R. Woods.

Escort: D, 1st Ohio Cav. (relieved June 18th), Lieut. James W. Kirkendall.

First Brigade, Brig.-Gen. Manning F. Force, Col. George E. Bryant: 20th Ill., Lieut.-Col. Daniel Bradley, Maj. George W. Kennard, Capt. John H. Austin; 30th Ill., Col. Warren Shedd, Lieut.-Col. William C. Rhoads, Capt. John L. Nichols; 31st Ill., Col. Edwin S. McCook, Lieut.-Col. Robert N. Pearson, Capt. Simpson S. Stricklin; 45th Ill. (detached at Etowah Bridge), Lieut.-Col. Robert P. Sealy; 16th Wis., Col. Cassius Fairchild, Maj. William F. Dawes. *Second Brigade,* Col. Robert K. Scott, Lieut.-Col. Greenberry F. Wiles: 20th Ohio, Lieut.-Col. John C. Fry, Maj. Francis M. Shaklee; 32d Ohio, (transferred to First Brigade, Fourth Division, July 10th), Col. Benjamin F. Potts, Capt. William M. Morris, Lieut.-Col. Jeff. J. Hibbets; 68th Ohio, Lieut.-Col. George E. Welles; 78th Ohio, Lieut.-Col. G. F. Wiles, Maj. John

T. Rainey. *Third Brigade,* Col. Adam G. Malloy: 17th Wis., Lieut.-Col. Thomas McMahon, Maj. Donald D. Scott; Worden's Battalion (detachments 14th Wis., and 81st and 95th Ill.), Maj. Asa Worden. *Artillery,*[2] Capt. William S. Williams: D, 1st Ill., Capt. Edgar H. Cooper; H, 1st Mich., Capt. Marcus D. Elliott, Lieut. William Justin; 3d Ohio, Lieut. John Sullivan.

FOURTH DIVISION, Brig.-Gen. Walter Q. Gresham, Col. William Hall, Brig.-Gen. Giles A. Smith.

First Brigade, Col. William L. Sanderson, Col. Benjamin F. Potts: 32d Ill. (transferred to Second Brigade July 18th), Col. John Logan, Lieut.-Col. George H. English; 23d Ind., Lieut.-Col. William P. Davis, Lieut.-Col. George S. Babbitt; 53d Ind., Lieut.-Col. William Jones, Maj. Warner L. Vestal, Capt. George H. Beers; 3d Iowa (3 co's), Capt. Daniel McLennon, Capt. Pleasant T. Mathes, Lieut. Lewis T. Linnell, Lieut. D. W. Wilson; 12th Wis. (transferred to First Brigade, Third Division, July 10th), Col. George E. Bryant, Lieut.-Col. James K. Proudfit. *Second Brigade* (at Allatoona, Kenesaw, Ackworth, and other points in rear from June 8th), Col. George C. Rogers, Col. Isaac C. Pugh, Col. John Logan: 14th Ill.,[3] Capt. Charles C. Cox; 15th Ill.,[3] Maj. Rufus C. McEathron; 41st Ill. (joined July 5th), Maj. Robert H. McFadden; 53d Ill. (transferred to First Brigade, July 18th), Lieut.-Col. John W. McClanahan. *Third Brigade,* Col. William Hall, Col. John Shane, Col. William Hall, Brig.-Gen. William W. Belknap: 11th Iowa, Lieut.-Col. John C. Abercrombie; 13th Iowa, Col. John Shane, Maj. W. A. Walker, Col. John Shane; 15th Iowa, Col. W. W. Belknap, Maj. George Pomutz; 16th Iowa, Lieut.-Col. Addison H. Sanders, Capt. Crandall W. Williams. *Artillery,* Capt. Edward Spear, Jr., Capt. William Z. Clayton: F, 2d Ill., Lieut. Walter H. Powell, Lieut. George R. Richardson, Lieut. Wendolin Meyer; 1st Minn., Capt. W. Z. Clayton, Lieut. Henry Hunter; C, 1st Mo. (at Allatoona and Kenesaw), Capt. John L. Matthaei; 10th Ohio (at Kenesaw from July 11th), Capt. Francis Seaman; 15th Ohio, Lieut. James Burdick.

ARMY OF THE OHIO (Twenty-third Corps), Maj.-Gen. John M. Schofield, Brig.-Gen. Jacob D. Cox (temporarily May 26th and 27th), Maj.-Gen. John M. Schofield.

Escort: G, 7th Ohio Cav., Capt. John A. Ashbury.

FIRST DIVISION,[4] Brig.-Gen. Alvin P. Hovey.

First Brigade, Col. Richard F. Barter: 120th Ind., Lieut.-Col. Allen W. Prather; 124th Ind., Col. James Burgess, Col. John M. Orr; 128th Ind., Col. Richard P. De Hart, Lieut.-Col. Jasper Packard. *Second Brigade,* Col. John C. McQuiston, Col. Peter T. Swaine: 123d Ind., Lieut.-Col. William A. Cullen, Col. J. C. McQuiston; 129th Ind., Col. Charles Case, Col. Charles A. Zollinger; 130th Ind., Col. Charles S. Parrish; 99th Ohio, Lieut.-Col. John E. Cummins. *Artillery:* 23d Ind., Lieut. Luther M. Houghton, Lieut. Aaron A. Wilber; 24th Ind. (assigned to cavalry division July 6th), Capt. Alexander Hardy, Lieut. Hiram Allen.

SECOND DIVISION, Brig.-Gen. Henry M. Judah, Brig.-Gen. Milo S. Hascall.

First Brigade, Brig.-Gen. Nathaniel C. McLean, Brig.-Gen. Joseph A. Cooper: 80th Ind. (transferred to Second Brigade June 8th), Lieut.-Col. Alfred D. Owen, Maj. John W. Tucker, Lieut.-Col. A. D. Owen, Maj. J. W. Tucker, Capt. Jacob Ragle, Maj. J. W. Tucker; 13th Ky. (transferred to Second Brigade June 8th), Col. William E. Hobson, Lieut.-Col. Benjamin P. Estes; 25th Mich., Lieut.-Col. Benjamin F. Orcutt, Capt. Samuel L. Demarest, Capt. Edwin Childs; 3d Tenn., Col. William Cross, Maj. R. H. Dunn, Col. Wm. Cross, Maj. R. H. Dunn; 6th Tenn., Col. J. A. Cooper, Maj. Edward Maynard, Capt. Marcus D. Bearden, Capt. William Ausmus; 91st Ind. (transferred to Third Brigade, Second Division, August 11th), Lieut.-Col. Charles H. Butterfield, Col. John Mehringer. *Second Brigade,* Brig.-Gen. Milo S. Hascall, Col. John R. Bond, Col. William E. Hobson, Col. J. R. Bond: 107th Ill., Maj. Uriah M. Laurance, Lieut.-Col.

[1] Maj. William H. Ross, chief of corps artillery.
[2] Chiefs of corps artillery: Maj. Thomas D. Maurice, Lieut.-Col. Albert M. Powell, Maj. John T. Cheney, Capt. Edward Spear, Jr.

[3] Consolidated July 5th, under Col. G. C. Rogers.
[4] Discontinued August 11th, and troops assigned to Second and Third Divisions, to which they were temporarily attached from June 9th.

Francis H. Lowry; 23d Mich., Lieut.-Col. Oliver L. Spaulding, Maj. William W. Wheeler; 45th Ohio (transferred to First Brigade, June 8th, and to Second Brigade, First Division, Fourth Corps, June 22d), Col. Benjamin P. Runkle, Lieut.-Col. Charles H. Butterfield, Capt. John H. Humphrey; 111th Ohio, Col. John R. Bond, Lieut.-Col. Isaac R. Sherwood; 118th Ohio, Lieut.-Col. Thomas L. Young, Capt. Edgar Sowers, Capt. William Kennedy, Capt. Rudolph Reul, Capt. Edgar Sowers. *Third Brigade* (joined May 28th and designated as Provisional Brigade to June 8th), Col. Silas A. Strickland: 14th Ky. (transferred to First Brigade August 11th), Col. George W. Gallup; 20th Ky., Lieut.-Col. Thomas B. Waller; 27th Ky., Lieut.-Col. John H. Ward, Capt. Andrew J. Bailey; 50th Ohio, Lieut.-Col. George R. Elstner, Maj. Hamilton S. Gillespie. *Artillery:* Capt. Joseph C. Shields: 22d Ind., Capt. B. F. Denning, Lieut. E. W. Nicholson; F, 1st Mich., Capt. Byron D. Paddock, Lieut. Marshall M. Miller; 19th Ohio, Capt. J. C. Shields. THIRD DIVISION, Brig.-Gen. Jacob D. Cox, Col. James W. Reilly (temporarily May 26–27), Brig.-Gen. J. D. Cox. *First Brigade*, Col. James W. Reilly, Col. James W. Gault, Brig.-Gen. James W. Reilly: 112th Ill. (joined May 11th, and transferred to Third Brigade August 11th), Col. Thomas J. Henderson, Lieut.-Col. Emery S. Bond, Maj. T. T. Dow, Col. T. J. Henderson, Maj. T. T. Dow; 16th Ky. (joined May 11th, and transferred to Third Brigade August 11th), Col. James W. Gault, Maj. John S. White, Col. James W. Gault, Maj. J. S. White, Capt. Jacob Miller, Maj. J. S. White; 100th Ohio, Col. Patrick S. Slevin, Capt. Frank Rundell; 104th Ohio, Col. Oscar W. Sterl; 8th Tenn., Col. Felix A. Reeve, Maj. William J. Jordan, Capt. Robert A. Ragan, Capt. James W. Berry. *Second Brigade*, Brig.-Gen. Mahlon D. Manson, Col. John S. Hurt, Brig.-Gen. Milo S. Hascall, Col. John S. Hurt, Col. John S. Casement, Col. Daniel Cameron, Col. John S. Casement: 65th Ill. (joined from veteran furlough June 4th), Lieut.-Col. William S. Stewart; 63d Ind. (transferred to Third Brigade August 11th), Col. Israel N. Stiles, Lieut.-Col. Daniel Morris; 65th Ind., Lieut.-Col. Thomas Johnson, Capt. Walter G. Hodge, Capt. William F. Stillwell, Capt. Edward A. Baker; 24th Ky., Col. John S. Hurt, Lieut.-Col. Lafayette North, Col. John S. Hurt; 103d Ohio, Capt. William W. Hutchinson, Capt. Philip C. Hayes, Lieut.-Col. James T. Sterling, Col. J. S. Casement, Capt. P. C. Hayes; 5th Tenn. (transferred to Third Brigade June 5th), Col. James T. Shelley, Maj. David G. Bowers, Col. James T. Shelley. *Third Brigade* (organized June 5th), Brig.-Gen. N. C. McLean, Col. Robert K. Byrd, Col. Israel N. Stiles: 11th Ky. (transferred to First Brigade August 11th), Col. S.

Palace Love, Lieut.-Col. E. L. Mottley, Col. S. P. Love; 12th Ky. (transferred to First Brigade August 11th), Lieut.-Col. Laurence H. Rousseau; 1st Tenn. (relieved for muster-out August 11th), Col. R. K. Byrd, Lieut.-Col. John Ellis. *Dismounted Cavalry Brigade* (assigned June 21st; transferred to cavalry division August 22d), Col. Eugene W. Crittenden: 16th Ill., Capt. Hiram S. Hanchett; 12th Ky., Lieut.-Col. James T. Bramlette, Maj. James B. Harrison. *Artillery*, Maj. Henry W. Wells: 15th Ind., Capt. Alonzo D. Harvey; D, 1st Ohio, Capt. Giles J. Cockerill.

CAVALRY DIVISION,[1] Maj.-Gen. George Stoneman, Col. Horace Capron.

Escort: D, 7th Ohio, Lieut. Samuel Murphy, Lieut. W. W. Manning.

First Brigade (joined army in the field July 27th), Col. Israel Garrard: 9th Mich., Col. George S. Acker; 7th Ohio, Lieut.-Col. George C. Miner. *Second Brigade* (designated as the *First Brigade* until July 31st), Col. James Biddle, Col. Thomas H. Butler, Col. James Biddle: 16th Ill., Capt. Hiram S. Hanchett; 5th Ind., Col. Thomas H. Butler, Maj. Moses D. Leeson; 6th Ind., Lieut.-Col. C. C. Matson, Maj. William W. Carter; 12th Ky., Col. Eugene W. Crittenden, Maj. James B. Harrison. *Third Brigade* (joined army in the field June 28th), Col. Horace Capron: 14th Ill., Lieut.-Col. David P. Jenkins; 8th Mich., Lieut.-Col. Elisha Mix, Maj. William L. Buck, Maj. Edward Coates; McLaughlin's Ohio Squadron, Maj. Richard Rice. *Independent Brigade*, Col. Alex. W. Holeman, Lieut.-Col. Silas Adams: 1st Ky., Lieut.-Col. Silas Adams; 11th Ky., Lieut.-Col. Archibald J. Alexander.

EFFECTIVE STRENGTH OF THE UNION ARMY.

DATE.	*Infantry.*	*Artillery.*	*Cavalry.*	*Total.*
May 1st..............	88,188	4460	6,149	98,797
June 1st (17th Corps joined June 8th......)	94,310	5601	12,908	112,819
July 1st..............	88,086	5945	12,039	106,070
August 1st..............	75,659	5499	10,517	91,675
September 1st..... ...	67,674	4690	9,394	81,758

Losses: killed, 4423; wounded, 22,822; captured or missing, 4442 = 31,687. (Major E. C. Dawes, of Cincinnati, who has made a special study of the subject, estimates the Union loss at about 40,000, and the Confederate loss at about the same.)

THE CONFEDERATE ARMY.

ARMY OF TENNESSEE, General Joseph E. Johnston, General John B. Hood.

Escort, Capt. Guy Dreux.

HARDEE'S CORPS, Lieut.-Gen. William J. Hardee,[2] Maj.-Gen. P. R. Cleburne.

Escort, Capt. W. C. Raum.

CHEATHAM'S DIVISION, Maj.-Gen. B. F. Cheatham, Brig.-Gen. George Maney, Brig.-Gen. John C. Carter.

Escort, Capt. T. M. Merritt.

Maney's Brigade, Brig.-Gen. George Maney, Col. George C. Porter: 1st and 27th Tenn., Col. H. R. Feild, Capt. W. C. Flournoy, Lieut.-Col. John L. House; 4th Tenn. (Confed.) and 24th Tenn. Batt'n, Lieut.-Col. O. A. Bradshaw; 6th and 9th Tenn., Lieut.-Col. J. W. Buford,

Lieut.-Col. John L. Harris; 19th Tenn., Col. F. M. Walker, Maj. J. G. Deaderick; 50th Tenn., Col. Stephen H. Colms. *Wright's Brigade*, Brig.-Gen. John C. Carter: 8th Tenn., Col. J. H. Anderson; 16th Tenn., Maj. Benjamin Randals; 28th Tenn., Col. S. S. Stanton, Lieut.-Col. D. C. Crook, Capt. L. L. Dearman, Capt. John B. Holman; 38th Tenn., Lieut.-Col. A. D. Gwynne, Maj. H. W. Cotter; 51st and 52d Tenn., Lieut.-Col. John G. Hall, Lieut.-Col. J. W. Estes, Maj. T. G. Randle. *Strahl's Brigade*, Brig.-Gen. O. F. Strahl: 4th and 5th Tenn., Col. J. J. Lamb, Maj. H. Hampton; 24th Tenn., Lieut.-Col. S. E. Shannon, Col. J. A. Wilson, Lieut.-Col. S. E. Shannon; 31st Tenn., Maj. Samuel Sharp, Lieut.-Col. F. E. P. Stafford; 33d Tenn., Col. W. P. Jones, Maj. R. N. Payne,

---

[1] Reorganized August 11th, with Col. Israel Garrard as division commander, and formed into two brigades. The "Mounted Brigade" was commanded by Col. George S. Acker, except from August 16th to 23d, when Col. W. D. Hamilton was in command. It consisted of the 9th Mich., Lieut.-Col. W. B. Way; 7th Ohio, Lieut.-Col. G. C. Miner; detachment 9th Ohio, Capt. L. H. Bowlus; McLaughlin's Ohio Squadron, Maj. Richard Rice; and the 24th Ind. Battery, Lieut. Hiram Allen. The "Dismounted Brigade," com-

manded by Col. Horace Capron, was composed of the 14th and 16th Ill., 5th and 6th Ind., and 12th Ky. The 16th Ill. was detailed as provost guard Twenty-third Corps from August 16th, and the 12th Ky. as cattle guard from August 21st. The 6th Ind., under Maj. William H. Carter, was ordered to Nashville for remount August 23d.

[2] In command of his own and Lee's corps August 31st–September 2d.

Capt. W. F. Marberry; 41st Tenn., Lieut.-Col. James D. Tillman, Capt. A. M. Kieth. *Vaughan's Brigade,* Brig.-Gen. A. J. Vaughan, Jr., Col. M. Magevney, Jr., Brig.-Gen. G. W. Gordon: 11th Tenn., Col. G. W. Gordon, Maj. J. E. Burns; 12th and 47th Tenn., Col. W. M. Watkins, Capt. W. S. Moore, Lieut.-Col. V. G. Wynne; 29th Tenn., Col. Horace Rice; 13th and 154th Tenn., Col. M. Magevney, Jr., Lieut.-Col. B. L. Dyer, Col. M. Magevney, Jr. CLEBURNE'S DIVISION, Maj.-Gen. P. R. Cleburne, Brig.-Gen. M. P. Lowrey.

Escort, Capt. C. F. Sanders.

Polk's Brigade,[1] Brig.-Gen. Lucius E. Polk: 1st and 15th Ark., Col. J. W. Colquitt, Lieut.-Col. W. H. Martin, Capt. F. G. Lusk, Capt. W. H. Scales; 5th Confederate, Capt. W. A. Brown, Maj. R. J. Person, Capt. A. A. Cox; 2d Tenn., Col. W. D. Robison, Capt. Isaac P. Thompson; 35th and 48th Tenn., Capt. H. G. Evans, Lieut.-Col. A. S. Godwin, Col. B. J. Hill. *Lowrey's Brigade,* Brig.-Gen. M. P. Lowrey, Col. John Weir: 16th Ala., Col. F. A. Ashford; 33d Ala., Col. Samuel Adams, Lieut.-Col. R. F. Crittenden; 45th Ala., Col. H. D. Lampley, Lieut.-Col. R. H. Abercrombie; 32d Miss., Col. W. H. H. Tison; 45th Miss., Col. A. B. Hardcastle; 3d Miss. Battalion, Lieut.-Col. J. D. Williams. *Govan's Brigade,* Brig.-Gen. D. C. Govan, Col. Peter V. Green: 2d and 24th Ark., Col. E. Warfield, Maj. A. T. Meek, Capt. J. K. Phillips; 5th and 13th Ark., Col. J. E. Murray, Col. P. V. Green, Lieut.-Col. E. A. Howell; 6th and 7th Ark., Col. S. G. Smith, Capt. J. T. Robinson; 8th and 19th Ark., Col. G. F. Baucum, Maj. D. H. Hamiter; 3d Confederate, Capt. M. H. Dixon. *Granbury's Brigade,* Brig.-Gen. H. B. Granbury, Brig.-Gen. J. A. Smith, Lieut.-Col. R. B. Young, Brig.-Gen. H. B. Granbury: 6th and 15th Tex., Capt. R. Fisher, Capt. M. M. Houston, Capt. J. W. Terrill, Capt. R. B. Tyus, Capt. S. E. Rice, Lieut. T. L. Flint; 7th Tex., Capt. J. H. Collett, Capt. C. E. Talley, Capt. J. W. Brown; 10th Tex., Col. R. Q. Mills, Capt. J. A. Formwalt, Lieut.-Col. R. B. Young; 17th and 18th Tex. (dismounted cavalry), Capt. G. D. Manion, Capt. William H. Perry, Capt. F. L. McKnight; 24th and 25th Tex. (dismounted cavalry), Col. F. C. Wilkes, Lieut.-Col. W. M. Neyland, Maj. W. A. Taylor. WALKER'S DIVISION,[2] Maj.-Gen. W. H. T. Walker, Brig.-Gen. H. W. Mercer.

Escort: Capt. T. G. Holt.

Jackson's Brigade, Brig.-Gen. John R. Jackson: 5th Ga.,[3] Col. C. P. Daniel; 47th Ga.,[3] Col. A. C. Edwards; 65th Ga., Capt. W. G. Foster; 5th Miss., Col. John Weir, Lieut.-Col. John B. Herring; 8th Miss., Col. J. C. Wilkinson; 2d Ga. Battalion Sharp-shooters, Maj. R. H. Whiteley. *Gist's Brigade,* Brig.-Gen. States R. Gist, Col. James McCullough: 8th Ga. Battalion, Lieut.-Col. Z. L. Watters; 46th Ga., Maj. S. J. C. Dunlop, Capt. E. Taylor, Maj. S. J. C. Dunlop; 16th S. C., Col. James McCullough, Capt. J. W. Boling; 24th S. C., Col. Ellison Capers, Lieut.-Col. J. S. Jones, Col. Ellison Capers. *Stevens's (or Jackson's) Brigade,* Brig.-Gen. C. H. Stevens, Brig.-Gen. H. R. Jackson, Col. W. D. Mitchell: 1st Ga. (Confederate), Col. G. A. Smith; 25th Ga., Col. W. J. Winn, Maj. A. W. Smith, Capt. G. W. Holmes; 29th Ga., Lieut.-Col. W. D. Mitchell, Maj. J. J. Owen, Capt. J. W. Turner; 30th Ga., Lieut.-Col. J. S. Boynton, Maj. H. Hendrick; 66th Ga., Col. J. C. Nisbet, Capt. T. L. Langston; 1st Ga. Battalion Sharp-shooters, Maj. A. Shaaf, Capt. B. H. Hardee, Maj. A. Shaaf; 26th Ga. Battalion, Maj. J. W. Nisbet. *Mercer's Brigade,* Brig.-Gen. H. W. Mercer, Col. W. Barkuloo, Lieut.-Col. M. Rawls, Lieut.-Col. C. S. Guyton, Col. C. H. Olmstead: 1st Ga., Col. C. H. Olmstead, Maj. M. J. Ford; 54th Ga., Lieut.-Col. M. Rawls, Capt. T. W. Brantley; 57th Ga., Col. William Barkuloo, Lieut.-Col. C. S. Guyton; 63d Ga., Col. G. A. Gordon, Major W. F. Allen, Capt. E. J. Craven. BATE'S DIVISION, Maj.-Gen. William B. Bate, Maj.-Gen. John C. Brown.

Escort, Lieut. James H. Buck.

Lewis's Brigade,[4] Brig.-Gen. Joseph H. Lewis: 2d Ky., Col. J. W. Moss, Lieut.-Col. Philip Lee, Capt. Joel Higgins; 4th Ky., Lieut.-Col. T. W. Thompson; 5th Ky., Lieut.-Col. H. Hawkins, Lieut.-Col. G. W. Connor, Maj. William Mynhier; 6th Ky., Maj. G. W. Moxson, Col. M. H. Cofer, Capt. Richard P. Finn; 9th Ky., Col. J. W. Caldwell. *Tyler's (or Smith's) Brigade,* Brig.-Gen. T. B. Smith: 37th Ga., Lieut.-Col. J. T. Smith; 10th Tenn., Maj. J. O'Neill, Col. William Grace, Lieut. L. B. Donoho; 15th and 37th Tenn., Maj. J. M. Wall, Lieut.-Col. R. D. Frayser, Capt. M. Dwyer; 20th Tenn., Lieut.-Col. W. M. Shy; 30th Tenn., Lieut.-Col. J. J. Turner; 4th Ga. Battalion Sharp-shooters, Capt. W. M. Carter, Maj. T. D. Caswell. *Finley's Brigade,* Brig.-Gen. J. J. Finley, Col. R. Bullock: 1st and 3d Fla., Maj. G. A. Ball, Capt. M. H. Strain, Maj. G. A. Ball; 1st and 4th Fla., Lieut.-Col. E. Badger, Maj. J. A. Lash, Lieut.-Col. E. Badger; 6th Fla., Col. A. D. McLean, Lieut.-Col. D. L. Kenan, Capt. S. A. Cawthorn; 7th Fla., Lieut.-Col. T. Ingram, Col. R. Bullock, Maj. N. S. Blount. ARTILLERY, Col. Melancthon Smith.

Hoxton's Battalion, Maj. L. Hoxton: Ala. Battery, Capt. John Phelan, Lieut. N. Venable; Fla. Battery, Capt. Thomas J. Perry, Lieut. J. C. Davis; Miss. Battery, Capt. William B. Turner, Lieut. W. W. Henry. *Hotchkiss's Battalion,* Maj. T. R. Hotchkiss, Capt. Thomas J. Key: Ark. Battery, Capt. T. J. Key, Lieut. J. G. Marshall; Ala. Battery, Capt. R. W. Goldthwaite; Miss. Battery, Lieut. H. Shannon, Lieut. H. N. Steele. *Martin's Battalion:* Mo. Battery, Lieut. C. W. Higgins, Capt. H. M. Bledsoe, Lieut. R. L. Wood; S. C. Battery, Lieut. R. T. Beauregard, Lieut. J. A. Alston; Ga. Battery, Lieut. W. G. Robson; Capt. Evan P. Howell. *Cobb's Battalion,* Maj. Robert Cobb: Ky. Battery, Lieut. R. B. Matthews; Tenn. Battery, Capt. J. W. Mebane, Lieut. J. W. Phillips; La. Battery, Lieut. W. C. D. Vaught, Capt. C. H. Slocomb, Lieut. J. A. Chalaron. *Palmer's Battalion:* Ala. Battery, Capt. C. L. Lumsden; Ga. Battery, Capt. R. W. Anderson; Ga. Battery, Capt. M. W. Havis.

HOOD'S (or LEE'S) CORPS, Lieut.-Gen. John B. Hood, Maj.-Gen. C. L. Stevenson, Maj.-Gen. B. F. Cheatham, Lieut.-Gen. S. D. Lee. HINDMAN'S DIVISION, Maj.-Gen. T. C. Hindman, Brig.-Gen. John C. Brown, Maj.-Gen. Patton Anderson, Maj.-Gen. Edward Johnson.

Escort: B, 3d Ala. Cav., Capt. F. J. Billingslea.

Deas's Brigade, Brig.-Gen. Z. C. Deas, Col. J. G. Coltart, Brig.-Gen. G. D. Johnston, Col. J. G. Coltart, Lieut.-Col. H. T. Toulmin, Brig.-Gen. Z. C. Deas: 19th Ala., Col. S. K. McSpadden, Lieut.-Col. G. R. Kimbrough; 22d Ala., Col. B. R. Hart, Capt. Isaac M. Whitney, Col. H. T. Toulmin; 25th Ala., Col. G. D. Johnston, Capt. N. B. Rouse; 39th Ala., Lieut.-Col. W. C. Clifton, Capt. T. J. Brannon, Capt. A. J. Miller, Capt. A. A. Cassady; 50th Ala., Col. J. G. Coltart, Capt. G. W. Arnold, Capt. A. D. Ray, Col. J. G. Coltart; 17th Ala. Battalion Sharp-shooters, Capt. J. F. Nabers, Lieut. A. R. Andrews. *Manigault's Brigade,* Brig.-Gen. A. M. Manigault: 24th Ala., Col. N. N. Davis, Capt. S. H. Oliver, Col. N. N. Davis; 28th Ala., Lieut.-Col. W. L. Butler; 34th Ala., Col. J. C. B. Mitchell, Maj. J. N. Slaughter, Capt. H. J. Rix, Capt. J. C. Carter; 10th S. C., Col. J. F. Pressley, Lieut.-Col. C. Irvin Walker, Capt. R. Z. Harllee, Capt. C. C. White, Capt. B. B. McWhite; 19th S. C., Lieut.-Col. T. P. Shaw, Maj. J. L. White, Capt. T. W. Getzen, Capt. E. W. Horne, Col. T. P. Shaw. *Tucker's (or Sharp's) Brigade,* Brig.-Gen. W. F. Tucker, Brig.-Gen. Jacob H. Sharp: 7th Miss., Lieut.-Col. B. F. Johns, Col. W. H. Bishop; 9th Miss., Capt. S. S. Calhoun, Lieut.-Col. B. F. Johns; 10th Miss., Capt. R. A. Bell, Lieut.-Col. G. B. Myers; 41st Miss., Col. Byrd Williams, Capt. J. M. Hicks; 44th Miss., Col. Jacob H. Sharp, Lieut.-Col. R. G. Kelsey; 9th Miss. Battalion Sharp-shooters, Maj. W. C. Richards, Lieut. J. B. Downing. *Walthall's (or Brantly's) Brigade,* Brig.-Gen. E. C. Walthall, Col. Samuel Benton,

---

[1] Broken up in July and regiments assigned to other brigades.

[2] Discontinued July 24th, Jackson's brigade being consolidated with Gist's, and transferred to Cheatham's division;

Stevens's brigade went to Bate's division, and Mercer's brigade to Cleburne's division.

[3] Transferred with General Jackson to Savannah July 3d.

[4] Assigned to Jackson's cavalry division September 4th.

Brig.-Gen. W. F. Brantly: 24th and 27th Miss. Col. Samuel Benton, Col. R. P. McKelvaine, Lieut.-Col. W. L. Lyles; 29th and 30th Miss., Col. W. F. Brantly, Lieut.-Col. J. M. Johnson, Maj. W. G. Reynolds; 34th Miss., Capt. T. S. Hubbard, Col. Samuel Benton, Captain T. S. Hubbard.

STEVENSON'S DIVISION, Major.-Gen. C. L. Stevenson.

Escort, Capt. T. B. Wilson.

Brown's Brigade, Brig.-Gen. John C. Brown, Col. Ed. C. Cook, Col. Joseph B. Palmer: 3d Tenn., Col. C. H. Walker, Lieut.-Col. C. J. Clack, Capt. W. S. Jennings; 18th Tenn., Lieut.-Col. W. R. Butler, Maj. William H. Joyner; 26th Tenn., Capt. A. F. Boggess, Col. R. M. Saffell; 32d Tenn., Col. Ed. C. Cook, Maj. J. P. McGuire, Capt. C. G. Tucker, Maj. J. P. McGuire; 45th and 23d (battalion) Tenn., Col. A. Searcy. *Cumming's Brigade,* Brig.-Gen. Alfred Cumming, Col. C. M. Shelley: 34th Ga., Maj. J. M. Jackson, Capt. W. A. Walker, Maj. J. M. Jackson, Capt. R. A. Jones; 36th Ga., Col. C. E. Broyles; 39th Ga., Lieut.-Col. J. F. B. Jackson, Capt. W. P. Milton; 56th Ga., Col. E. P. Watkins, Capt. J. A. Grice, Capt. B. T. Spearman; 2d Ga. (State troops), Col. J. B. Willcoxson, Capt. Seaborn Saffold. *Reynolds's Brigade,* Brig.-Gen. A. W. Reynolds, Col. R. C. Trigg, Col. John B. Palmer: 58th N. C., Maj. T. J. Dula, Capt. S. M. Silver; 60th N. C., Lieut.-Col. J. T. Weaver, Col. W. M. Hardy, Lieut.-Col. J. T. Weaver; 54th Va., Col. R. C. Trigg, Lieut.-Col. J. J. Wade, Capt. W. G. Anderson, Col. R. C. Trigg; 63d Va., Capt. C. H. Lynch. *Pettus's Brigade,* Brig.-Gen. E. W. Pettus: 20th Ala., Col. J. N. Dedman, Capt. S. W. Davidson, Col. J. N. Dedman; 23d Ala., Lieut.-Col. J. B. Bibb; 30th Ala., Col. C. M. Shelley, Lieut.-Col. J. K. Elliott; 31st Ala., Col. D. R. Hundley, Capt. J. J. Nix, Maj. G. W. Mathieson; 46th Ala., Maj. George E. Brewer, Capt. J. W. Powell.

STEWART'S DIVISION, Maj.-Gen. Alexander P. Stewart, Maj.-Gen. H. D. Clayton.

Escort: C, 1st Ga. Cav., Capt. George T. Watts.

Stovall's Brigade, Brig.-Gen. M. A. Stovall, Col. Abda Johnson, Brig.-Gen. M. A. Stovall: 40th Ga., Col. Abda Johnson, Capt. J. N. Dobbs, Capt. J. F. Groover, Maj. R. S. Camp; 41st Ga., Maj. M. S. Nall, Capt. J. E. Stallings; 42d Ga., Col. R. J. Henderson, Maj. W. H. Hulsey, Capt. L. P. Thomas; 43d Ga., Lieut.-Col. H. C. Kellogg, Maj. W. C. Lester, Capt. H. R. Howard, Maj. W. C. Lester, Col. H. C. Kellogg; 52d Ga., Capt. R. R. Asbury, Capt. J. R. Russell, Capt. R. R. Asbury, Capt. J. R. Russell; 1st Ga. (State troops), Col. E. M. Galt, Capt. — Howell, Maj. William Tate. *Clayton's Brigade,* Brig.-Gen. H. D. Clayton, Brig.-Gen. J. T. Holtzclaw, Col. Bushrod Jones: 18th Ala., Col. J. T. Holtzclaw, Lieut.-Col. P. F. Hunley; 32d and 58th Ala., Col. Bushrod Jones, Maj. H. I. Thornton; 36th Ala., Col. L. T. Woodruff, Capt. J. A. Wemyss, Lieut.-Col. T. H. Herndon, Capt. N. M. Carpenter; 38th Ala., Col. A. R. Lankford, Capt. G. W. Welch, Capt. D. Lee, Capt. B. L. Posey. *Baker's Brigade,* Brig.-Gen. Alpheus Baker: 37th Ala., Lieut.-Col. A. A. Greene, Capt. T. J. Griffin; 40th Ala., Col. John H. Higley; 42d Ala., Lieut.-Col. T. C. Lanier, Capt. W. D. McNeill, Capt. R. K. Wells, Capt. W. B. Kendrick; 54th Ala., Lieut.-Col. J. A. Minter. *Gibson's Brigade,* Brig.-Gen. Randall L. Gibson: 1st La., Maj. S. S. Batchelor, Capt. W. H. Sparks, Lieut. C. L. Huger, Capt. W. Quirk; 4th La., Col. S. E. Hunter; 13th La., Lieut.-Col. F. L. Campbell; 16th and 25th La., Col. J. C. Lewis, Lieut.-Col. R. H. Lindsay, Col. J. C. Lewis, Lieut.-Col. R. H. Lindsay; 19th La., Lieut.-Col. H. A. Kennedy, Col. R. W. Turner, Capt. J. W. Jones, Capt. C. Flournoy; 20th La., Maj. S. L. Bishop, Capt. R. L. Keen, Col. Leon von Zinken, Capt. R. L. Keen, Capt. A. Dresel; 30th La., Lieut.-Col. Thomas Shields, Capt. H. P. Jones; 4th La. Battalion, Lieut.-Col. J. McEnery, Maj. Duncan Buie, Capt. W. J. Powell, Capt. T. A. Bisland; 14th La. Battalion Sharp-shooters, Maj. J. E. Austin.

ARTILLERY, Col. Robert F. Beckham, Lieut.-Col. J. H. Hallonquist.

Courtney's Battalion, Maj. A. R. Courtney: Ala. Battery, Capt. James Garrity, Lieut. Phil. Bond, Capt. James Garrity; Confed. Battery, Capt. S. H. Dent; Tex. Battery, Lieut. J. H. Bingham, Capt.

J. P. Douglas. *Eldridge's Battalion,* Maj. J. W. Eldridge: Ala. Battery, Capt. McD. Oliver, Capt. W. J. McKenzie; La. Battery, Capt. Charles E. Fenner; Miss. Battery, Capt. T. J. Stanford, Lieut. J. S. McCall. *Johnston's Battalion,* Maj. J. W. Johnston, Capt. Max. Van D. Corput; Ga. Battery, Capt. Max. Van D. Corput, Lieut. W. S. Hoge, Lieut. M. L. McWhorter; Ga. Battery, Capt. J. B. Rowan; Tenn. Battery, Capt. L. G. Marshall. *Williams's (or Kolb's) Battalion:* Ala. Bat'y, Capt. R. F. Kolb, Lieut. P. F. Power; Miss. Bat'y, Capt. Put. Darden; Va. Bat'y, Capt. Wm. C. Jeffress, Lieut. B. H. Todd.

CAVALRY CORPS, Maj.-Gen. Joseph Wheeler.

MARTIN'S DIVISION, Maj.-Gen. W. T. Martin.

Morgan's (or Allen's) Brigade, Brig.-Gen. John T. Morgan, Brig.-Gen. William W. Allen: 1st Ala., Maj. A. H. Johnson, Lieut.-Col. D. T. Blakey; 3d Ala., Col. T. H. Mauldin, Col. James Hagan; 4th Ala., Col. A. A. Russell; 7th Ala., Col. James C. Malone, Capt. George Mason; 51st Ala., Col. M. L. Kirkpatrick; 12th Ala. Batt'n, Capt. W. S. Reese. *Iverson's Brigade,* Brig.-Gen. Alfred Iverson: 1st Ga., Col. S. W. Davitte; 2d Ga., Col. C. C. Crews, Maj. J. W. Mayo, Col. C. C. Crews; 3d Ga., Col. R. Thompson; 4th Ga., Col. I. W. Avery, Maj. A. R. Stewart, Col. I. W. Avery; 6th Ga., Col. J. R. Hart.

KELLY'S DIVISION, Brig.-Gen. J. H. Kelly.

Allen's (or Anderson's) Brigade, Brig.-Gen. William W. Allen, Brig.-Gen. R. H. Anderson, Col. Edward Bird: 3d Confed., Col. P. H. Rice, Lieut.-Col. John McCaskill; 8th Confed., Lieut.-Col. J. S. Prather; 10th Confed., Col. C. T. Goode, Capt. T. G. Holt, Capt. W. J. Vason; 12th Confed., Capt. C. H. Conner; 5th Ga., Maj. R. J. Davant, Jr., Col. Edward Bird. *Dibrell's Brigade,* Brig.-Gen. George G. Dibrell: 4th Tenn., Col. W. S. McLemore; 8th Tenn., Capt. J. Leftwich; 9th Tenn., Col. J. B. Biffle, Capt. J. M. Reynolds; 10th Tenn., Col. W. E. DeMoss, Maj. John Minor; 11th Tenn., Col. D. W. Holman. *Hannon's Brigade,* Col. M. W. Hannon: 53d Ala., Lieut.-Col. J. F. Gaines; 24th Ala. Batt'n, Maj. R. B. Snodgrass.

HUMES'S DIVISION, Brig.-Gen. W. Y. C. Humes.

Humes's (old) Brigade, Col. J. T. Wheeler, Col. H. M. Ashby: 1st Tenn., Maj. J. J. Dobbins, Col. J. T. Wheeler; 2d Tenn., Capt. J. H. Kuhn, Capt. W. M. Smith; 5th Tenn., Col. G. W. McKenzie; 9th Tenn., Maj. J. H. Akin, Capt. J. W. Greene, Maj. J. H. Akin. *Harrison's Brigade,* Col. Thomas Harrison: 3d Ark., Col. A. W. Hobson; 4th Tenn., Lieut.-Col. P. F. Anderson; 8th Tex., Lieut.-Col. Gustave Cook, Maj. S. P. Christian, Lieut.-Col. Gustave Cook; 11th Tex., Col. G. R. Reeves. *Grigsby's (or Williams's) Brigade,* Col. J. Warren Grigsby, Brig.-Gen. John S. Williams: 1st Ky., Col. J. R. Butler, Lieut.-Col. J. W. Griffith, Col. J. R. Butler; 2d Ky., Maj. T. W. Lewis; 9th Ky., Col. W. C. P. Breckinridge; 2d Ky. Batt'n, Capt. J. B. Dortch; Allison's Squadron, Capt. J. H. Allison; Hamilton's Batt'n, Maj. Jo. Shaw.

RODDEY'S COMMAND, Brig.-Gen. P. D. Roddey. (The only mention of Roddey in the reports of this time speaks of his having 600 men.)

ARTILLERY, Lieut.-Col. Felix H. Robertson, Maj. James Hamilton: Ark. Battery, Lieut. J. P. Bryant, Lieut. J. W. Callaway; Ga. Battery (Ferrell's, one section), Lieut. W. B. S. Davis; Tenn. Battery, Capt. B. F. White, Lieut. A. Pue, Capt. B. F. White; Tenn. Battery, Lieut. D. B. Ramsey; Tenn. Battery, Capt. A. L. Huggins.

ENGINEER TROOPS, Lieut.-Col. S. W. Presstman.

POLK'S (or STEWART'S) CORPS, ARMY OF MISSISSIPPI, Lieut.-Gen. Leonidas Polk, Maj.-Gen. W. W. Loring, Lieut.-Gen. A. P. Stewart, Maj.-Gen. B. F. Cheatham, Lieut.-Gen. A. P. Stewart.

Escort: Orleans Light Horse, Capt. L. Greenleaf.

LORING'S DIVISION, Maj.-Gen. W. W. Loring, Brig.-Gen. W. S. Featherston, Maj.-Gen. W. W. Loring.

Escort: B, 7th Tenn. Cav., Capt. J. P. Russell.

Featherston's Brigade, Brig.-Gen. W. S. Featherston, Col. Robert Lowry, Brig.-Gen. W. S. Featherston: 1st Miss., Maj. M. S. Alcorn; 3d Miss. Col. T. A. Melton, Lieut.-Col. S. M. Dyer; 22d Miss., Maj. Martin A. Oatis, Lieut.-Col. H. J. Reid, Capt. J. T. Formby; 31st Miss., Col. M. D. L. Stephens, Lieut.-Col. J. W. Drane, Lieut. William D. Shaw, Capt. T. J. Pulliam, Col. M. D. L. Stephens; 33d Miss., Col. J. L. Drake, Capt. M. Jackson,

Maj. A. J. Hall; 40th Miss., Col. W. B. Colbert, Lieut.-Col. George P. Wallace, Capt. C. A. Huddleston; 1st Miss. Batt'n Sharp-shooters, Maj. G. M. Stigler. *Adams's Brigade,* Brig.-Gen. John Adams: 6th Miss., Col. Robert Lowry; 14th Miss., Lieut.-Col. W. L. Doss; 15th Miss., Col. M. Farrell, Lieut.-Col. J. R. Binford; 20th Miss., Col. William N. Brown; 23d Miss., Col. J. M. Wells, Maj. G. W. B. Garrett; 43d Miss., Col. Richard Harrison. *Scott's Brigade,* Brig.-Gen. Thomas M. Scott: 27th Ala.,[1] Col. James Jackson, Lieut.-Col. E. McAlexander; 35th Ala.,[1] Col. S. S. Ives; 49th Ala.,[1] Lieut.-Col. J. D. Weeden, Capt. W. B. Beeson; 55th Ala., Col. John Snodgrass, Maj. J. B. Dickey; 57th Ala., Col. C. J. L. Cuningham, Lieut.-Col. W. C. Bethune, Capt. A. L. Milligan, Maj. J. H. Wiley; 12th La., Col. N. L. Nelson, Capt. E. McN. Graham. FRENCH'S DIVISION, Maj.-Gen. Samuel G. French.

Ector's Brigade, Brig.-Gen. M. D. Ector, Brig.-Gen. Wm. H. Young: 29th N. C., Lieut.-Col. B. S. Proffitt; 39th N. C., Col. D. Coleman; 9th Tex., Col. William H. Young, Maj. J. H. McReynolds; 10th Tex. (dismounted cav.), Col. C. R. Earp; 14th Tex. (dismounted cav.), Col. J. L. Camp; 32d Tex. (dismounted cav.), Col. J. A. Andrews; Jaques's Battalion, Maj. J. Jaques. *Cockrell's Brigade,* Brig.-Gen. F. M. Cockrell, Col. Elijah Gates, Brig.-Gen. F. M. Cockrell: 1st and 3d Mo. (dismounted cav.), Col. Elijah Gates, Lieut.-Col. D. T. Samuels, Col. Elijah Gates; 1st and 4th Mo., Col. A. C. Riley, Lieut.-Col. H. A. Garland; 2d and 6th Mo., Col. P. C. Flournoy; 3d and 5th Mo., Col. James McCown. *Sears's Brigade,* Col. W. S. Barry, Brig.-Gen. C. W. Sears: 4th Miss., Col. T. N. Adaire; 35th Miss., Lieut.-Col. R. H. Shotwell, Col. W. S. Barry; 36th Miss., Col. W. W. Witherspoon; 39th Miss., Lieut.-Col. W. E. Ross, Maj. R. J. Durr; 46th Miss., Col. W. H. Clark; 7th Miss. Batt'n, Capt. W. A. Trotter, Capt. J. D. Harris.

CANTEY'S (or WALTHALL'S) DIVISION, Brig.-Gen. James Cantey, Maj.-Gen. E. C. Walthall.

Quarles's Brigade, Brig.-Gen. William A. Quarles: 1st Ala., Col. S. L. Knox; 42d Tenn., Col. Isaac N. Hulme, Capt. A. M. Duncan; 46th and 55th Tenn., Col. R. A. Owens, Lieut.-Col. G. B. Black; 48th Tenn., Lieut.-Col. A. S. Godwin, Lieut.-Col. H. G. Evans; 49th Tenn., Col. W. F. Young, Capt. T. H. Smith, Maj. T. M. Atkins; 52d Tenn., Col. J. R. White, Maj. William C. Richardson, Capt. J. J. Rittenbury, Capt. S. C. Orr. *Reynolds's Brigade,* Brig.-Gen. D. H. Reynolds: 1st Ark. Mounted Rifles (dismounted), Lieut.-Col. M. G. Galloway, Capt. J. S. Perry, Capt. R. P. Parks; 2d Ark. Mounted Rifles (dismounted), Lieut.-Col. J. T. Smith, Capt. W. E. Johnson, Maj. J. P. Eagle; 4th Ark., Col. H. G. Bunn, Capt. A. Kile, Maj. J. A. Ross; 9th Ark., Lieut.-Col. J. W. Rogers, Maj. J. C. Bratton; 25th Ark., Lieut.-Col. Eli Hufstedler, Maj. L. L. Noles, Capt. E. C. Woodson; Gholson's Brigade,[2] Col. John McQuirk; Youngblood's Battalion,[2] Maj. —— Youngblood. *Canty's Brigade,* Col. V. S. Murphey, Col. E. A. O'Neal: 17th Ala., Col. V. S. Murphey, Maj. T. J. Burnett, Capt. T. A. McCane; 26th Ala., Col. E. A. O'Neal, Maj. D. F. Bryan; 29th Ala., Col. J. F. Conoley, Capt. J. A. Foster; 37th Miss., Col. O. S. Holland, Lieut.-Col. W. W. Wier, Maj. S. H. Terral. ARTILLERY, Lieut.-Col. S. C. Williams.

Waddell's Battalion: Ala. Battery, Capt. W. D. Emery;

Ala. Battery, Lieut. F. A. O'Neal, Capt. R. H. Bellamy; Mo. Battery, Capt. O. W. Barret, Lieut. William Brown. *Myrick's Battalion,* Maj. J. D. Myrick: La. Battery, Capt. A. Bouanchaud, Lieut. E. C. Legendre; Miss. Battery, Capt. J. J. Cowan, Lieut. G. H. Tompkins; Tenn. Battery, Capt. R. L. Barry, Lieut. R. L. Watkins. *Storrs's Battalion,* Maj. George S. Storrs: Ala. Battery, Capt. John J. Ward, Lieut. G. W. Weaver; Miss. Battery, Capt. J. A. Hoskins; Mo. Battery, Capt. Henry Guibor, Lieut. A. W. Harris, Sergt. Raymond Burke. *Preston's (or Truehart's) Battalion,* Maj. W. C. Preston, Maj. D. Truehart: Ala. Battery, Lieut. C. W. Lovelace; Ala. Battery, Lieut. Seth Shepard, Capt. E. Tarrant; Miss. Battery, Capt. J. H. Yates.

CAVALRY DIVISION, Brig.-Gen. W. H. Jackson.

Armstrong's Brigade, Brig.-Gen. F. C. Armstrong: 1st Miss., Col. R. A. Pinson; 2d Miss., Maj. J. J. Perry; 28th Miss., Maj. J. T. McBee, Col. P. B. Starke; Ballentine's Miss., Capt. E. E. Porter, Lieut.-Col. W. C. Maxwell; A, 1st Confed. (Escort), Capt. James Ruffin. *Ross's Brigade,* Brig.-Gen. L. S. Ross: 1st Tex. Legion, Col. E. R. Hawkins; 3d Tex., Lieut.-Col. J. S. Boggess; 6th Tex., Lieut.-Col. Peter F. Ross; 9th Tex., Col. D. W. Jones, Capt. H. C. Dial. *Ferguson's Brigade,* Brig.-Gen. S. W. Ferguson, Col. W. Boyles: 2d Ala., Col. John N. Carpenter; 56th Ala., Col. W. Boyles, Lieut.-Col. William Martin; 9th Miss., Col. H. H. Miller; 11th Miss., Col. R. O. Perrin; 12th Miss. Batt'n, Col. W. M. Inge, Capt. G. F. Peek. *Artillery,* Capt. John Waties: Ga. Battery, Capt. Ed. Croft, Lieut. A. J. Young; Mo. Battery, Capt. Houston King; S. C. Battery, Lieut. R. B. Waddell.

FIRST DIVISION GEORGIA MILITIA, Maj.-Gen. Gustavus W. Smith (who has supplied the following paragraph):

First Brigade, Brig.-Gen. R. W. Carswell: 1st Regt., Col. E. H. Pottle; 2d Regt., Col. C. D. Anderson: 5th Regt., Col. S. S. Stafford; 1st Batt'n, Lieut.-Col. H. K. McCay. *Second Brigade,* Brig.-Gen. P. J. Phillips: 3d Regt., Col. Q. M. Hill; 4th Regt., Col. R. McMillan; 6th Regt., Col. J. W. Burney; Artillery Battalion, Col. C. W. Styles. *Third Brigade,* Brig.-Gen. C. D. Anderson. *Fourth Brigade,* Brig.-Gen. H. K. McCay. (The Third and Fourth Brigades were formed after the Reserves joined, during the siege of Atlanta. The organizations of these two brigades are not found in any accessible data.)

LOSSES.

According to the report of Medical Director A. J. Foard (See Johnston's "Narrative," pp. 576-578), the losses of the Confederate Army in the Atlanta campaign amounted to 3044 killed, 18,952 wounded = 21,996. The prisoners (including deserters) captured by the Union Army (See Sherman's "Memoirs," Vol. II., p. 134), numbered 12,983, which gives 34,979 as the aggregate loss of the Confederate Army. (Major E. C. Dawes of Cincinnati, who has made a special study of the subject, estimates the Confederate loss at about 40,000, and the Union loss at about the same.)

For statements relative to the strength of the Confederate army in the Atlanta campaign see General Johnston's paper, p. 260, and Major E. C. Dawes's comments, p. 282.

---

[1] Consolidated in July, under Col. S. S. Ives.

[2] Temporarily attached, July 28.

SAVING A GUN.

THE STRUGGLE FOR ATLANTA.

BY OLIVER O. HOWARD, MAJOR-GENERAL, U. S. A.

THE forces under General Grant after his appointment as general-in-chief were, the Army of the Potomac, under Meade; that of the Ohio, near Knoxville, under Schofield; ⌡ that of the Cumberland, under Thomas, ⚓ near Chattanooga; that of the Tennessee, under McPherson, scattered from Huntsville, Alabama, to the Mississippi; that of the Gulf, under Banks, in Louisiana; besides subordinate detachments, under Steele and others, in Arkansas and farther west.

Grant took the whole field into his thought. He made three parts to the long, irregular line of armies, which extended from Virginia to Texas. He gave to Banks the main work in the south-west; to Sherman the middle part, covering the hosts of McPherson, Thomas, Schofield, and Steele; and reserved to himself the remainder. The numbers were known, at least on paper; the plan, promptly adopted, was simple and comprehensive: To break and keep broken the connecting links of the enemy's opposing armies, beat them one by one, and unite for a final consummation. Sherman's part was plain. Grant's plan, flexible enough to embrace his own, afforded Sherman "infinite satisfaction." It looked like "enlightened war." He rejoiced at "this verging to a common center." "Like yourself," he writes to Grant, "you take the biggest load, and from me you shall have thorough and hearty coöperation."

Sherman made his calculations so as to protect most faithfully our line of supply which ran through Louisville, Nashville, and Chattanooga, guarding it against enemies within and without his boundaries, and against accidents. He segregated the men of all arms for this protection. Block-houses and intrenchments were put at bridges and tunnels along the railway. Loco-

⌡ General John M. Schofield succeeded General John G. Foster in the command of the Department, and Army, of the Ohio, February 9th, 1864.—EDITORS.

⚓ General George H. Thomas succeeded General W. S. Rosecrans in command of the Department, and Army, of the Cumberland, October 19th, 1863.—EDITORS.

motives and freight cars were gathered in, and a most energetic force of skilled railroad men was put at work or held in reserve under capable chiefs.

Besides an equal number of guards of his large depots and long line of supply, Sherman had an effective field force of 100,000,— 50,000 with Thomas, 35,000 with McPherson, 15,000 with Schofield.

Sherman was gratified at the number of his force; for two years before, he had been held up as worthy of special distrust because he had declared to Secretary Cameron that before they were done with offensive operations on the line from the Big Sandy to Paducah, 200,000 men would be required.

A few changes of organization were made. Slocum's corps, the Twelfth, and mine, the Eleventh, were consolidated, making a new Twentieth, and Hooker was assigned to its command. I went at once to Loudon, east Tennessee, to take the Fourth Corps and relieve General Gordon Granger, to enable him to have a leave of absence. Slocum was sent to Vicksburg, Mississippi, to watch the great river from that quarter; while Hooker, Palmer, and myself, under Thomas, were to control the infantry and artillery of the Army of the Cumberland. In a few days I moved Wagner's (afterward Newton's) division and T. J. Wood's of my new corps to Cleveland, east Tennessee. Rations, clothing, transportation, and ammunition came pouring in with sufficient abundance, so that when orders arrived for the next movement, on the 3d of May, 1864, my division commanders, Stanley, Newton, and Wood, reported everything ready. This very day Schofield's column, coming from Knoxville, made its appearance at Cleveland. There was now the thrill of preparation, a new life everywhere. Soldiers and civilians alike caught the inspiration.

Ringgold and Catoosa Springs, Georgia, were the points of concentration for Thomas's three corps. We of his army were all in that neighborhood by the 4th of May. It took till the 7th for McPherson to get into Villanow, a few miles to the south of us. Schofield meanwhile worked steadily southward from Cleveland, east Tennessee, through Red Clay, toward Dalton, Georgia. The three railway lines uniting Chattanooga, Cleveland, and Dalton form an almost equilateral triangle. Dalton, its south-east vertex, was the center of the Confederate army, under Joseph E. Johnston. Pushing out from Dalton toward us at Catoosa Springs, Johnston occupied the famous pass through Taylor's Ridge, Buzzard-Roost Gap, and part of the ridge itself; and held, for his extreme outpost in our direction, Tunnel Hill, near which our skirmish-line and his first exchanged shots. His northern lines ran along the eastern side of the triangle, between Dalton and Red Clay.

Johnston, according to his official return for April, had a force of 52,992. At Resaca, a few days later, after the corps of Polk had joined him, it numbered 71,235.↓ Our three field armies aggregated then, in officers and men, 98,797, with 254 pieces of artillery. The Confederate commander had about the same number of cannon. McPherson had thus far brought to Sherman but 24,465 men.

↓ See the article by Major E. C. Dawes, p. 281.— EDITORS.

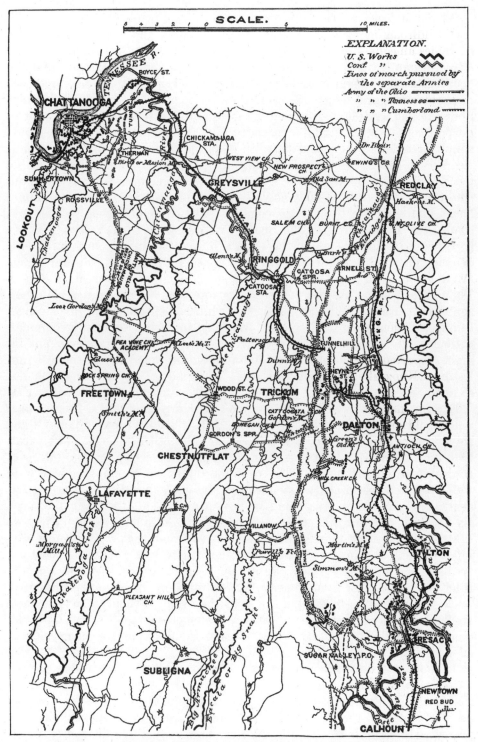

When the Army of the Cumberland was in line, facing the enemy, its left rested near Catoosa Springs, its center at Ringgold, the railway station, and its right at Leet's Tan-yard. My corps formed the left. Catoosa Springs was a Georgia watering-place, where there were several large buildings, hotel and boarding-houses, amid undulating hills, backed by magnificent mountain scenery. Here, on the morning of the 6th, I met Thomas and Sherman. Sherman had a habit of dropping in and explaining in a happy way what he purposed to do. At first he intended that Thomas and Schofield should simply breast the enemy and skirmish with him on the west and north, while McPherson, coming from Alabama, was to strike the Atlanta railroad at least ten miles below Resaca. McPherson, failing in getting some of his troops back from furlough, was not now deemed strong enough to operate alone; hence he was brought to Chattanooga instead, and sent thence to Villanow, soon after to pass through the Snake Creek Gap of Taylor's Ridge, all the time being kept near enough the other armies to get help from them in case of emergency. By this it was ardently hoped by Sherman that McPherson might yet succeed in getting upon Johnston's communications near Resaca. Thomas here urged his own views, which were to give Schofield and McPherson the skirmishing and demonstrations, while he (Thomas), with his stronger army, should pass through Snake Creek Gap and seize Johnston's communications. He felt sure of victory. Sherman, however, hesitated to put his main army twenty miles away beyond a mountain range on the enemy's line, lest he should thereby endanger his own. He could not yet afford an exchange of base. Still, in less than a week, as we shall see, he ran even a greater risk.

Early in the day, May 7th, the Fourth Corps, arranged for battle, was near a small farm-house in sight of Tunnel Hill. Two divisions, Stanley's and Newton's, abreast in long, wavy lines, and the other, Wood's, in the rear, kept on the *qui vive* to prevent surprises, particularly from the sweep of country to the north of us. The front and the left of the moving men were well protected by infantry skirmishers. It was a beautiful picture — that army corps, with arms glistening in the morning light, ascending the slope. By 8 o'clock the few rifle-shots had become a continuous rattle. First we saw far off, here and there, puffs of smoke, and then the gray horsemen giving back and passing the crest. Suddenly there was stronger resistance, artillery and musketry rapidly firing upon our advance. At 9 o'clock the ridge of Tunnel Hill bristled with Confederates, mounted and dismounted. A closer observation from Stanley's field-glass showed them to be only horse artillery and cavalry supports. In a few moments Stanley's and Newton's men charged the hill at a run and cleared the ridge, and soon beheld the enemy's artillery and cavalry galloping away. "The ball is opened," Stanley called out, as I took my place by his side to study Taylor's Ridge and its "Rocky Face," which was now in plain sight. We beheld it, a craggy elevation of about five hundred feet, extending from a point not far north of us, but as far as the eye could reach southward. Its perpendicular face presented a formidable wall and afforded us no favorable door of entrance.
[See also article, p. 278.]

Thomas's three corps, Palmer occupying the middle and Hooker the right, were now marched forward till my men received rifle-shots from the heights, Palmer's a shower of them from the defenders of the gap, and Hooker's a more worrisome fusillade from spurs of the ridge farther south. Thomas could not sit down behind this formidable wall and do nothing. How could he retain before him the Confederate host? Only by getting into closer contact.

On the 8th I sent Newton some two miles northward, where the ascent was not so abrupt. He succeeded by rushes in getting from cover to cover, though not without loss, till he had wrested at least one-third of the "knife edge" from those resolute men of gray. Quickly the observers of this sharp contest saw the bright signal flags up there in motion. Stanley and Wood gave Newton all possible support by their marksmen and by their efforts to land shells on the ridge. The enemy's signals were near Newton. He tried hard to capture them, but failed. In the night two pieces of artillery, after much toil, reached the top, and soon cleared away a few hundred yards more of this territory in bloody dispute. On May 9th Thomas put forth a triple effort to get nearer his foe. First, Stanley's division reconnoitered Buzzard-Roost Gap into the very "jaws of death," till it drew the fire from newly discovered batteries, and set whole lines of Confederate musketry-supports ablaze. At this time I had a

MAJOR-GENERAL JOHN M. PALMER.
FROM A PHOTOGRAPH.

narrow escape. Stanley, Captain G. C. Kniffin of his staff, several other officers, and myself were in a group, watching a reconnoissance. All supposed there were no Confederate sharp-shooters near enough to do harm, when *whiz* came a bullet which passed through the group; Kniffin's hat was pierced, three holes were made in my coat, and a neighboring tree was struck.

Thomas now made a second effort. Palmer sent Morgan's brigade up one of the spurs south of the gap. It encountered the hottest fire, and suffered a considerable loss in killed and wounded. One regiment drove back the enemy's first line, and, like Newton's men, came within speaking distance of their opponents. Here arose the story to the effect that a witty corporal proposed to read to them the President's Emancipation Proclamation, and that they kept from firing while he did so. Still farther south, with Hooker's Twentieth Corps, and almost beyond our hearing, Thomas made his third push. In this action fifty were reported killed, and a larger number wounded; among them every regimental commander engaged. Similarly, but with easier approaches than ours, Schofield kept Johnston's attention at the east and north. Such was the demonstration, while McPherson was making his long détour through Villanow, Snake Creek

PART OF THE BATTLE-FIELD OF RESACA, FROM A WAR-TIME PHOTOGRAPH

Gap, and out into Sugar Valley. He found the gap unoccupied; and so, with Kilpatrick's small cavalry detachment ahead, ♭ followed closely by Dodge's Sixteenth Corps, with Logan's Fifteenth well closed up, he emerged from the mountains on the morning of the 9th, at the eastern exit.

Immediately there was excitement — the cavalry advance stumbled upon Confederate cavalry, which had run out from Resaca to watch this doorway. Our cavalry followed up the retreating Confederates with dash and persistency, till they found shelter behind the deep-cut works and guns at Resaca. In plain view of these works, though on difficult ground, Logan and Dodge pressed up their men, under orders from McPherson "to drive back the enemy and break the railroad." And pray, why were not these plain orders carried out? McPherson answers in a letter that night sent to Sherman: "They [probably Polk's men] displayed considerable force and opened on us with artillery. After skirmishing [among the gulches and thickets] till nearly dark, and finding that I could not succeed in cutting the railroad before dark, or in getting to it, I decided to withdraw the command and take up a position for the night between Sugar Valley and the entrance to

♭ Lieutenant James Oates wrote to the editors on July 8th, 1887, from Cincinnati, Ark., as follows:

"General Howard is in error in the above statement. On May 1st the 9th Illinois Mounted Infantry broke camp at Decatur, Alabama, to take part in the Atlanta campaign. On the afternoon of May 8th the regiment came up with General McPherson at Villanow. Lieutenant-Colonel J. J. Phillips, who was in command, received orders to take the advance of the Army of the Tennessee, and did so at once, Company 'K,' Lieutenant James Oates in command, taking the lead through Snake Creek Gap. We advanced down into the open country of Sugar Valley on the evening of May 8th. No part of General Kilpatrick's command was there when we passed through Snake Creek Gap. On the morning of the 9th of May our regiment took the advance without any other cavalry support. The infantry was a considerable distance in the rear. Very early in the morning we engaged the Confederate cavalry, losing several men in killed and wounded — among the latter, Lieutenant-Colonel Phillips. The infantry came up at double-quick to our support and ended the fight. Our regiment followed up the retreating Confederates 'with dash and persistency.' It was during the advance that day that we came in contact with the Georgia Cadets from the Military Institute at Marietta, who had come out from the woods at Resaca and formed their line behind a rail fence. After a volley from the Cadets, which killed several of our men, our regiment charged them and did not give up the chase until it ran against the works at Resaca."

the gap." At the first news Sherman was much vexed, and declared concerning McPherson's failure to break the enemy's main artery: "Such an opportunity does not occur twice in a single life, . . . still he was perfectly justified by his orders."

Our commander, believing that Johnston would now speedily fall back to Resaca, at once changed his purpose. Leaving me at Rocky Face with the Fourth Corps and Stoneman's small division of cavalry to hold our line of supply, Sherman pressed after McPherson the armies of Thomas and Schofield. But Johnston was not in a hurry. He terrified me for two days by his tentative movements, till our skirmishing amounted at times almost to a battle. But the night of the 12th of May he made off in one of his clean retreats. At dawn of the 13th the formidable Buzzard-Roost Gap was open and safe, and our men passed through. Stoneman rushed into the village of Dalton from the north, and the Fourth Corps, eager and rapid, kept close to the chasing cavalry. Not far south of Dalton we came upon a bothersome Confederate rear-guard, which made our marching all that long day slow and spasmodic, yet before dark my command had skirted the eastern slope of Taylor's Ridge for eighteen miles and joined skirmishers with Sherman, who was already, with McPherson, abreast of Resaca. Thus we ended the combats of Tunnel Hill and Dalton, and opened up Resaca.

As soon as Johnston reached the little town of Resaca he formed a horse-shoe-shaped line, something like ours at Gettysburg. He rested Polk's corps on the Oostenaula River; placed Hardee's next, running up Milk Creek; and then curved Hood's back to strike the Connasauga River. After the

EXTREME LEFT (VIEW LOOKING SOUTH) OF THE CONFEDERATE LINES AT RESACA.
FROM A WAR-TIME PHOTOGRAPH.

The cluster of houses includes the railway station, the railway running generally parallel with the earth-works here seen, which in the distance descend to the Oostenaula River. The railway and wagon bridges mentioned in the notes on p. 266 are near the railway station.

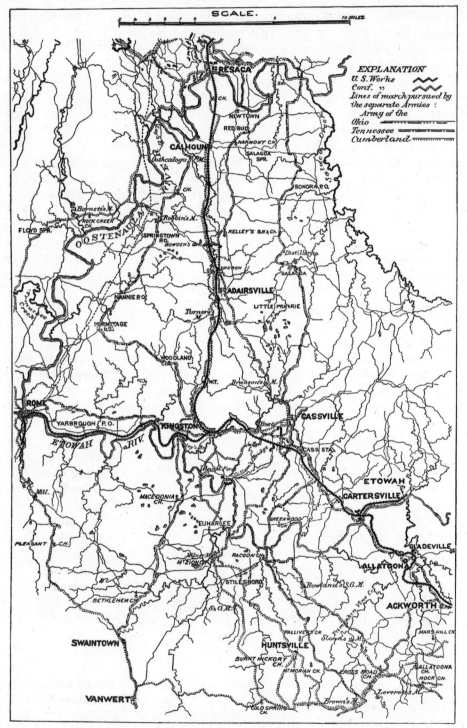

Confederates had thrown up the usual intrenchments, and put out one or two small advanced forts with cannon, the position was as strong as Marye's Heights had been against direct attack. We spent a part of the 14th of May creeping up among the bushes, rocks, and ravines.

Early that morning, while this was going on, Sherman, who had worked all night, was sitting on a log, with his back against a tree, fast asleep. Some men marching by saw him, and one fellow ended a slurring remark by: "A pretty way we are commanded!" Sherman, awakened by the noise, heard the last words. "Stop, my man," he cried; "while you were sleeping, last night,

BREVET BRIGADIER-GENERAL BENJAMIN HARRISON.
FROM A PHOTOGRAPH.

I was planning for you, sir; and now I was taking a nap." Thus, familiarly and kindly, the general gave reprimands and won confidence.

McPherson rested his right upon the Oostenaula River, opposite Polk. Thomas, with the corps of Palmer and Hooker, came next; and then that brave young officer, Cox, commanding the Twenty-third Corps, against a storm of bullets and shells swung his divisions round to follow the bend in the enemy's line. I watched the operation, so as to close upon his left. T. J. Wood's division moved up in a long line, with skirmishers well out, and then Stanley's carried us to the railway. Stanley's chief-of-artillery arranged two or three batteries to keep the enemy from walking around our unprotected left. The air was full of screeching shells and whizzing bullets, coming uncomfortably near, while line after line was adjusting itself for the deadly conflict. Our fighting at Resaca did not effect much. There might possibly have been as much accomplished if we had used skirmish-lines alone. In McPherson's front Logan had a battery well placed, and fired till he had silenced the troublesome foes on a ridge in his front; then his brave men, at a run, passed the ravine and secured the ridge. Here Logan intrenched his corps; and Dodge, abreast of him, did the same. Afterward, McPherson seized another piece of ground across Camp Creek, and held it. During the evening of the 14th a vigorous effort was made by Polk to regain this outpost, but he was repulsed with loss.

The detailed account gives great credit to Generals Charles R. Woods, Giles A. Smith, and J. A. J. Lightburn. One hundred prisoners and 1300 Confederates *hors de combat* were on Logan's list. This work forced Johnston to lay a new bridge over the Oostenaula. The divisions of Absalom Baird, R. W. Johnson, Jefferson C. Davis, and John Newton plunged into the thickets and worked their way steadily and bravely into the reëntrant angles on Hardee's front. Schofield's right division, under Judah, had a fearful struggle, losing six hundred men; the others, coming to its help, captured and secured a part of the enemy's intrenchments. Hood assailed my left after 3 P. M. The front attack was repulsed, but heavy columns came surging around Stanley's left. Everybody, battery men and supporting infantry, did

MAJOR-GENERAL E. C. WALTHALL, C. S. A.
FROM A PHOTOGRAPH.

wonders; still, but for help promptly rendered, Sherman's whole line, like the left of Wellington's at Waterloo, would soon have been rolled up and displaced. But Colonel Morgan of my staff, who had been sent in time, brought up Williams's division from Hooker's corps as quickly as men could march. Stanley's brave artillerymen were thus succored before they were forced to yield their ground, and Hood, disappointed, returned to his trenches. The next day, the 15th, came Hooker's attack. He advanced in a column of deployed brigades. Both armies watched with eager excitement this passage-at-arms. The divisions of Generals Butterfield, Williams, and Geary seized some trenches and cheered, but were stopped before a sort of lunette holding four cannon. The Confederates were driven from their trenches; but our men, meeting continuous and deadly volleys, could not get the guns till night. A color-bearer named Hess, of Colonel Benjamin Harrison's brigade, while his comrades were retiring a few steps for better cover, being chagrined at the defiant yell behind him, unfurled his flag and swung it to the breeze. He was instantly killed. A witness says: "There were other hands to grasp the flag, and it came back, only to return and wave from the very spot where its former bearer fell."

While the main battle was in progress, Dodge had sent a division under the one-armed Sweeny, to Lay's Ferry, a point below Resaca. Under the chief engineer, Captain Reese, he laid a bridge and protected it by a small force. Sweeny, being threatened by some Confederates crossing the river above him, and fearing that he might be cut off from the army, suddenly drew back about a mile beyond danger. On the 15th, however, he made another attempt and was more successful; formed a bridge-head beyond the river; threw over his whole force; and fought a successful battle against Martin's Confederate cavalry, before Walker's infantry, which was hastily sent against him from Calhoun, could arrive. Besides Sweeny's division, Sherman dispatched a cavalry force over the pontoons, instructing them to make a wider détour. The operations in this quarter being successful, there was nothing left to the Confederate commander but to withdraw his whole army from Resaca. This was effected during the night of the 15th, while our weary men were sound asleep. At the first peep of dawn Newton's skir-mishers sprang over the enemy's intrenchments to find them abandoned.

In the ensuing pursuit, Thomas, crossing the river on a floating bridge, hastily constructed, followed directly with the Fourth and the Fourteenth corps.

Stanley had some sharp fighting with Stewart's Confederate division, which was acting as Johnston's rear-guard. It was, in fact, a running skirmish, that lasted till evening, at the close of which we encamped for the night near the enemy's empty works at Calhoun. Meanwhile McPherson had been marching on parallel roads to the right toward Rome, Georgia, Jefferson C. Davis's division from Thomas's army sweeping farther still to the right, and Schofield, accompanied by Hooker, to the left toward Cassville.

Our enemy, between these columns with his entire force, made a brief stand on the 17th of May at Adairsville, and fortified. About 4 P. M. Newton and Wood, of my corps, Wood on the right, found the resistance constantly increasing as they advanced, till Newton's skirmishers, going at double-time through clumps of trees, awakened a heavy opposing fire. A little after this, while I was watching the developments from a high point, Sherman with his staff and escort joined me. Our showy group immediately drew upon it the fire of a battery, shells bursting over our heads with indescribable rapidity. Colonel Morgan's horse was very badly lamed; Fullerton, the adjutant-general, was set afoot, and several horses of the escort were killed or crippled. Captain Bliss, of Newton's staff, had one shoulder-strap knocked off by a fragment, which bruised him badly. The skirmishing of Newton and Wood kept increasing. In fact, both parties, though desiring to avoid a general battle, nevertheless reënforced, till the firing amounted to an engagement. It was not till after 9 o'clock that the rattling of the musketry had diminished to the ordinary skirmish, and the batteries had ceased, except an occasional shot, as if each were trying to have the last gun. The losses in my command in this combat were about two hundred killed and wounded. The morning of the 18th found the works in front of Adairsville with few reminders that an army had been there the night before. Hooker and Schofield had done the work. Johnston's scouts during the night brought him word that a large Federal force was already far beyond his right near Cassville, threatening his main crossing of the Etowah; and also that McPherson was camping below him at McGuire's Cross-roads, and that our infantry (Davis's division) was already in sight of the little town of Rome, where, under a weak guard, were foundries and important mills. We began now to perceive slight evidences of our opponent's demoralization. I captured a regiment and quite a large number of detached prisoners. The whole number taken, including many commissioned officers, was about four thousand.

The rapidity with which the badly broken railroad was repaired seemed miraculous. We had hardly left Dalton before trains with ammunition and other supplies arrived. While our skirmishing was going on at Calhoun, the locomotive whistle sounded in Resaca. The telegraphers were nearly as rapid : the lines were in order to Adairsville on the morning of the 18th. While we

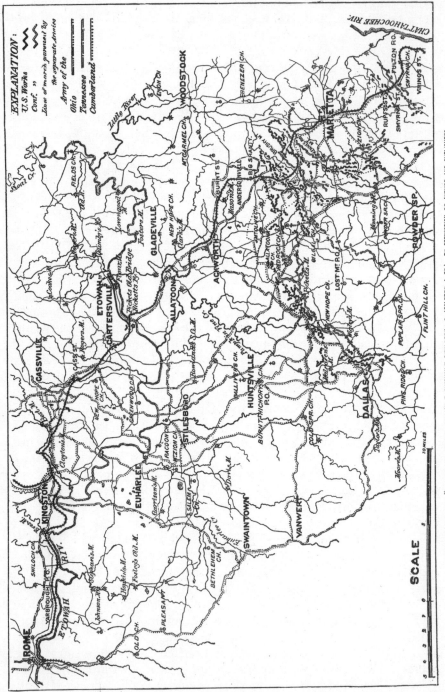

were breaking up the State arsenal at Adairsville, caring for the wounded and bringing in Confederate prisoners, word was telegraphed from Resaca that bacon, hard-bread, and coffee were already there at our service.

Johnston, by his speedy night-work, passed on through Kingston, and formed an admirable line of battle in the vicinity of Cassville, with his back to the Etowah River, protecting the selected crossing.

This was his final halt north of that river, so difficult with its mountain banks. Johnston remained here to obstruct and dispute our way one day only, for Schofield and Hooker had penetrated the forests eastward of him so far that Hood, still on Johnston's right, insisted that the Yankees were already beyond him and in force.

Upon this report, about which there has since been much controversy, Johnston ordered a prompt withdrawal. The morning of the 21st of May, bright and clear, showed us a country picturesque

MAJOR-GENERAL JACOB D. COX. FROM A PHOTOGRAPH.

in its natural features, with farm and woodland as quiet and peaceful as if there had been no war. So Sherman, taking up his headquarters at Kingston, a little hamlet on the railway, gave his armies three days' rest. ⟨

A glance at the map [see p. 251] shows the Etowah flowing nearly west thirty miles from Allatoona to Rome. Sherman's headquarters at Kingston were midway. While the armies were resting, the right (Davis's division) at Rome, the left (Schofield and Hooker) near Cartersville, and the remainder at Kingston, the railroad and telegraph lines were repaired to Kingston; baggage, temporarily abandoned, came back to officers and men; necessary supplies, at the hands of smiling quartermasters and commissaries, now found us. The dead were buried, the sick and wounded were made more comfortable, and everybody got his mail and wrote letters. Meanwhile Sherman and his army commanders were endeavoring to find the location of their enemy.

Johnston was holding the region south of the Etowah, including the pass

---

⟨ One of these days was Sunday. My friend E. P. Smith, of the Christian Commission, afterward Commissioner of Indian Affairs, was ringing the church bell at Kingston, when Sherman, being disturbed by the ringing, sent a guard to arrest the supposed "bummer."

Smith, in spite of his indignant protest, was marched to Sherman's anteroom and kept under guard for an hour. Then he was taken to Sherman, who looked up from his writing and asked abruptly:

"What were you ringing that bell for?"

"For service. It is Sunday, General," Smith replied.

"Oh! is it?" answered Sherman. "Didn't know it was Sunday. Let him go."— O. O. H.

of Allatoona, and extended his army along the ridge of Allatoona Creek toward the south-west. He was picketing a parallel ridge in front of his line, along another creek, the Pumpkin Vine. This is substantially where we found this able and careful commander; but he pushed a little to the left and forward as we came on, till Hardee was at Dallas and Hood at New Hope Church. Our march was resumed on the morning of the 24th of May, Thomas crossing on his own pontoons south of Kingston; Hooker, contrary to the plan, went in advance of Schofield's column over a bridge at Milam's, east of Kingston; Davis, being at Rome, went straightforward from that place, and McPherson did the same from his position, laying his bridges so as to take the road to Van Wert. Stoneman's cavalry covered the left; Garrard's division was near McPherson and Davis, while McCook's cleared the front for the center. The whole country between the Etowah and the Chattahoochee presented a desolate appearance, with few openings and very few farms, and those small and poor; other parts were covered with trees and dense underbrush, which the skirmishers had great difficulty in penetrating. Off the ordinary "hog-backs" one plunged into deep ravines or ascended abrupt steeps. There was much loose, shifting soil on the hills, and many lagoons and small streams bordered with treacherous quicksands.

Very soon on May 24th the usual skirmishing with the cavalry began, but there was not much delay. Hooker, coming into Thomas's road the next morning, the 25th, led our column, taking the direct road toward Dallas. It was showery all day, and the weather and bad roads had a disheartening effect on men and animals. To relieve the situation as much as possible Thomas had my corps take advantage of country roads to the right, that would bring us into Dallas by the Van Wert route. McPherson and Davis had already come together at Van Wert. Now, suddenly, Geary's division found a bridge over Pumpkin Vine Creek on fire, and hostile cavalry behind it. The cavalry soon fled, and the bridge was repaired. Hooker, thinking there was more force in that quarter, pushed up the road toward New Hope Church. He had gone but a short distance before he ran upon one of Hood's brigades. It was an outpost of Stewart's division, put there to create delay. Hooker soon dislodged this outpost and moved on, driving back the brigade through the woods, till he came upon the enemy's main line.

The sound of cannon speedily drew Sherman to the point of danger. He immediately ordered the necessary changes. Williams's division, having passed on, faced about and came back. Butterfield's hastened up. The two divisions, each forming in parallel lines, promptly assaulted Hood's position. Again and again Hooker's brave men went forward through the forest only to run upon log-barricades thoroughly manned and protected by well-posted artillery. During these charges occurred a thunder-storm, the heaviest shower of the day. I turned to the left by the first opportune road, and deployed Newton's division to the right of Hooker by 6 P. M. The remainder of my command came up over roads deep with mud and obstructed by wagons. In the morning all the troops were at hand. On that terrible night the nearest house to the field was filled with the wounded. Torch-lights and

CONFEDERATE INTRENCHMENTS NEAR NEW HOPE CHURCH. FROM A WAR-TIME PHOTOGRAPH.

candles lighted up dimly the incoming stretchers and the surgeons' tables and instruments. The very woods seemed to moan and groan with the voices of sufferers not yet brought in.

McPherson, with Davis for his left, took position at Dallas, having Logan on his right, and Garrard's cavalry still beyond. There must have been a gap of three miles between McPherson and us. Schofield was badly injured by the fall of his horse in that black forest while finding his way during the night to Sherman's bivouac, so that for a few days Cox took his command. Cox, with his Twenty-third Corps, and Palmer with the Fourteenth, swung in beyond me, as my men were moving up carefully into their usual positions in line of battle. Now the enemy kept strengthening his trench-barricades, which were so covered by thickets that at first we could scarcely detect them. As he did, so did we. No regiment was long in front of Johnston's army without having virtually as good a breastwork as an engineer could plan. There was a ditch before the embankment and a strong log revetment behind it, and a heavy "top-log" to shelter the heads of the men. I have known a regiment to shelter itself completely against musketry and artillery with axes and shovels, in less than an hour after it reached its position.

It would only weary the reader's patience to follow up the struggle step by step from New Hope Church to the Chattahoochee. Still, these were the hardest times which the army experienced. It rained continuously for seventeen days; the roads, becoming as broad as the fields, were a series of quagmires. And, indeed, it was difficult to bring enough supplies forward from Kingston to meet the needs of the army. Sherman began to pass his

UNION EARTH-WORKS IN FRONT OF BIG AND LITTLE KENESAW. FROM A WAR-TIME PHOTOGRAPH.

armies to the left. First, I was sent with two divisions to attempt to strike Johnston's right. I marched thither Wood's division, supported by R. W. Johnson's, and connected with the army by Cox on my right. At Pickett's Mill, believing I had reached the extreme of the Confederate line, at 6 P. M. of the 27th I ordered the assault. Wood encountered just such obstructions as Hooker had found at New Hope Church, and was similarly repulsed, suffering much loss. R. W. Johnson's division was hindered by a side-thrust from the hostile cavalry, so that we did not get the full benefit of his forward push. We believed that otherwise we should have lodged at least a brigade beyond Hindman's Confederate division. But we did what was most important: we worked our men all that weary night in fortifying. The Confederate commander was ready at daylight to take the offensive against us at Pickett's Mill, but he did not do so, because he found our position and works too strong to warrant the attempt. With a foot bruised by the fragment of a shell, I sat that night among the wounded in the midst of a forest glade, while Major Howard of my staff led regiments and brigades into the new position chosen for them. General R. W. Johnson had been wounded, Captain Stinson of my staff had been shot through the lungs, and a large number lay there, on a sideling slope by a faint camp-fire, with broken limbs or disfigured faces.

The next day, the 28th, McPherson made an effort to withdraw from Dallas, so as to pass beyond my left; but as Hardee at the first move quickly assailed him with great fury, he prudently advised further delay. This battle was the reverse of mine at Pickett's Mill. The enemy attacked mainly in columns of deployed regiments along the front of Dodge's and Logan's corps, and was repulsed with a dreadful loss, which Logan estimated at two thousand. Now, necessity pressing him in every direction, Sherman, mixing divisions somewhat along the line, gradually bore his armies to the left. The 1st of June put Stoneman into Allatoona, and on the 3d Schofield's infantry was across the railroad near Ackworth, having had a severe and successful combat *en route.*

Being now far beyond Johnston's right, and having seized and secured the Allatoona Creek from its mouth to Ackworth, Sherman was ready, from Allatoona as a new base, to push forward and strike a new and heavy blow, when, to his chagrin, in the night of the 4th of June Johnston abandoned his works and fell back to a new line. This line ran from Brush Mountain to Lost Mountain, with "Pine Top" standing out in a salient near the middle. He also held an outpost in front of Gilgal Church abreast of Pine Top. Slowly, with skirmishes and small combats, for the most part in dense woods, we continuously advanced. On my front we seized the skirmish-holes of the enemy, made epaulements for batteries there, and little by little extended our deep ditches or log-barricades close up to Johnston's. As we settled down to steady work again, McPherson was near Brush Mountain, having pushed down the railroad. F. P. Blair's corps (the Seventeenth) from Huntsville, Alabama, had now joined him, making up for our losses, which were already, from all causes, upward of nine thousand. This accession gave heart to us all. Thomas was next, advancing and bearing away toward Pine Top, and Schofield coming up against the salient angle near Gilgal Church. To tell the work of these two opposing hosts in their new position is a similar story to the last. There was gallant fighting here and there all along the lines. Here it was that my batteries, opening fire under the direct instruction of Sherman, drove back the enemy from the exposed intrenchments on Pine Top. It was at this time that General Polk was killed. McPherson, by overlapping Hood, skirmished heavily, and captured the 40th Alabama regiment entire. Schofield, brushing away the cavalry, penetrated between Lost Mountain and Gilgal Church, put his artillery on a prominent knoll, and, with rapid discharges, took Hardee in reverse.

That night, the 16th of June, Johnston again went back to a new line, already prepared, just behind Mud Creek. Our troops, being on the alert, followed at once with great rapidity. Just where the old lines joined the new (for Johnston's right wing was unchanged), I saw a feat the like of which never elsewhere fell under my observation. Baird's division, in a comparatively open field, put forth a heavy skirmish-line, which continued such a rapid fire of rifles as to keep down a corresponding hostile line behind its well-constructed trenches, while the picks and shovels behind the skirmishers fairly flew, till a good set of works was made four hundred yards distant from the enemy's and parallel to it. One of my brigades (Harker's), by a rush, did also a brave and unusual thing in capturing an intrenched and well-defended line of the enemy's works and taking their defenders captive. Again, another (Kirby's

CONFEDERATE WORKS ON THE SOUTH BANK OF THE CHATTAHOOCHEE. FROM A WAR-TIME PHOTOGRAPH.

brigade), having lost Bald Hill in a skirmish, retook it by a gallant charge in line, under a hot fire of artillery and infantry, and intrenched and kept it.

Hood, who had been massed opposite McPherson, made a forced night-march, and suddenly appeared on the other flank fronting Schofield and Hooker. With his known method of charging and firing, he delivered there a desperate attack on the 22d of June. After a hard battle he was repulsed with heavy loss. This was the "Battle of Culp's Farm." Here it was that Hooker received a reproof from Sherman for an exaggerated dispatch, which inferentially, but wrongly, blamed Schofield. ☆ Hooker was ever after incensed at Sherman.

Again, by the gradual pressure against Johnston's right and left, Sherman forced him to a new contraction of his lines. This time it was the famous Kenesaw position that he assumed. With his right still at Brush Mountain, he extended a light force over the crest of the Kenesaws, and placed a heavier one along the southern slope, reaching far beyond the Dallas and Marietta road. He drew back his left and fortified. The whole line was stronger in artificial contrivances and natural features than the cemetery at Gettysburg. The complete works, the slashings in front, and the difficulties of the slope toward us under a full sweep of cross-fire made the position almost impregnable.

For reasons similar to those which influenced Lee to strike twice for Little Round Top, Sherman ordered an assault here with the hope of carrying the southern slope of Kenesaw, or of penetrating Johnston's long front at some

☆ General Hooker signaled to General Sherman, on the evening of June 22d, that he [Hooker] was uneasy about his right flank, which Schofield had been ordered to protect.— EDITORS.

weak point. Schofield, well southward, advanced and crossed Olley's Creek, and kept up enough fire and effort to hold a large force in his front. Mc-Pherson, on the left, did the same, a serious engagement being sustained by Logan's corps advancing straight against the mountain. Logan lost heavily from the trenches in his front, and from artillery that raked his men as they advanced. Seven regimental commanders fell, killed or wounded. But the dreadful battle, hard to describe, was left to Thomas. He commanded two attacks, one opposite the Confederate General Loring's ‖ left, the other in front of Cheatham. Newton's division led my attack, and Davis that of Palmer. Like Pickett's charge at Gettysburg, the movement was preceded by a heavy cannonade. Then our skirmishers sprang forward and opened; and quickly the enemy's skirmish-line was drawn back to their main work. Harker, commanding one brigade, led his column rapidly over the open ground. Wagner did the same on Harker's left, and Kimball put his brigade in close support. The enemy's fire was terrific. Our men did not stop till they had gained the edge of the felled trees; a few penetrated, to fall close to the enemy's parapet; but most sought shelter behind logs and rocks, in rifle-holes, or depressions. Harker, moving with them, cheered on his men; when they were forced to stop, he rallied them again and made a second vigorous effort, in which he fell mortally wounded. Davis's effort was like Newton's; he met the same withering fire from rifle-balls and shells. But his men managed to make a shelter, which they kept, close up to the hostile works. Here they staid and intrenched. Among those who fell were brigade commanders Colonel Daniel McCook and Colonel O. F. Harmon. Our losses in this assault were heavy indeed, and our gain was nothing. We realized now, as never before, the futility of direct assaults upon intrenched lines already well prepared and well manned.

Plainly there was now nothing left for Sherman to do but to send his left army (McPherson's) to follow up the right (Schofield's) across Olley's Creek, and force his cavalry to Sandtown and the Chattahoochee far below Johnston's force. The first sign, namely, McPherson's starting, and Schofield's boldness, set the Confederates again in motion. On the morning of the 3d of July Sherman turned his spy-glass to the Kenesaw crest, and saw our pickets "crawling up the hill cautiously." The strong works were found vacant. Johnston had made new breastworks six miles below, at Smyrna Camp Ground, and another complete set, by the labor of slaves and new levies, where the railway crosses the Chattahoochee. Thomas, taking up the pursuit, followed his enemy through Marietta and beyond. My command skirmished up to the Smyrna works during the 3d. The next day Sherman paid us a Fourth of July visit. He could not at first believe that Johnston would make another stand north of the river. "Howard," he said to me, "you are mistaken; there is no force in your front; they are laughing at you!" We were in a thinnish grove of tall trees, in front of a farm-house. "Well, General," I

‖ General Loring remained with his division in the Department of Mississippi and East Louisiana until the Atlanta campaign was fairly opened by Sherman's advance, when all the infantry in Mississippi was ordered to Johnston. Polk, with Loring's division, reached Resaca May 11th. June 14th, Polk having been killed, Loring succeeded temporarily to the command of the corps.— EDITORS.

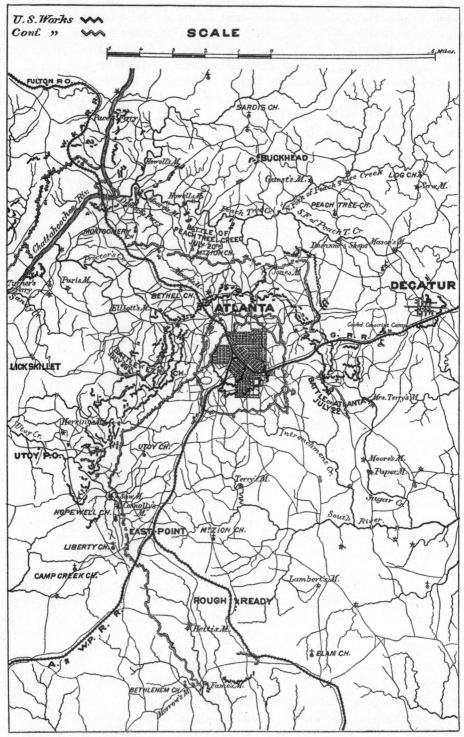

replied, "let us see." I called Stanley, whose division held the front. "General, double your skirmishers and press them." At once it was done. The lines sped forward, capturing the outlying pits of the enemy, and took many prisoners; but a sheet of lead instantly came from the hidden works in the edge of the wood beyond us, and several unseen batteries hurled their shot across our lines, some of them reaching our grove and forcing us to retire. Sherman, as he rode away, said that I had been correct in my report. While we kept the Confederates busy by skirmishing and battery firing, a set of demonstrations to the north and south of us finally resulted in gaining crossings of the river at Roswell, Soap Creek, Powers's and Paice's ferries. Schofield effected the first crossing by pushing out from Soap Creek boats loaded with men, crossing quickly, and surprising the Confederate cavalry and cannon in his front. This was done on the 9th of July. As soon as Johnston knew of it, he left his excellent works near the Chattahoochee, burned his bridges, and hastened his retreat to Atlanta. The weather had become good, and there was great animation and manifest joy on our side. It was gratifying to escape from such fastnesses and dismal forests as those which had hampered us for over a month, and we now firmly believed that the end of the campaign was sure.

GENERAL SHERMAN'S HEADQUARTERS AT THE HOWARD HOUSE, IN FRONT OF ATLANTA. FROM A SKETCH MADE AT THE TIME.

In his "Memoirs" General Sherman says that on July 21st (the day before General McPherson was killed), while he (Sherman) was at the head of Schofield's troops, expecting that the enemy would evacuate, McPherson and his staff rode up. "We went back," he says, "to the Howard House, a double frame-building with a porch, and sat on the steps discussing the chances of battle, and Hood's general character. McPherson had also been of the same class at West Point with Hood, Schofield, and Sheridan. We agreed that we ought to be unusually cautious, and prepared at all times for sallies and for hard fighting, because Hood, though not deemed much of a scholar, or of great mental capacity, was undoubtedly a brave, determined, and rash man."—EDITORS.

Our armies made a right wheel—Thomas, on the pivot, taking the shortest line to Atlanta; McPherson, on the outer flank, coming by Roswell to Decatur, with Schofield between.

As the several columns were crossing the famous Peach Tree Creek my corps was divided. I was sent, with Stanley and Wood, to connect with Schofield, causing a gap of two miles. Newton remained on Thomas's left; on Newton's right was Ward; next, Geary; then, Williams; last, Palmer's corps; all, having crossed over, were stretched out along the creek. There was at that point but little open ground, mostly woodland, and very uneven with cross-ravines.

Just at this time, much to our comfort and to his surprise, Johnston was removed, and Hood placed in command of the Confederate army. Johnston had planned to attack Sherman at Peach Tree Creek, expecting just such a division between our wings as we made.

Hood endeavored to carry out the plan. A. P. Stewart now had Polk's corps, and Cheatham took Hood's. Hardee on the right and Stewart on his left, in lines that overlapped Newton's position, at 3 o'clock of the 20th of July, struck the blow. They came surging on through the woods, down the gentle slope, with noise and fury like Stonewall Jackson's men at Chancellorsville. As to our men, some of them were protected by piles of rails, but the most had not had time to barricade.

Stewart's masses advanced successively from his right, so Newton was first assailed. His rifles and cannon, firing incessantly and with utmost steadiness, soon stopped and repulsed the front attack; but whole battalions went far east of him into the gap before described. Thomas, behind the creek, was watching; he turned some reserved batteries upon those Confederate battalions, and fired his shells into the thickets that bordered the

SPRAGUE'S BRIGADE PROTECTING THE WAGON TRAINS OF SHERMAN'S ARMY AT DECATUR, GEORGIA, JULY 22, 1864. FROM A SKETCH MADE AT THE TIME.

deep creek, sweeping the creek's valley as far as the cannon could reach. This was sufficient; in his own words, "it relieved the hitch." The hostile flankers broke back in confusion. In succession, Ward, Geary, Williams, and Palmer received the on-coming waves, and though their ranks were shaken in places, they each made a strong resistance, and soon rolled the Confederates back, shattered and broken. Hardee would have resumed the assault, but an order from Hood took away a whole division (Cleburne's), for McPherson was too rapidly approaching Cheatham and the defenses of Atlanta from the east.

The battle of the 20th did not end till Gresham's division, on McPherson's left, had gone diagonally toward Atlanta, sweeping the hostile cavalry of Wheeler before it past the Augusta railroad, and skirmishing up against an open knob denominated Bald Hill. General Gresham, a fine officer, was severely wounded during his brisk movement. Wheeler had made a desperate and successful stand here, and soon after, in the evening, the division (Cleburne's) which was taken from Newton's sorely handled front was brought hither and put into the trenches, in order to make secure the right of Hood's line. The Bald Hill was an important outpost.

The 21st, a fearfully hot day, was spent by all in readjustment. Thomas brought his three corps forward, near to the enemy. The gap in my lines was closed as we neared the city. Schofield filled the space between the Fourth (mine) and Logan's corps. McPherson, to get a better left, ordered Blair to seize Bald Hill. General Force, of Leggett's division, supported by Giles A. Smith, who now had Gresham's place, charged the hill and carried it, though with a heavy loss. No time ran to waste till this point was manned with batteries protected by thick parapets and well secured by infantry supports.

Atlanta appeared to us like a well-fortified citadel with outer and inner works. After Thomas had beaten him, Hood resolved to give up the Peach Tree line; so, after dark, he drew back two corps into those outer works.

Hardee, however, was destined to a special duty. About midnight he gathered his four divisions into Atlanta: Bate led the way; Walker came next; Cleburne, having now left the vicinity of Bald Hill (for he was soon to go beyond it), followed; then came Maney in rear. They pushed out far south and around Gresham's sleeping soldiers; they kept on eastward till Hardee's advance was within two miles of Decatur, and his rear was nearly past Sherman's extreme left. There, facing north, he formed his battle front; then he halted on rough ground, mostly covered by forest and thicket. He had made a blind night-march of fifteen miles; so he rested his men for a sufficient time, when, slowly and confidently, the well-disciplined Confederates in line took up their forward movement. Success was never more

SCENE OF GENERAL McPHERSON'S DEATH, ON THE BATTLE-FIELD OF JULY 22. FROM WAR-TIME PHOTOGRAPHS.

A 32-pounder cannon, set upon a granite block, now marks the spot of General McPherson's death.
A large pine stands within a few feet of the monument, which faces a partly improved
roadway that is called McPherson Avenue.

MAJOR-GENERAL JAMES B. McPHERSON, KILLED JULY 22, 1864. FROM A PHOTOGRAPH.

assured, for was not Sherman's cavalry well out of the way, breaking a railroad and burning bridges at and beyond Decatur? And thus far no Yankee
except a chance prisoner had discovered this Jacksonian march! The morning
showed us empty trenches from Bald Hill to the right of Thomas. We quickly
closed again on Atlanta, skirmishing as we went. McPherson's left was, however, near enough already, only a single valley lying between Blair's position
and the outer defensive works of the city. The Sixteenth Corps (Dodge), having sent a detachment under General Sprague to hold Decatur, to support the
cavalry and take care of sundry army wagons,—a thing successfully accomplished,—had marched, on the 21st, toward Atlanta. Dodge remained for the
night with head of column a mile or more in rear of Blair's general line.

Fuller's division was nearest Blair's left, and Sweeny's not far from the Augusta railroad, farther to the north. McPherson spent the night with Sweeny. His hospitals and main supply trains were between Sweeny and the front. About midday McPherson, having determined to make a stronger left, had set Dodge's men in motion. They marched, as usual, by fours, and were in long column pursuing their way nearly parallel to Hardee's battle front, which was hidden by the thick trees. Now danger threatened: at the first skirmish shots Dodge's troops halted and faced to the left and were in good line of battle. The Confederate divisions were advancing; fortunately for Dodge, after the firing began Hardee's approaching lines nearing him had to cross some open fields. McPherson was then paying a brief visit to Sherman near the Howard house. The attack was sudden, but Dodge's veterans, not much disturbed, went bravely to their work. It is easy to imagine the loud roar of artillery and the angry sounds of musketry that came to Sherman and McPherson when the sudden assault culminated and extended from Dodge to Blair's left. McPherson mounted, and galloped off toward the firing. He first met Logan and Blair near the railway; then the three separated, each to hasten to his place on the battle-line. McPherson went at once to Dodge; saw matters going well there; sent off aides and orderlies with dispatches, till he had but a couple of men left with him. He then rode forward to pass to Blair's left through the thick forest interval. Cheatham's division was just approaching. The call was made, "Surrender!" But McPherson, probably without a thought save to escape from such a trap, turned his horse toward his command. He was instantly slain, and fell from his horse. One of his orderlies was wounded and captured; the other escaped to tell the sad news. Our reënforcements were on the way, so that Cheatham was beaten back. While the battle raged, McPherson's body was brought to Sherman at the Howard house. I wrote next day: "We were all made sad yesterday by the death of General McPherson,—so young, so noble, so promising, already commanding a department!" I closed my report concerning him thus: "His death occasioned a profound sense of loss, a feeling that his place can never be completely filled. How valuable, how precious the country to us all, who have paid for its preservation such a price!" Logan immediately took the Army of the Tennessee, giving his corps to Morgan L. Smith. As soon as Hood, from a prominent point in front of Atlanta, beheld Hardee's lines emerging from the thickets of Bald Hill, and knew by the smoke and sound that the battle was fully joined, he hurried forward Cheatham's division to attack Logan all along the east front of Atlanta. At the time, I sat beside Schofield and Sherman near the Howard house, and we looked upon such parts of the battle as our glasses could compass. Before long we saw the line of Logan broken, with parts of two batteries in the enemy's hands. Sherman put in a cross-fire of cannon, a dozen or more, and Logan organized an attacking force that swept away the bold Confederates by a charge in double-time. Blair's soldiers repulsed the front attack of Cheatham's and Maney's divisions, and then, springing over their parapets, fought Bate's and Maney's men from the other side. The battle continued

BATTLE OF ATLANTA, JULY 22, 1864.—THE CONTEST ON BALD HILL [SEE PP. 317-328]: FOURTH DIVISION, FIFTEENTH CORPS, IN THE FOREGROUND. FROM THE PANORAMA OF "ATLANTA."

till night, when Hood again yielded the field to Sherman and withdrew. The losses on both sides in this battle of Atlanta were probably nearly even—about four thousand each. Our gain was in morale.

Sherman now drew his half-circle closer and closer, and began to manœuvre with a view to get upon the railways proceeding southward. The Army of the Tennessee (late McPherson's) was assigned to me by the President, and I took command on the 27th of July, while it was marching around by the rear of Schofield and Thomas, in order to throw itself forward close to Atlanta on the south-west side, near Ezra Church. Skirmishing briskly, Dodge was first put into line facing the city; next Blair, beside him; last, Logan, on the right, making a large angle with Blair. He was not at night quite up to the crest of the ridge that he was to occupy. In the morning of the 28th he was moving slowly and steadily into position. About 8 o'clock Sherman was riding with me through the wooded region in rear of Logan's forces, when the skirmishing began to increase, and an occasional shower of grape cut through the tree-tops and struck the ground beyond us. I said: "General, Hood will attack me here." "I guess not—he will hardly try it again," Sherman replied. I said that I had known Hood at West Point, and that he was indomitable. As the signs increased, Sherman went back to Thomas, where he could best help me should I need reënforcement. Logan halted his line, and the regiments hurriedly and partially covered their front with logs and rails, having only a small protection while kneeling or lying down. It was too late for intrenching. With a terrifying yell, Hood's men charged through the forest. They were met steadily and repulsed. But in the impulse a few Confederate regiments passed beyond Logan's extreme right. To withstand them four regiments came from Dodge; Inspector-General Strong led thither two from Blair, armed with repeating-rifles; and my chief-of-artillery placed several batteries so as to sweep that exposed flank. These were brought in at the exact moment, and after a few rapid discharges, the repeating-rifles being remarkable in their execution, all the groups of flankers were either cut down or had sought safety in flight. This battle was prolonged for hours. We expected help from Morgan's division of Palmer's corps, coming back from Turner's Ferry; but the Confederate cavalry kept it in check. Our troops here exhibited nerve and persistency; Logan was cheerful and hearty and full of enthusiasm. He stopped stragglers and sent them back, and gave every needed order. Blair was watchful and helpful, and so was Dodge. After the last charge had been repelled I went along my lines, and felt proud and happy to be intrusted with such brave and efficient soldiers. Hood, having again lost three times as many as we, withdrew within his fortified lines. Our skirmishers cleared the field, and the battle of Ezra Church was won; and with this result I contented myself. One officer, who was a little panic-stricken, ran with the first stragglers to Sherman, and cried substantially, as I remember, "You've made a mistake in McPherson's successor. Everything is going to pieces!" Sherman said, "Is General Howard there?" "Yes; I suppose he is." "Well, I'll wait before taking action till I hear from him!" So Sherman sustained and

MAJOR-GENERAL JOHN A. LOGAN. FROM A PHOTOGRAPH.

trusted me, and I was content. Of General Logan, who has so recently gone
from us, I wrote, after this battle:

> "Major-General Logan was spirited and energetic, going at once to the point where he appre-
> hended the slightest danger of the enemy's success. His decision and resolution animated and
> encouraged his officers and men to hold on at all hazards."

For a month Hood kept to a defensive attitude, and, like a long storm, the
siege operations set in. Sherman worked his right, with block after block,
eastward and southward. Schofield and part of Thomas's command had
passed beyond me, digging as they halted. Every new trench found a fresh
one opposite. The lines were near together. Many officers and men were

slain and many were wounded and sent back to the hospitals. Dodge, while reconnoitering, was badly hurt; T. E. G. Ransom took his corps, and J. M. Corse a division in it.

Hooker, already vexed at Sherman, was incensed at my assignment, resigned, and went home. Slocum came from Vicksburg to command the Twentieth Corps. Palmer, having a controversy concerning his seniority, left the Four-teenth Corps, and Jeff. C. Davis took his place. Hazen passed from a brigade in the Fourth (Stan-ley's) to M. L. Smith's divi-sion of Lo-gan's corps. F. P. Blair, in a report, con-densed the work of his corps in these

THE BATTLE OF EZRA CHURCH, JULY 28, 1864. FROM A SKETCH MADE AT THE TIME.

words: "The command was occupied for 28 days in making approaches, digging rifle-pits, and erecting batteries, being subjected day and night to a galling fire of artillery and musketry."

Sherman now having his supplies well up, beginning on the night of the 25th of August, intrenched Slocum's strong corps across his railroad commu-nication to defend it; then made another grand wheel of his armies. Schofield this time clung to the pivot. My command described an arc of 25 miles radius aiming at Jonesboro', while Thomas followed the middle course. Both southern railways were to be seized, and the stations and road destroyed.

Preceded by Kilpatrick, we made the march rapidly enough, considering the endless plague of the enemy's horse artillery supported by Wheeler's cavalry, and the time it took us to break up the West Point railroad. At Renfro Place we were to encamp on the night of the 30th of August. Finding no water there, and also hoping to secure the Flint River Bridge, six miles ahead, I called to Kilpatrick for a squadron. He sent me a most energetic young man, Captain Estes, and the horsemen needed. I asked Estes if he could keep the enemy in motion. He gave a sanguine reply, and galloped off at the head of his men. Wheeler's rear-guard was surprised, and hurried toward the river. Hazen's infantry followed, forgetting their fatigue in the excitement of pursuit. We reached the bridge as it was burning, extinguished the fire, crossed over in the dusk of the evening under an increasing fire from hostile cavalry and infantry, but did not stop till Logan had reached the wooded ridge beyond, near Jonesboro'. The command was soon put into position,

MAJOR-GENERAL JOHN M. CORSE, WHO "HELD THE
FORT" AT ALLATOONA. FROM A PHOTOGRAPH.

and worked all night and during the next morning to intrench, and build the required bridges. Hood had sent Hardee by rail, with perhaps half of his command, to hold Jonesboro'. My Confederate classmate, S. D. Lee, who had had the immediate assault at Ezra Church, here appeared again, commanding Cheatham's corps. At 3 P. M. on the 31st the Confederates came on with the usual vigor, but were met by Logan and Ransom, and thoroughly repulsed. Hood now abandoned Atlanta, and united with Hardee in the vicinity of Jonesboro', near Lovejoy's Station. Thomas, joining my left flank, fought mainly the battle of September 1st. During the rest that followed, Blair and Logan went home on leave of absence; the field-force of the Army of the Tennessee was consolidated into two corps, Osterhaus temporarily commanding the Fifteenth, and Ransom the Seventeenth. Thomas went to Chattanooga to defend the communications with Sherman's army. Wagner's division was sent to Chattanooga, and Corse's division to Rome. Colonel John E. Tourtellotte had a detachment garrisoning the works at Allatoona Pass.

Hood had been threatening for some time to break Sherman's long line of communication and supply. Sherman could not divine where the blow would fall. He was already arranging for a campaign southward; but he wanted Grant's formal sanction, and he wished to make proper provision for Hood.

At last, on the 2d of October, Hood had passed on his way back beyond the Chattahoochee. Sherman had waited for this till he was sure that the first attempt against his line would be south of the Etowah. Now, leaving one corps, Slocum's, at Atlanta, he followed Hood with the remainder of his force. Hood stopped near Dallas, and sent French's division to take the garrison of Allatoona and the depots there. From the top of Kenesaw, Sherman communicated with Corse,⎰ who had joined Tourtellotte at Allatoona, and

⎰ On the 4th of October General John M. Corse, commanding the Fourth Division, Fifteenth Corps, stationed in observation at Rome, Georgia, was ordered by General Sherman to move by railway to Allatoona to assist the garrison at that point against a heavy force of Hood's army, which was moving north from Kenesaw Mountain. With a part of his command Corse reached Allatoona at 1 A. M. on the 5th. The battle which took place that day is described in his report as follows:

"The ammunition being unloaded, and the train sent back [to Rome] for reënforcements, accompanied by Colonel Tourtellotte, the post commandant, I rode around and inspected the ground and made such disposition of the troops as, in my judgment, was necessary

to hold the place until daylight. I then learned from Colonel Tourtellotte that the garrison embraced the 4th Minnesota infantry, 450 men, Major J. C. Edson commanding; 93d Illinois infantry, 290 men, Major Fisher commanding; seven companies 18th Wisconsin infantry, 150 men, Lieutenant-Colonel Jackson commanding; 12th Wisconsin battery, six guns, Lieutenant Amsden commanding—furnishing a force of 890 men, commanded by Lieutenant-Colonel J. E. Tourtellotte, 4th Minnesota Volunteer infantry. I took with me, of Rowett's brigade of this division, eight companies 39th Iowa infantry, 280 men, Lieutenant-Colonel James Redfield commanding; nine companies 7th Illinois infantry, 291 men, Lieutenant-Colonel Hector Perrin commanding; eight companies 50th Illinois infantry, 267 men, Lieut.-Colonel Wm. Hanna commanding; two companies 57th Illinois infantry, 61 men, Captain Vanstienburg commanding; detachment

taken command. The popular hymn, "Hold the Fort," was based upon the messages between these chiefs and the noble defense that the garrison successfully made against a whole Confederate division. Sherman was coming,

12th Illinois, Adams brigade, 150 men, Capt. Koehler commanding; total, 1054 — making an aggregate of 1944. . . . Under a brisk cannonade, kept up for near two hours, with sharp skirmishing on our south front and our west flank, the enemy pushed a brigade of infantry around north of us, cut the railroad and telegraph, severing our communications with Cartersville and Rome. The cannonading and musketry had not ceased since, at half-past 8 A. M., I received by flag of truce, which came from the north on the Cartersville road, the following summons to surrender:

"'AROUND ALLATOONA, October 5th, 1864.

"'COMMANDING OFFICER UNITED STATES FORCES, Allatoona.

"'SIR : I have placed the forces under my command in such positions that you are surrounded, and to avoid a needless effusion of blood I call on you to surrender your forces at once and unconditionally. Five minutes will be allowed you to decide. Should you accede to this you will be treated in the most honorable manner as prisoners of war. I have the honor to be, very respectfully yours,   S. G. FRENCH,

"'Major-General Commanding Forces, Confederate States.'

"To which I made the following reply:

"'HEADQUARTERS, FOURTH DIVISION, FIFTEENTH ARMY CORPS, Allatoona, Georgia, 8:30 A. M., October 5th, 1864.

"'MAJOR-GENERAL S. G. FRENCH, Confederate States Army, etc. :

"'Your communication demanding surrender of my command I acknowledge receipt of, and respectfully reply that we are prepared for the "needless effusion of blood" whenever it is agreeable to you. I am, very respectfully, your obedient servant,   JOHN M. CORSE,

"'Brigadier-General Commanding Forces, United States.'

"I then hastened to my different commands, informing them of the object of the flag, etc., my answer, and the importance and necessity of their preparing for hard fighting. . . . I had hardly issued the incipient orders when the storm broke in all its fury. . . . The fighting up to . . . about 11 A. M. was of the most extraordinary character. . . . About 1 P. M. I was wounded by a rifle-ball, which rendered me insensible for some thirty or forty minutes, but managed to rally on hearing some person or persons cry, 'Cease firing,' which conveyed to me the impression that they were trying to surrender the fort. Again I urged my staff, the few officers left unhurt, and the men around me to renewed exertions, assuring them that Sherman would soon be there with reënforce-

ments. The gallant fellows struggled to keep their heads above the ditch and parapet, had the advantage of the enemy, and maintained it with such success that they [the Confederates] were driven from every position, and finally fled in confusion, leaving the dead and wounded and our little garrison in possession of the field." . . .

Corse's entire loss, officially reported, was:

Garrison.	Killed.	Wounded.	Missing.	Total.
Officers	6	23	6	35
Men	136	330	206	672
Total	142	353	212	707

General Sherman, in his "Memoirs," says:

"We crossed the Chattahoochee River during the 3d and 4th of October, rendezvoused at the old battle-field of Smyrna Camp, and the next day reached Marietta and Kenesaw. The telegraph wires had been cut above Marietta, and learning that heavy masses of infantry, artillery, and cavalry had been seen from Kenesaw (marching north), I inferred that Allatoona was their objective point; and on the 4th of October I signaled from Vining's Station to Kenesaw, and from Kenesaw to Allatoona, over the heads of the enemy, a message for General Corse at Rome, to hurry back to the assistance of the garrison at Allatoona. . . . Reaching Kenesaw Mountain about 8 A. M. of October 5th (a beautiful day), I had a superb view of the vast panorama to the north and west. To the south-west, about Dallas, could be seen the smoke of camp-fires, indicating the presence of a large force of the enemy, and the whole line of railroad, from Big Shanty up to Allatoona (full fifteen miles), was marked by the fires of the burning railroad. We could plainly see the smoke of battle about Allatoona, and hear the faint reverberation of the cannon. From Kenesaw I ordered the Twenty-third Corps (General Cox) to march due west on the Burnt Hickory road, and to burn houses or piles of brush as it progressed, to indicate the head of column, hoping to interpose this corps between Hood's main army at Dallas and the detachment then assailing Allatoona. The rest of the army was directed straight for Allatoona, north-west, distant eighteen miles. The signal-officer on Kenesaw reported that since daylight he had failed to obtain any answer to his call for Allatoona; but, while

ALLATOONA PASS, LOOKING NORTH — CORSE'S FORT ON THE LEFT (SEE P. 344). FROM A WAR-TIME PHOTOGRAPH.

THE BATTLE OF ALLATOONA, OCTOBER 5, 1864. FROM "THE MOUNTAIN CAMPAIGNS IN GEORGIA, OR WAR SCENES ON THE W. & A.," PUBLISHED BY THE WESTERN & ATLANTIC R. R. CO.

and French, several times repulsed with great loss, withdrew and joined Hood at New Hope Church.

Taking up his northward march, Hood avoided Rome and aimed for Resaca. Schofield was warned, and got ready to defend Chattanooga, while Sherman now made forced marches so as to overtake his enemy and force him to battle. Finding us on his heels, Hood, picking up two or three small garrisons, but leaving untouched those that showed great pluck, like that of the resolute Colonel Clark R. Wever at Resaca, ⚓ rushed through Sugar Valley and Snake Creek Gap, choking it behind him with trees. My command, following rapidly through the pass (October 16th), cut away or threw the gap obstructions to the right and left, and camped close up to Hood's rear-guard. He again refused battle, and we pursued him beyond Gaylesville, Alabama. Between Rome and Gaylesville, General Ransom, the gallant and promising young officer before mentioned, died from over-work and exposure due to our

BREVET MAJOR-GENERAL T. E. G. RANSOM.
FROM A PHOTOGRAPH.

forced marches. Taking advantage of a rich country, Sherman recuperated his men and moved slowly back to the Chattahoochee. Now, with the full consent of Grant, he hastened his preparations for his grand march to the sea.

I was with him, he caught a faint glimpse of the tell-tale flag through an embrasure, and after much time he made out these letters: 'C,' 'R,' 'S,' 'E,' 'H,' 'E,' 'R,' and translated the message, 'Corse is here.' It was a source of great relief, for it gave me the first assurance that General Corse had received his orders, and that the place was adequately garrisoned. I watched with painful suspense the indications of the battle raging there, and was dreadfully impatient at the slow progress of the relieving column, whose advance was marked by the smokes which were made according to orders, but about 2 P. M. I noticed with satisfaction that the smoke of battle about Allatoona grew less and less, and ceased altogether about 4 P. M. For a time I attributed this result to the effect of General Cox's march, but later in the afternoon the signal-flag announced the welcome tidings that the attack had been fairly repulsed, but that General Corse was wounded. The next day my aide, Colonel Dayton, received this characteristic dispatch:

"'ALLATOONA, GEORGIA, October 6th, 1864, 2 P. M.
"'CAPTAIN L. M. DAYTON, Aide-de-Camp:
"'I am short a cheek-bone and an ear, but am able to whip all h——l yet! My losses are very heavy. A force moving from Stilesboro' to Kingston gives me some anxiety. Tell me where Sherman is.   JOHN M. CORSE, Brigadier-General.'

"Inasmuch as the enemy had retreated south-west, and would probably next appear at Rome, I answered

General Corse with orders to get back to Rome with his troops as quickly as possible. . . .

"I esteemed this defense of Allatoona so handsome and important that I made it the subject of a general order, viz., No. 86, of October 7th, 1864:

"'The general commanding avails himself of the opportunity, in the handsome defense made at Allatoona, to illustrate the most important principle in war, that fortified posts should be defended to the last, regardless of the relative numbers of the party attacking and attacked. . . . The thanks of this army are due and are hereby accorded to General Corse, Colonel Tourtellotte, Colonel Rowett, officers, and men, for their determined and gallant defense of Allatoona, and it is made an example to illustrate the importance of preparing in time, and meeting the danger, when present, boldly, manfully, and well.

"'Commanders and garrisons of the posts along our railroad are hereby instructed that they must hold their posts to the last minute, sure that the time gained is valuable and necessary to their comrades at the front. By order of
"'MAJOR-GENERAL W. T. SHERMAN.
"'L. M. DAYTON, Aide-de-camp.'" EDITORS.

⚓ Hood had partly invested Resaca, and on the 12th of October he demanded the unconditional surrender of the garrison, which the commander, Colonel Wever, refused, saying, "In my opinion I can hold the post. If you want it, come and take it."—EDITORS.

HOOD'S SECOND SORTIE AT ATLANTA.

BY W. H. CHAMBERLIN, MAJOR, 81ST OHIO VOLUNTEERS.

GENERAL Sherman's line lay east and northeast of Atlanta, with McPherson's Army of the Tennessee forming the extreme left, and extending some distance south of the Augusta railroad. General Logan's Fifteenth Corps, which joined the left of the Army of the Ohio, extended across the Augusta railroad, and General Blair's Seventeenth Corps extended the line southward, touching the McDonough road beyond what is now McPherson Avenue. The Sixteenth Corps, commanded by General Grenville M. Dodge, had been in reserve in rear of the Fifteenth Corps, north of the railroad, until July 21st, when General Fuller's division was placed in the rear of the center of the Seventeenth Corps. On the morning of July 22d a movement was begun, which afterward proved to have been the most fortunate for the Union army that could have been ordered, even if the intention of the enemy had been known to us. It was to place the remainder of General Dodge's corps — General Sweeny's division — upon the left of the Seventeenth Corps. General Sweeny's division moved south of the railroad and halted, some time before noon, in open ground, sloping down toward a little stream, in the rear of General Fuller's division, which was in bivouac near the edge of a wood. Here, then, in the rear of the Seventeenth Corps, lay the two divisions of General Dodge's corps, as if in waiting for the approach of General Hardee's troops who had been marching nearly all night around Blair's left flank, and were even then making painfully slow progress, moving in line of battle through the thickets and obstructions that opposed their march. Our troops were really in waiting for the order to go to their new position. General Dodge had been out on the left of General Blair's corps to select a place for his troops, and had succeeded in drawing a shell or two from the enemy's nearest earth-work. He had returned to General Fuller's headquarters, and had accepted that officer's invitation to a noonday lunch with him. In a few minutes his command would have been in motion for the front. If that had happened, and his corps had vacated the space it then held, there would have been absolutely nothing but the hospital tents and the wagon trains to stop Hardee's command from falling unheralded directly upon the rear of the Fifteenth and Seventeenth corps in line. Upon what a slight chance, then, hung the fate of Sherman's army that day, for though such a catastrophe as this might not have wrought entire destruction, it is plain it would have put an entirely different phase on the battle.

Just here is a point upon which most of the accounts of the battle are wrong. They represent Dodge's corps to have been in motion. Fuller had bivouacked there the previous night. Sweeny's command, while technically in motion, had been halted, awaiting orders.

Just as General Dodge was about to dismount to accept General Fuller's hospitality, he heard firing in a south-easterly direction, to the rear of General Sweeny's division. He took no lunch. He was an intensely active, almost nervously restless, officer. He saw in an instant that something serious was at hand. He gave General Fuller orders to form his division immediately, facing south-eastwardly, and galloped off toward Sweeny's division. He had hardly reached that command when Hardee's lines came tearing wildly through the woods with the yells of demons. As if by magic, Sweeny's division sprang into line. The two batteries of artillery (Loomis's and Laird's) had stopped on commanding ground, and they were promptly in service. General Dodge's quick eye saw the proper disposition to be made of a portion of Colonel Mersy's brigade, and, cutting red tape, he delivered his orders direct to the colonels of the regiments. The orders were executed instantly, and the enemy's advance was checked. This act afterward caused trouble. General Dodge was not a West Point graduate, and did not revere so highly the army regulations as did General Sweeny, who had learned them as a cadet. Sweeny was much hurt by General Dodge's action in giving orders direct to regimental commanders, and pursued the matter so far as to bring on a personal encounter a few days after the battle, in which he came near losing his life at the hands of a hot-tempered officer. He was placed in arrest. The court-martial, however, did not consider his case until nearly the end of the war, when he was acquitted.

The battle of General Dodge's corps on this open ground, with no works to protect the troops of either side, was one of the fiercest of the war. General Dodge's troops were inspired by his courageous personal presence, for he rode directly along the lines, and must have been a conspicuous target for many a Confederate gun. His sturdy saddle-horse was worn out early in the afternoon, and was replaced by another. There was not a soldier who did not feel that he ought to equal his general in courage, and no fight of the war exhibited greater personal bravery on the part of an entire command than was shown here. Nor can I restrain a tribute to the bravery of the enemy. We had an advantage in artillery; they in numbers. Their assaults were repulsed, only to be fearlessly renewed, until the sight of dead and wounded lying in their way, as they charged again and again to break our lines, must have appalled the stoutest hearts. So persistent were their onslaughts that numbers were made prisoners by rushing directly into our lines.

When General Dodge rode from General Fuller's lunch toward the sound of the firing I rode with him. The first order he gave me was to return to General Fuller and direct him to close up his line on General Sweeny's right. Returning as soon as I could after delivering this order, I met General Dodge riding at full speed. As soon as he got

THE BATTLE OF ATLANTA, JULY 22. FROM THE PAINTING BY JAMES E. TAYLOR.

Fuller's division (of the Sixteenth Corps) rallying to hold their ground after being forced back by the first charge of the Confederates in their flank attack.

within hearing distance he called out to me, "Go at once to General McPherson, on Blair's left, and tell him I need troops to cover my left. The enemy is flanking us." Wheeling my horse, I started back. As I went, the attack on Dodge's corps was in full force. Out in open ground, in full view as it was, I could not resist checking my horse for a moment to see the grand conflict. I remember yet how the sight of our banners advancing amid the smoke thrilled me as it gave them a new beauty, and the sound of our artillery, though it meant death to the foe, fell upon our ears as the assurance of safety to us and to our flag.

General McPherson, from a point farther on, had witnessed the same scene. Lieutenant-Colonel W. E. Strong, his chief-of-staff, and the only staff-officer with him at that time, thus describes what they then saw:

"The enemy, massed in columns three or four lines deep, moved out of the dense timber several hundred yards from Dodge's position, and, after gaining fairly the open fields, halted and opened fire rapidly on the Sixteenth Corps. They, however, seemed surprised to find our infantry in line of battle prepared for attack, and, after facing for a few minutes the destructive fire from the divisions of Generals Fuller and Sweeny, fell back in disorder to the cover of the woods. Here, however, their lines were quickly re-formed, and they again advanced, evidently determined to carry

the position. The scene at this time was grand and impressive. It seemed to us that every mounted officer of the attacking column was riding at the front or at the right or left of the first line of battle. The regimental colors waved and fluttered in advance of the lines, and not a shot was fired by the rebel infantry, although their movement was covered by a heavy and well-directed fire of artillery which was posted in the woods and on higher ground, and which enabled the guns to bear upon our troops with solid shot and shell by firing over the attacking column. It seemed impossible, however, for the enemy to face the sweeping, deadly fire from Fuller's and Sweeny's divisions, and the guns of Laird's 14th Ohio and Welker's batteries fairly mowed great swaths in the advancing columns. They showed great steadiness, and closed up the gaps and preserved their alignments; but the iron and leaden hail that was poured upon them was too much for flesh and blood to stand, and before reaching the center of the open fields the columns were broken and thrown into great confusion. Taking advantage of this, a portion of Fuller's and Sweeny's divisions, with bayonets fixed, charged the enemy and drove them back to the woods, taking many prisoners. The 81st Ohio (Colonel Adams) charged first, then the 39th Ohio (Colonel McDowell) and the 27th Ohio (Colonel Churchill). General McPherson's admiration

BATTLE OF ATLANTA, JULY 22—RECAPTURE FROM THE CONFEDERATES OF DE GRESS'S BATTERY. I.

The view is west toward Atlanta; the Confederates in capturing the battery charged along the Georgia railroad from the rolling-mill [see map, p. 312], and took advantage of the cover of the railroad embankment and cut.

for the steadiness and determined bravery of the Sixteenth Corps was unbounded."

While I was riding to find General McPherson, he had just taken his eyes from the view of this splendid victory described by Colonel Strong, and had started ahead of me in the direction of Blair's left. Of course I did not find him. In a very few minutes after leaving Colonel Strong the brave general was dead, while I, following, was forced to deflect to the right, and reached our line at Giles A. Smith's division, at the point known then as Bald Hill. While in the act of asking there for a brigade for General Dodge's left, I heard a terrific yelling toward the left and rear, and, looking around, I saw a full Confederate line rushing out of the dense timber within easy hailing distance. I perceived at once that no brigade could be spared from that position for General Dodge. General Smith's troops quickly jumped to the other side of their works, prepared to meet this rear attack. The mounted officers, myself included, found some difficulty in getting their horses over the works before the firing began. I then rode to General Harrow's division, next on the right, but he had no reserve troops to spare. Proceeding to General Morgan L. Smith's division, I met General John A. Logan, commander of the Fifteenth Corps, and he directed General Smith to weaken

his front line by sending Martin's brigade to General Dodge's left.

Perhaps no better disposition of General Dodge's corps could have been made, if the intentions of General Hood had been known. But so much cannot be said of the position of General Blair's left. It has not escaped attention that Hood's ability to throw Hardee's corps into the position where it struck General Dodge that noonday, was aided materially by the fact that General Sherman's usual cavalry flanking pickets were wanting. The cavalry had nearly all been sent to break railroads in Hood's rear. Nor does it appear that General Blair's infantry outposts were far enough advanced to give timely warning of the approach of an enemy.

I happened to be with General Logan when he received the order to take command of the Army of the Tennessee in place of General McPherson. I shall not easily forget the ride I had with him as he made his way to the point of danger, the left. Although whizzing balls sped about our ears as we entered the open ground near Dodge's position, and shells now and then exploded overhead, General Logan moved on the most direct line, and with no delay, to General Dodge's headquarters. He heard, in a few terse sentences from General Dodge, how affairs stood there. Dodge's battle at

BATTLE OF ATLANTA, JULY 22—RECAPTURE FROM THE CONFEDERATES OF DE GRESS'S BATTERY. II.

This picture, in two parts, is a reproduction from the Panorama of the Battle of Atlanta.

that time was about won, and his command, after the enemy had spent its force in unsuccessful assaults, intrenched quickly, almost on the battle-line. Both General Fuller's and General Sweeny's divisions had captured battle-flags and prisoners. A part of General Fuller's command had changed front under fire with conspicuous bravery and steadiness, General Fuller having himself planted the colors of the 27th Ohio, to indicate the new line. Among the regiments engaged were the 27th, 39th, 43d, and 81st Ohio; the 7th, 9th, 12th, 50th, 52d, 57th, 64th, and 66th Illinois, and the 2d Iowa. The brigade (Martin's) from the Fifteenth Corps did not take part in the action, and was subsequently sent farther to the rear to assist in the defense of Decatur.

What may be considered a separate action, although intended by Hood to be simultaneous, was the attack on the Fifteenth Corps, one division of which (General Morgan L. Smith's) was driven from its line. This took place about 3 o'clock, after the Sixteenth Corps' fighting was mainly over. It was a part of the attack from the Atlanta defenses made by Hood on both the Seventeenth and Fifteenth corps.

When General Logan assumed command of the Army of the Tennessee he placed General Morgan L. Smith in command of the Fifteenth Corps, and General Lightburn succeeded to the command of

Smith's division. This all happened just before Hood's attack on the Fifteenth Corps. The line had been weakened as before indicated, and the enemy succeeding in pushing a column through a cut in the Augusta railroad line, and driving back a portion of General Lightburn's troops and flanking the rest, the whole division, to use the language of General Lightburn's official report, "broke in confusion to the rear." This left in the enemy's hands sections of an Illinois battery (A, 1st Artillery) stationed near the railroad, and also De Gress's famous battery of four 20-pounder Parrotts, placed on the right of this division. General Lightburn's report is very brief. He simply says he checked the retreat of his division at the line occupied by his troops on the morning of that day, re-formed, and, with the assistance of General Woods's division and one brigade of the Sixteenth Corps, commanded by Colonel Mersy, recaptured all the guns of Battery H, 1st Illinois (De Gress's), and two of Battery A. He had but six regiments in line when his division was driven back.

General Logan, in his report of the Army of the Tennessee, says that when he heard of the repulse of the Fifteenth Corps' division, he ordered Colonel Martin's brigade back to its position, and adds:

"I also ordered General Dodge to send a brigade of the Sixteenth Corps to the assistance of the right of our line. . . . The second brigade of the Second Division,

Sixteenth Corps, Colonel Mersy commanding, moved promptly out, and I conducted it to the rear of the old works of the Second Division of the Fifteenth Corps, where it deployed on the right of the railroad."

After detailing his orders to General Smith, and the disposition of troops by General Woods on the right, he continues:

"At the same time the Second Division, followed by Colonel Mersy's brigade, advanced upon the enemy's front. The movement was successful. Woods's division striking the enemy's flank, it began to break, and soon after, the Second Division charging his front, the old line of works, De Gress's battery, and two guns of Battery 'A' were recaptured."

Colonel Wells S. Jones, who succeeded to the command of Lightburn's brigade, after telling in his official report of the repulse of his brigade, says:

"It re-formed in a few minutes back at the works we had advanced from in the morning, and, supported by a brigade of the Sixteenth Corps, charged upon and drove the enemy from our works, turning our recaptured artillery upon the retreating enemy."

General C. R. Woods, who commanded the First Division, posted on the right of the Second, says in his official report:

"About 3 P. M. the rebels made a determined attack in heavy force upon the lines to my left, and, after having been several times repulsed, succeeded in breaking those lines and occupying the pits, which gave them a position three or four hundred yards to my rear and left. Finding my position untenable, I threw my left back, and formed a new line, facing the enemy's flank. At the same time I kept up a heavy artillery fire on the enemy, preventing them from taking off De Gress's battery of four 20-pounder Parrotts, of which they had possession. Shortly after having taken my new position I received a verbal order from General M. L. Smith, commanding Fifteenth Army Corps, to attack the enemy in flank and rear, while other troops moved up in front to retake the position. I immediately moved the Second Brigade forward to strike the enemy's flank and rear, and the First Brigade to attack them from front and flank. The movement proved successful, and in less than fifteen minutes I had retaken De Gress's battery and driven the enemy from their rifle-pits on their left as far as the railroad."

I was so well aware, at the time of the battle, that it was Colonel Mersy's brigade of General Sweeny's division of the Sixteenth Corps that retook De Gress's battery that I was astonished, years afterward, in reading accounts of the battle, to find that the honor was assigned to others. General Lightburn and Colonel Wells S. Jones, in their reports, mention the Sixteenth Corps' brigade, but do not specify the part it took, farther than to say it supported their troops; while General Woods makes no mention of it whatever. General Logan was evidently guided in his report by that of General Woods. To one not familiar with the numberless duties of an officer in General Logan's position at that time, it seems incredible that he should overlook the part taken by this

brigade, for he asked General Dodge in person for "the little Dutchman's brigade," meaning Colonel Mersy's brigade, and in person he rode at its head down the railroad until within range of the enemy, and then he gave Colonel Mersy orders to form his line along a board fence at right angles with the railroad, and in coöperation with General Woods to charge the enemy's line. He then left the brigade.|

Colonel Mersy had just given the order to leave the railroad, as directed, when a volley from the enemy struck the brigade, killing the colonel's horse and wounding him. He turned over the command to Colonel (afterward Brevet Brigadier-General) R. N. Adams, commanding the 81st Ohio, who had heard the instructions given by General Logan. The brigade was thrown into some confusion in leaving the railroad under a galling fire, but it quickly formed along the board fence, with its left resting on the railroad. Let me tell the remainder of the story in Colonel Adams's own words:

"I at once gave the command, 'Forward!' The brigade crossed the fence, and at 'trail arms' advanced under a moderate fire toward the line to be taken. On emerging from the ravine, and beginning the ascent of the hill, the enemy opened anew upon us, whereupon I gave the order, 'Charge!' and in apparently less than half a minute the line was ours. We captured some of the men who were manning the De Gress guns, and about fifty men in the works, who fired until they were captured. Among these was the only colored man I saw during the war shooting the wrong way. He was game; he fired till he was taken. *I detailed men at once to man the recovered guns,* but found them partly disabled. I am not sure, but it is my impression, that this detail succeeded in discharging one of the pieces. At any rate, they were endeavoring to use them when Captain De Gress and some of his men came and took charge of the recovered guns.

"Simultaneous with our action was that of General Charles Woods (I think it was), who charged the enemy on our right. It would not be fair to say that we could have succeeded without Woods's coöperation; nor is it fair for them to say that they could have succeeded without ours. Certain it is, we charged that line with the enemy in it, and that we recaptured the lost guns and had them in our possession some time before the men of any other command saw them, or before Captain De Gress himself came and took charge of them."

In another letter, General Adams, in answer to specific inquiries, says that his line, at the beginning of this movement, rested its left on the railroad; but during the movement it left a space between its left and the railroad, owing to the slight divergence of the road. No other troops advanced before, with, or behind his line over the

---

| Brevet Lieutenant-Colonel Edward Jones, of General Dodge's staff, writes to the editors that, by direction of General Dodge, he conducted General August Mersy's brigade to the scene of the charge. "After a rapid march of perhaps a mile," he says, "Mersy, at a run, deployed his brigade, charged and recaptured De Gress's battery and the line of works, having his horse

killed under him in the assault. The Fifteenth Corps men, who were present, joined Mersy, and were with him in the action; but the brigade (Mersy's) of the Sixteenth Corps led, and, if my memory does not fail me, Captain William S. Boyd, of the 66th Illinois, damaged one of the recaptured guns by attempting to discharge it upon the retreating enemy."—EDITORS.

space covered by his brigade. He does not speak of any simultaneous movement on his left. ⚓

No doubt the peculiar circumstances mentioned already, of the change in commanders of General Morgan L. Smith's division, gave rise to misleading accounts concerning the recovery of this battery. Shortly after the line was retaken, General Lightburn's troops relieved Mersy's brigade, and it marched back to its own division.

It should be remembered, in placing an estimate upon what was accomplished by these troops, that they had borne a part in an open field, at midday, under a scorching sun, in one of the fiercest fights of the war, and had afterward performed their share of the heavy work of throwing up intrenchments. They were still engaged at this when ordered to follow General Logan. The movement, under his leadership, was made at "double-quick" over the greater portion of the distance, which was more than a mile. There is not a man in that brigade who could be repaid by the pensions of a lifetime for the work of that single day and its attendant risks, nor could the country pay in pensions to the whole brigade, at the highest rates, for the actual value of its services rendered that day.

But I have not yet told the whole story of the service of General Dodge's command that day. When night fell, the Confederate line was intrenched almost within a stone's-throw of what was then called Bald Hill. That was a position which had been stubbornly fought for almost since General Leggett captured it, July 21st. It was the key to the situation, and was the point where an attack by Hood's forces was most likely to fall. General Leggett that night pleaded most earnestly to have his command relieved from duty at Bald Hill. His men, he said, were physically exhausted. They had been under almost constant fire for two days in such circumscribed limits that they were practically imprisoned in the trenches. General Logan answered that the entire army was worn — the Fifteenth Corps had been weakened, and had no reserves from which relief could be drawn; the Seventeenth Corps had been crushed, and was needed where it was. But General Leggett insisted that his men must be relieved; that it would be unwise to trust such an important

point in the hands of men in such a condition as his command was; and General Dodge was ordered to send a brigade to Bald Hill. It was long after nightfall when he designated Colonel Mersy's brigade, and for the third time that day these men were called to go into action. They went promptly, and though the assignment meant fighting and working on intrenchments during the remainder of the night, they did both so well that no serious night attack was made, and when morning came an attack would have been well-nigh hopeless, for Bald Hill was almost a Gibraltar. Its fortification was unique, and though engineered by the men who wielded the shovel, it was complete and invulnerable. General Hood's shattered forces, however, had spent their energies in that direction on the 22d, and no assaults were made on our lines on the 23d.

Colonel Mersy's term of service had expired shortly before this battle, but he had volunteered to lead his brigade while awaiting transportation. General Dodge gave him a letter of farewell, in which, speaking of his services on the 22d of July, he said:

"You leave at a time and under circumstances of which you and your command may justly be proud. Fighting as you did on three different fields the same day, and victorious on every one, forms the best and most honorable reward that you can take with you."

So far very little has been said of the action of the Seventeenth Corps. These troops occupied the line from Bald Hill to the McDonough road, and were attacked in flank, front, and rear, though in the inverse order. The first attack was from the rear, then upon the flank, and at last from the front. Their line was bent back at right angles, hinging at Bald Hill, and the wonder is that larger numbers were not captured. They fought with most heroic determination at close quarters. The next day I remember seeing Colonel Wm. W. Belknap of the 15th Iowa (afterward Brigadier-General and Secretary of War). He was a brawny, red-bearded giant in appearance, and it was told of him that he had captured a number of prisoners by pulling them over the breastworks by main force, so closely were the lines engaged.

⚓ Lieutenants Thomas H. Imes and William Pitman, and privates John Quigley and William E. McCreary, of the 81st Ohio (Mersy's brigade), have written me in corroboration of General Adams. Captain Edward Jonas, of General Dodge's staff, has written to the same effect in a letter which I have read.— W. H. C.

THE GEORGIA MILITIA ABOUT ATLANTA.

BY GUSTAVUS W. SMITH, MAJOR-GENERAL, C. S. A.

ABOUT the time that General Johnston crossed to the south of the Etowah, Governor Joseph E. Brown ordered the militia and the civil officers of the State of Georgia to assemble at Atlanta. These two classes of State officers were, by act of the Confederate Congress, exempt from conscription. Governor Brown's order was promptly obeyed, and these officers — about three thousand in number — were organized into companies, regiments, and two brigades, under the personal supervision of the Governor, by Major-General H. C. Wayne, Adjutant-General of the State. They were required to elect their own officers; and those not chosen had to take their places temporarily in the ranks. They were informed that if they were not willing to accede to this ruling, they would be deprived of their regular commissions in the State service and sent to the Confederate conscript camp. This action of Governor Brown gives a clear indication of the intense strain to which the States and the general government of the Confederacy were then being subjected. It will be seen later, that when General Johnston's army approached still closer to Atlanta, Governor Brown called into active service the old men of the State up to the age of fifty-five, and the boys down to sixteen years, armed in great part with flint-lock muskets, ordinary rifles, and shot-guns, and ordered them to report to me for service in the field.

Immediately after the two classes of State officers were organized, the Governor tendered their services to General Johnston, reserving the right, however, to withdraw them from the Confederate service whenever the interests of the State should require it. Their services were accepted on these terms, and General Wayne was ordered to report to General Johnston. The latter directed the larger portion of General Wayne's command to guard the crossings of the Chattahoochee River from Roswell to West Point, the distance being nearly one hundred miles. About one thousand men were left in camp of instruction near Atlanta.

A short time after, in order that General Wayne might resume his duties as Adjutant-General of the State, much to my surprise the troops elected me to command them in the field. At that time I was busily engaged in Macon, preparing for the manufacture of iron, the iron-works at Etowah, in north Georgia, under my charge, having been destroyed by General Sherman's army a few weeks before.

I took command of the Georgia militia on the 1st of June, and began to prepare them for the field. About the middle of June General Mansfield Lovell came from Marietta to explain to me the condition of affairs near that place and General Johnston's views in reference to the special service it was proposed should be performed by that portion of my command which was in camp of instruction. It seemed that whilst Johnston's army was strongly intrenched and capable of resisting direct attack, his lines were already so extended that no troops could safely be taken from the trenches to support the cavalry on the flanks. But it was believed by General Johnston that if the small cavalry force on his left could be supported by the militia, the extension of Sherman's army on that side might be checked, and the Confederates could permanently hold position near Marietta. I told General Lovell that I did not believe the small available force of raw militia, acting as a support to the cavalry, could stop Sherman's advance if he chose to move in force around Johnston's left flank; but if I received a positive order from General Johnston to move across the Chattahoochee for the purpose indicated, the order would be obeyed to the best of my ability, without regard to my opinion of the matter. In giving that order, General Lovell, in the name of General Johnston, directed me not to allow my command to become closely engaged with superior numbers.

Fortunately for this small body of militia, there was then in Atlanta a Confederate battery of light pieces, commanded by Captain R. W. Anderson. That battery had just been refitted for field service, and was awaiting orders to return to the front.

Without other authority than my own, but with the full consent of the officers and men, I took this battery with the militia when we crossed the Chattahoochee at James's Ferry, and assumed position in the open country, within close supporting distance of our small force of cavalry, five or six miles from the left of General Johnston's intrenched position.

We played "brag" with the Federals in the open country, on that side, for eight or ten days, giving way a little when they pressed, but still holding position well out until they advanced in earnest on the 3d of July, when it became apparent that they were moving close on us in large force. Against this advance our cavalry could do but little more than "get out of the way."

For a short time thereafter the "supporting force" was at a great disadvantage, but it was withdrawn in good order, and the line of cavalry pickets was again formed between the militia and the advancing Federal columns.

On the 4th, being farther pressed, the whole force was moved back to the crest of Nickajack ridge, about three miles north of Turner's Ferry. At the point where the road from that ferry crosses the ridge an embrasure battery for artillery had been previously constructed, and short lines of trenches for infantry extended on each side, but not far enough to give cover to more than five hundred men. In a very short time after the troops were formed in this defensive position, the Federals, in large force, advanced against our front.

The situation of the militia on the afternoon of the 4th will be better understood by reference to the movements that had been previously made in other portions of the theater of operations. July 1st, General Sherman reported to General Halleck: "Schofield is now south of Olley's Creek. . . . To-morrow night I propose to move McPherson from the left to the extreme right. . . . The movement is substantially . . . straight for Atlanta." One of McPherson's divisions moved on the 2d, the rest of his army followed that night, and on the 4th the armies of Schofield and McPherson were concentrated in front of the militia, four or five miles west and a little south of the position then occupied by General Johnston's army strongly intrenched at Smyrna Station, six or eight miles south of Marietta.

The affair at Smyrna Station, that day, is reported by General Sherman as follows:

"We celebrate our 4th of July by a noisy but not desperate battle, to hold the enemy there till Generals McPherson and Schofield can get well into position below him, near the Chattahoochee crossings."

When I took up a defensive position on the crest of Nickajack ridge I did not know that the armies of McPherson and Schofield were in my immediate front, but it was evident that the Federal forces pressing upon the militia were in large numbers, and if they passed us they would be within easy reach of the then unoccupied strong Confederate fortifications on the north bank of the Chattahoochee River. These works had been constructed some time before, under the supervision of an officer of General Johnston's staff, for the protection of the crossings of the Chattahoochee, including Turner's Ferry and the railroad bridge.

I understood the situation well enough to feel certain that the Federal forces in front of the militia should be held back if possible, and not permitted to reach the unoccupied works on the banks of the Chattahoochee whilst General Johnston's army remained at Smyrna Station. In making a stand on the crest of Nickajack ridge I intended to hold the position without regard to becoming closely engaged with superior numbers, and was determined to sacrifice the command, if necessary, in an earnest effort to prevent the Federals from crossing the ridge that afternoon.

Our position was strong against attack in front; but it could have been easily turned on either flank. About the middle of the afternoon the Federals approached our front, and, under cover of sharp firing of a strong skirmish-line, they made dispositions to attack in force. The firing soon became very heavy and continued so until night. No attempt was made to carry the position by assault, but they approached within good musket range, where they were held in check, principally, no doubt, by the very effective fire of Captain Anderson's battery. No effort was made against either of our flanks.

A little after nightfall I wrote to General Johnston, informed him of what had occurred, and stated that the enemy were in very large numbers and would, in all probability, attack again at daylight in such strength that my small force could not hold them back for more than a very short time. But, so long as he held his army at Smyrna Station, I should continue to resist the farther advance of the Federals, unless I received an order from him to withdraw.

Before that note was dispatched, General W. H. Jackson, the commander of the cavalry that I was supporting, and General Toombs, chief of my staff, joined me. At their earnest request I modified the note I had just written by adding: I would retire at daylight if I did not get orders during the night to hold the position as long as possible. At 1 A. M., July 5th, in reply, I received an order from General Johnston to withdraw my command at the dawn of day. When we arrived at the works on the north bank of the Chattahoochee we found them occupied by General Johnston's army.

I suppose that previously to the receipt of my note he must have known that the armies of McPherson and Schofield were on the left flank and rear of his intrenched position at Smyrna Station. Be that as it may, he withdrew his army to the works on the Chattahoochee before we retired from the crest of Nickajack ridge. The militia were proud of their début beyond the Chattahoochee; elated by the successful resistance they had made during the afternoon of July 4th; rather dissatisfied because of their being withdrawn at daylight on the 5th; but were reconciled to this when they found the main Confederate army had preceded them to the Chattahoochee.

In reference to these operations General Johnston says :|

"In the evening [July 4th] Major-General Smith reported that the Federal cavalry was pressing on him in such force that he would be compelled to abandon the ground he had been holding, and retire before morning to General Shoup's line of redoubts. As the position in question covered a very important route to Atlanta, and was nearer than the main body of our army to that place, the necessity of abandoning it involved the taking a new line. The three corps were accordingly brought to the intrenched position just prepared by General Shoup."

This "contribution of materials for the use of the future historian of the war between the States " ⚓ requires amendment. I did not report to General Johnston that the Federal cavalry was pressing me in such force that I would be compelled to abandon the ground I had been holding and retire before morning. It is true that the position in question did cover a very important route to Atlanta, and was nearer than the main body of our army to that place; but that position was pressed by the armies of McPherson and Schofield, and I held them in check until daylight of July 5th, thus enabling General Johnston to withdraw his army quietly from Smyrna Station during the night, after Sherman had held him there all day "by a noisy but not desperate battle."

If McPherson and Schofield had wiped out the small militia force opposing them on the 4th, and occupied the strong Confederate works that covered the crossings of the Chattahoochee, General Johnston would have had no opportunity to excuse his falling back from Smyrna Station by claiming that I *reported the Federal cavalry* was pressing on me in such force that I would be compelled to *abandon the ground* I had been holding and retire *before morning*. General Johnston fell back from Smyrna Station to the strong works on the north bank of the Chattahoochee because his left flank was turned by the armies of McPherson and Schofield. A few days later he fell back to the south side of the Chattahoochee because his right flank was turned by the Federal army. And on the 17th of July the Confederate Government relieved him from the command of the army he had led from Dalton to the gates of Atlanta without engaging in a decisive battle.

When he relinquished command on the 18th McPherson's army was closely approaching the east side of Atlanta, on the railroad leading to Augusta. Of the four railroads centering in Atlanta, two were already in the hands of the Federals, and that leading to Macon was within easy striking distance of McPherson.

In his "Narrative"—speaking of what he would have done if he had not been relieved from command—General Johnston says:↓

"I expected an opportunity to engage the enemy on terms of advantage while they were divided in crossing Peach Tree Creek. . . . If unsuccessful, we had a safe place of refuge in our intrenched lines close at hand. Holding it we could certainly keep back the enemy . . . until the State troops promised by Governor Brown were assembled. Then I intended to man

---

| Johnston's "Narrative," p. 345.   ⚓ Johnston's "Narrative," dedication.   ↓ Johnston's "Narrative," p. 350.

the works of Atlanta on the side toward Peach Tree Creek with those troops, and leisurely fall back with the Confederate troops into the town, and, when the Federal army approached, march out with the three corps against one of its flanks. . . . If unsuccessful, the Confederate army had a near and secure place of refuge in Atlanta, which it could hold forever, and so win the campaign of which that place was the object. The passage of Peach Tree Creek may not have given an opportunity to attack; but there is no reason to think that the second and far most promising plan might not have been executed."

In addition to the above claim, that he could have held Atlanta "forever" if he had not been relieved of command, General Johnston now says: "I assert that had one of the other lieutenant-generals of the army (Hardee or Stewart) succeeded me Atlanta would have been held." It is not proposed to discuss this assertion, nor to refer to the claim made by General Johnston in his own behalf, farther than may be necessary to elucidate briefly its connection with the Georgia militia.

At the time General Johnston was relieved the militia numbered about two thousand effectives, and the "troops promised by Governor Brown" were just beginning to assemble. Atlanta was not strongly fortified, and the Federal army on the east side was at the very gates of the city. In about two weeks the old men and boys called out by Governor Brown had arrived in sufficient numbers to increase the effective militia force in the trenches to five thousand. At no time did it exceed that number.

If the fortifications of Atlanta had been "impregnable," as General Johnston asserts, this would have given no assurance of his ability to prevent Sherman from turning the position, cutting off its railroad communications, and thus making it untenable for an army. It had neither provisions nor ammunition to enable it to resist a siege.

Suppose that General Johnston had not been relieved, and General Sherman had suspended his turning operations for two weeks "until the State troops promised by Governor Brown were assembled," what guarantee could be given that five thousand militia could hold Atlanta, whilst General Johnston with his army "leisurely" fell back "into the town," marched out against one of the flanks of the Federal army, and was "unsuccessful"? The Georgia militia were good fighters, but in the case supposed I do not think they could have held Atlanta as "a secure place of refuge" for Johnston's army. But if the militia had held the place whilst the three corps were "unsuccessful" on the outside Atlanta was no "secure place of refuge" for an army that could not, by hard and successful fighting, prevent the position from being turned.

On the afternoon of the 18th of July General Johnston gave up the command of the army to his successor, General John B. Hood. It will be borne in mind that General Johnston "expected an opportunity to engage the enemy on terms of advantage while they were crossing Peach Tree Creek." On the 19th General Hood gave orders for two corps to take position ready to attack Thomas's army on Peach Tree Creek, whilst one corps

watched and guarded against the movements of the armies of McPherson and Schofield, closely approaching Atlanta on the east side. On the night of the 19th Hood gave orders to the two corps then in the neighborhood of Peach Tree Creek to attack Thomas's army in that position at 1 P. M. on the 20th. At the time named Thomas's army was engaged in crossing the creek. The armies of Schofield and McPherson were not within good supporting distance, and it is safe to say that if Hood's order for the attack at 1 P. M. had been promptly obeyed by the two corps Thomas would have met with serious disaster before the forces of Schofield or McPherson could have reached him. Owing to mismanagement of the leading corps the Confederate attack was delayed until 4 P. M., and was then made without proper concert of action. In the meantime the advance of McPherson's army on the east of Atlanta was so threatening that it became necessary late in the afternoon to detach a division of the leading corps on Peach Tree Creek and send it to hold McPherson in check. That division was sent off before it had been put in action against Thomas. The Confederate attack on the latter was repulsed.

If Hood's orders had been promptly obeyed, this attack would probably have resulted in a staggering blow to Sherman. But Thomas had safely crossed Peach Tree Creek, and was strongly established on its south side. Schofield was again in fair communication with Thomas, and McPherson was extending his fortifications south of the railroad leading to Augusta, thus threatening the railroad leading to Macon. The militia occupied the unfinished lines of Atlanta, south of the Augusta road, closely confronted by McPherson's fortifications.

General Hood deemed it necessary that McPherson should be held back from the railroad leading to Macon. And he hoped by attacking the rear of McPherson's fortified lines to bring on a general engagement that might result in the defeat of the Federal army. On the 21st he ordered one corps to fall back at dusk and move rapidly from Peach Tree Creek, through the eastern suburb of Atlanta, pass out to the south, around McPherson's extreme left, and attack the fortified lines of the latter from the direction of Decatur. When the Federals were thus assailed in rear an attack was to be made on their front by the Confederates from the Atlanta side.

The corps that turned McPherson's left moved slowly, the attack was not made until late in the morning of the 22d, and was not then directed against the rear of the Federal lines, because the turning corps had not moved far enough in the direction of Decatur before being sent into action. When that corps became engaged General Hood ordered the corps on my left to advance from its lines around Atlanta and attack the front of the Federals. Seeing this movement on my left, I formed the militia in line of battle in the trenches, and without waiting for orders moved my command over the parapet against a strong embrasure battery in McPherson's line about one mile in front of our works. That battery had greatly annoyed us by its fire whilst we were engaged in completing our unfinished intrenchments. Anderson's battery accompanied this movement and took position in open ground, supported by the militia on the right and left, within about four hundred yards of the Federal lines. The effective fire of the enemy in our immediate front was soon silenced, and my command strongly desired that orders should be given for them to assault the embrasure battery. I would not permit this to be done at that time, because the firing on my right had ceased soon after the militia moved out of the lines and the Confederate troops on my left had been driven back several hundred yards in rear of the position held by command. I considered it useless to make an isolated attack with the militia — about two thousand men. But they were retained in the position they first assumed, and I awaited developments. About two hours later came an order from Hood to withdraw my command to the trenches.

In a letter to Governor Brown, July 23d, 1864, General Hood says: "The State troops, under General G. W. Smith, fought with great gallantry yesterday."

After the battle of the 22d of July Sherman withdrew his left from its position threatening the railroad leading to Macon, and extended his right in the direction of the railroad leading to West Point. In the meantime he pressed his lines closer to the city on the north and west.

On the 28th of July Hood fought the battle of Ezra Church, a few miles west of Atlanta, in order to prevent Sherman from seizing the West Point railroad. From that time Sherman continued to extend his right. On the 31st of August he succeeded in cutting off all railroad communications with Atlanta, and that place was consequently evacuated by Hood on the 1st of September, after he had held Sherman closely at bay for seventy-five days. It will be noticed that Sherman had succeeded in forcing Johnston back from Dalton to Atlanta in a somewhat less length of time.

My report of September 15th, 1864, says:

"A few days after the affair of the 22d of July I was ordered again to Poplar Spring, ⸮ . . . but was scarcely established in camp before we had to be placed in the trenches on the left of the Marietta road, and from that time until the end of the siege we continued under close fire night and day. We had to move from one portion of the lines to another, and had our full share of all the hardest places. . . . The militia, although poorly armed, very few having proper equipments, more than two-thirds of them without cartridge-boxes, almost without ambulances or other transportation, most of the reserves ['State troops promised by Governor Brown'] never having been drilled at all, and the others but a few days, all performed well every service required of them during an arduous and dangerous campaign. They have been in service about one hundred days, during at least fifty of which they have been under close fire of the enemy mostly night and day. . . . They have done good and substantial service in the cause of their country, and have established the fact that Georgia is willing and able to do something effective in her own name, besides furnishing more than her quota to the Confederate armies proper. . . . There being a lull in active operations, the Governor has . . . [temporarily] withdrawn the Georgia militia from Confederate service, and furloughed them for thirty days."

In his report Hood says: "This force rendered excellent and gallant service during the siege of Atlanta."

When again called into active service a few weeks later, the Georgia militia, although still under Hood's orders, did not form a part of his active operating army. During his Tennessee campaign the militia remained in Georgia and opposed Sherman's army in its march to Savannah.

As commander of a brigade, division, and corps, Hood had proved himself an aggressive, bold, determined, and *careful* fighter, perhaps a shade too sanguine, and disposed to assume that subordinates would carry instructions into effect as fully as he would have done if in their place. His high reputation as a brigade and division commander was acquired in the Army of Northern Virginia. At Gettysburg he was crippled in one arm; he lost a leg close up to the hip-joint on the field of Chickamauga. From these causes he was not physically as active as he had been in the early years of the war; but he was an excellent horseman and could ride nearly as well as most men who have two legs and two arms. It may be assumed, however, that many of the "slips" made by his subordinates whilst he commanded the army might have been corrected by him if he had then been as much "at home on horseback" as he was before he was so badly maimed. As an army commander his orders were judicious and well-timed in the operations around Atlanta; but he was compelled to evacuate that place, and the cry arose, "Atlanta was *impregnable* and if General Johnston had not been superseded he would have held it forever."

The fall of Atlanta was discouraging to the Confederates in a degree that called for the utmost exertion on the part of the commander of that army to force the Federals to abandon that city, and, if possible, make them give up all the territory in north Georgia which had been yielded to them by General Johnston.

The backing, digging, and constant service in trenches, from Dalton to Atlanta, had very perceptibly injured the *morale* of the Confederate forces before General Johnston was relieved from command. The condition of that army had not been improved by the loss of Atlanta, and its practical efficiency was likely to be ruined if the policy of "backing and digging" was continued. Hood determined to move against the railroad over which Sherman, in Atlanta, drew all his supplies from Nashville, then invade Tennessee, transfer the theater of operations to that State, and perhaps to Kentucky and the Ohio River. He believed that a change from the defensive, in trenches, to the active offensive would reëstablish the *morale* of his army, present many chances of success, free north Georgia, and probably arrest the previous tide of Federal successes in the West.

It seemed to him that the passive policy — waiting for Sherman to manœuvre the Confederate army back from one position to another — would result in the perhaps slow but certain subjugation and occupation of all Georgia by the Federals, and the consequent probable downfall of the Confederacy.

⸮ Near the south-western suburb of Atlanta.

VIEW OF THE BATTLE OF PEACH TREE CREEK FROM GENERAL HOOKER'S POSITION. FROM A SKETCH MADE AT THE TIME.

THE DEFENSE OF ATLANTA. ⸗

BY JOHN B. HOOD, GENERAL, C. S. A.

ABOUT 11 o'clock on the night of the 17th of July, 1864, I received a telegram from the War Office directing me to assume command of the Army of Tennessee. It is difficult to imagine a commander placed at the head of an army under more embarrassing circumstances than those against which I was left to contend. I was comparatively a stranger to the Army of Tennessee. The troops of the Army of Tennessee had for such length of time been subjected to the ruinous policy pursued from Dalton to Atlanta that they were unfitted for united action in pitched battle. They had, in other words, been so long habituated to security behind breastworks that they had become wedded to the "timid defensive" policy, and naturally regarded with distrust a commander likely to initiate offensive operations.

The senior corps commander [Hardee] considered he had been supplanted through my promotion, and thereupon determined to resign. In consequence, I have no doubt, of my application to President Davis to postpone the order transferring to me the command of the army, he, however, altered his decision, and concluded to remain with his corps.

The evening of the 18th of July found General Johnston comfortably quartered at Macon, whilst McPherson's and Schofield's corps were tearing up the Georgia railroad between Stone Mountain and Decatur; Thomas's army was hastening preparations to cross Peach Tree Creek, within about six miles of Atlanta; and I was busily engaged in hunting up the positions of, and establishing communication with, Stewart's and Hardee's corps.

After having established communication with the corps and the cavalry of the army during the forepart of the night, I found myself upon the morning of the 19th in readiness to fulfill the grave duties devolving upon me.

Our troops had awakened in me heartfelt sympathy, as I had followed their military career with deep interest from early in May of that year. I had witnessed their splendid condition at that period; had welcomed with pride the fine body of reënforcements under General Polk; but, with disappointment, I had seen them, day after day, turn their back upon the enemy, and lastly cross the Chattahoochee River on the night of the 9th of July with one-third of their number lost—the men downcast, dispirited, and demoralized. Stragglers and deserters, the captured and killed, could not now, however, be replaced by recruits, because all the recruiting depots had been drained to reënforce either Lee or Johnston. I could, therefore, but make the best dispositions in my power with the reduced numbers of the army, which opposed a force of 106,000 Federals, buoyant with suc-

⸗ Taken by permission and condensed from General Hood's work, "Advance and Retreat," published by General G. T. Beauregard for the Hood Orphan Memorial Fund, New Orleans, 1880.— EDITORS.

cess and hope, and who were fully equal to 140,-000 such troops as confronted Johnston at Dalton, by reason of their victorious march of a hundred miles into the heart of the Confederacy.

Accordingly, on the night of the 18th and morning of the 19th I formed line of battle facing Peach Tree Creek [see map, p. 312]; the left rested near Pace's Ferry road, and the right covered Atlanta. I was informed on the 19th that Thomas was building bridges across Peach Tree Creek; that McPherson and Schofield were well over toward, and even on, the Georgia railroad, near Decatur. I perceived at once that the Federal commander had committed a serious blunder in separating his corps or armies by such distance as to allow me to concentrate the main body of our army upon his right wing, whilst his left was so far removed as to be incapable of rendering timely assistance. General Sherman's violation of the established maxim that an army should always be held well within hand, or its detachments within easy supporting distance, afforded one of the most favorable occasions for complete victory which could have been offered; especially as it presented an opportunity, after crushing his right wing, to throw our entire force upon his left. In fact, such a blunder affords a small army the best, if not the sole, chance of success when contending with a vastly superior force.

Line of battle having been formed, Stewart's corps was in position on the left, Hardee's in the center, and Cheatham's [formerly Hood's] on the right. Orders were given to Generals Hardee and Stewart to observe closely and report promptly the progress of Thomas in the construction of bridges across Peach Tree Creek and the passage of troops. General Cheatham was directed to reconnoiter in front of his left; to erect, upon that part of his line, batteries so disposed as to command the entire space between his left and Peach Tree Creek, in order to completely isolate McPherson's and Schofield's forces from those of Thomas; and, finally, to intrench his line thoroughly. This object accomplished, and Thomas having partially crossed the creek and made a lodgment on the east side within the pocket formed by Peach Tree Creek and the Chattahoochee River, I determined to attack him with two corps — Hardee's and Stewart's, which constituted the main body of the Confederate army — and thus, if possible, crush Sherman's right wing, as we drove it into the narrow space between the creek and the river.

Major-General G. W. Smith's Georgia State troops were posted on the right of Cheatham, and it was impossible for Schofield or McPherson to assist Thomas without recrossing Peach Tree Creek in the vicinity of Decatur, and making on the west side a détour which necessitated a march of not less than ten or twelve miles, in order to reach Thomas's bridges across this creek. I immediately assembled the three corps commanders, Hardee, Stewart, and Cheatham, together with Major-General G. W. Smith, commanding Georgia State troops, for the purpose of giving orders for battle on the following day, the 20th of July.

The three corps commanders, together with General G. W. Smith, were assembled not only for the purpose of issuing to them orders for battle, but with the special design to deliver most explicit instructions in regard to their respective duties. I sought to "make assurance doubly sure" by direct interrogatory; each was asked whether or not he understood his orders. All replied in the affirmative. I was very careful in this respect, inasmuch as I had learned from long experience that no measure is more important, upon the eve of battle, than to make certain, in the presence of the commanders, that each thoroughly comprehends his orders. The usual discretion allowed these officers in no manner diminishes the importance of this precaution.

I also deemed it of equal moment that each should fully appreciate the imperativeness of the orders then issued, by reason of the certainty that our troops would encounter hastily constructed works, thrown up by the Federal troops which had been foremost to cross Peach Tree Creek. Although a portion of the enemy would undoubtedly be found under cover of temporary breastworks, it was equally certain a larger portion would be caught in the act of throwing up such works, and in just the state of confusion to enable our forces to rout them by a bold and persistent attack. With these convictions, I timed the assault at 1 P. M., so as to surprise the enemy in their unsettled condition.

The charge was unfortunately not made till about 4 o'clock P. M., on account of General Hardee's failure to obey my specific instructions in regard to the extension of the one-half division front to the right, in order to afford General Cheatham an advantageous position to hold in check McPherson and Schofield. The result was not, however, materially affected by this delay, since the Federals were completely taken by surprise.

General Stewart carried out his instructions to the letter; he moreover appealed in person to his troops before going into action, and informed them that orders were imperative they should carry everything, at all hazards, on their side of Peach Tree Creek; he impressed upon them that they should not halt before temporary breastworks, but charge gallantly over every obstacle and rout the enemy. It was evident that, after long-continued use of intrenchments, General Stewart deemed a personal appeal to his soldiers expedient.

General Stewart and his troops nobly performed their duty in the engagement of the 20th. At the time of the attack his corps moved boldly forward, drove the enemy from his works, and held possession of them until driven out by an enfilade fire of batteries placed in position by General Thomas.

Unfortunately, the corps on Stewart's right, although composed of the best troops in the army, virtually accomplished nothing. In lieu of moving promptly, attacking as ordered, and supporting Stewart's gallant assault, the troops of Hardee — as their losses on that day indicate — did nothing more than skirmish with the enemy. Instead of charging down upon the foe as Sherman represents Stewart's men to have done, many of the troops, when they discovered that they had come into contact

LIEUTENANT-GENERAL ALEX. P. STEWART, C. S. A.
FROM A PHOTOGRAPH.

with breastworks, lay down, and, consequently, this attempt at pitched battle proved abortive.

The failure on the 20th rendered urgent the most active measures, in order to save Atlanta even for a short period. Through the vigilance of General Wheeler I received information, during the night of the 20th, of the exposed position of McPherson's left flank; it was standing out in air, near the Georgia railroad between Decatur and Atlanta, and a large number of the enemy's wagons had been parked in and around Decatur. The roads were in good condition, and ran in the direction to enable a large body of our army to march, under cover of darkness, around this exposed flank and attack in rear.

I determined to make all necessary preparations for a renewed assault; to attack the extreme left of the Federals in rear and flank, and endeavor to bring the entire Confederate army into united action.

Accordingly, Hardee's and Stewart's corps resumed their former positions. Colonel Presstman, chief engineer, was instructed to examine at once the partially completed line of works toward Peach Tree Creek, which General Johnston had ordered to be constructed for the defense of Atlanta, and to report, at the earliest moment, in regard to their fitness to be occupied by Stewart's and Cheatham's corps, together with the Georgia State troops, under General G. W. Smith. The report was re-

ceived early on the morning of the 21st, to the effect that the line established by Johnston was not only too close to the city and located upon too low ground, but was totally inadequate for the purpose designed; that Sherman's line, which extended from the vicinity of Decatur almost to the Dalton railroad, north of Atlanta, rendered necessary the construction of an entirely new line, and upon more elevated ground.

The chief engineer was thereupon directed to prepare and stake off a new line, and to employ his entire force, in order that the troops might occupy the works soon after dark on the night of the 21st, and have time to aid in strengthening their position before dawn of next morning. This task was soon executed through the skill and energy of Colonel Presstman and his assistants. Generals Stewart, Cheatham, and G. W. Smith were instructed to order their division and brigade commanders to examine before dark the ground to be occupied by their respective troops, so as to avoid confusion or delay at the time of the movement.

General Hardee, who commanded the largest corps, and whose troops were comparatively fresh, as they had taken but little part in the attack of the previous day, was ordered to hold his forces in readiness to move promptly at dark that night — the 21st. I selected Hardee for this duty, because Cheatham had, at that time, but little experience as a corps commander, and Stewart had been heavily engaged the day previous.

The position of the enemy during the 21st remained, I may say, unchanged, with the exception that Schofield and McPherson had advanced slightly toward Atlanta. To transfer after dark our entire line from the immediate presence of the enemy to another line around Atlanta, and to throw Hardee, the same night, entirely to the rear and flank of McPherson — as Jackson was thrown, in a similar movement, at Chancellorsville and Second Manassas — and to initiate the offensive at daylight, required no small effort upon the part of the men and officers. I hoped, however, that the assault would result not only in a general battle, but in a signal victory to our arms.

It was absolutely necessary these operations should be executed that same night, since a delay of even twenty-four hours would allow the enemy time to intrench further, and afford Sherman a chance to rectify, in a measure, his strange blunder in separating Thomas so far from Schofield and McPherson.

I well knew he would seek to retrieve his oversight at the earliest possible moment; therefore I determined to forestall his attempt and to make another effort to defeat the Federal army. No time was to be lost in taking advantage of this second unexpected opportunity to achieve victory and relieve Atlanta.

I was convinced that McPherson and Schofield intended to destroy not only the Georgia railroad, but likewise our main line of communication, the railroad to Macon. It is now evident the blow on the 20th checked the reckless manner of moving, which had so long been practiced by the enemy, without fear of molestation, during the Dalton-Atlanta campaign. The rap of warning received by Thomas, on Peach Tree Creek, must have induced the Federal commander to alter his plan.

Thus was situated the Federal army at the close of night, on the 21st: it was but partially intrenched; Schofield and McPherson were still separated from Thomas, and at such distance as to compel them to make a détour of about twelve miles, in order to reach the latter in time of need.

The Confederate army occupied the same position, at dark, as prior to the attack of the 20th. The new line around the city, however, had been chosen; each corps commander fully advised of the ground assigned to him, and the special duty devolving upon him; working parties had been detailed in advance from the corps of Stewart and Cheatham, and from the Georgia State troops; rations and ammunition had been issued, and Hardee's corps instructed to be in readiness to move at a moment's warning.

The demonstrations of the enemy upon our right, and which threatened to destroy the Macon railroad,—our main line for receiving supplies,—rendered it imperative that I should check, immediately, his operations in that direction; otherwise Atlanta was doomed to fall at a very early day. Although the attack of the 20th had caused Sherman to pause and reflect, I do not think he would have desisted extending his left toward our main line of communication had not the events occurred which I am about to narrate.

As already stated, every preparation had been carefully made during the day of the 21st. I had summoned, moreover, to my headquarters the three corps commanders, Hardee, Stewart, and Cheatham, together with Major-General Wheeler, commanding cavalry corps, and Major-General G. W. Smith, commanding Georgia State troops. The following minute instructions were given in the presence of all assembled, in order that each might understand not only his own duty, but likewise that of his brother corps commanders. By this means I hoped each officer would know what support to expect from his neighbor in the hour of battle.

Stewart, Cheatham, and G. W. Smith were ordered to occupy soon after dark the positions assigned them in the new line round the city, and to intrench as thoroughly as possible. General Shoup, chief-of-artillery, was ordered to mass artillery on our right. General Hardee was directed to put his corps in motion soon after dusk; to move south on the McDonough road, across Entrenchment Creek at Cobb's Mills, and *completely* to turn the left of McPherson's army and attack at daylight, or as soon thereafter as possible. He was furnished guides from Wheeler's cavalry, who were familiar with the various roads in that direction; was given clear and positive orders to

detach his corps, to swing away from the main body of the army, and to march entirely around and to the rear of McPherson's left flank, even if he was forced to go to or beyond Decatur, which is only about six miles from Atlanta.

Major-General Wheeler was ordered to move on Hardee's right with all the cavalry at his disposal, and to attack with Hardee at daylight. General Cheatham, who was in line of battle on the right and around the city, was instructed to take up the movement from his right as soon as Hardee succeeded in forcing back, or throwing into confusion,

MAJOR-GENERAL W. H. T. WALKER, C. S. A., KILLED NEAR ATLANTA, JULY 22, 1864. FROM A PHOTOGRAPH.

the Federal left, and to assist in driving the enemy down and back upon Peach Tree Creek, from right to left. General G. W. Smith would, thereupon, join in the attack. General Stewart, posted on the left, was instructed not only to occupy and keep a strict watch upon Thomas, in order to prevent him from giving aid to Schofield and McPherson, but to engage the enemy the instant the movement became general, *i. e.*, as soon as Hardee and Cheatham succeeded in driving the Federals down Peach Tree Creek and near his right.

Thus orders were given to attack from right to left, and to press the Federal army down and against the deep and muddy stream in their rear. These orders were carefully explained again and again, till each officer present gave assurance that he fully comprehended his duties.

At dawn on the morning of the 22d, Cheatham, Stewart, and G. W. Smith had, by alternating working parties during the night previous, not only strongly fortified their respective positions, but had kept their men comparatively fresh for action, and were in readiness to act as soon as the battle was initiated by Hardee, who was supposed to be at that moment in rear of the adversary's flank.

I took my position at daybreak near Cheatham's right, whence I could observe the left of the enemy's intrenchments, which seemed to be thrown back a short distance on their extreme left. After awaiting nearly the entire morning, I heard, about 10 or 11 o'clock, skirmishing going on directly opposite the left of the enemy, which was in front of Cheatham's right and Shoup's artillery. A considerable time had elapsed when I discovered, with astonishment and bitter disappointment, a line of battle composed of one of Hardee's divisions advancing directly against the intrenched flank of the enemy. I at once perceived that Hardee had not only failed to turn McPherson's left, according to positive orders, but had thrown his men against the enemy's breastworks, thereby occasioning unnecessary loss to us, and rendering doubtful the great result desired. In lieu of completely turning the Federal left and taking the intrenched line of

It had rested in his power to rout McPherson's army by simply moving a little further to the right, and attacking in rear and flank instead of assaulting an intrenched flank. I hoped, nevertheless, this blunder would be remedied, at least in part, by the extreme right of his line lapping round, during the attack, to the rear of McPherson.

I anxiously awaited tidings from the scene of action while listening attentively to what seemed a spirited engagement upon that part of the field. This sound proceeded from the guns of the gallant Wheeler, in the direction of

1. EFFECT OF THE UNION FIRE ON THE POTTER HOUSE, ATLANTA.
2. VIEW OF THE CONFEDERATE LINE AT THE POTTER HOUSE, LOOKING EASTWARD.
3. VIEW OF CONFEDERATE DEFENSES OF ATLANTA, LOOKING NORTH-EAST.
FROM WAR-TIME PHOTOGRAPHS.

Decatur, whence I hoped, momentarily, to hear a continuous roar of musketry, accompanied by the genuine Confederate shout from Hardee's entire corps, as it advanced and drove the enemy down Peach Tree Creek between our general line of battle and that formidable

the enemy in reverse, he attacked the retired wing of their flank, having his own left almost within gunshot of our main line around the city. I then began to fear that his disregard of the fixed rule in war, that one danger in rear is more to be feared than ten in front,—in other words, that one thousand men in rear are equal to ten thousand in front,—would cause us much embarrassment, and place his corps at great disadvantage, notwithstanding he had held success within easy grasp.

stream. Although the troops of Hardee fought, seemingly, with determination and spirit, there were indications that the desired end was not being accomplished. The roar of musketry occurring only at intervals strengthened this impression, and a staff-officer was dispatched to General Hardee to know the actual result.

During the early afternoon I received information that the attack had been, in part, successful, but had been checked in consequence of our troops

coming in contact with different lines of intrenchments, several of which they had carried and held.
Fearing a concentration of the enemy upon Hardee,
I commanded General Cheatham, about 3 P. M., to
move forward with his corps and attack the position in his front, so as to, at least, create a diversion. The order was promptly and well executed,
and our troops succeeded in taking possession of
the enemy's defenses in that part of the field.
A heavy enfilade fire, however, forced Cheatham
to abandon the works he had captured.

Major-General G. W. Smith, perceiving that
Cheatham had moved out on his left, and having
thoroughly comprehended all the orders relative
to the battle, moved gallantly forward with his
State troops in support of Cheatham's attack, but
was eventually forced to retire on account of superiority of numbers in his front.

Hardee bore off as trophies eight guns and thirteen stand of colors, and, having rectified his line,
remained in the presence of the enemy. Cheatham
captured five guns and five or six stand of colors.

Notwithstanding the non-fulfillment of the brilliant result anticipated, the partial success of that
day was productive of much benefit to the army.
It greatly improved the *morale* of the troops, in-
fused new life and fresh hopes, arrested desertions, which had hitherto been numerous, defeated
the movement of McPherson and Schofield upon
our communications in that direction, and demonstrated to the foe our determination to abandon
no more territory without at least a manful effort
to retain it.

It became apparent almost immediately after the
battle of the 22d that Sherman would make an attack upon our left, in order to destroy the Macon
railroad; and, from that moment, I may say, began the siege of Atlanta. The battles of the 20th
and 22d checked the enemy's reckless manner of
moving, and illustrated effectually to Sherman the
danger of stretching out his line in such a manner
as to form extensive gaps between his corps or
armies as he admits he did at Rocky Face Ridge
and New Hope Church.

On the 26th of July the Federals were reported
to be moving to our left. This movement continued during the 27th, when I received the additional information that their cavalry was turning
our right, in the direction of Flat Rock, with the
intention, as I supposed, of interrupting our main
line of communication, the Macon railroad. We
had lost the road to Augusta previous to the departure of General Johnston on the 18th, and, by
the 22d, thirty miles or more thereof had been
utterly destroyed.

The Federal commander continued to move by
his right flank to our left, his evident intention
being to destroy the only line by which we were
still able to receive supplies. The railroad to
West Point, because of its proximity to the Chattahoochee River, was within easy reach of the
enemy whenever he moved far enough to the right
to place his left flank upon the river. Therefore,
after the destruction of the Augusta road, the
holding of Atlanta — unless some favorable opportunity offered itself to defeat the Federals in

battle — depended upon our ability to hold intact
the road to Macon.

General Wheeler started on the 27th of July in
pursuit of the Federal cavalry which had moved
around our right; and General [W. H.] Jackson,
with the brigades of [Thomas] Harrison and [L.
S.] Ross, was ordered, the following day, to push
vigorously another body of the enemy's cavalry
which was reported to have crossed the river,
at Campbellton, and to be moving, via Fairburn,
in the direction of the Macon road. On the 28th
it was apparent that Sherman was also moving
in the same direction with his main body. Lieutenant-General S. D. Lee was instructed to move
out with his corps upon the Lick-Skillet road,
and to take the position most advantageous to
prevent or delay the extension of the enemy's
right flank. This officer promptly obeyed orders,
and in the afternoon, unexpectedly, came in contact with the Federals in the vicinity of Ezra
Church, where a spirited engagement ensued. The
enemy was already in possession of a portion of
the ground Lee desired to occupy, and the struggle
grew to such dimensions that I sent Lieutenant-
General Stewart to his support. The contest lasted
till near sunset without any material advantage
having been gained by either opponent. Our
troops failed to dislodge the enemy from their
position, and the Federals likewise to capture the
position occupied by the Confederates.

Whilst these operations were in progress, Wheeler
and Jackson were in hot pursuit of the Federal
cavalry; General Lewis's infantry brigade having
been sent to Jonesboro', the point about which I
supposed the raiders would strike our communications.

At an early hour on the 29th dispatches were
received from various points upon the Macon road
to the effect that General Wheeler had successfully checked the enemy at Latimer's, and was
quietly awaiting developments. On our left, the
Federals succeeded in eluding our cavalry, for a
time, by skirmishing with our main body, whilst
their main force moved round to the rear and cut
the telegraph lines at Fairburn and Palmetto.
General Jackson, however, soon discovered the
ruse, and marched rapidly toward Fayetteville and
Jonesboro', the direction in which the Federals
had moved. The enemy succeeded in destroying
a wagon-train at the former place, in capturing
one or two quartermasters who afterward made
their escape, and in striking the Macon road about
four miles below Jonesboro', when the work of
destruction was begun in earnest.

General Lewis, within three hours after receiving
the order, had placed his men on the cars and was
in Jonesboro' with his brigade ready for action.
Meantime Jackson was coming up with his cavalry,
when the Federals became alarmed and abandoned their work, but not without having destroyed about a mile and a half of the road,
which was promptly repaired.

While Jackson followed in pursuit and Lewis
returned to Atlanta, Wheeler moved across from
Latimer's, with a portion of his command, in rear
of this body of the enemy, leaving General Iverson

to pursue General Stoneman, who, after somewhat further damaging the Augusta road and burning the bridges across Walnut Creek and the Oconee River, had moved against Macon.

These operations had been ordered by General Sherman upon a grand scale; picked men and horses had been placed under the command of Generals McCook and Stoneman, with the purpose to destroy our sole line of communication, and to release, at Andersonville, 34,000 Federal prisoners.

These raiders, under McCook, came in contact with General Roddey's cavalry at Newnan, and were there held in check till Wheeler's and Jackson's troops came up; whereupon the combined forces, directed by General Wheeler, attacked the enemy with vigor and determination, and finally routed them. Whilst these operations were progressing in the vicinity of Newnan, General Cobb was gallantly repelling the assault of Stoneman at Macon, when Iverson came up and engaged the enemy with equal spirit and success.

The flanks of the Federal army were at this juncture so well protected by the Chattahoochee and the deep ravines which run down into the river, that my antagonist was enabled to throw his entire force of cavalry against the Macon road; and but for the superiority of the Confederate cavalry he might have succeeded to such extent as to cause us great annoyance and subject our troops to short rations for a time.

After the utter failure of this experiment General Sherman perceived that his mounted force, about twelve thousand in number, in concert with a corps of infantry as support, could not so effectually destroy our main line of communication as to compel us to evacuate Atlanta.

Wheeler and Iverson having thus thoroughly crippled the Federal cavalry, I determined to detach all the troops of that arm that I could possibly spare, and expedite them, under the command of Wheeler, against Sherman's railroad to Nashville; at the same time to request of the proper authorities that General Maury, commanding at Mobile, be instructed to strike with small bodies the line at different points, in the vicinity of the Tennessee River, and also that Forrest be ordered, with the whole of his available force, into Tennessee for the same object. I intended Wheeler should operate, in the first instance, south of Chattanooga.

I was hopeful that this combined movement would compel Sherman to retreat for want of supplies, and thus allow me an opportunity to fall upon his rear with our main body.

In accordance with my determination to attempt, with cavalry, the destruction of Sherman's road, I ordered General Wheeler, with 4500 men, to begin operations at once. He succeeded in burning the bridge over the Etowah; recaptured Dalton and Resaca; destroyed about 35 miles of railroad in the vicinity, and captured about 300 mules and 1000 horses; he destroyed in addition about 50 miles of railroad in Tennessee. General Forrest, with his usual energy, struck shortly afterward the Federal line of supplies in this State, and inflicted great damage upon the enemy. Forrest and Wheeler accomplished all but the impossible with

their restricted numbers, and the former, finally, was driven out of Tennessee by superior forces.

So vast were the facilities of the Federal commander to reënforce his line of skirmishers, extending from Nashville to Atlanta, that we could not bring together a sufficient force of cavalry to accomplish the desired object. I thereupon became convinced that no sufficiently effective number of cavalry could be assembled in the Confederacy to interrupt the enemy's line of supplies to an extent to compel him to retreat.

A heavy demonstration was made on the 6th against Bate's division, which was twice assaulted; twice the foe were driven back in great confusion, with a loss of two stand of colors, eight hundred killed and wounded, some small-arms and intrenching tools.

On the 7th General Cleburne's division was transferred to our extreme left, and the 9th was made memorable by the most furious cannonade which the city sustained during the siege. Women and children fled into cellars, and were forced to seek shelter a greater length of time than at any period of the bombardment.

The 19th, nigh two weeks after Wheeler's departure with about one-half of our cavalry force, General Sherman took advantage of the absence of these troops, and again attempted a lodgment on the Macon road with cavalry. At 3:30 A. M. General Kilpatrick was reported to be moving, via Fairburn, in the direction of Jonesboro'. General Jackson quickly divined his object, moved rapidly in pursuit, overtook him at an early hour, attacked and forced him to retreat after sustaining considerable loss in killed, wounded, and prisoners. The Federals had previously destroyed a mile and a half of the Macon road, and they had cut the wires and burned the depot at Jonesboro'.

Our cavalry also drove a brigade of the enemy from the Augusta road on the 22d, which affair, together with the happy results obtained in the engagement with Kilpatrick, demonstrated conclusively that, the absence of one-half of our mounted force notwithstanding, we had still a sufficient number, with Jackson, to protect not only the flanks of the army, but likewise our communications against similar raids, and, moreover, to defend our people against pillaging expeditions.

The severe handling by Wheeler and Iverson of the troops under Stoneman and McCook, together with Jackson's success, induced me not to recall Wheeler's 4500 men, who were still operating against the railroad to Nashville. I had, moreover, become convinced that our cavalry was able to compete successfully with double their number. Our cavalry were not cavalrymen *proper*, but were mounted riflemen, trained to dismount and hold in check or delay the advance of the enemy, and who had learned by experience that they could without much difficulty defeat the Federal cavalry.

The bombardment of the city continued till the 25th of August; it was painful, yet strange, to mark how expert grew the old men, women, and children in building their little underground forts, in which to fly for safety during the storm of shell and shot. Often 'mid the darkness of night were they constrained to seek refuge in these dungeons beneath the earth; albeit, I cannot recall one word from their lips expressive of dissatisfaction or willingness to surrender.

Sherman had now been over one month continuously moving toward our left and thoroughly fortifying, step by step, as he advanced in the direction of the Macon railroad. On the night of the 25th he withdrew from our immediate front; his works, which at an early hour the following morning we discovered to be abandoned, were occupied at a later hour by the corps of Stewart and Lee.

On the 27th General G. W. Smith's division was ordered to the left to occupy the position of Stevenson's division which, together with Maury's command, was held in reserve. Early the following morning the enemy were reported by [F. C.] Armstrong in large force at Fairburn, on the West Point road. It became at once evident that Sherman was moving with his main body to destroy the Macon road, and that the fate of Atlanta depended upon our ability to defeat this movement. Reynolds's and Lewis's brigades were dispatched to Jonesboro' to coöperate with Armstrong. General Adams, at Opelika, was directed to guard the defenses of that place with renewed vigilance, while General Maury was requested to render him assistance, if necessary. The chief quartermaster, ordnance officer, and commissary were given most explicit instructions in regard to the disposition of their respective stores. All surplus property, supplies, etc., were ordered to the rear, or to be placed on cars in readiness to move at any moment the railroad became seriously threatened. Armstrong was instructed to establish a line of couriers to my headquarters, in order to report every hour, if requisite, the movements of the enemy. In fact, every precaution was taken not only to hold our sole line of communication unto the last extremity, but also, in case of failure, to avoid loss or destruction of stores and material.

On the 29th the Federals marched slowly in the direction of Rough and Ready and Jonesboro'. A portion of Brown's division was directed to take position at the former place and fortify thoroughly, in order to afford protection to the road at that point. General Hardee, who was at this juncture in the vicinity of East Point, was instructed to make such disposition of his troops as he considered most favorable for defense; and, in addition, to hold his corps in readiness to march at the word of command. Jackson and Armstrong received orders to report the different positions of the corps of the enemy at dark every night.

The morning of the 30th found our general line extended farther to the left—Hardee being in the vicinity of Rough and Ready with Lee's corps on his right, near East Point. Information from our cavalry clearly indicated that the enemy would strike our road at Jonesboro'. After consultation with the corps commanders, I determined upon the following operations as the last hope of holding on to Atlanta.

A Federal corps crossed Flint River, at about 6 P. M., near Jonesboro', and made an attack upon Lewis's brigade, which was gallantly repulsed.

This action became the signal for battle. General Hardee was instructed to move rapidly with his troops to Jonesboro', whither Lieutenant-General Lee, with his corps, was ordered to follow during the night. Hardee was to attack with the entire force early on the morning of the 31st, and drive the enemy, at all hazards, into the river in their rear. In the event of success, Lee and his command were to be withdrawn that night back to Rough and Ready; Stewart's corps, together with Major-General G. W. Smith's State troops, were to form line of battle on Lee's right, near East Point, and the whole force move forward the following morning, attack the enemy in flank, and drive him down Flint River and the West Point railroad. In the meantime the cavalry was to hold in check the corps of the enemy, stationed at the railroad bridge across the Chattahoochee, near the mouth of Peach Tree Creek, whilst Hardee advanced from his position near Jonesboro', or directly on Lee's left.

Such were the explicit instructions delivered. I impressed upon General Hardee that the fate of Atlanta rested upon his ability, with the aid of two corps, to drive the Federals across Flint River, at Jonesboro'. I also instructed him in the event of failure—which would necessitate the evacuation of the city—to send Lee's corps, at dark, back to or near Rough and Ready, in order to protect our retreat to Lovejoy's Station.

The attack was not made till about 2 P. M., and then resulted in our inability to dislodge the enemy. The Federals had been allowed time, by the delay, to strongly intrench; whereas had the assault been made at an early hour in the morning the enemy would have been found but partially protected by works.

General Hardee transmitted to me no official report at that period, nor subsequently, of his operations whilst under my command. I find, however, from the diary in my possession that his corps succeeded in gaining a portion of the Federal works; the general attack, notwithstanding, must have been rather feeble, as the loss incurred was only about 1400 in killed and wounded—a small number in comparison to the forces engaged. Among the wounded were General Patton Anderson and General Cumming, who were disabled whilst gallantly leading their troops into action.

This failure gave to the Federal army the control of the Macon road, and thus necessitated the evacuation of Atlanta at the earliest hour possible.

I was not so much pained by the fall of Atlanta as by the *recurrence* of retreat, which I full well knew would further demoralize the army and renew desertions. The loss of over 4000, sustained from this same cause during the change from Kenesaw Mountain to and across the Chattahoochee, augmented my great reluctance to order the army to again turn its back to the foe. Howbeit, the presence of 34,000 Federal prisoners at Andersonville rendered it absolutely incumbent to place the army between Sherman and that point, in order to prevent the Federal commander from turning loose this large body. . . Thus the proximity of these prisoners to Sherman's army not only forced me to remain in a position to guard the country against the fearful calamity aforementioned, but also thwarted my design to move north, across Peach Tree Creek and the Chattahoochee, back to Marietta, where I would have destroyed the enemy's communications and supplies, and then have taken position near the Alabama line, with the Blue Mountain railroad in rear, by which means the Confederate army could, with ease, have been provisioned.

In lieu of the foregoing operations, the battle of Jonesboro' was fought, and on the following day, September 1st, at 2 A. M., Lieutenant-General Lee, with his corps, marched from Jonesboro' to the vicinity of Rough and Ready, and so posted his troops as to protect our flank, whilst we marched out of Atlanta at 5 P. M. the same day, on the McDonough road, in the direction of Lovejoy's Station. Generals Morgan and Scott, stationed at East Point, received similar orders to protect our flank during the retreat.

Upon our uninterrupted march, information reached me that Hardee's corps was engaged with a large force of the enemy. His position upon a ridge with an open country in rear relieved me from special anxiety in regard to the safety of himself and command. Lieutenant-General Stewart, nevertheless, was instructed to hasten forward to his support, and General Lee to follow promptly with his corps. When these reënforcements reached the scene of action the contest had ceased. Hardee's troops had been attacked by a considerable force; but in consequence of the protection afforded by their breastworks their loss in killed and wounded was small in comparison to that of the enemy. The Federals, who largely exceeded them in numbers, forced them back a short distance from the position they primarily occupied, and necessitated the abandonment of two four-gun batteries. This engagement was the only

event of importance which occurred during our continuous march from Atlanta to Lovejoy's Station. I have often thought it strange Sherman should have occupied himself with attacking Hardee's intrenched position, instead of falling upon our main body on the march round to his rear.

Notwithstanding full and positive instructions, delivered prior to the evacuation of the city, and ample time and facilities afforded to move all stores, cars, and engines, the chief quartermaster grossly neglected to send off a train of ordnance stores and five engines, although they were on the track and in readiness to move. This negligence entailed the unnecessary loss of these stores, engines, and about eighty cars. The stores which had been abandoned were blown up at about 2 o'clock on the morning of the 2d September, and the rear-guard soon thereafter marched out of Atlanta. That night, and the morning of the 3d, our troops filed into position in Sherman's front, which was then near Jonesboro'. By the 4th our entire army was at this point, on the Macon road.

On the 6th the Federals withdrew from our immediate front and moved off in the direction of Atlanta. General Sherman published orders stating that his army would retire to East Point, Decatur, and Atlanta, and repose after the fatigue of the campaign through which it had passed. We were apprised of these instructions soon after their issuance — as well as of nigh every important movement of the enemy — through the vigilance of our cavalry, spies, and scouts, and from information received through Federal prisoners. Upon this date it may be justly considered that the operations round Atlanta ceased. We had maintained a defense, during forty-six days, of an untenable position, and had battled almost incessantly, day and night, with a force of about 45,000 against an army of 106,000 effectives, flushed with victory upon victory from Dalton to Atlanta.

UNION DEFENSES AT ALLATOONA PASS (SEE ALSO P. 323). FROM A WAR-TIME PHOTOGRAPH.

A. J. SMITH'S AND PORTER'S EXPEDITION STARTING FROM VICKSBURG FOR THE RED RIVER.   FROM A WAR-TIME SKETCH.

THE RED RIVER CAMPAIGN.

BY RICHARD B. IRWIN, LIEUTENANT-COLONEL, U. S. V., ASSISTANT ADJUTANT-GENERAL, DEPARTMENT OF THE GULF.

AFTER the fall of Port Hudson on the 8th of July, 1863, the forces of the Department of the Gulf, instead of going at once against Mobile as urged by General Grant, General Banks,[and Admiral Farragut, and thus lending an effective support to the main operations about Chattanooga at a critical period, were occupied in attempting to carry out the orders of the Government to restore the flag in Texas. General Banks was informed by General Halleck that the Government fully appreciated the importance of the proposed operations against Mobile, ↕ but there were important reasons, reasons other than military, why the Texas movement should be made first and with the least possible delay, by sea or land. A combined naval and military operation by the Red River was indicated as the best mode of carrying out the object; the selection of the route was, however, left to General Banks, but as to the movement itself he was distinctly told there was no choice and that the views of the Government must be carried out. ↓

The first attempt to carry them out led to the unfortunate expedition to Sabine Pass, in September [see Vol. III., p. 598], the object of which was to gain a footing on the coast by surprise. Its summary failure put that idea out

↓ Banks to Halleck, July 23d, 30th, and August 1st, 1863.   And see General Grant's article, Vol. III., p. 679, of this work.

↕ Halleck to Banks, July 24th, August 6th, 10th, and 12th.   There is some reason for thinking that the idea may have originated with Presi-

dent Lincoln himself: see Lincoln to Stanton, July 29th, 1863.

↓ General Halleck's own opinion of the relative value of the Mobile and Texas campaigns is indicated in his dispatch to General Banks of July 24th: "I think Texas much the most important."

of the question, and the route proposed by General Halleck being at that moment quite impracticable, because the Red River is only navigable during a few weeks in the spring, General Banks at once concentrated his troops on the Teche for a renewal of the attempt by moving directly west across the prairie by way of Niblett's Bluff. However, it did not take long to realize that to march an army three hundred miles across a barren country, with no water in the summer and fall, and plenty of water but no road in the winter and spring, was really not to be thought of, especially when the column would have to guard against an active enemy on its flank and rear during the march and to meet and overcome another at its end.

Accordingly, General Banks reverted to his first idea of making the attempt by sea, and selected the Thirteenth Corps, then commanded by Major-General C. C. Washburn, ♭ for the service. To Major-General N. J. T. Dana was assigned the duty of effecting the first landing at Brazos Santiago, at the mouth of the Rio Grande. The expedition, General Banks himself accompanying it, sailed from New Orleans on the 26th of October, under convoy of the *Monongahela, Owasco,* and *Virginia.* After encountering a severe "norther" on the 30th, from which the men, animals, and transports suffered greatly, on the 2d of November Dana landed on Brazos Island, drove off the small Confederate force on the mainland on the 3d, and on the 6th occupied Brownsville, thirty miles up the river. Point Isabel was occupied on the 8th. With the foot-hold thus gained, General Banks's plan was to occupy successively all the passes or inlets that connect the Gulf of Mexico with the land-locked lagoons or sounds of the Texas coast from the Rio Grande to the Sabine. Leaving Dana in command on the Rio Grande, a strong detachment, under Brigadier-General T. E. G. Ransom, embarked on the 16th, landed at Corpus Christi, occupied Mustang Island, crossed Aransas Pass, and moved on Pass Cavallo, where the Confederates had a strong work called Fort Esperanza, commanding the entrance to Matagorda Bay. This was captured on the 30th of December, the Confederates retiring to the mainland.

These operations, though completely successful so far and at small cost, being, indeed, almost unopposed, were not satisfactory to the Government. However, General Banks, being committed to the movement, was proceeding to complete the conquest of the Texas coast by moving in force against the strong Confederate positions at Galveston and the mouth of the Brazos when General Halleck on the 4th of January renewed his instructions of the previous summer for the naval and military operation on the Red River; this time it was to be on a larger scale, for Steele was also to advance to the Red River from the line of the Arkansas, and General Grant was to coöperate with such troops as he could spare during the winter from the military division of the Mississippi. Since it has been claimed that these instructions were not positive, that they *only* required General Banks to communicate with General Sherman, General Steele, and Admiral Porter, it may be enough to

---

♭ Major-General E. O. C. Ord, who had succeeded Major J. A. McClernand in command of the Thirteenth Army Corps, before Vicksburg, was on sick leave at this time and did not return to the Department of the Gulf, being assigned to duty with the Army of the James in the summer of 1864.

observe that they *did* instruct General Banks to communicate with the officers named, that each of those generals as well as General Grant received corresponding instructions, that Admiral Porter read those addressed to General Banks, and that all five commanders understood and executed these orders in the same sense.\ General Banks replied, expressing his concurrence in Halleck's plan. This may have been a mistake. Yet, though a soldier may often be excused, and sometimes even praised, for disobeying orders, he can never be blamed for obeying them when all the conditions are known to his superior, and it is unnecessary to burrow in search of a motive for the cheerful performance of duty. In an elaborate and carefully prepared memoir by his chief engineer, Major D. C. Houston, General Banks presented a clear view of the difficulties to be encountered and the conditions deemed essential to success. These conditions (all of which except the fourth, in the result, shared the general fate of "ifs," by being completely disregarded) were, in brief, five: 1. Complete preliminary organization, so as to avoid delay in movement. 2. A line of supply by land from the Mississippi, or, in other words, the reconstruction of the railway from De Soto to Monroe, and a good and safe wagon-road thence to Shreveport. 3. The expulsion of the Confederates from Arkansas and northern Louisiana. 4. The enemy to be kept fully employed, so as to be prevented from undertaking raids and diversions. 5. One general to command the whole force. The usual time of highest water in the upper Red River fixed the date for the movement as about the middle of March.

General Sherman came to New Orleans on the 1st of March and promptly arranged to send ten thousand men to join Admiral Porter at the mouth of the Red River, and, accompanied by the fleet, to be at Alexandria by the 17th of March, simultaneously with the arrival of Banks's troops marching north by the Teche. Thus two armies and a fleet, hundreds of miles apart, were to concentrate on a given day at a remote point far within the enemy's lines, situated, moreover, on a river always difficult and uncertain of navigation and now obstructed and fortified. And here, especially in Sherman's ready agreement to overlook a fundamental rule of the art of war, we see clearly the earliest sign of that general disregard of the enemy's power of resistance that was so soon to wreck the campaign. It is noteworthy that the same error was repeated on a greater scale when it was arranged that after once concentrating within the enemy's lines at Alexandria, the united forces of Banks, Sherman, and Porter should meet those of Steele within the enemy's lines at Shreveport, where, roughly speaking, Kirby Smith was within three hundred miles of either Banks or Steele, while the two Federal commanders, separated from each other at the start by nearly five hundred miles of hostile territory, could only communicate by the rivers in their rear over a long circuit, lengthening as they approached their common enemy in his central stronghold.

\ General Grant says [p. 108]: "General Banks had gone on an expedition up the Red River long before my promotion to general command. I had opposed the movement strenuously, but acquiesced because it was the order of my superior at the time. . . . It is but just to Banks, however, to say that his expedition was ordered from Washington. . . . He opposed the expedition."—EDITORS.

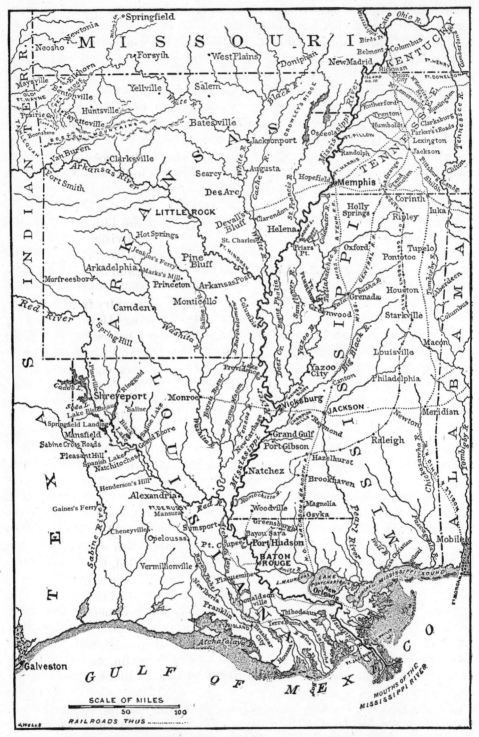

MAP OF THE RED RIVER, AND ARKANSAS AND MISSOURI CAMPAIGNS, OF 1864.

In estimating the forces at Kirby Smith's disposal to meet this triple invasion at 25,000 men, Banks was, as he had been the year before in the Port Hudson campaign, virtually correct, although on both occasions the Government regarded his figures as exaggerated. Since the forces told off for the Red River expedition numbered 42,000 officers and men of all arms, of whom Sherman was to furnish 10,000, Steele 15,000, and Banks 17,000, it is obvious that by concentrating his whole force, Kirby Smith would be stronger than either column separately, nearly as strong as the whole of Sherman's force and Banks's when united and before being weakened by detachments, and therefore possibly stronger than their combined force after providing for the heavy details indispensable to such a movement.

Porter's fleet entered the mouth of the Red River on the 12th of March, convoying Sherman's detachment on transports. On the 13th two divisions of the Sixteenth Corps under Mower, and Kilby Smith's division of the Seventeenth Corps, the whole under command of Brigadier-General A. J. Smith, landed at Simsport, near the head of the Atchafalaya, and the next morning marched on Fort de Russy. Walker's division of the Confederate army, under General Richard Taylor, which was holding the country from Simsport to Opelousas, at once fell back to Bayou Bœuf, covering Alexandria. A. J. Smith's march was therefore unmolested. He arrived before Fort de Russy on the afternoon of the 14th, and promptly carried the works by assault, with a loss of 34 killed and wounded, capturing 260 prisoners, eight heavy guns, and two field-pieces. Meantime the advance of Porter's fleet had burst through the dam and raft nine miles below, and was thus able to proceed at once up the river, arriving off Alexandria on the 15th. Kilby Smith followed on the transports with the remainder of the fleet, landed at Alexandria on the 16th, and occupied the town, Taylor having retired toward Natchitoches and called in Mouton's division from the country north of the river to join Walker's. A. J. Smith, with Mower, followed on the 18th. Thus Porter and A. J. Smith were at Alexandria ahead of time.

Banks himself was detained at New Orleans by the necessity of giving personal attention to special duties confided to him by the President in connection with the election and the installation, on the 4th of March, of the governor and other officers of the new or, as it was called, the "free State" Government of Louisiana. Some criticism and much ridicule have been wasted on this; the fact being that General Banks simply carried out the orders of President Lincoln, just as, for example, was done by General Gillmore in Florida and General Steele in Arkansas, only that more attention was naturally drawn to Louisiana as a greater State, and containing the most important city in the South. Banks therefore confided to Franklin, under whom the Nineteenth Corps had been reorganized and brought up to a high state of discipline and efficiency, the task of preparing and putting in motion the troops of the Department of the Gulf, designated to form part of the expedition. Franklin, when selected for this service, was the second officer in rank in the department, and, in any case, a better selection could not have been made.] His forces consisted of Emory's division, and Grover's two brigades of the Nineteenth Corps, about 10,500 strong, Cameron's and Ransom's divisions of the Thirteenth Corps, about 4800, and the newly organized division of cavalry and newly mounted infantry, under Brigadier-General Albert L. Lee, numbering 4600. Bad weather had ruined the roads; but on the 13th of March Lee led the advance of the column from Franklin, on the Teche, and, moving by Opelousas and Bayou Bœuf, marched into Alexandria, distant 175 miles, on the 19th, followed by the infantry and artillery on the 25th and 26th.

Banks himself made his headquarters at Alexandria on the 24th, and there on the 27th he received fresh orders that imposed a new and well-nigh impossible condition on the campaign. These were the instructions of Lieutenant-General Grant, dated the 15th of March, on taking command of the army of the United States, looking to the coöperation of the whole effective force of or in the Department of the Gulf in the combined movement early in May of all the armies between the Mississippi and the Atlantic. A. J. Smith was to join the Army of the Tennessee for the Atlanta campaign, and Banks was to go against Mobile. If Shreveport were not to be taken by the 25th of April, at latest, then A. J. Smith's corps was to be returned to Vicksburg by the 10th, " even if it should lead to the abandonment of the expedition." Yet Halleck's orders for the expedition were not revoked; it was to go on — only, to make sure that it should not be gone too long, it was put in irons. Banks might well have given up the campaign then and there; yet there was a chance that Kirby Smith might not be able to concentrate in time to save Shreveport; another, still more remote, that he might give the place up without a fight, and a third, more unlikely than either, that Steele might join Banks in time to make short work of it. There were twenty-six days left before the latest time at which A. J. Smith must leave him; so in his dilemma Banks decided to take these chances.

His delay made no real difference, for the river, though slowly rising, was still so low that the gun-boats had not been able to pass the difficult rapids that obstruct the navigation just above Alexandria. The leading gun-boat, *Eastport*, hung nearly three days on the rocks; the hospital steamer, *Woodford*, following her, was wrecked, and it was not until the 3d of April that the last of the thirteen gun-boats↓ and thirty transports that were finally taken above the rapids had succeeded in making the difficult passage. Seven gun-boats and the larger transports staid below; the only communication with the upper fleet was by the road around the falls; all supplies had therefore to be landed, hauled round in wagons, and reshipped; and this made it necessary to establish depots and to leave Grover's division, four thousand strong, at Alexandria for the protection of the stores and the carry. At the same time General McPherson, commanding the Seventeenth Corps, recalled Ellet's

---

↓ The following summer, even after the Red River failure, General Grant considered that he would be strengthened by having Franklin to command the right wing of his army [see p. 106].—R. B. I.

↓ The 13 gun-boats sent up were the *Eastport, Chillicothe, Carondelet, Louisville, Mound City, Pittsburgh, Osage, Ozark, Neosho, Fort Hindman, Cricket, Juliet,* and *Lexington.* See " The Navy in the Red River," p. 363.— EDITORS.

Marine Brigade to Vicksburg, and thus the expedition lost a second detachment of three thousand. This loss was partly made up by the arrival of a brigade of 1500 colored troops, under Colonel W. H. Dickey, from Port Hudson. Taylor, retiring before the advance of the columns ascending the Red River and the Teche under A. J. Smith and Franklin, had evacuated Alexandria, removing all the munitions of war and material except three guns and passing all the transports above the Falls, and on the 18th of March was with Walker's and Mouton's divisions at Carroll Jones's plantation, in the pine forest covering the roads to Shreveport and the Sabine, about thirty-six miles above Alexandria and forty-six below Natchitoches. After the arrival of Lee's cavalry, A. J. Smith sent Mower with his two divisions and Lucas's brigade of Lee's division on the 21st to Henderson's Hill, near Cotile, twenty-three miles above Alexandria, to clear the way across Bayou Rapides. Here, the same night, in a heavy rain-storm, Mower skillfully surprised the only cavalry force Taylor had, the 2d Louisiana, Colonel William G. Vincent, and with trifling loss captured nearly the whole regiment, about 250 men and 200 horses, together with the four guns of Edgar's battery. This was a heavy blow to Taylor, since it deprived him of the means of scouting until Green's cavalry, long looked for, should arrive from Texas. Mower returned to Alexandria and Taylor withdrew to Natchitoches.

While the navy was occupied in passing the rapids, the advance of the army, on the 27th, took up the line of march, and on the 3d of April the whole force was concentrated near Natchitoches, the gun-boats and the twenty-six transports carrying A. J. Smith's corps and the stores having arrived at Grand Ecore, four miles distant, on the same day. Here General John M. Corse overtook the expedition, bearing renewed and very special orders from Sherman for the return of A. J. Smith's corps by the 10th of April; but the expedition was now within four marches of Shreveport, and it was agreed to go on. Kilby Smith's division, 1700 strong, remained with the transports, under orders to proceed under convoy as far as Loggy Bayou, opposite Springfield, 110 miles by the river above Grand Ecore, while A. J. Smith with Mower's divisions, numbering about 7000, moved by land with the rest of the army, now reduced to less than 26,000 officers and men of all arms, including the 2200 colored infantry and engineers, and 1700 cavalry presently detached for service on the north bank. Franklin marched on the 6th of April, Lee's cavalry in advance, followed by the Thirteenth Corps under Ransom, Emory's division of the Nineteenth, and Dickey's colored brigade. A. J. Smith with Mower marched on the 7th, and the same day Admiral Porter, with Kilby Smith and six light-draught gun-boats carrying about seventeen guns, got under way for Loggy Bayou. On the night of the 7th, Lee's cavalry, after a sharp skirmish with Major's brigade of Green's division of Texas cavalry, bivouacked on Bayou St. Patrice, seven miles beyond Pleasant Hill, Ransom and Emory at Pleasant Hill, thirty-three miles from Natchitoches, and A. J. Smith a day's march in their rear; the march of the infantry having been retarded by a heavy storm that broke over the rear of the column and cut up the road.

MAJOR-GENERAL NATHANIEL P. BANKS. FROM A PHOTOGRAPH.

Meanwhile Taylor, who had continued to fall back, found himself on the 5th at Mansfield, covering the roads to Marshall, Texas, and to Shreveport, with Green's cavalry coming up at last, and Churchill's Arkansas division and Parsons's Missouri division of Price's army in supporting distance at Keachie, about half-way between Mansfield and Shreveport, which are forty-two miles apart. This gave Taylor 16,000 men with whom he might give battle in a chosen position, while Banks's force was stretched out to the length of a day's march on a single narrow road in the pine forest and encumbered and weakened by guarding twelve miles of wagons bearing all his ammunition and provisions through a barren wilderness, deep in the heart of the enemy's country. Such, indeed, was Kirby Smith's plan. However, Taylor did not wait for that, but, sending back orders for Churchill and Parsons to join him early on the morning of the 8th moved out three miles to Sabine Cross-roads, and there formed line of battle with Walker's, Mouton's, and Green's divisions, 11,000 strong, and awaited the approach of the Federals in a well-selected position, in the edge of the wood, commanding on both sides of the road one of the few clearings to be found in that region. This clearing was about 1200 yards long, 900 wide, and through the middle ran a deep ravine.

Lee's bivouac of the night before was but twelve miles away. Accompanied by Vance's brigade of Landram's division, Lee marched at daylight, and after meeting with a spirited resistance from three of Green's regiments, designed to give time for Taylor to form his line, arrived about noon on the hill at the eastern edge of the clearing that was to be the field of battle. The main body of the army marched at daybreak and halted between 10 and 11, Ransom two miles beyond Bayou St. Patrice and Emory on its banks, to wait for his provision train, which had not come up the night before. A. J. Smith moved up to within two miles of Pleasant Hill. Banks sent Ransom forward with Emerson's brigade, and rode to the front himself at an early hour. Finding the enemy before him in force, he ordered Lee to hold his ground and sent back " to hurry forward the column."

About 4 o'clock, when the two lines had been skirmishing and looking at each other for a couple of hours, Taylor suddenly delivered his attack ♭ by a vigorous charge of Mouton's division on the left of the Pleasant Hill road, supported on his left by Major's and Bagby's brigades of cavalry dismounted. Walker followed astride and on the right of the road, with Bee's brigade of cavalry on his right. The Federal line formed on the cleared slope, and, composed from left to right of the brigades of Dudley, Vance, Emerson, and Lucas, with four batteries, about 4500 in all, met with spirit the fierce onset of more than double their numbers, but were soon overcome. The artillery was powerless in the woods. Nims's splendid battery, with its honorable record on every field from Baton Rouge to Port Hudson, was taken by Walker's men in the first rush. Franklin, whose headquarters were with Cameron in front of Bayou St. Patrice, received Banks's orders to move to the front at a quarter-past three. He at once sent for Emory and led forward Cameron, whose division, advancing at the double-quick, arrived on the field, five miles away, an hour later, just in time to witness and for a brief interval to check the disaster, but not to retrieve it. The whole Union line was again driven back. To complete the confusion a wild panic ensued among the teamsters of the cavalry train, which was close behind. ⸜ This caused the loss of the guns of two fine batteries, the Chicago Mercantile and the 1st Missouri, as well as of many prisoners and wagons. Emory had received the order to advance at twenty minutes to four while in his bivouac on Bayou St. Patrice, and had instantly put his division in motion. Three miles in rear of the field of battle he met the routed column pressing in great disorder to the rear. Quickening their pace, his men forced their way through the confused mass of fugitives, negroes, cavalry, camp followers, wagons, and ambulances, and formed line in

♭ The Confederate accounts of this engagement (called by the Confederates the battle of Mansfield — by us, Sabine Cross-roads; see p. 369) cannot be quite reconciled without reading between the lines. Kirby Smith says the reconnoissance ordered by him was " converted into a decisive engagement." Taylor says, "Becoming impatient at the delay, . . . I ordered Mouton to open the attack. . . ." Lieutenant Edward Cunningham, A. D. C., and Chief-of-Artillery, in a very clear and outspoken letter to his brother, which was intercepted by our troops, says that Mouton attacked "without the knowledge or orders of General Taylor."— R. B. I.

⸜ This order of march has been severely criticised, but a little reflection will show that it did not cause but only aggravated a disaster really brought about by accepting battle at the head of a column twenty miles long, at the hands of an enemy formed in complete order of battle, in a position previously chosen by him, where our artillery could not be used.— R. B. I.

a good position to check the pursuit, Dwight on the right of the road, covered by the 161st New York deployed as skirmishers, Benedict on the left, and McMillan in reserve behind Dwight. Hardly was the line formed when Taylor's victorious troops attacked with great energy, pressing heavily on Dwight's right; but McMillan was brought up to his support, and when night shortly fell the attack had been thrown off. Emory's division held the ground it fought for, ☆ the retreat was covered and the army was saved—the army that had set out so confidently to take Shreveport, only two marches beyond; saved by a triumph of valor and discipline on the part of a single division, and of skill on the part of its intrepid commander, from complete destruction at the hands of an enemy inferior in everything, whose entire force ours outnumbered almost as two to one.

MAJOR-GENERAL A. J. SMITH. FROM A PHOTOGRAPH.

But the campaign was lost. All hope of taking or even reaching Shreveport within the time fixed for the breaking up of the expedition was at an end. Banks at once ordered a retreat, and sent messengers to notify Kilby Smith and Porter. Emory marched at midnight, and at 8 o'clock the next morning, the 9th of April, the army came into position at Pleasant Hill, where A. J. Smith had been left, and where what remained of Lee's cavalry, of Ransom's corps, now under Cameron,⌡ and of Dickey's colored brigade had been re-formed during the night. The train, escorted by Dickey's brigade, was put in motion toward Grand Ecore, followed by Cameron. Emory and A. J. Smith remained in position, covering the retreat and approaches to Pleasant Hill, including the important cross-road to Blair's Landing on the Red River,↓ where it would be easy and might be found best to reunite the army and the fleet.

Meanwhile Churchill's and Parsons's divisions having arrived at Mansfield

☆ Taylor says he drove the enemy five miles. "*Here* the Thirteenth Corps gave way entirely and was replaced by the Nineteenth hurriedly brought up to support the fight. The Nineteenth shared the fate of the Thirteenth." (The italics are mine.) This is a mistake ; the Nineteenth Corps never reached the position of the Thirteenth. Taylor's next paragraph describes the fight with the Nineteenth : "Just as night closed the enemy massed heavily on a ridge overlooking a small creek. . . . The

fighting was severe for a time, but . . . we encamped on the creek as night fell, the enemy forced back some four hundred yards beyond,"—*i. e.*, the skirmish-line was driven back to Emory's line of battle on the rising ground overlooking the creek. —R. B. I.

⌡ Ransom having been wounded at Sabine Cross-roads.

↓ Sixteen miles from Pleasant Hill and forty-five, by the river, above Grand Ecore.

after a march of twenty miles from Keachie, too late in the evening to take part in the battle of Sabine Cross-roads, Taylor ordered Churchill to march both divisions to the front at 2 A. M., meaning to renew the fight; but when daylight disclosed the retreat of the Union forces, Taylor promptly moved forward with his whole force in pursuit — Green with the cavalry leading, Churchill next with his own division under Tappan, then Parsons's, Walker's, and Mouton's divisions, the last now under Polignac.] It was afternoon when the Confederates found themselves confronted by Emory and Mower in order of battle. Churchill's men were so fagged by their early start and their long march of forty-five miles since the morning of the 8th that they were given two hours' rest. Taylor then formed line of battle, Bee with two brigades of cavalry on the left of the Mansfield road, with Polignac in support, Walker on the right of the road, and Churchill, with three regiments of cavalry on his right, moving under cover on the right of the Sabine River road. Major, with his own brigade and Bagby's dismounted, was sent to turn the Federal right and hold the Blair's Landing road.

The Union troops had rather the advantage of ground, except that the position was easily turned and that they could not stay in it for want of water, of which there was none to be had, and for want of provisions, which were rolling on the way to Grand Ecore; the Confederates were fresh and slightly superior in numbers,\ besides being, with good reason, elated by their signal victory of the day before;

however, I think this last advantage may fairly be offset by the steadiness with which the Northern soldier accepted and the sternness with which he avenged a defeat.

About 5 o'clock Churchill opened his attack, Parsons on the right, Tappan on his left, and fell vigorously on the left of the Union line, which happened to be the weakest part of Emory's position. Here was posted Benedict's brigade, supported on the left by Lynch's brigade and on the right by Moore's brigade of Mower's division. Benedict fell dead and his brigade was outflanked and crushed. At the sound of Churchill's guns, Walker, *en échelon*

MAJOR-GENERAL J. A. MOWER. FROM A PHOTOGRAPH.

of brigades on the right, fell upon Shaw of Mower's division (who had relieved McMillan of Emory's in the front line), enveloped both his flanks, and drove him back; but Emory quickly ordered a charge of McMillan's

---

] Mouton having been killed in the first onset on the 8th.

\ After the battle, each side claimed to have fought superior numbers. I cannot make out that the Union troops, including Gooding's cavalry, which was not engaged, numbered more than 11,000, nor that the Confederate force was less than 13,000: Taylor says he had 12,000 and attacked "twenty odd thousand," and that "the third army of the enemy in point of numbers on the theater of war was routed and driven from the field with a loss of at least 10,000 men."—R. B. I.

ALEXANDRIA, ON THE RED RIVER. FROM A WAR-TIME PHOTOGRAPH.

brigade, withdrawn from the right and rear and joined by some of Fessenden's men, who had rallied to his support, while others rallied upon Lynch,
who attacked and broke Parsons's right; A. J. Smith then advanced his
whole line in a fine charge led by Mower and completed the overthrow of
Parsons before Tappan could come to his aid.   Tappan, finding himself
exposed to a front and flank fire by the giving way of Parsons, fell back
to re-form.   Dwight, who was strongly posted in the woods, stood firm
against the combined attacks of Walker in his front and Bee on his right.
Taylor ordered up Polignac to their assistance, but the whole Confederate
line was now falling back in confusion and the battle was lost.☆   Walker
and Churchill with most of the cavalry retreated six miles to the nearest
water, while Polignac with one brigade of cavalry remained about two miles
from the field to cover the retreat.   After the close of the action, Kirby
Smith joined Taylor, having hurried to the front as soon as he heard of the
engagement at Sabine Cross-roads.   Kirby Smith now determined to move
against Steele in Arkansas; accordingly, during the 10th and 11th, Taylor
withdrew his infantry to Mansfield, leaving the cavalry under Green to watch
and, if possible, harass the enemy.

At first Banks was for resuming the advance, but during the night he
decided to continue the retreat to Grand Ecore.⎮ The whole army was
reunited there on the 11th.   Banks then intrenched, threw a pontoon-bridge

☆ The earliest Confederate dispatches and
orders claimed a signal and glorious victory, but
Kirby Smith's report of August 28th, 1864, to
President Davis, says that "Taylor's troops were
repulsed and thrown into confusion. . . . The
Missouri and Arkansas troops, with a brigade of
Walker's division, were broken and scattered.
The enemy recovered artillery which we had taken,
and two of our pieces were left in his hands. . . .
To my great relief I found in the morning that the
enemy had fallen back during the night. . . .
Our troops were completely paralyzed by the repulse at
Pleasant Hill." (Italics mine.) In the letter already

cited, Lieutenant Cunningham says: "That it
was impossible for us to pursue Banks immediately — under four or five days — cannot be gain-
said. . . . It was impossible . . . because
we had been beaten, demoralized, paralyzed, in
the fight of the 9th."—R. B. I. [And see p. 370.]

⎮ General A. J. Smith strongly opposed this.
General Franklin proposed to march to Blair's
Landing to await the return of the fleet.   This
was probably sound advice, though it would have
separated the army· temporarily from its train
and from the troops that had already gone on to
Grand Ecore.—R. B. I.

across the river, placed a strong detachment on the north side, sent to New Orleans and Texas for reënforcements, and waited for the fleet, now in great peril. The fleet arrived at Loggy Bayou on the afternoon of the 10th, and two hours later received the news of the misfortune at Pleasant Hill. The next morning Kilby Smith received written orders to return to Grand Ecore. On the 12th Green, with three or four regiments of cavalry and three guns, posted in ambush on the bluff near Blair's Landing, attacked the fleet and the transports as they were descending the river. A brisk fight followed; the Confederates were soon driven off, and their leader killed, by the guns of the *Lexington* and *Osage* and the fire of Kilby Smith's infantry and part of his artillery on the transports. On the 13th Porter and Kilby Smith re-turned to Grand Ecore, and by the 15th all the gun-boats were back. The river was falling, and as fast as the vessels could pass the bar they made their way toward Alexandria. The *Eastport* was sunk by a torpedo eight miles below Grand Ecore on the 15th, but was got afloat on the 21st; on the 26th, after grounding several times, she ran hard and fast on a raft of logs fifty miles farther down, and had to

BREVET MAJOR-GENERAL JOSEPH BAILEY.
FROM A PHOTOGRAPH.

be abandoned and blown up. The other vessels, though several times seri-ously molested by parties of the enemy on the river bank, reached the falls above Alexandria in safety.

When he heard from Admiral Porter that the *Eastport* was afloat, Banks, on the 22d, marched from Grand Ecore on Alexandria, and bivouacked the same night at Cloutierville, after a march of thirty-seven miles. Kirby Smith had taken the whole of Taylor's force to go against Steele in Arkansas, except Polignac's division, reduced to about 2000 men, and Green's division of cavalry augmented by a fresh brigade from Texas, and now commanded by General John A. Wharton, of Tennessee fame. The road on which Banks was marching twice crosses the western arm of the Red River, called Cane River, the second time at Monette's Ferry, thirty-six miles below Natchitoches. Here Bee, with four brigades and four batteries, had taken up a position to contest the pas-sage, while Wharton and Polignac (to use Taylor's expression) worried Banks's rear. On the 23d Emory↓ sent Birge with his own brigade and Fessenden's, supported by Cameron's division, to ford the river three miles above the ferry, turn Bee's left flank, while Emory engaged his attention in front, and drive him away. Birge performed this service handsomely, overcoming many difficulties with great skill, and finally leading the brilliant assault of

↓ Franklin having been wounded on the 8th.

Fessenden's brigade that dislodged Bee from his strong position, and sent him off to Beasley's, thirty miles away.♭   The way being thus cleared, the army marched into Alexandria on the 25th and 26th, without further serious molestation.   Here General Hunter was met, bearing fresh, and this time very positive, orders from Lieutenant-General Grant to bring the expedition to an end.☖   These orders were afterward suspended (April 30th); but in any case it was now impossible to abandon the navy in its perilous situation above the rapids, with the river falling, and an active enemy on both banks.

From this danger the navy, from this reproach the army, from this irreparable disaster the country was saved by the genius and skill of Lieutenant-Colonel Joseph Bailey, of the 4th Wisconsin regiment, then serving on General Franklin's staff as chief engineer, and by hard and willing work on the part of the officers and men of the army.   After the capture of Port Hudson, Bailey, by means of wing dams and a central boom, had floated and released the Confederate transports *Starlight* and *Red Chief*, found lying on their sides in the mud of Thompson's creek.   He now proposed to rescue the fleet in the same way.   Stupendous as the work looked, the engineer officers of the army reported it practicable.☆   General Franklin, himself a distinguished engineer, approved it, and General Banks gave orders to carry it out.

In the month that had elapsed since the fleet had, even then with some difficulty, ascended the rapids, the river had fallen more than six feet; for a mile and a quarter the rocks were now bare; there were but three feet four inches of water, the gun-boats needing at least seven feet; and in some places the channel, shallow as it was, was narrowed to a mere thread.   The current ran nine miles an hour, the total fall was thirteen feet, and at the point just above the lower chute, where Bailey proposed to construct his dam, the river

♭ The Union losses in this affair were about 200, of which 153 were in Fessenden's brigade. Colonel Fessenden was severely wounded.—R. B. I.

☖ The records show that General Grant wished Hunter to be sent out to relieve Banks, on the strength of private information received, but that the President was not ready for this.—R. B. I.

☆ Especially Captain John C. Palfrey, United States Engineers, who had made a careful and complete survey of the rapids.—R. B. I.

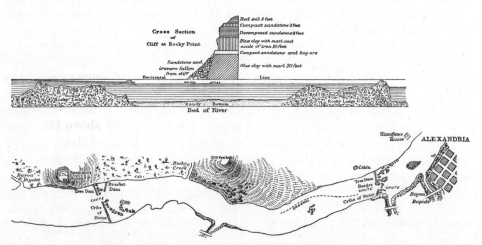

MAP AND SECTIONS OF THE RED RIVER DAMS ABOVE ALEXANDRIA.

was 758 feet wide, with a fall of six feet below the dam. The problem was to raise the water above the dam seven feet, backing it up so as to float the gun-boats over the upper fall. From the north bank a wing dam was constructed of large trees, the butts tied by cross-logs, the tops toward the current, and kept in place by weighting with stone, brick, and brush. From the cultivated south bank, where large trees were scarce, a crib was made of logs and timbers, filled in with stone and with bricks and heavy pieces of machinery taken from the neighboring sugar-houses and cotton-gins. The space of about 150 feet between the wings was closed by sinking across it four of the large coal barges belonging to the navy.

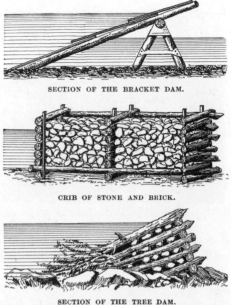

SECTION OF THE BRACKET DAM.

CRIB OF STONE AND BRICK.

SECTION OF THE TREE DAM.
FEATURES OF THE RED RIVER DAM.

The work was begun on the 30th of April and finished on the 8th of May. The water having been thus raised five feet four and a half inches, three of the light-draught boats passed the upper fall on that day. On the morning of the 9th the tremendous pressure of the pent-up waters drove out two of the barges, making a gap sixty-six feet wide, and swung them against the rocks below. Through the gap the river rushed in a torrent. The admiral at once galloped round to the upper fall and ordered the *Lexington* to run the rapids. With a full head of steam she made the plunge, watched in the breathless silence of suspense by the army and the fleet, and greeted with a mighty cheer as she rode in safety below. The three gun-boats (the *Osage, Neosho,* and *Fort Hindman*) that were waiting just above the dam followed her down the chute; but six gun-boats and two tugs were still imprisoned by the falling waters.

So far Bailey had substantially followed the same plan that had worked so successfully the year before at Port Hudson,⹋ but it was now plainly shown to be not altogether applicable against such a weight and volume and velocity of water as had to be encountered here. He therefore promptly remedied the defect by constructing three wing dams at the upper fall: a stone crib on the south side, and a tree dam on the north side just above the upper rocks, and just below them, also on the north side, a bracket dam, made of logs raised at the lower end on trestles and sheathed with plank. Thus the whole current was turned into one narrow channel, a further rise of fourteen inches was obtained, making six feet six and a half inches in all; and this

⹋ There the gap between the two wings was closed by a boom of logs, to which, when all was ready, a hawser was attached and carried to the capstan of one of the steamers. With a slow strain the boom was hauled up against the current; then the hawser was cut with an axe, the boom carried away the dam, and the boats, under full headway, steamed out into the Mississippi.— R. B. I.

THE "LEXINGTON" PASSING OVER THE FALLS AT THE DAM.   FROM A WAR-TIME SKETCH.

new task, by incredible exertions, being completed in three days and three nights, on the 12th and 13th the remaining gun-boats passed free of the danger. ↓

This accomplished and the reunited fleet being on its way to the Mississippi, the army at once marched out of Alexandria on Simsport, where the column arrived, without serious molestation, on the 16th of May. Bailey improvised a bridge of steamboats across the Atchafalaya, ♭ here between six and seven hundred yards wide, and thus, by the 19th, the whole command crossed in safety. On the day before, however, the rear-guard under Mower had rather a sharp encounter with Wharton and Polignac on Yellow Bayou, the Confederates losing 452 killed and wounded to our loss of about 267.

At Simsport a third messenger was waiting, this time bearing the bowstring, disguised as a silken cord, for though Banks was for a time left in command of the Department of the Gulf, Canby was placed over him and took control of his troops as the commander of the newly made Trans-Mississippi division. A. J. Smith's troops embarked for Vicksburg on the 22d of May, forty-two days after the date first set for their return and two weeks after the opening of the Atlanta campaign, in which they were to have been employed. The Government decided that it was too late to use Banks's army against Mobile, and ordered the Nineteenth Corps, consolidated into two divisions, with part of the Thirteenth Corps incorporated, to join the Army of the Potomac. They arrived just in time to be sent to Washington to aid in repelling Early's invasion. Of Steele's operations, since they belong to another chapter [see p. 375], it is only necessary to say here that he entered Camden, Arkansas, ninety miles in a north-easterly direction from Shreveport, on the 15th of April, just when Banks got back to Grand Ecore. Kirby Smith then left Taylor with Wharton and Polignac to watch and

---

↓ Bailey was made a brigadier-general and received the thanks of Congress. The cribs were soon washed away, but it is said the main tree dam survives to this day, having driven the channel toward the south shore and washed away a large slice of the bank at the upper end of the town.— R. B. I.

♭ General Banks speaks of this use of steamboats to form a bridge as the first attempt of the kind; but when we moved on Port Hudson, the year before, the last of the troops and trains crossed over at the same place in substantially the same way.— R. B. I.

worry Banks, and, concentrating all the rest of his army against Steele, forced him to retreat to Little Rock.

On both sides this unhappy campaign of the Red River raised a great and bitter crop of quarrels. Taylor was relieved by Kirby Smith, as the result of an angry correspondence; Banks was overslaughed, and Franklin quitted the department in disgust; Stone was replaced by Dwight as chief-of-staff, and Lee as chief-of-cavalry by Arnold; A. J. Smith departed more in anger than in sorrow; while between the admiral and the general commanding, recriminations were exchanged in language well up to the limits of "parliamentary" privilege. I have nothing to do with any of these things, but I feel it a duty to express my entire disbelief in all the many tales that seek to cast upon the army or its commander the shadow of a great cotton speculation. These stories, as ample in insinuation as they are weak in specification, are in the last resort found to be vouched for by nobody. I am convinced they are false. The speculators who certainly went with the army as far as Alexandria, had for the most part passes from Washington; the policy under which they were permitted to go was avowedly encouraged by the Government, for reasons of state. When General Banks sent them all back from Alexandria, without their sheaves, they returned to New Orleans furious against him and mouthing calumnies. All the cotton gathered by the army was turned over first to the chief quartermaster, and by him to the special agent of the Treasury Department designated to receive it.⸔ All the cotton seized by the navy ☆ was sent to Cairo, was adjudged "lawful prize of war," and its proceeds distributed as prescribed by the statute. At one time it was supposed that the extensive seizures made by the navy led to the burning of the cotton by the Confederates; the truth is, however, that Kirby Smith ordered the burning of all the cotton in Louisiana east of the Ouachita and south of Alexandria, estimated by him at 150,000 bales, and then worth $60,000,000, on the 14th of

⸔ In a statement presented to the Committee on the Conduct of the War (1865, Vol. II., p. 347) General Banks says:

"During the Red River campaign, all the property that came into the hands of the army was turned over to the quartermaster, and by him to the Treasury officers. There was no exception to this rule. Every person who accompanied the expedition . . . was notified that trade was prohibited, and the quartermaster and the supervising agent of the Treasury Department informed that whatever property should fall into our hands would be disposed of according to the orders of the Government and the laws of Congress, subject to such claims as should be recognized at Washington."

R. B. I.

☆ About 6000 bales, Admiral Porter states.

UNITED STATES HOSPITAL SHIP, "RED ROVER." FROM A WAR-TIME PHOTOGRAPH.

March, as soon as he became satisfied that Banks's army meant to advance once more up the Teche. Porter and A. J. Smith had then just entered the mouth of the Red River, but as yet Kirby Smith neither knew nor expected their coming.

After the Red River campaign no important operation was undertaken by either side in Louisiana. The Confederate forces in that State held out until the end of the war, when, on the surrender of Kirby Smith, May 26th, 1865, they were finally disbanded.

THE NAVY IN THE RED RIVER.

BY THOMAS O. SELFRIDGE, CAPTAIN, U. S. N.

THE Red River expedition was essentially a movement of the Army of the Gulf to control more thoroughly Louisiana and eastern Texas, in which Admiral Porter was called upon to coöperate with the naval forces of the Mississippi.

For this purpose, early in March, 1864, he assembled at the mouth of the Red River the ironclads *Eastport, Essex, Benton, Lafayette, Choctaw, Chillicothe, Ozark, Louisville, Carondelet, Pittsburgh, Mound City, Osage, Neosho,* and the light-draught gun-boats *Ouachita, Lexington, Fort Hindman, Cricket, Gazelle, Juliet,* and *Black Hawk,* bearing the admiral's flag.

This was the most formidable force that had ever been collected in the western waters. It was under a courageous and able commander, full of energy and fertile in resources, and was manned by officers and men who, from a long series of conflicts on the Mississippi, had become veterans in river warfare. With a powerful army, reënforced by ten thousand of Sherman's old soldiers under General A. J. Smith, the navy felt there would be but few laurels left for them to win, and little did it dream of the dangers, hardships, and possible loss of a portion of this splendid squadron that the future had in store for it, owing to the treacherous nature of this crooked, narrow, and turbid stream, whose high banks furnished the most favorable positions for artillery and for the deadly sharp-shooter. That the naval portion did not meet with greater loss of life is owing to the skill, derived from long experience, with which the officers prepared and fought their vessels.

The active coöperation of the navy was dependent to a considerable extent upon the usual spring rise ; but this year the rise did not come, and the movements of the army, which forced the navy to risk its vessels in insufficient depths of water, were the main causes of the almost insurmountable difficulties it had to contend with. Had the river been bank-full no force that the Confederates could have controlled could have stood for a moment against the fleet; its movement to Shreveport would have been but a holiday excursion. But against nature it could not contend, and the very low stage of water soon reduced the active squadron to three iron-clads and a half-dozen light-draughts.

On the 12th of March the fleet and transports moved up the Red River. The greater part turned off at the Atchafalaya to cover the landing of Smith's force at Simsport; from which point they were to march by land to Alexandria, where the junction with Banks's army was to be made. The *Eastport* (Lieutenant-Commander S. L. Phelps), *Osage* (Lieutenant-Commander T. O. Selfridge), *Fort Hindman* (Acting-Master John Pearce), and *Cricket* (Lieutenant H. H. Gorringe) were ordered to go ahead and clear the obstructions that were known to exist below Fort De Russy, a strong fortification constructed by the Confederates earlier in the war, recently strengthened, and now armed with heavy guns in casemates protected with railroad iron.⌡ These obstructions were reached March 14th, and were found to consist of a row of piles across the river, supported by a second row bolted to the first ; a forest of trees had been cut and floated against them, with their branches interlaced with the piles. It was slow work clearing a passage, owing to the strength of the current and to the raft of logs and the snags above the piling, so that a day was consumed ; and before the squadron had finally pushed through and had arrived in proximity to the fort the guns of the Union forces were heard, so that for fear of injury to them the fleet could only fire a few rounds at the water-battery.

The capture of Fort De Russy was a most gallant feat, General Mower actually riding into the fort at the head of his attacking column. Porter's orders to Phelps to push ahead were delayed by the dispatch vessel getting entangled in the obstructions, or else we should have captured the Confederate transports, which were just out of sight as we reached Alexandria, about ten miles above the fort.

On the morning of March 16th nine gun-boats had arrived. I was directed, with 180 men from the fleet, to occupy the town until the arrival of the land forces under General A. J. Smith. It had been agreed that General Banks should be at Alexandria by March 17th, but the cavalry did not arrive till the 19th, and his whole force was not assembled till the 26th. [See p. 350.]

On March 29th fourteen of the squadron left Alexandria for the upper river, the *Eastport* and

⌡ Fort De Russy was captured by the navy in the first movement up the Red River in May, 1863, but was afterward abandoned when the army marched to Port Hudson (see Vol. III., p. 592).— EDITORS.

Osage being in the advance; thus fourteen days of precious time had been lost, allowing the Confederates to concentrate their forces for the defense of Shreveport, our objective point. As we advanced the enemy's scouts set fire to all the cotton within ten miles of the river-bank. Millions of dollars worth of it were destroyed, and so dense was the smoke that the sun was obscured, and appeared as though seen through a smoked glass. One Sunday morning a man was seen waving a white handkerchief in front of a handsome dwelling. Captain Phelps and myself stopped and went ashore to inquire the reason. He told us his name was Colhoun; that he was a brother of Captain Colhoun of the United States navy; that, being over age, he had taken no part in the conflict, but had remained at home cultivating his plantation. With tears in his eyes he told us that that night his cotton pile, of 5000 bales, had been set on fire, and his ginhouse, costing $30,000, destroyed. He was a rich man the night before, and the morning found him penniless. A bale of cotton was worth at that time $400 in New Orleans, so that he had lost at a single blow $2,000,000. He was but one of many innocent persons who suffered the loss of all their property through this indiscriminate destruction. [See p. 372.]

Our supply of coals having given out, we were dependent upon fence rails for fuel. Two hours before sunset the fleet and transports would tie up to the bank, and whole crews and companies of soldiers would range over the country, each man loading himself with two rails, and in an incredibly short time the country would be denuded of fences as far as the eye could see. So dependent were we upon these rails for fuel that it was a saying among the Confederates that they should have destroyed the fences and not the cotton. Had they done so, our progress would have been much slower. As it was, it proved a laborious task for the crews of the gun-boats to cut up these cotton-wood rails in lengths to fit the furnaces, which were much shorter than those of the transports.

On April 3d, Acting Volunteer Lieutenant J. P. Couthouy, commanding the iron-clad *Chillicothe*, was shot by a guerrilla a few miles above Grand Ecore. He was a brave officer, and his loss was much lamented in the squadron.

April 7th, Admiral Porter, on the *Cricket*, bearing his flag, left Grand Ecore for Shreveport, accompanied by the *Osage*, *Neosho*, *Fort Hindman*, *Lexington*, and *Chillicothe*, convoying twenty transports, containing General Kilby Smith's division of the Sixteenth Army Corps; a rendezvous being agreed upon with the army within three days at Springfield Landing, 110 miles by the river below Shreveport. The river was stationary, at a lower stage than usual at this season, and there was barely water to float the gun-boats.

April 10th, the fleet, as agreed upon, arrived at Springfield Landing, about 30 miles, as the crow flies, from its destination, meeting with no obstruction beyond the usual amount of bushwhacking. Here the channel was found obstructed by the sinking of a large steamboat, the *New Falls City*, ⚓ across the channel, both ends resting upon the banks. Of the disastrous results of the battles of Sabine Cross-roads and Pleasant Hill, April 8th and 9th, the fleet were entirely ignorant until a courier reached Admiral Porter from General Banks stating that the army was falling back upon Grand Ecore.

Signal was made for commanding officers to repair on board the flag-ship, when the repulse and retreat of the army was first made known to them. It was announced that it would be necessary for the fleet to go back. The gun-boats were distributed through the transports, and my vessel, the *Osage*, was directed to bring up the rear.

The return of the fleet was fraught with peril: The Confederates, being relieved by the falling back of the army, were now free to attack us at any point of the river. There were but half-a-dozen gun-boats to defend the long line, two of which were light-draughts, known as "tin-clads," from the lightness of their defensive armor, which was only bullet-proof. The river was falling; its narrowness and its high banks afforded the best possible opportunities for harassing attacks, and the bends of the river were so short that it was with the greatest difficulty they were rounded by vessels of the *Osage* type. Steaming with the current, the *Osage* was almost unmanageable, and on the morning of April 12th the transport *Black Hawk* ↓ was lashed to her starboard quarter, and thus the descent was successfully made till about 2 P. M., when the *Osage* ran hard aground opposite Blair's Plantation, or Pleasant Hill Landing, the bows down stream and the starboard broadside bearing on the right bank. While endeavoring to float her, the pilot of the *Black Hawk* reported a large force gathering in the woods some three miles off dressed in Federal uniforms. I ascended to the pilot-house, and scanning them carefully made sure they were Confederates, and at the same time directed Lieutenant Bache of the *Lexington* to go below and open an enfilading fire upon them. Every preparation being made, the attack was quietly awaited. The battery unlimbered near the *Lexington*, but a caisson being blown up they quickly withdrew. The enemy came up in column of regiments, and, protected by the high and almost perpendicular banks, opened a terrific musketry fire, and at a distance not exceeding one hundred yards. Shell-firing under the circumstances was almost useless. The great guns of the *Osage* were loaded with grape and canister, and, when these were exhausted, with shrapnel having fuses cut to one second. Our fire was reserved till the heads of the enemy were seen just above the bank, when both guns were fired. Everything that was made of wood on the *Osage* and *Black Hawk* was pierced with bullets. Upon the iron shield in the pilot-house of the latter were the marks of sixty bullets, a proof

⚓ This steamer was sunk, as stated in the text, on the 5th of April by Captain James McCloskey, acting under the orders of Generals E. K. Smith and Taylor. After the return of the fleet to Grand Ecore, the obstruction had to be removed before the Confederates could recover the use of the river.— EDITORS.

↓ Not to be confounded with the naval steamer of the same name, which remained at Alexandria.— EDITORS.

"BLACK HAWK" AND "OSAGE."   "LEXINGTON."

THE FIGHT AT BLAIR'S PLANTATION. FROM A WAR-TIME SKETCH.

of the hotness of the fire. This unequal contest could not continue long, and after an hour and a half the enemy retreated with a loss of over four hundred killed and wounded, as afterward ascertained. Among the former was General Thomas Green, their foremost partisan fighter west of the Mississippi. ♪ The *Osage* sustained a loss of seven wounded. Company A of the 90th Illinois were on board and behaved most gallantly.

The Confederates did not again molest the fleet until the 25th of April, when they attacked Admiral Porter in the light-draught gunboat *Cricket*. At this late period the low condition of the river had forced him to send the *Osage* and *Neosho* down the river, or the rebels would have suffered as severely as at Blair's Plantation.

The 15th of April found the squadron with its fleet of transports safe back at Grand Ecore, not much the worse for their encounters with the enemy and the snags and sand bars of the river. Admiral Porter was called to Alexandria by the affairs of the Mississippi squadron, leaving the *Osage* and *Lexington* at Grand Ecore. The larger iron-clads had with great difficulty been forced over the bar below Grand Ecore and sent on toward Alexandria, whither the *Osage* and *Lexington* followed them.

The *Eastport* (Lieutenant-Commander Phelps), the largest of our iron-clads, which had joined the squadron for the first time on this expedition, unfortunately struck a torpedo eight miles below Grand Ecore, and her bottom was so badly injured

that she sank. Captain Phelps was very proud of his ship, and went to work with a will to save her. After the most untiring efforts he succeeded in bulkheading the leak, and, assisted by two steam-pump boats which the admiral had brought to his assistance, succeeded in getting her some forty miles down the river. Here she grounded again, but after strenuous efforts, assisted by the admiral, who remained behind, she was floated, but after proceeding a few miles again grounded on a pile of snags. From the 21st to the 25th of April Captain Phelps, one of the bravest and most competent commanders in the squadron, had worked day and night with his officers and crew to save his ship, but the retreat of the army had left the banks of the river unprotected [see p. 357], and the low stage of water had compelled the admiral to send his squadron to Alexandria. There was no longer a chance to save the *Eastport*, and he reluctantly gave the order to blow her up. Hardly had this been done when the little squadron was attacked by a large force of infantry, which was quickly driven off. It was evident that serious work was ahead. The squadron now consisted of the light-draught gun-boats *Cricket* (flag-ship), *Juliet*, and *Fort Hindman*. They had proceeded some twenty miles when the enemy opened upon them with twenty pieces of artillery. Nineteen shells went crashing through the *Cricket*, and during the five minutes she was under fire she was struck thirty-eight times and lost twelve killed and nineteen wounded out of a crew of fifty, one-third of

♪ Of this action Admiral Porter, in his "Naval History of the Civil War," writes as follows: "Selfridge conducted this affair in the handsomest manner, inflicting such a punishment on the enemy that their infantry gave no more trouble, having come to the conclusion that fighting with muskets against iron-clads did not pay. To say nothing of the loss in men inflicted upon

the enemy, the *Osage* had killed the best officer the Confederates had in this quarter, who, judging from his energy on this occasion, would have given no end of trouble had he lived. Lieutenant [George M.] Bache managed the *Lexington* beautifully and did great execution with his guns, though less exposed to the infantry fire than the *Osage*."— EDITORS.

whom were negroes. The escape of the *Cricket* was almost miraculous, and was largely owing to the coolness and skill of the admiral. ⸿ The remainder of the squadron turned up stream, except the two pump-boats, *Champion No.* 3 and *No.* 5, which being unarmed were destroyed.

Captain Phelps concluded to wait till the next day to run the batteries, which was successfully accomplished under a heavy fire, the *Juliet* sustaining a loss of 15 killed and wounded, and the *Fort Hindman* 7. ☆

April 27th found the fleet once more assembled at Alexandria. During all this hazardous and harassing return from Springfield Landing there had been no instance in which the navy had withheld support from the army when called upon; of which there is no better proof than that every transport returned safely, though by delaying the return to the last possible moment the safety of the fleet was jeopardized, and the *Eastport* and the two pump-boats were lost.

Twelve of the squadron were now assembled above the falls, the rocks of which were bare, while the channel between them was hardly twenty feet wide, and three feet deep. No spring rise had come, and General Banks with the army was anxious to leave Alexandria and the region where no laurels had been gained. What should be done with the squadron stopped by this seemingly impassable barrier, the falls of the Red River? At this critical moment Lieutenant-Colonel Joseph Bailey, chief engineer of the Nineteenth Army Corps, came forward with the proposition to construct a dam at the falls. It seemed almost an impossibility to accomplish what had before been attempted without success in more peaceful times; but it was only necessary to propose the plan for both army and navy to enter into the scheme with characteristic American energy.⸗ While the work was in progress, the side armor was stripped from the larger iron-clads, taken up the river after nightfall, and dropped in a deep hole, while the lighter guns, 32-pounders, some dozen altogether, were put ashore. In about ten days the unique and Herculean work was completed. All the credit is due to the gallant men of the army, who for eight days worked good-humoredly in water, and exposed to a hot sun.

The current was now rushing through the gap in the dam at a rate of nine miles an hour, and yet upon the falls there lacked a foot of water to float the larger boats. To close the gate, two strong loaded coal-barges were shipped into it, secured by lines from the banks. After all but the largest vessels had descended safely over the falls, it seemed assured that the morning would show enough water to float the whole squadron over. But during the night the lines parted, and the barges were swept away and struck a ledge of rocks below the dam and bilged. What then seemed a great misfortune, however, proved our salvation, for the *Lexington*, the first gun-boat to go through, though carried against this very ledge and striking the sides of the barges, caromed off down stream, when, but for them, she would doubtless have been sunk, most seriously obstructing the channel against the passage of the others.⚓ Colonel Bailey, as a next resource, proceeded to construct below the upper falls wing dams from each bank, by which a further rise of a few inches was obtained. Hawsers were run out from the gun-boats to the shore, and these manned by a brigade, and the united force of three thousand men, enlivened with a band of music, dragged them over the bottom till they floated in the deeper water below, and both army and navy breathed more freely in this rescue of the squadron upon seeing them anchored in the stream below Alexandria. On the morning of May 13th I was dispatched to the upper falls to destroy the 32-pounders left behind, the army having already begun its march for the Mississippi. Just as the last one was blown to pieces, a rebel cavalry regiment galloped down the road and fired a volley which happily did no damage, and before it could be repeated the swift current had carried the boat out of their range.

During the building of the dam a gallant but disastrous action took place between the small light-draught gun-boats *Signal* (Acting-Master Morgan) and *Covington* (Acting Volunteer Lieutenant Lord), at Dunn's Bayou, below Alexandria, while convoying the *Warner*, a quartermaster's boat, down the river. The rebels, having passed round the rear of our forces at Alexandria with six thousand men and twenty-five pieces of artillery, established themselves on the river and opened on the *Warner* when she came in sight. The gun-boats rounded to immediately and opened the fight, but the fire was so severe that the steam-pipes were cut and the boilers perforated. Though virtually disabled, they continued this unequal contest for five hours, when Lieutenant Lord landed his crew and set fire to his vessel. The *Signal* had too many wounded to permit her commander to pursue a like course, and she fell into the hands of the enemy, who, after removing the guns, sunk her in the river as an obstruction.

⸿ When the pilot was wounded, Admiral Porter piloted the vessel himself. See Mahan's "The Gulf and Inland Waters," p. 201.— EDITORS.

☆ The destruction of the *Eastport* and the action of the *Cricket* occurred on the 26th. While the *Cricket* was running the gauntlet of the Confederate position, the pump-boat *Champion No.* 3 received a shot in her boiler, causing it to explode. The captain, Stewart, three engineers, and all the crew, composed of some 200 negroes, were scalded to death, with the exception of 15. The *Champion No.* 5 retreated with the *Hindman* and *Juliet*, above the Confederate battery, and on the 27th attempted to make the passage down in their company.

Unable to get by, she was guided to the opposite bank by her pilot, Maitland, who remained at the wheel after having received eight wounds. The boat finally sank, and most of the crew were captured.— EDITORS.

⸗ For a description of the dam, see p. 359.— EDITORS.

⚓ The *Osage*, *Neosho*, and *Fort Hindman* passed the falls on the 8th, the other vessels remaining above. On the 9th, after the barges had been carried away, and thus had opened the break in the dam, these three gun-boats and the *Lexington* passed through the opening. The vessels remaining above, which passed through on the 11th and 12th, were the *Carondelet*, *Louisville*, *Mound City*, *Pittsburgh*, *Ozark*, *Chillicothe*, and two tugs.—EDITORS.

Of this action, Admiral Porter writes :

"The brave men in their light vessels, only musket-proof, defended them for four or five hours, and many of the actions heralded to the world during the late war were much less worthy of notice than this contest between two little gun-boats and twenty pieces of artillery, most of which had been captured from the army at Pleasant Hill [meaning Sabine Cross-roads]."

On the 21st of May, the squadron and transports reached the Mississippi. And thus ended the Red River expedition, one of the most humiliating and disastrous that had to be recorded during the war. The vessels lost were the *Eastport*, sunk by a torpedo ; the two pump-boats, *Champion No. 3* and *No. 5*, and the small gun-boats *Covington* and *Signal*. The total casualties of the navy in killed, wounded, and missing were about 120, exclusive of the crews of the pump-boats, which lost upward of 200.

THE MISSISSIPPI FLOTILLA IN THE RED RIVER EXPEDITION.

Rear-Admiral David D. Porter, commanding.

IRON-CLADS.— *Essex*, Com. Robert Townsend, 2 100-pounder Parrotts, 6 9-inch, 4 12-pounder howitzers. *Benton*, Lieut.-Com. James A. Greer, 2 100-pounder Parrotts, 8 9-inch, 2 50-pounder Dahlgren rifles, 4 32-pounders. *Lafayette*, Lieut.-Com. J. P. Foster, 2 11-inch, 2 9-inch, 2 100-pounder Parrotts, 2 24-pounder howitzers, 2 12-pounder howitzers. *Choctaw*, Lieut.-Com. F. M. Ramsay, 1 100-pounder Parrott, 3 9-inch, 2 30-pounder Parrotts, 2 12-pounder howitzers. *Chillicothe*, Act. V. Lieut. Joseph P. Couthouy, Lieut.-Com. Watson Smith (temporarily), 2 11-inch, 1 12-pounder. *Ozark*, Act. V. Lieut. George W. Brown, 2 11-inch, 1 12-pounder rifled howitzer. *Louisville*, Lieut.-Com. E. K. Owen, 1 100-pounder Parrott, 4 9-inch, 2 30-pounder Parrotts, 4 32-pounders. *Carondelet*, Lieut.-Com. J. G. Mitchell, 2 100-pounder Parrotts, 3 9-inch, 4 8-inch, 1 50-pounder rifle, 1 30-pounder rifle. *Eastport*, Lieut.-Com. S. L. Phelps, 2 100-pounder Parrotts, 4 9-inch, 2 50-pounder Dahlgren rifles. *Pittsburgh*, Act. V. Lieut. W. R. Hoel, 4 9-inch, 1 100-pounder Parrott, 2 30-pounder Parrotts. *Mound City*, Act. V. Lieut. A. R. Langthorne, 1 100-pounder Parrott, 4 9-inch, 3 8-inch, 1 50-pounder rifle, 1 30-pounder rifle, 2 32-pounders. *Osage*, Lieut.-Com. T. O. Selfridge, 2 11-inch, 1 12-pounder howitzer. *Neosho*, Act. V. Lieut. Samuel Howard, 2 11-inch, 2 12-pounder howitzers.

TIN-CLADS.— *Cricket*, Acting Master H. H. Gorringe, 2 20-pounder Parrotts, 4 24-pounder howitzers, 1 12-pounder howitzer. *Gazelle*, Acting Master Charles Thatcher, 6 12-pounder rifled howitzers. *Signal*, Act. V. Lieutenant E. Morgan, 4 24-pounder S. B. howitzers, 2 12-pounder rifled howitzers, 2 30-pounder Parrotts. *Juliet*, Acting Master J. S. Watson, 6 24-pounder S. B. howitzers.

OTHER VESSELS.— *Lexington*, Lieut. George M. Bache, 4 8-inch, 2 30-pounder Parrotts, 1 32-pounder. *Black Hawk* (flag-ship), Lieut.-Com. K. R. Breese, 2 30-pounder Parrotts, 8 24-pounder S. B. howitzers, 2 12-pounder rifled howitzers, 1 12-pounder S. B. howitzer, 2 Union repeating guns, 1 Parmenter battery gun. *Benefit* (naval transport), Lieut.-Com. S. W. Terry. *Covington*, Act. V. Lieut. George P. Lord, 4 24-pounder howitzers, 1 12-pounder howitzer, 2 30-pounder Parrotts, 2 50-pounder Dahlgren rifles. *Ouachita*, Lieut.-Com. Byron Wilson, 5 30-pounder Parrotts, 18 24-pounder S. B. howitzers, 15 12-pounder S. B. howitzers, 1 12-pounder rifled howitzer. *Fort Hindman*, Act. V. Lieut. John Pearce, 6 8-inch, 1 12-pounder howitzer.

ON THE MISSISSIPPI RIVER HOSPITAL-BOAT "D. A. JANUARY." FROM A WAR-TIME SKETCH.

THE OPPOSING FORCES IN THE RED RIVER CAMPAIGN.[1]

THE UNION ARMY.— Major-General Nathaniel P. Banks.

Headquarters Troops (Guard): A and B, Capt. Richard W. Francis. *(Escort):* C, Capt. Frank Sayles.

THIRTEENTH ARMY CORPS (detachment), Brig.-Gen. Thomas E. G. Ransom (w), Brig.-Gen. Robert A. Cameron.

THIRD DIVISION, Brig.-Gen. Robert A. Cameron.

First Brigade, Lieut.-Col. Aaron M. Flory: 46th Ind., Capt. William M. De Hart; 29th Wis., Maj. Bradford Hancock. *Second Brigade,* Col. William H. Raynor: 24th Iowa, Maj. Edward Wright; 28th Iowa, Maj. John Connell; 56th Ohio, Capt. Maschil Manring. *Artillery:* A, 1st Mo., Lieut. Elisha Cole; 2d Ohio, Lieut. Wm. H. Harper.

FOURTH DIVISION, Col. William J. Landram.

First Brigade, Col. Frank Emerson (w and c): 77th Ill., Lieut.-Col. Lysander R. Webb; 67th Ind. (non-veterans of 60th Ind. attached), Maj. Francis A. Sears; 19th Ky., Lieut.-Col. John Cowan; 23d Wis., Maj. Joseph E. Greene. *Second Brigade,* Col. Joseph W. Vance (k): 97th Ill., Col. Friend S. Rutherford; 130th Ill., Maj. John B. Reid; 48th Ohio, Lieut.-Col. Joseph W. Lindsey; 83d Ohio, Lieut.-Col. William H. Baldwin; 96th Ohio, Lieut.-Col. Albert H. Brown. *Artillery:* Chicago (Ill.) Mercantile Battery, Capt. Patrick H. White (chief of artillery detachment Thirteenth Army Corps), Lieut. Pinckney S. Cone; 1st Ind., Capt. Martin Klauss.

SIXTEENTH AND SEVENTEENTH ARMY CORPS (detachment from the Army of the Tennessee), Brig.-Gen. Andrew J. Smith.

SIXTEENTH ARMY CORPS.

FIRST AND THIRD DIVISIONS, Brig.-Gen. Jos. A. Mower.

FIRST DIVISION.

Second Brigade, Col. Lucius F. Hubbard: 47th Ill., Col. John D. McClure; 5th Minn., Maj. John C. Becht; 8th Wis., Lieut.-Col. John W. Jefferson. *Third Brigade,* Col. Sylvester G. Hill: 35th Iowa, Lieut.-Col. William B. Keeler; 33d Mo., Lieut.-Col. William H. Heath.

THIRD DIVISION.

First Brigade, Col. William F. Lynch: 58th Ill., Maj. Thomas Newlan; 119th Ill., Col. Thomas J. Kinney; 89th Ind., Col. Charles D. Murray. *Second Brigade,* Col. William T. Shaw: 14th Iowa, Lieut.-Col. Joseph H. Newbold; 27th Iowa, Col. James I. Gilbert; 32d Iowa, Col. John Scott; 24th Mo. (non-veterans of 21st Mo. attached), Maj. Robert W. Fyan. *Third Brigade,* Col. Risdon M. Moore: 49th Ill., Maj. Thomas W. Morgan; 117th Ill., Lieut.-Col. Jonathan Merriman; 178th N. Y., Col. Edward Wehler. *Artillery:* 3d Ind., Capt. James M. Cockefair; 9th Ind., Capt. George R. Brown.

SEVENTEENTH ARMY CORPS, Brig.-Gen. T. Kilby Smith.

First Brigade, Col. Jonathan B. Moore: 41st Ill., Lieut.-Col. John H. Nale; 3d Iowa, Lieut.-Col. James Tullis; 33d Wis., Maj. Horatio H. Virgin. *Second Brigade,* Col. Lyman M. Ward: 81st Ill., Col. Andrew W. Rogers; 95th Ill., Col. Thos. W. Humphrey; 14th Wis., Capt. C. M. G. Mansfield. *Artillery:* M, 1st Mo., Lieut. John H. Tiemeyer.

NINETEENTH ARMY CORPS, Maj.-Gen. William B. Franklin (w), Brig.-Gen. William H. Emory.

FIRST DIVISION, Brig.-Gen. William H. Emory, Brig.-Gen. J. W. McMillan.

First Brigade, Brig.-Gen. William Dwight, Jr., Col. Geo. L. Beal: 29th Me., Col. George L. Beal; 114th N. Y., Lieut.-Col. Henry B. Morse; 116th N. Y., Col. George M. Love; 153d N. Y., Col. Edwin P. Davis; 161st N. Y., Lieut.-Col. William B. Kinsey. *Second Brigade,* Brig.-Gen. James W. McMillan: 13th Me., Col. Henry Rust, Jr.; 15th Me., Col. Isaac Dyer; 160th N. Y., Lieut.-Col. John B. Van Petten; 47th Pa., Col. Tilghman H. Good. *Third Brigade,* Col. Lewis Benedict (k), Col. Francis Fessenden (w): 30th Me., Col. Francis Fessenden, Lieut.-Col. Thomas H. Hubbard; 162d N. Y., Lieut.-Col. Justus W. Blanchard; 165th N. Y., Lieut.-Col. Gouverneur Carr;

173d N. Y., Col. Lewis M. Peck. *Artillery,* Capt. George T. Hebard: 25th N. Y., Lieut. Irving D. Southworth; L, 1st U. S., Lieut. Franck E. Taylor; 1st Vt., Capt. George T. Hebard.

SECOND DIVISION, Brig.-Gen. Cuvier Grover.

First Brigade, [2] Brig.-Gen. F. S. Nickerson. *Second Brigade,* Brig.-Gen. Henry W. Birge, [3] Col. Edward L. Molineux: 13th Conn., Col. Charles D. Blinn; 1st La., Col. William O. Fiske; 90th N. Y. (3 co's), Maj. John C. Smart; 159th N. Y., Lieut.-Col. Edward L. Gaul. *Third Brigade,* Col. Jacob Sharpe: 38th Mass., Lieut.-Col. James P. Richardson; 128th N. Y., Col. James Smith; 156th N. Y., Capt. James J. Hoyt; 175th N. Y. (batt'n), Capt. Charles McCarthey. *Artillery,* Capt. George W. Fox: 7th Mass., Capt. Newman W. Storer; 26th N. Y., Capt. George W. Fox; F, 1st U. S., Lieut. Hardman P. Norris; C, 2d U. S., Lieut John I. Rodgers. *Cavalry:* 3d Md., Col. C. Carroll Tevis.

ARTILLERY RESERVE, Capt. Henry W. Closson (chief of corps artillery): 1st Del., Capt. Benjamin Nields; D, 1st Ind. Heavy, Capt. William S. Hinkle.

CAVALRY DIVISION, Brig.-Gen. Albert L. Lee, Brig.-Gen. Richard Arnold.

First Brigade, Col. Thomas J. Lucas: 16th Ind. (mounted inf'y), Lieut.-Col. James H. Redfield; 2d La (mounted inf'y), Maj. Alfred Hodsdon; 6th Mo. (Howitzer battery under Capt. Herbert H. Rottaken, attached), Capt. Sidney A. Breese; 14th N. Y., Maj. Abraham Bassford. *Third Brigade,* Col. Harai Robinson: 87th Ill. (mounted inf'y), Lieut.-Col. John M. Crebs; 1st La., Maj. Algernon S. Badger. *Fourth Brigade,* Col. Nathan A. M. Dudley: 2d Ill., Maj. Benjamin F. Marsh, Jr.; 3d Mass., Lieut.-Col. Lorenzo D. Sargent; 31st Mass. (mounted inf'y), Capt. Elbert H. Fordham; 8th N. H. (mounted inf'y), Lieut.-Col. George A. Flanders. *Fifth Brigade,* Col. Oliver P. Gooding: 2d N. Y. Veteran, Col. Morgan H. Chrysler; 18th N. Y., Col. James J. Byrne; 3d R.I. (detachment), Maj. George R. Davis. *Artillery:* 2d Mass., Capt. Ormand F. Nims; G, 5th U. S., Lieut. Jacob B. Rawles.

CORPS D'AFRIQUE.

First Brigade, Col. William H. Dickey: 1st Infantry (73d U. S. C. T.), Maj. Hiram E. Perkins; 3d Infantry (75th U. S. C. T.), Col. Henry W. Fuller; 12th Infantry (84th U. S. C. T.), Capt. James H. Corrin; 22d Infantry (92d U. S. C. T.), Col. Henry N. Frisbie.

In his testimony before the Committee on the Conduct of the War (p. 21, Vol. II.), General Banks says:

" We started with the idea that we were to have a concentrated command of at least 35,000 to 40,000 men, when in fact we had less than 20,000, and but little more than 15,000 for actual battle with the enemy."

The returns for March 31st, 1864, however, show a total present for duty of 31,303 officers and men, viz.: Headquarters, 67; Engineers, 721; 13th Corps, 4773; 19th Corps, 10,619; Corps d'Afrique, 1535; Cavalry, 4653,— total Army of the Gulf, 22,368; detachment Army of the Tennessee, 8935,—grand total, 31,303. Deducting Grover's division left at Alexandria (3846), and Kilby Smith's division, which moved with the fleet (1721), it will be seen that the marching column consisted on the 31st of March of 25,736 officers and men of all arms.

In his official report Banks says:

" In these operations (up to April 26th), in which my own command had marched by land nearly 400 miles, the total loss sustained was 3980 men, of whom 289 were killed, 1541 wounded, and 2150 missing. A large portion of the latter were captured."

On the return march from Alexandria the loss approximated 165 killed, 650 wounded, and 450 captured or missing.

[1] As constituted about April 1st, 1864, with subsequent changes of Union commanders partly indicated.
[2] Also commanded the troops engaged at the battles of Sabine Cross-roads and Pleasant Hill.
[3] Joined the army at Alexandria (from New Orleans) after the battle of Pleasant Hill.
[4] Also commanded at Monette's Ferry a temporary division of his own brigade and the Third Brigade, First Division.

THE CONFEDERATE ARMY.— General E. Kirby Smith.

DISTRICT OF WEST LOUISIANA, Lieut.-Gen. Richard Taylor.

WALKER'S DIVISION, Maj.-Gen. John G. Walker.
Brigade Commanders: Brig.-Gens. T. N. Waul, W. R. Scurry, and Col. Horace Randal.

MOUTON'S DIVISION, Brig.-Gen. Alfred Mouton, Brig.-Gen. C. J. Polignac.
Brigade Commanders: Brig.-Gen. C. J. Polignac and Col. Henry Gray.

SUB-DISTRICT OF NORTH LOUISIANA, Brig.-Gen. St. John R. Liddell.

CAVALRY DIVISION, Brig.-Gen. Thomas Green and Maj.-Gen. John A. Wharton.
Brigade Commanders: Brig.-Gens. Hamilton P. Bee, J. P. Major, and Arthur P. Bagby.

UNATTACHED CAVALRY: 2d La., Col. W. G. Vincent; 4th La., Col. Louis Bush.

DETACHMENT OF PRICE'S ARMY, Brig.-Gen. Thomas J. Churchill.

MISSOURI DIVISION, Brig.-Gen. M. M. Parsons.
Brigade Commanders: Brig.-Gen. John B. Clark, Jr., and Col. S. P. Burns.

ARKANSAS DIVISION (Churchill's), Brig.-Gen. John C. Tappan.
Brigade Commanders: Cols. H. L. Grinsted and L. C. Gause.

ARTILLERY (attached to brigades and divisions).

General Taylor says:

"The army I had the honor to command in this campaign numbered, at its greatest strength, about 13,000 of all arms, including Liddell's force on the north bank of Red River; but immediately after the battle of Pleasant Hill it was reduced to 5200 by the withdrawal of Walker's and Churchill's divisions. . . . Our total loss in killed, wounded, and missing was 3976." (See p. 191, "Destruction and Reconstruction," D. Appleton & Co., New York.)

General E. Kirby Smith, in his official report, says:

"Taylor had at Mansfield, after the junction of Green, 11,000 effectives, with 5000 infantry from Price's army in one day's march of him."

According to General Parsons's report, his division at Pleasant Hill numbered "2200 muskets."

THE OPPOSING FORCES IN ARKANSAS, APRIL 20, 1864.

THE UNION ARMY.

DEPARTMENT OF ARKANSAS, Maj.-Gen. Frederick Steele.

THIRD DIVISION, Brig.-Gen. Frederick Salomon.
First Brigade, Brig.-Gen. Samuel A. Rice: 50th Ind., Lieut.-Col. Samuel T. Wells; 29th Iowa, Col. Thomas H. Benton, Jr.; 33d Iowa, Col. Cyrus H. Mackey; 9th Wis., Col. Charles E. Salomon. *Second Brigade,* Col. William E. McLean: 43d Ind., Maj. Wesley W. Norris; 36th Iowa, Col. C. W. Kittredge; 77th Ohio, Col. William B. Mason. *Third Brigade,* Col. Adolph Engelmann: 43d Ill., Lieut.-Col. Adolph Dengler; 40th Iowa, Col. John A. Garrett; 27th Wis., Col. Conrad Krez. *Artillery:* Ill. Battery, Capt. T. F. Vaughn; 3d Iowa, Lieut. M. C. Wright; K, 1st Mo., Capt. James Marr; E, 2d Mo., Lieut. Charles Peetz.

FRONTIER DIVISION, Brig.-Gen. John M. Thayer.
First Brigade, Col. John Edwards: 1st Ark., Lieut.-Col. E. J. Searle; 2d Ark., Maj. M. L. Stephenson; 18th Iowa, Capt. William M. Duncan; 2d Ind. Battery, Lieut. Hugh Espey. *Second Brigade,* Col. Charles W. Adams:

1st Kan. (colored), Col. James M. Williams; 2d Kan. (colored), Col. Samuel J. Crawford; 12th Kan., Lieut.-Col. Josiah E. Hayes; 1st Ark. Battery, Capt. Denton D. Stark. *Third Brigade* (cavalry), Col. Owen A. Bassett: 2d Kan., Maj. Julius G. Fisk; 6th Kan., Lieut.-Col. William T. Campbell; 14th Kan., Lieut.-Col. John G. Brown.

CAVALRY DIVISION, Brig.-Gen. Eugene A. Carr.
First Brigade, Col. John F. Ritter: 3d Ark., Maj. George F. Lovejoy; 1st Mo., Capt. Miles Kehoe; 2d Mo., Capt. William H. Higdon; 13th Ill. and 3d Iowa (detachment), Capt. Adolph Bechaud. *Third Brigade,* Lieut.-Col. Joseph W. Caldwell: 1st Iowa, Capt. James P. Crosby; 10th Ill. (detachment), Lieut. R. J. Bellamy; 3d Mo., Maj. John A. Lennon.

INDEPENDENT CAVALRY BRIGADE, Col. Powell Clayton: 1st Ind., Maj. Julian D. Owen; 5th Kan., Lieut.-Col. Wilton A. Jenkins. Effective force (estimated), 13,000; total loss about 2,500.

THE CONFEDERATE ARMY.—General E. Kirby Smith.

DISTRICT OF ARKANSAS, Maj.-Gen. Sterling Price.‡
Escort: Mo. Battalion, Maj. R. C. Wood.

FAGAN'S CAVALRY DIVISION, Brig.-Gen. J. F. Fagan.
Cabell's Brigade, Brig.-Gen. W. L. Cabell: 1st Ark., Col. J. C. Monroe; 2d Ark., Col. T. J. Morgan; 4th Ark., Col. A. Gordon; 7th Ark., Col. John F. Hill; Ark. Battalion, Lieut.-Col. T. M. Gunter; Blocher's Battery, ——. *Dockery's Brigade,* Brig.-Gen. T. P. Dockery: 18th Ark., ——; 19th Ark., Lieut.-Col. H. G. P. William; 20th Ark., ——; Ark. Battalion, ——. *Crawford's Brigade,* Col. W. A. Crawford: 2d Ark., Capt. O. B. Tebbs; Crawford's Reg't, ——; Wright's Reg't, Col. John C. Wright; Poe's Battalion, Maj. J. T. Poe; Ark. Battalion, Maj. E. L. McMurtrey. *Artillery:* Ark. Battery, Capt. W. M. Hughey.

MARMADUKE'S CAVALRY DIVISION, Brig.-Gen. John S. Marmaduke.
Greene's Brigade, Col. Colton Greene: 3d Mo., Lieut.-Col. L. A. Campbell; 4th Mo., Lieut.-Col. W. J. Preston; 7th Mo., ——; 8th Mo., Col. W. L. Jeffers; 10th Mo., Col. R. R. Lawther; Mo. Battery, Capt. —— Harris. *Shelby's Brigade,* Brig.-Gen. Joseph O. Shelby: 1st Mo., Battalion, Maj. Benjamin Elliott; 5th Mo., Col. B. F. Gordon; 11th Mo., Col. M. W. Smith; 12th Mo., Col. David Shanks; Hunter's Reg't, Col. D. C. Hunter; Mo. Battery, Capt. R. A. Collins.

MAXEY'S CAVALRY DIVISION, Brig.-Gen. Saml. B. Maxey.
Gano's Brigade, Col. Charles De Morse: 29th Tex., Maj.

J. A. Carroll; 30th Tex., Lieut.-Col. N. W. Battle; 31st Tex., Maj. M. Looscan; Welch's Co., Lieut. Frank M. Gano; Tex. Battery, Capt. W. B. Krumbhaar. *Choctaw Brigade,* Col. Tandy Walker: 1st Regiment, Lieut.-Col. James Riley; 2d Regiment, Col. Simpson W. Folsom.

WALKER'S DIVISION, Maj.-Gen. John G. Walker.
Brigade Commanders: Brig.-Gens. T. N. Waul, W. R. Scurry, and Col. Horace Randal.

ARKANSAS DIVISION, Brig.-Gen. Thomas J. Churchill.
Tappan's Brigade, Brig.-Gen. J. C. Tappan: 24th and 30th Ark., Lieut.-Col. W. R. Hardy; 27th and 38th Ark., Col. R. G. Shaver; 33d Ark., Col. H. L. Grinsted. *Hawthorn's Brigade,* Brig.-Gen. A. T. Hawthorn: . . . *Gause's Brigade,* Col. L. C. Gause: 26th Ark., Lieut.-Col. Iverson L. Brooks; 32d Ark., Lieut.-Col. William Hicks; 36th Ark., Col. J. M. Davie.

MISSOURI DIVISION, Brig.-Gen. M. M. Parsons.
First Brigade, Brig.-Gen. John B. Clark, Jr.: 8th Mo., Col. Charles S. Mitchell; 9th Mo., Col. R. H. Musser; Mo. Battery, Capt. S. T. Ruffner. *Second Brigade,* Col. S. P. Burns: 10th Mo., Col. William Moore; 11th Mo., Lieut.-Col. Thomas H. Murray; 12th Mo., ——; 16th Mo., Lieut.-Col. P. W. H. Cumming; 9th Mo. Battalion Sharp-shooters, Maj. L. A. Pindall; Mo. Battery, Capt. A. A. Lesueur.

Maximum effective strength (estimated), 14,000; total loss (estimated), 1200.

‡ Assumed command of the Arkansas and Missouri divisions April 26.

THE DEFENSE OF THE RED RIVER.┃

BY E. KIRBY SMITH, GENERAL, C. S. A.

SOON after my arrival in the Trans-Mississippi Department ⚓ I became convinced that the valley of the Red River was the only practicable line of operations by which the enemy could penetrate the country. This fact was well understood and appreciated by their generals.

I addressed myself to the task of defending this line with the slender means at my disposal. Fortifications were erected on the lower Red River; Shreveport and Camden were fortified, and works were ordered on the Sabine and the crossings of the upper Red River. Depots were established on the shortest lines of communication between the Red River valley and the troops serving in Arkansas and Texas. Those commands were directed to be held ready to move with little delay, and every preparation was made in advance for accelerating a concentration, at all times difficult over long distances, and through a country destitute of supplies and with limited means of transportation.

In February, 1864, the enemy were preparing in New Orleans, Vicksburg, and Little Rock for offensive operations. Though 25,000 of the enemy were reported on the Texas coast, my information convinced me that the valley of the Red River would be the principal theater of operations and Shreveport the objective point of the columns moving from Arkansas and Louisiana.

On the 21st of February General Magruder, commanding in Texas, was ordered to hold Green's division of cavalry in readiness to move at a moment's warning, and on the 5th of March the division was ordered to march at once to Alexandria and report to General Taylor, who had command in Louisiana. About that time the enemy commenced massing his forces at Berwick Bay.

On the 12th of March a column of ten thousand men, composed of portions of the Sixteenth and Seventeenth Army Corps under General A. J. Smith, moved down from Vicksburg to Simsport, and advanced with such celerity on Fort De Russy, taking it in reverse, that General Taylor was not allowed time to concentrate and cover this important work, our only means of arresting the progress of the gun-boats. The fall of this work and the immediate movement of the enemy, by means of his transports, to Alexandria, placed General Taylor in a very embarrassing position. He extricated himself with his characteristic tact by a march of seventy miles through the pine woods. Banks now pressed forward from Berwick Bay, by the line of the Teche, and by the aid of steamers, on both the Mississippi and Red rivers, concentrated at Alexandria a force of over 30,000 men, supported by the most powerful naval armament ever employed on a river.

┃ I have found amongst my war papers two letters upon the Red River campaign which I believe have never been published. They were written by me to Mr. Davis, the President of the Confederacy, immediately after the occurrence of those events, and are official and have the merit of being written when events were fresh and before either prejudice or personal feeling could have biased. From these, chiefly, I take this narrative.—E. K. S.

⚓ General E. Kirby Smith took command of all the Confederate forces west of the Mississippi River March 7th, 1863, and held it until the end of the war.—EDITORS.

As soon as I received intelligence of the debarkation of the enemy at Simsport, I ordered General Price, who commanded in Arkansas, to dispatch his entire infantry, consisting of Churchill's and Parsons's divisions, to Shreveport, and General Maxey to move toward General Price, and, as soon as Steele advanced, to join Price with his whole command, Indians included. The cavalry east of the Ouachita was directed to fall back toward Natchitoches, and subsequently to oppose, as far as possible, the advance of the enemy's fleet. It was under the command of General St. John R. Liddell. All disposable infantry in Texas was directed on Marshall, and although the enemy still had a force of several thousand on the coast, I reduced the number of men holding the defenses to an absolute minimum. General Magruder's field report shows that but 2300 men were left in Texas. Except these, every effective soldier in the department was put in front of Steele or in support of Taylor.

LIEUTENANT-GENERAL RICHARD TAYLOR.
FROM A PHOTOGRAPH.

The enemy was operating with a force, according to my information, of full 50,000 effective men; with the utmost powers of concentration not 25,000 men of all arms could be brought to oppose his movements. Taylor had at Mansfield, after the junction of Green, 11,000 effectives with 5000 infantry from Price's army in one day's march of him at Keachie. Price, with 6000 or 8000 cavalry, was engaged in holding in check the advance of Steele, whose column, according to our information, did not number less than 15,000 of all arms. Shreveport was made the point of concentration; with its fortifications covering the depots, arsenals, and shops at Jefferson, Marshall, and above, it was a strategic point of vital importance. All the infantry not with Taylor, opposed to Banks, was directed on Shreveport. Price with his cavalry command was instructed to delay the march of Steele's column whilst the concentration was being made. Occupying a central position at Shreveport, with the enemy's columns approaching from opposite directions, I proposed drawing them within striking distance, when, by concentrating upon and striking them in detail, both columns might be crippled or destroyed.

Banks pushed on to Natchitoches. It was expected he would be detained there several days in accumulating supplies. Steele on the Little Missouri and Banks at Natchitoches were but about one hundred miles from Shreveport or Marshall. The character of the country did not admit of their forming a junction above Natchitoches, and if they advanced I hoped, by refusing one of them, to fight the other with my whole force.

It seemed probable at this time that Steele would advance first. When he reached Prairie d'Ane, two routes were open to him: the one to Marshall,

THE CONFEDERATE FORT DE RUSSY, ABOUT TEN MILES BELOW ALEXANDRIA.
FROM A SKETCH MADE SOON AFTER IT WAS CAPTURED.

crossing the river at Fulton, the other direct to Shreveport. I consequently held Price's infantry, under Churchill, a few days at Shreveport. Steele's hesitation and the reports of the advance of Banks's cavalry caused me, on the 4th of April, to move Churchill to Keachie, a point twenty miles in rear of Mansfield, where the road divides to go to Marshall and Shreveport. He was directed to report to General Taylor. I now visited and conferred with General Taylor. He believed that Banks could not yet advance his infantry across the barren country lying between Natchitoches and Mansfield. I returned to Shreveport and wrote General Taylor not to risk a general engagement, but to select a position in which to give battle should Banks advance, and by a reconnoissance in force to compel the enemy to display his infantry, and to notify me as soon as he had done so and I would join him in the front.

The reconnoissance was converted into a decisive engagement near Mansfield, on the 8th of April, with the advance of the enemy (a portion of the Thirteenth Corps and his cavalry), and by the rare intrepidity of Mouton's division resulted in a complete victory over the forces engaged. The battle of Mansfield was not an intentional violation of my instructions on General Taylor's part. The Federal cavalry had pushed forward so far in advance of their column as to completely cover its movement, and General Taylor reported to me by dispatch at 12 meridian of the day on which the battle took place, that there was no advance made from Grand Ecore except of cavalry. In fact, however, General Franklin with his infantry was on the march and at once pushed forward to the support of the cavalry. When General Mouton with his division drove in the cavalry, he struck the head of Franklin's troops, and by a vigorous and able attack, without waiting for orders from Taylor, repulsed and drove back Franklin's advance and opened the battle of Mansfield, which, when Taylor came to the front, with his accustomed boldness and vigor he pushed to a complete success. [See p. 353.]

Churchill, with his infantry under Tappan and Parsons joined Taylor that night. The next morning Taylor, advancing in force, found the enemy in position at Pleasant Hill. Our troops attacked with vigor and at first with success, but, exposing their right flank, were finally repulsed and thrown into confusion. The Missouri and Arkansas troops, with a brigade of Walker's division, were broken and scattered. The enemy recovered cannon which we had captured the day before, and two of our pieces with the dead and wounded were left on the field. Our repulse at Pleasant Hill was so complete and our command was so disorganized that had Banks followed up his success vigorously he would have met but feeble opposition to his advance on Shreveport.

Having ridden forward at 2 A. M. on receipt of Taylor's report of the battle of Mansfield, I joined Taylor after dark on the 8th, a few yards in rear of the battle-field of that day. Polignac's (previously Mouton's) division of Louisiana infantry was all that was intact of Taylor's force. Assuming command, I countermanded the order that had been given for the retreat of Polignac's division, and was consulting with General Taylor when some stragglers from the battle-field, where our wounded were still lying, brought the intelligence that Banks had precipitately retreated after the battle, converting a victory which he might have claimed into a defeat. Our troops in rear rallied, and the field was next day occupied by us.

Banks continued his retreat to Grand Ecore, where he intrenched himself and remained until the return of his fleet and its safe passage over the bars, made especially difficult this season by the unusual fall of the river.

Our troops were completely paralyzed and disorganized by the repulse at Pleasant Hill, and the cavalry, worn by its long march from Texas, had been constantly engaged for three days, almost without food or forage. Before we could reorganize at Mansfield and get into condition to advance over the fifty-five miles of wilderness that separated our armies, the enemy had been reënforced and intrenched at Grand Ecore. The enemy held possession of the river until he evacuated Grand Ecore.

Steele was still slowly advancing from the Little Missouri to the Prairie d'Ane. I deemed it imprudent to follow Banks below Grand Ecore with my whole force, and leave Steele so near Shreveport. Even had I been able to throw Banks across the Atchafalaya, the high water of that stream would have arrested my farther progress. An intercepted dispatch from General Sherman to General A. J. Smith, directing the immediate return of his force to Vicksburg, removed the last doubt in my mind that Banks would withdraw to Alexandria as rapidly as possible, and it was hoped the falls would detain his fleet there until we could dispose of Steele, when the entire force of the department would be free to operate against him. I confidently hoped, if I could reach Steele with my infantry, to beat him at a distance from his depot, in a poor country, and with my large cavalry force to destroy his army. The prize would have been the Arkansas Valley and the powerful fortifications of Little Rock. Steele's defeat or retreat would leave me in position promptly to support Taylor's operations against Banks.

Leaving Taylor with his cavalry, now under Wharton, and the Louisiana division of infantry under Polignac, to follow up Banks's retreat, and taking the Texas, Arkansas, and Missouri divisions of infantry, I moved against Steele's column in Arkansas. Steele entered Camden, where he was too strong for assault, but the capture of his train at the battle of Marks's Mill on the 25th of April forced him to evacuate Camden on the 28th, and the battle of Jenkins's Ferry on the Saline, April 30th, completed his discomfiture. [See p. 375.] He retreated to Little Rock. Churchill, Parsons, and Walker were at once marched across country to the support of Taylor, but before the junction could be effected Banks had gone.

To return to Taylor, after the enemy left Grand Ecore General Taylor attacked his rear at Cloutierville, whilst a detachment under Bee held the Federal advance in check at Monette's Ferry. General Taylor's force was, however, too weak to warrant the hope that he could seriously impede the march of Banks's column. After the latter reached Alexandria, General Taylor transferred a part of his command to the river below Alexandria, and with unparalleled audacity and great ability and success operated on the enemy's gun-boats and transports.

The construction of the dam, aided by a temporary rise in Red River, enabled Admiral Porter to get his fleet

BRIGADIER-GENERAL C. J. POLIGNAC, C. S. A.
FROM A PHOTOGRAPH.

over the falls. Had he delayed but one week longer, our whole infantry force would have been united against him.

Banks evacuated Alexandria on the 12th and 13th of May, the fleet quitted the Red River, and the campaign ended with the occupation of all the country we had held at its beginning, as well as of the lower Teche.

The operations of Taylor on Red River and Marmaduke on the Mississippi prevented A. J. Smith from obeying Sherman's order to return to Vicksburg in time for the Atlanta campaign.↓

Through the courtesy of the editors of this work, I have carefully read a statement in which are grouped in detail the covert insinuations, the gossip of camps and capitals, and the misstatements of well-known facts that go to make up the old story of many versions of "an arrangement at Washington whereby Kirby Smith's army was to recede before the army of General Banks, falling back through the State of Texas, and finally to disband. In anticipation of this," the story continues, "Confederate cotton to an amount

↓ A. J. Smith did not rejoin Sherman, but, after Sherman had set out for Savannah, he joined Thomas in time to take part in the battle of Nashville.— EDITORS.

named, believed to be 25,000 bales, was to be gathered at points convenient for transportation and taken by three commissioners, residents of New Orleans, who would accompany the expedition under Banks, and sold by them; the proceeds to be divided like naval prize money, and to go to make a fund for the benefit of such Confederate officers and men as might expatriate themselves in Brazil or some other country. General Banks was instructed to carry out this arrangement. General Dick Taylor was assigned to the command of the Army of the West Mississippi *after* this arrangement was entered into and before its execution, was not a party to it, and purposely prevented its being carried out by bringing on an engagement at Mansfield. After the navy commenced taking the cotton, claiming it as prize of war, a wrangle began over it and its destruction commenced."

I remark in passing that neither the emphatic statement in regard to General Taylor, nor the equally explicit one about the destruction of cotton, can stand the test of dates; for General Taylor had been in command since 1862,— in fact before either General Banks or myself,—and I ordered the cotton to be burned, in accordance with the settled policy of the Confederacy, as soon as I heard of Banks's movement, and before I knew of the approach of the navy. There is not the least foundation upon which this story could rest. The circumstances alleged are impossible to have happened without my having been a party to them. My power in the Trans-Mississippi Department was almost absolute. I bought cotton through my Cotton Bureau at three and four cents a pound, and sold it at fifty cents a pound in gold. It passed in constant streams by several crossings of the Rio Grande, as well as through Galveston, to the agents abroad. It would have been absurd in me to have called in the devious and uncertain agency of a Federal army, and of cotton speculators from within the Union lines, when I could at any time have safely exported and placed to my credit abroad thousands of bales of cotton.

RÉSUMÉ OF MILITARY OPERATIONS IN MISSOURI AND ARKANSAS, 1864–65.

BY WILEY BRITTON, 6TH KANSAS CAVALRY.

THE capture of Fort Smith by General Blunt, and of Little Rock by General Steele, early in September, 1863 [see "The Conquest of Arkansas," Vol. III., p. 441], put the Arkansas River, from its mouth to its junction with the Grand and Verdigris rivers, into the possession of the Federal forces. This general advance of the Federal line forced General Price to fall back with his army from his fortified positions around Little Rock to Camden and Arkadelphia, in the southern part of the State. Having now no threatened positions of importance to hold, the Confederate generals in Arkansas were free to use their mounted troops and light artillery in attacking and threatening with attack the small posts and lines of communication in the rear of the Federal army. On his retreat from Little Rock [see map, p. 348],

Price detached General Joseph O. Shelby with a brigade from Marmaduke's cavalry division and a battery of light artillery to make a raid into Missouri, hoping by this diversion to cause the withdrawal of at least part of the Federal troops from the Arkansas valley. Shelby, with his brigade of upward of two thousand men,‡ and with two pieces of artillery, crossed the Arkansas River on the 27th of September, moved north rapidly, entered south-west Missouri near Cassville about the 1st of October, and captured the post of Neosho with a detachment of the Missouri State militia stationed there, and paroled them. From Neosho he moved north, and, with scarcely any opposition, reached the vicinity of Marshall in central Missouri, where he encountered General E. B. Brown with a force of the State militia. On

‡ Shelby reported his force as 600. There were four colonels, Shelby, Hunter, Gordon, and Coffee. The writer's father was captured at Neosho, and stated the force as 2000, an estimate which is supported by four Union reports quoted in Moore's "Rebellion Record."— EDITORS.

the 13th of October, after a sharp fight of several hours, Shelby was defeated, his artillery captured, and his command dispersed. General Thomas Ewing, Jr., commanding the District of the Border, on hearing of the advance of the Confederate raiding force into central Missouri, marched with a force of about two thousand men from Kansas City to join General Brown, and picked up some of Shelby's demoralized command in their retreat toward the Kansas border. Having suffered this reverse, Shelby's next object was to get out of the State in as good shape as possible, and at once he commenced a hasty retreat south. He was pursued day and night by Ewing and Brown, in an exciting chase of upward of two hundred miles, and until his command lost all cohesion in the mountainous regions of Arkansas. Thus western Missouri was not only relieved for the remainder of the year 1863 of Shelby's raiding force, but also of Quantrill's murderous band of guerrillas, who, on the 20th of August, had burned the city of Lawrence, Kansas, and murdered 150 of her citizens in cold blood; and on the 6th of October had killed some 80 of Blunt's escort at Baxter Springs, Kansas, most of whom were first wounded and fell into his hands.

During the winter of 1863–64 the forces of Generals Steele and Blunt held the Arkansas River as a Federal line of advance. The winter was so cold that no important aggressive operations were attempted. During this period of inactivity, however, Steele was making preparations for a vigorous spring campaign. It was decided that the column under General Banks and the columns under General Steele from Little Rock and Fort Smith should converge toward Shreveport, Louisiana. The Federal columns under Steele left Little Rock and Fort Smith the latter part of March, moved toward the southern part of the State, and after some fighting and manœuvring drove General Price's forces from Camden, Arkadelphia, and Washington.

In the midst of these successful operations, Steele received information that Banks's army had been defeated and was retreating ⚓ [see p. 354], and that Price had received reënforcements from Kirby Smith of 8000 infantry and a complement of artillery, and would at once assume the offensive. Not feeling strong enough to fight the combined Confederate forces, Steele determined to fall back upon Little Rock. He had scarcely commenced his retrograde movement when Smith and Price began to press him vigorously. A retreating fight was kept up for several days, until the Federal army reached Jenkins's Ferry on the Saline River. Here the swollen condition of the stream and the almost impassable swamp on the opposite side held Steele's forces until his trains were crossed over on the pontoons. While he was thus detained, on the 30th of April, Smith and Price came up and

attacked him with great energy. The battle raged furiously nearly half a day, when the Confederate army was repulsed with heavy loss and withdrew from the field. Steele crossed the river without further opposition and retired leisurely to Little Rock, with all his army except the division under General John M. Thayer, which was sent back to Fort Smith. Price was so badly beaten that he made no effort to pursue the Federal forces north of Saline River.

After the battle of Jenkins's Ferry, instead of making preparations to attack the Federal forces at Little Rock and Fort Smith, Price commenced organizing his forces for an expedition into Missouri, to be led by him in person. The Confederate troops under Cooper, Maxey, and Gano, in the Indian Territory and western Arkansas, were to make demonstrations against Fort Smith and Fort Gibson, and the line of communication between those points and Kansas, while another part of the Confederate army was to threaten Little Rock. Price's army for the invasion of Missouri numbered some 15,000↓ men and 20 pieces of artillery before crossing the Arkansas River, and consisted of three divisions, commanded by Generals Fagan, Marmaduke, and Shelby. These troops were mostly veterans, having been in active service since the first year of the war. About the 1st of September, while strong demonstrations were being made against Fort Smith and Little Rock, Price, with his army, crossed the Arkansas River about half-way between those points at Dardanelle, and marched to the northern part of the State without opposition, and, in fact, without his movements being definitely known to General Rosecrans, who then commanded the Department of the Missouri at St. Louis. ♭ When the Confederate forces entered Missouri they were met by detachments of the State militia, who captured several Confederate prisoners, from whom it was ascertained that the invading force was much larger than had been supposed, and that Price was marching direct for St. Louis. Rosecrans at once commenced collecting his forces to meet and check the enemy. General Thomas Ewing, Jr., was in command of the District of South-east Missouri. Pilot Knob, near Iron Mountain [see map, Vol I., p. 263], was a post of importance, with fortifications of considerable strength, and was on Price's direct line of march to St. Louis, which was only eighty-six miles distant.

Finding that General Price was certainly advancing toward St. Louis, Ewing, in order to defend Pilot Knob, drew in the detachments of his command stationed at different points in south-east Missouri. As the Federal forces around and in the vicinity of St. Louis were considered inadequate to defend the city against the reported strength of Price's veteran army, on the request of Rosecrans General A. J. Smith's veteran division of the Army

---

⚓ "On learning the defeat and consequent retreat of General Banks on Red River . . . General Steele determined to fall back to the Arkansas River." [Report of General U. S. Grant. Appendix to "Memoirs," p. 592.]

↓ This follows Steele's report, but Colonel Snead, of Price's staff, places the force at 12,000, of whom only 8000 were armed, and 14 guns.— EDITORS.

♭ General William S. Rosecrans, who was relieved of command at Chattanooga, October 19th, 1863, assumed command of the Department of the Missouri, January 28th, 1864, and remained in command of that department until December 9th, 1864. For the remainder of the war he was at Cincinnati on waiting orders.— EDITORS.

of the Tennessee, 4500 strong, passing up the Mississippi River to join Sherman's army, was detained at Cairo to assist in checking the advance of the Confederate army.

Price arrived before Pilot Knob in the afternoon of September 26th, and skirmished until night with detachments of Federal cavalry, which had been thrown out to meet his advance. Ewing had 1051 men at that post, which were only enough to man the works. Having got his troops and artillery all up, Price opened the attack on the fort at daylight on the 27th, and kept it up all day with great resolution. But Ewing's well-served artillery of eleven pieces and his thousand small-arms repulsed every assault made by the Confederates. When night came, however, Ewing was satisfied that he could not hold out another day against the superior attacking force, and he determined to evacuate the fort. Shortly after midnight his troops marched out, and a few moments later his magazine was blown up, and the ammunition which could not be taken along was destroyed. Ewing then marched with his force and joined the troops engaged in the defense of St. Louis and of Jefferson City. On hearing the explosion of the magazine, Price suspected the retreat of the garrison, and immediately ordered his generals to start in pursuit. Continuing his march north with his army he came up and attacked the defenses of St. Louis some miles south of the city, but was repulsed by General A. J. Smith's veterans and other troops, and then changed his line of march and moved westward toward Jefferson City, the State capital. While Price's plans were not definitely known, his movements indicated that he would endeavor to take Jefferson City. But Rosecrans determined not to allow the State capital to fall into the hands of the invader, and not only called out the enrolled militia of central Missouri for its defense, but also ordered General John B. Sanborn, commanding the District of South-west Missouri at Springfield, and General John McNeil, commanding the District of Rolla, to march to its defense with their available forces, with the least possible delay. General E. B. Brown and General Clinton B. Fisk, commanding districts in central and north Missouri, were also directed to bring forward to Jefferson City all the State militia that could be spared from their respective districts. General Price moved forward and attacked the capital, but as he was closely pursued by the Federal forces from St. Louis he was soon driven off, and continued his march westward up the south side of the Missouri River.

↓ As this statement has been questioned, I quote the following documents from Colonel R. J. Hinton's "Invasion of Missouri and Kansas in 1864":

"NOTICE. HEADQUARTERS, LEXINGTON, MISSOURI, October 14th [1864].

"I hereby notify the citizens of Lexington and vicinity that I am here now for the purpose of enlisting *all* those who are subject to military duty, and organizing them into companies, battalions, etc., with authority from Major-General Price. *All* those subject to duty will report to me at the Court House immediately.

"L. L. BEDINGER, Captain and Recruiting Officer."

"GENERAL ORDER. HEADQUARTERS, SHELBY'S BRIGADE. LEXINGTON, MISSOURI, October 14th [1864].

"II. *All* male white citizens between the ages of 17 and 50

His next objects were understood to be the capture of Kansas City, and Fort Leavenworth, Kansas, and more particularly the invasion and desolation of Kansas. He conscripted and pressed into service every man and youth found at home able to bear arms.↓ Major-General S. R. Curtis, commanding the Department of Kansas and the Indian Territory, the moment he was advised of the approaching storm, began collecting all his forces along the eastern border of the State south of Kansas City, and urged Governor Carney, of Kansas, to call out the militia to coöperate with the volunteers in resisting the threatened invasion. In response to the governor's call, twenty-four regiments of militia were hastily organized, and took position along the eastern line of the State. Early in these preparatory operations for the defense of the border, Major-General George Sykes,⟩ commanding the District of South Kansas, was, at his own request, relieved, and Major-General James G. Blunt was placed in command. As soon as information was received that Price had been driven from Jefferson City and was moving westward, Curtis and Blunt took the field in person to direct the operations of their forces in defense of the border. Blunt took the available force of the volunteers and several sections of artillery, and moved down to Lexington, some forty miles, to meet and hold the enemy as long as possible, so that Rosecrans's forces in pursuit from St. Louis and Jefferson City, under Generals Alfred Pleasonton ⟨ and A. J. Smith, could come up and attack Price in the rear.

On the afternoon of October 20th Price's advance under Shelby came within sight of Lexington on the south side of the city. Sharp fighting at once commenced between the opposing forces, and lasted until night, when Blunt, having ascertained the strength of the enemy, fell back to Little Blue River, a few miles east of Independence, to form a new line of battle. As this stream was fordable at different points above and below where the Independence and Lexington road crossed it, Blunt's forces, under Colonel Thomas Moonlight, were obliged, on the 21st, to abandon the position taken up behind it after an engagement with Shelby's division, lasting several hours, and fall back behind the Big Blue River, a few miles west of Independence. Here a new line of battle was formed with all Curtis's available troops, including most of the Kansas State militia, who had consented to cross the State line into Missouri. Curtis and Blunt determined to hold Price's army

are ordered to report to headquarters at the Court House within 24 hours after issuing this order.

"GEO. S. RATHBUN, Captain Commanding Detachment Shelby Brigade Recruiting Service."   W. B.

⟩ General Sykes, who was relieved from the command of the Fifth Corps (Army of the Potomac) in March, 1864, was on duty in the Department of Kansas from April 20th, 1864, until June 7th, 1865. For a part of this time (September 1st–October 10th, 1864) he was in command of the District of South Kansas.— EDITORS.

⟨ General Pleasonton, who was relieved from the command of the Cavalry Corps of the Army of the Potomac in March, 1864, served in the Department of Missouri from March 23d, 1864, until the close of the war.— EDITORS.

east of the Big Blue as long as practicable in the hope of receiving assistance from Rosecrans, who, it was thought, was following close upon the rear of the Confederate army. While Curtis's forces were thus fighting and skirmishing with the enemy over nearly every foot of the ground from Lexington to Big Blue, Pleasonton's provisional cavalry division of Rosecrans's army was marching day and night from Jefferson City to overtake the invading force. On the 22d, just as Curtis's troops were being driven from the line of the Big Blue back upon the State line and Kansas City, Pleasonton's cavalry came up and attacked the rear of Price's army, east of Independence, and routed it and drove it in great disorder through the town. Pleasonton at once sent a messenger to Curtis, announcing his presence upon the field. The night of the 22d Price's army encamped on the west side of the Big Blue, just south of Westport. Pleasonton's cavalry encamped that night around and in the neighborhood of Independence, east of the Big Blue. Curtis's forces were encamped from Kansas City to Westport and along the State line west of Westport.

At daylight on the 23d the columns of Pleasonton began to move west, and those of Curtis to move south, and in a short time afterward they became warmly engaged with the Confederates, who were drawn up in the line of battle two and a half miles south of Westport. The opposing armies fought over an area of five or six square miles, and at some points the fighting was furious. At times there were as many as forty or fifty guns throwing shot and shell and grape and canister. About the middle of the afternoon Price's lines began to give way, and by sundown the entire Confederate army was in full retreat southward along the State line, closely pursued by the victorious Federal forces.

In the meanwhile General A. J. Smith was bringing forward his division of veteran infantry on forced marches from Lexington, but, receiving information that the Confederate army was retreating down the border, changed his line of march to move via Pleasant Hill and Harrisonville, to head off Price and bring him to a stand. When, however, General Smith's division reached a point some four miles south-west of Harrisonville, he ascertained that Price had already passed on southward down the line road. After the battle near Westport the cavalry of Curtis and Pleasonton kept up the pursuit and was constantly engaged in skirmishing with the Confederate rear column until the Southern forces arrived at the Marais des Cygnes River. Here Price was obliged to make a stand to get his artillery and trains across the river. After being driven from this position he formed a line of battle on the 25th, a few miles south of the Marais des Cygnes, near Mine Creek, in Linn County, Kansas, placing his artillery, supported by a large force, on a high mound in the prairie. The Federal cavalry coming up charged his position with great gallantry, broke his line, captured nearly all his artillery, ten pieces, and a large number of prisoners, among them Generals Marmaduke and Cabell and many other officers of lower rank. In his retreat from this position Price was closely pursued by the Federal cavalry, his rear-guard being almost constantly under fire. His army encamped that night on the Marmiton River, about eight miles nearly east of Fort Scott, which place he had intended to capture with the large depot of Government supplies. Having lost most of his artillery, about midnight he blew up such of his artillery ammunition as was unsuitable for the guns which he still had. The troops of Curtis and Pleasonton, who reached Fort Scott that night and replenished their haversacks and cartridge-boxes, heard the loud explosion. From Fort Scott the pursuit was continued by Curtis's forces under Blunt, and by Rosecrans's cavalry under Sanborn and McNeil. At Newtonia in south-west Missouri, on the 28th of October, Price made another stand, and was attacked by the pursuing forces named, and finally driven from the field with heavy loss. This was next to the severest battle of the campaign. Blunt, and some of the Missouri troops, continued the pursuit to the Arkansas River, but Price did not again attempt to make a stand. His line of march from Westport to Newtonia was strewn with the débris of a routed army. He crossed the Arkansas River above Fort Smith with a few pieces of artillery, with his army demoralized and reduced by captures and dispersion to perhaps less than 5000 men. Most of the noted guerrilla bands followed him from the State.

The "Price raid," as it was called in the West, was the last military operation of much consequence that took place in Missouri and Arkansas. It is certain that Price lost more than he gained in war material and that the raid did not tend to strengthen the Confederate cause in the West. He did not capture and take off a single piece of cannon on his raid. Large numbers of the men he conscripted and pressed into service during the raid left him at the first opportunity and returned to their homes, or were picked up by the Federal cavalry and paroled.

[In General Price's report occurs the following summary of the campaign: "I marched 1434 miles, fought 43 battles and skirmishes, captured and paroled over 3000 Federal officers and men, captured 18 pieces of artillery, 3000 stand of small-arms, 16 stand of colors, . . . a great many wagons and teams, large numbers of horses, great quantities of subsistence and ordnance stores, . . . and destroyed property to the cost of $10,000,000. . . . I lost 10 pieces of artillery, 2 stand of colors, 1000 small-arms, while I do not think I lost 1000 prisoners. . . . I brought with me at least 5000 recruits."—EDITORS.]

"LACKAWANNA,"   "OSSIPEE."   "BROOKLYN,"   "RICHMOND,"   "HARTFORD."   "CHICKASAW,"
  "WINNEBAGO,"   "TENNESSEE,"   "ITASCA,"   FORT MORGAN,

SURRENDER OF THE "TENNESSEE," BATTLE OF MOBILE DAY.

"GALENA."   "ITASCA."
THE "BROOKLYN" AFTER THE BATTLE OF MOBILE.   FROM A SKETCH MADE AT THE TIME.

FARRAGUT AT MOBILE BAY.

BY JOHN CODDINGTON KINNEY, FIRST LIEUTENANT, 13TH CONNECTICUT INFANTRY,
AND ACTING SIGNAL OFFICER, U. S. A.

AFTER the Mississippi was opened in July, 1863, by the capture of Vicksburg and the consequent surrender of Port Hudson, Admiral Farragut devoted a large share of his attention to the operations against Mobile Bay. He was aware that the Confederates were actively engaged in the construction of rams and iron-clads at Mobile and above, and it was his earnest desire to force the entrance into Mobile Bay and capture the forts that guarded it, before the more powerful of the new vessels could be finished and brought down to aid in the defense. In January, 1864, he made a reconnoissance of Forts Gaines and Morgan, at which time no Confederate vessels were in the lower bay, except one transport. In letters to the Navy Department he urged that at least one iron-clad be sent to help his wooden fleet, and asked for the coöperation of a brigade of five thousand soldiers to enable him, after running into the bay, to reduce the forts at his leisure. It is easy to see now the wisdom of his plan. Had the operations against Mobile been undertaken promptly, as he desired, the entrance into the bay would have been effected with much less cost of men and materials, Mobile would have been captured a year earlier than it was, and the Union cause would have been saved the disaster of the Red River campaign of 1864. At this late day it is but justice to Farragut to admit the truth.

His position at the time was one of great anxiety. He saw the ease with which the forts could be captured if a few thousand troops could be obtained

Based upon the author's paper in "The Century" for May, 1881, entitled "An August Morning with Farragut," revised and extended for the present work.—EDITORS.

to coöperate with his fleet. He knew that the Confederates were bending all their energies to the construction of three or more powerful rams, to meet which he had until late in the summer nothing but wooden vessels. Every day was strengthening the Confederate situation and making his own position more perilous. With the necessary coöperation he would run inside the bay, prevent any iron-clads from crossing Dog River bar (over which they had to be floated with " camels "), put a stop to the planting of torpedoes, effectually prevent blockade-running, and easily capture the garrisons of the forts.

But, much to his regret, the army under General Banks started up the Red River, and he was left alone with his little fleet to watch the operations he could not prevent. At last, about May 20th, the great ram *Tennessee* made her appearance in the lower bay. Just before she arrived, and when it was known that Admiral Buchanan was engaged in efforts to float the ram over the bar, eight miles up the bay, Farragut wrote to Secretary Welles:

"I fully understand and appreciate my situation. The experience I had of the fight between the *Arkansas* and Admiral Davis's vessels on the Mississippi showed plainly how unequal the contest is between iron-clads and wooden vessels, in loss of life, unless you succeed in destroying the iron-clad. I therefore deeply regret that the department has not been able to give me *one* of the many iron-clads that are off Charleston and in the Mississippi. I have always looked for the latter, but it appears that it takes us twice as long to build an iron-clad as any one else. It looks as if the contractors and the fates were against us. While the rebels are bending their whole energies to the war our people are expecting the war to close by default ; and if they do not awake to a sense of their danger soon it will be so. But be assured, sir, that the navy will do its duty, let the issue come when it may, or I am greatly deceived."

A few days later the *Tennessee* came down and anchored near Fort Morgan. From that time until the battle was fought, Farragut never left the *Hartford* except when making inspections. It was expected that the rebel admiral would attack the blockading fleet before the iron-clads arrived, and Farragut made his preparations accordingly, even arranging extemporized torpedoes to place himself in this respect on a par with the enemy. This he did very reluctantly, writing on May 25th:

"Torpedoes are not so agreeable when used on both sides ; therefore, I have reluctantly brought myself to it. I have always deemed it unworthy a chivalrous nation, but it does not do to give your enemy such a decided superiority over you."

In the same letter he speaks of the discouraging news just received of Banks's defeat, and adds:

"I see by the rebel papers Buchanan is advertised to raise the blockade as soon as he is ready. As I have before informed the department, if I had the military force . . . and one or two iron-clads, I would not hesitate to run in and attack him ; but if I were to run in and in so doing get my vessels crippled, it would be in his power to retire to the shoal water with his iron-clads (in fact, all their vessels draw much less water than ours), and thus destroy us without our being able to get at him. But if he takes the offensive and comes out of port, I hope to be able to contend with him. The department has not yet responded to my call for the iron-clads in the Mississippi."

After the Red River disaster, General Grant decided that the majority of the fighting men of the army could be used to better advantage in Virginia, and the force in the Department of the Gulf was largely reduced. It was not

THE "RICHMOND" AND THE "LACKAWANNA" STRIPPED FOR THE FIGHT. FROM A WAR-TIME SKETCH.

until the latter part of July, 1864, that General Canby could make his arrangements to coöperate with Farragut at Mobile Bay. On the 3d of August a division of troops, under General Gordon Granger, landed on the west end of Dauphine Island and began preparations for a siege of Fort Gaines. Meantime, also, three monitors had arrived and a fourth was daily expected, and at last the time, for which Admiral Farragut had so long been praying, arrived.

On the morning of August 4th a detachment of army signal officers, under command of the late Major Frank W. Marston, arrived by tug from New Orleans. They were distributed among the principal vessels of the fleet, for the purpose of communicating with General Granger's force after the entrance into the bay had been effected, and it was the good fortune of the writer to be assigned to duty on the *Hartford*. In the afternoon of the same day Admiral Farragut, with the commanding officers of the different vessels, made a reconnoissance on the steam-tender *Cowslip*, running inside of Sand Island, where the three monitors were anchored, and within easy range of both the forts. On the left, some three miles distant, was Fort Gaines, a small brick and earth work, mounting a few heavy guns, but too far away from the ship channel to cause much uneasiness to the fleet. Fort Morgan was on the right, one of the strongest of the old brick forts, and greatly strengthened by immense piles of sand-bags, covering every portion of the exposed front. The fort was well equipped with three tiers of heavy guns, one of the guns, at least, of the best English make, imported by the Confederates. In addition, there was in front a battery of seven powerful guns, at the water's edge on the beach. All the guns, of both fort and water-battery, were within point-blank range of the only channel through which the fleet could pass. The Confederates considered the works impregnable, but they did not depend solely upon them. Just around the point of land, behind Fort Morgan, we could see that afternoon three saucy-looking gun-boats and the famous ram *Tennessee*. The latter was then considered the strongest and most powerful iron-clad ever put afloat. She looked like a great turtle; her sloping sides were covered with iron plates

six inches in thickness, thoroughly riveted together, and she had a formidable iron beak projecting under the water. Her armament consisted of six heavy Brooke rifles, each sending a solid shot weighing from 95 to 110 pounds — a small affair compared with the heavy guns of the present time, but irresistible then against everything but the turrets of the monitors. In addition to these means of resistance, the narrow channel to within a few hundred yards of the shore had been lined with torpe-

FORT MORGAN.
FROM WAR-TIME PHOTOGRAPHS.

1. Light-house, Mobile Point. 2. The south-east bastion. 3. The citadel, from the north side.

does. These were under the water, anchored to the bottom. Some of them were beer-kegs filled with powder, from the sides of which projected numerous little tubes containing fulminate, which it was expected would be exploded by contact with the passing vessels, but the greater part were tin cones fitted with caps.

Except for what Farragut had already accomplished on the Mississippi, it would have been considered a foolhardy experiment for wooden vessels to attempt to pass so close to one of the strongest forts on the coast; but when to the forts were added the knowledge of the strength of the ram and the supposed deadly character of the torpedoes, it may be imagined that the coming event impressed the person taking his first glimpse of naval warfare as decidedly hazardous and unpleasant. So daring an attempt was never made in any country but ours, and was never successfully made by any commander except Farragut, who, in this, as in his previous exploits in passing the forts of the Mississippi, proved himself one of the greatest naval commanders the world has ever seen. It was the confidence reposed in him, the recollection that he had not failed in his former attempts, and his manifest faith in the success of the projected movement, that inspired all around him.

The scene on the *Cowslip* that afternoon of the 4th of August was a notable one, as she steamed within range of the forts. The central figure was the grand old admiral, his plans all completed, affable with all, evidently not thinking of failure as among the possibilities of the morrow, and filling every one with his enthusiasm. He was sixty-three years old, of medium height, stoutly built, with a finely proportioned head and smoothly shaven face, with an expression combining overflowing kindliness with iron will and invincible determination, and with eyes that in repose were full of sweetness and light, but, in emergency, could flash fire and fury.

Next in prominence to the admiral was the tall, commanding form of Fleet-Captain Percival Drayton, the man of all men to be Farragut's chief-of-staff, gentlemanly and courteous to all, but thoughtful and reserved, a man of marked intellect and power, in whose death, a few years later, our navy lost one of its very brightest stars, and the cause of liberty and human rights a most devoted friend. I have digressed to this extent to pay my humble tribute to one of the bravest and most patriotic men I ever met, and to a native South Carolinian of bluest blood, and proud of his ancestry, who in his love of country had learned to look beyond State lines and to disregard the ties of kinship.

As we steamed slowly along inside Sand Island, inspecting every hostile point, a Confederate transport landed at Fort Gaines, and began discharging cargo. At a signal from the admiral, one of the monitors, by way of practice, opened fire at long range, and, as the huge fifteen-inch shell dropped uncomfortably near, the work of unloading was stopped, and the transport suddenly left—the last Confederate transport that ever crossed the bay.

After the reconnoissance the final council of war was held on board the *Hartford*, when the positions of the various vessels were assigned, and the order of the line was arranged. Unfortunately Captain (now Rear-Admiral) Thornton A. Jenkins was absent, his vessel, the *Richmond*, having been unavoidably delayed at Pensacola, whither she had gone for coal and to escort the monitor *Tecumseh*. Had he been present he certainly would have been selected to take the lead, in which event the perilous halt of the next day would not have occurred. Much against his own wish Admiral Farragut yielded to the unanimous advice of his captains and gave up his original determination of placing his flagship in the advance, and, in the uncertainty as to the arrival of the *Richmond*, assigned the *Brooklyn*, Captain Alden, to that position. ⚓

⚓ According to Admiral Farragut's report the *Brooklyn* was appointed to lead, because she had four chase-guns and apparatus for picking up torpedoes.— EDITORS.

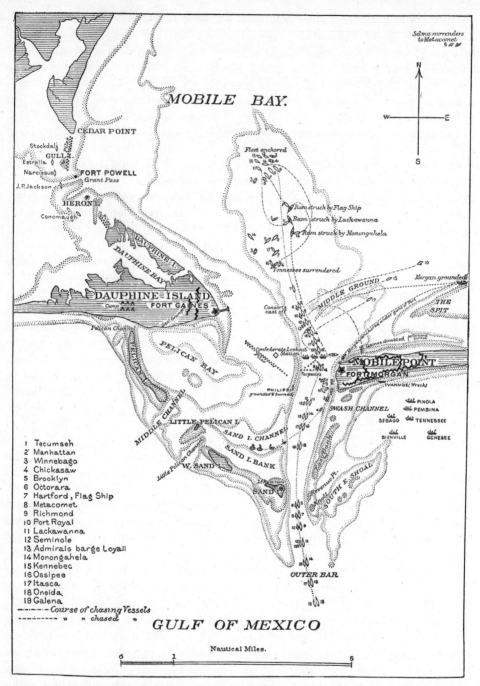

MOBILE BAY.

Selma surrenders to Metacomet

CEDAR POINT

Stockdale
GULL I.
Estrella
Narcissus
J.P.Jackson

FORT POWELL
Grant Pass

HERON
Conmaugh

Fleet anchored

Ram struck by Flag Ship
Ram struck by Lackawanna
Ram struck by Monongahela

DAUPHINE I.

DAUPHINE BAY

DAUPHINE ISLAND
FORT GAINES

Tennessee surrendered

MIDDLE GROUND

Morgan grounded

THE SPIT

PELICAN BAY

Confederate Lookout Station

MOBILE POINT
FORT MORGAN

Philippi grounded & burned

IVANHOE (Wreck)

PELICAN CHANNEL

MIDDLE CHANNEL

LITTLE PELICAN I.

SAND I. CHANNEL

SAND I. BANK

W. SAND I.

SAND I.

SWASH CHANNEL

PINOLA
PEMBINA
SEBAGO
TENNESSEE
BIENVILLE
GENESEE

SOUTH E. SHOAL

1 Tecumseh
2 Manhattan
3 Winnebago
4 Chickasaw
5 Brooklyn
6 Octorara
7 Hartford, Flag Ship
8 Metacomet
9 Richmond
10 Port Royal
11 Lackawanna
12 Seminole
13 Admirals barge Loyall
14 Monongahela
15 Kennebec
16 Ossipee
17 Itasca
18 Oneida
19 Galena
——— *Course of chasing Vessels*
-------- " " chased "

OUTER BAR

GULF OF MEXICO

Nautical Miles.

GULF OF MEXICO

NOTE.—The *Tecumseh*, the leading monitor, moved from the position shown on the map under Fort Morgan, to the left toward the right of the line marked "Torpedoes," where she was blown up. The distance traversed by the *Metacomet*, after casting off from the *Hartford* and until she came up with the *Selma*, is estimated by Admiral Jouett at nine miles. The time elapsed, as noted in the various reports, sustains this estimate. Owing to the limited size of the page, the map fails to show this distance, but it indicates the direction of the course of the gun-boats. The capture of the *Selma*, as well as the grounding of the *Morgan*, occurred some distance to the north-east of the edge of the map.—EDITORS.

A few hours later, just before sunset, the *Richmond* arrived with the *Tecumseh*, and the cause of her delay was satisfactorily explained, but the admiral decided to make no change in the order of the line, which was settled upon as follows: *Brooklyn* and *Octorara*, *Hartford* and *Metacomet*, *Richmond* and *Port Royal*, *Lackawanna* and *Seminole*, *Monongahela* and *Kennebec*, *Ossipee* and *Itasca*, *Oneida* and *Galena*. The first-named of each pair was on the starboard or more exposed side.

The four monitors were to go a little in advance, and on the right flank of the wooden vessels. The *Tecumseh* and *Manhattan* were single-turreted, each with two 15-inch guns. The *Winnebago* and *Chickasaw* were of lighter draught, with two turrets each, and four 11-inch guns.

Before attempting to narrate the events of the next day, it may be well to give an idea of the situation. Mobile Bay gradually widens from the city to the gulf, a distance of thirty miles. The entrance is protected by a long, narrow arm of sand, with Fort Morgan on the extreme western point. Across the channel from Fort Morgan, and perhaps three miles distant, is Dauphine Island, a narrow strip of sand with Fort Gaines at its eastern end. Further to the west is little Fort Powell, commanding a narrow channel through which light-draught vessels could enter the bay. Between Dauphine Island and Fort Morgan, and in front of the main entrance to the bay, is Sand Island, a barren spot, under the lee of which three of our monitors were lying. The army signal officers were sent on board the fleet, not with any intention of having their services used in passing the forts, but in order to establish communication afterward between the fleet and the army, for the purpose of coöperating in the capture of the forts. The primary objects of Admiral Farragut in entering the bay were to close Mobile to the outside world, to capture or destroy the *Tennessee*, and to cut off all possible means of escape from the garrisons of the forts. Incidentally, also, he desired to secure the moral effect of a victory, and to give his fleet, which had been tossed on the uneasy waters of the Gulf for many months, a safe and quiet anchorage. There was no immediate expectation of capturing the city of Mobile, which was safe by reason of a solid row of piles and torpedoes across the river, three miles below the city. Moreover, the larger vessels of the fleet could not approach within a dozen miles of the city, on account of shallow water. But the lower bay offered a charming resting-place for the fleet, with the additional attraction of plenty of fish and oysters, and an occasional chance to forage on shore.

At sunset the last orders had been issued, every commander knew his duty, and unusual quiet prevailed in the fleet. The sea was smooth, a gentle breeze relieved the midsummer heat, and the night came on serenely and peacefully, and far more quietly than to a yachting fleet at Newport. For the first hour after the candles were lighted below the stillness was almost oppressive. The officers of the *Hartford* gathered around the ward-room table, writing letters to loved ones far away, or giving instructions in case of death. As brave and thoughtful men, they recognized the dangers that they did not fear, and made provision for the possibilities of the morrow. But this occupied little

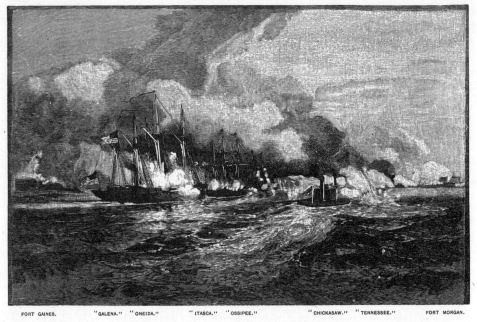

FORT GAINES.　"GALENA."　"ONEIDA."　"ITASCA."　"OSSIPEE."　"CHICKASAW."　"TENNESSEE."　FORT MORGAN.

THE BATTLE OF MOBILE. FROM A WAR-TIME SKETCH.

time, and then, business over, there followed an hour of unrestrained jollity. Many an old story was retold and ancient conundrum repeated. Old officers forgot, for the moment, their customary dignity, and it was evident that all were exhilarated and stimulated by the knowledge of the coming struggle. There was no other "stimulation," for the strict naval rules prevented. Finally, after a half-hour's smoke under the forecastle, all hands turned in. The scene on the flag-ship was representative of the night before the battle throughout the fleet.

It was the admiral's desire and intention to get under way by daylight, to take advantage of the inflowing tide; but a dense fog came on after midnight and delayed the work of forming line.

It was a weird sight as the big ships "balanced to partners," the dim outlines slowly emerging like phantoms in the fog. The vessels were lashed together in pairs, fastened side by side by huge cables. All the vessels had been stripped for the fight, the top-hamper being left at Pensacola, and the starboard boats being either left behind or towed on the port side. The admiral's steam-launch, the *Loyall*, named after his son,↓ steamed alongside the flag-ship on the port side.

It was a quarter of six o'clock before the fleet was in motion. Meantime a light breeze had scattered the fog and left a clear, sunny August day. The line moved slowly, and it was an hour after starting before the opening gun was fired. This was a 15-inch shell from the *Tecumseh*, and it exploded over Fort Morgan. Half an hour afterward the fleet came within range and the firing from the starboard vessels became general, the fort and the Confed-

↓ Mrs. Farragut's maiden name was Loyall.— EDITORS.

erate fleet replying. The fleet took position across the entrance to the bay and raked the advance vessels fore and aft, doing great damage, to which it was for a time impossible to make effective reply. Gradually the fleet came into close quarters with Fort Morgan, and the firing on both sides became terrific. The wooden vessels moved more rapidly than the monitors, and as the *Brooklyn* came opposite the fort, and approached the torpedo line, she came nearly alongside the rear monitor. To have kept on would have been to take the lead, with the ram *Tennessee* approaching and with the unknown danger of the torpedoes underneath. At this critical moment the *Brooklyn* halted and began backing and signaling with the army signals. The *Hartford* was immediately behind and the following vessels were in close proximity, and the sudden stopping of the *Brooklyn* threatened to bring the whole fleet into collision, while the strong inflowing tide was likely to carry some of the vessels to the shore under the guns of the fort.

On the previous night the admiral had issued orders that the army signal officers were not to be allowed on deck during the fight, but were to go into the cockpit, on the lower deck, and assist the surgeons. The reason assigned was that these officers would not be needed during the passage of the forts, but would be wanted afterward to open communication with the army, and that therefore it would be a misfortune to have any of them disabled. The two army signal officers on the *Hartford* disrelished this order exceedingly, and, after consulting together, decided that in the confusion of the occasion their presence on deck would probably not be noticed, and that they would evade the command if possible. In this they were successful until shortly before passing Sand Island and coming within range of Fort Morgan. Then the executive officer, Lieutenant-Commander Lewis A. Kimberly, who never allowed anything to escape his attention, came to them very quietly and politely, and told them the admiral's order must be obeyed. We were satisfied from his manner that the surgeons had need of us, and, without endeavoring to argue the matter, made our way to the stifling hold, where Surgeon Lansdale and Assistant-Surgeon Commons, with their helpers, were sitting, with their paraphernalia spread out ready for use.

Nearly every man had his watch in his hand awaiting the first shot. To us, ignorant of everything going on above, every minute seemed an hour, and there was a feeling of great relief when the boom of the *Tecumseh's* first gun was heard. Presently one or two of our forward guns opened, and we could hear the distant sound of the guns of the fort in reply. Soon the cannon-balls began to crash through the deck above us, and then the thunder of our whole broadside of nine Dahlgren guns kept the vessel in a quiver. But as yet no wounded were sent down, and we knew we were still at comparatively long range. In the intense excitement of the occasion it seemed that hours had passed, but it was just twenty minutes from the time we went below, when an officer shouted down the hatchway: " Send up an army signal officer immediately; the *Brooklyn* is signaling." In a moment the writer was on deck, where he found the situation as already described. Running on to the forecastle, he hastily took the *Brooklyn's* message, which

"TENNESSEE."   FORT MORGAN.   "HARTFORD."   "BROOKLYN."   SAND ISLAND LIGHT.

THE BATTLE OF MOBILE, LOOKING SOUTH AND EASTWARD. FROM A WAR-TIME SKETCH.

imparted the unnecessary information, "The monitors are right ahead; we cannot go on without passing them." The reply was sent at once from the admiral, "Order the monitors ahead and go on." But still the *Brooklyn* halted, while, to add to the horror of the situation, the monitor *Tecumseh*, a few hundred yards in the advance, suddenly careened to one side and almost instantly sank to the bottom, carrying with her Captain Tunis A. M. Craven and the greater part of his crew, numbering in all 114 officers and men. ⸥ The pilot, John Collins, and a few men who were in the turret jumped into

⸥ In Farragut's Supplementary General Order (No. 11) of July 29th, occurs the following:

"There are certain black buoys placed by the enemy from the piles on the west side of the channel across it towards Fort Morgan. It being understood that there are torpedoes and other obstructions between the buoys, the vessels will take care to pass eastward of the easternmost buoy, which is clear of all obstructions."

The easternmost buoy was the famous red buoy which figures in all accounts of the battle. As the fleet approached, the *Tennessee* was lying in the rear of the torpedo obstructions, and therefore to the westward of the red buoy. When Craven, in the *Tecumseh*, drew near to the buoy, influenced by the narrowness of the channel to the eastward, as his remark to the pilot would indicate (Mahan, "Gulf and Inland Waters," p. 231), or by a desire to get at the *Tennessee* more quickly, as Parker suggests ("Battle of Mobile Bay," p. 26), he disregarded the instructions, and, shaping his course to the westward of the buoy, struck the torpedoes. His course crowded the main column to the westward,

and left no choice to Alden and the fleet following in his wake, but to pass over the obstructions also. Of 114 officers and men on board the *Tecumseh*, 21 were saved. Of these two officers and five men escaped in one of the *Tecumseh's* boats, four swam to Fort Morgan where they were made prisoners, and ten, including Ensign Zettick and John Collins, the pilot, were rescued by Acting-Ensign Nields. It is to the statement of Collins that the world is indebted for the account of that heroic act which will forever be associated with Craven's name. Commodore Parker thus tells the story:

"Craven and Mr. John Collins, the pilot of the *Tecumseh*, met, as their vessel was sinking beneath them, at the foot of the ladder leading to the top of the turret. . . . It may be, then, that Craven, in the nobility of his soul,—for all know he was one of nature's noble men,—it may be, I say, that, in the nobility of his soul, the thought flashed across him that it was through no fault of his pilot that the *Tecumseh* was in this peril; he drew back. 'After you, pilot,' said he, grandly. 'There was nothing after me,' relates Mr. Collins; 'when I reached the upmost round of the ladder, the vessel seemed to drop from under me.'"   EDITORS.

the water and were rescued by a boat from the *Metacomet*, which, under charge of Acting Ensign Henry C. Nields, rowed up under the guns of the fort and through a deadly storm of shot and shell and picked them up.\ Meantime the *Brooklyn* failed to go ahead, and the whole fleet became a stationary point-blank target for the guns of Fort Morgan and of the rebel vessels. It was during these few perilous moments that the most fatal work of the day was done to the fleet.

Owing to the *Hartford's* position, only her few bow guns could be used, while a deadly rain of shot and shell was falling on her, and her men were being cut down by scores, unable to make reply. The sight on deck was sickening beyond the power of words to portray. Shot after shot came through the side, mowing down the men, deluging the decks with blood, and scattering mangled fragments of humanity so thickly that it was difficult to stand on the deck, so slippery was it. The old expressions of the " scuppers running blood," " the slippery deck," etc., give but the faintest idea of the spectacle on the *Hartford*. The bodies of the dead were placed in a long row on the port side, while the wounded were sent below until the surgeons' quarters would hold no more. A solid shot coming through the bow struck a gunner on the neck, completely severing head from body. One poor fellow (afterward an object of interest at the great Sanitary Commission Fair in New York) lost both legs by a cannon-ball; as he fell he threw up both arms, just in time to have them also carried away by another shot. At one gun, all the crew on one side were swept down by a shot which came crashing through

\ The gallantry of Nields's conduct was all the more striking in view of the fact that in pulling to the *Tecumseh's* wreck it was necessary to pass around the stern and under the broadside of the *Hartford* and across the *Brooklyn's* bow, thus placing the boat directly in the line of fire of the fleet as well as of the fort. In fact, as the boat at first carried no flag, Acting Ensign Whiting, in charge of the forecastle guns on board the *Hartford*, was about to fire at her, when some one standing by informed him of her character and errand. A moment later, Nields himself observed the omission, and took the flag from its case and shipped it. The rescued men were placed on board the *Winnebago*, and Nields and his boat's crew, unable to regain their ship, joined the *Oneida*, where they served during the remainder of the battle.—EDITORS.

THE "GALENA" AFTER THE FIGHT IN MOBILE BAY. FROM A WAR-TIME SKETCH.

CAPTAIN TUNIS A. M. CRAVEN. FROM A PHOTOGRAPH.

the bulwarks. A shell burst between the two forward guns in charge of Lieutenant Tyson, killing and wounding fifteen men. The mast upon which the writer was perched was twice struck, once slightly, and again just below the foretop by a heavy shell, from a rifle on the Confederate gun-boat *Selma*. Fortunately the shell came tumbling end over end, and buried itself in the mast, butt-end first, leaving the percussion-cap protruding. Had it come point first, or had it struck at any other part of the mast than in the reënforced portion where the heel of the topmast laps the top of the lower mast, this contribution to the literature of the war would probably have been lost to the world, as the distance to the deck was about a hundred feet. As it was, the sudden jar would have dislodged any one from the crosstrees had not the shell been visible from the time it left the *Selma*, thus giving time to prepare for it by an extra grip around the top of the mast. Looking out over the water, it was easy to trace the course of every shot, both from the guns of the *Hartford* and from the Confederate fleet. Another signal message from the *Brooklyn* told of the sinking of the *Tecumseh*, a fact known already, and another order to "go on" was given and was not obeyed.

Soon after the fight began, Admiral Farragut, finding that the low-hanging smoke from the guns interfered with his view from the deck, went up the rigging of the mainmast as far as the futtock-shrouds, immediately below the maintop. The pilot, Martin Freeman, was in the top directly overhead, and the fleet-captain was on the deck below. Seeing the admiral in this exposed position, where, if wounded, he would be killed by falling to the deck, Fleet-Captain Drayton ordered Knowles, the signal-quartermaster, to fasten a rope around him so that he would be prevented from falling. [See p. 407.]

Finding that the *Brooklyn* failed to obey his orders, the admiral hurriedly inquired of the pilot if there was sufficient depth of water for the *Hartford* to pass to the left of the *Brooklyn*. Receiving an affirmative reply, he said: " I will take the lead," and immediately ordered the *Hartford* ahead at full speed. ☆ As he passed the *Brooklyn* a voice warned him of the torpedoes, to which he returned the contemptuous answer, " Damn the torpedoes." This is the current story, and may have some basis of truth. But as a matter of fact, there was never a moment when the din of the battle would not have drowned any attempt at conversation between the two ships, and while it is quite probable that the admiral made the remark it is doubtful if he shouted it to the *Brooklyn*. ∤

Then was witnessed the remarkable sight of the *Hartford* and her consort, the *Metacomet*, passing over the dreaded torpedo ground and rushing ahead far in advance of the rest of the fleet, the extrication of which from the con- fusion caused by the *Brooklyn's* halt required many minutes of valuable time. ∤ The *Hartford* was now moving over what is called the " middle ground," with shallow water on either side, so that it was impossible to move except as the channel permitted. Taking advantage of the situation, the Confederate gun- boat *Selma* kept directly in front of the flag-ship and raked her fore and aft, doing more damage in reality than all the rest of the enemy's fleet. The other gun-boats, the *Gaines* and the *Morgan*, were in shallow water on our starboard bow, but they received more damage from the *Hartford's* broadsides than they were able to inflict. Meanwhile the ram *Tennessee*, which up to this time had contented herself with simply firing at the approaching fleet, started for the *Hartford*, apparently with the intention of striking her amidships. She came on perhaps for half a mile, never approaching nearer than a hundred yards, and then suddenly turned and made for the fleet, which, still in front of the fort, was gradually getting straightened out and following the *Hartford*. This change of course on the part of the ram has always been a mystery. The captain of the ram, in papers published since the war, denies that any such move was made, but it was witnessed by the entire fleet, and is mentioned by both Admiral Farragut and Fleet-Captain Drayton in their official reports. ∤

The *Hartford* had now run a mile inside the bay, and was suffering chiefly from the raking fire of the *Selma*, which was unquestionably managed more skillfully than any other Confederate vessel. Captain (now Admiral) Jouett, commanding the *Hartford's* escort, the *Metacomet*, repeatedly asked permission

---

☆ In turning to clear the *Brooklyn's* stern, the *Hartford* went ahead, while the *Metacomet* backed.— EDITORS.

∤ The period of delay between the halting of the *Brooklyn* and the decision of the admiral to take the lead could hardly have been less than ten minutes, and may have been longer. The first signal message from the *Brooklyn* was taken from the forecastle of the *Hartford*. Then the smoke from the *Hartford's* bow guns interfered, and I started up the foremast, intending to make a signal-station of the foretop. Finding a howitzer crew at work there I kept on to the foretop-gallant crosstrees, where I received and replied to two messages before the *Hartford* passed the *Brooklyn*. As I was not a sailor and had never before been so far up in the rigging of a ship,

it could hardly have taken me less then five min- utes to shift from the forecastle to the crosstrees. It was while going up the mast that I witnessed the sinking of the *Tecumseh*.— J. C. K.

∤ Farragut, when he had altered his course, had every reason to suppose that there were torpedoes directly in his path. It was known that they had been placed west of the red buoy, the *Brooklyn* had seen them, and the fate of the *Tecumseh* was con- clusive evidence. In fact the officers both of the *Hartford* and the *Richmond* heard the snapping of torpedo-primers under the bottom of the ships as they passed, but the torpedoes failed to explode, having probably been corroded by lying a long time in the water.— EDITORS.

∤ See Captain Johnston's account, p. 401.— EDITORS.

UNITED STATES STEAMSHIP "MONONGAHELA," SHOWING INJURIES RECEIVED IN THE FIGHT.
FROM A SKETCH MADE AFTER THE BATTLE OF MOBILE.

of the admiral to cut loose and take care of the *Selma*, and finally, at five minutes past eight, consent was given. In an instant the cables binding the two vessels were cut, and the *Metacomet*, the fastest vessel in the fleet, bounded ahead. The *Selma* was no match for her, and, recognizing her danger, endeavored to retreat up the bay. But she was speedily overhauled, and when a shot had wounded her captain and killed her first lieutenant she surrendered. Before this the *Gaines* had been crippled by the splendid marksmanship of the *Hartford's* gunners, and had run aground under the guns of the fort, where she was shortly afterward set on fire, the crew escaping to the shore. The gunboat *Morgan*, after grounding for a few moments on the shoals to the east of Navy Cove, retreated to the shallow water near the fort, whence she escaped the following night to Mobile. The *Hartford*, having reached the deep water of the bay, about three miles north of Dauphine Island, came to anchor.

Let us now return to the other vessels of the fleet, which we left massed in front of Fort Morgan by the remarkable action of the *Brooklyn* in stopping and refusing to move ahead. When the ram *Tennessee* turned away from the *Hartford*, as narrated, she made for the fleet, and in their crowded and confused condition it seemed to be a matter of no difficulty to pick out whatever victims the Confederate commander (Admiral Franklin Buchanan) might desire, as he had done in 1861 when commanding the *Merrimac* in Hampton Roads. Before he could reach them the line had become straightened, and the leading vessels had passed the fort. Admiral Jenkins, who commanded the *Richmond* during the fight, writing of this part of the fight, for the use of the present writer, says:

"During the delay under the guns of Fort Morgan and the water-battery by the backing of the *Brooklyn*, the vessels astern had remained apparently stationary, so that the nearest one to the *Richmond* was about half a mile off, and some of them paid very dearly, for the men of the water-battery, who had been driven away from their guns and up the sand hills by the fire of the *Richmond* and *Chickasaw*, had time to return and attack them. When the *Hartford* 'cut adrift' from the *Brooklyn* and *Richmond* — the only safe thing possible to do — the

Tennessee and the three gun-boats pursued her. That is, the *Tennessee*, after getting above the lines of torpedoes, turned into the main ship-channel and followed the *Hartford*, while the gun-boats were in shallow water to the northward, where our heavy vessels could not go after them. When the *Tennessee* was within probably half a mile of the *Hartford*, she suddenly turned her head toward the *Brooklyn* and *Richmond* (both close together). As she approached, every one on board the *Richmond* supposed that she would ram the *Brooklyn*; that, we thought, would be our opportunity, for if she struck the *Brooklyn* the concussion would throw her port side across our path, and being so near to us, she would not have time to 'straighten up,' and we would strike her fairly and squarely, and most likely sink her.

"The guns were loaded with solid shot and heaviest powder charge; the forecastle gun's crew were ordered to get their small-arms and fire into her gun-ports; and as previously determined, if we came in collision at any time, the orders were to throw gun charges of powder in bags from the fore and main yard-arms down her smoke-stack (or at least try to do so). To our great surprise, she sheered off from the *Brooklyn*, and at about one hundred yards put two shot or shells through and through the *Brooklyn*'s sides (as reported), doing much damage.

"Approaching, passing, and getting away from the *Richmond*, the ram received from us three full broadsides of 9-inch solid shot, each broadside being eleven guns. They were well aimed and all struck, but when she was examined next day, no other indications were seen than scratches. The musketry fire into the two ports prevented the leveling of her guns, and therefore two of her shot or shell passed harmlessly over the *Richmond*, except the cutting of a ratline in the port main-shroud, just under the feet of the pilot, while the other whistled unpleasantly close to Lieutenant Terry's head.

REAR-ADMIRAL THORNTON A. JENKINS.
FROM A PHOTOGRAPH.

The *Tennessee* passed toward the *Lackawanna*, the next vessel astern, and avoided her — wishing either to ram Captain Strong's vessel *(Monongahela)*, or cross his bow and attack McCann's vessel (the *Kennebec*, Strong's consort). Strong was ready for her, and, anticipating her object, made at her, but the blow (by the quick manœuvring of the *Tennessee)* was a glancing one, doing very little damage to either Strong's or McCann's vessel. Thence the *Tennessee*, after firing two broadsides into the *Oneida*, proceeded toward the fort, and for a time entirely disappeared from our sight. During this time the three gun-boats were proceeding, apparently, up the bay, to escape. The *Hartford* was closely watched with our glasses, and soon after the *Tennessee* had left Strong the *Metacomet* (Jouett) was seen to cast off; and divining the purpose, the *Port Royal* (Gherardi) was ordered to cast off from the *Richmond* and go in chase of the enemy, pointing in the direction of the three gun-boats of the enemy. George Brown (in the *Itasca*) cast off from the *Ossipee* and (I believe) McCann did also, and steered for the enemy. By this time Jouett had come up with the *Selma*, and the fight commenced. A very few minutes after Gherardi had left the side of the *Richmond*, and the other small vessels had left their consorts, a thick mist, with light rain (just enough to wet the deck), passed over the *Richmond*, obscuring from sight every object outside the vessel; indeed, for a few minutes the bowsprit of the *Richmond* could not be seen from the poop-deck. This mist and rain, in a cloudless sunshiny day, were slowly wafted over the waters toward the fort and pilot town, enabling John W. Bennett, commanding one of the enemy's gun-boats, and George W. Harrison, commanding the other, to shape their courses for safety, in shoal water, and finally under Fort Morgan. Gherardi in the *Port Royal* (as soon as he could see) saw only the *Selma* and *Metacomet*, and continued his course for them."

CAPTURE OF THE CONFEDERATE GUN-BOAT "SELMA" BY THE "METACOMET." FROM A WAR-TIME SKETCH.

Whatever damage was done by the *Tennessee* to the fleet in passing the fort was by the occasional discharge of her guns. She failed to strike a single one of the Union vessels, but was herself run into by the *Monongahela*, Captain Strong, at full speed. ⁊　The captain says in his report:

"After passing the forts I saw the rebel ram *Tennessee* head on for our line. I then sheered out of the line to run into her, at the same time ordering full speed as fast as possible. I struck her fair, and swinging around poured in a broadside of solid 11-inch shot, which apparently had little if any effect upon her."

This modest statement is characteristic of the gallant writer, now dead, as are so many others of the conspicuous actors in that day's work. The *Monongahela* was no match for the *Tennessee*, but she had been strengthened by an artificial iron prow, and being one of the fastest — or rather, *least slow* — of the fleet, was expected to act as a ram if opportunity offered. Captain Strong waited for no orders, but seeing the huge ram coming for the fleet left his place in the line and attacked her, as narrated. It was at this time that the *Monongahela's* first lieutenant, Roderick Prentiss, a brave and gifted young officer, received his death wound, both legs being shattered.

At last all the fleet passed the fort, and while the ram ran under its guns the vessels made their way to the *Hartford* and dropped their anchors, except the *Metacomet*, *Port Royal*, *Kennebec*, and *Itasca*. After the forts were passed, the three last named had cut loose from their escorts and gone to aid the *Metacomet* in her struggle with the *Selma* and *Morgan*. ☆

⁊ The *Tennessee*, after colliding with the *Monongahela*, grazed the bow of the *Kennebec*, injured slightly the latter's planking, and dropped one of her boats on the deck of the gun-boat.—EDITORS.

☆ The *Oneida*, the last ship in the line, suffered more severely than any other of the fleet in the passage. One shell exploded in the boiler, another cut the wheel-ropes, and a third disabled the forward pivot-gun. The list of casualties was very large, Commander Mullany being among the wounded. The crippled vessel was carried on by her consort, the *Galena*.—EDITORS.

The thunder of heavy artillery now ceased. The crews of the various vessels had begun to efface the marks of the terrible contest by washing the decks and clearing up the splinters. The cooks were preparing breakfast, the surgeons were busily engaged in making amputations and binding arteries, and under canvas, on the port side of each vessel, lay the ghastly line of dead waiting the sailor's burial. As if by mutual understanding, officers who were relieved from immediate duty gathered in the ward-rooms to ascertain who of their mates were missing, and the reaction from such a season of tense nerves and excitement was just setting in when the hurried call to quarters came and the word passed around, " The ram is coming."

The *Tennessee*, after remaining near Fort Morgan while the fleet had made its way four miles above to its anchorage,—certainly as much as half an hour,—had suddenly decided to settle at once the question of the control of the bay. Single-handed she came on to meet the whole fleet, consisting now of ten wooden vessels and the three monitors. At that time the *Tennessee* was believed to be the strongest vessel afloat, and the safety with which she carried her crew during the battle proved that she was virtually invulnerable. Fortunately for the Union fleet she was weakly handled, and at the end fell a victim to a stupendous blunder in her construction—the failure to protect her rudder-chains. The spectacle afforded the Confederate soldiers, who crowded the ramparts of the two forts,—the fleet now being out of range,— was such as has very rarely been furnished in the history of the world. To the looker-on it seemed as if the fleet was at the mercy of the ram, for the monitors, which were expected to be the chief defense, were so destitute of speed and so difficult to manœuvre that it seemed an easy task for the *Tennessee* to avoid them and sink the wooden vessels in detail. Because of the slowness of the monitors, Admiral Farragut selected the fastest of the wooden vessels to begin the attack. While the navy signals for a general attack of the enemy were being prepared, the *Monongahela* (Captain Strong) and the *Lackawanna* (Captain Marchand) were ordered by the more rapid signal system of the army to "run down the ram," the order being immediately repeated to the monitors.

The *Monongahela*, with her prow already somewhat weakened by the previous attempt to ram, at once took the lead, as she had not yet come to anchor. The ram from the first headed for the *Hartford*, and paid no attention to her assailants, except with her guns. The *Monongahela*, going at full speed, struck the *Tennessee* amidships — a blow that would have sunk almost any vessel of the Union navy, but which inflicted not the slightest damage on the solid iron hull of the ram. (After the surrender it was almost impossible to tell where the attacking vessel had struck.) Her own iron prow and cutwater were carried away, and she was otherwise badly damaged about the stern by the collision. The *Lackawanna* was close behind and delivered a similar blow with her wooden bow, simply causing the ram to lurch slightly to one side. As the vessels separated the *Lackawanna* swung alongside the ram, which sent two shots through her and kept on her course for the *Hartford*, which was now the next vessel in the attack. The two flag-ships approached each other, bow to bow, iron against oak. It was impossible for the *Hartford*, with her lack of speed, to circle around and strike the ram on the side; her only safety was in keeping pointed directly for the bow of her assailant. The other vessels of the fleet were unable to do anything for the defense of the admiral except to train their guns on the ram, on which as yet they had not the slightest effect.

It was a thrilling moment for the fleet, for it was evident that if the ram could strike the *Hartford* the latter must sink. But for the two vessels to strike fairly, bows on, would probably have involved the destruction of both, for the ram must have penetrated so far into the wooden ship that as the *Hartford* filled and sank she would have carried the ram under water. Whether for this reason or for some other, as the two vessels came together the *Tennessee* slightly changed her course, the port bow of the *Hartford* met the port bow of the ram, and the ships grated against each other as they passed. The *Hartford* poured her whole port broadside against the ram, but the solid shot merely dented the side and bounded into the air. The ram tried to return the salute, but owing to defective primers only one gun was discharged. This sent a shell through the berth-deck, killing five men and wounding eight. The muzzle of the gun was so close to the *Hartford* that the powder blackened her side.

The admiral stood on the quarter-deck when the vessels came together, and as he saw the result he jumped on to the port-quarter rail, holding

CAPTAIN GEORGE H. PERKINS.
FROM A PHOTOGRAPH.

to the mizzen-rigging, a position from which he might have jumped to the deck of the ram as she passed. Seeing him in this position, and fearing for his safety, Flag-Lieutenant Watson slipped a rope around him and secured it to the rigging, so that during the fight the admiral was twice "lashed to the rigging," each time by devoted officers who knew better than to consult him before acting. Fleet-Captain Drayton had hurried to the bow of the *Hartford* as the collision was seen to be inevitable, and expressed keen satisfaction when the ram avoided a direct blow.

The *Tennessee* now became the target for the whole fleet, all the vessels of which were making toward her, pounding her with shot, and trying to run her down. As the *Hartford* turned to make for her again, we ran in front of the *Lackawanna*, which had already turned and was moving under full headway with the same object. She struck us on our starboard side, amidships, crushing half-way through, knocking two port-holes into one, upsetting one of the Dahlgren guns, and creating general consternation. For a time it was thought that we must sink, and the cry rang out over the deck: "Save the admiral! Save the admiral!" The port boats were ordered lowered, and in their haste some of the sailors cut the "falls," and two of the cutters dropped into the water wrong side up, and floated astern. But the admiral sprang into the starboard mizzen-rigging, looked over the side of the ship, and, finding there were still a few inches to spare above the water's edge, instantly ordered the ship ahead again at full speed, after the ram. The unfortunate *Lackawanna*, which had struck the ram a second blow, was making for her once more, and, singularly enough, again came up on our starboard side, and another collision seemed imminent. And now the admiral became a trifle excited. He had no idea of whipping the rebels to be himself sunk by a friend, nor did he realize at the moment that the *Hartford* was as much to blame as the *Lackawanna*. Turning to the writer he inquired. "Can you say 'For God's sake' by signal?" "Yes, sir," was the reply. "Then say to the *Lackawanna*, 'For God's sake get out of our way and anchor!'"

REAR-ADMIRAL JAMES E. JOUETT.
FROM A PHOTOGRAPH.

In my haste to send the message, I brought the end of my signal flag-staff down with considerable violence upon the head of the admiral, who was standing nearer than I thought, causing him to wince perceptibly. It was a hasty message, for the fault was equally divided, each ship being too eager to reach the enemy, and it turned out all right, by a fortunate accident, that Captain Marchand never received it. The army signal officer on the *Lackawanna*, Lieutenant Myron Adams (now pastor of Plymouth Congregational Church in Rochester, N. Y.), had taken his station in the foretop, and just as he received the first five words, "For God's sake get out"—— the wind flirted the large United States flag at the mast-head around him, so that he was unable to read the conclusion of the message.

The remainder of the story is soon told. As the *Tennessee* left the *Hartford* she became the target of the entire fleet, and at last the concentration of solid shot from so many guns began to tell. The flag-staff was shot away, the smoke-stack was riddled with holes, and finally disappeared. The monitor *Chickasaw*, Lieutenant-Commander Perkins, succeeded in coming up astern and began pounding away with 11-inch solid shot, and one shot from a 15-inch gun of the *Manhattan* crushed into the side sufficiently to prove that a few more such shots would have made the casemate untenable. Finally, one of the *Chickasaw's* shots cut the rudder-chain of the ram and she would no longer mind her helm.‖   At this time, as Admiral Farragut says in his report, "she was sore beset.   The *Chickasaw* was pounding away at her stern, the *Ossipee* was approaching her at full speed, and the *Monongahela*, *Lackawanna*, and this ship were bearing down upon her, determined upon her destruction." From the time the *Hartford* struck her she did not fire a gun.   Finally the Confederate admiral, Buchanan, was severely wounded by an iron splinter or a piece of a shell, and just as the *Ossipee* was about to strike her the *Tennessee* displayed a white flag, hoisted on an improvised staff through the grating over her deck.   The *Ossipee* (Captain Le Roy) reversed her engine, but was so near that a harmless collision was inevitable.   Suddenly the terrific cannonading ceased, and from every ship rang out cheer after cheer, as the weary men realized that at last the ram was conquered and the day won. ⚓ The *Chickasaw* took the *Tennessee* in tow and brought her to anchor near the *Hartford*. The impression prevailed at first that the *Tennessee* had been seriously injured by the ramming she had received and was sinking, and orders were signaled to send boats to assist her crew, but it was soon discovered that this was unnecessary.   Admiral Buchanan surrendered his sword to Lieutenant Giraud, of the *Ossipee*, who was sent to take charge of the captured *Tennessee*.   Captain Heywood, of the Marine Corps, was sent on board the ram with a guard of marines.   On meeting Admiral Buchanan he could not

‖ The admiral says in his report:

"I cannot give too much praise to Lieutenant-Commander Perkins, who, though he had orders from the Department to return north, volunteered to take command of the *Chickasaw*, and did his duty nobly."

According to the pilot of the *Tennessee*, "the *Chickasaw* hung close under our stern.   Move as

we would, she was always there, firing the two 11-inch guns in her forward turret like pocket-pistols, so that she soon had the plates flying in the air."— EDITORS.

⚓ The first gun of the day was fired at 6:47 A. M.   The surrender of the ram occurred at 10 o'clock.— EDITORS.

FIGHT BETWEEN THE "CHICKASAW" AND FORT POWELL, AUGUST 5, 1864.   FROM A WAR-TIME SKETCH.
The picture appears to represent the blowing up of Fort Powell, which did not occur until after 10 o'clock that night, when the fort was evacuated.— EDITORS.

resist the temptation to inform him that they had met before under different circumstances, the captain having been on the frigate *Cumberland* when she was sunk in Hampton Roads by Buchanan in the *Merrimac.*↓

Late in the afternoon the *Metacomet* was sent to Pensacola with the wounded of both sides, including Admiral Buchanan. In his report he accuses Captain Harrison of the *Morgan* of deserting the *Selma.* Captain Harrison in his report, on the other hand, charges Captain Murphy of the *Selma* with running away and with bad seamanship. Those who witnessed the fight at close quarters will not accept Captain Harrison's view, and the record of killed and wounded tells the story. On the *Morgan* one man was slightly wounded, on the *Selma* eight were killed and seven wounded; and there is no doubt that the *Selma* was better managed and did more harm to the Union fleet than the two other rebel gun-boats combined. Captain Murphy of the *Selma*, in his official report, written like those of Buchanan and Johnston from the Pensacola hospital, tells very briefly the story of his part in the fight and makes no insinuations or complaints against brother officers. The total casualties in the rebel fleet were 12 killed and 20 wounded, as follows:

	Killed.	Wounded.
Ram *Tennessee*	2	9
Gun-boat *Selma*	8	7
" *Gaines*	2	3
" *Morgan*	—	1
Total	12	20

[To the above should be added those captured on board the surrendered vessels, including, according to Farragut's report, 190 in the *Tennessee* and 90 in the *Selma.*— EDITORS.]

The *Gaines*, according to the official report of her captain, was disabled by a shot or shell from the *Hartford*, "which broke in the outer planking under the port quarter about the water-line, and which from the marks seemed to have glanced below in the direction of the stern-post." This caused a leak in the after-magazine that could not be stopped, and made it necessary to beach the vessel as already described. The captain succeeded in removing the ammunition, supplies, and small-arms to the shore, for the use of Fort Morgan, and during the next night made his escape with his crew to Mobile, pulling up the bay in six cutters, which in the darkness easily evaded the Union gun-boats that were on guard. The *Morgan* also succeeded in making her way through without difficulty, covering all her lights and running very slowly until she had passed the Union vessels. The writer of this sketch has

↓ The casualties of the Union fleet, as reported by Admiral Farragut, were 52 killed and 170 wounded, as follows:

	Killed.	Wounded.		Killed.	Wounded.
Hartford	25	28	*Ossipee*	1	7
Brooklyn	11	43	*Richmond*	0	2
Lackawanna	4	35	*Galena*	0	1
Oneida	8	30	*Octorara*	1	10
Monongahela	♭0	6	*Kennebec*	1	6
Metacomet	1	2			

To the above should be added the casualties on board the *Tecumseh*, viz., 93 drowned and 4 captured, making the total losses 145 killed, 170 wounded and 4 captured.— EDITORS.

♭ First-Lieutenant Roderick Prentiss died a day later, as already mentioned.

never been able to understand why the *Morgan* and the boats belonging to the *Gaines* were not destroyed during the afternoon following the fight, as might have been done with ease and safety by any one of the monitors. This was supposed to have been the object of a little excursion of the *Winnebago* in the afternoon, which, however, aside from firing a few harmless and unnecessary shots at Fort Morgan, accomplished nothing. The *Chickasaw* (Lieutenant-Commander Perkins) at the same time shelled Fort Powell, which was evacuated about 10 P. M. that night, the officers and men escaping to the mainland. The *Chickasaw* also tackled Fort Gaines on the 6th, and speedily convinced the commanding officer that it would be folly to attempt to withstand a siege. The result was a surrender to the army and navy the next morning.

Fort Morgan was at once invested, and surrendered on the 23d of August.

THE OPPOSING FORCES AT MOBILE.

THE UNION FLEET IN THE BATTLE OF MOBILE BAY.

Rear-Admiral D. G. Farragut, Commanding.   Fleet-Captain, Captain Percival Drayton.

MONITORS.— *Tecumseh*, Com. T. A. M. Craven, 2 15-inch guns; *Manhattan*, Com. J. W. A. Nicholson, 2 15-inch; *Winnebago*, Com. Thomas H. Stevens, 4 11-inch; *Chickasaw*, Lieut.-Com. George H. Perkins, 4 11-inch.

SCREW-SLOOPS.— *Hartford* (flag-ship), Capt. Percival Drayton, 2 100-pounder Parrott rifles, 1 30-pounder Parrott, 18 9-inch, 3 howitzers; *Brooklyn*, Capt. James Alden, 2 100-pounder Parrotts, 2 60-pounder rifles, 20 9-inch, 1 howitzer; *Richmond*, Capt. Thornton A. Jenkins, 1 100-pounder rifle, 1 30-pounder rifle, 18 9-inch, 2 howitzers; *Lackawanna*, Capt. J. B. Marchand, 1 150-pounder Parrott pivot, 1 50-pounder Dahlgren pivot, 2 11-inch, 4 9-inch, 6 howitzers; *Monongahela*, Com. James H. Strong, 1 150-pounder Parrott, 2 11-inch, 5 32-pounders, 3 howitzers; *Ossipee*, Com. William E. Le Roy, 1 100-pounder Parrott, 1 11-inch, 6 32-pounders, 2 30-pounder Parrotts, 2 howitzers; *Oneida*, Com. J. R. M. Mullany, 2 11-inch, pivot,

3 30-pounder Parrotts, 4 32-pounders, 1 howitzer; *Seminole*, Com. Edward Donaldson, 1 11-inch pivot, 1 30-pounder Parrott, 6 32-pounders.

SCREW-STEAMER.— *Galena*, Lieut.-Com. Clark H. Wells. 1 100-pounder Parrott pivot, 1 30-pounder, 8 9-inch, 1 howitzer.

DOUBLE-ENDERS.— *Octorara*, Lieut.-Com. Charles H. Greene, 1 100-pounder Parrott pivot, 3 9-inch, 2 32-pounders, 4 howitzers; *Metacomet*, Lieut.-Com. James E. Jouett, 2 100-pounder Parrotts, 4 9-inch, 4 howitzers; *Port Royal*, Lieut.-Com. B. Gherardi, 1 100-pounder Parrott pivot, 1 10-inch, 2 9-inch, 2 50-pounder Dahlgren rifles, 2 howitzers.

GUN-BOATS.— *Kennebec*, Lieut.-Com. W. P. McCann, 1 11-inch, 1 20-pounder, 3 howitzers; *Itasca*, Lieut.-Com. George Brown, 1 11-inch, 2 32-pounders, 2 20-pounders, 1 howitzer.

CONFEDERATE FLEET.—Admiral Franklin Buchanan, Commanding.

IRON-CLAD RAM.— *Tennessee* (flag-ship), Com. J. D. Johnston, 2 7-inch Brooke rifles, 4 6.4-inch Brooke rifles.

SIDE-WHEEL GUN-BOATS.— *Morgan*, Com. George W.

Harrison, 2 7-inch rifles, 4 32-pounders; *Gaines*, Lieut. J. W. Bennett, 1 8-inch rifle, 5 32-pounders; *Selma*, Com. P. U. Murphy, 1 6-inch rifle, 3 8-inch shell guns.

LAND OPERATIONS AGAINST MOBILE.—August 5th–23d, 1864.

THE UNION FORCES were immediately commanded by Maj.-Gen. Gordon Granger (with Maj.-Gen. E. R. S. Canby as his superior), and consisted of the following organizations: *Infantry:* 77th Ill., 94th Ill., 67th Ind., 20th Iowa, 34th Iowa, 38th Iowa, 161st N. Y., 96th Ohio, 20th Wis., 23d Wis., 96th U. S. C. T., and 97th U. S. C. T. *Cavalry:* 3d Md.; A, 2d Me.; M, 14th N. Y. *Artillery:* 1st Ind. Heavy (battalion); 6th Mich. Heavy; Battery A, 2d Ill.; 2d Conn. Battery; 17th Ohio Battery.

The brigade commanders were Colonels Joseph Bailey, Joshua J. Guppey, George W. Clark, Henry Bertram, and George D. Robinson.

The effective strength of this command was about 5500; loss in the bombardment of Fort Morgan, 7 wounded.

THE CONFEDERATE FORCES: Maj.-Gen. Dabney H. Maury was the Confederate commander at Mobile, with Brig.-Gen. Richard L. Page in command of the defensive works at Fort Morgan, etc. Fort Morgan was garrisoned by a portion of the 1st Ala. battalion of artillery, one company of the 21st Ala., and the 1st Tenn. Fort Gaines, commanded by Col. Charles D. Anderson, was garrisoned by six companies of the 21st Ala., two companies 1st Ala. battalion of artillery, the Pelham Cadets, some reserves and marines; in all about 600. Lieut.-Col. James M. Williams was in command of Fort Powell, which was garrisoned by two companies 21st Ala. and a part of Culpeper's S. C. battery.

Confederate loss in Fort Morgan: 1 killed, 3 wounded.

THE CONFEDERATE IRON-CLAD "TENNESSEE." FROM A WAR-TIME SKETCH.

THE RAM "TENNESSEE" AT MOBILE BAY.

BY JAMES D. JOHNSTON, COMMANDER, C. S. N.

THE Confederate naval force at Mobile at the time of Admiral Farragut's attack was commanded by Admiral Franklin Buchanan, of *Merrimac* fame, and consisted of the iron-clad ram *Tennessee*, armed with four 6.4-inch rifled guns in broadside, and two 7-inch rifles, one at each end of the shield; the gun-boats *Morgan* and *Gaines*, carrying six guns each, chiefly of smaller caliber; and the *Selma*, carrying only four, making in all 22 guns. The entire force of officers and men was about 470. Admiral Farragut's fleet consisted of six first-class steam sloops of war, eight smaller sloops and gun-boats, and four monitors, two of which had double turrets. The total number of guns carried by these vessels was 159, and 33 howitzers; and the officers and crews numbered about 3000.

The hull of the *Tennessee* was constructed on a high bluff near the Alabama River, a short distance above the city of Selma, and all the timber used was cut in the immediate vicinity. She was 209 feet in length and 48 feet in breadth of beam. The shield for the protection of her battery and crew was 78 feet 8 inches long and 8 feet high above the deck, which at each end of the shield was only about 18 inches above the surface of the water when the vessel had been prepared for service. Sponsons of heavy timber projected about five feet from the sides in a line with the deck, extending seven feet below it, the lower edge of the shield covering the outer angle or apex of the sponsons. The sides of the shield were of yellow pine and white oak, 23 inches thick, placed at an angle of 33 degrees with the deck.

When she was prepared for launching, I was ordered by Admiral Buchanan to charter two steamboats and proceed with them to Selma, to tow her down to Mobile, as soon as she was launched. I found on arrival at Selma that every preparation had been made for that purpose by the naval constructor in charge (Mr. Henry Pearce). She was immediately taken in tow by the steamboats and towed down to Mobile, to receive her machinery and battery, the latter having been cast at the Government foundry in Selma, under the superintendence of Commander Catesby ap Roger Jones, late commander of the *Merrimac*, who had acquired great distinction as an ordnance officer of the United States navy. The armor plating had been prepared at the rolling-mills of Atlanta, and was rapidly arriving. It consisted of plates of exceedingly tough and malleable iron seven inches wide, two inches thick, and 21 feet long. Three layers of the 2-inch plates were bolted on the forward end of the shield as far as the after end of the pilot-house (which extended about two feet above the top of the shield), and from that point to the termination of the shield two plates of 2-inch and one of 1-inch were used.

While this tedious work was progressing, the machinery and guns were placed in position, and about the 1st of April, 1864, the vessel was ready to receive her crew. As executive officer of the station under the admiral, I had superintended the completion of the vessel, and by his request I was now selected for the command, being immediately afterward promoted to the grade of commander.

But as the draught of the vessel was over thirteen feet, and there were only nine feet of water on Dog River bar, at the mouth of the Mobile River, it became a serious problem to solve as to the means of floating her over this bar. Naval Constructor Thomas Porter conceived the idea of building heavy camels or floats, to be made fast to the sides of the ram; the surfaces in contact with the ram to conform to the model of the hull; and the camels were to contain a sufficient weight of water to counterbalance in part the weight of the vessel. This plan was immediately adopted, but the timber for the purpose had yet to pass from the forest, through the saw-mill, some ten miles up the river, down to Mobile. Time was precious, and the newspapers were beginning to express the impatience of the people to see the powerful ram of which so much was expected taken down the bay to attack the blockading fleet. The camels were being constructed with all possible dispatch, but just as they were nearly ready they were totally destroyed by fire. Undaunted by this calamity, Admiral Buchanan, with his usual energy and pluck, soon had them rebuilt, and about the middle of May the *Tennessee*, drawing less than nine feet of water, was towed over the bar by two steamboats, one of which contained her coal, and the other her ammunition. Her crew were employed during the passage down the bay in transferring these supplies, and by the time she reached a sufficient depth of water to float without the aid of the camels, she was quite prepared for action. But unfortunately it was now near midnight, and by the time the camels had been sent adrift, the tide had fallen so much that she was found to be hard and fast aground. Here was an insurmountable and most unlooked-for end to the long-cherished hope of taking the enemy by surprise, dispersing the blockading fleet, and capturing Fort Pickens, at the entrance of Pensacola Bay. Such was the work Buchanan had mapped out for the ram, and but for the fact that her presence in the bay was soon revealed by daylight, this attempt would certainly have been made.

When the tide rose sufficiently to float the ship, she was moved down to an anchorage near Fort Morgan, where she remained nearly three months, engaged in exercising the crew at their guns. Having realized from the first that the running of the steering gear was very defective, I addressed a letter to the admiral soon after reaching our anchorage, suggesting certain necessary alterations therein, and he sent the naval constructor down from the city to make plans for the purpose; but before they could be perfected we were compelled to take the consequences of the defect, which proved to be disastrous.

On the evening of the 4th of August, 1864, it was plainly to be seen that the blockading fleet, which had recently been augmented by the arrival of the heavier wooden vessels and the monitors, was making preparations to attempt the passage of Forts Morgan and Gaines, situated on either side of the entrance to the bay, and to attack the Confederate squadron. Similar preparations were made by our vessels, which had been anchored just within the bay for nearly three months, in daily expectation of the impending encounter. During the

night a blockade-runner entered the bay and was boarded by the executive officer of the *Tennessee*.

At about 6 o'clock on the morning of the 5th, the fleet was discovered to be under way toward the bay, the monitors on the right and the wooden vessels lashed together two and two, each of the heavier ships having a gun-boat lashed alongside. All the light spars had been sent down, leaving only the lower and top masts standing, while the boats had been hauled upon the beach at Sand Island just within the bar, on the morning previous.

All hands were immediately called on board the Confederate vessels, and after hurriedly taking coffee, the crew were set to work to slip the cable and buoy the anchor. This being done, they were assembled at their quarters for action, as the distance from the bar to the entrance of the bay is only about three miles, and the Federal vessels were already within range of the guns of Fort Morgan and were receiving its fire without damage.

As the leading monitor, the *Tecumseh*, reached the center of the channel between the forts, the *Tennessee* steamed out to meet her, but the speed of both vessels was so slow that the steam-sloops advanced beyond them, and the *Tennessee* was directed toward the leading ship, with the hope of reaching her in time to run into her broadside and sink her; but by slightly changing her course, and with her superior speed, the ship easily avoided the intended ramming, and seemed to fly up the bay. This was the admiral's flag-ship *Hartford*, and while she passed ahead of the ram, the *Brooklyn*, leading the other vessels of the fleet, passed astern and followed the admiral. I learned after the fight that her commander had obtained the admiral's permission to take the lead, but an event occurred just after the *Tennessee* had moved down to the

THE "MONONGAHELA" RAMMING THE "TENNESSEE." FROM A WAR-TIME SKETCH.

THE "HARTFORD" IN COLLISION WITH THE "TENNESSEE." FROM A WAR-TIME SKETCH.

middle of the channel⸗ which disconcerted him for a moment and caused him to stop his ship, thus compelling the admiral to take the lead himself. This event was the most startling and tragic of the day, causing the almost instantaneous loss of 93 lives. The monitor *Tecumseh*, at her commander's special request, had been detailed to "take care of the *Tennessee*," and had reserved her fire until she had approached that vessel within a quarter of a mile, when she was suddenly struck by a torpedo, and disappeared beneath the water. But for the cheering of my men as they saw her sinking I should not have seen her go down. Twenty-one of her crew escaped from her, of whom four landed at Fort Morgan.

Meantime the other vessels of the Confederate squadron were doing their duty faithfully by raking the enemy's ships as they advanced head on, and they killed and wounded a large number of men.

As soon as Admiral Buchanan realized that his enemy had escaped for the moment he ordered me to follow him up the bay; but meanwhile the lashings between each two vessels of the fleet had been cast off, and four gun-boats went immediately in pursuit of the three hastily improvised wooden vessels of our squadron. The *Selma* was speedily captured by one of these, the *Metacomet*, after a gallant resistance, during which seven of her crew and her executive officer were killed, and her commander, Lieutenant P. U. Murphy, was slightly wounded. The *Gaines*, commanded by Lieutenant John W. Bennett, which was run ashore near Fort

Morgan to prevent her from sinking, had received several shots below the water-line, and at night was burned by her own crew. The *Morgan*, Commander George W. Harrison, ran alongside the wharf at the fort to escape capture, and during the night passed safely through the enemy's fleet up to the city of Mobile. She afterward rendered good service in the defense of the city.

While this sort of by-play was in progress the heavier ships of the fleet, together with the monitors, steamed up the bay to a point about four miles above Fort Morgan, where they were in the act of anchoring when it was discovered that the ram was approaching with hostile intent. Upon this apparently unexpected challenge the fleet was immediately put in motion, and the heavier vessels seemed to contend with each other for the glory of sinking the daring rebel ram, by running themselves up on her decks, which extended some thirty feet at each end of the shield, and were only about eighteen inches above the surface of the water. So great was their eagerness to accomplish this feat that the *Lackawanna*, one of the heaviest steamers, ran bows on into the *Hartford*, by which both vessels sustained greater damage than their united efforts in this direction could have inflicted upon their antagonist.

Early in the action, the pilot of the *Tennessee* had been wounded by having the trap-door on the top of the pilot-house knocked down upon his head by a shot from one of the enemy's ships, which struck it on the edge while it was thrown back to admit of his seeing more clearly the posi-

⸗ In this statement, Captain Johnston's chronology is undoubtedly at fault. The testimony of eye-witnesses makes it certain that the *Brooklyn* had stopped before the sinking of the *Tecumseh*.—EDITORS.

tion of the vessel. Thereafter I remained in the pilot-house, for the purpose of directing the movements of the ram.

The monitors kept up a constant firing at short range. The two double-turreted monitors (*Chickasaw* and *Winnebago*) were stationed under the stern of the *Tennessee*, and struck the after end of her shield so repeatedly with 11-inch solid shot that it was found at the close of the action to be in a rather shaky condition. One of these missiles had struck the iron cover of the stern port and jammed it against the shield so that it became impossible to run the gun out for firing, and Admiral Buchanan, who superintended the battery during the entire engagement, sent to the engine room for a machinist to back out the pin of the bolt upon which the port cover revolved. While this was being done a shot from one of the monitors struck the edge of the port cover, immediately over the spot where the machinist was sitting, and his remains had to be taken up with a shovel, placed in a bucket, and thrown overboard. The same shot caused several iron splinters to fly inside of the shield, one of which killed a seaman, while another broke the admiral's leg below the knee. The admiral sent for me, and as I approached he quietly remarked, "Well, Johnston, they've got me. You'll have to look out for her now. This is your fight, you know." I replied, "All right, sir. I'll do the best I know how." While returning to the pilot-house I felt the vessel careen so suddenly as nearly to throw me off my feet. I discovered that the *Hartford* ⚓ had run into the ram amidships, and that while thus in contact with her the Federal crew were using their small-arms by firing through the open ports. However, only one man was wounded in this way, the cause of all our other wounds being iron splinters from the washers on the inner ends of the bolts that secured the plating. I continued on my way to the pilot-house, and upon looking through the narrow peep-holes in its sides to ascertain the position of the enemy's ships, I discovered that the wooden vessels had mostly withdrawn from the action, leaving it to the monitors to effect the destruction of the ram at their leisure.‡ At this time both of my most efficient guns had been placed in broadside, because both the after and forward port covers had been so effectually jammed against the shield as to block up the ports. The steering apparatus had been completely destroyed, as it had been plainly visible on the after deck, and the smoke-stack had fallen, destroying the draught in such a degree as to render it impossible to keep steam enough to stem the tide, which was running out at the rate of over four miles an hour.

Realizing the impossibility of directing the firing of the guns without the use of the rudder, and that the ship had been rendered utterly helpless, I went to the lower deck and informed the admiral of her condition, and that I had not been able to bring a gun to bear upon any of our antagonists for nearly half an hour, to which he replied: "Well, Johnston, if you cannot do them any further damage you had better surrender." With this sanction of my own views I returned to the gun-deck, and after another glance about the bay to see if there was any chance of getting another shot, and seeing none of the enemy's ships within range of our broadside guns, I went to the top of the shield and took down the boat-hook to which the flag had been lashed after having been shot away several times during the fight. While I was thus engaged repeated shots came from the enemy's vessels, but as soon as I returned to the gun-deck and had a flag of truce attached to the boat-hook the firing ceased. Having returned to the top of the shield, I saw one of the heaviest ships of the fleet approaching rapidly, apparently for the purpose of making another attempt to sink the ram. Seeing the flag of truce, the commander stopped his ship, but her momentum was too great to be overcome in the short intervening space, and she struck the ram on the starboard quarter, but without injuring it. As she did so her commander hailed, saying: "This is the United States steamer *Ossipee*. Hello, Johnston, how are you? Le Roy—don't you know me? I'll send a boat alongside for you." The boat came and conveyed me on board the *Ossipee*, at whose gangway I was met by her genial commander, between whom and myself a lifelong friendship had existed. When I reached the deck of his ship, he remarked, "I'm glad to see you, Johnston. Here's some ice-water for you—I know you're dry; but I've something better than that for you down below." I thanked him cordially, but was in no humor for receiving hospitalities graciously, and quietly followed him to his cabin, where he placed a bottle of "navy sherry" and a pitcher of ice-water before me and urged me to help myself. Calling his steward, he ordered him to attend to my wishes as he would his own. I remained on board six days, during which time I was visited by nearly all the commanding officers of the fleet.

Within an hour after I was taken on board the *Ossipee* Admiral Farragut sent for me to be brought on board his flag-ship, and when I reached her deck he expressed regret at meeting me under such circumstances, to which I replied that he was not half as sorry to see me as I was to see him.

⚓ All the official reports show that the only contact between the *Hartford* and the ram was bows on, a glancing blow (see Report of the Secretary of the Navy, 1864, pp. 402, 407, and 410). Captain Johnston undoubtedly mistook the *Lackawanna* for the *Hartford*. Admiral Farragut in his report (ibid., p. 402) says:

"The *Lackawanna*, Captain Marchand, was the next vessel to strike her, which she did at full speed; but, though her stern was cut and crushed to the plank ends for the distance of three feet above the water's edge to five feet below, the only perceptible effect on the ram was to *give her a heavy list*."　　　EDITORS.

‡ This statement is not sustained by the official records of the fight. Admiral Farragut in his report says:

"She [the ram] was at this time sore beset; the *Chickasaw* was pounding away at her stern, the *Ossipee* was approaching her at full speed, and the *Monongahela*, *Lackawanna*, and this ship [*Hartford*] were bearing down upon her."

Here is direct mention of four wooden ships, and the *Brooklyn*, *Richmond*, and others were not out of the fight.　　　EDITORS.

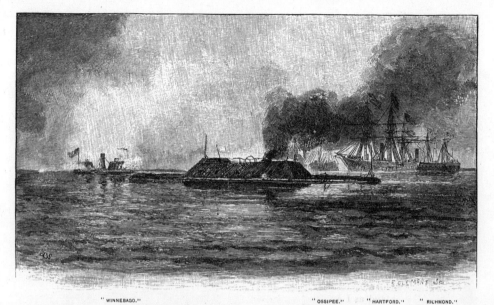

"WINNEBAGO."   "OSSIPEE." "HARTFORD." "RICHMOND."

SURRENDER OF THE "TENNESSEE." FROM A WAR-TIME SKETCH.

His flag-captain, Percival Drayton, remarked, "You have one consolation, Johnston; no one can say that you have not nobly defended the honor of the Confederate flag to-day." I thanked him, but gave all the honor due to its defense to Admiral Buchanan, who was the true hero of the battle; and when the disparity between the forces engaged is duly considered, I am constrained to believe that history will give him his just meed of praise.

The casualties on board the *Tennessee* were two killed and nine wounded. Her armor was never penetrated, although she was under the heaviest fire for nearly four hours. One solid 15-inch shot struck her shield, at point-blank range, between two of the ports and caused an indentation of about twelve inches, but did not break the iron plating. ⸜ Her speed did not exceed six knots under full steam in slack water, owing to her heavy draught, which exceeded the original calculation by more than a foot. Her engine had been removed from an old Mississippi River steamboat and adapted to a propeller, and its power was totally inadequate to the performance of the work expected of it.

After I left the *Tennessee* Admiral Buchanan was transferred to a small transport steamer and taken to the hospital in the navy yard at Pensacola, where he was accompanied by his own fleet-surgeon, Dr. D. B. Conrad, and his aides. Five days after the admiral's departure I was trans-

ported to Pensacola and transferred to the receiving-ship *Potomac*, lying off the navy yard; but as soon as Admiral Farragut's fleet-surgeon, Dr. James C. Palmer, heard of my arrival he had me removed to the hospital, owing to the fact of my suffering at the time with a painful disease. On reaching the hospital I found myself placed in a room near to that occupied by Admiral Buchanan, and immediately adjoining that of Captain J. R. M. Mullany, who had commanded the steamer *Oneida* of the fleet, and had had the misfortune to have his left arm shot away during the action. I had known him long before the war, and called upon him at once to offer my condolence.

After remaining in the hospital about three weeks I was placed on board a small ordnance steamer in company with Lieutenant-Commanding Murphy, late of the *Selma*, with Lieutenants Bradford and Wharton of the *Tennessee*, accompanied by my servant (whom Admiral Farragut had kindly allowed me to retain), for transportation to the Brooklyn Navy Yard. We reached our destination after a pleasant passage of five or six days, and on arrival the commander of the steamer, Captain Tarbox, reported to Admiral Hiram Paulding, commandant of the yard. On returning to the steamer he informed me that he had obtained the admiral's permission to escort the party to the navy yard at Boston, and that it was his intention to take us all down to his home at Cape Ann to spend a few days

⸜ The Board of Survey appointed by Admiral Farragut, and consisting of Captain T. A. Jenkins, Captain James Alden, Commander W. E. Le Roy, and Chief-Engineer Thomas Williamson, reported in part as follows on the injuries received in the action, by the *Tennessee:*

"On the port side of the casemate the armor is also badly damaged from shot. On that side nearly amidship of the

casemate, and between the two broadside guns, a 15-inch solid shot *knocked a hole through the armor and backing*, leaving on the inside an undetached mass of oak and pine splinters, about three by four feet, and projecting inside of the casemate about two feet from the side. This is the only shot that penetrated the wooden backing of the casemate, although there are numerous places on the inside giving evidence of the effect of the shot."

(Report of the Secretary of the Navy, 1864, p. 455.)

with him before turning us over to the officer commanding Fort Warren, which was to be our abode until we were exchanged. We were all delighted at the prospect of this pleasing respite from prison life, and expressed our gratitude to the kind-hearted captain. But we were awakened early on the following morning by the announcement from the distressed captain, who had had a second interview with the admiral, that we were all to be placed in irons and conveyed to Boston by rail. We remonstrated gently against this unprecedented mode of treating prisoners of war, but to no purpose.

When we reached the wharf at Fort Warren, the commanding officer, Major A. A. Gibson, inquired the cause of our being in irons, and upon being informed that they were placed upon us by order of Admiral Paulding, he made the further inquiry whether or not we had been guilty of any rebellious conduct as prisoners of war; this being answered in the negative, he replied that he had never heard of such treatment, and that we could not be landed on the island until the irons were removed.

Soon after becoming settled in my new quarters I addressed a communication to the Secretary of the Navy, inquiring whether or not he had authorized the action of Admiral Paulding, which was answered by Assistant-Secretary Fox, who disavowed the act, but excused it on the ground of repeated attempts of prisoners to escape.

An order for the exchange of all the prisoners in the fort had reached the commanding officer previous to our arrival, and after ten days we left for City Point on the steamer *Assyrian*. We naturally supposed that on our arrival at City Point we would be immediately forwarded to the landing on James River, at which exchanges were usually made. But when General B. F. Butler, whose lines were between us and that point, was advised of our presence he refused to allow us to pass through them, on account of President Davis's proclamation declaring him an outlaw. The Commissioner of Exchange informed General Grant of the fact, and he came alongside the *Assyrian* with his steamer, and informed us that we should be forwarded to Richmond on the following day. True to his promise, he had us landed near Dutch Gap the next morning, whence we were conveyed

COMMANDER J. D. JOHNSTON, C. S. N.

in ambulances to Varina Landing, where we found a Confederate steamer awaiting us with the Federal prisoners on board. We soon exchanged places to the tune of "Dixie." After a delightful visit of five days at the house of Mrs. Stephen R. Mallory, the charming wife of the Secretary of the Confederate Navy, I was ordered to return to Mobile and report for duty under Commodore Ebenezer Farrand, who had succeeded Admiral Buchanan in command of that station.

THE LASHING OF ADMIRAL FARRAGUT IN THE RIGGING. ‖

I. BY J. CRITTENDEN WATSON, CAPTAIN, U. S. N.

At the commencement of the action [in Mobile Bay] Admiral Farragut was standing in the port main-rigging, which position enabled him to overlook the other vessels of the fleet while at the same time it gave him perfect command of both his own flag-ship and the *Metacomet*, the latter vessel being lashed on that side of the *Hartford* for the purpose of carrying the flag-ship inside the bay in case of the disabling of her own machinery. A slight wind was blowing the smoke from our guns on to Fort Morgan. As the wind fell lighter (which it frequently does during heavy firing), the smoke gradually obscured the admiral's view, and he almost unconsciously climbed the rigging, ratline by ratline, in order to see over it, until finally he found himself in the futtock-shrouds, some little distance below the maintop. Here he could lean either backward or forward in a comfortable position, having the free use of both hands for his spy-glass, or any other purpose. Captain Drayton, commanding the *Hartford*, and also chief-of-staff to the admiral, becoming solicitous lest even a slight wound, a blow from a splinter, or the cutting away of a portion of the rigging, might throw the admiral to the deck, sent the signal-quartermaster aloft with a small rope, to secure him to the rigging. The admiral at first declined to allow the quartermaster to do this, but quickly admitted the wisdom of the precaution, and himself passed two or three turns of the rope around his body, and secured one end while the quartermaster (Knowles) fastened the other. The admiral remained aloft until after we had passed Fort Morgan.

‖ From "The Century Magazine" (old series), June, 1881.

While leaning against the futtock-shrouds, he was near enough to the pilot — who was in the maintop, just over his head — to communicate with him. He was at all times visible to Captain Drayton and the flag-lieutenant (myself), who were standing on the poop-deck, and conversed with him several times during the action. Lieutenant A. R. Yates, now Commander in the United States Navy, who was acting as a volunteer aide, was stationed underneath the admiral, and carried his orders to the other parts of the ship.

After the passage of the forts was accomplished, and the vessels were anchored and anchoring, the Confederate ram *Tennessee* was observed to be moving out from under the guns of Fort Morgan. Captain Drayton reported this fact to the admiral, who was then on the poop, stating that Buchanan, the Confederate admiral, was going outside to destroy the outer fleet. The admiral immediately said, "Then we must follow him out!" though he suspected that Buchanan, becoming desperate, had resolved to sink or destroy the flag-ship *Hartford*, and do us as much injury as possible before losing his own vessel. Immediately after the above remark, Farragut said, "No! Buck's coming here. Get under way at once; we must be ready for him!" Captain Drayton could not believe this, and we were a little slow about getting up our anchor, in spite of the admiral's impatience.

In Lieutenant Kinney's interesting account of the battle, the subsequent events are described. [See p. 379.] I have only to add that when the *Hartford* rammed the *Tennessee* the admiral was standing in the port *mizzen*-rigging, near the rail, where I secured him with a rope's-end, having first remonstrated with him, and begged him not to stand in so exposed a place, — as he was only a few feet from and above the deck of the ram, which scraped her whole length along that side of the *Hartford*.

There could never have been any dispute as to the admiral's having been lashed in the main-rigging, had the fact been generally known that the admiral himself told Captain Drayton and me, shortly after the battle, exactly what took place when the quartermaster came up to him with the rope and the message from the captain, just as I have related it. He was afterward amused and amazed at the notoriety of the incident. When a comic picture of the scene, in one of the illustrated weeklies, came to hand, a few days after the battle, he said to Captain Drayton and myself in conversation, "How curiously some trifling incident catches the popular fancy! My being in the main-rigging was a mere accident, owing to the fact that I was driven aloft by the smoke. The lashing was the result of your own fears [Captain Drayton's] for my safety." At the close of the war he yielded to the solicitations of Mr. Page to stand for a historical portrait in the position in which he was first lashed.

New York, September 6th, 1880.

II. BY JOSEPH MARTHON, LIEUTENANT-COMMANDER, U. S. N. ⚓

In regard to the truth of the statements made by various people at different times, whether Admiral Farragut was, or was not, lashed to the rigging of the United States flag-ship *Hartford* during the battle of the 5th of August, 1864, passing the forts at the entrance of Mobile Bay, my position placed me in a situation to be able to see and know as much in that respect as any one at that time. I was in charge of the howitzer placed in the maintop of the *Hartford*, was at my station, and used the gun while in range of Fort Morgan in passing.

The admiral climbed into the port main-rigging, and stood on the upper sheer ratline (about five or six ratlines up). Captain Drayton sent a quartermaster with a piece of lead-line to lash him to the shroud to prevent his falling, in case of injury. After a short time the smoke grew more dense, when the admiral cast off the lashing, climbed up to the futtock-rigging, taking the lashing with him, where he lashed himself and remained during the action, and till we passed well up the bay, when he came into the top and I went up to the maintopsail-yard. Just then a heavy north-west squall of wind and rain struck us, making it very dark, and the order was given to anchor. As the squall slowly passed off I reported each ship as they came in sight coming up the bay, and catching sight of black smoke, thought it must be the ram *Tennessee* heading up the bay. For a short time, owing to the darkness of the squall and rain, I was in doubt as to her movements, but soon noticed she was steaming against the wind by the way the smoke left the smoke-stack, as nothing of her was visible. I said to the admiral, "The ram is coming for us." For a few moments he was in doubt, for he believed the ram would either go outside and attack the vessels on blockade, or else go under the guns of the fort, and compel the admiral to make another attack on him or stand a night attack from the ram. When I convinced the admiral the ram was coming he said, "I did not think old Buck was such a fool." He then went on deck, and orders were given to up anchor, get under way, and ram the enemy at full speed. The ram, after a good fight, surrendered.

My station was in the maintop, right over the head of the admiral, only a few feet distant, for the admiral without any trouble reached his hand through the lubber's hole, and pressed the pilot's foot, to attract the pilot's attention on one or two occasions. My attention was called to the admiral's position by his hailing the top in a low tone of voice, just before the *Tecumseh* was sunk, asking, "where this water was coming from." Upon looking about I found that the water-breaker, placed in the hole of a coil of rigging I was sitting on, had been capsized by a piece of shell knocking a hole in the top, and the water was running down on the admiral's head. I informed him of the fact. He replied, "I noticed it is not salt."

After passing the forts the admiral came into

⚓ A revision and extension of a letter of December 5th, 1877, to Mr. Loyall Farragut.

the top, and I went up to the maintopsail-yard and reported the vessels as they passed the forts, and the position and movements of the rebel ram *Tennessee.*

Doubt having been expressed as to the ability of the admiral to reach the pilot with his hand, in July, 1877, while the *Hartford* was at the Norfolk navy yard, I went on board and requested Lieutenant-Commander C. H. Black, who was the executive officer at that time, to send some one aloft to take the measure of the distance. He sent for the boatswain and explained what I wanted.

The boatswain and one man went aloft, taking a tape-line, and made the proper measure of the distance. Mr. Black and I stood on the quarter-deck and saw the measure taken. The distance from the crossing of the futtock-shrouds with the main-rigging is six feet to the platform of the maintop.

I made my last cruise in the old *Hartford*, and this question often came up. Many times, in going aloft, I have stood in the same place and reached my hand above the platform of the maintop.

NEW YORK, October 18th, 1888.

FORT MORGAN, MOBILE BAY. FROM A WAR-TIME SKETCH.

THE DEFENSE OF FORT MORGAN.

BY R. L. PAGE, BRIGADIER-GENERAL, C. S. A., COMMANDER OF THE FORT.

EARLY on the morning of the 5th of August, 1864, I observed unusual activity in the Federal fleet off Mobile Bay, indicating, as I supposed, that they were about to attempt the passage of the fort. After an early breakfast the men were sent to the guns. Everybody was in high spirits. In a short time preparations were ended, and then followed perfect silence, before the noise of battle.

At 6 o'clock A. M. the enemy's ships began to move in with flags flying. They gradually fell into a line, consisting of twenty-three vessels, four of which were monitors. Each of the first four of the largest wooden ships had a smaller one lashed on the side opposite the fort, and was itself protected by a monitor between it and the fort. The smaller ships followed in line.

As they approached with a moderate wind and on the flood tide, I fired the first gun at long range, and soon the firing became general, our fire being briskly returned by the enemy. For a short time the smoke was so dense that the vessels could not be distinguished, but still the firing was incessant.

When abreast of the fort the leading monitor, the *Tecumseh*, suddenly sank. Four of the crew swam ashore and a few others were picked up by a boat from the enemy. Cheers from the garrison now

rang out, which were checked at once, and the order was passed to sink the admiral's ship and then cheer.

Here I must note a little incident which challenged my admiration. As the *Tecumseh* was going down, a boat was observed to shoot out from under the bow of the leading ship, with oars up and boat-hook in hand. Seeing her, I gave directions, "Pass the order not to fire on that boat; she is saving drowning men."

At this moment the *Brooklyn*, the leading ship, stopped her engine, apparently in doubt; whereupon the order was passed to concentrate on her, in the hope of sinking her, my belief being that it was the admiral's ship, the *Hartford.* As I learned afterward, he was on the second ship. Farragut's coolness and quick perception saved the fleet from great disaster and probably from destruction. While the *Brooklyn* hesitated, the admiral put his helm to starboard, sheered outside the *Brooklyn*, and took the lead, the rest following, thus saving the fouling and entanglement of the vessels and the danger of being sunk under my guns. When, after the fight, the *Brooklyn* was sent to Boston for repairs, she was found to have been struck over seventy times in her hull and masts, as was shown by a drawing that was sent me while I was a prisoner of war at Fort Lafayette.

The ships continued passing rapidly by, no single vessel being under fire more than a few moments. Shot after shot was seen to strike, and shells to explode, on or about the vessels, but their sides being heavily protected by chain cables, faked along the sides and abreast the engines, no vital blow could be inflicted, particularly as the armament of the fort consisted of guns inadequate

BRIGADIER-GENERAL RICHARD L. PAGE, C. S. A.
FROM A PHOTOGRAPH.

in caliber and numbers for effective service against a powerful fleet in rapid motion. The torpedoes in the channel were also harmless; owing to the depth of the water, the strong tides, and the imperfect moorings none exploded. Four of the enemy's fleet turned from the fire they would have to encounter in passing, and joined the other vessels in the enfilading fire from the gulf side.♭ One small gun-boat (the *Philippi*) attempting to run by alone, after the fleet passed in, was sunk at the second shot, in shoal water, the crew saving themselves in boats. She was burned by a boat sent from the Confederate States gun-boat *Morgan*. One man was found on board. He was severely wounded, and died while the officer was on board.

During the passage of the fleet 491 projectiles were fired from the fort, without derangement of any kind to guns or gun-carriages. But little damage was done to the fort, and but small loss of life, owing to the fact that the guns of the fleet were too much elevated; most of the projectiles passing over our heads. The spirit displayed by the garrison was fine; the guns were well served, and all did their duty nobly.

As the fleet passed the fort and out of range of my guns, they were immediately attacked by the Confederate vessels under Admiral Buchanan, who fought most gallantly until he was disabled and overpowered by the Federal fleet.

After the entrance of the Federal fleet into the bay and the evacuation of Fort Powell (a small battery which was untenable), and after the surrender

of Fort Gaines, six miles distant on the opposite side of the bay, I felt confident that the whole naval and land forces of the enemy would be brought against Fort Morgan. I began at once to prepare the fort for as determined a defense as possible.

It had been demonstrated by the fire of the enemy that the *enceinte* or outer rampart of the fort (in which was its main strength) protected the scarp of the main wall of masonry only about one-half its height from curvated shot, and that it would be in the power of the enemy to open fire from any point of the compass, and consequently none of the casemates without heavy traverses in their front would be safe. It was manifest that by the concentration of fire my heavy guns could soon be dismounted, and the length of my resistance would depend upon my ability to protect my men from the heavy fire and to hold the fort from the flank casemates against assault. With these views, I employed my men day and night, most of the time under fire, in erecting traverses to protect my guns on the main wall, to render the casemates selected for the sick and wounded secure, and provide safe quarters for themselves in their rest from the constant and arduous duties they would have to endure. I found it necessary also to build a large traverse at the sally-port, which was entirely exposed. Thus absolutely to prevent the probability of Fort Morgan being reduced at the first severe test by the heavy guns of the enemy, it was necessary for my garrison of 400 men to labor hard night and day.

On the morning of the 9th the enemy proceeded with monitors and transports to land troops and guns at Navy Cove, commencing at once their first work of investment by land.

By my order the "redoubt" (2700 yards from the fort) called "Battery Bragg," from which the guns had been removed, was destroyed by burning the wood-work. The buildings about the fort, hospitals, quarters, stables, etc., were fired and cleared away as far as possible.

During the day, two monitors, three sloops of war, and some gun-boats engaged the fort for several hours—the wooden vessels at long range—with but little damage on either side. Soon after, a flag of truce was reported from the fleet, bringing me a communication to this effect:

"BRIGADIER-GENERAL R. L. PAGE,
"Commanding Fort Morgan.

"SIR: To prevent the unnecessary sacrifice of human life which must follow the opening of our battteries, we demand the unconditional surrender of Fort Morgan and its dependencies.

"We are, respectfully, your obedient servants,
"D. G. FARRAGUT, Rear-Admiral.
"GORDON GRANGER, Major-General."

To which I sent the following reply:

"SIRS: I am prepared to sacrifice life, and will only surrender when I have no means of defense. I do not understand that while being communicated with under the flag of truce, the *Tennessee* should be towed within range of my guns.♯

"Respectfully, etc.,
"R. L. PAGE, Brigadier-General."

♭ The enfilading vessels were the *Genesee, Tennessee, Bienville, Pembina, Sebago,* and *Pinola.*—EDITORS.
♯ Acknowledged to have been done by mistake; the vessel was towed back immediately.—R. L. P.

After this time, day and night, we were engaged by the fleet, sometimes in a brisk fight of several hours' duration, at others in desultory firing without any material damage being done to the fort, save a demonstration of the fact that our brick walls were easily penetrable by the heavy missiles of the enemy, and that a systematic concentrated fire would soon breach them.

On the 15th three of the 15-inch shells, striking the right-flank face of bastion No. 4, breached the wall and disabled the howitzers therein. By this time the enemy had erected several batteries of heavy guns on the land approach and opened fire, which was kept up pretty continuously; and in the interval of serving the guns my men were engaged in the work, before mentioned, for their protection, in anticipation of a vigorous bombardment.

The sharp-shooters in our front had become very numerous and active, and with them encircling us on the land and the fire being delivered from the fleet on the flanks our guns had to be served with care and under great difficulty. The land forces of the enemy completed their first line of approach across the peninsula on the 10th, and the second and third on the 14th to within 700 yards of the fort. This work continued until the 21st, when they had approached to within 200 yards of our glacis. Such guns as could be used on this intrenching force were employed, especially at night, and as far as possible retarded their work, though nothing very effective could be accomplished by this firing, as their working parties were well concealed and protected behind the sand-banks; when our fire was concentrated on any particular point they would remove to some other.

Up to the morning of the 22d our efforts were with the heavy guns that could be used against the investing forces. The topography of the country afforded the enemy great advantages, and they made a steady advance, covering it with an irregular fire from the batteries already in position, and lining their works with sharp-shooters to pick off our gunners. At daylight of the 22d the fleet was reported moving up and encircling the fort, the iron-clads and the captured *Tennessee* included, and shortly its guns and all the batteries on land opened a furious fire, which came from almost every point of the compass, and continued unabated throughout the day, culminating in increased force at sundown; after which the heavy calibers and mortars kept it up during the night.

During this heavy bombardment I found it use-less to attempt to fire my guns, as the sharp-shooters could pick off my men as fast as they would appear at the guns. This bombardment disabled all my guns, save two, partly breached the walls in several places, cutting up the fort to such an extent as to make the whole work a mere mass of débris. Their mortar-firing in the night from the land side was particularly accurate. Apprehensive now, from the decided effect already produced on the walls, that my magazines, containing eighty thousand pounds of powder, were in great danger by the continuation of the bombardment at night, with great care and under continuous fire I had the powder brought out and flooded. The guns of the water and lunette batteries, now unserviceable and in jeopardy from the enemy, I ordered to be spiked and otherwise effectually damaged, and all the guns dismounted by the enemy on the main rampart were destroyed as of no further avail in defense. Early in the night the wood-work of the citadel was fired by the mortar shells, and burned furiously for some hours; the enemy during the conflagration pouring in his missiles with increased vigor. With great efforts the fire was arrested and prevented from extending around near the magazines, which would have been in imminent danger of explosion. In the gallant endeavor to stay this disaster I must be allowed to record the names of privates Murphy, Bembough, and Stevens, 1st Tennessee regiment, distinguished for extraordinary courage and daring.

At daybreak on the 23d, accompanied by the engineer, I inspected the fort to determine its condition for further defense. The report was made by some of the company captains that of the casemates, which had been made as safe for the men as my means allowed, some had been breached, others partly so, and that another shot on them would bring down the walls. A resumption of the fire would thus inflict heavy loss of life, as there was no bomb-proof in the fort. The enemy's approach was very near the glacis, my guns and powder were destroyed, the citadel had been set on fire the second time and entirely consumed; the commissariat and quartermaster's stores had been destroyed by the shells of the enemy. It was evident that "I had no means left of defense," and that under a renewed bombardment unnecessary loss of life would result.

At 6 o'clock A. M. the white flag was displayed from the ramparts, and at 2 o'clock P. M. I capitulated. I am proud to say that throughout this severe test the garrison behaved like brave men.

LAND OPERATIONS AGAINST MOBILE.

BY RICHARD B. IRWIN, LIEUTENANT-COLONEL AND ASSISTANT ADJUTANT-GENERAL, U. S. V.

IN the last days of July, 1864, General E. R. S. Canby sent General Gordon Granger[|] with 1800 men from New Orleans to coöperate with Admiral Farragut. On August 3d Granger landed on Dauphine Island, and the next morning, the appointed time, was in position before Fort Gaines.

At once crossing the bay, now held by Farragut's fleet, Granger landed in the rear of Fort Morgan and began a siege. A siege train was sent from New Orleans, and three more regiments of infantry. On the 22d of August, twenty-five guns and sixteen mortars being in

[|] General Granger relinquished the command of the Fourth Corps, Army of the Cumberland, April 10th, 1864, and, on ⸱ ⸱ne 21st, was ordered to report to General Canby.— EDITORS.

position, ♯ a general bombardment by the army and the fleet began at daylight. At 6 o'clock the next morning, the 23d, the white flag was shown, and the fort surrendered at 2:30 P. M. About five hundred prisoners were taken and about fifty guns. ↓

After Thomas had overthrown Hood at Nashville (December 16th, 1864), Grant ordered him to follow Hood south, but when in January the badness of the roads stopped the movement at Eastport, Grant detached A. J. Smith with the reorganized Sixteenth Corps ♭ and sent him to join Canby at New Orleans. In anticipation of this, on the 18th of January, Grant ordered Canby to move against Mobile. The main lines of fortification, three in number, and very strong, being on the western side, Canby determined to approach Mobile on the east, where he would have the full benefit of the coöperation of the navy, and the principal works he would have to reduce were Spanish Fort commanding the mouth, and Blakely commanding the head of the Appalachee, where the Tensas leaves it.

The movement was made in two columns: one from Dauphine Island, under Canby himself, the other from Pensacola, under Major-General Frederick Steele. Canby's own force was about 32,000 strong, and consisted of Veatch's and Benton's divisions and Bertram's brigade of the reorganized Thirteenth Corps, ⸗ under Major-General Gordon Granger, the Sixteenth Corps, under A. J. Smith, and a siege train under Brigadier-General Richard Arnold, chief-of-artillery. Steele's force was composed of C. C. Andrews's division of the Thirteenth Corps (except Bertram's brigade), Hawkins's division of colored troops, and Lucas's brigade of cavalry, and numbered 13,000. When united, Canby had 45,000 men of all arms. Mobile was defended by about ten thousand ☆ troops, with three hundred field and siege guns, commanded by Major-General Dabney H. Maury; there were also five gun-boats ╵ under Commodore Ebenezer Farrand.

Canby's movement began on the 17th of March. The Sixteenth Corps moved by water from Fort Gaines; the Thirteenth Corps marched from Fort Morgan. Uniting at Danley's Ferry, near the mouth of Fish River, they laid siege to Spanish Fort on the 27th of March. Smith, with Carr's and Mc-Arthur's divisions, held the right, and Granger, with Benton's and Veatch's ♯ ♯ divisions and Bertram's brigade, the left of the Federal line. From left to right the defense was upheld by the brigades of Ector, Holtzclaw, and Gibson. By the 8th of April the trenches were well advanced and a bombard-

ment was begun by ninety guns in position, joined by all the gun-boats within range. In the evening a lodgment was effected on the right of the Confederate lines, and during the night the garrison made good its retreat, with the loss of about 500 prisoners captured. Nearly fifty guns fell into the possession of the besiegers.

Steele set out from Pensacola on the 20th of March, and, as if Montgomery were his object, moved first to Pollard on the Escambia, fifty miles to the northward of Pensacola. There he turned toward Mobile, and on the 1st of April, after a march of a hundred miles over very bad roads, deployed before Blakely. His supplies had run so short that Veatch's division of the Thirteenth Corps had to be sent out on the 31st of March with a commissary train of seventy-five wagons. The siege of Blakely began on the 2d of April. From left to right the lines of attack were held by Garrard's division of the Sixteenth Corps, Veatch's and Andrews's of the Thirteenth Corps, and Hawkins's colored division. Thomas's brigade of "boy reserves" had the right, and Cockrell's division the left, of the defenses. On the afternoon of the 9th, twenty-eight guns being in position, and Spanish Fort having fallen, the Confederate works were captured by a general assault of 16,000 men; 3423 prisoners were taken and more than forty guns.

Forts Tracy and Huger, two small works, were evacuated and blown up on the night of the 11th.

The rivers were swept for torpedoes; the fleet gained the rear of Mobile by the Blakely and Tensas; and Granger crossed the bay under convoy and entered the city on the morning of the 12th, Maury having marched out with the remainder of his force, numbering 4500 infantry and artillery, together with twenty-seven field-pieces and all his transportation. ↓ ↓

Maury retreated to Meridian, the cavalry sent out from Pensacola to cut him off being prevented by high water from crossing the Alabama and Tombigbee. Meanwhile Wilson, with a reorganized and freshly equipped force of 12,500 cavalry, setting out from the Tennessee on the 18th of March, had completely defeated Forrest and taken Selma, with its fortifications, foundries, and workshops, on the 2d of April, and entered Montgomery on the day Canby gained Mobile.

On the news of Johnston's capitulation Taylor surrendered to Canby, on the 4th of May, 1865, at Citronelle, all the remaining forces of the Confederacy east of the Mississippi; on the 26th Kirby Smith followed with the Trans-Mississippi, and the war was ended.

♯ Manned by the 1st Indiana Heavy Artillery, 38th Iowa, Rawles's battery, 5th U. S., and a naval detachment under Lieutenant Tyson, of the *Hartford*. General Richard Arnold was the chief-of-artillery.— R. B. I.

↓ General Grant, in his official report, says: "The total captures [at the three forts] amounted to 1464 prisoners and 104 pieces of artillery."— EDITORS.

♭ The original Sixteenth Corps, constituted December 18th, 1862, and first commanded by Major-General S. A. Hurlbut, was broken up November 7th, 1864. It was reorganized February 18th, 1865, under Major-General Andrew J. Smith.— EDITORS.

⸗ The original Thirteenth Corps, constituted October 24th and December 18th, 1862, and first commanded by

Grant, afterward by McClernand, was broken up June 11th, 1864. The new corps was organized February 18th, 1865.— EDITORS.

☆ Or 9200 *enlisted men* "effective," which is General Maury's estimate.— EDITORS.

╵ Including the *Morgan*, the partly completed ironclads *Tuscaloosa* and *Huntsville*, and the steamers *Nashville* and *Baltic*.— EDITORS.

♯. ♯. Till March 30th.— EDITORS.

↓ ↓ The Union loss during these operations was 189 killed, 1201 wounded, and 27 captured,— a total of 1417. General Randall L. Gibson, the Confederate commander at Spanish Fort, reported a loss of 93 killed, 395 wounded, and 250 missing.— EDITORS.

CLOSING OPERATIONS IN THE GULF AND WESTERN RIVERS.

BY PROFESSOR JAMES RUSSELL SOLEY, U. S. N.

IN the operations against Mobile, in March and April, 1865, the navy bore its full share of the work, and met with heavy losses. The West Gulf squadron, after Farragut's retirement from the command in September, 1864, had been under the direction of Commodore James S. Palmer, who was in turn relieved at the end of February by Acting Rear-Admiral Henry K. Thatcher. Palmer, however, an officer of great energy and skill, continued to serve with the squadron. Admiral Thatcher took personal direction of the closing operations against Mobile in coöperation with General Canby. His force included among other vessels the iron-clads *Cincinnati, Winnebago, Chickasaw, Milwaukee, Osage,* and *Kickapoo.* Among the wooden vessels were the double-enders *Genesee, Sebago, Octorara,* and *Metacomet,* the gun-boats *Itasca* and *Sciota,* the tin-clads *Rodolph, Elk, Meteor, Tallahatchie, Nyanza,* and *Stockdale* (flag-ship). The upper waters of the bay were thickly sown with stationary torpedoes, and great numbers of floating mines were sent down from above, so that the naval operations were full of danger.

The Confederate torpedo service at Mobile was particularly efficient, and the lighter vessels of the Union fleet were constantly employed in sweeping for torpedoes. In the closing attacks on Fort Alexis and Spanish Fort, which resulted in their capture, the gun-boats joined in the bombardment, while a naval battery on shore under Lieutenant-Commander Gillis rendered efficient service. Previous to this attack, and while it was in progress, 150 large submerged torpedoes were removed from Blakely River and the adjacent waters by the *Metacomet,* Commander Pierce Crosby. On the following days Forts Huger and Tracy were shelled by the gun-boats, causing their evacuation on the evening of the 11th of April. On the 12th the fleet convoyed 8000 troops under General Granger to the western shore of the bay above Mobile, while the monitors took position in front of the city. In the afternoon the mayor of Mobile made a formal surrender to the army and navy. The Confederate iron-clads *Huntsville* and *Tuscaloosa* had already been sunk in Spanish River, and the other vessels, the *Morgan, Nashville,* and *Baltic,* had taken refuge in the Tombigbee, whither they were presently pursued and where they were finally captured. The surrender of Commodore Farrand and the naval forces under his command was agreed to Admiral Thatcher was agreed upon at Citronelle on May 4th, at the same time as the surrender of Taylor to Canby. The formal surrender, in accordance with the agreement, was made to Fleet-Captain Edward Simpson, on May 10th, at Nanna Hubba Bluff, on the Tombigbee. It included four vessels, 112 officers, 285 enlisted men, and 24 marines.

The loss of vessels during the campaign was unusually large. On March 28th the *Milwaukee,* Lieutenant-Commander James H. Gillis, returning to the fleet from an attack on a transport lying near Spanish Fort, exploded a torpedo, and sank in three minutes. Next day the *Osage* struck a torpedo under her bow and went down almost immediately. A similar accident resulted in the loss of the tin-clad *Rodolph* on April 1st. A fortnight later, immediately after the surrender of Mobile, the gun-boat *Sciota* was lost in the same way, as were also the tugs *Ida* and *Althea,* and a launch belonging to the *Cincinnati.* These disasters resulted in a loss of 23 killed and 32 wounded.

In the Mississippi squadron, now under the command of Acting Rear-Admiral S. P. Lee, the last months were chiefly occupied in convoy duty and keeping up communication on the Mississippi, in blockading the Red River, and in active operations in conjunction with the army by the fleets on the Tennessee and Cumberland rivers, the former under Lieutenant-Commander Shirk and the latter under Lieutenant-Commander Fitch. Both these officers displayed great energy and resource in an exacting and difficult service, and they were ably seconded by the volunteer officers who commanded the light gun-boats in frequent and hotly contested engagements with the Confederate batteries and troops on the banks.

The last effort of the Confederate navy on the Western rivers was the brilliant but unsuccessful dash of the ram *Webb,* under Commander C. W. Read, out of Red River in April with a load of cotton. Read's plan was to run the Mississippi blockade and carry his vessel and cotton to Havana. It was one of the boldest exploits of the war. The *Webb* made a rush through the fleet at the Red River mouth and escaped without injury. Her approach was telegraphed to New Orleans, but under the disguise of an army transport she nearly passed the vessels lying off the city before they discovered her character, too late to stop her progress. Twenty miles below the city she met the *Richmond,* and finding farther advance impossible Read ran her ashore and burnt her. On the 3d of June Lieutenant-Commander W. E. Fitzhugh received the surrender of Lieutenant J. H. Carter and the Confederate naval forces under his command in the Red River.

On the west Gulf coast the blockade continued until the end, several important cutting-out expeditions occurring during January and February. Among these the most noteworthy were the capture of the *Delphina,* January 22d, in Calcasieu River, by Lieutenant-Commander R. W. Meade; of the *Pet* and the *Anna Sophia,* February 7th, at Galveston, by an expedition organized by Commander J. R. M. Mullany; and of the *Anna Dale,* February 18th, at Pass Cavallo, by a party sent in by Lieutenant-Commander Henry Erben. After the surrender of Mobile, Admiral Thatcher turned his attention to the coast of Texas, and on May 25th Sabine Pass was evacuated. On the 2d of June Galveston surrendered, and the war on the Texas coast came to an end.

THE LEVEE AT NASHVILLE, LOOKING DOWN THE CUMBERLAND. FROM A WAR-TIME PHOTOGRAPH.

CAVALRY OPERATIONS IN THE WEST UNDER ROSECRANS AND SHERMAN.

BY THOMAS SPEED, CAPTAIN, U. S. V.

UNTIL General W. S. Rosecrans took command of the Army of the Cumberland, October 30th, 1862, the Union cavalry in Kentucky and Tennessee had not been organized in a separate command, but its various regiments and brigades were attached to the several infantry divisions. There being no such organization, there was of course no commander of cavalry to direct the movements of the entire body of these troops, but the commander of a cavalry brigade was the ranking colonel present who received orders from the army commander direct, or through subordinate commanders of the infantry. With Rosecrans came an effort toward a better organization. Rosecrans divided his army into three grand divisions known as "The Center," "The Right Wing," and "The Left Wing." The cavalry was all placed under one commander, General D. S. Stanley, who at once proceeded to get the cavalry in condition for efficient service. He formed it in three brigades. The First was under Colonel R. H. G. Minty, of the 4th Michigan Cavalry; the Second under Colonel Lewis Zahm, of the 3d Ohio Cavalry; the Third he kept under his personal charge, while Colonel John Kennett was made commander of the cavalry division. Such was the organization when Rosecrans began the campaign which resulted in the Battle of Stone's River, December 31st, 1862, to January 2d, 1863.

In the autumn of 1862, while Rosecrans was making his preparations at Nashville, a number of cavalry regiments were being recruited in Kentucky, and that State became a general camp of instruction for new regiments on their way to the front from other States. They were not able, however, to protect the country from the raids of the Confederate cavalry. On the 7th of December, 1862, John H. Morgan attacked the Federals at

Hartsville, Tennessee, and captured the garrison. On the 9th General Joseph Wheeler attacked unsuccessfully a Federal brigade under Colonel Stanley Matthews, on the road leading to Murfreesboro'. A little later in December Morgan moved into Kentucky and destroyed bridges on the Louisville and Nashville Railroad. The Federal cavalry was in condition at this time to operate successfully against these efforts of the Confederates.

In the same month of December, 1862, a bold movement was made by a force of Federal cavalry under General S. P. Carter, composed of three regiments—the 9th Pennsylvania, 2d Michigan, and 8th Ohio. Carter made his way through the mountains into east Tennessee, and destroyed the track and bridges on the railroad leading from Virginia to Knoxville. This successful dash showed that raiding was not to be left wholly to one side.

The cavalry under General Stanley was actively used in the advance upon Murfreesboro'. While numbering only about four thousand effective men, and consequently not expected to cope with the enemy's infantry, it covered the flanks of Rosecrans's army and also kept well to the front, developing the positions of the enemy, and by bold scouting obtained information of movements. During the fighting at Stone's River, December 31st, the Confederate cavalry made its way to the Federal rear for the purpose of cutting communications and destroying supplies. Much damage might then have occurred had not General Stanley's cavalry met and repulsed the raiders. In the fighting which ensued the 3d Kentucky Cavalry, under Colonel E. H. Murray, particularly distinguished itself, also the 1st Ohio Cavalry, under Colonel Minor Milliken, who was killed. After the battle General Stanley kept his command posted in the country between the opposing armies until active operations began in the spring of 1863. General Rosecrans endeavored unsuccessfully to increase this branch of his army materially. The authorities at Washington do not seem to have appreciated the necessities of the case as fully as himself. Some increase, however, was made, by the coming of new regiments. And while General Stanley was on the alert for all the necessary purposes of the army in position, General Rosecrans organized, in the spring of 1863, for a cavalry raid around the rear of Bragg's army. For this purpose seventeen hundred men were placed under Colonel A. D. Streight, with directions to embark on transports on the Tennessee River at Fort Henry and proceed to Eastport, Mississippi. Colonel Streight reached Eastport and set out thence April 21st. He reached Tuscumbia, Alabama, April 24th, and by May 1st was at Blountsville, Alabama. His objective was Rome, Georgia; but when near Cedar Bluffs, Alabama, twenty-eight miles from Rome, he was attacked and defeated by Forrest. Colonel Streight himself and thirteen

hundred men were captured and carried as prisoners to Richmond. While this raid was in progress Colonel J. T. Wilder with a body of 2600 cavalry was destroying the railroads south of Murfreesboro' and capturing a number of prisoners, and other similar movements were being made by Colonels Louis D. Watkins and A. P. Campbell in the direction of Columbia, Tennessee.

At this time, also, another celebrated cavalry raid took place in Mississippi. Colonel B. H. Grierson of the 6th Illinois Cavalry, taking his own regiment, the 7th Illinois, Colonel Edward Prince, and the 2d Iowa, Colonel Edward Hatch, left La Grange, Tennessee, April 17th, and in sixteen days traversed six hundred miles of the enemy's country and reached Baton Rouge, where a Federal force was stationed. [See map, Vol. III., p. 442.] Hatch's regiment destroyed the railroads east of Columbus, Mississippi, and returned to La Grange, while the remainder of Grierson's force destroyed much of the Mobile and Ohio and Vicksburg and Meridian railroads. This bold and successful raid produced

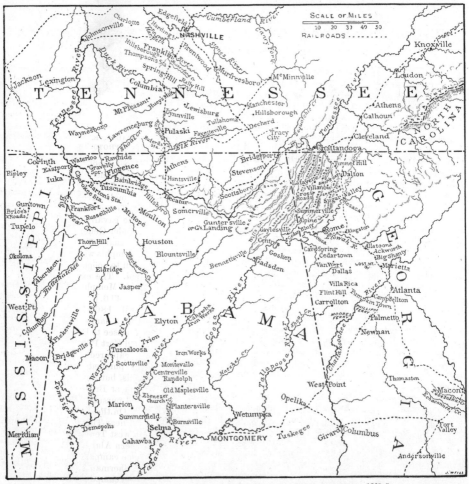

MAP OF OPERATIONS IN MIDDLE TENNESSEE AND NORTH ALABAMA, 1863-5.

a profound sensation, and was of great benefit to General Grant in the Vicksburg campaign.

The great activity of the Union cavalry at this period is further shown by the fact that General Stanley in the month of June led a strong force in rear of Bragg's position at Tullahoma, cutting the railroads at Decherd Station, whereupon Bragg fell back to Bridgeport. In July Stanley again made a movement upon Huntsville. Proceeding by several roads, the separate brigades of General J. B. Turchin and Colonels Eli Long and Robert Galbraith all reached Huntsville, Alabama, and, after capturing prisoners, supplies, and stock, returned without serious loss.

The Confederates on their part also made a celebrated raid at this time. On the 27th of June Morgan crossed the Cumberland River at Burksville, Kentucky, with about 2500 men. He passed northwardly through Columbia, Kentucky, and, reaching Green River at Tebbs's Bend on the 4th of July, demanded the surrender of Colonel O. H. Moore, who was stationed there with a portion of his regiment—the 25th Michigan. Colonel Moore returned the famous reply that the 4th of July was not a good day to surrender, and was instantly attacked. After a severe fight Moore drove off his assailants, and saved the bridge over Green River at that point. Morgan crossed below the bridge and passed through Lebanon and Bardstown and on to Brandenburg on the Ohio River; there, seizing a steamboat, he crossed into Indiana, and dashed through that State into Ohio and was captured near Salineville July 26th. [See map and article, Vol. III., p. 635.] This raid has become famous for many reasons, but one of the most notable things pertaining to it was the pursuit and capture of the raider and his men. The pursuit began at Burksville immediately upon Morgan's passage of Cumberland River. The night of the passage four Kentucky cavalry regiments, the 1st, 8th, 9th, and 12th, under Generals J. M. Shackelford and E. H. Hobson, both Kentuckians, were concentrated at Marrow Bone, only a few miles west of Burksville. Four noted Kentucky officers commanded these regiments, Frank Wolford, B. H. Bristow, R. T. Jacob, and E. W. Crittenden. At Bardstown the pursuers were joined by three Ohio regiments.

A month later this same Federal cavalry and several other regiments were organized at Camp Nelson in Kentucky by Burnside for an expedition to east Tennessee. It was placed under command of Shackelford, who led it through Williamsburg and Big Creek Gap to Kingston. The infantry force under Burnside moved out at the same time and took possession of Knoxville. Shackelford's cavalry then hastened to Cumberland Gap and captured the place, with 2500 men under the Confederate General Fraser. They then made their way to the borders of Virginia, clearing the valley of Confederates, and returned to Knoxville, where Burnside was concentrating to resist the advance of Longstreet. For three weeks the cavalry was shut up in Knoxville with the infantry. After the siege it pursued Longstreet up the valley, fighting a hard battle at Bean's Station. Winter coming on, active movements ceased.

The cavalry under Stanley coöperated with Rosecrans's infantry in the advance to Chattanooga, bearing its full share of the burdens at Chickamauga. After the battle of Missionary Ridge, November 25th, 1863, General W. L. Elliott was assigned to the command of the cavalry.

Elliott dispatched Colonel Long's brigade to the relief of Knoxville, and during the months of

LIEUTENANT-GENERAL N. B. FORREST, C. S. A.
FROM A PHOTOGRAPH.

November and December, among the various dashes made at this season was one by Colonel Watkins, with 250 men, as far as Lafayette, Georgia. Also Colonel Long, with a small force, defeated General Wheeler at Calhoun, Tennessee, December 27th. During the winter the cavalry was principally at Athens, Tennessee, under General Elliott.

On the 11th of February, 1864, General Sooy Smith started from Memphis with a mounted force of seven thousand men to coöperate with Sherman in eastern Mississipni. The expedition proved a failure, and returned to Memphis. [See foot-note, p. 247, and article, p. 416.]

In March and April, 1864, Forrest advanced from Mississippi with a large force, and passed through western Tennessee to Paducah, Kentucky. Returning, he reached Fort Pillow on the morning of April 12th, and captured the fort. [See p. 418.] Forrest was pursued by General S. D. Sturgis from Memphis, but turned upon him, and signally defeated him at Brice's Cross Roads on the 10th of June, and pursued him back to Memphis. [See p. 420.] On the 14th of July Forrest was in turn defeated near Tupelo by A. J. Smith. Forrest remained in west Tennessee and northern Mississippi and northern Alabama, until he joined Hood in the Tennessee campaign.

The cavalry which Sherman assembled at Chattanooga for the Atlanta campaign numbered about

15,000 in four divisions. [For organization, see pp. 286 and 289.] In the new organization General Stanley was assigned to duty with the infantry in the Army of the Cumberland. The details of the service of the cavalry in the Atlanta campaign cannot be given here. It participated in all the movements and engagements from May to August, 1864. When the lines were drawn closely about Atlanta the cavalry became very active.

Meanwhile Major-General L. H. Rousseau, who had been stationed at Nashville for the protection of Sherman's rear, and who had succeeded in preventing Wheeler from injuring the Nashville and Chattanooga Railroad, was ordered to execute a very important duty. On the 10th of July, 1864, he started from Decatur, Alabama, with two brigades of cavalry, under Colonels T. J. Harrison, 8th Indiana, and William D. Hamilton, 9th Ohio. In nine days he had traveled 300 miles, and was 100 miles in rear of Johnston's army. He destroyed railroads and supplies, and safely joined Sherman in Georgia near Atlanta.

On the 27th of July General McCook moved down the right bank of the Chattahoochee to Campbelltown, and crossing pushed boldly into the Macon road, damaging it, burning trains, and capturing four hundred prisoners. On his return he encountered the enemy in strong force, and was not only compelled to give up his prisoners, but lost many of his own men.

On the same date General Stoneman moved from the other flank and destroyed the railroads leading from Macon to Augusta, but he, too, suffered greatly, Stoneman himself and part of his command being captured. Colonel Silas Adams of the 1st Kentucky Cavalry successfully fought his way back with the brigade he commanded.

After the fall of Atlanta a portion of the cavalry, under General Kilpatrick, accompanied General Sherman on his march to the sea; the remainder was placed under General Thomas for the protection of Tennessee against the expected movements of Hood, and went to Tuscumbia early in November, 1864, commanded by General Edward Hatch.

During the Atlanta campaign Kentucky was protected against guerrillas and raiders by General S.

G. Burbridge. In May he started for Virginia with a large mounted force, and at the same time Morgan came into Kentucky through Pound Gap. This was Morgan's last raid. He was attacked at Cynthiana, Mount Sterling, and Augusta, Kentucky, by the Federal cavalry under Colonel John Mason Brown, Colonel Wickliffe Cooper, and others, and finally was driven into east Tennessee, where he was killed, at Greenville, on the 4th of September, 1864. [See article by General Duke, p. 243.]

In October, 1864, General Hood, having led his army from Georgia into northern Alabama, was organizing for his expedition into Tennessee. At the same time Forrest was operating with his usual energy and activity. On the 30th of October he suddenly appeared with a strong force on the Tennessee River, near Johnsonville, where he captured a gun-boat, the *Undine*, and two transports — an exploit which excited very general admiration. He then joined Hood near Decatur. At this time General John T. Croxton, with a brigade of Union cavalry, was watching along the north bank of the Tennessee, and on the 7th of November was joined by General Edward Hatch with a division. This body, numbering about three thousand men, kept a sharp lookout for indications of Hood's advance. On the 20th it became apparent that Hood was moving in the direction of Lawrenceburg. Hatch skirmished with Forrest, and while the infantry under Schofield fell back from Pulaski to Columbia, Hatch also backed steadily until that point was reached.

At Columbia General J. H. Wilson, who had been transferred from the cavalry corps of the Army of the Potomac and assigned to the command of all the cavalry in General Thomas's department, came up and took personal charge. [See p. 466.]

The fame of Forrest, Morgan, and Wheeler was accented by the widespread heralding of all their exploits. On the other hand the services of the Union cavalry, being far southward and beyond the reach of newspapers, excited less notice; but for boldness and effectiveness, devotion to duty, endurance, celerity of movement, and accomplishment of results the Federal cavalry in the West made a proud record, and its history, when written in detail, will be full of thrilling interest.

THE SOOY SMITH EXPEDITION (FEBRUARY, 1864).

BY GEORGE E. WARING, JR., COLONEL, 4TH MISSOURI CAVALRY, U. S. V., COMMANDING BRIGADE.

IN January, 1864, General Sherman arranged for an expedition from Vicksburg to Meridian with 20,000 infantry, under his own command, and a coöperating cavalry expedition, 7000 mounted men and 20 pieces of artillery, under the command of General W. Sooy Smith, chief-of-cavalry on General Grant's staff. This cavalry force was ordered to start from Collierville, east of Memphis, on the 1st of February, and to join Sherman at Meridian as near the 10th as possible, destroying public property and supplies and the Mobile and Ohio Railroad, from Okolona south. [See map, p. 348.] Sherman's orders to Smith were, "Attack any force of cavalry you may meet

and follow them south. . . . Do not let the enemy draw you into minor affairs, but look solely to the greater object — to destroy his communications from Okolona to Meridian and then east toward Selma." Reference was made to previous verbal instructions covering all points.

Sherman left Vicksburg with his force February 3d, reached Meridian on the 14th, remained there until the 20th, and in Canton until the 28th, hoping to receive word of Smith's whereabouts. None coming, he then returned to Vicksburg.

Smith's command comprised three brigades of cavalry: First, Waring's; Second, Hepburn's; Third, McCrillis's; and a battalion of the 4th (regular) Cavalry, commanded by Captain Bowman. The main command was ready to start at the appointed time. The First Brigade had left Union City, Tenn., January 22d, but was prevented from reaching Collierville until February 8th by the flooded condition of the difficult country, with its broad swamps and overflowing rivers. ⎰ Three days were occupied in arranging a pack-train, which might have been made ready in advance, and on the 11th the command continued its march.

The heavy rains had made the country nearly impassable, and Okolona was not reached until the 18th. Here we entered the beautiful prairie region of eastern Mississippi. A finer country for cavalry is nowhere to be found.

There was a little skirmishing, but no material opposition, until we reached West Point, thirty miles south of Okolona, on the afternoon of the 20th. Here we were confronted by Forrest's command, in a position of considerable strength, protected by swamps and rivers. On the morning of the 21st, without an engagement worthy of the name, we were ordered to return to Okolona. As we fully believed at that time, and as the publication of General Forrest's report shows, we could have proceeded on our way, driving him before us; there was, however, much to be said in favor of drawing him out on to the prairie for an engagement in the open country. But it soon became evident that we were not to "retire," but to "retreat." Forrest had only his "escort and a portion of Faulkner's regiment." With this force he drove our seven thousand men without difficulty, the First and Third brigades receiving constant orders from Smith to hasten on and give the road to the Second Brigade for its retreat. It was an unwilling retreat, and but for its orders, the command could easily have held its position at any moment. We proceeded in this manner to the camp of the division about three miles south of Okolona.

At 5 A. M. on the 22d the First Brigade was ordered to form line and prepare for a fight. It formed in the open country, with the enemy in sight, about a mile away across the prairie. Later we were ordered to take up our line of march on the road for Memphis. As we passed to the left of Okolona, one regiment, the 7th Indiana, was ordered to fall out and support the 4th Regulars, which had been stationed at the edge of the town to watch the movements of the enemy. The Third Brigade had the rear of the column. Before it had passed, the regulars and the 7th Indiana were engaged, and this brigade was ordered to the attack. It soon broke in disgraceful flight and confusion, abandoning five guns of its battery without firing a shot. Nothing can be said in excuse of its behavior, but the explanation of it is not far to seek. It had taken part in the hurried retreat of the day before, and, having seen no cause for it, imagined itself in the toils of an overwhelming enemy. It had lost all confidence in the commanding general, and its discipline dissolved. After entering the wooded country, the checking of the enemy's advance became easier. No attempt was made to stop him or to defeat him, only to hold him back by maintaining temporary lines, formed by the leading brigade, until the others could pass through. In this manner we retreated nine miles between 11 A. M. and 5 P. M.

At 5 o'clock, without orders, portions of the First and Second brigades formed in order of battle on open, gently sloping ground, determined to end the pursuit. Until this time Smith had been in advance. By design or by accident, he now came on the field. The feeling that had governed him for two days, and caused him to abandon such an opportunity as no antagonist of Forrest ever had before, was gone. In the actual presence of the first real personal danger that he had encountered, he became brave and cool.

The enemy was approaching rapidly and swarming toward both our flanks. Our little battery was doing good service, and an attempt was made to deploy and fight on foot. It soon became obvious that this would be futile, and the 4th Missouri Cavalry was speedily mounted and formed for a charge. The charge was made in good order, and with great moral effect, in spite of a high stake-and-rider fence, which made it impossible to reach the main body of the enemy. It, however, drove back his straggling advance and sent them over the fence in such panic as to turn back the main line. The fence in their front, and the heavy firing at close range, broke the charging line, which turned and fled. It was rallied and formed by its own officers before its starting-point was reached, wheeling into line in good order, ready for a second charge. This stopped the pursuit, and we gradually got on to the road in marching order and went finally on our way.

In his preliminary report, written that night, Forrest said the battle was ended by a cavalry charge of the enemy which was repulsed. In his final report, written March 8th, he says:

"As we moved up, the whole force ⚓ charged down at a gallop, and I am proud to say that my men did not disappoint me. Standing firm, they repulsed the grandest cavalry charge I ever witnessed.

"The 2d and 7th Tennessee drove back the advance line, and as it wheeled in retreat poured upon them a destructive fire. Each successive line of the enemy shared the same fate and fled the field in dismay and confusion, losing another piece of artillery and leaving it strewn with dead and wounded men and horses. . . ."

Forrest estimates our loss in the whole engagement, killed, wounded, and missing, at 800,⎰ with six pieces of artillery and 33 stand of colors, and says: "My force in the fight did not exceed 2500 men, while that of the enemy was 27 regiments of cavalry and infantry, estimated at 7000 strong."

⎰ Sherman says that Smith, under his orders, was not justified in waiting for the First Brigade, as he had a sufficient force without it.— G. E. W. In a letter to General Sherman, dated July 9th, 1875, General Smith says, referring to Waring's brigade, "I asked you if I should wait its arrival, and you answered, 'Certainly; if you go without it, you will be too weak, and I want you strong enough to go where you please.'"—EDITORS.

⚓ It was not the "whole force" that charged, only the 4th Missouri Cavalry, less than 600 strong.— G. E. W.

⎰ The official list of the Union loss was: killed, 47; wounded, 152; missing, 120,— total, 319.— EDITORS.

The retreat to Memphis was a weary, disheartened, almost panic-stricken flight, in the greatest disorder and confusion, through a most difficult country. The First Brigade reached its camping-ground, outside the city, five days after the engagement, with the loss of all of its heart and spirit and of over 1500 fine cavalry horses.

The expedition filled every man connected with it with burning shame. It gave Forrest the most glorious achievement of his career. ♭

♭ General Sherman in his report said: "I inclose herewith my instructions to General Smith, with a copy of his report, and must say it is unsatisfactory. The delay in his start to the 11th of February, when his orders contemplated his being at Meridian on the 10th, and when he knew I was marching from Vicksburg, is unpardonable, and the mode and manner of his return to Memphis was not what I expected from the intended bold cavalry movement." In his "Memoirs," Sherman says Smith "has appealed to me to relieve him of that censure, but I could not do it, because it would falsify history."— G. E. W.

In a letter to General Sherman dated July 14th, 1875 [see Sherman's "Memoirs," Vol. I., Appendix, p. 455], General Smith says of the delay: "In the conversation that occurred between us at Nashville [after the campaign ended], while all the orders, written and verbal, were still fresh in your memory, you did not censure me for waiting for Waring, but for allowing myself to be encumbered with fugitive negroes to such an extent that my command was measurably unfit for active movement or easy handling, and for turning back from West Point, instead of pressing on toward Meridian. Invitations had been industriously circulated, by printed circulars and otherwise, to the negroes to come into our lines, and to seek our protection wherever they could find it, and I considered ourselves pledged to receive and protect them." In a letter of July 9th, 1875 [Sherman, Vol. I., Appendix, p. 453], General Smith says: "To have attempted to penetrate farther into the enemy's country, with the cavalry of Polk's army coming up to reënforce Forrest, would have insured the destruction of my entire command, situated as it was." The "Cavalry of Polk's Army" refers to the command of General S. D. Lee which joined Forrest within a day or two after Smith began his retreat.— EDITORS.

THE CAPTURE OF FORT PILLOW (April 12th, 1864).

MAJOR LIONEL F. BOOTH, 6th United States Heavy Artillery, who commanded Fort Pillow April 12th, 1864, was killed in the battle of that date of which there is no circumstantial official Union report. From the data attainable it appears that the garrison consisted of 557 soldiers (about half of them colored troops), and that the killed, wounded, and captured numbered about 400. According to the Confederate reports the prisoners, including wounded, numbered 237. The percentage of killed was extraordinarily large. The news of this fight created much excitement in the North and led to an investigation by the Committee on the Conduct of the War, which reported that the Confederates entered the works shouting "No quarter," and that they then began "an indiscriminate slaughter, sparing neither age nor sex, white or black, soldier or civilian."

On June 17th, 1864 (in view of "the Fort Pillow Massacre"), General C. C. Washburn, the Union commander of the District of West Tennessee, wrote to General S. D. Lee, then the Confederate commander of the Department of Alabama, Mississippi, and East Louisiana, asking for information as to the intention of the Confederates concerning colored soldiers who might fall into their hands as prisoners of war. General Lee replied, June 28th, in part as follows:

"The version [of Fort Pillow] given by you and your Government is untrue, and not sustained by the facts to the extent that you indicate. The garrison was summoned in the usual manner, and its commanding officer assumed the responsibility of refusing to surrender after having been informed by General Forrest of his ability to take the fort, and of his fears as to what the result would be in case the demand was not complied with. The assault was made under a heavy fire and with considerable loss to the attacking party. Your colors were never lowered, and your garrison never surrendered, but retreated under cover of a gun-boat with arms in their hands and constantly using them. This was true particularly of your colored troops, who had been firmly convinced by your teachings of the certainty of slaughter in case of capture. Even under these circumstances, many of your men, white and black, were taken prisoners. I respectfully refer you to history for numerous cases of indiscriminate slaughter after successful assault, even under less aggravated circumstances. It is generally conceded by all military precedent that where the issue had been fairly presented and the ability displayed, fearful results are expected to follow a refusal to surrender.

"The case under consideration is almost an extreme one. You had a servile race armed against their masters, and in a country which had been desolated by almost unprecedented outrages. I assert that our officers, with all the circumstances against them, endeavored to prevent the effusion of blood, and as an evidence of this I refer you to the fact that both white and colored prisoners were taken, and are now in our hands."

The following are extracts from Forrest's report, dated April 26th, 1864 [see also p. 107]:

". . . My command consisted of McCulloch's brigade of Chalmers's division and Bell's brigade of Buford's division, both placed for the expedition under the command of Brigadier-General James R. Chalmers, who, by a forced march, drove in the enemy's pickets, gained possession of the outer works, and by the time I reached the field, at 10 A. M., had forced the enemy to their main fortifications, situated on the bluff or bank of the Mississippi River at the mouth of Coal Creek. . . . Assuming command, I ordered General Chalmers to advance his line and gain position on the slope, where our men would be perfectly protected from the heavy fire of artillery and musketry, as the enemy could not depress their pieces so as to rake the slopes, nor could they fire on them with small-arms except by mounting the breastworks and exposing themselves to the fire of our sharp-shooters, who, under cover of stumps and logs, forced them to keep down inside the works. After several hours' hard fighting the desired position was gained, not, however, without considerable loss. Our main line was now within an average distance of one hundred yards from the fort, and extended from Coal Creek on the right to the bluff or bank of the Mississippi River on the left.

"During the entire morning the gun-boat [*New Era*—gun-boat No. 7—Captain James Marshall] kept up a continued fire in all directions, but without effect, and being confident of my ability to take [the] fort by assault, and desiring to prevent further loss of life, I sent, under flag of truce, a demand for the unconditional surrender of the garrison. . . . [Major Booth, in reply, asked an hour for consultation with his officers and Captain Marshall.] . . . The gun-boat had ceased firing, but the smoke of three other boats ascending the river was in view, the foremost apparently crowded with troops; and believing the request for an hour was to gain time for reënforcements to arrive, and that the desire to consult the officers of the gun-boat was a pretext by which they desired improperly to communicate with her, I at once sent this reply . . . [giving twenty minutes in which to surrender] . . . directing Captain [W. A.] Goodman, assistant adjutant-general of Brigadier General Chalmers, who bore the flag, to remain until he received a reply or until the expiration of the time proposed.

"My dispositions had all been made, and my forces were in a position that would enable me to take the fort with less loss than to have withdrawn under fire, and it seemed [to] me so perfectly apparent to the garrison that such was the case, that I deemed their capture without further bloodshed a certainty. After some little delay, seeing a message delivered to Captain Goodman, I rode up myself to where the notes were received and delivered. The answer was handed me, written in pencil on a slip of paper, without envelope, and was, as well as I remember, in these words: 'Negotiations will not attain the desired object.' As the officers who were in charge of the Federal flag of truce had expressed a doubt as to my presence, and had pronounced the demand a trick, I handed them back the note, saying, 'I am General Forrest; go back and say to Major Booth that I demand an answer in plain, unmistakable English: Will he fight or surrender?' Returning to my original position, before the expiration of twenty minutes I received a reply . . . [Major Booth replied, 'We will not surrender.'] . . .

"While these negotiations were pending the steamers from below were rapidly approaching the fort. The foremost was the *Olive Branch*, whose position and movements indicated her intention to land. A few shots fired into her caused her [to] leave the shore and make for the opposite. One other boat passed up on the far side of the river; the third one turned back. The time having expired, I directed Brigadier-General Chalmers to prepare for the assault. . . Everything being ready, the bugle sounded the charge, which was made with a yell, and the works carried without a perceptible halt in any part of the line. As our troops mounted and poured into the fortification, the enemy retreated toward the river, arms in hand, and firing back, and their colors flying; no doubt expecting the gun-boat to shell us away from the bluff and protect them until they could be taken off or reënforced. As they descended the bank an enfilading and deadly fire was poured into them by the troops under Captain Anderson on the left, and Barteau's detachment on the right. Until this fire was opened upon them, at a distance varying from thirty to one hundred yards, they were evidently ignorant of any force having gained their rear. The regiment who had

stormed and carried the fort also poured a destructive fire into the rear of the retreating, and now panic-stricken, and almost decimated, garrison. Fortunately for those of the enemy who survived this short but desperate struggle, some of our men cut the halyards, and the United States flag, floating from a tall mast in the center of the fort, came down. The forces stationed in the rear of the fort could see the flag, but were too far under the bluff to see the fort, and when the flag descended they ceased firing. But for this, so near were they to the enemy that few, if any, would have survived unhurt another volley. As it was, many rushed into the river and were drowned, and the actual loss of life will perhaps never be known, as there were quite a number of refugee citizens in the fort, many of whom were drowned and several killed in the retreat from the fort. In less than twenty minutes from the time the bugles sounded the charge, firing had ceased, and the work was done. One of the Parrott guns was turned on the gun-boat. She steamed off without replying. She had, as I afterward understood, expended all her ammunition, and was therefore powerless in affording the Federal garrison the aid and protection they doubtless expected of her when they retreated toward the river. Details were made, consisting of the captured Federals and negroes, in charge of their own officers, to collect together and bury the dead, which work continued until dark.

"I also directed Captain Anderson to procure a skiff and take with him Captain [John T.] Young, a captured Federal officer, and deliver to Captain Marshall, of the gun-boat, the message, copy of which is appended ↓ . . . All the boats and skiffs having been taken off by citizens escaping from the fort during the engagement, the message could not be delivered, although every effort was made to induce Captain Marshall to send his boat ashore by raising a white flag, with which Captain Young walked up and down the river in vain signaling her to come in or send out a boat. She finally moved off and disappeared around the bend above the fort. General Chalmers withdrew his forces from the fort before dark and encamped a few miles east of it. On the morning of the 13th I again dispatched Captain Anderson to Fort Pillow for the purpose of placing, if possible, the Federal wounded on board their transports, and report to me on his return the condition of affairs at the river ♭ . . .

"We captured six pieces of artillery, viz., two 10-pounder Parrott guns, two 12-pounder howitzers, and two brass 6-pounder guns, and about 350 stand of small-arms. The balance of the small-arms had been thrown in the river. All the small-arms were picked up where the enemy fell or threw them down. A few were in the fort, the balance scattered from the top of the hill to the water's edge. We captured 164 Federals, 75 negro troops, and about 40 negro women and children, and after removing everything of value as far as able to do so, the warehouses, tents, etc., were destroyed by fire."

↓ HEADQUARTERS, FORREST'S CAVALRY, FORT PILLOW, April 12, 1864. CAPTAIN —— MARSHALL, Commanding U. S. Gun-boat. SIR: My aide-de-camp, Captain Charles W. Anderson, is fully authorized to negotiate with you for the delivery of the wounded of the Federal garrison at this place. upon your own or any other United States vessel. Respectfully, N. B. FORREST, Major-General.

♭ The report of Captain Anderson shows that on the 13th he delivered on board the U. S. Steamer *Silver Cloud* (Acting Master W. Ferguson) three officers, 43 white soldiers, and 14 colored soldiers, and received an acknowledgment in writing. The Confederate loss, according to the latest compilation in the War Department, was 14 killed and 86 wounded.— EDITORS.

FORREST'S DEFEAT OF STURGIS AT BRICE'S CROSS-ROADS (June 10th, 1864).

BY E. HUNN HANSON, ADJUTANT, 4TH MISSOURI CAVALRY, U. S. V., A. D. C. WARING'S BRIGADE.

IN May, 1864, in order to protect his long line of communication, General Sherman ordered an expedition from Memphis to defeat Forrest's cavalry, then in northern Mississippi, and thereby prevent its descent upon his line of advance. Accordingly, on the 1st of June, a small but well-organized force began its march from White's

Station, near Memphis. On the following day General Samuel D. Sturgis was placed in command. Some weeks earlier he had commanded an expedition sent out from Memphis to intercept Forrest on his march southward after his capture of Fort Pillow and the massacre of its garrison, but had been unable to do so. On the 8th of June, before the enemy had been met, Sturgis, although he had supplies sufficient for eleven days, desired to give up the expedition, but was dissuaded.

The cavalry was commanded by General B. H. Grierson, and consisted of two brigades: Waring's, 1600 men, two rifled guns, and four small howitzers, and Winslow's, 1800 men and a light battery. There were three brigades of infantry, two white and one colored. In all, over five thousand men with two 6-gun batteries. The whole, as a division, was commanded by Colonel W. L. McMillen.

The expedition had a new and complete supply train with eighteen days' rations. Adding regimental wagons, there were in all 250, exclusive of ambulances and medical wagons.

June 8th the command reached Ripley, about eighty miles from its starting-point, and on the following night it encamped at Stubb's Farm, fourteen miles south from Ripley.

At 5 o'clock on the morning of June 10th Waring's brigade, in advance, moved southward in the direction of Brice's plantation, followed by Winslow's brigade, the infantry, and the train, the latter guarded by the brigade of colored troops. The advance found the fences down, as if for an engagement, and two small bridges over the road taken up. About half-past nine o'clock it reached Brice's Cross-roads, about eleven miles from Stubb's Farm. [See map, p. 414.]

The road on which the command was marching ran nearly north and south, and about a mile and a half north of the cross-roads it passed through a wooded bottom and over a swampy piece of ground and took somewhat the character of a causeway, in length nearly three-quarters of a mile. After passing this, and for about a third of a mile, the ground rose somewhat, so that at the cross-roads it was perhaps twenty feet above the causeway. At Brice's house a road crossed at right angles. Waring's brigade was halted at the cross-roads and a squadron sent forward on the direct road southward, and one each on the roads to the west and to the east; the latter led in the direction of the Mobile and Ohio Railroad, distant about six miles, at which point was Guntown — a station and small village. The last-mentioned squadron, after going about a mile, commenced to skirmish with a small mounted force, some of which dismounted and occupied a house by the roadside, and stopped the advancing squadron by their fire.

From the southern end of the causeway to the cross-roads, and for about a third of a mile, the land had been cleared, at the cross-roads in each direction, and for nearly a mile there was standing timber and brush, to the east and south of which there were open fields. Waring's brigade was moved on the road to the east and deployed in line, dismounted, at the edge of the timber and on both sides of the road. The rifled guns and howitzers were placed in position on the road, along the fence of which, and in advance of the guns, a detachment of about one hundred men with revolving rifles were placed as skirmishers. On the right of Waring's brigade, in line, dismounted, with its right somewhat refused, Winslow's brigade took position covering the road which ran from the cross-

roads to the south. Soon after these lines were formed the enemy moved from the cover of a wood to the east and south of the open fields, and a third of a mile away, in two lines of skirmishers, followed by a line of battle with some troops massed upon the left flank. The enemy's right rested near the road on which were the guns and the skirmishers of Waring's brigade, and the enemy's left was in front of the left and center of Winslow's line. In other words, the line of the enemy was somewhat shorter than that of the cavalry in position. The enemy in view did not exceed 2500 men. They advanced until the right of their line came under the rapid and flanking fire at short range of the skirmishers with revolving rifles, when it wavered and halted, and with but little disorder the entire force fell back to the wood.

No effort was made to follow and turn the retreat into rout, and none to throw troops upon either flank, the right flank being vulnerable from Waring's brigade and the left from Winslow's. A skirmish fire was kept up at long range, and a small force, less than three hundred, moved against the extreme left of Waring's brigade, but was easily repulsed.

An officer who rode with the squadron sent eastward on the Guntown road had remarked as it emerged from the timber, and about a mile to the northward, a road which seemed to lead to the right and rear of the enemy's position. This fact was brought to Colonel Waring's notice, who directed that it be reported to Grierson. This was done by the officer in question, and half an hour later, and before noon, to Grierson's adjutant-general. To neither did it seem of moment, and no action was taken with regard to it.

While the engagement described was in progress General Grierson sent word of it to General Sturgis, who was with the infantry five miles north of the cross-roads, stopped by a very bad piece of wet and sunken road, and by officer and orderly again and again urged that the infantry be hurried forward. A ride of half an hour would have brought an aide or the general commanding himself on the field, and would have enabled him to judge if it were expedient or otherwise to give battle where the cavalry was, or to select a position where the infantry was and direct the cavalry to fall back to that. This course was not taken, but, yielding to the representations and urgency of Grierson, Sturgis ordered the infantry forward as fast as was practicable, and, riding in advance of them, arrived at the cross-roads less than half an hour before the head of the infantry column appeared. In the meantime, and about the time that General Sturgis arrived at the cross-roads, the enemy, disposed as before, again marched upon the cavalry; again their line wavered, but by the exertion of their officers the men moved forward with spirit and resolution. When near, and within from fifty to seventy-five paces of the edge of the wood, along which Waring's brigade was, the center of that command slowly gave way. As a result, the entire brigade fell back. This uncovered Winslow's left flank and caused his brigade also to fall back. A line was hastily formed about half-way between that first taken up and the cross-roads. With a knowledge of this it was even then possible to have halted the infantry on the north side of the causeway and there to have formed line of battle. It is true the position was far from good, but it was incomparably better than that taken. About 2 o'clock, or a little later, and after the cavalry had retreated from its first position, the head of the infantry column appeared at the cross-roads, the Second Brigade in advance. The day was very sultry and hot; the men had for five miles been hurried forward. Some had fallen exhausted and all were distressed by the march. In this condition, and under a skirmish fire from the successful enemy, the Second Brigade of infantry, followed by the First, was placed on the cramped line to which the cavalry had retreated, and the section of a battery was unlimbered and sent into action on the ground to the north of the cross-roads. The cavalry, partly by order and partly without, withdrew. Some of it was placed on the right flank of the infantry, and much of it was held as a reserve on the field near where the battery was in action, but to the westward of the road. Each flank of the infantry line was unprotected, and first the right was seriously threatened and then the left. With these difficulties, and those before mentioned, the infantry struggled for nearly three hours. During this time the train had come on the causeway, preceded by the artillery and a number of ambulances; so far as was possible some of these were parked on the field near the cross-roads before mentioned as that to which the greater part of the cavalry had gone. About 5 o'clock the efforts of the enemy on the left of the line succeeded, and it yielded to a flanking fire and retreated the very short distance between it and the cross-roads; about the same time the right of the line was enveloped by the enemy's skirmishers, and their artillery got with precision the range of the cross-roads. At first sullenly, and then rapidly, the whole line fell back to the cross-roads, and with cavalry, ambulances, artillery, and wagons of the train began a disordered retreat along the causeway. The enemy followed with eagerness, and utter disorganization succeeded disorder as piece after piece of artillery became the spoil of the fast-pursuing enemy, some of which was turned upon the huddled mass of fleeing men.

Sturgis and McMillen made strenuous efforts to form a line some two miles northward of the lost field with the colored brigade and a part of the troops that had been longer in action. This line stayed the pursuit for but a space and then became a part of the retreating force. Through the hours of the late afternoon and all through the night the beaten men kept on their way, reaching Ripley, 24 miles from the field, by early morning of June 11th. During the retreat the enemy had captured 14 pieces of artillery, the entire train of 250 wagons, with 10 days' rations and a large supply of ammunition, and over 1500 prisoners.

At Ripley an attempt was made to form the command gathered there into companies and regiments, but the enemy appeared on two sides and were checked only until the retreat could be resumed. It continued via Collierville to Memphis. The bitter humiliation of this disaster rankles after a quarter of a century.

Our loss in killed and wounded was 23 officers and 594 men. The captured or missing amounted to 52 officers and 1571 men, making a total loss of 2240. The enemy may have numbered more than 3500 or 4000, but it must be reluctantly confessed that not more than this number is believed to have been in action. If there was, during the war, another engagement like this, it is not known to the writer; and in its immediate results there was no success among the many won by Forrest comparable to that of Guntown.

A. J. SMITH'S DEFEAT OF FORREST AT TUPELO (July 14th, 1864).

BY W. S. BURNS, CAPTAIN, 4TH MISSOURI CAVALRY, U. S. V.

ON the 9th of June, 1864, General A. J. Smith arrived at Memphis with his command from the "Red River Expedition." His men were scarcely settled in camp when the vanguard of Sturgis's retreating army made its appearance, having just been thoroughly defeated by Forrest at Brice's Cross-roads.

General C. C. Washburn, then nominally in command of the large Union department of which Forrest had the real control (excepting the headquarters at Memphis), immediately ordered General Smith to make preparations for an expedition into "Forrest's country."

On July 1st we had assembled at La Grange, fifty miles east of Memphis. Our forces consisted of the First and Third divisions of the right wing of the Sixteenth Army Corps, commanded respectively by General J. A. Mower and Colonel David Moore, with a division of cavalry, commanded by General B. H. Grierson, and a brigade of colored troops, commanded by Colonel Edward Bouton—in all about 14,000 men with twenty guns.

On July 5th the command started on its march southward, pushing on day after day, with Forrest hovering on our front and flanks. On the 11th, after a sharp skirmish, we entered Pontotoc (Mississippi), driving Forrest through and beyond the village. Having now arrived within striking distance of the Mobile and Ohio Railroad, early in the morning of the 13th, we moved out of Pontotoc eastward, as if to strike the railroad at Tupelo, 19 miles distant, thereby "flanking" Forrest, who, with his army numbering about 12,000 men, was in a good fighting position 10 miles south awaiting Smith. Forrest soon discovered this move, and started to intercept us before we could reach the railroad, which he did six miles from Tupelo, attacking Mower's division in the rear. He was soon repulsed. An hour later he made another attack upon the same division and met the same fate,

Mower's men charging, and capturing some prisoners and a battle-flag. About dark we encamped at Harrisburg, a small hamlet, one mile from Tupelo. Smith was now in position to compel an attack from Forrest.

Next morning (14th), at a very early hour, Grierson was sent to Tupelo with orders to destroy the railroad north and south, while Smith placed his troops for the impending battle. They occupied a knoll almost clear of trees for a mile or more to the south, west, and north-west, beyond which was a growth of timber. The road over which the troops had marched led to the center of the position. Mower was stationed on the right or north of this (Pontotoc) road, looking west, and Moore on the left or south. Bouton's colored brigade was on the extreme left.

About 6 o'clock Forrest made his attack, the brunt falling upon Moore's division and the left wing of Mower's. The onset was made with Forrest's characteristic impetuosity, but it was impossible for his men to reach our lines. Smith's command was in the open, without any protection, excepting part of Moore's division, in front of which was a "worm fence," and beyond this a wide gully. Here the attacking force was rallied. Four times they attacked, each time without success. Between the assaults Forrest's artillery was very active, one battery being handled with great accuracy, throwing its shot and shell into the 21st Missouri, 58th Illinois, and 89th Indiana, until an Illinois and an Indiana battery engaged their attention. These batteries so annoyed the enemy that Colonel W. W. Faulkner charged upon them for their capture but he was met by an enfilading fire from the 119th Illinois, and a direct fire and a charge from the 21st Missouri, 58th Illinois, and 89th Indiana, the 122d Illinois charging to the right. Faulkner's line broke and fled, leaving many of their wounded and dead upon the field, among them the leader, Colonel Faulkner.

For an hour and a half the struggle continued, until the enemy were driven from the front of Moore, leaving the ground covered with their dead and dying. Instead of retiring to the woods (where their horses were held in reserve, for Forrest's army was always "mounted infantry") they moved in what at first appeared a confused mass to their left, crossed to the north of the Pontotoc road, turned, and, in good line of battle, swept down upon Mower, whose men (under orders) reserved their fire until the enemy were quite near, when they opened upon them with musketry and canister-shot. Human beings could not stand such a storm, and the attacking line fell back, but only to return to some seemingly exposed part of Mower's line. For two hours and a half the battle raged on this part of the field, the enemy attacking and our men keeping their positions and repelling all attacks. At last Mower ordered his division to advance, which they did, capturing many prisoners and driving the enemy into the woods, where they mounted their horses and moved off. It was useless to pursue them farther.

The afternoon was spent bringing in and caring for the wounded of both armies, and burying the dead of our own. Our loss was about 650, of which number 82 were killed. That of Forrest could only be estimated.⎰ Of his dead alone there were left on the field about 350.

Smith had defeated Forrest as he had never been defeated before. But our rations and ammunition were low, and Grierson's cavalry having destroyed the railroad, Smith could, from a military point of view, do no more, so he decided to return to Memphis.

About 9 o'clock in the evening Forrest attacked our extreme left, including Bouton's colored brigade, and the 14th, 27th, and 32d Iowa, and 24th Missouri, but it was rather a feeble attempt and was soon repulsed. At an early hour next morning the enemy again made their appearance, advancing from the cover of the woods, but as they did not approach with much energy Mower charged upon them, when they fled to their horses. In the meantime troops were seen advancing upon the scene of last night's attempt, where the colored brigade was still in position. Smith hurried to the spot, and for two hours there was artillery firing. Forrest, under cover of his guns, then advanced, determined to have a parting blow at the colored troops. These, by command of General Smith, held their fire until he gave the word, after which he personally led them in a charge, which was made with spirit and in excellent order, the enemy breaking and fleeing in confusion.

Believing that this was the last of the foe, General Smith moved slowly northward five miles, and went into camp at "Old Town Creek." The men were just settling themselves for the rest they needed when the sound of artillery was heard in our rear and a few shells fell and burst among them. Mower quickly repelled this attack, made by a few horsemen and one piece of artillery, and no more was seen of them. We continued our march, and by easy stages reached Memphis July 23d.

⎰ Forrest's loss was officially reported as 153 killed, 794 wounded, and 49 missing,— total, 996.— EDITORS.

JOHN MORGAN IN 1864.

BY BASIL W. DUKE, BRIGADIER-GENERAL, C. S. A.

GENERAL JOHN H. MORGAN escaped from the prison at Columbus, Ohio, November 27th, 1863,⎰ and reached the Confederate lines early in December. He was not ordered upon active service during that winter, but in April was virtually placed in command of the Department of South-western Virginia, which embraced also a portion of east Tennessee. The forces at his

⎰ Generals Morgan and Duke and sixty-eight other officers of Morgan's command, captured in Ohio, at the close of July, 1863 [see Vol. III., p. 634], were confined in the State penitentiary at Columbus. On the night of November 27th, Morgan and Captains J. C. Bennett, L. D. Hockersmith, C. S. Magee, Ralph Sheldon,

disposal for the defense of the department, exclusive of the militia or "reserves" of that territory, numbered about three thousand. Of these nearly one thousand were men of his former division, who had either been left in Tennessee when their comrades set out upon the Ohio raid, or had escaped capture in that expedition. Five or six hundred of these troops were mounted, and were organized into two battalions, commanded respectively by Captains Cassell and Kirkpatrick. Some four hundred were dismounted and were temporarily employed as infantry. Two brigades of Kentucky cavalry, under H. L. Giltner and George B. Cosby, of excellent material, although numerically depleted by hard and constant service, had been stationed in that region for two years previously, and the thorough acquaintance of their officers and men with the country rendered them especially valuable.

On the 8th of May intelligence came of the simultaneous advance of two strong Federal columns. General Averell, with a body of cavalry, threatened the salt-works, and General Crook, with infantry and cavalry, was approaching Dublin Depot, near New River Bridge. It was of vital importance to repulse both. The Confederacy was largely dependent upon the works at Saltville for its salt supply, and the lead-works at Wytheville, not far distant, were nearly as valuable. If Crook should be successful he would be able to damage the railroad in that vicinity to such an extent that communication with Richmond might be permanently destroyed and the transmission of supplies from all that region prevented. It was necessary, therefore, at once to confront and cripple, if not completely defeat, both columns. General A. G. Jenkins, with his cavalry brigade, detached from the Army of Northern Virginia, put himself in front of Crook, but was not strong enough to cope with him. Morgan hastened the four hundred dismounted men of his command to the assistance of General Jenkins. Colonel D. H. Smith, commanding them, reached Dublin on the morning of the 10th and found General Jenkins there, hard pressed by the enemy, and that gallant officer severely wounded. Smith at once reported to Colonel John McCausland, who had taken command, and the timely reënforcement restored the battle, which had been sorely against the Confederates. Holding the enemy in check until sunset, the Confederates retreated to New River Bridge and encamped in a position to protect that structure. [See map, p. 478.]

In the meantime General Morgan, with Giltner's brigade and the two battalions of Cassell and Kirkpatrick, sought Averell. He was convinced on the 9th, by the reports of his scouts, that Averell's first blow would not be delivered at Saltville, but that he was striking at Wytheville. Pressing rapidly on past Saltville he fell on Averell's track and followed it to the junction of the roads leading respectively to Crab Orchard and Wytheville. Averell had taken the road to Crab Orchard, and doubtless wished and expected to be closely pursued by that route. In that event, by a judicious employment of a part of his command, he could have held his opponent at bay in that very rugged country long enough to have thrown a detachment into Wytheville (which was garrisoned only by a small provost guard), and could have destroyed the military stores there and the neighboring lead-mines, besides rendering the railroad useless for many weeks. Morgan, believing this to be his skillful adversary's plan, marched directly to Wytheville by the shorter road through Burke's Garden, arriving there on the afternoon of the 11th. Colonel George B. Crittenden, taking command of a small detachment of W. E. Jones's cavalry brigade, which had reached Wytheville the day before, was instructed to occupy a small pass or gap in the mountain, through which alone the enemy's approach to the town, from the road on which he was marching, was practicable. Crittenden was attacked soon after he reached the position assigned him, but Morgan marching to his assistance with all of the troops, Averell fell back to a commanding ridge, about eight hundred yards from the gap. He was immediately attacked and, after a sharp combat, dislodged. The fighting continued, however, until after nightfall, in a succession of attacks on the one side and retreats on the other. At length Averell withdrew from the field, which he had very gallantly and obstinately contested. Morgan lost in killed and wounded fifty or sixty. Averell's loss was somewhat more, besides nearly one hundred prisoners.

Notwithstanding these successes, the department was by no means out of danger; for neither Crook nor Averell was materially weakened, and both continued to menace it. It soon became apparent that when supported by a movement already in progress from Kentucky they would return to the attack with greater determination. Burbridge and Hobson were reported en route for south-western Virginia, with all of the Federal forces in Kentucky available for active service. General Morgan had no hope of successfully resisting a combined onset of these various forces; but he was confident that he could avert the invasion of his own territory by himself assuming the offensive. His plan can be best explained in his own words. On the 31st of May, after commencing his march, he wrote General Samuel Cooper (Adjutant-General):

"While General Buckner was in command of this department he instructed me to strike a blow at the

Samuel Taylor, and Thomas H. Hines escaped from their cells, having cut a way through the cell-walls into an air-chamber, and tunneled the outer foundation-walls of the prison at the end of the chamber. The tools used in cutting away the masonry and the earth were two small knives, and the work was accomplished in twenty days, of five hours' labor each day. After leaving the prison the party separated. General Morgan and Captain Hines took the cars at Columbus for Cincinnati. At

Cincinnati they crossed into Kentucky, and, passing southward through New Castle and Bardstown, reached the Cumberland, near Burkesville, on December 5th. Soon afterward they fell in with a detachment of Morgan's men that had not taken part in the Ohio raid, and on the 13th crossed the Tennessee near Kingston. After several adventures with scouting parties of Union cavalry, in one of which Captain Hines was retaken, Morgan reached the Confederate lines.— EDITORS.

enemy in Kentucky. As I was on the eve of executing this order, the rapid movement of the enemy from the Kanawha valley, in the direction of the Tennessee and Virginia Railroad, made it necessary that I should remain to coöperate with the other forces for the defense of this section. . . . I have just received information that General Hobson left Mount Sterling on the 23d inst. with six regiments of cavalry (about 3000 strong), for Louisa, on the Sandy. This force he has collected from all the garrisons in middle and south-eastern Kentucky. At Louisa there is another force of about 2500 cavalry, under a colonel of a Michigan regiment recently sent to that vicinity. It is the reported design of General Hobson to unite with this latter force and coöperate with Generals Averell and Crook in another movement upon the salt-works and lead-mines of south-western Virginia. This information has determined me to move at once into Kentucky, and thus distract the plans of the enemy by initiating a movement within his lines. My force will be about 2000 men."

Morgan accordingly entered Kentucky with Giltner's brigade, the mounted men of the old Morgan division, and 800 dismounted men from the various cavalry commands stationed in the department. It was impossible to carry artillery over the roads by which he expected to march. The column reached Pound Gap on the 2d of June, dislodged a small Federal garrison occupying it, and pushed through. More than 150 miles of the most rugged regions of the Kentucky mountains were then traversed in seven days. The dismounted men, whose numbers were constantly augmented as horses broke down from fatigue and lack of forage, kept pace with their comrades in the saddle. Giltner's brigade lost more than 200 horses. On the 7th of June detachments were sent forward to destroy the bridges on the Louisville and Lexington and Kentucky Central railroads, to prevent troops from being sent from Indiana and Ohio to the defense of central Kentucky. Night fell on the 8th while the column was still struggling in the gloomy and difficult wilderness through which wound the "rebel trace"; but on the morning of the 9th they had reached the confines of the beautiful blue-grass country, and were not far from Mount Sterling. That day the town was attacked and captured, and 380 prisoners were taken. Leaving Giltner to destroy the captured stores and property, and provide for mounting the foot-men, Morgan promptly moved upon Lexington with the greater part of the mounted troops. That night the first disaster of the expedition befell him, and it was visited on the brave men who had made the long and painful march on foot.

The Federal movement from Kentucky was made as Morgan had anticipated. Burbridge, with the Fifth Division of the Twenty-third Corps, had proceeded some distance east of Louisa when Morgan passed through Pound Gap. The respective columns were distant from each other, but it was impossible to conceal all evidence of the Confederate advance, and Colonel John Mason Brown, commanding the Second Brigade of the Fifth Federal Division, became convinced of its character and urged Burbridge to return, and, if possible, intercept Morgan at Mount Sterling. His advice was taken and the Federal troops countermarched with extraordinary celerity. They reached Mount Sterling at midnight of the 9th, and at 3 P. M. of the 10th attacked the camp of the dismounted men, which was very inefficiently picketed. Colonel Brown's brigade, supported by Hanson's, rode over the picket detail and into the encampment. A desperate fight at close quarters ensued. Giltner was not near enough to render prompt assistance, and Colonel R. M. Martin, commanding the body assaulted, with great difficulty extricated it and effected a junction with Giltner after three or four hours of combat. Martin's loss was 14 officers and between two and three hundred men; he was twice wounded. The Federal loss was about two hundred. On the same morning, the 10th, General Morgan captured Lexington, and found in the Government stables there a sufficient number of horses to mount the survivors of the dismounted brigade, who, with Giltner's brigade, rejoined him that night. He immediately marched on Cynthiana, taking that place, after a brisk skirmish with the garrison, on the 11th. That afternoon, General Hobson, coming to the relief of the town, approached with 1500 cavalry. He was immediately attacked in front by Giltner, while Morgan, assailing him in the rear with Cassell's battalion, compelled his surrender. On the 12th Morgan was attacked at Cynthiana by Burbridge at the head of 5200 men. Morgan's effective strength was now reduced, by losses in battle and details to guard prisoners and destroy railroad track and bridges, to less than 1300, and his ammunition was nearly exhausted. After some hours of hard fighting he was defeated and forced to retreat, with a loss of fully one half of his remaining command in killed, wounded, and prisoners. He destroyed all of his captured stores and paroled the prisoners he had taken, and marching instantly back to Virginia, via Flemingsburg and West Liberty, and thence through the mountains, reached Abingdon, Va., June 20th. Disastrous as this raid was, in some respects, it accomplished its purpose, and delayed the apprehended incursion into south-western Virginia for several months, and until measures were concerted to frustrate it. ⚓

From this period until the date of his death, September 4th, 1864, General Morgan was engaged in no military operation of consequence. He was killed at Greenville while advancing to attack Gillem at Bull's Gap in Tennessee, with the intention, if successful, of marching into middle Tennessee. He was succeeded in the command of the department by General John C. Breckinridge.

⚓ General S. G. Burbridge reported officially that the losses in his command during these operations amounted to 53 killed, 156 wounded, and 205 captured or missing = 414.— EDITORS.

THE INVASION OF TENNESSEE.

BY J. B. HOOD, GENERAL, C. S. A.

UNLESS the army could be heavily reënforced, there was but one plan to be adopted [after withdrawing from Atlanta. See p. 343]: by manœuvres, to draw Sherman back into the mountains, then beat him in battle, and at least regain our lost territory. Therefore, after anxious reflection and consultation with the corps commanders, I determined to communicate with the President, and ascertain whether or not reënforcements could be obtained from any quarter.

The reply from His Excellency conveyed no hope of assistance:

"RICHMOND, September 5th, 1864.
" . . . The necessity for reënforcements was realized, and every effort made to bring forward reserves, militia, and detailed men for the purpose. . . . No other resource remains. It is now requisite that absentees be brought back, the addition required from the surrounding country be promptly made available, and that the means in hand be used with energy proportionate to the country's need. JEFFERSON DAVIS."

I thereupon decided to operate at the earliest moment possible in the rear of Sherman, as I became more and more convinced of our inability successfully to resist an advance of the Federal army.

I recalled General Wheeler from Tennessee to join immediately the left of the army, whilst Colonel Presstman, of the engineer corps, made ready to move with the pontoon-train and a sufficient number of boats to meet any emergency.

Upon the morning of the 18th the army began to move in the direction of the West Point Railroad, which the advance reached on the 19th. Upon the 20th, line of battle was formed, with the right east of the railroad, and the left resting near the river, with army headquarters at Palmetto.

On the 28th I issued instructions to commence the movement across the Chattahoochee at Pumpkin Town and Phillips's Ferry, and on the following morning I directed that our supplies from Newnan cross the river at Moore's Ferry. At noon I rode over the pontoon-bridge in advance of the infantry, and that night established my headquarters at Pray's Church, along with General W. H. Jackson, commanding the cavalry.

The morning of the 1st of October Brigadier-General Jackson advanced with the cavalry, sending a detachment at the same time to operate against the railroad between the Chattahoochee and Marietta. That night the army went into bivouac eight miles north of Pray's Church, after having effected an undisturbed and safe passage of the Chattahoochee. Information was here received that Kilpatrick's cavalry was north of the river, and that Garrard's cavalry had moved in the direction of Rome.

The night of the 2d the army rested near Flint Hill Church. On the morning of the 3d Lieutenant-General Stewart was instructed to move with his corps and take possession of Big Shanty; to send, if practicable, a detachment for the same purpose to Ackworth, and to destroy as great a portion of the railroad in the vicinity as possible; also to send a division to Allatoona to capture that place, if, in the judgment of the commanding officer, the achievement was feasible. The main body of the army in the meantime moved forward and bivouacked near Carley's house, within four miles of Lost Mountain.

On the 4th General Stewart captured, after a slight resistance, about 170 prisoners at Big Shanty, and at 9:30 A. M. the garrison at Ackworth, numbering 250 men, surrendered to General Loring. The forces under these officers joined the main body near Lost Mountain on the morning of the 5th, having, in addition, destroyed about ten or fifteen miles of the railroad.

I had received information that the enemy had in store at Allatoona large supplies which were guarded by two or three regiments. As one of the objects of the campaign was to deprive the enemy of provisions, Major-General French was ordered to move with his division, capture the garrison, if practicable, and gain possession of the supplies. Accordingly, on the 5th, at 10 A.M., after a refusal to surrender, he attacked the Federal forces at Allatoona, and succeeded in capturing a portion of the works; at that juncture he received intelligence that large reënforcements were advancing in support of the enemy, and fearing he would be cut off from the main body of the army, he retired and abandoned the attempt. Our soldiers fought with great courage; during the engagement Brigadier-General Young, a brave and efficient officer, was wounded and captured by the enemy. General Corse won my admiration by his gallant resistance, and not without reason the Federal commander complimented this officer, through a general order, for his handsome conduct in the defense of Allatoona. [See pp. 322, 323, and 324.]

Our presence upon his communications compelled Sherman to leave Atlanta in haste and cross the Chattahoochee on the 3d and 4th of October with, according to our estimate at that time, about 65,000 infantry and artillery and two divisions of cavalry. He left one corps to guard the city and the railway bridge across the river, and telegraphed to Grant he would attack me if I struck his road south of the Etowah.

On the 6th my army reached Dallas; our right rested at New Hope Church, where intelligence was received that the enemy was advancing from Lost Mountain. From Dallas we marched to Coosaville, ten miles south-west of Rome, via Van Wert, Cedartown, and Cave Spring. At the latter place Major-General Wheeler, with a portion of his command, joined me from Tennessee. We arrived at Coosaville on the 10th.

In a dispatch to General [Richard] Taylor, October 7th, I requested that Forrest be ordered to operate at once in Tennessee:

"Your dispatch of the 6th received. This army being in motion, it is of vital importance that Forrest should

⸗ Taken by permission (and condensed) from General Hood's work, "Advance and Retreat," published by General G. T. Beauregard for the Hood Orphan Memorial Fund: New Orleans, 1880.

move without delay, and operate on the enemy's railroad. If he cannot break the Chattanooga and Nashville Railroad he can occupy their forces there and prevent damage being repaired on the other road. He should lose no time in moving."

On the 11th the army crossed the Coosa River, marched in the direction of Resaca and Dalton, and bivouacked that night fourteen miles above Coosaville and ten miles north-west of Rome. That same day Major-General Arnold Elzey, chief-of-artillery, was directed to move to Jacksonville with the reserve artillery and all surplus wagons, and General Jackson was instructed to retard the enemy as much as possible, in the event of his advance from Rome.

Having thus relieved the army of all incumbance, and made ready for battle, we marched rapidly to Resaca, and thence to Dalton, via Sugar Valley Post-Office. Lieutenant-General Lee moved upon Resaca, with instructions to display his forces and demand the surrender of the garrison, but not to attack unless, in his judgment, the capture could be effected with small loss of life. He decided not to assault the Federal works, and commenced at once the destruction of the railroad.

On the 13th I demanded the surrender of Dalton, which, in the first instance, was refused, but was finally acceded to at 4 P. M. The garrison consisted of about one thousand men. As the road between Resaca and Tunnel Hill had been effectually destroyed, the army was put in motion the next morning in the direction of Gadsden, and camped that night near Villanow.

From Villanow the army passed through the gaps in the mountains, and halted on the 15th at Cross Roads, in a beautiful valley about nine miles south of Lafayette. At this time I received intelligence that on the 13th Sherman had reached Snake Creek Gap, where the right of his line had rested in the early spring of this year; also that he was marching in our pursuit, whilst General Wheeler was endeavoring to retard his advance as much as possible. I here determined to advance no farther toward the Tennessee River, but to select a position and deliver battle, since Sherman, at an earlier date than anticipated, had moved as far north as I had hoped to allure him; moreover, I was again in the vicinity of the Alabama line, with the Blue Mountain Railroad in my rear, and I thought I had discovered that improvement in the morale of the troops which would justify me in delivering battle. In accordance with information received from our cavalry, Sherman had, however, made no further division of his forces after leaving Atlanta. I therefore estimated his strength to be about 65,000 effectives.

Upon the eve of action I considered it important to ascertain by personal inquiry and through the aid of officers of my staff,—not alone from corps commanders, but from officers of less rank,— whether or not my impressions after the capture of

Dalton were correct, and I could rely upon the troops entering into battle at least hopeful of victory. I took measures to obtain likewise the views of Lieutenant-General S. D. Lee, who at this juncture was with his corps in rear, at or near Ship's Gap. He agreed with all the officers consulted; the opinion was unanimous that although the army had much improved in spirit, it was not in condition to risk battle against the numbers reported by General Wheeler.

The renouncement of the object for which I had so earnestly striven brought with it genuine disappointment; I had expected that a forward movement of one hundred miles would re-inspirit the officers and men in a degree to impart to them confidence, enthusiasm, and hope of victory, if not strong faith in its achievement.

I remained two days at Cross Roads in serious thought and perplexity. I could not offer battle while the officers were *unanimous* in their opposition. Neither could I take an intrenched position with likelihood of advantageous results, since Sherman could do the same, repair the railroad, amass a large army, place Thomas in my front in command of the forces he afterward assembled at Nashville, and then, himself, move southward; or, as previously suggested, he could send Thomas into Alabama, whilst he marched through Georgia, and left me to follow in his rear. This last movement upon our part would be construed by the troops into a retreat, and could but result in disaster. In this dilemma I conceived the plan of marching into Tennessee with the hope to establish our line eventually in Kentucky, and determined to make the campaign which followed, unless withheld by General Beauregard ⚓ or the authorities at Richmond. I decided to make provision for twenty days' supply of rations in the haversacks and wagons; to order a heavy reserve of artillery to accompany the army, in order to overcome any serious opposition by the Federal gun-boats; to cross the Tennessee at or near Guntersville, and again destroy Sherman's communications at Stevenson and Bridgeport; to move upon Thomas and Schofield, and to attempt to rout and capture their army before it could reach Nashville. I intended then to march upon that city, where I would supply the army and re-enforce it, if possible, by accessions from Tennessee. I was imbued with the belief that I could accomplish this feat, afterward march north-east, pass the Cumberland River at some crossing where the gun-boats, if too formidable at other points, were unable to interfere, then move into Kentucky, and take position with our left at or near Richmond, and our right extending toward Hazel Green, with Pound and Stony gaps in the Cumberland Mountains at our rear.

In this position I could threaten Cincinnati, and recruit the army from Kentucky and Tennessee; the former State was reported, at this juncture, to be more aroused and embittered against the Federals than at any other period of the war. While

⚓ On the 28th of September General Beauregard had been placed in control of the operations in the departments commanded by Generals Hood and Taylor. His

previous operations in defense of Petersburg are described by General Beauregard later in this work.— EDITORS.

Sherman was debating between the alternatives of following our army or marching through Georgia, I hoped, by rapid movements, to achieve these results.

If Sherman should cut loose and move south — as I then believed he would do after I left his front *without previously worsting him in battle* — I would occupy at Richmond, Kentucky, a position of superior advantage, as Sherman, upon his arrival at the sea-coast, would be forced to go on board ship, and, after a long détour by water and land, repair to the defense of Kentucky and Ohio or march direct to the support of Grant. If he should return to confront my forces, or follow me directly from Georgia into Tennessee and Kentucky, I hoped then to be in condition to offer battle; and, if blessed with victory, to send reënforcements to General Lee, in Virginia, or to march through the gaps in the Cumberland Mountains and attack Grant in rear. This latter course I would pursue in the event of defeat or of inability to offer battle to Sherman. If, on the other hand, he should march to join Grant, I could pass through the Cumberland gaps to Petersburg, and attack Grant in rear at least two weeks before he, Sherman, could render him assistance. This move, I believed, would defeat Grant, and allow General Lee, in command of our combined armies, to march upon Washington or turn upon and annihilate Sherman.

Such is the plan which during the 15th and 16th, as we lay in bivouac near Lafayette, I maturely considered, and determined to carry out.

On the 17th the army resumed its line of march, and that night camped three miles from the forks of the Alpine, Gaylesville, and Summerville roads; thence it proceeded towards Gadsden. I proposed to move directly on to Guntersville and to take into Tennessee about one-half of Wheeler's cavalry (leaving the remainder to look after Sherman) and to have a depot of supplies at Tuscumbia in the event that I should meet with defeat in Tennessee.

Shortly after my arrival at Gadsden, General Beauregard reached the same point; I at once unfolded to him my plan, and requested that he confer apart with the corps commanders, Lieutenant-Generals Lee and Stewart and Major-General Cheatham. If after calm deliberation he deemed it expedient we should remain upon the Alabama line and attack Sherman, or take position, intrench, and finally follow on his rear when he should move south, I would of course acquiesce, albeit with reluctance. If, contrariwise, he should agree to my proposed plan to cross into Tennessee, I would move immediately to Guntersville, thence to Stevenson, Bridgeport, and Nashville.

This important question at issue was discussed during the greater part of one night, with maps before us. General Beauregard at length took the ground that, if I should engage in the projected campaign, it would be necessary to leave in Georgia all the cavalry at present with the army, in order to watch and harass Sherman in case he should move south, and to instruct Forrest to join me as soon as I should cross the Tennessee River. To this proposition I acceded. After he had held a separate conference with the corps commanders, we again

debated several hours over the course of action to be pursued; and, during the interview, I discovered that he had gone to work in earnest to ascertain, in person, the true condition of the army; that he had sought information not only from the corps commanders, but from a number of officers, and had reached the same conclusion I had formed at Lafayette: that we were not competent to offer pitched battle to Sherman, nor could we follow him south without causing our retrograde movement to be construed by the troops into *a recurrence* of retreat, which would entail desertions and render the army of little or no use in its opposition to the enemy's march through Georgia. After two days' deliberation General Beauregard authorized me, on the evening of the 21st of October, to proceed to the execution of my plan of operations into Tennessee. General Beauregard's approval of a forward movement into Tennessee was soon made known to the army. The prospect of again entering that State created great enthusiasm, and from the different encampments arose at intervals that genuine Confederate shout so familiar to every Southern soldier, and which then betokened an improved state of feeling among the troops.

With twenty days' rations in the haversacks and wagons, we marched, on the 22d of October, upon all the roads leading from Gadsden in the direction of Guntersville, on the Tennessee River, and bivouacked that night in the vicinity of Bennettsville.

I here received information that General Forrest was near Jackson, Tennessee, and could not reach the middle portion of this State, as the river was too high. It would, therefore, be impossible for him to join me if I crossed at Guntersville; as it was regarded as essential that the whole of Wheeler's cavalry should remain in Georgia, I decided to deflect westward, effect a junction with Forrest, and then cross the river at Florence. General Beauregard sent orders to him to join me without delay, and also dispatched a messenger to hasten forward supplies to Tuscumbia.

The succeeding day the movement was continued toward Florence, in lieu of Guntersville as I had expected. Lieutenant-General Lee's corps reached the Tennessee, near Florence, on the 30th; [Edward] Johnson's division crossed the river and took possession of that town. My headquarters were during the 27th and 28th at the house of General Garth, near Decatur, where General Beauregard also stopped. While the army turned Decatur, I ordered a slight demonstration to be made against the town till our forces passed safely beyond, when I moved toward Tuscumbia, at which place I arrived on the 31st of October. Johnson's division, which held possession of Florence, was reënforced the same day by Clayton's division.

Thus the Confederate army rested upon the banks of the Tennessee one month after its departure from Palmetto. It had been almost continuously in motion during the interim; by rapid moves and manœuvres, and with only a small loss, it had drawn Sherman as far north as he stood in the early spring. The killed and wounded at Allatoona had been replaced by absentees who returned to ranks, and, as usual in such operations, the number of desertions became of no consequence.

Notwithstanding my request as early as the 9th of October that the railroad to Decatur be repaired, nothing had been done on the 1st of November toward the accomplishment of this important object. I had expected upon my arrival at Tuscumbia to find additional supplies, and to cross the river at once. Unfortunately, I was constrained to

MAJOR-GENERAL WILLIAM B. BATE, C. S. A.
FROM A PHOTOGRAPH.

await repairs upon the railroad before a sufficient amount of supplies could be received to sustain the army till it was able to reach middle Tennessee.

General Beauregard remained two weeks at Tuscumbia and in its vicinity, during which interval the inaugurated campaign was discussed anew at great length. General Sherman was still in the neighborhood of Rome, and the question arose as to whether we should take trains and return to Georgia to oppose his movements south, or endeavor to execute the projected operations into Tennessee and Kentucky. I adhered to the conviction I had held at Lafayette and Gadsden, and a second time desired General Beauregard to consult the corps commanders, together with other officers, in regard to the effect a return to Georgia would produce upon the army. I also urged the consideration that Thomas would immediately overrun Alabama, if we marched to confront Sherman. I had fixedly determined, unless withheld by Beau-

regard or the authorities at Richmond, to proceed, as soon as supplies were received, to the execution of the plan submitted at Gadsden.

At this juncture I was advised of the President's opposition to the campaign into Tennessee previous to a defeat of Sherman in battle. ↓ The President was evidently under the impression that the army should have been equal to battle by the time it had reached the Alabama line, and was averse to my going into Tennessee. He was not, as were General Beauregard and myself, acquainted with its true condition. Therefore, a high regard for his views notwithstanding, I continued firm in the belief that the only means to checkmate Sherman, and coöperate with General Lee to save the Confederacy, lay in speedy success in Tennessee and Kentucky, and in my ability finally to attack Grant in rear with my entire force.

Although every possible effort was made to expedite the repairs upon the railroad, the work progressed slowly. Heavy rains in that section also interfered with the completion of the road. On the 13th I established my headquarters in Florence, upon the north branch of the Tennessee, and the following day General Forrest, with his command, reported for duty. On the 15th the remainder of Lee's corps crossed the river and bivouacked in advance also of Florence. Stewart's and Cheatham's corps were instructed to cross. About the time all necessary preparations verged to a completion, and I anticipated to move forward once more, heavy rains again delayed our supplies. Working parties were at once detailed and sent to different points on the railroad; wagons were also dispatched to aid in the transportation of supplies. The officer in charge was instructed to require the men to labor unceasingly for the accomplishment of this important object. In the meantime information had reached me that Sherman was advancing south, from Atlanta. He marched out of that fated city on the 16th. Thus were two opposing armies destined to move in opposite directions, each hoping to achieve glorious results.

I well knew the delay at Tuscumbia would accrue to the advantage of Sherman, as he would thereby be allowed time to repair his railroad, and at least start to the rear all surplus material. I believed, however, that I could still get between Thomas's forces and Nashville, and rout them; furthermore, effect such manœuvres as to insure to our troops an easy victory. These convictions counterbalanced my regret that Sherman was permitted to traverse Georgia unopposed.

General Beauregard had moved in the direction of Georgia to assemble all available forces to oppose Sherman's advance.

↓ "RICHMOND, November 7th, 1864.
"Via Meridian.

"GENERAL J. B. HOOD: No troops can have been sent by Grant or Sheridan to Nashville. The latter has attempted to reënforce the former, but Early's movements prevented it. That fact will assure you as to their condition and purposes. The policy of taking advantage of the reported division of his [Sherman's] forces, where he cannot reunite his army, is too obvious to have been overlooked by you. I therefore take it for granted that

you have not been able to avail yourself of that advantage during his march northward from Atlanta. Hope the opportunity will be offered before he is extensively recruited. If you keep his communications destroyed, he will most probably seek to concentrate for an attack on you. But if, as reported to you, he has sent a large part of his force southward, you may first beat him in detail, and, subsequently, without serious obstruction or danger to the country in your rear, advance to the Ohio River. JEFFERSON DAVIS."

On the 19th the cavalry was ordered to move forward. The succeeding day Lee's corps marched to the front about ten miles on the Chisholm road, between the Lawrenceburg and Waynesboro' roads. On the 20th of November, Stewart's corps having crossed the Tennessee and bivouacked several miles beyond on the Lawrenceburg road, orders were issued that the entire army move at an early hour the next morning. Lee's and Stewart's corps marched upon the Chisholm and the Lawrenceburg roads, and Cheatham's upon the Waynesboro' road. Early dawn of the 21st found the army in motion. I hoped by a rapid march to get in rear of Schofield's forces, then at Pulaski, before they were able to reach Duck River. That night headquarters were established at Rawhide, twelve miles north of Florence, on the Waynesboro' road. The march was resumed on the 22d and continued till the 27th, upon which date the troops, having taken advantage of every available road, reached Columbia, via Mount Pleasant. Forrest operated in our front against the enemy's cavalry, which he easily drove from one position to another.

The Federals at Pulaski became alarmed, and, by forced marches, reached Columbia, upon Duck River, in time to prevent our troops from cutting them off.

Colonel Presstman and his assistants laid the pontoons [over Duck River] during the night of the 28th, about three miles above Columbia; orders to move at dawn the following day having been issued to the two corps and the division above mentioned, I rode with my staff to Cheatham's right, passed over the bridge soon after daybreak, and moved forward at the head of Granbury's Texas brigade, of Cleburne's division, with instructions that the remaining corps and divisions follow, and at the same time keep well closed up during the march.

General Forrest had crossed, the evening previous, and moved to the front and right. I threw forward a few skirmishers who advanced at as rapid a pace as troops could possibly proceed.

During the march the Federal cavalry appeared on the hills to our left; not a moment, however, was lost on that account, as the army was marching by the right flank and was prepared to face at any instant in their direction. No attention, therefore, was paid to the enemy, save to throw out a few sharp-shooters in his front. ▷

Thus I led the main body of the army to within about two miles and in full view of the pike from Columbia to Spring Hill and Franklin. I here halted about 3 P. M., and requested General Cheatham, commanding the leading corps, and

Major-General Cleburne to advance to the spot where, sitting upon my horse, I had in sight the enemy's wagons and men passing at double-quick along the Franklin pike. As these officers approached, I spoke to Cheatham in the following words, which I quote almost verbatim, as they have remained indelibly engraved upon my memory ever since that fatal day: "General, do you see the enemy there, retreating rapidly to escape us?" He answered in the affirmative. "Go," I continued, "with your corps, take possession of and hold that pike at or near Spring Hill. Accept whatever comes, and turn all those wagons over to our side of the house." Then, addressing Cleburne, I said, "General, you have heard the

A SOUTHERN PRIVATE. FROM AN AMBROTYPE.

orders just given. You have one of my best divisions. Go with General Cheatham, assist him in every way you can, and do as he directs." Again, as a parting injunction to them, I added, "Go and do this at once. Stewart is near at hand, and I will have him double-quick his men to the front." ◁

They immediately sent staff-officers to hurry the men forward, and moved off with their troops at a quick pace in the direction of the enemy. I sent several of my staff with orders to Stewart and Johnson to make all possible haste. Meantime I rode to one side and looked on at Cleburne's division, followed by the remainder of Cheatham's corps, as it marched by, seemingly ready for battle.

Within about one-half hour from the time Cheatham left me skirmishing began with the enemy, when I rode forward to a point nearer the pike, and again sent a staff-officer to Stewart and Johnson to push forward. At the same time I dispatched a

▷ In the "Southern Bivouac" for April, 1885, General Cheatham, in an article dated November 30th, 1881, says, in reply to the above paragraph:

"General John C. Brown states that 'at or near Bear Creek the commanding general, apprehending an attack on our left flank, ordered your (Cheatham's) corps, in its march from that point, to move in two parallel columns, so that it could come instantly into action in two lines of battle.' General Brown's division marched · five or six miles through fields and woods and over rough ground' some four hundred yards to the right of the road, necessarily causing more or less delay. General Brown further states that 'about the commencement of this movement, or soon afterward, by the orders of the commanding general in person, the whole of Gist's and about one-half of Strahl's brigade were detached for picket duty.'" EDITORS.

◁ "At the hour named, 3 P. M., there was no movement of 'wagons and men' in the vicinity of Spring Hill. Moreover, from the crossing at Duck River to the point referred to by General Hood, the turnpike was never in view, nor could it be seen until I had moved up to within three-quarters of a mile of Spring Hill. Only a mirage would have made possible the vision." . . . —GENERAL CHEATHAM, in the "BIVOUAC."

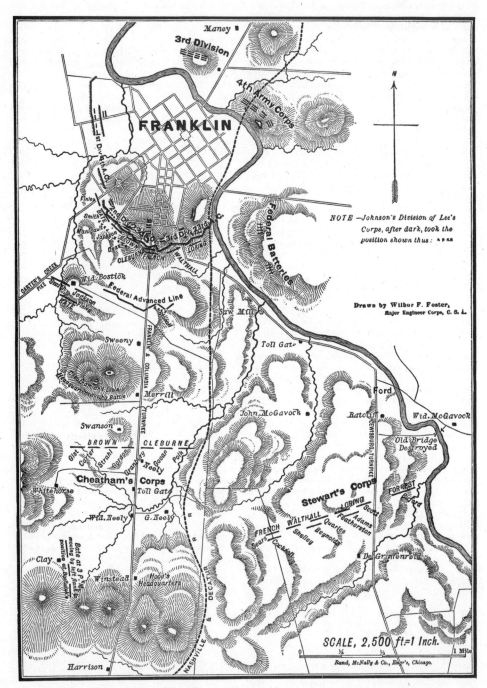

MAP OF THE BATTLE-FIELD OF FRANKLIN, TENNESSEE. FROM THE "BIVOUAC" FOR JUNE, 1885.

messenger to General Cheatham to lose no time in gaining possession of the pike at Spring Hill. It was reported back that he was about to do so. ☆

Listening attentively to the fire of the skirmishers in that direction I discovered there was no continued roar of musketry, and being aware of the quick approach of darkness, about 4 o'clock at that season of the year, I became somewhat uneasy, and again ordered an officer to go to General Cheatham, inform him that his supports were very near at hand ; that he must attack at once, if he had not already so done, and take and hold possession of the pike. Shortly afterward I intrusted another officer with the same message, and, if my memory is not treacherous, finally requested the governor of Tennessee, Isham G. Harris, to hasten forward and impress upon Cheatham the importance of action without delay. I knew no large force of the enemy could be at Spring Hill, as couriers reported Schofield's main body still in front of Lee, at Columbia, up to a late hour in the day. I thought it probable that Cheatham had taken possession of Spring Hill without encountering material opposition, or had formed line across the pike, north of the town, and intrenched without coming in serious contact with the enemy, which would account for the little musketry heard in his direction. However, to ascertain the truth, I sent an officer to ask Cheatham if he held the pike, and to inform him of the arrival of Stewart, whose corps I intended to throw on his left, in order to assail the Federals in flank that evening or the next morning, as they approached and formed to attack Cheatham. At this juncture the last messenger returned with the report that the road had not been taken possession of. General Stewart was then ordered to proceed to the right of Cheatham and place his corps across the pike north of Spring Hill.

By this hour, however, twilight was upon us, when General Cheatham rode up in person. I at once directed Stewart to halt, and, turning to Cheatham, I exclaimed with deep emotion, as I felt the golden opportunity fast slipping from me, "General, why in the name of God have you not attacked the enemy and taken possession of that pike ?" He replied that the line looked a little too long for him, and that Stewart should first form on his right. ⌡ I could hardly believe it possible that this brave old soldier, who had given proof of such courage and ability upon so many hard-fought fields, would even make such a report. After leading him within full view of the enemy, and pointing

out to him the Federals retreating in great haste and confusion along the pike, and then giving explicit orders to attack, I would as soon have expected midday to turn into darkness as for him to have disobeyed my orders. I then asked General Cheatham whether or not Stewart's corps, if formed on the right, would extend across the pike. He answered in the affirmative. Guides were at once furnished to point out Cheatham's right to General Stewart, who was ordered to form thereon, with his right extending across the pike. Darkness, however, which was increased by large shadetrees in that vicinity, soon closed upon us, and Stewart's corps, after much annoyance, went into bivouac for the night, near, but not across, the pike, at about 11 or 12 o'clock.

It was reported to me about this hour that the enemy was marching along the road, almost under the light of the camp-fires of the main body of the army. I sent anew to General Cheatham to know if at least a line of skirmishers could not be advanced, in order to throw the Federals in confusion, to delay their march, and allow us a chance to attack in the morning. Nothing was done. The Federals, with immense wagon-trains, were permitted to march by us the remainder of the night, within gunshot of our lines. I could not succeed in arousing the troops to action, when one good division would have sufficed to do the work. One good division, I reassert, could have routed that portion of the enemy which was at Spring Hill; could have taken possession of and formed line across the road; and thus could have made it an easy matter to Stewart's corps, Johnson's division, and Lee's two divisions, from Columbia, to have enveloped, routed, and captured Schofield's army that afternoon and the ensuing day. General Forrest gallantly opposed the enemy farther down to our right to the full extent of his power ; beyond this effort nothing whatever was done, although never was a grander opportunity offered to utterly rout and destroy the Federal army. Had I dreamed for one moment that Cheatham would have failed to give battle, or at least to take position across the pike and force the enemy to assault him, I would myself have ridden to the front and led the troops into action. ⚓

In connection with this grave misfortune, I must here record an act of candor and nobility upon the part of General Cheatham, which proves him to be equally generous-hearted and brave. I was, necessarily, much pained by the disappointment suffered, and, a few days later, telegraphed to Rich-

☆ "General Hood conveniently forgot to mention, in his account of this affair, the facts as to his orders to me at Rutherford's Creek. [See p. 438.] And he also forgot that, at the very moment he claims to have sent staff-officers to the rear with orders to Stewart and Johnson to make all possible haste, Stewart was forming line of battle on the south side of Rutherford's Creek, in pursuance of orders from him; nor did he remember that Stewart's corps was not ordered forward until about dusk."— GENERAL CHEATHAM, in the "BIVOUAC."

⌡ "Here, again, General Hood's memory proved treacherous. As to the preliminary statements of this paragraph, I refer to that portion of my account [see p. 438] which covers the doings of the hours from 4 to 6 P. M., during most of which time General Hood was on

the ground and in frequent personal communication with me. The dramatic scene with which he embellishes his narrative of the day's operations only occurred in the imagination of General Hood."— GENERAL CHEATHAM, in the "BIVOUAC."

⚓ "The next order, in the shape of a suggestion that I had better have my pickets fire upon straggling troops passing along the pike in front of my left, was received and was immediately communicated to General Johnson, whose division was on my left and nearest the pike. This note from Major Mason, received about midnight, was the only communication I had from General Hood after leaving him at his quarters at Captain Thompson's."— GENERAL CHEATHAM, in the "BIVOUAC."

mond, to withdraw my previous recommendation for his promotion, and to request that another be assigned to the command of his corps. Before the receipt of a reply, this officer called at my headquarters — then at the residence of Mr. Overton, six miles from Nashville — and, standing in my presence, spoke an honest avowal of his error, in the acknowledgment that he felt we had lost a brilliant opportunity at Spring Hill to deal the enemy a crushing blow, and that he was greatly to blame. I telegraphed and wrote to the War Department to withdraw my application for his removal, in the belief that, inspired with an ambition to retrieve his shortcoming, he would prove in the future doubly zealous in the service of his country. The following are the dispatches above referred to :

"HEADQUARTERS, six miles from Nashville, on Franklin Pike, December 7, 1864.

"HON. J. A. SEDDON : I withdraw my recommendation in favor of the promotion of Major-General Cheatham, for reasons which I will write more fully.

"J. B. HOOD, General."

"HEADQUARTERS, six miles from Nashville, on Franklin Pike, December 8, 1864.

"HON. J. A. SEDDON, Secretary of War ; GENERAL G. T. BEAUREGARD, Macon, Ga.: A good lieutenant-general should be sent here at once to command the corps now commanded by Major-General Cheatham. I have no one to recommend for the position.

"J. B. HOOD, General."

"HEADQUARTERS, six miles from Nashville, on Franklin Pike, December 8, 1864.

"HON. J. A. SEDDON : Major-General Cheatham made a failure on the 30th of November which will be a lesson to him. I think it best he should remain in his position for the present. I withdraw my telegrams of yesterday and to-day on this subject.

"J. B. HOOD, General."

On the 11th of December I wrote the Hon. Mr. Seddon :

. . . "Major-General Cheatham has frankly confessed the great error of which he was guilty, and attaches

↓ "In order to make clear what I have to say in this connection I will quote Governor Isham G. Harris :

"'GOVERNOR JAMES D. PORTER.

"'DEAR SIR : . . . General Hood, on the march to Franklin, spoke to me, in the presence of Major [Lieut.-Colonel A. P.] Mason [Assistant Adjutant-General, Army of Tennessee], of the failure of General Cheatham to make the night attack at Spring Hill, and censured him in severe terms for his disobedience of orders. Soon after this, being alone with Major Mason, the latter remarked that "General Cheatham was not to blame about the matter last night. I did not send him the order." I asked if he had communicated the fact to General Hood. He answered that he had not. I replied that "it is due General Cheatham that this explanation should be made." Thereupon Major Mason joined General Hood and gave him the information. Afterward General Hood said to me that he had done injustice to General Cheatham, and requested me to inform him that he held him blameless for the failure at Spring Hill, and on the day following the battle of Franklin I was informed by General Hood that he had addressed a note to General Cheatham assuring him that he did not censure him with the failure to attack.

"'Very respectfully,　　ISHAM G. HARRIS.
"'MEMPHIS, TENNESSEE, May 20, 1877.'

"The first intimation made to me, from any source, that my conduct at Spring Hill, on the 29th of November, 1864, or during the night of that day, was the subject of criticism, was the receipt of a note from General Hood, written and received on the morning of the 3d of December. This is the communication referred to in the letter of Governor Harris, above quoted. This note was read, so far as I know, by only four persons besides myself — my chief-of-staff, James D. Porter, Governor

much blame to himself. While his error lost so much to the country, it has been a severe lesson to him, by which he will profit in the future. In consideration of this, and of his previous conduct, I think that it is best that he should retain for the present the command he now holds."↓

The best move in my career as a soldier I was thus destined to behold come to naught. The discovery that the army, after a forward march of one hundred and eighty miles, was still, seemingly, unwilling to accept battle unless under the protection of breastworks, caused me to experience grave concern. In my inmost heart I questioned whether or not I would ever succeed in eradicating this evil. It seemed to me I had exhausted every means in the power of one man to remove this stumbling-block to the Army of Tennessee. On the morning of the 30th of November, Lee was on the march up the Franklin pike, when the main body of the army, at Spring Hill, awoke to find the Federals had disappeared.

I hereupon decided, before the enemy would be able to reach his stronghold at Nashville, to make that same afternoon another and final effort to overtake and rout him, and drive him into the Big Harpeth River at Franklin, since I could no longer hope to get between him and Nashville, by reason of the short distance from Franklin to that city, and the advantage which the Federals enjoyed in the possession of the direct road.

At early dawn the troops were put in motion in the direction of Franklin, marching as rapidly as possible to overtake the enemy before he crossed the Big Harpeth, eighteen miles from Spring Hill. Lieutenant-General Lee had crossed Duck River after dark the night previous, and, in order to reach Franklin, was obliged to march a distance of thirty miles. The head of his column arrived at Spring Hill at 9 A. M. on the 30th, and, after a short rest, followed in the wake of the main body.

Isham G. Harris, Major J. F. Cumming, of Georgia, and John C. Burch. Not having been in the habit of carrying a certificate of military character, I attached no special value to the paper, and it was lost somewhere during the campaign in North Carolina. Governor Porter and Major Cumming agree with me that the following was the substance of the note :

"　'December 3d, 1864.

"'MY DEAR GENERAL : I do not censure you for the failure at Spring Hill. I am satisfied you are not responsible for it. I witnessed the splendid manner in which you delivered battle at Franklin on the 30th ult. I now have a higher estimate of you as a soldier than I ever had. You can rely upon my friendship. Yours very truly,　J. B. HOOD, General.
"'TO GENERAL B. F. CHEATHAM.'

"On the morning of the 4th of December I went to the headquarters of General Hood, and, referring to his note and the criticism of my conduct that had evidently been made by some one, I said to him : 'A great opportunity was lost at Spring Hill, but you know that I obeyed your orders there, as everywhere, literally and promptly.' General Hood not only did not dissent from what I said, but exhibited the most cordial manner, coupled with confidence and friendship. The subject was never again alluded to by General Hood to myself, nor, so far as I know, to any one. When he wrote, under date of December 11th, 1864, to Mr. Seddon, that 'Major-General Cheatham has frankly confessed the great error of which he was guilty, and attaches much blame to himself,' he made a statement for which there was not the slightest foundation."— GENERAL CHEATHAM, in the "BIVOUAC."

Stewart's corps was first in order of march; Cheatham followed immediately, and Lieutenant-General Lee in rear. Within about three miles of Franklin, the enemy was discovered on the ridge over which passes the turnpike. As soon as the Confederate troops began to deploy, and skirmishers were thrown forward, the Federals withdrew slowly to the environs of the town.

It was about 3 P. M. when Lieutenant-General Stewart moved to the right of the pike and began to establish his position in front of the enemy. Major-General Cheatham's corps, as it arrived in turn, filed off to the left of the road, and was also disposed in line of battle. The artillery was instructed to take no part in the engagement, on account of the danger to which women and children in the village would be exposed. ♭ General Forrest was ordered to post cavalry on both flanks, and, if the assault proved successful, to complete the ruin of the enemy by capturing those who attempted to escape in the direction of Nashville. Lee's corps, as it arrived, was held in reserve, owing to the lateness

MAJOR-GENERAL PATRICK R. CLEBURNE, C. S. A., KILLED AT FRANKLIN, NOVEMBER 30, 1864. FROM A PHOTOGRAPH.

of the hour and my inability, conseqently, to post it on the extreme left. Schofield's position was rendered favorable for defense by open ground in front, and temporary intrenchments which the Federals had had time to throw up, notwithstanding the Confederate forces had marched in pursuit with all possible speed. At one or two points, along a short space, a slight abatis had been hastily constructed, by felling some small locust saplings in the vicinity.

Soon after Cheatham's corps was massed on the left, Major-General Cleburne came to me where I was seated on my horse in rear of the line, and asked permission to form his division in two, or, if I remember correctly, three lines for the assault. I at once granted his request, stating that I desired the Federals to be driven into the river in their immediate rear, and directing him to advise me as soon as he had completed the new disposition of his troops. Shortly afterward Cheatham and Stewart reported all in readiness for action, and received orders to drive the enemy from his position into the river *at all hazards*. About that time Cleburne returned, and, expressing himself with an enthusiasm which he had never before betrayed in our intercourse, said, "General, I am ready, and have more hope in the final success of

our cause than I have had at any time since the first gun was fired." I replied, "God grant it!" He turned and moved at once toward the head of his division; a few moments thereafter he was lost to my sight in the tumult of battle. These last words, spoken to me by this brave and distinguished soldier, I have often recalled; they can never leave my memory, as within forty minutes after he had uttered them he lay lifeless upon or near the breastworks of the foe.

The two corps advanced in battle array at about 4 P. M., and soon swept away the first line of the Federals, who were driven back upon the main line. At this moment resounded a concentrated roar of musketry, which recalled to me some of the deadliest struggles in Virginia, and which now proclaimed that the possession of Nashville was once more dependent upon the fortunes of war. The conflict continued to rage with intense fury; our troops succeeded in breaking the main line at one or more points, capturing and turning some of the guns on their opponents.

Just at this critical moment of the battle, a brigade of the enemy, reported to have been Stanley's, ¶ gallantly charged, and restored the Federal line, capturing at the same time about one thousand of our troops within the intrenchments. Still

♭ General J. D. Cox has pointed out that the reports confirm his own observation that Hood's artillery was used in the battle.— EDITORS.

¶ Opdycke's brigade of Stanley's Fourth Corps, and the second line of Reilly's brigade of Cox's Twenty-third Corps.— EDITORS.

MAP OF
THE BATTLE-FIELD
OF NASHVILLE.
Dec. 15-16th, 1864.

Drawn by Wilbur F. Foster,
Major Engineer Corps, C. S. A.

EXPLANATIONS.

Confederate Advanced Lines.
Confederate Lines, Morning, Dec. 15th.
Confederate Lines, 1 P. M., Dec. 15th.
Confederate Lines, from Morn to 4 P. M., Dec. 16th.
Federal Lines, 3 P. M., Dec. 15th.
Federal Lines, 4 P. M., Dec. 16th.

Scale of Miles.

Rand, McNally & Co., Engr's, Chicago.

FROM THE "BIVOUAC" FOR AUGUST, 1885.

434

OVERTON'S HOUSE, HOOD'S HEADQUARTERS AT NASHVILLE.   FROM A PHOTOGRAPH TAKEN IN 1884.

the ground was obstinately contested, and at several points upon the immediate sides of the breastworks the combatants endeavored to use the musket upon one another, by inverting and raising it perpendicularly, in order to fire ; neither antagonist, at this juncture, was able to retreat without almost a certainty of death. It was reported that soldiers were even dragged from one side of the breastworks to the other by men reaching over hurriedly and seizing their enemy by the hair or the collar.

Just before dark Edward Johnson's division of Lee's corps moved gallantly to the support of Cheatham ; although it made a desperate charge and succeeded in capturing three stand of colors, it did not effect a permanent breach in the line of the enemy. Unfortunately, the two remaining divisions could not become engaged owing to the obscurity of night. The struggle continued with more or less violence until 9 P. M., when skirmishing and much desultory firing followed until about 3 A. M. the ensuing morning. The enemy then withdrew, leaving his dead and wounded upon the field. Thus terminated one of the fiercest conflicts of the war.

Nightfall, which closed in upon us so soon after the beginning of the battle, prevented the formation and participation of Lee's entire corps on the extreme left. This, it may safely be asserted, saved Schofield's army from destruction. I might, with equal assurance, assert that had Lieutenant-General Lee been in advance at Spring Hill the previous afternoon Schofield's army never would have passed that point.

☆ As shown by Colonel Mason's official report, made on the 10th of December, ten days after the battle, our effective strength was : Infantry, 18,342 ; artillery, 2405 ; cavalry, 2306,—total, 23,053. This last number, subtracted from 30,600, the strength of the army at Florence, shows a total loss from all causes of 7547, from the 6th of November to the 10th of December, which period includes the engagements at Columbia, Franklin, and of Forrest's cavalry. The enemy's estimate of our losses, as well as of the number of Confederate colors captured, is errone-

Major-General Cleburne had been distinguished for his admirable conduct upon many fields, and his loss at this moment was irreparable. He was a man of equally quick perception and strong character, and was, especially in one respect, in advance of many of our people. He possessed the boldness and the wisdom earnestly to advocate, at an early period of the war, the freedom of the negro and the enrollment of the young and able-bodied men of that race. This stroke of policy and additional source of strength to our armies would, in my opinion, have given us our independence.

After the failure of my cherished plan to crush Schofield's army before it reached its strongly fortified position around Nashville, I remained with an effective force of only 23,053. ☆ I was therefore well aware of our inability to attack the Federals in their new stronghold with any hope of success, although Schofield's troops had abandoned the field at Franklin, leaving their dead and wounded in our possession, and had hastened with considerable alarm into their fortifications — which latter information, in regard to their condition after the battle, I obtained through spies. I knew equally well that in the absence of the prestige of complete victory I could not venture with my small force to cross the Cumberland River into Kentucky, without first receiving reënforcements from the Trans-Mississippi Department. I felt convinced that the Tennesseans and Kentuckians would not join our forces, since we had failed in the first instance to defeat the Federal army and capture Nashville. The President was still urgent in his instructions relative to the transference of

ous, as will be seen by my telegram of December 15th to the Secretary of War :

"The enemy claim that we lost thirty colors in the fight at Franklin. We lost thirteen, capturing nearly the same number. The men who bore ours were killed on or within the enemy's interior line of works." J. B. H.

General J. D. Cox states in his "Franklin and Nashville" that the capture of 22 colors by Reilly and 10 by Opdycke was officially reported and verified at the time.— EDITORS.

troops to the Army of Tennessee from Texas, and I daily hoped to receive the glad tidings of their safe passage across the Mississippi River.

Thus, unless strengthened by these long-looked-for reënforcements, the only remaining chance of success in the campaign, at this juncture, was to take position, intrench about Nashville, and await Thomas's attack, which, if handsomely repulsed, might afford us an opportunity to follow up our advantage on the spot, and enter the city on the heels of the enemy.

I could not afford to turn southward, unless for the *special* purpose of forming a junction with the

MAJOR-GENERAL J. B. STEEDMAN. FROM A PHOTOGRAPH.

expected reënforcements from Texas, and with the avowed intention to march back again upon Nashville. In truth, our army was in that condition which rendered it more judicious the men should face a decisive issue rather than retreat— in other words, rather than renounce the honor of their cause, without having made a last and manful effort to lift up the sinking fortunes of the Confederacy.

I therefore determined to move upon Nashville, to intrench, to accept the chances of reënforcements from Texas, and, even at the risk of an attack in the meantime by overwhelming numbers, to adopt the only feasible means of defeating the enemy with my own reduced numbers, viz., to await his attack, and, if favored by success, to follow him into his works. I was apprised of each accession to Thomas's army, but was still unwilling to abandon the ground as long as I saw a shadow of probability of assistance from the Trans-Mississippi Department, or of victory in battle ;

and, as I have just remarked, the troops would, I believed, return better satisfied even after defeat if, in grasping at the last straw, they felt that a brave and vigorous effort had been made to save the country from disaster. Such, at the time, was my opinion, which I have since had no reason to alter.

In accordance with these convictions I ordered the army to move forward on the 1st of December in the direction of Nashville ; Lee's corps marched in advance, followed by Stewart's and Cheatham's corps, and the troops bivouacked that night in the vicinity of Brentwood. On the morning of the 2d the march was resumed, and line of battle formed in front of Nashville. Lee's corps was placed in the center and across the Franklin pike ; Stewart occupied the left and Cheatham the right — their flanks extending as near the Cumberland as possible, whilst Forrest's cavalry filled the gap between them and the river.

General Rousseau occupied Murfreesboro' in rear of our right, with about eight thousand men, heavily intrenched. General Bate's division and Sears's and Brown's brigades were ordered, on the 5th, to report at that point to General Forrest, who was instructed to watch closely that detachment of the enemy. The same day information was received of the capture of 100 prisoners, two pieces of artillery, 20 wagons and teams by Forrest's cavalry at La Vergne ; of the capture and destruction of three block houses on the Chattanooga Railroad by Bate's division ; and of the seizure the day previous by Chalmers of two transports on the Cumberland River with 300 mules on board.

We had in our possession two engines and several cars, which ran as far south as Pulaski. Dispatches were sent to Generals Beauregard and Maury to repair the railroad from Corinth to Decatur, as our trains would be running in a day or two to the latter point. This means of transportation was of great service in furnishing supplies to the army. When we reached middle Tennessee our troops had an abundance of provisions, although sorely in need of shoes and clothing.

General Bate's division was ordered to return to the army ; Forrest was instructed to direct Palmer's and Mercer's infantry brigades to thoroughly intrench on Stewart's Creek, or at La Vergne, according as he might deem more judicious, to constitute, with these troops and his cavalry, a force in observation of the enemy at Murfreesboro', and, lastly, to send a brigade of cavalry to picket the river at Lebanon.

The Federals having been reported to be massing cavalry at Edgefield, Forrest was instructed to meet and drive them back, if they attempted to cross the Cumberland. The same day, the 10th of December, Generals Stewart and Cheatham were directed to construct detached works in rear of their flanks, which rested near the river, in order to protect these flanks against an effort by the Federals to turn them. Although every possible exertion was made by these officers, the works were not completed when, on the 15th, the Federal army moved out and attacked both flanks, whilst the main assault was directed against our left. It was my intention to have made these defenses self-sustaining, but time was not allowed, as the enemy attacked on the morning of the 15th. Throughout that day they were repulsed at all points of the general line with heavy loss, and only succeeded toward evening in capturing the infantry outposts on our left, and with them the small force together with the artillery posted in these unfinished works. Finding that the main movement of the Federals was directed against our left, the chief engineer was instructed carefully to select a line in prolongation of the left flank; Cheatham's corps was withdrawn from the right during the night of the 15th and posted on the left of Stewart — Cheatham's left resting near the Brentwood Hills. The men were ordered to construct breastworks there during that same night.

The morning of the 16th found us with Lee's right on Overton's Hill. At an early hour the enemy made a general attack along our front, and were again and again repulsed at all points with heavy loss, especially in Lee's front. About 3:30 P. M. the Federals concentrated a number of guns against a portion of our line, which passed over a mound on the left of our center, and which had been occupied during the night. This point was favorable for massing troops for an assault under cover of artillery. Accordingly the enemy availed himself of the advantage presented, massed a body of men — apparently one division — at the base of this mound, and, under the fire of artillery, which prevented our men from raising their heads above the breastworks, made a sudden and gallant charge up to and over our intrenchments. Our line, thus pierced, gave way; soon thereafter it broke at all points, and I beheld for the first and only time a Confederate army abandon the field in confusion. I was seated upon my horse not far in rear when the breach was effected, and soon discovered that all hope to rally the troops was vain.

I did not, I might say, anticipate a break at that time, as our forces up to that moment had repulsed the Federals at every point, and were waving their colors in defiance, crying out to the enemy, "Come on, come on." Just previous to this fatal occurrence I had matured the movement for the next morning. The enemy's right flank, by this hour, stood in air some six miles from Nashville, and I had determined to withdraw my entire force during the night, and attack this exposed flank in rear. I could safely have done so, as I still had open a line of retreat.

The day before the rout, the artillery posted in the detached works had been captured; a number of guns in the main line were abandoned for the reason that the horses could not be brought forward in time to remove them. Thus the total number of guns captured amounted to fifty-four. We had fortunately still remaining a sufficient number of pieces of artillery for the equipment of the army, since, it will be remembered. I had taken with me at the outset of the campaign a large reserve of artillery to use against gun-boats. Our losses in killed and wounded in this engagement were comparatively small, as the troops were protected by breastworks.

Order among the troops was in a measure restored at Brentwood, a few miles in rear of the scene of disaster, through the promptness and gallantry of Clayton's division, which speedily formed and confronted the enemy, with Gibson's brigade and McKenzie's battery, of Fenner's battalion, acting as rear-guard of the rear-guard. General Clayton displayed admirable coolness and courage that afternoon and the next morning in the discharge of his duties. Gibson, who evinced conspicuous gallantry and ability in the handling of his troops, succeeded, in concert with Clayton, in checking and staying the first and most dangerous shock which always follows immediately after a rout. The result was that even after the army passed the Big Harpeth, at Franklin, the brigades and divisions were marching in regular order.

General S. D. Lee displayed his usual energy and skill in handling his troops on the 17th, whilst protecting the rear of our army. Unfortunately, in the afternoon he was wounded and forced to leave the field. General C. L. Stevenson then assumed command of Lee's corps, and ably discharged his duties during the continuance of the retreat to and across the Tennessee River.

General Walthall, one of the most able division commanders in the South, was here ordered to form a rear-guard with eight picked brigades and Forrest's cavalry; the march was then resumed in the direction of Columbia, Stewart's corps moving in front, followed by those of Cheatham and Stevenson. The army bivouacked in line of battle near Duck River on the night of the 18th.

The following day we crossed the river and proceeded on different roads leading toward Bainbridge on the Tennessee. I entertained but little concern in regard to being further harassed by the enemy. I therefore continued to march leisurely, and arrived at Bainbridge on the 25th of December. The following day the march was continued in the direction of Tupelo, at which place Cheatham's corps, the last in the line of march, went into camp on the 10th of January, 1865.

On the 13th of January I sent the following dispatch to the Secretary of War: "I request to be relieved from the command of this army."

Upon General Beauregard's arrival at Tupelo, on the 14th of January, I informed him of my application to be relieved from the command of the army. I again telegraphed the authorities in Richmond, stating that the campaigns to the Alabama line and into Tennessee were my own conception; that I alone was responsible; that I had striven hard to execute them in such manner as to bring victory to our people, and at the same time repeated my desire to be relieved. The President finally complied with my request, and I bade farewell to the Army of Tennessee on the 23d of January, 1865, after having served with it somewhat in excess of eleven months, and having performed my duties to the utmost of my ability.

GENERAL CHEATHAM AT SPRING HILL.

BY B. F. CHEATHAM, MAJOR-GENERAL, C. S. A.

IN pursuance of orders my command [formerly Hardee's] crossed Duck River on the morning of the 29th of November, 1864, the division of Major-General [P. R.] Cleburne in advance, followed by that of Major-General [W. B.] Bate, the division of Major-General [J. C.] Brown in the rear. The march was made as rapidly as the condition of the roads would allow, and without occurrence of note, until about 3 o'clock P. M., when I arrived at Rutherford's Creek, two and one-half miles from Spring Hill. At this point General Hood gave me verbal orders as follows: That I should get Cleburne across the creek and send him forward toward Spring Hill, with instructions to communicate with General Forrest, who was near the village, ascertain from him the position of the enemy, and attack immediately; that I should remain at the creek, assist General Bate in crossing his division, and then go forward and put Bate's command in to support Cleburne; and that he would push Brown forward to join me. [See p. 432.]

As soon as the division of General Bate had crossed the creek, I rode forward, and at a point on the road about one and a half miles from Spring Hill I saw the left of Cleburne's command just disappearing over a hill to the left of the road. Halting here, I waited a few minutes for the arrival of Bate, and formed his command with his right upon the position of Cleburne's left, and ordered him forward to the support of Cleburne. Shortly after Bate's division had disappeared over the same range of hills, I heard firing toward Cleburne's right, and just then General Brown's division had come up. I thereupon ordered Brown to proceed to the right, turn the range of hills over which Cleburne and Bate had crossed, and to form line of battle and attack to the right of Cleburne. The division of General Brown was in motion to execute this order, when I received a message from Cleburne that his right brigade had been struck in the flank by the enemy and had suffered severely, and that he had been compelled to fall back and re-form with a change of front.

It so happened that the direction of Cleburne's advance was such as had exposed his right flank to the enemy's line. When his command was formed on the road by which he had marched from Rutherford's Creek, neither the village of Spring Hill nor the turnpike could be seen. Instead of advancing directly upon Spring Hill his forward movement was a little south of west and almost parallel with the turnpike toward Columbia, instead of north-west upon the enemy's lines south and east of the village. General Cleburne was killed in the assault upon Franklin the next day, and I had no opportunity to learn from him how it was that the error of direction occurred. Meanwhile, General Bate, whom I had placed in position on the left of Cleburne's line of march, continued to move forward in the same direction

until he had reached the farm of N. F. Cheairs, one and a half miles south of Spring Hill.

After Brown had reached the position indicated to him and had formed a line of battle, he sent to inform me that it would be certain disaster for him to attack, as the enemy's line extended beyond his right several hundred yards. I sent word to him to throw back his right brigade and make the attack. I had already sent couriers after General Bate to bring him back and direct him to join Cleburne's left. Going to the right of my line, I found Generals Brown and Cleburne, and the latter reported that he had re-formed his division. I then gave orders to Brown and Cleburne that, as soon as they could connect their lines, they should attack the enemy, who were then in sight; informing them at the same time that General Hood had just told me that Stewart's column was close at hand, and that General Stewart had been ordered to go to my right and place his command across the pike. I furthermore said to them that I would go myself and see that General Bate was placed in position to connect with them, and immediately rode to the left of my line for that purpose.

During all this time I had met and talked with General Hood repeatedly, our field headquarters being not over one hundred yards apart. After Cleburne's repulse I had been along my line, and had seen that Brown's right was outflanked several hundred yards. I had urged General Hood to hurry up Stewart and place him on my right, and had received from him the assurance that this would be done; and this assurance, as before stated, I had communicated to Cleburne and Brown.

When I returned from my left, where I had been to get Bate in position, and was on the way to the right of my line, it was dark; but I intended to move forward with Cleburne and Brown and make the attack, knowing that Bate would be in position to support them. Stewart's column had already passed by on the way toward the turnpike, and I presumed he would be in position on my right.

On reaching the road where General Hood's field headquarters had been established I found a courier with a message from General Hood requesting me to come to him at Captain Thompson's house, about one and a fourth miles back on the road to Rutherford's Creek. I found General Stewart with General Hood. The commanding general there informed me that he had concluded to wait until the morning, and then directed me to hold my command in readiness to attack at daylight. I was never more astonished than when General Hood informed me that he had concluded to postpone the attack till daylight. The road was still open — orders to remain quiet until morning — and nothing to prevent the enemy from marching to Franklin.

About 11 o'clock that night General Hood sent

Reprinted from the "Southern Bivouac" for April, 1885. Dated November 30th, 1881.

438

Major-General [Edward] Johnson, whose division had marched in rear of Stewart's corps, to report to me. I directed Major Bostick, of my staff, to place Johnson on my extreme left. About midnight Major Bostick returned and reported that he had been near to the turnpike, and could hear straggling troops passing northward. While he was talking about this to Colonel Porter, my chief-of-staff, a courier from headquarters brought a note from Major [A. P.] Mason [Assistant-Adjutant General], to the effect that General Hood had just learned that stragglers were passing along the road in front of my left, and "the commanding general says you had better order your picket line to fire on them." Upon reading the note I ordered Major Bostick to return to General Johnson, whose command was on my left and nearest the pike, and say to him that he must take a brigade, or, if necessary, his whole division, and go on to the pike and cut off anything that might be passing. Major Bostick afterward informed me that General Johnson commenced complaining bitterly at having been "loaned out," and asked why General Cheatham did not order one of his own divisions to go in; but at length ordered his horse and rode with Major Bostick close up to the turnpike, where they found everything quiet and no one passing. General Johnson came with Major Bostick to my quarters, and informed me of what

they had done. It was now about 2 o'clock on the morning of the 30th.

This suggestion that I had better order my pickets to fire upon stragglers passing in front of my left was the only order, if that can be called an order, that I received from General Hood after leaving him at his quarters early in the night, when he had informed me of his determination to wait until daylight to attack the enemy. What reason General Stewart gave for not reaching the turnpike I do not know. As I have already stated, General Hood said to me repeatedly, when I met him between 4 and 6 o'clock in the afternoon, "Stewart will be here in a few minutes." Stewart's column did not come up until about dark.

General Stewart says he was at Rutherford's Creek before General Brown's division crossed that stream. He also says that General Hood there ordered him to form line of battle on the south side of the creek, and that he was not allowed to move thence until dusk. If General Stewart had followed Brown he would have been in position on my right, across the turnpike, before dark. That he would have executed an order to make such disposition of his command, no one who knows that officer will doubt; and he would have done it in the darkness of midnight as surely and as certainly as in the day.

THE DEATH OF GENERALS CLEBURNE AND ADAMS.

IN the "Bivouac" for October, 1885, James Barr, of Company E, 65th Illinois Volunteers, writing from Barwell, Kansas, said:

"I was somewhat interested in that terrible affair at Franklin. I was a prisoner near the cotton-gin for about three or four minutes, was ordered to the rear by some of the Confederates, and would have had a trip to Andersonville had it not been for that 'devil-may-care' counter-charge made by Illinoisans and Kentuckians. Our Colonel Stewart (65th Illinois) tried hard to save the life of General John Adams, of Mississippi. Colonel Stewart called to our men not to fire on him, but it was too late. Adams rode his horse over the ditch to the top of the parapet, undertook to grasp the 'old flag' from the hands of our color-sergeant, when he fell, horse and all, shot by the color-guard.

"I was a reënlisted veteran, and went through twenty-seven general engagements, but I am sure that Franklin was the hardest-fought field that I ever looked upon. General J. D. Cox [in his 'Franklin and Nashville'] censures General Wagner for holding to his advanced position too long, calls his action a gross blunder, etc.; but, as one of Cox's men, I looked upon the matter in a different light. I think if Cleburne had not struck Wagner's two brigades as he did that his brave lads would have broken our line successfully; but, as it was, his men were badly winded with his work with Wagner, which gave Opdycke's and White's men a better chance to check him at the cotton-gin. The way I saw it was this: I was acting as orderly and standing a few paces east of the cotton-gin. The first Confederate troops that came in view were Stewart's corps on our left with Cheatham's corps to the left of Stewart. The Confederate line moved easily and steadily on, until Cleburne

was checked for the time by Wagner. The short time lost by Cleburne threw Stewart's line too far in advance. Stewart was first to receive the fire from our main line, and was unable to carry our works, his men who were not killed or wounded being compelled to retire. Now Cleburne, who had been delayed by Wagner, came up just in time to receive a heavy right oblique fire from the men who had repulsed Stewart's corps. I never saw men put in such a terrible position as Cleburne's division was in for a few minutes. The wonder is that any of them escaped death or capture."

In the "Bivouac" for November, 1885, John McQuaide, of Vicksburg, Miss., wrote:

"Some time since I called attention to the inaccuracies of current history in regard to the manner of General Patrick Cleburne's death at Franklin. The subject has been brought to my mind again by Mr. James Barr's letter. It has been stated that Cleburne and horse were killed on top of the works, which is incorrect. It was General John Adams, of Loring's division, Stewart's corps. Early next morning I assisted in putting his body in an ambulance; also the body of General Cleburne. Adams's horse was a bay. It was dead upon the works, with its front legs toward the inner side of the works. Adams's body was lying outside, at the base of the works, when I helped to pick it up. Cleburne's body was not less than fifty or sixty yards from the works, and on nearly a straight line from where Adams fell. This may appear strange, as the two generals belonged to different divisions and different corps; but there were repeated charges made upon the works. When one command was repulsed another would be thrown forward."

DEFENDING AN EMBRASURE.

REPELLING HOOD'S INVASION OF TENNESSEE.

BY HENRY STONE, BREVET COLONEL, U. S. V., MEMBER OF THE STAFF OF GENERAL THOMAS.

ON September 28th, 1864, less than four weeks from the day the Union forces occupied Atlanta, General Sherman, who found his still uncon-quered enemy, General Hood, threatening his communications in Georgia, and that formidable raider, General Forrest, playing the mischief in west Tennessee, sent to the latter State two divisions — General Newton's of the Fourth Corps, and General J. D. Morgan's of the Fourteenth — to aid in destroying, if possible, that intrepid dragoon. To make assurance doubly sure, the next day he ordered General George H. Thomas, his most capable and experienced lieutenant, and the commander of more than three-fifths of his grand army, "back to Stevenson and Decherd . . . to look to Tennessee."

No order could have been more unwelcome to General Thomas. It removed him from the command of his own thoroughly organized and harmonious army of sixty thousand veterans, whom he knew and trusted, and who knew and loved him, and relegated him to the position of super-visor of communications. It also sent him to the rear just when great preparations were making for an advance. But, as often happens, what seemed an adverse fate opened the door to great, unforeseen opportunity. The task of expelling Forrest and reopening the broken communications was speedily completed, and on the 17th of October General Thomas wrote to General Sherman, "I hope to join you very soon." Sherman, however, had other views, and the hoped-for junction was never made. On the 19th he wrote to General Thomas:

"I will send back to Tennessee the Fourth Corps, all dismounted cavalry, all sick and wounded, and all incumbrances whatever except what I can haul in our wagons. . . . I want you to remain in Tennessee and take command of all my [military] division not actually present with me. Hood's army may be set down at forty thousand (40,000) of all arms, fit for duty. . . . If you can defend the line of the Tennessee in my absence of three (3) months, it is all I ask."

With such orders, and under such circumstances, General Thomas was left to play his part in the new campaign.

General Hood, after a series of daring adventures which baffled all Sherman's calculations ("he can turn and twist like a fox," said Sherman, "and wear out my army in pursuit"), concentrated his entire force, except Forrest's cavalry, at Gadsden, Alabama, on the 22d of October, while General Sherman established his headquarters at Gaylesville,— a "position," as he wrote to General Halleck, "very good to watch the enemy." In spite of this "watch," Hood suddenly appeared on the 26th at Decatur, on the Tennessee River, seventy-five miles north-west of Gadsden. This move was a complete surprise, and evidently "meant business." The Fourth Corps, numbering about twelve thousand men, commanded by Major-General D. S. Stanley, was at once ordered from Gaylesville, to report to General Thomas. On the 1st of November its leading division reached Pulaski, Tennessee, a small town on the railroad, about forty miles north of Decatur, where it was joined four days later by the other two.

Making a slight though somewhat lengthened demonstration against Decatur, General Hood pushed on to Tuscumbia, forty-five miles west. Here he expected to find — what he had weeks before ordered — ample supplies, and the railroad in operation to Corinth. But he was doomed to disappointment. Instead of being in condition to make the rapid and triumphant march with which he had inflamed the ardor of his troops, he was detained three weeks, a delay fatal to his far-reaching hopes. Placing one corps on the north side of the river at Florence, he waited for supplies and for Forrest, who had been playing havoc throughout west Tennessee, from the line of the Mississippi border, northward to Kentucky, and was under orders to join him.

Convinced now of Hood's serious intentions, General Sherman also ordered the Twenty-third Corps, ten thousand men, under command of Major-General J. M. Schofield, to report to General Thomas. Reaching Pulaski, with one division, on the 14th of November, General Schofield, though inferior in rank to Stanley, assumed command by virtue of being a department commander. The whole force gathered there was less than 18,000 men; while in front were some 5000 cavalry, consisting of a brigade of about 1500, under General Croxton, and a division of some 3500, under General Edward Hatch, the latter being fortunately intercepted while on his way to join Sherman.

The Confederate army in three corps (S. D. Lee's, A. P. Stewart's, and B. F. Cheatham's) began its northward march from Florence on the 19th of November, in weather of great severity. It rained and snowed and hailed and froze, and the roads were almost impassable. Forrest had come up, with about six thousand cavalry, and led the advance with indomitable energy. Hatch and Croxton made such resistance as they could; but on the 22d the head of Hood's column was at Lawrenceburg, some 16 miles due west of Pulaski, Tennessee and on a road running direct to Columbia, where the railroad and turn-

MAJOR-GENERAL GEORGE H. THOMAS. FROM A PHOTOGRAPH.

pike to Nashville cross Duck River, and where there were less than 800 men to
guard the bridges. The situation at Pulaski, with an enemy nearly three times
as large fairly on the flank, was anything but cheering. Warned by the reports
from General Hatch, and by the orders of General Thomas, who, on the 20th,
had directed General Schofield to prepare to fall back to Columbia, the two
divisions of General J. D. Cox and General George D. Wagner (the latter
Newton's old division) were ordered to march to Lynnville—about half-way

to Columbia — on the 22d. On the 23d the other two divisions, under General Stanley, were to follow with the wagon-trains. It was not a moment too soon. On the morning of the 24th General Cox, who had pushed on to within nine miles of Columbia, was roused by sounds of conflict away to the west. Taking a cross-road, leading south of Columbia, he reached the Mount Pleasant pike just in time to interpose his infantry between Forrest's cavalry and a hapless brigade, under command of Colonel Capron, which was being handled most unceremoniously.⏐ In another hour Forrest would have been in possession of the crossings of Duck River, and the only line of communication with Nashville would have been in the hands of the enemy. General Stanley, who had left Pulaski in the afternoon of the 23d, reached Lynnville after dark. Rousing his command at 1 o'clock in the morning, by 9 o'clock the head of his column connected with Cox in front of Columbia — having marched thirty miles since 2 o'clock of the preceding afternoon. These timely movements saved the little army from utter destruction.

When General Sherman had finally determined on his march to the sea, he requested General Rosecrans, in Missouri, to send to General Thomas two divisions, under General A. J. Smith, which had been lent to General Banks for the Red River expedition, and were now repelling the incursion of Price into Missouri. As they were not immediately forthcoming, General Grant had ordered General Rawlins, his chief-of-staff, to St. Louis, to direct, in person, their speedy embarkation. Thence, on the 7th of November, two weeks before Hood began his advance from Florence, General Rawlins wrote to General Thomas that Smith's command, aggregating nearly 14,000, would begin to leave that place as early as the 10th. No news was ever more anxiously awaited or more eagerly welcomed than this. But the promise could not be fulfilled. Smith had to march entirely across the State of Missouri; and instead of leaving St. Louis on the 10th, he did not arrive there until the 24th. Had he come at the proposed time, it was General Thomas's intention to place him at Eastport, on the Tennessee River, so as to threaten Hood's flank and rear if the latter advanced. With such disposition, the battles of Franklin and Nashville would have been relegated to the category of "events which never come to pass." But when Smith reached St. Louis, Hood was threatening Columbia; and it was an open question whether he would not reach Nashville before the reënforcements from Missouri.

⏐ Major Henry C. Connelly, of the 14th Illinois cavalry, on August 8th, 1887, wrote to the editors as follows:

"When General Hood advanced from the Tennessee River, General Capron's brigade was on the extreme right of our army, and from the 19th of November until the 24th, the day Columbia was reached, we fought Forrest's cavalry. I was with the rear-guard on the occasion referred to; it fell back and found the brigade in good position in line of battle. I rode to General Capron and expressed the opinion that he could not hold his position a moment against the troops pressing us in the rear and on the flanks, which we could easily see advancing rapidly to attack us. General Capron replied that he had been ordered to make a decided stand if it sacrificed every man in his brigade; that we must hold the advancing forces in check to enable the infantry to arrive and get in position. I replied, 'We are destroyed and captured if we remain here.' At this moment General Capron gave the order to retire. While passing through a long lane south of Columbia, Forrest's forces charged the brigade in rear and on both flanks with intrepid courage. Our command was confined to a narrow lane, with men and horses in the highest state of excitement. We were armed with Springfield rifles, which after the first volley were about as serviceable to a cavalryman thus hemmed in as a good club. The men could not reload while mounted, in the excitement of horses as well as soldiers. The only thing that could be done was to get out as promptly as possible, and before Forrest's forces should close in and capture the command.

"This was done successfully. The brigade was composed of the 14th and 16th Illinois cavalry and the 8th Michigan cavalry."

As fast as the Union troops arrived at Columbia, in their hurried retreat from Pulaski, works were thrown up, covering the approaches from the south, and the trains were sent across the river. But the line was found to be longer than the small force could hold; and the river could easily be crossed, above or below the town. Orders were given to withdraw to the north side on the night of the 26th, but a heavy storm prevented. The next night the crossing was made, the railroad bridge was burned, and the pontoon boats were scuttled. This was an all-night job, the last of the pickets crossing at 5 in the morning. It was now the fifth day since the retreat from Pulaski began, and the little army had been exposed day and night to all sorts of weather except sunshine, and had been almost continually on the move. From deserters it was learned that Hood's infantry numbered 40,000, and his cavalry, under Forrest, 10,000 or 12,000. But the Union army was slowly increasing by concentration and the arrival of recruits. It now numbered at Columbia about 23,000 infantry and some 5000 cavalry — of whom only 3500 were mounted. General James H. Wilson, who had been ordered by General Grant to report to General Sherman,— and of whom General Grant wrote, "I believe he will add fifty per cent. to the effectiveness of your cavalry,"— had taken command personally of all General Thomas's cavalry, which was trying to hold the fords east and west of Columbia. [See article by General Wilson, to follow.]

In spite of every opposition, Forrest succeeded in placing one of his divisions on the north side of Duck River before noon of the 28th, and forced back the Union cavalry on roads leading toward Spring Hill and Franklin. At 1 o'clock on the morning of the 29th General Wilson became convinced that the enemy's infantry would begin crossing at daylight, and advised General Schofield to fall back to Franklin. At 3:30 the same morning General Thomas sent him similar orders. Daylight revealed the correctness of Wilson's information. Before sunrise Cheatham's corps, headed by Cleburne's division,— a division unsurpassed for courage, energy, and endurance by any in the Confederate army,— was making its way over Duck River at Davis's Ford, about five miles east of Columbia. The weather had cleared, and it was a bright autumn morning, the air full of invigorating life. General Hood in person accompanied the advance.

When General Schofield was informed that the Confederate infantry were crossing, he sent a brigade, under Colonel P. Sidney Post, on a reconnoissance along the river-bank, to learn if the report was true. He also ordered General Stanley to march with two divisions, Wagner's and Kimball's, to Spring Hill, taking the trains and all the reserve artillery. In less than half an hour after receiving the order, Stanley was on the way. On reaching the point where Rutherford Creek crosses the Franklin Pike, Kimball's division was halted, by order of General Schofield, and faced to the east to cover the crossing against a possible attack from that quarter. In this position Kimball remained all day. Stanley, with the other division, pushed on to Spring Hill. Just before noon, as the head of his column was approaching that place, he met "a cavalry soldier who seemed to be badly scared," who reported that Buford's division of Forrest's cavalry was approaching from the east. The troops were at once double-quicked into the town, and the leading brigade, deploying as it advanced, drove off the enemy just as they were expecting, unmolested, to occupy the place. As the other brigades came up, they also were deployed, forming nearly a semicircle,—Opdycke's brigade stretching in a thin line from the railroad station north of the village to a point some distance east, and Lane's from Opdycke's right to the pike below. Bradley was sent to the front to occupy a knoll some three-fourths of a mile east, commanding all the approaches

VIEW OF THE WINSTEAD HILLS, FRANKLIN, WHERE HOOD FORMED HIS LINE OF BATTLE.   FROM A PHOTOGRAPH.
The right of Wagner's two brigades, in the advanced position, was posted behind the stone wall in the fore-ground.   The Columbia Pike is shown passing over the hills on the left of the picture.

from that direction. Most of the artillery was placed on a rise south of the town. The trains were parked within the semicircle.

From Spring Hill roads radiate to all points, the turnpike between Colum-bia and Franklin being there intersected by turnpikes from Rally Hill and Mount Carmel, as well as by numerous country roads leading to the neigh-boring towns. Possession of that point would not only shut out the Union army from the road to Nashville, but it would effectually bar the way in every direction. Stanley's arrival was not a moment too soon for the safety of the army, and his prompt dispositions and steady courage, as well as his vigorous hold of all the ground he occupied, gave his little command all the moral fruits of a victory.

Hardly had the three brigades, numbering, all told, less than four thousand men, reached the positions assigned them, when Bradley was assailed by a force which the men declared fought too well to be dismounted cavalry. At the same time, at Thompson's Station, three miles north, an attack was made on a small wagon train heading for Franklin; and a dash was made by a detachment of the Confederate cavalry on the Spring Hill station, north-west of the town. It seemed as if the little band, attacked from all points, was threatened with destruction. Bradley's brigade was twice assaulted, but held its own, though with considerable loss, and only a single regiment could be spared to reënforce him. The third assault was more successful, and he was driven back to the edge of the village, Bradley himself receiving a disabling wound in rallying his men. While attempting to follow up this temporary advantage, the enemy, in crossing a wide corn-field, was opened upon with spherical case-shot from eight guns posted on the knoll, and soon scattered in considerable confusion. These attacks undoubtedly came from Cleburne's division, and were made under the eye of the corps commander, General Cheatham, and the army commander, General Hood. That they were not successful, especially as the other two divisions of the same corps, Brown's and Bate's, were close at hand, and Stewart's corps not far off, seems un-

BREVET MAJOR-GENERAL EMERSON OPDYCKE.
FROM A PHOTOGRAPH.

accountable. Except this one small division deployed in a long thin line to cover the wagons, there were no Union troops within striking distance; the cavalry were about Mount Carmel, five miles east, fully occupied in keeping Forrest away from Franklin and the Harpeth River crossings. The nearest aid was Kimball's division, seven miles south, at Rutherford Creek. The other three divisions of infantry which made up Schofield's force — Wood's, Cox's, and Ruger's (in part) — were still at Duck River. Thus night closed down upon the solitary division, on whose boldness of action devolved the safety of the whole force which Sherman had spared from his march to the sea to breast the tide of Hood's invasion. When night came, the danger increased rather than diminished. A single Confederate brigade, like Adams's or Cockrell's or Maney's,— veterans since Shiloh,— planted squarely across the pike, either south or north of Spring Hill, would have effectually prevented Schofield's retreat, and daylight would have found his whole force cut off from every avenue of escape by more than twice its numbers, to assault whom would have been madness, and to avoid whom would have been impossible.

Why Cleburne and Brown failed to drive away Stanley's one division before dark; why Bate failed to possess himself of the pike south of the town; why Stewart failed to lead his troops to the pike at the north; why Forrest, with his audacious temper and his enterprising cavalry, did not fully hold Thompson's Station or the crossing of the West Harpeth, half-way to Franklin: these are to this day disputed questions among the Confederate commanders; and it is not proposed to discuss them here. The afternoon and night of November 29th, 1864, may well be set down in the calendar of

CARTER HOUSE (UNDER STEEPLE). GIN-HOUSE. ROPER'S KNOB.

THE BATTLE-FIELD OF FRANKLIN, TENNESSEE, LOOKING NORTH FROM GENERAL CHEATHAM'S HEADQUARTERS. FROM A PHOTOGRAPH.

lost opportunities. The heroic valor of the same troops the next day, and their frightful losses as they attempted to retrieve their mistake, show what might have been.

By 8 o'clock at night — two hours only after sunset, on a moonless night — at least two corps of Hood's army were in line of battle facing the turnpike, and not half a mile away. The long line of Confederate camp-fires burned

MAJOR-GENERAL D. S. STANLEY.
FROM A PHOTOGRAPH.

bright, and the men could be seen standing around them or sauntering about in groups. Now and then a few would come almost to the pike and fire at a passing Union squad, but without provoking a reply. General Schofield, who had remained at Duck River all day, reached Spring Hill about 7 P. M., with Ruger's division and Whitaker's brigade. Leaving the latter to cover a cross-road a mile or two below the town, he started with Ruger about 9 P. M. to force a passage at Thompson's Station, supposed to be in the hands of the enemy. At 11 P. M. General Cox arrived with his division, and soon after Schofield returned to Spring Hill with the welcome news that the way was open. From Thompson's Station he sent his engineer officer, Captain William J. Twining, to Franklin, to telegraph the situation to General Thomas, all communication with whom had been cut off since early morning. Captain Twining's dispatch shows most clearly the critical condition of affairs: "The general says he will not be able to get farther than Thompson's Station to-night. . . . He regards his situation as extremely perilous. . . . Thinking the troops under A. J. Smith's command had reached Franklin, General Schofield directed me to have them pushed down to Spring Hill by daylight to-morrow." This was Tuesday. The day before, General Thomas had telegraphed to General Schofield that Smith had not yet arrived, but would be at Nashville in three days — that is, Thursday. The expectation of finding him at Franklin, therefore, was like a drowning man's catching at a straw.

Just before midnight Cox started from Spring Hill for Franklin, and was ordered to pick up Ruger at Thompson's Station. At 1 A. M. he was on the road, and the train, over five miles long, was drawn out. At the very outset it had to cross a bridge in single file. So difficult was this whole movement, that it was 5 o'clock in the morning before the wagons were fairly under way. As the head of the train passed Thompson's Station, it was attacked by the Confederate cavalry, and for a while there was great consternation. Wood's division, which had followed Cox from Duck River, was marched along to the east of the pike, to protect the train, and the enemy were speedily driven off. It was near daybreak when the last wagon left Spring Hill. Kimball's division followed Wood's, and at 4 o'clock Wagner drew in his lines, his skirmishers remaining till it was fairly daylight. The rear-guard was commanded by Colonel Emerson Opdycke, who was prepared, if necessary, to sacrifice the last man to secure the safety of the main body. So efficiently did his admirable brigade do its work, that, though surrounded by a cloud of the enemy's cavalry, which made frequent dashes at its lines, not a straggler nor a wagon was left behind. The ground was strewn with knapsacks cut from the shoulders of a lot of raw recruits weighed down with their unaccustomed burden.

The head of the column, under General Cox, reached the outskirts of Franklin about the same hour that the rear-guard was leaving Spring Hill. Here the tired, sleepy, hungry

1. THE CARTER HOUSE, FROM THE SIDE TOWARD THE TOWN. 2. THE CARTER HOUSE, FROM THE CONFEDERATE SIDE. 3. FRONT VIEW OF THE CARTER HOUSE. FROM PHOTOGRAPHS TAKEN IN 1884.

men, who had fought and marched, day and night, for nearly a week, threw up a line of earth-works on a slight eminence which guards the southern approach to the town, even before they made their coffee. Then they gladly dropped anywhere for the much-needed "forty winks." Slowly the rest of the weary column, regiment after regiment of worn-out men, filed into the works, and continued the line, till a complete bridge-head, from the river-bank above to the river-bank below, encircled the town. By noon of the 30th all the troops had come up, and the wagons were crossing the river, which was already fordable, notwithstanding the recent heavy rainfalls. The rear-guard was still out, having an occasional bout with the enemy. [See map of the field, p. 430.]

The Columbia Pike bisected the works, which at that point were built just in front of the Carter house, a one-story brick dwelling west of the pike, and a large gin-house on the east side. Between the gin-house and the river the works were partly protected in front by a hedge of Osage orange, and on the knoll, near the railroad cut close to the bank, were two batteries belonging to the Fourth Corps. Near the Carter house was a considerable thicket of locust trees. Except these obstructions, the whole ground in front was entirely unobstructed and fenceless, and, from the works, every part of it was in plain sight. General Cox's division of three brigades, commanded that day, in order from left to right, by Colonels Stiles and Casement and General Reilly, occupied the ground between the Columbia Pike and the river above the town. The front line consisted of eight regiments, three in the works and one in reserve for each of the brigades of Stiles and Casement, while Reilly's brigade nearest the pike had but two regiments in the works, and two in a second line, with still another regiment behind that. West of the pike, reaching to a ravine through which passes a road branching from the Carter's Creek Pike, was Ruger's division of two brigades — the third, under General Cooper, not having come up from Johnsonville. Strickland's brigade, of four regiments, had two in the works and two in reserve. Two of these regiments, the 72d Illinois and 44th Missouri, belonged to A. J. Smith's corps, and had reported to General Schofield only the day before. A third, which was in reserve, the 183d Ohio, was a large and entirely new regiment, having been mustered into service only three weeks before, and having joined the army for the first time on the 28th. Moore's brigade, of six regiments, had four in the works and two in reserve. Beyond Ruger, reaching from the ravine to the river below, was Kimball's division of the Fourth Corps,— all veterans,— consisting of three brigades commanded by Generals William Grose and Walter C. Whitaker and Colonel Isaac M. Kirby. All the troops in the works were ordered to report to General Cox, to whom was assigned the command of the defenses.⚓ General Wood's division of the Fourth Corps had gone over the river with the trains; and two brigades of Wagner's division, which had so valiantly stood their ground at Spring Hill and covered the rear since, were halted on a slope about half a mile to the front. Opdycke had brought his brigade within the works, and held them massed, near the pike, behind the Carter house. Besides the guns on the knoll, near the railroad cut, there were six pieces in Reilly's works; four on Strickland's left; two on Moore's left, and four on Grose's left — in all, twenty-six guns in that part of the works, facing south, and twelve more in reserve, on or near the Columbia Pike.

As the bright autumn day, hazy with the golden light of an Indian summer atmosphere, wore away, the troops that had worked so hard looked hopefully forward to a prospect of ending it in peace and rest, preparatory either to a night march to Nashville, or to a reënforcement by Smith's corps and General Thomas. But about 2 o'clock, some suspicious movements on the hills a mile or two away — the waving of signal flags and the deployment of the enemy in line of battle — caused General Wagner to send his adjutant-general, from the advanced position where his two brigades had halted, to his commanding general, with the information that Hood seemed to be preparing for attack. In a very short time the whole Confederate line could be

⚓ General D. S. Stanley, who commanded the Fourth Corps, takes exception to this statement. Some of his troops as they arrived were assigned to positions by General Cox. General Stanley, in the performance of his duty, went with General Schofield to the north side of the river, but returned when the firing began and assisted in rallying Wagner's brigades, of his corps, during which he was wounded. General Schofield said in his report of December 31st, 1864: "The troops were placed in position and intrenched under his [Cox's] immediate direction, and the greater portion of the line engaged was under his command during the battle."— EDITORS.

seen, stretching in battle array, from the dark fringe of chestnuts along the river-bank, far across the Columbia Pike, the colors gayly fluttering and the muskets gleaming brightly, and advancing steadily, in perfect order, dressed on the center, straight for the works. Meantime General Schofield had retired to the fort, on a high bluff on the other side of the river, some two miles away, by the road, and had taken General Stanley with him. From the fort the whole field of operations was plainly visible. Notwithstanding all these demonstrations, the two brigades of Wagner were left on the knoll where they had been halted, and, with scarcely an apology for works to

FRONT VIEW OF THE GIN-HOUSE.

The line of the Union works ran in front of the Gin-house, and only a few feet from it; in 1886 a faint depression along the edge of the field still indicated the position. Near the tree seen in the lower picture there is a round, deep hollow which afforded protection to the Union soldiers. The lower view was taken from the same point on the pike, looking a little to the right, as the view of "The Carter House, from the Confederate side," on p. 449.

VIEW OF THE GIN-HOUSE, FROM THE PIKE.

protect them, had waited until it was too late to retreat without danger of degenerating into a rout.

On came the enemy, as steady and resistless as a tidal wave. A couple of guns, in the advance line, gave them a shot and galloped back to the works. A volley from a thin skirmish-line was sent into their ranks, but without causing any delay to the massive array. A moment more, and with that wild "rebel yell" which, once heard, is never forgotten, the great human wave swept along, and seemed to ingulf the little force that had so sturdily awaited it.

The first shock came, of course, upon the two misplaced brigades of Wagner's division, which, through some one's blunder, had remained in their false position until too late to retire without disaster. They had no tools to throw up works; and when struck by the resistless sweep of Cleburne's and Brown's divisions, they had only to make their way, as best they could, back to the works. In that wild rush, in which friend and foe were intermingled, and the piercing "rebel yell" rose high above the "Yankee cheer," nearly seven hundred were made prisoners. But, worst of all for the Union side, the men of Reilly's and Strickland's brigades dared not fire, lest they should shoot down their own comrades, and the guns, loaded with grape and canister, stood silent in the embrasures. With loud shouts of "Let's go into the works with them," the triumphant Confederates, now more like a wild, howling mob than an organized army, swept on to the very works, with hardly a check from any quarter. So fierce was the rush that a number of the fleeing soldiers—officers and men—dropped exhausted into the ditch, and lay there while the terrific contest raged over their heads, till, under cover of darkness, they could crawl safely inside the intrenchments.

On Strickland's left, close to the Columbia Pike, was posted one of the new infantry regiments. The tremendous onset, the wild yells, the whole infernal din of the strife, were too much for such an undisciplined body. As they saw their comrades from the advance line rushing to the rear, they too turned and fled. The contagion spread, and in a few minutes a disorderly stream was pouring down the pike past the Carter house toward

BRIDGE AT FRANKLIN OVER THE HARPETH RIVER, LOOKING UP-STREAM.

The left of the picture is the north bank of the stream; Franklin is upon the south bank. Fort Granger, where General Schofield had his headquarters, occupied the site of the buildings on the north bank.

the town. The guns, posted on each side the Columbia Pike, were abandoned, and the works, for the space of more than a regimental front, both east and west of the pike, were deserted. Into the gap thus made, without an instant's delay, swarmed the jubilant Confederates, urged on by Cleburne and Brown, and took possession of both works and guns. For a moment it looked as though these two enterprising divisions, backed by the mass of troops converging toward the pike, would sweep down the works in both directions, and, taking Strickland and Reilly on the flank, drive them out, or capture them. Fortunately, there were at hand reserves of brave men who were not demoralized by the momentary panic. Colonel Emerson Opdycke, of Wagner's division, as already stated, had brought his brigade inside the works, and they were now massed near the Carter house, ready for any contingency. Two regiments of Reilly's brigade, the 12th and 16th Kentucky, which had reached Franklin about noon, had taken position a little in rear of the rest of the brigade, and thrown up works. As soon as the break was made in the lines all these reserves rushed to the front, and, after a terrific struggle, succeeded in regaining the works. Opdycke's brigade, deploying as it advanced, was involved in as fierce a hand-to-hand encounter as ever soldiers engaged in. The two Kentucky regiments joined in the fight with equal ardor and bravery. A large part of Conrad's and Lane's men, as they came in, though wholly disorganized, turned about and gave the enemy a hot reception. Opdycke's horse was shot under him, and he fought on foot at the head of his brigade. General Cox was everywhere present, encouraging and cheering on his men. General Stanley, who, from the fort where he had gone with General Schofield, had seen the opening clash, galloped to the front as soon as possible and did all that a brave man could until he was painfully wounded. Some of Opdycke's men manned the abandoned guns in Reilly's works; others filled the gap in Strickland's line. These timely movements first checked and then repulsed the assaulting foe, and soon the entire line of works was reoccupied, the enemy sullenly giving up the prize which was so nearly won. Stewart's corps, which was on Cheatham's right, filling the space to the river, kept abreast of its valiant companion, and, meeting no obstacle, reached the works near the Union left before Cheatham made the breach at the Columbia Pike. Owing to the peculiar formation of the field, the left of Stewart's line was thrown upon the same ground with the right of Cheatham's; the two commands there became much intermingled. This accounts for so many of General Stewart's officers and men being killed in front of Reilly's and Casement's regiments.

Where there was nothing to hinder the Union fire, the muskets of Stiles's and Casement's brigades made fearful havoc; while the batteries at the railroad cut plowed furrows through the ranks of the advancing foe. Time after time they came up to the very works, but they never crossed them except as prisoners. More than one color-bearer was shot down on the parapet. It is impossible to exaggerate the fierce energy with which the Confederate soldiers, that short November afternoon, threw themselves against the works, fighting with what seemed the very madness of despair. There was not a breath of wind, and the dense smoke settled down upon the field, so that, after the first assault, it was impossible to see at any distance. Through this blinding medium, assault after assault was made, several of the Union officers declaring in their reports that their lines received as many as thirteen distinct attacks. Between the gin-house and the Columbia Pike the fighting was fiercest, and the Confederate losses the greatest. Here fell most of the Confederate generals, who, that fateful afternoon, madly gave up their lives; Adams of Stewart's corps—his horse astride the works, and himself within a few feet of them. Cockrell and Quarles, of the same corps, were severely wounded. In Cheatham's corps, Cleburne and Granbury were killed near the pike. On the west of the pike Strahl and Gist were killed, and Brown was severely wounded. General G. W. Gordon was captured by Opdycke's brigade, inside the works. The heaviest loss in all the Union regiments was in the 44th Missouri, the advance guard of Smith's long-expected reënforcement, which had been sent to Columbia on the 27th, and was here stationed on the right of the raw regiment that broke and ran at the first onset of the enemy. Quickly changing front, the 44th held its ground, but with a loss of 34 killed, 37 wounded, and 92 missing, many of the latter being wounded. In the 72d Illinois, its companion, every field-officer was wounded, and the entire color-guard, of one sergeant and eight corporals, was shot down. Its losses were 10 killed, 66 wounded, and 75 missing.

While this infantry battle was going on, Forrest had crossed the river with his cavalry some distance east of the town, with the evident purpose of getting at Schofield's wagons. But he reckoned without his host. Hatch and Croxton, by General Wilson's direction, fell upon him with such vigor that he returned to the south side and gave our forces no further trouble. At nightfall the victory was complete on every part of the Union lines. But here and there on the Confederate side desultory firing was kept up till long after dark, though with little result.

At 3 o'clock in the afternoon, as the Confederate lines were forming for their great assault, General Schofield, in reply to a telegram from General Thomas, asking him if he could "hold Hood at Franklin for three days longer," replied, "I do not think I can. . . . It appears to me I ought to take position at Brentwood at once." Accordingly General Thomas, at 3:30, directed him to retire to Brentwood, which he did that night, bringing away all the wagons and other property in safety. Among the spoils of war were thirty-three Confederate colors, captured by our men from the enemy. The morning found the entire infantry force safe within the friendly shelter of the works at Nashville, where they also welcomed the veterans of A. J. Smith, who were just arriving from Missouri. Soon after, a body of about five thousand men came in from Chattanooga, chiefly of General Sherman's army, too late for their proper commands. These were organized into a provisional division under General J. B. Steedman, and were posted between the Murfreesboro' Pike and the river. Cooper's brigade also came in after a narrow escape from capture, as well as several regiments of colored troops from the railroad between Nashville and Johnsonville. Their arrival completed the force on which General Thomas was to rely for the task he now placed before himself—the destruction of Hood's army. It was an ill-assorted and heterogeneous mass, not yet welded into an army, and lacking a great proportion of the outfit with which to undertake an aggressive campaign. Horses, wagons, mules, pontoons, everything needed to mobilize an army, had to be obtained. At that time they did not exist at Nashville. [See map, p. 434.]

The next day Hood's columns appeared before the town and took up their positions on a line of hills nearly parallel to those occupied by the Union army, and speedily threw up works and prepared to defend their ground.

Probably no commander ever underwent two weeks of greater anxiety and distress of mind than General Thomas during the interval between Hood's arrival and his precipitate departure from the vicinity of Nashville. The story is too painful to dwell upon, even after the lapse of twenty-three years. From the 2d of December until the battle was fought on the 15th, the general-in-chief did not cease, day or night, to send him from the headquarters at City Point, Va., most urgent and often most uncalled-for orders in regard to his operations, culminating in an order on the 9th relieving him, and directing him to turn over his command to General Schofield, who was assigned to his place—an order which, had it not been revoked, the great captain would have obeyed with loyal single-heartedness. This order, though made out at the Adjutant-General's office in Washington, was not sent to General Thomas, and he did not know of its existence until told of it some years later by General Halleck, at San Francisco. He felt, however, that something of the kind was impending. General Halleck dispatched to him, on morning of the 9th: "Lieutenant-General Grant expresses much dissatisfaction at your delay in attacking the enemy." His reply shows how entirely he understood the situation: "I feel conscious I have done everything in my power, and that the troops could not have been gotten ready before this. *If General Grant should order me to be relieved, I will submit without a murmur.*" As he was writing this,—2 o'clock in the afternoon of December 9th,—a terrible storm of freezing rain had been pouring down since daylight, and it kept on pouring and freezing all that day and a part of the next. That night General Grant notified him that the order relieving him—which he had divined—was suspended. But he did not know who had been designated as his successor. With this threat hanging over him; with the utter impossibil-

HILL NEAR NASHVILLE FROM WHICH BATE'S CONFEDERATE DIVISION WAS DRIVEN ON DECEMBER 16. FROM A PHOTOGRAPH TAKEN IN 1884.

ity, in that weather, of making any movement; with the prospect that the labors of his whole life were about to end in disappointment, if not disaster,— he never, for an instant, abated his energy or his work of preparation. Not an hour, day and night, was he idle. Nobody—not even his most trusted staff-officers—knew the contents of the telegrams that came to him. But it was very evident that something greatly troubled him. While the rain was falling and the fields and roads were ice-bound, he would sometimes sit by the window for an hour or more, not speaking a word, gazing steadily out upon the forbidding prospect, as if he were trying to will the storm away. It was curious and interesting to see how, in this gloomy interval, his time was occupied by matters not strictly military. Now, it was a visit from a delegation of the city government, in regard to some municipal regulation; again, somebody whose one horse had been seized and put into the cavalry; then, a committee of citizens, begging that wood might be furnished, to keep some poor families from freezing; and, of evenings, Governor Andrew Johnson— then Vice-President elect—would unfold to him, with much iteration, his fierce views concerning secession, rebels, and reconstruction. To all he gave a patient and kindly hearing, and he often astonished Governor Johnson by his knowledge of constitutional and international law. But, underneath all, it was plain to see that General Grant's dissatisfaction keenly affected him, and that only by the proof which a successful battle would furnish could he hope to regain the confidence of the general-in-chief.

So when, at 8 o'clock on the evening of December 14th, after having laid his plans before his corps commanders, and dismissed them, he dictated to General Halleck the telegram, "The ice having melted away to-day, the enemy will be attacked to-morrow morning," he drew a deep sigh of relief, and for the first time for a week showed again something of his natural buoyancy and cheerfulness. He moved about more briskly; he put in order all the little last things that remained to be done; he signed his name where it was needed in the letter-book, and then, giving orders to his staff-officers to be ready at 5 o'clock the next morning, went gladly to bed.

The ice had not melted a day too soon; for, while he was writing the telegram to General Halleck, General Logan was speeding his way to Nashville, with orders from General Grant that would have placed him in command of all the Union forces there assembled. General Thomas, fortunately, did not then learn this second proof of General Grant's lack of confidence; and General Logan, on reaching Louisville, found that the work intended for him was already done — and came no farther. At the very time when these orders were made out at Washington, in obedience to General Grant's directions, a large part of the cavalry was unmounted; two divisions were absent securing horses and proper outfit; wagons were unfinished and mules lacking or unbroken; pontoons unmade and pontoniers untrained; the ground was covered with a glare of ice which made all the fields and hillsides impassable for horses and scarcely passable for foot-men. The natives declared that the Yankees brought their weather as well as their army with them. Every corps commander in the army protested that a movement under such conditions would be little short of madness, and certain to result in disaster.

THE CAPITOL, NASHVILLE.

Strong works, set with cannon, inclosed the foundations of the Capitol. Cisterns within the building held a bountiful supply of water. Owing to its capacity and the massiveness of the lower stories, the Capitol was regarded as a citadel, in which a few thousand men could maintain themselves against an army.

A very considerable reorganization of the army also took place during this enforced delay. General Stanley, still suffering from his wound, went North, and General T. J. Wood, who had been with it from the beginning, succeeded to the command of the Fourth Corps. General Ruger, who had commanded a division in the Twenty-third Corps, was also disabled by sickness, and was succeeded by General D. N. Couch, formerly a corps commander in the Army of the Potomac, and who had recently been assigned to duty in the Department of the Cumberland.ⵔ General Wagner was retired from command of his division, and was succeeded by General W. L. Elliott, who had been chief of cavalry on General Thomas's staff in the Atlanta campaign. General Kenner Garrard, who had commanded a cavalry division during the Atlanta campaign, was assigned to an infantry division in Smith's corps. In all these cases, except in that of General Wood succeeding to the command of the Fourth Corps, the newly assigned officers were entire strangers to the troops over whom they were placed.

On the afternoon of the 14th of December General Thomas summoned his corps commanders, and, delivering to each a written order containing a

---

ⵔ General Couch was in command of the Department of the Susquehanna from June 11th, 1863, to December 1st, 1864. On December 8th, 1864, he took command of the Second Division of the Twenty-third Corps.— EDITORS.

detailed plan of the battle, went with them carefully and thoroughly over the whole ground, answering all questions and explaining all doubts. Never had a commander a more loyal corps of subordinates or a more devoted army. The feeling in the ranks was one of absolute and enthusiastic confidence in their general. Some had served with him since his opening triumph at Mill Springs; some had never seen his face till two weeks before. But there was that in his bearing, as well as in the confidence of his old soldiers, which inspired the new-comers with as absolute a sense of reliance upon him as was felt by the oldest of his veterans.

The plan, in general terms, was for General Steedman, on the extreme left, to move out early in the morning, threatening the rebel right, while the cavalry, which had been placed on the extreme right, and A. J. Smith's corps were to make a grand left wheel with the entire right wing, assaulting and, if possible, overlapping the left of Hood's position. Wood was to form the pivot for this wheel, and to threaten and perhaps attack Montgomery Hill; while General Schofield was to be held in reserve, near the left center, for such use as the exigency might develop.

It was not daylight, on the morning of the 15th of December, when the army began to move. In most of the camps reveille had been sounded at 4 o'clock, and by 6 everything was ready. It turned out a warm, sunny, winter morning. A dense fog at first hung over the valleys and completely hid all movements, but by 9 o'clock this had cleared away. General Steedman, on the extreme left, was the first to draw out of the defenses, and to assail the enemy at their works between the Nolensville and Murfreesboro' pikes. It was not intended as a real attack, though it had that effect. Two of Steedman's brigades, chiefly colored troops, kept two divisions of Cheatham's corps constantly busy, while his third was held in reserve; thus one Confederate corps was disposed of. S. D. Lee's corps, next on Cheatham's left, after sending two brigades to the assistance of Stewart, on the Confederate left, was held in place by the threatening position of the garrison troops, and did not fire a shot during the day. Indeed, both Cheatham's and Lee's corps were held, as in a vise, between Steedman and Wood. Lee's corps was unable to move or to fight. Steedman maintained the ground he occupied till the next morning, with no very heavy loss.

When, about 9 o'clock, the sun began to burn away the fog, the sight from General Thomas's position was inspiring. A little to the left, on Montgomery Hill, the salient of the Confederate lines, and not more than six hundred yards distant from Wood's salient, on Lawrens Hill, could be seen the advance line of works, behind which an unknown force of the enemy lay in wait. Beyond, and along the Hillsboro' Pike, were stretches of stone wall, with here and there a detached earth-work, through whose embrasures peeped the threatening artillery. To the right, along the valley of Richland Creek, the dark line of Wilson's advancing cavalry could be seen slowly making its difficult way across the wet, swampy, stumpy ground. Close in front, and at the foot of the hill, its right joining Wilson's left, was A. J. Smith's corps, full of cheer and enterprise, and glad to be once more in the open field. Then

VIEWS OF FORT NEGLEY ON THE LEFT OF THE
UNION INTRENCHMENTS, NASHVILLE, BETWEEN THE FRANKLIN
AND NOLENSVILLE PIKES. FROM PHOTOGRAPHS.

The lower picture shows a casemate protected with railroad iron. The hills in the
distance were the Confederate center and left at the opening of the fight.

came the Fourth Corps, whose left, bending back toward the north, was hidden behind Lawrens Hill. Already the skirmishers were engaged, the Confederates slowly falling back before the determined and steady pressure of Smith and Wood.

By the time that Wilson's and Smith's lines were fully extended and brought up to within striking distance of the Confederate works, along the Hillsboro' Pike, it was noon. Post's brigade of Wood's old division (now commanded by General Sam Beatty), which lay at the foot of Montgomery Hill, full of dash and spirit, had since morning been regarding the works at the summit with covetous eyes. At Post's suggestion, it was determined to see which party wanted them most. Accordingly, a charge was ordered — and in a moment the brigade was swarming up the hillside, straight for the enemy's advanced works. For almost the first time since the grand assault on Missionary Ridge, a year before, here was an open field where everything could be seen. From General Thomas's headquarters everybody looked on with breathless suspense, as the blue line, broken and irregular, but with steady persistence, made its way up the steep hillside against a fierce storm of musketry and artillery. Most of the shots, however, passed over the men's heads.

It was a struggle to keep up with the colors, and, as they neared the top, only the strongest were at the front. Without a moment's pause, the color-bearers and those who had kept up with them, Post himself at the head, leaped the parapet. As the colors waved from the summit, the whole line swept forward and was over the works in a twinkling, gathering in prisoners and guns. Indeed, so large was the mass of the prisoners that a few minutes later was seen heading toward our own lines, that a number of officers at General Thomas's headquarters feared the assault had failed and the prisoners were Confederate reserves who had rallied and retaken the works. But the fear was only momentary; for the wild outburst of cheers that rang across the valley told the story of complete success.

Meanwhile, farther to the right, as the opposing lines neared each other, the sound of battle grew louder and louder, and the smoke thicker and thicker, until the whole valley was filled with the haze. It was now past noon, and, at every point the two armies were so near together that an assault was inevitable. Hatch's division of Wilson's cavalry, at the extreme right of the continuous line, was confronted by one of the detached works which Hood had intended to be "impregnable"; and the right of McArthur's division of A. J. Smith's infantry was also within striking distance of it. Coon's cavalry brigade was dismounted and ordered to assault the work, while Hill's infantry brigade received similar orders. The two commanders moved forward at the same time, and entered the work together, Colonel Hill falling dead at the head of his command. In a moment the whole Confederate force in that quarter was routed and fled to the rear, while the captured guns were turned on them.

With the view of extending the operations of Wilson's cavalry still farther to the right, and if possible gaining the rear of the enemy's left, the two divisions of the Twenty-third Corps that had been in reserve near Lawrens Hill were ordered to Smith's right, while orders were sent to Wilson to gain, if possible, a lodgment on the Granny White Pike. These orders were promptly obeyed, and Cooper's brigade on reaching its new position got into a handsome fight, in which its losses were more than the losses of the rest of the Twenty-third Corps during the two days' battle.

But though the enemy's left was thus rudely driven from its fancied security, the salient at the center, being an angle formed by the line along Hillsboro' Pike and that stretching toward the east, was still firmly held. Post's successful assault had merely driven out or captured the advance forces; the main line was intact. As soon as word came of the successful assault on the right, General Thomas sent orders to General Wood, commanding the Fourth Corps, to prepare to attack the salient. The staff-officer by whom this order was sent did not at first find General Wood; but seeing the two division commanders whose troops would be called upon for the work, gave them the instructions. As he was riding along the line he met one of the brigade commanders — an officer with a reputation for exceptional courage and gallantry — who, in reply to the direction to prepare for the expected assault, said, "You don't mean that we've got to go in here and attack the works on that hill?" "Those are the orders," was the answer. Looking earnestly across the open valley, and at the steep hill beyond, from which the enemy's guns were throwing shot and shell with uncomfortable frequency and nearness, he said, "Why, it would be suicide, sir; perfect suicide." "Nevertheless, those are the orders," said the officer; and he rode on to complete his work. Before he could rejoin General Thomas the assault was made, and the enemy were driven out with a loss of guns, colors, and

prisoners, and their whole line was forced to abandon the works along the Hillsboro' Pike and fall back to the Granny White Pike. The retreating line was followed by the entire Fourth Corps (Wood's), as well as by the cavalry and Smith's troops; but night soon fell, and the whole army went into bivouac in the open fields wherever they chanced to be.

At dark, Hood, who at 12 o'clock had held an unbroken, fortified line from the Murfrees-

VIEW OF A PART OF THE UNION LINES AT NASHVILLE. FROM A PHOTOGRAPH.

boro' to the Hillsboro' Pike, with an advanced post on Montgomery Hill and five strong redoubts along the Hillsboro' Pike, barely maintained his hold of a line from the Murfreesboro' Pike to the Granny White Pike, near which on two large hills the left of his army had taken refuge when driven out of their redoubts by Smith and Wilson. These hills were more than two miles to the rear of his morning position. It was to that point that Bate, who had started from Hood's right when the assault was first delivered on the redoubts, now made his way amidst, as he says, "streams of stragglers, and artillerists, and horses, without guns or caissons — the sure indications of defeat."

General Hood, not daunted by the reverses which had befallen him, at once set to work to prepare for the next day's struggle. As soon as it was dusk Cheatham's whole corps was moved from his right to his left; Stewart's was retired some two miles and became the center; Lee's also was withdrawn and became the right. The new line extended along the base of a range of hills two miles south of that occupied during the day, and was only about half as long as that from which he had been driven. During the night the Confederates threw up works along their entire front, and the hills on their flanks were strongly fortified. The flanks were also further secured by return works, which prevented them from being left "in the air." Altogether, the position was naturally far more formidable than that just abandoned.

At early dawn the divisions of the Fourth Corps moved forward, driving out the opposing skirmishers. The men entered upon the work with such ardor that the advance soon quickened into a run, and the run almost into a

SOUTH-WEST FRONT OF THE CAPITOL AT
NASHVILLE. FROM A PHOTOGRAPH.
The view is toward the battle-field. Near the
base of the first column is seen in the
distance the flag of Fort Negley.

charge. They took up their posi-
tions in front of the enemy's new line, at one point coming within 250 yards
of the salient at Overton's Hill. Here they were halted, and threw up works,
while the artillery on both sides kept up a steady and accurate fire. Steedman also moved forward and about noon joined his right to Wood's left,
thus completing the alignment.

On his way to the front General Thomas heard the cannonading, and, as
was his custom, rode straight for the spot where the action seemed heaviest.
As he was passing a large, old-fashioned house, his attention was attracted by
the noise of a window closing with a slam. Turning to see the cause, he was
greeted by a look from a young lady whose expression at the moment was
the reverse of angelic. With an amused smile, the general rode on, and soon
forgot the incident in the excitement of battle. But this trifling event had a
sequel. The young lady, in process of time, became the wife of an officer
then serving in General Thomas's army,—though he did not happen to be
a witness of this episode.

The ground between the two armies for the greater part of the way from
the Franklin to the Granny White Pike is low, open, and crossed by frequent
streams running in every direction, and most of the fields were either newly
plowed or old corn-fields, and were heavy, wet, and muddy from the recent
storms. Overton's Hill, Hood's right, is a well-rounded slope, the top of
which was amply fortified, while hills held by the left of his line just west of
the Granny White Pike are so steep that it is difficult to climb them, and
their summits were crowned with formidable barricades, in front of which

were abatis and masses of fallen trees. Between these extremities the works in many places consisted of stone walls covered with earth, with head-logs on the top. To their rear were ample woods, sufficiently open to enable troops to move through them, but thick enough to afford good shelter. Artillery was also posted at every available spot, and good use was made of it.

The morning was consumed in moving to new positions. Wilson's cavalry, by a wide détour, had passed beyond the extreme Confederate left, and secured a lodgment on the Granny White Pike. But one avenue of escape was now open for Hood—the Franklin Pike. General Thomas hoped that a vigorous assault by Schofield's corps against Hood's left would break the line there, and thus enable the cavalry, relieved from the necessity of operating against the rebel flank, to gallop down the Granny White Pike to its junction with the Franklin, some six or eight miles below, and plant itself square across the only remaining line of retreat. If this scheme could be carried out, nothing but capture or surrender awaited Hood's whole army.

Meantime, on the National left, Colonel Post, who had so gallantly carried Montgomery Hill the morning before, had made a careful reconnoissance of Overton's Hill, the strong position on Hood's right. As the result of his observation, he reported to General Wood, his corps commander, that an assault would cost dear, but he believed it could be made successfully; at any rate he was ready to try it. The order was accordingly given, and everything prepared. The brigade was to be supported on either side by fresh troops to be held in readiness to rush for the works the moment Post should gain the parapet. The bugles had not finished sounding the charge, when Post's brigade, preceded by a strong line of skirmishers, moved forward, in perfect silence, with orders to halt for nothing, but to gain the works at a run. The men dashed on, Post leading, with all speed through a shower of shot and shell. A few of the skirmishers reached the parapet; the main line came within twenty steps of the works, when, by a concentrated fire of musketry and artillery from every available point of the enemy's line, the advance was momentarily checked, and, in another instant, Post was brought down by a wound, at first reported as mortal. This slight hesitation and the disabling of Post were fatal to the success of the assault. The leader and animating spirit gone, the line slowly drifted back to its original position, losing in those few minutes nearly 300 men; while the supporting brigade on its left lost 250.

Steedman had promised to coöperate in this assault, and accordingly Thompson's brigade of colored troops was ordered to make a demonstration at the moment Post's advance began. These troops had never before been in action and were now to test their mettle. There had been no time for a reconnoissance, when this order was given, else it is likely a way would have been found to turn the enemy's extreme right flank. The colored brigade moved forward against the works east of the Franklin Pike and nearly parallel to it. As they advanced, they became excited, and what was intended merely as a demonstration was unintentionally converted into an actual assault. Thompson, finding his men rushing forward at the double-quick, gallantly led them to the very slope of the intrenchments. But, in their advance across the open field, the continuity of his line was broken by a large fallen tree. As the men separated to pass it, the enemy opened an enfilading fire on the exposed flanks of the gap thus created, with telling effect. In consequence, at the very moment when a firm and compact order was most needed, the line came up ragged and broken. Meantime Post's assault was repulsed, and the fire which had been concentrated on him was turned against Thompson. Nothing was left, therefore, but to withdraw as soon as possible to the original position. This was done without panic or confusion, after a loss of 467 men from the three regiments composing the brigade.

When it was seen that a heavy assault on his right, at Overton's Hill, was threatened, Hood ordered Cleburne's old division to be sent over to the exposed point, from the extreme left, in front of Schofield. About the same time General Couch, commanding one of the divisions of the Twenty-third Corps, told General Schofield that he believed he could carry the hill in his front, but doubted if he could hold it without assistance. The ground in front of General Cox, on Couch's right, also offered grand opportunities for a successful assault. Meantime the cavalry, on Cox's right, had made its way beyond the extreme left flank of the enemy, and was moving northward over the wooded hills direct to the rear of the extreme rebel left.

General Thomas, who had been making a reconnoissance, had no sooner reached Schofield's front than General McArthur, who commanded one of Smith's divisions, impatient at the long waiting, and not wanting to spend the second night on the rocky hill he was occupying, told Smith that he could carry the high hill in front of Couch,—the same that Couch himself had told Schofield he could carry,—and would undertake it unless forbidden. Smith silently acquiesced, and McArthur set to work. Withdrawing McMillen's (his right) brigade from the trenches, he marched it by the flank in front of General Couch's position, and with orders to the men to fix bayonets, not to fire a shot and neither to halt nor to cheer until they had gained the enemy's works, the charge was sounded. The gallant brigade, which had served and fought in every part of the South-west, moved swiftly down the slope, across the narrow valley, and began scrambling up the steep hillside, on the top of which was the redoubt, held by Bate's division, and mounted also with Whitworth guns. The bravest onlookers held their breath as these gallant men steadily and silently approached the summit amid the crash of musketry and the boom of the artillery. In almost the time it has taken to tell the story they gained the works, their flags were wildly waving from the parapet, and the unmistakable cheer, "the voice of the American people," as General Thomas called it, rent the air. It was an exultant moment; but this was only a part of the heroic work of that afternoon. While McMillen's brigade was preparing for this wonderful charge, Hatch's division of cavalry, dismounted, had also pushed its way through the woods, and had gained the tops of two hills that commanded the rear of the enemy's works. Here, with incredible labor, they had dragged, by hand, two pieces of artillery, and, just as McMillen began his charge, these opened on the hill where Bate was, up the opposite slope of which the infantry were scrambling. At the same time

Coon's brigade of Hatch's division with resounding cheers charged upon the enemy and poured such volleys of musketry from their repeating-rifles as I have never heard equaled. Thus beset on both sides, Bate's people broke out of the works, and ran down the hill toward their right and rear as fast as their legs could carry them. It was more like a scene in a spectacular drama than a real incident in war. The hillside in front, still green, dotted with the boys in blue swarming up the slope; the dark background of high hills beyond; the lowering clouds; the waving flags; the smoke slowly rising through the leafless tree-tops and drifting across the valleys; the wonderful outburst of musketry; the ecstatic cheers; the multitude racing for life down into the valley below,—so exciting was it all, that the lookers-on instinctively clapped their hands, as at a brilliant and successful transformation scene, as indeed it was. For, in those few minutes, an army was changed into a mob, and the whole structure of the rebellion in the South-west, with all its possibilities, was utterly overthrown. As soon as the other divisions farther to the left saw and heard the doings on their right, they did not wait for orders. Everywhere, by a common impulse, they charged the works in front, and carried them in a twinkling. General Edward Johnson and nearly all his division and his artillery were captured. Over the very ground where, but a little while before, Post's assault had been repulsed, the same troops now charged with resistless force, capturing fourteen guns and one thousand prisoners. Steedman's colored brigades also rallied and brought in their share of prisoners and other spoils of war. Everywhere the success was complete.

Foremost among the rejoicing victors was General Steedman, under whose command were the colored troops. Steedman had been a life-long Democrat and was one of the delegates, in 1860, to the Charleston convention, at which ultimately Breckinridge was nominated for President. As he rode over the field, immediately after the rout of the enemy, he asked, with a grim smile, as he pointed to the fleeing hosts, "I wonder what my Democratic friends over there would think of me if they knew I was fighting them with 'nigger' troops?"

I have not space to tell the story of the pursuit, which only ended, ten days later, at the Tennessee River. About a month before, General Hood had triumphantly begun his northward movement. Now, in his disastrous retreat, he was leaving behind him, as prisoners or deserters, a larger number of men than General Thomas had been able to place at Pulaski to hinder his advance — to say nothing of his terrific losses in killed at Franklin. The loss to the Union army, in all its fighting,— from the Tennessee River to Nashville and back again,— was less than six thousand killed, wounded, and missing. At so small a cost, counting the chances of war, the whole Northwest was saved from an invasion that, if Hood had succeeded, would have more than neutralized all Sherman's successes in Georgia and the Carolinas; saved by the steadfast labors, the untiring energy, the rapid combinations, the skillful evolutions, the heroic courage and the tremendous force of one man, whose name will yet rank among the great captains of all time.

THE UNION CAVALRY IN THE HOOD CAMPAIGN.

BY JAMES HARRISON WILSON, MAJOR-GENERAL, U. S. V., AND BREVET MAJOR-GENERAL, U. S. A.

BRIDGE OVER THE CUMBERLAND AT NASHVILLE.

UNTIL after Sheridan's victory of the Opequon, September 19, 1864, I had led the Third Cavalry Division. Toward the close of October, 1864, I reported to Sherman at Gaylesville, Alabama, at which place the latter had suspended his northward pursuit of Hood, and after a full and interesting conference I was announced, on October 24th, as chief-of-cavalry, and placed in absolute command of all the mounted forces of the three armies, only a small proportion of which were actually with the colors for duty. This force was by the same order detached entirely from the control of the army commanders and designated as the Cavalry Corps of the Military Division of the Mississippi. General Sherman, after issuing all the necessary instructions and unfolding his plans for the operations of the army, and especially of this new corps, generously added: "Do the best you can with it, and if you make any reputation out of it I shall not undertake to divide it with you." Thus the paper organization had its origin; but inasmuch as most of the force was dismounted and detachments of it were scattered from east Tennessee to south-western Missouri, much the greater part of the real work of reorganization had yet to be done.

By special orders Kilpatrick's division of something over five thousand men, and a full complement of horses taken from other divisions and brigades, was detached from the corps and marched down to the sea with Sherman, while the nuclei of the six other divisions into which the corps was divided, commanded then or afterward by Generals E. M. McCook, Eli Long, Emory Upton, Edward Hatch, R. W. Johnson, and Joseph F. Knipe, in the order named, took part in the campaign against Hood and in the final overthrow of the rebellion. Meanwhile the work went on of collecting, remounting, and reëquipping these troops and disposing them so as to cover the operations of the Federal infantry and to develop the plans and movements of Hood.

On the 30th of October, 1864, Hood's army crossed the Tennessee on its northward march, three miles below Bainbridge, and this circumstance was promptly detected by General Croxton, commanding the First Brigade of McCook's division, lately remounted at Louisville, and was reported at once to General Thomas, who had just taken post at Nashville. Without waiting for orders Croxton then made haste to collect his brigade and lead it against the enemy; but as he could not muster over a thousand troopers for duty, he failed

to check the rebel advance and was soon forced to take up a position of observation behind Shoal Creek, where he was joined on the 5th of November by General Hatch, with the Fifth Division, which had but recently come from west Tennessee. A few days later these united forces, under Hatch, with not over 3000 men in the saddle, took the offensive, recrossed Shoal Creek, and drove the rebel cavalry sharply back upon the infantry at Florence, capturing a part of the unfinished field-works at that place. By great activity and vigilance, General Hatch discovered every movement of the enemy and promptly and correctly reported every indication of his intentions to Stanley, Schofield, or Thomas, or to me. After becoming convinced that Hood would soon advance, Hatch employed his force in felling trees in the roads and obstructing the fords so as to delay his march as much as possible.

I arrived at Nashville on the 6th of November, and by the aid of a large staff, mostly from the regular army, pressed forward the preparations of the corps for the campaign which it was now evident that the resolute Hood was about to begin for the capture of Nashville and the possession of middle Tennessee. The Federal forces in that region, infantry as well as cavalry, were widely scattered. They were the remnants of three armies, and although the supreme command had been conferred on Thomas, a host in himself, aided by such able lieutenants as Generals Stanley, Schofield, Steedman, Cox, and Thomas J. Wood, and finally by A. J. Smith, it was by no means certain that their forces could be welded into an efficient army in time to check the onset of Hood's fleet-footed and fiercely aggressive veterans.

On the 19th of November the enemy was reported by the cavalry pickets as marching north in force on the west side of Shoal Creek, and this was confirmed without delay by a cavalry reconnoissance in force, which resulted in the capture of the head-quarters trains belonging to Chalmers's and Buford's divisions, and in a severe engagement with those commands. Constant marching, accompanied by heavy fighting and many skirmishes, followed. The Federal cavalry, under the immediate direction of Hatch, who showed great coolness and steadiness, slowly fell back through Lexington, Lawrenceburg, Pulaski, and Lynnville to Columbia, where all its detachments then in that theater of operations were for the first time collected under my command. Having as far as possible completed my arrangements at Nashville, I had taken the field in person a few days before. At this juncture Hatch's division had been reduced to 2500 men and horses for duty, Croxton's brigade to about 1000, and Capron's to 800 — in all only 4300 men.

After the concentration of the National forces in the strongly fortified camp at Columbia, where Schofield had paused to give the army a breathing-spell and to insure the safety of its *matériel*, the cavalry withdrew to the north side of Duck River, and was so disposed as to watch the enemy's movements either to the right or the left. It was here strengthened by the arrival of several regiments from the remount camp at Louisville, and notwithstanding the terrible work and waste of the campaign that followed, it grew stronger and stronger till after the battle of Nashville.

At noon of November 28th the pickets of Croxton's and Capron's brigades gave notice of the appearance of the Confederate cavalry at the various fords of the Duck River between Columbia and the crossing of the Lewisburg turnpike. Shortly afterward the pickets were driven in, and at 2:10 P. M., on the same day, I notified General Schofield of the enemy's determined advance and that I should therefore concentrate the cavalry that night on the Lewisburg turnpike near Rally Hill, so as to prevent the enemy from occupying that highway and marching rapidly to Franklin, at the crossing of the Harpeth River, and also at the junction of the Lewisburg and the Columbia turnpikes. I assumed, as a matter of course, that Schofield would fall back on the last-mentioned turnpike, and that this arrangement would force the enemy to advance slowly and with caution, by either of these roads, or still move slowly by the dirt road, from Huey's Mills to Spring Hill. By 7 P. M. the entire cavalry, after much skirmishing and rapid marching, was concentrated at Hurt's Cross-roads, near Rally Hill, and by midnight it had become certain that Forrest's entire command, followed by the infantry of Hood's army, were crossing at Huey's Mills, and would probably move at early dawn toward Spring Hill. Accordingly, at 1 A. M. of that night, I sent a dispatch by courier to General Schofield informing him of these facts, and suggesting that he should reach Spring Hill, only twelve miles away, with the infantry of his army, by 10 A. M., because Hood's advance-guard would probably get there by noon. This dispatch was received at daylight on the 29th, and thereupon Stanley, with one division, was ordered to march at once to that place, while the remainder of the army held on at Columbia, and in its vicinity, till the next night. Meanwhile Hood had marched in the direction and by the road indicated in my dispatch, but fortunately he was met by the gallant and capable Stanley already in position covering Spring Hill and held at bay till Schofield, under cover of darkness, was enabled to rescue his imperiled command and make good his retreat into the fortified camp at Franklin. Forrest followed me along the Lewisburg turnpike, as had also been foreseen, but, thanks to the steadiness of the imperturbable Croxton (who declined all assistance from Hatch, and coolly declared that he needed nobody's help to cover a retreat, if the rest of the corps would only get out of the way and give him a clear road), the Confederate cavalry commander not only gained no advantage but was foiled in all his efforts to overthrow the rearguard, or to strike the retreating column in flank.

The battle of Franklin occurred the next day, and, as is well known, resulted in a signal victory for the National arms, and also in irreparable loss of men and officers to Hood's gallant army. On the Union side the heroes were Stanley and Cox and Opdycke. Their prompt action neutralized the faults of others, and wrested victory from the intrepid Cleburne and his no less intrepid companions.

One important circumstance connected with this battle has been persistently dwarfed or neglected altogether by historians. Simultaneously with Hood's infantry assault, his cavalry under Chalmers advanced to the attack, driving back Croxton and his pickets from the Lewisburg turnpike to the north side of the Harpeth River, where Hatch, Johnson, and Harrison's troopers had been disposed so as to cover and watch the fords and protect the left and rear of Schofield's army. Realizing the importance of holding this position, as soon as the rebel cavalrymen had made their appearance on the north side of the river, which properly formed the real line of defense for the Union army, I ordered Hatch and Croxton to attack with vigor, and drive the enemy into the river if possible, while Harrison with Capron's old brigades would look well to the left and rear. The field was broken by hills, covered with woods and small clearings, not specially unfavorable to mounted men; but the occasion was a grave one. It indicated either the advance of Hood's whole army, as at Duck River, or a turning movement by his cavalry; and in either case, from the fact that the National infantry and artillery were still on the south side of the river, it was absolutely necessary for their safety that my orders should be carried out to the letter. My subordinate commanders dismounted every man that could be spared, and went in with a rush that was irresistible. The fight was at first somewhat desultory, but toward the middle of the afternoon it became exceedingly sharp. The enemy's troopers fought with their accustomed gallantry, but the Union cavalrymen, outnumbering their antagonists for the first time and skillfully directed, swept everything before them. So closely did they press the enemy that they drove them into the water wherever they reached it. No time was allowed them to find the fords, and no rest was given them till the last man was driven to the south side of the river. Upon this occasion Hood made a fatal mistake, for it will be observed that he had detached Forrest with two divisions of his corps on a side operation, which left him only Chalmers's division to coöperate as described with the main attack of his infantry. Had his whole cavalry force advanced against me it is possible that it would have succeeded in driving us back.

Immediately after the close of the cavalry battle, and when it was certain that there was no further attack to be expected that night, I rode to General Schofield's headquarters, which I found in the square redoubt on the north side of the river. It was then dark and the arrangements for the withdrawal of the army to Nashville had been completed. Schofield and Stanley, the latter severely wounded, were together discussing the events of the day. After I had made my report Schofield thanked me for my services, and added: "Your success is most important; it insures the safety of this army, for, notwithstanding our great victory to-day over Hood, we should not have been able to withdraw from Franklin, or to maintain ourselves there, but for the defeat and repulse of Forrest's cavalry, which was evidently aiming to turn our left flank and throw itself upon our line of retreat." He then gave me orders to hold the position till daylight the next morning, after which I should withdraw, covering the rear and flanks of the infantry as it marched toward Nashville. This duty was successfully performed with but little skirmishing. The infantry had already occupied the fortifications at Nashville, and, there being no room for the cavalry immediately behind them, late on the evening of December 2d it crossed the Cumberland and went into camp at Edgefield.

For forty days my force had been constantly engaged in marching and fighting or in watching the enemy, and therefore it was in great need of rest. It had lost heavily, especially in horses. Many troopers had been dismounted, and many more were coming from furlough or detached service without horses or equipments; hence it was necessary to make the most extraordinary efforts to obtain remounts and otherwise to fit the corps for the field.

General Thomas now resolved to take a few days for repairing the losses and perfecting the organization of his hastily improvised army, especially the cavalry, upon which so much depended. He frankly made his plans and views known to the War Department and to the general-in-chief, but without receiving their proper sympathy and support. [See p. 454.] General Grant issued positive orders to march out and attack Hood in his intrenched position without further delay. In spite, however, of the doubts at first, and of the urgent orders afterward, Thomas stood fast behind his intrenchments. I sent out through Tennessee and Kentucky to impress horses, which the Secretary of War had cheerfully and promptly authorized me to do at the first intimation of a necessity for such an extreme measure. The cavalry officers did their duty well and rapidly, sparing no man's horses provided they were fit for cavalry service. Governor Johnson, then vice-president elect, no less than the farmers, the street-car companies, and the circuses, was called upon to give up his horses, and did so without a murmur. It was a busy time for the division, brigade, and regimental commanders as well as for the cavalry corps staff. Every man and officer did his best. A. J. Alexander, chief-of-staff; E. B. Beaumont, the adjutant-general; L. M. Hosea, the mustering officer; E. B. Carling, the quartermaster; J. C. Read, the commissary of subsistence; Bowman, Green, and H. E. Noyes, the inspectors; J. N. Andrews, W. W. Van Antwerp, G. H. Kneeland, Webster, and Pool, the aides-de-camp,—all officers of rare experience and intelligence,—threw themselves into the work and kept it up night and day till it was completed. Clothing was drawn

for the men, the horses were shod, extra shoes were fitted, and every horse in the corrals or hospitals fit for service, or that could be found in the country, cities, towns, and villages, was taken and issued to the troopers, who were now flocking in from all quarters. In just seven days the effective force of the corps was reported to General Thomas at 12,000 men, mounted, armed, and equipped, besides about 3000 for whom it was impossible to find remounts, but who were organized as infantry. They were all present for the impending struggle, except the brigades of La Grange and Watkins, which had been sent to drive a raiding party under Lyon and Crossland out of Kentucky.

At a meeting of the corps commanders, called by General Thomas the night of the 10th, the feasibility of carrying out General Grant's urgent orders to fight was fully considered. The plan of battle, which had already been outlined by General Thomas, involved a grand turning movement by the cavalry, and the active coöperation of that arm with the infantry at every stage of the engagement. I fully understood this, when, as the junior officer present, I was asked to speak first. I gave it as my decided opinion that it was folly to jeopard the chances of success by moving in such a storm and over the ground covered, as it then was, by a continuous glare of ice. I added that if the movement were delayed till the thaw, which in that climate might be expected soon, had set in, success was certain, and, in conclusion, declared that if I were occupying such an intrenched line as Hood's, with my dismounted cavalrymen, each armed with nothing more formidable than a basket of brickbats, I would agree to defeat the whole Confederate army if it should advance to the attack under such circumstances. At this remark the assembled officers, including Thomas, broke into a smile, whereupon the veteran Thomas J. Wood, commanding the Fourth Corps, a much older and more experienced cavalryman of the regular army than I, expressed his hearty concurrence. This was also entirely in accord with Thomas's own opinion, and, inasmuch as no one in that meeting expressed a different one or made a different suggestion, the meeting was dismissed with the information that no movement would be made for the time being. I was asked to remain after the others had gone, and it was upon that occasion that General Thomas, after repeating the orders he had received and the reply he had made to them *before* he had consulted his officers, added, with a depth of feeling and emotion which he did not attempt to conceal: "Wilson, they [meaning General Grant and the War Department] treat me as though I were a boy and incapable of planning a campaign or fighting a battle. If they will let me alone I will fight this battle just as soon as it can be done, and will surely win it; but I will not throw the victory away nor sacrifice the brave men of this army by moving till the thaw begins. I will surrender my command without a murmur, if they wish it; but I will not act against my judgment when I know I am right, and in such a grave emergency."

Fortunately for him and for the country the thaw set in on the night of the 13th, and had so far progressed that the action was begun on the morning of the 15th, just as he had planned it. The story of what followed has been told and retold many times, and never better than by Colonel Stone [see p. 456], but even he has failed, for want of space, to set forth the decisive part performed by the cavalry corps in the great events which followed.

The official reports reveal how it was arranged on the night of the 14th that the cavalry, which had recrossed to the south side of the river and encamped in the suburbs of the city, behind the right wing of the infantry, should sally from the fortified line against the Confederate left as soon as it was light enough to see, and how A. J. Smith's veterans of the Sixteenth Corps should move to their position in line of battle by the rear of the cavalry rather than across its front, so as not to delay it, but failed to carry out the arrangement, and thereby delayed the beginning of the battle an hour and a half longer than the time of delay due to the fog which prevailed in the early morning.☆ Fortunately, however, this did not derange the plan of operations, though it cut an hour and a half off the period of daylight in which to press the advantages of the first day, and the pursuit after Hood's lines were broken and put to flight on the evening of the second day.

Most historians of the Rebellion have followed the official reports of the great battle which ensued, but these reports were written too soon afterward, especially that of General Thomas, to give a strictly accurate account of the various movements, and of the results produced by them, or to consider properly the delay caused by the fog, and by Smith's movement. They have also fallen into error in giving McArthur's gallant infantry credit for entering the Confederate works on the first day, simultaneously with or ahead of the dismounted cavalry, while the fact is that the infantry joined in the charge against the works because they saw Hatch's men on their right advancing gallantly and successfully to the assault. The conduct of the infantry on that occasion was all that could be desired ; it did not hold back for orders, but led by the intrepid McArthur it sprang gallantly to the attack, and did its best to overtake and outstrip the dismounted cavalrymen, as they swept up the steep hillsides and over the enemy's works, after having broken through and driven back his attenuated left wing. The race for victory which followed between rival arms of the service was an unusual scene in that or any other army. Up to that time the cavalry in the West had been reserved for independent operations, and had rarely been seen assaulting fortified positions. Such work had been, by common consent, left for the infantry ; but now, under the influence of organization and discipline, the cavalry, with their Spencer repeating rifles, felt themselves equal to any task. And so well did they perform the one before them that McArthur and his gallant men, in the heat and exultation of the moment, were loud in their praises of the dismounted cavalrymen, and generously

awarded them the trophies of victory, together with the honor of being first to enter the works.

It is impossible within the limits of a single chapter to give any adequate account of the gallant deeds of Hatch, Croxton, Hammond, Johnson, Knipe, Coon, Stewart, Spalding, and their nameless but invincible followers upon that glorious day. Using the horses, which they had called for so lustily, for the purpose of moving the fighting force of the corps with celerity, but without fatigue, across the hills and plowed fields, now softened by thawing weather, to the vital points in the enemy's line, they were everywhere successful. Neither artillery nor musketry, nothing but darkness, could stay their onward progress, and after their first onset they looked upon fortifications and breastworks, abatis and entanglements, as new incitements to victory. Night found the bulk of their force a united and compact mass, bivouacked in the left and rear of the enemy's position, six miles from Nashville, and facing that city, with a firm grip on the Harding and Hillsborough turnpikes, and ready to press on toward the Granny White turnpike and the enemy's left center and rear at dawn the next day. They had captured sixteen field-guns from behind breastworks and redoubts and had taken many flags and prisoners.

Early on the 16th the cavalry resumed its operations in accordance with General Thomas's original plan ; Hatch continuing to press the enemy's extreme left and rear, Hammond moving farther to the right, and Croxton in position to support either, as might be required, while Johnson was sweeping in the same direction from the Charlotte turnpike on a wider circle. The country was still more hilly and densely covered with timber, and the enemy's line more compact and better able than the day before to resist attack from any quarter. As a consequence it was again necessary for the National cavalry to dismount and fight on foot, and its progress was correspondingly slow, except in Hammond's front. Indeed, Hood, discerning at an early hour that his principal danger lay in the direction of the cavalry attack, made extra exertions to hold it in check, and so stubbornly did his men bar the way that it seemed for a while impossible to advance farther. The exact dispositions made by Hood were concealed by the thick woods and undergrowth of the Brentwood Hills, and it was surmised that his new position might be found to be impregnable. To meet this contingency I suggested to General Thomas, about 10 A. M., that it might be well to transfer the whole or a part of the cavalry corps to the left, to see what effect it could produce upon the enemy's right flank. General Thomas agreed to the proposition, should another determined push from the various positions then occupied by the cavalry not be followed by satisfactory results. Fortunately, however, while this suggestion was being considered, the dismounted men, urged on by their gallant officers, continued their pressure, and by noon had driven the skirmishers close in upon Hood's main line, and had formed a continuous line

☆ See General Wilson's report, "Report of the Congressional Committee on the Conduct of the War," Supplement, Part I., pp. 409-422.—J. H. W.

from the right of Schofield's corps to and beyond the Granny White turnpike, which passed north and south through Hood's left center. Thus it will be seen that Hood's entire left wing was enveloped front and rear, and would be obliged to give way whenever it was vigorously and simultaneously assailed from opposite sides. Riding close up to the front, and perceiving the advantageous position which my men had gained, I sent my staff-officers, one after another, to Generals Schofield and Thomas with information of the success, accompanied by suggestions that the infantry should attack with vigor. It was during this stage of the battle that a most important dispatch from Hood to Chalmers (Forrest was still absent) was captured and brought to me, and forwarded by me at once to General Thomas. This dispatch seems to have been lost after the battle; at all events it has disappeared, but its character impressed it upon the memory of all who saw it. It ran, in substance, as follows: "For God's sake drive the Yankee cavalry from our left and rear, or all is lost." I found Thomas with Schofield in rear of the right of the line, and explained to them the situation, which was fortunately made entirely clear to them by the sight of the dismounted cavalrymen in full view, skirmishing heavily with the Confederate left, and also by the fire of a section of horse artillery, which had been dragged up the steep hillsides to a commanding position in rear of the Confederate works, and was pouring a heavy fire into them. Occasionally a shot would pass over the heads of the enemy and fall into our own lines. Seeing all this Thomas turned to Schofield and indicated that the time had come for the infantry to advance.

This was between half-past three and four o'clock. Schofield ordered his men forward at once, and as they charged the Confederate lines in front Hatch's dismounted cavalrymen entered them from the rear. Pressed on all sides, and perceiving that further resistance was futile if not impossible, the Confederates broke and fled in confusion from the field, leaving nearly all their artillery and many prisoners to fall into our hands. The cavalrymen had, however, become separated from their horses by an unusual distance, and, although the latter were hurried forward as rapidly as possible, and Croxton, who was most available, was ordered to mount and push without delay through Brentwood, to be followed by Hatch and Hammond as soon as they could mount, it had become so dark before they were well under way in pursuit that the men could scarcely see their horses' ears. It was a rainy and disagreeable night, but nevertheless Hatch, Knipe, Croxton, Hammond, Coon, and Spalding dashed forward, each vying with the other for the advance, and each doing his best to reach the Franklin turnpike that night so as to drive the now thoroughly disorganized

MAJOR-GENERAL JAMES H. WILSON. FROM A PHOTOGRAPH.

enemy from his last line of retreat. Orders were also sent to Johnson to move rapidly by the Hillsborough turnpike, and after crossing the Harpeth to turn up its south bank and fall upon the enemy at or near Franklin. Every one obeyed orders with alacrity, but darkness and distance were against them. Hatch's column had not gone more than two miles when its advance under Colonel Spalding encountered Chalmers's cavalry strongly posted across the road behind a fence-rail barricade. They charged it at once, and a spirited hand-to-hand mêlée ensued, in which many men were killed and wounded on each side. Colonel Spalding had the honor of capturing Brigadier-General Rucker, in a personal encounter, in which each had seized and wrested the other's saber from him, and used it against its owner. It was a scene of pandemonium, in which every challenge was answered by a saber stroke or pistol shot, and the flash of the carbine was the only light by which the combatants could recognize each other's position. The gallant Confederates were driven in turn from every fresh position taken up by them, and the running fight was kept up till nearly midnight. Chalmers had, however, done the work cut out for him gallantly and well. He was overborne and driven back, it is true, but the delay which he forced upon the Federal cavalry by the stand he had made was sufficient to enable the fleeing Confederate infantry to sweep by the danger-point that night, to improvise a rear-guard, and to make good their retreat the next day.

During the hurrying night ride down the Granny

White turnpike I was overtaken by General Thomas after it was so dark that men could recognize each other only by their voices. Thomas, riding up on my right, exclaimed in a tone of exultation never to be forgotten: "Didn't I tell you we could lick 'em? didn't I tell you we could lick 'em, if they would only let us alone?" (referring of course to the Washington authorities). After a few words of congratulation he turned about and leisurely rode back into camp.

The pursuit was resumed at the earliest dawn next morning and was kept up throughout the day, with a succession of sharp engagements, in which the Union cavalry was always victorious.

Late in the evening, apparently exhausted with rapid marching, the enemy took up a strong position in the open fields about a mile north of the West Harpeth River. It was then so dark from fog and approaching night that the men of Hatch's division, who had become somewhat intermingled with the sullen and taciturn Confederate stragglers, began to doubt that the ranks which were now looming up in their front were really those of the enemy's rear-guard. The momentary hesitation caused by this doubt gave Forrest an opportunity to straighten his lines and to post his single remaining battery in position so as to sweep the turnpike. Hatch on the left and Knipe on the right were at once ordered to charge the enemy's flanks, while the Fourth regular cavalry, under Lieutenant Hedges, was directed straight against his center. Seeing what was about to burst upon him, the battery commander opened with canister at short range, but had hardly emptied his guns before the storm broke upon him as well as upon the entire rebel line. Forrest did his best to hold his ground, but it was impossible. Hedges rode headlong over the battery and captured a part of his guns, while Hatch's horsemen, under a counter-fire from their own guns, with irresistible fury swept everything before them. Before the fight was over night closed in and covered the field with a pall of impenetrable darkness. The scene, like that of the night before, was one of great confusion, but every musket-flash and every defiant shout was a guide to the gallant and unrelenting pursuers. Hammond, passing around the enemy's left, forded the West Harpeth, and with the Tenth Indiana Cavalry, Lieutenant-Colonel Ben. Gresham commanding, struck a new line, formed a short distance south of the river, and in a desperate hand-to-hand fight, mounted men against footmen, saber and pistol against stout hearts and clubbed muskets, with the pall of darkness still over all, again scattered the enemy, capturing their remaining guns, and spreading confusion and terror throughout the retreating mass of now completely disorganized Confederates. It was 10 o'clock before the National cavalry ceased the pursuit, and an hour later before order could be restored to its ranks. Men and horses were ravenously hungry and almost worn out with three days of continuous marching and fighting, and there was nothing left them but to bivouac on the field. At early dawn the next morning, the 19th, the cavalry corps, although entirely out of rations, resumed the pursuit, Hatch and Knipe

pressing close upon the enemy's rear-guard, which had again been formed and was now commanded by Forrest in person, while Croxton and Johnson endeavored to reach around it and strike the retreating Confederates at Spring Hill. The densely wooded hills, the muddy roads, the plowed fields, rendered almost impassable by the constant rains, and, above all, the now rapidly rising streams made it impossible for the flanking columns traveling through the open country to overtake the enemy and again bring him to action. Late in the afternoon, in a violent winter rain-storm, the advanced guard was halted at Rutherford Creek, a considerable stream, now full to the hills on either side. The enemy had succeeded in destroying the bridges. The country had been entirely denuded of supplies for both men and horses; the haversacks and forage-bags were empty, and there was no alternative but to wait for the supply trains which had been ordered forward, and which joined late in the night. But during the night the rain turned into a snow-storm, and by order of General Thomas the larger part of the cavalry corps remained in bivouac the next day, while Hatch was trying to repair the railroad bridge.

The pontoon-train was also behind, and did not arrive till the next day. Meanwhile the pioneers of the cavalry were not idle. Those of Hatch's division, by dint of hard work, soon made the railroad bridge passable for skirmishers, and by the morning of the 20th had built a floating bridge out of the débris of another railroad bridge. This enabled him to cross the creek with his whole command, but a few miles beyond he was again stopped by the Duck River, which was also at flood. The delay of the pursuit at Rutherford Creek was short, but it gave the enemy a breathing-spell, which was of great value to him. It enabled him to get safely across the last considerable river between him and the Tennessee, to destroy the bridges which he had maintained at Columbia for the purpose of keeping communication open with the South, and, what was of still greater importance, to form all of his infantry that had not thrown their arms away into an effective rear-guard of eight brigades, each about five hundred strong. The Duck River proved impassable for the National cavalry till the single pontoon-train of the army could be brought forward, and this, owing to the condition of the roads and a mistake which had started it in the wrong direction, involved a further delay of twenty-four hours.

However, the bridge was completed by the evening of the 23d, and that night the whole corps, except the dismounted men who had been sent back to Nashville, crossed to the south side of the river, and early next morning resumed the pursuit. Hood's reorganized rear-guard, under the redoubtable Forrest, was soon encountered by the cavalry advanced guard, and he was a leader not to be attacked by a handful of men, however bold. The few remaining teams and the rabble of the army had been hurried on toward the Tennessee, marching to Pulaski by turnpike and thence to Bainbridge by the dirt roads of the country. The rear-guard had thus a clear road, and when hard pressed could fall back rapidly. The open country to the right and left of the turnpike was much broken, heavily wooded, and almost impassable, while the turnpike itself, threading the valleys, depressions, and gorges, offered many advantageous positions for defense; hence with a few men the pursuing force could be made to develop a front almost anywhere, and hence its progress was at times comparatively slow. But, withal, the enemy was closely pressed and every opportunity was seized upon to bring him to bay. In the vicinity of Lynnville, the country being somewhat more open, he was driven back rapidly, and at Buford's station, while General Hatch was engaging him upon the turnpike, General Croxton struck him in the flank, captured one flag and a number of prisoners, wounded General Abram Buford, and drove his cavalry rapidly beyond Richland Creek.

Just before sundown on Christmas day Forrest, in a fit of desperation, made a stand on a heavily wooded ridge at the head of a ravine, and by a rapid and savage counter-thrust drove back the skirmishers of Thomas Harrison's brigade, capturing one gun, which he succeeded in carrying away, as the sole trophy of that desperate campaign. This was the last flicker of aggressive temper shown by any part of Hood's beaten and demoralized army. Hammond, Hatch, and Croxton hastened to the front, and falling upon the flanks of the gallant Confederates drove them from the field into the cover and safety of darkness.

From that time till the Tennessee River was reached Forrest made a frequent show of resistance, each of which ended with nothing more serious than an insignificant skirmish. The weather had become worse and worse; it was cold and freezing during the nights, and followed by days of rain, snow, and thaw. The country, which was poor and thinly settled at best, had been absolutely stripped of forage and provisions by the march of contending armies. The men of both forces suffered dreadfully, but the poor cavalry horses fared still worse than their riders. Scarcely a withered corn-blade could be found for them, and thousands, exhausted by overwork, famished with hunger, or crippled so that death was a mercy, with hoofs dropping off from frost and mud, fell by the roadside never to rise again. By the time the corps found rest on the Tennessee River it could muster scarcely 7000 horses fit for service.

The failure of the light-draught gun-boats on the Tennessee River to reach and destroy the pontoon-bridge which Hood had kept in position insured his safe retreat. The cavalry advanced

guard, under the active and enterprising Spalding, reached the north bank of the river just as the bridge had been swung to the south side and the last of the rebels were disappearing in the distance. Another part of the cavalry corps under General W. J. Palmer sallied out from Decatur with General Steedman and finally overtook the remnant of Hood's army, destroyed his pontoon-train, with all of his remaining wagons, and captured several hundred prisoners.

The report of the provost-marshal shows that, during the operations beginning at Nashville on the 15th, and ending at the Tennessee River 175 miles south, on the 28th of December, the cavalry corps captured 32 field-guns, 11 caissons, 12 colors, 3332 prisoners, including one general officer, one train of 80 pontoons, and 125 wagons, and compelled the enemy besides to abandon or destroy a large number of wagons. Its own losses were one field-gun, 122 officers and men killed, 521 wounded, and 259 missing.

It may be fairly claimed that the organization of the cavalry corps of the Military Division of the Mississippi, during the progress of an active campaign, and in the presence of an invading army, the increase of that part of its force left in Tennessee from 4500 to 12,000 mounted men, the increase of its effective horses by impressment, the successes it gained in battle, and the persistency with which it pursued the flying enemy, are without a parallel in the history of this or any other war. It may also be fairly claimed that there was no success gained over the enemy's left wing on either the first or second day of the battle of Nashville which was not primarily and directly due to the operations of the cavalry, and this is particularly true of the final assault which broke the enemy's lines and sent his army to the rear in confusion.

It has been said in criticism of General Thomas, whose reputation as a great general as well as a winner of battles is more firmly founded upon his defeat of Hood at Nashville than upon any other event in his glorious career, that he made a mistake in waiting to rest and especially to remount his cavalry. The same writer also cites the fact that the cavalry fought mostly on foot as full justification for this remarkable criticism. It is sufficiently answered by the statement that the horses were used upon that occasion, as in all modern wars where cavalry has appeared, mainly for the transportation of the fighting men, and not to fight themselves, and by the further and conclusive fact that Hood's army was effectually destroyed by the defeat at Nashville and the subsequent pursuit. ↓

↓ When Hood reached Tupelo his whole army numbered about 21,000. Forrest took his cavalry to Mississippi, and the infantry brigades of Gibson, Holtzclaw, Ector, Cockrell, and Sears, with some batteries of artillery, went to General Maury, at Mobile. Of the re-

mainder, perhaps five thousand joined General Johnston in North Carolina the next spring. General Hood ("Advance and Retreat," p. 510) says that nine thousand left the ranks between Tupelo and North Carolina.— EDITORS.

THE OPPOSING FORCES AT NASHVILLE, DEC. 15-16, 1864.

THE UNION ARMY, Major-General George H. Thomas.

FOURTH ARMY CORPS, Brig.-Gen. Thomas J. Wood.
FIRST DIVISION, Brig.-Gen. Nathan Kimball.
First Brigade, Col. Isaac M. Kirby: 21st Ill., Capt. William H. Jamison; 38th Ill., Capt. Andrew M. Pollard; 31st Ind., Col. John T. Smith; 81st Ind., Maj. Edward G. Mathey; 90th Ohio, Lieut.-Col. Samuel N. Yeoman; 101st Ohio, Lieut.-Col. Bedan B. McDanald. Brigade loss: k, 20; w, 100 = 120. *Second Brigade*, Brig.-Gen. Walter C. Whitaker: 96th Ill., Maj. George Hicks; 115th Ill., Col. Jesse H. Moore; 35th Ind., Lieut.-Col. Augustus G. Tassin; 21st Ky., Col. James C. Evans; 23d Ky., Lieut.-Col. George W. Northup; 45th Ohio, Lieut.-Col. John H. Humphrey; 51st Ohio, Lieut.-Col. Charles H. Wood. Brigade loss: k, 10; w, 38; m, 1 = 49. *Third Brigade*, Brig.-Gen. William Grose: 75th Ill., Col. John E. Bennett; 80th Ill., Capt. James Cunningham; 84th Ill., Lieut.-Col. Charles H. Morton; 9th Ind., Col. Isaac C. B. Suman; 30th Ind., Capt. Henry W. Lawton; 36th Ind. (1 co.), Lieut. John P. Swisher; 84th Ind., Maj. John C. Taylor; 77th Pa., Lieut.-Col. Thomas E. Rose. Brigade loss: k, 6; w, 75; m, 1 = 82.
SECOND DIVISION, Brig.-Gen. Washington L. Elliott.
First Brigade, Col. Emerson Opdycke: 36th Ill., Maj. Levi P. Holden; 44th Ill., Capt. Alonzo W. Clark; 73d Ill., Capt. Wilson Burroughs; 74th and 88th Ill., Lieut.-Col. George W. Smith; 125th Ohio, Maj. Joseph Bruff; 24th Wis., Capt. William Kennedy. Brigade loss: k, 8; w, 39; m, 4 = 51. *Second Brigade*, Col. John Q. Lane: 100th Ill., Lieut.-Col. Charles M. Hammond; 40th Ind., Lieut.-Col. Henry Leaming; 57th Ind., Lieut.-Col. Willis Blanch; 28th Ky., Lieut.-Col. J. Rowan Boone; 26th Ohio, Capt. William Clark; 97th Ohio, Lieut.-Col. Milton Barnes. Brigade loss: k, 4; w, 57; m, 1 = 62. *Third Brigade*, Col. Joseph Conrad: 42d Ill., Lieut.-Col. Edgar D. Swain; 51st Ill., Capt. Albert M. Tilton; 79th Ill., Col. Allen Buckner; 15th Mo., Capt. George Ernst; 64th Ohio, Lieut.-Col. Robert C. Brown; 65th Ohio, Maj. Orlow Smith. Brigade loss: k, 8; w, 47; m, 2 = 57.
THIRD DIVISION, Brig.-Gen. Samuel Beatty.
First Brigade, Col. Abel D. Streight: 89th Ill., Lieut.-Col. William D. Williams; 51st Ind., Capt. William W. Scearce; 8th Kan., Lieut.-Col. John Conover; 15th Ohio, Col. Frank Askew, Lieut.-Col. John McClenahan; 49th Ohio, Maj. Luther M. Strong, Capt. Daniel Hartsough. Brigade loss: k, 40; w, 204 = 244. *Second Brigade*, Col. P. Sidney Post, Lieut.-Col. Robert L. Kimberly: 59th Ill., Maj. James M. Stookey; 41st Ohio, Lieut.-Col. Robert L. Kimberly, Capt. Ezra Dunham; 71st Ohio, Lieut.-Col. James H. Hart, Capt. William H. McClure; 93d Ohio, Lieut.-Col. Daniel Bowman; 124th Ohio, Lieut.-Col. James Pickands. Brigade loss: k, 36; w, 263; m, 13 = 312. *Third Brigade*, Col. Frederick Knefler: 79th Ind., Lieut.-Col. George W. Parker; 86th Ind., Col. George F. Dick; 13th Ohio (4 co's), Maj. Joseph T. Snider; 19th Ohio, Lieut.-Col. Henry G. Stratton. Brigade loss: k, 1; w, 7 = 8.
ARTILLERY, Maj. Wilbur F. Goodspeed: 25th Ind., Capt. Frederick C. Sturm; 1st Ky., Capt. T. S. Thomasson; E, 1st Mich., Capt. Peter De Vries; G, 1st Ohio, Capt. Alexander Marshall; 6th Ohio, Lieut. Aaron P. Baldwin; B, Pa., Capt. Jacob Ziegler; M, 4th U. S., Lieut. Samuel Canby. Artillery loss: k, 2; w, 4 = 6.
TWENTY-THIRD ARMY CORPS, Maj.-Gen. John M. Schofield.
SECOND DIVISION, Maj.-Gen. Darius N. Couch.
First Brigade, Brig.-Gen. Joseph A. Cooper: 130th Ind., Col. Charles S. Parrish; 26th Ky., Col. Cicero Maxwell; 25th Mich., Capt. Samuel L. Demarest; 99th Ohio, Lieut.-Col. John E. Cummins; 3d Tenn., Col. William Cross; 6th Tenn., Lieut.-Col. Edward Maynard. Brigade loss: k, 7; w, 82 = 89. *Second Brigade*, Col. Orlando H. Moore: 107th Ill., Capt. John W. Wood; 80th Ind., Lieut.-Col. Alfred D. Owen; 129th Ind., Col. Charles A.

Zollinger; 23d Mich., Col. Oliver L. Spaulding; 111th Ohio, Col. Isaac R. Sherwood; 118th Ohio, Maj. Edgar Sowers. Brigade loss: k, 2; w, 34 = 36. *Third Brigade*, Col. John Mehringer: 91st Ind., Lieut.-Col. Charles H. Butterfield; 123d Ind., Col. John C. McQuiston; 50th Ohio, Lieut.-Col. Hamilton S. Gillespie; 183d Ohio, Col. George W. Hoge. Brigade loss: k, 2; w, 20 = 22. *Artillery:* 15th Ind., Capt. Alonzo D. Harvey; 19th Ohio, Capt. Frank Wilson.
THIRD DIVISION, Brig.-Gen. Jacob D. Cox.
First Brigade, Col. Charles C. Doolittle: 12th Ky., Col. Laurence H. Rousseau; 16th Ky., Capt. Jacob Miller; 100th Ohio, Lieut.-Col. Edwin L. Hayes; 104th Ohio, Lieut.-Col. Oscar W. Sterl; 8th Tenn., Capt. James W. Berry. Brigade loss: w, 5. *Second Brigade*, Col. John S. Casement: 65th Ill., Lieut.-Col. W. Scott Stewart; 65th Ind., Lieut.-Col. John W. Hammond; 124th Ind., Col. John M. Orr; 103d Ohio, Capt. Henry S. Pickands; 5th Tenn., Lieut.-Col. Nathaniel Witt. Brigade loss: w, 9. *Third Brigade*, Col. Israel N. Stiles: 112th Ill., Maj. Tristam T. Dow; 63d Ind., Lieut.-Col. Daniel Morris; 120th Ind., Maj. John M. Barcus; 128th Ind., Lieut.-Col. Jasper Packard. Brigade loss: w, 3. *Artillery:* 23d Ind., Lieut. Aaron A. Wilber; D, 1st Ohio, Capt. Giles J. Cockerill.
ARMY OF THE TENNESSEE (Detachment), Maj.-Gen. Andrew J. Smith.
FIRST DIVISION, Brig.-Gen. John McArthur.
First Brigade, Col. William L. McMillen: 114th Ill., Capt. John M. Johnson; 93d Ind., Col. De Witt C. Thomas, Capt. Charles A. Hubbard; 10th Minn., Lieut.-Col. Samuel P. Jennison, Capt. Edwin C. Sanders; 72d Ohio, Lieut.-Col. Charles G. Eaton; 95th Ohio, Lieut.-Col. Jefferson Brumback; Ill. Battery (Cogswell's), Lieut. S. H. McClaury. Brigade loss: k, 22; w, 96 = 118. *Second Brigade*, Col. Lucius F. Hubbard: 5th Minn., Lieut.-Col. William B. Gere; 9th Minn., Col. Josiah F. Marsh; 11th Mo., Lieut.-Col. Eli Bowyer, Maj. Modesta J. Green; 8th Wis., Lieut.-Col. William B. Britton; 2d Iowa Battery, Capt. Joseph R. Reed. Brigade loss: k, 33; w, 281; m, 1 = 315. *Third Brigade*, Col. Sylvester G. Hill, Col. William R. Marshall: 12th Iowa, Lieut.-Col. John H. Stibbs; 35th Iowa, Maj. William Dill, Capt. Abraham N. Snyder; 7th Minn., Col. William R. Marshall, Lieut.-Col. George Bradley; 33d Mo., Lieut.-Col. William H. Heath; I, 2d Mo. Art'y, Capt. Stephen H. Julian. Brigade loss: k, 12; w, 133 = 145.
SECOND DIVISION, Brig.-Gen. Kenner Garrard.
First Brigade, Col. David Moore: 119th Ill., Col. Thomas J. Kinney; 122d Ill., Lieut.-Col. James F. Drish; 89th Ind., Lieut.-Col. Hervey Craven; 21st Mo. (detachment 24th Mo. attached), Lieut.-Col. Edwin Moore; 9th Ind. Battery, Lieut. Samuel G. Calfee. Brigade loss: k, 2; w, 47 = 49. *Second Brigade*, Col. James I. Gilbert: 58th Ill., Maj. Robert W. Healy; 27th Iowa, Lieut.-Col. Jed. Lake; 32d Iowa, Lieut.-Col. Gustavus A. Eberhart; 10th Kan. (4 co's), Capt. William C. Jones; 3d Ind. Battery, Lieut. Thomas J. Ginn. Brigade loss: k, 1; w, 62 = 63. *Third Brigade*, Col. Edward H. Wolfe: 49th Ill., Col. Phineas Pease; 117th Ill., Lieut.-Col. Jonathan Merriam; 52d Ind., Lieut.-Col. Zalmon S. Main; 178th N. Y., Capt. John B. Gandolfo; G, 2d Ill. Art'y, Capt. John W. Lowell. Brigade loss: k, 5; w, 46; m, 1 = 52.
THIRD DIVISION, Col. Jonathan B. Moore.
First Brigade, Col. Lyman M. Ward: 72d Ill., Capt. James A. Sexton; 40th Mo., Col. Samuel A. Holmes; 14th Wis., Maj. Eddy F. Ferris; 33d Wis., Lieut.-Col. Frederick S. Lovell. Brigade loss: w, 3. *Second Brigade*, Col. Leander Blanden: 81st Ill., Lieut.-Col. Andrew W. Rogers; 95th Ill., Lieut.-Col. William Avery; 44th Mo., Lieut.-Col. Andrew J. Barr. Brigade loss: w, 1. *Artillery:* 14th Ind., Capt. Francis W. Morse; A, 2d Mo., Lieut. John Zepp. Artillery loss: k, 1.

PROVISIONAL DETACHMENT, Maj.-Gen. James B. Steedman.

PROVISIONAL DIVISION, | Brig.-Gen. Charles Cruft.

First Brigade, Col. Benjamin Harrison. *Second Brigade*, Col. John G. Mitchell. *Third Brigade*, Lieut.-Col. Charles H. Grosvenor. Loss in these three brigades : k, 19 ; w, 68 ; m, 32 = 119. *Second Brigade* (Army Tenn.), Col. A. G. Malloy. *Miscellaneous :* 68th Ind. (attached to Third Brigade), Lieut.-Col. H. J. Espy ; 18th Ohio, Capt. Ebenezer Grosvenor, Capt. J. M. Benedict, Lieut. Chas. Grant. Loss : k, 12 ; w, 47 ; m, 9 = 68. *Artillery :* 20th Ind., Capt. M. A. Osborne ; 18th Ohio, Capt. Chas. C. Aleshire. Artillery loss : w, 8. *First Colored Brigade*, Col. Thos. J. Morgan ; 14th U. S. C. T., Lieut.-Col. H. C. Corbin ; 16th U. S. C. T., Col. William B. Gaw ; 17th U. S. C. T., Col. Wm. R. Shafter ; 18th U. S. C. T. (battalion), Maj. Lewis D. Joy ; 44th U. S. C. T., Col. Lewis Johnson. Brigade loss : k, 21 ; w, 118 ; m, 23 = 162. *Second Colored Brigade*, Col. Chas. R. Thompson : 12th U. S. C. T., Lieut.-Col. Wm. R. Sellon, Capt. Henry Hegner ; 13th U. S. C. T., Col. J. A. Hottenstein ; 100th U. S. C. T., Maj. Collin Ford ; 1st Kan. Battery, Capt. Marcus D. Tenney, Brigade loss : k, 77 ; w, 390 ; m, 1 = 468.

POST OF NASHVILLE, Brig.-Gen. John F. Miller.

Second Brigade, Fourth Division, Twentieth Corps, Col. Edwin C. Mason : 142d Ind., Col. John M. Comparet ; 45th N. Y., Col. Adolphus Dobke ; 176th Ohio, Lieut.-Col. William B. Nesbitt ; 179th Ohio, Col. Harley H. Sage ; 182d Ohio, Col. Lewis Butler. *Unattached :* 3d Ky., —— ; 28th Mich., Col. William W. Wheeler ; 173d Ohio, Col. John R. Hurd ; 78th Pa. (detachment), Lieut.-Col. Henry W. Torbett ; Veteran Reserve Corps, Col. Frank P. Cahill ; 44th Wis. (battalion), Lieut.-Col. Oliver C. Bissell ; 45th Wis. (battalion), ——.

GARRISON ARTILLERY, Maj. John J. Ely : 2d Ind., Capt. James S. Whicher ; 4th Ind., Capt. Benjamin F. Johnson ; 12th Ind., Capt. James E. White ; 21st Ind., Capt. Abram P. Andrew ; 22d Ind., Capt. Edward W. Nicholson ; 24th Ind., Lieut. Hiram Allen ; F, 1st Mich., Capt. Byron D. Paddock ; E, 1st Ohio, Lieut. Frank B. Reckard ; 20th Ohio, Capt. William Backus ; C, 1st Tenn., Lieut. Joseph Grigsby ; D, 1st Tenn., Capt. Samuel D. Leinart ; A, 2d U. S. Colored, Capt. Josiah V. Meigs.

QUARTERMASTER'S DIVISION (composed of quartermaster's employees), Col. James L. Donaldson.

CAVALRY CORPS, Brig.-Gen. James H. Wilson.

Escort : 4th U. S., Lieut. Joseph Hedges.

FIRST DIVISION (Second and Third Brigades, under Brig.-Gen. E. M. McCook, absent in western Kentucky).

First Brigade, Brig.-Gen. John T. Croxton : 8th Iowa, Col. Joseph B. Dorr ; 4th Ky. (mounted infantry), Col. Robert M. Kelly ; 2d Mich., Lieut.-Col. Benjamin Smith ; 1st Tenn, Lieut.-Col. Calvin M. Dyer ; Ill. Battery, Capt. George I. Robinson. Brigade loss : w, 2.

FIFTH DIVISION, Brig.-Gen. Edward Hatch.

First Brigade, Col. Robert R. Stewart : 3d Ill., Lieut.-Col. Robert H. Carnahan ; 11th Ind., Lieut.-Col. Abram Sharra ; 12th Mo., Col. Oliver Wells ; 10th Tenn., Maj. William P. Story, Maj. James T. Abernathy. Brigade loss : k, 14 ; w, 108 = 122. *Second Brigade*, Col. Datus E.

Coon : 6th Ill., Lieut.-Col. John Lynch ; 7th Ill., Maj. John M. Graham ; 9th Ill., Capt. Joseph W. Harper ; 2d Iowa, Maj. Charles C. Horton ; 12th Tenn., Col. George Spalding ; I, 1st Ill. Art'y, Lieut. Joseph A. McCartney. Brigade loss : k, 14 ; w, 98 ; m, 1 = 113.

SIXTH DIVISION, Brig.-Gen. Richard W. Johnson.

First Brigade, Col. Thomas J. Harrison : 16th Ill., Maj. Charles H. Beeres ; 5th Iowa, Lieut.-Col. Harlon Baird ; 7th Ohio, Col. Israel Garrard. Brigade loss : k, 2 ; w, 9 ; m, 9 = 20. *Second Brigade*, Col. James Biddle : 14th Ill., Maj. Haviland Tompkins ; 6th Ind., Maj. Jacob S. Stephens ; 8th Mich., Col. Elisha Mix ; 3d Tenn., Maj. Benjamin Cunningham. Brigade loss : w, 7 ; m, 1 = 8. *Artillery :* I, 4th U. S., Lieut. Frank G. Smith.

SEVENTH DIVISION, Brig.-Gen. Joseph F. Knipe.

First Brigade, Brevet Brig.-Gen. John H. Hammond : 9th Ind., Col. George W. Jackson ; 10th Ind., Lieut.-Col. B. Q. A. Gresham ; 19th Pa., Lieut.-Col. Joseph C. Hess ; 2d Tenn., Lieut.-Col. William R. Cook ; 4th Tenn., Lieut.-Col. Jacob M. Thornburgh. Brigade loss : k, 5 ; w, 42 ; m, 10 = 57. *Second Brigade*, Col. Gilbert M. L. Johnson : 12th Ind., Col. Edward Anderson ; 13th Ind., Lieut.-Col. William T. Pepper ; 6th Tenn., Col. Fielding Hurst. Brigade loss : k, 1 ; w, 4 ; m, 2 = 7. *Artillery :* 14th Ohio, Capt. William C. Myers.

Total Union loss : killed, 387 ; wounded, 2558 ; captured or missing, 112 = 3057. The casualties at Franklin, November 30th, amounted to 189 killed ; 1033 wounded ; and 1104 captured or missing = 2326. General Thomas reported that the losses of his army in the entire campaign did not exceed 10,000 in killed, wounded, and missing. According to official returns the effective force of Thomas's *whole command* was as follows : October 31st, 53,415 ; November 20th, 59,534 ; November 30th, 71,452 ; December 10th, 70,272. In his official report, General Thomas says that his effective force early in November " consisted of the Fourth Corps, about 12,000, under General D. S. Stanley ; the Twenty-third Corps, about 10,000, under General J. M. Schofield ; Hatch's division of cavalry, about 4000 ; Croxton's brigade, 2500, and Capron's brigade of about 1200 [total, 29,700]. The balance of my force was distributed along the railroad, and posted at Murfreesboro', Stevenson, Bridgeport, Huntsville, Decatur, and Chattanooga, to keep open our communications and hold the posts above named, if attacked, until they could be reënforced, as up to this time it was impossible to determine which course Hood would take — advance on Nashville, or turn toward Huntsville." It is estimated that the *available* Union force of all arms in and about Nashville on December 15th aggregated at least 55,000. Col. Henry Stone, of General Thomas's staff, furnishes the following estimate of the number of Union troops *actually engaged* in the battle (not including the garrison force and dismounted cavalry, viz. : Fourth Corps, 13,350 ; Twenty-third Corps, 8830 ; Detachment Army of the Tennessee, 9210 ; Steedman's Detachment, 5270 ; Cavalry Corps (mounted men), 6600, or an aggregate, including artillery, of 43,260. General J. H. Wilson says the cavalry numbered 12,000.

THE CONFEDERATE ARMY.

ARMY OF TENNESSEE. — General John B. Hood.

LEE'S CORPS (Hood's), Lieut.-Gen. S. D. Lee.

JOHNSON'S DIVISION, Maj.-Gen. Edward Johnson.

Deas's Brigade, Brig.-Gen. Z. C. Deas : 19th Ala., Lieut.-Col. R. Kimbrough ; 22d Ala., Capt. H. W. Henry ; 25th Ala., Capt. N. B. Rouse ; 39th Ala., Lieut.-Col. W. C. Clifton ; 50th Ala., Col. J. G. Coltart. *Manigault's Brigade*, Lieut.-Col. W. L. Butler : 24th Ala., Capt. T. J. Kimball ; 28th Ala., Capt. W. M. Nabors ; 34th Ala., Lieut.-Col. J. C. Carter ; 10th S. C., Lieut.-Col. C. Irvin Walker ; 19th S. C., Capt. T. W. Getzen. *Sharp's Brigade*, Brig.-Gen. J. H. Sharp : 7th and 9th Miss., Maj. H. Pope ; 10th and 44th Miss., and 9th Miss. Batt'n Sharp-

shooters, Capt. R. A. Bell ; 41st Miss., Capt. J. M. Hicks. *Brantly's Brigade*, Brig.-Gen. W. F. Brantly : 24th and 34th Miss., Capt. C. Dancy ; 27th Miss., Capt. S. M. Pegg ; 29th and 30th Miss., Capt. R. W. Williamson ; Dismounted Cavalry, Capt. D. W. Alexander.

ARTILLERY, Lieut.-Col. L. Hoxton (Chief Corps Art'y).

Courtney's Battalion, Capt. J. P. Douglas : Ala. Battery, Capt. S. H. Dent ; Ala. Battery, Lieut. H. Ferrell ; Tex. Battery, Lieut. Ben. Hardin.

STEVENSON'S DIVISION, Maj.-Gen. C. L. Stevenson.

Cumming's Brigade, Col. E. P. Watkins : 34th Ga., Capt. R. A. Jones ; 36th Ga., Col. Charles E. Broyles ; 39th Ga.,

---

| Composed mainly of detachments belonging to the 14th, 15th, 17th, and 20th corps, which had been unable to rejoin their proper commands, serving with Sherman's army on the march through Georgia.

Capt. W. P. Milton; 56th Ga., Capt. B. T. Spearman. *Pettus's Brigade*, Brig.-Gen. E. W. Pettus: 20th Ala., Col. J. N. Dedman; 23d Ala., Lieut.-Col. J. B. Bibb; 30th Ala., Lieut.-Col. J. R. Elliott; 31st Ala., Lieut.-Col. T. M. Arrington; 46th Ala., Capt. G. E. Brewer. *Artillery Battalion* (Johnston's), Capt. J. B. Rowan: Ga. Bat'y, Lieut. W. S. Hoge; Ga. Bat'y, Lieut. W. L. Ritter.
CLAYTON'S DIVISION, Maj.-Gen. H. D. Clayton.

Stovall's Brigade, Brig.-Gen. M. A. Stovall: 40th Ga., Col. A. Johnson; 41st Ga., Capt. J. E. Stallings; 42d Ga., Col. R. J. Henderson; 43d Ga., Col. H. C. Kellogg; 52d Ga., Capt. R. R. Asbury. *Gibson's Brigade*, Brig.-Gen. Randall L. Gibson: 1st La., Capt. J. C. Stafford; 4th La., Col. S. E. Hunter; 13th La., Col. F. L. Campbell; 16th La., Lieut.-Col. R. H. Lindsay; 19th La., Maj. C. Flournoy; 20th La., Capt. A. Dresel; 25th La., Col. F. C. Zacharie; 30th La., Maj. A. Picolet; 4th La. Battalion, Capt. T. A. Bisland; 14th La. Battalion Sharp-shooters, Lieut. A. T. Martin. *Holtzclaw's Brigade*, Brig.-Gen. J. T. Holtzclaw: 18th Ala., Lieut.-Col. P. F. Hunley; 32d and 58th Ala., Col. Bushrod Jones; 36th Ala., Capt. N. M. Carpenter; 38th Ala., Capt. C. E. Bussey. *Artillery Battalion* (Eldridge's), Capt. C. E. Fenner: Ala. Battery, Capt. W. J. McKenzie; Miss. Bat'y, Lieut. J. S. McCall.
STEWART'S CORPS (Polk's), Lieut.-Gen. A. P. Stewart.
LORING'S DIVISION, Maj.-Gen. W. W. Loring.

Featherston's Brigade, Brig.-Gen. W. S. Featherston: 1st Miss., Capt. O. D. Hughes; 3d Miss., Capt. O. H. Johnston; 22d Miss., Maj. M. A. Oatis; 31st Miss., Capt. R. A. Collins; 33d Miss., Capt. T. L. Cooper; 40th Miss., Col. W. B. Colbert; 1st Miss. Batt'n, Maj. J. M. Stigler. *Adams's Brigade*, Col. Robert Lowry: 6th Miss., Lieut.-Col. Thomas J. Borden; 14th Miss., Col. W. L. Doss; 15th Miss., Lieut.-Col. J. R. Binford; 20th Miss., Maj. Thomas B. Graham; 23d Miss., Maj. G. W. B. Garrett; 43d Miss., Col. Richard Harrison. *Scott's Brigade*, Col. John Snodgrass: 55th Ala., Maj. J. B. Dickey; 57th Ala., Maj. J. H. Wiley; 27th, 35th, and 49th Ala., Lieut.-Col. J. D. Weeden; 12th La., Capt. J. T. Davis.
ARTILLERY, Lieut.-Col. S. C. Williams (Chief Corps Art'y). *Myrick's Battalion:* La. Battery (Bouanchaud's); Miss. Battery (Cowan's); Miss. Battery (Darden's).
FRENCH'S DIVISION (temporarily attached to Walthall's division).

Sears's Brigade, Brig.-Gen. C. W. Sears: 4th Miss., ——; 35th Miss., ——; 36th Miss., ——; 39th Miss., ——; 46th Miss., ——; 7th Miss. Battalion, ——. *Ector's Brigade*, Col. D. Coleman: 29th N. C., Maj. E. H. Hampton; 39th N. C., Capt. J. G. Crawford; 9th Texas, Maj. J. H. McReynolds; 10th Tex. (dismounted cavalry), Col. C. R. Earp; 14th Tex. (dismounted cavalry), Capt. R. H. Harkey; 32d Texas (dismounted cavalry), Maj. W. E. Estes. *Artillery Battalion* (Storrs's): Ala. Battery (Kolb's); Miss. Battery (Hoskins's); Mo. Bat'y (Guibor's).
WALTHALL'S DIVISION, Maj.-Gen. E. C. Walthall.

Quarles's Brigade, Brig.-Gen. George D. Johnston: 1st Ala., Lieut. C. M. McRae; 42d, 46th, 49th, 53d, and 55th Tenn., Capt. A. M. Duncan; 48th Tenn., Col. W. M. Voorhies. *Cantey's Brigade*, Brig.-Gen. C. M. Shelley: 17th Ala., Capt. John Bolling; 26th Ala., Capt. D. M. Gideon; 29th Ala., Capt. S. Abernathy; 37th Miss., Maj. S. H. Terral. *Reynolds's Brigade*, Brig.-Gen. D. H. Reynolds: 1st Ark. Mounted Rifles (dismounted), Capt. R. P. Parks; 2d Ark. Mounted Rifles (dismounted), Maj. J. P. Eagle; 4th Ark., Maj. J. A. Ross; 9th Ark., Capt. W. L. Phefer; 25th Ark., Lieut. T. J. Edwards. *Artillery Battalion* (Truehart's): Ala. Battery (Lumsden's); Ala. Battery (Selden's); Ala. Battery (Tarrant's).
CHEATHAM'S CORPS (formerly Hardee's), Lieut.-Gen. B. F. Cheatham.
BROWN'S DIVISION.

Gist's Brigade, Lieut.-Col. Z. L. Walters: 46th Ga., Capt. Malcolm Gillis; 65th Ga. and 8th Ga. Battalion, Capt. W. W. Grant; 2d Ga. Battalion Sharp-shooters, Capt. William H. Brown; 16th S. C., Capt. J. W. Boling; 24th S. C., Capt. W. C. Griffith. *Maney's Brigade*, Col. H. R. Feild: 4th Confed., and 6th, 9th, and 50th Tenn., Lieut.-Col. G. W. Pease; 1st and 27th Tenn., Lieut.-Col. J. L. House; 8th, 16th, and 28th Tenn., Col. J. H. Ander-

son. *Strahl's Brigade*, Col. A. J. Kellar: 4th, 5th, 31st, 33d, and 38th Tenn., Lieut.-Col. L. W. Finlay; 19th, 24th, and 41st Tenn., Capt. D. A. Kennedy. *Vaughan's Brigade*, Col. W. M. Watkins: 11th and 29th Tenn., Maj. J. E. Burns; 12th and 47th Tenn., Capt. C. N. Wade; 13th, 51st, 52d, and 154th Tenn., Maj. J. F. Williamson.
ARTILLERY, Col. Melancthon Smith (Chief Corps Art'y).
Artillery Battalion: Ala. Battery (Phelan's); Fla. Battery (Perry's); Miss. Battery (Turner's).
CLEBURNE'S DIVISION, Brig.-Gen. J. A. Smith.

Lowrey's Brigade, Brig.-Gen. M. P. Lowrey: 16th, 33d, and 45th Ala., Lieut.-Col. R. H. Abercrombie; 5th Miss. and 3d Miss. Battalion, Capt. F. M. Woodward; 8th and 32d Miss., Maj. A. E. Moody. *Govan's Brigade*, Brig.-Gen. D. C. Govan, Col. Peter V. Green: 1st, 2d, 5th, 13th, 15th, and 24th Ark., Col. Peter V. Green; 6th and 7th Ark., Lieut.-Col. P. Snyder; 8th and 19th Ark., Maj. D. H. Hamiter. *Granbury's Brigade*, Capt. E. T. Broughton: 35th Tenn., ——; 6th and 15th Tex., Capt. B. R. Tyus; 7th Tex., Capt. O. P. Forrest; 10th Tex., Capt. R. D. Kennedy; 17th and 18th Tex. (dismounted cavalry), Capt. F. L. McKnight; 24th and 25th Texas (dismounted cavalry), Capt. J. F. Matthews; La. Cav. Co., Capt. L. M. Nutt. *Artillery Battalion* (Hotchkiss's): Ala. Battery (Goldthwaite's); Ark. Battery (Key's); Mo. Battery (Bledsoe's).
BATE'S DIVISION, Maj.-Gen. William B. Bate. *Escort*, Capt. J. H. Buck.

Tyler's Brigade, Brig.-Gen. T. B. Smith: 37th Ga., Capt. J. A. Sanders; 4th Ga. Battalion Sharp-shooters, Maj. T. D. Caswell; 2d, 10th, 15th, 20th, 30th, and 37th Tenn., Col. W. M. Shy, Maj. H. C. Lucas. *Finley's Brigade*, Maj. G. A. Ball: 1st and 3d Fla., Capt. M. H. Strain; 6th Fla., Capt. A. M. Williams; 7th Fla., Capt. R. B. Smith; 1st Fla. Cav. (dismounted) and 4th Fla., Maj. Jacob A. Lash. *Jackson's Brigade*, Brig.-Gen. H. R. Jackson: 1st Ga. (Confed.) and 66th Ga., Lieut.-Col. J. C. Gordon; 25th Ga., Capt. J. E. Fulton; 29th and 30th Ga., Col. W. D. Mitchell; 1st Ga. Battalion Sharp-shooters, Lieut. R. C. King. *Artillery Battalion*, Capt. R. T. Beauregard: La. Battery (Slocomb's); S. C. Battery (Ferguson's); Tenn. Battery (Mebane's).
CAVALRY DIVISION, Brig.-Gen. James R. Chalmers. *Escort*, Capt. C. T. Smith.

Rucker's Brigade, Col. E. W. Rucker, Lieut.-Col. R. R. White: 7th Ala., ——; 5th Miss., ——; 7th Tenn., ——; 14th Tenn., Lieut.-Col. R. R. White; 15th Tenn., ——; 26th Tenn. Battalion, ——. *Biffle's Brigade*, Col. J. B. Biffle: 9th Tenn., ——; 10th Tenn., ——.

At the time of the battle of Nashville, Forrest, with Jackson's and Buford's divisions of cavalry and Mercer's and Palmer's brigades of infantry, was detached from the main army and operating on its flanks. Hood reported that he began the campaign with "an 'effective total' of 40,403." On November 6th his strength was 44,729. By the arrival of Forrest's cavalry, on November 15th, the army aggregated 53,938. Exclusive of Palmer's brigade of Lee's corps, Mercer's brigade of Cheatham's corps, and Sears's and Cockrell's brigades of Stewart's corps, and Forrest's cavalry (not included in Hood's return), the "present for duty" on December 10th was 26,877. These omitted commands probably numbered 12,000, which would give Hood an aggregate effective force at that date of nearly 39,000. But Col. Henry Stone estimates that Hood's army at Nashville numbered 37,937, including some who were reported as on "extra duty," but who he (Stone) claims were with their commands, and (Hood being on the defensive) were, as occasion required, put in the ranks to fight. According to Hood's official report his loss at Franklin in killed, wounded, and prisoners was 4500. The loss at Nashville is not stated. He reached Tupelo, at the close of the campaign, with about 21,000. General Hood reported officially: "Losses, including prisoners, during the entire campaign do not exceed 10,000 men." On the other hand, General Thomas states in his official report that during the campaign he "captured 13,189 prisoners of war," and that "during the same period over 2000 deserters from the enemy were received."

REVEILLE.

OPERATIONS IN EAST TENNESSEE AND SOUTH-WEST VIRGINIA.

BY THE REV. EDWARD O. GUERRANT, ASSISTANT ADJUTANT-GENERAL TO
GENERAL HUMPHREY MARSHALL, C. S. A.

BETWEEN the two great Confederate armies in Virginia and Tennessee lay a long stretch of country, principally covered by the Alleghany and Cumberland mountains. The only means of direct communication and transportation between these armies was the East Tennessee, Virginia, and Georgia Railroad. Near this road were the great King's salt-works, in Smyth County, and the lead mines of Wythe County, Virginia, and along this route lay many very fertile valleys and rich uplands, which furnished the Confederate armies a large part of their provisions. For these and other reasons the defense of this line was a matter of the first importance to the Confederate Government, and its control of equal importance to the Federal armies.

As the mountainous nature of the country rendered its occupation by a large army impracticable, numerous invasions by smaller forces, principally of cavalry, were made in order to destroy the salt-works and the railroad communications. The very extent of the frontier and its broken surface made it difficult of defense, and rendered necessary a larger force of occupation than was generally available.

General Garfield's campaign early in 1862 against General Humphrey Marshall has already been described in this work. [See Vol. I., p. 393.]

In December, 1862, General Samuel P. Carter, of Tennessee, and Colonel T. T. Garrard, of Kentucky, crossed the Cumberland Mountains from Kentucky with a large force of Federal cavalry and made a raid upon the railroad in east Tennessee, and destroyed the bridges over the Holston and Watauga rivers. General Humphrey Marshall was at that time in command of the Department of Western Virginia and Eastern Kentucky. His troops were widely scattered over the country in order to obtain subsistence, and before they could be concentrated the enemy had retreated across the mountains into Kentucky. The raiders were prevented from occupying Bristol and doing further damage by the timely arrival of General Marshall's force, which pursued to Jonesville.

In May, 1862, a much larger invading force of infantry, cavalry, and artillery, numbering several thousand, was led up the Kanawha and New

rivers, West Virginia, by General J. D. Cox. This column was met at Princeton, in Mercer County, and arrested by General Marshall in an engagement on the 16th of May, which resulted in the repulse and retreat of the invading force, whose killed and wounded were left behind. [See Vol. II., p. 280.]

On the 3d of September, 1863, Burnside occupied Knoxville, Tennessee, with his army corps. ⌡ Nearly all the available Confederate forces had been ordered to reënforce Bragg at Chattanooga. A small force under Brigadier-General Alfred E. Jackson occupied the upper portion of east Tennessee. Marshall had been transferred to the Western army, and Colonel Henry L. Giltner, of the 4th Kentucky Cavalry, with a handful of troops, occupied the Department of South-western Virginia. On the 7th of September about five hundred of Burnside's infantry advanced as far east as Telford's Depot, in Washington County. On the 8th they were attacked by about an equal force, under General Jackson and Colonel Giltner. After a short engagement the Federals retreated to Limestone Depot, where, after a stubborn resistance, 350 surrendered, about 100 escaped, and 60 were killed and wounded.

The Federal forces, under Colonel Foster, advancing again into upper east Tennessee, were met by Colonel James E. Carter, of the 1st Tennessee Cavalry, at Blountsville, where a stubborn fight ensued on the 22d of September. The Federal batteries shelled the town, and by superior numbers compelled the withdrawal of Colonel Carter's force.

In the latter part of September, 1863, Brigadier-General John S. Williams assumed command of the Confederate forces in east Tennessee and advanced as far as Blue Springs. Burnside's forces occupied Bull's Gap, nine miles in front. Williams was ordered "not to give up an inch of ground until driven from it." He had only about seventeen hundred effective men, with two batteries of artillery. Brigadier-General Alfred E. Jackson, with about five hundred men, mostly recruits, was at Greenville. There was no other support within nearly one hundred miles. To maintain his ground against a force so largely superior, General Williams took a strong position on a ridge crossing the road east of Blue Springs. By multiplying camp-fires and beating drums he made an exhibition of force he did not possess. But this *ruse de guerre* did not hold the enemy in check. On the 10th of October they

⌡ General J. M. Shackelford commanded Burnside's cavalry force in the Knoxville campaign.—EDITORS.

advanced in force and attacked General Williams's position. Every inch of ground was stubbornly disputed, but the greater number of the Federals compelled the lengthening of the Confederate lines until they became little more than a skirmish-line. About 5 P. M. a heavy column of infantry broke the center of Williams's line, but was arrested by a heavy fire of artillery from the high ridge. The engagement lasted until dark, with but little change of position. To avoid capture by a force probably treble his own, General Williams withdrew during the night and retired toward Virginia. The next morning at daylight he was intercepted at Henderson's Mill by a large force of Federal cavalry, which had passed around him the day before. By a gallant charge this force was driven from the field, but continued to pursue and attack the Confederates until they reached the neighborhood of Leesburg.

On the 4th of November, 1863, General Williams, at his own request, was relieved of the command, and the brigade was placed under Colonel Henry L. Giltner. Major-General Robert Ransom, who was then in command of the department, ordered Colonel Giltner to coöperate with Brigadier-General William E. Jones in an attack upon General Carter, whose brigade was camped at Big Creek, near Rogersville, Tennessee. On the night of the 5th of November Colonel Giltner's brigade crossed the Holston River at Kingsport and advanced to Big Creek. This brigade numbered 1063 men, besides Lowry's battery. General Jones's command, probably, was not so large. At daylight next morning Colonel Giltner attacked General Carter's brigade, consisting of about one thousand men, and captured most of the force with all their camp-equipage, horses, artillery, and transportation. General Jones, who had gone around to the rear of the Federals, intercepted some two hundred fugitives. A few escaped across the river.

BRIGADIER-GENERAL JACOB AMMEN, U. S. V.
FROM A PHOTOGRAPH.

General Ammen commanded the District of East Tennessee, April 10, 1864, to January 14, 1865.

In May, 1864, a formidable force under General Crook advanced up the Kanawha and New rivers and reached the railroad at Dublin, in Pulaski County. An inferior force, commanded by General Albert G. Jenkins, engaged the advancing Federals on the 9th of May at Cloyd's Mountain, and Jenkins was mortally wounded and his force defeated. General Crook destroyed the depot at Dublin and the large bridge over New River.

On the 10th of May a large cavalry force, under General Averell, made an advance on Wytheville, but was met at Crockett's Cove by General John H. Morgan and defeated, leaving forty dead on the field.

In June, 1864, Colonel E. F. Clay, of the 1st Kentucky Mounted Rifles, in command of a small brigade of Confederate cavalry, was sent into Kentucky

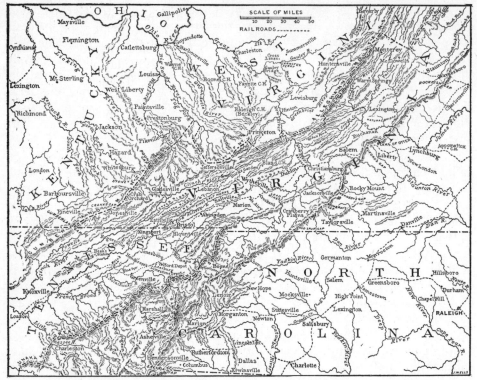

MAP OF OPERATIONS AGAINST THE VIRGINIA AND TENNESSEE RAILROAD, LYNCHBURG, VA., TO KNOXVILLE, TENN.

from the Department of South-western Virginia to secure forage and cover other military movements. Colonel Clay first advanced upon Paintsville, with a view of capturing some four hundred Federals who were camped there. Difficulties in the way of his advance delayed his arrival until the enemy had received large reënforcements, which deterred him from making an attack. Retiring upon Licking River, he camped in the narrow valley of a little stream known as Puncheon. Though he had taken every precaution to guard against surprise, an important order had not been executed, and at 2 P. M. the enemy in force surprised his camp, attacking it from the surrounding mountains. After a desperate resistance he was forced to withdraw, leaving thirty-seven prisoners in the enemy's hands — nine wounded, two of them mortally. Colonel Clay lost his right eye during the engagement.

Late in September, 1864, General Stephen G. Burbridge, with a force estimated at 5000 men, advanced upon King's salt-works, through eastern Kentucky, and up the Big Sandy River. He was met at Liberty Hill, Virginia, by Colonel H. L. Giltner, in command of a small brigade of cavalry. At that time not over 1000 men interposed between General Burbridge and the salt-works, only about 23 miles distant. But by dint of strategy and stubborn resistance Giltner detained the Federal army two days on the road, so that when Burbridge arrived there about an equal force confronted him, commanded by General John C. Breckinridge. On October 2d Burbridge attacked the forces at the salt-works. A battalion of Virginia Reserves (the 13th), composed of boys and old men, received the first shock of battle at "Governor" Saunders's house, in advance of the main line. This little company fought desperately and suffered severely before being driven back. The engagement continued with varying fortunes during the day, and when night came Burbridge was not in sight at the salt-works. The next morning he was 20 miles away. He left Colonel Charles S. Hanson (wounded) and many other wounded men and prisoners in the hands of the Confederates. General Williams and Colonel Giltner pursued him to the head of the Louisa fork of the Big Sandy. The 10th Kentucky Cavalry (Confederate) lost its colonel, Edwin Trimble, and nearly every officer above lieutenant was either killed or wounded. It had borne the brunt of battle at the ford of Holston River.

In December, 1864, General Stoneman, with a force of cavalry estimated at four thousand, entered south-west Virginia through east Tennessee, and proceeded to take possession of the country. The department had been drained of most of its troops by increasing demands from the armies east and west, so that Breckinridge found himself in command of only about 1000 or 1500 men in a department large enough to require an army corps to defend it. This handful was concentrated at the salt-works in hopes of defending a position naturally very strong, even against so large an opposing force. Stoneman, doubtless aware of this fact, and knowing the defenseless condition of the country, changed the ordinary tactics and devoted himself to capturing the towns and destroying the railroad. He occupied Bristol and Abingdon, and passing by the salt-works advanced upon Wytheville and the lead-mines. In hopes of arresting his course Breckinridge moved from the salt-works to Marion, on the railroad, where he intercepted Stoneman on Sunday, the 18th of December, and fought an engagement which lasted through the day and resulted in a substantial victory for the Confederates, who held their position against largely superior numbers. But during the day Stoneman sent a force down another road to the salt-works, now without defenders, except a few militia and teamsters, and destroyed as much of the works as possible before Breckinridge's forces could reach there. Having accomplished this long-desired object, the Federal forces withdrew across the mountains.⚓ The weather was very cold and wet, and all the troops suffered great hardships and privations. During the engagement at Marion on the 17th and 18th of December they stood in the rain and mud, without fire, food, or shelter, for over thirty-six hours. Yet they bore it all uncomplainingly and heroically.

⚓ On the 27th of February, 1865, General Grant instructed General Thomas, commanding the Department of the Cumberland, to direct General Stoneman "to repeat the raid of last fall, destroying the railroad as far toward Lynchburg as he can." Stoneman set out from Knoxville about the 20th of March, and moved, via Morristown and Bull's Gap, across Iron Mountain to Boone, North Carolina. Stoneman's force consisted of General A. C. Gillem's division. The brigade commanders were Colonels S. B. Brown, W. J. Palmer, and J. K. Miller. From Boone the command crossed the Blue Ridge to Wilkesboro', and then turned toward south-western Virginia, destroying the Virginia and Tennessee Railroad from Wytheville nearly to Lynchburg. On the 9th of April Stoneman moved again into North Carolina, via Jacksonville, Taylorsville, and Germantown. At Germantown the force divided, Palmer's brigade going to Salem, and the main body to Salisbury. Palmer destroyed the railroad between Greensboro' and Danville, Virginia, and also south of Greensboro'. The main body entered Salisbury on the 12th of April, capturing 14 pieces of artillery and 1364 prisoners. General Stoneman now returned to Tennessee with the artillery and prisoners, leaving the force, under command of General Gillem, to do scouting service on the east side of the mountains.—EDITORS.

THE BATTLE OF NEW MARKET, VA., MAY 15TH, 1864.

BY JOHN D. IMBODEN, BRIGADIER-GENERAL, C. S. A.

CADET OF THE VIRGINIA MILITARY INSTITUTE IN MARCHING OUTFIT.

ON the retreat of General Lee from Gettysburg, in July, 1863, he was not pursued by the Federal army into the Shenandoah Valley. After resting there and recuperating his shattered forces for a short time he crossed to the east side of the Blue Ridge. On the 21st of July, 1863, he assigned me to the command of "the Valley District," comprising the ·country west of the Blue Ridge and as far south as James River in Botetourt County. This district had been constituted a separate territorial command in 1861–62 for "Stonewall" Jackson, and its boundaries were not changed during the war. When I took the command it was so little menaced that I had only my own brigade of cavalry and mounted infantry and General Gabriel C. Wharton's infantry brigade, McClanahan's six-gun battery, McNeill's Rangers, and two small battalions of cavalry under Major Harry Gilmor and Major Sturgis Davis, of Maryland; in all not exceeding three thousand effective men of all arms. I was a native of the valley, acquainted with nearly all its leading inhabitants, and perfectly familiar with the natural features and resources of the entire district.

After General Lee retired to the Upper Rappahannock in the latter part of July, 1863, the Federal troops that were left in my front were posted to protect the Baltimore and Ohio Railroad, and rarely ventured more than a few miles from it. In this state of quietude General Lee shortly ordered General Wharton with his brigade to rejoin his division east of the Blue Ridge.

During the fall of 1863 and winter of 1863–64 nothing of much importance occurred in the valley. We frequently raided the railroad, destroying bridges and trains as we could, and capturing some small detachments posted and fortified on the railroad or found scouting too far from it. In December, 1863, General Averell made a daring raid from New Creek with about four thousand cavalry. We prevented his getting into the Shenandoah Valley to strike at Staunton. But in "shying" him off from that point we caused him to sweep on behind the North Mountain range, where he struck the Virginia and Tennessee Railroad sixty odd miles west of Lynchburg, and destroyed the army stores accumulated there, and then made his escape back to his base.

By the month of April, 1864, information reached us that General Sigel had established himself at Winchester, and was preparing for a forward movement with over eight thousand infantry, twenty-five hundred cavalry, and three or four field-batteries. On the 2d of May I broke camp at Mount Crawford, in Rockingham County, something over seventy miles from Winchester, and moved to meet Sigel and find out as far as possible his strength and designs and report the facts to General Lee. I had with me the 62d Virginia Infantry, mounted, Colonel Geo. H. Smith; the 23d Virginia Cavalry, Colonel Robert White; the 18th Virginia Cavalry, Colonel George W. Imboden; Major Harry Gilmor's Maryland battalion of cavalry; a part of Major Sturgis Davis's Maryland battalion of cavalry, Captain J. H. McNeill's Rangers, Captain J. H. McClanahan's excellent six-gun battery of horse artillery, and Captain Bartlett's Valley District Signal Corps. I had ordered General Wm. H. Harman at Staunton to notify the "reserves" (militia) of Rockingham and Augusta Counties, consisting of men over forty-five and boys between sixteen and eighteen years of age, and all detailed men on duty in shops, at furnaces, etc., to be ready to move at a moment's notice. A similar notification was sent to General Francis H. Smith, Commandant of the Virginia Military Institute at Lexington, where there were about three hundred cadets under eighteen years of age at school.[J] My veteran troops, "effective present," numbered but 1492 men when we left Mount Crawford on the 2d of May, to which should be added about 100 men scouting either in front of or behind Sigel. Harman's "reserves" did not amount to one thousand men, and these were undisciplined and armed mostly with hunting-rifles and shot-guns. This was the total scattered and incongruous force in front of Sigel in the valley the first week in May. The 1500 or 1600 veterans, with their horses, were in splendid condition for hard service.

On May 5th we reached Woodstock, Sigel then being at Strasburg, only about twelve miles distant. By the aid of my scouts and the citizens, almost the exact strength of Sigel had been ascertained, and all his preparations made known to us; these were very fully and promptly reported by wire from New Market to General Lee. I also made the most earnest appeals to him to send more troops to the valley at once. About eleven thousand men were reported in my front. The Signal Corps in the mountains west of us reported a force of 7000 men at Lewisburg, only a little over 100 miles

---

[J] As the war progressed conscription had to be resorted to to fill the Confederate ranks. It embraced all classes between eighteen and forty-five years of age. Conscription was therefore, for the time, almost fatal to the colleges and the institutes. Colonel Smith, however, resolved to keep open his school. He reduced the regulation age for admission from eighteen to sixteen years. This was below the conscript age, and soon the institute was filled to repletion with three hundred boys, all it would hold. But under State laws even they were a part of the "reserves," a militia force liable to be called out in emergencies.—J. D. I.

west from Staunton, apparently awaiting Sigel's movements to coöperate with him. General Lee's reply was to the effect that he was sorely pressed by Grant and needed all his men, at least for a few days, and he ordered me to retard Sigel's advance in every way I could, taking care not to be surrounded and captured. But fortune favored us in a most unexpected way. Early in the afternoon of Sunday, the 8th of May, Captain Bartlett announced from his signal station on top of the Massanutten Mountain, overlooking Strasburg, that two bodies of cavalry, which he estimated at one thousand men each, had left General Sigel's camp in the forenoon, the one moving across the North Mountain westward on the Moorefield road, and the other eastward through Front Royal, passing that town and taking the road leading through Chester Gap in the Blue Ridge. These facts convinced me that Sigel, before venturing to advance, meant to ascertain whether he had enemies in dangerous force within striking distance on either flank; an investigation which would consume several days. As there were no troops, except my little band, nearer than General Lee's army, it was manifestly important to attack these detachments as far from Strasburg as possible and delay their return as long as possible. I summoned Colonel Smith, of the 62d, to my headquarters, and informed him confidentially of my intention to take the 18th Regiment, Colonel Imboden's, McNeill's Rangers, and two guns of McClanahan's battery and that night cross the North Mountain through a pass called "The Devil's Hole," and intercept the enemy on the Moorefield road on Lost River in Hardy County, more than twenty miles from Strasburg, and either capture or defeat them; knowing that in the latter event we could drive them via Romney across the Potomac and into Maryland. Leaving Colonel Smith in command at Woodstock, it was given out that I was about to move camp some five or six miles back toward the North Mountain in search of better grazing for our horses. This ruse was practiced to prevent any Union man (and there were plenty around us) from taking the information of the movement to Sigel that night. We set out from Woodstock about 4 P. M. on Sunday across the North Mountain, and, having accomplished the purposes of the expedition, on Monday, late in the night, reached Mount Jackson, where I found Colonel Smith, who, in the exercise of a sound discretion, had fallen back from Woodstock, leaving only a mounted picket at Fisher's Hill, and relays of couriers to report any advance by Sigel.

Immediately on my return to Mount Jackson I learned from Major Harry Gilmor, who had been sent across by Luray to get tidings of the other body of cavalry that had left Sigel on Sunday morning, that he had been to the top of the Blue Ridge and had there met fleeing citizens from Rappahannock County who said that this expedition consisted of the 1st New York Cavalry under Colonel Boyd, five hundred strong, and that they had been taking things leisurely and without molestation, on the east side of the mountain, and had stated to citizens where they camped that they were coming on to New Market by the middle of the week to rejoin General Sigel at that place. Upon this information we laid a trap for Colonel Boyd, and on Wednesday we captured 464 men, nearly all of this force. [See p. 488.] These mishaps to General Sigel's flanking parties of cavalry, sent out the previous Sunday, secured us the all-important few days' respite from his dreaded advance, and enabled General John C. Breckinridge, from south-western Virginia, to reach the valley with something over 2500 of his best veteran troops to be united with mine for a battle with Sigel wherever we might chance to meet him.

In 1864 the village of New Market had a population of about one thousand. Its site is one of the most beautiful in the far-famed Shenandoah Valley. The north fork of the Shenandoah River flows behind a range of hills that rise gently to a height of perhaps four hundred feet north-west of the town. These hills were cleared and in cultivation on their slope facing the town, and at their foot runs the valley turnpike, the main street of New Market and the great highway of the valley during the war. About a mile east and south of the turnpike flows Smith's Creek, a mill-stream, at the foot of the rugged Massanutten Mountain, which, from Strasburg to near Port Republic, separates the Luray or Page Valley from the Shenandoah Valley for a distance of over forty miles. Luray and New Market are connected by a mudpike which crosses the Massanutten Mountain through a slight depression or gap four miles from New Market. Five miles north-east of New Market the valley turnpike crosses the north fork of the Shenandoah, on the boundary of the celebrated "Meem Plantation." Rude's Hill, one mile nearer New Market than the river at the bridge, overlooks the whole of the Meem bottoms from an elevation of perhaps seventy-five or one hundred feet. No place in the great valley was the scene of more conflicts than the Meem bottoms and Rude's Hill. From this hill to New Market, four miles, the country is undulating, and was cleared and in a high state of cultivation. Between New Market and Smith's Creek, where the road to Luray crosses it, there was in 1864 a body of perhaps one hundred acres or more of woodland, and the town and its outskirts were ornamented with many orchards. From about the center of the town a deep little valley, or rather ravine, leads to the north fork of the Shenandoah River, and cuts the range of hills back of the town at right angles, the hills being higher on the south-west side of this ravine than those on the north-east side. This description of the town and country is necessary to a clear understanding of the movements on both sides in the battle of May 15th.

On Thursday, the 12th, General Breckinridge telegraphed me his arrival at Staunton on his way to my assistance, and sent forward a staff-officer to inform me more fully of his strength and movements. We spent Thursday and Friday in perfect quiet at New Market, awaiting Sigel from the north-east and Breckinridge from the south-west, being well-informed of the movements of each.

General Sigel's advance was so slow and cautious that on Saturday morning, the 14th, information from the front indicated that he would not attempt to pass Meem's bottoms or Rude's Hill that day. Learning about 10 o'clock that Breckinridge and his staff would reach Lacy Springs, ten miles from New Market, by noon, I mounted and rode there to meet and confer with him, leaving Colonel Smith of the 62d in command during my absence. The general came as expected and invited me to remain for dinner. Whilst we were at table a courier arrived with a message from Colonel Smith to me that Sigel's cavalry, 2500 strong, had reached Rude's Hill, and that Colonel Imboden of the 18th was falling back skirmishing, but was so vigorously pressed that he, Smith, had formed line of battle just west of the town to cover the 18th in its retreat. The courier had come rapidly, but before we left the table the booming of McClanahan's guns broke upon us, and a moment afterward the roar of an opposing battery was distinctly heard. I instantly mounted to go to my men, with orders from Breckinridge to hold New Market at all hazards till dark, and then fall back four miles to the position mentioned above, where he would join me during the night with his troops. One of his staff accompanied me, and in an hour we had ridden the ten miles, stimulated at every jump by the rapid artillery firing, indicating, as we had but six guns there, that they were opposed by at least double their number.

Arriving on the field I found that Colonel George H. Smith had made an admirable disposition of the little command

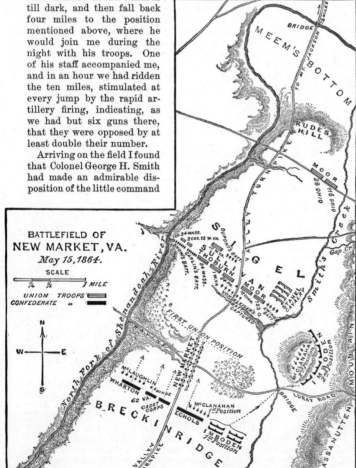

BATTLEFIELD OF
NEW MARKET, VA.
May 15, 1864.
SCALE
¼   ½   1 MILE
UNION TROOPS
CONFEDERATE   "

on the west side of the town, forming it in single ranks, and not too close, so as to present the appearance of a much larger force than it was in reality. His line extended from about half-way up the hillside west of the town, away across the turnpike toward Smith's Creek, his right being concealed by the forest in its front. McClanahan was posted on the extreme left, near the top of the hill, which gave him a plunging fire across the town and down upon the enemy's guns occupying ground from one to two hundred feet lower, putting them to the disadvantage of having to shoot up, at a high angle, to reach him at all. On arriving at his battery I had a full view of the enemy for a long distance, and from what I saw felt no apprehension of any attempt to dislodge us that evening, and that nothing more serious than an artillery duel was impending. Except their advanced cavalry and artillery no troops had been formed in line. It was afterward reported that a negro from beyond Lacy Springs had made his way down Smith's Creek, and informed General Sigel of the rapid approach of an army from Staunton. He had seen Breckinridge's brigades, and exaggerated their numbers. This false information would naturally have caused General Sigel to advance with great caution after passing Rude's Hill.

Night terminated the artillery firing, and with no serious damage to either side. We still held the town. A rain coming up, it became intensely dark, and favorable to our withdrawal. Under cover of the darkness Sigel moved a large body of his infantry to a plateau north-west of the town, and beyond the ravine running from it to the river. Their camp-fires disclosed their exact position to us.

About two hours before daybreak I was aroused by the light of a tin lantern shining in my face. It was carried by one of the camp guard, who knew where to find me on the roadside. I was immediately accosted by General Breckinridge. He informed me that his troops would reach that point before sunrise.

About daylight Breckinridge's troops came up, weary, wet, and muddy, and were halted for rest. The general looked over the ground, selected his line of battle, and intended to await Sigel's assault there, expecting, of course, it would occur early in the day. Whilst our horses were feeding, and the men getting something to eat, the general explained to me his plan of the approaching battle. He had brought with him two small infantry brigades, commanded respectively by Brigadier-Generals John Echols and Gabriel C. Wharton. These were veteran troops, and equal to any in the Confederate army, and were ably commanded. He also had Major William McLaughlin's artillery — six guns — and a section of the cadet battery from the Virginia Military Institute, temporarily attached to McLaughlin. He had also ordered out the full corps of cadets,— boys from 16 to 18 years old,— and they were present to the number of 225, under command of Colonel Ship, one of their professors, and an excellent soldier in every sense. The "reserves" from Augusta and Rockingham Counties had also been ordered out, but had not had time to assemble from their scat- tered homes, and were not up. The entire force, above enumerated and present, of all arms, did not exceed three thousand men. My whole effective force, then present, did not exceed 1600 additional men. My largest regiment, the 62d Virginia Infantry, mounted, had present that day not quite 550 men. They were nearly all three-years' veterans, and never had been whipped, though they had been in many a hard fight. General Breckinridge ordered me to dismount them for the day's work, and said that he would place them and the Cadet Corps together, on the flank of either Echols's or Wharton's brigade, in the center of his infantry line of battle. ⚓ The rest of my command of about one thousand cavalry and McClanahan's horse artillery were to form the extreme right wing south of the turnpike, and near Smith's Creek.

An hour after daybreak had passed, and the report from New Market was that only a desultory cavalry skirmish was going on in and around the town. The whole country for two or three miles lay before and below, like a map, and a few words of explanation from me as to roads, streams, etc., enabled General Breckinridge to grasp it all; and he remarked after five minutes' study of the scene, "We can attack and whip them here, and I'll do it." He sent orders at once for all the troops to advance as rapidly as possible, and for Major McLaughlin not to wait for the infantry, but to bring on his guns to the hill where we were. I was ordered, as soon as the artillery and infantry came up, to concentrate all my cavalry and with McClanahan's battery take position on our extreme right next to Smith's Creek, to cover that flank. Within little more than an hour these dispositions were all made and McLaughlin "opened the ball." The left flank of our infantry line was well up on the hillside south-west of the town, and probably about 2500 men, infantry and artillery, formed the line on that side of the turnpike, and 1000 on the lower side, McLaughlin's eight guns being on the hillside, or on its summit. With something under

one thousand cavalry and McClanahan's battery, I was still nearer Smith's Creek, forming the extreme right, and concealed from the enemy by the woods in our front, which I took care to fill pretty well with mounted skirmishers several hundred yards in advance of our main line.

The battle began in earnest. McLaughlin was working his guns "for all they were worth" under a tremendous fire from the other side. At this stage of the fight the town lay between the contending forces, but owing to its low situation the shot and shells passed over it. For an hour, perhaps, no small-arms were used. Breckinridge was steadily advancing his infantry line in splendid order notwithstanding an occasional gap made in it by a solid shot or an exploding shell. Sigel had brought up his infantry steadily into line on his side of the little valley or ravine running from the town to the river, where he occupied a wide and high plateau, and from which his artillery was playing upon our line.

Whilst General Breckinridge was advancing the brigades of Echols and Wharton, and the 62d Virginia under Colonel Smith and the cadets under Colonel Ship, and in the face of a most galling artillery fire steadying them everywhere by his personal presence, we on the extreme right were only treated to an occasional random shell thrown through the woods from an invisible battery.

When the infantry had reached the edge of the town, I rode into the woods in my front to ascertain what force, if any, the enemy had immediately beyond the woods, with which we would have to cope when Breckinridge passed beyond the town, as it was evident he would do in the next half hour. I was rewarded by the discovery of Sigel's entire cavalry force massed in very close order in the fields just beyond the woods. It was from a battery of theirs that the few stray shots, aimed at random, had reached us through the woods. I moved my command at a "trot march." We swept down Smith's Creek to the bridge on the Luray road, McClanahan's battery following. Moving down the east side of the creek we gained the top of a little hill [see map, p. 482] and unlimbered "in battery" before we were discovered, or at least before a shot was fired at us. The position was a magnificent one for our purpose. It was less than one thousand yards from the enemy's cavalry, and a little in rear of the prolongation of his line. A large part of his cavalry, and that nearest to us, was massed in column, close order, squadron front, giving our gunners a target of whole acres of men and horses. The guns were rapidly worked, whilst my cavalry kept on slowly down the creek as if aiming to get in the enemy's rear. The effect was magical. The first discharge of the guns threw his whole body of cavalry into confusion. They could not change front and face us without great slaughter. They did the next best thing. Being ignorant that the woods in their front were only held by a skirmish-line, they turned to the right

wish to put the cadets in if he could avoid it, but that should occasion require it, he would use them very freely."— EDITORS.

about and retired rapidly till beyond our range. In doing this they uncovered one of their batteries, which changed front to the left and exchanged a few rounds with McClanahan. But the rapid retrograde movement of the discomfited cavalry and our flank fire was observed by General Breckinridge, who immediately pushed forward his infantry with great energy under cover of the excellent service of McLaughlin's guns, aided by McClanahan, whose shot and shell, now that the

BREVET MAJOR-GENERAL WILLIAM W. AVERELL.
FROM A PHOTOGRAPH.

cavalry were out of the way, began to fall upon Sigel's infantry flank. Thus pressed in front, and harassed in flank, General Sigel retired his whole line to a new position half a mile farther back, pressed all the time by Echols's and Wharton's brigades, Smith's 62d, and the Cadet Corps. The town was thus passed by our troops, and a little after noon McLaughlin occupied the ground on which the enemy's batteries had been planted the day before, and from which they had been gallantly served all that forenoon.

Every moment the conflict became more desperate. There was one six-gun battery on elevated ground west of the turnpike that was particularly destructive in its fire upon Breckinridge's infantry, and he decided to dislodge or capture it. Its position was directly in front of Smith's 62d regiment of my brigade and the Cadet Corps, and it fell to their lot to silence it by a charge in the very face of its terrible guns. The order to advance upon it was given by Breckinridge to Colonels Smith and Ship. It so happened that when they came to within about three hundred yards of the

battery they had to cross a deep rocky gulch, grown up with scrub cedars, thorns and briers, and filled here and there with logs and old stumps. Many men had fallen before Smith and Ship had reached this gulch, but whilst in it they were sheltered by its banks. As it was difficult to get through, Smith and his veterans took their time, gaining thereby a slight breathing-spell before making the deadly run necessary to reach the hostile battery. The boys from the Military Institute were more agile and ardent than Smith's veterans, and got out on the bank first. They suffered severely in the two or three minutes while Smith was getting the 62d out of the gulch, but still they kept their formation till the order was given to charge at "double-quick." The work was then soon done. The guns were captured and also most of the gunners, who stood to them till overpowered. Lieutenant-Colonel W. S. Lincoln, of the 34th Massachusetts, was terribly wounded and fell into our hands. ↓

A wild yell went up when a cadet mounted a caisson and waved the Institute flag in triumph over it. The battery was taken, but at a fearful cost. Neither the 62d nor the cadets had suffered very much loss during the day till that terrible charge. Then the ground was soon strewn with their dead and wounded. The cadets lost 8 killed and 46 wounded, out of 225. ♭

Colonel Smith went into action with about 550 men of the 62d. Seven of his ten captains fell between the gulch and the battery, four of whom were instantly killed and three crippled for life. He reported the next day the total casualties of his regiment at 241 officers and men killed and wounded; and nearly all these fell in passing over that deadly three hundred yards up "to the cannon's mouth." My recollection is distinct that the losses in killed and wounded of the 62d and the Cadet Corps constituted over one-half of the casualties of the day in the whole of our little army of about 4500 men.

McLaughlin ran his guns through the town on the smooth, hard macadamized main street, loaded with canister ready for emergencies, and it was well they were loaded, for a cavalry charge was made upon him before the enemy had all left, under McClanahan's fire from across the creek. In an instant as they charged McLaughlin came "into battery," and gave them a blizzard that sent them back hastily to their comrades. Simultaneously with the capture of the battery on the hill, Echols and Wharton charged the whole infantry line, and it gave way. From that time on till night the fighting was desultory and at long range.

When Breckinridge had pursued the enemy about three miles and had come in sight of Rude's Hill, General Sigel halted his batteries on its crest and began shelling our advancing lines. Breckinridge ordered a halt and stationed his batteries in an orchard, on the right of the pike, to return the fire. It was then perhaps 5 P. M. As I had not

<hr>

↓ Colonel Lincoln had been caught under his horse, which was killed. The colonel in that sad predicament tried to use his pistol, and only desisted when a cadet threatened to plunge a bayonet through him.—J. D. I.

♭ I had a boy brother, J. P. Imboden, in that corps who was knocked down and disabled for the time by a spent canister-shot as the command advanced from the gulch.—J. D. I.

seen General Breckinridge since the fight began, I rode to the left in search of him. He was soon found at about one hundred yards immediately in rear of McLaughlin's guns, on foot and muddy to the waist. I learned that he had been much of the time off his horse during the whole day, mingling with and cheering his brave, tired, hungry, drenched, and muddy infantry and artillery, to whose lot had fallen the hard fighting all the day long. The general explained the reason for his halting. Nearly every cartridge-box had been empty for an hour. He had sent back for the ordnance-wagons, but kept on pursuing the enemy till the wagons should overtake him. The wagons had come up and the line was halted, and the men were engaged in filling their cartridge-boxes, preparatory to a final charge on Rude's Hill. Whilst we were talking over the events of the day, several shells, aimed at McLaughlin, passed over him and exploded in the orchard near us. I expostulated with the general for so unnecessarily exposing himself, when, by moving one hundred yards to the right or left, he would be out of the line of fire. He laughed and said it was too muddy anywhere else than in that orchard, where the ground was covered with a dense, closely grazed greensward, and that he would rather risk stray shells than wade in the mud again, and that he had sent for his horse to be brought to him there.

At this moment he was informed that all his men had been supplied with ammunition and at once ordered the whole line forward, directing me to oblique the cavalry to the left and move toward Rude's Hill, to which he ordered McClanahan's battery to proceed rapidly down the turnpike. As soon as Sigel discovered this general forward movement on our side his troops disappeared over Rude's Hill and were lost to view in Meem's Bottoms. McClanahan's battery, under Lieutenant Carter Berkeley, charging like cavalry, on the hard road, reached the hill first and was unsupported for some time, we having a greater distance to go, all the way up to our horses' knees in the mud. When his battery reached the hill the enemy's rear-guard was crossing the bridge over the river. He fired a few times at them, but it was getting too dark to see with what effect. In a little while flames shot up from dry combustibles that had been brought to the bridge and set on fire. The bridge was completely destroyed and further pursuit rendered impossible that night.

If Sigel had beaten Breckinridge on the 15th of May General Lee could not have spared the men to check his progress (as he did that of Hunter, a month later) without exposing Richmond to immediate, and almost inevitable, capture. In view of these probable consequences, there was no secondary battle of the war of more importance than that of New Market. The necessities of General Lee were such, that on the day after the battle he ordered Breckinridge to join him near Richmond with the brigades of Echols and Wharton and what remained of my 62d regiment, leaving me with but about one thousand men at New Market to con-

front the force we had with so much difficulty defeated on the 15th, causing it to fall back to Strasburg, where, however, it began to reorganize and recuperate for a more formidable advance two weeks later.

We picketed on Rude's Hill, but sent small scouting parties as far as Strasburg, and even beyond. On the 21st General Hunter had superseded Sigel, and at the close of May his advance appeared at Mount Jackson just beyond the burnt bridge at Meem's Bottoms. The enemy placed a picket at the river.

On the 1st of June Hunter, with his army reënforced to at least eleven thousand ⸶ men of all arms, drove me out of New Market with my handful of cavalry and six guns. I again reported the perils of the valley to General Lee. Over eleven thousand men were driving me before them up the valley. Generals Crook and Averell, with ten thousand more, were known to be rapidly coming down upon my rear from Lewisburg, and would form a junction with Hunter at Staunton within five or six days unless sufficient reënforcements were sent to the valley at once to defeat one or both of these columns. General Lee replied, as he had done in May, that he could not immediately spare any troops. He directed me again to call out all the "reserves," and to telegraph Brigadier-General William E. Jones, then in south-west Virginia, beyond Lynchburg, to come to my aid with all the men he could collect from that part of the State or in east Tennessee. Jones responded promptly that he would join me via Lynchburg and Staunton by the 4th with about three thousand men.

Late in the afternoon of June 2d I was driven through Harrisonburg with some loss. That night I took position on the south bank of the North River fork of the Shenandoah River at Mount Crawford, eight miles from Harrisonburg and seventeen from Staunton. On the 3d Hunter rested at Harrisonburg. That night Jones's troops began to arrive in small detachments, just as they had been posted at many points along the line of the Virginia and Tennessee Railroad west of Lynchburg. My staff and I were up nearly all night organizing these detachments into two small brigades.

At sunrise of the 4th General Jones and staff rode up, having traveled from Staunton during the night. An hour or two later Brigadier-General J. C. Vaughn came up with less than one thousand of his Tennessee brigade of cavalry. The reserves of Augusta and Rockingham counties had assembled to the number of five or six hundred. We thus had, of all sorts of troops, veterans and militia, something less than 4500 men. ☆ Of artillery, we had McClanahan's six guns, and an improvised battery of six guns from Staunton, manned by a company of reserves under Captain J. C. Marquis.

On comparing dates of commission with Jones and Vaughn they were both found to be my seniors. Jones, holding the oldest commission, took command. On the 5th our forces were concentrated about half a mile north-east of the village of Piedmont. Without going into details it suffices to say

---

⸶ The official records say 8500.—EDITORS.

☆ But General Vaughn telegraphed to Bragg on June

6th: "Went into the fight yesterday with an aggregate of 5600."—EDITORS.

MAJOR-GENERAL GEORGE CROOK.
FROM A PHOTOGRAPH.

General Crook served in West Virginia and the Shenandoah Valley from February, 1864, till February, 1865, being for part of this time in command of the Department of West Virginia.

now that battle was joined. After repelling two assaults, our left wing was doubled up by a flank attack, Jones was killed, and we were disastrously beaten. Our loss was not less than 1500 men.

Our defeat opened the way to Hunter to effect a junction with Crook and Averell at Staunton on the 6th. Their combined forces numbered about 18,000 men of all arms. Vaughn and I fell back in good order, and on the 6th occupied Waynesboro', eleven miles east of Staunton, and the neighboring (Rockfish) gap in the Blue Ridge, where the Chesapeake and Ohio Railroad passes through the mountain. Hunter remained two or three days at Staunton resting his troops and burning both public and private property, especially the latter.

On hearing of our defeat General Lee again sent Breckinridge to our aid. He brought but few troops, and with these occupied the defensive position of Rockfish Gap, thus interposing a barrier to Hunter's direct march on Lynchburg. Hunter decided to push his column forty or fifty miles farther up the great valley, and then, crossing the Blue Ridge, swoop down upon Lynchburg from the west. Successful resistance to his progress in the valley being impossible, Breckinridge directed Brigadier-General McCausland to take position in Hunter's front and obstruct his march as much as possible, and report his daily progress, while Breckinridge moved all the rest of his troops directly to Lynchburg to defend the place. Hunter threw a

brigade of cavalry across the Blue Ridge from Staunton, through an unfrequented gap, at the head of Back Creek, twelve or fifteen miles southwest of Rockfish Gap. To my command was assigned the duty of looking after this brigade. With the exception of one or two light skirmishes, no collision occurred between us. Our rapid movement on Lynchburg doubtless saved it from capture by this cavalry force, as the town was then virtually defenseless. The second day after reaching the eastern base of the Blue Ridge in Nelson County this brigade retired through White's Gap, and rejoined Hunter at Lexington about the 12th of June.

Hunter halted a day at Lexington to burn the Virginia Military Institute, Governor Letcher's residence, and other private property, and ordered the torch to be applied to Old Washington College, that had been endowed by the "Father of His Country." This was too much for many of his officers, and they protested, and thus the old college was saved, and is now "The Washington and Lee University," where General R. E. Lee quietly ended his days as its President.

From Lexington Hunter proceeded to Buchanan in Botetourt County, only slightly impeded by McCausland, who gallantly fought his advance at almost every mile as best he could. At Buchanan the torch again did its work. Colonel John T. Anderson, an old gray-haired man, with his aged wife, occupied a palatial brick mansion a mile above the town. The grand old house, its splendid library and collection of pictures, the furniture and all the family wearing-apparel, made a bonfire that was seen for many a mile around. From Buchanan Hunter crossed the Blue Ridge via the lofty Peaks of Otter, and moved by the shortest route direct to Lynchburg.

To defend that place and drive Hunter back General Lee had sent there the Second Corps of his army, "Stonewall" Jackson's old corps, under Lieutenant-General Jubal A. Early. Breckinridge was already there with his small force from Rockfish Gap, when (on Friday, June 17th) Early made his appearance with the advance division of his army corps. That day I had been ordered, with my own and Brigadier-General William L. Jackson's brigade of cavalry, to go ten miles out to New London, reënforce McCausland, and assume command of the three brigades, and retard Hunter as much as possible, to give time for the whole of Early's corps to come up by rail from Richmond. About sunset we had a skirmish at New London, and that night fell back to the "Quaker Meeting House," four miles out from Lynchburg on the Salem or Liberty turnpike, upon which the enemy was approaching. In the afternoon of Friday we were attacked in this position, and after a sharp resistance, entailing a loss on our side of over one hundred men in killed and wounded, fell back upon the fortifications of the city unpursued by the enemy. [See p. 493.]

SIGEL IN THE SHENANDOAH VALLEY IN 1864.

BY FRANZ SIGEL, MAJOR-GENERAL, U. S. V.

ON the 8th of March, 1864, while in command of the District of Lehigh, with headquarters at Reading, Pennsylvania, I received an order from the President appointing me to the command of the Department of West Virginia, and on the 10th of the same month I arrived at Cumberland, the headquarters of the department.

As this was the time when General Grant assumed the chief command of the armies and began his preparations for the campaign of 1864, it seemed to me necessary to subordinate all military arrangements in the department to the paramount object of making the bulk of our forces available as an auxiliary force in the prospective campaign. It was also necessary to protect the Baltimore and Ohio Railroad, the shortest line of communication between Washington and Cincinnati. To reach these ends a system of defensive measures was applied to the line of that road, and the troops were concentrated at certain points on the road to be reorganized, disciplined, and provided with all the necessary material for active service. The intrenchments at Harper's Ferry were extended and strengthened, and the construction of detached works was begun at Martinsburg, Cumberland, Grafton, and Clarksburg, to protect these places against raiding parties. There were block-houses at the most important points on the Baltimore and Ohio, and iron-clad railroad cars were brought into requisition, each of them armed with a small piece. A pontoon-bridge was laid over the river at Falling Waters, between Harper's Ferry and Williamsport.

At the middle of March there were about 24,000 men in the department, most of them guarding the railroad from Monocacy and Harper's Ferry to Parkersburg and Wheeling, while about 3500 under General Crook were in the Kanawha Valley. Amid great difficulties the work of organization went on tolerably well, so that I expected to have, after the middle of April, a force of about 20,000 men ready for "active service in the field." On the 29th of March General E. O. C. Ord arrived at my headquarters at Cumberland with a letter from General Grant, saying in substance that I should immediately assemble 8000 infantry, 1500 cavalry ("picked men"), besides artillery, provided with ten days' rations, at Beverly, for the purpose of marching by Covington to Staunton; the troops to be under the command of General Ord, who supplemented the letter by saying, on the authority of General Grant, that the column should start within ten days. General Crook was to move from Charleston against the Virginia and Tennessee Railroad, destroy as much of it as possible, and then turn toward Lynchburg or await further orders. Crook had been summoned to Grant's headquarters about a week before, where this "raid" had been discussed and decided upon. In another letter I was directed to have a large train ready and to move up the Valley and meet the expedition of Ord and Crook as soon as it should reach Staunton. The most energetic measures were immediately taken to put this plan into operation. All the troops that could be spared were concentrated at Webster and Clarksburg to move to Beverly as soon as the necessary material should be collected at that point. But continuous rains had made the roads so bad that it was almost impossible to move even empty wagons to Beverly, and only about 6500 troops could be assembled for the expedition, unless the whole region from Harper's Ferry and Martinsburg to Cumberland and Parkersburg were to be left unprotected and exposed to hostile enterprises. Of all these circumstances General Grant was informed, and General Ord, who was every day in my headquarters, became so diffident in regard to the whole matter that he asked General Grant to be relieved. His request was granted on the 17th of April, and on the same day Colonel O. E. Babcock arrived with instructions from General Grant to confer with me about the best way of solving the "raiding" problem. It was decided that General Crook should move against the Virginia and Tennessee Railroad and New River Bridge with the best and strongest part of our forces, about 10,000 men, while the remainder, about 7000, should advance in the Shenandoah Valley, at least as far as Cedar Creek, with the double object of protecting the eastern part of the department, from Harper's Ferry to Cumberland, and at the same time facilitating the operations of General Crook by inducing his opponent to detach a part of his forces from south-west Virginia against the troops advancing in the Shenandoah Valley. This arrangement was approved by General Grant. Reënforcements of infantry and the best mounted cavalry were sent to General Crook on the Kanawha by way of Parkersburg and the Kanawha River; one division of infantry of eight regiments, besides the remnants of General Averell's cavalry division and three batteries (later on increased to five), was concentrated at Martinsburg and put under the command of General Julius Stahel, the senior officer. Besides these troops there remained on the Baltimore and Ohio, from Monocacy and Harper's Ferry to Parkersburg and Wheeling, a total distance of 300 miles, for local defense and other duties, seven regiments of infantry, several batteries, and a few hundred cavalry.

It was understood that Crook should commence his movement on the 2d of May, while the troops in the Shenandoah should start a few days earlier to divert the enemy's attention from south-west Virginia. General Averell, who had distinguished himself by his successful raid against the Virginia and Tennessee Railroad, in December, 1863 [see p. 480], was especially assigned by General Grant to the command of the cavalry division to operate with General Crook.

In conformity with these arrangements I left Cumberland on the 25th of April for Martinsburg, inspected the troops assembled there, and moved to

Bunker Hill on the 29th, and to Winchester on the 1st of May, while the cavalry advanced to Cedar Creek and Strasburg. To meet the wishes of General Crook, the cavalry force left at Beverly was sent forward into Pocahontas County, spreading false rumors as to our strength and movements. General Crook, with the principal force, of from 7000 to 8000 men, left Fayette, not far from the mouth of New River, on the 2d of May, moving by Raleigh Court House and Princeton toward Newbern, "meeting and beating" the enemy at Cloyd's Mountain, then again near Dublin and Newbern, and after destroying the bridge over New River and the Virginia and Tennessee Railroad for a considerable distance, returned by Union and Lewisburg to Meadow Bluff, where he arrived on the 19th of May. General Averell, at the head of two thousand cavalry, moved on a more western line against Saltville, with the intention of destroying the saltworks at that place, but, in spite of fighting bravely at that point and at Wytheville, was forced to withdraw, and followed Crook on his homeward march to Union.

The expedition from the Kanawha, although not attaining all that was proposed, was excellently planned and executed, and its moral effect was great; but it would have been of much greater importance if it had been undertaken before Longstreet had rejoined Lee's army. About the time that Babcock arrived at my headquarters at Cumberland the two divisions of Longstreet passed over the Virginia and Tennessee road and New River bridge to the east, and took their position at Gordonsville, forming the extreme left of the Army of Northern Virginia.

From our position at Winchester and Cedar Creek we learned that there was no hostile force in the Shenandoah Valley, except General Imboden's cavalry and mounted infantry, reported to be about 3000 strong. It seemed to me, therefore, necessary to advance farther south toward Staunton, in order to induce Breckinridge to send a part of his forces against us, and thereby facilitate the operations of Crook and Averell. Before leaving Winchester, a force of 500 cavalry, under Colonel Jacob Higgins, was sent toward Wardensville to protect our right flank, and Colonel William H. Boyd, with 300 select horsemen, into the Luray Valley to cover our left flank, especially against Mosby; but Colonel Higgins was attacked and beaten by a detachment of Imboden's brigade between Wardensville and Moorefield on the 9th of May, and pursued north toward Romney. Colonel Boyd was ambuscaded on his way from the Luray Valley to New Market on the 13th and defeated, suffering a loss of 125 men [General Imboden, p. 481, says 464 men] and 200 horses.

Meanwhile Sullivan's division at Winchester joined the troops at Cedar Creek on May 9th, and on the 10th our cavalry, after some skirmishing, occupied Woodstock. Here the whole telegraphic correspondence between Breckinridge and Imboden and the commander of Gilmor's cavalry, stationed at Woodstock, fell into our hands. Among the dispatches was one signed by Breckinridge, and dated Dublin Station, May 5th, saying that 4000 men were *en route* for Jackson River depot; also that the quartermaster should furnish transportation for Breckinridge and staff and 16 horses. Another and later dispatch, dated Staunton, and signed by Breckinridge, directed Captain Davis, at Woodstock, to find out the strength of our forces. A third dispatch directed Captain Davis to watch particularly any movement of ours in the direction of Grant's army. Another dispatch, dated Staunton, May 10th, also to Captain Davis, stated that General Lee was driving the enemy at every point.

The anxiety of Breckinridge to know whether there was any movement in the direction of Grant's army suggested such a movement on our part, while the unfavorable news relative to the great struggle between Grant and Lee could not fail to prompt me to energetic action.

To gain more detailed information, two regiments of infantry, under Colonel Augustus Moor, assisted by five hundred of the 1st New York (Lincoln) Cavalry, under Major Timothy Quinn, were sent forward on the 13th. This force met a part of Imboden's troops near Mount Jackson on the 14th, forced them across the Shenandoah, took possession of the bridge, and, animated by this success, followed them as far as New Market, seven miles beyond Mount Jackson, or nineteen miles from the position of our forces at Woodstock. Having received information of this little exploit late at night of the 14th, and also that Breckinridge was on his march down the Valley, and considering that in case of an attack the position of Mount Jackson would afford many advantages as a defensive point, I ordered the troops to move at 5 A. M. on the 15th. They arrived at Mount Jackson at about 10 o'clock A. M. I rode forward to reconnoiter the ground and to decide whether we should advance farther or meet the enemy's attack at Mount Jackson. During this time I received information from Colonel Moor that he was in a very good position. Major T. F. Lang,—an officer of General Averell's staff, and temporarily attached to my headquarters,—whom I had ordered to the front, sent me a note, saying that our troops were in a good position and "eager for the fight." Captain Carl Heintz, of the staff of General Stahel, reported to me that Breckinridge was in force in our front, and that "if I would send two batteries they would be of excellent use." Believing that a retreat would have a bad effect on our troops, and well aware of the strategical value of New Market, commanding, as it did, the road to Luray, Culpeper, and Charlottesville, as well as the road to Brock's Gap and Moorefield, I resolved to hold the enemy in check until the arrival of our main forces from Mount Jackson and then accept battle.

We had 5500 infantry and artillery, with 28 guns and 1000 cavalry. Breckinridge's and Imboden's force I estimated, from what we could know, at 5000 infantry and 2000 cavalry. [See p. 491.] We were about equal, and from what had happened the day before I thought that the advantage was on our side. I therefore hastened forward to New Market, with Captain Alexander and Major T. A. Meysenburg (of my staff), where I arrived about noon, and before the enemy began his attack. It now became clear to me that all the troops could not reach the position close to New Market. I therefore ordered Colonel Moor to evacuate his position slowly, covered by cavalry, under Captain J. C. Battersby, and to fall back into a new position, which was selected about three-quarters of a mile north of New Market, right and left of the pike leading to Mount Jackson. During this time I sent two officers, Captain McEntee and Captain T. G. Putnam, back to General Sullivan, with orders to bring forward all his troops without delay; and at the same moment, when Colonel Moor was approaching the new line from his position in advance, it was reported to me by Captain R. G. Prendergast, commander of my escort, that all the infantry and artillery of General Sullivan had arrived, the head of the column being in sight, and that they were waiting for orders. Supposing this report to be correct, two batteries — Captain Carlin's and Captain Snow's — were posted on the extreme right of the line [see map, p. 482], Thoburn's brigade (34th Massachusetts, 1st West Virginia, and 54th Pennsylvania) was deployed on the left of the batteries, while Colonel Moor was ordered to form on the left of Thoburn; but unfortunately only two of his regiments (the 18th Connecticut and 123d Ohio) came into position on the right and left of Von Kleiser's battery, and a short distance in advance of Thoburn's line. The 12th West Virginia and Du Pont's battery took position behind the right of Thoburn's brigade as a reserve, and four companies of that regiment were posted behind the batteries on the right for their support. One company of the 34th Massachusetts was placed on the extreme right, between the batteries and the river, to watch any movement of the enemy through the woods and along the river. Ewing's battery was on the extreme left, and some distance behind it the cavalry. Skirmishers were deployed in our front. I personally directed and superintended this arrangement of the right wing, and was about to proceed to the left to see whether all the troops were in their proper positions, when my attention was directed to the approach of the enemy, whose lines appeared on the crest of the hills opposite our front, north-west of New Market.

Our skirmishers began to fall back, and fire was opened by Snow's battery on our right. I ordered the 34th Massachusetts to kneel down and deliver their fire by file as soon as the enemy came near enough to make it effective. A very severe conflict now followed at short range, the enemy charging repeatedly and with great determination against our line of infantry and the batteries, and being repulsed by the coolness and bravery of the 34th Massachusetts, 1st West Virginia, and 54th Pennsylvania, and the batteries. The smoke from the infantry fire on the left and the batteries on the right became so dense that I could not distinguish friend from foe.[note] There was an interruption of a few minutes, when the enemy's lines recoiled, and our men cheered; then the fire began again and lasted about thirty minutes; the enemy again charged, this time especially against our batteries; he came so near that Lieutenant Ephraim Chalfant of Carlin's battery rode up to me and said that he could not hold his position. I immediately ordered two companies of the 12th West Virginia to advance and protect the pieces, but to my surprise there was no disposition to advance; in fact, in spite of entreaties and reproaches, the men could not be moved an inch! At this moment Major Meysenburg of my staff came up to me, [note] and, to save the guns, I determined to make a counter-charge of the whole right wing, and requested him to transmit the order to Colonel Thoburn, who was not far from me toward the center. Bayonets were fixed and the charge was made in splendid style, but the enemy rallied, received our line with a destructive fire, and forced it back to its position. Before the charge was made, our extreme left wing had given way; two pieces of Von Kleiser's battery fell into the enemy's hands, and a part of his forces moved against the left and rear of Thoburn's brigade. When Thoburn's regiments came back, strewing the ground with their killed and wounded, the enemy, close on their heels, now again turned against the batteries on the right, filling the air with their high-pitched yells. I saw that the battery would be lost, as men and horses were falling.

I therefore reluctantly gave orders to Captain Carlin, through Lieutenant Chalfant, who was nearest to me, to withdraw his pieces successively, by sections from the right, and take position on an eminence, a short distance in the rear. Suddenly Carlin, who acted as chief-of-artillery, galloped back in hot haste, and his whole command followed him immediately. As some of the horses of two pieces had been killed, the guns were abandoned. Our whole position now became untenable, and the infantry retreated, pursued for a short distance by the enemy.[note] During the retreat, and while the artillery were crossing a

[note] During the battle rain fell in torrents and the wind drove clouds of smoke from our own and the enemy's lines against us, giving the latter the advantage in distinguishing our position and rendering his fire more effective, thus accounting in part for the greater number of killed on our side. — F. S.

[note] I was chained to my advanced position on the right by a circumstance that is unpleasant to record. Desiring to know what was going on to the left, I soon turned to ride out of the smoke, and to gain a survey of the whole field. As I did so, the companies placed behind the batteries quickly rose from the ground and followed me, as if by command. I immediately turned around, brought them back to their position, and remained at my post. In spite of the seriousness of the situation, it seemed to me almost comical that a major-general commanding a department and an "army" was condemned to the function of a "watchman." Then came the charge I ordered from our right. The disagreeable incident mentioned prevented me from performing an important duty. — F. S.

[note] The battle was well fought by the Southern troops, especially as to the timely and skillful manœuvre of Imboden, by which he gained a position with his battery, which enfiladed our line on the left, without a chance on our side, on account of the intervening creek, to attack or dislodge him. But better fighting was never done than by the 34th Massachusetts, under Colonel Wells and Lieutenant-Colonel Lincoln, who were both wounded in the battle; and by the 1st West Virginia, and by the 54th Pennsylvania under Colonel Campbell. The 34th Massachusetts lost 202

creek, another piece had to be abandoned, the horses being unable to bring it along. I tried my best to save it, and was nearly made a prisoner by the enemy's skirmishers who followed us. There was some confusion and scattering of our retreating forces, but very soon order was restored. They rallied again and formed a line opposite the Dunker Church, and west of the turnpike leading to Mount Jackson, about three-quarters of a mile from the battle-field. Here we could see a dark line on Rude's Hill, and discovered that it was the line of the 28th and 116th Ohio, the two regiments that were unfortunately not with us during the battle. After remaining in our position about half an hour, we marched back toward Rude's Hill, and the whole command formed in line, with the 28th and 116th Ohio on its extreme left.

When this new and last line was forming I met General Sullivan, and after some consultation we came to the conclusion not to await another attack, for the reason that our losses were severe ; that the regiments that had sustained the brunt of the fight were nearly out of ammunition and would have no time to receive it from the train, which was in the rear, beyond the bridge ; that our position was not a good one, being commanded by the enemy's guns, posted on the hill in front of our left; and that in case of defeat we could not cross the swollen river, except by the bridge. There was some cannonading, but nothing else was undertaken by the enemy for at least half an hour. I therefore directed the troops to withdraw to Mount Jackson, which was done slowly and in perfect order, under the immediate supervision of Generals Sullivan and Stahel, Captain Battersby's company being the last to cross the bridge. We would have remained at that place, but since the cavalry on our flank, under Colonels Boyd and Higgins respectively, had been beaten, flanks and rear were unprotected. We had a supply train of two hundred wagons with us, destined for General Crook in case we should have joined him. All our ambulances and a part of the train were filled with wounded, who could not have been sent back without being protected by a large detachment. It was therefore thought best to bring our little army back to Cedar Creek, disengage it from its impediments, receive the reënforcements that were expected and on their way, and, according to circumstances, remain there or advance again. As to General Crook, the battle of New Market did not affect his movements at that time, since, after his raid against the Virginia and Tennessee Railroad, he fell back to Lewisburg and Meadow Bluff, where, on the 19th of May, he found my dispatch, saying that he should advance to Staunton.

We arrived with all our troops behind the Shenandoah, at Mount Jackson, a little before 7 o'clock in the evening, and took position behind Mill Creek. We were perfectly safe there, as the creek was high and could not be forded, nor could the enemy venture to pass it in the face of our line ; but in order to retard his forward movement, if he

should try it, to give our troops the necessary rest, without molestation, to gain time for preparation after our arrival at Cedar Creek, and also for the purpose of deceiving Breckinridge in regard to our intention to come back, the bridge over the north branch of the Shenandoah was destroyed. We remained in our position for two hours, during which time (to use the words of Lieutenant-Colonel Lincoln in his "Life with the 34th Massachusetts Regiment"):

"the men ate their suppers, while the injured were looked up, their wounds examined and dressed, and the slightly wounded placed in ambulances for transportation. Those more severely wounded were disposed of in the hospital buildings at Mount Jackson, and left under charge of Assistant Surgeon Allen, of the 34th. These arrangements completed, at about 9 P. M., the column was again put in motion, the 34th bringing up the rear."

It will be seen from these statements that we did not "flee in disorder" from our position at Rude's Hill to Mount Jackson and Cedar Creek, nor lose or burn any wagons, nor "forsake" our sick and wounded, as was publicly proclaimed at the time, and often repeated, but we deliberately retreated to Mount Jackson in perfect order. All our wounded, with the exception of those that could not be carried away from the battle-field or transported from Mount Jackson, were with us on the retreat to Cedar Creek. The enemy captured no muskets, except those of our killed and severely wounded, left on the field ; and of the five pieces of artillery, two (of von Kleiser's battery) were taken in the first attack on our left — the other three were abandoned and taken on account of the horses having been killed or being unable to bring them along. The losses on both sides [see p. 491] were great in proportion to the forces engaged, which shows that the struggle was severe and was maintained with courage and tenacity.

From Mount Jackson we reached Edinburg by a night's march at 7 o'clock in the morning of the 16th, and after a two-hours' rest proceeded to Strasburg, where we arrived at 5 o'clock in the evening. Early in the morning of the 17th we crossed Cedar Creek and encamped on the same heights we had left just a week before. The troops were disappointed, but not the least "demoralized." The commander of the 12th West Virginia acknowledged the bad conduct of a part of his troops that failed to do their duty; but this regiment, under the same commander, redeemed its honor by its gallant behavior in the battle of Piedmont, and on other occasions.

On the 18th a detachment of infantry, cavalry, and artillery, under Colonel Wells of the 34th Massachusetts, was sent to Strasburg and the cavalry advanced to Fisher's Hill, the pickets of the enemy retiring before them. The Union flag was hoisted in the little fort at Strasburg, and patriotic speeches were made by Colonel Wells and others. On the 19th, at Cedar Creek, I received two dispatches, one from General Crook and the other from General Averell, bringing the news of

officers and men in killed and wounded, the 1st West Virginia 55, and the 54th Pennsylvania 132; I therefore have no doubt that the battle would have ended

differently if the two regiments, which I had good reason to believe were near, had arrived in time to assist us.— F. S.

their exploits, which of course created much enthusiasm. As I had already instructed General Weber at Harper's Ferry to send all the troops that were not absolutely necessary for the defense of the forts, and also those that were stationed at Martinsburg, to Cedar Creek, I now telegraphed to General Crook to march to Staunton, while I would advance again and try to meet him as soon as he was ready for coöperation. ⸘ He answered on the 19th from Meadow Bluff, that on account of certain difficulties he could not move before a week, but that he would move on the 1st of June and be in Staunton in six days. On the same day I was informed that General Hunter had been assigned to the department and would take command of the troops. This he did at Cedar Creek on the 21st of May. After a friendly conversation with him in which he expressed his desire that I should remain in the department and accept either the command of the Infantry Division or of the Reserve Division, comprising all the troops at Harper's Ferry and the lines of the Baltimore and Ohio, the matter was deferred to the next day,

when I accepted and was assigned to the latter command. I took leave of the troops on the same day and proceeded to Martinsburg, where the headquarters of the division were established.

Considering the different raids, and minor enterprises in West Virginia and the Shenandoah Valley, from the beginning of the campaign of 1864 until the appearance of Early before Washington, and including the subsequent engagements at Snicker's Gap and Bunker Hill, they represent in their totality, and in spite of partial successes of Averell, Crook, and Hunter, an utter failure, because Lee, having the advantage of a central position between the Army of the Potomac and the Shenandoah Valley, was always ready and able to turn the scales in his favor, whenever his communications leading west and north-west were seriously threatened; and so it came to pass that finally an army of at least 40,000 had to be applied to a problem that could not be solved by 5000 or 10,000. What should have been done at the beginning of the campaign in May, 1864, with a force of 20,000, in August demanded twice as many.

⸘ A dispatch from General Grant was received in the evening of that day, saying that I should march to Staunton.— F. S.

THE OPPOSING FORCES AT NEW MARKET, VA.,

MAY 15, 1864.

THE UNION ARMY.— Major-General Franz Sigel.

FIRST INF'NTRY DIVISION, Brig.-Gen. Jeremiah C. Sulliv.
First B. ade, Col. Augustus Moor: 18th Conn., Maj. Henry Pe ; 28th Ohio, Lieut.-Col. Gottfried Becker; 116th Ohio, ol. James Washburn; 123d Ohio, Maj. Horace Kellogg. *Second Brigade,* Col. Joseph Thoburn: 1st W. Va., Lieut.-Col. Jacob Weddle; 12th W. Va., Col. William B. Curtis; 34th Mass., Col. George D. Wells; 54th Pa., Col. Jacob M. Campbell.
FIRST CAVALRY DIVISION, Maj.-Gen. Julius Stahel.
First Brigade, Col. William B. Tibbits: 1st N. Y. (Veteran), Col. R. F. Taylor; 1st N. Y. (Lincoln), Lieut.-Col. Alonzo W. Adams; 1st Md., P. H. B. (detachment), Maj. J. T. Daniel; 21st N. Y., Maj. C. G. Otis; 14th Pa. (detach-

ment), Capt. Ashbel F. Duncan, Lieut.-Col. William Blakely. *Second Brigade,* Col. John E. Wynkoop: Small detachments of the 15th N. Y., ——; 20th Pa., ——; 22d Pa., ——. Total strength of the two cavalry brigades about 1000 men.
ARTILLERY: B, Md., Capt. Alonzo Snow; 30th N. Y., Capt. Albert von Kleiser; D, 1st W. Va., Capt. John Carlin; G, 1st W. Va., Capt. C. T. Ewing; B, 5th U. S., Capt. Henry A. Du Pont.
The effective strength of Sigel's command was about 6500, about 5150 men and 22 guns being available in the battle. (The 28th and 116th Ohio were not engaged.) The losses were 93 killed, 552 wounded, and 186 captured or missing $= 831$.

THE CONFEDERATE ARMY.— Major-General John C. Breckinridge.

Echols's Brigade, Brig.-Gen. John Echols: 22d Va., ——; 23d Va., ——; 26th Va., ——. *Wharton's Brigade,* Brig.-Gen. G. C. Wharton: 45th Va., ——; 51st Va., ——; 30th Va. Battalion, ——. *Cadet Corps* (four companies from the Virginia Military Institute), Lieut.-Col. Scott Ship. *Artillery,* McLaughlin's Battalion, Maj. William McLaughlin; Cadet Battery Section, Lieut. C. H. Minge. *Cavalry,* Imboden's Brigade, Brig.-Gen. John D. Imboden: 62d Va. (mounted infantry), Col. George H. Smith; 23d Va., Col. Robert White; 18th Va., Col. George W. Imboden; Gilmor's Maryland Battalion, Maj. Harry Gilmor; Davis's Maryland Battalion (detachment), Maj. Sturgis Davis; Partisan Rangers, Capt. John H. McNeill; McClanahan's Va. Battery, Capt. J. H. McClanahan.
In an address delivered at the anniversary celebration of the battle General Echols referred to the bravery of

a company of Missourians who were in the battle. They were 70 in number, and, according to the "Rockingham Register" of May 20th, 1864, they lost 47 in killed and wounded.
The strength of Breckinridge's forces was about 5000. General Sigel, in an estimate based on the official reports, places Breckinridge's strength at 4816, as follows: Wharton's brigade, 1578; Echols's brigade, 1622; engineer co., 56; cadet corps, 227; company of Missourians, 70; Jackson's battery, 100; Chapman's battery, 135; Callahan's battery, 93; cadet's section, 35; Imboden's cavalry (not including the 62d Va., with Wharton), 900. The losses were 42 killed, 522 wounded, and 13 missing $= 577$. These figures include the losses of the cadet corps, which numbered 225, and sustained a loss of 8 killed and 46 wounded.

THE OPPOSING FORCES IN THE LYNCHBURG EXPEDITION.

THE UNION ARMY.—Maj.-Gen. David Hunter.

FIRST INFANTRY DIVISION, Brig.-Gen. Jeremiah C. Sullivan.

First Brigade, Col. Augustus Moor, Col. Geo. D. Wells: 34th Mass. (transferred from 2d Brigade June 8th), Col. George D. Wells, Capt. George W. Thompson; 28th Ohio (sent to the rear with prisoners, etc., June 8th), Lieut.-Col. Gottfried Becker; 116th Ohio, Col. James Washburn; 123d Ohio, Col. William T. Wilson; A, B, C, and D, 5th N. Y. Hy. Arty., Lieut.-Col. Edward Murray. *Second Brigade,* Col. Joseph Thoburn: 18th Conn. (transferred from 1st Brigade June 8th), Col. William G. Ely; 1st W. Va., Lieut.-Col. Jacob Weddle; 12th W. Va., Col. William B. Curtis. *Unassigned:* 2d Md. (Eastern Shore), Col. Robert S. Rodgers; 2d Md. (Potomac Home Brigade), Lieut.-Col. G. Ellis Porter.

SECOND INFANTRY DIVISION, Brig.-Gen. George Crook.

First Brigade, Col. Rutherford B. Hayes: 23d Ohio, Lieut.-Col. James M. Comly; 36th Ohio, Col. Hiram F. Duval; 5th W. Va., Col. A. A. Tomlinson; 13th W. Va., Col. William R. Brown. *Second Brigade,* Col. Carr B. White: 12th Ohio, Lieut.-Col. Jonathan D. Hines; 91st Ohio, Col. John A. Turley, Lieut.-Col. Benjamin F. Coates; 9th W. Va., Col. Isaac H. Duval; 14th W. Va., Col. Daniel D. Johnson. *Third Brigade,* Col. Jacob M. Campbell: 54th Pa. (transferred from 2d Brigade, 1st Division, June 9th), Col. Jacob M. Campbell, Maj. Enoch

D. Yutzy; 3d and 4th Pa. Reserves (battalion), Capt. Abel T. Sweet; 11th W. Va. (6 co's), Col. Daniel Frost; 15th W. Va., Lieut.-Col. Thomas Morris. *Artillery:* 1st Ky., Capt. Daniel W. Glassie; 1st Ohio, Lieut. George P. Kirtland.

ARTILLERY, Capt. Henry A. Du Pont: B, Md., ——; 30th N. Y., Capt. Alfred von Kleiser; D, 1st W. Va., Capt John Carlin; B, 5th U. S., ——.

FIRST CAVALRY DIVISION, Maj.-Gen. Julius Stahel, Brig.-Gen. Alfred N. Duffié.

First Brigade, Col. William B. Tibbits: 1st N. Y. (Lincoln), ——; 1st N. Y. (Veteran), ——; 21st N. Y., ——; 1st Md., P. H. B., ——. *Second Brigade,* Col. John E. Wynkoop: 15th N. Y., ——; 20th Pa., ——; 22d Pa., ——.

SECOND CAVALRY DIVISION, Brig.-Gen. William W. Averell.

First Brigade, Col. James N. Schoonmaker: 8th Ohio, Col. Alpheus S. Moore; 14th Pa., ——. *Second Brigade,* Col. John H. Oley: 34th Ohio (m't'd infantry), ——; 3d W. Va., ——; 5th W. Va., ——; 7th W. Va., ——. *Third Brigade,* Col. William H. Powell: 1st W. Va., ——; 2d W. Va., ——.

Hunter started on this expedition with about 8500 men of all arms. After uniting with Crook and Averell at Staunton his force was about 18,000 strong.

THE CONFEDERATE ARMY.

The forces resisting Hunter's advance were commanded by Generals W. E. Jones (killed at Piedmont), J. C. Vaughn, John McCausland, W. L. Jackson, and J.

D. Imboden. General John C. Breckinridge's division and Jubal A. Early's corps arrived at Lynchburg in time to defend the place against Hunter's meditated attack.

EARLY'S MARCH TO WASHINGTON IN 1864.|

BY JUBAL A. EARLY, LIEUTENANT-GENERAL, C. S. A.

ON the 12th of June, 1864, while the Second Corps (Ewell's) of the Army of Northern Virginia was lying near Gaines's Mill, in rear of Hill's line at Cold Harbor, I received orders from General Lee to move the corps, with two of the battalions of artillery attached to it, to the Shenandoah Valley; to strike Hunter's force ⚓ in the rear and, if possible, destroy it; then to move down the valley, cross the Potomac near Leesburg, in Loudoun County, or at or above Harper's Ferry, as I might find most practicable, and threaten Washington city.| I was further directed to communicate with General Breckinridge, who would coöperate with me in the attack on Hunter and the expedition into Maryland.

The Second Corps now numbered a little over eight thousand muskets for duty. It had been on active and arduous service in the field for forty days. Divisions were not stronger than brigades ought to have been, nor brigades than regiments. On the morning of the 13th, at 2 o'clock, we

commenced the march, and on the 16th arrived at the Rivanna River, near Charlottesville, having marched over eighty miles in four days. At Charlottesville I received a telegram from Breckinridge, dated at Lynchburg, informing me that Hunter was then in Bedford County about twenty miles from that place and moving on it. The railroad and telegraph between Charlottesville and Lynchburg had been, fortunately, but slightly injured by the enemy's cavalry, and had been repaired. I ordered all the trains of the two roads to be sent to me with all dispatch, for the purpose of transporting my troops to Lynchburg. The trains were not in readiness to take the troops on board until sunrise on the morning of the 17th, and then only enough were furnished to transport about half my infantry. I accompanied Ramseur's division, going on the front train; but the road and rolling stock were in such bad condition that I did not reach Lynchburg until about 1 o'clock in the afternoon, and the other trains were much later.

| Condensed from General Early's "Memoir of the Last Year of the War for Independence in the Confederate States of America." Lynchburg: Published by Charles W. Button for the Virginia Memorial Association, 1867; here printed by permission of the author.

⚓ See p. 485, et seq.

| In a letter to the editors under date of November 23d, 1888, General Early says: "General Lee did not expect me to be able to enter Washington. His orders were merely to threaten the city, and when I suggested to him the idea of capturing it he said it would be impossible."

As General Breckinridge was in bed, suffering from an injury received near Cold Harbor, at his request General D. H. Hill, who happened to be in town, had made arrangements for the defense of the city with such troops as were at hand. Slight works had been hastily thrown up on College Hill, covering the turnpike and Forest roads from Liberty, manned by Breckinridge's infantry and the dismounted cavalry of the command [Jones's and Vaughn's brigades] which had been with Jones at Piedmont. The reserves, invalids from the hospitals, and the cadets from the Military Institute at Lexington occupied other parts of the line. My troops, as they arrived, had been ordered in front of the works to bivouac, and I immediately sent orders for them to move out on the turnpike, and two brigades of Ramseur's division arrived just in time to be thrown across the road at a redoubt about two miles from the city as Imboden's command was driven back by vastly superior numbers. These brigades, with two pieces of artillery in the redoubt, arrested the progress of the enemy, and Ramseur's other brigade, and the part of Gordon's division which had arrived, took position on the same line. The enemy opened a heavy fire of artillery on us, but as night soon came on he went into camp on our front.

Orders had been given for the immediate return of the trains for the rest of my infantry, but it did not get to Lynchburg until late in the afternoon of the 18th, and meanwhile I contented myself with acting on the defensive. There was artillery firing and skirmishing along the line, and in the afternoon an attack was made to the right of the turnpike, which was handsomely repulsed with considerable loss to the enemy. A demonstration of the enemy's cavalry on the Forest road was checked by part of Breckinridge's infantry under Wharton, and McCausland's cavalry. As soon as the remainder of my infantry arrived by the railroad, though none of my artillery had gotten up, arrangements were made for attacking Hunter at daylight on the 19th; but after midnight it was discovered that he was moving, and at light it was observed that he was in retreat, and pursuit commenced. The enemy's rear was overtaken at Liberty, twenty-five miles from Lynchburg, just before night, and driven through that place, after a brisk skirmish, by Ramseur's division. The day's march on the old turnpike, which was very rough, had been terrible. The pursuit was resumed early on the morning of the 20th, and the enemy was pursued into the mountains at Buford's Gap, but he had taken possession of the crest of the

Blue Ridge, and put batteries in position commanding a gorge through which the road passes. On the 21st the pursuit was resumed very shortly after sunrise. The enemy had turned off from Salem toward Lewisburg, and McCausland had struck his column and captured ten pieces of artillery, but was compelled to fall back, carrying off, however, the prisoners and also a part of the artillery, and disabling the rest. As the enemy had got into the mountains, where nothing useful could be accomplished by pursuit, I did not deem it proper to continue it farther. A great part of my command had had nothing to eat for the last two days, except a little bacon which was obtained at Liberty. It had marched sixty miles in the three days' pursuit, over very rough roads. I determined, therefore, to rest on the 22d, so as to enable the wagons and artillery to get up, and prepare the men for the long march before them. ♭

At Lynchburg I had received a telegram from General Lee, directing me, after disposing of Hunter, either to return to his army or to carry out the original plan, as I might deem most expedient. After the pursuit had ceased I received another dispatch from him, submitting it to my judgment whether the condition of my troops would permit the expedition across the Potomac to be carried out, and I determined to take the responsibility of continuing it. On the 23d the march was resumed, and we reached Buchanan that night. On the 26th I reached Staunton in advance of the troops, and the latter came up next day, which was spent in reducing transportation and getting provisions from Waynesboro'. The official reports at this place showed about two thousand mounted men for duty in the cavalry, which was composed of four small brigades, to wit: Imboden's, McCausland's, Jackson's, and Jones's (now Johnson's). The official reports of the infantry showed ten thousand muskets for duty, including Vaughn's dismounted cavalry. Besides Breckinridge's own infantry division, under Elzey (now under Vaughn, afterward under Echols), Gordon's division of the Second Corps was assigned to General Breckinridge, in order to give him a command commensurate with his proper one. Nearly half the troops were barefoot, or nearly so, and shoes were sent for. But without waiting for them the march was resumed on the 28th, with five days' rations in the wagons and two days' in haversacks. Imboden was sent through Brock's Gap to the South Branch of the Potomac to destroy the railroad bridge over that stream, and all the bridges on the Baltimore and Ohio Railroad from that point to Martinsburg. On

---

♭ Grant, in his report, says "General Hunter, owing to a want of ammunition to give battle, retired from before the place" [Lynchburg]. This is a little remarkable, as it appears that this expedition had been long contemplated and was one of the prominent features of the campaign of 1864. Sheridan, with his cavalry, was to have united with Hunter at Lynchburg, and the two together were to have destroyed Lee's communications and depots of supplies, and then have joined Grant. Can it be believed that Hunter set out on so important an expedition with an insufficient supply of ammunition? Had Sheridan defeated Hampton at Trevilian's, he would have reached Lynchburg after destroying the

railroad on the way, and I could not have reached there in time to do any good. But Hampton defeated Sheridan. Had Hunter moved on Lynchburg with energy, that place would have fallen before it was possible for me to get there.—J. A. E.

The notification of Secretary Stanton to General Stahel on the subject was as follows: "General Sheridan, who was sent by General Grant to open communication with General Hunter by way of Charlottesville, has just returned to York River without effecting his object. It is therefore very probable that General Hunter will be compelled to fall back into West Virginia."—Editors.

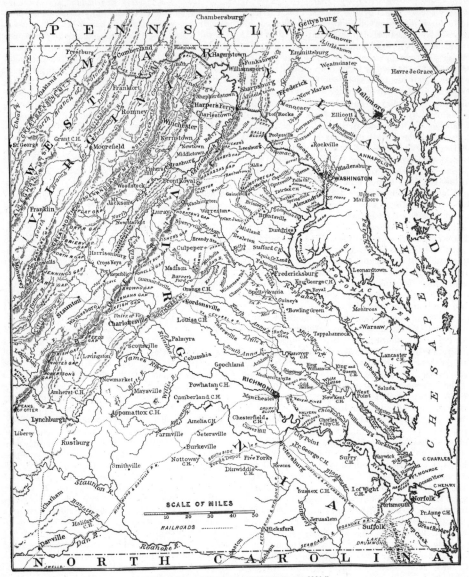

MAP OF THE VIRGINIA CAMPAIGNS OF 1864-5.

the 2d of July we reached Winchester, and here I received a dispatch from General Lee, directing me to remain in the lower valley until everything was in readiness to cross the Potomac, and to destroy the Baltimore and Ohio Railroad and the Chesapeake and Ohio Canal as far as possible. This was in accordance with my previous determination, and its policy was obvious. My provisions were nearly exhausted, and if I had moved through Loudoun it would have been necessary for me to halt and thresh wheat and have it ground, as neither bread nor flour could be otherwise obtained; which would have caused much greater delay than was required on the other route, where we could take provisions

from the enemy. Moreover, unless the Baltimore and Ohio Railroad was torn up the enemy would have been able to move troops from the West over that road to Washington.

On the morning of the 3d Sigel, with a considerable force, after slight skirmishing, evacuated Martinsburg, leaving considerable stores in our hands. McCausland burned the bridge over Back Creek, capturing the guard at North Mountain depot, and succeeded in reaching Hainesville; but Bradley T. Johnson, after driving Mulligan, with hard fighting at Leetown, across the railroad, was himself forced back, when Sigel united with Mulligan, upon Rodes's and Ramseur's divisions, which arrived at Leetown after a march of twenty-four miles. During the night Sigel retreated across the Potomac at Shepherdstown to Maryland Heights.

During the night of the 4th the enemy evacuated Harper's Ferry, burning the railroad and pontoon bridges across the Potomac. It was not possible to occupy the town of Harper's Ferry, except with skirmishers, as it was thoroughly commanded by the heavy guns on Maryland Heights; and the 5th was spent by Rodes's and Ramseur's divisions in demonstrating at that place. In the afternoon Breckinridge's command moved to Shepherdstown and crossed the Potomac, followed by Rodes's and Ramseur's divisions early on the 6th. Gordon's division advanced toward Maryland Heights, and drove the enemy into his works. Working parties were employed in destroying the aqueduct of the canal over the Antietam, and the locks and canalboats. On the 7th Rodes moved through Rohrersville on the road to Crampton's Gap in South Mountain, and skirmished with a small force of the enemy, while Breckinridge demonstrated against Maryland Heights. McCausland had occupied Hagerstown and levied a contribution of $20,000, and Boonsboro' had been occupied by Johnson's cavalry. A letter from General Lee had informed me that an effort would be made to release the prisoners at Point Lookout, and directing me to take steps to unite them with my command. My desire had been to manœuvre the enemy out of Maryland Heights, so as to move directly to Washington; but he had taken refuge in his strongly fortified works, and I therefore determined to move through the gaps of South Mountain north of the Heights. On the 7th the greater portion of the cavalry was sent in the direction of Frederick; and that night the expected shoes arrived and were distributed.

Early on the morning of the 8th the whole force moved: Rodes through Crampton's Gap to Jefferson; Breckinridge through Fox's Gap; and Ramseur, with the trains, through Boonsboro' Gap, followed by Lewis's brigade, which had started from Harper's Ferry the night before, after burning the trestle-work on the railroad and the stores which had not been brought off. Early on the 9th Johnson, with his brigade of cavalry and a battery of horse artillery, moved to the north of Frederick,

with orders to strike the railroads from Baltimore to Harrisburg and Philadelphia, burn the bridges over the Gunpowder, also to cut the railroad between Washington and Baltimore, and threaten the latter place; and then to move toward Point Lookout for the purpose of releasing the prisoners, if we should succeed in getting into Washington. The other troops also moved forward toward Monocacy Junction, and Ramseur's division passed through Frederick, driving a force of skirmishers before it.

The enemy in considerable force, under General Lew Wallace,[✝] was found strongly posted

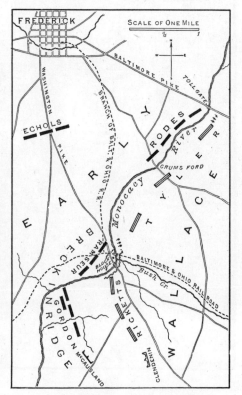

MAP OF THE BATTLE OF THE MONOCACY.

[✝] In his "Personal Memoirs" (Vol. II., pp. 304-6), General Grant writes as follows of the battle of Monocacy and its effect:

"In the absence of Hunter, General Lew Wallace, with headquarters at Baltimore, commanded the department in which the Shenandoah lay. His surplus of troops with which to move against the enemy was small in number. Most of these were raw, and, consequently, very much inferior to our veterans and to the veterans which Early had with him; but the situation of Washington was precarious, and Wallace moved with commendable promptitude to meet the enemy at the Monocacy. He could hardly have expected to defeat him badly, but he hoped to cripple and delay him until Washington could be put into a state of preparation for his reception. I had previously ordered General Meade to send a division to Baltimore for the purpose of adding to the defenses of Washington, and he had sent Ricketts's division of the Sixth Corps (Wright's), which arrived in Baltimore on the 8th of July. Finding that Wallace had gone to the front with his command, Ricketts immediately took the cars and followed him

to the Monocacy with his entire division. They met the enemy and, as might have been expected, were defeated; but they succeeded in stopping him for the day on which the battle took place. The next morning Early started on his march to the capital of the nation, arriving before it on the 11th.

"Learning of the gravity of the situation, I had directed General Meade to also order Wright, with the rest of his corps, directly to Washington for the relief of that place, and the latter reached there the very day that Early arrived before it. The Nineteenth Corps, which had been stationed in Louisiana, having been ordered up to reënforce the armies about Richmond, had about this time arrived at Fortress Monroe, on their way to join us. I diverted them from that point to Washington, which place they reached almost simultaneously with Wright, on the 11th. The Nineteenth Corps was commanded by Major-General Emory.

"Early made his reconnoissance with a view of attacking on the following morning, the 12th; but the next morning he found our intrenchments, which were very strong, fully manned. He at once commenced to retreat, Wright following. [The retreat began on the night of the 12th. See

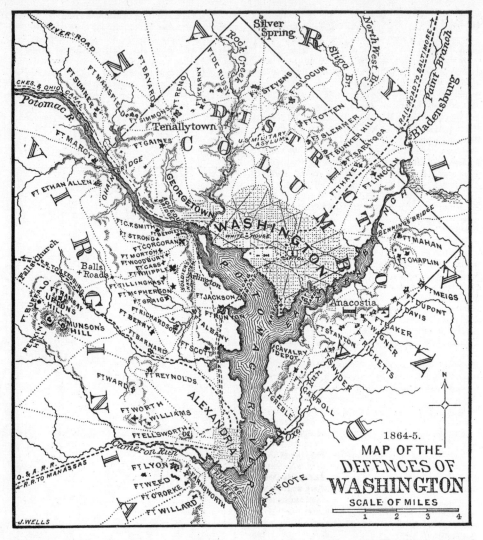

1864-5.

MAP OF THE
DEFENCES OF
WASHINGTON

SCALE OF MILES

1   2   3   4

J. WELLS

on the eastern bank of the Monocacy, near the junction, with an earth-work and two block-houses commanding both the railroad bridge and the bridge on the Georgetown pike. McCausland, crossing the river with his brigade, dismounted his men and advanced rapidly against the enemy's left flank, which he threw into confusion, but he was then gradually forced back. McCausland's movement, which was very brilliantly executed, solved the problem for me, and orders were sent to Breckinridge to move up rapidly with Gordon's division to McCausland's assistance, and, striking the enemy's left, to drive him from the positions commanding the crossings in Ramseur's front, so

that the latter might cross. This division crossed under the personal superintendence of General Breckinridge, and while Ramseur skirmished with the enemy in front, the attack was made by Gordon in gallant style, and with the aid of several pieces of King's artillery, which had been crossed over, and Nelson's artillery from the opposite side, he threw the enemy into great confusion and forced him from his position. Ramseur immediately crossed on the railroad bridge and pursued the enemy's flying forces, and Rodes crossed on the left and joined in the pursuit. Between 600 and 700 unwounded prisoners fell into their hands, and the enemy's loss in killed and wounded

quotation from General Grant's report (in relation to the time of Early's withdrawal), foot-note, p. 499.—EDITORS.] There is no telling how much this result was contributed to by General Lew Wallace's leading what might well be considered almost a forlorn-hope. If Early had been but one day earlier, he might have entered the capital before the

arrival of the reënforcements I had sent. Whether the delay caused by the battle amounted to a day or not, General Wallace contributed on this occasion, by the defeat of the troops under him, a greater benefit to the cause than often falls to the lot of a commander of an equal force to render by means of a victory."

FORT STEVENS, WASHINGTON. FROM A WAR-TIME PHOTOGRAPH.

was very heavy. Our loss in killed and wounded was about 700. The action closed about sunset, and we had marched about fourteen miles before it commenced. All the troops and trains were crossed over the Monocacy that night, so as to resume the march early the next day. During the operations at Monocacy, a contribution of $200,000 in money was levied on the city of Frederick, and some much-needed supplies were obtained.

On the 10th the march was resumed at daylight, and we bivouacked four miles from Rockville, on the Georgetown pike, having marched twenty miles. McCausland, moving in front, drove a body of the enemy's cavalry before him, and had a brisk engagement at Rockville, where he encamped after defeating and driving off the enemy.

We moved at daylight on the 11th, McCausland on the Georgetown pike, while the infantry, preceded by Imboden's cavalry under Colonel Smith, turned to the left at Rockville, so as to reach the 7th street pike which runs by Silver Springs into Washington. Jackson's cavalry moved on the left flank. The previous day had been very warm, and the roads were exceedingly dusty, as there had been no rain for several weeks. The heat during the night had been very oppressive, and but little rest had been obtained. This day was an exceedingly hot one, and there was no air stirring. While marching, the men were enveloped in a suffocating cloud of dust, and many of them fell by the way from exhaustion. Our progress was therefore very much impeded, but I pushed on as rapidly as possible, hoping to get into the fortifications around Washington before they could be manned. Smith drove a small body of cavalry before him into the works on the 7th street pike, and dismounted his men and deployed them as skirmishers. I rode ahead of the infantry, and

arrived in sight of Fort Stevens on this road a short time after noon, when I discovered that the works were but feebly manned.

Rodes, whose division was in front, was immediately ordered to bring it into line as rapidly as possible, throw out skirmishers, and move into the works if he could. My whole column was then moving by flank, which was the only practicable mode of marching on the road we were on, and before Rodes's division could be brought up we saw a cloud of dust in the rear of the works toward Washington, and soon a column of the enemy filed into them on the right and left, and skirmishers were thrown out in front, while an artillery fire was opened on us from a number of batteries. This defeated our hopes of getting possession of the works by surprise, and it became necessary to reconnoiter.

Rodes's skirmishers were thrown to the front, driving those of the enemy to the cover of the works, and we proceeded to examine the fortifications in order to ascertain if it was practicable to carry them by assault. They were found to be exceedingly strong, and consisted of what appeared to be inclosed forts for heavy artillery, with a tier of lower works in front of each, pierced for an immense number of guns, the whole being connected by curtains with ditches in front, and strengthened by palisades and abatis. The timber had been felled within cannon range all around and left on the ground, making a formidable obstacle, and every possible approach was raked by artillery. On the right was Rock Creek, running through a deep ravine which had been rendered impassable by the felling of the timber on each side, and beyond were the works on the Georgetown pike which had been reported to be the strongest of all. On the left, as far as the eye could reach, the works appeared to be of the same impregnable character. ⚓ This reconnoissance consumed the balance of the day.

The rapid marching and the losses at Harper's Ferry, Maryland Heights, and Monocacy had reduced my infantry to about 8000 muskets.↓ Of these a very large number were greatly exhausted by the last two days' marching, some having fallen by sunstroke, and not more than one-third of my force could have been carried into action. I had about forty pieces of artillery, of which the largest were 12-pounder Napoleons, besides a few pieces of horse-artillery with the cavalry. McCausland reported the works on the Georgetown pike too strongly manned for him to assault. After dark on the 11th I held a consultation with Major-Generals Breckinridge, Rodes, Gordon, and Ramseur, in which I stated to them the necessity of doing something immediately, as the passes of South Mountain and the fords of the Upper Potomac would soon be closed against us. After interchanging views with them, I determined to make an assault on the enemy's works at daylight next morning. But during the night a dispatch was received from General Bradley T. Johnson from near Baltimore, that two corps had arrived from General Grant's army, and that his whole army was probably in motion. As soon as it was light enough to see, I rode to the front, and found the parapet lined with troops. I had, therefore, reluctantly to give up all hopes of capturing Washington, after I had arrived in sight of the dome of the Capitol, and given the Federal authorities a terrible fright.

Some of the Northern papers stated that, between Saturday and Monday, I could have entered the city; but on Saturday I was fighting at Monocacy, thirty-five miles from Washington, a force which I could not leave in my rear; and after disposing of that force and moving as rapidly as it was possible for me to move, I did not arrive in front of the fortifications until after noon on

Monday, and then my troops were exhausted, and it required time to bring them up into line. I had then made a march, over the circuitous route by Charlottesville, Lynchburg, and Salem, down the valley and through the passes of the South Mountain, which, notwithstanding the delays in dealing with Hunter's, Sigel's, and Wallace's forces, is, for its length and rapidity, I believe, without a parallel in this or any other modern war. My small force had been thrown up to the very walls of the Federal capital, north of a river which could not be forded at any point within forty miles, and with a heavy force and the South Mountain in my rear—the passes through which mountain could be held by a small number of troops. A glance at the map, when it is recollected that the Potomac is a wide river, and navigable to Washington for the largest vessels, will cause the intelligent reader to wonder, not why I failed to take Washington, but why I had the audacity to approach it as I did, with the small force under my command. It was supposed by some, who were not informed of the facts, that I delayed in the lower valley longer than was necessary; but an examination of the foregoing narrative will show that not one moment was spent in idleness. I could not move across the Potomac and through the passes of the South Mountain, with any safety, until Sigel was driven from, or safely housed in, the fortifications at Maryland Heights.

After abandoning the idea of capturing Washington I determined to remain in front of the fortifications during the 12th, and retire at night. Johnson had burned the bridges over the Gunpowder, on the Harrisburg and Philadelphia roads, threatened Baltimore, and started for Point Lookout; but the attempt to release the prisoners was not made, as the enemy had received notice of it in some way. On the afternoon of the 12th a heavy reconnoitering force was sent out by the

---

⚓ General Barnard, in his "Defences of Washington," thus describes the works (see map, p. 496):

"Every prominent point, at intervals of eight hundred to one thousand yards, was occupied by an inclosed field-fort; every important approach or depression of ground, unseen from the forts, swept by a battery for field-guns; and the whole connected by rifle-trenches which were in fact lines of infantry parapets, furnishing emplacement for two ranks of men, and affording covered communication along the line, while roads were opened wherever necessary, so that troops and artillery could be moved rapidly from one point of the immense periphery to another, or, under cover, from point to point along the line. The counterscarps were surrounded by abatis; bomb-proofs were provided in nearly all the forts; all guns not solely intended for distant fire placed in embrasures and well traversed. All commanding points on which an enemy would be likely to concentrate artillery to overpower that of one or two of our forts or batteries were subjected not only to the fire, direct and cross, of many points along the line, but also from heavy rifled guns from distant points unattainable by the enemy's field-guns. With all these developments, the lines certainly approximated to the maximum degree of strength which can be attained from unrevetted earth-works. Inadequately manned as they were, the fortifications compelled at least a concentration and an arraying of force on the part of the assailants, and thus gave time for the arrival of succor."

General Barnard gives this account of the local forces prior to the arrival of the Sixth and Nineteenth corps:

"The effective forces were 1819 infantry, 1834 artillery, and

63 cavalry north of the Potomac, and 4064 infantry, 1772 artillery, and 51 cavalry south thereof. There were besides, in Washington and Alexandria, about 3900 effectives and about 4400 (six regiments) of Veteran Reserves. The foregoing constitute a total of about 20,400 men. Of that number, however, but 9600, mostly perfectly raw troops, constituted the *garrison* of the defenses. Of the other troops, a considerable portion were unavailable, and the whole would form but an inefficient force for service on the lines."

Of the troops sent by Grant, Ricketts's division of the Sixth Corps was with Wallace at Baltimore; the other two divisions, under General Wright, and the first steamer-load, amounting to 800 men, of the Nineteenth Corps, reached Washington before 2 P. M. of the 11th. At 4:10 P. M. of that day Wright sent this dispatch to General Augur from Fort Stevens: "The head of my column has nearly reached the front." That night the Sixth Corps relieved the provisional forces on the picket line. The remainder of Emory's division of the Nineteenth Corps continued to come by installments.—EDITORS.

↓ Writing on November 23d, 1888, General Early adds:

"A considerable number of my men had broken down on the march, from exhaustion and want of shoes, and on my return to the Valley I found some 1800 or 2000 collected at Winchester by Colonel Goodwin, and others who had been temporarily disabled in the campaign from the Wilderness to Richmond also returned."—EDITORS.

enemy, which, after severe skirmishing, was driven back by Rodes's division with but slight loss to us.) About dark we commenced retiring, and did so without molestation. Passing through Rockville and Poolesville, we crossed the Potomac

) Grant says: "On the 12th a reconnoissance was thrown out in front of Fort Stevens to ascertain the enemy's position and force. A severe skirmish ensued, in which we lost 280 in killed and wounded. The enemy's loss was probably greater. He commenced retiring during the night." The above is correct, with the exception of the estimate placed on our loss.— J. A. E.

) General Wright, with about 15,000 men of the Sixth and Nineteenth corps, followed by several thousand more, under Ricketts and Kenly, pursued General Early, who, however, after resting on the 14th and 15th at Leesburg, reached the Shenandoah Valley safely through

at White's Ford, above Leesburg, in Loudoun County, on the morning of the 14th, bringing off the prisoners captured at Monocacy, and our captured beef cattle and horses, and everything else, in safety.)

Snicker's Gap, losing some loaded wagons at Purcellville to the cavalry of Hunter's field forces. These latter had returned from the Kanawha Valley to Harper's Ferry, and moved out under Crook against the flank of Early's column. Thoburn's division of Crook's command, crossing at Snicker's Gap, was repulsed by Early with a loss of 422 on the 18th of July. On the 20th Averell, with a mixed infantry and cavalry force, 2350 strong, attacked and defeated Ramseur's division near Winchester, inflicting a loss of about 400, and suffering a loss of 214. On July 22d General Early established himself at Strasburg.— EDITORS.

THE OPPOSING FORCES AT THE MONOCACY, MD.

July 9th, 1864.

THE UNION ARMY.—Major-General Lewis Wallace.

First Separate Brigade (Eighth Army Corps), Brig.-Gen. Erastus B. Tyler: 1st Md., Potomac Home Brigade (5 co's), Capt. Charles J. Brown; 3d Md., P. H. B., Col. Charles Gilpin; 11th Md., Col. William T. Landstreet; 144th Ohio (3 co's) and 149th Ohio (7 co's), Col. Allison L. Brown; Baltimore (Md.) Battery, Capt. F. W. Alexander.

Cavalry, Lieut.-Col. D. R. Clendenin: 8th Ill., Lieut.-Col. D. R. Clendenin; Detachment 159th Ohio (m't'd inf.), Capt. Edward H. Leib and Capt. Henry S. Allen; Detachment Mixed Cavalry, Maj. Charles A. Wells; Loudoun (Va.) Rangers.

THIRD DIVISION (Sixth Corps), Brig.-Gen. James B. Ricketts.

First Brigade, Col. William S. Truex: 14th N. J., Lieut.-Col. C. K. Hall; 106th N. Y., Capt. Edward M. Paine; 151st N. Y., Col. William Emerson; 87th Pa., Lieut.-Col. James A. Stahle; 10th Vt., Col. William W. Henry. *Second Brigade*, Col. Matthew R. McClennan: 9th N. Y. Heavy Art'y, Col. William H. Seward; 110th Ohio, Lieut.-Col. Otho H. Binkley; 122d Ohio (detachment), Lieut. Charles J. Gibson; 126th Ohio, Lieut.-Col. Aaron W. Ebright; 138th Pa., Maj. Lewis A. May. The 6th Md., 67th Pa., and part of the 122d Ohio, of this brigade, did not reach the battle-field. Union loss: k, 98; w, 594; m, 1188 = 1880.

Effective strength (estimated): Eighth Corps troops, 2700; Ricketts's division (on the field), 3350 = 6050.

THE CONFEDERATE ARMY.—Lieutenant-General Jubal A. Early.

GORDON'S DIVISION,) Maj.-Gen. John B. Gordon.

Evans's Brigade, Brig.-Gen. C. A. Evans, Col. E. N. Atkinson: 13th Ga., ——; 26th Ga., Col. E. N. Atkinson; 31st Ga., ——; 38th Ga., ——; 60th Ga., ——; 61st Ga., Col. J. H. Lamar; 12th Ga. Battalion, ——. *Hays's Brigade*, ‡ Col. W. R. Peck: 5th La., ——; 6th La., ——; 7th La., ——; 8th La., ——; 9th La., ——. *Stafford's Brigade*, ‡ 1st La., ——; 2d La., ——; 10th La., ——; 14th La., ——; 15th La., ——. *Terry's Brigade*, ↓ Brig.-Gen.. William Terry: 2d, 4th, 5th, 27th, and 33d Va. (Stonewall Brigade), Col. J. H. S. Funk; 21st, 25th, 42d, 44th, 48th, and 50th Va. (J. M. Jones's brigade), Col. R. H. Dungan; 10th, 23d, and 37th Va. Steuart's brigade), Lieut.-Col. S. H. Saunders.

BRECKINRIDGE'S DIVISION, ☆ Brig.-Gen. John Echols. [Consisted of Echols's, Wharton's, and Vaughn's brigades, the latter being dismounted cavalry.]

RODES'S DIVISION, Maj.-Gen. R. E. Rodes.

Grimes's Brigade: 32d N. C., ——; 43d N. C., ——; 45th N. C., ——; 53d N. C., ——; 2d N. C. Batt'n, ——. *Cook's Brigade:* 4th Ga., ——; 12th Ga., ——; 21st Ga., ——; 44th Ga., ——. *Cox's Brigade:* 1st N. C., ——; 2d N. C., ——; 3d N. C., ——; 4th N. C., ——; 14th N. C., ——; 30th N. C., ——. *Battle's Brigade:* 3d

Ala., ——; 5th Ala., ——; 6th Ala., ——; 12th Ala., ——; 61st Ala., ——.

RAMSEUR'S DIVISION, Maj.-Gen. S. D. Ramseur.

Lilley's Brigade: 13th Va., ——; 31st Va., ——; 49th Va., ——; 52d Va., ——; 58th Va., ——. *Johnston's Brigade:* 5th N. C., ——; 12th N. C., ——; 20th N. C., ——; 23d N. C., ——. *Lewis's Brigade:* 6th N. C., ——; 21st N. C., ——; 54th N. C., ——; 57th N. C., ——; 1st N. C. Batt'n, ——.

CAVALRY, Maj.-Gen. Robert Ransom.

[Composed of the brigades of McCausland, Imboden, W. L. Jackson, and Bradley T. Johnson. The latter brigade was not before the battle " to cut the Northern Central and the Philadelphia and Baltimore railroads."]

ARTILLERY, Lieut.-Col. J. Floyd King.

[Composed of Nelson's, Braxton's, and McLaughlin's battalions.]

With the forces above enumerated General Early continued his movement on Washington. In his official report he says that in the action at the Monocacy " our entire loss was between 600 and 700, including the cavalry," and that when in front of Washington " my infantry force did not exceed 10,000."

) Maj.-Gen. John C. Breckinridge commanded Gordon's and Echols's divisions.

‡ United under the command of Brigadier-General Zebulon York.

↓ Composed of " the fragmentary remains of fourteen of the regiments of Edward Johnson's division, most of which was captured by the enemy May 12th, 1864."

☆ Composition not clearly indicated.

PART OF SHERIDAN'S WAGON TRAIN. FROM A WAR-TIME SKETCH.

SHERIDAN IN THE SHENANDOAH VALLEY.

BY WESLEY MERRITT, MAJOR-GENERAL, U. S. V., BRIGADIER-GENERAL, U. S. A.

UP to the summer of 1864 the Shenandoah Valley had not been to the Union armies a fortunate place either for battle or for strategy. A glance at the map will go far toward explaining this. The Valley has a general direction from south-west to north-east. The Blue Ridge Mountains, forming its eastern barrier, are well defined from the James River above Lynchburg to Harper's Ferry on the Potomac. Many passes (in Virginia called "gaps") made it easy of access from the Confederate base of operations; and, bordered by a fruitful country filled with supplies, it offered a tempting highway for an army bent on a flanking march on Washington or the invasion of Maryland or Pennsylvania. For the Union armies, while it was an equally practicable highway, it led away from the objective, Richmond, and was exposed to flank attacks through the gaps from vantage-ground and perfect cover.

It was not long after General Grant completed his first campaign in Virginia, and while he was in front of Petersburg, that his attention was called to this famous seat of side issues between Union and Confederate armies. With quick military instinct he saw that the Valley was not useful to the Government for aggressive operations. He decided that it must be made untenable for either army. In doing this he reasoned that the advantage would be with us, who did not want it as a source of supplies, nor as a place of arms, and against the Confederates, who wanted it for both. Accordingly, instructions were drawn up for carrying on a plan of devastating the Valley in a way least injurious to the people. These instructions, which were intended for Hunter, were destined to be carried out by another, and how well this was accomplished it is my purpose to recount.

Hunter's failure to capture Lynchburg in the spring of 1864 [see p. 492] and his retreat by a circuitous line opened the Valley to General Early, who had gone to the relief of Lynchburg. Marching down the Valley and taking possession of it without serious opposition, Early turned Harper's

Ferry, which was held by a Union force under Sigel, and crossed into Maryland at Shepherdstown. The governors of New York, Pennsylvania, and Massachusetts were called on for hundred-days men to repel the invasion, and later the Army of the Potomac supplied its quota of veterans as a nucleus around which the new levies could rally. General Early marched on Washington, and on the 11th of July was in front of the gates of the capital. The following day, after a severe engagement in which the guns of Fort Stevens took part, he withdrew his forces through Rockville and Poolesville, and, crossing the Potomac above Leesburg, entered the Valley of Virginia through Snicker's Gap. Afterward, crossing the Shenandoah at the ferry of the same name, he moved to Berryville, and there awaited developments.

After the immediate danger to Washington had passed it became a question with General Grant and the authorities in Washington to select an officer who, commanding in the Valley, would prevent further danger from invasion. After various suggestions,┊ Major-General Philip H. Sheridan was selected temporarily for this command. His per-

MAJOR-GENERAL WESLEY MERRITT.
FROM A PHOTOGRAPH.

manent occupation of the position was opposed by Secretary Stanton on the ground that he was too young for such important responsibility. On the 7th of August, 1864, Sheridan assumed command of the Middle Military Division and of the army for the protection of the Valley, afterward known as the "Army of the Shenandoah."

Naturally, on assuming command, Sheridan moved with caution. He was incited to this by his instructions, and inclined to it by his unfamiliarity with the country, with the command, and with the enemy he had to deal with. On the other hand, Early, who had nothing of these to learn, save the mettle of his new adversary, was aggressive, and at once manœuvred with a bold front, seemingly anxious for a battle. The movements of the first few days showed, however, that Early was not disposed to give battle unless he could do so on his own conditions.

On the morning of the 10th of August Sheridan, who had massed his army at Halltown, in front of Harper's Ferry, marched toward the enemy's communications, his object being to occupy Early's line of retreat and force him to fight before reënforcements could reach him. The march of my cavalry toward the Millwood-Winchester road brought us in contact with the

┊ On the 18th of July General Grant suggested Franklin for the command of the projected Middle Military Division, and, on this being objected to, proposed the assignment of Meade, with Hancock to command the Army of the Potomac and Gibbon for the Second Corps.—EDITORS.

enemy's cavalry on that road, and it was driven toward Kernstown. At the same time a brigade under Custer, making a reconnoissance on the Berryville-Winchester road, came on the enemy holding a defile of the highway while "his trains and infantry were marching toward Strasburg." As soon as the retreat of the enemy was known to General Sheridan the cavalry was ordered to pursue and harass him. Near White Post, Devin came upon a strongly posted force, which, after a sharp fight, he drove from the field, and the division took position on the Winchester-Front Royal pike. The same day my division had a severe affair with infantry near Newtown, in which the loss to my Second Brigade was considerable.

On the 12th of August, the enemy having retired the night before, the cavalry pursued to Cedar Creek, when it came up with Early's rear-guard and continued skirmishing until the arrival of the head of the infantry column. The day following, the reconnoissance of a brigade of cavalry discovered the enemy strongly posted at Fisher's Hill. About this time Early received his expected reënforcements. General Sheridan, being duly informed of this, made preparations to retire to a position better suited for defense and adapted to the changed conditions of the strength of the two armies.

On the 13th of August General Devin's brigade of the First Division was ordered to Cedarville on the Front Royal pike, and on the 14th I

marched with the rest of my division to the same point, Gibbs taking position near Nineveh. On the arrival of his reënforcements Early had requested General R. H. Anderson, in command, to take station at Front Royal, it being a convenient point from which to make a flank movement in case of attack on Sheridan's command, which Early undoubtedly contemplated. At the same time it constituted a guard to the Luray Valley.

About 2 P. M. on the 16th an attack was made by this command on the First Cavalry Division, which resulted in the battle of Cedarville. A force of cavalry under Fitz Lee, supported by a brigade of Kershaw's division, made a descent on Devin's brigade. General Fitz Lee drove in the cavalry pickets and attacked Devin with great violence. This force was scarcely repulsed when a brigade of infantry was discovered moving on the opposite bank of the Shenandoah River toward the left of the cavalry position. One regiment of Custer's brigade, dismounted, was moved up to the crest of a hill near the river-bank to meet this force, while the rest of the brigade, mounted, was stationed to the right of the hill. At the same time the Reserve Brigade under General Gibbs was summoned to the field. The enemy advanced boldly, wading the river, and when within short carbine range was met by a murderous volley from the dismounted men, while the remainder of the command charged mounted. The Confederates were thrown into confusion and retreated, leaving 300 prisoners, together with two stand of colors. Anderson hurried reënforcements to his beaten brigades, but no further attempt to cross the river was made. The loss to the Union cavalry was about 60 in killed and wounded. The loss to the enemy was not less than 500.

These affairs between the Union cavalry and the enemy's infantry were of more importance than might appear at first glance. They

GENERAL PHILIP H. SHERIDAN. FROM A PHOTOGRAPH TAKEN IN 1864.

gave the cavalry increased confidence, and made the enemy correspondingly doubtful even of the ability of its infantry, in anything like equal numbers, to contend against our cavalry in the open fields of the Valley.

On the night of the 16th Sheridan withdrew toward his base, and on the following day the cavalry marched, driving all the cattle and live stock in the Valley before it, and burning the grain from Cedar Creek to Berryville. No other private property was injured, nor were families molested.

On the afternoon of the 17th the Third Division of cavalry, under General James H. Wilson, reported to General Torbert, chief-of-cavalry, who with it and Lowell's brigade and the Jersey brigade (Penrose's) of the Sixth Corps was ordered to cover the flank of the army which marched and took position near Berryville. General Early, who on the morning of the 17th discovered the withdrawal of Sheridan's force, pursued rapidly, Anderson advancing from Front Royal with his command. Early struck Torbert's force with such vigor and with such overwhelming numbers as completely to overthrow it, with considerable loss, and drive it from Winchester. In this affair Penrose's brigade lost about 300 men in killed, wounded, and prisoners, and Wilson's cavalry lost

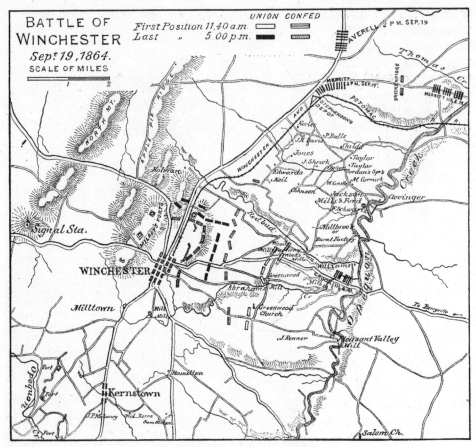

MAP OF THE BATTLE OF WINCHESTER, SEPTEMBER 19, 1864.

in prisoners some 50 men. At this time, information having reached Sheridan that the reënforcements that had come to Early under Anderson were only part of what might be expected, Sheridan concluded still further to solidify his lines. On the 21st of August Early moved with his army to attack Sheridan. His own command marched through Smithfield toward Charlestown, and Anderson on the direct road through Summit Point. Rodes's and Ramseur's infantry were advanced to the attack, and heavy skirmishing was continued for some time with a loss to the Sixth Corps, principally Getty's division, of 260 killed and wounded. In the meantime Anderson was so retarded by the Union cavalry that he did not reach the field, and night overtaking him at Summit Point, he there went into camp. That night Sheridan drew in the cavalry, and, carrying out the resolution already formed, withdrew his army to Halltown. During the three days following the Confederates demonstrated in front of Sheridan's lines, but to little purpose except to skirmish with Crook's and Emory's pickets. On the 25th, leaving Anderson's force in front of Sheridan, Early moved with his four divisions and Fitzhugh Lee's cavalry to Leetown, from which place he dispatched Lee toward Williamsport while he crossed the railroad at Kearneysville and moved

SPROUT'S SPRING MILL, OPEQUON RIVER, VA., HOSPITAL OF THE SIXTH ARMY CORPS DURING THE
BATTLE OF WINCHESTER, SEPTEMBER 19, 1864. FROM A WAR-TIME SKETCH.

toward Shepherdstown. Between Kearneysville and Leetown he was met
by Torbert with the cavalry. A sharp fight followed, in the first shock of
which Early's advance, consisting of Wharton's division, was driven back
in confusion, but upon discovering the strength of the enemy, Torbert withdrew in good order, though Custer's brigade was pressed so closely that he
was forced to cross the Potomac. A charge on the flank of the pursuing
infantry relieved Custer from danger, and the next morning he returned, as
ordered, via Harper's Ferry to the army at Halltown. Early's movement
ended with this affair, and during the following two days he returned to
the vicinity of Winchester.

During the absence of Early, R. H. Anderson's position was reconnoitered by
Crook with two divisions and Lowell's cavalry brigade, who carried Anderson's
lines, driving two brigades from their earth-works and capturing a number
of officers and men, after which Anderson withdrew from Sheridan's front.

In a dispatch to Halleck Sheridan said: "I have thought it best to be prudent, everything considered." Grant commended Sheridan's conduct of
affairs in general terms, and predicted the withdrawal from the Valley of all
of Early's reënforcements. This the pressure of Grant's lines at Petersburg finally accomplished.

On the 28th of August Sheridan moved his army forward to Charlestown.
My division of cavalry marched to Leetown, and drove the enemy's cavalry
to Smithfield and across the Opequon. The next day Early's infantry, in
turn, drove my division from Smithfield; whereupon Sheridan, advancing
with Ricketts's division, repulsed the enemy's infantry, which retired to the
west bank of the Opequon. On this day the cavalry had some severe fighting with Early's infantry, but not until in hand-to-hand fighting the Confederate cavalry had been driven from the field.

On the 3d of September Rodes's Confederate division proceeded to Bunker
Hill, and in conjunction with Lomax's cavalry made a demonstration which

was intended to cover the withdrawal of Anderson's force from the Valley. But on marching toward the gap of the Blue Ridge, via Berryville, Anderson came upon Crook's infantry just taking station there. The meeting was a surprise to both commands and resulted in a sharp engagement which continued till nightfall. On the following morning Early moved with part of his infantry to Anderson's assistance, and demonstrating toward the right of Sheridan's lines, he made show of giving battle, but only long enough to extricate Anderson and his trains, when the entire command retired to the country near Winchester. On the 14th Anderson withdrew from Early's army, and this time unmolested pursued his march through the Blue Ridge to Culpeper Court House. Fitzhugh Lee's cavalry remained with Early.

FAC-SIMILE (REDUCED) OF PRESIDENT LINCOLN'S
LETTER TO GENERAL SHERIDAN.

About this time General Grant visited the Valley and found everything to his satisfaction. Sheridan was master of the situation, and he was not slow in showing it to his chief. On the 12th of September Sheridan had telegraphed Grant to the effect that it was exceedingly difficult to attack Early in his position behind the Opequon, which constituted a formidable barrier; that the crossings, though numerous, were deep, and the banks abrupt and difficult for an attacking force; and, in general, that he was waiting for the chances to change in his favor, hoping that Early would either detach troops or take some less defensible position. His caution was fortunate at this time, and his fearlessness and hardihood were sufficiently displayed thereafter. In the light of criticisms, then, it is curious that the world is now inclined to call Sheridan reckless and foolhardy.

At 2 A. M. of September 19th Sheridan's army was astir under orders to attack Early in front of Winchester. My cavalry was to proceed to the fords of the Opequon, near the railroad crossing, and, if opposed only by cavalry, was to cross at daylight and, turning to the left, attack Early's left flank. Wilson's division was to precede the infantry and clear the crossing of the Opequon, on the Berryville road, leading to Winchester. The infantry of the army, following Wilson, was to cross the Opequon, first Wright and then Emory, while Crook's command, marching across country, was to take position in reserve, or be used as circumstances might require. South of Winchester, running nearly east and emptying into the Opequon, is Abraham's Creek, and nearly parallel to it, on the north of Winchester, is Red Bud Creek. These two tributaries flanked the usual line of the Confederates, when in position, covering Winchester, and on this line, across the Berryville-Winchester road, Ramseur was stationed with his infantry, when Sheridan's forces debouched from the defile and deployed for attack. Sheridan's plan was to attack and overthrow this part of Early's force before the rest of the army, which a day or two before was known to be scattered to the north as far as Martinsburg, could come to its assistance. At daylight Wilson advanced across the Opequon, and carried the earth-work which covered the defile and captured part of the force that held it. The infantry followed— Wright's corps first, with Getty leading, and Emory next. Between two and three miles from the Opequon, Wright came up with Wilson, who was waiting in the earth-work he had captured. There the country was suitable for the deployment of the column, which commenced forming line at once. Ramseur, with the bulk of the Confederate artillery, immediately opened on Wright's troops, and soon the Union guns were in position to reply. Wilson took position on the left of the Sixth Corps. Then followed a delay that thwarted the part of the plan which contemplated the destruction of Early's army in detail. Emory's command was crowded off the road in its march, and so delayed by the guns and trains of the Sixth Corps that it was slow getting on the field, and it was hours before the lines were formed. ⚓ This delay gave the Confederates time to bring up the infantry of Gordon and Rodes. Gordon, who first arrived, was posted on Ramseur's left near the Red Bud, and when Rodes arrived with three of his four brigades, he was given the center. This change in the situation, which necessitated fighting Early's army in his chosen position, did not disconcert the Union commander. He had come out to fight, and though chafing at the unexpected delay, fight he would to the bitter end.

In the meantime the cavalry, which had been ordered to the right, had not been idle. Moving at the same time as did the rest of the army, my division reached the fords of the Opequon near the railroad crossing at early dawn. Here I found a force of cavalry supported by Breckinridge's infantry. After sharp skirmishing the stream was crossed at three different points, but the enemy contested every foot of the way beyond. The cavalry, however, hearing Sheridan's guns, and knowing the battle was in progress, was satisfied with the work it was doing in holding from Early a considerable force of infantry. The battle here continued for some hours, the cavalry making charges on foot or mounted according to the nature of the country, and steadily though slowly driving the enemy's force toward Winchester. Finally Breckinridge, leaving one brigade to assist the cavalry in retarding our advance, moved to the help of Early, arriving on the field about 2 P. M.

It was 11:30 A. M. before Sheridan's lines were ready to advance. When they moved forward Early, who had gathered all his available strength, met them with a front of fire, and the battle raged with the greatest fury. The advance was pressed in the most resolute manner, and the resistance by the enemy being equally determined and both sides fighting without cover, the

⚓ In an unpublished narrative, addressed to the Adjutant-General, and dated May 30th, 1872, Emory states that all the infantry was placed under command of Wright; that Wright ordered the column to march at 2 A. M., the Sixth Corps leading, followed by its train, the Nineteenth Corps next, followed by its train, then the Eighth Corps; that he (Emory) moved with the Nineteenth Corps at the appointed hour, and at the crossing of the Opequon was halted by General Wright in person, the head of the Sixth Corps not having passed yet; that the subsequent march was obstructed by the trains of the Sixth Corps [see above]; that, hearing a lively cannonade, after sending forward all his staff-officers in succession for instructions, he finally disregarded the order of march, and putting his corps in motion rode on to General Sheridan, who at once confirmed his action. The Sixth Corps was still engaged in crossing the Opequon. Owing to these delays, it was midday before the Nineteenth Corps reached its position.— EDITORS.

THE BATTLE OF WINCHESTER—RICKETTS'S ADVANCE AGAINST RODES'S DIVISION ON THE MORNING OF SEPTEMBER 19, 1864.

casualties were very great. Wright's infantry forced Ramseur and Rodes steadily to the rear, while Emory on the right broke the left of the enemy's line and threw it into confusion. At this time the Confederate artillery opened with canister at short range, doing fearful execution. This, coupled with the weakening of the center at the junction between Emory and Wright, and with a charge delivered on this junction of the lines by a part of Rodes's command, just arrived on the field, drove back the Union center. At this critical moment Russell's division of Wright's corps moved into the breach on Emory's left, and, striking the flank of the Confederate troops who were pursuing Grover, restored the lines and stayed the Confederate advance.↓ The loss to both sides had been heavy. General Russell of the Union army and Generals Rodes and Godwin of the Confederate were among the killed.

A lull in the battle now followed, which General Sheridan improved to restore his lines and to bring up Crook, who had not yet been engaged. It had been the original purpose to use Crook on the left to assist Wilson's cavalry in cutting off Early's retreat toward Newtown. But the stress of battle compelled Sheridan to bring his reserve in on the line, and accordingly Crook was ordered up on Emory's right, one brigade extending to the north of Red Bud Creek. At the same time Early re-formed his lines, placing Breckinridge's command in reserve. At this time Merritt, who with his cavalry had followed Breckinridge closely to the field, approached on the left rear of the Confederates, driving their flying and broken cavalry through the infantry lines. The cavalry then charged repeatedly into Early's infantry, first striking it in the rear, and afterward face to face as it changed front to repel the attack.♭ These attacks were made by the cavalry without any knowledge of the state of the battle except what was apparent to the eye. First Devin charged with his brigade, returning to rally, with three battle-flags and over three hundred prisoners. Next Lowell charged with his

↓ General Emory, in his official narrative, says of the action on the right at this point:

"Grover's division was placed in line of battle on the right of the Sixth Corps, and Dwight's division was placed in échelon on the right of Grover's. Not many minutes elapsed before receiving orders to charge the enemy. I ordered Grover's division to charge, holding Dwight's in reserve. The charge was made with great bravery, dispersing the enemy's first line; but this first success seemed to throw our men off their guard, and give them too much confidence, and they rushed, without orders, with impetuosity upon the second line of the enemy, which had the protection of woods and stone walls, and they met with a bloody repulse.

"Simultaneously with this repulse, and a moment or two preceding it, I saw that the charge of the Sixth Corps, on my left, had been repulsed. Quickly drawing a brigade of Dwight's division from the right, I placed it on the line occupied by Grover's division, behind which that division rallied in good order, considering the terrible repulse they had met. The enemy rose from their sheltered position and charged in mass on our lines. A small point of woods projected at right angles from the right of my line; in this I posted Colonel Nicholas W. Day, 131st New York Volunteers, with his regiment, and as the enemy came down on our lines with loud yells they received the fire of this regiment in the flank and rear, and at the same time receiving a very spirited fire in front, they broke and fled." EDITORS.

♭ "Breckinridge was scarcely in position before our cavalry on the left was discovered coming back in great confusion followed by the enemy's, and Breckinridge's force was ordered to the left to repel this cavalry force, which had gotten in rear of my left, and this with the assistance of the artillery he succeeded in doing. But as soon as the firing was heard in rear of our left flank the infantry commenced falling back along the whole line, and it was very difficult to stop them. I succeeded, however, in stopping enough of them in the old rifle-pits, constructed by General Johnston, to arrest the progress of the enemy's infantry, which commenced advancing again when confusion in our ranks was discovered, and would still have won the day if our cavalry would have stopped the enemy's; but so overwhelming was the latter, and so demoralized was the larger part of ours, that no assistance was received from it.

"The enemy's cavalry again charged around my left flank and the men began to give way again, so that it was necessary for me to retire through the town."—LETTER FROM GENERAL EARLY TO GENERAL LEE, DATED OCTOBER 9TH, 1864.

brigade, capturing flags, prisoners, and two guns. After this the entire division was formed and charged to give the final coup.\

At the time of this last charge the Union infantry advanced along the entire line and the enemy fled in disorder from the field, and night alone (for it was now dark) saved Early's army from capture.

At daylight on the morning of the 20th the army moved rapidly up the main Valley road in pursuit of the enemy. Early had not stopped on the night of the battle until he reached the shelter of Fisher's Hill. This is admirably situated for defense for an army resisting a movement south. Here the Valley is obstructed by the Massanutten Mountains and its width virtually reduced to four or five miles. In this position Early's right was protected by impassable mountains and by the north fork of the Shenandoah, and he at once took means to protect his left artificially.

"On the evening of the 20th," reports Sheridan, "Wright and Emory went into position on the heights of Strasburg, Crook north of Cedar Creek, the cavalry on the right and rear of Emory, extending to the back road."

On the 21st Sheridan occupied the day in examining the enemy's lines and improving his own. Accompanied by General Wright, he directed changes in the lines of the Sixth Corps, so that it occupied the high lands to the north of Tumbling Run. Wright did not secure this vantage-ground without a severe struggle, in which Warner's brigade was engaged, finally holding the heights after a brilliant charge. Sheridan decided on turning Early's impregnable position by a movement on the Little North Mountain. On the night of the 21st he concealed Crook's command in the timber north of Cedar Creek. In making his disposition Sheridan did not attempt to cover the entire front, it being his intention to flank the enemy by Crook's march, and then, by advancing the right of Wright's and Emory's line, to form connection and make his line continuous. On the morning of the 22d, Crook, being still concealed, was marched to the timber near Little North Mountain and massed in it. Before this, Torbert, with his two divisions of cavalry, except one brigade (Devin's), was ordered via Front Royal into Luray Valley, with a view to reëntering the Valley of the Shenandoah at New Market. This design was not accomplished. ☆

Not long before sundown Crook's infantry, which had not yet been discov-

---

\ An officer who was in this last charge, and who had the misfortune to fall into the hands of the enemy in consequence of the breaking of his bridle-curb, says: "The confusion, disorder, and actual rout produced by the successive charges of Merritt's division would appear incredible did not the writer actually witness them. To the right a battery with guns disabled and caissons shattered was trying to make to the rear, the men and horses impeded by broken regiments of cavalry and infantry; to the left, the dead and wounded, in confused masses, around their field-hospitals — many of the wounded, in great excitement, seeking shelter in Winchester; directly in front, an ambulance, the driver nervously clutching the reins,

while six men in great alarm were carrying to it the body of General Rodes." General Torbert, chief of cavalry, also says in his report of the battle of Winchester: "This day the First Division (Brigadier-General Merritt) alone captured 775 prisoners, about 70 officers, seven battle-flags, and two pieces of artillery."— W. M.

☆ It may be here remarked that Sheridan was, as a rule, opposed to combinations involving long marches. He had no faith in their successful accomplishment. It is therefore easy to believe that he looked upon this movement of the cavalry as a means of turning the Confederates out of the position at Fisher's Hill, provided his infantry was not successful in the present project.— W. M.

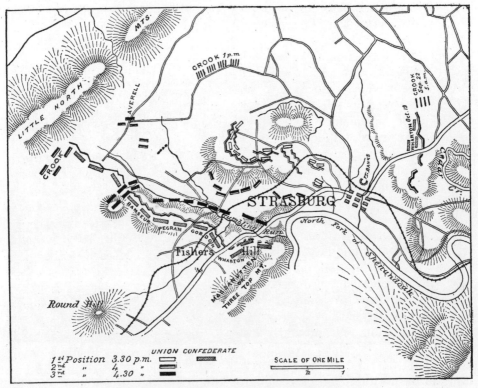

MAP OF THE BATTLE OF FISHER'S HILL, SEPTEMBER 22, 1864.

ered by the enemy, struck Early's left and rear so suddenly as to cause his
army to break in confusion and flee. The rout was complete, the whole of
Sheridan's troops uniting in the attack. That night, though the darkness
made the marching difficult, Sheridan followed Early as far as Woodstock,
some fifteen miles, and the following day up to Mount Jackson, where he
drove the enemy, now to some extent reorganized, from a strong position
on the opposite bank of the river. From this point the enemy retreated
in line of battle. But every effort to make him fight failed. No doubt
Sheridan in this pursuit regretted the absence of his cavalry, which, with
Torbert, was striving, by a circuitous and obstructed march, to reach the
enemy's rear.

A few miles beyond New Market Early abandoned the main road, which
leads on through Harrisonburg; turning to the east, he pursued the road
that leads thence to Port Republic. This direction was taken to receive the
reënforcements which were to reach him through one of the gaps of the Blue
Ridge. For it appears that Kershaw and his command had not proceeded
beyond Culpeper in his march to Lee's army before he was ordered to return
to Early, the news of whose overthrow at Winchester, and afterward at
Fisher's Hill, had reached the authorities at Richmond.

On the 25th of September Torbert with the cavalry rejoined General Sheridan, and was at once put to work doing what damage was possible to the

THE REAR-GUARD—GENERAL CUSTER'S DIVISION RETIRING FROM MOUNT JACKSON, OCTOBER 7, 1864.
FROM A WAR-TIME SKETCH.

Central Railway. After proceeding to Staunton and destroying immense
quantities of army stores, Torbert moved to Waynesboro', destroying the
railway track, and after burning the railway bridges toward the Blue Ridge,
and on being threatened by Early's forces, which had moved thither to attack
him, he retired to Bridgewater.

Naturally a question now arose between Sheridan, the authorities in
Washington, and General Grant as to the future theater of the campaign and
the line of operations. Sheridan was opposed to the proposition submitted
by the others, which was to operate against Central Virginia from his base
in the Valley. The general reasons for his opposition were the distance from
the base of supplies, the lines of communication, which in a country infested
by guerrillas it would take an army to protect, and the nearness, as the
campaign progressed, if successful, to the enemy's base, from which large
reënforcements could easily and secretly be hurried and the Union army be
overwhelmed. But before the plan was finally adopted a new turn was given
to affairs, and the plan originally formed was delayed in its execution if not
changed altogether.

When the army commenced its return march, the cavalry was deployed
across the Valley, burning, destroying, or taking away everything of value,
or likely to become of value, to the enemy. It was a severe measure, and
appears severer now in the lapse of time; but it was necessary as a measure
of war. The country was fruitful and was the paradise of bushwhackers and
guerrillas. They had committed numerous murders and wanton acts of

cruelty on all parties weaker than themselves. Officers and men had been murdered in cold blood on the roads, while proceeding without a guard through an apparently peaceful country. The thoughtless had been lured to houses only to find, when too late, that a foe was concealed there, ready to take their lives if they did not surrender. It is not wonderful, then, that the cavalry sent to work the destruction contemplated did not at that time shrink from the duty. It is greatly to their credit that no personal violence on any inhabitant was ever reported, even by their enemies. The Valley from Staunton to Winchester was completely devastated, and the armies thereafter occupying that country had to look elsewhere for their supplies. There is little doubt, however, that enough was left in the country for the subsistence of the people, for this, besides being contemplated by orders, resulted of necessity from the fact that, while the work was done hurriedly, the citizens had ample time to secrete supplies, and did so.

The movement north was conducted without interruption for two days, except that the enemy's cavalry, made more bold by the accession to its strength of a command under General T. L. Rosser, followed our cavalry, dispersed across the Valley as already described. On the 8th of October the enemy's cavalry harassed Custer's division on the back road during the day, taking from him some battery-forges and wagons. The cavalry also showed itself on the main road upon which Merritt was retiring, but dispersed upon being charged by a brigade which was sent to develop their strength. That night Sheridan gave orders to his chief-of-cavalry, Torbert, to attack and beat the enemy's cavalry the following day " or to get whipped himself," as it was expressed.

On the morning of the 9th Torbert's cavalry moved out to fight that of the enemy under Generals Rosser and Lomax. Merritt's division moved on the pike and extended across to the back road where Custer was concentrated. A stubborn cavalry engagement commenced the day, but it was not long before the Confederate cavalry was broken and routed, and from that time till late in the day it was driven a distance of twenty-six miles, losing everything on wheels, except one gun, and this at one time was in possession of a force too weak to hold it. At one time General Lomax was a prisoner, but made his escape by personally overthrowing his captor. In this affair the advantage of pluck, dash, and confidence, as well as of numbers, was on the Union side. From the time of the occupation of the Valley by Sheridan's force the cavalry had been the active part of his command. Scarcely a day passed that they were not engaged in some affair, and often with considerable loss, as is shown by the fact that in twenty-six engagements, aside from the battles, the cavalry lost an aggregate of 3205 men and officers.

In reporting the result of the cavalry battle of October 9th, Early says:

" This is very distressing to me, and God knows I have done all in my power to avert the disasters which have befallen this command ; but the fact is the enemy's cavalry is so much superior to ours, both in numbers and equipment, and the country is so favorable to the operations of cavalry, that it is impossible for ours to compete with his."

He further says in this same connection:

"Lomax's cavalry is armed entirely with rifles and has no sabers, and the consequence is they cannot fight on horseback, and in this open country they cannot successfully fight on foot against large bodies of cavalry."

This is a statement on which those who think our cavalry never fought mounted and with the saber should ponder. The cavalry had scant justice done it in reports sent from the battle-field; and current history, which is so much made up of first reports and first impressions, has not to a proper extent been impressed with this record.

On the return of the army after the pursuit of the scattered remnants of Early's force, General Sheridan placed it in position on Cedar Creek north of the Shenandoah, Crook on the left, Emory in the center, and Wright in reserve. The cavalry was placed on the flanks. The occupation of Cedar Creek was not intended to be permanent; there were many serious objections to it as a position for defense. The approaches from all points of the enemy's stronghold at Fisher's Hill were through wooded ravines in which the growth and undulations concealed the movement of troops, and for this reason and its proximity to Fisher's Hill the pickets protecting its front could not be thrown, without danger of capture, sufficiently far to the front to give ample warning of the advance of the enemy. We have already seen how Sheridan took advantage of like conditions at Fisher's Hill. Early was now contemplating the surprise of his antagonist.

On the 12th of October Sheridan received a dispatch from Halleck saying that Grant wished a position taken far enough south to serve as a base for operations upon Gordonsville and Charlottesville. On the 13th and the 16th he received dispatches from the Secretary of War and from General Halleck pressing him to visit Washington for consultation.

On the 15th General Sheridan, taking with him Torbert with part of the cavalry, started for Washington, the design being to send the cavalry on a raid to Gordonsville and vicinity. The first camp was made near Front Royal, from which point the cavalry was returned to the army, it being considered safer to do so in consequence of a dispatch intercepted by our signal officers from the enemy's station on Three Top Mountain, and forwarded to General Sheridan by General Wright. This dispatch was as follows:

"To LIEUTENANT-GENERAL EARLY: Be ready to move as soon as my forces join you, and we will crush Sheridan.— LONGSTREET, Lieutenant-General."

In sending back the cavalry General Sheridan wrote to General Wright, directing caution on his part, so that he might be duly prepared to resist the attack in case the above dispatch was genuine.| Sheridan continued to Washington, and the cavalry resumed its station in the line of defense at Cedar Creek. At this time everything was quiet — suspiciously so.

|General Wright wrote to General Sheridan, October 16th, inclosing Longstreet's intercepted message, and adding:

"If the enemy should be strongly reënforced in cavalry he might, by turning our *right*, give us a great deal of trouble. . . . I shall only fear an attack on my *right*."

To this Sheridan replied, the same day, from Front Royal:

"The cavalry is all ordered back to you. . . . Close

THE SURPRISE AT CEDAR CREEK. FROM A WAR-TIME SKETCH.

The right of the picture shows the Confederate flanking column attacking the left of the Nineteenth Corps
from the rear. The Union troops, after a determined resistance, took position
on the outer side of their rifle-pits.

On the 16th Custer made a reconnoissance in his front on the back road,
but found no enemy outside the lines at Fisher's Hill. This absence of the
enemy's cavalry was accounted for the next morning just before daylight by
the appearance of Rosser in the rear of Custer's picket line with his cavalry
and one brigade of infantry. Rosser carrying the infantry behind his cavalry troopers had made a march of thirty-two miles to capture an exposed
brigade of Custer's division on the right; but a change in the arrangements
of the command (the return of Torbert) thwarted the scheme, and it resulted
only in the capture of a picket guard. On the 18th reconnoissances on both
flanks discovered no sign of a movement by the enemy.

The result of the destruction of supplies in the Valley was now being felt
by Early's troops. About this time he writes: "I was now compelled to
move back for want of provisions and forage, or attack the enemy in his
position with the hope of driving him from it; and I determined to attack."
From reports made by General Gordon and a staff-officer who ascended
Three Top Mountain to reconnoiter the Union position, and the result of a

in Colonel Powell, who will be at this point. . . . Look
well to your ground, and be well prepared."

In his official report of the campaign General
Sheridan says:

"During my absence the enemy had gathered all his
strength, . . . striking Crook, who held the *left* of
our line, in flank and rear, so unexpectedly and forcibly

as to drive in his outposts, invade his camp, and turn
his position. This surprise was owing, probably, to not
closing in Powell, or that the cavalry divisions of Merritt and Custer were placed on the *right* of our line,
where, it had always occurred to me, there was but
little danger of attack."

The italics in these quotations are not in the
originals. — EDITORS.

HILL AT CEDAR CREEK OCCUPIED BY SHERIDAN'S LEFT, OCTOBER 19, 1864, AS SEEN FROM KERSHAW'S FORD.
FROM A PHOTOGRAPH TAKEN IN 1865.

reconnoissance made at the same time by General Pegram toward the right flank of the Union army, General Early concluded to attack by secretly moving a force to turn Sheridan's left flank at Cedar Creek.

The plan of this attack was carefully made; the routes the troops were to pursue, even after the battle had commenced, were carefully designated. [See General Early's article, p. 526.] The attack was made at early dawn. The surprise was complete. Crook's camp, and afterward Emory's, were attacked in flank and rear and the men and officers driven from their beds, many of them not having the time to hurry into their clothes, except as they retreated half awake and terror-stricken from the overpowering numbers of the enemy. Their own artillery, in conjunction with that of the enemy, was turned on them, and long before it was light enough for their eyes, unaccustomed to the dim light, to distinguish friend from foe, they were hurrying to our right and rear intent only on their safety. Wright's infantry, which was farther removed from the point of attack, fared somewhat better, but did not offer more than a spasmodic resistance. The cavalry on the right was on the alert. The rule that in the immediate presence of the enemy the cavalry must be early prepared for attack resulted in the whole First Division being up with breakfast partly finished, at the time the attack commenced. A brigade sent on reconnoissance to the right had opened with its guns some minutes before the main attack on the left, for it had met the cavalry sent by Early to make a demonstration on our right.

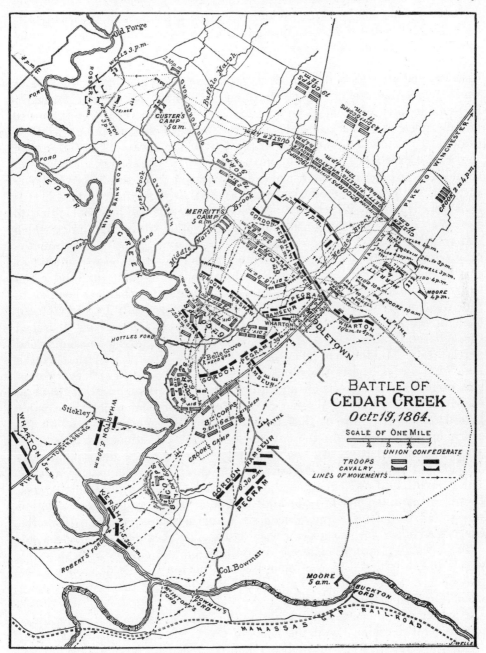

BATTLE OF
CEDAR CREEK
Oct. 19, 1864.

SCALE OF ONE MILE

UNION CONFEDERATE

TROOPS
CAVALRY
LINES OF MOVEMENTS

The disintegration of Crook's command did not occupy many minutes. With a force of the enemy passing through its camp of sleeping men, and another powerful column well to their rear, it was not wonderful that the men as fast as they were awakened by the noise of battle thought first and only of saving themselves from destruction. The advance of Gordon deflected this fleeing throng from the main road to the rear, and they passed over to the right of the army and fled along the back road. Emory made an attempt to form line facing along the main road, but the wave of Gordon's advance on his left, and the thunders of the attack along the road from Strasburg, rendered the position untenable, and he was soon obliged to withdraw to save his lines from capture. ⚓

At this time there were hundreds of stragglers moving off by the right to the rear, and all efforts to stop them proved of no avail. A line of cavalry was stretched across the fields on the right, which halted and formed a respectable force of men, so far as numbers were concerned, but these fled and disappeared to the rear as soon as the force which held them was withdrawn. By degrees the strength of the battle died away. The infantry of the Sixth Corps made itself felt on the advance of the enemy, and a sort of confidence among the troops which had not fled from the field was being restored. A brigade of cavalry was ordered to the left to intercept the enemy's advance to Winchester. Taylor's battery of artillery, belonging to the cavalry, moved to the south, and, taking position with the infantry which was retiring, opened on the enemy. The artillery with the cavalry was the only artillery left to the army. The other guns had either been captured or sent to the rear. This battery remained on the infantry lines and did much toward impeding the enemy's advance until the cavalry changed position to the Winchester-Strasburg road. This change took place by direction of General Torbert about 10 o'clock. In making it the cavalry marched through the broken masses of infantry direct to a point on the main road north-east of Middletown. The enemy's artillery fire was terrific. Not a man of the cavalry left the ranks unless he was wounded, and everything was done with the precision and quietness of troops on parade. General Merritt informed Colonel Warner of Getty's division, near which the cavalry passed, and which was at that time following the general retreat of the army, of the point where the cavalry would take position and fight, and Warner promised to notify General Getty, and no doubt did so, for that division of the Sixth Corps advanced to the position on the cavalry's right. Then Devin and Lowell charged and drove back the advancing Confederates. Lowell dismounted his brigade and held some stone walls whose position was suited to defense. Devin held on to his advance ground. Here the enemy's advance was checked for the first time, and beyond this it did not go.

The enemy's infantry sheltered themselves from our cavalry attacks in the woods to the left, and in the inclosures of the town of Middletown. But they opened a devastating fire of artillery. This was the state of affairs when Sheridan arrived.

Stopping at Winchester over night on the 18th, on his way from Washington, General Sheridan heard the noise of the battle the following morning,

⚓ General Emory states in his "Narrative" that the Nineteenth Corps promptly repulsed the first attack on them but, the enemy having gained their rear through the capture of Crook's camps, then fell back about a mile and a half to a new line that "under the circumstances would have done honor to the best regular troops in the world." They were not again attacked, but by order of General Wright fell back in perfect order, about a mile, when "the Nineteenth Corps was again halted, and the men immediately facing about commenced throwing off their kits and stripping to renew the fight." About noon General Emory says he was again ordered by General Wright to retire to the position in which General Sheridan found the army on his arrival.—EDITORS.

and hurried to the field. His coming restored confidence. A cheer from the cavalry, which awakened the echoes of the valley, greeted him and spread the good news of his coming over the field. ↓

He rapidly made the changes necessary in the lines, and then ordered an advance. The cavalry on the left charged down on the enemy in their front, scattering them in all directions. The infantry, not to be outdone by the mounted men, moved forward in quick time and charged impetuously the lines of Gordon, which broke and fled. ◗ It took less time to drive the enemy from the field than it had for them to take it. They seemed to feel the changed conditions in the Union ranks, for their divisions broke one after another and disappeared toward their rear. The cavalry rode after them and over them, until

REDUCED FAC-SIMILE OF PRESIDENT LINCOLN'S CONGRATULATIONS TO GENERAL SHERIDAN ON THE BATTLE OF CEDAR CREEK.

↓ In his "Personal Memoirs" (New York: C. L. Webster & Co., 1888), Vol. II., General Sheridan says that toward 6 A. M. of October 19th word was brought to him (at Winchester) of the artillery firing at Cedar Creek. Between half-past 8 and 9 o'clock, while he was riding along the main street of Winchester, toward Cedar Creek, the demeanor of the people who showed themselves at the windows convinced him that the citizens had received secret information from the battle-field, "and were in raptures over some good news." The narrative continues:

"For a short distance I traveled on the road, but soon found it so blocked with wagons and wounded men that my progress was impeded, and I was forced to take to the adjoining fields to make haste. . . .

"My first halt was made just north of Newtown, where I met a chaplain digging his heels into the sides of his jaded horse, and making for the rear with all possible speed. I drew up for an instant, and inquired of him how matters were going at the front. He replied, 'Everything is lost; but all will be right when you get there'; yet, notwithstanding this expression of confidence in me, the parson at once resumed his breathless pace to the rear. At Newtown I was obliged to make a circuit to the left, to get around the village. I could not pass through it, the streets were so crowded, but meeting on this detour Major McKinley, of Crook's staff, he spread the news of my return through the motley throng there.

"When nearing the Valley pike, just north of Newtown, I saw about three-fourths of a mile west of the pike a body of troops, which proved to be Ricketts's and Wheaton's divisions of the Sixth Corps, and then learned that the Nineteenth Corps had halted a little to the right and rear of these; but I did not stop, desiring to get to the extreme front. Continuing on parallel with the pike, about midway between Newtown and Middletown I crossed to the west of it, and a little later came up in rear of Getty's division of the Sixth Corps. When I arrived, this division and the cavalry were the only troops in the presence of the enemy; they were apparently acting as a rear-guard at a point about three miles north of the line we held at Cedar Creek when the battle began. General Torbert was the first officer to meet me, saying as he rode up, 'My God! I am glad you've come.' . . .

"Jumping my horse over the line of rails, I rode to the crest of the elevation, and there, taking off my hat, the men rose up from behind their barricade with cheers of recognition. . . . I then turned back to the rear of Getty's division, and as I came behind it a line of regimental flags rose up out of the ground, as it seemed, to welcome me. They were mostly the colors of Crook's troops, who had been stampeded and scattered in the surprise of the morning. The color-bearers, having withstood the panic, had formed behind the troops of Getty. The line with the colors was largely composed of officers, among whom I recognized Colonel R. B. Hayes, since President of the United States, one of the brigade commanders. At the close of this incident I crossed the little narrow valley, or depression, in rear of Getty's line, and, dismounting on the opposite crest, established that point as my headquarters. . . . Returning to the place where my headquarters had been established, I met near them Ricketts's division, under General Keifer, and General Frank Wheaton's division, both marching to the front. When the men of these divisions saw me they began cheering and took up the double-quick to the front, while I turned back toward Getty's line to point out where these returning troops should be placed.

"All this had consumed a great deal of time, and I concluded to visit again the point to the east of the Valley pike, from where I had first observed the enemy, to see what he was doing. Arrived there, I could plainly see him getting ready for attack, and Major Forsyth now suggested that it would be well to ride along the line of battle before the enemy assailed us, for although the troops had learned of my return, but few of them had seen me. Following his suggestion I started in behind the men, but when a few paces had been taken I crossed to the front, hat in hand, passed along the entire length of the infantry line; and it is from this circumstance that many of the officers and men who then received me with such heartiness have since supposed that that was my first appearance on the field. But at least two hours had elapsed since I reached the ground, for it was after midday when this incident of riding down the front took place, and I arrived not later, certainly, than half-past ten o'clock." EDITORS.

◗ General Emory says in his "Narrative":

"This electric message from General Sheridan put every man on his feet. . . . Very soon the pickets came in, quickly followed by the enemy's infantry. Our first line [Grover] then rose up *en masse* and delivered their fire, and the enemy disappeared. There was not a sound of musket or gun for twenty minutes following. The night fell and ended the fray at the foot of Fisher's Hill. Three battle-flags and twenty-two guns were added to the trophies of the cavalry that day. Early lost almost all his artillery and trains, besides everything that was captured from the Union army in the morning.↑

COLONEL CHARLES RUSSELL LOWELL.
FROM A PHOTOGRAPH.

The victory was dearly bought. The killed or mortally wounded included General Bidwell and Colonels Thoburn and Kitching, besides many other officers and men. Among the killed in the final charge by the cavalry at Cedar Creek was Colonel Charles Russell Lowell. He had been wounded earlier in the day, but had declined to leave the field.

The battle of Cedar Creek has been immortalized by poets and historians. The transition from defeat, rout, and confusion to order and victory, and all this depending on one man, made the country wild with enthusiasm.

The victory was a fitting sequel to Winchester, a glorious prelude to Five Forks and Appomattox. In this battle fell mortally wounded on the Confederate side Major-General Stephen D. Ramseur, four years before a classmate of the writer at West Point. A Union officer — a friend — watched by his side in his last moments and conveyed to his southern home his last words of affection.

There is little more to record of events in the Valley. Part of the night after its defeat Early's army rested in the intrenchments on Fisher's Hill, but before dawn the next day it retreated to New Market. Rosser, with the Confederate cavalry, acted as rear-guard, and was driven by the Union cavalry beyond Woodstock. While Early remained at New Market reënforcements were sent him in the way of convalescents and one brigade from south-western Virginia. He contented himself, however, with remaining on the defensive.

The winter of 1864-65 was passed by Sheridan's command at Kernstown, where better protection could be given the troops and a short line of supplies secured. He moved to this position in November. About this time I moved under orders with my division of cavalry into Loudoun Valley and reduced it to a state of destitution, so far as supplies for the enemy were concerned, as had been done in other parts of the valley. On December 19th Torbert with two divisions of cavalry marched through Chester Gap in another raid on

First Division was deployed to the right of the Second, and the charge commenced. . . . The enemy resisted at every strong fence and ditch and other obstacle with great bravery, but still the line swept on. The First Brigade (Colonel Edwin P. Davis) of the First Division (Dwight's), which was on the extreme right, with unparalleled intrepidity and fleetness completely enveloped the enemy, so that one hour before the sun set . . . the troops were in complete command . . . of the camp they had occupied in the morning." . . .

↑ It may be here remarked of this battle, as well as that at Winchester, that General Early [see pp. 523 and 528] speaks of the repulse of cavalry charges where no repulse occurred. Cavalry, even after successful charges, from the nature of the arm, is oftentimes obliged to retire and reform preparatory to making a new charge, or allowing other cavalry to charge.— W. M.

the Virginia Central Railway; but this attempt, like the others, was unsuccessful. The local troops and Valley cavalry succeeded in delaying Torbert until infantry was hurried by rail from Richmond, when he was forced to retire. As a diversion in favor of Torbert's expedition Custer's cavalry was moved up the Valley to engage the cavalry of Early. Near Harrisonburg he was attacked and surprised and was forced to retreat.

In making these expeditions the troops suffered intensely from cold, bad roads, and miserable camps. This was especially so with Torbert's column in crossing the mountains. It is difficult to imagine a more disagreeable duty for a mounted soldier than marching over sleety, slushy, snowy or icy roads in winter, and bivouacking without the means of protection. It is demoralizing to men and ruinous to horses.

After the failure of these expeditions no further movements were attempted in the Valley, and most of the infantry of Sheridan's army was sent either to the Army of the Potomac at Petersburg, or elsewhere where it was needed. In February Sheridan made arrangements to march from the Valley with the cavalry with a view to interrupting and destroying, as far as possible, the lines of supply through central Virginia. After accomplishing this it was intended that he should either move west of Richmond and join Sherman's army, or return to the Valley, or join Meade's army in front of Petersburg, as might be most practicable. February 27th the movement commenced, the command consisting of two superb divisions of cavalry which had been recruited and remounted during the winter, under myself, as chief-of-cavalry. The march to Staunton was made without noticeable opposition. On the morning of March 2d

BRIGADIER-GENERAL BRADLEY T. JOHNSON, C. S. A. FROM A PHOTOGRAPH.

Early was found posted on a ridge west of Waynesboro'. The veteran soldier was full of pluck and made a bold front for a fight, but his troops were overcome, almost without even perfunctory resistance, by the advance regiments of the column, and Early, with a few general officers, barely escaped capture by flight. All Early's supplies, all transportation, all the guns, ammunition and flags, and most of the officers and men of the army were captured and sent to the rear.

From this point Sheridan moved unmolested to the Virginia Central Railroad, which was destroyed for miles, large bridges being wrecked, the track torn up, and the rails heated and bent. The command was divided and sent to the James River Canal, which was destroyed as effectually as the railroad. This done, the cavalry proceeded to White House, on the Pamunkey River, where it arrived on March 19th, 1865.

VIEW ON THE VALLEY TURNPIKE WHERE SHERIDAN JOINED THE ARMY AT CEDAR CREEK.   FROM A PHOTOGRAPH TAKEN IN 1885.

WINCHESTER, FISHER'S HILL, AND CEDAR CREEK. ↕

BY JUBAL A. EARLY, LIEUTENANT-GENERAL, C. S. A.

THE object of my presence in the lower valley during the two months after our return from Washington ⚓ was to keep up a threatening attitude toward Maryland and Pennsylvania, and prevent the use of the Baltimore and Ohio Railroad and the Chesapeake and Ohio Canal, as well as to keep as large a force as possible from Grant's army to defend the Federal capital. Had Sheridan, by a prompt movement, thrown his whole force on the line of my communications, I would have been compelled to attempt to cut my way through, as there was no escape for me to the right or left, and my force was too weak to cross the Potomac while he was in my rear. If I had moved up the valley at all, I could not have stopped short of New Market, for between that place and the country in which I was there was no forage for my horses; and this would have enabled the enemy to resume the use of the railroad and canal, and return all the troops from Grant's army to him.

Being compelled to occupy the position where I was, and being aware of its danger as well as apprised of the fact that very great odds were opposed to me, my only resource was to use my forces so as to display them at different points with great rapidity, and thereby keep up the impression that they were much larger than they really were. The events of the last month had satisfied me that the commander opposed to me was without enterprise, and possessed an excessive caution which amounted to timidity.

Having been informed that a force was at work on the railroad at Martinsburg, I moved on the afternoon of the 17th of September, with Rodes's and Gordon's divisions and Braxton's artillery, to Bunker Hill, and on the morning of the 18th, with Gordon's division and a part of the artillery, to Martinsburg, preceded by a part of Lomax's cavalry. Averell's division of cavalry was driven from the town across the Opequon in the direction

↕ Condensed from General Early's "Memoir of the Last Year of the War for Independence in the Confederate States of America" (Lynchburg: Published by Charles W. Button for the Virginia Memorial Association, 1867); here printed by permission of the author.— EDITORS.

⚓ The chief events of these two months, as described by General Early in his "Memoir," to which readers are referred for much that is here necessarily omitted or summarized, were his defeat of Crook and Averell with heavy loss at Kernstown, July 24th; his cavalry expedition under McCausland into Pennsylvania and burning of Chambersburg in retaliation for Hunter's burning of houses in the valley; Averell's surprise and

defeat of McCausland's and Bradley Johnson's cavalry at Moorefield, August 7th; Sheridan's arrival in command with large reënforcements, August 7th, which necessitated Early's withdrawal to Fisher's Hill, when Sheridan advanced; Sheridan's withdrawal in turn to Halltown, near Harper's Ferry, when General Early received at Strasburg reënforcements of Kershaw's division of infantry and Fitz Lee's of cavalry; finally, General Early's stay of a month, from August 17th to September 17th, in the lower valley, at and near Winchester, keeping the Baltimore and Ohio Railroad and the canal obstructed, and threatening Maryland and Pennsylvania.— EDITORS.

of Charlestown, and we then returned to Bunker Hill. Gordon was left at Bunker Hill, with orders to move to Stephenson's Depot by sunrise next morning, and Rodes's division moved to the latter place that night, to which I also returned. At Martinsburg, where the enemy had a telegraph office, I learned that Grant was with Sheridan that day, and I expected an early move.

At light on the morning of the 19th our cavalry pickets at the crossing of the Opequon on the Berryville road were driven in, and Ramseur's troops, which were in line across the Berryville road about one and one-half miles out from Winchester, on an elevated plateau between Abraham's Creek and Red Bud Run, were soon skirmishing with the enemy. Nelson's artillery was on Ramseur's line, and Lomax's cavalry occupied the right and Fitz Lee the left. I sent orders for Breckinridge and Rodes to move up as rapidly as possible. Gordon's division arrived first, at a little after 10 A. M., and was placed on Ramseur's left, and Rodes was then placed on Gordon's right, both under cover of woods. While this movement was being executed, we discovered very heavy columns of the enemy, which had been massed under cover between the Red Bud and the Berryville road, moving to attack Ramseur on his left flank, while another force pressed him in front. Rodes and Gordon were ordered forward and attacked with great vigor, while Nelson's artillery on the right and Braxton's on the left opened a destructive fire. But Evans's brigade of Gordon's division, which was on the extreme left of our infantry, received a check from a column of the enemy, and was forced back through the woods from behind which it had advanced, the enemy following to the very rear of the woods, and to within musket range of seven pieces of Braxton's artillery which were without support. This caused a pause in our advance, and the position was most critical, for it was apparent that unless this force were driven back the day was lost. Braxton's guns, in which now was our only hope, resolutely stood their ground, and under the personal superintendence of Lieutenant-Colonel C. M. Braxton and Colonel T. H. Carter, then my chief-of-artillery, opened with canister on the enemy. This fire was so rapid and well-directed that the enemy staggered, halted, and commenced falling back, leaving a battle-flag on the ground, whose bearer was cut down by a canister shot. Just then Battle's brigade of Rodes's division, which had arrived and been formed in line for the purpose of advancing to the support of the rest of the division, moved forward and swept through the woods, driving the enemy before it, while Evans's brigade was rallied and brought back to the charge. Our advance, which had been suspended for a moment, was resumed, and the enemy's attacking columns were thrown into great confusion and driven from the field. Lomax and Lee had aided, while Ramseur had received the enemy's shock and recovered. This affair had occurred about 11 A. M., and a splendid victory had been gained. But on our side Major-General Rodes had been killed, in the very moment of

triumph, while conducting the attack of his division with great gallantry and skill, and this was a heavy blow to me. Brigadier-General A. C. Godwin of Ramseur's division had been killed, and Brigadier-General Zebulon York of Gordon's division had lost an arm.

When the order was sent for the troops to move from Stephenson's Depot, General Breckinridge had moved to the front, with Wharton's division and King's artillery, to meet a cavalry force which had driven our pickets from the Opequon on the Charlestown road, and that division had become heavily engaged with the enemy, and had sustained and repulsed several determined charges of his cavalry, while its own flanks were in great danger from the enemy's main force on the right, and a column of his cavalry moving up the Martinsburg road on the left.

After much difficulty and some hard fighting General Breckinridge succeeded in extricating his force and moving up the Martinsburg road to join me, but he did not reach the field until about 2 o'clock. Late in the afternoon two divisions of the enemy's cavalry drove in the small force which had been watching it on the Martinsburg road, and Crook's corps, which had not been engaged, advanced at the same time on that flank, on the north side of the Red Bud, and before this overwhelming force Patton's brigade of infantry and Payne's brigade of cavalry, under Fitz Lee, were forced back. A considerable force of the enemy's cavalry then swept along the Martinsburg road to the very skirts of Winchester, thus getting in the rear of our left flank. Wharton's two other brigades were moved in double-quick time to the left and rear, and twice repulsed the cavalry. But Crook advanced against our left, and again the enemy's cavalry succeeded in getting around our left, so that nothing was left for us but to retire through Winchester; and Ramseur's division, which maintained its organization, was moved on the east of the town to the south side of it, and put in position, forming the basis for a new line, while the other troops moved back through the town. Wickham's brigade, with some pieces of horse artillery on Fort Hill, covered this movement and checked the pursuit of the enemy's cavalry. When the new line was formed the enemy's advance was checked until night-fall, and we then retired to Newtown without serious molestation. Lomax had held the enemy's cavalry on the Front Royal road in check, and a feeble attempt at pursuit was repulsed by Ramseur near Kernstown.

A skillful and energetic commander of the enemy's forces would have crushed Ramseur before any assistance could have reached him, and thus insured the destruction of my whole force; and, later in the day, when the battle had turned against us, with the immense superiority in cavalry which Sheridan had, and the advantage of the open country, would have destroyed my whole force and captured everything I had. As it was, considering the immense disparity in numbers and equipment, the enemy had very little to boast of. I had lost a few pieces of artillery and some very valuable officers and men, but the main part of my force and all my trains had been saved, and the enemy's loss in killed and wounded was far greater than mine. When I look back to this battle, I can but attribute my escape from utter annihilation to the incapacity of my opponent. ↓

At light on the morning of the 20th my troops moved to Fisher's Hill without molestation, and the cavalry of Fitz Lee (who was severely wounded at Winchester), now under Wickham, was sent up to Millford Pass to hold Luray valley. In the afternoon Sheridan's forces appeared on the banks of Cedar Creek, about four miles from Fisher's Hill, and the 21st, and the greater part of the 22d, were consumed by him in reconnoitering and gradually moving his forces to my front under cover of breastworks. After some skirmishing he attained a strong position immediately in my front and fortified it, and I began to think he was satisfied with the advantage he had gained and would not probably press it further; but on the afternoon of the 22d I discovered that another attack was contemplated, and orders were given for my troops to retire, after dark, as I knew my force was not strong enough to resist a determined assault. Just before sunset, however, Crook's corps, which had moved to our left on the side of Little North Mountain, and, under cover of the woods, had forced back Lomax's dismounted cavalry, advanced against Ramseur's left. Ramseur made an attempt to meet this movement by throwing his brigades successively into line to the left, and Wharton's division was sent for from the right, but it did not arrive. Pegram's brigades were also thrown into line in the same manner as Ramseur's, but the movement produced some disorder in both divisions, and as soon as it was observed by the enemy he advanced along his whole line, and the mischief could not be remedied. After a very brief contest my whole force retired in

considerable confusion, but the men and officers of the artillery behaved with great coolness, fighting to the very last, and I had to ride to some of the officers and order them to withdraw their guns before they would move. In some cases they had held out so long, and the roads leading from their positions into the pike were so rugged, that eleven guns fell into the hands of the enemy. Vigorous pursuit was not made, and my force fell back through Woodstock to a place called the Narrow Passage, all the trains being carried off in safety. ♭

We moved up the valley during the succeeding days, followed by the enemy, Wickham, with his own and Payne's brigades, having detained the enemy at Millford Pass until we had passed New Market in safety. On the 25th, between Port Republic and Brown's Gap, Fitz Lee's and Lomax's cavalry joined us, and on the 26th Kershaw's division with Cutshaw's battalion of artillery came up, after having crossed through Swift Run Gap, and encountered and repulsed, below Port Republic, a body of the enemy's cavalry. There was likewise heavy skirmishing on my front on the 26th with the enemy's cavalry, which made two efforts to advance toward Brown's Gap, both of which were repulsed after brisk fighting in which artillery was used.

Thence I moved for Waynesboro' and Rockfish Gap, where the enemy was engaged in destroying the railroad bridge and tunnel, and Wickham drove the enemy's working parties from Waynesboro'. On the 1st of October I moved my whole force across the country to Mount Sidney on the valley pike. ↘ On the 5th Rosser's brigade arrived, but it did not exceed six hundred mounted men for duty when it joined me. Kershaw's division numbered 2700 muskets for duty, and he had brought with him Cutshaw's battalion of artillery. These reënforce-

↓ The battle of Winchester, or of the Opequon, as General Sheridan calls it, was fought September 19th. The strength of Early's infantry August 31st, exclusive of Kershaw (who was not engaged at Winchester), as shown by the abstract from monthly returns, was as follows: Present for duty, 1076 officers and 9570 men,—aggregate present for duty, 10,646. Fitz Lee's (cavalry) strength on July 10th was 115 officers and 1591 men; but it had probably been decreased by over two months of hard service, and General Early's "Memoir" gives its number of mounted men on September 19th as "about 1200," and also the mounted men of Lomax as "about 1700." To the artillery are ascribed on September 10th, in the best available returns, 39 officers and 818 men. Taking the official figures for the infantry, General Early's figures for the cavalry, and the indicated returns for the artillery, the total "present for duty" with his army would be about 13,288 enlisted men of all three arms, with, in round numbers, about 1200 officers. But for the infantry only do we find the "War Records" statistics vouching.

General Early, in a note to the editors, dated November 9th, 1888, says, regarding the returns of 9570 men, August 31st, that between that time and September 19th "there had been considerable loss in several engagements, which, with the men who had broken down and given out, and with the men required to guard the trains, etc., reduced my available force to 8500 muskets."

The "field return of troops in the field" of Sheridan's command for September 10th is as follows: Present for duty, 43,284 enlisted men, 2225 officers. In signing and forwarding this field return, General Sheridan wrote:

"The inclosed return does not include the cavalry under Averell, about 2500, or the troops of the Departments of Washington, Susquehanna, or Middle." Sheridan's return includes 204 officers and 4611 men, ascribed to the "Military District, Harper's Ferry," who were not in the battle at Winchester.

The Confederate losses in the battle were about 4000; the Union losses about 5000. The Confederate losses were more than half in prisoners and missing; but the Union losses showed nearly 4400 killed and wounded and only about 600 missing.—EDITORS.

♭ Early's dispatch to Lee as to his losses at Fisher's Hill says: "The loss in the infantry and artillery was 30 killed, 210 wounded, and 995 missing,—total, 1235. I have been able to get no report of the loss in the cavalry, but it was slight." Sheridan's loss was 52 killed, 457 wounded, and 19 captured or missing,—a total of 528. Making allowance for the slight cavalry loss of Early, his total losses in the two battles of Winchester and Fisher's Hill were about 5300, and those of Sheridan in the same two battles were 749 killed, 4440 wounded, and 357 captured or missing = 5546. In the two battles Sheridan captured twenty-one guns.—EDITORS.

↘ Grant says that, after the fight at Fisher's Hill, "Sheridan pursued him [Early] with great energy through Harrisonburg, Staunton, and the gaps of the Blue Ridge." I did not leave the valley at all. Had Sheridan moved his infantry to Port Republic, I would have been compelled to retire through Brown's Gap, to get provisions and forage, and it would have been impossible for me to return to the valley until he evacuated the upper part of it.—J. A. E.

LIEUTENANT-GENERAL JOHN B. GORDON, C. S. A. FROM A PHOTOGRAPH.

ments about made up my losses at Winchester and Fisher's Hill, and I determined to attack the enemy in his position at Harrisonburg, and for that purpose made a reconnoissance on the 5th, but on the morning of the 6th it was discovered that he had retired during the night down the valley. ☆

When it was discovered that the enemy was retiring, I moved forward at once and arrived at New Market with my infantry on the 7th. Rosser pushed forward on the back and middle roads in pursuit of the enemy's cavalry, which was engaged in burning houses, mills, barns, and stacks of wheat and hay, and had several skirmishes with it,

☆ While Sheridan's forces were near Harrisonburg, and mine were watching them, three of our cavalry scouts, in their uniforms and with arms, got around his lines near a little town called Dayton, and encountered Lieutenant [John R.] Meigs, a Federal engineer officer, with two soldiers. These parties came upon each other suddenly, and Lieutenant Meigs was ordered to surrender by one of our scouts, to which he replied by shooting and wounding the scout, who in his turn fired and killed

while Lomax also moved forward on the valley pike and the roads east of it. I halted at New Market with the infantry, but Rosser and Lomax moved down the valley in pursuit, and skirmished successfully with the enemy's cavalry on the 8th; but on the 9th they encountered his whole cavalry force at Tom's Brook, in rear of Fisher's Hill, and both of their commands were driven back in considerable confusion, with a loss of some pieces of artillery; nine were reported to me as the number lost, but Grant claims eleven.

Having heard that Sheridan was preparing to send part of his troops to Grant, I moved down

the lieutenant. One of the men with Lieutenant Meigs was captured and the other escaped. For this act Sheridan ordered the town of Dayton to be burned, but for some reason that order was countermanded and another substituted for burning a large number of private houses in the neighborhood, which was executed, thus inflicting on non-combatants and women and children a most wanton and cruel punishment for a justifiable act of war.— J. A. E.

the valley again on the 12th. On the morning of the 13th we reached Fisher's Hill, and there remained until the 16th. The enemy was found posted on the north bank of Cedar Creek, in a very strong position and in strong force. I was now compelled to move back for want of provisions and forage, or attack the enemy in his position with the hope of driving him from it, and I determined to attack. General Gordon and Captain Jed. Hotchkiss, my topographical engineer, were sent to the signal station on the end of Massanutten Mountain, which had been reëstablished, for the purpose of examining the enemy's position from that point, and General John Pegram was ordered to go as near as he could to Cedar Creek on the enemy's right flank and see whether it was practicable to surprise him on that flank. Captain Hotchkiss returned to my headquarters after dark and reported the result of his and General Gordon's examination, and he gave me a sketch of the enemy's position and camps. He informed me that the enemy's left flank, which rested near Cedar Creek, a short distance above its mouth, was lightly picketed, and that there was but a small cavalry picket on the north fork of the Shenandoah, below the mouth of the creek, and he stated that, from information he had received, he thought it was practicable to move a column of infantry between the base of the mountain and the river to a ford below the mouth of the creek. He also informed me that the main body of the enemy's cavalry was on his right flank on the back road to Winchester. The sketch made by Captain Hotchkiss, which proved to be correct, designated the roads in the enemy's rear, and the house of a Mr. Cooley as a favorable point for forming an attacking column, after it crossed the river, in order to move against the enemy and strike him on the valley pike in rear of his works. The next morning General Gordon confirmed the report of Captain Hotchkiss, expressing confidence that the attack could be successfully made on the enemy's left and rear, and General Pegram reported that a movement on the enemy's right flank would be attended with great difficulty, as the banks of Cedar Creek on that flank were high and precipitous and were well guarded. General Gordon and Captain Hotchkiss were then sent to examine and ascertain the practicability of the route at the base of the mountain, and reported it to be practicable for infantry but not for artillery, and a temporary bridge was constructed, under Captain Hotchkiss's superintendence, at the first crossing of the river on our right. The plan of attack on which I determined was to send the three divisions of the Second Corps, to wit, Gordon's, Ramseur's, and Pegram's, under General Gordon, over the route which has been specified to the enemy's rear; to make the attack at 5 o'clock in the morning — which would be a little before daybreak; to move myself, with Kershaw's and Wharton's divisions, and all the artillery, along the pike through Strasburg, and attack the enemy on the front and left flank as soon as Gordon should become engaged, and for Rosser to move with his own and Wickham's brigade on the back road across Cedar Creek and attack the enemy's

cavalry simultaneously with Gordon's attack, while Lomax should move by Front Royal, cross the river, and come to the valley pike, so as to strike the enemy wherever he might be, of which he was to judge by the sound of the firing. The artillery was ordered to concentrate where the pike passed through the lines at Fisher's Hill, and, at the hour appointed for the attack, to move at a gallop to Hupp's Hill — the movement of the artillery being thus delayed for fear of attracting the attention of the enemy by the rumbling of the wheels over the macadamized roads. Swords and canteens were directed to be left in camp, so that there would be as little noise as possible.

Gordon moved at the appointed time, and after he had started General Pegram reported to me that he had discovered from the signal station on the mountain what he supposed to be an intrenchment thrown up across the road over which Gordon would have to advance after crossing the river the second time, and that the signal operators had informed him that it had been thrown up since Gordon and Hotchkiss made their examination; and he suggested the propriety of attacking the enemy's left flank at the same time Gordon made his attack, as he would probably have more difficulty than had been anticipated. I adopted this suggestion, and at 1 o'clock on the morning of the 19th Kershaw and Wharton went forward, the former moving at Strasburg to the right on the road to Bowman's Mill, while Wharton moved along the pike to Hupp's Hill, with instructions not to display his forces, but to avoid the enemy's notice until the attack began, when he was to move forward, support the artillery when it came up, and send a force to get possession of the bridge on the pike over the creek. I accompanied Kershaw's division, and we got in sight of the enemy's fires at half-past three o'clock. The moon was now shining and we could see the camps. The division was halted under cover to await the arrival of the proper time, and I pointed out to Kershaw and the commander of his leading brigade the enemy's position and described the nature of the ground, and directed them how the attack was to be made and followed up. Kershaw was directed to cross his division over the creek as quietly as possible, and to form it into column of brigades as he did so, and advance in that manner against the enemy's left breastwork, extending to the right or left as might be necessary. At half-past four he was ordered forward, and a very short time after he started the firing from Rosser on our left and the picket firing at the ford at which Gordon was crossing were heard. Kershaw crossed the creek without molestation and formed his division as directed, and precisely at 5 o'clock his leading brigade, with little opposition, swept over the enemy's left work, capturing seven guns, which were at once turned on the enemy. As soon as this attack was made, I rode as rapidly as possible to the position on Hupp's Hill, to which Wharton and the artillery had been ordered. I found the artillery just arriving, and a very heavy fire of musketry was now heard in the enemy's rear from Gordon's column. Wharton had advanced his skirmishers to the creek, capturing some prisoners, but the enemy still held the works on our left of the pike, commanding that road and the bridge, and opened on us with his artillery. Our artillery was immediately brought into action and opened on the enemy, but he soon evacuated his works, and our men from the other columns rushed into them. Just then the sun rose, and Wharton's division and the artillery were immediately ordered forward. I rode in advance of them across the creek, and met General Gordon on the opposite hill. Kershaw's division had swept along the enemy's works on the right of the pike, which were occupied by Crook's corps, and he and Gordon had united at the pike, and their divisions had pushed across it in pursuit of the enemy. The rear division of Gordon's column (Pegram's) was crossing the river at the time Kershaw's attack was made, and General Gordon moved rapidly to Cooley's house, formed his troops and advanced against the enemy with his own division on the left, under Brigadier-General C. A. Evans, and Ramseur's on the right, with Pegram's in the rear supporting them. There had been a delay of an hour at the river before crossing it, either from a miscalculation of time in the dark, or because the cavalry which was to precede his column had not gotten up, and the delay thus caused, for which no blame is to be attached to General Gordon, enabled the enemy partially to form his lines after the alarm produced by Kershaw's attack, and Gordon's attack, which was after light, was therefore met with greater obstinacy by the enemy than it would otherwise have encountered, and the fighting had been severe. Gordon, however, pushed his attack with great energy, and the Nineteenth and Crook's corps were in complete rout, and their camps, with a number of pieces of artillery and a considerable quantity of small-arms, abandoned. The Sixth Corps, which was on the enemy's right, and some distance from the point attacked, had had time to get under arms and take position so as to arrest our progress. General Gordon briefly informed me of the condition of things, and stated that Pegram's division, which had not been previously engaged, had been ordered in. He then rode to take command of his division, and I rode forward on the pike to ascertain the position of the enemy, in order to continue the attack. There was now a heavy fog, and that, with the smoke from the artillery and small-arms, so obscured objects that the enemy's position could not be seen; but I soon came to Generals Ramseur and Pegram, who informed me that Pegram's division had encountered a division of the Sixth Corps on the left of the valley pike, and, after a sharp engagement, had driven it back on the main body of that corps, which was in their front in a strong position. They further informed me that their divisions were in line confronting the Sixth Corps, but that there was a vacancy in the line on their right which ought to be filled. I ordered Wharton's division forward at once, and directed Generals Ramseur and Pegram to put it where it was required.

In a very short time, and while I was endeavoring to discover the enemy's line through the obscurity, Wharton's division came back in some confusion, and General Wharton informed me that, in advancing to the position pointed out to him by Generals Ramseur and Pegram, his division had been driven back by the Sixth Corps, which, he said, was advancing. He pointed out the direction from which he said the enemy was advancing, and some pieces of artillery which had come up were brought into action. The fog soon rose sufficiently for us to see the enemy's position on a ridge to the west of Middletown, and it was discovered to be a strong one. After driving back Wharton's division, he had not advanced, but opened on us with artillery, and orders were given for concentrating all our guns on him. In the meantime a force of cavalry was advancing along the pike and through the fields to the right of Middletown, thus placing our right and rear in great danger, and Wharton was ordered to form his division at once and take position to hold the enemy's cavalry in check. Wofford's brigade of Kershaw's division, which had become separated from the other brigades, was ordered up for the same purpose. Discovering that the Sixth Corps could not be attacked with advantage on its left flank, because the approach in that direction was through an open flat and across a boggy stream with deep banks, I directed Captain Powell, serving on General Gordon's staff, who rode up to me while the artillery was being placed in position, to tell the general to advance against the enemy's right flank and attack it in conjunction with Kershaw, while a heavy fire of artillery was opened from our right; but as Captain Powell said he did not know where General Gordon was, and expressed some doubt about finding him, immediately after he started I sent Lieutenant Page, of my own staff, with orders for both Generals Gordon and Kershaw to make the attack. In a short time Colonel Carter concentrated eighteen or twenty guns on the enemy, and he was soon in retreat. Ramseur and Pegram advanced at once to the position from which the enemy was driven, and just then his cavalry commenced pressing heavily on the right, and Pegram's division was ordered to move to the north of Middletown and take position across the pike against the cavalry. Lieutenant Page had returned and informed me that he delivered my order to General Kershaw, but the latter informed him that his division was not in a condition to make the attack, as it was very much scattered, and there was a cavalry force threatening him in front. Lieutenant Page also stated that he had seen Gordon's division in Kershaw's rear re-forming, and that it was also much scattered, and that he had not delivered the order to General Gordon, because he saw that neither his division nor Kershaw's was in a condition to execute it. As soon as Pegram moved Kershaw was ordered from the left to supply his place. I then rode to Middletown to make provision against the enemy's cavalry, and discovered a large body of it seriously threatening that flank, which was very much exposed. Wharton's division and Wofford's brigade were put in position on Pegram's right, and several charges of the enemy's cavalry were repulsed. I had no cavalry on that flank except Payne's very small brigade, which had accompanied Gordon and made some captures of prisoners and wagons. Lomax had not arrived, but I received a message from him informing me that he had crossed the river after some delay from a cavalry force guarding it, and I sent a message to him requiring him to move to Middletown as quickly as possible, but, as I subsequently ascertained, he did not receive that message. Rosser had attacked the enemy promptly at the appointed time, but he had not been able to surprise him, as he was found on the alert on that flank, doubtless owing to the attempt at a surprise on the night of the 16th. There was now one division of cavalry threatening my right flank, and two were on the left, near the back road, held in check by Rosser. The force of the latter was too weak to make any impression on the enemy's cavalry, and all he could do was to watch it. As I passed across Cedar Creek after the enemy was driven from it, I had discovered a number of men in the enemy's camps plundering, and one of Wharton's battalions was ordered to clear the camps and drive the men to their commands. It was reported to me subsequently that a great number were at the same work, and I sent all my staff-officers who could be spared to stop it if possible, and orders were sent to the division commanders to send for their men.

After he was driven from his second position the enemy had taken a new position about two miles north of Middletown, and, as soon as I had regulated matters on the right so as to prevent his cavalry from getting in rear of that flank, I rode to the left for the purpose of ordering an advance. I found Ramseur and Kershaw in line with Pegram, but Gordon had not come up. In a short time, however, I found him coming up from the rear, and I ordered him to take position on Kershaw's left and advance for the purpose of driving the enemy from his new position — Kershaw and Ramseur being ordered to advance at the same time. As the enemy's cavalry on our left was very strong, and had the benefit of an open country to the rear of that flank, a repulse at this time would have been disastrous, and I therefore directed General Gordon, if he found the enemy's line too strong to attack with success, not to make the assault. The advance was made for some distance, when Gordon's skirmishers came back reporting a line of battle in front behind breastworks, and General Gordon did not make the attack. It was now apparent that it would not do to press my troops further. They had been up all night and were much jaded. In passing over rough ground to attack the enemy in the early morning their own ranks had been much disordered and the men scattered, and it had required time to re-form them. Their ranks, moreover, were much thinned by the absence of the men engaged in plundering the enemy's camps. The delay which had unavoidably occurred had enabled the enemy to rally a portion of his routed troops, and his immense force of cavalry, which

remained intact, was threatening both of our flanks in an open country, which of itself rendered an advance extremely hazardous. I determined, therefore, to try and hold what had been gained, and orders were given for carrying off the captured and abandoned artillery, small-arms, and wagons. A number of bold attempts were made during the subsequent part of the day by the enemy's cavalry to break our line on the right, but they were invariably repulsed. Late in the afternoon the enemy's infantry advanced against Ramseur's, Kershaw's, and Gordon's lines, and the attack on Ramseur's and Kershaw's fronts was handsomely repulsed in my view, and I hoped that the day was finally ours, but a portion of the enemy had penetrated an interval which was between Evans's brigade, on the extreme left, and the rest of the line, when that brigade gave way and Gordon's other brigades soon followed. General Gordon made every possible effort to rally his men and lead them back against the enemy, but without avail. The information of this affair, with exaggerations, passed rapidly along Kershaw's and Ramseur's lines, and their men, under the apprehension of being flanked, commenced falling back in disorder, though no enemy was pressing them, and this gave me the first intimation of Gordon's condition. At the same time the enemy's cavalry, observing the disorder in our ranks, made another charge on our right, but was again repulsed. Every effort was made to stop and rally Kershaw's and Ramseur's men, but the mass of them resisted all appeals and continued to go to the rear without waiting for any effort to retrieve the partial disorder. Ramseur, however, succeeded in retaining with him two or three hundred men of his division, and Major Goggin, of Kershaw's staff, who was in command of Conner's brigade, about the same number from that brigade ; and these men, aided by several pieces of artillery, held the enemy's whole force on our left in check for one hour and a half, until Ramseur was shot down mortally wounded and the ammunition of those pieces of artillery was exhausted. While the latter were being replaced by other guns the force that had remained with Ramseur and Goggin gave way also. Pegram's and Wharton's divisions and Wofford's brigade had remained steadfast on the right, and resisted all efforts of the enemy's cavalry, but no portion of this force could be moved to the left without leaving the pike open to the cavalry, which would have destroyed all hope at once. Every effort to rally the men in the rear having failed, I had now nothing left for me but to order these troops to retire also. When they began to move the disorder soon extended to them, but General Pegram succeeded in bringing back a portion of his command across Cedar Creek in an organized condition, holding the enemy in check; but this small force soon dissolved. A part of Evans's brigade had been rallied in the rear, and held a ford above the bridge for a short time, but it followed the example of the rest. I tried to rally the men immediately after crossing Cedar Creek and at Hupp's Hill, but without success. Could five hundred men have been rallied at either of these places, who would have stood by me, I am satisfied that all my artillery and wagons and the greater part of the captured artillery could have been saved, as the enemy's pursuit was very feeble. As it was, a bridge broke down on a very narrow part of the road between Strasburg and Fisher's Hill, just above Strasburg, where there was no other passway, thereby blocking up all the artillery, ordnance, and medical wagons and ambulances which had not passed that point; and, as there was no force to defend them, they were lost, a very small body of the enemy's cavalry capturing them.

The greater part of the infantry was halted at Fisher's Hill, and Rosser, whose command had retired in good order on the back road, was ordered to that point with his cavalry. The infantry moved back toward New Market at three o'clock next morning, and Rosser was left at Fisher's Hill to cover the retreat of the troops, and hold that position until they were beyond pursuit. He remained at Fisher's Hill until after ten o'clock on the 20th, and the enemy did not advance to that place while he was there. He then fell back without molestation to his former position, and established his line on Stony Creek, across from Columbia Furnace to Edinburg, seven miles below Mount Jackson. My other troops were halted at New Market, about seven miles from Mount Jackson, and there was an entirely open country between the two places, they being very nearly in sight of each other. |

Lomax had moved on the day of the battle, on the Front Royal road toward Winchester, under the impression that the enemy was being forced back toward that place, and he did not reach me. When he ascertained the reverse which had taken place in the latter part of the day, he retired up the Luray Valley to his former position at Millford, without molestation.

My loss in the battle of Cedar Creek was twenty-three pieces of artillery, some ordnance and medical wagons and ambulances, which had been carried to the front for the use of the troops on the field; about 1860 in killed and wounded, and something over 1000 prisoners. ⚓ Major-General Ramseur fell into the hands of the enemy mortally wounded, and in him not only my command,

LIEUTENANT-GENERAL JUBAL A. EARLY, C. S. A.
FROM A PHOTOGRAPH.

but the country sustained a heavy loss. He was a most gallant and energetic officer whom no disaster appalled, but his courage and energy seemed to gain new strength in the midst of confusion and disorder. He fell at his post fighting like a lion at bay, and his native State has reason to be proud of his memory. Brigadier-General C. A. Battle was wounded at the beginning of the fight, and other valuable officers were lost. Fifteen hundred prisoners were captured from the enemy and brought off, and his loss in killed and wounded in this action was very heavy.

This was the case of a glorious victory given up by my own troops after they had won it, and it is to be accounted for on the ground of the partial demoralization caused by the plunder of the enemy's camps, and from the fact that the men undertook to judge for themselves when it was proper to retire.

Had my cavalry been sufficient to contend with

| Grant says in his account of the battle of Cedar Creek: "The enemy was defeated with great slaughter, and the loss of the most of his artillery and trains, and the trophies he had captured in the morning. The wreck of his army escaped during the night, and fled in the direction of Staunton and Lynchburg. Pursuit was made to Mount Jackson." Stanton, who seems to have thought it was his duty to improve on all Grant's statements, says: "The routed forces of the enemy were pursued to Mount Jackson, where he arrived without an organized regiment of his army. All of his artillery and thousands of prisoners fell into Sheridan's hands. These successes closed military operations in the Shenandoah Valley, and *a rebel force appeared there no more during the war.*" The recklessness of these statements, of both

Grant and Stanton, will appear from the above narrative, as well as from my subsequent operations in the Shenandoah Valley. Would it be believed that this "wreck" of my army, which fled in such wild dismay before its pursuers, carried from the battle-field 1500 prisoners,— who were sent to Richmond,— subsequently confronted Sheridan's whole force north of Cedar Creek, for two days, without his attacking it, and sent out expeditions which captured two important posts, with over 1000 prisoners and several pieces of artillery, in the limits of Sheridan's command? Yet such was the case.
J. A. E.

⚓ Sheridan's loss in this battle was 644 killed, 3430 wounded, 1591 captured or missing,—aggregate, 5665. Early's was about 3000.— EDITORS.

that of the enemy, the rout in the morning would have been complete; as it was, I had only about 1200 cavalry on the field under Rosser; Lomax's force, which numbered less than 1700, did not get up. My infantry and artillery were about the same strength as at Winchester. The reports of the ordnance officers showed in the hands of my troops about 8800 muskets, in round numbers as follows: in Kershaw's division, 2700; Ramseur's, 2100; Gordon's, 1700; Pegram's, 1200, and Wharton's, 1100. Making a moderate allowance for the men left to guard the camps and the signal station on the mountain, as well as for a few sick and wounded, I went into this battle with about 8500 muskets and a little over forty pieces of artillery.

Sheridan was absent in the morning at the beginning of the fight, and returned in the after-

noon before the change in the fortunes of the day. Nevertheless, I saw no reason to change the estimate I had formed of him. ☽

It may be asked, why with my small force I made the attack. I can only say we had been fighting large odds during the whole war, and I knew there was no chance of lessening them. It was of the utmost consequence that Sheridan should be prevented from sending troops to Grant, and General Lee, in a letter received a day or two before, had expressed an earnest desire that a victory should be gained in the valley if possible, and it could not be gained without fighting for it. I did hope to gain one by surprising the enemy in his camp, and then thought and still think I would have had it, if my directions had been strictly complied with, and my troops had awaited my orders to retire. ☆

☽ The retreat of the main body of his army had been arrested, and a new line formed behind breastworks of rails, before Sheridan arrived on the field; and he still had immense odds against me when he made the attack in the afternoon.— J. A. E.

☆ A silly story was circulated and even published in the papers, that this battle was planned and conducted by one of my subordinates up to a certain point, when my arrival on the field stopped the pursuit and arrested the victory. No officer or soldier on that day received an order from me to halt, unless he was going to the rear. My orders were to press the enemy from the beginning and give him no time to form, and when I found that my troops had halted, I endeavored to advance

again, but I discovered it would not do to press them further. Those who have known me from my youth, as well as those who came in contact with me during the war, know that I was not likely to permit any other to plan a battle for me, or assume my duties in any particular. Yet I was always willing to receive and adopt valuable suggestions from any of my officers.— J. A. E.

After the battle of Cedar Creek Early established his army at New Market. On the 9th of November Sheridan established his at Kernstown. Early in December Lee called back to Richmond his Second Corps, and Grant called to Petersburg the Sixth Corps. Early remained, moving back to Staunton, with Wharton's division and cavalry and artillery.— EDITORS.

THE OPPOSING FORCES AT CEDAR CREEK, VA., OCT. 19, 1864.

THE UNION ARMY.

ARMY OF THE SHENANDOAH, Maj.-Gen. Philip H. Sheridan.

Escort: 17th Pa. Cavalry (detachment), Maj. Weidner H. Spera; 6th U. S. Cavalry, Capt. Ira W. Claflin.

SIXTH ARMY CORPS, Brig.-Gen. James B. Ricketts (w), ☽ Brig.-Gen. George W. Getty, Maj.-Gen. Horatio G. Wright. ☽ Staff loss: w, 2.

Escort: G, 1st Mich. Cavalry, Lieut. William H. Wheeler.

FIRST DIVISION, Brig.-Gen. Frank Wheaton.

First Brigade, Col. William H. Penrose (w), Lieut.-Col. Edward L. Campbell, Capt. Baldwin Hufty: 4th N. J., Capt. Baldwin Hufty; 10th N. J., Maj. Lambert Boeman, Capt. Charles D. Claypool; 15th N. J., Lieut.-Col. Edward L. Campbell, Capt. James W. Penrose. Brigade loss: k, 17; w, 129; m, 19 = 165. *Second Brigade,* Joseph E. Hamblin, Col. Ranald S. Mackenzie (w), Lieut.-Col. Egbert Olcott: 2d Conn. Heavy Artillery, Col. Ranald S. Mackenzie, Maj. Edward W. Jones; 65th N. Y., Lieut.-Col. Thomas H. Higginbotham, Capt. Henry C. Fisk; 121st N. Y., Lieut.-Col. Egbert Olcott, Capt. Daniel D. Jackson; 95th and 96th Pa., Capt. John Harper. Brigade loss: k, 52; w, 272; m, 80 = 404. *Third Brigade* (at Winchester and not engaged in the battle), Col. Oliver Edwards: 37th Mass., Lieut.-Col. George L. Montague; 49th Pa., Lieut.-Col. Baynton J. Hickman; 82d Pa., Col. Isaac C. Bassett; 119th Pa., Lieut.-Col. Gideon Clark; 2d R. I. (batt'n), Capt. Elisha H. Rhodes; 5th Wis. (batt'n), Maj. Charles W. Kempf; 17th Pa. Cavalry, Maj. Coe Durland.

SECOND DIVISION, Brig.-Gen. George W. Getty, Brig.-Gen. Lewis A. Grant, Brig.-Gen. George W. Getty.

First Brigade, Col. James M. Warner: 62d N. Y., Lieut.-Col. Theodore B. Hamilton; 93d Pa., Capt. David C. Keller; 98th Pa., Lieut.-Col. John B. Kohler, Capt. Gottfried Bauer; 102d Pa., Maj. James H. Coleman, Capt. James Patchell; 139th Pa., Lieut.-Col. John G. Parr. Brigade loss: k, 36; w, 189; m, 4 = 229. *Second Brigade,* Brig.-Gen. Lewis A. Grant, Lieut.-Col. Amasa S. Tracy, Brig.-Gen. Lewis A. Grant: 2d Vt., Lieut.-Col. Amasa S. Tracy, Capt. Elijah Wales, Lieut.-Col. Amasa S. Tracy; 3d Vt. (batt'n), Maj. Horace W. Floyd; 4th Vt., Maj. Horace W. Floyd, Col. George P. Foster; ☟ 5th Vt., Maj. Enoch E. Johnson; 6th Vt. (batt'n), Capt. Edwin R. Kinney, Capt. William J. Sperry; 11th Vt. (1st Heavy Artillery), Lieut.-Col. Charles Hunsdon. Brigade loss: k, 34; w, 209; m, 41 = 284. *Third Brigade,* Brig.-Gen. Daniel D. Bidwell (k), Lieut.-Col. Winsor B. French: 1st Me. (Veteran), Maj. Stephen C. Fletcher; 43d N. Y. (batt'n), Maj. Charles A. Milliken; 49th N. Y. (batt'n), Lieut.-Col. Erastus D. Holt; 77th N. Y., Lieut.-Col. Winsor B. French; 122d N. Y., Lieut.-Col. Augustus W. Dwight, Maj. Jabez M. Brower; 61st Pa. (batt'n), Capt. David J. Taylor. Brigade loss: k, 37; w, 172; m, 16 = 225.

THIRD DIVISION, Col. J. Warren Keifer.

First Brigade, Col. William Emerson: 14th N. J., Capt. Jacob J. Janeway; 106th N. Y., Capt. Alvah W. Briggs, Capt. Peter Robertson; 151st N. Y., Capt. Browning N. Wiles, Capt. Hiram A. Kimball; 184th N. Y. (batt'n), Maj. William D. Ferguson; 87th Pa. (batt'n), Capt. Edgar M. Ruhl, Capt. John A. Salsbury; 10th Vt., Col. William W. Henry, Capt. Henry H. Dewey. Brigade loss: k, 39; w, 210; m, 21 = 270. *Second*

☟ This roster may be incomplete as regards the indication of officers who were killed (k) or wounded (w).

☽ Commanded the army during General Sheridan's temporary absence in the early part of the battle.

☟ Corps officer of the day at the beginning of the battle; later rejoined brigade and commanded the left of its line.

Brigade, Col. William H. Ball: 6th Md., Maj. Joseph C. Hill; 9th N. Y. Heavy Artillery, Maj. James W. Snyder; 110th Ohio, Lieut.-Col. Otho H. Binkley; 122d Ohio, Lieut.-Col. Moses M. Granger; 126th Ohio, Maj. George W. Voorhes, Capt. George W. Hoge; 67th Pa., Lieut. John F. Young; 138th Pa., Maj. Lewis A. May. Brigade loss: k, 69; w, 352; m, 15 = 436.

ARTILLERY BRIGADE, Col. Charles H. Tompkins: 5th Me., Capt. Greenleaf T. Stevens; 1st N.Y., Lieut. Orsamus R. Van Etten; C, 1st R. I., Lieut. Jacob H. Lamb; G, 1st R. I., Capt. George W. Adams; M, 5th U. S., Capt. James McKnight. Brigade loss: k, 14, w, 93; m, 4 = 111.

NINETEENTH ARMY CORPS, Brig.-Gen. William H. Emory. Staff loss: w, 2.

FIRST DIVISION, Brig.-Gen. James W. McMillan, Brig.-Gen. William Dwight.

First Brigade, Col. Edwin P. Davis: 29th Me., Maj. George H. Nye, Capt. Alfred L. Turner; 30th Mass., Capt. Samuel D. Shipley; 90th N. Y., Lieut.-Col. Nelson Shaurman, Capt. Henry de La Paturelle; 114th N. Y., Lieut.-Col. Henry B. Morse; 116th N. Y., Col. George M. Love; 153d N. Y., Lieut.-Col. Alexander Strain, Capt. George H. McLaughlin. Brigade loss: k, 71; w, 443; m, 49 = 563. *Second Brigade,* Col. Stephen Thomas, Brig.-Gen. James W. McMillan: 12th Conn., Lieut.-Col. George N. Lewis; 160th N. Y., Capt. Henry P. Underhill; 47th Pa., Maj. J. P. Shindel Gobin; 8th Vt., Maj. John B. Mead, Capt. Moses McFarland, Col. Stephen Thomas. Brigade loss: k, 85; w, 246; m, 167 = 498. *Third Brigade* (guarding wagon trains, and not engaged in the battle), Col. Leonard D. H. Currie: 30th Me., Col. Thomas H. Hubbard; 133d N. Y., Maj. Anthony J. Allaire; 162d N. Y., Col. Justus W. Blanchard; 165th N. Y. (6 companies), Lieut.-Col. Gouverneur Carr; 173d N. Y., Maj. George W. Rogers.

Artillery: 5th N. Y., Capt. Elijah D. Taft.

SECOND DIVISION, Brig.-Gen. Cuvier Grover (w), Brig.-Gen. Henry W. Birge. Staff loss: w, 1.

First Brigade, Brig.-Gen. Henry W. Birge, Col. Thomas W. Porter: 9th Conn. (batt'n), Capt. John G. Healy; 12th Me., Lieut.-Col. Edwin Ilsley; 14th Me., Col. Thomas W. Porter, Capt. John K. Laing; 26th Mass. (batt'n), Lieut. John S. Cooke; 14th N. H., Capt. Theodore A. Ripley, Capt. Oliver H. Marston; 75th N. Y., Maj. Benjamin F. Thurber. Brigade loss: k, 28; w, 152; m, 169 = 349. *Second Brigade,* Col. Edward L. Molineux: 13th Conn., Col. Charles D. Blinn; 11th Ind., Lieut.-Col. William W. Darnall; 22d Iowa, Col. Harvey Graham; 3d Mass. Cavalry (dismounted), Col. Lorenzo D. Sargent; 131st N. Y., Col. Nicholas W. Day; 159th N. Y., Lieut.-Col. William Waltermire. Brigade loss: k, 19; w, 171; m, 97 = 287. *Third Brigade,* Col. Daniel Macauley, Lieut.-Col. Alfred Neafie: 38th Mass., Maj. Charles F. Allen; 128th N. Y., Capt. Charles R. Anderson; 156th N. Y., Lieut.-Col. Alfred Neafie, Captain Alfred Cooley; 175th N. Y. (batt'n), Capt. Charles McCarthey; 176th N. Y., Maj. Charles Lewis. Brigade loss: k, 20; w, 87; m, 191 = 298. *Fourth Brigade,* Col. David Shunk: 8th Ind., Lieut.-Col. Alexander J. Kenny, Maj. John R. Polk; 18th Ind., Lieut.-Col. William S. Charles; 24th Iowa, Lieut.-Col. John Q. Wilds, Capt. Leander Clark, Maj. Edward Wright; 28th Iowa, Lieut.-Col. Bartholomew W. Wilson, Maj. John Meyer. Brigade loss: k, 26; w, 200; m, 103 = 329.

Artillery: 1st Me., Lieut. Eben D. Haley, Lieut. John S. Snow. Artillery loss: k, 3; w, 17; m, 8 = 28.

RESERVE ARTILLERY, Maj. Albert W. Bradbury: 17th Ind., Lieut. Hezekiah Hinkson; D, 1st R. I., Lieut. Fred'k Chase. Artillery Reserve loss: k, 5; w, 17; m, 6 = 28.

ARMY OF WEST VIRGINIA, Brig.-Gen. George Crook. Staff loss: k, 1.

FIRST DIVISION, Col. Joseph Thoburn (k), Col. Thomas M. Harris. Staff loss: k, 1.

First Brigade, Lieut.-Col. Thomas F. Wildes: 34th Mass., Capt. Andrew Potter; 5th N. Y. Heavy Artillery (2d Battalion), Capt. Frederick C. Wilkie; 116th Ohio, Capt. Wilbert B. Teters; 123d Ohio, Maj. Horace Kellogg. Brigade loss: k, 1; w, 36; m, 371 = 408. *Second*

Brigade (at Winchester and not engaged in the battle), Col. William B. Curtis: 1st W. Va., Lieut.-Col. Jacob Weddle; 4th W. Va., Capt. Benjamin D. Boswell; 12th W. Va., Lieut.-Col. Robert S. Northcott. *Third Brigade,* Col. Thomas M. Harris, Col. Milton Wells: 23d Ill. Battalion (not in action), Capt. Samuel A. Simison; 54th Pa., Capt. John Suter; 10th W. Va., Lieut.-Col. Moses S. Hall, Maj. Henry H. Withers; 11th W. Va., Lieut.-Col. Van H. Bukey; 15th W. Va., Col. Milton Wells, Maj. John W. Holliday. Brigade loss: k, 12; w, 61; m, 103 = 176.

SECOND DIVISION, Col. Rutherford B. Hayes.

First Brigade, Col. Hiram F. Duval: 23d Ohio, Lieut.-Col. James M. Comly; 36th Ohio, Lieut.-Col. William H. G. Adney; 5th W. Va. (batt'n), Lieut.-Col. William H. Enochs; 13th W. Va., Col. William R. Brown, Lieut.-Col. James R. Hall. Brigade loss: k, 22; w, 105; m, 8 = 135. *Second Brigade,* Lieut.-Col. Benjamin F. Coates: 34th Ohio (batt'n), Lieut.-Col. Luther Furney; 91st Ohio, Maj. Lemuel Z. Cadot; 9th W. Va., Capt. John S. P. Carroll; 14th W. Va., Maj. Shriver Moore. Brigade loss: k, 3; w, 52; m, 31 = 86.

ARTILLERY BRIGADE, Capt. Henry A. Du Pont: L, 1st Ohio, Capt. Frank C. Gibbs; D, 1st Pa., Lieut. William Munk; B, 5th U. S., Lieut. Henry F. Brewerton, Lieut. Charles Holman. Brigade loss: k, 8; w, 16; m, 27 = 51.

PROVISIONAL DIVISION, 〕 Col. J. Howard Kitching (m w). Loss: k, 12; w, 72; m, 18 = 102.

CAVALRY, Brig.-Gen. Alfred T. A. Torbert.

Escort: 1st R. I., Maj. William H. Turner, Jr.

FIRST DIVISION, Brig.-Gen. Wesley Merritt.

First Brigade, Col. James H. Kidd: 1st Mich., Capt. Andrew W. Duggan; 5th Mich., Maj. Smith H. Hastings; 6th Mich., Maj. Charles W. Deane; 7th Mich., Maj. Daniel H. Darling; 6th N. Y. Battery, Capt. Joseph W. Martin. Brigade loss: k, 10; w, 45; m, 33 = 88. *Second Brigade,* Col. Thomas C. Devin: 4th N. Y., 〕 Maj. Edward Schwartz; 6th N. Y., Capt. George E. Farmer; 9th N. Y., Col. George S. Nichols; 19th N. Y. (1st Dragoons), Col. Alfred Gibbs; K and L, 1st U. S. Art'y, Lieut. Franck E. Taylor. Brigade loss: k, 5; w, 19 = 24. *Reserve Brigade,* Col. Charles R. Lowell, Jr. (k), Lieut.-Col. Casper Crowninshield: 2d Mass., Lieut.-Col. Casper Crowninshield, Capt. Archibald McKendry; 1st U. S., Capt. Eugene M. Baker; 2d U. S., Capt. Robert S. Smith; 5th U. S., Lieut. Gustavus Urban. Brigade loss: k, 9; w, 27; m, 1 = 37.

SECOND DIVISION, ☆ Col. William H. Powell.

First Brigade, Col. Alpheus S. Moore: 8th Ohio (detachment), ——; 14th Pa., Maj. Thomas Gibson; 22d Pa., Lieut.-Col. Andrew J. Greenfield. Brigade loss: w, 7. *Second Brigade,* Col. Henry Capehart: 1st N. Y., Maj. Timothy Quinn; 1st W. Va., Maj. Harvey Farabee; 2d W. Va., Lieut.-Col. John J. Hoffman; 3d W. Va., Lieut.-Col. John L. McGee. Brigade loss: k, 1; w, 1; m, 1 = 3. *Artillery:* L, 5th U. S., Lieut. Gulian V. Weir.

THIRD DIVISION, Brig.-Gen. George A. Custer.

First Brigade, Col. Alexander C. M. Pennington, Jr.: 1st Conn., Capt. Edwin W. French; 3d N. J., Lieut.-Col. Charles C. Suydam; 2d N. Y., Capt. Andrew S. Glover; 5th N. Y., Maj. Theodore A. Boice; 2d Ohio, Lieut.-Col. George A. Purington; 18th Pa., Maj. John W. Phillips. Brigade loss: k, 2; w, 17; m, 8 = 27. *Second Brigade,* Col. William Wells: 3d Ind. (2 co's), Lieut. Benjamin F. Gilbert; 1st N. H. (batt'n), Col. John L. Thompson; 8th N. Y., Lieut.-Col. William H. Benjamin; 22d N. Y., Maj. Charles C. Brown; 1st Vt., Lieut.-Col. John W. Bennett. Brigade loss: w, 7.

HORSE ARTILLERY: B and L, 2d U. S., Capt. Charles H. Peirce; C, F, and K, 3d U. S., Capt. Dunbar R. Ransom. Artillery loss: k, 2; w, 1 = 3.

Sheridan's field forces present for duty in the Valley, September 10th, 1864, were about 43,000 officers and men. He had, also, in garrison at Harper's Ferry, Martinsburg, and other points, probably 7000. General Early puts Sheridan's aggregate, September 1st, at 56,618, but this includes troops subsequently left in garrisons at

---

〕 Only a small detachment from the First Brigade, and the 6th N. Y. H. Art'y, from the Second Brigade, engaged in the battle.
〕 Detailed for duty at General Sheridan's headquarters.   ☆ From Department of West Virginia.

Harper's Ferry, Martinsburg, and further west on the Baltimore and Ohio Railroad, and in West Virginia.

His losses in the principal engagements were: Winchester, or the Opequon, 697 killed, 3983 wounded, 338 captured or missing,— total, 5018; Fisher's Hill, 52 killed,

457 wounded, 19 captured or missing,— total, 528; Cedar Creek, 644 killed, 3430 wounded, 1591 captured or missing,— total, 5665. During the campaign the Union loss aggregated 1938 killed, 11,893 wounded, and 3121 captured or missing = 16,952.

THE CONFEDERATE ARMY.— Lieut.-Gen. Jubal A. Early.

RAMSEUR'S DIVISION, Maj.-Gen. S. D. Ramseur (k).

Battle's Brigade, Brig.-Gen. C. A. Battle, Lieut.-Col. E. L. Hobson: 3d Ala. ——; 5th Ala., Lieut.-Col. E. L. Hobson; 6th Ala., Capt. J. Green; 12th Ala., Capt. P. D. Rose; 61st Ala., Maj. W. E. Pinckard. *Cook's Brigade*, Brig.-Gen. Phil. Cook: 4th Ga., Lieut.-Col. W. H. Willis; 12th Ga., Capt. James Everett; 21st Ga., Capt. H. T. Battle; 44th Ga., Lieut.-Col. J. W. Beck. *Grimes's Brigade*, Brig.-Gen. Bryan Grimes: 32d and 53d and 2d N. C. Battalion, Col. D. G. Cowand; 43d and 45th N. C., Col. John R. Winston. *Cox's Brigade*, Brig.-Gen. William R. Cox: 1st N. C., Capt. W H. Thomson; 2d N. C., Capt. T. B. Beall; 3d N. C., Capt. W. H. Thomson; 4th N. C. ——; 14th N. C., Capt. Joseph Jones; 30th N. C., Capt. J. C. McMillan.

PEGRAM'S (Early's) DIVISION, Brig.-Gen. John Pegram.

Godwin's Brigade : 6th N. C. ——; 21st N. C. ——; 54th N. C. ——; 57th N. C. ——. *Johnston's Brigade*, Brig.-Gen. Robert D. Johnston: 5th N. C. ——; 12th N. C. ——; 20th N. C., Col. T. F. Toon; 23d N. C. ——; 1st N. C. Battalion Sharp-shooters, Capt. R. E. Wilson. *Pegram's Brigade*, Col. John S. Hoffman: 13th Va., Capt. Felix Heiskell; 31st Va., Lieut.-Col. J. S. K. McCutchen; 49th Va., Capt. John G. Lobban; 52d Va., Capt. J. M. Humphreys; 58th Va., Capt. L. C. James.

GORDON'S DIVISION, Maj.-Gen. John B. Gordon.

Evans's Brigade, Brig.-Gen. C. A. Evans: 13th Ga. ——; 26th Ga. ——; 31st Ga. ——; 38th Ga. ——; 60th Ga. ——; 61st Ga. ——; 12th Ga. Battalion, ——. *Hays's Brigade*, 5th, 6th, and 7th La. ——; 8th La. ——; 9th La. ——. *Terry's Brigade* (composed of the fragmentary remains of fourteen of the regiments of Edward Johnson's division, most of which was captured by the enemy, May 12th, 1864), Brig.-Gen. William Terry: 2d, 4th, 5th, 27th, and 33d Va. [Stonewall Brigade], Col. J. H. S. Funk; 21st, 25th, 42d, 44th, 48th, and 50th Va. [J. M. Jones's Brigade], Col. R. H. Dungan; 10th, 23d, and 37th Va. [Steuart's brigade], Lieut.-Col. S. H. Saunders. *Stafford's Brigade* : 1st and 14th La. ——; 2d La. ——; 10th and 15th La. ——.

KERSHAW'S DIVISION, Maj.-Gen. J. B. Kershaw.

Conner's Brigade, Brig.-Gen. James Conner, Maj. James M. Goggin: 2d S. C., Maj. B. R. Clyburn; 3d S. C., Maj. R. T. Todd; 7th S. C. ——; 8th S. C. ——; 15th S. C. ——; 20th S. C., Col. S. M. Boykin; 3d S. C. Battalion, ——. *Wofford's Brigade* : 16th Ga. ——; 18th Ga. ——; 24th Ga. ——; 3d Ga. Battalion, ——; Cobb's Ga. Legion, ——; Phillips's Ga. Legion. *Humphreys's Brigade*, Brig.-Gen. Benjamin G. Humphreys: 13th Miss. ——; 17th Miss. ——; 18th Miss. ——; 21st Miss. ——. *Bryan's Brigade*, Col. James P. Simms: 10th Ga., Col. W. C. Holt; 50th Ga., Col. P. McGlashan; 51st Ga., Col. E. Ball; 53d Ga. ——.

WHARTON'S DIVISION, Brig.-Gen. G. C. Wharton.

Wharton's Brigade : 45th Va. ——; 50th Va. ——; 51st Va. ——; 30th Va. Battalion Sharp-shooters, ——. *Echols's Brigade* : 22d Va. ——; 23d Va. Battalion, ——; 26th Va. Battalion, ——. *Smith's Brigade*, Col. Thomas Smith: 36th Va. ——; 60th Va., Capt. A. G. P. George; 45th Va. Battalion, Capt. W. B. Hensly; Thomas Legion, Lieut.-Col. James R. Lowe.

CAVALRY.

LOMAX'S DIVISION, Maj.-Gen. Lunsford L. Lomax.

Imboden's Brigade : 18th Va. ——; 23d Va. ——; 62d Va. ——. *McCausland's Brigade*, Brig.-Gen. John McCausland: 14th Va. ——; 16th Va. ——; 17th Va.

——; 25th Va. ——; 37th Va. Battalion, ——. *B. T. Johnson's Brigade* : 8th Va. ——; 21st Va. ——; 22d Va. ——; 34th Va. Battalion, ——; 36th Va. Battalion, ——. *Jackson's Brigade*, Brig.-Gen. H. B. Davidson: 1st Md. ——; 19th Va. ——; 20th Va. ——; 46th Va. Battalion, ——; 47th Va. Battalion. ——.

ROSSER'S (Fitz Lee's) DIVISION, Maj. Gen. Thos. L. Rosser.

Wickham's Brigade : 1st Va. ——; 2d Va. ——; 3d Va. ——; 4th Va. ——. *Rosser's Brigade* : 7th Va. ——; 11th Va. ——; 12th Va. ——; 35th Va. Battalion, ——. *Payne's Brigade* : 5th Va. ——; 6th Va. ——; 15th Va ——.

ARTILLERY, Col. T. H. Carter.

Braxton's Battalion : Va. Battery (Carpenter's) ; Va. Battery (Hardwicke's) ; Va. Battery (Cooper's). *Carter's Battalion* : Ala. Battery (Reese's), Va. Battery (W. P. Carter's) ; Va. Battery (Pendleton's) ; Va. Battery (Fry's). *Cutshaw's Battalion* : Va. Battery (Carrington's) ; Va. Battery (Tanner's) ; Va. Battery (Garber's). *Nelson's Battalion*, Lieut.-Col. William Nelson : Ga. Battery (Milledge's) ; Va. Battery (Kirkpatrick's) ; Va. Battery (Massie's). *King's Battalion*, Lieut.-Col. J. Floyd King: Va. Battery (Bryan's) ; Va. Battery (Chapman's) ; Va. Battery (Lowry's). *Horse Artillery* : Md. Battery (Griffin's) ; Va. Battery (Jackson's) ; Va. Battery (Lurty's) ; Va. Battery (McClanahan's) ; Va. Battery (Johnston's) ; Va. Battery (Shoemaker's) ; Va. Battery (Thomson's).

The maximum effective strength of Early's army in the Valley is estimated at about 20,000 of all arms, about August 15th, 1864 ; but at the battle of Winchester, September 19th, his force had been reduced by the departure of Kershaw, who on August 31st had been 3822 strong, officers and men. [See foot-note, p. 524.] According to Early's official report the losses in killed and wounded from September 1st to October 1st were 291 killed and 2023 wounded = 2314. The loss (including the missing) of the infantry and artillery at the Opequon is stated at 3611. At Fisher's Hill the infantry and artillery lost 30 killed, 210 wounded, and 995 missing = 1235. At Cedar Creek 700 or 800 were killed and wounded. In his "Memoir," p. 112, General Early says that his losses at Cedar Creek were "about 1860 in killed and wounded and something over 1000 prisoners."

Colonel B. W. Crowninshield, who was provost-marshal of Sheridan's command, says in his "Cedar Creek," that he "had on his books, record of 7000 unwounded prisoners who were soldiers," and Colonel E. B. Parsons, who succeeded Crowninshield as provost-marshal, reported about 13,000 Confederate prisoners received by him from August 1st, 1864, to March 1st, 1865. This statement is denied by General Early, who says ("Memoir," p. 118): "My loss in killed, wounded, and prisoners, at Winchester and Fisher's Hill, had been less than 4000, and, at Cedar Creek, about 3000, but the enemy has attempted to magnify it to a much larger figure, claiming as prisoners several thousand more than my entire loss. How he makes out his estimate is not for me to explain. . . I know that a number of prisoners fell into the enemy's hands who did not belong to my command ; such as cavalrymen on details to get fresh horses, soldiers on leave of absence, conscripts on special details, citizens not in the service, men employed in getting supplies for the departments, and stragglers and deserters from other commands."

UNION BATTERY NEAR DUNN'S HOUSE PETERSBURG. FROM A WAR-TIME PHOTOGRAPH.

OPERATIONS SOUTH OF THE JAMES RIVER.

I. FIRST ATTEMPTS TO CAPTURE PETERSBURG. BY AUGUST V. KAUTZ, BREVET MAJOR-GENERAL, U. S. A.

THE Cavalry Division of the Army of the James was organized in the last days of April, 1864. Through the personal application of Lieutenant-General Grant I was selected and promoted to be Brigadier-General of Volunteers to organize and command it. I found the troops of which it was to be made up encamped in rear of Portsmouth, Va., picketing the line of the Blackwater River, on the 20th of April. As first organized it was arranged as follows: First Brigade, 3d New York, and 1st District of Columbia Cavalry, Colonel S. H. Mix commanding. Second Brigade, 11th and 5th Pennsylvania Cavalry, Colonel S. P. Spear commanding. A section of 3-inch rifles of the 4th

Wisconsin Battery was temporarily assigned. The division numbered less than 2800 men, all told.

When I reported to General Butler he informed me what he expected the division to do after it should be organized. Its task was to cut the Weldon Railroad, and this was to be done by crossing the Blackwater at Franklin, and proceeding direct to Hicksford and destroying the large bridge across the Meherrin River at that point; the object being to delay reënforcements from the south while the Army of the James was making a lodgment at Bermuda Hundred and City Point. While organizing the division I studied up the situation, and at the end of a week I reported to General Butler that I

Previous operations in south-eastern Virginia have been referred to by General Longstreet in Vol. III., p. 244, and in the foot-note, p. 265. General John J. Peck, whose division of the Fourth Army Corps (Keyes's) remained on the Peninsula when the Army of the Potomac was withdrawn (see p. 438, Vol. II.), and who took command at Suffolk soon after, gives the following account of events on the Nansemond and the Blackwater, between September, 1862, and May, 1863 [see map, p. 494]:

"On the 22d September, 1862, I was ordered to Suffolk, with about 9000 men, to repel the advance of Generals Pettigrew and French from the Blackwater with 15,000 [5000] men. . . . Situated at the head of the Nansemond River, with the railway to Petersburg and Weldon, Suffolk is the key to all the approaches to the mouth of the James River on the north of the Dismal Swamp. Regarding the James as second only in importance to the Mississippi for the Confederates, . . . I prepared a system, and on the 25th commenced Fort Dix. . . . My labors alarmed the authorities at Richmond, who believed I was preparing a base for a grand movement upon the rebel capital, and the whole of the Blackwater was fortified, as well as Cypress Swamp and Birchen and Chipoak rivers. This line rests upon the James, near Fort Powhatan. About the 26th of February Lieutenant-General Longstreet was detached from Lee's army, and placed in command of the Department of Virginia [and North Carolina], with headquarters at Petersburg; of his corps 15,000 [12,000] were on the Blackwater, and 15,000 [12,000] between Petersburg and the river, near the railway. This distribution enabled him to concentrate in twenty-four hours within a few miles of Suffolk. . . . Early in April deserters reported troops moving to the Blackwater; that many bridges were being constructed; and that a pontoon-train had arrived from Petersburg."

On the 17th of April, 1863, Longstreet wrote to the Secretary of War regarding his operations on the Blackwater as follows:

"I am very well convinced that we could reduce it [Suffolk] in two or three days, but doubt if we can afford to expend the powder and ball. To take it by assault would cost us three thousand men. . . The principal object of the expedition was to draw out supplies for our army. I shall confine myself to this unless I find a fair opportunity for something more."

On the 30th of April Longstreet was ordered to rejoin Lee with his command, and on the 4th of May he withdrew his whole force across the Blackwater. There is no report by General Longstreet on file. General John A. Dix, commanding the Department of Virginia, which included General Peck's command, reported to General Halleck on the 23d of May:

"On April 11th the enemy suddenly advanced with a large force commanded by Lieutenant-General Longstreet, which had been quietly assembled on the Blackwater, intending to take Suffolk by assault; but finding the place well prepared for defense, after repeated unsuccessful attempts on our lines, in all of which he was signally repulsed, he sat down before it and commenced an investment according to the most improved principles of military science."

The chief engagements during the siege were an attack, April 14th, by the Confederate land batteries on the gun-boats in the Nansemond, and the capture, April 19th, of Battery Huger, at the mouth of the West Branch, by a combined force from the Union army and navy, under General George W. Getty and Lieutenant R. H. Lamson, commanding the flotilla in the upper Nansemond. The force under General Longstreet at the time of the closest investment numbered 20,000. March 31st, General Peck had 15,000, and April 30th nearly 25,000.— EDITORS.

did not consider the task laid out a feasible one with the means at my command. The reasons I advanced were considered good, and the duty then assigned to us was to destroy the bridges across Stony Creek and the Nottoway River, which I thought we could do by rapid marching, and by heading the Blackwater.

The command moved on the 5th of May, and on the afternoon of the 7th reached Stony Creek Station and captured the guard, of about fifty men

MAJOR-GENERAL M. C. BUTLER, C. S. A.
FROM A PHOTOGRAPH.

of the Holcombe Legion, under Major M. G. Zeigler, and the same evening destroyed the bridge, station, water-tank, railroad buildings and cars, and a large amount of railroad material, as well as a good portion of the track. On the 8th the bridge across the Nottoway was burned, and also Jarrett's Station and water-tank, and the track was torn up between Jarrett's and the bridge. The bridge was fortified and had a strong guard, under Colonel W. B. Tabb of the 59th Virginia, which might have prevented us from burning the bridge. The division reached City Point on the 10th, with about 130 prisoners, having seriously impeded the movement of the Confederate reënforcements moving north under General Beauregard.

On the 11th the division crossed to Bermuda Hundred, and on the 12th moved out under cover of the advance of the Army of the James on Drewry's Bluff, and the same night reached Coalfield and destroyed the station and railroad property and tore up the track, thus cutting the Danville road ten miles from Richmond. On the 12th we moved to Powhatan Station, and burnt it and a

train loaded with bacon and forage. Mattoax bridge, across the Appomattox, we found fortified and too strongly guarded to justify an attempt to capture it, and the march was continued to Chula Station. During the night of the 13th we destroyed it and tore up a portion of the track. On the 14th we crossed over to the Petersburg and Lynchburg Railroad, and destroyed the stations of Wilson's, Blacks and Whites, and Wellville, and tore up more or less of the track. On the 15th and 16th we marched upon Hicksford and threatened that point, but found it too strongly fortified and guarded; but the concentration at that point enabled us to pass without molestation at Jarrett's, where we found a new water-tank, replacing the one destroyed a week before, and which, in turn, we destroyed. The division reached City Point again on the 17th, with about fifty prisoners, all very much worn and fatigued. We had marched from forty to fifty miles daily for about two weeks, and heavy rains during the last week had greatly embarrassed the command. The loss of the division during this time was, as officially reported, 14 killed, 60 wounded, and 27 missing. The moral effect on the enemy of having all the railroads from the south into Richmond interrupted at one time, was, perhaps, the principal justification for the extraordinary exertion and expense incurred.

On the night of the 8th of June, General Butler having perfected a plan for the capture of Petersburg, the cavalry moved in conjunction with a brigade of white troops under Colonel J. R. Hawley and a part of Hinks's colored division; the whole commanded by General Gillmore. [See p. 148.] The infantry was expected to threaten Petersburg from the City Point road, while the cavalry made a detour to the Jerusalem plank-road, where the enemy's line was believed to be weak. It was agreed that if the cavalry carried this line, General Gillmore was to assault the line in his front. The distance the cavalry had to march took up more time than was anticipated, and the line was not carried until just before noon of the 9th, and General Gillmore, having exhausted his patience, was far on his way back to City Point at that time. ‡ The line, where the Jerusalem road entered it, was held by about two hundred Second Class militia, and was easily carried, and had the infantry been at hand to support the cavalry Petersburg could have been taken and held at this time. The Cavalry Division, however, had only about thirteen hundred serviceable men on this occasion, and could not hold the advantage gained without sufficient infantry support. The advance penetrated to the water-works, where it was confronted by a battery in position, and the rear of the cavalry was threatened by the enemy holding the line on the City Point front, and was therefore compelled to retire with the captured prisoners, and returned to Bermuda Hundred, where we arrived after dark. Shortly after this affair General Gillmore was relieved from the command of the Tenth Corps.

‡ General A. A. Humphreys, in "The Virginia Campaign of '64 and '65," page 197, says that General Kautz attacked the intrenchments at half-past eleven, and that at half-past one General Gillmore, "receiv-

ing no communication from General Kautz during the day," withdrew from the front of the intrenchments and began his return march to City Point at 3 o'clock.— EDITORS.

On the 15th of June, the Eighteenth Corps under General W. F. Smith having rejoined Butler, after its detachment to Cold Harbor, another effort was made to take Petersburg, with this difference in the plan, that while the cavalry should distract the enemy as much as possible in the direction of the Jerusalem plank-road, the Eighteenth Corps was to carry the line on the City Point side. The cavalry, having driven in the enemy's pickets on the City Point road, moved to the left and was engaged the entire day exposed mainly to artillery fire, without any apparent action on the part of the Eighteenth Corps. We believed ourselves again deserted, and at seven in the evening the cavalry was withdrawn, and the column was just fairly on the return when the noise of the assault so long expected broke upon us about four miles to our right. It was all over in a few moments, and, as we subsequently learned, General Smith had carried the entire line in his front. The Army of the Potomac began to arrive on the night of the 15th, and was on hand to support the Eighteenth Corps in the position it had captured.

On the 20th I received orders to report to General James H. Wilson for the purpose of coöperating in his raid against the Danville Railroad. At 2 o'clock on the morning of the 22d the Cavalry Division of the Army of the James took the advance, with orders to proceed, via Reams's Station on the Weldon Railroad, to Sutherland's Station on the South-side Railroad. Reams's Station was captured at 7 in the morning, but General W. H. F. Lee with the Confederate cavalry was found to be encamped on our route to Sutherland's, and that route involved a battle that might have been fatal to the object of the expedition even if Lee had been beaten. The head of the column was therefore directed south, as if the Weldon road were the object of the expedition. We marched eight miles south, and then turned west to Dinwiddie Court House, and

then north through Five Forks, and evening found us on the South-side road between Sutherland's and Ford's stations with the enemy's cavalry in front. This was the initial success of the raid, for it enabled us to get inside of the enemy's line and to accomplish the object of the expedition. A battle might, and probably would, have caused our immediate return. The Cavalry Division of the Army of the James remained on the advance, down the Richmond and Danville Railroad, which was destroyed for a distance of thirty miles. When the command started on the return, the division brought up the rear until the advance was confronted by the enemy's forces at Stony Creek, when it took the advance to Reams's Station, where, also, it was confronted by the enemy on the morning of the 29th. By noon it was becoming evident that we were being surrounded, and General Wilson decided to retreat the way we came, and I was directed by him to bring up the rear with my division. Before my command could get on the road Wilson's lines were broken by two brigades of Hampton's cavalry under General M. C. Butler, and I decided to retreat on a different line with my command. Keeping in the timbered region to the south-east, we were soon out of the enemy's range, and then changed direction to the north-east, and by 9 P. M. went into camp within the lines of the Army of the Potomac. General Wilson retreated by Jarrett's Station and came in at Cabin Point on the James, several days after. The successful destruction of the Danville road was quite equaled by our retreat after being almost completely surrounded. The loss of the division in this remarkable raid was about five hundred in killed, wounded, and missing, quite one-fourth of the command. The official table prepared in the War Department shows the loss of the division from June 15th to 30th, inclusive, to have been 48 killed, 153 wounded, and 429 captured or missing = 630. ↓

II. REPELLING THE FIRST ASSAULT ON PETERSBURG.   BY R. E. COLSTON, BRIGADIER-GENERAL, C. S. A.

At the end of April, 1864, I was transferred from the Department of Georgia to that of Virginia and was assigned by General H. A. Wise to the provisional command of the post of Petersburg, which I had already held from January to March, 1863. General Wise returned to Petersburg about June 1st, and I remained there while waiting for another assignment.

At that time the lines covering Petersburg on the south side of the Appomattox formed a semi-circle of about eight miles development, resting upon the river at each extremity. With the exception of a few lunettes and redoubts at the most commanding positions, they were barely marked out, and a horseman could ride over them without the least difficulty almost everywhere, as I

myself had done day after day for weeks just before the fight. They differed *in toto* from the shortened and formidable works constructed later by General Lee's army.

On the 9th of June the lines were entirely stripped of regular troops, with the exception of Wise's brigade on our extreme left, and of Sturdivant's battery of four guns. Every other regiment had been ordered across the James to aid General Lee on the north side. A few skeleton companies of home guards (less than 150 men) occupied the redoubts half a mile from the river on the left, which were armed with heavy artillery. Then came a gap of a mile and a half to lunette 16, occupied by 30 home guards with 4 pieces of stationary artillery. One mile farther to the

↓ In his official report of the operations of June 28th and 29th General Wade Hampton says:

"The pursuit of the enemy, which ended near Peters's bridge, closed the active operations which began on June 8th, when the movement against Sheridan [see p. 233] commenced. During that time, a period of twenty-two days, the command had no rest, was badly supplied with rations and

forage, marched upward of four hundred miles, fought the greater portion of six days and one entire night, captured upward of 2000 prisoners, many guns, small-arms, wagons, horses, and other materials of war, and was completely successful in defeating two of the most formidable and well-organized expeditions of the enemy. This was accomplished at a cost in my division of 719 killed, wounded, and missing. . . ."   EDITORS.

right were two howitzers of Sturdivant's battery; one mile farther still were lunettes 26, 27, and 28, at the intersection of the lines with the Jerusalem road; but neither there nor for four miles more to the river on our right was there a man or gun.

During the night of June 8th-9th General Kautz and Colonel Spear, with four regiments of cavalry and 4 pieces of artillery, crossed the Appomattox on a pontoon-bridge, about 7 miles below Petersburg, and on the morning of the 9th they made their appearance in front of the left of our lines, while the Federal gun-boats opened a heavy fire upon Fort Clifton and other positions on the river. The alarm-bell was rung in the city about 9 o'clock, and every man able to shoulder a musket hurried out to the lines. Colonel F. H. Archer, a veteran of the Mexican war, who had commanded a Confederate battalion in my brigade in 1862, but now commanding the Home Guards, hastened to take position at lunettes Nos. 27 and 28 on the Jerusalem road with 125 men. This force was composed of Second Class Reserves, men exempted from active service on account of age or infirmities, and boys under conscription age, who had had no military training. Very few of them wore a uniform, and they were armed with inferior muskets and rifles, for all the best arms had to be reserved for troops in the field.

At the first sound of alarm I mounted my horse, hastened to report to General Wise and to offer my services. He thanked me warmly, saying that he was just going across the river to bring back his brigade as promptly as possible, together with other reënforcements, and directed me to take command of all the forces in the lines and use them according to my judgment, with only one specific order, viz., that lunette No. 16 must be held at any hazard. He added as he turned his horse's head: "For God's sake, General, hold out till I come back, or all is lost!"

At lunette No. 16 I found the men at their guns, but the enemy were not yet in sight. They had reconnoitered from a distance the positions on our left; seeing heavy guns on the works, and not aware of the very small number of the defenders, they had continued their reconnoissance toward the right, nearly hidden from our view by the wooded and undulating character of the ground. We had no scouts or mounted men to send out for information. I had been at lunette 16 about an hour, and it was nearly 11 o'clock, when a courier arrived from Petersburg with a note from General Wise, saying that the enemy were advancing by the Jerusalem road upon Colonel Archer's position, and that reënforcements were on the way. I left my aide, Lieutenant J. T. Tosh, in command at lunette 16, with orders not to leave that position until relieved. I galloped on alone toward the Jerusalem road, and when half-way there I heard the rattle of musketry from that point. Being just then at the position of Sturdivant's section, I ordered the sergeant to bring on one of his howitzers to lunette 28, and hastened toward it, catching glimpses of Federal cavalry still moving to our right, parallel to our intrenchments. Arrived at lunettes 27 and 28 I found that Colonel Archer had disposed his

small force very judiciously in the low trenches. A wagon had been overturned across the road and, together with a hastily built rail-fence, formed a pretty good barricade. A detachment of Federal cavalry had just made a spirited charge and been checked by this obstruction and by the scattering fire of the militia. Several dead horses, some sabers and carbines, and a couple of prisoners were the tokens of the repulse, and the men were in high spirits at their success in this their first fight. It was evident, however, that the enemy had only been feeling the position and were preparing for a more serious attack. Their line was visible on the edge of the woods back of the Gregory house, and our slender ranks were extended to the right and left to present an equal front. In a few minutes the howitzer that I had ordered up came in sight and was welcomed with cheers by our men. I placed it in lunette 28, and took my position in the trenches, which did not cover us more than waist-high.

Very soon an advance was made by the enemy's dismounted skirmishers, while a mounted line in close order appeared behind the Gregory house. I impressed upon the men the necessity of holding their fire until the enemy were at close range, and this direction was well observed. But the howitzer opened fire and the Federal skirmishers fell back under cover and commenced a continuous fire of small-arms. A number of their men had taken position in the Gregory house and were shooting, some from the windows and others from the garret, and firing through openings made by knocking off the shingles. I directed the artillery sergeant to send a few shells at the house to dislodge them, but the distance was so short that the shells passed through the building before exploding, and failed to set it on fire as I had hoped. Meanwhile the mounted line, some three hundred yards back, presented a tempting mark and I told the sergeant to give them canister. To my intense vexation he replied that he had not a single charge of canister with his piece. I then directed him to shell the mounted line, but several shells passed over the line and burst harmlessly beyond it. I now ordered him to cut the fuse at the closest notch, and, pointing the piece myself very low, I had the satisfaction of seeing the shell explode just in front of the line of cavalry and make a great gap in its ranks, causing its immediate retreat.

All this time the bullets were flying uncomfortably thick and close, but I saw no signal of another advance. Meanwhile our men, closely hugging the low breastworks and holding back their fire, were suffering no harm. In about half an hour a cannon shot was fired at us, then another, followed by others in quick succession. The enemy had paused while waiting for the arrival of their battery. So far from being dismayed, the brave civilians around me, with Colonel Archer at their head, offered to charge the battery, but I knew that the moment they left the cover of the trenches to cross the open ground they would be destroyed by the breech-loading carbines of the dismounted men supporting the battery and far overlapping our front. Our only hope was in delay. I called for a volunteer

RESERVOIR HILL, WHERE KAUTZ'S ADVANCE WAS STOPPED, JUNE 9, 1864. FROM A PHOTOGRAPH MADE IN 1886.

The spires of Petersburg are seen to the left of the reservoir. In front of the reservoir is the ravine of Lieutenant's Creek that encircles the eastern outskirts of the city and afforded the Confederates a concealed and convenient way by which either wing of their lines could be reënforced by troops from the other.

to mount my horse, find General Wise, and let him know that we could hold out but a very short time longer. A lieutenant of the Junior Reserves, Wales Hurt, a youth of eighteen, promptly offered to go, and I watched him galloping away until hidden from view by the bend of the road, while the bullets were knocking up the dust all around him and under his horse's feet.

By this time our ability to retain the position was a question of minutes only, but on these few minutes hung the rescue or the capture of the city. I knew that if we were driven in before a sufficient Confederate force recrossed the Appomattox the enemy would at once ride into the town and burn the bridges, after which they would have no difficulty in holding the place until their infantry came up, and then all of General Lee's army would be unable to force a recrossing. With the town would be lost the main lines of railway upon which our army depended almost entirely for its supplies.

But the end was very near. The enemy, sheltered by the Gregory house and the defective construction of our works, which allowed approach under cover to within fifty yards, redoubled the fire of their skirmishers and artillery; while a line in open order, overlapping both our flanks, advanced, firing rapidly. The brave militia discharged their pieces at close range. Numbers of them fell killed or wounded, and before the survivors could reload the enemy turned our left flank and more of our men fell by bullets that struck us in the rear from lunette No. 26, which we had not had men enough to occupy. Yet those heroic citizens held their ground. In the heat of the fight I picked up and discharged at the enemy two or three of the muskets dropped by our fallen men. We were now hemmed in on three sides, and only a narrow path leading through an abrupt ravine offered a way of escape. The howitzer, which continued its fire to the last, was captured while limbering up, the horses being shot in their

traces, and two artillerymen killed. Some of the militia were killed or wounded with the bayonet or carbine butts, and many were captured. Our shattered remnants made their way down and across the ravine and re-formed at my command on Reservoir Hill, in order, if needed, to support Graham's battery, which had just arrived and unlimbered on the top of the hill. ♩

After driving us from the trenches the enemy paused awhile to call in their dismounted men and to send to their rear our wounded and prisoners. They then formed in mounted column, with a few files thrown forward in open order. They advanced upon the main road, evidently expecting to enter the city without further opposition. ♯

The moments gained at such fearful cost barely gave time for Graham's battery to cross the bridge. They came up Sycamore street at full gallop and unlimbered on the summit of Reservoir Hill just as the head of the Federal column was coming down the opposite slope into the hollow. The battery opened fire, and with rapidity and precision hurled a storm of shell and canister upon the approaching cavalry. The enemy, who thought themselves already in possession of the city, halted in surprise. But just at this moment, while they were yet hesitating, Dearing's cavalry, which had followed after Graham's battery, charged upon Kautz's and Spear's column with irresistible impetuosity. The latter wheeled about, but re-formed on the top of the next hill and gallantly endeavored to make a stand there, being joined by another column advancing upon the Blandford road. But this also was checked by a section of Sturdivant's battery, which came on their flank from another road. Under the fire of artillery and the charge of Dearing's cavalry the enemy retreated. In Jackson's field, about a mile beyond Blandford church, our cavalry captured a howitzer, complete, with its team, and in the subsequent pursuit killed or captured a number of the enemy.

♩ The loss of the militia in this conflict was 12 killed (not counting the 2 artillerymen), 20 wounded, and 30 prisoners,—62 out of 125.—R. E. C.

♯ Lieutenant Hurt had delivered his message and was returning at this time by the same road. Coming suddenly upon the leading Federal files he was shot dead.—R. E. C.

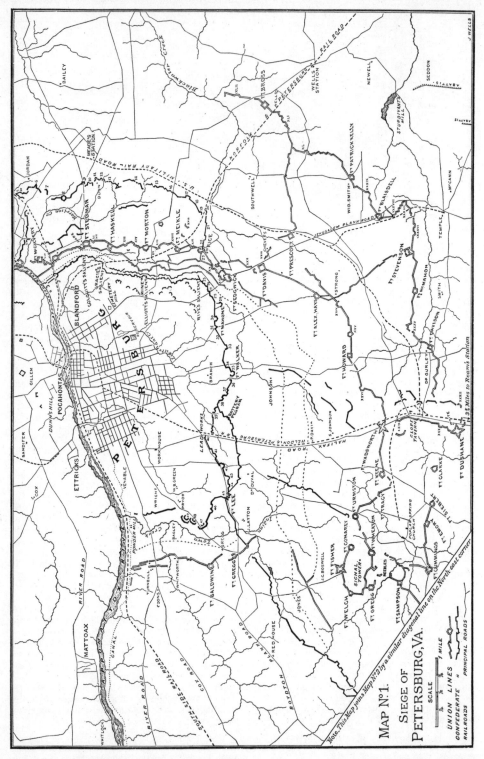

MAP Nº1.
SIEGE OF
PETERSBURG, VA.

SCALE
½   ¼   0   1 MILE

UNION LINES
CONFEDERATE   "
RAILROADS   PRINCIPAL ROADS

Note. This Map joins Map Nº2 by a similar diagonal line on the North east corner.

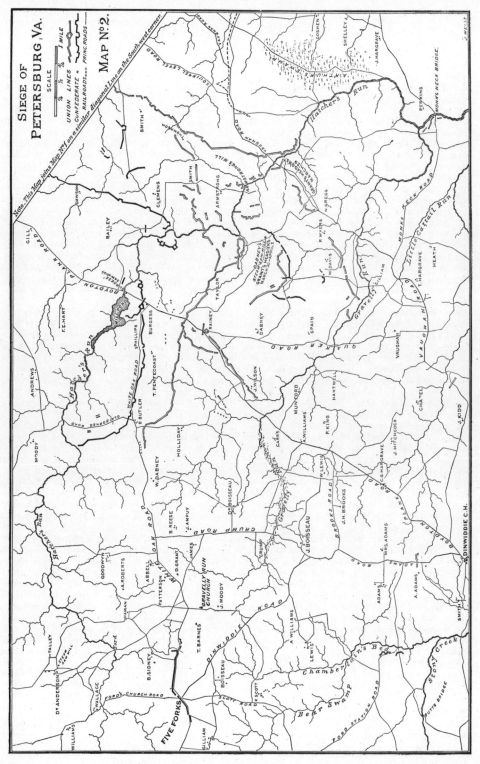

SIEGE OF
PETERSBURG, VA.

SCALE
¼   ½   ¾   1 MILE

UNION LINES ━━━
CONFEDERATE " ━━━
RAILROADS ┅┅┅
PRINC. ROADS ━━━

MAP Nº 2.

Note.—This Map joins Map Nº1 on a similar diagonal Line on the South-west corner.

FOUR DAYS OF BATTLE AT PETERSBURG. ⌡

BY G. T. BEAUREGARD, GENERAL, C. S. A.

THE movement of the Army of the Potomac to the south side of the James ⌡⚓ began on the evening of the 12th of June, and Smith's corps (the Eighteenth) was at Bermuda Hundred in the early afternoon of the 14th. From Point of Rocks it crossed the river that night and was pushed forward without delay against Petersburg. Kautz's cavalry and Hinks's command of colored troops had been added to it. ⌡

It was with a view to thwart General Grant in the execution of such a plan that I proposed to the War Department [June 9th] the adoption — should the emergency justify it, and I thought it did — of the bold and, to me, safer plan of concentrating all the forces we could readily dispose of to give battle to Grant, and thus decide at once the fate of Richmond and of the cause we were fighting for, while we still possessed a comparatively compact, well-disciplined, and enthusiastic army in the field.

From Swift Creek, early on June 14th, I telegraphed to General Bragg: "Movement of Grant's across Chickahominy and increase of Butler's force render my position here critical. With my present forces I cannot answer for consequences. Cannot my troops sent to General Lee be returned at once? . . ." No answer came. Late in the evening of the same day, having further reason to believe that one corps at least of General Grant's army was already within Butler's lines, I telegraphed to General Lee: "A deserter from the enemy reports that Butler has been reënforced by the Eighteenth and a part of the Tenth Army Corps." To this dispatch, likewise, there came no response. But, as prompt and energetic action became more and more imperative, and as I could no longer doubt the presence of Smith's corps with Butler's forces, I sent one of my aides, Colonel Samuel B. Paul, to General Lee with instructions to explain to him the exact situation. General Lee's answer to Colonel Paul was not encouraging. He said that I must be in error in believing the enemy had thrown a large force on the south side of the James; that the troops referred to by me could be but a few of Smith's corps going back to Butler's lines. Strange to say, at the very time General Lee was thus expressing himself to Colonel Paul, the whole of Smith's corps was actually assaulting the Petersburg lines. But General Lee finally said that he had already issued orders for the return of Hoke's division; that he would do all he could to aid me, and even come himself should the necessity arise.

The Confederate forces opposed to Smith's corps on the 15th of June consisted of the 26th, 34th, and 46th Virginia regiments, the 64th Georgia, the 23d South Carolina, Archer's militia, Battle's and Wood's battalions, Sturdivant's battery, Dear-

ing's small command of cavalry, and some other transient forces, having a real effective for duty of 2200 only. These troops occupied the Petersburg line on the left from Battery No. 1 to what was called Butterworth's Bridge, toward the right, and had to be so stationed as to allow but one man for every 4½ yards. From that bridge to the Appomattox — a distance of fully 4½ miles — the line was defenseless.

Early in the morning — at about 7 o'clock — General Dearing, on the Broadway and City Point roads, reported his regiment engaged with a large force of the enemy. The stand made by our handful of cavalry, near their breastworks, was most creditable to themselves and to their gallant commander, and the enemy's ranks, at that point, were much thinned by the accurate firing of the battery under Graham. But the weight of numbers soon produced its almost inevitable result, and, in spite of the desperate efforts of our men, the cavalry breastworks were flanked and finally abandoned by us, with the loss of one howitzer. Still, Dearing's encounter with the enemy, at that moment and on that part of the field, was of incalculable advantage to the defenders of our line, inasmuch as it afforded time for additional preparation and the distribution of new orders by Wise.

At 10 o'clock A. M. the skirmishing had assumed very alarming proportions. To the urgent demands of General Wise for reënforcements, I was enabled at last to answer that part of Hoke's division was on the way from Drewry's Bluff and would be in time to save the day, if our men could stand their ordeal, hard as it was, a little while longer. Then all along the line, from one end to the other, the order was given "to hold on at all hazards!" It was obeyed with the resolute fortitude of veterans, though many of the troops thus engaged, with such odds against them, had hardly been under fire before. At 12 M., and as late as 2 P. M., our center was vigorously pressed, as though the Norfolk and Petersburg Railroad were the immediate object of the onset. General Wise now closed the line from his right to strengthen Colonel J. T. Goode and, with him, the 34th Virginia; while, at the same time and with equal perspicacity, he hurried Wood's battalion toward the left in support of Colonel P. R. Page and his command.

The enemy, continuing to mass his columns toward the center of our line, pressed it more and more and concentrated his heaviest assaults upon Batteries Nos. 5, 6, and 7. Thinned out and exhausted as they were, General Wise's heroic forces resisted still, with such unflinching stubbornness as to equal the veterans of the Army of Northern Virginia. I was then on the field and only left it when darkness set in. Shortly after 7 P. M. the

---

⌡ Taken by permission from the "North American Review" for December, 1887, and condensed.

⚓ For the particulars of the previous attempt on Petersburg, see the article by General Beauregard, p. 195, and that by General William F. Smith, p. 206.— EDITORS.

⌡ The Ninth Corps (Burnside's) and the Sixth (Wright's) moved by way of Jones's Bridge and Charles City Court House road. The Second Corps (Hancock's) and the Fifth (Warren's) were marched from Long Bridge to Wilcox's Landing.— G. T. B.

enemy entered a ravine between Batteries 6 and 7, and succeeded in flanking Battery No. 5. ♭

But just then very opportunely appeared, advancing at double-quick, Hagood's gallant South Carolina brigade, followed soon afterward by Colquitt's, Clingman's, and, in fact, by the whole of Hoke's division. They were shown their positions, on a new line selected at that very time by my orders, a short distance in the rear of the captured works, and were kept busy the greatest part of the night throwing up a small epaulement for their additional protection.

Strange to say, General Smith contented himself with breaking into our lines, and attempted nothing further that night. All the more strange was this inaction on his part, since General Hancock, with his strong and well-equipped Second Army Corps, had also been hurried to Petersburg, and was actually there, or in the immediate vicinity of the town, on the evening of the 15th. He had informed General Smith of the arrival of his command and of the readiness of two of his divisions — Birney's and Gibbon's — to give him whatever assistance he might require. Petersburg at that hour was clearly at the mercy of the Federal commander, who had all but captured it, and only failed of final success because he could not realize the fact of the unparalleled disparity between the two contending forces. Although the result of the fighting of the 15th had demonstrated that 2200 Confederates successfully withheld nearly a whole day the repeated assaults of at least 18,000 Federals,⸮ it followed, none the less, that Hancock's corps, being now in our front, with fully 28,000 ☆ men,— which raised the enemy's force against Petersburg to a grand total of 46,000,↓— our chance of resistance, the next morning and in the course of the next day, even after the advent of Hoke's division, was by far too uncertain to be counted on, unless strong additional reënforcements could reach us in time.

Without awaiting an answer from the authorities at Richmond to my urgent representations, I ordered General Bushrod R. Johnson to evacuate the lines in front of Bermuda Hundred at the dawn of day on the 16th, leaving pickets and skirmishers to cover the movement until daylight, or later if necessary, and to march as rapidly as possible with his entire force to the assistance of Petersburg. The emergency justified this action. I had previously [1:45 P. M.] communicated with General Bragg

upon this point, and had asked the War Department to elect between the Bermuda Hundred line and Petersburg, as, under the present circumstances, I could no longer hold both. The War Department had given me no answer, clearly intending that I should assume the responsibility of the measure, which I did. Scarcely two hours after Johnson's division had abandoned its position at Bermuda Hundred, Butler's forces drove off the Confederate pickets left there, as already stated, and took full possession of the lines. ⚓

By the 16th of June three Federal corps,— Smith's, Hancock's, and Burnside's,— aggregating about 66,000↓ men, confronted our lines. Opposed to them I had, after the arrival of Johnson's division, about 10 A. M., an effective of not more than 10,000 men of all arms.

Through a sense of duty I addressed the following telegram, June 16th, 7:45 A. M., to General Lee: "Prisoner captured this A. M. reports that he belongs to Hancock's corps (Second), and that it crossed day before yesterday and last night from Harrison's Landing. Could we not have more reenforcements here?"

No direct answer was received to the above. But in reply to another dispatch of mine, June 16th, 4 P. M., relative to tugs and transports of the enemy reported to have been seen that day by Major Terrett, General Lee sent this message: "The transports you mention have probably returned Butler's troops. Has Grant been seen crossing James River?" This shows that Lee was still uncertain as to his adversary's movements, and, notwithstanding the information already furnished him, could not realize that the Federals had crossed the James, and that three of their corps were actually assaulting the Petersburg lines.

General Hancock, the ranking Federal officer present, had been instructed by General Meade not to begin operations before the arrival of Burnside's command. Hence the tardiness of the enemy's attack, which was not made till after 5 o'clock P. M., though Burnside had reached Petersburg, according to his own report, at 10 o'clock A. M.

The engagement lasted fully three hours, much vigor being displayed by the Federals, while the Confederates confronted them with fortitude, knowing that they were fighting against overwhelming odds, constantly increasing. Birney's division of Hancock's corps finally broke into part of our line and effected a lodgment. The

♭ Gen. Wise, in his report, says : "The line then broke, from No. 3 to No. 11 inclusive. The whole line on the right was then ordered to close to the left, up to Battery No. 14; Batteries 1 and 2 being still ours. The 59th Virginia, arriving at that time, was sent on the City Point road toward Battery No. 2, to arrest the retreat of the line on the left."— G. T. B.

⸮ If the strength of Smith's corps as given by General Badeau (Vol. II., Chap. xx., p. 354) be the correct one, and not my own computation of 22,000.— G. T. B. [More probably 18,000.— EDITORS.]

☆ A later estimate (1888), based on official returns, places Hancock's corps at 20,000.— EDITORS.

↓ More probably 38,000.— EDITORS.

⚓ It is clear, from the preceding narrative, that no troops from General Lee's army were at Petersburg on the 15th of June, despite the assertions of a few writers

to that effect, among whom, strange to say, is Mr. Davis himself. It is true that Hoke's division had been sent from Drewry's Bluff at that date, and had arrived late in the evening and been placed in position on our new line, a fact which had given a feeling of unequivocal relief to all who had seen or taken part in the unequal contest of that memorable day. But Hoke's division, composed then of Colquitt's, Hagood's, and Clingman's brigades, with the addition later on of Martin's, had never belonged to the Army of Northern Virginia, though sent temporarily to reënforce it after the battle of Drewry's Bluff, on the 16th and 17th of May. They formed part of my new command, as did also Bushrod R. Johnson's division, including Matthew W. Ransom's brigade, transferred north of the James River on or about the 4th of June.— G. T. B.

↓ Later compilation makes the total more probably 53,000.— EDITORS.

COLQUITT'S SALIENT.

GRACIE'S SALIENT.

THE RAILWAY CULVERT BECAME A UNION PICKET POST.

VIEW OF THE CONFEDERATE LINE TAKEN UP BY GENERAL BEAUREGARD, JUNE 18. FROM A POINT ON THE UNION PICKET LINE TO THE FRONT AND LEFT OF FORT HASKELL. [SEE MAP, P. 538.] FROM A SKETCH MADE IN 1886.

contest, with varying results, was carried on until after nightfall, with advantage to us on the left and some serious loss on the right. It then slackened and gradually came to an end. In the meantime Warren's corps, the Fifth, had also come up, but too late to take a part in the action of the day. Its presence before our lines swelled the enemy's aggregate to about 90,000,[>] against which stood a barrier of not even 10,000 exhausted, half-starved men, who had gone through two days of constant hard fighting and many sleepless nights in the trenches.

Hostilities began early on the 17th. I here quote from "Military Operations of General Beauregard," Vol. II., p. 232:

"Three times were the Federals driven back, but they as often resumed the offensive and held their ground. About dusk a portion of the Confederate lines was wholly broken and the troops in that quarter were about to be thrown into a panic, which might have ended in irreparable disaster, when happily, as General Beauregard, with his staff, was endeavoring to rally and re-form the troops, Gracie's brigade, of Johnson's division, consisting of about twelve hundred men,— the return of which to his command General Beauregard had been urgently asking,— came up from Chaffin's Bluff, whence, at last, the War Department had ordered it to move. It was promptly and opportunely thrown into the gap on the lines and drove back the Federals, capturing about two thousand prisoners. The conflict raged with great fury until after 11 o'clock at night."

Anticipating the inevitable result of such a pressure upon our weak defenses, and knowing that at any moment they might be irrevocably lost to us, I had — accompanied by Colonel D. B. Harris, of the Engineers — selected the site of another and shorter line, near Taylor's Creek, at a convenient distance toward the rear. I caused it to be carefully staked out during the battle, and shown to the adjutants, quartermasters, and other staff-officers of Hoke's and Johnson's divisions, and through them to all the available regimental adjutants on the field; so that each command, at the appointed hour, even at dead of night, might easily retire upon the new line with order and precision, and unperceived by the enemy. Meanwhile, the order to "hold on at any cost" remained unchanged all down the line. There was no reason to hope for assistance of any kind. The Army of Northern Virginia was yet far distant, and I had failed to convince its distinguished commander of the fact that I was then fighting Grant's whole army with less than eleven thousand men. On the 17th, from Clay's House, at 12 o'clock M., General Lee answered as follows one of my telegrams of that morning: "Telegram of 9 A. M. received. Until I can get more definite information of Grant's movements, I do not think it prudent to draw more troops to this side of the river." And, acting on the desire for additional information, at 3:30 P. M., on the same day, he telegraphed W. H. F. Lee, then at Malvern Hill, as follows: "Push after the enemy, and endeavor to ascertain what has become of Grant's army." Later on — *i. e.*, at 4:30 P. M., on the same day — he sent this message to A. P. Hill, at Riddle's shop: "General Beauregard reports large numbers of Grant's troops crossed James River, above Fort Powhatan, yesterday. If you have nothing contradictory of this, move to Chaffin's Bluff." Just at that time, however [5 P. M.], I sent another telegram to General Lee, reiterating my former assertions, with the addition of other particulars:

"Prisoners just taken represent themselves as belonging to Second, Ninth, and Eighteenth corps. They state that Fifth and Sixth corps are behind coming on. Those from Second and Eight-

[>] A careful reckoning, based on official data, makes this aggregate 67,000.— EDITORS.

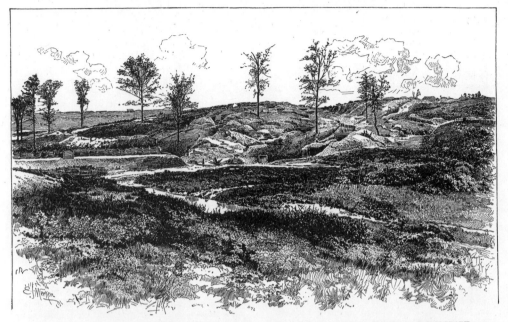

INTERIOR VIEW OF THE CONFEDERATE LINES AT GRACIE'S SALIENT. FROM A WAR-TIME PHOTOGRAPH.

eenth came here yesterday, and arrived first. Others marched night and day from Gaines's Mill, and arrived yesterday evening. The Ninth crossed at Turkey Bend, where they have a pontoon-bridge. They say Grant commanded on the field yesterday. All are positive that they passed him on the road seven miles from here."

The firing lasted, on the 17th, until a little after 11 o'clock P. M. Just before that time I had ordered all the camp-fires to be brightly lighted, with sentinels well thrown forward and as near as possible to the enemy's. Then, at about 12:30 A. M., on the 18th, began the retrograde movement, which, notwithstanding the exhaustion of our troops and their sore disappointment at receiving no further reënforcements, was safely and silently executed, with uncommonly good order and precision, though the greatest caution had to be used in order to retire unnoticed from so close a contact with so strong an adversary.

The digging of trenches was begun by the men as soon as they reached their new position. Axes, as well as spades; bayonets and knives, as well as axes,—in fact, every utensil that could be found,— were used. And when all was over, or nearly so, with much anxiety still, but with comparative relief, nevertheless, I hurried off this telegram to General Lee [18th, 12:40 A. M.]: "All quiet at present. I expect renewal of attack in morning. My troops are becoming much exhausted. Without immediate and strong reënforcements, results may be unfavorable. Prisoners report Grant on the field with his whole army."

But General Lee, although not wholly convinced even at that hour that the Army of the Potomac was already on the south side of the James, long before the dawn of day, on the 18th, and immedi-

ately after his conference with Major Cooke, sent me this message: "Am not yet satisfied as to General Grant's movements; but upon your representations will move at once to Petersburg." And, in fact, even previous to that hour, on the same night, he had concluded to send Kershaw's division to my assistance. The next step taken by General Lee was to endeavor to procure sufficient means for the immediate transportation of his troops. The same morning he communicated with General Early [at Lynchburg], who had not yet returned from his Shenandoah campaign: "Strike as quick as you can, and, if circumstances authorize, carry out the original plan, or move upon Petersburg without delay." Late as had been the credence given by General Lee to my representations of Grant's movements, it was, fortunately, not yet too late, by prompt and energetic action, to save Petersburg—and, therefore, Richmond.

General Kershaw's division, which proved to be the vanguard of General Lee's army, reached Petersburg early Saturday morning, June 18th; it numbered about 5000 men, and, by my orders, was placed on the new line already occupied by our forces with its right on or near the Jerusalem plank-road, extending across the open field and bending back toward the front of the cemetery. Field's division, of about equal strength, came in some two hours after Kershaw's. It had not yet been assigned to its place on the line when Lee in person arrived at 11:30 o'clock A. M. on that day.

When, early in the morning, the enemy was pushed forward to make the "grand attack ordered for 4 A. M. on the 18th,"⸶ the retirement of our forces on the previous night from their first posi-

⸶ General Meade's report, dated November 1st, 1864.— G. T. B.

tions to the new line of defenses selected by me, as already explained, had so much surprised the assaulting columns as to induce their immediate commanders to additional prudence in their advance and to a complete halt in their operations.

On that morning the troops arrayed against us consisted of Hancock's, Burnside's, and Warren's corps, with the larger portion of Smith's under General Martindale, and finally Neill's division from Wright's corps (the Sixth), strengthened by its whole artillery. This gave the enemy an aggregate of over 90,000 effectives. We had on our side, after Kershaw's arrival, but 15,000 men, no deduction being made for the casualties of the three preceding days. It was only later on, somewhere between 12 M. and 1 P. M., that Field's command was put in position on the line, and from that moment to the end of the day our grand total amounted to about 20,000 men. At noon — or thereabout — the predetermined "grand attack" was renewed, although partial disconnected assaults had been made before that hour on several parts of our line, but with no tangible result of any kind. This renewed attack was mainly led by Gibbon's division of Hancock's corps. It proved to be entirely ineffectual. And still another grand attempt was made at 4 P. M., with at least three full Federal corps coöperating: Hancock's on the right, Burnside's in the center, and Warren's on the left. General Meade, in his report, says it was "without success." And he adds these words: "Later in the day attacks were made by the Fifth and Ninth corps with no better results." The truth is that, despite the overwhelming odds against us, every Federal assault, on the 18th, was met with most signal defeat, "attended," says Mr. Swinton, the Federal historian, "with another mournful loss of life." This was, in fact, very heavy, and exceeded ours in the proportion of nine to one. ☆

My welcome to General Lee was most cordial. He was at last where I had, for the past three days, so anxiously hoped to see him — within the limits of Petersburg! Two of his divisions had preceded him there, and his whole army would be in by evening of the next day, namely, the 19th of June. I felt sure, therefore, that, for the present at least, Petersburg and Richmond were safe. Not that our forces would be numerically equal to those of the enemy, even after the arrival of the last regiment of the Army of Northern Virginia; but I was aware that our defensive line would now count more than one man per every four and a half yards of its length; and I felt relieved to know that, at last, the whole of our line — not portions of it only, as heretofore — would be guarded by veteran troops, alike, if not superior, in mettle to the veteran troops opposing them.

Scarcely two hours after General Lee's arrival I rode with him to what was known as the City Reservoir, on a commanding elevation, toward the right of our line. A good view of the surrounding country could be had from this point, and the whole field was there spread out before us like a map. I explained to General Lee and showed him the relative positions of our troops and of those of the enemy. I also pointed out to him the new and shorter line then occupied by us, and gave my reasons for its location there. They were these:

"*First.* That it kept the enemy's batteries at a greater distance from the besieged town.

"*Second.* That it would act as a covered way (as the phrase is in the regular fortifications) should we deem it advisable to construct better works on the higher ground in the rear. In the meantime we could construct a series of batteries to protect our front line by flanking and over-shooting fires; and we could throw up infantry parapets for our reserves, whenever we should have additional troops.

"*Third.* That the new line gave a close infantry and artillery fire on the reverse slope of Taylor's Creek and ravine, which would prevent the construction of *boyaux* of approaches and parallels for a regular attack."

General Lee, whose capacity as a military engineer was universally acknowledged,— and none appreciated it more than I did,— was entirely of my opinion. Thus the new defensive line selected by me, which my own troops had been holding for twelve hours before the arrival of General Lee at Petersburg, and which his troops occupied as they came in, was maintained unchanged as to location — though much strengthened and improved thereafter — until the end of the war.

After those explanations to General Lee, and while still examining the field, I proposed to him that, as soon as Hill's and Anderson's corps should arrive, our entire disposable force be thrown upon the left and rear of the Federal army before it began to fortify its position. General Lee, after some hesitation, pronounced himself against this plan. He thought it was wiser, under the circumstances, to allow some rest to his troops (those present as well as those still coming up) after the long march all would have gone through with; and he stated as a further reason for his objection, that our best policy — one, he said, which had thus far proved successful to him — would be to maintain the defensive as heretofore. I urged that the Federal troops were at least as much exhausted as ours, and that their ignorance of the locality would give us a marked advantage over them; that their spirits were jaded, and ours brightened just then by the fact of the junction of his army with my forces; and that the enemy was not yet intrenched. But I was then only second in command, and my views did not prevail.

The evening of the 18th was quiet. There was no further attempt on the part of General Meade to assault our lines. He was "satisfied," as he said in his report, that there was "nothing more to be gained by direct attacks." The spade took the place of the musket, and the regular siege was begun. It was only raised April 2, 1865.

No event of our war was more remarkable than the almost incredible resistance of the men who served under me at Petersburg, on the 15th, 16th, 17th, and 18th of June, before the arrival of Lee.

☆ General Humphreys, in his "Virginia Campaign, 1864 and 1865," places the Union losses from the 15th to the 18th of June at 9964 killed, wounded, and missing. — EDITORS.

CRATER.

THE APPROACH TO THE CRATER AS SEEN FROM A POINT SOUTH-EAST OF THE MOUTH OF THE MINE.   FROM A SKETCH MADE IN 1886.

THE BATTLE OF THE PETERSBURG CRATER.

BY WILLIAM H. POWELL, MAJOR, U. S. A.

BY the assaults of June 17th and 18th, 1864, on the Confederate works at Petersburg, the Ninth Corps, under General Burnside, gained an advanced position beyond a deep cut in the railroad, within 130 yards of the enemy's main line and confronting a strong work called by the Confederates Elliott's Salient, and sometimes Pegram's Salient. In rear of that advanced position was a deep hollow. [See map, p. 538.] A few days after gaining this position Lieutenant-Colonel Henry Pleasants, who had been a mining engineer and who belonged to the 48th Pennsylvania Volunteers, composed for the most part of miners from the upper Schuylkill coal region, suggested to his division commander, General Robert B. Potter, the possibility of running a mine under one of the enemy's forts in front of the deep hollow. This proposition was submitted to General Burnside, who approved of the measure, and work was commenced on the 25th of June. If ever a man labored under disadvantages, that man was Colonel Pleasants. In his testimony before the Committee on the Conduct of the War, he said:

"My regiment was only about four hundred strong. At first I employed but a few men at a time, but the number was increased as the work progressed, until at last I had to use the whole regiment—non-commissioned officers and all. The great difficulty I had was to dispose of the material got out of the mine. I found it impossible to get any assistance from anybody; I had to do all the work myself. I had to remove all the earth in old cracker-boxes; I got pieces of hickory and nailed on the boxes in which we received our crackers, and then iron-clad them with hoops of iron taken from old pork and beef barrels. . . . Whenever I made application I could not get anything, although General Burnside was very favorable to it. The most important thing was to ascertain how far I had to mine, because if I fell short of or went beyond the proper place, the explosion would have no practical effect. Therefore I wanted an accurate instrument with which to make the necessary triangulations. I had to make them on the farthest front line, where the enemy's sharp-shooters could reach me. I could not get the instrument I wanted, although there was one at army headquarters, and General Burnside had to send to Washington and get an old-fashioned theodolite, which was given to me. . . . General Burnside told me that General Meade and Major Duane, chief engineer of the Army of the Potomac, said the thing could not be done—that it was all clap-trap and nonsense; that such a length of mine had never been excavated in military operations, and could not be; that I would either get the men smothered, for want of air, or crushed by the falling of the earth; or the enemy would find it out and it would amount to nothing. I could get no boards or lumber supplied to me for my operations. I had to get a pass and send two companies of my own regiment, with wagons, outside of our lines to rebel saw-mills, and get lumber in that way, after having previously got what lumber I could by tearing down an old bridge. I had no mining

CRATER.

I. PROFILE OF THE GROUND BETWEEN THE CRATER AND THE MOUTH OF THE MINE.

picks furnished me, but had to take common army picks and have them straightened for my mining picks. . . . The only officers of high rank, so far as I learned, that favored the enterprise were General Burnside, the corps commander, and General Potter, the division commander."

On the 23d of July Colonel Pleasants had the whole mine ready for the placing of the powder. With proper tools and instruments it could have been done in one-third or one-fourth of the time. The greatest delay was occasioned by taking out the material, which had to be carried the whole length of the gallery. Every night the pioneers of Colonel Pleasants's regiment had to cut bushes to cover the fresh dirt at the mouth of the gallery; otherwise the enemy could have observed it from trees inside his own lines.

The main gallery was $510\frac{8}{10}$ feet in length. The left lateral gallery was thirty-seven feet in length and the right lateral thirty-eight feet. The magazines, eight in number, were placed in the lateral galleries — two at each end a few feet apart in branches at nearly right angles to the side galleries, and two more in each of the side galleries similarly placed by pairs, situated equidistant from each other and the end of the galleries.

It had been the intention of General Grant to make an assault on the enemy's works in the early part of July; but the movement was deferred in consequence of the work on the mine, the completion of which was impatiently awaited. As a diversion Hancock's corps and two divisions of cavalry had crossed to the north side of the James at Deep Bottom and had threatened Richmond. A part of Lee's army was sent from Petersburg to checkmate this move, and when the mine was ready to be sprung Hancock was recalled in haste to Petersburg. When the mine was ready for the explosives General Meade requested General Burnside to submit a plan of attack. This was done in a letter dated July 26th, 1864, in which General Burnside said:

" . . . It is altogether probable that the enemy are cognizant of the fact that we are mining, because it is mentioned in their papers, and they have been heard at work on what are supposed to

BREVET BRIGADIER-GENERAL HENRY PLEASANTS.
FROM A PHOTOGRAPH.

UNION BREASTWORKS.

MOUTH OF THE MINE.

II. [FOR TITLE, SEE PREVIOUS PAGE.] FROM SKETCHES MADE IN 1886.

be shafts in close proximity to our galleries. But the rain of night before last has, no doubt, much retarded their work. We have heard no sound of workmen in them either yesterday or to-day; and nothing is heard by us in the mine but the ordinary sounds of work on the surface above. This morning we had some apprehension that the left lateral gallery was in danger of caving in from the weight of the batteries above it and the shock of their firing. But all possible precautions have been taken to strengthen it, and we hope to preserve it intact. The placing of the charges in the mine will not involve the necessity of making a noise. It is therefore probable that we will escape discovery if the mine is to be used within two or three days. It is, nevertheless, highly important, in my opinion, that the mine should be exploded at the earliest possible moment consistent with the general interests of the campaign. . . . But it may not be improper for me to say that the advantages reaped from the work would be but small if it were exploded without any coöperative movement.

"My plan would be to explode the mine just before daylight in the morning or at about 5 o'clock in the afternoon; mass the two brigades of the colored division in rear of my first line, in columns of division,—'double-columns closed in mass,'—the head of each brigade resting on the front line, and, as soon as the explosion has taken place, move them forward, with instructions for the divisions to take half distance, and as soon as the leading regiments of the two brigades pass through the gap in the enemy's line, the leading regiment of the right brigade to come into line perpendicular to the enemy's line by the 'right companies on the right into line, wheel,' the left companies on the right into line, and proceed at once down the line of the enemy's works as rapidly as possible; and the leading regiment of the left brigade to execute the reverse movement to the left, moving up the enemy's line. The remainder of the columns to move directly toward the crest in front as rapidly as possible, diverging in such a way as to enable them to deploy into column of regiments, the right column making as nearly as possible for Cemetery Hill; these columns to be followed by the other divisions of the corps as soon as they can be thrown in. This would involve the necessity of relieving these divisions by other troops before the movement, and of holding columns of other troops in readiness to take our place on the crest, in case we gain it, and sweep down it. It would, in my opinion, be advisable, if we succeed in gaining the crest, to throw the colored division right into the town. There is a necessity for the coöperation, at least in the way of artillery, by the troops on our right and left. Of the extent of this you will necessarily be the judge. I think our chances of success, in a plan of this kind, are more than even." . . .

With a view of making the attack, the division of colored troops, under General Edward Ferrero, had been drilling for several weeks, General Burnside thinking that they were in better condition to head a charge than either of the white divisions. They had not been in any very active service. On the other hand, the white divisions had performed very arduous duties since the beginning of the campaign, and before Petersburg had been in such proximity to the enemy that no man could raise his head above the parapets without being fired at.   They had been in the habit of using every possible means of covering themselves from the enemy's fire.

General Meade objected to the use of the colored troops, on the ground, as he stated, that they were a new division and had never been under fire, while this was an operation requiring the very best troops.   General Burnside, however, insisted upon his programme, and the question was referred to General Grant, who confirmed General Meade's views, although he subsequently said in his evidence before the Committee on the Conduct of the War:

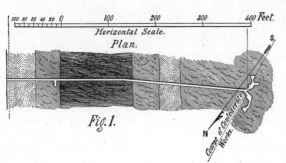

Fig. 1.

"General Burnside wanted to put his colored division in front, and I believe if he had done so it would

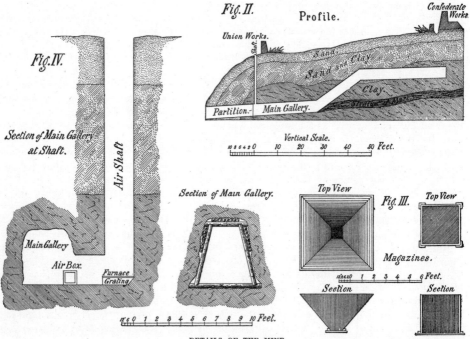

DETAILS OF THE MINE.

have been a success. Still I agreed with General Meade as to his objections to that plan. General Meade said that if we put the colored troops in front (we had only one division) and it should prove a failure, it would then be said, and very properly, that we were shoving these people ahead to get killed because we did not care anything about them.   But that could not be said if we put white troops in front."

The mine was charged with only 8000 pounds of powder, instead of 14,000, as asked for, the amount having been reduced by order of General Meade; and while awaiting the decision of General Grant on the question of the colored troops, precise orders for making and supporting the attack were issued by General Meade.

In the afternoon of the 29th of July, Generals Potter and O. B. Willcox met together at General Burnside's headquarters, to talk over the plans of the attack, based upon the idea that the colored troops would lead the charge, and while there the message was received from General Meade that General Grant disapproved of that plan, and that General Burnside must detail one of his white divisions to take the place of the colored division. This was the first break in the original plan. There were then scarcely twelve hours, and half of these at night, in which to make this change—and no possible time in which the white troops could be familiarized with the duties expected of them in connection with the assault.

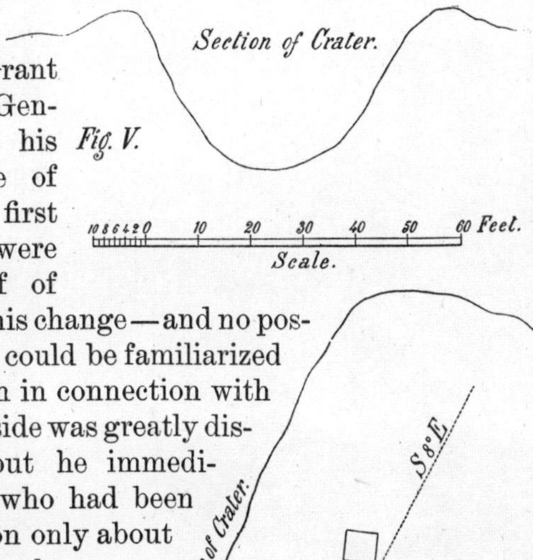

Section of Crater.

Fig. V.

10 8 6 4 2 0   10   20   30   40   50   60 Feet.

Scale.

General Burnside was greatly disappointed by this change; but he immediately sent for General Ledlie, who had been in command of the First Division only about six weeks. Upon his arrival General Burnside determined that the three commanders of his white divisions should "pull straws," and Ledlie was (as he thought) the unlucky victim. He, however, took it good-naturedly, and, after receiving special instructions from General Burnside, proceeded with his brigade commanders to ascertain the way to the point of attack. This was not accomplished until after dark on the evening before the explosion.

The order of attack, as proposed by General Burnside, was also changed by direction of General Meade with the approval of General Grant. Instead of moving down to the right and left of the crater of the mine, for the purpose of driving the enemy from their intrenchments, and removing to that extent the danger of flank attacks, General Meade directed that the troops should push at once for the crest of Cemetery Hill.

Fig. VI.

Outline of Crater.   S 8° E.   *Magazines.*   End of Tamping   Tamping Tube in Tube.   *Course of Confederate Works.*   *Magazines.*   *Outline of Crater.*

DIAGRAM OF THE CRATER.

The approaches to the Union line of intrenchments at this particular point were so well covered by the fire of the enemy that they were cut up into a network of covered ways almost as puzzling to the uninitiated as the catacombs of Rome.⌋

⌋The writer of this article was serving as judge-advocate of Ledlie's division, and also performed the duties of aide-de-camp to General Ledlie at the time of the explosion. When the orders were pub-

Upon General Ledlie's return from the front orders were issued, and the division was formed at midnight. Shortly afterward it advanced through the covered ways, and was in position some time before daybreak, behind the Union breastworks, and immediately in front of the enemy's fort, which was to be blown up. The orders were that Ledlie's division should advance first, pass over the enemy's works, and charge to Cemetery Hill, four hundred yards to the right, and approached by a slope comparatively free from obstacles; as soon as the First Division should leave the works, the next division (Willcox's) was to advance to the left of Cemetery Hill, so as to protect the left flank of the First Division; and the next division (Potter's) was to move in the same way to the right of Cemetery

CARRYING POWDER TO THE MINE. FROM A SKETCH MADE AT THE TIME.

Hill. The Ninth Corps being out of the way, it was intended that the Fifth and Eighteenth corps should pass through and follow up the movement.

At 3:30 A. M. Ledlie's division was in position, the Second Brigade, Colonel E. G. Marshall, in front, and that of General W. F. Bartlett behind it, the men and officers in a feverish state of expectancy, the majority of them having been awake all night. Daylight came slowly, and still they stood with every nerve strained prepared to move forward the instant an order should be given. Four o'clock arrived, officers and men began to get nervous, having been on their feet four hours; still the mine had not been exploded. General Ledlie then directed me to go to General Burnside and report to him that the command had been in readiness to move since 3:30 A. M., and to inquire the cause of the delay of the explosion. I found General Burnside in rear of the fourteen-gun battery, delivered my message, and received the reply from the general information that there was some trouble with the fuse dying out, but

lished for the movement he and Lieutenant George M. Randall, also of the regular army, and aide-de-camp to General Ledlie, were informed that they must accompany the advance troops in the attack, but that the volunteer staff would remain with General Ledlie, all of whom did so during the entire engagement, in or near a bomb-proof within the Union lines.—W. H. P.

that an officer had gone into the gallery to ignite it again, and that the explosion would soon take place. ⚓

I returned immediately, and just as I arrived in rear of the First Division the mine was sprung. It was a magnificent spectacle, and as the mass of earth went up into the air, carrying with it men, guns, carriages, and timbers, and spread out like an immense cloud as it reached its altitude, so close were the Union lines that the mass appeared as if it would descend immediately upon the troops waiting to make the charge. This caused them to break and scatter to the rear, and about ten minutes were consumed in re-forming for the attack.↓ Not much was lost by this delay, however, as it took nearly that time for the cloud of dust to pass off. The order was then given for the advance. As no part of the Union line of breastworks had been removed (which would have been an arduous as well as hazardous undertaking), the troops clambered over them as best they could. This in itself broke the ranks, and they did not stop to re-form, but pushed ahead toward the crater, about 130 yards distant, the débris from the explosion having covered up the abatis and *chevaux-de-frise* in front of the enemy's works.

Little did these men anticipate what they would see upon arriving there: an enormous hole in the ground about 30 feet deep, 60 feet wide, and 170 feet long, filled with dust, great blocks of clay, guns, broken carriages, projecting timbers, and men buried in various ways—some up to their necks, others to their waists, and some with only their feet and legs protruding from the earth. One of these near me was pulled out, and proved to be a second lieutenant of the battery which had been blown up. The fresh air revived him, and he was soon able to walk and talk. He was very grateful and said that he was asleep when the explosion took place, and only awoke to find himself wriggling up in the air; then a few seconds afterward he felt himself descending, and soon lost consciousness.

The whole scene of the explosion struck every one dumb with astonishment as we arrived at the crest of the débris. It was impossible for the troops of the Second Brigade to move forward in line, as they had advanced; and, owing to the broken state they were in, every man crowding up to look into the hole, and being pressed by the First Brigade, which was immediately in rear, it was equally impossible to move by the flank, by any command, around the crater. Before the brigade commanders could realize the situation, the two brigades became inextricably mixed, in the desire to look into the hole.

However, Colonel Marshall yelled to the Second Brigade to move forward, and the men did so, jumping, sliding, and tumbling into the hole, over the débris of material, and dead and dying men, and huge blocks of solid clay. They were followed by General Bartlett's brigade. Up on the other side of the crater they climbed, and while a detachment stopped to place two of the

⚓ Sergeant Henry Rees entered the mine and found that the fuse had died out at the first splicing. He cut the fuse above the charred portion; on his way out for materials he met Lieutenant Jacob Douty, who assisted in making a fresh splice, which was a success.— EDITORS.

↓ Immediately following the explosion the heavy guns along the line opened a severe fire.— W. H. P.

THE CHARGE TO THE CRATER. FROM A SKETCH MADE AT THE TIME.

dismounted guns of the battery in position on the enemy's side of the crest of the crater [see p. 562], a portion of the leading brigade passed over the crest and attempted to re-form. In doing so members of these regiments were killed by musket-shots from the rear, fired by the Confederates who were still occupying the traverses and intrenchments to the right and left of the crater. These men had been awakened by the noise and shock of the explosion, and during the interval before the attack had recovered their equanimity, and when the Union troops attempted to re-form on the enemy's side of the crater, they had faced about and delivered a fire into the backs of our men. This coming so unexpectedly caused the forming line to fall back into the crater.

Had General Burnside's original plan, providing that two regiments should sweep down inside the enemy's line to the right and left of the crater, been sanctioned, the brigades of Colonel Marshall and General Bartlett could and would have re-formed and moved on to Cemetery Hill before the enemy realized fully what was intended; but the occupation of the trenches to the right and left by the enemy prevented re-formation, and there being no division, corps, or army commander present to give orders to other troops to clear the trenches, a formation under fire from the rear was something no troops could accomplish.

After falling back into the crater a partial formation was made by General Bartlett and Colonel Marshall with some of their troops, but owing to the precipitous walls the men could find no footing except by facing inward, digging their heels into the earth, and throwing their backs against the side of the crater, or squatting in a half-sitting, half-standing posture, and some of the men were shot even there by the fire from the enemy in the traverses. It was at this juncture that Colonel Marshall requested me to go to General Ledlie and explain the condition of affairs, which he knew that I had seen and understood perfectly well. This I did immediately.

While the above was taking place the enemy had not been idle. He had brought a battery from his left to bear upon the position, and as I started on my errand the crest of the crater was being swept with canister. Special attention was given to this battery by our artillery, but for some reason or other the enemy's guns could not be silenced. Passing to the Union lines under this storm of canister, I found General Ledlie and a part of his staff ensconced in a protected angle of the works. I gave him Colonel Marshall's message, explained to him the situation, and Colonel Marshall's reasons for not being able to move forward. General Ledlie then directed me to return at once and say to Colonel Marshall and General Bartlett that it was General Burnside's order that they should move forward immediately. This message was delivered. But the firing on the crater now was incessant, and it was as heavy a fire of canister as was ever poured continuously upon a single objective point. It was as utterly impracticable to re-form a brigade in that crater as it would be to marshal bees into line after upsetting the hive; and equally as impracticable to re-form outside of the crater, under the severe fire in front and rear, as it would be to hold a dress parade in front of a charging enemy. Here, then, was the second point of advantage lost by the fact that there was no person present with authority to change the programme to meet the circumstances. Had a prompt attack of the troops to the right and left of the crater been made as soon as the leading brigade had passed into the crater, or even fifteen minutes afterward, clearing the trenches and diverting the fire of the enemy, success would have been inevitable, and particularly would this have been the case on the left of the crater, as the small fort immediately in front of the Fifth Corps was almost, if not entirely, abandoned for a while after the explosion of the mine, the men running away from it as if they feared that it was to be blown up also.

Whether General Ledlie informed General Burnside of the condition of affairs as reported by me I do not know; but I think it likely, as it was not long after I had returned to the crater that a brigade of the Second Division (Potter's) under the command of Brigadier-General S. G. Griffin advanced its skirmishers and followed them immediately, directing its course to the right of the crater. General Griffin's line, however, overlapped the crater on the left, where two or three of his regiments sought shelter in the crater. Those on the right passed over the trenches, but owing to the peculiar character of the enemy's works, which were not single, but complex and involuted and filled with pits, traverses, and bomb-proofs, forming a labyrinth as difficult of passage as the crater itself, the brigade was broken up, and, meeting the severe fire of canister, also fell back into the crater, which was then full to suffocation. Every organization melted away, as soon as it entered this hole in the ground, into a mass of human beings clinging by toes and heels to the

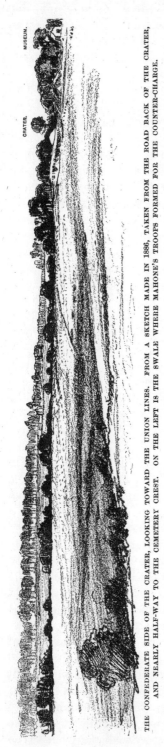

THE CONFEDERATE SIDE OF THE CRATER, LOOKING TOWARD THE UNION LINES. FROM A SKETCH MADE IN 1886, TAKEN FROM THE ROAD BACK OF THE CRATER, AND NEARLY HALF-WAY TO THE CEMETERY CREST. ON THE LEFT IS THE SWALE WHERE MAHONE'S TROOPS FORMED FOR THE COUNTER-CHARGE.

almost perpendicular sides. If a man was shot on the crest he fell and rolled to the bottom of the pit.

From the actions of the enemy, even at this time, as could be seen by his moving columns in front, he was not exactly certain as to the intentions of the Union commander; he appeared to think that possibly the mine explosion was but a feint and that the main attack would come from some other quarter. However, he massed some of his troops in a hollow in front of the crater, and held them in that position.

Meantime General Potter, who was in rear of the Union line of intrenchments, being convinced that something ought to be done to create a diversion and distract the enemy's attention from this point, ordered Colonel Zenas R. Bliss, commanding his First Brigade, to send two of his regiments to support General Griffin, and with the remainder to make an attack on the right. Subsequently it was arranged that the two regiments going to the support of General Griffin should pass into the crater, turn to the right, and sweep down the enemy's lines. Colonel Bliss was partly successful, and obtained possession of some 200 or 300 yards of the line, and one of the regiments advanced to within 20 or 30 yards of the battery whose fire was so severe on the troops; but it could make no further headway for lack of support — its progress being impeded by slashed timber, while an unceasing fire of canister was poured into the men. They therefore fell back to the enemy's traverses and intrenchments.

At the time of ordering forward Colonel Bliss's command General Potter wrote a dispatch to General Burnside, stating that it was his opinion, from what he had seen, and from the reports he had received from subordinate officers, that too many men were being forced in at this one point; that the troops there were in confusion, and it was absolutely necessary that an attack should be made from some other point of the line, in order to divert the enemy's attention and give time to straighten out our line. To that dispatch he never received an answer. Orders were, however, being constantly sent to the three division commanders of the white troops to push the men forward as

THE CRATER, AS SEEN FROM THE UNION SIDE. FROM A SKETCH MADE AT THE TIME.

In October, 1887, Major James C. Coit, of Cheraw, South Carolina, wrote as follows with regard to this picture, and the Confederate battery, under his command, bearing on the crater:

"I am satisfied that I made that sketch of the crater. I had sent the sketch home after the battle, and had given some of the officers on the lines copies. It was made when I was in front of the Federal lines under the flag of truce for burying the dead. One gun that was blown up by the explosion fell between the lines, as represented in the sketch.

"My guns [Coit's battalion] were all upon the front line up to the time of the explosion of the mine. After that time one of my batteries was placed upon a second line, upon the Jerusalem plank-road immediately in rear of the crater. I also had a mortar-battery between the crater and the cemetery, about 150 yards in rear of the battery that was so effective on the day of the explosion. This battery [Wright's], where I was during the engagement, was just across the ravine to our left of the crater and just in rear of our infantry line, about three hundred yards distant from the crater. It was erected there to defend Elliott's salient. It bore directly upon the crater, and was the only battery which could reach the Federal troops in advancing to our lines and after they occupied the crater. It commanded the ground from the Federal main line to the Jerusalem plank-road in rear of the crater. General Potter was unable to silence it, or even to do us any serious injury, because he could not fire directly upon its front. From this position, which was very elevated, I had a view of the whole field from the Federal main line to the ridge or plank-road. I saw all the movements of the Federal troops from the beginning to the end of the fight. I remember particularly being struck with the gallantry of one of the Federal officers, with a flag in one hand and waving his sword in the other, mounting our works."

fast as could be done, and this was, in substance, about all the orders that were received by them during the day up to the time of the order for the withdrawal.

When General Willcox came with the Third Division to support the First, he found the latter and three regiments of his own, together with the regiments of Potter's Second Division which had gone in on the right, so completely filling up the crater that no more troops could be got in there, and he therefore ordered an attack with the remainder of his division on the works of the enemy to the left of the crater. This attack was successful, so far as to carry the intrenchments for about 150 yards; but they were held only for a short time.

Previous to this last movement I had again left the crater and gone to General Ledlie, and had urged him to try to have something done on the right and left of the crater—saying that every man who got into the trenches to the right or left of it used them as a means of escape to the crater, and the enemy was reoccupying them as fast as our men left. All the satisfaction I received was an order to go back and tell the brigade commanders to get their men out and press forward to Cemetery Hill. This talk and these orders, coming from a commander sitting in a bomb-proof inside the Union lines, were disgusting. I returned again to the crater and delivered the orders, which I knew beforehand could not possibly be obeyed; and I told General Ledlie so before I left him. Upon my return to the crater I devoted my attention to the movements of the enemy, who was evidently making dispositions for an assault.

About two hours after the explosion of the mine (7 o'clock) and after I had returned to the crater for the third time, General Edward Ferrero, commanding the colored division of the Ninth Corps, received an order to advance his division, pass the white troops which had halted, and move on to carry the crest of Cemetery Hill at all hazards. General Ferrero did not think it advisable to move his division in, as there were three divisions of white troops already huddled together, and he so reported to Colonel Charles G. Loring, of General Burnside's staff. Loring requested Ferrero to wait until he could report to General Burnside. General Ferrero declined to wait, and then Colonel Loring gave him an order, in General Burnside's name, to halt without passing over the Union works, which order he obeyed. Colonel Loring went off to report to General Burnside, came back, and reported that the order was peremptory for the colored division to advance at all hazards.

The division then started in, moved by the left flank, under a most galling fire, passed around the crater on the crest on the débris, and all but one regiment passed beyond the crater. The fire upon them was incessant and severe, and many acts of personal heroism were done here by officers and men. Their drill for this object had been unquestionably of great benefit to them, and had they led the attack, fifteen or twenty minutes from the time the débris of the explosion had settled would have found them at Cemetery Hill, before the enemy could have brought a gun to bear on them.

But the leading brigade struck the enemy's force, which I had previously reported as massed in front of the crater, and in a sharp little action the colored troops captured some two hundred prisoners and a stand of colors, and recaptured a stand of colors belonging to a white regiment of the Ninth Corps. In this almost hand-to-hand conflict the colored troops became somewhat disorganized, and some twenty minutes were consumed in re-forming; then they made the attempt to move forward again. But, unsupported, subjected to a galling fire from batteries on the flanks, and from infantry fire in front and partly on the flank, they broke up in disorder and fell back to the crater, the majority passing on to the Union line of defenses, carrying with them a number of the white troops who were in the crater and in the enemy's intrenchments.\

Had any one in authority been present when the colored troops made their

\ A field-officer of one of the colored regiments [Lieutenant-Colonel John A. Bross] seized a stand of United States colors as he saw his men faltering when they first met the withering fire of the enemy, and mounting the very highest portion of the crest of the crater waved the colors zealously amid the storm of shot and canister. The gallant fellow was soon struck to the earth.

While this was taking place an amusing occurrence happened in the crater. As the colored column was moving by the left flank around the edge of the crater to the right, the file-closers, on account of the narrowness of the way, were compelled to pass through the mass of white men inside the crater. One of these file-closers was a massively built, powerful, and well-formed ser-

THE CONFEDERATE LINE AS RECONSTRUCTED AT THE CRATER. FROM A DRAWING MADE
BY LIEUTENANT HENDERSON AFTER THE BATTLE.

charge, and had they been supported, even at that late hour in the day, there would have been a possibility of success; but when they fell back and broke up in disorder, it was the closing scene of the tragedy. The rout of the colored troops was followed up by a feeble attack from the enemy, more in the way of a reconnoissance than a charge; but the attack was repulsed by the troops in the crater and in the intrenchments connected therewith, and the Confederates retired.

It was now evident that the enemy did not fear a demonstration from any other quarter, as they began to collect their troops for a decisive assault. On observing this I left the crater and reported to General Ledlie, whom I found seated in a bomb-proof with General Ferrero, that some means ought to be devised for withdrawing the mass of men from the crater without exposing them to the terrific fire which was kept up by the enemy; that if some shovels and picks could be found, the men in an hour could open a covered way by which they could be withdrawn; that the enemy was making every preparation for a determined assault on the crater, and, disorganized as the troops were, they could make no permanent resistance. Not an implement of any kind could be found; indeed, the proposition was received with disfavor. Matters remained *in statu quo* until about 2 P. M., when the enemy's anticipated assault was made.

About 9:30 A. M. General Meade had given positive orders to have the troops withdrawn from the crater. To have done so under the severe fire of

geant, stripped to the waist — his coal-black skin shining like polished ebony in the strong sunlight. As he was passing up the slope to emerge on the enemy's side of the crest he came across one of his own black fellows, who was lagging behind his company, evidently with the intention of remaining inside the crater, out of the way of the bullets. He was accosted by the sergeant with "None ob yo' d——n skulkin', now," with which remark he seized the culprit with one hand, and, lifting him up in his powerful grasp by the waistband of his trousers, carried him to the crest of the crater, threw him over on the enemy's side, and quickly followed.— W. H. P.

the enemy would have produced a stampede, which would have endangered the Union lines, and might possibly have communicated itself to the troops that were massed in rear of the Ninth Corps. General Burnside thought, for these and other reasons, that it would be possible to leave his command there until nightfall, and then withdraw it. There was no means of getting food or water to them, for which they were suffering. The midsummer sun caused waves of moisture produced by the exhalation from this mass to rise above the crater. Wounded men died there begging piteously for water, and soldiers extended their tongues to dampen their parched lips until their tongues seemed to hang from their mouths. Finally, the enemy, having taken advantage of our inactivity to mass his troops, was seen to emerge from the swale [see cut, p. 554] between the hill on which the crater was situated and that of the cemetery. On account of this depression they could not be seen by our artillery, and hence no guns were brought to bear upon them. The only place where they could be observed was

MAJOR-GENERAL ROBERT B. POTTER.
FROM A PHOTOGRAPH.

from the crater. But there was no serviceable artillery there, and no infantry force sufficiently organized to offer resistance when the enemy's column pressed forward. All in the crater who could possibly hang on by their elbows and toes lay flat against its conical wall and delivered their fire; but not more than a hundred men at a time could get into position, and these were only armed with muzzle-loading guns, and in order to re-load they were compelled to face about and place their backs against the wall.

The enemy's guns suddenly ceased their long-continued and uninterrupted fire on the crater, and the advancing column charged in the face of feeble resistance offered by the Union troops. At this stage they were perceived by our artillery, which opened a murderous fire, but too late. Over the crest and into the crater they poured, and a hand-to-hand conflict ensued. It was of short duration, however; crowded as our troops were, and without organization, resistance was vain. Many men were bayoneted at that time—some probably that would not have been, except for the excitement of battle. About 87 officers ☆ and 1652 men of the Ninth Corps were captured, the remainder retiring to our own lines, to which the enemy did not attempt to advance.

☆ Among the captured was General William F. Bartlett. Earlier in the war he had lost a leg, which he replaced with one of cork. While he was standing in the crater, a shot was heard to strike with the peculiar thud known to those who have been in action, and the general was seen to

In the engagements of the 17th and 18th of June, in order to obtain the position held by the Ninth Corps at the time of the explosion, the three white divisions lost 29 officers and 348 men killed; 106 officers and 1851 men wounded; and 15 officers and 554 men missing,—total, 2903. From the 20th of June to the day before the crater fight of July 30th these same divisions lost in the trenches 12 officers and 231 men killed; 44 officers and 851 men wounded; and 12 men missing,— total, 1150. These casualties were caused by picket and shell firing, and extended pretty evenly over the three divisions. The whole of General Willcox's division was on the line for thirty days or more without relief. General Potter's and General Ledlie's divisions had slight reliefs, enabling those officers to draw some of their men off at intervals for two or three days at a time.

In the engagement of July 30th the four divisions of the Ninth Corps had 52 officers and 376 men killed; 105 officers and 1556 men wounded; and 87 officers and 1652 men captured,— total, 3828.

It was provided in General Meade's order for the movement that the cavalry corps should make an assault on the left. Two divisions of the cavalry were over at Deep Bottom. They could not cross the

RELICS IN THE CRATER MUSEUM.

1. Musket-barrel with bullet-hole at the muzzle. 2. Musket burst by two bullets meeting in the barrel, a bullet having entered the muzzle as the gun was discharged. 3. Musket struck by six bullets, one embedding itself in the barrel near the bayonet. 4. Musket bent after having been cocked and capped. 5. Musket-stock covered with blood, found in a bomb-proof. 6. Sword found in a bomb-proof. 7. Broken sword. 8. Lining of a cartridge-box. 9. Canteen perforated by bullets. 10. Shovel having bullet-holes, found on the Union picket line in front of the crater. 11. Frying-pan having bullet-holes; taken out of the crater.

river until after the Second Corps had crossed, so that it was late in the day before they came up. Indeed, the head of the column did not appear before the offensive operations had been suspended. As General James H. Wilson had been ordered to be in readiness, and in view of the unavoidable delay of General Sheridan, orders were sent to Wilson not to wait for General

totter and fall. A number of officers and men immediately lifted him, when he cried out, "Put me any place where I can sit down." "But you are wounded, General, aren't you?" was the inquiry. "My leg is shattered all to pieces," said he. "Then you can't sit up," they urged; "you'll have to lie down." "Oh, no!" exclaimed the general, "*it's only my cork leg that's shattered!*"—W. H. P.

Sheridan, but to push on himself to the Weldon railroad. But the length of the march prevented success; so no attack was made by the cavalry, except at Lee's Mills, where General Gregg, encountering cavalry, drove them away in order to water his horses. The Fifth Corps and the Eighteenth Corps remained inert during the day, excepting Turner's division of the Tenth Corps (temporarily attached to the Eighteenth), which made an attempt on the right of the crater, but it happened to be just at the time that the colored troops broke up; so his command was thrown into confusion, and fell back to the trenches.

SIDES AND EDGE OF TWO BULLETS THAT MET POINT TO POINT AT THE CRATER—THE SIDES FROM PHOTOGRAPHS OF THE ORIGINAL IN MAJOR GRIFFITH'S MUSEUM AT THE CRATER.

In this affair the several efforts made to push troops forward to Cemetery Hill were as futile in their results as the dropping of handfuls of sand into a running stream to make a dam. With the notable exception of General Robert B. Potter, there was not a division commander in the crater or connecting lines, nor was there a corps commander on the immediate scene of action; the result being that the subordinate commanders attempted to carry out the orders issued prior to the commencement of the action, when the first attack developed the fact that a change of these plans was absolutely necessary. ↓

↓ A revised table that has been prepared for publication in the "Official Records" shows the loss of the Ninth Corps to have been 50 officers and 423 men killed, 124 officers and 1522 men wounded, and 79 officers and 1277 men captured or missing = 3475. The total loss at the mine (including Turner's division of the Tenth Corps) was 504 killed, 1881 wounded, and 1413 captured or missing = 3798. General Mahone states that the number of prisoners taken was 1101. The loss in Lee's army is not fully reported. Elliott's brigade lost 677, and that was probably more than half of the casualties on the Confederate side.—EDITORS.

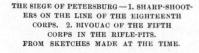

THE SIEGE OF PETERSBURG—1. SHARP-SHOOTERS ON THE LINE OF THE EIGHTEENTH CORPS. 2. BIVOUAC OF THE FIFTH CORPS IN THE RIFLE-PITS. FROM SKETCHES MADE AT THE TIME.

EXPLOSION OF THE MINE. FROM A SKETCH MADE AT THE TIME.

IN THE CRATER.

BY CHARLES H. HOUGHTON, BREVET MAJOR, 14TH NEW YORK HEAVY ARTILLERY.

ON the evening of July 29th, 1864, we of the Ninth Corps in front of Petersburg knew that an important movement was to take place, as we were ordered out for inspection and dress parade, and soon after returning to our place in the trenches, orders came to prepare three days' cooked rations, and ammunition was distributed. Soon we were relieved by troops from the Eighteenth Corps and marched back to the open ground several rods in rear of our works and halted, lying down in the sand till about 3 o'clock in the morning of the 30th. We now marched toward the left, and passing out through covered ways advanced to the front line of works. The men were cautioned to prevent the rattling of tin cups and bayonets, because we were so near the enemy that they would discover our movements. We marched with the stillness of death; not a word was said above a whisper. We knew, of course, that something very important was to be done and that we were to play a prominent part. We formed our lines of battle in the trenches of General Potter's division. Our brigade, commanded by Colonel E. G. Marshall of the 14th New York Artillery, was first in line and formed three lines of battle, the 2d Pennsylvania Provisional Artillery in the first line, the 14th New York Artillery in the second line, and the 179th New York and 3d Maryland in the third line. Our regiment, originally composed of three battalions, had been consolidated into two of six companies each, the 1st Battalion commanded by Captain L. J. Jones, and the 2d Bat-

talion by myself. Each battalion was acting as an independent regiment.

While waiting quietly and anxiously for the explosion, men had been allowed to lie down in line. I was lying on the ground resting my head on my hand and thinking of the probable result, when the denouement came. I shall never forget the terrible and magnificent sight. The earth around us trembled and heaved — so violently that I was lifted to my feet. Then the earth along the enemy's lines opened, and fire and smoke shot upward seventy-five or one hundred feet. The air was filled with earth, cannon, caissons, sand-bags and living men, and with everything else within the exploded fort. One huge lump of clay as large as a hay-stack or small cottage was thrown out and left on top of the ground toward our own works. Our orders were to charge immediately after the explosion, but the effect produced by the falling of earth and the fragments sent heavenward that appeared to be coming right down upon us, caused the first line to waver and fall back, and the situation was one to demoralize most troops. I gave the command "Forward," but at the outset a serious difficulty had to be surmounted. Our own works, which were very high at this point, had not been prepared for scaling. But scale them in some way we must, and ladders were improvised by the men placing their bayonets between the logs in the works and holding the other end at their hip or on shoulders, thus forming steps over which men climbed. I with others stood on top of the works

561

pulling men up and forming line; but time was too precious to wait for this, and Colonel Marshall, who was standing below within our works, called to me to go forward. This was done very quickly and our colors were the first to be planted on the ruined fort. We captured several prisoners and two brass field-pieces, light twelve-pounders, which were in the left wing (their right) of the fort and had not been buried beneath the ruins. Prisoners stated that about one thousand men were in the fort. If so, they were massed there over night, expecting an attack, as the fort could not accommodate so many men; but nearly all who were within it were killed or buried alive. We succeeded in taking out many — some whose feet would be waving above their burial-place; others, having an arm, hand, or head only, uncovered; others, alive but terribly shaken. Being convinced that a magazine was near the two pieces of artillery, I detailed a sergeant and some men to search for it and to man the guns. The magazine, containing a supply of ammunition, was found. We then hauled back the pieces of artillery to get a range over the top of works on a Confederate gun on our left that was throwing canister and grape into us. We loaded and fired and silenced the gun, and at our first fire forty-five prisoners came in, whom I sent to our lines. We loaded and placed the other piece in position to use on the advance of the enemy if a counter-charge should be attempted. A charge was made upon us, and the fire from this piece did terrible execution on their advancing lines, and with the fire of our men they were repulsed. On the repulse of this charge we captured a stand of colors. Sergeant James S. Hill of Company C of our regiment secured the flag in a hand-to-hand encounter.] At this time General Hartranft, who stood within the crater, called for three cheers for the members of the 14th New York Artillery who were handling the guns, at the same time requesting me to continue in command of them. But other work had to be done. We charged and captured the works behind the crater, but our supports had not come. The delay in getting them over our own works gave the enemy a chance to recover their surprise and resume their stations at their guns, which they opened upon our men then crossing the field. When the colored troops advanced they could not be forced beyond the "crater" for some time, and when they were, were driven back to our lines, or into the pit.

When our brigade line was forced back from the enemy's breastworks to the crater, the colored division and other troops having previously fallen back, I stopped at the crater. Only a few of the 14th were there, most of them wounded. I went through the crater to the wing of the fort where I had left the guns in charge of a sergeant, and while I was passing through a narrow entrance General Hartranft, who had preceded me, called to me to drop down and crawl in, as sharp-shooters were

picking off every one passing that point, which was in full view of the enemy. I escaped their bullets, but the next officer who came received a serious if not mortal wound. In this wing of the fort were Generals Potter, Hartranft, and S. G. Griffin, and myself, with one or two other officers. Bartlett, who was in the pit of the crater, had received a shot, disabling his artificial leg, and he could not be carried to the rear. Colonel E. G. Marshall, commanding our brigade, was then on the outside of the fort. After remaining there some time and knowing that if the stay was prolonged we would go to Richmond and to Confederate prisons, or be killed, as the enemy were on the right flank and front of the crater then, I decided to get back to our works. The generals tried to dissuade me, predicting sure death to any one crossing that field, which was swept by both artillery and infantry fire of the enemy from both directions and was so thickly strewn with killed and wounded, both white and black, that one disposed to be so inhuman might have reached the works without stepping on the ground. The generals thought that a covered way back to our lines could be dug, or if we could hold the breach till night we could escape. The sun was pouring its fiercest heat down upon us and our suffering wounded. No air was stirring within the crater. It was a sickening sight: men were dead and dying all around us; blood was streaming down the sides of the crater to the bottom, where it gathered in pools for a time before being absorbed by the hard red clay.

Corporal Bigelow of Company L was that day serving me as orderly. When asked which he preferred, to remain in the crater or attempt to reach the works, he replied that he would follow his commander whichever way he decided upon. So we passed through the embrasure looking toward our own line to prepare for the attempt. Colonel Marshall asked what I intended doing, and when informed, he also said it was sure death to go. I replied that it would be sure death or starvation in Confederate prisons to remain, and that if I could reach our lines I could release all of them by opening fire so that the smoke would obscure the field and all could come out. I gave the word that when the next shell came, Corporal Bigelow and I would start, keeping a little apart. We did so, and, passing through showers of bullets, we reached our line in safety and I ordered my men to open fire on the enemy's line. They replied by a furious fire, and soon the smoke settled over the field, and under cover of that fire all the general officers but Bartlett escaped. Bartlett and Colonel Marshall were captured.

The loss of our regiment that day was as follows: One lieutenant (Hartley) killed, two wounded; Colonel Marshall and Lieutenants George H. Wing (Company L), Fauss, and Grierson prisoners; and 126 men killed, wounded, and missing — this from less than 400 taken into the charge.

] Adjutant C. H. VanBrackle and Sergeant Hill presented the flag to General Ledlie to be forwarded to the War Department, and then returned to the front. When the regiment was forced back to our own works, Sergeant Hill was missing; he was probably killed.

For his bravery that day he was awarded a medal by Congress, which was afterward presented by General Meade in person to his company for him. He was also commissioned a lieutenant in the regiment. Both medal and commission were sent to his mother.—C. H. H.

THE COLORED TROOPS AT PETERSBURG.

BY HENRY GODDARD THOMAS, BREVET MAJOR-GENERAL, U. S. V.

GUIDON OF THOMAS'S BRIGADE OF THE COLORED DIVISION --- SHADED PARTS, GREEN ; THE FIELD, WHITE.

EAST of Petersburg, on high ground, protruding like the ugly horn of a rhinoceros, stood the Confederate earthwork, fortified as a battery, which we undermined and exploded July 30th, 1864. It did a good deal of goring before we destroyed it. Its position enabled the garrison to throw a somewhat enfilading fire into our lines, under which many fell, a few at a time.

For some time previous to the explosion of the mine it was determined by General Burnside that the colored division ⸗ should lead the assault. The general tactical plan had been given to the brigade commanders (Colonel Sigfried and myself), with a rough outline map of the ground, and directions to study the front for ourselves. But this latter was impracticable except in momentary glimpses. The enemy made a target of every head that appeared above the work, and their marksmanship was good. The manner of studying the ground was this : Putting my battered old hat on a ramrod and lifting it above the rampart just enough for them not to discover that no man was under it, I drew their fire ; then stepping quickly a few paces one side, I took a hasty observation.

We were all pleased with the compliment of being chosen to lead in the assault. Both officers and men were eager to show the white troops what the colored division could do. We had acquired confidence in our men. They believed us infallible. We had drilled certain movements, to be executed in gaining and occupying the crest. It is an axiom in military art that there are times when the ardor, hopefulness, and enthusiasm of new troops, not yet rendered doubtful by reverses or chilled by defeat, more than compensate, in a dash, for training and experience. General Burnside, for this and other reasons, most strenuously urged his black division for the advance. Against his most urgent remonstrance he was overruled. About 11 P. M., July 29th, a few hours before the action, we were officially informed that the plan had been changed, and our division would not lead.

We were then bivouacking on our arms in rear of our line, just behind the covered way leading to the mine. I returned to that bivouac dejected

and with an instinct of disaster for the morrow. As I summoned and told my regimental commanders, their faces expressed the same feeling.

Any striking event or piece of news was usually eagerly discussed by the white troops, and in the ranks military critics were as plenty and perhaps more voluble than among the officers. Not so with the blacks ; important news such as that before us, after the bare announcement, was usually followed by long silence. They sat about in groups, "studying," as they called it. They waited, like the Quakers, for the spirit to move ; when the spirit moved, one of their singers would uplift a mighty voice, like a bard of old, in a wild sort of chant. If he did not strike a sympathetic chord in his hearers, if they did not find in his utterance the exponent of their idea, he would sing it again and again, altering sometimes the words, more often the music. If his changes met general acceptance, one voice after another would chime in ; a rough harmony of three parts would add itself ; other groups would join his, and the song would become the song of the command.

The night we learned that we were to lead the charge the news filled them too full for ordinary utterance. The joyous negro guffaw always breaking out about the camp-fire ceased. They formed circles in their company streets and were sitting on the ground intently and solemnly "studying." At last a heavy voice began to sing,

> "We-e looks li-ike me-en a-a-marchin' on,
> We looks li-ike men-er-war."

Over and over again he sang it, making slight changes in the melody. The rest listened to him intently ; no sign of approval or disapproval escaped their lips or appeared on their faces. All at once, when his refrain had struck the right response in their hearts, his group took it up, and shortly half a thousand voices were upraised extemporizing a half dissonant middle part and bass. It was a picturesque scene — these dark men, with their white eyes and teeth and full red lips, crouching over a smoldering camp-fire, in dusky shadow, with only the feeble rays of the lanterns of the first sergeants and the lights of the candles dimly showing through the tents. The sound was as weird as the scene, when all the voices struck the low E (last note but one), held it, and then rose to A with a *portamento* as sonorous as it was clumsy. Until we fought the battle of the crater they sang this

⸗ There was but one division of colored troops in the Army of the Potomac — the Fourth Division of the Ninth Corps, organized as follows :

Brigadier-General Edward Ferrero, commanding division. *First Brigade*, Colonel Joshua K. Sigfried (of the 48th Penn.) : 27th U. S. colored troops, Lieutenant-Colonel Charles J. Wright ; 30th U. S. colored troops, Colonel Delevan Bates ; 39th U. S. colored troops, Colonel Ozora P. Stearns ; 43d U. S. colored troops, Lieutenant-Colonel H. Seymour Hall. *Second Brigade*, Colonel Henry Goddard Thomas, 19th U. S. colored troops : 19th U. S. colored troops, Lieutenant-Colonel Joseph G.

Perkins ; 23d U. S. colored troops, Colonel Cleaveland J. Campbell ; Battalion of six companies 28th U. S. colored troops, Lieutenant-Colonel Charles S. Russell ; 29th U. S. colored troops, Lieutenant-Colonel John A. Bross ; 31st U. S. colored troops, Lieutenant-Colonel W. E. W. Ross.

This made a division of only nine regiments, divided into two brigades, yet it was numerically a large division. The regiments were entirely full, and a colored deserter was a thing unknown. On the day of the action the division numbered 4300, of which 2000 belonged to Sigfried's brigade and 2300 to mine.— H. G. T.

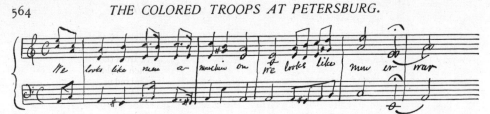

We looks like men a-marchin on, we looks like men er war

SONG OF THE COLORED DIVISION BEFORE CHARGING INTO THE CRATER.

every night to the exclusion of all other songs. After that defeat they sang it no more.

About 3 A. M. the morning of the battle we were up after a short sleep under arms. Then came the soldiers' hasty breakfast. "Never fight on an empty stomach" was a proverb more honored in that army than any of Solomon; for the full stomach helps the wounded man to live through much loss of blood. This morning our breakfast was much like that on other mornings when we could not make fires: two pieces of hard-tack with a slice of raw, fat salt pork between — not a dainty meal, but solid provender to fight on. By good fortune I had a bottle of cucumber pickles. These I distributed to the officers about me. They were gratefully accepted, for nothing cuts the fat of raw salt pork like a pickle. We moistened our repast with black coffee from our canteens. The privates fared the same, barring the luxury of the pickle.

We had been told that the mine would be fired at 3:45 A. M. But 4 o'clock arrived, and all was quiet. Not long after that came a dull, heavy thud, not at all startling; it was a heavy, smothered sound, not nearly so distinct as a musket-shot. Could this be the mine? No; impossible. There was no charging, no yells—neither the deep-mouthed bass growl of the Union troops, nor the sharp, shrill, fox-hunting cry of the Confederates. Here was a mine blown up, making a crater from 150 to 200 feet long, 60 wide, and 30 deep, and the detonation and the concussion were so inconsiderable to us, not over a third of a mile away, that we could hardly believe the report of a staff-officer, back from the line, that the great mine had been exploded.

At about 5:30 A. M. a fairly heavy musketry fire from the enemy had opened. Shortly after, as we lay upon our arms awaiting orders, a quiet voice behind me said, "Who commands this brigade?" "I do," I replied. Rising, and turning toward the voice, I saw General Grant. He was in his usual dress: a broad-brimmed felt hat and the ordinary coat of a private. He wore no sword. Colonel Horace Porter, his aide-de-camp, and a single orderly accompanied him. "Well," said the general, slowly and thoughtfully, as if communing with himself rather than addressing a subordinate, "why are you not in?" Pointing to the First Brigade just in my front, I replied, "My orders are to follow that brigade." Feeling that golden opportunities might be slipping away from us, I added, "Will you give me the order to go in now?" After a moment's hesitation he answered in the same slow and ruminating manner, "No, you may keep the orders you have." Then, turning his horse's head, he rode away at a walk.

Fifteen minutes later an aide to the division commander gave us the order, and we moved into the covered way, my brigade following Sigfried's. This was about 6 A. M. For an hour or more we lay here inactive, the musketry growing quicker and sharper all the time. A heavy cannonading opened. We sat down at first, resting against the walls of the covered way. Soon, however, we had to stand to make room for the constantly increasing throng of wounded who were being brought past us to the rear. Some few, with flesh-wounds merely, greeted us with such jocularity as, "I'm all right, boys! This is good for a thirty days' sick-leave." Others were plucky and silent, their pinched faces telling the effort they were making to suppress their groans; others, with the ashy hue of death already gathering on their faces, were largely past pain. Many, out of their senses through agony, were moaning or bellowing like wild beasts. We stood there over an hour with this endless procession of wounded men passing. There could be no greater strain on the nerves. Every moment changed the condition from that of a forlorn hope to one of forlorn hopelessness. Unable to strike a blow, we were sickened with the contemplation of revolting forms of death and mutilation.

Finally, about 7:30 A. M., we got the order for the colored division to charge. My brigade followed Sigfried's at the double-quick. Arrived at the crater, a part of the First Brigade entered. The crater was already too full; that I could easily see. I swung my column to the right and charged over the enemy's rifle-pits connecting with the crater on our right. These pits were different from any in our lines — a labyrinth of bomb-proofs and magazines, with passages between. My brigade moved gallantly on right over the bomb-proofs and over the men of the First Division. [‡] As we mounted the pits, a deadly enfilade from eight guns on our right and a murderous cross-fire of musketry met us. Among the officers, the first to fall was the gallant Fessenden of the 23d Regiment. Ayres and Woodruff of the 31st dropped within a few yards of Fessenden, Ayres being killed, and Woodruff mortally wounded. Liscomb of the 23d then fell to rise no more; and then Hackhiser of the 28th and Flint and Aiken of the 29th. Major Rockwood of the 19th then mounted the crest and fell back dead, with a cheer on his lips. Nor were these all; for at that time hundreds of heroes "carved in ebony" fell. These black men commanded the admiration and respect of every beholder.

The most advantageous point for the purpose,

‡ Major Van Buren's testimony, "Report of Committee on the Conduct of the War," Vol. I.

about eight hundred feet from the crater, having been reached, we leaped from the works and endeavored to make a rush for the crest. Captain Marshall L. Dempcy, and Lieutenant Christopher Pennell, of my staff, and four white orderlies with the brigade guidon accompanied me, closely followed by Lieutenant-Colonel Ross, leading the 31st Regiment. At the instant of leaving the works Ross was shot down; the next officer in rank, Captain Wright, was shot as he stooped over him. The men were largely without leaders, and their organization was destroyed. Two of my four orderlies were wounded: one, flag in hand; the remaining two sought shelter when Lieutenant Pennell, rescuing the guidon, hastened down the line outside the pits. With his sword uplifted in his right hand and the banner in his left, he sought to call out the men along the whole line of the parapet. In a moment, a musketry fire was focused upon him, whirling him round and round several times before he fell. Of commanding figure, his bravery was so conspicuous that, according to Colonel Weld's testimony, a number of his (Weld's) men were shot because, spell-bound, they forgot their own shelter in watching this superb boy, who was an only child of an old Massachusetts clergyman, and to me as Jonathan was to David. Two days later, on a flag of truce, I searched for his body in vain. He was doubtless shot literally to pieces, for the leaden hail poured for a long time almost incessantly about that spot, killing the wounded and mutilating the dead; and he probably sleeps among the unknown whom we buried in the long deep trench we dug that day.‡

The men of the 31st making the charge were being mowed down like grass, with no hope of any one reaching the crest, so I ordered them to scatter and run back. The fire was such that Captain Dempcy and myself were the only officers who returned, unharmed, of those who left the works for that charge.♭

We were not long back within the honeycomb of passages and bomb-proofs near the crater before I received this order from the division commander: "Colonels Sigfried and Thomas, if you have not already done so, you will immediately proceed to take the crest in your front." My command was crowded into the pits, already too full, and were sandwiched, man for man, against the men of the First Division. They were thus partly sheltered from the fire that had reduced them coming up; but their organization was almost lost. I had already sent word to General Burnside by Major James L. Van Buren, of his staff, that unless a movement simultaneous with mine was made to the right, to stop the enfilading fire, I thought not a man would live to reach the crest; but that I would try another charge in about ten minutes, and I hoped to be supported. I then

directed the commanders of the 23d, 28th, and 29th regiments to get their commands as much together and separated from the others as possible in that time, so that each could have a regimental following, for we were mixed up with white troops, and with one another to the extent of almost paralyzing any effort. We managed to make the charge, however, Colonel Bross of the 29th leading. The 31st had been so shattered, was so diminished, so largely without officers, that I got what was left of them out of the way of the charging column as

BREVET MAJOR-GENERAL HENRY G. THOMAS.
FROM A PHOTOGRAPH.

much as possible. This column met the same fate in one respect as the former. As I gave the order, Lieutenant-Colonel John A. Bross, taking the flag into his own hands, was the first man to leap from the works into the valley of death below. He had attired himself in full uniform, evidently with the intent of inspiring his men. He had hardly reached the ground outside the works before he fell to rise no more. He was conspicuous and magnificent in his gallantry. The black men followed into the jaws of death, and advanced until met by a charge in force from the Confederate lines.

The report of the Confederate General Bushrod R. Johnson (commanding the opposing forces at that point), to which I have had access, says that the Confederate troops in this charge were the First Brigade of Mahone's division, with the 25th and 49th North Carolina and the 26th and part of the 17th South Carolina regiments. It was no dis-

‡ While the contemplation of one death so softens the heart, the sight of the myriad dead of a battle-field blunts the sensibilities. During the burial of the dead, a stretcher-bearer, seeing that the trousers-pocket of a soldier long dead contained tobacco, deliberately cut it out, and took a chew with an air of relish.— H. G. T.

♭ My brigade guidon, which Lieutenant Pennell held when killed, was captured by Private John W. Niles. Company D, 41st Virginia, was stored in Richmond, and there retaken by our troops when we entered that city on April 3d, 1865, and is now stored in the War Department. —H. G. T.

UNION TROOPS.

THE BATTLE OF THE CRATER. FROM AN OIL PAINTING.

CONFEDERATES CHARGING.

credit to what was left of three regiments that they were repulsed by a force like that.

I lost in all 36 officers and 877 men,—total, 913. The 23d Regiment entered the charge with eighteen officers; it came out with seven. The 28th entered with eleven officers, and came out with four. The 31st had but two officers for duty that night. Colonel Sigfried says in his official report:

"The First Brigade worked its way through the crater, and was halted behind the honeycomb of bomb-proofs. Here the 43d charged the intrenchments, but owing to the crowded condition of the bomb-proofs, it was impossible to get the rest of the brigade on. Too much praise cannot be awarded to the bravery of officers and men; the former fearlessly led, while the latter as fearlessly followed, through a fire hot enough to cause the best troops to falter. But few of the field-officers escaped. Colonel Delevan Bates fell, shot in the face. Major Leeke stood, urging the men on, with the blood gushing from his mouth. Captain Wright of the 43d Regiment himself captured a Confederate stand of colors and five prisoners, and brought them in. Lieutenant-Colonel Wright, with two bullet wounds, retained the command of his regiment. . . . Had it not been for the almost impassable crowd of troops of the other divisions in the crater and intrenchments, Cemetery Hill would have been ours without a falter on the part of my brigade."

Nor was the giving way a willing movement on the part of the colored troops. One little band, after my second charge was repulsed, defended the intrenchments we had won from the enemy, exhibiting fighting qualities that I never saw surpassed in the war. This handful stood there without the slightest organization of company or regiment, each man for himself, until the enemy's banners waved in their very faces. Then they made a dash for our own lines, and that at my order. Speaking of this stand, General Burnside says in his official report: "But not all of the colored troops retired; some held the pits behind which they had advanced, severely checking the enemy until they were nearly all killed."

The engagement was over. We had not only lost about forty per cent., but had been repulsed. The enemy having retaken their former lines, the troops, black and white, in the crater were cut off from our army. Squads there occasionally made a dash for our lines, but as many fell as reached

LIEUTENANT CHRISTOPHER PENNELL.
FROM A PHOTOGRAPH.

three charges. They were weak, exhausted, and suffering from want of water. They succumbed, and most of them fell into the hands of the enemy. Of this last scene in the battle the Confederate General Bushrod R. Johnson says in his official report:

"Between 11 and 12 A. M., a second unsuccessful charge having been made by Wright's brigade of Mahone's division, I proceeded to concert a combined movement on both flanks of the crater. . . . A third charge a little before 2 P. M. gave us entire possession of the crater and adjacent lines. This charge on the left [our right] and rear of the crater was made by Sanders's brigade of Mahone's division, the 61st North Carolina of Hoke's division, and the 17th South Carolina of this division. . . . These movements were all conducted by General Mahone, while I took the 22d and 23d South Carolina into the crater and captured three colors and 130 prisoners. Previous to this charge the incessant firing kept up by our troops on both flanks and in rear had caused many of the enemy to run the gauntlet of our cross-fires in front of the breach, but a large number still remained unable to advance, and perhaps afraid to retreat."

Thus ended in disaster what had at first promised to be a grand success. We were back within our old lines and badly cut up. We had inflicted a heavy, but by no means equal, loss on the enemy.

Brevet Brigadier-General H. Seymour Hall, who commanded the 43d United States colored troops, writes to the editors, under date of April 5th, 1888, as follows:

"After an inspection of the division by an officer of General Burnside's staff, the 43d was selected to lead the assault which was to follow the explosion of the mine, in the first plan of attack, and still had the advance when the division finally went into action. I drilled the command, and carefully inspected the ground over which we were to advance. When the order to lead out from the covered way was given me, we moved by the flank, scrambled, climbed, or jumped as best we could over our outer works double-quick, swept up the slope, already the center of a tornado of shot and shell, through which, leading my command directly to the crater, and mounting the crest of the débris, saw at once the utter hopelessness of passing the enemy's lines through and over the mass of soldiers in the yawning gulf. The 43d moved to our right around on the crest of the crater's rim, till within a few yards of the enemy's main line of intrenchments on our right, which was at that time fully manned by the rebel forces, who were concentrating upon us a deadly fire of musketry, and flaunting their colors defiantly almost in our very faces. Still at the double-quick, changing direction,

to the right, leading the command in front of and parallel to the intrenchments held by the enemy, as soon as sufficient distance was taken I gave the command to march by the left flank, and as the line thus formed moved toward the enemy, gave the order to charge. Officers and men swept resistlessly on, over the enemy's intrenchments, without an instant's halt or waver, capturing nearly all the force in our immediate front, probably about one hundred prisoners, the stand of rebel colors mentioned, and recapturing a stand of national colors. All this occupied scarcely five minutes from the time we left the covered way, but we were exposed to the most terrific concentration of infantry and artillery fire it had ever been my lot to encounter.

"We had opened a gateway, but the crest of the ridge in rear of the mine, our objective, was not yet gained. Just as I was about to give the order to advance my right arm fell nerveless to my side, pierced and shattered near the shoulder by a musket-ball. Recovering my saber, which had dropped from my hand, I retired from the field to the amputating-table.

"The 43d had not more than 15 officers and 350 enlisted men present for duty. One officer and 28 men were killed, 10 officers and 94 men were wounded, 12 men missing,—total, 145. The colors were tattered, and the color-lance splintered and shivered into a dozen pieces by musket-balls." EDITORS.

ACTIONS ON THE WELDON RAILROAD.

BY ORLANDO B. WILLCOX, BREVET MAJOR-GENERAL, U. S. A.

I. GLOBE TAVERN.

THE operations on the railroad connecting Petersburg with Weldon, North Carolina, were a bit of strategy conceived by Grant in connection with Hancock's and Butler's movements north of the James, in order to force a withdrawal of the enemy's troops operating against Sheridan in the valley, and were intended by Meade to cut off one more avenue of supplies to Petersburg. Meade also wanted to attack the intrenchments on the south side of the James, believing that Hancock's move had drawn off all but two divisions from the defenses; but in this he was overruled by Grant.

The movement therefore became a reconnoissance in force, with instructions to the commander, General G. K. Warren, to make the best of any advantages that might be developed, to effect a lodgment on the railroad as near the enemy's fortifications as practicable, and to destroy the road as far down as possible. The track had already been pretty badly cut up by our cavalry, but only in spots and not beyond speedy repair. Warren started out early on the morning of August 18th, 1864, with his own (Fifth) corps, and a brigade of General A. V. Kautz's division of cavalry, under Colonel Samuel P. Spear. The heat was intense and the country so drenched with rain that the fields were well-nigh impassable for artillery. Griffin took the lead, with his division and Spear's cavalry, met the enemy's pickets a mile from the road,—which was guarded by General James Dearing's brigade of cavalry,—deployed his skirmish-line, and advanced rapidly on the road in column of brigades, then turned to the south and west. Ayres followed, but wheeled toward the city, with Crawford's division in column on his right and Cutler's division in reserve.

A report by Dearing to General Beauregard,

commanding the defenses of Petersburg, enabled that commander to get troops on the road, and after a mile's march Ayres found himself confronted by General Heth's division of Hill's corps, in position, with artillery. At the first encounter Ayres was forced to fall back a little to prevent the turning of his left flank, but he quickly rallied and finally, by the help of Hofmann's brigade of Cutler's division, drove Heth from the ground, though with very heavy loss. To what extent this advantage might have been immediately followed up is a disputed question. Crawford's left was somewhat engaged, but his passage through the thick woods and swampy ground, cut up with ravines, was found difficult. He could not keep up with Ayres, and Warren halted within a mile or two from the Vaughn road intersection.

The intersection was the point Meade most wanted Warren to gain. However, he was pleased sufficiently as it was, and ordered Warren to maintain his hold on the road " at all hazards." He directed Mott's division, Second Corps, to establish a connection with the new works, and ordered out Willcox's, White's,[‡] and afterward Potter's divisions from the Ninth Corps' works to reënforce Warren; these to be followed finally by Gregg's cavalry brigade and two hundred railroad men to destroy the tracks toward Reams's Station. My division being nearest was first to arrive next morning, and was ordered to bivouac near the " Globe Tavern," where Warren had his headquarters. When White came up he was posted farther to the right.

Beauregard likewise ordered out reënforcements, under Lieutenant-General A. P. Hill, viz., three brigades under Mahone, Pegram's batteries, and W. H. F. Lee's cavalry — all of whom, with Heth's brigades, were concentrated at the Vaughn road

---

‡ General Julius White had commanded a division in the Twenty-third Corps, in Burnside's army in east Tennessee. Immediately after the mine explosion, July 30th, he relieved General James H. Ledlie in command of the First Division, Ninth Corps.— EDITORS.

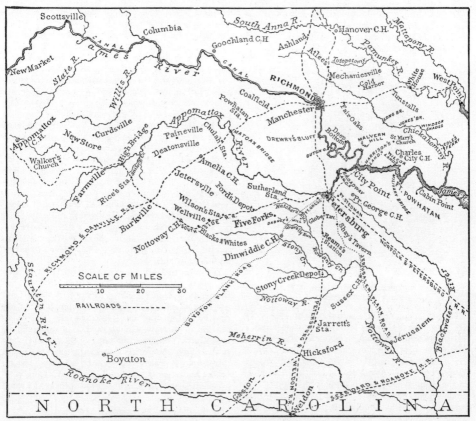

MAP OF THE PETERSBURG AND APPOMATTOX CAMPAIGNS.

junction for an attack during the afternoon of the 19th.

Heth opened on Ayres's front, while Mahone, who was best acquainted with the woods, burst in Ayres's right and swept down on Crawford in column of fours, carrying off Crawford's skirmishers, and seizing parts of the main line, and compelling Ayres's right and Crawford's line to fall back. For a short time chaos and confusion reigned, Crawford fighting on all sides, and pieces of artillery of both armies pouring their fire into the intermingled mass of friend and foe — ranks there were none. Crawford himself was at one moment a prisoner and escaped "by miracle," while of the other prisoners captured, some were secured and others fled or were rescued. In this mêlée Captain Newbury was shot by a rebel officer to prevent his rescue, and died in the arms of his own men with the avowal on his lips. The confusion was scarcely over before our Ninth Corps got up.

Hearing the attack on Ayres my division was first ordered in his direction, toward the left. But as the firing quickly became general along the line and men came streaming out everywhere, I ordered my First Brigade, General John F. Hartranft, forward into the woods, and Colonel William Humphrey with the Second Brigade to support him in the direction of Crawford's right front.

Hartranft encountered a line of troops, probably Clingman's brigade, coming through a strip of timber. They had penetrated some six hundred yards in the right and rear of Crawford's works, and through a corn-field, giving them full view of the space around Globe Tavern and all our movements. Hartranft threw forward his right regiments, and advancing thus drove the fellows back through the edge of the woods and into the field, capturing a good lot of prisoners. The enemy, collecting in the corn-field again, came forward, while Hartranft brought up his left wing, and now drove them "under a terrific fire of musketry" across that field into the farther woods; there they once more rallied and came out, this time to within seventy-five yards of us, but were again driven to cover just as Humphrey's brigade closed up.

About this time I received orders from Warren to send a brigade to the left of Crawford and right of Ayres, and Humphrey was started over. Humphrey fell foul of the enemy, one of Mahone's brigades, coming through the trees. Both sides halted and commenced firing, but the Confederates soon fell back to the captured works. Moving a little further to the left. Humphrey formed his men in two lines and made a charge, in which he succeeded in driving the enemy from the works at the point designated by Warren, capturing a battle-flag and quite a number of prisoners. In this charge fell Major Horatio Belcher, of the 8th Michigan, while waving on his "Wolverines" with his wonted enthusiasm.

MAJOR-GENERAL HENRY HETH, C. S. A.
FROM A PHOTOGRAPH.

The achievement of these works,— more strictly, rifle-pits,— says Colonel Humphrey, a most truthful and unassuming man, was effected without connection with other troops, on either flank, where the works were recaptured later, as will be seen further on, when Ayres on his left and Crawford on the right came up with their troops.♆

Meanwhile, the battle began to rage again on our right. Scarcely had Hartranft started over to support and connect with Humphrey, leaving the ground that he had gained to be occupied by White, when White was attacked by Colquitt. Warren ordered me to assume command of both divisions and I ordered Hartranft to support White. His support was scarcely needed, for, refusing his right wing, as he had been previously directed by Warren, to prevent another such disaster as had opened the proceedings, White repulsed the attack completely. Beauregard telegraphed Lee, with reference to the attacks on Hartranft and White, that "Colquitt and Clingman, in advancing through the thick undergrowth, lost their organizations, and were ordered to their camps to rally them."

Meantime, Edward S. Bragg's brigade of Cutler's division had been ordered up to support and help reëstablish Ayres's broken right, which it gallantly did, encountering a small force on its way; Crawford also had somewhat re-formed his broken battalions. These preparations being made, Warren ordered us all to attack and recapture the lost rifle-pits yet remaining in the enemy's hands, and about the time that White was driving Colquitt the general advance was handsomely made. Not only were our rifle-pits everywhere retaken, but rows of

muskets in stacks—perhaps those left by our own men — were captured as they stood. Heth alone held his grip in front of Ayres, and remained unbroken. He had made two assaults during the day, both without shaking Ayres, and at a loss of some prisoners as well as a flag. Just before dark — a favorite hour for the enemy's assaults — the stubborn Heth made his third, last, and most desperate attack. But Ayres was stronger, both in troops and position. His volunteers emulated his regulars in their enthusiastic bravery, and such isolated assaults on intrenched lines hardly ever prove successful. Besides the reënforcements mentioned Griffin had sent over a brigade to strengthen his classmate.↓ And it was now classmate against classmate. With the odds so much on one side the result might have been, and probably was, anticipated; but "war is a game of chances." Heth was ignorant of the reënforcements and calculated on Ayres's weakness from his shifting back his right. He made a most gallant charge, was repulsed, and, strange to say, was suffered to retire without a counter-charge.

Down on the left and rear General W. H. F. Lee had made strenuous attempts to turn our flank, but Spear, supported by Griffin at the end of the line, not only stood him off there, but reported at night that he had driven Lee to within a mile of Reams's Station. There was much jubilation in our camps that night. Warren felt happy and was lavish in praise of all, generously thanking me and the Ninth Corps troops present for what he was kind enough to say had "saved the day." General Meade telegraphed that " he was delighted to hear the good

MAJOR-GENERAL W. H. F. LEE, C. S. A.
FROM A PHOTOGRAPH.

♆ This incident is overlooked by Warren in his report, which I find in the "War Records" Publication Office, and which was written before he received copy of my own report through Ninth Corps headquarters.—O. B. W.

↓ Ayres, Griffin, and myself were members of the same graduating class at the Military Academy, West Point, and so were two of our opponents on this field, A. P. Hill and Heth.—O. B. W.

GENERAL WARREN'S HEADQUARTERS AT GLOBE TAVERN. FROM A SKETCH MADE AT THE TIME.

news, and congratulated Warren and his brave officers and men on their success," adding, "it will serve greatly to inspirit the whole army, and proves that we only want a fair chance to defeat the enemy. I hope he will try it again." Well did that army need cheering up, for it had been under a black cloud ever since the fatal mine affair, and felt the long strain of the trenches on its nerves.

On the 20th Warren drew back his line about a mile to more open ground, where his artillery might play its part; and on the 21st Hill reappeared before him to "try it again" with his own corps and W. H. F. Lee's cavalry, reënforced by part of Hoke's division of Ewell's corps. Hill was a dashing general, and he made a gallant effort on Warren's lines, now pretty well intrenched,

assaulting under cover of a cannonade of thirty guns. But Griffin and Ayres were both old artillerists, and Hill's long, serried lines were smashed by our guns before they got within reach of our musketry. Later in the day Mahone selected a point, and "hurled" his division with his well-known fiery energy fairly up to our works on the left, but in vain. Hagood's brigade alone got inside, and were there made prisoners in a body, though part of them, in the confusion and delay to take them in, re-opened fire and made their escape. Besides all the wounded, over two hundred Confederates lay dead upon the field in front of our defenses — a sad sight, for, enemies as they were, they were bone of our bone and flesh of our flesh. Thus ended the last and most reckless attempt to dislodge Warren.

II. REAMS'S STATION.

EVER since the first investment of Petersburg both sides had appreciated the importance of the Weldon Railroad, and every attempt on our part was fiercely contested by the rebels. Wilson's cavalry raid was started off against that and the Lynchburg Railroad on June 22d by General Meade. [See p. 535.] Late in August, in view of the success of the Fifth and Ninth corps at Globe Tavern, it was determined to continue the work of destruction down on this much-fought-for railway. For this purpose Hancock was ordered over from Deep Bottom with two divisions to Reams's Station. He arrived there on the 22d, after a most fatiguing march, and set to work at once with his accustomed promptitude and energy, and without rest. He found the station house burnt, and some sorry intrenchments in a flat, woody country, where two roads crossed, which had been hastily thrown up during the June opera-

tions, but which he did not stop to improve: one from the Jerusalem plank-road, by which he had marched; the other from the Vaughn road, running from Petersburg to Dinwiddie Court House. He found the roads picketed by Spear's brigade of cavalry, and to this he added D. McM. Gregg's cavalry, which he had brought along.

Hancock had torn up and burned some miles of the track, when, on the evening of August 24th, Meade notified him that bodies of troops, estimated at ten thousand, were seen by the signal men moving within the Confederate lines to our left, and advancing down the Halifax-Vaughn road. It might be intended to attack either Warren's left, or Reams's Station. Meade thought the latter the more likely.

For some time next morning nothing appeared before Hancock but the usual parties of W. H. F. Lee's cavalry, that had sought to interrupt the

The total Union loss was 251 killed, 1148 wounded, and 2879 captured or missing = 4278. The Confederate loss is not officially stated. — EDITORS.

work of our men, but were easily kept off by Gregg, who held the roads toward Dinwiddie Court House and Petersburg. Gibbon's division was about to proceed down the track to resume its labors when Spear, farther down to the left, reported the enemy advancing in force. Gregg deployed and advanced to meet them, and developed the fact that their cavalry was supported by infantry. During the skirmish a party broke through Gregg's pickets to the left and rear. This party was driven back by a regiment of our cavalry with its infantry supports, and the whole demonstra-

MAJOR-GENERAL JOHN GIBBON.
FROM A PHOTOGRAPH.

tion — probably a reconnoissance — was over. Prisoners taken in the skirmish proved to be from C. M. Wilcox's, Heth's, and Field's divisions, of A. P. Hill's command. In fact, there were nine brigades, including two of Mahone's, and Pegram's artillery, present or coming up. Developments so far were reported to army headquarters and preparations were made for a vigorous defense. Gibbon's division was drawn into the left breastworks, which were strengthened and extended somewhat to the rear, and Miles, with Barlow's division, occupied the right. Both flanks were exposed to reverse fire from the front, as may be easily seen from Hancock's map. Until 12 o'clock all communications with Meade were by couriers through Warren's headquarters. At noon the field telegraph line was brought down to within half a mile. It was not until 2 o'clock that the enemy made another move, when they attacked Miles,

were repulsed, and again attacked more vigorously, and were again repulsed, this time leaving their killed and wounded within a few yards of Miles's front.

Meantime Meade had ordered all the available troops from Mott's division that were on Warren's right to move down the plank-road to its intersection with the Reams's Station cross-road, four miles back from the station, and report from there to Hancock. And now, since this last attack at 2:45 P. M., Willcox's division of the Ninth Corps, held in reserve on Warren's center, was ordered to the same point. Hancock had been advised by telegraph from Warren's headquarters, where Meade had come to be in closer communication: "Call him [Willcox] up if necessary"; and the dispatch adds: "I hope you'll give the enemy a good thrashing. All I apprehend is his being able to interpose between you and Warren."

I proposed to the officer who brought me my orders — I forget whether it was General Parke, commanding the Ninth Corps, ≀ or a staff-officer — to march straight down the railroad, four or five miles at most, and join Hancock at once, instead of marching round twelve miles by the plank-road, but was told that there was some apprehension of the enemy's getting round Hancock's left and rear, and that I must look out for that side. We passed the Gurley House at 3:55, marched across lots to the plank-road, and down to the cross-roads at Shay's Tavern, where we arrived before 6, and received a message from Hancock calling me up rapidly. My troops were in good spirits. They heard the cannon-firing and felt that, having assisted Warren of late materially and in the nick of an extremity, they were rather honored by this call from the grand old Second Corps, and we pushed ahead at a swinging gait. Very soon we began to meet stragglers from the front, and some wagons and ambulances. Farther on an orderly handed me an order ☆ from Hancock to arrest the stragglers and "form them according to their regiments," for which I had to deploy and leave the 20th Michigan Infantry, and that delayed us a little of course. With the rest of the division I pushed on, without halting, until 7 o'clock, when I received word that if one or two brigades could be got up in time the day might yet be saved. This was communicated to the troops, who threw off their blanket rolls and started at a double-quick, which they kept up, with few breathing intervals, the rest of the way until I reported to Hancock.

Meantime a bitter fight had been going on. After the 2 o'clock affair everything looked promising to Hancock for an hour or two. However, the rest of Hill's troops were coming up, and the chopping of trees and the rumble of artillery were heard in the forest. Hancock only felt solicitous to keep the road open leading to the plank-road, up which he looked for aid, "if necessary," and by which he must retreat if worsted. At 4:15 he became more anxious, and telegraphed Meade

---

≀ On August 13th General Burnside was granted a leave of absence and General John G. Parke was assigned to the command of the Ninth Corps. General Burnside resigned April 15th, 1865.— EDITORS.

☆ This order was intended for the officer commanding Mott's troops, still at Shay's Tavern.— O. B. W.

that heavy skirmishing was going on, and an attack pending, probably, on the left. He desired, as he said to Meade, "to know as soon as possible whether you wish me to retire from this station in case we can get through safe — think it too late for Willcox; had he come down the railroad he would have been in time. Have ordered up Mott's division by way of precaution." Evidently he expected Mott first at the junction.

At 5 o'clock Hill had opened with his artillery, both shot and shell, some of which took the works, so-called, in reverse, but did little actual damage other than demoralizing the men, of whom there were many, even in the old regiments, who never had come to fight, but to run on the first chance, or get into the hospital, and, ho! for a pension afterward! "Some of their officers could not speak a word of English," says Hancock in his report, and were therefore without that mutual intelligence and support which battle demands, and with nothing in common with their men but panic.

The first assault came on Miles, opposite his Fourth Brigade, and at a part of the line held by the consolidation of material of different regiments. For a time the severity of Miles's fire, the slashing and other obstacles on the ground, staggered the assaulting column, and they must have baffled it completely if the fire had continued only a few minutes longer. As it was, the assailants were thrown into considerable confusion when, suddenly, our recruits gave way, and a break occurred of two regiments on the right, and though Miles ordered up what little reserve he had these men would neither move forward nor fire. Still Lieutenant George K. Dauchy, of McKnight's 12th New York Battery, turned his guns on the breach with effect, until the enemy crept along the silent rifle-pits, captured the battery, and turned a gun inside our lines. Murphy's brigade of the Second Division being likewise driven off, the enemy captured the 10th Massachusetts Battery, and Battery B, 1st Rhode Island Artillery, on his front, though it was served with "marked gallantry" to the last.

Gibbon's division was ordered to retake the works that were thus lost, but the men responded feebly, and fell back to their other works. Here, however, they were exposed to such an interior fire that they were compelled to throw themselves over to the outside of their parapet. Affairs looked desperate. But the gallant and indefatigable Miles, rallying

some brave men of the 61st New York, formed line at right angles, swept down, recaptured considerable of the ground lost, including McKnight's battery, and threw two hundred men across the railroad, threatening the enemy's rear. This force was insufficient to hold their advantage, and Gibbon's fellows were ordered to reënforce it. But in vain. "They could not be got to go up," said the veteran, who, with his staff, tried his best, with sword and expostulations. His own side was soon attacked "by dismounted cavalry, and driven from their breastworks with little or no resistance," until some dismounted regiments of Gregg's and Spear's cavalry, fighting with bravery that shamed our infantry, rescued the prize from the enemy, who finally fell back. Gibbon partially rallied his men behind the right wing, and formed a new line of pits a short distance to his rear, on the left of which Gregg withdrew his troopers.

Every attempt subsequently made by the enemy was successfully repelled. ⸸ In one assault Miles made a counter-charge and recaptured part of his lost line and a gun, and so matters stood at my arrival near the scene of action some time before dark. With the assistance of my division it did not seem too late to recover everything that had been lost. But, considering the utter demoralization of one of his divisions, and the fatigue of all the brave men that had stood, Hancock did not think it wise to renew the fight that evening, though both Miles and Gregg offered to retake their portions of the works. Nor did he think it worth while to sacrifice any more men for an object that was so far accomplished that, previous to the action, he had telegraphed Meade his own intention to withdraw that night anyhow. Nothing more could be done to destroy the railroad now, and consequently there was nothing to keep Hancock at the station. "Had our troops behaved as they used to I could have beaten Hill," he said to me. "But some were new, and all were worn out with labor. Or had your force been sent down the railroad to attack the enemy's flank we would have whipped him; or a small reserve about 6 o'clock would have accomplished the same object." These points were also mentioned in his report. ⸸ He requested me to draw up my division as a rearguard and let his troops pass by after dark. I never had seen him in better form. It was more like abdication than defeat.

The enemy did not attempt to follow us. ⸸

⸸ Captain Christian Woerner's 3d New Jersey Battery rendered important service at this time.— EDITORS.

⸸ General Humphreys in a letter to me of October 9th, 1883, says:

"I considered your not having taken part in the fight to be due entirely to the route you were ordered to take, as indeed it was. Meade was at Warren's headquarters. I was at headquarters Army of the Potomac. The telegrams were all taken off for me and I was sorely tempted to telegraph Meade to send you down the railroad to hit the enemy in flank, but refrained from delicacy, to my great regret ever since."

The general also furnished me with copies of notes intended to correct mistakes and fill omissions which occurred in his history, "The Virginia Campaign of 1864 and 1865," and which are corrected and supplied in these articles, so far as the Weldon Railroad fights and my division are concerned.— O. B. W.

⸸ The Union loss was 140 killed, 529 wounded, and 2073 captured or missing = 2742.
The loss of the Confederates reached a total of 720, mostly in killed and wounded.— EDITORS.

GENERAL GRANT ON THE SIEGE OF PETERSBURG.

EXTRACT FROM LIEUTENANT-GENERAL U. S. GRANT'S REPORT, DATED JULY 22D, 1865.
[SEE ALSO PP. 145–151.]

ON the 16th [of June, 1864], the enemy, to re-enforce Petersburg, withdrew from a part of his intrenchment in front of Bermuda Hundred, expecting, no doubt, to get troops from north of the James to take the place of those withdrawn before we could discover it. General Butler, taking advantage of this, at once moved a force on the railroad between Petersburg and Richmond. As soon as I was apprised of the advantage thus gained, to retain it I ordered two divisions of the Sixth Corps, General Wright commanding, that were embarking at Wilcox's Landing, under orders for City Point, to report to General Butler at Bermuda Hundred, of which General Butler was notified, and the importance of holding a position in advance of his present line urged upon him.

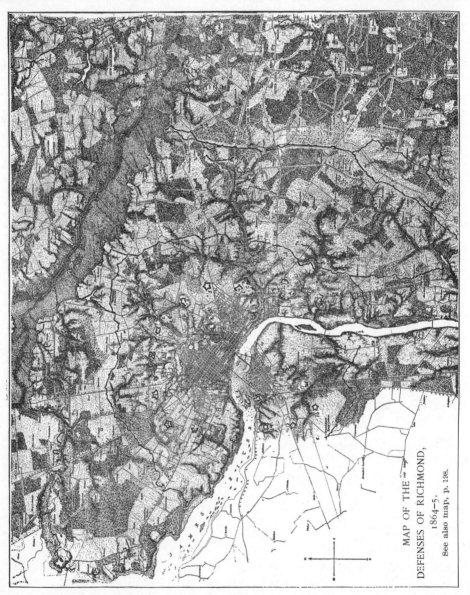

MAP OF THE
DEFENSES OF RICHMOND,
1864–5.

See also map, p. 198.

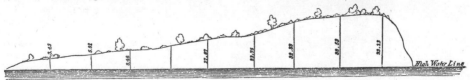

EXCAVATING THE DUTCH GAP CANAL.
FROM A SKETCH MADE AT THE TIME.

At the request of the editors, the following account of the Dutch Gap Canal has been prepared by General P. S. Michie, engineer in charge of the work:

"The strong defensive lines of Bermuda Hundred, behind which the Army of the James retreated after its repulse at Drewry's Bluff, May 16th, 1864, were badly chosen, as their location permitted the Confederates to occupy an equally strong line, and thus to prevent any active operations on the part of this army against the Richmond and Petersburg Railroad. The powerful Confederate battery Dansler completely commanded Trent Reach — a wide, shallow part of the James River on the north flank of the contending lines. This barred all approach toward Richmond on the part of the United States war vessels. General Butler, conceiving the idea of cutting a canal through the narrow neck of land, known as Dutch Gap, for the passage of the monitors, directed me to report on the practicability of this project. The report being favorable, ground was broken August 10th, 1864. The canal, cutting off 4¾ miles of river navigation, was only 174 yards long — the excavation being 43 yards wide at the top, 27 yards at water-level, and 13.5 yards at a depth of 15 feet below water-level; 31 yards deep at the north-west end and nearly 12 yards at the south-east end; the total excavation being very nearly 67,000 cubic yards. While no serious civil-engineering difficulties occurred, the troops employed were constantly subjected to a severe continuous fire, first of heavy rifled guns and afterward of mortars. The casualties were continuous throughout, on one occasion resulting in twelve killed and forty wounded; in addition, great losses in mules, horses, and carts were sustained. The dredge (after being once sunk) and the steam-pump were bombproofed for protection. This constant vertical fire from mortar-batteries only twelve hundred yards distant delayed the work beyond anticipation, causing frequent suspension of all labor. The troops seeking cover in earthen dug-outs that covered the site of the work were also undergoing constant discomfort and exposure. The greater part of the excavation was done by colored troops, who displayed the greatest courage and fortitude, and maintained under the most trying circumstances their usual good humor and cheerful disposition. Owing to various causes, and especially to the capture by General Butler of the outer line of the Richmond defenses on the 29th of September, the importance of the canal project sensibly diminished; therefore the work was much delayed, was subject to indifferent management, and was not ultimately completed until December 30th, 1864. The rather large bulkhead containing nearly 6000 cubic yards of earth was mined and charged with 12,000 pounds of powder, distributed in four charges, one being 25 feet, and three 15 feet, below the water-level. At 3:50 P. M., January 1st, 1865, these mines were exploded by means of a Gomez fulminate fuse so arranged as to give a point of ignition for every one hundred pounds of powder. The condition of the canal in November is well delineated in the accompanying cut. The bomb-proof steam-pump is shown in the far corner, and the bulkhead, separated from the adjacent embankment by vertical trenches, is that which was mined and blown up. After the explosion the débris at the north-west end was partially removed by means of a steam-dredge. This canal was not of service during the war, but was subsequently enlarged and perfected, and became the usual channel for the passage of vessels."

VERTICAL PLAN OF THE DUTCH GAP CANAL.

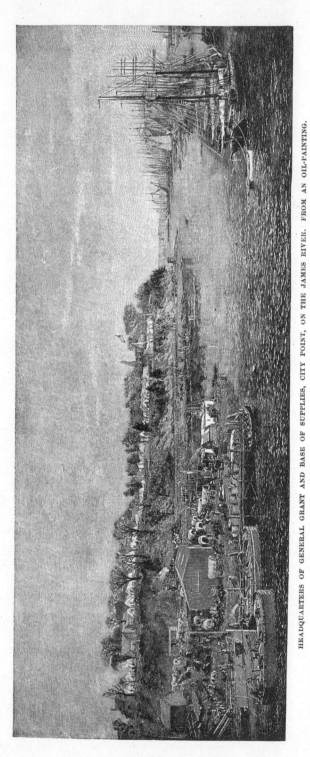

HEADQUARTERS OF GENERAL GRANT AND BASE OF SUPPLIES, CITY POINT, ON THE JAMES RIVER. FROM AN OIL-PAINTING.

About 2 o'clock in the afternoon General Butler was forced back to the line the enemy had withdrawn from in the morning. General Wright, with his two divisions, joined General Butler on the forenoon of the 17th, the latter still holding with a strong picket-line the enemy's works. But instead of putting these divisions into the enemy's works to hold them he permitted them to halt and rest some distance in the rear of his own line. Between 4 and 5 o'clock in the afternoon the enemy attacked and drove in his pickets and re-occupied his old line.

On the night of the 20th and morning of the 21st a lodgment was effected by General Butler, with one brigade of infantry, on the north bank of the James, at Deep Bottom, and connected by pontoon-bridge with Bermuda Hundred.

On the 19th General Sheridan, on his return from his expedition against the Virginia Central Railroad [see p. 233], arrived at the White House just as the enemy's cavalry was about to attack it, and compelled it to retire. . . . After breaking up the depot at that place he moved to the James River, which he reached safely after heavy fighting. He commenced crossing on the 25th, near Fort Powhatan, without further molestation, and rejoined the Army of the Potomac.

On the 22d [of June] General Wilson, with his own division of cavalry of the Army of the Potomac and General Kautz's division of cavalry of the Army of the James, moved against the enemy's railroads south of Richmond. [See p. 535.] . . .

With a view of cutting the enemy's railroad from near Richmond to the Anna rivers, and making him wary of the situation of his army in the Shenandoah, and, in the event of failure in this, to take advantage of his necessary withdrawal of troops from Petersburg, to explode a mine that had been prepared in front of the Ninth Corps and assault the enemy's lines at that place, on the night of the 26th of July the Second Corps and two divisions of the cavalry corps and Kautz's cavalry were crossed to the north bank of the James River and joined the force General Butler had there. On the 27th the enemy was driven from his intrenched position, with the loss of four pieces of artillery. [See map, p. 198.] On the 28th our lines were extended from Deep Bottom to New Market road, but in getting this position were attacked by the enemy in heavy force. The fighting lasted for several hours, resulting in considerable loss to both sides. The first object of this move having failed, by reason of the very large force thrown there by the enemy, I determined to take advantage of the diversion made by assaulting Petersburg before he could get his force back there. One division of the Second Corps was withdrawn on the night of the 28th, and moved during the night to the rear of the Eighteenth Corps, to relieve that corps in the line, that it might be foot-loose in the assault to be made. The other two divisions of the Second Corps and Sheridan's cavalry were crossed over on the night of the 29th and moved in front of Petersburg. On the morning of the 30th, between 4 and 5 o'clock, the mine was sprung, blowing up a battery and most of a regiment, and the advance of the assaulting column, formed of the Ninth Corps, immediately took possession of the crater made by the explosion, and the line for some distance to the right and left of it, and a detached line in front of it, but for some cause failed to advance promptly to the ridge beyond. [See p. 540, *et seq.*] Had they done this, I have every reason to believe that Petersburg would have fallen. Other troops were immediately pushed forward, but the time consumed in getting them up enabled the enemy to rally from his surprise (which had been complete) and get forces to this point for its defense. The captured line thus held being untenable, and of no advantage to us, the troops were withdrawn, but not without heavy loss. Thus terminated in disaster what promised to be the most successful assault of the campaign. . . .

Reports from various sources led me to believe that the enemy had detached three divisions from Petersburg to reënforce Early in the Shenandoah Valley. [See pp. 500 and 522.] I therefore sent the Second Corps and Gregg's division of cavalry, of the Army of the Potomac, and a force of General Butler's army, on the night of the 13th of August, to threaten Richmond from the north side of the James, to prevent him from sending troops away, and, if possible, to draw back those sent. [See map, p. 198.] In this move we captured six pieces of artillery and several hundred prisoners, detained troops that were under marching orders, and ascertained that but one division (Kershaw's) of the three reputed detached had gone.

The enemy having withdrawn heavily from Petersburg to resist this movement, the Fifth Corps, General Warren commanding, was moved out on the 18th, and took possession of the Weldon Railroad. [See p. 568.] During the day he had considerable fighting. To regain possession of the road

the enemy made repeated and desperate assaults, but was each time repulsed with great loss. On the night of the 20th the troops on the north side of the James were withdrawn, and Hancock and Gregg returned to the front at Petersburg. On the 25th the Second Corps and Gregg's division of cavalry, while at Reams's Station destroying the railroad, were attacked, and after desperate fighting a part of our line gave way and five pieces of artillery fell into the hands of the enemy. [See p. 571.]

By the 12th of September a branch railroad was completed from the City Point and Peters-

UNION RAILROAD BATTERY, PETERSBURG.
FROM A PHOTOGRAPH.

burg Railroad to the Weldon Railroad, enabling us to supply, without difficulty, in all weather, the army in front of Petersburg. [See map, p. 538.]

The extension of our lines across the Weldon Railroad compelled the enemy to so extend his that it seemed he could have but few troops north of the James for the defense of Richmond. On the night of the 28th the Tenth Corps, Major-General [D. B.] Birney, and the Eighteenth Corps, Major-General [E. O. C.] Ord commanding, of General Butler's army, were crossed to the north side of the James, and advanced on the morning of the 29th, carrying the very strong fortifications and intrenchments below Chaffin's Farm, known as Fort Harrison, capturing fifteen pieces of artillery and the New Market road and intrenchments. This success was followed up by a gallant assault upon Fort Gilmer, | immediately in front of the Chaffin Farm fortifications, in which we were repulsed with heavy loss. [See map, p. 198.] Kautz's cavalry was pushed forward on the road to the right of this, supported by infantry, and reached the enemy's inner line, but was unable to get farther. The position captured from the enemy was. so threatening to Richmond that I determined to hold it. The enemy made several desperate attempts to dislodge us, all of which were unsuccessful, and for which he paid dearly.⚓ On the morning of the 30th [of September] General Meade sent out a

---

| The assault on Fort Gilmer was made by General Adelbert Ames's division, and Brigadier-General William Birney's colored brigade of the Tenth Corps.— EDITORS.

⚓ The assaults on Fort Harrison were made by the brigades of Clingman, Colquitt, Law, G. T. Anderson,

and Bratton, under General R. H. Anderson, commanding Longstreet's corps. The Confederate loss in killed and wounded was about two thousand. General George J. Stannard, commander of the Union troops at Fort Harrison, lost his arm, and General Hiram Burnham, a brigade commander, was killed.— EDITORS.

reconnoissance with a view to attacking the enemy's line if it was found sufficiently weakened by withdrawal of troops to the north side. In this reconnoissance we captured and held the enemy's works near Poplar Spring Church. In the afternoon troops moving to get to the left of the point gained were attacked by the enemy in heavy force and compelled to fall back until supported by the

MAJOR-GENERAL ORLANDO B. WILLCOX.
FROM A PHOTOGRAPH.

forces holding the captured works. Our cavalry under Gregg was also attacked, but repulsed the enemy with great loss.

On the 7th of October the enemy attacked Kautz's cavalry north of the James and drove it back with heavy loss in killed, wounded, and prisoners, and the loss of all the artillery — eight or nine pieces.⧫ This he followed up by an attack on our intrenched infantry line, but was repulsed with severe slaughter. On the 13th a reconnoissance was sent out by General Butler, with a view to drive the enemy from some new works he was constructing, which resulted in very heavy loss to us.⧫

On the 27th [of October] the Army of the Potomac, leaving only sufficient men to hold its fortified line, moved by the enemy's right flank. The

Second Corps, followed by two divisions of the Fifth Corps, with the cavalry in advance and covering our left flank, forced a passage of Hatcher's Run, and moved up the south side of it toward the South Side Railroad, until the Second Corps and part of the cavalry reached the Boydton plank-road where it crosses Hatcher's Run. At this point we were six miles distant from the South Side Railroad, which I had hoped by this movement to reach and hold. But finding that we had not reached the end of the enemy's fortifications, and no place presenting itself for a successful assault by which he might be doubled up and shortened, I determined to withdraw to within our fortified line. Orders were given accordingly. Immediately upon receiving a report that General Warren had connected with General Hancock I returned to my headquarters. Soon after I left the enemy moved out across Hatcher's Run, in the gap between Generals Hancock and Warren, which was not closed as reported, and made a desperate attack on General Hancock's right and rear. General Hancock immediately faced his corps to meet it, and after a bloody combat drove the enemy within his works, and withdrew that night to his old position.

In support of this movement General Butler made a demonstration on the north side of the James, and attacked the enemy on the Williamsburg road, and also on the York River Railroad. In the former he was unsuccessful; in the latter he succeeded in carrying a work which was afterward abandoned, and his forces had withdrawn to their former positions.

From this time forward the operations in front of Petersburg and Richmond, until the spring campaign of 1865, were confined to the defense and extension of our lines, and to offensive movements for crippling the enemy's lines of communication, and to prevent his detaching any considerable force to send south. By the 7th of February our lines were extended to Hatcher's Run, and the Weldon Railroad had been destroyed to Hicksford. . . .↾

After the long march by General Sheridan's cavalry, from the Shenandoah Valley, over winter roads it was necessary to rest and refit at White House. At this time the greatest source of uneasiness to me was the fear that the enemy would leave his strong lines about Petersburg and Richmond for the purpose of uniting with Johnston, before he was driven from them by battle or I

⧫ General Kautz writes to the editors, November, 1888:

"The new lines which resulted from the success of General Butler at Fort Harrison on the 29th of September, gave my division the duty of guarding the right flank of the Army of the James with pickets as far as White's Tavern on the Charles City road. The headquarters of the division were at Darbytown, two miles in front of the intrenched infantry line, located in the forks of the swamp which forms Four Mile Creek. The error of the position was duly represented. When the enemy at 4 A. M. on the 7th of October tried to extend his lines, the weight of the assault fell upon the cavalry. Two divisions of infantry under Longstreet engaged my force in front, while a superior force of Confederate cavalry under General Gary, covered by the timber, penetrated to the rear. The cavalry sustained the attack until 8 o'clock, giving the Tenth Corps ample time to prepare to punish the enemy very severely."

⧫ General Kautz writes:

"On the 13th of October the Cavalry Division participated in a movement under General Terry, then in command of the Tenth Corps. We engaged the Confederate cavalry on the Charles City road, while the Tenth Corps troops attacked the enemy's intrenched line on the Darbytown road."

↾ Among the movements on the left were the expedition, December 7th to 10th, under Warren, by which the Weldon Railroad was destroyed as far as Hicksford, and the combined movement, February 5th to 7th, under Warren and Humphreys (who on the 28th of November succeeded to the command of the Second Corps, Hancock having been detailed to organize the Veteran Corps),— which resulted in extending the Union intrenchments to Hatcher's Run, after some severe fighting with the troops of A. P. Hill and Gordon.—EDITORS.

was prepared to make an effectual pursuit. On the 24th of March General Sheridan moved from White House [see p. 494], crossed the James River at Jones's Landing, and formed a junction with the Army of the Potomac in front of Petersburg on the 27th. During this move General Ord ⚓ sent forces to cover the crossings of the Chickahominy. On the 24th of March . . . instructions for a general movement [on March 29th] of the armies operating against Richmond were issued. . . .

Early on the morning of the 25th the enemy assaulted our lines in front of the Ninth Corps (which held from the Appomattox River toward our left)

⚓ On the 8th of January, 1865, General E. O. C. Ord succeeded General B. F. Butler in command of the Army of the James, and the Department of Virginia and North Carolina, the designation of which was changed, February 8th, to the Department of Virginia.—EDITORS.

☆ General A. A. Humphreys, in his history, "The Virginia Campaign of '64 and '65," gives the following account of the object of the Confederate movement:

"General Lee proposed . . . to make a sortie in order to gain some of the works on the right of the line held by the Army of the Potomac, near the Appomattox River, and the ridge in their rear. . . . General Gordon was selected for

and carried Fort Stedman and a part of the line to the right and left of it, established themselves and turned the guns of the fort against us; ☆ but our troops on either flank held their ground until the reserves were brought up, when the enemy was driven back with a heavy loss in killed and wounded, and 1900 prisoners. . . . General Meade at once ordered the other corps to advance and feel the enemy in their respective fronts. Pushing forward, they captured and held the enemy's strongly intrenched picket-line in front of the Second and Sixth corps, and 834 prisoners. The enemy made desperate attempts to retake this line, but without success. . . .

the service, and his corps was brought to the intrenchments nearest Petersburg, with its left on the Appomattox. The point of attack was Fort Stedman, where the opposing lines were only 150 yards apart, the pickets 50 yards apart. General Gordon was sanguine that this redoubt could be taken by a night assault, and that through the breach thus made a sufficient force could be thrown to disorganize and destroy Grant's left wing before he could recover and concentrate his forces from the right. General Gordon says that General Lee placed at his disposal, in addition to his own corps, a portion of A. P. Hill's and a portion of Longstreet's, and a detachment of cavalry, in all about one-half of the army." EDITORS.

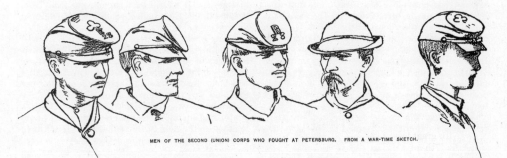

MEN OF THE SECOND (UNION) CORPS WHO FOUGHT AT PETERSBURG. FROM A WAR-TIME SKETCH.

GORDON'S ATTACK AT FORT STEDMAN.

BY GEORGE L. KILMER, COMPANY I, 14TH NEW YORK HEAVY ARTILLERY.

ON the 25th of March, 1865, General O. B. Willcox's division, of the Ninth Corps, was formed on the Petersburg lines in the following order from right to left [see map, p. 538]: Second Brigade (Lieutenant-Colonel Ralph Ely), from the Appomattox to Battery IX, near the City Point Railroad; Third Brigade (Colonel N. B. McLaughlen), from Battery IX to Fort Haskell; First Brigade (Colonel Samuel Harriman), from Fort Haskell to Fort Morton, directly facing Cemetery Hill. Fort Morton was a bastioned work, high and impregnable. Fort Haskell, the next down the line, on lower ground and quite under the best guns that Lee had

on the crest, was a small field redoubt mounting six rifled guns and holding a feeble infantry gar-

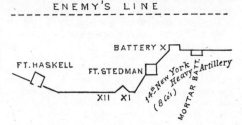

ENEMY'S LINE

The Third Brigade was formed on the lines as follows: Eight companies of the 14th New York Heavy Artillery garrisoned Fort Stedman and Battery X, and guarded the trenches from the fort to a point one hundred yards to the right of the battery, and the 57th Massachusetts occupied the trenches on the right of the 14th; a detachment of Company K, 1st Connecticut Heavy Artillery, served a Coehorn mortar-battery near Battery X, and one section of the 14th Massachusetts Battery, Light Artillery, was stationed in the battery. Two sections of the 19th New York Battery occupied Fort Stedman. The

29th and 59th Massachusetts garrisoned the trenches and occupied Batteries XI and XII, where, also, Company L, 1st Connecticut Heavy Artillery served, with batteries of 8-inch and Coehorn mortars. The 100th Pennsylvania occupied the trenches from Battery XII to Fort Haskell, and the 3d Maryland those for a short distance on the left of that work. The garrison of Fort Haskell consisted of four companies (I, K, L, and M) of the 14th New York Heavy Artillery, Captain Christian Woerner's 3d New Jersey Battery, and a detachment of the 1st Connecticut Heavy Artillery with Coehorn mortars.—G..L. K.

rison. Eighty rods farther was Fort Stedman, a stronger work than Haskell, and not so well commanded from Cemetery Hill. Two hundred rods from Stedman was Fort McGilvery, near the river and out of range of Lee's heavy ordnance. In front of Haskell there were woods, marshes, and a sluggish stream completely obstructing the passage of men and guns from the enemy's works eastward, but at Stedman, where the lines were but forty rods apart, the ground of both lines and all between was solid, and feasible for rapid movements of bodies of every arm of service, even to cavalry, and so here was a road that a master-stroke might open.

The headquarters of the 14th were at Stedman, where our acting colonel, Major George M. Randall, had command. Captain Charles H. Houghton, of Company L, commanded at Fort Haskell.

About 3 o'clock on the morning of March 25th Lieutenants C. A. Lochbrunner and Frank M. Thomson, who were on night duty at Fort Stedman, informed Major Randall of an unusual commotion in front of the works. Lieutenant Thomson was directed to arouse the command at once and have the men moved to the works as quickly and as quietly as possible. The attack fell first upon Battery X and the breastworks on the right of it, and at that time the most of the officers and men of the garrison were in their places. Captain J. P. Cleary, Lieutenant Thomson, and Sergeant John Delack (who had been on guard duty during the night) had hauled a gun to the sally-port on the face of the fort toward Battery X, and it was opened upon the assailants. Many of the Confederates were captured and sent to the rear.[*] The guns on this face were fired several times under command of the officers of the battery. The artillerymen in Battery X attempted to defend their guns, and Lieutenant E. B. Nye, commanding the section, was shot down beside his pieces.

A second attack was immediately made on the rear of Fort Stedman by an overwhelming force that entered the breach at Battery X. The Confederates climbed over the parapets and in at the embrasures, and it was so dark that the garrison could not distinguish their own men from the enemy. Finding it impossible to hold the fort, the officers and men of the garrison who could get away took shelter on the outside of the parapets, and continued the fight with muskets. After daylight some of the officers and men of the 14th made their way along the moat of the trenches to Fort Haskell, and others fell back in line down the road toward Meade's Station, and formed on the slope within rifle range of their old works. Major Randall was captured just outside of Fort

Stedman, but managed to get away from his captors and reach Fort Haskell. The Confederates had silenced the pickets in front of Fort Stedman by taking advantage of General Grant's order of amnesty to deserters from the enemy. This order encouraged these deserters to bring in their arms, by offering payment for them.[‡] On this occasion Confederates claiming to be deserters came in in large numbers, and very soon overpowered the pickets and passed on to the first line of works.

It was the intention of the Confederates to surprise Fort Haskell also.[♭] This work was guarded by two rows of abatis, and at the gap where the pickets filed out and in a sentinel was on duty all night. The man who served the last watch that morning on this outer post was Sylvester E. Hough, Company M, 14th Regiment, and soon after he went on post (at 3 o'clock) he saw blue-lights flash up along the picket-pits. He also heard the sound of chopping at the abatis on the lines between Stedman and the Confederate works on its front. He hallooed to the second sentinel at Haskell, whose post was at the bridge across the moat, and an alarm was called out in the fort. Hough then advanced down the picket trail toward the outposts, and as he did so the first cannon was fired from Stedman, and the muffled sounds of the fighting there were heard.

There was a long slope between Fort Haskell and the picket-pits, and on this slope Hough met a column of men moving stealthily up toward our western front. The enemy were in two ranks, and had filed into our lines through the gap in front of Stedman, and were moving upon us unopposed, for they were between us and our pickets. If some traitor had divulged their secret movement hours in advance the men of this column could not have been at greater disadvantage than they now were by the chances of war. Hough, unseen by the enemy, ran back to the fort to advise the gunners. Three howitzers, double-shotted with grape, were trained upon the ground. The garrison had been called to arms, and the firing at Fort Stedman aroused the cry on all sides, "They have taken Fort Stedman." The story told by Hough confirmed our suspicions that we were to be attacked, also; we had not long to wait. When the assailants neared the abatis we could hear their tread and their suppressed tones. "Wait," said Captain Houghton; "wait till you see them, then fire." A breath seemed an age, for we knew nothing of the numbers before us. Finally, the Confederate leader called out, "Steady! We'll have their works. Steady, my men!" Our nerves rebelled, and like a flash the thought passed along the parapet, "Now!" Not a word was spoken, but in

[*] The flag of the 26th South Carolina was taken by one of the men of the 14th, and delivered to Major Randall.— G. L. K.

[‡] Copies of the order referred to had been distributed in quantities, inside of the Confederate lines, during the autumn previous, and had the effect of inducing deserters to plan to get away in squads. My diary states that on the night of February 24th nine deserters came in on our brigade front, and on the next night fourteen, including a commissioned officer, many of them fully armed and equipped.— G. L. K.

[♭] The Reverend Charles A. Mott, now (1888) pastor of the Calvary Baptist Church, Philadelphia, was a corporal in Company I, 14th Regiment, and had charge of a vidette picket-post on the right of Fort Haskell, on the night of the 24th and 25th. In a letter now in my possession, written November 1st, 1888, he states that at the opening of the attack a cannon-shot from Fort Stedman plowed the ground near his post, and very soon afterward he heard the tread of a column of the enemy advancing toward our lines.— G. L. K.

perfect concert the cannon and muskets were discharged upon the hapless band. It must have been a surprise for the surprisers, though fortunately for them we had been too hasty, and, as they were moving by the flank along our front, only the head of their column received the fire. But this repulse did not end it; the survivors closed up and tried it again. Then they divided into squads and moved on the flanks, keeping up the by-play until there were none left. Daylight soon gave us perfect aim, and their game was useless.

This stunning blow to the assailants in front of Haskell occurred just as another column of Confederates, that had filed into the works at Stedman, started on a rapid conquest along the trenches toward Fort McGilvery. We could see from Haskell the flashing of rifles as these men moved on and on through the camps of the parapet guards. Another column started also from Stedman along the breastworks linking our two forts. This division aimed to take Haskell in the right rear. At the very outset, this last movement met with a momentary check, for it fell upon two concealed batteries, XI

artillery. He placed one piece in the right rear angle, where the embrasure admitted the working of it with an oblique as well as a direct range. About the same time some officers and men of the 100th Pennsylvania and 3d Maryland regiments, who previous to the attack had occupied the breastworks adjoining, came in and were posted on the rear works by Captain George Brennan, of Company

FORT HASKELL FROM GRACIE'S SALIENT.

FORT STEDMAN FROM COLQUITT'S SALIENT.

FROM SKETCHES MADE IN 1886.

On the morning of March 25th, General Gordon's column (advancing from Colquitt's salient) moved over the level ground shown on the left, in the lower picture. Fort Stedman was located in front of the clump of trees.

and XII, and the 59th and 29th Massachusetts regiments, stationed near and now under arms.

Meanwhile there was a lull around Haskell; but it was of short duration, for it was now so light that the enemy could observe from his main line every point on the scene of conflict. He opened on Haskell with Stedman's guns, and also with his own in front. Our little garrison divided, one half guarding the front parapet, the remainder rallying along the right wall to meet the attack threatened by the division coming against it from Stedman. At this juncture, Captain Christian Woerner, of the 3d New Jersey Battery, who had been on duty at the headquarters of the artillery brigade, in the rear, came into the fort and took charge of the

M, who commanded in that quarter. ≀ The venturesome Confederate column had borne down all opposition, captured batteries XI and XII, and driven all the infantry from the trenches, and, with closed-up ranks, came bounding along. ☆ At a point thirty rods from us the ground was cut by a ravine, and from there it rose in a gentle grade up to the fort. Woerner's one angle gun and about 50 muskets were all we could summon to repel this column, and there were probably an even 60 cannon and 1000 muskets at Stedman and on the main Confederate line concentrating their fire upon Haskell to cover this charge. ↓ The advancing troops reserved their fire. Our thin line mounted the banquettes — the wounded and sick men

≀ Lieutenant J. H. Stevenson, of Company K, 100th Pennsylvania, writes under date of December 2d, 1887:

"A little after the alarm was given, all the companies on my right and left were taken to the rear as skirmishers, and I spread my company out in a thin line along our breastworks. Here we stood waiting for the enemy. When the bullets began to come in from the rear I moved my company out for the purpose of being ready to face to the rear. I formed at right angles with the breastworks, but soon found that this was no place for the men and took them into Fort Haskell. My men were posted along the north-east parapet. Only a few could be of service in firing, and the others loaded the muskets."

J. C. Stevenson, of the same regiment, writes that he

was in action in the north-east angle, and was temporarily disabled by the enemy's fire.— G. L. K.

☆ Among the prisoners taken by this column was our brigade commander, Colonel McLaughlen (the proper colonel of the 57th Massachusetts). After the repulse of the column on the west front of Fort Haskell, Colonel McLaughlen reached the fort, and, learning the situation, started toward Fort Stedman, attempting to rally the infantry in the trenches on the way. He was captured near Fort Stedman, where he arrived almost alone.— G. L. K.

↓ In an artillery duel shortly before this we counted twenty-four mortar bombs in the air at once with pathway directly over the fort.— G. L. K.

loading the muskets, while those with sound hands stood to the parapets and blazed away. The foremost assailants recoiled and scattered. The Confederate forts opposite us gave a response more fierce than ever, and a body of sharp-shooters posted within easy range sent us showers of minies. The air was full of shells, and on glancing up one saw, as it were, a flock of blackbirds with blazing tails beating about in a gale. At first the shells did not explode. Their fuses were too long, so they fell intact, and the fires went out. Sometimes they rolled about like foot-balls, or bounded along the parapet and landed in the watery ditch. But when at last the Confederate gunners got the range, their shots became murderous. We held the battalion flag in the center of the right parapet, and a shell aimed there exploded on the mark. A sergeant of the color company was hoisted bodily into the air by the concussion. Strange to say, he was unharmed, but two of his fellow-soldiers, Sergeant Thomas Hunton and Corporal Stanford Bigelow, were killed, and the commandant, Houghton, who stood near the flag, was prostrated with a shattered thigh. This was all the work of one shell. Before our commander could be removed, a second shell wounded him in the head and in the hand.

The charging column was now well up the slope, and Captain Woerner aided our muskets by some well-directed case-shot. Each check on this column by our effective firing was a spur to the Confederates at a distance to increase their fire upon us. They poured in solid and case shot, and had twelve Coehorn mortar-batteries sending up bombs, and of these Fort Haskell received its complement. Lieutenant Julius G. Tuerk, of Woerner's battery, had an arm torn off by a shell while he was sighting that angle gun. Captain Woerner relieved him, and mounted the gun-carriage, glass in hand, to fix a more destructive range. He then left the piece with a corporal, the highest subordinate fit for duty, with instruction to continue working it on the elevation just set, while he himself went to prepare another gun for closer quarters. The corporal leaped upon the gun-staging and was brained by a bullet before he could fire a shot. The Confederate column was preceded, as usual, by sharp-shooters, and these, using the block-houses of the cantonments along the trenches for shelter, succeeded in getting their bullets into the fort, and also in gaining command of our rear sally-port. All of our outside supports had been driven off, and we were virtually surrounded. The flag-pole had been shot away, and the post colors were down. To make matters still worse, one of our own batteries, a long range siege-work away back on the bluff near the railroad, began to toss shell into the fort. We were isolated, as all could see; our flag was from time to time depressed below the ramparts, or if floating was enveloped in smoke; we were reserving our little stock of ammunition for the last emergency, the hand-to-hand struggle that seemed inevitable. The rear batteries interpreted the situation with us as a sign that Haskell had yielded, or was about to yield. ⚓

Our leader at Haskell, Captain Houghton, was permanently disabled, but Major Randall had come into the fort soon after Houghton fell. With the men of the Stedman battalion who had reached us, he now joined in the defense. When the fire from our rear batteries became serious, Major Randall called for a volunteer guard to sally with the colors, in rear of the fort, to show the troops behind us that Haskell was still holding on. Our color-bearer, Robert Kiley, and eight men responded. Randall led the way along the narrow bridge-stringers over the moat (the planks having been removed to prevent a sudden rush of the enemy) and the flag was waved several times in the faces of the Confederates, who hung about the rear of the fort, and who opened fire upon the colors. Four of the guard were hit, one being mortally wounded, but the fire from our rear batteries ceased.

The ranks of the enemy soon broke under the fire of our muskets and Woerner's well-aimed guns, but some, of the boldest came within speaking distance and hailed us to surrender. The main body hung back beyond canister range near the ravine at the base of the slope, but within range of our bullets. Captain Woerner at last held his fire, having three pieces on the north front loaded with grape. Suddenly a great number of little parties or squads, of three to six men each, rose with a yell from their hidings down along those connecting parapets, and dashed toward us. The parapets joined on to the fort, and upon these the Confederates leaped, intending thus to scale our walls. But Woerner had anticipated this; the rear angle embrasure had been contrived for the emergency, and he let go his grape. Some of the squads were cut down, others ran off to cover, and not a few passed on beyond our right wall to the rear of the work and out of reach of the guns. With this the aggressive spirit of that famous movement melted away forever.

To Gordon, the dashing leader of the sortie, it was now no longer a question of forging ahead, but of getting back out of the net into which he had plunged in the darkness. The way of retreat was back over the ridge in front of Stedman. This was swept by two withering fires, for Fort Haskell commanded the southern slope of the ridge, and Battery IX ↓ and Fort McGilvery the northern. With

<hr>

⚓ A message to this effect was taken to one of the distant siege batteries, with the request to fire upon us. The commandant refused.—G. L. K.

↓ George M. Buck, 20th Michigan Volunteers, sends us the following concerning the action on the right of Fort Stedman:

"Between Forts Stedman and McGilvery [see map, p. 538] there was an earth-work known to the troops investing Petersburg as Battery IX. It was occupied during the closing weeks of the siege by the 20th Michigan Infantry, two guns of Batteries C and I, 5th United States Artillery, and three Coehorn mortars served by Company K, 1st Connecticut Heavy Artillery, with the 2d Michigan Infantry in the rifle-pits immediately to the left. Both of these regiments belonged to the Second Brigade, of Willcox's division, commanded by Colonel Ralph Ely. Between Battery IX and Fort McGilvery ran the City Point and Petersburg road. On the morning of March 25th, before daybreak, the soldiers of the 2d and 20th Michigan learned that Fort Stedman was in the hands of the enemy, and the former retired within Battery IX, and with the 20th Michigan and the two guns of the

either slope uncovered the retreat would be comparatively easy and safe for Gordon, and the Haskell battery was the one at once able to effect the severest injury to his retreating ranks, and apparently the easiest to silence. The rifle and mortar batteries and sharp-shooters in our front took for a target the right forward angle of Haskell, the only point from which Woerner's guns could reach that coveted slope. A heavy fire was poured into this angle, while the Confederates in Stedman began to scramble back to their own lines. Woerner removed his ammunition to the magazine, out of reach of the bombs that were dropping all about the gun. His men cut fuses below and brought up the shell as needed. The brave soldier mounted the breastworks with his field-glass and signaled to the gunner for every discharge, and he made the slope between Stedman and the Confederate salient (Colquitt's) a place of fearful slaughter. My mind sickens at the memory of it — a real tragedy in war — for the victims had ceased fighting, and were now struggling between imprisonment on the one hand, and death or home on the other. Suddenly an officer on a white horse rode out under the range of Woerner's gun and attempted to rally the panic-stricken mass. He soon wheeled about, followed by some three hundred men whom he drew back out of range, halted, and formed for a charge to silence the gun. The movement was distinctly observed by us in Haskell, and Woerner continued to pound away at the slope, while the infantry once more formed on the parapets. The

storming-party moved direct on our center, as if determined now to avoid contact with the guns of either angle. But our muskets were well aimed, and the new ranks were thinned out with every volley. The party crossed the ravine, and there the leader fell, shot through the head. Many of his men fell near him, and the last spasm of the assault was ended. Gradually the fire on both sides slackened, and many of the Confederates that were still within our lines laid down their arms.

Major Randall now resolved to recapture Fort Stedman, and taking a number of the men of the 14th Regiment, belonging to the Stedman battalion, formed on the parade in rear of Haskell. He was soon joined by detachments of officers and men from the 3d Maryland, 100th Pennsylvania, and 29th Massachusetts regiments, and the column charged down the breastworks to Fort Stedman, the 3d Maryland men, led by Captain Joseph F. Carter, being the first to enter the work and demand its surrender. At the same time Major N. J. Maxwell, of the 100th Pennsylvania, and a number of his men, mounted the parapet and planted their colors there. This column re-occupied Fort Stedman and Battery X and the breastworks, and the prisoners and rifles captured were awarded to the officers of McLaughlen's brigade, who led the counter-charge from Fort Haskell. Randall and his men took possession of the recaptured works and continued to garrison them. ♪ [See, also, General Hartranft's article, p. 584 and following.]

battery repulsed no less than three vigorous and determined assaults of the enemy. In repelling these assaults Fort McGilvery rendered efficient assistance. Captain Jacob Roemer, commanding the artillery there, finding at one time that he could not incline his guns sufficiently to reach the assaulting column, had two pieces hauled out of the fort and planted them near the City Point road. Battery IX endured for several hours the incessant and concentrated fire of the "Chesterfield" and "Gooseneck" batteries, the mortar-batteries in front, and the guns of Spring Hill on the left, besides the desperate and stubborn attacks of infantry greatly superior in numbers to those within the battery. And while the attempt to capture Battery IX was probably not so furious or sanguinary as that upon Fort Haskell, it was sufficient to test to the highest degree the courage and endurance of the men. In his official report of the battle, General Willcox, the division commander, says: 'The 2d Michigan fought the enemy on this flank . . . in the most spirited manner, until they were drawn in by order of their brigade commander (Colonel Ralph Ely) to Battery No. IX.' And when ordered into Battery IX, the movement was executed in order, with steadiness and without confusion, though the regiment was heavily pressed by the skirmishers of the enemy, in both flank and rear. On the morning of the 25th, after the final assault and repulse, a Confederate captain, who was one of the prisoners taken from the enemy, told me

that the column making the last assault on Battery IX was composed of two brigades, Ransom's and another, the name of the commander of which I have forgotten. He stated that the orders to the attacking party were to move upon the flank and rear of our line, clear the works to McGilvery, and take the fort by assault in the rear. As he expressed it, the assailants got along well enough till they 'came to this rise (indicating Battery IX), where you-uns sort of discouraged us.' Mention should be made of the service performed by the other regiments in our brigade, and also by Fort McGilvery, Battery V, and Battery IV, the two latter being batteries firing at long range." EDITORS.

♪ The loss in the four companies of the 14th New York, in Fort Haskell, was 4 killed and 23 wounded. The 3d New Jersey Battery lost 1 killed and 7 wounded. The eight companies of the 14th New York stationed at Fort Stedman lost 8 killed, 22 wounded, and 201 captured or missing. The two sections of the 19th New York Battery, in Fort Stedman, lost 1 killed and 14 missing. The section of the 14th Massachusetts Battery, in Battery X, lost 1 killed (Lieut. Nye), 2 wounded, and 11 missing. The loss of the Ninth Corps in repulsing the attack on Stedman, Haskell, etc., was 70 killed, 424 wounded, and 523 captured,— in all, 1017.— EDITORS.

GENERAL HOSPITAL AT CITY POINT. FROM A WAR-TIME PHOTOGRAPH.

THE RECAPTURE OF FORT STEDMAN. |

BY JOHN F. HARTRANFT, BREVET MAJOR-GENERAL, U. S. V.

O F the Union intrenchments in front of Petersburg, Fort Stedman, with Batteries X and IX on its right and Batteries XII and XI and Fort Haskell on its left, covered Meade's Station on the United States Military Railroad, the supply route of the Army of the Potomac. [See map, p. 538.] Meade's Station was the depot of the Ninth Army Corps. This part of the line—about a mile in length—was garrisoned principally by the Third Brigade of the First Division of the Ninth Corps, commanded by Colonel N. B. McLaughlen.

The First Division, commanded by General Willcox, was intrusted with the defense of the whole line from the Appomattox to somewhat beyond Fort Morton, and the Second Division (Potter's) continued the defense of the line about to Fort Alexander Hays. The Third Division, under my command, was in reserve to these two divisions. The division covered four miles, with headquarters at the Avery House, in the center, the right resting at the Friend House, a mile in rear of the works, north-east of Fort Stedman, and the left behind Fort Prescott.

From the Avery House a ravine ran northerly about two-thirds of a mile in rear of the works, to the Friend House, approaching Fort Stedman to within less than one-third of a mile. From this ravine the ground rose gently to the works on the west, and more sharply to a ridge of irregular hills, on the east, behind which ran the army railroad. About one hundred yards behind Fort Stedman, between the fort and the ravine, there was a slight rise in the slope, upon which was encamped the 57th Massachusetts, and to the left of this, some old works which the enemy had abandoned as our forces pressed upon the city. Between this camp and these works ran an old country road, somewhat sunken, from the rear of Stedman to Meade's Station. All the undergrowth and fences had long since disappeared, and the ground was generally open.

Before dawn on the morning of March 25th, 1865, Major-General Gordon, of the Confederate Army, with his corps and two brigades, numbering probably 10,000 or 12,000 effectives, by a sudden and impetuous attack carried the line from Battery IX on the right to Fort Haskell on the left. This space included Fort Stedman and Batteries X, XI, and XII, and the bomb-proofs and covered ways connecting these works. It was, to a certain extent, a surprise, and the enemy captured some hundreds of prisoners, including Colonel McLaughlen. But before they were driven out of the works or captured, the troops inflicted considerable injury upon the enemy, and the attack upon Fort Haskell, made at the same time, was repulsed with heavy loss. Fortunately, upon the line taken, the enemy could not easily deploy for their farther advance upon Meade's Station and the railroad, the enfilad-

| Condensed, with revisions by the author, from the "Philadelphia Press" for March 17th, 1886.

ing fires of Battery IX and Fort Haskell forcing their troops into the bomb-proofs of the captured lines to the right and left of Fort Stedman, which was thus the only opening for their columns to enter and deploy to the rear. Great credit is justly due to the garrisons of these two points for their steadiness in holding them in the confusion and nervousness of a night attack. If they had been lost the enemy would have had sufficient safe ground on which to recover and form their ranks, the reserves would have been overwhelmed and beaten in detail by a greatly superior force, and the destruction of the railroad and supplies of the army would have delayed its final movements for a long time. The tenacity with which these points were held, therefore, saved the Union army great loss of men, time, and materials.

The alarm of General Gordon's attack reached the headquarters of the division at 4:30 A. M., just before daybreak.

Upon receipt of this information, and of orders received from corps headquarters about 5 o'clock, the 208th Pennsylvania, the regiment nearest, was ordered to report to Colonel McLaughlen, and at the same time written orders were sent to Colonel

MAJOR-GENERAL JOHN G. PARKE. FROM A PHOTOGRAPH.

J. A. Mathews, commanding the Second Brigade, to hold his brigade in readiness to move to the right, if needed.✠ On the way over to General Willcox's headquarters, at the Friend House on the extreme right, I met the 209th Regiment moving *from* Meade's Station toward that point, and the 200th, drawn out of camp with its right resting on the Dunn House battery. These movements were by order of General Willcox, these regiments having instructions to obey orders direct from him in case of attack, to avoid delay in communicating through my headquarters, which were two miles away, owing to the great length of the line covered by my command. This movement apparently uncovered the objective point of the enemy's attack, viz., Meade's Station, and, although the détour of the 209th finally brought it into effective position on the extreme right, the 200th was, for the moment, the only regiment left in any position to strike the enemy.

While I was talking with General Willcox I called his attention to the puffs of smoke issuing from the wood in the rear and to the right and left of Fort Stedman. It was not yet light enough to see the enemy, nor could any

---

✠ General Hartranft's division was composed of the 200th, 208th, and 209th Pennsylvania, forming the First Brigade, under Lieutenant-Colonel W. H. H. McCall, and the 205th, 207th, and 211th Pennsylvania, forming the Second Brigade, under Colonel Joseph A. Mathews.— EDITORS.

INTERIOR OF FORT STEDMAN. FROM A PHOTOGRAPH.

The fort was named after Colonel Griffin A. Stedman, Jr., of the 11th Connecticut, who was mortally wounded in front of Petersburg on August 5, 1864.

sound be heard, owing to the direction of the wind, but the white puffs indicated musketry-firing, and, being in the rear of our lines, disclosed unmistakably an attack in force, and not a feint. It was a skirmish line followed by an assaulting column or a line of battle.↓ It was equally evident that time must be gained, at any cost, to bring up the extended division in reserve to meet it. Requesting General Willcox to designate one of his staff-officers to conduct the 209th into position on the right, I rode down to Colonel W. H. H. McCall, of the 200th, as the one immediately in hand. A small body of the 57th Massachusetts, which had been driven from its camp, had rallied just in front of the 200th and were feebly replying to the enemy. This detachment was ordered forward to its old camp, and the 200th pushed forward to that point also without serious loss. Intending to force the fighting, no time was lost in feeling the enemy or fighting his skirmishers, but the regiment advanced in line of battle. This movement broke the enemy's line of skirmishers, and those directly in front were driven in; but in the old country road to Meade's Station, running from the rear of Fort Stedman, by the left of the camp, and in some old rebel works beyond the road on our left, the line was strong and the enemy was in force, while the guns of Fort Stedman just captured, turned against us, were on our right. Sending Major George Shorkley, of my staff, to hurry up the 209th to form connection on the right of the 200th, the latter was immediately led to the attack. It advanced bravely; but the enemy was too strong to be pushed, and the fire from the supports and Fort Stedman was very severe. The momentum was lost a little beyond the camp, and after a momentary wavering the 200th was forced back through the camp and took shelter in an old

↓ General Parke, in his report, calls these the enemy's skirmishers; General A. A. Humphreys, in "The Virginia Campaign of 1864–65," says: "Those whom General Parke calls skirmishers were probably the three detachments of Gordon's troops sent to capture the rear forts." General Gordon has since told me that he never heard from these detachments; not one of them returned to report. They must have been the ones who cut the telegraph lines to City Point, and I must have ridden on my way to General Willcox's headquarters, between them and the enemy in the forts. What the 200th attacked was, in my judgment, a heavy line and groups of skirmishers.—J. F. H.

line of works about forty yards in its rear and to the right. From horse-back at this point the enemy's officers could now plainly be seen urging their men through Fort Stedman, and endeavoring to deploy them in the rear. To prevent or delay this would justify another attack, although the position of the enemy on the left, whose flag could be seen in the continuation of the old works on the other side of the road, not seventy yards away, and the supporting fire of the captured works on the front and right, plainly showed at what cost it must be made. It was better to attack than be attacked. The 200th was again led forward and responded gallantly. In the face of a galling fire in front and flanks it succeeded in reaching a fairly defensible position, and for a few moments the troops struggled tenaciously to hold it. Fighting under the eye of the general, every officer and man stood up nobly, and for twenty minutes struggled desperately to hold their own in the face of supporting batteries within a hundred yards and superior forces pressing on all sides.

BREVET MAJOR-GENERAL JOHN F. HARTRANFT.
FROM A PHOTOGRAPH.

This was the heaviest fighting of the day, and under a tremendous fire of small-arms and artillery the loss in twenty minutes was over one hundred killed and wounded. The regiment finally staggered and receded. But when its desperate grasp on the position was broken it fell back without confusion and rallied and re-formed at the call of its officers and myself in the old works from which it had advanced.

While the enemy was shaking off these fierce assaults, the 209th had been able to push its way to a good position, its left resting on the old works to which the 200th had fallen back, with the right of which it now connected and its right toward Battery IX, with which it was connected by the 2d and 17th Michigan Volunteers, two small regiments of the First Division, which also had thus had time to come up and complete the line. This information was brought to me, while ordering the operations of the 200th, by Captain L. C. Brackett, the staff-officer designated by General Willcox, as requested, for that purpose—who also brought word of the wounding of Major Shorkley, of my staff, on the same errand. The 20th Michigan on the line to the right of Battery IX had also been crowded forward into the work, which was now fully manned, and had opened fire vigorously and effectively. A solid line was thus formed against the advance of the enemy in this direction. A ride around the line to Colonel McLaughlen's headquarters on the left showed that a corresponding line had been formed on the south. While the enemy was engaged with the 200th this had been done without interruption or difficulty. Captain Prosper Dalien had succeeded in placing the 208th, which had been ordered in the morning to report to Colonel Mc-

Laughlen, in a good position, its left connected with Fort Haskell ⑂ by about 200 men mostly from the 100th Pennsylvania, and some few from the 3d Maryland, who had been driven from Batteries XI and XII and were now formed on the left of the 208th. The 205th and 207th regiments, which had promptly reported at division headquarters, were conducted by Captain J. D. Bertolette, of my staff, by the right through the ravine toward the road leading to Meade's Station. This he was doing in consequence of orders direct from corps headquarters to cover Meade's Station with the Second Brigade. They were halted in continuation of the southern line, when the left of the 207th connected with the 208th. The 211th, encamped three miles from the field of action, had been notified and was rapidly approaching. The field-artillery, directed by Brevet Brigadier-General Tidball, commanding the artillery brigade of the corps, had taken position on the hills in the rear of Fort Stedman, and with Fort Haskell and Battery IX opened on the captured works and the space around, driving the enemy to the bomb-proofs and materially interfering with the deployment of a line of battle. There was still a distance of three hundred yards between the left of the 200th and the right of the 205th, through which ran the road to Meade's Station, uncovered. A short time before, Colonel Loring, of General Parke's staff, had delivered to me, on the way over from the right to the left, orders to put the Second Brigade in position on the hills directly covering Meade's Station. But the positions of the 205th and 207th of this brigade were so favorable, and the spirit of the order had been so effectually carried out, that it was unnecessary to obey it literally, and only the 211th, now at hand after a three-miles march, was ordered to deflect to the right and take post on the hills covering the station and in support of the artillery.

The time and opportunity to make these dispositions were due entirely to the stubborn courage of the 200th Regiment.⑂ Its courage and steadiness undoubtedly saved that part of the army severe punishment; and although we did not know it at the time, and were apparently awaiting the attack of a superior force, it had recaptured Fort Stedman in its twenty-minutes fight.

Riding along on the other flank, the whole scene of operations on the opposite slope was spread out before me. On a semicircle of a mile and a half, five regiments and detachments, nearly 4000 men, were ready to charge.

At 7;30 o'clock the long line of the 211th lifted itself with cadenced step over the brow of the hill and swept down in magnificent style toward Fort Stedman. The success of the manœuvre was immediate and complete. The enemy, apparently taken by surprise and magnifying the mass pouring down the hill into the sweep of a whole brigade, began to waver, and the rest of the Third Division, responding to the signal, rose with loud cheers and sprang forward to the charge. So sudden and impetuous was the advance that many of the enemy's skirmishers and infantry in front of the works, throwing down their arms and rushing in to get out of the fire between

---

⑂ But see p. 582.— EDITORS.

⑂ Officers and men of the 14th New York Heavy Artillery, who escaped from Fort Stedman, say that they formed a line at this point, fought, and captured prisoners. Major Mathews, commanding 17th Michigan, of the Second Brigade makes a similar statement regarding his regiment.— EDITORS.

the lines, looked in the distance like a counter-charge, and the rest were forced back into the works in such masses that the victors were scarcely able to deploy among the crowds of their prisoners. The 208th stormed Batteries XI and XII ☆ and the lines to the fort; the 207th carried the west angle of Fort Stedman, the 205th and 211th the rear, the 200th the east angle, and the 209th Battery X and the remaining line to the right. These were taken almost simultaneously, and it is impossible to say which flag was first planted on the works. There was a momentary hand-to-hand struggle for the rebel flags in the batteries and fort. The substantial trophies of the victory were some 1600 prisoners and a large number of small-arms. The prisoners were mostly passed through the lines to the rear, to be picked up and claimed by other commands, and all but one of the captured flags were claimed and taken from the soldiers by unknown officers.

Just as the 211th moved I received orders to delay the assault until the arrival of a division of the Sixth Army Corps, on its way to support me. As the movement was begun, it was doubtful whether the countermand would reach the regiments on the extreme right and left in time. Besides, I had no doubt of the result, and therefore determined to take the responsibility.

The losses in the assault were unexpectedly light. Then was reaped the full advantage of the work of the gallant 200th. This regiment lost in killed and wounded — mostly in its fight in the morning — 122 out of a total loss for the division of 260. ⎮ The losses of the enemy must have been very heavy. ⛏

☆ Lieutenant Stevenson's letter (see foot-note, page 581) contains the statement that Company K, of the 100th Pennsylvania, was in possession of Battery XII when General Hartranft's men charged, having left Fort Haskell some time before. See also p. 583.— EDITORS.

⎮ A writer in "The Century" magazine for September, 1887, claims for the troops in Fort Haskell, reënforced by the 14th New York Heavy Artillery, the merit of recapturing Fort Stedman, and that the Third Division of Pennsylvanians merely advanced at 8 o'clock and re-occupied the positions. Such a claim is extravagantly absurd, and disproved at once by a reference to the official table of losses. The Ninth Corps lost 507 in killed and wounded; of these 260 were in the Third Division, 73 in the 100th Pennsylvania, and 37 in the 57th Massachusetts, of the First Division, and 37 in the Artillery Brigade,— in all, 407, showing conclusively who did the bulk of the fighting. The losses of the 14th New York were comparatively light in killed and wounded, the greater part happening in Fort Stedman, where 201 of them were captured. [See note, p. 583.] The veteran steadiness and good fighting of the 100th Pennsylvania saved Fort Haskell, as the reports and returns clearly indicate. Since the publication of the article in "The Century" I have seen General Gordon and his adjutant-general, Colonel Hy. Kyd. Douglas, who assure me that for the moment, whatever desultory attacks may have been made on Fort Haskell, they were paying no attention to that work, but were endeavoring to deploy their troops in the rear of the captured line and hurry over supports. [But see p. 585.] They ascribe their failure to the delay of the latter to come up, to the promptness with which the Third Division was assembled, and to the sudden attack of the 200th Pennsylvania.

In making this criticism and correction I do not wish to be understood as detracting from the merits of the garrison at Fort Haskell, to whose nerve in holding on, under trying circumstances, I had done full justice in the above article long before September, 1887.— J. F. H.

It should be noted that the losses of the several Union organizations, cited by General Hartranft, include those sustained before the movement to re-occupy the lines began.— EDITORS.

⛏ I transcribe the following receipt, found among the memoranda of the fight. It tells its own story:

"Received of Major Bertolette 120 dead and 15 wounded in the engagement of the 25th March, 1865.
"For MAJ.-GEN. GORDON,
"HY. KYD DOUGLAS, A. A. Gen."

If the same proportion held between their dead and wounded as between ours, their total loss would have been a little over four thousand. The ratio in our case was, however, unusually high. The Confederate loss was probably over three thousand. Two thousand (1949) of these were prisoners, the rest killed and wounded.— J. F. H.

THE OPPOSING FORCES AT PETERSBURG AND RICHMOND.

December 31st, 1864.

THE UNION ARMY.—Lieutenant-General Ulysses S. Grant.

Escort: B, F, and K, 5th U. S. Cav., Capt. Julius W. Mason; 4th U. S. Inf., Capt. Avery B. Cain.

ARMY OF THE POTOMAC.—Maj.-Gen. George G. Meade (on leave), Maj.-Gen. John G. Parke.

Provost Guard, Brig.-Gen. Marsena R. Patrick: 8th Del. (3 co's), Capt. Robert I. Holt; K, 1st Ind. Cav., Lieut. William O. Hedrick; C and D, 1st Mass. Cav., Capt. Edward A. Flint; 80th N. Y. (20th militia), Lieut.-Col. John McEntee; 3d Pa. Cav. (8 co's), Lieut.-Col. James W. Walsh; 68th Pa., Col. Andrew H. Tippin; 114th Pa., Col. Charles H. T. Collis.

Engineer Brigade and Defenses of City Point, Brig.-Gen. Henry W. Benham: 1st Me. Sharp-shooters (2 co's), Capt. George R. Abbott; 61st Mass. (6 co's), Lieut.-Col. Charles F. Walcott; Hall's Batt'n Mich. Sharp-shooters (2 co's), Capt. Nathaniel P. Watson; 18th N. H. (6 co's), Lieut.-Col. Joseph M. Clough; 15th N. Y. Engr's, Col. Wesley Brainerd; 50th N. Y. Engr's, Col. William H. Pettes. *Battalion U. S. Engineers*, Maj. Franklin Harwood. *Guards and Orderlies:* Oneida (N. Y.) Cav., Lieut. Frank Vane.

ARTILLERY, Brig.-Gen. Henry J. Hunt (chief of artillery). *Siege Artillery*, Col. Henry L. Abbot: 1st Conn. Heavy (5 co's), Maj. George B. Cook; 1st Conn. Heavy (7 co's), Maj. Albert F. Brooker; 3d Conn. Battery, Capt. Thomas S. Gilbert. *Artillery Reserve*, Capt. Ezekiel R. Mayo: 14th Mass., Capt. Joseph W. B. Wright; 2d Me., Capt. Albert F. Thomas; 3d Me., Capt. Ezekiel R. Mayo; F, 15th N. Y. Heavy, Capt. Calvin Shaffer; H, 1st R. I., Capt. Crawford Allen, Jr.; 3d Vt., Capt. Romeo H. Start.

SECOND ARMY CORPS, Maj.-Gen. Andrew A. Humphreys.

FIRST DIVISION, Brig.-Gen. Nelson A. Miles.

First Brigade, Col. George N. Macy: 26th Mich., Maj. Nathan Church; 5th N. H., Lieut.-Col. Welcome A. Crafts; 2d N. Y. Heavy Art'y, Lieut.-Col. George Hogg; 61st N. Y., Col. George W. Scott; 81st Pa., Lieut.-Col. William Wilson; 140th Pa., Capt. William A. F. Stockton; 183d Pa., Col. George T. Egbert. *Second Brigade*, Col. Robert Nugent: 28th Mass. (5 co's), Capt. John Connor; 7th N. Y. Heavy Art'y, Maj. Samuel L. Anable; 63d N. Y. (6 co's), Lieut.-Col. John H. Gleason; 69th N. Y., Maj. Richard Moroney; 88th N. Y. (5 co's), Lieut.-Col. Denis F. Burke. *Third Brigade*, Col. Clinton D. MacDougall: 7th N. Y., Col. George W. von Schack; 39th N. Y., Capt. David A. Allen; 52d N. Y., Lieut.-Col. Henry M. Karples; 111th N. Y., Lieut.-Col. Lewis W. Husk; 125th N. Y., Lieut.-Col. Joseph Hyde; 126th N. Y. (5 co's), Capt. John B. Geddis. *Fourth Brigade*, Col. William Glenny: 4th N. Y. Heavy Art'y, Maj. Frank Williams; 64th N. Y. (6 co's), Capt. Victor D. Renwick; 66th N. Y., Capt. Nathaniel P. Lane; 53d Pa., Lieut.-Col. George C. Anderson; 116th Pa., Capt. David W. Megraw; 145th Pa., Capt. Peter W. Free; 148th Pa., Capt. James F. Weaver.

SECOND DIVISION, Maj.-Gen. John Gibbon (on leave), Brig.-Gen. Thomas A. Smyth.

Provost Guard: 2d Co. Minn. Sharp-shooters, Capt. Mahlon Black.

First Brigade, Col. James M. Willett: 19th Me., Col. Isaac W. Starbird; 19th Mass., Lieut.-Col. Edmund Rice; 20th Mass., Maj. John Kelliher; 7th Mich., Lieut.-Col. George W. La Point; 1st Minn. (2 co's), Capt. James C. Farwell; 59th N. Y., Col. William A. Olmsted; 152d N. Y., Capt. Charles H. Dygert; 184th Pa., Maj. George L. Ritman; 36th Wis., Lieut.-Col. Clement E. Warner. *Second Brigade*, Col. Mathew Murphy: 8th N. Y. Heavy Art'y, Maj. Joel B. Baker; 155th N. Y., Capt. Michael Doheny; 164th N. Y., Lieut.-Col. William DeLacy; 170th N. Y., Col. James P. McIvor; 182d N. Y. (69th N. Y. N. G. A.), Capt. Michael McGuire. *Third Brigade*, Lieut.-

Col. Francis E. Pierce: 14th Conn., Lieut.-Col. Samuel A. Moore; 1st Del., Lieut.-Col. Daniel Woodall; 12th N. J., Capt. Henry F. Chew; 10th N. Y. (batt'n), Capt. Joseph La Fuira; 108th N. Y., Capt. William H. Andrews; 4th Ohio (batt'n), Lieut.-Col. Charles C. Calahan; 69th Pa., Maj. Patrick S. Tinen; 106th Pa. (batt'n), Capt. John H. Gallager; 7th W. Va., Lieut.-Col. Isaac B. Fisher.

THIRD DIVISION, Brig.-Gen. Gershom Mott.

First Brigade, Brig.-Gen. P. Regis de Trobriand: 20th Ind., Maj. William Orr; 1st Me. Heavy Art'y, Col. Russell B. Shepherd; 17th Me., Capt. William Hobson; 40th N. Y., Lieut.-Col. Madison M. Cannon; 73d N. Y., Lieut.-Col. Michael W. Burns; 86th N. Y., Lieut.-Col. Nathan H. Vincent; 124th N. Y., Lieut.-Col. Charles H. Weygant; 99th Pa., Lieut.-Col. Peter Fritz, Jr.; 110th Pa., Capt. William Stewart; 2d U. S. Sharp-shooters, Maj. James E. Doughty. *Second Brigade*, Brig.-Gen. Byron R. Pierce: 1st Mass. Heavy Art'y, Maj. Nathaniel Shatswell; 5th Mich., Col. John Pulford; 93d N. Y., Lieut.-Col. Benjamin C. Butler; 57th Pa., Lieut.-Col. Lorenzo D. Bumpus; 84th Pa. (4 co's), Capt. Samuel Bryan; 105th Pa., Capt. James Miller; 141st Pa., Col. Henry J. Madill; 1st U. S. Sharp-shooters (2 co's), Capt. Benjamin M. Peck. *Third Brigade*, Col. John Ramsey: 11th Mass. (batt'n), Lieut.-Col. Charles C. Rivers; 7th N. J. (batt'n), Col. Francis Price; 8th N. J. (batt'n), Capt. Louis M. Morris; 11th N. J., Lieut.-Col. John Schoonover; 120th N. Y., Maj. Abram L. Lockwood.

ARTILLERY BRIGADE, Maj. John G. Hazard: 6th Me., Lieut. William H. Rogers; 10th Mass., Capt. J. Henry Sleeper; M, 1st N. H., Capt. Frederick M. Edgell; 2d N. J. (or B, 1st N. J.), Capt. A. Judson Clark; 3d N. J. (or C, 1st N. J.), Capt. Christian Woerner; G, 1st N. Y., Capt. Samuel A. McClellan; C, 4th N. Y. Heavy, Capt. James H. Wood; L, 4th N. Y. Heavy, Lieut. Richard Kennedy; 11th N. Y., Lieut. George W. Davey; 12th N. Y., Lieut. William S. Bull; F, 1st Pa., Lieut. John F. Campbell; B, 1st R. I., Capt. T. Fred. Brown; K, 4th U. S., Lieut. John W. Roder; C and I, 5th U. S., Lieut. William B. Beck.

FIFTH ARMY CORPS, Maj.-Gen. Gouverneur K. Warren.

Escort: Detachment 4th Pa. Cav., Capt. Napoleon J. Horrell.

Provost Guard: E and F, 5th N. Y., Capt. Paul A. Oliver; 104th N. Y., Capt. William W. Graham.

FIRST DIVISION, Brig.-Gen. Charles Griffin (on leave), Brig.-Gen. Joseph J. Bartlett.

First Brigade, Brig.-Gen. Joshua L. Chamberlain: 185th N. Y., Lieut.-Col. Gustavus Sniper; 198th Pa., Col. Horatio G. Sickel. *Second Brigade*, Col. Edgar M. Gregory: 187th N. Y., Lieut.-Col. Daniel Myers; 188th N. Y., Lieut.-Col. Isaac Doolittle; 189th N. Y., Maj. Joseph G. Townsend. *Third Brigade*, Col. Alfred L. Pearson: 20th Me., Lieut.-Col. Charles D. Gilmore; 32d Mass., Lieut.-Col. James A. Cunningham; 1st Mich., Maj. George Lockley; 16th Mich. (Brady's and Jardine's co's Sharp-shooters attached), Capt. Charles H. Salter; 83d Pa. (6 co's), Lieut.-Col. Chauncey P. Rogers; 91st Pa., Lieut.-Col. Eli G. Sellers; 118th Pa., Maj. Henry O'Neill; 155th Pa., Lieut.-Col. John Ewing.

SECOND DIVISION, Brig.-Gen. Romeyn B. Ayres (on leave), Col. James Gwyn.

First Brigade, Col. Frederick Winthrop: 5th N. Y., Capt. Charles S. Montgomery; 15th N. Y. Heavy Art'y, Lieut.-Col. Michael Wiedrich; 140th N. Y., Capt. William S. Grantsynn; 146th N. Y., Maj. James Grindlay. *Second Brigade*, Col. Andrew W. Denison: 1st Md., Col. John W. Wilson; 4th Md., Col. Richard N. Bowerman; 7th

Md., Lieut.-Col. David T. Bennett; 8th Md., Lieut.-Col. John G. Johannes. *Third Brigade,* Col. William Sergeant: 3d Del., Maj. James E. Bailey; 4th Del., Maj. Moses B. Gist; 157th Pa. (4 co's), Maj. Edmund T. Tiers; 190th and 191st Pa., Lieut.-Col. Joseph B. Pattee; 210th Pa., Lieut.-Col. Edward L. Witman.

THIRD DIVISION, Brig.-Gen. Samuel W. Crawford.

Sharp-shooters: 1st N. Y. (batt'n), Capt. Clinton Perry. *First Brigade,* Col. Henry A. Morrow: 24th Mich., Maj. William Hutchinson; 143d Pa., Maj. Chester K. Hughes; 149th Pa., Maj. James Glenn; 150th Pa., Maj. George W. Jones; 6th Wis., Col. John A. Kellogg; 7th Wis., Lieut.-Col. Hollon Richardson. *Second Brigade,* Brig.-Gen. Henry Baxter: 16th Me., Col. Charles W. Tilden; 39th Mass., Lieut.-Col. Henry M. Tremlett; 97th N. Y., Col. Charles Wheelock; 11th Pa., Col. Richard Coulter; 88th Pa., Lieut.-Col. Benjamin F. Haines; 107th Pa., Col. Thomas F. McCoy. *Third Brigade,* Col. J. William Hofmann: 76th N. Y. (2 co's), Lieut. George W. Steele; 94th N. Y., Capt. Henry H. Fish; 95th N. Y., Lieut.-Col. James Creney; 147th N. Y., Capt. James Coey; 56th Pa., Maj. John T. Jack; 121st Pa., Capt. Adam Zinnel; 142d Pa., Lieut.-Col. Horatio N. Warren.

ARTILLERY BRIGADE, Col. Charles S. Wainwright (on leave), Maj. Robert H. Fitzhugh: 5th Mass., Capt. Charles A. Phillips; 9th Mass., Lieut. Richard S. Milton; B, 1st N. Y., Lieut. Robert E. Rogers; C, 1st N. Y., Capt. David F. Ritchie; D, 1st N. Y., Capt. James B. Hazelton; E, 1st N. Y., Capt. Angell Matthewson; H, 1st N. Y., Capt. Charles E. Mink; L, 1st N. Y., Capt. George Breck; B, 1st Pa., Lieut. William McClelland; B, 4th U. S., Lieut. John Mitchell; D and G, 5th U. S., Lieut. Jacob B. Rawles.

SIXTH ARMY CORPS, Maj.-Gen. Horatio G. Wright.

Escort: E, 21st Pa. Cav., Capt. William H. Boyd, Jr.

FIRST DIVISION, Brig.-Gen. Frank Wheaton.

First Brigade, Capt. Baldwin Hufty: 1st N. J. (3 co's), Lieut. Jacob L. Hutt; 2d N. J. (1 co.), Lieut. Adolphus Weiss; 4th N. J., Capt. Ebenezer W. Davis; 10th N. J., Capt. James W. McNeely; 15th N. J. (1 co. 3d N. J. attached), Capt. James W. Penrose; 40th N. J. (2 co's), Capt. John Edelstein. *Second Brigade,* Brig.-Gen. Ranald S. Mackenzie: 2d Conn. Heavy Art'y, Lieut.-Col. James Hubbard; 65th N. Y., Lieut.-Col. Henry C. Fisk; 121st N. Y., Capt. James W. Cronkite; 95th Pa. (6 co's), Maj. John Harper. *Third Brigade,* Col. Thomas S. Allen: 37th Mass., Maj. Rufus P. Lincoln; 49th Pa., Lieut.-Col. Baynton J. Hickman; 82d Pa., Lieut.-Col. James R. Neiler; 119th Pa., Lieut.-Col. Gideon Clark; 2d R. I. (6 co's), Capt. Elisha H. Rhodes; 5th Wis., Lieut.-Col. James M. Bull.

SECOND DIVISION, Brig.-Gen. George W. Getty (on leave), Brig.-Gen. Lewis A. Grant.

First Brigade, Col. James M. Warner (on leave), Col. George P. Foster: 62d N. Y., Maj. William H. Baker; 93d Pa., Lieut.-Col. Charles W. Eckman; 98th Pa., Capt. Peter Beisel; 102d Pa., Lieut.-Col. James Patchell; 139th Pa., Lieut.-Col. John G. Parr. *Second Brigade,* Lieut.-Col. Charles Hunsdon: 1st Vt. Heavy Art'y, Maj. Aldace F. Walker; 2d Vt., Maj. Enoch E. Johnson; 3d and 4th Vt., Lieut.-Col. Horace W. Floyd; 5th Vt., Capt. Ronald A. Kennedy; 6th Vt. (6 co's), Maj. Sumner H. Lincoln. *Third Brigade,* Col. Thomas W. Hyde: 1st Me., Lieut.-Col. Stephen C. Fletcher; 43d N. Y. (5 co's), Lieut.-Col. Charles A. Milliken; 49th N. Y. (5 co's), Lieut.-Col. Erastus D. Holt; 77th N. Y. (5 co's), Capt. David J. Caw; 122d N. Y., Maj. Alonzo H. Clapp; 61st Pa., Capt. Charles H. Clausen.

THIRD DIVISION, Brig.-Gen. Truman Seymour.

First Brigade, Col. William S. Truex: 14th N. J., Lieut.-Col. Jacob J. Janeway; 106th N. Y., Capt. Alvah W. Briggs; 151st N. Y. (5 co's), Capt. Browning N. Wiles; 87th Pa. (5 co's), Capt. James Tearney; 10th Vt., Capt. George B. Damon. *Second Brigade,* Col. Benjamin F. Smith: 6th Md., Lieut.-Col. Joseph C. Hill; 9th N. Y. Heavy Art'y, Lieut.-Col. James W. Snyder; 110th Ohio, Lieut.-Col. Otho H. Binkley; 122d Ohio, Col. William H. Ball; 126th Ohio, Capt. Thomas W. McKinnie; 67th Pa., Lieut. John F. Young; 138th Pa., Col. Matthew R. McClennan.

ARTILLERY BRIGADE, Col. Charles H. Tompkins: 4th Me., Lieut. Charles W. White; 1st N. J. (or A, 1st N. J.), Capt. Augustin N. Parsons; 3d N. Y., Lieut. Alexander S. McLain; H, 1st Ohio, Capt. Stephen W. Dorsey; E, 1st R. I., Lieut. Ezra K. Parker; E, 5th U. S., Lieut. John R. Brinckle.

NINTH ARMY CORPS, Brig.-Gen. Orlando B. Willcox.

Escort: Detachment 2d Pa. Cav., Sergeant Charles O'Brien. *Provost Guard:* 79th N. Y. (4 co's), Capt. Andrew D. Baird.

FIRST DIVISION, Col. Napoleon B. McLaughlen.

First Brigade, Col. Samuel Harriman: 8th Mich., Lieut.-Col. Ralph Ely; 27th Mich. (1st and 2d co's Sharpshooters attached), Lieut.-Col. Charles Waite; 109th N. Y., Maj. George W. Dunn; 51st Pa., Col. William J. Bolton; 37th Wis., Lieut.-Col. John Green; 38th Wis., Col. James Bintliff. *Second Brigade,* Col. Byron M. Cutcheon: 1st Mich. Sharp-shooters, Maj. Asahel W. Nichols; 2d Mich., Lieut.-Col. Edwin J. March; 20th Mich., Maj. Claudius B. Grant; 46th N. Y., Capt. Victor Traxmarer; 60th Ohio, Lieut.-Col. Martin P. Avery; 50th Pa., Capt. George W. Brumm. *Third Brigade,* Lieut.-Col. Gilbert P. Robinson: 3d Md. (4 co's), Capt. Joseph F. Carter; 29th Mass., Capt. Charles T. Richardson; 57th Mass., Lieut.-Col. Julius M. Tucker; 59th Mass., Lieut.-Col. Joseph Colburn; 14th N. Y. Heavy Art'y, Maj. George M. Randall; 100th Pa., Lieut.-Col. Joseph H. Pentecost.

Acting Engineers: 17th Mich., Lieut.-Col. Frederick W. Swift.

SECOND DIVISION, Brig.-Gen. Robert B. Potter (on leave), Brig.-Gen. Simon G. Griffin.

First Brigade, Col. John I. Curtin: 35th Mass., Col. Sumner Carruth; 36th Mass., Lieut.-Col. Thaddeus L. Barker; 58th Mass., Lieut.-Col. John C. Whiton; 39th N. J., Col. Abram C. Wildrick; 51st N. Y., Capt. Thomas B. Marsh; 45th Pa., Capt. Roland C. Cheeseman; 48th Pa., Lieut.-Col. George W. Gowan; 4th and 7th R. I., Lieut.-Col. Percy Daniels. *Second Brigade,* Col. Herbert B. Titus: 31st Me., Maj. George A. Bolton; 2d Md., Lieut.-Col. Benjamin F. Taylor; 56th Mass., Lieut.-Col. Horatio D. Jarves; 6th N. H., Lieut.-Col. Phin. P. Bixby; 9th N. H., Capt. John B. Cooper; 11th N. H., Col. Walter Harriman; 179th N. Y., Col. William M. Gregg; 186th N. Y., Col. Bradley Winslow; 17th Vt., Col. Francis V. Randall.

THIRD DIVISION, Brig.-Gen. John F. Hartranft.

First Brigade, Col. Charles W. Diven: 200th Pa., Lieut.-Col. W. H. H. McCall; 208th Pa., Col. Alfred B. McCalmont; 209th Pa., Lieut.-Col. George W. Frederick. *Second Brigade,* Col. Joseph A. Mathews: 205th Pa., Lieut.-Col. William F. Walter; 207th Pa., Col. Robert C. Cox; 211th Pa., Col. James H. Trimble.

ARTILLERY BRIGADE, Col. John C. Tidball: 7th Me., Capt. Adelbert B. Twitchell; 11th Mass., Capt. Edward J. Jones; 19th N. Y., Lieut. Alfred B. Losee; 27th N. Y., Capt. John B. Eaton; 34th N. Y., Capt. Jacob Roemer; D, Pa., Capt. Samuel H. Rhoads.

CAVALRY.

SECOND DIVISION, Brig.-Gen. David McM. Gregg (on leave), Brig.-Gen. Henry E. Davies.

First Brigade, Col. Hugh H. Janeway: 1st Mass. (8 co's), Lieut.-Col. Samuel E. Chamberlain; 1st N. J., Maj. James H. Hart; 10th N. Y., Col. M. Henry Avery; 24th N. Y., Lieut.-Col. Walter C. Newberry; 1st Pa. (5 co's), Maj. Richard J. Falls; A, 2d U. S. Art'y, Lieut. John H. Calef. *Second Brigade,* Col. J. Irvin Gregg: 2d Pa., Maj. George F. McCabe; 4th Pa., Lieut.-Col. S. B. M. Young; 8th Pa., Lieut.-Col. William A. Corrie; 13th Pa., Col. Michael Kerwin; 16th Pa., Lieut.-Col. John K. Robison; H and I, 1st U. S. Art'y, Lieut. T. B. von Michalowski. *Third Brigade,* Col. Charles H. Smith: 1st Me., Lieut.-Col. Jonathan P. Cilley; 2d N. Y. Mounted Rifles, Capt. Samuel D. Stevenson; 6th Ohio, Lieut.-Col. George W. Dickinson; 21st Pa., Maj. Robert Bell. *Unattached:* 13th Ohio, Maj. Stephen R. Clark.

ARMY OF THE JAMES, Maj.-Gen. Benjamin F. Butler.

Engineers: 1st N. Y., Col. Edward W. Serrell.
Naval Brigade, Brig.-Gen. Charles K. Graham.

TWENTY-FOURTH ARMY CORPS, Maj.-Gen. E. O. C. Ord (on leave), Brig.-Gen. Alfred H. Terry.

Headquarters' Guard : 8th Conn., Col. John E. Ward. *Provost Guard and Orderlies :* F and K, 4th Mass. Cav. (detachments), Capt. Joseph J. Baker.

FIRST DIVISION, Brig.-Gen. Robert S. Foster.

First Brigade, Col. Thomas O. Osborn : 39th Ill., Capt. Homer A. Plympton ; 62d Ohio, Lieut.-Col. Henry R. West ; 67th Ohio, Lieut.-Col. Henry S. Commager ; 199th Pa., Col. James C. Briscoe. *Second Brigade,* Brig.-Gen. Joseph R. Hawley : 6th Conn., Col. Alfred P. Rockwell ; 7th Conn., Capt. Henry B. Gill ; 3d N. H., Capt. William H. Trickey ; 7th N. H., Col. Joseph C. Abbott ; 16th N. Y. Heavy Art'y (6 co's), Maj. Frederick W. Prince. *Third Brigade,* Col. Harris M. Plaisted : 10th Conn., Lieut.-Col. Edwin S. Greely ; 11th Me., Lieut.-Col. Jonathan A. Hill ; 24th Mass., Maj. Albert Ordway ; 100th N. Y., Col. George B. Dandy ; 206th Pa., Col. Hugh J. Brady. *Fourth Brigade,* Col. James Jourdan : 8th Me., Lieut.-Col. William M. McArthur ; 89th N. Y., Col. Harrison S. Fairchild ; 148th N. Y., Col. John B. Murray ; 158th N. Y., Lieut.-Col. William H. McNary ; 55th Pa., Lieut.-Col. George H. Hill.

SECOND DIVISION, Brig.-Gen. Adelbert Ames.

First Brigade, Col. N. Martin Curtis : 3d N. Y., Capt. George W. Warren ; 112th N. Y., Lieut.-Col. John F. Smith ; 117th N. Y., Col. Rufus Daggett ; 142d N. Y., Lieut.-Col. Albert M. Barney. *Second Brigade,* Col. Galusha Pennypacker : 47th N. Y., Capt. Joseph M. McDonald ; 48th N. Y., Lieut.-Col. William B. Coan ; 76th Pa., Col. John S. Littell ; 97th Pa., Lieut. John Wainwright ; 203d Pa., Col. John W. Moore. *Third Brigade,* Col. Louis Bell : 13th Ind. (5 co's), Capt. Samuel M. Zent ; 9th Me., Col. G. Frederick Granger ; 4th N. H., Capt. John H. Roberts ; 115th N. Y., Maj. Ezra L. Walrath ; 169th N. Y., Col. Alonzo Alden.

THIRD DIVISION, Brig.-Gen. Charles Devens, Jr.

First Brigade, Lieut.-Col. John B. Raulston : 11th Conn., Lieut.-Col. Randall H. Rice ; 13th N. H., Lieut.-Col. Normand Smith ; 81st N. Y., Capt. Edward A. Stimson ; 98th N. Y., Lieut.-Col. William Kreutzer ; 139th N. Y., Capt. Theodore Miller ; 19th Wis., Maj. Samuel K. Vaughan. *Second Brigade,* Col. Joseph H. Potter : 5th Md., Lieut.-Col. William W. Bamberger ; 10th N. H., Lieut.-Col. John Coughlin ; 12th N. H., Lieut.-Col. Thomas E. Barker ; 96th N. Y., Col. Edgar M. Cullen ; 118th N. Y., Maj. John S. Cunningham ; 9th Vt., Col. Edward H. Ripley. *Third Brigade,* Col. Guy V. Henry : 21st Conn., Lieut.-Col. James F. Brown ; 40th Mass., Capt. John Pollack ; 2d N. H., Maj. John D. Cooper ; 58th Pa., Maj. Robert C. Redmond ; 188th Pa., Maj. Francis H. Reichard.

FIRST INFANTRY DIVISION ⌐ (Army of West Virginia), Col. Thomas M. Harris.

First Brigade, Lieut.-Col. Thomas F. Wiles : 34th Mass., Lieut.-Col. Andrew Potter ; 116th Ohio, Capt. Wilbert B. Teters ; 123d Ohio, Maj. Horace Kellogg. *Second Brigade,* Col. William B. Curtis : 23d Ill. (5 co's), Capt. Martin Wallace ; 54th Pa., Capt. Franklin B. Long ; 12th W. Va., Maj. Richard H. Brown. *Third Brigade,* Col. Milton Wells : 10th W. Va., Lieut.-Col. Moses S. Hall ; 11th W. Va., Capt. Dixon R. King ; 15th W. Va., Lieut.-Col. John W. Holliday.

ARTILLERY BRIGADE, Maj. Charles C. Abell : E, 3d N. Y., Capt. George E. Ashby ; H, 3d N. Y., Capt. William J. Riggs ; K, 3d N. Y., Capt. James R. Angel ; M, 3d N. Y., Capt. John H. Howell ; 7th N. Y., Lieut. Martin V. McIntyre ; 16th N. Y., Capt. Richard H. Lee ; 17th N. Y., Lieut. Hiram D. Smith ; A, 1st Pa., Capt. William Stitt ; F, 1st R. I., Lieut. Robert B. Smith ; L, 4th U. S., Lieut. Richard Wilson ; A, 5th U. S., Lieut. Charles P. Muhlenberg ; F, 5th U. S., Lieut. Leonard Martin.

TWENTY-FIFTH ARMY CORPS, ⚓ Maj.-Gen. Godfrey Weitzel.

Provost Guard : E and H, 4th Mass. Cav., Maj. Atherton H. Stevens, Jr.

FIRST DIVISION, Brig.-Gen. Charles J. Paine.

First Brigade, Col. Delevan Bates : 1st U. S., Lieut.-

Col. Giles H. Rich ; 27th U. S., Col. Albert M. Blackman ; 30th U. S., Col. Hiram A. Oakman. *Second Brigade,* Col. John W. Ames : 4th U. S., Lieut.-Col. George Rogers ; 6th U. S., Lieut.-Col. Clark E. Royce ; 39th U. S., Col. Ozora P. Stearns. *Third Brigade,* Col. Elias Wright : 5th U. S., Col. Giles W. Shurtleff ; 10th U. S., Lieut.-Col. Edward H. Powell ; 37th U. S., Col. Nathan Goff, Jr. ; 107th U. S., Lieut.-Col. David M. Sells.

SECOND DIVISION, Brig.-Gen. William Birney.

First Brigade, Col. Charles S. Russell : 7th U. S., Col. James Shaw, Jr. ; 109th U. S., Col. Orion A. Bartholomew ; 116th U. S., Col. William W. Woodward ; 117th U. S., Col. Lewis G. Brown. *Second Brigade,* Col. Ulysses Doubleday : 8th U. S., Col. Samuel C. Armstrong ; 45th U. S. (6 co's), Lieut.-Col. Edelmiro Mayer ; 127th U. S., Lieut.-Col. James Given. *Third Brigade,* Col. Henry C. Ward : 28th U. S., Lieut.-Col. Thomas H. Logan ; 29th U. S., Maj. T. Jeff. Brown ; 31st U. S., Maj. Thomas Wright.

THIRD DIVISION, Brig.-Gen. Edward A. Wild.

First Brigade, Col. Alonzo G. Draper : 22d U. S., Lieut.-Col. Ira C. Terry ; 36th U. S., Maj. William H. Hart ; 38th U. S., Lieut.-Col. Dexter E. Clapp ; 118th U. S., Col. John C. Moon. *Second Brigade,* Col. Edward Martindale : 29th Conn., Col. William B. Wooster ; 9th U. S., Lieut.-Col. David Torrence ; 41st U. S., Col. Llewellyn F. Haskell. *Third Brigade,* Brig. Gen. Henry G. Thomas : 19th U. S., Lieut.-Col. Joseph G. Perkins ; 23d U. S., Lieut.-Col. Marshall L. Dempcy ; 43d U. S., Col. Stephen B. Yeoman.

UNASSIGNED : 2d U. S. Colored Cavalry (dismounted), Capt. Edward P. Wilson.

ARTILLERY BRIGADE, Lieut.-Col. Richard H. Jackson : 1st Conn., Capt. James B. Clinton ; 4th N. J. (or D, 1st N. J.), Capt. Charles R. Doane ; 5th N. J. (or E, 1st N. J.), Lieut. Henry H. Metcalf ; detachment 16th N. Y. Heavy, Lieut. Silas J. Truax ; E, 1st Pa., Capt. Henry Y. Wildey ; C, 3d R. I., Capt. Martin S. James ; D, 1st U. S., Lieut. Redmond Tully ; M, 1st U. S., Capt. Loomis L. Langdon ; E, 3d U. S., Lieut. John R. Myrick ; D, 4th U. S., Capt. Frederick M. Follett.

CAVALRY DIVISION, Brig.-Gen. August V. Kautz.

First Brigade, Col. Robert M. West : 20th N. Y., Col. Newton B. Lord ; 5th Pa., Lieut.-Col. Christopher Kleinz. *Second Brigade,* Col. Samuel P. Spear : 1st D. C. (4 co's), Maj. J. Stannard Baker ; 11th Pa., Lieut.-Col. Franklin A. Stratton. *Third Brigade,* Col. Andrew W. Evans : 1st Md., Lieut.-Col. Jacob H. Counselman ; 1st N. Y. M't'd Rifles, Col. Edwin V. Sumner. *Artillery :* 4th Wis., Capt. Dorman L. Noggle ; B, 1st U. S., Lieut. Theodore K. Gibbs.

DEFENSES OF BERMUDA HUNDRED, Brig.-Gen. Edward Ferrero.

First Brigade, Col. William Heine : 41st N. Y. (6 co's), Lieut.-Col. Detleo von Einsiedel ; 103d N. Y., Lieut.-Col. Andrew Wettstein ; 104th Pa. (5 co's), Capt. Theophilus Kephart. *Second Brigade,* Lieut.-Col. G. De Peyster Arden : 6th N. Y. Heavy Art'y, Maj. George C. Kibbe ; 10th N. Y. Heavy Art'y, Maj. James B. Campbell. *Provisional Brigade,* Col. William M. McClure : detachment C, 13th N. H., Lieut. Royal B. Prescott ; 2d Pa. Heavy Art'y (batt'n), Capt. Nicholas Baggs. *Siege Artillery :* A and H, 13th N. Y. Heavy, Capt. William Prendell ; E and G, 3d Pa. Heavy, Capt. Samuel Hazard, Jr. ; M, 3d Pa. Heavy, Capt. Frederick Korte. *Pontoniers :* I, 3d Mass. Heavy Art'y, Lieut. Oliver J. Bixby.

SEPARATE BRIGADE, Col. Wardwell G. Robinson.

Fort Pocahontas, Maj. William H. Tantum : 38th N. J. (4 co's), Maj. William H. Tantum ; 16th N. Y. Heavy Art'y (2 co's), Capt. Henry C. Thompson ; 33d N.Y. Batt'y, Capt. Alger M. Wheeler ; detachment 1st U. S. Col'd Cav., Capt. David Vandevort. *Harrison's Landing,* Lieut.-Col.William P. McKinley : detachment 4th Mass. Cav., Lieut. Thomas Miles ; 184th N. Y., Lieut.-Col. W. P. McKinley ; detachment 3d Pa. Heavy Art'y, Lieut. Frederick Grill. *Fort Powhatan,* Col. William J. Sewell : 38th N. J. (6 co's) Lieut.-Col. Ashbel W. Angel ; detachment 3d Pa. Heavy Art'y ; E, 1st U. S. Col'd Cav., Capt. Charles W. Emerson.

⌐ Temporarily attached to Twenty-fourth Corps.

⚓ All the infantry were colored troops.

According to the official returns the effective force of the armies operating against Petersburg and Richmond, from June to December, 1864, was as follows:

DATE.	Cavalry.	Artillery.	Infantry.	Total.
June 30th	14,044	8,005	85,370	107,419
July 31st	8,559	8,952	59,810	77,321
August 31st.......	5,827	7,200	45,896	58,923
September 30th...	6,799	8,858	61,118	76,775
October 31st	6,295	7,508	71,243	85,046
November 30th ...	8,554	7,964	70,205	86,723
December 31st....	9,974	9,582	90,808	110,364

The total losses from June 15th to December 31st, 1864, were as follows:

MONTH.	Killed.	Wounded.	Captured or Missing.	Total.
June..............	2,013	9,935	4,621	16,569
July..............	915	3,808	1,644	6,367
August............	876	4,151	5,969	10,996
September........	644	3,503	2,871	7,018
October	528	2,946	2,094	5,568
November	57	258	108	423
December........	66	278	269	613
Aggregate	5,099	24,879	17,576	47,554

THE CONFEDERATE ARMY. ↓

General Robert E. Lee.

Provost Guard, etc.: 1st Va. Batt'n, Maj. D. B. Bridgford; 39th Va. Batt'n Cav., Maj. John H. Richardson. *Engineer Troops:* 1st Reg't, Col. T. M. R. Talcott.

FIRST ARMY CORPS, Lieut.-Gen. James Longstreet.

PICKETT'S DIVISION, Maj.-Gen. George E. Pickett.

Steuart's Brigade, Brig.-Gen. George H. Steuart: 9th Va., Col. J. J. Phillips; 14th Va., Col. William White; 38th Va., Col. George K. Griggs; 53d Va., Col. W. R. Aylett; 57th Va., Col. C. R. Fontaine. *Corse's Brigade,* Brig.-Gen. Montgomery D. Corse: 15th Va., Col. T. P. August; 17th Va., Col. Arthur Herbert; 29th Va., Col. James Giles; 30th Va., Col. R. S. Chew; 32d Va., Col. E. B. Montague. *Hunton's Brigade,* Brig.-Gen. Eppa Hunton: 8th Va., Col. N. Berkeley; 18th Va., Col. H. A. Carrington; 19th Va., Col. Henry Gantt; 28th Va., Col. William Watts; 56th Va., Col. William E. Green. *Terry's Brigade,* Brig.-Gen. William R. Terry: 1st Va., Col. Frederick G. Skinner; 3d Va., Col. Joseph Mayo, Jr.; 7th Va., Col. C. C. Flowerree; 11th Va., Col. M. S. Langhorne; 24th Va., Lieut.-Col. Richard L. Maury.

FIELD'S DIVISION, Maj.-Gen. Charles W. Field.

Anderson's Brigade, Brig.-Gen. G. T. Anderson: 7th Ga., Col. G. H. Carmical; 8th Ga., Col. J. R. Towers; 9th Ga., Lieut.-Col. E. F. Hoge; 11th Ga., Col. F. H. Little; 59th Ga., Col. J. Brown. *Law's Brigade,* Col. W. F. Perry: 4th Ala., Col. P. D. Bowles; 15th Ala., Col. A. A. Lowther; 44th Ala., Col. ——; 47th Ala., Col. M. J. Bulger; 48th Ala., Lieut.-Col. W. M. Hardwick. *Gregg's Brigade,* Col. F. S. Bass: 3d Ark., Col. Van H. Manning; 1st Tex., Capt. W. A. Bedell; 4th Tex., Col. J. P. Bane; 5th Tex., Col. R. M. Powell. *Benning's Brigade,* Brig.-Gen. H. L. Benning: 2d Ga., Lieut.-Col. W. S. Shepherd; 15th Ga., Lieut.-Col. S. Z. Hearnsberger; 17th Ga., Col. Wesley C. Hodges; 20th Ga., Col. J. D. Waddell. *Bratton's Brigade,* Brig.-Gen. John Bratton: 1st S. C., Col. James R. Hagood; 5th S. C., Col. A. Coward; 6th S. C., Col. J. M. Steedman; 2d S. C. Rifles, Col. R. E. Bowen; Palmetto (S. C.) Sharp-shooters, Col. Joseph Walker.

KERSHAW'S DIVISION, Maj.-Gen. J. B. Kershaw.

Wofford's Brigade, Brig.-Gen. Dudley M. DuBose: 16th Ga., Maj. J. H. Skelton; 18th Ga., Col. Joseph Armstrong; 24th Ga., Col. C. C. Sanders; 3d Ga. Batt'n Sharp-shooters, Lieut.-Col. N. L. Hutchins, Jr.; Cobb's Ga. Legion, Lieut.-Col. Luther J. Glenn; Phillips Ga. Legion, Lieut.-Col. Joseph Hamilton. *Humphreys's Brigade,* Brig.-Gen. B. G. Humphreys: 13th Miss., Lieut.-Col. A. G. O'Brien; 17th Miss., Capt. J. C. Cochran; 18th Miss., Lieut.-Col. William H. Luse; 21st Miss., Col. D. N. Moody. *Bryan's Brigade,* Brig.-Gen. Goode Bryan: 10th Ga., Col. Willis C. Holt; 50th Ga., Col. P. McGlashan; 51st Ga., Lieut.-Col. James Dickey; 53d Ga., Col. J. P. Simms. *Conner's Brigade,* Brig.-Gen. James Conner: 2d S. C., Col. J. D. Kennedy; 3d S. C., Lieut.-Col. R. C. Moffett; 7th S. C., Capt. E. J. Goggans; 8th S. C., Col. J. W. Henagan; 15th S. C., Col. J. B. Davis; 20th S. C., Col. S. M. Boykin; 3d S. C. Batt'n, Lieut.-Col. W. G. Rice.

ARTILLERY, ▷ Brig.-Gen. E. P. Alexander.

Cabell's Battalion, Col. H. C. Cabell: Va. Batt'y, Capt.

R. M. Anderson; Ga. Batt'y, Lieut. Morgan Callaway; Ga. Batt'y, Capt. H. H. Carlton; N. C. Batt'y, Capt. Basil C. Manly. *Huger's Battalion,* Lieut.-Col. F. Huger: S. C. Batt'y, Capt. W. W. Fickling; La. Batt'y (Moody's), Lieut. J. C. Parkinson; Va. Batt'y, Capt. W. W. Parker; Va. Batt'y, Capt. John D. Smith; Va. Batt'y, Capt. O. B. Taylor; Va. Batt'y, Lieut. James Woolfolk. *Hardaway's Battalion* (detached from the Second Corps), Lieut.-Col. R. A. Hardaway: Va. Batt'y, Capt. Willis J. Dance; Va. Batt'y, Capt. Archibald Graham; Va. Batt'y, Capt. Charles B. Griffin; Va. Batt'y, Capt. B. H. Smith, Jr. *Haskell's Battalion,* Maj. John C. Haskell: N. C. Batt'y, Capt. H. G. Flanner; N. C. Batt'y, Capt. John A. Ramsay; S. C. Batt'y, Capt. H. R. Garden; Va. Batt'y, Capt. J. N. Lamkin. *Stark's Battalion,* Lieut.-Col. A. W. Stark: La. Batt'y, Capt. Charles A. Green; Va. Batt'y, Capt. A. D. Armistead; Va. Batt'y, Capt. David A. French.

SECOND ARMY CORPS, Maj.-Gen. John B. Gordon.

RODES'S DIVISION.

Battle's Brigade: 3d Ala., ——; 5th Ala., ——; 6th Ala., ——; 12th Ala., ——; 61st Ala., ——. *Grimes's Brigade:* 32d N. C., ——; 43d N. C., ——; 45th N. C., ——; 53d N. C., ——; 2d N. C. Batt'n, ——. *Cox's Brigade:* 1st N. C., ——; 2d N. C., ——; 3d N. C., ——; 4th N. C., ——; 14th N. C., ——; 30th N. C., ——. *Cook's Brigade:* 4th Ga., ——; 12th Ga., ——; 21st Ga., ——; 44th Ga., ——.

EARLY'S DIVISION, Brig.-Gen. John Pegram.

Johnston's Brigade: 5th N. C., ——; 12th N. C., ——; 20th N. C., ——; 23d N. C., ——; 1st N. C. Batt'n, ——. *Lewis's Brigade:* 6th N. C., ——; 21st N. C., ——; 54th N. C., ——; 57th N. C., ——. *Pegram's Brigade:* 13th Va., ——; 31st Va., ——; 49th Va., ——; 52d Va., ——; 58th Va., ——.

GORDON'S DIVISION, Brig.-Gen. C. A. Evans.

Evans's Brigade: 13th Ga., ——; 26th Ga., ——; 31st Ga., ——; 38th Ga., ——; 60th Ga., ——; 61st Ga., ——; 12th Ga. Batt'n, ——. *Terry's Brigade,* Brig.-Gen. William Terry: 2d Va., ——; 4th Va., ——; 5th Va., ——; 10th Va., ——; 21st Va., ——; 23d Va., ——; 25th Va., ——; 27th Va., ——; 33d Va., ——; 37th Va., ——; 42d Va., ——; 44th Va., ——; 48th Va., ——. *York's Brigade:* 1st La., ——; 2d La., ——; 5th La., ——; 6th La., ——; 7th La., ——; 8th La., ——; 9th La., ——; 10th La., ——; 14th La., ——; 15th La., ——. [With the exception of Hardaway's battalion, attached to the First Corps, the artillery of the Second Corps was "still in the Valley."]

THIRD ARMY CORPS, Lieut.-Gen. Ambrose P. Hill.

HETH'S DIVISION, Maj.-Gen. Henry Heth.

Davis's Brigade, Brig.-Gen. Joseph R. Davis: 1st Confederate Batt'n, Maj. F. B. McClung; 2d Miss., Col. J. M. Stone; 11th Miss., Lieut.-Col. W. B. Lowry; 26th Miss., Col. A. E. Reynolds; 42d Miss., Col. A. M. Nelson. *Cooke's Brigade,* Brig.-Gen. J. R. Cooke: 15th N. C., Lieut.-Col. W. H. Yarborough; 27th N. C., Col. J. A. Gilmer, Jr.; 46th N. C., Col. W. L. Saunders; 48th N. C., Col. S. H. Walkup; 55th N. C., Col. John K. Connally.

↓ Some of the regimental and battery commanders mentioned were not in actual command on December 31st.

▷ Brig.-Gen. W. N. Pendleton commanded the artillery of the army.

MacRae's Brigade, Brig.-Gen. William MacRae: 11th N. C., Col. W. J. Martin; 26th N. C., Col. J. R. Lane; 44th N. C., Col. T. C. Singeltary; 47th N. C., Col. G. H. Faribault; 52d N. C., Col. M. A. Parks. *Archer's Brigade,* Col. R. M. Mayo (also in command of Walker's brigade, following): 13th Ala., Col. James Aiken; 1st Tenn. (Prov. Army), Col. N. J. George; 7th Tenn., Col. J. A. Fite; 14th Tenn., Col. Wm. McComb. *Walker's Brigade:* 2d Md. Batt'n, Lieut.-Col. J. R. Herbert; 22d Va. Batt'n, Lieut.-Col. E. P. Tayloe; 40th Va., Lieut.-Col. A. S. Cunningham; 47th Va., Capt. C. J. Green; 55th Va., Col. W. S. Christian. *Johnson's Brigade:* 17th and 23d Tenn., ———; 25th and 44th Tenn., ———; 63d Tenn., ———.

WILCOX'S DIVISION, Maj.-Gen. Cadmus M. Wilcox.

Thomas's Brigade, Brig.-Gen. E. L. Thomas: 14th Ga., Col. R. P. Lester; 35th Ga., Col. B. H. Holt; 45th Ga., Col. T. J. Simmons; 49th Ga., Col. John T. Jordan. *Lane's Brigade,* Brig.-Gen. James H. Lane: 7th N. C., Col. E. G. Haywood; 18th N. C., Col. J. D. Barry; 28th N. C., Capt. T. V. Apperson; 33d N. C., Col. R. V. Cowan; 37th N. C., Lieut.-Col. W. G. Morris. *McGowan's Brigade,* Brig.-Gen. Samuel McGowan: 1st S. C. (Prov. Army), Col. C. W. McCreary; 12th S. C., Lieut.-Col. T. F. Clyburn; 13th S. C., Col. Isaac F. Hunt; 14th S. C., Col. J. N. Brown; Orr's (S. C.) Rifles, Col. G. McD. Miller. *Scales's Brigade,* Brig.-Gen. Alfred M. Scales: 13th N. C., Col. J. H. Hyman; 16th N. C., Col. W. A. Stowe; 22d N. C., Col. T. S. Gallaway; 34th N. C., Col. W. L. J. Lowrance; 38th N. C., Col. John Ashford.

MAHONE'S DIVISION, Maj.-Gen. William Mahone.

Sanders's Brigade, Brig.-Gen. J. C. C. Sanders: 8th Ala., Col. Y. L. Royston; 9th Ala., Col. J. H. King; 10th Ala., Col. W. H. Forney; 11th Ala., Col. G. E. Tayloe; 13th Ala., Col. James Aiken; 14th Ala., Col. L. Pinckard. *Weisiger's Brigade,* Brig.-Gen. D. A. Weisiger: 6th Va., Col. George T. Rogers; 12th Va., Lieut.-Col. E. M. Feild; 16th Va., Col. Joseph H. Ham; 41st Va., Col. W. A. Parham; 61st Va., Col. V. D. Groner. *Harris's Brigade,* Brig.-Gen. Nathaniel H. Harris: 12th Miss., Col. M. B. Harris; 16th Miss., Col. E. C. Councell; 19th Miss., Col. R. W. Phipps; 48th Miss., Col. J. M. Jayne. *Sorrel's Brigade,* Brig.-Gen. G. M. Sorrel: 3d Ga., Col. E. J. Walker; 22d Ga., Col. George H. Jones; 48th Ga., Col. William Gibson; 64th Ga., Col. W. H. Weems; 2d Ga. Batt'n, Maj. C. J. Moffett; 10th Ga. Batt'n, Capt. J. D. Frederick. *Finegan's Brigade,* Brig.-Gen. Joseph Finegan: 2d Fla., Maj. W. R. Moore; 5th Fla., Col. T. B. Lamar; 8th Fla., Col. David Lang; 9th Fla., Col. J. M. Martin; 10th Fla., Col. C. F. Hopkins; 11th Fla., Col. T. W. Brevard.

ARTILLERY, Col. R. L. Walker: Ala. Battery, Capt. W. B. Hunt; Md. Battery, Capt. W. F. Dement; Md. Battery, Capt. W. S. Chew; Va. Battery, Capt. W. K. Donald; Va. Battery, Capt. B. Z. Price; Va. Battery (Clutter's), Lieut. Lucas McIntosh. *Pegram's Battalion,* Col. W. J. Pegram: Miss. Battery, Capt. T. J. Richards; S. C. Battery, Capt. Thomas E. Gregg; Va. Battery (Braxton's), Lieut. J. G. Pollock; Va. Battery, Capt. T. A. Brander; Va. Battery, Capt. George M. Cayce; Va. Battery, Capt. T. Ellett. *Poague's Battalion,* Col. W. T. Poague: N. C. Battery, Capt. A. B. Williams; Va. Battery, Capt. C. F. Johnston; Va. Battery, Capt. A. W. Utterback. *Eshleman's Battalion,* Lieut.-Col. B. F. Eshleman: La. Battery, Capt. Edward Owen; La. Battery, Capt. J. B. Richardson; La. Battery, Capt. Andrew Hero, Jr.; La. Battery, Capt. Joe Norcom. *Richardson's Battalion,* Lieut.-Col. Charles Richardson: La. Battery, Capt. R. P. Landry; Va. Battery, Capt. J. D. Moore; Va. Battery, Capt. C. R. Grandy; Va. Battery, Capt. Nathan Penick. *Lane's Battalion,* Maj. John Lane: Ga. Battery, Capt. J. T. Wingfield; Ga. Battery, Capt. G. M. Patterson; Ga. Batt'y, Capt. H. M. Ross. *Owen's Battalion,* Maj. W. M. Owen: Va. Batt'y, Capt. J. H. Chamberlayne; Va. Batt'y, Capt. Crispin Dickenson; Va. Batt'y, Capt. D. N. Walker.

ANDERSON'S CORPS, Lieut.-Gen. R. H. Anderson.

HOKE'S DIVISION (started for Wilmington, N. C., Dec. 20th, 1864), Maj.-Gen. R. F. Hoke.

Hagood's Brigade, Brig.-Gen. Johnson Hagood: 11th S. C., Col. F. H. Gantt; 21st S. C., Col. R. F. Graham; 25th S. C., Col. C. H. Simonton; 27th S. C., Col. P. C. Gaillard; 7th S. C. Batt'n, Maj. J. H. Rion. *Colquitt's*

Brigade, Brig.-Gen. A. H. Colquitt: 6th Ga., Lieut.-Col. S. W. Harris; 19th Ga., Col. J. H. Neal; 23d Ga., Col. M. R. Ballenger; 27th Ga., Capt. E. D. Graham; 28th Ga., Capt. J. A. Johnson. *Clingman's Brigade:* 8th N. C., Lieut.-Col. R. A. Barrier; 31st N. C., Lieut.-Col. C. W. Knight; 51st N. C., Col. Hector McKethan; 61st N. C., Lieut.-Col. Wm. S. Devane. *Kirkland's Brigade,* Brig.-Gen. W. W. Kirkland: 17th N. C., Lieut.-Col. T. H. Sharpe; 42d N. C., Col. J. E. Brown; 66th N. C., Col. John H. Nethercutt.

JOHNSON'S DIVISION, Maj.-Gen. Bushrod R. Johnson.

Wise's Brigade, Brig.-Gen. Henry A. Wise: 26th Va., Capt. W. R. Perrin; 34th Va., Col. J. T. Goode; 46th Va., Capt. J. H. White; 59th Va., Maj. R. G. Mosby. *Elliott's Brigade,* Brig.-Gen. Stephen Elliott, Jr.: 17th S. C., Col. F. W. McMaster; 18th S. C., Lieut.-Col. W. B. Allison; 22d S. C., Col. W. G. Burt; 23d S. C., Col. H. L. Benbow; 26th S. C., Col. A. D. Smith; Holcombe S. C. Legion, Capt. A. B. Woodruff. *Gracie's Brigade,* Brig.-Gen. A. Gracie, Jr.: 41st Ala., Col. M. L. Stansel; 43d Ala., Lieut.-Col. J. J. Jolly; 59th Ala., Lieut.-Col. G. W. Huguley; 60th Ala., Col. J. W. A. Sanford; 23d Ala. Batt'n, Maj. N. Stallworth. *Ransom's Brigade,* Brig.-Gen. M. W. Ransom: 24th N. C., Lieut.-Col. J. L. Harris; 25th N. C., Col. H. M. Rutledge; 35th N. C., Col. J. T. Johnson; 49th N. C., Col. L. M. McAfee; 56th N. C., Col. Paul F. Faison.

ARTILLERY, Col. H. P. Jones. *Moseley's Battalion:* Ga. Batt'y, Capt. C. W. Slaten; N. C. Batt'y, Capt. J. D. Cumming; Va. Batt'y, Capt. John Miller; Va. Batt'y, Capt. E. R. Young. *Blount's Battalion:* Va. Batt'y, Capt. J. W. Dickerson; Va. Batt'y, Capt. W. C. Marshall; Va. Batt'y, Capt. M. C. Macon; Va. Batt'y, Capt. J. E. Sullivan. *Coit's Battalion:* La. Batt'y, Capt. S. T. Wright; Miss. Batt'y, Capt. W. D. Bradford; Va. Batt'y, Capt. R. G. Pegram. *Martin's Battalion:* Va. Batt'y (Martin's), Lieut. S. H. Pulliam; Va. Batt'y (Sturdivant's), Lieut. W. H. Weisiger.

CAVALRY CORPS, Maj.-Gen. Wade Hampton.

BUTLER'S DIVISION, Maj.-Gen. M. C. Butler.

Butler's Brigade, Col. H. K. Aiken: 4th S. C., Lieut.-Col. William Stokes; 5th S. C., Capt. Z. Davis; 6th S. C., Lieut.-Col. L. P. Miller. *Young's Brigade,* Col. J. F. Waring: 10th Ga., Capt. L. F. Smith; Cobb's Ga. Legion, Lieut.-Col. B. S. King; Phillips Ga. Legion, Lieut.-Col. W. W. Rich; Jeff. Davis's Miss. Legion, Maj. J. F. Lewis.

LEE'S DIVISION, Maj.-Gen. W. H. F. Lee.

Barringer's Brigade, Brig.-Gen. Rufus Barringer: 1st N. C., Col. W. H. Cheek; 2d N. C., Col. W. P. Roberts; 3d N. C., Col. J. A. Baker; 5th N. C., Maj. J. H. McNeill. *Beale's Brigade,* Brig.-Gen. R. L. T. Beale: 9th Va., Col. T. Waller; 10th Va., Lieut.-Col. R. A. Caskie; 13th Va., Col. J. C. Phillips. *Dearing's Brigade,* Brig.-Gen. J. Dearing: 8th Ga., Col. J. R. Griffin; 4th N. C., Col. D. D. Ferebee; 16th N. C. Batt'n, Lieut.-Col. J. T. Kennedy.

HORSE ARTILLERY, Maj. R. Preston Chew: S. C. Batt'y (Hart's), Lieut. E. L. Halsey; Va. Batt'y, Capt. Edward Graham; Va. Batt'y, Capt. William M. McGregor.

RICHMOND AND DANVILLE DEFENSES, Brig.-Gen. J. A. Walker. [Consisted mainly of several battalions of Virginia Reserves, second-class militia, and small detachments of cavalry and artillery.]

The following exhibit of Lee's strength at Richmond and Petersburg is compiled from official returns:

DATE.	Cavalry.	Artillery.	Infantry.	Total.
June 30th	7421	5520	41,810	54,751
July 10th	8962	5569	42,566	57,097
August 31st	6739	3631	24,307	34,677
September 10th	7110	4976	23,002	35,088
October 31st	5654	5057	36,596	47,307
November 30th	6208	6144	44,072	56,424
December 20th	6438	5456	54,639	66,533

In the return for June 30th the strength of Dearing's cavalry (estimated at 1800) is not included, and the return for November 30th indicates that 1290 of the cavalry were dismounted. The numbers given above are the "present for duty" on June 30th, July 10th, September 10th, and December 20th, and the "effective total" on August 31st, October 31st, and November 30th.

THE CONFEDERATE CRUISERS.

BY PROFESSOR JAMES RUSSELL SOLEY, U. S. N.

THE first of the ocean cruisers of the Confederate navy, as distinguished from the privateers, was the *Sumter*. This steamer, formerly the *Habana*, of the New Orleans and Havana line, was altered into a ship-of-war in April and May, 1861, and, under the command of Captain Raphael Semmes, escaped from the Mississippi early in July, after an unsuccessful chase by the *Brooklyn*, which was at the time blockading the mouth of the river. Her cruise lasted six months, during which she made fifteen prizes. Of these seven were destroyed, one was ransomed, one recaptured, and the remaining six were sent into Cienfuegos, where they were released by the Cuban authorities. In January the *Sumter* arrived at Gibraltar, where she was laid up and finally sold.

The Confederate Government early recognized that in order to attack the commerce of the United States with any hope of success it must procure cruisers abroad. For this purpose it sent several agents to Europe. The foremost of these was Captain James D. Bulloch, of the Confederate navy, who arrived in England and established himself at Liverpool in June, 1861. Having satisfied himself as to the scope and bearing of the neutrality laws, he lost no time in closing a contract with the firm of Fawcett & Preston, engine builders, of Liverpool, for a screw gun-vessel. The steamer was named the *Oreto*, and it was announced that she was being built for a firm at Palermo; presumably for the Italian Government. She was a duplicate of the gun-vessels of the English navy. The construction of the vessel proceeded without interruption during the fall and winter of 1861–62. The American Minister, Mr. Charles Francis Adams, twice called the attention of the Foreign Office to her suspected character, and *pro formá* inquiries were set on foot, but they failed to show evidence of her real destination. The *Oreto* therefore cleared without difficulty for Palermo and Jamaica, a Liverpool merchant, representing the Palermo firm, having sworn that he was the owner, and an English captain having been appointed to the command. On the 22d of March the vessel sailed from Liverpool. At the same time the steamer *Bahama* left Hartlepool for Nassau, carrying the *Oreto's* battery.

The new cruiser arrived at Nassau April 28th, consigned to Adderly & Co., the Confederate agents at that port, and a few days later she was joined by the *Bahama*. The consignees immediately set about transferring the arms and ammunition, but on the representations of the United States consul at Nassau the *Oreto* was inspected by Captain Hickley, of H. M. ship *Greyhound*, who reported that she was in every respect fitted as a man-of-war. She was thereupon libelled in the vice-admiralty court, and after a trial, in which the sympathies of the court were plainly apparent, she was released on the 7th of August. The *Oreto*, or *Florida*, as she was henceforth called, now sailed for Green Cay, took on board her battery, consisting of two 7-inch rifles and six 6-inch guns,

and became a veritable Confederate cruiser, under the command of Commander J. N. Maffitt, of the Confederate navy. Her course was first shaped for Cuba. Here Maffitt hoped to obtain certain essential parts of his ordnance which had not been supplied at Nassau, and also to ship a crew. The authorities in Cuba, however, prohibited any shipment of men or supply of equipments, and presently the crew, which numbered only twenty-two, was attacked by yellow fever, until nearly every one on board, including the captain, was prostrated by the disease. After delaying a week at Cardenas and Havana, Maffitt determined to attempt to run the blockade at Mobile.

The squadron, at this time off Mobile, was composed of the sloop-of-war *Oneida* and the gun-boat *Winona*, under Commander George H. Preble. The *Oneida* was just completing repairs to her boilers, and was working at a reduced speed. At 5 o'clock on the afternoon of the 4th of September the *Florida* was sighted in the distance. At this moment the *Winona* was just returning from a chase in company with the schooner *Rachel Seaman*. From the appearance of the stranger, and from her English ensign and pennant, Preble was satisfied that she was an English gun-vessel inspecting the blockade. When she came abreast of the *Oneida*, as she showed no signs of stopping, Preble fired across her bow three times. The *Florida* continued at full speed, but made no reply. Upon this Preble fired into her, the *Winona* and *Rachel Seaman* joining in from a distance. The *Florida* received some damage from shot and shell, but she was not disabled, and in a few moments she had passed out of range, and was making her way up the main ship-channel to Fort Morgan.

The *Florida* remained four months at Mobile completing her repairs and equipment and filling up her crew. On the night of January 15th, 1863, she ran the blockade outward. It was a dark, stormy night. Seven vessels now composed the blockading squadron, several of which had been selected for their size and speed, with the view of preventing the escape of the *Florida*. Although her coming was expected, she succeeded in passing directly between the flag-ship *Susquehanna* and the *Cuyler*, the fastest of the blockaders. The *Cuyler* started in pursuit and chased the *Florida* during the whole of the next day, but at night lost sight of her.

Within ten days after leaving Mobile the *Florida* captured and burnt three vessels. Maffitt then put into Nassau, where he was warmly received and, in violation of the neutrality regulations, permitted to remain thirty-six hours and to take on board a three-months' supply of coal. During the next five months, comprising the spring and early summer of 1863, fourteen prizes were captured, one of which, the brig *Clarence*, was fitted out as a tender and placed under the command of Lieutenant Charles W. Read. Proceeding northward on a roving cruise in the *Clarence*, Read captured, during the month of June, five vessels off the coast of the United States, between the Chesapeake and Portland. The fifth was the schooner *Tacony*, and finding her better suited to his purpose, Read burned the *Clarence*, after transferring his guns and men to the new cruiser. His four other prizes were also destroyed. During the next fortnight the *Tacony* made ten prizes. The last of these, the *Archer*, then became a ship-of-war, and the *Tacony* and the other prizes were burned. Read now made a raid into Portland harbor and cut out the reve-

CAPTAIN JAMES D. BULLOCH, C. S. N.
FROM A PHOTOGRAPH.

nue-cutter *Cushing*, but the inhabitants of Portland fitted out all the available steamers in port, and Read was overtaken and captured.

Soon after these events the *Florida* proceeded to Brest, where she remained for six months undergoing repairs. She sailed in February, 1864, under the command of Captain C. M. Morris. After cruising for four months in the North Atlantic, she visited Bermuda, where she obtained supplies of coal. During the summer she continued her cruise in the Atlantic, destroying merchantmen in the neighborhood of the United States coast.

On the 5th of October the *Florida* arrived at Bahia, in Brazil, where she found the United States sloop-of-war *Wachusett*, Commander N. Collins. She took a position near the shore about half a mile from the *Wachusett*. A Brazilian corvette, as a precaution, took a berth between the two vessels.

The temptation to violate the neutrality of the port of Bahia was too great for Captain Collins, and he resolved to run down the *Florida* and sink her at her anchorage. It was his design to give the act the appearance of an accident, but the plan was so badly carried out that the capture of the vessel assumed the character of a perfectly unjustifiable outrage. Before daylight, on the morning of October 7th, the *Wachusett* got under way, passed

the Brazilian corvette, and ran into the *Florida*, striking her on the starboard quarter, cutting down her bulwarks and carrying away her mizzen-mast. As the *Wachusett* backed off, and the *Florida* was clearly not in a sinking condition, Collins fired one or two volleys of small-arms, and also two discharges from his heavy guns, upon which the *Florida* surrendered. At the time of the capture, the captain and a large part of the crew of the *Florida* were on shore; the remainder were taken prisoners. The *Florida* was taken to Hampton Roads, where she was afterward sunk by collision with a transport. The United States made the *amende honorable* to Brazil, and Captain Collins was tried by court-martial.

The second cruiser built in England, through the agency of Captain Bulloch, was the *Alabama*, whose career is described in another place. [See p. 600.] Notwithstanding the very urgent representations of Mr. Adams, accompanied by depositions which left no doubt as to the character and objects of the vessel, she was permitted to escape through the extreme dilatoriness of the English officials who had the matter in hand at the critical moment. On the 29th of July, 1862, the law officers of the Crown rendered the opinion that the vessel was clearly intended for warlike use against the United States, and recommended that she be seized without loss of time; but on that very day she left Liverpool, ostensibly on a trial trip, and, after completing her preparations at Point Lynas, made her way to the North Atlantic.

The third of the Confederate vessels obtained abroad was the *Georgia*. In the latter part of 1862, Commander Matthew F. Maury, who had acquired great distinction as a scientific man while in the old navy, was sent to England partly to influence public opinion in favor of the Confederacy, and also with a general authority to fit out ships of war. In March, 1863, he purchased on the Clyde the *Japan*, a new iron screw steamer. She was an excellent vessel, although built for the merchant service, but she was seriously defective as a commerce-destroyer, from the lack of auxiliary sail-power, a defect which Bulloch, in his contracts and purchases, had uniformly avoided.

The *Japan* cleared from Greenock on the 1st of April, 1863, in ballast, as a merchant vessel, bound for the East Indies. A shipping firm of Liverpool was employed as the intermediary to cover all the transactions. One member of the firm was the ostensible owner, and the *Japan* was registered in his name as a British vessel, and remained so for three months, though engaged during this time in active hostilities against the United States. Another member of the firm shipped the crew, and took charge of a small steamer which cleared about the same time from Newhaven, with a cargo of guns and ammunition. The two vessels met off the coast of France, the cargo was transferred, the officers proceeded on board, and the Confederate cruiser *Georgia*, though still registered as the British steamer *Japan*, started on her cruise. Her career extended over a year, during which she cruised in the Atlantic under Lieutenant William L. Maury. During her cruise she captured only eight vessels, her movements being restricted by her want of sail-power and her limited coal capacity.

The operations of the Confederate cruisers having their base in Europe were now under the principal direction of Commodore Samuel Barron, senior officer at Paris. Barron, having no further use for the *Georgia*, sent her to Liverpool in May, 1864, to be disposed of by Bulloch. She was sold on June 1st to Mr. Edwin Bates, a Liverpool merchant, who took her under a bill of sale signed by Bulloch. After the transfer was completed, the ship was chartered by the Portuguese Government, and she set out on her voyage to Lisbon. At the instance of Mr. Adams, the *Niagara*, under Commodore Thomas T. Craven, proceeded to Liverpool, and, learning the proposed destination of the *Georgia*, took measures to intercept her. Meeting her outside of Lisbon, Craven seized her and sent her into Boston, where she was condemned. The claim for damages subsequently entered on behalf of Mr. Bates before the Mixed Commission at Washington was unanimously disallowed.

The members of the Liverpool firm which had been engaged in fitting out the *Georgia* and securing her crew were afterward indicted under the Foreign Enlistment Act, and, being found guilty, were sentenced to pay a fine of £50 each. The Confederate operations in England did not suffer so much from the penalty inflicted upon the guilty parties as from the scandal and notoriety caused by the prosecution and the light which it threw upon the methods of the purchasing agents. Notwithstanding all this, Commander Maury was not deterred from making a second attempt, which was even less profitable.

During the latter part of 1863, several condemned dispatch boats belonging to the royal navy were offered for sale at Sheerness; one of these, the *Victor*, was bought by an agent of Maury's. In such cases it was usual to allow the purchaser to put in the equipment of the vessel and overhaul her machinery at the dock-yard; but, whatever the practice may be, it is of course necessary that a neutral government should take care that it is not thereby instrumental in turning over a ship-of-war to a belligerent. The real ownership of the *Victor* was carefully concealed, and, wittingly or unwittingly, the dock-yard officials were superintending her equipment. It was intended that the *Rappahannock*, as the new cruiser was named, should receive her battery from the *Georgia* after she got to sea, but suspicion was aroused at the United States Legation, inquiries were set on foot, Maury took alarm, and one night in the winter the ship was hurried off with the workmen still on board, and with only a fragment of a crew. In the Channel she was joined by a party of Confederate officers and put in commission, and the next morning she entered Calais in the guise of a Confederate ship-of-war in distress, which had been driven by the need of repairs to seek the hospitality of the port. She was allowed to enter, but placed under close observation. After much discussion, the French Government decided that it would place no obstacle in the way of her departure, but would allow no increase of the crew or

the supply of warlike equipment, and a French gun-boat was anchored close by to enforce the prohibition. No further attempt was made to remove the vessel, and she remained at Calais as a depot ship. In March, 1865, Barron turned her over to Bulloch, and an attempt was made to sell her; but as the Confederacy had now come to an end, Bulloch could give no legal title, and the ship was eventually delivered to the United States.

In the latter part of 1862 a new cruiser, of the same type as the *Florida*, was projected by the Confederate agents in Liverpool. She was launched on the 7th of March, 1863, and was called the *Alexandra*. The suspicions of Mr. Dudley, United States consul at Liverpool, were aroused, and near the end of March Mr. Adams brought the subject to the notice of the Foreign Office, at the same time forwarding affidavits that left no doubt of the vessel's character. As a result she was seized by the customs officers, and the case was tried in the following June before the Court of Exchequer. The court, in interpreting the Foreign Enlistment Act, held that there was no offense under the statute unless the vessel was *armed* for hostile purposes, and unless the arming was done within British jurisdiction. The jury, in consequence, brought in a verdict of not guilty. Appeals and motions for a new trial followed, but were defeated upon various technical grounds, and the vessel was eventually released. The protracted series of trials, however, kept the vessel in custody until it was too late to make use of her as a cruiser, and she became a blockade-runner.

Another vessel, the *Pampero*, built by Lieutenant George T. Sinclair, on the Clyde, was seized by the Scottish officials in November, 1863. To avoid the litigation and delay which had attended the *Alexandra* case a compromise was arranged between the owners—that is, the builders—and the Government, by which a verdict was entered for the Crown, and the owners were allowed to retain the vessel, provided they should not sell her for two years without the consent of the Crown. This simple arrangement, if it had been adopted in the case of the other cruisers, would have obviated the whole controversy over the so-called *Alabama* claims.

Secretary Mallory attached a high importance to the construction of iron-clads, and already, in June, 1862, he had directed Bulloch to procure them. The latter immediately made a contract with the Lairds, the builders of the *Alabama*, to build two double-turret iron-clads, of 1800 tons each, fitted with rams and with powerful engines, and carrying $5\frac{1}{2}$ inches of armor and a battery of four 9-inch rifles. They were probably superior to any vessels at that time in the possession of the United States. The main object for which they were intended was the recovery of the Mississippi. In the spring of 1863 Bulloch began to feel apprehensive that measures might be taken to stop the building of the rams. He accordingly arranged with a mercantile firm in Paris, Messrs. Bravay & Co., that they should become the purchasers of the vessels, ostensibly for the Viceroy of Egypt, and that they should subsequently sell them to him. This plan was carried out with every formality, and the rams became the property of the firm of Bravay.

Early in June the first of the rams was launched. Mr. Adams had for some time been observing their progress, and on the 11th of that month he wrote an urgent letter to Earl Russell, detailing the circumstances, and inclosing four affidavits, which gave conclusive evidence of the character and destination of the rams. More forcible protests, accompanied by further affidavits, were made on the 16th, and again on the 24th of July, on the 14th of August, and on the 3d and 4th of September.

All these letters met with no response from the Foreign Office other than simple acknowledgment.

COMMANDER JOHN M. BROOKE, C. S. N.
FROM A PHOTOGRAPH.

On the 29th of August the second ram was launched. It had been Mr. Adams's belief at the beginning that in so clear a case it would only be necessary to recite the facts to induce the Government to take action. As the days and weeks passed by and no answer came, his appeals grew more and more earnest and forcible, until in the later letters they had reached a tone of solemn warning.

At last a reply came, which had been written on the 1st of September, and therefore before the receipt of the last two communications. It repeated the usual formula of the Foreign Office that the evidence was insufficient for legal proceedings, and quoted the belief of the collector at Liverpool that the vessels were not intended for the Confederates. It was in reply to this letter that Mr. Adams sent the dispatch containing his famous ultimatum: "It would be superfluous in me to point out to your lordship that this is war."

In consequence of this letter, or at least directly upon its receipt, instructions were issued by the British Government to detain the rams. Shortly afterward they were seized, a guard was placed on board, and a squadron of the royal navy was detailed to watch them. After a detention lasting several months, the vessels were finally purchased by the Admiralty for the royal navy, on whose list they appeared as the *Scorpion* and the *Wivern*. Only one attempt was made to procure ships of

war for the Confederates in France. From intimations received by Mr. Slidell, the commissioner at Paris, it was believed that the French emperor would place no obstacle in the way of Confederate operations in France. A contract was therefore made with Arman, an influential ship-builder, of Bordeaux, early in 1863, for four corvettes, and in the following July for two powerful iron-clad rams, each carrying a 300-pounder Armstrong rifle in a casemate and two 70-pounders in a turret. Before the work was far advanced, however,— that is, in September, 1863,— the United States Minister, Mr. Dayton, was informed of the whole transaction, through certain letters which came into the possession of John Bigelow, Consul-General at Paris. The letters formed a complete exposure of the business, and the Government was forced to interpose; and although during the next six months the work of construction was permitted to go on, at the end of that time the ships were ordered to be sold under penalty of seizure.

Of the four corvettes, two were bought by Prussia and two by Peru. One of the rams was sold to Prussia and the other, known as the *Sphinx*, to Denmark. Before her arrival in Copenhagen the Schleswig-Holstein war was over, and the Danes, having no use for her, were well satisfied to have her taken off their hands without inquiring too closely into the character of the purchaser. In this way Bulloch got possession of her, and on the 30th of January, 1865, she was commissioned in the English Channel as the *Stonewall*, and started on a cruise under Captain T. J. Page.

The *Stonewall* had not gone far before she sprang a leak and put into Ferrol for repairs. Here she was found by the *Niagara* and *Sacramento*, under Commodore T. T. Craven, who took up a position in the adjoining port of Coruña. On the 24th of March the *Stonewall* steamed out of Ferrol and lay for several hours off the entrance of Coruña; Craven, however, declined to join battle, under the belief that the odds against him were too great, although the *Niagara* carried ten heavy rifles, and the *Sacramento* two 11-inch guns. The *Stonewall* steamed that night to Lisbon, thence to Teneriffe and Nassau, and finally to Havana. It was now the middle of May, and the Confederacy was breaking up; Captain Page therefore made an agreement with the Captain-General of Cuba, by which the latter advanced $16,000 to pay off his officers and men and received possession of the vessel. She was subsequently turned over to the United States, and finally sold to Japan.

Another cruiser, the *Tallahassee*, was originally the English blockade-runner *Atlanta*, and made two trips from Bermuda to Wilmington in the summer of 1864. She was then fitted out and armed as a cruiser, and on the 6th of August sailed from Wilmington under Commander John T. Wood. Her cruise lasted less than three weeks, but was remarkably successful. It extended along the United States coast and so on to Halifax. The small coasters and fishing vessels were totally unprepared for an enemy, and over thirty of them were captured, nearly all being destroyed. At one time the *Tallahassee* was not far from New York, and several cruisers were sent out in pursuit of her, but without success. At Halifax the authorities were not inclined to permit repairs or supplies of coal. Wood put to sea again, and on the 26th ran the blockade into Wilmington. On the 29th of October the *Tallahassee*, now called the *Olustee*, made another short cruise along the coast as far as Sandy Hook, under Lieutenant Ward, making seven prizes, and returning again to Wilmington after a slight brush with the blockading vessels. Her battery was now removed, and, after a fictitious sale to the navy agent at Wilmington, she was renamed the *Chameleon*. She sailed with a cargo of cotton on December 24th, while the first attack on Fort Fisher was in progress. Captain John Wilkinson of the navy commanded her, and his object was to obtain supplies at Bermuda for Lee's army. She returned late in January, but was unable to enter either Wilmington or Charleston, and after landing her stores at Nassau she proceeded to Liverpool. Here she was seized by the authorities, and ultimately she was delivered to the United States.

The last of the Confederate commerce-destroyers was the *Sea King*, or *Shenandoah*. Commander John M. Brooke, the Confederate ordnance officer at Richmond, devised the plan which was afterward adopted on her cruise. Brooke's service in the North Pacific Exploring Expedition of 1855 had familiarized him with the movements of the New Bedford whaling fleet, and it was against this fleet that the proposed cruise was to be made. The whalers generally cruised in the South Pacific in winter, going in the spring to Behring Strait, where they remained during the summer season, returning in October to the Sandwich Islands. As the *Alabama* and her consorts had nearly swept American commerce from the seas, the whaling fleet was the only remaining object of naval attack.

The summer of 1864 was now nearly over, and it was evident to Bulloch that no ships specially fitted for war could safely be purchased in England. He therefore turned his attention to securing a merchant vessel which should answer the requirements of the commerce-destroying service : speed, sail-power, and sufficient strength for a battery and room for a crew. Such vessels were difficult to find, but Bulloch, by good luck, discovered one that answered his purpose,—the *Sea King*, a vessel built for the Bombay trade, which had made only one voyage; and in September she was purchased, her ostensible owner being a British subject who acted privately as Bulloch's agent. On the 8th of October the *Sea King* cleared from London for Bombay, carrying coal as ballast, and with Lieutenant Whittle of the Confederate navy on board as a passenger. On the same day the *Laurel*, a fast steamer, purchased ostensibly for a blockade-runner, sailed from Liverpool with a cargo containing six guns and their appurtenances, and nineteen passengers, who consisted of Captain James I. Waddell and eighteen other Confederate officers. The two vessels proceeded directly to Madeira. On their arrival they withdrew to the Desertas, a group of barren islands in the neighborhood, where the passengers and cargo were transferred, and the *Sea King* was put in commission as the Confederate States ship *Shenandoah*, under the command of Waddell. Contrary to his expectation, most of the seamen who had been shipped for a voyage to Bombay refused to join the *Shenandoah's* crew when her real character was known. She was therefore obliged to start with only 23 seamen instead of 120, which was her complement.

The *Shenandoah* proceeded first to Melbourne. On her way she met nine American vessels, seven of which were destroyed and the others ransomed. From the crews of the captured prizes, Waddell succeeded in obtaining twenty-four seamen who consented to enlist on board the *Shenandoah*, making her total number forty-seven.

The *Shenandoah* arrived at Melbourne on the 25th of January, 1865. Here she was admitted to a building slip on the ground that she needed repairs. She was also allowed to remain at Melbourne nearly four weeks, to put her machinery in thorough order at her leisure, and to take on board 300 tons of coal. Her crew, which had now been reduced by desertions to thirty men, was reënforced with an addition of forty-two new recruits, the authorities showing extreme slackness in preventing the enlistments, notwithstanding the urgent representations of the United States Consul. Leaving Melbourne on February 18th, the *Shenandoah* pursued her course to the northward. Three vessels were captured in April and one in May.

In the latter part of June, approaching Behring Strait, she fell in with the New Bedford whaling fleet. In the course of one week, from the 21st to the 28th, twenty-five whalers were captured, of which four were ransomed, and the remaining twenty-one were burnt.

The loss on these twenty-one whalers was estimated at upwards of $3,000,000, and considering that it occurred in June, 1865, two months after the Confederacy had virtually passed out of existence, it may be characterized as the most useless act of hostility that occurred during the whole war.

The first intimation received by Waddell of the progress of events at home was on June 22d, when the captain of one of the whalers told him that he believed the war was over; the statement was, however, unsupported by other evidence, and Waddell declined to believe it. On the 23d he received from one of his prizes San Francisco newspapers of a sufficiently late date to contain news of the fall of Richmond. The war was not yet ended, however, and subsequently to the receipt of these newspapers fifteen whalers were destroyed. On the 28th, the work of destroying the fleet having been completed, Waddell started to return home. On his way southward, on August 2d, he met the British bark *Barracouta*, from which he received positive information that the Confederacy was at an end; he thereupon dismounted his battery and shaped his course for Liverpool, where he arrived on the 5th of November, having made his voyage of 17,000 miles without speaking a vessel. The *Shenandoah* was surrendered on her arrival to the British Government, which in turn delivered her to the United States.

CRUISE AND COMBATS OF THE "ALABAMA."

BY HER EXECUTIVE OFFICER, JOHN McINTOSH KELL.

THE Confederate cruiser *Alabama* was built by the Lairds, of Birkenhead, England, for the Confederate States Government. In the House of Commons the senior partner of the constructors stated "that she left Liverpool a perfectly legitimate transaction." Captain James D. Bulloch, as agent for the Confederacy, super-intended her construction. As a "ruse" she was sent on a trial trip, with a large party of ladies and gentle-men. A tug met the ship in the channel and took off the guests, while the two hundred and ninetieth ship built in the Laird yard proceeded on her voyage to the island of Terceira, one of the Azores, whither a transport had preceded her with war material. Cap-tain Raphael Semmes, with his officers, carried by the *Bahama*, met her there. Under the lee of the island, outside the marine league, we lashed our ships together, and made the transfer of armament and stores.

Arriving on Wednesday, August 20th, 1862, by Saturday night we had completed the transfer, and on Sunday morning, under a cloudless sky, upon the broad Atlantic, a common heritage, we put the *Alabama* in commission, by authority of the Confederate States Government. Thus empowered, we proceeded to ship such men from the crews of the several ships as were willing to sign the articles. Eighty men signed, and these formed the nucleus of our crew, the full complement being soon made up from the crews of our prizes. We then commenced our cruise of twenty-two months, during which she more successfully accomplished the work for which she was constructed than had any single ship of any nation in any age.

The *Alabama* was built for speed rather than battle. Her lines were sym-metrical and fine; her material of the best. In fifteen minutes her propeller could be hoisted, and she could go through every evolution under sail with-out any impediment. In less time her propeller could be lowered; with sails furled, and yards braced within two points of a head-wind, she was a perfect steamer. Her speed, independent, was from ten to twelve knots; combined, and under favorable circumstances, she could make fifteen knots. When ready for sea she drew fifteen feet of water. She was barkentine-rigged, with long lower masts, which enabled her to carry an immense spread of lower canvas, and to lay close to the wind. Her engines were of three hundred horse-power, with a condensing apparatus that was indispensable. Since we lived principally upon provisions taken from our prizes, their water-supply was never sufficient. Our condenser enabled us to keep the sea for long periods, as we had to seek a port only for coals.

THE CONFEDERATE CRUISER "ALABAMA."

This sketch was made from a photograph (of a drawing) which Captain Semmes gave to a friend, with the remark that it was a correct picture of his ship. On the stocks, and until she went into commission, the *Alabama* was known as "No. 290," that being her number on the list of ships built by the Lairds. According to the volume, "Our Cruise in the Confederate States' War Steamer *Alabama*," she was a bark-rigged wooden propeller, of 1040 tons register; length of keel, 210 feet; length over all, 220; beam, 32; depth, 17. She carried two horizontal engines, each of 300 horse-power; she had stowage for 350 tons of coal. All her standing rigging was of wire. She had a double wheel placed just before the mizzen-mast, and on it was inscribed the motto, "*Aide toi et Dieu t'aidera.*"

The bridge was in the center, just before the funnel. She carried five boats : cutter and launch amidships, gig and whale-boat between the main and mizzen mast, and dingey astern. The main deck was pierced for twelve guns. She had an elliptic stern, billet head, and high bulwarks. Her cabin accommodations were first-class ; and her ward-room was furnished with a handsome suite of state-rooms. The starboard steerage was for midshipmen, the port for engineers. Next came the engine-room, coal-bunkers, etc. ; then the berth-deck, accommodating 120 men. Under the ward-room were store-rooms and under the steerage were shell-rooms. Just forward of the fire-room came the hold, next the magazines, and, forward of all, the boatswain's and sailmaker's store-rooms. The hold was all under the berth-deck.— EDITORS.

Our armament consisted of eight guns : one Blakely 100-pounder rifled gun, pivoted forward ; one 8-inch solid-shot gun, pivoted abaft the mainmast ; and six 32-pounders in broadside. Our crew numbered about 120 men and 24 officers. The commander, Captain Semmes, had been an officer of high standing in the old navy, had studied law, paying particular attention to the international branch, and had been admitted to the bar in Alabama, of which State he was a citizen. Thus he was eminently qualified for the position he was now called upon to assume. During the Mexican war he commanded the brig *Somers* in the blockade of Vera Cruz, and lost that unfortunate vessel in chase, during a norther, and narrowly escaped drowning. He afterward accompanied the army to the city of Mexico. The writer, his executive officer, had served twenty years in the old navy, and had accompanied every expedition of a warlike nature fitted out by the United States during that period. In the Mexican war, on the coast of California, I served ashore and afloat ; then with the gallant Commodore Perry, in his expedition to Japan, and again in the Paraguay expedition. Our second lieutenant, R. F. Armstrong, from Georgia, and third lieutenant, J. D. Wilson, from Florida, came out with us in the *Sumter*. They were just from Annapolis, having resigned on the secession of their respective States. Both the father and the grandfather of our fourth lieutenant, Arthur Sinclair, Jr., of Virginia, had been captains in the United States navy. Our fifth lieutenant, John Lowe, of Georgia, had seen some service, and was a most efficient officer ;

REAR-ADMIRAL RAPHAEL SEMMES, C. S. N., CAPTAIN OF THE "ALABAMA."   FROM A PHOTOGRAPH
TAKEN IN ENGLAND AFTER THE LOSS OF HIS SHIP.

our Acting Master, I. D. Bulloch, of Georgia, was a younger brother of
Captain James D. Bulloch. A few months' active service gave confidence
to the watch-officers of the ward-room, and it may safely be affirmed that
older heads could not have filled their places with greater efficiency. The
remainder of our ward-room mess was made up of our surgeon, Dr. F. L.
Galt, of Virginia, also of the old service; Dr. D. H. Llewellyn, of Wilt-
shire, England, who, as surgeon, came out in the ship when under English
colors, and joined us as assistant surgeon. First Lieutenant B. K. Howell, of
the Marine Corps, brother-in-law of President Davis, was from Mississippi,

and Mr. Miles J. Freeman, our chief engineer, had been with us in the *Sumter*. The steerage mess was made up of three midshipmen—E. M. Anderson, of Georgia; E. A. Maffitt, of North Carolina, son of the captain of the Confederate States steamer *Florida;* and George T. Sinclair, of Virginia. The latter was afterward detached from the *Alabama* and made executive officer to Lieutenant Lowe on the *Tuscaloosa,* a tender that we captured and commissioned. Upon our arrival at Cherbourg, Sinclair came at once to join his old ship, having heard of the contemplated engagement. Accompanying him came also Lieutenant William C. Whittle, Jr., of Virginia, a gallant young son of Commodore W. C. Whittle of the old navy, and Lieutenant John Grimball, a South Carolinian, offering their services for any position during the engagement. They were not permitted to join us, on the ground that it would be a violation of French neutrality. The remainder of the steerage mess was made up of young master's mates and engineers, most of whom had come out with us in the *Sumter*. |

The eleventh day after going into commission we captured our first prize, not one hundred miles from where we hoisted our flag. After working round the Azores for some weeks, with fine breezes, we shaped our course for Sandy Hook; but we encountered frequent gales off the Newfoundland banks, and on the 16th of October lost our main-yard in a cyclone. Being considerably shaken up, we decided to seek a milder latitude. Running down to the Windward Islands, we entered the Caribbean Sea. Our prizes gave us regularly the mails from the United States, from which we learned of the fitting out of the army under General Banks for the attack on Galveston and the invasion of Texas, and the day on which the fleet would sail; whereupon Captain Semmes calculated about the time they would arrive, and shaped his course accordingly, coaling and refitting ship at the Arcas Keys. He informed me of his plan of attack, which was to sight the shipping off Galveston about the time that General Banks was due with his large fleet of transports, under the convoy perhaps of a few vessels of war. The entire fleet would anchor in the outer roadstead, as there is only sufficient water on the bar for light-draughts. All attention at such a time would be given to the disembarkation of the army, as there were no enemy's cruisers to molest them, our presence in the Gulf not being known. We were to take the bearing of the fleet, and, after the mid-watch was set and all was quiet, silently approach, steam among them with both batteries in action, slowly steam through the midst of them, pouring in a continuous discharge

| Of the crew of the *Alabama* I cannot say too much. It was made up from all the seafaring nations of the globe, with a large sprinkling of Yankee tars (among whom are to be found the best sailors), and with a nucleus of Southern pilots and seamen from the ports of Savannah, Charleston, and New Orleans. The pilots were given the positions of petty officers, and sustained their reputation nobly, materially aiding in the discipline of the crew, for upon our peculiar service, and with our ports locked against us, we were compelled to observe the strictest discipline, both with officers and crew. As the executive officer who enforced this discipline I may say that a nobler set of young men filling the position of officers, and a braver and more willing crew, never floated. As an evidence of their attachment to the captain and the service, I will state that after the sinking of the *Alabama*, upon our visit to Liverpool, where the crew were paid off, a large deputation of them called upon Captain Semmes, and pleaded with him to get command of another ship the equal of the *Kearsarge*, promising that they would join him to a man.—J. McI. K.

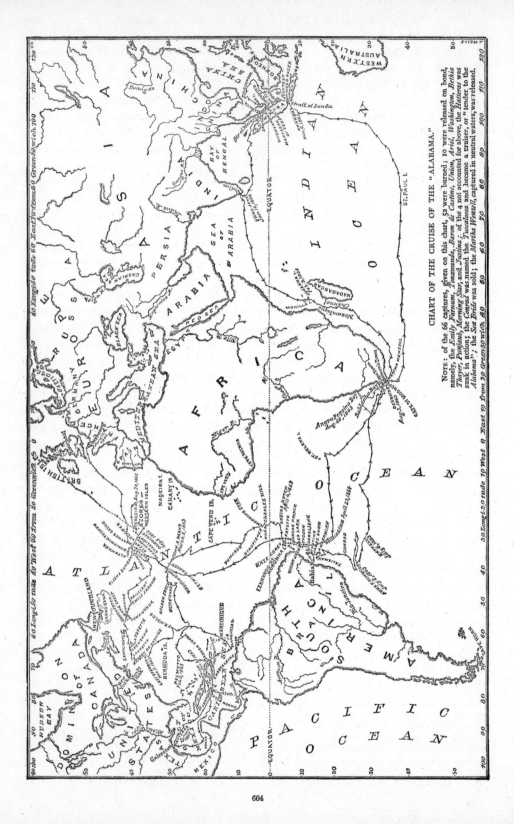

CHART OF THE CRUISE OF THE "ALABAMA."

NOTE: of the 66 captures, given on this chart, 10 were released on bond, namely, the *Emily Farnum*, *Tonawanda*, *Baron de Castine*, *Union*, *Ariel*, *Washington*, *Bethia Thayer*, *Punjaub*, *Morning Star*, and *Justina*; of the 4 not accounted for above, the *Hatteras* was sunk in action; the *Conrad* was named the *Tuscaloosa* and became a cruiser, or "tender to the *Alabama*"; the *Sea Bride* was sold; the *Martha Wenzell*, captured in neutral waters, was released.

of shell to fire and sink them as we went; thus we expected to accomplish our work and be off on another cruise before the convoys could move.

But instead of sighting General Banks's fleet of transports we sighted five vessels of war at anchor, and soon after our lookout reported a steamer standing out for us. We were then under topsails only, with a light breeze, heading off shore, and gradually drawing our pursuer from the squadron. It was the *Hatteras*, and about dark she came up with us, and in an action of thirteen minutes we sank her. The action closed about twilight, when Captain Semmes, who always took his position on the weather horse-block, above the rail of the ship, to enable him to see all the surroundings, and to note the effect of our shot in action, or at exercise at general quarters, called to me and said, "Mr. Kell, the enemy have fired a gun to leeward; cease firing." We were then about seventy-five yards from the enemy, and could hear distinctly their hail, saying they "were fast sinking and on fire in three places, and for God's sake to save them." We immediately sent boats, and in the darkness took every living soul from her. These events occurred in the presence of the enemy's fleet, bearing the pennant of Commodore Bell within signal-distance.⚓ The *Hatteras* went down in a few minutes. She carried a larger crew than our own. Knowing that the Federal squadron would soon be upon us, every light on board ship was put under cover and we shaped our course for broader waters. During the night a fearful norther came sweeping after us, but under the circumstances it was a welcome gale. Hoisting our propeller, we crowded all the sail we could bear, and soon were out of harm's way. As Captain Blake of the *Hatteras* (whom I had known in the old service) came on deck, he remarked upon the speed we were making, and gracefully saluted me with, "Fortune favors the brave, sir!" I wished him a pleasant voyage with us; and I am sure he, with his officers and men, received every attention while on board the *Alabama*.⚓

We paroled the officers and crew of the *Hatteras* at Kingston, Jamaica, and after repairing a few shot-holes and coaling ship, we passed on to our work in the South Atlantic, taking our position at the cross-roads of the homeward-bound East India and Pacific trade. After a few weeks of good work in that locality and along the coast of Brazil, we crossed over to the Cape of Good Hope, where we played "hide and seek" with the United States steamer *Vanderbilt*, whose commander, Charles H. Baldwin, had explained to Sir Baldwin Walker, the English Admiral of the station at Simon's Town, "that he did not intend to fire a gun at the *Alabama*, but to run her down and sink her." We were not disposed to try issues with the *Vanderbilt;* so one night about 11 o'clock, while it blew a gale of wind from the south-east, we hove anchor and steamed out of Simon's Bay. By morning we had made a good offing, and, setting what sail we could carry, hoisted our propeller and made a due south course. We ran down to the fortieth degree

⚓ The *Hatteras*, when destroyed, was 16 to 20 miles from the fleet. She had been a river excursion boat, and was no match for her adversary. Her heaviest rifle was a 30-pounder, and her heaviest smooth-bore was a 32-pounder.— EDITORS.

⚓ As the reader will see, this was quite in contrast with the treatment received by us from the *Kearsarge* upon the sinking of the *Alabama*.— J. McI. K.

See also pages 620 and 621.— EDITORS.

CAPTAIN JOHN McINTOSH KELL, EXECUTIVE OFFICER OF THE "ALABAMA."
FROM A PHOTOGRAPH TAKEN IN SOUTHAMPTON IMMEDIATELY AFTER THE FIGHT.

south latitude, where we fell in with westerly gales and bowled along nearly due east, until we shaped our course for the Straits of Java. Our long stretch across the Indian Ocean placed us in the China Sea, where we were least expected, and where we soon fell in with the China trade. In a few weeks we had so paralyzed the enemy's commerce that their ships were absolutely locked up in port, and neutrals were doing all the carrying trade. Having thus virtually cleared the sea of the United States flag, we ran down to Singapore, coaled ship, and then turned westward through the Straits of Malacca, across to India, thence to the east coast of Africa. Passing through the Mozambique Channel, we again touched at the Cape of Good Hope, and thence crossed to the coast of Brazil. ♭

♭ The prisoners on board the *Alabama* as a general practice were *not* put in irons, but were simply confined to an allotted space with a guard over them. The prisoners of the first half-dozen prizes were put in irons, including the captains and mates, at which the captains were very indignant. Captain Semmes replied that he confined them in irons in retaliation for the manner in which the agents of the United States Government had treated the purser of the Confederate States steamer *Sumter.* The purser, under orders, was *en route* from Gibraltar to Cadiz in a French merchant steamer. Walk-

Our little ship was now showing signs of the active work she had been doing. Her boilers were burned out, and her machinery was sadly in want of repairs. She was loose at every joint, her seams were open, and the copper on her bottom was in rolls. We therefore set our course for Europe, and on the 11th of June, 1864, entered the port of Cherbourg, and applied for permission to go into dock. There being none but national docks, the Emperor had first to be communicated with before permission could be granted, and he was absent from Paris. It was during this interval of waiting, on the third day after our arrival, that the *Kearsarge* steamed into the harbor, for the purpose, as we learned, of taking on board the prisoners we had landed from our last two prizes. Captain Semmes, however, objected to this on the ground that the *Kearsarge* was adding to her crew in a neutral port. The authorities conceding this objection valid, the *Kearsarge* steamed out of the harbor, without anchoring. During her stay we examined her closely with our glasses, but she was keeping on the opposite side of the harbor, out of the reach of a very close scrutiny, which accounts for our not detecting the boxing to her chain armor. After she left the harbor Captain Semmes sent for me to his cabin, and said: "I am going out to fight the *Kearsarge;* what do you think of it?" We discussed the battery, and especially the advantage the *Kearsarge* had over us in her 11-inch guns. She was built for a vessel of war, and we for speed, and though she carried one gun less, her battery was more effective at point-blank range. While the *Alabama* carried one more gun, the *Kearsarge* threw more metal at a broadside; and while our heavy guns were more effective at long range, her 11-inch guns gave her greatly the advantage at close range. She also had a slight advantage in her crew, she carrying 163, all told, while we carried 149. Considering well these advantages, Captain Semmes communicated through our agent to the United States consul that if Captain Winslow would wait outside the harbor he would fight him as soon as we could coal ship.

Accordingly, on Sunday morning, June 19th, between 9 and 10 o'clock, we weighed anchor and stood out of the western entrance of the harbor, the French iron-clad frigate *Couronne* following us. The day was bright and beautiful, with a light breeze blowing. Our men were neatly dressed, and our officers in full uniform. The report of our going out to fight the *Kearsarge* had been circulated, and many persons from Paris and the surrounding country had come down to witness the engagement. With a large number of the inhabitants of Cherbourg they collected on every prominent point on the shore that would afford a view seaward. As we rounded the breakwater we discovered the *Kearsarge* about seven miles to the northward and eastward. We immediately shaped our course for her, called all hands to quarters, and cast loose the starboard battery. Upon reporting to the captain that the ship was ready for action, he directed me to send all hands aft,

ing ashore at Tangier, in a neutral country, he was seized by the United States consul at the head of an armed force, and brutally imprisoned, with heavy manacles, and finally sent to New York in irons. The purser was a gentleman of unimpeach-able character and high position. Again, there were occasions during the cruise when the number of prisoners warranted placing some in irons, but never were captains put in irons after that first measure of retaliation.—J. McI. K.

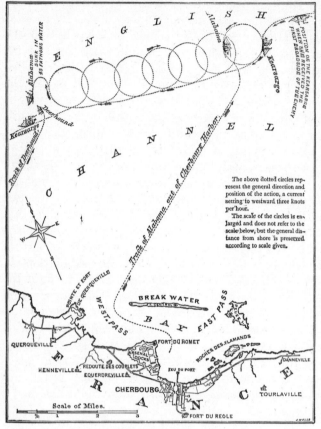

The above dotted circles represent the general direction and position of the action, a current setting to westward three knots per hour.

The scale of the circles is enlarged and does not refer to the scale below, but the general distance from shore is preserved according to scale given.

CHART OF THE ACTION OFF CHERBOURG.

and mounting a gun-carriage, he made the following address:

"OFFICERS AND SEAMEN OF THE 'ALABAMA': You have at length another opportunity of meeting the enemy—the first that has been presented to you since you sank the *Hatteras!* In the meantime you have been all over the world, and it is not too much to say that you have destroyed, and driven for protection under neutral flags, one-half of the enemy's commerce, which at the beginning of the war covered every sea. This is an achievement of which you may well be proud, and a grateful country will not be unmindful of it. The name of your ship has become a household word wherever civilization extends! Shall that name be tarnished by defeat? The thing is impossible! Remember that you are in the English Channel, the theater of so much of the naval glory of our race, and that the eyes of all Europe are at this moment upon you. The flag that floats over you is that of a young Republic, which bids defiance to her enemy's whenever and wherever found! Show the world that you know how to uphold it! Go to your quarters."

In about forty-five minutes we were somewhat over a mile from the *Kearsarge*, when she headed for us, presenting her starboard bow. At a distance of a mile we commenced the action with our 100-pounder pivot-gun from our starboard bow. Both ships were now approaching each other at high speed, and soon the action became general with broadside batteries at a distance of about five hundred yards. To prevent passing, each ship used a strong port helm. Thus the action was fought around a common center, gradually drawing in the circle. At this range we used shell upon the enemy. Captain Semmes, standing on the horse-block abreast the mizzen-mast with his glass in hand, observed the effect of our shell. He called to me and said: "Mr. Kell, use solid shot; our shell strike the enemy's side and fall into the water." We were not at this time aware of the chain armor of the enemy, and attributed the failure of our shell to our defective ammunition. ↿ After using solid shot

↿ On the coast of Brazil we had had some target practice at one of our prizes. Many of our fuses proved defective. Upon visiting the target I found that one of the 100-pound shells had exploded on the quarter-deck, and I counted fifteen marks from its missiles, which justifies me in asserting that

"KEARSARGE."   FIGHTING IN A CIRCLE.   "ALABAMA."

for some time, we alternated shell and shot. The enemy's 11-inch shells were now doing severe execution upon our quarter-deck section. Three of them successively entered our 8-inch pivot-gun port: the first swept off the forward part of the gun's crew; the second killed one man and wounded several others; and the third struck the breast of the gun-carriage, and spun around on the deck till one of the men picked it up and threw it overboard. Our decks were now covered with the dead and the wounded, and the ship was careening heavily to starboard from the effects of the shot-holes on her water-line.

Captain Semmes ordered me to be ready to make all sail possible when the circuit of fight should put our head to the coast of France; then he would notify me at the same time to pivot to port and continue the action with the port battery, hoping thus to right the ship and enable us to reach the coast of France. The evolution was performed beautifully, righting the helm, hoisting the head-sails, hauling aft the fore try-sail sheet, and pivoting to port, the action continuing almost without cessation.

This evolution exposed us to a raking fire, but, strange to say, the *Kearsarge* did not take advantage of it. The port side of the quarter-deck was so encumbered with the mangled trunks of the dead that I had to have them thrown overboard, in order to fight the after pivot-gun. I abandoned the after 32-pounder, and transferred the men to fill up the vacancies at the

had the 100-pound shell which we placed in the stern-post of the *Kearsarge* exploded, it would have changed the result of the fight. I at once examined every fuse and cap, discarding the apparently defective, and at the same time made a thorough overhauling of the magazine, as I thought; but the action with the *Kearsarge* proved that our entire supply of powder was damaged. The report from the *Kearsarge's* battery was clear and sharp, the powder burning like thin vapor, while our guns gave out a dull report, with thick and heavy vapor.— J. McI. K.

pivot-gun under the charge of young Midshipman Anderson, who in the midst of the carnage filled his place like a veteran. At this moment the chief engineer came on deck and reported the fires put out, and that he could no longer work the engines. Captain Semmes said to me, "Go below, sir, and see how long the ship can float." As I entered the ward-room the sight was indeed appalling. There stood Assistant-Surgeon Llewellyn at his post, but the table and the patient upon it had been swept away from him by an 11-inch shell, which opened in the side of the ship an aperture that was fast filling the ship with water.

It took me but a moment to return to the deck and report to the captain that we could not float ten minutes. He replied to me, "Then, sir, cease firing, shorten sail, and haul down the colors; it will never do in this nine-teenth century for us to go down, and the decks covered with our gallant wounded." The order was promptly executed, after which the *Kearsarge* deliberately fired into us five shot. ☆ I ordered the men to stand to their quarters and not flinch from the shot of the enemy; they stood every man to his post most heroically. With the first shot fired upon us after our colors were down, the quartermaster was ordered to show a white flag over the stern, which order was executed in my presence. When the firing ceased Captain Semmes ordered me to dispatch an officer to the *Kearsarge* to say that our ship was sinking, and to ask that they send boats to save our wounded, as our boats were disabled. The dingey, our smallest boat, had escaped damage. I dispatched Master's-mate Fullam with the request. No boats appearing, I had one of our quarter-boats lowered, which was slightly injured, and I ordered the wounded placed in her. Dr. Galt, the surgeon who was in charge of the magazine and shell-room division, came on deck at this moment and was at once put in charge of the boat, with orders to "take

☆ In Captain Winslow's letter (dated Cherbourg, June 21st, 1864) to the Secretary of the Navy, he says: "Toward the close of the action between the *Alabama* and this vessel, all available sail was made on the former for the purpose of again reaching Cherbourg. When the object was apparent the *Kearsarge* was steered across the bow of the *Alabama* for a raking fire; but before reaching this point the *Alabama* struck. Uncertain whether Captain Semmes was using some *ruse*, the *Kearsarge* was stopped"—and, I may add, continued his fire, for by his own words he thought Captain Semmes was making some ruse. The report that the *Alabama* fired her guns after the colors were down and she had shortened sail is not correct. There was a cessation in the firing of our guns when we shifted our battery to port, after which we renewed the action.

Almost immediately afterward the engineer reported the fires put out, when we ceased firing, hauled down the colors, and shortened sail. There was *no* gun fired from the *Alabama* after that. Captain Winslow may have thought we had surren-dered when we ceased firing and were in the act of shifting the battery; but the idle report that junior officers had taken upon themselves to con-tinue the action after the order had been given to cease firing is not worthy of notice. I did not hear the firing of a gun, and the discipline of the *Alabama* would not have permitted it.—J. McI. K.

In the letter from which Captain Kell quotes Captain Winslow does not speak of "continuing his fire." But in his detailed report (dated July 30th, 1864) Captain Winslow says of the *Alabama*, after she had winded and set sail: "Her port broadside was presented to us, with only two guns bearing, not having been able, as I learned after-ward, to shift over but one. I saw now that she was at our mercy, and a few more guns well directed brought down her flag. I was unable to ascertain whether it had been hauled down or shot away; but a white flag having been displayed over the stern our fire was reserved. Two minutes had not more than elapsed before she again opened on us with the two guns on the port side. This drew our fire again, and the *Kearsarge* was immediately steamed ahead and laid across her bows for rak-ing. The white flag was still flying, and our fire was again reserved. Shortly after this her boats were seen to be lowering, and an officer in one of them came alongside and informed us the ship had surrendered and was fast sinking."—EDITORS.

the wounded to the *Kearsarge*." They shoved off just in time to save the poor fellows from going down in the ship.

I now gave the order for every man to jump overboard with a spar and save himself from the sinking ship. To enforce the order, I walked forward and urged the men overboard. As soon as the decks were cleared, save of the bodies of the dead, I returned to the stern-port, where stood Captain Semmes with one or two of the men and his faithful steward, who, poor fellow! was doomed to a watery grave, as he could not swim. The *Alabama's* stern-port was now almost at the water's edge. Partly undressing, we plunged into the sea, and made an offing from the sinking ship, Captain Semmes with a life-preserver and I on a grating.

The *Alabama* settled stern foremost, launching her bows high in the air. Graceful even in her death-struggle, she in a moment disappeared from the face of the waters. The sea now presented a mass of living heads, striving for their lives. Many poor fellows sank for the want of timely aid. Near me I saw a float of empty shell-boxes, and called to one of the men, a good swimmer, to examine it; he did so and replied, "It is the doctor, sir, dead." Poor Llewellyn! he perished almost in sight of his home. The young midshipman, Maffitt, swam to me and offered his life-preserver. My grating was not proving a very buoyant float, and the white-caps breaking over my head were distressingly uncomfortable, to say the least. Maffitt said: "Mr. Kell, take my life-preserver, sir; you are almost exhausted." The gallant boy did not consider his own condition,

ASSISTANT-SURGEON DAVID HERBERT LLEWELLYN. FROM A PORTRAIT IN THE "ILLUSTRATED LONDON NEWS."

but his pallid face told me that his heroism was superior to his bodily suffering, and I refused it. After twenty minutes or more I heard near me some one call out, "There is our first lieutenant," and the next moment I was pulled into a boat, in which was Captain Semmes, stretched out in the stern-sheets, as pallid as death. He had received during the action a slight contusion on the hand, and the struggle in the water had almost exhausted him. There were also several of our crew in the boat, and in a few moments we were alongside a little steam-yacht, which had come among our floating men, and by throwing them ropes had saved many lives. Upon reaching her deck, I ascertained for the first time that she was the yacht *Deerhound*, owned by Mr. John Lancaster, of England. In looking about I saw two French pilot-boats engaged in saving our crew, and finally two boats from the *Kearsarge*. To my surprise I found on the yacht Mr. Fullam, whom I had dispatched in the dingey to ask that boats be sent to save our wounded. He reported to me that our shot had literally torn

RETURNING FOR THE WOUNDED.

the casing from the chain armor of the *Kearsarge*, indenting the chain in many places, which explained Captain Semmes's observation of the effect of our shell upon the enemy, "that they struck the sides and fell into the water."

Captain Winslow, in his report, states that his ship was struck twenty-five or thirty times, and I doubt if the *Alabama* was struck a greater number of times. I may not, therefore, be bold in asserting that had not the *Kearsarge* been protected by her iron cables, the result of the fight would have been different. Captain Semmes felt the more keenly the delusion to which he fell a victim (not knowing that the *Kearsarge* was chain-clad) from the fact that he was exceeding his instructions in seeking an action with the enemy; but to seek a fight with an iron-clad he conceived to be an unpardonable error. However, he had the satisfaction of knowing she was classed as a wooden gun-boat by the Federal Government; also that he had inspected her with most excellent glasses, and so far as outward appearances showed she displayed no chain armor. At the same time it must be admitted that Captain Winslow had the right unquestionably to protect his ship and crew. In justice to Captain Semmes I will state that the battle would never have been fought had he known that the *Kearsarge* wore an armor of chain beneath her outer covering. Thus was the *Alabama* lost by an error, if you please, but, it must be admitted, a *most pardonable* one, and not until "Father Neptune" claimed her as his own did she lower her colors.

The 11-inch shells of the *Kearsarge* did fearful work, and her guns were served beautifully, being aimed with precision, and deliberate in fire. She came into action magnificently. Having the speed of us, she took her own position and fought gallantly. But she tarnished her glory when she fired upon a fallen foe. It was high noon of a bright, beautiful day, with a moderate breeze blowing to waft the smoke of battle clear, and nothing to obstruct the view at five hundred yards. The very fact of the *Alabama* ceasing to fire, shortening sail, and hauling down her colors simultaneously, must have attracted the attention of the officer in command of the *Kearsarge*. Again, there is no reason given why the *Kearsarge* did not steam immediately into the midst of the crew of the *Alabama*, after their ship had been sunk, and, like a brave and generous foe, save the lives of her enemies, who had fought

Surgeon Browne points out [p. 624], that the advantage derived from the chain armor was immaterial. It was a device that Captain Semmes also might have employed.— EDITORS.

nobly as long as they had a plank to stand upon. Were it not for the timely presence of the kind-hearted Englishman and the two French pilot-boats, who can tell the number of us that would have rested with our gallant little ship beneath the waters of the English Channel? I quote the following from Mr. John Lancaster's letter to the London "Daily News": "I presume it was because he [Captain Winslow] *would* not or could not save them himself. The fact is that if the captain and crew of the *Alabama* had depended for safety altogether upon Captain Winslow, not one-half of them would have been saved." ⚓

When Mr. Lancaster approached Captain Semmes, and said, "I think every man has been picked up; where shall I land you?" Captain Semmes replied, "I am now under the English colors, and the sooner you put me with my officers and men on English soil, the better." The little yacht moved rapidly

⚓ In his report of June 21st, 1864, Captain Winslow said:

"It was seen shortly afterward that the *Alabama* was lowering her boats, and an officer came alongside in one of them to say that they had surrendered and were fast sinking, and begging that boats would be dispatched immediately for the saving of life. The two boats not disabled were at once lowered, and as it was apparent the *Alabama* was settling, this officer was permitted to leave in his boat to afford assistance. An English yacht, the *Deerhound*, had approached near the *Kearsarge* at this time, when I hailed and begged the commander to run down to the *Alabama*, as she was fast sinking and we had but two boats, and assist in picking up the men. He answered affirmatively, and steamed toward the *Alabama*, but the latter sank almost immediately."

The following is an extract from Mr. John Lancaster's log, dated "Steam-yacht *Deerhound*, off Cowes":

"Sunday, June 19th, 9 A. M. Got up steam, and pro-

ceeded out of Cherbourg harbor. Half-past ten, observed the *Alabama* steaming out of the harbor toward the Federal steamer *Kearsarge*. Ten minutes past eleven, the *Alabama* commenced firing with her starboard battery, the distance between the contending vessels being about one mile. The *Kearsarge* immediately replied with her starboard guns. A very sharp, spirited fire was kept up, shot sometimes being varied by shells. In manœuvring, both vessels made seven complete circles at a distance of from a quarter to half a mile. At 12 a slight intermission was observed in the *Alabama's* firing, the *Alabama* making head-sail, and shaping her course for the land, distant about nine miles. At 12:30, observed the *Alabama* to be disabled and in a sinking state. We immediately made toward her, and in passing the *Kearsarge* were requested to assist in saving the *Alabama's* crew. At 12:50, when within a distance of two hundred yards, the *Alabama* sunk. We then lowered our two boats, and with the assistance of the *Alabama's* whale-boat and dingey, succeeded in saving about forty men, including Captain Semmes and thirteen officers. At 1 P. M. we started for Southampton."   EDITORS.

THE SINKING OF THE "ALABAMA."

away at once, under a press of steam, for Southampton. Armstrong, our second lieutenant, and some of our men who were saved by the French pilot-boats, were taken into Cherbourg. Our loss was 9 killed, 21 wounded, and 10 drowned.

It has been charged that an arrangement had been entered into between Mr. Lancaster and Captain Semmes, previous to our leaving Cherbourg, that in the event of the *Alabama* being sunk the *Deerhound* would come to our rescue. Captain Semmes and myself met Mr. Lancaster for the first time when rescued by him, and he related to us the circumstance that was the occasion of his coming out to see the fight. Having his family on board, his intention was to attend church with his wife and children, when the gathering of the spectators on the shore attracted their attention, the report having been widely circulated that the *Alabama* was to go out that morning and give battle to the *Kearsarge*. The boys were clamorous to see the fight, and after a family discussion as to the propriety of going out on the Sabbath to witness a naval combat, Mr. Lancaster agreed to put the question to vote at the break-fast-table, where the youngsters carried their point by a majority. Thus many of us were indebted for our lives to that inherent trait in the English character, the desire to witness a " passage at arms."

That evening we landed in Southampton, and were received by the people with every demonstration of sympathy and kindly feeling. Thrown upon their shores by the chances of war, we were taken to their hearts and homes with that generous hospitality which brought to mind with tenderest feeling our own dear Southern homes in *ante-bellum* times. To the Rev. F. W. Tremlett, of Belsize Park, London, and his household, I am indebted for a picture of English home life that time cannot efface, and the memory of which will be a lasting pleasure till life's end.

THE UNITED STATES SCREW-SLOOP "KEARSARGE" AT THE TIME OF THE ENCOUNTER WITH THE "ALABAMA."

When the *Kearsarge* was at the Azores, a few months before the fight with the *Alabama*, Midshipman Edward
E. Preble made a mathematically correct drawing of the ship, and from a photograph of that
drawing the above picture was made. After the fight alterations were made in
the *Kearsarge* which considerably changed her appearance.— EDITORS.

THE DUEL BETWEEN THE "ALABAMA" AND THE "KEARSARGE."

BY JOHN M. BROWNE, SURGEON OF THE "KEARSARGE."

ON Sunday, the 12th of June, 1864, the *Kearsarge*, Captain John A. Winslow, was lying at anchor in the Scheldt, off Flushing, Holland. The cornet suddenly appeared at the fore, and a gun was fired. These were unexpected signals that compelled absent officers and men to return to the ship. Steam was raised, and as soon as we were off, and all hands called, Captain Winslow gave the welcome news of a telegram from Mr. Dayton, our minister to France, announcing that the *Alabama* had arrived the day previous at Cherbourg; hence the urgency of departure, the probability of an encounter, and the expectation of her capture or destruction. The crew responded with cheers. The succeeding day witnessed the arrival of the *Kearsarge* at Dover for dispatches, and the day after (Tuesday) her appearance off Cherbourg, where we saw the Confederate flag flying within the breakwater. As we approached, officers and men gathered in groups on deck, and looked intently at the "daring rover" that had been able for two years to escape numerous foes and to inflict immense damage on our commerce. She was a beautiful specimen of naval architecture. The surgeon went on shore and obtained *pratique* (permission to visit the port) for boats. Owing to the neutrality limitation, which would not allow us to remain in the harbor longer than twenty-four hours, it was inexpedient to enter the port. We placed a vigilant watch by turns at each of the harbor entrances, and continued it to the moment of the engagement.

On Wednesday Captain Winslow paid an official visit to the French admiral commanding the maritime district, and to the United States commercial agent, bringing on his return the unanticipated news that Captain Semmes had declared his intention to fight. At first the assertion was barely credited, the policy of the *Alabama* being regarded as opposed to a conflict, and to escape rather than to be exposed to injury, perhaps destruction; but the doubters were half convinced when the so-called challenge was known to read as follows:

"C. S. S. 'ALABAMA,' CHERBOURG, June 14th, 1864.

"To A. BONFILS, Esq., CHERBOURG. SIR: I hear that you were informed by the U. S. Consul that the *Kearsarge* was to come to this port solely for the prisoners landed by me, and that she was to depart in twenty-four hours. I desire you to say to the U. S. Consul that my intention is to fight the *Kearsarge* as soon as I can make the necessary arrangements. I hope these will not detain me more than until to-morrow evening, or after the morrow morning at furthest. I beg she will not depart before I am ready to go out.

"I have the honor to be, very respectfully,

"Your obedient servant,

"R. SEMMES, Captain.

This communication was sent by Mr. Bonfils, the Confederate States Commercial Agent, to Mr. Liais, the United States Commercial Agent, with a request that the latter would furnish a copy to Captain Winslow for his guidance. There was no other challenge to combat. The letter that passed between the commercial agents *was* the challenge about which so much has been said. Captain Semmes informed Captain Winslow through Mr. Bonfils of his intention to fight; Captain Winslow informed Captain Semmes through Mr. Liais that he came to Cherbourg to fight, and had no intention of leaving. He made no other reply.

Captain Winslow assembled the officers and discussed the expected battle. It was probable the two ships would engage on parallel lines, and the *Alabama* would seek neutral waters in event of defeat; hence the necessity of beginning the action several miles from the breakwater. It was determined not to surrender, but to fight until the last, and, if need be, to go down with colors flying. Why Captain Semmes should imperil his ship was not understood, since he would risk all and expose the cause of which he was a selected champion to a needless disaster, while the *Kearsarge*, if taken or destroyed, could be replaced. It was therefore concluded that he would fight because he thought he would be the victor.

Preparations were made for battle, with no relaxation of the watch. Thursday passed; Friday came; the *Kearsarge* waited with ports down, guns pivoted to starboard, the whole battery loaded, and shell, grape, and canister ready to use in any mode of attack or defense; yet no *Alabama* appeared. French pilots came on board and told of unusual arrangements made by the enemy, such as the hurried taking of coals, the transmission of valuable articles to the shore, such as captured chronometers, specie, and the bills of ransomed vessels; and the sharpening of swords, cutlasses, and boarding-pikes. It was reported that Captain Semmes had been advised not to give battle; that he replied. he would prove to the world that his ship was not a privateer, intended only for attack upon merchant vessels, but a true man-of-war; further, that he had consulted French officers, who all asserted that in his situation they would fight. Certain newspapers declared that he ought to improve the opportunity afforded by the presence of the enemy to show that his ship was not a "corsair," to prey upon defenseless merchantmen, but a real ship-of-war, able and willing to fight the "Federal" waiting outside the harbor. It was said the *Alabama* was swift, with a superior crew, and it was known that the ship, guns, and ammunition were of English make.

A surprise by night was suggested, and precautionary means were taken; everything was well planned and ready for action, but still no *Alabama* came. Meanwhile the *Kearsarge* was cruising to and fro off the breakwater. A message was brought from Mr. Dayton, our minister to Paris, by his son, who with difficulty had obtained permission from the French admiral to visit the *Kearsarge*. Communication with either ship was prohibited, but the permission was given upon the promise of Mr. Dayton to return on shore directly after the delivery of the message. Mr. Dayton expressed the opinion that Captain Semmes would not fight, though acknowledging the prevalence of a contrary belief in Cherbourg. He was told that, in the event of battle, if we were successful the colors would be displayed at the mizzen as the flag of victory. He went on shore with the intention of leaving for Paris without delay. In taking leave

THE CREW OF THE "KEARSARGE" AT QUARTERS.
FROM A PHOTOGRAPH.

of the French admiral the latter advised Mr. Dayton to remain over night, and mentioned the fixed purpose of Captain Semmes to fight on the following day, Sunday ; and he gave the intelligence that there could be no further communication with the *Kearsarge*. Mr. Dayton passed a part of Saturday night trying to procure a boat to send off the acquired information, but the vigilance along the coast made his efforts useless. He remained, witnessed the battle, telegraphed the result to Paris, and was one of the first to go on board and offer congratulations.

At a supper in Cherbourg on Saturday night, several officers of the *Alabama* met sympathizing friends, the coming battle being the chief topic of conversation. Confident of victory, they proclaimed the intent to sink the "Federal" or gain a "corsair." They rose with promises to meet the following night to repeat the festivity as victors, were escorted to the boat, and departed with cheers and best wishes for a successful return. ⸗

Sunday, the 19th, came ; a fine day, atmosphere somewhat hazy, little sea, light westerly wind. At 10 o'clock the *Kearsarge* was near the buoy marking the line of shoals to the eastward of Cherbourg, at a distance of about three miles from the entrance. The decks had been holystoned, the bright work cleaned, the guns polished, and the crew were dressed in Sunday suits. They were in-

spected at quarters and dismissed to attend divine service. Seemingly no one thought of the enemy ; so long awaited and not appearing, speculation as to her coming had nearly ceased. At 10:20 the officer of the deck reported a steamer approaching from Cherbourg,— a frequent occurrence, and consequently it created no surprise. The bell was tolling for service when some one shouted, "She's coming, and heading straight for us!" Soon, by the aid of a glass, the officer of the deck made out the enemy and shouted, "The *Alabama!*" and calling down the ward-room hatch repeated the cry, "The *Alabama!*" The drum beat to general quarters ; Captain Winslow put aside the prayer-book, seized the trumpet, ordered the ship about, and headed seaward. The ship was cleared for action, with the battery pivoted to starboard.

The *Alabama* approached from the western entrance, escorted by the French iron-clad frigate *Couronne*, flying the pennant of the commandant of the port, followed in her wake by a small fore-and-aft-rigged steamer, the *Deerhound*, flying the flag of the Royal Mersey Yacht Club. The commander of the frigate had informed Captain Semmes that his ship would escort him to the limit of the French waters. The frigate, having convoyed the *Alabama* three marine miles from the coast, put down her helm, and steamed back into port without delay.

The steam-yacht continued on, and remained near the scene of action.

Captain Winslow had assured the French admiral that in the event of an engagement the position of the ship should be far enough from shore to prevent a violation of the law of nations. To avoid a question of jurisdiction, and to avert an escape to neutral waters in case of retreat, the *Kearsarge* steamed to sea, followed by the enemy, giving the appearance of running away and being pursued. Between six and seven miles from the shore the *Kearsarge*, thoroughly ready, at 10:50 wheeled, at a distance of one and a quarter miles from her opponent, presented the starboard battery, and steered direct for her, with the design of closing or of running her down. The *Alabama* sheered and presented her starboard battery. More speed was ordered, the *Kearsarge* advanced rapidly, and at 10:57 received a broadside of solid shot at a range of about eighteen hundred yards. This broadside cut away a little of the rigging, but the shot mostly passed over or fell short. It was apparent that Captain Semmes intended to fight at long range.

The *Kearsarge* advanced with increased speed, receiving a second and part of a third broadside, with similar effect. Captain Winslow wished to get at short range, as the guns were loaded with five-second shell. Arrived within nine hundred yards, the *Kearsarge*, fearing a fourth broadside, and

⸗ This incident, and others pertaining to the *Alabama*, were told the writer by the officers who were
taken prisoners.— J. M. B.

REAR-ADMIRAL JOHN A. WINSLOW, CAPTAIN OF THE "KEARSARGE."
FROM A PHOTOGRAPH TAKEN SOON AFTER THE FIGHT, IN POSSESSION OF PAYMASTER-GENERAL J. A. SMITH, U. S. N.

apprehensive of a raking, sheered and broke her silence with the starboard battery. Each ship was now pressed under a full head of steam, the position being broadside, both employing the starboard guns.

Captain Winslow, fearful that the enemy would make for the shore, determined with a port helm to run under the *Alabama's* stern for raking, but was prevented by her sheering and keeping her broad-side to the *Kearsarge*, which forced the fighting on a circular track, each ship, with a strong port helm, steaming around a common center, and pour-ing its fire into its opponent a quarter to half a mile away. There was a current setting to west-ward three knots an hour.

The action was now fairly begun. The *Alabama* changed from solid shot to shell. ⚓ A shot from an early broadside of the *Kearsarge* carried away the

⚓ Commander Kell [see p. 608] says the *Alabama* began with shell.—EDITORS.

CAPTAIN JAMES S. THORNTON, EXECUTIVE OFFICER OF THE "KEARSARGE."
FROM A PHOTOGRAPH TAKEN IN 1864.

spanker-gaff of the enemy, and caused his ensign to come down by the run. This incident was regarded as a favorable omen by the men, who cheered and went with increased confidence to their work. The fallen ensign reappeared at the mizzen. The *Alabama* returned to solid shot, and soon after fired both shot and shell to the end. The firing of the *Alabama* was rapid and wild, getting better near the close; that of the *Kearsarge* was deliberate, accurate, and almost from the beginning productive of dismay, destruction, and death.‡ The *Kearsarge* gunners had been cautioned against firing without direct aim, and had been advised to point the heavy guns below rather than above the water-line, and to clear the deck of the enemy with the lighter ones. Though subjected to an incessant storm of shot and shell, they kept their stations and obeyed instructions.

The effect upon the enemy was readily perceived, and nothing could restrain the enthusiasm of our men. Cheer succeeded cheer; caps were thrown in the air or overboard; jackets were discarded; sanguine of victory, the men were shouting, as each projectile took effect: "That is a good one!" "Down, boys!" "Give her another like the last!" "Now we have her!" and so on, cheering and shouting to the end.

After the *Kearsarge* had been exposed to an uninterrupted cannonade for eighteen minutes, a 68-pounder Blakely shell passed through the starboard bulwarks below the main rigging, exploded upon the quarter-deck, and wounded three of the crew of the after pivot-gun. With these exceptions, not an officer or man received serious injury. The three unfortunate men were speedily taken below, and so quietly was the act done that at the termination of the fight a large number of the men were unaware that any of their comrades were wounded. Two shots entered the ports occupied by the thirty-twos, where several men were stationed, one

‡ Captain Semmes in his official report says: "The firing now became very hot, and the enemy's shot and shell soon began to tell upon our hull, knocking down, killing, and disabling a number of men in different parts of the ship."—J. M. B.

taking effect in the hammock-netting, the other going through the opposite port, yet none were hit. A shell exploded in the hammock-netting and set the ship on fire; the alarm calling for fire-quarters was sounded, and men who had been detailed for such an emergency put out the fire, while the rest staid at the guns.

It is wonderful that so few casualties occurred on board the *Kearsarge*, considering the number on the *Alabama* — the former having fired 173 shot and shell, and the latter nearly double that number. The *Kearsarge* concentrated her fire, and poured in the 11-inch shells with deadly effect. One penetrated the coal-bunker of the *Alabama*, and a dense cloud of coal-dust arose. Others struck near the water-line between the main and mizzen masts, exploded within board, or, passing through, burst beyond. Crippled and torn, the *Alabama* moved less quickly and began to settle by the stern, yet did not slacken her fire, but returned successive broadsides without disastrous result to us.

Captain Semmes witnessed the havoc made by the shells, especially by those of our after pivot-gun, and offered a reward to any one who would silence it. Soon his battery was turned upon this particular offending gun. It was in vain, for the work of destruction went on. We had completed the seventh rotation on the circular track and had begun the eighth, when the *Alabama*, now settling, sought to escape by setting all available sail (fore-trysail and two jibs), left the circle amid a shower of shot and shell, and headed for the French waters; but to no purpose. In winding, the *Alabama* presented the port battery, with only two guns bearing, and showed gaping sides, through which the water washed. The *Kearsarge* pursued,

JAMES R. WHEELER, ACTING MASTER OF THE "KEARSARGE," IN CHARGE OF THE FORWARD PIVOT-GUN. FROM A PHOTOGRAPH OF THE OFFICERS TAKEN IN 1864.

keeping on a line nearer the shore, and with a few well-directed shots hastened the sinking. Then the *Alabama* was at our mercy. Her colors were struck, and the *Kearsarge* ceased firing. I was told by our prisoners that two of the junior officers swore they would never surrender, and in a mutinous spirit rushed to the two port guns and opened fire upon the *Kearsarge*. [See page 610.] Captain Winslow, amazed at this extraordinary conduct of an enemy who had hauled down his flag in token of surrender, exclaimed, "He is playing us a trick; give him another broadside." Again the shot and shell went crashing through her sides, and the *Alabama* continued to settle by the stern. The *Kearsarge* was laid across her bows for raking, and in position to use grape and canister.

A white flag was then shown over the stern of the *Alabama* and her ensign was half-masted, union down. Captain Winslow for the second time gave orders to cease firing. Thus ended the fight, after a duration of one hour and two minutes. Captain Semmes, in his report, says: "Although we were now but four hundred yards from each other, the enemy fired upon me five times after my colors had been struck. It is charitable to suppose that a ship-of-war of a Christian nation could not have done this intentionally." He is silent as to the renewal by the *Alabama* of the fight after his surrender — an act which, in Christian warfare, would have justified the *Kearsarge* in continuing the fire until the *Alabama* had sunk beneath the waters.

Boats were now lowered from the *Alabama*. Her master's-mate, Fullam, an Englishman, came alongside the *Kearsarge* with a few of the wounded, reported the disabled and sinking condition of his ship, and asked for assistance. Captain Winslow inquired, "Does Captain Semmes surrender his ship?" "Yes," was the reply. Fullam then solicited permission to return with his boat and crew to assist in rescuing the drowning, pledging his

WILLIAM SMITH, QUARTERMASTER OF THE "KEARSARGE" AND CAPTAIN OF THE AFTER PIVOT-GUN, WHICH IT WAS SAID INFLICTED THE MOST DAMAGE ON THE "ALABAMA." FROM A PHOTOGRAPH TAKEN IN 1864.

THE ELEVEN-INCH FORWARD PIVOT-GUN ON THE "KEARSARGE," IN ACTION.

word of honor that when this was done he would come on board and surrender. Captain Winslow granted the request. With less generosity he could have detained the officer and men, supplied their places in the boat from his ship's company, secured more prisoners, and afforded equal aid to the distressed. The generosity was abused, as the sequel shows. Fullam pulled to the midst of the drowning, rescued several officers, went to the yacht *Deerhound*, and cast his boat adrift, leaving a number of men struggling in the water.

It was now seen that the *Alabama* was settling fast. The wounded, and the boys who could not swim, were sent away in the quarter-boats, the waist-boats having been destroyed. Captain Semmes dropped his sword into the sea and jumped overboard with the remaining officers and men.

Coming under the stern of the *Kearsarge* from the windward, the *Deerhound* was hailed, and her commander requested by Captain Winslow to run down and assist in picking up the men of the sinking ship. Or, as her owner, Mr. John Lancaster, reported: "The fact is, that when we passed the *Kearsarge* the captain cried out, 'For God's sake, do what you can to save them'; and that was my warrant for interfering in any way for the aid and succor of his enemies." The *Deerhound* was built by the Lairds at the same time and in the same yard with the *Alabama*. Throughout the action she kept about a mile to the windward of the contestants. After being hailed she steamed toward the *Alabama*, which sank almost immediately after. This was at 12:24. The *Alabama* sank in forty-five fathoms of water, at a distance of about four and a half miles from the breakwater, off the west entrance. She was severely hulled between the main and mizzen masts, and settled by the stern; the mainmast, pierced by a shot at the very last, broke off near the head and went over the side, the bow lifted high from the water, and then came the end. Suddenly assuming a perpendicular position, caused by the falling aft of the battery and stores, straight as a plumb-line, stern first, she went down, the jibboom being the last to appear above water. Thus sank the terror of merchantmen, riddled through and through, and as she disappeared to her last resting-place there was no cheer; all was silent.

The yacht lowered her two boats, rescued Captain Semmes (wounded in the hand by broken iron rigging), First Lieutenant Kell, twelve officers, and twenty-six men, leaving the rest of the survivors to the two boats of the *Kearsarge*. Apparently aware that the forty persons he had rescued would be claimed, Mr. Lancaster steamed away as fast as he could, direct for Southampton, without waiting for such surgical assistance as the *Kearsarge* might render. Captain Winslow permitted the yacht to secure his prisoners, anticipating their subsequent surrender. Again his confidence was misplaced, and he afterward wrote: "It was my mistake at the moment that I could not recognize an enemy who, under the garb of a friend, was affording assistance." The aid of the yacht, it is presumed, was asked in a spirit of chivalry, for the *Kearsarge*, comparatively uninjured, with but three wounded, and a full head of steam, was in condition to engage a second enemy. Instead of remaining at a distance of about four hundred yards from the *Alabama*, and from this position sending two boats, the other boats being injured, the *Kearsarge* by steaming close to the settling ship, and in the midst of the defeated, could have captured all — Semmes, officers, and men. Captain Semmes says: "There was no appearance of any boat coming to me from the enemy after the ship went down. Fortunately, however, the steam-yacht *Deerhound*, owned by a gentleman of Lancashire, England, Mr. John Lancaster, who was himself on board, steamed up in the midst of my drowning men, and rescued a number of both officers and men from the water. I was fortunate enough myself thus to escape to the shelter of the neutral flag, together with about forty others, all told. About this time the *Kearsarge* sent one, and then, tardily, another boat."

This imputation of inhumanity is contradicted by Mr. Lancaster's assertion that he was requested to do what he could to save "the poor fellows who were struggling in the water for their lives."

The *Deerhound* edged to the leeward and steamed rapidly away. An officer approached Captain Winslow and reported the presence of Captain Semmes and many officers on board the English yacht. Believing the information authentic, as it was obtained from the prisoners, he suggested the expediency of firing a shot to bring her to, and asked permission. Captain Winslow declined, saying "it was impossible; the yacht was simply coming round." Meanwhile the *Deerhound* increased the distance from the *Kearsarge*; another officer spoke to him in similar language, but with more positiveness. Captain Winslow replied that no Englishman who carried the flag of the Royal Yacht Squadron could so act. The *Deerhound* continued her flight, and yet another officer urged the necessity of firing a shot. With undiminished confidence Captain Winslow refused, saying the yacht was "simply coming round," and would not go away without communicating. The escape of the yacht and her coveted prize was manifestly regretted. The famed *Alabama*, "a formidable ship, the terror of American commerce, well armed, well manned, well handled," was destroyed, "sent to the bottom in an hour," but her commander had escaped; the victory seemed already lessened. It was held by the Navy Department that Captain Semmes violated the usages of war in surrendering to Captain Winslow through the agency of one of his officers and then effecting an escape during the execution of the commission; that he was a prisoner of the United States Government from the moment he sent the officer to make the surrender. ⟩

⟩ The controversy in reference to the *Deerhound* is summarized thus in a letter to the editors from Professor James Russell Soley, U. S. N.:

"A neutral ship, in general, could have no right to take part in hostilities even to the extent of rescuing the drowning sailors of a belligerent, their situation being a part and a consequence of the battle. In the case of the *Deerhound*, however, the interference was directly authorized by Captain Winslow's request, addressed to Mr. Lancaster, and, there-

The wounded of the survivors were brought on board the *Kearsarge* for surgical attendance. Seventy men, including five officers (Surgeon F. L. Galt, acting paymaster, Second Lieutenant J.

SEAMAN WILLIAM GOUIN, MORTALLY WOUNDED ON THE "KEARSARGE."

D. Wilson, First Assistant-Engineer M. J. Freeman, Third Assistant-Engineer Pundt, and Boatswain McCloskey), were saved by the *Kearsarge's* boats and a French pilot-boat. Another pilot-boat saved Second Lieutenant Armstrong and some men, who were landed at Cherbourg. Lieutenant Wilson was the only officer who delivered up his sword. He refused to go on board the *Deerhound*, and because of his honorable conduct Captain Winslow on taking his parole gave him a letter of recommendation. Our crew fraternized with their prisoners, and shared their clothes, supper, and grog with them. The conduct of the

Alabama's Assistant-Surgeon Llewellyn, son of a British rector, deserves mention. He was unremitting in attention to the wounded during battle, and after the surrender superintended their removal to the boats, refusing to leave the ship while one remained. This duty performed, being unable to swim, he attached two empty shell-boxes to his waist as a life-preserver and jumped overboard. Nevertheless, he was unable to keep his head above water.

When the *Kearsarge* was cleared for action every man on the sick-list went to his station. The *Kearsarge* had three wounded, of whom one died in the hospital a few days after the fight. This was William Gouin, ordinary seaman, whose behavior during and after battle was worthy of the highest praise. Stationed at the after pivot-gun he was seriously wounded in the leg by the explosion of a shell; in agony, and exhausted from the loss of blood, he dragged himself to the forward hatch, concealing the severity of his injury, so that his comrades might not leave their stations for his assistance; fainting, he was lowered to the care of the surgeon, and when he revived he greeted the surgeon with a smile, saying, "Doctor, I can fight no more, and so come to you, but it is all right; I am satisfied, for we are whipping the *Alabama*"; and afterward, "I will willingly lose my leg or my life, if it is necessary." Lying upon his mattress, he paid attention to the progress of the fight, so far as could be known by the sounds on the deck, his face showing satisfaction whenever the cheers of his shipmates were heard; with difficulty he waved his hand over his head, and joined in each cheer with a feeble voice. When a wounded shipmate on

fore, the latter committed no breach of neutrality in taking the prisoners on board. Once on board the English yacht, however, they were as free as air. So far from its being the obligation of the *Deerhound* to surrender them, the obligation was exactly the other way. Their surrender would have been as gross a violation of neutrality toward the Confederates as their unauthorized rescue would have been toward the Union Government. Captain Winslow was therefore perfectly right in refusing to detain the *Deerhound*, since the conduct of the yacht was the necessary and logical consequence of his

own act. The point where he was clearly in the wrong was in making the request in the first place. What he should have done, as Surgeon-General Browne clearly intimates, was to have steamed up close to the sinking *Alabama*, and saved her people himself, instead of remaining four hundred yards off."

It will be noticed that this statement leaves untouched the question of the right of a prisoner to escape after surrender and before delivering himself up.— EDITORS.

CLOSE OF THE COMBAT—THE "KEARSARGE" GETTING INTO POSITION TO RAKE THE "ALABAMA."

either side of him complained, he reproved him, saying, "Am I not worse hurt than you? and I am satisfied, for we are whipping the *Alabama*." Directly after the enemy's wounded were brought on board he desired the surgeon to give him no further attention, for he was "doing well," requesting that all aid be given to "the poor fellows of the *Alabama*." In the hospital he was patient and resigned, and happy in speaking of the victory. "This man, so very interesting by his courage and resignation," wrote the French surgeon-in-chief, "received general sympathy; all desired his recovery and lamented his death." At a dinner given by loyal Americans in Paris to Captain Winslow and two of his officers, a telegram was received announcing the death of Gouin. His name was honorably mentioned, his behavior eulogized, and his memory drunk in silence.

THE BOAT FROM THE "ALABAMA" ANNOUNCING THE SURRENDER AND ASKING FOR ASSISTANCE.

The picture shows shot-marks in the thin deal covering of the chain armor amidships.

At 3:10 P. M. the *Kearsarge* anchored in Cherbourg harbor close by the ship-of-war *Napoléon*, and was soon surrounded by boats of every description filled with excited and inquisitive people. Ambulances, by order of the French admiral, were sent to the landing to receive the wounded, and thence they were taken to the Hôpital de la Marine, where arrangements had been made for their reception. Dr. Galt and all the prisoners except four officers were paroled and sent on shore before sunset. Secretary Welles soon after expressed his disapprobation of this action.

An incident that occasioned gratification was the coincidence of the lowering of the enemy's colors by an early shot from the *Kearsarge*, already mentioned, and the unfolding of the victorious flag by a shot from the *Alabama*. The *Kearsarge's* colors were "stopped" at the mizzen, that they might be displayed if the ensign were carried away, and to serve as the emblem of victory in case of success. A shot from the last broadside of the *Alabama* passed high over the *Kearsarge*, carried away the halyards of the colors, stopped at the mizzen, and in so doing pulled sufficiently to break the stop, and thereby unfurled the triumphant flag.

The *Kearsarge* received twenty-eight shot and shell, of which thirteen were in the hull, the most efficient being abaft the mainmast. A 100-pounder

rifle shell entered at the starboard quarter and lodged in the stern-post. The blow shook the ship from stem to stern. Luckily the shell did not explode, otherwise the result would have been serious, if not fatal. A 32-pounder shell entered forward of the forward pivot port, crushing the waterways, raising the gun and carriage, and lodged, but did not explode, else many of the gun's crew would likely have been injured by the fragments and splinters. The smoke-pipe was perforated by a rifle shell, which exploded inside and tore a ragged hole nearly three feet in diameter, and carried away three of the chain guys. Three boats were shattered. The cutting away of the rigging was mostly about the mainmast. The spars were left in good order. A large number of pieces of burst shell were gathered from the deck and thoughtlessly thrown overboard. During the anchorage in Cherbourg harbor no assistance was received from shore except that rendered by a boiler-maker in patching up the smoke-stack, every other repair being made by our own men.

Captain Semmes in his official report says:

"At the end of the engagement it was discovered, by those of our officers who went alongside the enemy's ship with the wounded, that her midship section on both sides was thoroughly iron-coated. The planking had been ripped off in every direction by our shot and shell, the chain broken and indented in many places, and forced partly into the ship's side. The enemy was heavier than myself, both in ship, battery, and crew; but I did not know until the action was over that she was also iron-clad."

The ships were well matched in size, speed, armament, and crew, showing a likeness rarely seen in naval battles.↓ The number of the ship's company of the *Kearsarge* was 163. That of the *Alabama*, from the best information, was estimated at 150.

The chain plating was made of one hundred and twenty fathoms of sheet-chains of one and seven-tenths inch iron, covering a space amidships of forty-nine and one-half feet in length by six feet

THE SHELL IN THE STERN-POST OF THE "KEARSARGE."

The charge was withdrawn from the shell, which was boxed in, and in that condition it remained for months, until the ship reached Boston, where, when the vessel was repaired, a section of the stern-post containing the embedded shell was cut away and sent to the Navy Department, and was finally deposited in the Ordnance Museum, at the Navy Yard, Washington.—J. M. B.

two inches in depth, stopped up and down to eye-bolts with marlines, secured by iron dogs, and employed for the purpose of protecting the engines when the upper part of the coal-bunkers was empty, as happened during the action. The chains were concealed by one-inch deal-boards as a finish. The chain plating was struck by a 32-pounder shot in the starboard gangway, which cut the chain and bruised the planking; and by a 32-pounder shell, which broke a link of the chain, exploded, and tore away a portion of the deal covering. Had the shot been from the 100-pounder rifle the result would have been different, though without serious dam-

age, because the shot struck five feet above the water-line, and if sent through the side would have cleared the machinery and boilers. It is proper therefore to assert that in the absence of the chain armor the result would have been nearly the same, notwithstanding the common opinion at the time that the *Kearsarge* was an "iron-clad" contending with a wooden ship. The chains were fastened to the ship's sides more than a year previous to the fight, while at the Azores. It was the suggestion of the executive officer, Lieutenant-Commander James S. Thornton, to hang the sheet-chain (or spare anchor-cable) over the sides, so as to protect the midship section, he having served with Admiral Farragut in passing the forts to reach New Orleans, and having observed its benefit on that occasion. The work was done in three days, at a cost for material not exceeding seventy-five dollars. In our visit to European ports, the use of sheet-chains for protective purposes had attracted notice and caused comment. It is strange that Captain Semmes did not know of the chain armor; supposed spies had been on board and had been shown through the ship, as there was no attempt at concealment; the same pilot had been employed by both ships, and had visited each during the preparation for battle. The *Alabama* had bunkers full of coal, which brought her down in the water. The *Kearsarge* was deficient in seventy tons of coal of her proper supply, but the sheet-chains stowed outside gave protection to her partly-filled bunkers.

The battery of the *Kearsarge* consisted of seven guns: two 11-inch pivots, smooth bore, one 30-pounder rifle, and four light 32-pounders; that of the *Alabama* of eight guns: one 68-pounder pivot, smooth bore, one 100-pounder pivot rifle, and six heavy 32-pounders. Five guns were fought by the *Kearsarge* and seven by the *Alabama*, each with the starboard battery. Both ships had made thirteen knots an hour under steam; at the time of the battle the *Alabama* made ten knots. The masts of the *Kearsarge* were low and small; she never carried more than top-sail yards, depending upon her engines for speed. The greater size and height of the masts of the *Alabama* and the heaviness of her rig (barque) gave the appearance of a larger vessel than her antagonist.

Most of the line officers of the *Kearsarge* were from the merchant service, and of the crew only eleven men were of foreign birth. Most of the officers of the *Alabama* were formerly officers in the United States Navy; nearly all the crew were English, Irish, and Welsh, a few of whom were said to belong to the "Royal Naval Reserve." Captain Semmes said, "Mr. Kell, my first lieutenant, deserves great credit for the fine condition in which the ship went into action with regard to her battery, magazine, and shell-rooms"; and he assuredly had confidence in the speed and strength of his ship, as shown by the eagerness and dash with which he opened the fight. The prisoners declared that the best practice during the action was by the

↓	Alabama.	Kearsarge.
Length over all	220 ft.	232 ft.
Length at water-line	210 "	198½ "
Beam	32 "	33 "

	Alabama.	Kearsarge.
Depth	17 ft.	16½ ft.
2 Engines apiece, each of	300 h. p.	400 h. p.
Tonnage	1040	1031

gunners who had been trained on board the *Excellent* in Portsmouth harbor. The Blakely rifle was the most effective gun. The *Alabama* fought bravely until she could no longer fight or float.

The contest was decided by the superiority of the 11-inch Dahlgrens, especially the after-pivot, together with the coolness and accuracy of aim of the gunners of the *Kearsarge*, and notably by the skill of William Smith, the captain of the after-pivot, who in style and behavior was like Long Tom Coffin in Cooper's "Pilot."

To the disparagement of Captain Winslow it has been said that Lieutenant-Commander Thornton commanded the ship during the action. This is not true. Captain Winslow, standing on the horse-block abreast the mizzen-mast, fought his ship gallantly and, as is shown by the result, with excellent judgment. In an official report he wrote:

"It would seem almost invidious to particularize the conduct of any one man or officer, in which all had done their duty with a fortitude and coolness which cannot be too highly praised, but I feel it due to my executive officer, Lieutenant-Commander Thornton, who superin-

tended the working of the battery, to particularly mention him for an example of coolness and encouragement of the men while fighting which contributed much toward the success of the action."

This Sunday naval duel was fought in the presence of more than 15,000 spectators, who, upon the heights of Cherbourg, the breakwater, and rigging of men-of-war, witnessed "the last of the *Alabama*." Among them were the captains, their families, and crews of two merchant ships burnt by the daring cruiser a few days before her arrival at Cherbourg, where they were landed in a nearly destitute condition. Many spectators were provided with spy-glasses and camp-stools. The *Kearsarge* was burning Newcastle coals, and the *Alabama* Welsh coals, the difference in the amount of smoke enabling the movements of each ship to be distinctly traced. An excursion train from Paris arrived in the morning, bringing hundreds of pleasure-seekers, who were unexpectedly favored with the spectacle of a sea-fight. A French gentleman at Boulogne-sur-Mer assured me that the fight was the conversation of Paris for more than a week.

NOTE.— Twelve Confederate cruisers figured in the so-called "Alabama" Claims" settlement with England. Named in the order of the damage inflicted by each, these cruisers were: the *Alabama, Shenandoah, Florida, Tallahassee, Georgia, Chickamauga, Sumter, Nashville, Retribution, Jeff. Davis, Sallie,* and *Boston.* The actual losses inflicted by the *Alabama* ($7,050,293.76, according to claims for ships and cargoes filed up to March 15th, 1872) were only about $400,000 greater than those inflicted by the *Shenandoah.* The sum total of the claims filed against the twelve cruisers for ships and cargoes, up to March 15th, 1872, was $19,782,917.60, all but about six millions of it being charged to the account of the *Alabama* and *Shenandoah.*

On May 8th, 1871, the Treaty of Washington was concluded, in accordance with which a Tribunal of Arbitration was appointed, which assembled at Geneva. It consisted of Count Frederick Sclopis, named by the King of Italy; Mr. Jacob Staempfli, named by the President of

the Swiss Confederation; Viscount d'Itajuba, named by the Emperor of Brazil; Mr. Charles Francis Adams, named by the President of the United States; and Sir Alexander Cockburn, named by the Queen of Great Britain. The Counsel of Great Britain was Sir Roundell Palmer (afterward Lord Selborne). The United States was represented by William M. Evarts, Caleb Cushing, and Morrison R. Waite. Claims were made by the United States for indirect and national losses, as well as for the actual private losses represented by nearly twenty millions on ships and cargoes.

The Tribunal decided that England was in no way responsible for the $1,781,915.43 of losses inflicted by the *Tallahassee, Georgia, Chickamauga, Nashville, Retribution, Jeff. Davis, Sallie, Boston,* and *Sumter;* and on September 14th, 1872, it awarded $15,500,000 damages for actual losses of ships and cargoes and interest, on account of the *Alabama,* the *Florida* and her tenders, and the *Shenandoah* after she left Melbourne.— EDITORS.

THE FIRST BATTLE OF THE CONFEDERATE RAM "ALBEMARLE."

BY HER BUILDER, GILBERT ELLIOTT.

IN the spring of 1864 it was decided at Confederate headquarters that an attempt should be made to recapture Plymouth. ☆ General Hoke was placed in command of the land forces, and Captain J. W. Cooke received orders to coöperate with the *Albemarle,* an iron-clad then nearly finished.

☆ For an account of the capture of New Berne and Plymouth, North Carolina, by the Union forces, see Vol. I., pp. 647–659. The Confederates made three attempts to recapture New Berne. On March 14th, 1863, General D. H. Hill sent General J. J. Pettigrew with infantry and seventeen guns to attack Fort Anderson, an earthwork on the Neuse opposite the town, and garrisoned by 300 men of the 92d New York. After a bombardment of several hours Pettigrew withdrew and Hill abandoned the project. During the action the gun-boats *Hetzel* and *Hunchback* opened upon the Confederate batteries, drove the enemy from the field, and covered the landing of the 85th New York, in aid of the garrison. On January 30th, 1864, an expedition, under General George E. Pickett, set out from Kinston, North Carolina, to capture New Berne, the defenses of which were garrisoned by 3000 men under General I. N. Palmer. A flotilla, composed of the steamers *Lockwood, Commodore Hull,* and

Accordingly Hoke's division proceeded to the vicinity of Plymouth and surrounded the town from the river above to the river below, and preparation was made to storm the forts and breastworks as soon as the *Albemarle* could clear the river front of the Federal war vessels protecting the place with their guns.

Underwriter, under Acting Volunteer Lieutenant G. W. Graves, was stationed in the Neuse and the Trent. General Pickett's force consisted of three brigades of infantry, 14 guns, and 600 cavalry, in all numbering about 4500 men, and a fleet of ten row-boats, manned by 300 men armed with rifles and cutlasses, under Colonel John Taylor Wood. On the night of February 1st Wood's force boarded the *Underwriter* as she lay at anchor in the Neuse under the guns of Fort Stevenson, killing her commander, Acting Master Jacob Westervelt, and three of the crew, and capturing a third of the remainder. Finding the boilers of the *Underwriter* cold, Colonel Wood set fire to the vessel. After some skirmishing General Pickett abandoned the enterprise on the 3d. On May 5th, 1864, a third demonstration was made against New Berne, but the Confederates retired without having accomplished any results of importance.— EDITORS.

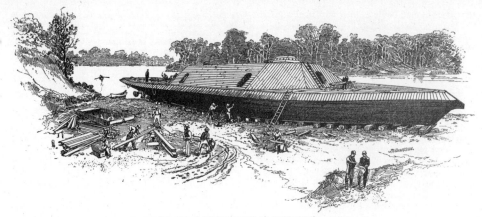

BUILDING THE "ALBEMARLE" AT EDWARDS'S FERRY.

On the morning of April 18th, 1864, the *Albemarle* left the town of Hamilton and proceeded down the river toward Plymouth, going stern foremost, with chains dragging from the bow, the rapidity of the current making it impracticable to steer with her head down-stream. She came to anchor about three miles above Plymouth, and a mile or so above the battery on the bluff at Warren's Neck, near Thoroughfare Gap, where torpedoes, sunken vessels, piles, and other obstructions had been placed. An exploring expedition was sent out, under command of one of the lieutenants, which returned in about two hours, with the report that it was considered impossible to pass the obstructions. Thereupon the fires were banked, and the officers and crew not on duty retired to rest.

Having accompanied Captain Cooke as a volunteer aide, and feeling intensely dissatisfied with the apparent intention of lying at anchor all that night, and believing that it was "then or never" with the ram if she was to accomplish anything,

and that it would be foolhardy to attempt the passage of the obstructions and batteries in the daytime, I requested permission to make a personal investigation. Captain Cooke cordially assenting, and Pilot John Luck and two of the few experienced seamen on board volunteering their services, we set forth in a small lifeboat, taking with us a long pole, and arriving at the obstructions proceeded to take soundings. To our great joy it was ascertained that there was ten feet of water over and above the obstructions. This was due to the remarkable freshet then prevailing; the proverbial "oldest inhabitant" said, afterward, that such high water had never before been seen in Roanoke River. Pushing on down the stream to Plymouth, and taking advantage of the shadow of the trees on the north side of the river, opposite the town, we watched the Federal transports taking on board the women and children who were being sent away for safety, on account of the approaching bombardment. With muffled oars, and almost afraid to

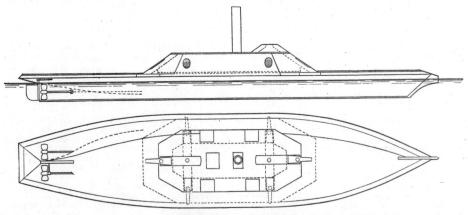

PLAN OF THE "ALBEMARLE."

The *Albemarle*, built at Edwards's Ferry, on the Roanoke, thirty miles below Weldon, by Gilbert Elliott, according to the plans of Chief Constructor John L. Porter, C. S. N., was of solid pine frame timbers, each 8 x 10 inches thick, dovetailed together, and sheathed with 4-inch plank. The *Albemarle* was 122 feet long, 45 feet beam, and drew 8 feet. The *Albemarle's* shield, octagonal in form, was 60 feet long, and was protected by two layers of 2-inch iron plating. The prow, or "ram," was of solid oak, plated with 2-inch iron, tapering to an edge. She had two engines of 200 horse-power each.

CAPTAIN J. W. COOKE, C. S. N.

breathe, we made our way back up the river, hugging the northern bank, and reached the ram about 1 o'clock, reporting to Captain Cooke that it was practicable to pass the obstructions provided the boat was kept in the middle of the stream. Captain Cooke instantly aroused his men, gave the order to get up steam, slipped the cables in his impatience to be off, and started down the river. The obstructions were soon reached and safely passed, under a fire from the fort at Warren's Neck which was not returned. Protected by the iron-clad shield, to those on board the noise made by the shot and shell as they struck the boat sounded no louder than pebbles thrown against an empty barrel. At Boyle's Mill, lower down, there was another fort upon which was mounted a very heavy gun. This was also safely passed, and we then discovered two steamers coming up the river. They proved to be the *Miami* and the *Southfield*. ⚓

The two ships were lashed together with long spars, and with chains festooned between them. The plan of Captain Flusser, who commanded, was to run his vessels so as to get the *Albemarle* between the two, which would have placed the ram at a great disadvantage, if not altogether at his mercy; but Captain Cooke ran the ram close to the southern shore, and then suddenly turning toward the middle of the stream, and going with the current, the throttles, in obedience to his bell, being wide open, he dashed the prow of the *Albemarle* into the side of the *Southfield*, making an opening large enough to carry her to the bottom in much less time than it takes to tell the story. Part of her crew went down with her.‡

The chain-plates on the forward deck of the *Albemarle* became entangled in the frame of the sinking vessel, and her bow was carried down to such a depth that water poured into her port-holes

in great volume, and she would soon have shared the fate of the *Southfield*, had not the latter vessel reached the bottom, and then, turning over on her side, released the ram, thus allowing her to come up on an even keel. The *Miami*, right alongside, had opened fire with her heavy guns, and so close were the vessels that a shell with a ten-second fuse, fired by Captain Flusser, after striking the *Albemarle* rebounded and exploded, killing the gallant man who pulled the lanyard, tearing him almost to pieces. Notwithstanding the death of Flusser, an attempt was made to board the ram, which was heroically resisted by as many of the crew as could be crowded on the top deck, who were supplied with loaded muskets passed up by their comrades below. The *Miami*, a very fast side-wheeler, succeeded in eluding the *Albemarle* without receiving a blow from her ram, and retired below Plymouth, into Albemarle Sound.

Captain Cooke having successfully carried out his part of the programme, General Hoke attacked the fortifications the next morning and carried them; not, however, without heavy loss, Ransom's brigade alone leaving five hundred dead and wounded on the field, in their most heroic charge upon the breastworks protecting the eastern front of the town. General Wessells, commanding the Federal forces, made a gallant resistance, and surrendered only when further effort would have been worse than useless. During the attack the *Albemarle* held the river front, and all day long poured shot and shell into the resisting forts with her two guns.

COMMANDER C. W. FLUSSER, U. S. N.

‡ The *Miami* carried six 9-inch guns, one 100-pounder Parrott rifle, and one 24-pounder smooth-bore howitzer, and the ferry-boat *Southfield* five 9-inch, one 100-pounder Parrott, and one 12-pounder howitzer.—EDITORS.

‡ Of the officers and men of the *Southfield*, seven of

the former, including Acting Volunteer Lieutenant C. A. French, her commander, and forty-two of her men were rescued by the *Miami* and the other vessels of the Union fleet; the remainder were either drowned or captured.—EDITORS.

THE "ALBEMARLE" AND THE "SASSACUS."

BY EDGAR HOLDEN, U. S. N.

ON the 5th of May, 1864, the *Albemarle*, with the captured steamer *Bombshell*, and the steamer *Cotton Plant*, laden with troops, came down the Roanoke River. The double-enders *Mattabesett*, *Sassacus*, *Wyalusing*, and *Miami*, together with the smaller vessels, *Whitehead*, *Ceres*, and *Commodore Hull*, steamed up Albemarle Sound to give battle.⌇

The *Sassacus* was one of the several wooden side-wheel ships, known as "double-enders," built for speed, light draught, and ease of manœuvre. She carried four 9-inch Dahlgren guns and two 100-pounder Parrott rifles, and was under the command of Lieutenant-Commander F. A. Roe.

The Union plan of attack was for the large vessels to pass as close as possible to the ram without endangering their wheels, deliver their fire, and then round to for a second discharge. The smaller vessels were to take charge of thirty armed launches, which were expected to accompany the iron-clad. The *Miami* carried a torpedo to be exploded under the enemy, and a strong net, or seine, to foul her propeller.

⌇ The Union force under Captain Melancton Smith in the action of May 5th, 1864, was: Double-enders: *Mattabesett*, Commander John C. Febiger; *Sassacus*, Lieutenant-Commander Francis A. Roe; *Wyalusing*, Lieutenant-Commander Walter W. Queen; *Miami*, Acting Volunteer Lieutenant Charles A. French. Ferryboat: *Commodore Hull*, Acting Master Francis Josselyn. Gun-boats: *Whitehead*, Acting Ensign G. W. Barrett; *Ceres*, Acting Master H. H. Foster. The losses were: *Mattabesett*, k, 2; w, 6,— total, 8; *Sassacus*, k, 1; w, 19 (13 of these were scalded),— total, 20; *Wyalusing*, k, 1,— in all 29.— EDITORS.

All eyes were fixed on this second *Merrimac* as, like a floating fortress, she came down the bay. A puff of smoke from her bow port opened the ball, followed quickly by another, the shells being aimed skillfully at the pivot-rifle of the leading ship, *Mattabesett*, cutting away rail and spars, and wounding six men at the gun. The enemy then headed straight for her, in imitation of the *Merrimac*, but by a skillful management of the helm the *Mattabesett* rounded her bow,⚓ closely followed by our own ship, the *Sassacus*, which at close quarters gave her a broadside of solid 9-inch shot. The guns might as well have fired blank cartridges, for the shot skimmed off into the air, and even the 100-pound solid shot from the pivot-rifle glanced from the sloping roof into space with no apparent effect. The rapid firing from the different ships produced clouds of smoke. Changes of position were necessary to avoid being run down, and constant watchfulness to get a shot into the ports of the ram, as they quickly opened to deliver their well-directed fire. There was also danger of

⚓ If the *Mattabesett* rounded the bow of the *Albemarle*, the latter must have been heading up the sound at the time; in other words, she must have turned previous to the advance of the Union fleet. Upon this point the reports of the captains of the double-enders give conflicting testimony. Commander Febiger represents the ram as retreating toward the Roanoke, while Lieutenant-Commander Roe describes her as in such a position that she would necessarily have been heading toward the advancing squadron. The conflict of opinion was doubtless due to the similarity in the two ends of the ram.— EDITORS.

our ships firing into or entangling each other. As our own ship delivered her broadside, and fired the pivot-rifle with great rapidity at roof, and port, and hull, and smoke-stack, trying to find a weak spot, the ram headed for us and narrowly passed our stern. She was foiled in this attempt, as we were under full headway; and swiftly rounding her with a hard-a-port helm, we delivered a broadside at her consort, the *Bombshell*, each shot hulling her. We now headed for the latter ship, going within hail.

Thus far in the action our pivot-rifle astern had had but small chance to fire, and the captain of the gun, a broad-shouldered, brawny fellow, was now wrought up to a pitch of desperation at holding his giant gun in leash, and as we came up to the *Bombshell* he mounted the rail, and, naked to the waist, he brandished a huge boarding-pistol and shouted, "Haul down your flag and surrender, or we'll blow you out of the water!" The flag came down, and the *Bombshell* was ordered to drop out of action and anchor, which she did.

Now came the decisive moment, for by this action we had acquired a distance from the ram of about four hundred yards, and the latter, to evade the *Mattabesett*, had sheered off a little and lay broadside to us. The Union ships were now on both sides of the ram, with engines stopped. Commander Roe cried to the engineer, "Crowd waste and oil in the fires and back slowly! Give her all the steam she can carry!" To Acting Master Boutelle he said, "Lay her course for the junction of the casemate and the hull!" Then came four bells, and with full steam and open throttle the ship sprang forward like a living thing. It was a moment of intense strain and anxiety. The guns ceased firing, the smoke lifted from the ram, and we saw that every effort was being made to evade the shock. Straight as an arrow we shot forward to the designated spot. Then came the order, "All hands, lie down!" and with a crash that shook the ship like an earthquake, we struck full and square on the iron hull, careening it over and tearing away our own bows,

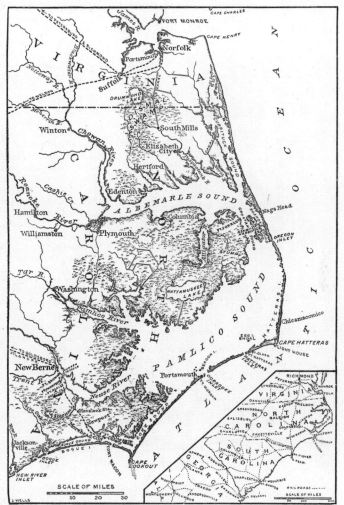

MAPS OF THE COAST OF THE CAROLINAS.

ripping and straining our timbers at the water-line.

The enemy's lights were put out, and his men were hurled from their feet, and, as we learned afterward, it was thought for a moment that all was over with them. Our ship quivered for an instant, but held fast, and the swift plash of the paddles showed that the engines were uninjured. Through the starboard shutter, which had been partly jarred off by the concussion, I saw the port of the ram not ten feet away. It opened, and like a flash of lightning I saw the grim muzzle of a cannon, the gun's-crew naked to the waist and blackened with powder; then a blaze, a roar and the rush of the shell as it crashed through, whirling me round and dashing me to the deck.

Both ships were under headway, and as the ram advanced, our shattered bows clinging to the iron casemate were twisted round, and a second shot from a Brooke gun almost touching our side crashed through, followed immediately by a cloud of steam and boiling water that filled the forward decks as our

overcharged boilers, pierced by the shot, emptied their contents with a shrill scream that drowned for an instant the roar of the guns. The shouts of command and the cries of scalded, wounded, and blinded men mingled with the rattle of small-arms that told of a hand-to-hand conflict above. The ship surged heavily to port as the great weight of water in the boilers was expended, and over the cry, "The ship is sinking!" came the shout, "All hands, repel boarders on starboard bow!"

The men below, wild with the boiling steam, sprang to the ladder with pistol and cutlass, and gained the bulwarks; but men in the rigging with muskets and hand-grenades, and the well-directed fire from the crews of the guns, soon baffled the attempt of the Confederates to gain our decks. To send our crew on the grated top of the iron-clad would have been madness. The horrid tumult, always characteristic of battle, was intensified by the cries of agony from the scalded and frantic men. In the midst of all this, when every other man had left the engine-room, our chief engineer, Mr. Hobby, although badly scalded, stood with heroism at his post; nor did he leave it till after the action, when he was brought up, blinded a helpless, to the deck. An officer of the *Wyalusing* says that when the dense smoke and steam enveloped us they thought we had sunk, till the flash of our guns burst through the clouds, followed by flash after flash in quick succession as our men recovered from the shock of the explosion.

To us, at least, there seemed time enough for the other ships to close in on the ram and sink her, or sink beside her, and it was thirteen minutes as timed by an officer of the *Wyalusing*; but the other ships were silent, and with stopped engines looked

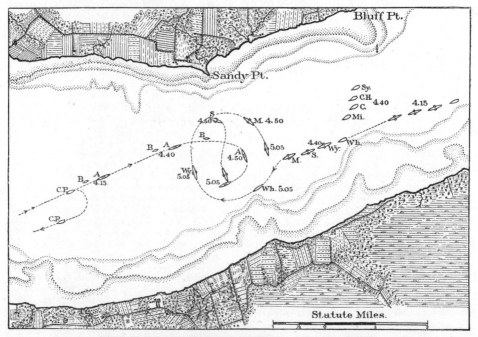

CHART OF THE ENGAGEMENT IN ALBEMARLE SOUND, MAY 5, 1864.

A, *Albemarle*; B, *Bombshell*; C P, *Cotton Plant*; M, *Mattabesett*; S, *Sassacus*; Wy, *Wyalusing*; Mi, *Miami*; C, *Ceres*; Wh, *Whitehead*; C H, *Commodore Hull*.

THE "SASSACUS" RAMMING THE "ALBEMARLE."

THE "SASSACUS" DISABLED AFTER RAMMING.

on as the clouds closed over us in the grim and final struggle. ↓

Captain French, of the *Miami*, who had bravely fought his ship at close quarters, and often at the ship's length, vainly tried to get bows on, to come to our assistance and use his torpedo; but his ship steered badly, and he was unable to reach us before we dropped away. In the meantime the *Wyalusing* signaled that she was sinking — a mistake, but one that affected materially the outcome of the battle. We struck exactly at the spot for which we had aimed; and, contrary to the diagram given in the naval report for that year, the headway of both ships twisted our bows, and brought us broadside to broadside — our bows at the enemy's stern and our starboard paddle-wheel on the forward starboard angle of his casemate. ♭ At length we drifted off the ram, and our pivot-gun, which had been fired incessantly by Ensign Mayer, almost muzzle to muzzle with the enemy's guns, was kept at work till we were out of range.

The official report says that the other ships then got in line and fired at the enemy, also attempting to lay the seine to foul his propeller — a task that proved, alas, as impracticable as that of injuring him by the fire of the guns. While we were alongside, and had drifted broadside to broadside, our 9-inch Dahlgren guns had been depressed till the shot would

↓ There was no lack of courage on the other ships, and the previous loss of the *Southfield*, the signal from the *Wyalusing* that she was sinking, the apparent loss of our ship, and the loss of the sounds of North Carolina if more were disabled, dictated the prudent course they adopted.— E. H.

♭ Against the report mentioned, I not only place my own observation, but I have in my possession the written statement of the navigator, Boutelle, now a member of Congress from Maine.— E. H.

strike at right angles, and the solid iron would bound from the roof into the air like marbles. Fragments even of our 100-pound rifle-shots, at close range, came back on our own decks.

Commander Roe was asked to correct his report as to the speed of our ship. He had said we were going at a speed of ten knots, and the naval report says, "He was not disposed to make the original correction." I should think not!— when the speed could

PAYMASTER GEORGE DE F. BARTON, ACTING AIDE AND SIGNAL OFFICER TO COMMANDER ROE DURING THE ENGAGEMENT WITH THE "ALBEMARLE." FROM A PHOTOGRAPH.

ACTING MASTER CHARLES A. BOUTELLE, U. S. N.

COMMANDER W. B. CUSHING, U. S. N.

only be estimated by his own officers, and the navigator says clearly in his report *eleven* knots. We had, perhaps, the swiftest ship in the navy. We had backed slowly to increase the distance; with furious fires and a gagged engine working at the full stroke of the pistons,—a run of over four hundred yards, with eager and excited men counting the revolutions of our paddles; who should give the more correct statement?

Another part of the official report states that the bows of the double-enders were all frail, and had they been armed would have been in-

sufficient to have sunk the ram. Our bow, however, was shod with a *bronze beak*, weighing fully three tons, well secured to prow and keel; and this was twisted and almost entirely torn away in the collision.

At dusk the ram steamed into the Roanoke River, never again to emerge for battle, and the object of her coming on the day of our engagement, viz., to aid the Confederates in an attack on New Berne, was defeated; but her ultimate destruction was reserved for the gallant Lieutenant Cushing, of glorious memory.

NOTE.— The Navy Department was not satisfied with the first official reports, and new and special reports were called for. As a result of investigation, promotions of many of the officers were made.— EDITORS.

THE "ALBEMARLE" READY FOR ACTION.

THE DESTRUCTION OF THE "ALBEMARLE."

BY W. B. CUSHING, COMMANDER, U. S. N.

IN September, 1864, the Government was laboring under much anxiety in regard to the condition of affairs in the sounds of North Carolina. Some months previous (April 19th) a rebel iron-clad had made her appearance, attacking and recapturing Plymouth, beating our fleet, and sinking the *Southfield*. Some time after (May 5th), this iron-clad, the *Albemarle*, had steamed out into the open sound and engaged seven of our steamers, doing much damage and suffering little. The *Sassacus* had attempted to run her down, but had failed, and had had her boiler exploded. [See p. 628.] The Government had no iron-clad that could cross Hatteras bar and enter the sounds, ‡ and it was impossible for any number of our vessels to injure the ram at Plymouth.

PART OF THE SMOKE-STACK OF THE "ALBEMARLE."

At this stage of affairs Admiral S. P. Lee ♱ spoke to me of the case, when I proposed a plan for her capture or destruction. I submitted in writing two plans. The first was based upon the fact that through a thick swamp the iron-clad might be approached to within a few hundred yards, whence India-rubber boats, to be inflated and carried upon men's backs, might transport a boarding-party of a hundred men; in the second plan the offensive force was to be conveyed in two very small low-pressure steamers, each armed with a torpedo and a howitzer. In the latter (which had my preference), I intended that one boat should dash in, while the other stood by to throw canister and renew the attempt if the first should fail. It would also be useful to pick up our men if the attacking boat were disabled. Admiral Lee believed that the plan was a good one, and ordered me to Washington to submit it to the Secretary of the Navy. Mr. Fox, Assistant Secretary of the Navy, doubted the merit of the project, but concluded to order me to New York to "purchase suitable vessels."

Finding some boats building for picket duty, I selected two, and proceeded to fit them out. They were open launches, about thirty feet in length, ‡ with small engines, and propelled by a screw. A 12-pounder howitzer was fitted to the bow of each, and a boom was rigged out, some fourteen feet in length, swinging by a goose-neck hinge to the bluff of the bow. [See p. 636.] A topping lift, carried to a stanchion inboard, raised or lowered it, and the torpedo was fitted into an iron slide at the end. This was intended to be detached from the boom by means of a heel-jigger leading inboard, and to be exploded by another line, connecting with a pin, which held a grape shot over

---

‡ Several light-draught monitors were in course of construction at this time, but were not yet completed.—EDITORS.

♱ On September 5th, 1862, Acting Rear-Admiral S. P. Lee relieved Rear-Admiral Goldsborough of the command of the North Atlantic Squadron; he in turn was relieved by Rear-Admiral D. D. Porter, October 12th, 1864.—EDITORS.

‡ According to Engineer-in-Chief W. W. Wood the launches were "45 to 47 feet long, 9 feet 6 inches beam. . . . Draught of water about 40 to 42 inches."—EDITORS.

a nipple and cap. The torpedo was the invention of Engineer Lay of the navy, and was introduced by Chief-Engineer Wood. Everything being completed, we started to the southward, taking the boats through the canals to Chesapeake Bay. My best boat having been lost in going down to Norfolk, I proceeded with the other through the Chesapeake and Albemarle canal. Half-way through, the canal was filled up, but finding a small creek that emptied into it below the obstruction, I endeavored to feel my way through. Encountering a mill-dam, we waited for high water, and ran the launch over it; below she grounded, but I got a flat-boat, and, taking out gun and coal, succeeded in two days in getting her through. Passing with but seven men through the canal, where for thirty miles there was no guard or Union inhabitant, I reached the sound, and ran before a gale of wind to Roanoke Island.

In the middle of the night I steamed off into the darkness, and in the morning was out of sight. Fifty miles up the sound I found the fleet anchored off the mouth of the river, and awaiting the ram's appearance. Here, for the first time, I disclosed to my officers and men our object, and told them that they were at liberty to go or not, as they pleased. These, seven in number, all volunteered. One of them, Mr. Howarth of the *Monticello*, had been with me repeatedly in expeditions of peril. ‡

The Roanoke River is a stream averaging 150 yards in width, and quite deep. Eight miles from the mouth was the town of Plymouth, where the ram was moored. Several thousand soldiers occupied town and forts, and held both banks of the stream. A mile below the ram was the wreck of the *Southfield*, with hurricane deck above water, and on this a guard was stationed. Thus it seemed impossible to surprise them, or to attack with hope of success.

Impossibilities are for the timid: we determined to overcome all obstacles. On the night of the 27th of October § we entered the river, taking in tow a small cutter with a few men, whose duty was to dash aboard the wreck of the *Southfield* at the first hail, and prevent a rocket from being ignited.

We passed within thirty feet of the pickets without discovery, and neared the vessel. I now thought that it might be better to board her, and "take her alive," having in the two boats twenty men well armed with

‡ Cushing had already obtained a unique reputation in the service. His first notable exploit was a successful raid in November, 1862, up New River Inlet, in North Carolina, in the tugboat *Ellis*. In January, 1863, he captured by surprise an earth-work at Little River, his force consisting of 25 men in three cutters. In April he commanded the flotilla in the Lower Nansemond. (See "Closing Operations in the James River," to follow.) Two important raids were made in Cape Fear River. The first was in February, 1864. Its object was to capture General Hébert at Smithville. Taking two boats and twenty men, Cushing rowed past Fort Caswell in the darkness, landed at the town, and, concealing his men, took a small party with him to Hébert's headquarters. The general happened to be away, but one of his staff-officers was taken prisoner and carried to the boats. In June Cushing took one cutter with fifteen men and went up nearly to Wilmington. Hiding his men during the day in a swamp, at night he embarked and made a reconnoissance of the obstructions below the city. At daybreak he landed again, and taking a party through the woods to the high road between Fort Fisher and Wilmington, he captured the courier with the mail from the fort. His third night was devoted to an examination of the Confederate gun-boat *Raleigh*, which was found to have been destroyed. On his way out he found a large force of guard-boats. His coolness and good judgment enabled him to elude them, and he returned without losing a man. On the strength of these exploits the Department intrusted him with the expedition against the *Albemarle*. — EDITORS.

§ The first attempt was made on the previous night, but the launch grounded.— EDITORS.

revolvers, cutlasses, and hand-grenades. To be sure, there were ten times our number on the ship and thousands near by; but a surprise is everything, and I thought if her fasts were cut at the instant of boarding, we might overcome those on board, take her into the stream, and use her iron sides to protect us afterward from the forts. Knowing the town, I concluded to land at the lower wharf, creep around, and suddenly dash aboard from the bank; but just as I was sheering in close to the wharf, a hail came, sharp and quick, from the iron-clad, and in an instant was repeated. I at once directed the cutter to cast off, and go down to capture the guard left in our rear, and, ordering all steam, went at the

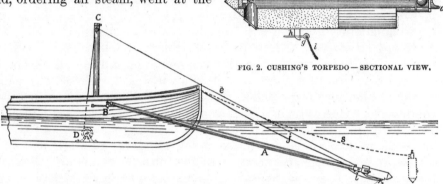

FIG. 2. CUSHING'S TORPEDO—SECTIONAL VIEW.

FIG. 1. CUSHING'S LAUNCH AND TORPEDO—SHOWING METHODS OF WORKING.

A long spar A (Fig. 1) was pivoted by means of a universal joint on its inboard end into the bracket B, the bracket being securely fastened to the outside of the boat. The spar was raised or lowered by means of a halliard e, which passed through a block at the head of the stanchion C, and thence down to the drum of a small windlass D, situated in the bottom of the boat, directly abaft the stanchion. On the outboard end of the spar was a socket, or head, which carried the shell. The shell was held in place only by a small pin g, which passed through a lug h, protruding from the lower side of the shell, and thence through an inclined plane i, which was attached to the socket. The lug and pin are clearly shown in Fig. 2. To detach the shell the pin g was pulled, and the shell forced gently out of the socket. This was accomplished by a lanyard j, which led from the boat to the head of the socket, passing back of the head of the shell through the lugs a a, so that when the lanyard was tautened it would force the shell out. A smaller lanyard l, leading to the pin g, was spliced to the lanyard j in such a manner that when the lanyard j was pulled, first the pin and then the shell would come out.

The shell (Fig. 2) contained an air chamber X and a powder chamber Z. The result of this arrangement was that when the shell was detached it assumed a vertical position, with the air chamber uppermost, and, being lighter than its volume of water, it floated gradually toward the surface. At the top of its central shaft or tube was a grape-shot, held in place by a pin p, to which was attached the lanyard s. The pin was a trigger, and the lanyard was known as the trigger-line. Upon pulling the lanyard the pin came out, the shot fell by its own weight upon the nipple, which was covered by a percussion-cap and connected directly with the powder chamber, whereupon the torpedo exploded.

When the spar was not in use it was swung around by means of a stern line, bringing the head of the spar to the stern of the boat. To use the apparatus, the shell was put in place and the spar was swung around head forward; it was then lowered by means of the halliard e to the required depth; the lanyard j was pulled, withdrawing the pin g, and forcing out the shell; finally, when the floating shell had risen to its place, the trigger-line s was pulled and the torpedo fired.

dark mountain of iron in front of us. A heavy fire was at once opened upon us, not only from the ship, but from men stationed on the shore. This did not disable us, and we neared them rapidly. A large fire now blazed upon the bank, and by its light I discovered the unfortunate fact that there was a circle of logs around the *Albemarle*, boomed well out from her side, with the very intention of preventing the action of torpedoes. To examine them more closely, I ran alongside until amidships, received the enemy's fire, and sheered off for the purpose of turning, a hundred yards away, and going at the booms squarely, at right angles, trusting to their having been long enough in the water to have become slimy — in which case my boat, under full headway, would bump up against them and slip over into the pen with the ram. This was my only chance of success, and once over the obstruction my boat would never get out again. As I turned, the whole back of my coat was torn out by buckshot, and the sole of my shoe was carried away. The fire was very severe.

In a lull of the firing, the captain hailed us, again demanding what boat it was. All my men gave comical answers, and mine was a dose of canister from the howitzer. In another instant we had struck the logs and were over, with headway nearly gone, slowly forging up under the enemy's quarter-port. Ten feet from us the muzzle of a rifle gun looked into our faces, and every word of command on board was distinctly heard.

My clothing was perforated with bullets as I stood in the bow, the heel-jigger in my right hand and the exploding-line in the left. We were near enough then, and I ordered the boom lowered until the forward motion of the launch carried the torpedo under the ram's overhang. A strong pull of the detaching-line, a moment's waiting for the torpedo to rise under the hull, and I hauled in the left hand, just cut by a bullet.☆

The explosion took place at the same instant that 100 pounds of grape, at 10 feet range, crashed among us, and the dense mass of water thrown out by the torpedo came down with choking weight upon us.

Twice refusing to surrender, I commanded the men to save themselves; and, throwing off sword, revolver, shoes, and coat, struck out from my disabled and sinking boat into the river. It was cold, long after the frosts, and the water chilled the blood, while the whole surface of the stream was plowed up by grape and musketry, and my nearest friends, the fleet, were twelve miles away; but anything was better than to fall into rebel hands, so I swam for the opposite shore. As I neared it a man [Samuel Higgins, fireman], one of my crew, gave a great gurgling yell and went down.

The rebels were out in boats, picking up my men; and one of the boats, attracted by the sound, pulled in my direction. I heard my own name

☆ In considering the merits of Cushing's success with this exceedingly complicated instrument, it must be remembered that nothing short of the utmost care in preparation could keep its mechanism in working order; that in making ready to use it, it was necessary to keep the end of the spar elevated until the boat had surmounted the boom of logs, and to judge accurately the distance in order to stop the boat's headway at the right point; that the spar had then to be lowered with the same precision of judgment; that the detaching lanyard had then to be pulled firmly, but without a jerk; that, finally, the position of the torpedo under the knuckle of the ram had to be calculated to a nicety, and that by a very gentle strain on a line some twenty-five or thirty feet long the trigger-pin had to be withdrawn. When it is reflected that Cushing had attached to his person four separate lines, viz., the detaching lanyard, the trigger-line, and two lines to direct the movements of the boat, one of which was fastened to the wrist and the other to the ankle of the engineer; that he was also directing the adjustment of the spar by the halliard; that the management of all these lines, requiring as much exactness and delicacy of touch as a surgical operation, where a single error in their employment, even a pull too much or too little, would render the whole expedition abortive, was carried out directly in front of the muzzle of a 100-pounder rifle, under a fire of musketry so hot that several bullets passed through his clothing, and carried out with perfect success, it is safe to say that the naval history of the world affords no other example of such marvelous coolness and professional skill as were shown by Cushing in the destruction of the *Albemarle.*— J. R. SOLEY.

Lieutenant Cushing was a brother of Lieutenant Alonzo H. Cushing, 4th U. S. Artillery, a West Point officer, who was killed at Gettysburg (see Vol. III., p. 390) at the age of twenty-two, having there displayed the greatest gallantry.— EDITORS.

THE BLOWING-UP OF THE "ALBEMARLE."

mentioned, but was not seen. I now "struck out" down the stream, and was soon far enough away again to attempt landing. This time, as I struggled to reach the bank, I heard a groan in the river behind me, and, although very much exhausted, concluded to turn and give all the aid in my power to the officer or seaman who had bravely shared the danger with me.

Swimming in the night, with eye at the level of the water, one can have no idea of distance, and labors, as I did, under the discouraging thought that no headway is made. But if I were to drown that night, I had at least an opportunity of dying while struggling to aid another. Nearing the swimmer, it proved to be Acting Master's Mate Woodman, who said that he could swim no longer. Knocking his cap from his head, I used my right arm to sustain him, and ordered him to strike out. For ten minutes at least, I think, he managed to keep afloat, when, his physical force being completely gone, he sank like a stone.

Again alone upon the water, I directed my course toward the town side of the river, not making much headway, as my strokes were now very feeble, my clothes being soaked and heavy, and little chop-seas splashing with choking persistence into my mouth every time I gasped for breath. Still, there was a determination not to sink, a will not to give up; and I kept up a sort of mechanical motion long after my bodily force was in fact expended. At last, and not a moment too soon, I touched the soft mud, and in the excitement of the first shock I half raised my body and made one step forward; then fell, and remained half in the mud and half in the water until daylight, unable even to crawl on hands and knees, nearly frozen, with my brain in a whirl, but with one thing strong in me—the fixed determination to escape.

As day dawned I found myself in a point of swamp that enters the suburbs of Plymouth, and not forty yards from one of the forts. The sun came out bright and warm, proving a most cheering visitant, and giving me back a good portion of the strength of which I had been deprived before. Its light showed me the town swarming with soldiers and sailors, who moved about excitedly, as if angry at some sudden shock. It was a source of satisfaction to me to know that I had pulled the wire that set all these figures moving, but as I had no desire of being discovered my first object was to get into a dry fringe of rushes that edged the swamp; but to do this required me to pass over thirty or forty feet of open ground, right under the eye of a sentinel who walked the parapet.

Watching until he turned for a moment, I made a dash to cross the space, but was only half-way over when he again turned, and forced me to drop down right between two paths, and almost entirely unshielded. Perhaps I was unobserved because of the mud that covered me and made me blend with the earth; at all events the soldier continued his tramp for some time while I, flat on my back, lay awaiting another chance for action. Soon a party of four men came down the path at my right, two of them being officers, and passed so close to me as almost to tread upon my arm. They were conversing upon the events of the previous night, and were wondering " how it was done," entirely unaware of the presence of one who could give them the information. This proved to me the necessity of regaining the swamp, which I did by sinking my heels and elbows into the earth and forcing my body, inch by inch, toward it. For five hours then, with bare feet, head, and hands, I made my way where I venture to say none ever did before, until I came at last to a clear place, where I might rest upon solid ground. The cypress swamp was a network of thorns and briers that cut into the flesh at every step like knives; frequently, when the soft mire would not bear my weight, I was forced to throw my body upon it at length, and haul myself along by the arms. Hands and feet were raw when I reached the clearing, and yet my difficulties were but commenced. A working-party of soldiers was in the opening, engaged in sinking some schooners in the river to obstruct the channel. I passed twenty yards in their rear through a corn furrow, and gained some woods below. Here I encountered a negro, and after serving out to him twenty dollars in greenbacks and some texts of Scripture (two powerful arguments with an old darkey), I had confidence enough in his fidelity to send him into town for news of the ram.

When he returned, and there was no longer doubt that she had gone down, I went on again, and plunged into a swamp so thick that I had only the sun for a guide and could not see ten feet in advance. About 2 o'clock in the afternoon I came out from the dense mass of reeds upon the bank of one of the deep, narrow streams that abound there, and right opposite to the only road in the vicinity. It seemed providential, for, thirty yards above or below, I never should have seen the road, and might have struggled on until, worn out and starved, I should find a never-to-be-discovered grave. As it was, my fortune had led me to where a picket party of seven soldiers were posted, having a little flat-bottomed, square-ended skiff toggled to the root of a cypress-tree that squirmed like a snake in the inky water. Watching them until they went back a few yards to eat, I crept into the stream and swam over, keeping the big tree between myself and them, and making for the skiff. Gaining the bank, I quietly cast loose the boat and floated behind it some thirty yards around the first bend, where I got in and paddled away as only a man could whose liberty was at stake.

Hour after hour I paddled, never ceasing for a moment, first on one side, then on the other, while sunshine passed into twilight and that was swallowed up in thick darkness only relieved by the few faint star rays that penetrated the heavy swamp curtain on either side. At last I reached the mouth of the Roanoke, and found the open sound before me. My frail boat could not have lived in the ordinary sea there, but it chanced to be very calm, leaving only a slight swell, which was, however, sufficient to influence my boat, so that I was forced to paddle all upon one side to keep her on the intended course.

THE WRECK OF THE "ALBEMARLE." FROM A PHOTOGRAPH.

After steering by a star for perhaps two hours for where I thought the fleet might be, I at length discovered one of the vessels, and after a long time got within hail. My "Ship ahoy!" was given with the last of my strength, and I fell powerless, with a splash, into the water in the bottom of my boat, and awaited results. I had paddled every minute for ten successive hours, and for four my body had been "asleep," with the exception of my arms and brain. The picket-vessel, *Valley City*, upon hearing the hail, at once got under way, at the same time lowering boats and taking precaution against torpedoes. It was some time before they would pick me up, being convinced that I was the rebel conductor of an infernal machine, and that Lieutenant Cushing had died the night before. At last I was on board, had imbibed a little brandy and water, and was on my way to the flag-ship.

As soon as it became known that I had returned, rockets were thrown up and all hands were called to cheer ship; and when I announced success, all the commanding officers were summoned on board to deliberate upon a plan of attack. In the morning I was well again in every way, with the exception of hands and feet, and had the pleasure of exchanging shots with the batteries that I had inspected the day before. I was sent in the *Valley City* to report to Admiral Porter at Hampton Roads, and soon after Plymouth and the whole district of the Albemarle, deprived of the iron-clad's protection, fell an easy prey to Commander Macomb and our fleet. ‖

‖ The list of officers and men on board Picket-boat No. 1, on the expedition of October 27th, 1864, with the vessels to which they were officially attached, was as follows: Lieutenant William B. Cushing, commanding, *Monticello;* Acting Assistant Paymaster Francis H. Swan, *Otsego;* Acting

Ensign William L. Howarth, *Monticello;* Acting Master's Mate John Woodman, *Commodore Hull;* Acting Master's Mate Thomas S. Gay, *Otsego;* Acting Third Assistant Engineer William Stotesbury, Picket-boat; Acting Third Assistant Engineer Charles L. Steever, *Otsego;* Samuel Higgins, first-class fireman, Picket-boat; Richard Hamilton, coal-heaver, *Shamrock;* William Smith, ordinary seaman, *Chicopee;* Bernard Harley, ordinary seaman, *Chicopee;* Edward J. Houghton, ordinary seaman, *Chicopee;* Lorenzo Deming, landsman, Picket-boat; Henry Wilkes, landsman, Picket-boat; Robert H. King, landsman, Picket-boat. Cushing and Howarth, together with those designated as attached to the "Picket-boat," were the original seven who brought the boat down from New York. Cushing and Houghton escaped, Woodman and Higgins were drowned, and the remaining eleven were captured.

For his exploit Lieutenant Cushing received the congratulations of the Navy Department, and also the thanks of Congress, and was promoted to the grade of lieutenant-commander.

The *Albemarle* was afterward raised, towed to Norfolk, and in 1867 there stripped and sold.

EDITORS.

Lieutenant Cushing reached the *Valley City* about midnight on the night of October 28th-29th. On the next day, the 29th, at 11:15 A. M., Commander Macomb got under way, and his fleet proceeded up the Roanoke River. Upon the arrival of the fleet at the wreck of the *Southfield*, after exchanging shots with the lower batteries, it was found that the enemy had effectually obstructed the channel by sinking schooners alongside the wreck, and the expedition was therefore compelled to return.

On the next day, Commander Macomb, having ascertained from a reconnoissance by the *Valley City* that Middle River offered a clear passage, determined to approach Plymouth by that route. The expedition threaded the channel, shelling Plymouth across the woods on the intervening neck of land on its way up, until it reached the head of Middle River and passed into the Roanoke, where it lay all night.

At 9:30 on the morning of the 31st of October the line was formed, the *Commodore Hull* being placed in advance, as her ferry-boat construction enabled her to fire ahead. The *Whitehead*, which had arrived with stores just before the attack, was lashed to the *Tacony*, and the tugs *Bazley* and *Belle* to the *Shamrock* and *Otsego*, to afford motive power in case of accident to the machinery. Signal was

made to "Go ahead fast," and soon after 11 the fleet was hotly engaged with the batteries on shore, which were supported by musketry from rifle-pits and houses. After a spirited action of an hour at

CAPTAIN ALEXANDER F. WARLEY, C. S. N.

short range, receiving and returning a sharp fire of shell, grape, and canister, the *Shamrock* planted a shell in the enemy's magazine, which blew up, whereupon the Confederates hastily abandoned their works. In a short time Plymouth was entirely in possession of the Union forces. The casualties on the Union side were six killed and nine wounded.

The vessels engaged were as follows: DOUBLE-ENDERS: *Shamrock*, Commander W. H. Macomb, commanding division, Lieutenant Rufus K. Duer, executive officer; *Otsego*, Lieutenant-Commander H. N. T. Arnold; *Wyalusing*, Lieutenant-Commander Earl English; *Tacony*, Lieutenant-Commander W. T. Truxtun. FERRY-BOAT: *Commodore Hull*, Acting Master Francis Josselyn. GUN-BOAT: *Whitehead*, Acting Master G. W. Barrett. TUGS: *Belle*, Acting Master James G. Green; *Bazley*, Acting Master Mark D. Ames. The *Chicopee*, Commander A. D. Harrell, and *Valley City*, Acting Master J. A. J. Brooks, were not present at the second and final demonstration.—J. R. SOLEY.

NOTE ON THE DESTRUCTION OF THE "ALBEMARLE."

BY HER CAPTAIN, A. F. WARLEY, C. S. N.

WHEN I took command of the Confederate States iron-clad *Albemarle* I found her made fast to the river bank nearly abreast of the town of Plymouth. She was surrounded by a cordon of single cypress logs chained together, about ten feet from her side. There was no reason why the place might not be recaptured any day: the guns com-

manding the river were in no condition for use, and the troops in charge of them were worn down by ague, and were undrilled and worthless.

When I had been about a month at Plymouth the troops were relieved by a new set. On the day of their arrival I heard of a steam-launch having been seen in the river, and I informed the officer in command of the fact, and at the same time told him that the safety of the place depended on the *Albemarle,* and the safety of the *Albemarle* depended on the watchfulness of his pickets.

The crew of the *Albemarle* numbered but sixty, too small a force to allow me to keep an armed watch on deck at night and to do outside picketing besides. Moreover, to break the monotony of the life and keep down ague, I had always out an expedition of ten men, who were uniformly successful in doing a fair amount of damage to the enemy.

The officer in command of the troops was inclined to give me all assistance, and sent a picket of twenty-five men under a lieutenant; they were furnished with rockets and had a field-piece. This picket was stationed on board of a schooner about gun-shot below the *Albemarle,* where an attempt was being made to raise a vessel (the *Southfield*) sunk at the time of Commander Cooke's dash down the river. Yet on the night of the 27th of October Cushing's steam-launch ran alongside the schooner unobserved by the picket, without a sound or signal, and then steamed up to the *Albemarle.*

It was about 3 A. M. The night was dark and slightly rainy, and the launch was close to us when we hailed and the alarm was given — so close that the gun could not be depressed enough to reach her; so the crew were sent in the shield with muskets, and kept up a heavy fire on the launch as she slowly forced her way over the chain of logs and ranged by us within a few feet. As she reached the bow of the *Albemarle* I heard a report as of an unshotted gun, and a piece of wood fell at my feet. Calling the carpenter, I told him a torpedo had been exploded, and ordered him to examine and report to me, saying nothing to any one else. He soon reported "a hole

in her bottom big enough to drive a wagon in." By this time I heard voices from the launch: "We surrender," etc., etc., etc. I stopped our fire and sent out Mr. Long, who brought back all those who had been in the launch except the gallant captain and three of her crew, all of whom took to the water. Having seen to their safety, I turned my attention to the *Albemarle* and found her resting on the bottom in eight feet of water, her upper works above water.

That is the way the *Albemarle* was destroyed, and a more gallant thing was not done during the war. After her destruction, failing to convince the officer in command of the troops that he could not hold the place, I did my best to help defend it. Half of my crew went down and obstructed the river by sinking the schooner at the wreck, and with the other half I had two 8-inch guns commanding the upper river put into serviceable order, relaid platforms, fished out tackles from the *Albemarle,* got a few shells, etc., and waited. I did not have to wait long. The fleet steamed up to the obstructions, fired a few shells over the town, steamed down again, and early next morning rounding the island were in the river and opened fire.

The two 8-inch guns worked by Mr. Long and Mr. Shelley did their duty, and I think did all that was done in the defense of Plymouth. The fire of the fleet was concentrated on us, and one at least of the steamers was so near that I could hear the orders given to elevate or depress the guns. When I felt that by hanging on I could only sacrifice my men and achieve nothing, I ordered our guns spiked and the men sent round to the road by a ravine. The crew left me by Captain Maffitt were good and true men, and stuck by me to the last.

THE DEFENSE OF FORT FISHER.

BY ITS COMMANDER, WILLIAM LAMB, COLONEL, C. S. A.

THE capture of Fort Fisher, N. C., on the 15th of January, 1865, was followed so quickly by the final dissolution of the Southern Confederacy that the great victory was not fully realized by the American people. The position commanded the last gateway between the Confederate States and the outside world. [See outline map, p. 629; also map, p. 694.] Its capture, with the resulting loss of all the Cape Fear River defenses, and of Wilmington, the great importing depot of the South, effectually ended all blockade-running. Lee sent me word that Fort Fisher must be held, or he could not subsist his army.

The indentation of the Atlantic Ocean in the Carolina coast known as Onslow Bay and the Cape Fear River running south from Wilmington form the peninsula known as Federal Point, which, during the civil war, was called Confederate Point. Not quite seven miles north of the end of this peninsula stood a high sand-hill called the "Sugar Loaf." Here there was an intrenched camp for the Army of Wilmington, under General Braxton Bragg, the department commander, that was hid from the sea by forest and sand-hills. From this intrenched camp the river bank, with a neighboring ridge

of sand-dunes, formed a covered way for troops to within a hundred yards of the left salient of Fort Fisher. Between this road and the ocean beach was an arm of Masonboro' Sound, and where it ended, three miles north of the fort, were occasional fresh-water swamps, generally wooded with scrub growth, and in many places quite impassable. Along the ocean shore was an occasional battery formed from a natural sand-hill, behind which Whitworth guns were carried from the fort to cover belated blockade-runners, or to protect more unfortunate ones that had been chased ashore. About half a mile north of the fort there was a rise in the plain forming a hill some twenty feet above the tide on the river side, and on this was a redoubt commanding the approach to the fort by the river road. Thus Nature, assisted by some slight engineering work, had given a defense to Confederate Point which would have enabled an efficient commander at the intrenched camp, co-operating with the garrison of Fort Fisher, to have rendered the Point untenable for a largely superior force at night when the covering fire of the Federal navy could not distinguish between friend and foe. [See General Bragg's statement, note, p. 654.]

At the land-face of Fort Fisher, five miles from the intrenched camp, the peninsula was about half a mile wide. This face commenced about a hundred feet from the river with a half bastion, and extended with a heavy curtain to a full bastion on the ocean side, where it joined the sea-face. The work was built to withstand the heaviest artillery fire. There was no moat with scarp and counterscarp, so essential for defense against storming parties, the shifting sands rendering its construction impossible with the material available. The outer slope was twenty feet high from the berme to the top of the parapet, at an angle of 45°, and was sodded with marsh grass, which grew luxuriantly. The parapet was not less than twenty-five feet thick, with an inclination of only one foot. The revetment was five feet nine inches high from the floor of the gun-chambers, and these were some twelve feet or more from the interior plane. The guns were all mounted in barbette, on Columbiad carriages; there was not a single case-mated gun in the fort. Experience had taught that casemates of timber and sand-bags were a delusion and a snare against heavy projectiles; and there was no iron to construct them with. Between the gun-chambers, containing one or two guns each (there were twenty heavy guns on the land-face), there were heavy traverses, exceeding in size any known to engineers, to protect from an enfilading fire. They extended out some twelve feet on the parapet, and were twelve feet or more in height above the parapet, running back thirty feet or more. The gun-chambers were reached from the rear by steps. In each traverse was an alternate magazine or bomb-proof, the latter ventilated by an air-chamber. Passageways penetrated the traverses in the interior of the work, forming additional bomb-proofs for the reliefs for the guns.

The sea-face for a hundred yards from the north-east bastion was of the same massive character as the land-face. A crescent battery [see p. 649], intended for four guns, joined this. It had been originally built of palmetto logs and tarred sand-bags and sand revetted with sod; but the logs had decayed, and it was converted into a hospital bomb-proof. In its rear a heavy curtain was thrown up to protect the chambers from fragments of shells. From this bomb-proof a series of batteries extended for three-quarters of a mile along the sea, connected by an infantry curtain. These batteries had heavy traverses, but were not more than ten or twelve feet high to the top of the parapets, and were built for ricochet firing. On this line was a bomb-proof electric battery connected with a system of submarine torpedoes. Farther along, where the channel ran close to the beach, inside the bar, a mound battery 60

feet high was erected, with two heavy guns, which had a plunging fire on the channel; this was connected with the battery north of it by a light curtain. Following the line of the works, it was over one mile from the mound to the north-east bastion at the angle of the sea and land faces, and upon this line twenty-four heavy guns were mounted. From the mound for nearly a mile to the end of the point was a level sand-plain scarcely three feet above high tide, and much of it was submerged during gales. At the point was Battery Buchanan, four guns, in the shape of an ellipse, commanding the inlet, its two 11-inch guns covering the approach by land. It was garrisoned by a detachment from the Confederate States navy. An advanced redoubt with a 24-pounder was added after the attack by the forces under General Butler and Admiral Porter on Christmas, 1864. A wharf for large steamers was in close proximity to these works. Battery Buchanan was a citadel to which an overpowered garrison might retreat and with proper transportation be safely carried off at night, and to which reënforcements could be sent under the cover of darkness.

Thus Fort Fisher, being designed to withstand the heaviest bombardment, was extremely difficult to defend against assault after its guns were destroyed. The soldiers in the gun-chambers could not see the approach in front for a hundred feet, and to repel assailants they had to leave all cover and stand upon the open parapet.

As a defense against infantry there was a system of sub-terra torpedoes extending across the peninsula, five to six hundred feet from the land-face, and so disconnected that the explosion of one would not affect the others; inside the torpedoes, about fifty feet from the berme of the work, extending from river bank to sea-shore, was a heavy palisade of sharpened logs nine feet high pierced for musketry, and so laid out as to have an enfilading fire on the center, where there was a redoubt, guarding a sally-port, from which two Napoleons were run out, as occasion required. At the river end of the palisade was a deep and muddy slough, across which was a bridge, the entrance of the river road into the fort; commanding this bridge was a Napoleon gun. There were three mortars in rear of the land-face.

It was after a careful reconnoissance on December 25th, 1864, having drawn our fire by an advance of his skirmish-line to within 75 yards of the fort, that General Godfrey Weitzel, finding the works substantially uninjured by the explosion of the powder-ship [see p. 655] and the two days' terrific bombardment of Porter's great armada, reported to Butler that the fort could not be carried by assault.‡ In the works on that afternoon were

---

§ When I assumed command of Fort Fisher, July 4th, 1862, it was composed of several detached earth-works, with a casemated battery of sand and palmetto logs, mounting four guns and with only one heavy gun in the works. The frigate *Minnesota* could have destroyed the works and driven us out in a few hours. I immediately went to work. and with 500 colored laborers, assisted by the garrison, constructed the largest earth-work in the Southern Confederacy, of heavy timbers covered by sand from 15 to 20 feet deep and sodded with

turf. The fort was far from complete when it was attacked, especially as against an assault by land; the sides exposed to the sea being first constructed, on the theory that the Army of Wilmington would prevent an investment.—W. L.

‡ General B. F. Butler in his report of the operations of his troops, says in part:

"Brevet Brigadier-General [N. M.] Curtis, who deserves well for his gallantry and conduct, immediately pushed up his brigade within a few hundred yards of Fort Fisher, captur-

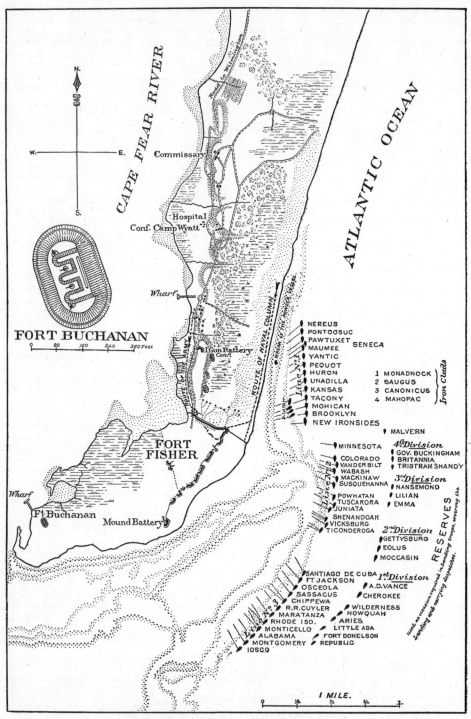

MAP OF THE NAVAL AND MILITARY ATTACKS ON FORT FISHER, JANUARY 15, 1865, SHOWING
DIRECTION OF FIRE OF UNION VESSELS.

NOTE.—The flag-ship *Malvern* (placed on the map behind the *New Ironsides*) had no fixed position.

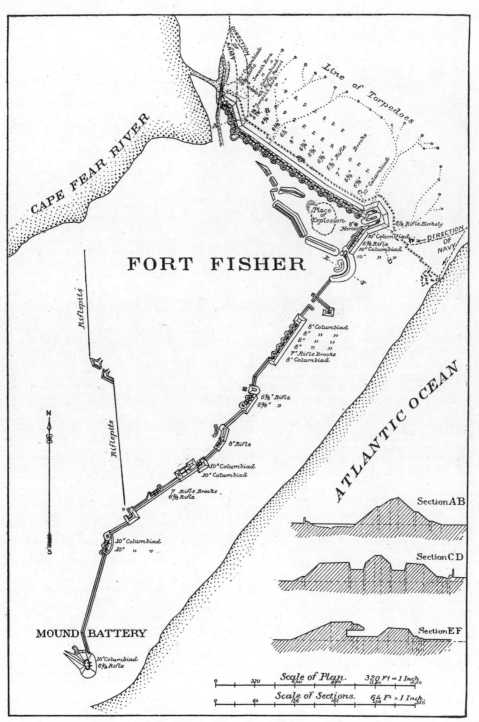

CAPE FEAR RIVER

FORT FISHER

DIRECTION OF ARMY

Line of Torpedoes

Place of Explosion

Mortar

6⅜" Rifle Blakely

10" Columbiad
6⅜" Rifle
10" Columbiad
10" "

DIRECTION OF NAVY

8" Columbiad
8" " "
8" " "
8" " "
7" Rifle Brooks
8" Columbiad

6⅜" Rifle
6⅜" "

8" Rifle

10" Columbiad
10" Columbiad

7" Rifle Brooks
6⅜" Rifle

10" Columbiad
10" " "

Riflepits

Riflepits

N

S

ATLANTIC OCEAN

Section A B

Section C D

Section E F

MOUND BATTERY

10" Columbiad
6⅜" Rifle

Scale of Plan.
320 Ft = 1 Inch

Scale of Sections.
64 Ft = 1 Inch

PLAN AND SECTIONS OF FORT FISHER.

COLONEL WILLIAM LAMB, C. S. A. FROM A PHOTOGRAPH.

over 900 veteran troops and 450 junior reserves, reënforced after dark by 60 sailors and marines. As soon as the fire of the fleet ceased, the parapets were not only manned, but half the garrison was

stationed outside the work behind the palisades. There was no fear of an assault in front; what most disturbed the defenders was a possible landing from boats between the Mound Battery and Battery Buchanan. Admiral Porter was as much to blame as General Butler for the repulse. ↓

The garrison of Fort Fisher was composed altogether of North Carolinians. For two years and a half the force had been under my command, and in that time only two companies, temporarily there, were from outside the State. After the repulse of Butler and Porter, although some important guns were destroyed by the bombardment and by explosion, little or nothing was done to repair damages or strengthen the armament of the work. Requisitions were made for additional ammunition, especially for hand-grenades, to repel assault, but it was impossible to obtain what was needed. Application was made for the placing of marine torpedoes where the iron-clads had anchored, and whither they returned, but no notice was taken of it. Although we heard on January 8th that the fleet had returned to Beaufort, and we knew that Fort Fisher was still its objective point, General Braxton Bragg [see note, Vol. III., p. 711] withdrew the supporting army from Sugar Loaf and marched it to a camp sixteen miles distant, north

ing the Half-moon battery and its men, who were taken off by the boats of the navy. In the meantime the remainder of Ames's division had captured 218 men and 10 commissioned officers of the North Carolina reserves and other prisoners. From them I learned that Kirkland's and Hagood's brigades of Hoke's division had left the front of the Army of the James, near Richmond, and were then within two miles of the rear of my forces, and their skirmishers were then actually engaged, and that the remainder of Hoke's division had come the night before to Wilmington, and were then on the march, if they had not already arrived. General Weitzel reported to me that to assault the work, in his judgment, and in that of the experienced officers of his command who had been on the skirmish-line, with any prospect of success, was impossible. This opinion coincided with my own, and much as I regretted the necessity of abandoning the attempt, yet the path of duty was plain. Not so strong a work as Fort Fisher had been taken by assault during the war, and I had to guide me the experience of Port Hudson, with its slaughtered thousands in the repulsed assault, and the double assault of Fort Wagner, where thousands were sacrificed in an attempt to take a work less strong than Fisher, after it had been subjected to a more continued and fully as severe fire. And in neither of the instances I have mentioned had the assaulting force in its rear, as I had, an army of the enemy larger than itself. I therefore ordered that no assault should be made, and that the troops should re-embark."   EDITORS.

↓ General Butler was blamed by contemporaneous writers for not capturing the works. For this criticism he had himself to blame. On the evening of the 25th, before waiting for official reports, he listened to camp gossip and wrote to Admiral Porter:

"General Weitzel advanced his skirmish-line within fifty yards of the fort, while the garrison was kept in their bomb-proofs by the fire of the navy, and so closely that three or four men of the picket-line ventured upon the parapet and through the sally-port of the work, capturing a horse,

which they brought off, killing the orderly, who was the bearer of a dispatch from the chief of artillery of General Whiting, to bring a light battery within the fort, and also brought away from the parapet the flag of the fort."

This piece of romance was sent North, and has gotten a lodgment in current history, and is actually repeated by General Grant in his "Memoirs," though General Butler corrected the error in his official report of January 3d, 1865. No Federal soldier entered Fort Fisher Christmas day, except as a prisoner. The courier was sent out of the fort without my knowledge, and was killed and his horse captured within the enemy's lines. The flag captured was a small company flag, placed on the extreme left of the work, and which was carried away and thrown off the parapet by an enfilading shot from the navy. It was during a terrific bombardment of the land-face, when I had ordered my men to cover themselves behind parapet and traverses as well as in the bomb-proofs. Amid the smoke of bursting shells, Captain W. H. Walling, of the 142d New York, gallantly crawled through the broken palisade and carried off the flag, doing what two or more men could not have done without observation. The angle of the work hid him from the sharp-shooters on the front, who, from behind traverses, were watching for an advance.

When Butler's skirmish-line approached I purposely withheld the fire of infantry and artillery until an attack should be made in force. Only one gun on the land-face had been seriously disabled [see p. 658], and I could have opened a fire of grape and canister on the narrow beach, which no troops could have survived. In the second attack by the army, as the reader will see, all my heavy guns on the land-face but one were disabled; my torpedoes were useless, and my palisades were so torn up and cut down that they furnished a protection to the assailants instead of a formidable impediment.—W. L.

VIEW OF THE LAND FRONT FROM THE SECOND TRAVERSE OF THE NORTH-WEST SALIENT.
FROM A PHOTOGRAPH TAKEN AFTER THE CAPTURE.

The indentation of the palisades in the middle-ground marks the position of the sally-port. Beyond is seen
the north-east salient, overlooking the sea.

of Wilmington, and there had a grand review. The fort was not even advised of the coming of the fleet, which should have been seen off Masonboro' during the day; and its arrival was reported from Fort Fisher to headquarters in Wilmington.

The night of the 12th of January, from the ramparts of Fort Fisher, I saw the great armada returning. My mounted pickets had informed me of its coming. I began at once to put my works in order for action. I had but 800 men,—the 36th North Carolina,—at least 100 of whom were not fit for duty. Sunrise the next morning revealed to us the most formidable armada the world had ever known, supplemented by transports carrying about 8500 troops. Suddenly that long line of floating fortresses rained shot and shell, upon fort and beach and wooded hills, causing the very earth and sea to tremble. I had telegraphed for reënforcements, and during the day and night following about 700 arrived,—companies of light and heavy artillery, North Carolina troops, and some 50 sailors and marines of the Confederate States navy,—giving me 1500, all told, up to the morning of January 15th, including the sick and slightly wounded. On Friday, the 13th, in the midst of the bombardment, General W. H. C. Whiting, the district commander, and his staff, arrived in the fort. They had walked up from Battery Buchanan. I did not know of their approach until the general came to me on the works and remarked, "Lamb,

my boy, I have come to share your fate. You and your garrison are to be sacrificed." I replied, "Don't say so, General; we shall certainly whip the enemy again." He then told me that when he left Wilmington General Bragg was hastily removing his stores and ammunition, and was looking for a place to fall back upon.♭ I offered him the command, although he came unarmed and without orders; but he refused, saying he would counsel with me, but would leave me to conduct the defense.

In the former bombardment the fire of the fleet had been diffuse, not calculated to effect any particular damage, and so wild that at least one-third of the missiles fell in the river beyond the fort or in the bordering marshes; but now the fire was concentrated, and the definite object of the fleet was the destruction of the land defenses by enfilade and direct fire, and the ships took position accordingly. When attacked in December, I had had for my 44 heavy guns and three mortars not over 3600 shot and shell; and for the most effective gun in the work, the 150-pounder Armstrong, there were but 13 shells, and we had no other ammunition that could be used in it. The frigates *Minnesota* and *Wabash* each had an armament superior to ours, and these two vessels alone fired more shot and shell at the works in the last attack than we had, all told or on hand, in both engagements. During the time between the two expeditions we had begged for more ammunition, but

♭ In a report to General Lee, dictated at Fort Fisher January 18th, 1865, and in another (inclosing the first one) dated Fort Columbus, New York Harbor, February 19th, 1865, General Whiting blames General Bragg for the loss of Fort Fisher, and asks that the latter's conduct be investigated. He says: "I went into the fort with the conviction that it was to be sacrificed, for the last I heard General Bragg say, was to point out

a line to fall back on if Fort Fisher fell." General Bragg was "charged with the command and defense of Wilmington," by the Secretary of War, on January 13th; and General Whiting concludes with a feeling reference to the fact that he was not allowed to conduct the defense of "a harbor on which I had expended for two years all the labor and skill I had."— EDITORS.

INTERIOR VIEW OF THE THREE TRAVERSES OF THE NORTH-WEST SALIENT, ADJOINING THE RIVER ROAD. [SEE MAP, P. 645.] FROM A PHOTOGRAPH.

none came except a few useless bolts designed for the Armstrong gun. In the former fight we had fired 1272 shot and shell; leaving about 2328, exclusive of grape and shrapnel, to resist a passage of the ships and an assault by land. I was obliged to husband my ammunition even more than in the previous battle, and therefore gave the same orders that each gun should be fired only once every half-hour until disabled or destroyed, except when special orders were given to concentrate on a particular vessel, or in case an attempt were made to cross the bar and run in, when every available gun should be used with all possible effectiveness. It was this slow firing from the fort, at times not over forty-four guns in thirty minutes, compared to the naval fire of from one to two guns a second, that gave the navy the erroneous idea that they had silenced the fort. But no attempt was made to run by the fort, which was a great surprise to us. Occasionally a wooden vessel, more daring than her consorts, would come close in, when the guns of several batteries would be concentrated upon her and she would be quickly withdrawn more or less injured.

All day and night on the 13th and 14th of January the navy continued its ceaseless torment; it was impossible to repair damages at night on the land-face. The *Ironsides* and monitors bowled their eleven and fifteen inch shells along the parapet, scattering shrapnel in the darkness. We could scarcely gather up and bury our dead without fresh casualties. At least two hundred had been killed and wounded in the two days since the fight began. Only three or four of my land guns were of any service. The Federal army had been approaching on the river side during the day; but they were more or less covered by the formation of the land, and we could only surmise their number. I had seen them pass Craig's Landing near my cottage and occupy the redoubt about half a mile from the fort. We had fired some shot and shell at their approaching columns, but it was at a fearful cost of limb and life that a land gun was discharged; for to fire from that face was to draw upon the gunners the fury of the fleet. Early in the afternoon, to my astonishment, I saw a Confederate flat-bottomed steam-transport, loaded with stores,

approaching Craig's Landing, which was now in the enemy's lines. I had a gun fired toward her to warn her off, but on she came, unconscious of her danger, and she fell an easy captive in the enemy's hands. Shortly after, the Confederate steamer *Chickamauga*, which had been annoying the enemy from the river, fired into and sank the stupid craft. This incident gave me the first intimation that we were deserted. From the conformation of the Cape Fear River, General Bragg could have passed safely from Sugar Loaf toward Smithfield, and with a glass could have seen everything on the beach and in the fort, and in person or through an aide, with the steamers at his command, could have detected every movement of the enemy; but now, thirty-six hours after the fight had commenced, several hours after Craig's Landing had been in the possession of the enemy, he

LIEUTENANT WILEY H. WILLIFORD, C. S. A.
FROM A PHOTOGRAPH.

sent into the enemy's lines a steamer full of sorely needed stores, which at night could have gone to Battery Buchanan in safety. We had both telegraphic and signal communication between Fort Fisher and Sugar Loaf, Bragg's headquarters, and I got General Whiting to telegraph him to attack the enemy under cover of night when the fleet could not coöperate, and we would do the same from the fort, and that thus we could capture a portion or the whole of the force, or at least demoralize it. No reply was received. Still I thought General Bragg could not fail to respond; so, after the dead were buried, ten companies were put in readiness for a sortie, and I carried Captain Patterson's company out in front of the work beyond the palisade line and the range of the enemy's fire, and threw them out as skirmishers with orders to discover the position of the enemy. We

the order, and with effectiveness, but at a sad sacrifice in killed and wounded. At the same time on the ocean side a column of sailors and marines were seen approaching, throwing up slight trenches to protect their advance. On these we brought to bear our single heavy gun, while the two guns on the mound battery turned their attention from the sailors afloat to the sailors on shore, but at too long range to be very effective. Hagood's brigade, sent by Bragg, was now arriving at Battery Buchanan, but the steamer bearing them was driven off by the fire of the fleet after it had succeeded in landing two South Carolina regiments, which came at a double-quick to the mound under a heavy fire. The number of these reënforcements was

INTERIOR VIEW OF THE NORTH-EAST ANGLE. FROM A PHOTOGRAPH.

On the left is the interior slope of the land-face, adjoining the north-east salient. The crescent battery is shown on the right, its bomb-proofs being used as a hospital. In the foreground, toward the right, was the reserve magazine that was exploded.

found none on the sea-shore within half a mile, but on the river-shore they were occupying the redoubt, where their skirmishers extended toward the left of the fort. Some of them fired on us, but we remained there awaiting a message from Bragg, or the sound of his guns from the north, but in vain, and before daylight we retired to the fort.

With the rising sun, on the 15th, the fleet, which had been annoying us all through the night, redoubled its fire on the land-face. The sea was calm, the naval gunners had become accurate by practice, and before noon but one heavy gun, protected by the angle of the north-east bastion, remained serviceable on that face. The harvest of wounded and dead was increased, and at noon I had not 1200 men to defend the long line of works. The enemy were now preparing to assault; we saw their skirmish-line on the left digging rifle-pits close to our torpedo lines and their columns along the river-shore massing for the attack, while their sharp-shooters were firing upon every head that showed itself upon our front. Despite the imminent danger to the gunners I ordered the two Napoleons at the central sally-port and the Napoleon on the left to fire grape and canister upon the advancing skirmish-line. They fearlessly obeyed

reported to me by the officer in command as 350. They reached the fort less than thirty minutes before the attacking columns came like avalanches upon our right and left. The South Carolinians were out of breath and more or less disorganized and demoralized by the ordeal through which, by Bragg's neglect, they had been forced to pass. I sent them to an old commissary bomb-proof to recover breath.

My headquarters during the fight were the pulpit battery on the sea-face, one hundred yards from the north-east salient and adjoining the hospital bomb-proof, commanding the best view of the approaches to the land-face. At half-past two, as I was returning from another battery, Private Arthur Muldoon, one of my lookouts, called to me, "Colonel, the enemy are about to charge." I informed General Whiting, who was near, and at my request he immediately telegraphed General Bragg, at "Sugar Loaf":

"The enemy are about to assault; they outnumber us heavily. We are just manning our parapets. Fleet have extended down the sea-front outside and are firing very heavily. Enemy on the beach in front of us in very heavy force, not more than seven hundred yards from us. Nearly all land guns disabled. Attack! Attack! It is all I can say and all you can do." ¶

¶ The original, in Whiting's handwriting, is in possession of Dr. Geo. L. Porter, Bridgeport, Conn.—W. L.

THE BOMBARDMENT OF FORT FISHER, AS SEEN FROM THE MOUND BATTERY. FROM A WAR-TIME SKETCH.

I then passed hurriedly down in rear of the land-face and through the galleries, and although the fire of the fleet was terrific, I knew it must soon cease, and I ordered additional sharp-shooters to the gun-chambers with instructions to pick off the officers in the assaulting columns, and directed the battery commanders to form their detachments and rush to the top of the parapets when the firing stopped and drive the assailants back. As I returned, I instructed the squads that were forming under cover to rally to the parapets as soon as the order should be given, to which they responded with enthusiasm. I had determined to allow the assailants to reach the berme of the work before exploding a line of torpedoes, believing it would enable us to kill or capture the first line, while destroying or demoralizing their supporting lines of assault. I had not quite reached my headquarters when the roar of artillery suddenly ceased, and instantly the steam-whistles of the vast fleet sounded a charge. It was a soul-stirring signal both to besiegers and besieged.

I ordered my aide, Lieutenant Charles H. Blocker, to double-quick the 21st and 25th South Carolina to reënforce Major James Reilly, whom I had put in command on the left, while I went to the north-east salient, which I believed to be the vital point of the work and the one which needed most protection. I rallied there the larger portion of the garrison of the main work, putting 300 men on top of the bastion and adjoining parapets and holding some 200 more in the adjoining batteries. About 250 remained for defense on the left, to which I supposed the 350 South Carolinians would immediately be added, and these with the Napoleon and the torpedoes I felt sure would successfully defend that portion of the work. The assaulting line on the right was directed at the angle or point of the L, and consisted of two thousand sailors and marines, ☆ the greater portion of whom had flanked my torpedo lines by keeping close to the sea. Ordering the mound battery, and any other on the sea-face that could do so, to fire upon them, and the two Napoleons at the sally-port to join our Columbiad in pouring grape and canister into their ranks, I held in reserve the infantry fire. Whiting stood upon the brink of the parapet inspiring those about him. The sailors and marines reached the berme and some sprang up the slope, but a murderous fire greeted them and swept them down. Volley after volley was poured into their faltering ranks by cool, determined men, and in half an hour several hundred dead and wounded lay at the foot of the bastion. The bravery of the officers could not restrain their men from panic and retreat, and with small loss to ourselves we witnessed what had never been seen before, a disorderly rout of American sailors and marines. Had the fleet helped their own column as they did afterward that of the army, theirs would have been the glory of victory.

As our shouts of triumph went up I turned to look at the western salient, and saw, to my astonishment, three Federal battle-flags upon our ramparts. General Whiting saw them at the same moment, and, calling on the men to pull down those flags and drive the enemy from the work, rushed toward them on the parapet. Among those who followed Whiting, and who gave his young life upon those ramparts, I must mention the brave Lieutenant Williford, who commanded the Blakely battery.

In order to make a careful reconnoissance of the position of the enemy, I passed through the sally-port, and outside of the work witnessed a savage hand-to-hand conflict for the possession of the fourth gun-chamber from the left bastion. My men, led by Whiting, had driven the standard-bearer from the top of the traverse and the enemy from the parapet in front. They had recovered the gun-chamber with great slaughter, and on the parapet and on the long traverse of the next gun-chamber the contestants were savagely firing into each other's faces, and in some cases clubbing their guns, being too close to load and fire. Whiting had quickly been wounded by two shots and had been carried to the hospital bomb-proof. I saw that the Confederates were exposed not only to the fire in front, but to a galling infantry fire from the captured salient. I saw also a fresh force pouring into the left of the work, now offering no resistance. I doubt if ever before the commander of a work went outside of it and looked back upon the conflict for its possession; but from the peculiar construction of the works it was necessary to do so in order to see the exact position of affairs. I was in front of the sally-port and concealed from the army by a fragment of the palisade. ⏐

extreme left and had been repulsed by the fire of the Napoleon and by the infantry; that the torpedo wires had been cut by the fire of the fleet and the electrician had tried in vain to execute my orders; that, driven from the extreme left, the enemy had found a weak defense between the left salient and the sally-port in their third charge, and had gained the parapet and, capturing two gun-chambers, had attacked the force in the left bastion on the flank, simultaneously with a direct charge of a fresh column, and that our men after great slaughter, especially those at the Napoleon, had been forced to surrender just as we had repulsed the naval column; that to add to the discomfiture of the Confederates, as soon as the Federal battle-flags appeared on the ramparts, Battery Buchanan had opened with its two heavy guns on the left of the work, killing and wounding friend and foe alike. Major Reilly had failed to lead the men to the top of the parapet on the right of the western salient, firing instead from the two gun-chambers on the assailants, who were not within range until they reached the parapet. Had the parapet been manned by fifty determined men at this point, I do not believe the enemy could have got into the fort before reënforcements had arrived. Reilly was a veteran soldier, and showed his indomitable courage later in the day, but his mistake was fatal.

1. THE MOUND BATTERY FROM THE FORT SIDE. 2. THE SEA-FACE OF THE SIXTH TO THE ELEVENTH TRAVERSES. 3. BATTERY BUCHANAN. FROM PHOTOGRAPHS.

Ordering Captain Z. T. Adams to turn his Napoleons on the column moving into the fort (the gallant Mayo had already turned his Columbiad upon them), I returned into the work, and, placing men behind every cover that could be found, poured at close range a deadlier fire into the flank of the enemy occupying the gun-chambers and traverses than they were able to deliver upon my men from the left salient. While thus engaged I met my aide, who informed me that the South Carolinians had failed to respond to my order, although their officers had pleaded with them, and with a few of them had gone into the fight; that the assaulting column had made two distinct charges upon the

This was disheartening, but I told Captain Blocker if we could hold the enemy in check until dark I would then drive them out, and I sent a telegram by him to Bragg, imploring him to attack, and saying that I could still save the fort.

Notwithstanding the loss of a portion of the work and a part of the garrison, the men were in good spirits and seemed determined to recover the fort. We had retaken one gun-chamber in the charge on the parapet, and since we had opened on their flank we had shot down all their standard-bearers, and the Federal battle-flags had disappeared from our ramparts. I was encouraged to believe that before sundown we could recover

⏐ I was told, several years after the war, by a United States marine named Clark, that I was distinctly seen and recognized by a comrade and himself who had feigned death in front of the north-east salient, and that

his comrade rose from his place of concealment to shoot me, but before he could fire was shot in the head by a soldier in the fort. I never thought of danger from that direction.— W. L.

all the gun-chambers to the east of the western salient. Just as the tide of battle seemed to have turned in our favor the remorseless fleet came to the rescue of the faltering Federals. Suddenly the bombardment, which had been confined to the sea-face, turned again on our land-front, and with deadly precision; the iron-clads and heavy frigates drove in our Napoleons and exploded shells in the interior of the sally-port, which had heretofore escaped. They also swept the gun-chamber occupied by Confederates in front of those occupied by the enemy, and their shells rolled down within the works and exploded in most unexpected quarters,

BREVET MAJOR-GENERAL NEWTON M. CURTIS.
FROM A PHOTOGRAPH.

preventing even company formation. They drove from the front of the enemy all assailants except those so near that to have fired on them would have been to slaughter the Federals.

We had now to contend with a column advancing around the rear of the left bastion into the interior plane of the fort. It moved slowly and cautiously, apparently in column of companies and in close order. I met it with an effective infantry fire, my men using the remains of an old work as a breastwork and taking advantage of every object that would afford cover, for we were now greatly outnumbered. The fire was so unexpected and destructive on the massed columns of the Federals, that they halted when an advance would have been fatal to us. With orders to the officers to dispute stubbornly any advance until my return, I went rapidly to the extreme southern limit of my work and turned the two mound guns on the column in the fort. As I passed the different batteries I ordered the guns turned on the assailants, but on returning found that only two besides those on the mound would bear upon them, and these had to be fired over my men. I ordered them, notwithstanding,

to be fired carefully with properly cut fuses, which was done, but it made some of my men very nervous. I brought back with me to the front every man except a single detachment for each gun. I was gone from the front at least thirty minutes, and on my return found the fighting still continuing over the same traverse for the possession of the gun-chamber, despite the fire of the fleet. As my men would fall others would take their places. It was a soldier's fight at that point, for there could be no organization; the officers of both forces were loading and firing with their men. If there has ever been a longer or more stubborn hand-to-hand encounter, I have failed to meet with it in history. The Federal column inside had advanced no farther, and seemed demoralized by the fire of the artillery and the determined resistance of the garrison. I had brought back with me more than a hundred of my old garrison, and I threw them in front with those already engaged. Those who had been driven from the parapet had taken position behind the old work. I went to the bomb-proof where the South Carolinians were and appealed to them to help save the fort; they were in a position to flank a part of the column, and they promised to do so. I proceeded to the sally-port and ordered the gallant Adams to bring his guns out and open fire on the head of the column, and if he had not men left to serve the guns to get volunteers from other companies. I went along the galleries and begged the sick and wounded who had retreated from the captured bomb-proofs to come and make one supreme effort to dislodge the enemy. As I passed through my work the last time, the scene was indescribably horrible. Great cannon were broken in two, and over their ruins were lying the dead; others were partly buried in graves dug by the shells which had slain them.

Still no tidings from Bragg. The enemy's advance had ceased entirely; protected by the fleet, they held the parapet and gun-chambers, but their massed columns refused to move and appeared to be intrenching in the work. I believed a determined assault with the bayonet upon their front would drive them out. I had cautioned the gunners not to fire on our men, and had sent Lieutenant Jones, of the navy, to Battery Buchanan, asking for all the force they could spare, and to be careful not to fire on us if we became closely engaged with the enemy. The head of the column was not over one hundred feet from the portion of our breast-work which I occupied; I passed quickly in rear of the line and asked the officers and men if they would follow me; they all responded fearlessly that they would. I returned to my post, and, giving the order "Charge bayonets," sprang upon the breast-work, waved my sword, and, as I gave the command "Forward! double-quick, march!" fell on my knees, a rifle-ball having entered my left hip. We were met by a heavy volley, aimed too high to be effective; but our column wavered and fell back behind the breastworks. A soldier raised me up; I turned the command over to Captain Daniel Munn and told him to keep the enemy in check, and that I would bandage my wound and soon return. Before I could reach the hospital I was made to realize that I was incapacitated from joining my men again. In the hospital I found General Whiting suffering uncomplainingly from his two wounds. He told me that Bragg had ignored his presence in the fort and had not noticed his messages. I perceived that the fire of my men had slackened, and sent my acting adjutant, John N. Kelly, for Major Reilly, next in command (Major James M. Stevenson being too ill for service). Reilly came and promised me that he would continue the fight as long as a man or a shot was left, and nobly did he keep his promise. I again sent a message to Bragg begging him to come to the rescue. Shortly after my fall the Federals made an advance, and, capturing several more of the gun-chambers, reached the sally-port. The column in the work advanced, but Major Reilly, rallying the men, among them the South Carolinians, who had all become engaged, drove them back. About 8 o'clock at night my aide came to me and said the ammunition was giving out; that he and Chaplain McKinnon had gathered all on the dead and wounded in a blanket and had distributed it; that the enemy had possession of nearly all of the land-face; that it was impossible to hold out much longer, and suggested that it would be wise to surrender, as a further struggle might be a useless sacrifice of life. I replied that so long as I lived I would not surrender the fort; that Bragg must soon come to the rescue, and it would save us. General Whiting remarked, "Lamb, when you die I will assume command, and I will not surrender the fort." In less than an hour a fourth brigade (three were already in the fort under General Ames) entered the sally-port and swept the defenders from the remainder of the land-face. Major Reilly had General Whiting and myself hurriedly removed on stretchers to Battery Bu-

BREVET MAJOR-GENERAL GALUSHA PENNYPACKER.
FROM A PHOTOGRAPH.

chanan, where he purposed to make a stand. When we left the hospital the men were fighting over the adjoining traverse and the spent balls

fell like hail-stones around us. The garrison then fell back in an orderly retreat along the sea-face, the rear-guard keeping the enemy engaged

BREVET MAJOR-GENERAL ADELBERT AMES.
FROM A PHOTOGRAPH.

as they advanced slowly and cautiously in the darkness as far as the Mound Battery, where they halted. Some of the men, cut off from the main body, had to retreat as best they could over the river marsh, while some few unarmed artillerists barely eluded the enemy by following the sea-shore. When we reached Battery Buchanan there was a mile of level beach between us and our pursuers, swept by two 11-inch guns and a 24-pounder, and in close proximity to the battery, a commodious wharf where transports could have come to carry the men off. We expected to cover with this battery the retreat of the remnant of the garrison, but we found the guns spiked, and every means of transportation, even the barge and crew of the colonel commanding, taken by Captain R. F. Chapman, of our navy, who, following the example of General Bragg, had abandoned us to our fate. None of the guns of Fort Fisher were spiked, the men fighting them until they were destroyed or their defenders were killed, wounded, or driven out of the batteries by overwhelming numbers. The enemy threw out a heavy skirmish-line and sent their fourth brigade to Battery Buchanan, where it arrived about 10 P. M. and received the surrender of the garrison from Major James H. Hill and Lieutenant George D. Parker. Some fifteen minutes or more before the surrender, while lying on a stretcher near General Whiting in front of the battery, and witnessing the grand pyrotechnic display of the fleet over the capture of Fort Fisher, I was accosted by General A. H. Colquitt, who had been ordered to the fort to take command. I had a few moments' hurried conversation with him, informed him of the assault, of the early loss of a portion of the work and garrison, and that when I fell it had for a time demoralized the men, but that the enemy was equally demoralized by our unexpected resistance; and I assured him that if Bragg would even then attack, a fresh brigade landed at Battery Buchanan could retake the work. Some officer suggested that the general should take me with him, as I was probably fatally wounded, but I refused to leave, wishing to share the fate of my garrison; and desiring that my family, anxiously awaiting tidings across the river, where they had

COLONEL LOUIS BELL. FROM A PHOTOGRAPH.

watched the battle, should not be alarmed, I spoke lightly of my wound. I asked him to carry General Whiting to a place of safety, as he had come to the fort a volunteer. Just then the approach of the enemy was reported, and Colquitt made a precipitate retreat, leaving Whiting behind. ⚓

One more distressing scene remains to be chronicled. The next morning after sunrise a frightful explosion occurred in my reserve magazine, killing and wounding several hundred of the enemy and some of my own wounded officers and men. The magazine was a frame structure 20 x 60 feet and 6 feet high, covered with 18 feet or more of sand, luxuriantly turfed, and contained probably 13,000 pounds of powder. It made an artificial mound most inviting to a wearied soldier, and after the fight was occupied for the night by Colonel Alden's 169th New York and by some of my suffering soldiers. Two sailors from the fleet, stupefied by liquor which they had found in the hospital, and looking for booty, were seen to enter the structure with lights, and a moment after the green mound blew up. The telegraph wires, running from a bomb-proof near this magazine across the river to Battery Lamb, gave rise to the impression that it had been purposely exploded from the opposite shore, but an official investigation traced it to the drunken sailors.

So stoutly did those works resist the 50,000 shot and shell thrown against them in the two bombardments that not a magazine or bomb-proof was injured, and after the land armament, with palisades and torpedoes, had been destroyed, no assault would have been practicable in the presence of Bragg's force, had it been under a competent officer. ‡ One thousand tons of iron were gathered by the United States from the works.

Had there been no fleet to assist the army at Fort Fisher the Federal infantry could not have dared assault it until its land defenses had been destroyed by gradual approaches. For the first time in the history of sieges the land defenses of the works were destroyed, not by any act of the besieging army, but by the concentrated fire, direct and enfilading, of an immense fleet poured upon them without intermission, until torpedo wires were cut, palisades breached so that they actually afforded cover for assailants, and the slopes of the work were rendered practicable for assault.

⚓ General Whiting died a prisoner at Fort Columbus, New York Harbor, March 10th, 1865.

‡ In Vol. X., p. 346, of the "Southern Historical Society Papers" may be found a letter from General Braxton Bragg to his brother, dated Wilmington, five days after the fall of Fort Fisher (first published in 1881); also an article by Colonel Lamb, controverting most of General Bragg's statements. General Bragg says (more emphatically but substantially as in his official report):

"Two hours before hearing of the certain fall of the fort, I felt as confident as ever man did of successfully defending it. . . . No human power could have prevented the enemy from landing, covered as he was by a fleet of ships carrying 600 heavy guns. Anywhere beyond the range of our heavy guns on the fort our land force could not approach him. Once landed, our only chance was to keep him, if possible, from the fort. With less than half his numbers, had we extended far enough toward the fort to prevent his movement that way he could have crossed the narrow peninsula north of us and cut us off entirely, when the fort and all must have gone."

General Bragg, after explaining that his cavalry pickets failed to report the movement by night of Terry's force to its intrenched position near Fort Fisher, says:

"I put the command in motion, and ordered the enemy dislodged if it was at all practicable. General Hoke and his brigadiers made a close reconnoissance and expressed to me the opinion that their troops were unequal to the task. I moved forward with them, and made a close examination, confirmed their opinion, and after a conference decided not to attack. An attack and failure would have insured the fall of the fort, and would also have opened the whole State. We could not have succeeded without defeating double our numbers behind intrenchments, while at the same time exposed to a raking fire from their fleet. [See p. 642.] . . . Believing myself that Grant's army could not storm and carry the fort if it was defended, I felt perfect confidence that the enemy had assumed a most precarious position, from which he would escape with great difficulty. I accordingly ordered Hoke to intrench immediately in his front, and push his lines close on him so as to keep him engaged and closely observed. . . . Had the cavalry done its duty and promptly reported the enemy's movements, I do not think the result would have been different. Such was the configuration of the country and the obstacles, that he would have accomplished his object with the force he had. Our only safe reliance was in his repulse, we being the weak and assailed party. . . . The defense of the fort ought to have been successful against *this* attack, but it had to fall eventually. The expedition brought against it was able to reduce it in spite of all I could do. . . ."

EDITORS.

THE NAVY AT FORT FISHER.

BY THOMAS O. SELFRIDGE, JR., CAPTAIN, U. S. N.

WHEN the Secretary of the Navy, Mr. Welles, recognizing the importance of closing the port of Wilmington, urged upon President Lincoln to direct a coöperation of the army, General Grant was requested to supply the necessary force from the troops about Richmond. As Fort Fisher lay within the territorial jurisdiction of General Butler, commanding the Department of Virginia and North Carolina, the troops were detailed from his command, and in the first attack Butler, with General Weitzel in immediate command of the troops, had control of the land operations. The naval command of the expedition having been declined by Admiral Farragut, on account of ill-health, Rear-Admiral Porter, who had so successfully coöperated with the army in opening the Mississippi, was selected, and was allowed to bring with him five of his officers, of whom the writer was one, being detailed for the command of the gun-boat *Huron*. The Atlantic and Gulf coasts being almost entirely in our possession, the Navy Department was able to concentrate before Fort Fisher a larger force than had ever before assembled under one command in the history of the American navy—a total of nearly 60 vessels [see p. 662], of which five were iron-clads, including the *New Ironsides*, besides the three largest of our steam-frigates, viz., the *Minnesota*, *Colorado*, and *Wabash*. The fleet arrived in sight of the fort on the morning of December 20th.

A novel feature of this first attack was the explosion of a powder-boat near the fort on the night of December 23d. The vessel was the *Louisiana*, an old gun-boat no longer serviceable. The more sanguine believed that Fort Fisher, with its garrison, guns, and equipment, would be leveled to the ground, while others were equally certain it would prove a fizzle. Commander A. C. Rhind, with a crew of volunteers, successfully performed the perilous duty, and, applying the match at midnight, the crew rowed safely away to the *Wilderness*, a

swift gun-boat, in waiting. The whole fleet having moved off shore, under low steam, awaited the result in anxiety. A glare on the horizon and a dull report were the indications that the floating mine had been sprung. In the morning, when the fleet steamed in, all eyes were toward the fort. There it was, as grim as ever, apparently uninjured, with its flag floating as defiantly as before. In these days, with better electrical appliances, the explosion could have been made more nearly instantaneous, but I doubt if the general result would have been different.

The powder-boat proving an ignominious failure, the fleet stood in toward the fort in close order of divisions, the iron-clads leading. At 11:30 the signal was thrown out from the flag-ship *Malvern*: "Engage the enemy." The *Ironsides*, followed by

CAPTAIN T. O. SELFRIDGE, JR. FROM A PHOTOGRAPH.

⸬ The total number of guns and howitzers in the fleet was over 600, and the total weight of projectiles at a single discharge of all the guns (both broadsides) was over 22 tons.—EDITORS.

THE BOMBARDMENT OF FORT FISHER, JANUARY 15, 1865. TAKEN FROM LITHOGRAPHS.

the monitors, took position as close in as their draught would permit, engaging the north-east face. The *Ironsides* was followed by the *Minnesota*, *Colorado*, and *Wabash*. The enemy replied briskly, but when these frigates found the range and commenced firing rapidly nothing could withstand their broadsides of twenty-five 9-inch guns. It was a magnificent sight to see these frigates fairly engaged, and one never to be forgotten. Their sides seemed a sheet of flame, and the roar of their guns like a mighty thunderbolt. Meanwhile all the other ships took positions as detailed, and so perfect were the plans of the admiral, and so well were they carried out by his captains, that not a mishap took place. Nothing could withstand such a storm of shot and shell as was now poured into this fort. The enemy took refuge in their bomb-proofs, replying sullenly with an occasional gun. The enemy's fire being silenced, signal was made to fire with deliberation, and attention was turned to the dismounting of the guns. So quickly had the guns of Fort Fisher been silenced ⚓ that not a man had been injured by their fire, though several ships had sustained losses by the bursting of their 100-pounder Parrott rifles. The *Mackinaw*, however, had had her boiler exploded by a shot, and several of her crew had been scalded, and the *Osceola* was struck by a shell near her magazine, but was saved from sinking by her captain, Commander Clitz.

During the bombardment the transports, with troops, arrived from Beaufort. On Christmas day, as agreed upon between Admiral Porter and General Butler, the smaller vessels were engaged in covering the disembarkation of the troops, while the iron-clads and frigates were sent in to resume the bombardment of the fort. The larger portion of the army was landed by the boats of the fleet and advanced with little or no opposition to within a short distance of the fort, the skirmish-line within

MAJOR GENERAL A. H. TERRY. FROM A PHOTOGRAPH.

fifty yards. Butler and Weitzel decided that it could not be taken by assault. Orders were issued to reëmbark after being on shore but a few hours. Some seven hundred men were left on shore, the sea being too rough to get them off, but the demoralized enemy did not attempt to attack them. They were taken off in the morning, and the transports steamed away for Hampton Roads, the fleet returning to Beaufort. Thus ended the first attack upon Fort Fisher. Words cannot express the bitter feeling and chagrin of the navy. We all felt the fruit was ripe for plucking and with little exertion would have fallen into the hands of the army.

SECOND ATTACK UPON FORT FISHER.

Upon receiving Admiral Porter's dispatches, Mr. Welles again sought the coöperation of the army, to which General Grant at once acceded, sending back the same force of white troops, reënforced

⚓ In a note to the editors Colonel Lamb says:

"The guns of Fort Fisher were not silenced. On account of a limited supply of ammunition, I gave orders to fire each gun not more than once in thirty minutes, except by special order, unless an attempt should be made to run by the fort, when discretion was given each gun commander to use his piece effectively. There were forty-four guns. On the 24th of December 672 shots were expended; a detailed report was received from each battery. Only three guns were rendered unserviceable, and these by the fire of the fleet disabling the carriages. On the 25th of December six hundred shots were expended, exclusive of grape and canister. Detailed reports were made. Five guns were disabled by the fire of the fleet, making eight in all. Besides, two 7-inch Brooke rifled guns exploded, leaving thirty-four heavy guns on Christmas night. The last guns on the 24th and 25th were fired by Fort Fisher on the retiring fleet. In the first fight the total casualties were 61, as follows: December 24th, mortally wounded, 1; seriously 3; slightly, 19 = 23. December 25th, killed, 3; mortally wounded, 2; severely, 7; slightly, 26. These included those wounded by the explosion of the Brooke rifled guns = 38."

CAPTAIN K. R. BREESE. FROM A PHOTOGRAPH.

ASSAULT OF THE NAVAL COLUMN ON THE NORTH-EAST SALIENT OF FORT FISHER.

by two colored brigades under General Charles J. Paine, the whole under the command of Major-General Alfred H. Terry. While lying at Beaufort, Admiral Porter determined to assist in the land attack of the army by an assault upon the sea-face of Fort Fisher with a body of seamen. In a general order volunteers from the fleet were called for, and some two thousand officers and men offered themselves for this perilous duty.

General Terry arrived off Beaufort [see map, p. 629] with his forces on the 8th of January, 1865, a plan of operations was agreed upon, and the 12th was fixed for the sailing of the combined force.

Upon the morning of the 13th the iron-clads were sent in to engage the fort. Going in much closer than before, the monitors were within twelve hundred yards of the fort. Their fire was in consequence much more effective.

The remainder of the fleet were occupied till 2 P. M. in landing the troops and stores. This particular duty, the provisioning of the army, and the protection of its flank was afterward turned over to the lighter gun-boats, whose guns were too small to employ them in the bombardment of the fort, the whole under the charge of Commander J. H. Upshur, commanding the gun-boat *A. D. Vance.*

On the afternoon of the 13th the fleet, excepting the iron-clads, which had remained in their first positions close to the fort, steamed into the several positions assigned them and opened a terrific fire. By placing a buoy close to the outer reef, as a guide, the leading ship, the *Minnesota,* was enabled to anchor nearer, and likewise the whole battle-line was much closer and their fire more effective, the best proof of which is the large number of guns upon the land-face of the fort that was found to be destroyed or dismounted.‡ The weight of fire was

such that the enemy could make but a feeble reply. At nightfall the fleet hauled off, excepting the iron-clads, which kept up a slow fire through the night.

During the 14th a number of the smaller gun-boats carrying 11-inch guns were sent in to assist in dismounting the guns on the land-face. Their fire was necessarily slow, and the presence of these small craft brought the enemy out of their bomb-proofs to open upon them, during which the *Huron* had her main-mast shot away. Upon seeing this renewal of fire, the *Brooklyn, Mohican,* and one or two other vessels were ordered in by Porter, and with this reënforcement the fire of the fort slackened. The bombardment from the smaller gun-boats and iron-clads was kept up during the night. This constant duty day and night was very hard upon these small vessels, and the officers and crew of my own vessel, the *Huron,* were worn out.

Fort Fisher was at this time much stronger than at the first attack. The garrison had been reënforced by veteran troops, damages by the first bombardment had been repaired, and new defenses added; among which was a battery of light pieces in a half-moon around the sally-port, from whose fire the sailors suffered heavily in their assault.♭

It was arranged that the grand bombardment should begin on the morning of the 15th, and the separate assaults of soldiers and sailors should take place at 3 P. M. A code of signals was agreed upon between the two commanders, and the assault was to be signaled to the fleet by a blowing of steam-whistles, whereupon their fire would be directed to the upper batteries. After the assault of the sailors had failed the *Ironsides* used her 11-inch guns with great effect in firing into the traverses filled with Confederates resisting the advance of the Union forces. At 9 A. M. the fleet was directed

‡ According to the report of General C. B. Comstock, General Terry's chief engineer, there were 21 guns and 3 mortars on the land front; "of these three-fourths were rendered unserviceable." General H. L. Abbot states ("Defence of the Sea Coast of the United States," p. 31), as a result of personal inspection immediately after the capture, that out of 20 guns on the land-face "8 guns and 8 carriages (16 in all) were disabled."—EDITORS.

♭ Colonel Lamb, writing, December, 1888, says:

"There were never in Fort Fisher, including sick, killed, and wounded, over 1900 men. [See detailed statement, p. 661.] The sailors and marines, etc., captured from Battery Buchanan, and those captured in front of the work, while swelling the list of prisoners, cannot rightly be counted among the defenders of the work. No new defense was added to the face of the fort between the battles. The redoubt in front of the sally-port was there in December and had been used against Butler's skirmish-line."

by signal to move in three divisions, and each ship took its prescribed place as previously indicated to her commander; consequently there was no disorder.

All felt the importance of this bombardment, and while not too rapid to be ineffective such a storm of shell was poured into Fort Fisher, that forenoon, as I believe had never been seen before in any naval engagement. The enemy soon ceased to make any reply from their heavy guns, excepting the "Mound Battery," which was more difficult to silence, while those mounted on the land-face were by this time disabled. [See note, p. 658.]

Before noon the signal was made for the assaulting column of sailors and marines to land. From thirty-five of the sixty ships of the fleet boats shoved off, making, with their flags flying as they pulled toward the beach in line abreast, a most spirited scene. The general order of Admiral Porter required that the assaulting column of sailors should be armed with cutlasses and pistols. It was also intended that trenches or covered ways should be dug for the marines close to the fort and that our assault should be made under the cover of their fire; but it was impossible to dig such shelter trenches near enough to do much good under fire in broad daylight.

The sailors as they landed from their boats were a heterogeneous assembly, companies of two hundred or more from each of the larger ships, down to small parties of twenty each from the gun-boats. They had been for months confined on shipboard, had never drilled together, and their arms, the old-fashioned cutlass and pistol, were hardly the weapons to cope with the rifles and bayonets of the enemy. Sailor-like, however, they looked upon the landing in the light of a lark, and few thought the sun would set with a loss of one-fifth of their number.

After some discussion between the commander, Lieutenant-Commander K. R. Breese, and the senior officers, it was decided to form three divisions, each composed of the men from the corresponding division squadrons of the fleet; the first division, under the command of Lieutenant-Commander C. H. Cushman, the second under Lieutenant-Commander James Parker (who was Breese's senior but waived his rank, the latter being in command as the admiral's representative), the third under Lieutenant-Commander T. O. Selfridge, Jr.;

a total of 1600 blue jackets, to which was added a division of 400 marines under Captain L. L. Dawson.

The whole force marched up the beach and lay down under its cover just outside rifle range, awaiting the movements of the army. We were formed by the flank, and our long line flying numerous flags gave a formidable appearance from the fort, and caused the Confederates to divide their forces, sending more than one-half to oppose the naval assault.

At a preconcerted signal the sailors sprang forward to the assault, closely following the water's edge, where the inclined beach gave them a

COMMANDER JAMES PARKER. FROM A PHOTOGRAPH.

slight cover. We were opened upon in front by the great mound battery, and in flank by the artillery of the half-moon battery, and by the fire of a thousand rifles. Though many dropped rapidly under this fire, the column never faltered, and when the angle where the two faces of the fort unite was reached the head halted to allow the rear to come up. This halt was fatal, for as the others came up they followed suit and lay down till the space between the parapet and the edge of the water was filled. As the writer approached with the Third Division he shouted to his men to come on, intending to lead them to where

NORTH-EAST SALIENT OF FORT FISHER, SHOWING ON THE LEFT THE GROUND OVER WHICH THE NAVAL COLUMN CHARGED. FROM A PHOTOGRAPH.

there was more space; but, looking back, he discovered that his whole command, with few exceptions, had stopped and joined their comrades.

LIEUTENANT SAMUEL W. PRESTON.
FROM A PHOTOGRAPH.

Making his way to the front, close to the palisade, he found several officers, among whom were Lieutenant-Commanders Parker and Cushman. The situation was a very grave one. The rush of the sailors was over; they were packed like sheep in a pen, while the enemy were crowding the ramparts not forty yards away, and shooting into them as fast as they could fire. There was nothing to reply with but *pistols*. Something must be done, and speedily. There were some spaces in the palisade where it was torn away by the fire of the fleet, and an attempt was made to charge through, but we found a deep, impassable ditch, †‡ and those who got through were shot down. Flesh and blood could not long endure being killed in this slaughter-pen, and the rear of the sailors broke, followed by the whole body, in spite of all efforts to rally them. It was certainly mortifying, after charging for a mile, ☆ under a most galling fire, to the very foot of the fort, to have the whole force retreat down the beach. It has been the custom, unjustly in my opinion, to lay the blame on the marines for not keeping down the fire till the sailors could get in. But there were but 400 of them against 1200 of the garrison: the former in the open plain, and with no cover; the latter under the shelter of their ramparts. ǀ The mistake was in expecting a body of sailors, collected hastily from different ships, unknown to each other, armed

with swords and pistols, to stand against veteran soldiers armed with rifles and bayonets. Another fatal mistake was the stopping at the sea angle. Two hundred yards farther would have brought us to a low parapet without palisade or ditch, where, with proper arms, we could have intrenched and fought. Some sixty remained at the front, at the foot of the parapet, under cover of the palisade, until nightfall enabled them to withdraw. Among the number I remember Lieutenant-Commanders Breese, Parker, Cushman, Sicard; Lieutenants Farquhar, Lamson, S. W. Nichols, and Bartlett.

A loss of some three hundred in killed and wounded attests the gallant nature of the assault. Among these were several prominent officers, including Lieutenants Preston and Porter, killed; Lieutenant-Commanders C. H. Cushman, W. N. Allen, Lieutenant G. M. Bache, wounded.

After their repulse the sailors did good service with the marines by manning the intrenchments thrown up across the peninsula, which enabled General Terry to send Abbott's brigade and Blackman's (27th U. S.) colored regiment to the assistance of the troops fighting in the fort. Here they remained till morning, when they returned to their respective ships. When the assault of the marine column failed, the *Ironsides* and the monitors were directed to fire into the gun traverses in advance of the positions occupied by the army, and by doing so greatly demoralized the enemy. About 8 P. M. that night the fort fell into our hands after the hardest fighting by our gallant troops, and with its capture fell the last strong-

LIEUTENANT BENJAMIN H. PORTER.
FROM A PHOTOGRAPH.

ǀ Colonel Lamb says on this point: "There was no ditch, merely a dry depression in front of the berme where sand had been dug out to repair work."—EDITORS.

☆ General Terry writes to the editors that he thinks that the head of the column of sailors was within 600 or 800 yards of the work before they began to charge.
                                        EDITORS.

ǀ Colonel Lamb, writing to the editors on the subject of the numbers defending the north-east salient, says:

"Five hundred effective men will cover all engaged in repulsing the naval column, and the destructive fire was from the three hundred, who, from the top of the ramparts and traverses, fired upon the assailants. The gallant navy need not exaggerate the number opposing them, assisted by the artillery. No apology or defense is necessary to excuse the repulse. The unorganized and improperly armed force failed to enter the fort, but their gallant attempt enabled the army to enter and obtain a foothold, which they otherwise could not have done."

hold of the Southern Confederacy on the Atlantic coast.

I will not go so far as to say the army could not have stormed Fort Fisher without the diversion afforded by the naval assault, for no soldiers during the war showed more indomitable pluck than the gallant regiments that stormed the fort on that afternoon; but I do say our attack enabled them to get into the fort with far less loss than they would otherwise have suffered.

As a diversion the charge of sailors was a success; as an exhibition of courage it was magnificent; but the material of which the column was composed, and the arms with which it was furnished, left no reasonable hope after the first onslaught had been checked that it could have succeeded.

While kept under the walls of the fort, I was an eye-witness to an act of heroism on the part of Assistant-Surgeon William Longshaw, a young officer of the medical staff, whose memory should ever be kept green by his corps, and which deserves more than this passing notice. A sailor too severely wounded to help himself had fallen close to the water's edge, and with the rising tide would have drowned. Dr. Longshaw, at the peril of his life, went to his assistance and dragged him beyond the incoming tide. At this moment he heard a cry from a wounded marine, one of a small group who, behind a little hillock of sand close to the parapet, kept up a fire upon the enemy. Longshaw ran to his assistance, and while attending to his wounds was shot dead. What made the action of this young officer even more heroic was the fact that on that very day he had received a leave of absence, but had postponed his departure to volunteer for the assault.

THE OPPOSING FORCES AT FORT FISHER, N. C.

January 13–15, 1865.

THE UNION ARMY.— Major-General Alfred H. Terry.

SECOND DIVISION, TWENTY-FOURTH ARMY CORPS, Brig.-Gen. Adelbert Ames.

First Brigade, Col. N. Martin Curtis: 3d N. Y., Capt. James H. Reeve, Lieut. Edwin A. Behan; 112th N. Y., Col. John F. Smith; 117th N. Y., Lieut.-Col. Francis X. Meyer; 142d N. Y., Lieut.-Col. Albert M. Barney. *Second Brigade,* Col. Galusha Pennypacker, Maj. Oliver P. Harding: 47th N. Y., Capt. Joseph M. McDonald; 48th N. Y., Lieut.-Col. William B. Coan, Maj. Nere A. Elfwing; 76th Pa., Col. John S. Littell, Maj. Charles Knerr; 97th Pa., Lieut. John Wainwright; 203d Pa., Col. John W. Moore, Lieut.-Col. Jonas W. Lyman, Maj. Oliver P. Harding, Capt. Heber B. Essington. *Third Brigade,* Col. Louis Bell, Col. Alonzo Alden: 13th Ind., Lieut.-Col. Samuel M. Zent; 4th N. H., Capt. John H. Roberts; 115th N. Y., Lieut.-Col. Nathan J. Johnson; 169th N. Y., Col. Alonzo Alden, Lieut.-Col. James A. Colvin. *Second Brigade, First Division* (temporarily attached to Second Division), Col. Joseph C. Abbott: 6th Conn., Col. Alfred P. Rockwell; 7th Conn., Capt. John Thompson, Capt. William S. Marble; 3d N. H., Capt. William H. Trickey; 7th N. H., Lieut.-Col. Augustus W. Rollins; 16th N. Y. Heavy Artillery (detachment), Lieut. F. F. Huntington.

THIRD DIVISION, TWENTY-FIFTH ARMY CORPS (colored troops), Brig.-Gen. Charles J. Paine.

Second Brigade, Col. John W. Ames: 4th U. S., Lieut.-Col. George Rogers; 6th U. S., Maj. A. S. Boernstein; 30th U. S., Lieut.-Col. H. A. Oakman; 39th U. S., Col. O. P. Stearns. *Third Brigade,* Col. Elias Wright: 1st U. S., Lieut.-Col. Giles H. Rich; 5th U. S., Maj. William R. Brazie; 10th U. S., Lieut.-Col. Edward H. Powell; 27th U. S., Col. A. M. Blackman; 37th U. S., Colonel Nathan Goff, Jr.

ARTILLERY: B, G, and L, 1st Conn. Heavy, Capt. William G. Pride; 16th N. Y. Battery, Capt. Richard H. Lee; E, 3d U. S., Lieut. John R. Myrick.

ENGINEERS: A, and I, 15th N. Y., Lieut. K. S. O'Keefe.

The effective strength of the force above enumerated was nearly 8000. The loss aggregated 184 killed, 749 wounded, and 22 missing = 955. By the explosion of a magazine the day after the capture there were 25 killed, 66 wounded, and 13 missing.

THE CONFEDERATE ARMY.

GENERAL BRAXTON BRAGG (department commander);

MAJOR-GENERAL W. H. C. WHITING (district commander).

DEFENSES, MOUTH OF CAPE FEAR RIVER, Brig.-Gen. Louis Hébert.

Garrison of Fort Fisher, Col. William Lamb, Maj. James M. Stevenson (too ill for duty), Maj. James Reilly: 10th N. C. (1st Artillery), Maj. James Reilly (2 companies: Co. F, Capt. E. D. Walsh, Co. K, Capt. William Shaw); 36th N. C. (2d Artillery), Maj. James M. Stevenson (ill), Capt. Daniel Munn (10 companies: Co. A, Capt. R. J. Murphy, Co. B, Capt. Daniel Munn, Co. C, Capt. K. J. Braddy, Co. D, Capt. E. B. Dudley, Co. E, Capt. O. H. Powell, Co. F, Lieut. E. L. Hunter, Co. G, Capt. William Swain, Co. H, Capt. Daniel Patterson, Co. I, Capt. J. F. Melvin, Co. K, Capt. William F. Brooks); 40th N. C. (4 companies: Co. D, Capt. James L. Lane, Co. E, Capt. M. H. McBryde, Co. G, Capt. George C. Buchan, Co. K, Capt. D. J. Clarke); D, 1st N. C. Artillery Battalion, Capt. James L. McCormick; C, 3d N. C. Artillery Battalion, Capt. John M. Sutton; D, 13th N. C. Artillery Battalion, Capt. Z. T. Adams; Naval detachment, Capt. A. C. Van Benthuysen.

Battery Buchanan: Capt. R. F. Chapman, C. S. N.

HOKE'S DIVISION, Major.-Gen. Robert F. Hoke.

Clingman's Brigade: 8th N. C., ——; 31st N. C., ——; 57th N. C., ——; 61st N. C., ——. *Colquitt's Brigade,* Brig.-Gen. A. H. Colquitt: 6th Ga., Col. T. J. Lofton; 19th Ga., ——; 23d Ga., ——; 27th Ga., ——; 28th Ga., ——. *Hagood's Brigade:* 11th S. C., ——; 21st S. C., ——; 25th S. C., ——; 27th S. C., ——; 7th S. C. Battalion, ——. *Kirkland's Brigade:* 17th N. C., ——; 42d N. C., ——; 50th N. C., ——; 66th N. C., ——.

CAVALRY: 2d S. C., Col. T. J. Lipscomb.

According to General Bragg's official report the garrison of Fort Fisher (including reënforcements from the adjacent forts) numbered 1800, and the movable force under General Hoke, including reserves and cavalry, was about 6000. In regard to the losses, the same authority says: "After the enemy entered the fort our loss is represented to have been about 500 killed and wounded. The garrison consisted of about 110 commissioned officers and 2400 or 2500 men." The strength thus stated probably included the 21st and 25th South Carolina sent from Hagood's Brigade. General Terry reported the capture of 112 officers and 1971 men. Colonel Lamb writes that all present in Fort Fisher, Jan. 13th-15th, including sick, killed, and wounded, numbered 1900.

NAVAL FORCE AT FORT FISHER, DEC. 23-26, 1864, AND JAN. 13-16, 1865.

NORTH ATLANTIC SQUADRON: Rear-Admiral David D. Porter, Commanding. Lieutenant-Commander K. R. Breese, Fleet Captain. Lieut. M. W. Sanders, Signal Officer. Lieutenant S. W. Terry and Lieutenant S. W. Preston (k), Aides.

FIRST DIVISION, Commodore Henry K. Thatcher; SECOND DIVISION, Commodore Joseph Lanman; THIRD DIVISION, Commodore Jas. Findlay Schenck; FOURTH DIVISION, Commodore S. W. Godon; IRON-CLAD DIVISION, Commodore Wm. Radford.

FLAG-SHIP.—*Malvern*, Lieut. William B. Cushing (1st attack); Lieut. B. H. Porter (k), (2d attack).

IRON-CLADS.—*Canonicus*, Lieut.-Com. George E. Belknap. *Mahopac*, Lieut.-Com. E. E. Potter (1st attack); Lieut.-Com. A. W. Weaver (2d attack). *Monadnock*, Com. E. G. Parrott. *New Ironsides*, Commo. William Radford. *Saugus*, Com. E. R. Colhoun.

SCREW FRIGATES.—*Colorado*, Commo. H. K. Thatcher. *Minnesota*, Commo. Joseph Lanman. *Wabash*, Capt. M. Smith.

SIDE-WHEEL STEAMERS (1st class). — *Powhatan*, Commo. J. F. Schenck. *Susquehanna*, Commo. S. W. Godon.

SCREW SLOOPS.—*Brooklyn*, Capt. James Alden. *Juniata*, Capt. W. R. Taylor (1st attack); Lieut.-Com. T. S. Phelps (2d attack). *Mohican*, Com. D. Ammen. *Shenandoah*, Capt. D. B. Ridgely. *Ticonderoga*, Capt. C. Steedman. *Tuscarora*, Com. J. M. Frailey.

SCREW GUN-VESSELS.—*Kansas*, Lieut.-Com. P. G. Watmough. *Maumee*, Lieut.-Com. R. Chandler. *Nyack*, Lieut.-Com. L. H. Newman. *Pequot*, Lieut.-Com. D. L. Braine. *Yantic*, Lieut.-Com. T. C. Harris.

SCREW GUN-BOATS.— *Chippewa*, Lieut.-Com. A. W. Weaver (1st attack); Lieut.-Com. E. E. Potter (2d attack). *Huron*, Lieut.-Com. T. O. Selfridge. *Seneca*, Lieut.-Com. M. Sicard. *Unadilla*, Lieut.-Com. F. M. Ramsay.

DOUBLE-ENDERS.—*Iosco*, Com. John Guest. *Mackinaw*, Com. J. C. Beaumont. *Maratanza*, Lieut.-Com. G. W. Young. *Osceola*, Com. J. M. B. Clitz. *Pawtuxet*, Com. J. H. Spotts. *Pontoosuc*, Lieut.-Com. Wm. G. Temple. *Sassacus*, Lieut.-Com. J. L. Davis. *Tacony*, Lieut.-Com. W. T. Truxtun.

MISCELLANEOUS VESSELS.—*Fort Jackson*, Capt. B. F. Sands. *Monticello*, Act. V.-Lieut. D. A. Campbell (1st attack); Lieut. W. B. Cushing (2d attack). *Nereus*, Com. J. C. Howell. *Quaker City*, Com. W. F. Spicer. *Rhode Island*, Com. S. D. Trenchard. *Santiago de Cuba*, Capt. O. S. Glisson. *Vanderbilt*, Capt. C. W. Pickering.

POWDER VESSEL.—*Louisiana*, Com. A. C. Rhind (1st attack; blown up).

RESERVE.—*A. D. Vance*, Lieut.-Com. J. H. Upshur. *Alabama*, Act. V. Lieut. Frank Smith (1st attack); Act. V. Lieut. A. R. Langthorne (2d attack). *Britannia*, Act. V. Lieut. Samuel Huse (1st attack); Act. V. Lieut. W. A. Sheldon (2d attack). *Cherokee*, Act. V. Lieut. W. E. Denison. *Emma*, Act. V. Lieut. T. C. Dunn (1st attack); Act. V. Lieut. J. M. Williams (2d attack). *Gettysburg*, Lieut. Com. R. H. Lamson (w). *Governor Buckingham*, Act. V. Lieut. J. McDiarmid. *Howquah*, Act. V. Lieut. J. W. Balch. *Keystone State*, Com. H. Rolando. *Lilian*, Act. V. Lieut. T. A. Harris. *Little Ada*, Acting Master S. P. Crafts. *Moccasin*, Act. Ens. James Brown. *Nansemond*, Act. Master J. H. Porter. *Tristram Shandy*, Act. Ens. Ben. Wood (1st attack); Act. V. Lieut. F. M. Green (2d attack). *Wilderness*, Acting Master H. Arey.

At the second attack the fleet was composed of the same vessels, with the exception of the *Nyack*, *Keystone State*, and *Quaker City*. The following additions were also made to the fleet: *Montgomery*, Act. V. Lieut. T. C. Dunn; *R. R. Cuyler*, Com. C. H. B. Caldwell; *Aries*, Act. V. Lieut. F. S. Wells; *Eolus*, Acting Master E. S. Keyser; *Fort Donelson*, Acting Master G. W. Frost; and *Republic*, Act. Ens. J. W. Bennett.

ARMAMENT OF THE FLEET.

In the first attack the armament of the fleet was 10 15-inch S. B., 27 11-inch S. B., 1 10-inch S. B., 255 9-inch S. B., 30 8-inch S. B., 31 32-pounders S. B., 10 150-pounders R., 37 100-pounders R., 5 60-pounders R., 1 50-pounder R., 43 30-pounders R., 28 20-pounders R.; total guns, 478. Howitzers: 68 24-pounders, 73 12-pounders; total howitzers, 141; grand total, 619.

In the second attack there were 1 more 10-inch S. B., 2 fewer 9-inch S. B., 2 more 8-inch S. B., 8 more 32-pounders S. B., 8 fewer 100-pounders R., 1 fewer 50-pounder R., 5 more 30-pounders R., 1 fewer 20-pounder R., 4 more 12-pounder howitzers; making 4 more guns and 4 more howitzers; grand total, 627.

LANDING PARTY AT FORT FISHER, JAN. 15, 1865: 2261 OFFICERS, SEAMEN, AND MARINES.— Lieut.-Com. K. R. Breese, Fleet Captain, commanding.

FIRST DIVISION, Capt. L. L. Dawson, U. S. M. C.; SECOND DIVISION, Lieut.-Com. C. H. Cushman (w); THIRD DIVISION, Lieut.-Com. James Parker; FOURTH DIVISION, Lieut.-Com. T. O. Selfridge. PIONEERS, Lieut. S. W. Preston (k). — *Malvern*, 60 men, Lieut. B. H. Porter (k). *Colorado*, 218 men, Lieut. H. B. Robes· . *Minnesota*, 241 men, Lieut.-Com. James Parker. `·` bash, 188 men, Lieut.-Com. C. H. Cushman (w). *Powhatan*, 100 men, Lieut. George M. Bache (w). *Susquehanna*, 75 men, Lieut.-Com. F. B. Blake. *Brooklyn*, 70 men (estimated), Act. Ens. D. Cassell; *Juniata*, 69 men, Acting Master C. H. Hamilton (w). *Mohican*, 52 men, Acting Master W. Burdett. *Shenandoah*, 71 men, Lieut. S. W. Nichols. *Ticonderoga*, 60 men, Ensign G. W. Coffin (w). *Tuscarora*, 60 men, Lieut. Com. W. N. Allen (w). *Kansas*, 20 men, Act. Ens. Williams. *Pequot*, 44 men, Act. Ens. G. Lamb. *Yantic*, 45 men, Act. Ens. J. C. Lord. *Chippewa*, 24 men, Act. Ens. G. H. Wood. *Huron*, 34 men, Lieut.-Com. T. O. Selfridge. *Seneca*, 29 men, Lieut.-Com. M. Sicard. *Iosco*, 44 men, Act. Ens. W. Jameson. *Mackinaw*, 45 men, Acting Master A. J. Louch (w). *Maratanza*, 51 men, Acting Master J. B. Wood (w). *Osceola*, 39 men, Act. Ens. J. F. Merry (w). *Pawtuxet*, 40 men (estimated), Act. Ens. J. A. Slamm. *Pontoosuc*, 42 men, Act. Ens. L. R. Chester (w). *Sassacus*, 37 men, Act. Ens. W. H. Mayer. *Tacony*, 32 men, Act. Ens. J. B. Taney. *Fort Jackson*, 69 men, Lieut. S. H. Hunt. *Monticello*, 41 men, Lieut. W. B. Cushing. *Nereus*, 61 men, Act. Ens. E. G. Dayton. *Rhode Island*, 47 men, Lieut. F. R. Smith. *Santiago de Cuba*, 53 men, Lieut. N. H. Farquhar. *Vanderbilt*, 70 men (estimated), Act. V. Lieut. J. D. Daniels. *Gettysburg*, 71 men, Lieut. R. H. Lamson (w). *Tristram Shandy*, 22 men, Act. Ens. B. Wood (w). *Montgomery*, 37 men, Acting Master W. N. Wells. Total, 2261 men.

CASUALTIES.—The reports of casualties in the first attack, as collated by the Surgeon-General, give the following result: 19 killed, 1 mortally scalded, 31 severely wounded, 1 severely scalded, 31 slightly wounded or scalded. Total, 83.

CASUALTIES IN THE SECOND ATTACK.—*Malvern*, 3 killed, 1 wounded; *Canonicus*, 3 w; *Saugus*, 1 w; *Colorado*, 4 k, 17 w, 8 missing; *Minnesota*, 15 k, 26 w, 2 m; *Wabash*, 4 k, 22 w, 5 m; *Powhatan*, 4 k, 17 w, 8 m; *Susquehanna*, 3 k, 15 w; *Brooklyn*, 3 w, 2 m; *Juniata*, 5 k, 10 w; *Mohican*, 1 k, 11 w; *Shenandoah*, 6 w, 5 m; *Ticonderoga*, 2 k, 2 w; *Tuscarora*, 4 k, 12 w; *Kansas*, 1 w; *Pequot*, 3 k, 5 w; *Yantic*, 2 k, 1 w; *Chippewa*, 4 k, 4 w; *Huron*, 5 w; *Seneca*, 5 w; *Iosco*, 2 k, 12 w; *Mackinaw*, 2 w, 2 m; *Maratanza*, 3 w; *Osceola*, 3 w; *Pawtuxet*, 2 w; *Pontoosuc*, 7 w; *Tacony*, 4 k, 11 w; *Sassacus*, 3 k, 3 w; *Fort Jackson*, 1 k, 10 w; *Monticello*, 4 k, 4 w; *Nereus*, 3 k, 3 w; *Rhode Island*, 8 w, 2 m; *Santiago de Cuba*, 1 k, 9 w; *Vanderbilt*, 2 k, 13 w; *Gettysburg*, 6 k, 6 w; *Tristram Shandy*, 2 w, 1 m; *Montgomery*, 2 k, 4 w. Total, k, 82; w, 269; m, 35; grand total, 386.

MARCHING THROUGH GEORGIA.

SHERMAN'S ADVANCE FROM ATLANTA.

BY OLIVER O. HOWARD, MAJOR-GENERAL, U. S. A.

WHEN Sherman decided to march south from Atlanta, he ordered to Thomas at Nashville Schofield with the Twenty-third Corps, Stanley with the Fourth Corps, all the cavalry, except Kilpatrick's division, all the detachments drawn back from the railway line, and such other troops, including A. J. Smith's, as Sherman's military division could furnish. Sherman reserved for his right wing my two corps, the Fifteenth and Seventeenth; and for his left wing the Fourteenth and Twentieth under Slocum. Mine, the Army of the Tennessee, numbered 33,000; Slocum's, the "Army of Georgia," 30,000; Kilpatrick's division of cavalry, 5000; so that the aggregate of all arms was 68,000 men. All surplus stores and trains were sent back to Tennessee. The railway south of the Etowah was next completely demolished. Under the efficient management of Colonel O. M. Poe, Sherman's chief engineer, all that was of a public nature in Atlanta which could aid the enemy was destroyed. Wrecked engines, bent and twisted iron rails, blackened ruins and lonesome chimneys saddened the hearts of the few peaceful citizens who remained there.

Behold now this veteran army thus reorganized and equipped, with moderate baggage and a few days' supply of small rations, but with plenty of ammunition, ready to march anywhere Sherman might lead. Just before starting, Sherman had a muscular lameness in one arm that gave him great trouble. On a visit to him I found his servant bathing and continuously rubbing the arm. As I understood the general's ruling, I would command next to him, because I had from the President an assignment to an army and a department. I was therefore especially anxious to know fully his plans, and plainly told him so. While the rubbing went on he explained in detail what he proposed and pointed significantly to Goldsboro', North Carolina, on his map, saying, "I hope to get there." On November 15th we set forth in good earnest. Slocum, Sherman accompanying him, went by the Augusta Railroad, and passed on through Milledgeville. I followed the Macon Railroad, and for the first seven days had Kilpatrick with me.

Notwithstanding our reduction of the impedimenta, our wagon trains were still long, and always a source of anxiety. Pushing toward Macon, I found

some resistance from General G. W. Smith's new levies. The crossing of the Ocmulgee, with its steep and muddy banks, was hard enough for the trains. I protected them by a second demonstration from the left bank against Macon. Smith crossed the river and gave us battle at Griswoldville. It was an affair of one division,— that of Charles R. Woods,— using mainly Walcutt's bri-

HOOK USED BY GENERAL SHERMAN'S ARMY FOR TWISTING AND DESTROYING RAILROAD IRON.

gade. Smith was badly defeated, and during the mêlée our trains were hurried off to Gordon and parked there in safety. ⏐ Here, at Gordon, Sherman, from Milledgeville, came across to me. Slocum had enjoyed a fine march, having had but little resistance. The stories of the mock Legislature at the State capital, of the luxurious supplies enjoyed all along, and of the constant fun and pranks of "Sherman's bummers," rather belonged to that route than ours. Possibly we had more of the throngs of escaping slaves, from the baby in arms to the old negro hobbling pain-fully along the line of march — negroes of all sizes, in all sorts of patched costumes, with carts and bro-ken-down horses and mules to match.

We brought along our wounded (over 200, I believe) in am-bulances, and though

SHERMAN'S TROOPS DESTROYING RAILROADS AT ATLANTA. FROM A PHOTOGRAPH.

they were jolted over corduroy roads and were much exposed to hardship, and participated in the excitements of the march, they all reached Savannah without the loss of a life. Our system of foraging was sufficiently good for the army, but the few citizens, women and children, who remained at home,

⏐ The Union loss at Griswoldville was 13 killed, 69 wounded, and 2 missing = 84. General C. C. Walcutt was among the wounded. The total Confederate loss was over 600.— EDITORS.

GENERAL SHERMAN SENDING HIS LAST TELEGRAM BEFORE CUTTING THE WIRES AND ABANDONING ALL
COMMUNICATION WITH THE NORTH. FROM A SKETCH MADE AT THE TIME.

suffered greatly. We marched our divisions on parallel roads when we could
find them; but sometimes, using rails or newly cut poles, made our roads
through swamps and soft ground, employing thousands of men. Arriving at
the Oconee, Osterhaus found a wooded valley, with lagune bridges and a
narrow causeway, on his road. A division of Hardee's, who himself had
left Hood and gone to Savannah to command what Confederates he could
hastily gather, had marched out to meet us and was intrenched on the east
bank. Artillery and infantry fire swept our road. Osterhaus, excited by the
shots, came to me shaking his head and asking how we would get any further.
"Deploy your skirmishers more and more till there is no reply," I said. He
did so. A half mile above he was able to send over among the cypresses a
brigade in boats. The Confederate division gave way and fled. Then shortly
our bridge was laid on the main road and we marched on. Blair, who had
returned from his furlough before we left Atlanta, crossed and kept the left
bank of the Ogeechee, and Sherman usually accompanied him. Blair's knowledge and hospitality attracted him. So the armies went on meeting an increased resistance, but were not much delayed till we got to the Savannah

Canal. Captain Duncan from my cavalry escort had carried Sherman's messages down the Ogeechee in a boat past Confederate guards and topedoes, and gone out to sea. He was picked up by a United States vessel and his message taken to the admiral. Hence navy and provision ships were waiting off the headlands, uncertain just where Sherman would secure a harbor.

Owing to swamps and obstructed roads and Hardee's force behind them, we could not enter Savannah. Our food was getting low. True, Sherman had sent Kilpatrick to try and take Fort McAllister, a strong fort which held the mouth of the Ogeechee. But as its capture was too much for the cavalry, I asked Sherman to allow me to take that fort with infantry. Hazen's division was selected. My chief engineer, Reese, with engineers and pioneers and plenty of men to help him, in three days repaired the burnt bridge, over 1000 feet long, near King's house. Hazen, ready at the bridge, then marched over and took Fort McAllister by assault, ⚓ which Sherman and I witnessed from the rice mill, some miles away on the other bank of the Ogeechee. Now we connected with the navy, and our supplies flowed in abundantly. Slocum soon put a force beyond the Savannah. Hardee, fearing to be penned up, abandoned his works and fled during the night before Slocum had seized his last road to the east. On December 23d the campaign culminated as Sherman entered Savannah. He sent the following dispatch to President Lincoln, which he received Christmas Eve: "I beg to present to you, as a Christmas gift, the city of Savannah, with one hundred and fifty heavy guns and plenty of ammunition, and also about twenty-five thousand bales of cotton."

⚓ There seem to have been but 230 men in the work. Hazen's loss was 24 killed and 110 wounded.—EDITORS.

SHERMAN'S ARMY LEAVING ATLANTA. FROM A SKETCH MADE AT THE TIME.

THE GEORGIA MILITIA DURING SHERMAN'S MARCH TO THE SEA.[‡]

BY GUSTAVUS W. SMITH, MAJOR-GENERAL, C. S. A.

ON the 12th of October, 1864, I was ordered to assemble the State forces of Georgia at Lovejoy's Station, to support the small body of Confederate cavalry observing the Federal garrison of Atlanta, and, by threatening the latter, draw the attention of General Sherman to that place, whilst his army was in pursuit of Hood, who was moving on the Federal line of communications.

At Lovejoy's Station we were joined by two small regiments of Georgia State line troops that had previously served with the Confederate army, and by several detachments of home guards and work-shop troops, ordered to report to me by General Howell Cobb, commanding in Georgia.

On the 15th of November, when General Sherman's army started from Atlanta on its famous "march to the sea," I had at Lovejoy's Station 2800 infantry, 3 batteries, and 250 local reserve cavalry, supporting the very small Confederate cavalry force in observation around Atlanta. So far as I knew, or had reason to believe, mine was the only force, except the cavalry, that was likely to be brought into the field to oppose Sherman's march through the State.

That night I withdrew my command to the intrenchments at Griffin. Early on the 16th Wheeler's cavalry was jammed back to our position, and the Federals made serious demonstrations on our lines, but no real attack. Late in the afternoon it was ascertained that a large portion of their forces had passed through McDonough, ten miles or more to the east of us, and were nearer to Macon than we were. I fell back from Griffin at dark, and in less than twenty-four hours reached Forsythe, thirty-five miles distant, just in time to repel the advance of Sherman's cavalry and save the large depot of supplies at that place. In the meantime Sherman had commenced crossing to the east side of the Ocmulgee, and Wheeler had moved over that river. The next day I withdrew to Macon, in time to assist in repelling a formidable demonstration against East Macon, in which the Federals succeeded in forcing General Wheeler, with a portion of his command, to the bank of the Ocmulgee, in rear of our fortifications. During the night Wheeler extricated his forces, and passed out to the south and east, thus again placing his cavalry on the flank and in front of Sherman.

The militia had saved Griffin, Forsythe, and Macon; but as yet there had been no serious collision with the Federals. The face of the country was open, the roads were in good order, the weather was fine and bracing, the crops had been gathered, and were ready for use; in short, a combination of circumstances favored an easy march for Sherman's army. It was evidently no part of his purpose to attack the fortified places in the interior of the State. He was only passing through it to his ultimate destination—subsisting on the country along his route, and destroying a great deal of property, besides thoroughly breaking up

the railroads, thus cutting off communications between Richmond and the States of Alabama, Mississippi, Louisiana, and Florida.

When my command reached Macon, the work-shop troops, home guards, local reserve cavalry, and the artillery—except Anderson's battery—were ordered to report to General Cobb. In the meantime General Beauregard, Lieutenant-Generals Hardee and Richard Taylor, and other officers of prominence, reached Macon, but they brought no troops with them. General Hardee assumed the chief command. Whilst on the field in East Macon, he ordered one of the militia brigades to start at once to Augusta, and a few hours later he ordered me to move, next morning, with the remainder of my command and proceed to the same place. A few hours after I was ordered to move to Augusta General Hardee started to Savannah, and General Taylor succeeded to the command in Macon. Early on the morning of the 22d the militia moved in compliance with Hardee's order; I remained in Macon a few hours for the purpose of procuring ammunition, supplies, and transportation, having ordered the senior brigadier-general present with the troops to halt before reaching Griswoldville and wait for further orders. He was instructed not to engage the enemy, but, if pressed, to fall back to the fortifications of East Macon; or, if necessary, toward the south in the direction already taken by Wheeler's cavalry. Contrary to my instructions the militia became engaged about one mile beyond Griswoldville, and were badly cut up. They lost 51 killed and 472 wounded, but they remained in close contact with the enemy until dark. By authority of General Taylor I then withdrew them to Macon and moved by rail to Albany, thence across the country to Thomasville, and from the latter point by rail to Savannah. About one thousand of the command arrived at the latter place at 2 A. M. on the 30th of November.

Immediately upon the arrival of the leading train in Savannah, before I had left my seat in the car, an officer of Hardee's staff handed me two orders. The first, dated 10 P. M., November 29th, read:

"Lieutenant-General Hardee directs that you will proceed at once with the first two trains of your troops which may arrive at Savannah to-night, and in the same cars, to Grahamville and Coosawhatchie, on the Charleston and Savannah Railroad, which places are being threatened by raiding parties of the enemy, and if you find yourself the ranking officer present, that you assume command and drive the enemy back to their gun-boats."

The second order was dated one hour later:

"Lieutenant-General Hardee directs me to say that, from information received, he thinks it best that the first train of your troops which arrives shall go to Coosawhatchie, the farthest point, and the second to Grahamville."

On receipt of these orders I directed the troops to remain in the cars, and ordered the two trains

‡ A continuation of the article on p. 331.

to be transferred through the city, to the depot of the Charleston and Savannah Railroad, and there to await further orders from me. I at once called on General Hardee, whom I found in bed, in his room at a private house, and showed him my conditional authority, from Governor Brown, to withdraw my command from the Confederate service proper. I said to him: "You know that the militia of this State cannot be legally ordered beyond its limits without a special act of the Legislature. But if you can satisfy me that it is absolutely necessary that my command shall go into South Caro-

INCIDENT OF SHERMAN'S MARCH — THE FATE
OF THE RAIL FENCE.

lina I will endeavor to carry out your orders. If you do not satisfy me, and persist in your orders, I will be under the disagreeable necessity of withdrawing the State forces from your control."

General Hardee said that Governor Brown, being cut off from eastern Georgia by the advancing Federal forces, had been superseded by General Rantz Wright, the presiding officer of the State Senate; and that the latter, in view of the alleged disabilities of Governor Brown, had issued a proclamation from Augusta, declaring himself to be acting Governor of the State. The authority I held from Governor Brown was several days later in date than Wright's proclamation. General Hardee then explained the condition of affairs; upon which I told him I was satisfied that, in the existing emergency, it was right that the militia should be moved into South Carolina, although this was contrary to the laws of the State of Georgia. And I added that when the emergency was over the militia must be promptly brought back to their own State. To this he acceded.

On reaching the depot I found the troops all on board the cars. I called around me about a dozen representative men of the command, briefly explained the necessity for our going beyond the limits of the State, and told them to communicate this to the men, and let me know quickly what they said about it. The reply came in a few minutes. Nearly if not quite all of the officers said they were willing to go anywhere General Smith wanted them to go. But nearly all the privates said that, whilst they would like to do what General Smith wanted, they would not go into South Carolina even to please him, because the South Carolina militia for months remained on the heights of Hamburg, and refused to cross over to Augusta and relieve the home guards of that place, thereby enabling those guards to go to the front whilst Georgia was being invaded.

On receiving this message I told the representative men to go back and inform all concerned that they were going to South Carolina, because it was my order; and that they would start within ten minutes — would be engaged in a big fight before 12 o'clock — must win it — and would be brought back to Georgia within forty-eight hours. This message was promptly delivered. In a few moments I heard laughter from every car, and ordered the conductors to put both trains in motion immediately. The men understood that they were to protect the railroad from raiding parties, and thus enable the expected Confederate reënforcements to reach Savannah.

The leading train arrived at Grahamville Station on the Charleston and Savannah Railroad about 8 A. M. The men were immediately moved out on the road leading to the Broad River landing, along which route the Federals, in large force, were reported to be steadily advancing. The second train followed the first within half an hour.

About three miles south of the station, on the crest of the north bank of a small stream, a parapet for light guns had been previously constructed, and short trenches for infantry had been prepared. These earth-works were about one hundred yards from the little stream, and were located upon ground called Honey Hill, ten or twelve feet above the water-level. On the right of the battery there was a dense forest; on the left an open pine wood. The ground between the earth-works and the small stream was mostly open, with a skirt of bushes near the water. The road on which the Federals approached was bordered closely, on both sides, by dense forests.

There were five pieces of South Carolina light artillery in the battery; and about one thousand militia, partly in the trenches, were formed in line on the right and left. Dispositions to resist attack were completed about 10 A. M. In my official report it is stated:

"The 47th Georgia [expected earlier from Charleston] had not yet reached the field. Within five or ten minutes after these dispositions had been made, the battle began by an advance piece of our artillery firing upon the enemy. Their line of battle was soon formed, and from that time until near dark they made continuous efforts to carry our position. . . . In an hour the enemy had so extended and developed their attack that it became absolutely necessary for me to place in the front line of battle my last troops, the 47th Georgia regiment, making in all about 1400 effective muskets on the field, and all engaged. . . . While we could not from the dense wood accurately estimate the number of the enemy, it was very clear their force largely exceeded ours, and I awaited, with some anxiety, the arrival of the 32d Georgia, and the forces expected from North and South Carolina. . . . About 4:30 P. M. Brigadier-General Robertson arrived with a portion of the 32d Georgia from Charleston, a battery of artillery, and a company of cavalry. These constituted an effective reserve, but came up too late to be used in the action. During the night the enemy retired rapidly in the direction of their gun-boats. Our loss, in every arm of service, was 8 men killed and 42 wounded. . . . Lieutenant-General Hardee arrived at Grahamville Station between 8 and 9 o'clock on the morning of the 1st of December. The enemy having been beaten back on the 30th of November, and the Confederate forces [between 2000 and 3000 in number] having now arrived, there was, in my judgment, no longer any necessity for retaining the State troops of Georgia beyond their legal jurisdiction. I therefore asked and obtained permission to bring these exhausted troops back to their own State." |

In the meantime General Sherman's army was steadily moving through Georgia. The Confederate cavalry under General Wheeler restricted the eccentric movements and depredations of the Federal cavalry under General Kilpatrick, but could not materially, if at all, affect the regular daily progress of Sherman's main forces. If General Sherman purposed crossing the Savannah River, and thus reaching the sea-coast of South Carolina, he abandoned such intention after the defeat of Hatch's forces at Honey Hill. Sherman's army continued to move down the Savannah River on the Georgia side.

About fifteen thousand Confederate troops from the Carolinas had reached Savannah, and General Hardee sent large detachments out on the Georgia Central Railroad to delay Sherman's progress, but without success. On the 9th of December the Federals were close against the fortifications of Savannah.

During the siege of that place, the line occupied by my command — about two thousand men — was about three miles above the city, and extended from the Savannah River to the Ogeechee Canal. This line was nearly two and a half miles in length. Batteries had been constructed at the Central Railroad, the Augusta road, and at Williamson's plantation, near the bank of the river. Between the batteries there were some slight trenches or rifle-pits, leaving three-fourths of a mile on my front without earth cover.

A short distance in front of the left of my line there was a swamp, and, nearer the river, a rice-field, both of which were flooded by means of a dam at the river-bank; and this sheet of water formed a serious obstacle to the two Federal corps jammed close against our front. But there was nothing at the far end of the dam to prevent its being cut, thereby draining the swamp and the rice-field; in which case the position could easily have been carried. To prevent this a work was begun, under the direction of Colonel B. W. Frobel, in front of the rice-field, but before it was completed the enemy appeared in front. The small militia garrison made a gallant and successful resistance, and saved the dam from being cut.

The enemy, after the capture of Fort McAllister, on the Altamaha River, effected a permanent lodgment on Hutchinson's Island, crossed the Savannah River, and established works on the South Carolina shore, almost within range of our only line of retreat.

At my suggestion, by collecting boats and using the city wharves for flooring and car-wheels for anchors, Colonel Frobel constructed a pontoon-bridge, about half a mile in length, from Hutchinson's Island over the river, and on December 20th the city was evacuated. The artillery, baggage wagons, and all the troops, except the permanent garrisons of the forts below, passed over the bridge, the militia bringing up the rear and encamping on the sand-hills on the South Carolina side.

After the evacuation of Savannah my command was ordered to proceed through South Carolina to Augusta, Georgia, and were put in camp on the sand-hills west of that place. Later we were transferred to the lines on Briar Creek; and in the latter part of the winter took position for a short time in South Carolina, covering the approaches to Augusta on that side. ⚓

| The Federal forces engaged at Honey Hill consisted of about 5500 men and 10 guns, under General John P. Hatch, sent by General John G. Foster, commanding the Department of the South, to secure a foothold for Sherman's army and to cut off Confederate reënforcements from Savannah. The Federal loss was 88 killed, 623 wounded, 43 missing,— total, 754.— EDITORS.

⚓ In my lines in front of Savannah there was a small battalion made up of released Federal prisoners of war, who had taken the oath of allegiance to the Confederate Government, and were enlisted in the Confederate army. Because of suspicious circumstances reported to me, I had given orders to the troops in the line on the right and left of this battalion, to fire upon and destroy these renegades in case they committed any overt act of treachery to us. These enlisted prisoners were styled "galvanized Yankees." Shortly before the evacuation of Savannah, our troops on the extreme left needing reënforcements, these "galvanized Yankees" were detached from my command by General Hardee, and within a very few days several of them were put to death for overt acts of mutiny and attempted desertion. After the war the general by whose order this was done was tried for murder by a military commission, and acquitted.

G. W. S.

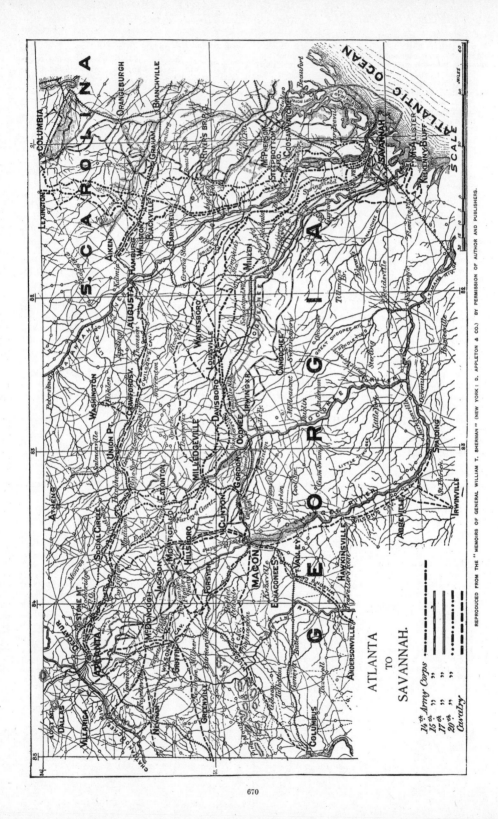

ATLANTA
TO
SAVANNAH.

14th Army Corps ....
15th   ,, ...
17th   ,, ...
20th   ,, ...
Cavalry ....

CAMP OF THE 2D MASS., CITY HALL SQUARE, ATLANTA. FROM A WAR-TIME PHOTOGRAPH.

MARCHING THROUGH GEORGIA AND THE CAROLINAS.

BY DANIEL OAKEY, CAPTAIN, 2D MASSACHUSETTS VOLUNTEERS.

To us of the Twelfth Corps who had gone West with the Eleventh Corps from the Army of the Potomac, the distant thunder of "the battle of the clouds" was the first sound of conflict in the new field. Some of our "Potomac airs," which had earned us the name of "Kid gloves and paper collars," | began to wear away as we better understood the important work to be done by the great army organizing around us, and of which we were to form a considerable part. A most interesting feature of these preparations was the reënlistment of the old three-years regiments. The two Potomac corps were consolidated, and we of the Twelfth who wore "the bloody star" were apprehensive lest different insignia should be adopted; but the star became the badge of the new (Twentieth) corps, the crescent men amiably dropping their Turkish emblem.

General W. H. Slocum, who had commanded the Twelfth so long, was assigned to command at Vicksburg, but was recalled to succeed Hooker in the command of the Twentieth Corps when toward the end of August, 1864, Hooker asked to be relieved because Howard, who was his junior, had been placed at the head of the Army of the Tennessee to fill the vacancy made by the death of McPherson at Atlanta. This temporary separation from our commander was hard, as all will remember who crowded to his headquarters on the evening of April 7th, 1864. But the sorrow of the hour was dispelled by the generous hospitality of his staff and his indulgent order to waive all rank for the occasion.

We observed in the Western troops an air of in-

dependence hardly consistent with the nicest discipline; but this quality appeared to some purpose at the battle of Resaca, where we saw our Western companions deliberately leave the line, retire out of range, clean their guns, pick up ammunition from the wounded, and return again to the fight. This cool self-reliance excited our admiration. On we went in a campaign of continual skirmishes and battles that ended in the capture of Atlanta. The morale of the troops had been visibly improved by this successful campaign.

On my way to army headquarters at Atlanta to call upon a staff friend, I met General Sherman, who acknowledged my salute with a familiar "How do you do, Captain." Scrutinizing the insignia on my cap, he continued, "Second Massachusetts? Ah, yes, I know your regiment; you have very fine parades over there in the park."

Sherman could be easily approached by any of his soldiers, but no one could venture to be familiar. His uniform coat, usually wide open at the throat, displayed a not very military black cravat and linen collar, and he generally wore low shoes and one spur. On the march he rode with each column in turn, and often with no larger escort than a single staff-officer and an orderly. In passing us on the march he acknowledged our salutations as if he knew us all, but hadn't time to stop. On "the march to the sea" a soldier called out to Sherman, "Uncle Billy, I guess Grant's waiting for us at Richmond." Sherman's acquaintance among his officers was remarkable, and of great advantage, for he learned the character of

| The Twelfth Corps of the Army of the Potomac was named "Kid gloves and paper collars" by the Fourteenth Corps of the Western Army owing to the careful discipline of the Twelfth Corps. It was originally the Fifth Corps (March, 1862), then it became the Second Corps, Army of Virginia (June, 1862), then the Twelfth Corps (September, 1862). The basis of it was Banks's old

division, and Banks was its first commander. Mansfield commanded the corps at Antietam, where he was killed and was succeeded by Slocum. The corps had as subordinate commanders such men as A. S. Williams, Charles S. Hamilton, John W. Geary, George H. Gordon, Ruger, Andrews, William Hawley, and the discipline they imparted continued to the end and affected other troops.—D. O.

every command, even of regiments, and could assign officers to special duties, with knowledge of those who were to fill the vacancies so made. The army appreciated these personal relations, and every man felt in a certain sense that Sherman had his eye on him.

Before the middle of November, 1864, the inhabitants of Atlanta, by Sherman's orders, had left the place. Serious preparations were making for the march to the sea. Nothing was to be left for the use or advantage of the enemy. The sick were sent back to Chattanooga and Nashville, along with every pound of baggage that could be dispensed with. The army was reduced, one might say, to its fighting weight, no man being retained who was not capable of a long march. Our communications were then abandoned by destroying the railroad and telegraph. There was something intensely exciting in this perfect isolation.

The engineers had peremptory orders to avoid any injury to dwellings, but to apply gunpowder and the torch to public buildings, machine-shops, depots, and arsenals. Sixty thousand of us witnessed the destruction of Atlanta, while our post band and that of the 33d Massachusetts played martial airs and operatic selections. It was a night never to be forgotten. Our regular routine was a mere form, and there could be no "taps" amid the brilliant glare and excitement.

The throwing away of superfluous conveniences began at daybreak. The old campaigner knows what to carry and what to throw away. Each group of messmates decided which hatchet, stewpan, or coffee-pot should be taken. The single wagon allowed to a battalion carried scarcely more than a grip-sack and blanket, and a bit of shelter tent about the size of a large towel, for each officer, and only such other material as was necessary for regimental business. Transportation was reduced to a minimum, and fast marching was to be the order of the day. Wagons to carry the necessary ammunition in the contingency of a battle, and a few days' rations in case of absolute need, composed the train of each army corps, and with one wagon and one ambulance for each regiment made very respectable "impedimenta," averaging about eight hundred wagons to a corps.

At last came the familiar "Fall in"; the great "flying column" was on the march, and the last regiment in Atlanta turned its back upon the smoking ruins. Our left wing (the Fourteenth and Twentieth corps under Slocum) seemed to threaten Macon, while the right wing (the Fifteenth and Seventeenth corps under Howard) bent its course as if for Augusta. Skirmishers were in advance, flankers were out, and foraging parties were ahead gathering supplies from the rich plantations. We were all old campaigners, so that a brush with the militia now and then or with Hardee's troops made no unusual delay; and Wheeler's cavalry was soon disposed of. We were expected to make fifteen miles a day; to corduroy the roads where necessary; to destroy such property as was designated by our corps commander, and to consume everything eatable by man or beast.

Milledgeville proved to be Sherman's first objective, and both wings came within less than supporting distance in and around the capital of the State. Our colored friends, who flocked to us in embarrassing numbers, told many stories about the fear and flight of the inhabitants at the approach of Sherman.

Cock-fighting became one of the pastimes of the "flying column." Many fine birds were brought in by our foragers. Those found deficient in courage and skill quickly went to the stew-pan in company with the modest barn-yard fowl, but those of redoubtable valor won an honored place and name, and were to be seen riding proudly on the front seat of an artillery caisson, or carried tenderly under the arm of an infantry soldier.

Our next objective was Savannah. Hazen's capture of Fort McAllister opened the gates of that beautiful city, while Hardee managed to escape with his little army; and Sherman, in a rather facetious dispatch, presented the city to Mr. Lincoln as a Christmas gift. Flushed with the success of our march, we settled down for a rest. Our uniforms were the worse for wear, but the army was in fine condition and fully prepared for the serious work ahead.

In the middle of December in the neighborhood of Savannah, after Hardee's troops had nearly exhausted the country, which was now mainly under water, there was little opportunity for the foragers to exercise their talents, and some of them returned to the ranks. The troops bivouacked here and there in comparatively dry spots, while picket duty had to be performed at many points in the water. In going from Sister's Ferry to Robertsville, where my regiment was in bivouac, I waded for a mile and a half in water knee-deep. At Purysburg the pickets were all afloat in boats and scows and on rafts, and the crestfallen foragers brought in nothing but rice, which became unpalatable when served three times a day for successive weeks. At length, when we left Savannah and launched cheerily into the untrodden land of South Carolina, the foragers began to assume their wonted spirit. We were proud of our foragers. They constituted a picked force from each regiment, under an officer selected for the command, and were remarkable for intelligence, spirit, and daring. Before daylight, mounted on horses captured on the plantations, they were in the saddle and away, covering the country sometimes seven miles in advance. Although I have said "in the saddle," many a forager had nothing better than a bit of carpet and a rope halter; yet this simplicity of equipment did not abate his power of carrying off hams and sweet-potatoes in the face of the enemy. The foragers were also important as a sort of advance guard, for they formed virtually a curtain of mounted infantry screening us from the inquisitive eyes of parties of Wheeler's cavalry, with whom they did not hesitate to engage when it was a question of a rich plantation.

When compelled to retire, they resorted to all the tricks of infantry skirmishers, and summoned reënforcements of foragers from other regiments to help drive the "Johnnies" out. When success crowned their efforts, the plantation was promptly

A BIVOUAC AMONG THE GEORGIA PINES.

DESTROYING A RAILROAD.

stripped of live stock and eatables. The natives were accustomed to bury provisions, for they feared their own soldiers quite as much as they feared ours. These subterranean stores were readily discovered by the practiced "Yankee" eye. The appearance of the ground and a little probing with a ramrod or a bayonet soon decided whether to dig. Teams were improvised; carts and vehicles of all sorts were pressed into the service and loaded with provisions. If any antiquated militia uniforms were discovered, they were promptly donned, and a comical procession escorted the valuable train of booty to the point where the brigade was expected to bivouac for the night. The regimentals of the past, even to those of revolutionary times, were often conspicuous.

On an occasion when our brigade had the advance, several parties of foragers, consolidating themselves, captured a town from the enemy's cavalry, and occupied the neighboring plantations. Before the arrival of the main column hostilities had ceased; order had been restored, and mock arrangements were made to receive the army. Our regiment in the advance was confronted by a picket dressed in continental uniform, who waved his plumed hat in response to the gibes of the men, and galloped away on his bareback mule to apprise his comrades of our approach. We marched into the town and rested on each side of the main street. Presently a forager, in ancient militia uniform indicating high rank, debouched from a side street to do the honors of the occasion. He was mounted on a raw-boned horse with a bit of carpet for a saddle. His old plumed chapeau in hand, he rode with gracious dignity through the street, as if reviewing the brigade. After him came a family carriage laden with hams, sweet-potatoes, and other provisions, and drawn by two horses, a mule, and a cow, the two latter ridden by postilions.

At Fayetteville, North Carolina, the foragers as usual had been over the ground several hours before the heads of column arrived, and the party from my regiment had found a broken-down grist-mill. Their commander, Captain Parker, an officer of great spirit and efficiency, and an expert machinist, had the old wheel hoisted into its place and put the mill in working order. Several parties from other regiments had been admitted as

SHERMAN'S FORAGERS ON A GEORGIA PLANTATION.

working members, and teams of all sorts were busy collecting and bringing in corn and carrying away meal for distribution. This bit of enterprise was so pleasing to the troops that plenty of volunteers were ready to relieve the different gangs, and the demand was so great as to keep the mill at work all night by the light of pine-knot fires and torches.

The march through Georgia has been called a grand military promenade, all novelty and excitement. But its moral effect on friend and foe was immense. It proved our ability to lay open the heart of the Confederacy, and left the question of what we might do next a matter of doubt and terror. It served also as a preliminary training for the arduous campaign to come. Our work was incomplete while the Carolinas, except at a few points on the sea-coast, had not felt the rough contact of war. But their swamps and rivers, swollen and spread into lakes by winter floods, presented obstructions almost impracticable to an invading army, if opposed by even a very inferior force.

The task before us was indeed formidable. It

involved exposure and indefatigable exertion. To succeed, our forward movement had to be continuous, for even the most productive regions would soon be exhausted by our 60,000 men and more, and 13,000 animals.

Although we were fully prepared, with our great trains of ammunition, to fight a pitched battle, our mission was not to fight, but to consume and destroy. Our inability to care properly for the wounded, who must necessarily be carried along painfully in jolting ambulances to die on the way from exhaustion and exposure, was an additional and very serious reason for avoiding collision with the enemy. But where he could not be evaded, his very presence across our path increased the velocity of our flying column. We repelled him by a decisive blow and without losing our momentum.

The beginning of our march in South Carolina was pleasant, the weather favorable, and the country productive. Sometimes at the midday halt a stray pig that had cunningly evaded the foragers would venture forth in the belief of having escaped "the cruel war," and would find his error, alas! too late, by encountering our column. Instantly an armed mob would set upon him, and his piercing shrieks would melt away in the scramble for fresh pork. But the midday sport of the main column and the happy life of the forager were sadly interrupted. The sun grew dim, and the rain came and continued. A few of our excellent foragers were reported captured by Wheeler's cavalry, while we sank deeper and deeper in the mud as we approached the Salkehatchie Swamp, which lay between us and the Charleston and Augusta railroad. As the heads of column came up, each command knew what it had to do. Generals Mower and G. A. Smith got their divisions across by swimming, wading, and floating, and effected lodgments in spite of the enemy's fire. An overwhelming mass of drenched and muddy veterans swept away the enemy, while the rest of our force got the trains and artillery over by corduroying, pontooning, and bridging. It seemed a grand day's work to have accomplished, as we sank down that night in our miry bivouac. The gallant General Wager Swayne lost his leg in this Salkehatchie encounter. Luckily for him and others we were not yet too far from our friends to send the wounded back, with a strong escort, to Pocotaligo.

We destroyed about forty miles of the Charleston and Augusta railroad, and, by threatening points beyond the route we intended to take, we deluded the enemy into concentrating at Augusta and other places, while we marched rapidly away, leaving him well behind, and nothing but Wade Hampton's cavalry, and the more formidable obstacle of the Saluda River and its swamps, between us and Columbia, our next objective. As the route of our column lay west of Columbia, I saw nothing of the oft-described and much-discussed burning of that city.

During the hasty removal of the Union prisoners from Columbia two Massachusetts officers managed to make their escape. Exhausted and almost naked, they found their way to my command. My mess begged for the privilege of caring for one of them. We gave him a mule to ride with a com-

fortable saddle, and scraped together an outfit for him, although our clothes were in the last stages. Our guest found the mess luxurious, as he sat down with us at the edge of a rubber blanket spread upon the ground for a table-cloth, and set with tin cups and platters. Stewed fighting-cock and bits of fried turkey were followed by fried corn-meal and sorghum. Then came our coffee and pipes, and we lay down by a roaring fire of pine-knots, to hear our guest's story of life in a rebel prison. Before daybreak the tramp of horses reminded us that our foragers were sallying forth. The red light from the countless camp-fires melted away as the dawn stole over the horizon, casting its wonderful gradations of light and color over the masses of sleeping soldiers, while the smoke from burning pine-knots befogged the chilly morning air. Then the bugles broke the impressive stillness, and the roll of drums was heard on all sides. Soon the scene was alive with blue coats and the hubbub of roll-calling, cooking, and running for water to the nearest spring or stream. The surgeons looked to the sick and footsore, and weeded from the ambulances those who no longer needed to ride.

It was not uncommon to hear shots at the head of the column. The foragers would come tumbling back, and ride alongside the regiment, adding to the noisy talk their account of what they had seen, and dividing among their comrades such things as they had managed to bring away in their narrow escape from capture. A staff-officer would gallop down the roadside like a man who had forgotten something which must be recovered in a hurry. At the sound of the colonel's ringing voice, silence was instant and absolute. Sabers flashed from their scabbards, the men brought their guns to the "carry," and the battalion swung into line at the roadside; cats, fighting-cocks, and frying-pans passed to the rear rank; officers and sergeants buzzed round their companies to see that the guns were loaded and the men ready for action. The color-sergeant loosened the water-proof cover of the battle-flag, a battery of artillery flew past on its way to the front, following the returning staff-officer, and we soon heard the familiar bang of shells. Perhaps it did not amount to much after all, and we were soon swinging into "route step" again.

At times when suffering from thirst it was hard to resist the temptation of crystal swamp water, as it rippled along the side of a causeway, a tempting sight for the weary and unwary. In spite of oft-repeated cautions, some contrived to drink it, but these were on their backs with malarial disease at the end of the campaign, if not sooner.

After passing Columbia there was a brief season of famine. The foragers worked hard, but found nothing. They made amends, however, in a day or two, bringing in the familiar corn-meal, sweet-potatoes, and bacon.

We marched into Cheraw with music and with colors flying. Stacking arms in the main street, we proceeded to supper, while the engineers laid the pontoons across the Pedee River. The railing of the town pump, and the remains of a buggy, said to belong to Mr. Lincoln's brother-in-law, Dr. Todd, were quickly reduced to kindling-wood to boil the

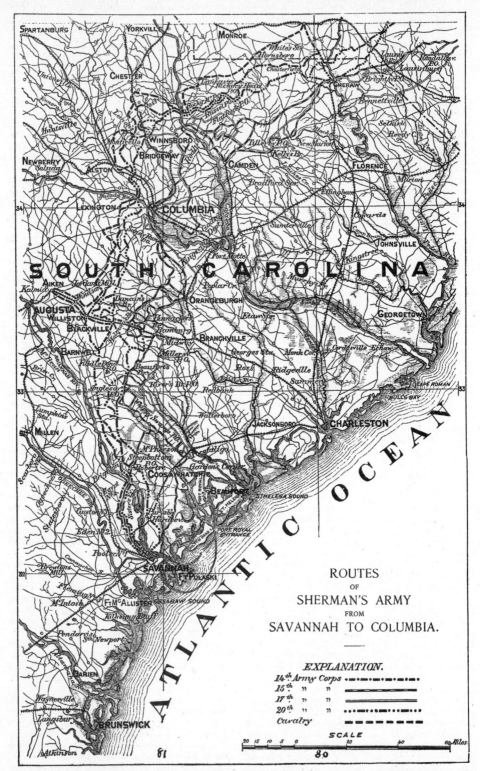

ROUTES
OF
SHERMAN'S ARMY
FROM
SAVANNAH TO COLUMBIA.

EXPLANATION.

14th Army Corps		
15th " "		
17th " "		
20th " "		
Cavalry		

SCALE
20 15 10 5 0   20   40   60 Miles
80

THE ROAD FROM McPHERSONVILLE. SHERMAN AND HIS STAFF PASSING THROUGH WATER AND MIRE. FROM A SKETCH MADE AT THE TIME.

coffee. The necessary destruction of property was quickly accomplished, and on we went. A mile from the Lumber River the country, already flooded ankle-deep, was rendered still more inhospitable by a steady down-pour of rain. The bridges had been partly destroyed by the enemy, and partly swept away by the flood. An attempt to carry heavy army wagons and artillery across this dreary lake might have seemed rather foolhardy, but we went to work without loss of time. The engineers were promptly floated out to the river, to direct the rebuilding of bridges, and the woods all along the line of each column soon rang with the noise of axes. Trees quickly became logs, and were brought to the submerged roadway. No matter if logs disappeared in the floating mud; thousands more were coming from all sides. So, layer upon layer, the work went bravely on. Soon the artillery and wagons were jolting over our wooden causeway.

As my regiment was the rear-guard for the day, we had various offices to perform for the train, and it was midnight before we saw the last wagon over the bridge by the light of our pine torches. It seemed as if that last wagon was never to be got over. It came bouncing and bumping along, its six mules smoking and blowing in the black, misty air. The teamster, mounted on one of the wheelers, guided his team with a single rein and addressed each mule by name, reminding the animal of his faults, and accusing him of having, among other peculiarities, "a black military heart." Every sentence of his oath-adorned rhetoric was punctuated with a dexterous whip-lash.

At last, drenched to the skin and covered with mud, I took my position on the bridge, seated in a chair which one of my men had presented to me, and waited for the command to "close up."

As we passed the wagon camp, there was the deafening, indescribable chorus of mules and teamsters, besides the hoarse shouting of quartermasters and wagonmasters plunging about on horseback through the mud, to direct the arriving teams into their places. But it all died away in the distance as we marched on to find the oozy resting-place of the brigade. The army had been in bivouac some hours, and countless camp-fires formed a vast belt of fire that spread out into the black night.

As we advanced into the wild pine regions of North Carolina the natives seemed wonderfully impressed at seeing every road filled with marching troops, artillery, and wagon trains. They looked destitute enough as they stood in blank amazement gazing upon the "Yanks" marching by. The scene before us was very striking; the resin pits were on fire, and great columns of black smoke rose high into the air, spreading and mingling together in gray clouds, and suggesting the roof and pillars of a vast temple. All traces of habitation were left behind, as we marched into that grand forest with its beautiful carpet of pine-needles. The straight trunks of the pine-tree shot up to a great height, and then spread out into a green roof, which kept us in perpetual shade. As night came on, we found that the resinous sap in the cavities cut in the trees to receive it, had been lighted by "bummers" in our advance.

THE STORMING OF THE LITTLE SALKEHATCHIE RIVER BY WEVER'S BRIGADE OF THE
FIFTEENTH CORPS. FROM A WAR-TIME SKETCH.

The effect of these peculiar watch-fires on every side, several feet above the ground, with flames licking their way up the tall trunks, was peculiarly striking and beautiful. But it was sad to see this wanton destruction of property, which, like the firing of the resin pits, was the work of "bummers," who were marauding through the country committing every sort of outrage. There was no restraint except with the column or the regular foraging parties. We had no communications, and could have no safeguards. The country was necessarily left to take care of itself, and became a "howling waste." The "coffee-coolers" of the Army of the Potomac were archangels compared to our "bummers," who often fell to the tender mercies of Wheeler's cavalry, and were never heard of again, earning a fate richly deserved.

On arriving within easy distance of the Cape Fear River, where we expected to communicate with the navy, detachments were sent in rapid advance to secure Fayetteville. Our division, after a hard day of corduroying in various spots over a distance of twelve miles, went into camp for supper, and then, taking the plank-road for Fayetteville, made a moonlight march of nine miles in three hours, but our friends from the right wing arrived there before us.

Hardee retired to a good position at Averysboro', where Kilpatrick found him intrenched and too strong for the cavalry to handle unassisted. It was the turn of our brigade to do special duty, so at about 8 o'clock in the evening we were ordered to join the cavalry. We were not quite sure it rained, but everything was dripping. The men furnished themselves with pine-knots, and our weapons glistened in the torch-light, a cloud of black smoke from the torches floating back over our heads. The regimental wits were as ready as ever, and amid a flow of lively badinage we toiled on through the mud.

When the column was halted for a few minutes to give us an opportunity of drawing breath, I found Sergeant Johnson with one arm in the mud up to the elbow. He explained that he was trying to find his shoe. We floundered on for five miles, and relieved a brigade of Kilpatrick's men whom we found in some damp woods. There was a comfort in clustering round their camp-fires, while they retired into outer darkness to prepare for the morning attack. But the cavalry fireside was only a temporary refuge from the storm, for we also had to depart into the impenetrable darkness beyond, to await in wet line of battle the unforeseen. Those who were exhausted sank down in the mud to sleep, while others speculated on the future.

The clear wintry dawn disclosed a long line of blue-coats spread over the ground in motionless groups. This was the roaring torch-light brigade of the night before. The orders "Fall in!" "Forward!" in gruff tones broke upon the chilly air, and brought us shivering to our feet. We moved to the edge of the woods with the cavalry. The skirmish line, under Captain J. I. Grafton, had already disappeared into the opposite belt of woods, and evidently were losing no time in developing the enemy and ascertaining his force. They were drawing his fire from all points, indicating a force more than double that of our brigade. Dismounted cavalry were now sent forward to prolong the skirmish-line. Captain Grafton was reported badly wounded in the leg, but still commanding with his usual coolness. Suddenly he appeared staggering out of the wood into the open space in our front, bareheaded, his face buried in his hands, his saber hanging by the sword-knot from his wrist, one leg bound up with a handkerchief, his uniform covered with blood; in a moment he fell toward the colors. Officers clustered about him in silence, and a gloom spread through the brigade as word passed that Grafton was dead.

The main column was now arriving, and as the troops filed off to the right and left of the road, and the field-guns galloped into battery, we moved forward to the attack. The enemy gave us a hot reception, which we returned with a storm of lead. It was a wretched place for a fight. At some points we had to support our wounded until they could be carried off, to prevent their falling into the swamp water, in which we stood ankle-deep. Here and there a clump of thick growth in the black mud broke the line as we advanced. No ordinary troops were in our front. They would not give way until a division of Davis's corps was thrown

upon their right, while we pressed them closely. As we passed over their dead and wounded, I came upon the body of a very young officer, whose handsome, refined face attracted my attention. While the line of battle swept past me I knelt at his side for a moment. His buttons bore the arms of South Carolina. Evidently we were fighting the Charleston chivalry. Sunset found us in bivouac on the Goldsboro' road, and Hardee in retreat.

As we trudged on toward Bentonville, distant sounds told plainly that the head of the column was engaged. We hurried to the front and went into action, connecting with Davis's corps. Little opposition having been expected, the distance between our wing and the right wing had been allowed to increase beyond supporting distance in the endeavor to find easier roads for marching as well as for transporting the wounded. The scope of this paper precludes a description of the battle of Bentonville, which was a combination of mistakes, miscarriages, and hard fighting on both sides. It ended in Johnston's retreat, leaving open the road to Goldsboro', where we arrived ragged and almost barefoot. While we were receiving letters from home, getting new clothes, and taking our regular doses of quinine, Lee and Johnston surrendered, and the great conflict came to an end.

SHERMAN'S "BUMMERS" CAPTURING FAYETTEVILLE COURT HOUSE, N. C.
FROM A SKETCH MADE AT THE TIME.

THE FAILURE TO CAPTURE HARDEE.

BY ALEXANDER ROBERT CHISOLM, COLONEL, C. S. A.

WHEN General Sherman in his march across Georgia had passed through Milledgeville, General Beauregard was hastily ordered from Mississippi to Charleston, there to assume command of the department then commanded by General Hardee, ‡ who had urgently asked for his presence.

When he arrived in Charleston Sherman was close to Savannah, the end of his march to the sea.

Here he lost an easy and brilliant opportunity to capture, with that city, Hardee's entire command of about 10,000 men. In his "Memoirs" he writes (Vol. II., p. 204) that General Slocum wanted to transfer a whole corps to the South Carolina bank of the Savannah River, the object being to cut off Hardee's retreat. At that time Hardee's only line of retreat was at Screven's Ferry to a causeway,

‡ Lieutenant-General W. J. Hardee was assigned to the command of the Department of South Carolina, Georgia, and Florida, on the 28th of September, 1864, succeeding Major-General Samuel Jones.— EDITORS.

over two miles in length, on the South Carolina bank. Without a pontoon-bridge or other means of getting away, he was relying only on three very small steamboats. The only troops he had on the Carolina bank were a small force of light artillery and Ferguson's brigade of Wheeler's cavalry, numbering not more than 1000 men. At this time Beauregard's "Military Division of the West" did not embrace the department of General Hardee, although he had authority and discretion there, in an emergency. Therefore he had gone to Charleston on December 7th, with a view of saving and concentrating the scattered Confederate forces in that region for some effective action against Sherman. He telegraphed Hardee (December 8th), advising him to hold Savannah as long as practicable, but under no circumstances to risk the garrison, and to be ready for withdrawal to a junction with Major-General Samuel Jones at Pocotaligo, South Carolina. At Hardee's urgent request Beauregard went to Savannah on the morning of the 9th. Finding no means prepared for the contingency of evacuation he directed the immediate construction of a pontoon-bridge, with the plantation rice-flats (collected at my suggestion) for pontoons. These, moored by old guns and car-wheels for anchors, were covered with flooring supplied by pulling down the wharves and wooden buildings. After giving instructions as to the plan of operations, Beauregard returned to Charleston. Instructions were also given for the best feasible defense of the causeway and road from Screven's Ferry. On the 14th Hardee telegraphed to Beauregard of the enemy's movements, his own doubts and his desire to have specific orders; and on the 15th he again telegraphed, urging Beauregard to return and determine the actual time for the evacuation and junction with Jones. Beauregard (whom I accompanied) went to Savannah on the night of the 16th, in my wagon, running the gauntlet of Foster's batteries near Pocotaligo so as to save the railroad from obstruction by an unlucky shot at his train, and traversing by like conveyance the distance along which the railroad had been broken by Sherman near Savannah, my wagon and pair of horses being transported between the breaks in freight-cars. He found the pontoon-bridge only about one-third constructed, some of Wheeler's cavalry having destroyed a number of rice-flats collected, supposing they had been gathered by Sherman for the crossing of the river. But the work was prosecuted with such vigor by the chief engineer, Colonel John G. Clarke, in person, that by daylight of the 19th General Beauregard found it all but completed, stretching from the city to Hutchinson's Island, over which a causeway was built; thence to Pennyworth Island, where another causeway was laid; thence across the Back River to a causeway that led over the swamps to the main-land of the Carolina bank. Beauregard ordered the movement to be made that night, though accident delayed it until the night of the 20th, when by this route — the only exit from Savannah — Hardee was safely withdrawn, with field-artillery, baggage, and stores, and the bridge then destroyed. This was one of the neatest achievements of the war, rivaling in decision, resource, and skill the evacuations of Corinth and of Morris Island by the same commander.

But meanwhile, cautiously leaving his 60,000 men concentrated on the Georgia bank of the river, General Sherman had gone in person around by the sea to Hilton Head in order to procure the assistance of Foster's army for the investment of Savannah from the Carolina bank. It is clear that, had Slocum's suggestion been adopted, or had even the single brigade of his corps that had crossed the river above Savannah been vigorously pushed against the thin line of Confederate pickets covering this causeway, all escape from Savannah must have been cut off. General Sherman saw his mistake too late, and, in his letter of December 24th, 1864, he excuses himself to Halleck: "I feel somewhat disappointed at Hardee's escape, but really am not to blame. I moved as quickly as possible to close up the Union causeway, but intervening obstacles were such that, before I could get troops on the road, Hardee had slipped out." The real point is that, having an overwhelming force, his movement should have been a prompt and vigorous one to the rear of Savannah, and not a voyage to Hilton Head to borrow forces from General Foster. ⚓ As to "intervening obstacles," they consisted of some light artillery and a very thin line of cavalry of which, in his letters, he saw fit to write in the most disparaging terms. In this case they seem to have sufficed to cover the retreat of about 10,000 men.

To estimate General Sherman's error we must here consider that the Confederate troops in Savannah formed the only substantial force then interposed, and the bulk of the only force afterward interposed, between him and Grant. From a military point of view, therefore, this failure was of importance. Beauregard had suggested to the Government a bold and rapid concentration of a portion of Lee's army with the forces that he was then assembling, in order to try a supreme and decisive blow against Sherman, and, if successful, then to concentrate all forces upon Grant.

⚓ In his "Memoirs," Vol. II., p. 216, General Sherman explains his action at this time as follows:

"On the 18th of December, at my camp by the side of the plank-road, eight miles back of Savannah, I received General Hardee's letter declining to surrender, when nothing remained but to assault. The ground was difficult, and, as all former assaults had proved so bloody, I concluded to make one more effort to completely surround Savannah on all sides, so as further to excite Hardee's fears, and in case of success to capture his whole army. We had already completely invested the place on the north, west, and south, but there remained to the enemy on the east the use of the old dyke or plank-road leading into South Carolina, and I knew that Hardee would have a pontoon-bridge across the river. On examining my maps I thought that the division of John P. Hatch, belonging to General Foster's command, might be moved from its then position at Broad River, by water, down to Bluffton, from which it could reach the plank-road, fortify and hold it, at some risk, of course, because Hardee could avail himself of his central position to fall on this detachment with his whole army."

To carry out the purpose Sherman went to Hilton Head, and on the way back was met with the announcement that Hardee had evacuated Savannah.—EDITORS.

ADVANCING UNDER DIFFICULTIES.

SHERMAN'S MARCH FROM SAVANNAH TO BENTONVILLE.

BY HENRY W. SLOCUM, MAJOR-GENERAL, U. S. V.

GENERAL SHERMAN'S army commenced its march from "Atlanta to the Sea" on the morning of November 15th, and arrived in front of the defenses of Savannah on the 10th of December, 1864. No news had been received from the North during this interval except such as could be gleaned from Southern papers picked up by the soldiers on the line of our march. Our fleet was in Ossabaw Sound with supplies of food and clothing, and an immense mail, containing letters from home for nearly every one in the army, from the commanding general down to the private soldier. All that blocked our communication with the fleet was Fort McAllister on the Ogeechee River. This fort was captured by Hazen's division of the Fifteenth Corps on December 13th, and the 15th brought us our mails and an abundant supply of food and ammunition, making this one of the happiest days experienced by the men of Sherman's army. Preparations were at once commenced for assaulting the Confederate works, and were nearly completed when the Confederates evacuated Savannah. Our troops entered the city before daybreak on the 21st of December. The fall of Fort McAllister placed General Sherman in communication with General Grant and the authorities at Washington. Prior to the capture of Savannah, the plan contemplated by General Grant involved the removal of the infantry of Sherman's army to City Point by sea. On December 6th General Grant wrote to Sherman:

"My idea now is that you establish a base on the sea-coast, fortify, and leave all your artillery and cavalry and enough infantry to protect them, and at the same time so threaten the interior

FROM A PHOTOGRAPH.

GENERAL WM. B. HAZEN. GENERAL W. T. SHERMAN. GENERAL HENRY W. SLOCUM.
GENERAL JOHN A. LOGAN. GENERAL JEFF. C. DAVIS. GENERAL J. A. MOWER.
GENERAL O. O. HOWARD.

that the militia of the South will have to be kept home.   With the balance of your command come here with all dispatch."

In reply, under date of December 13th, Sherman said:

"I had expected, after reducing Savannah, instantly to march to Columbia, South Carolina, thence to Raleigh, and then to report to you."

The fall of Savannah resulted in the adoption of the plan which Sherman had contemplated.   In a letter dated December 24th Sherman says:

"Many and many a person in Georgia asked me why I did not go to South Carolina, and when I answered that we were *en route* for that State, the invariable reply was, 'Well, if you will make those people feel the utmost severities of war we will pardon you for your desolation of Georgia.'"

About one month was spent in Savannah in clothing the men and filling the trains with ammunition and rations.   Then commenced the movement which was to make South Carolina feel the severities of war. ♱ The right wing, with the exception of Corse's division of the Seventeenth Corps, moved via Hilton Head to Beaufort.   The left wing with Corse's division and the cavalry moved up the west bank of the Savannah River to Sister's Ferry, distant about forty miles from Savannah.   Sherman's plan was similar to that adopted on leaving Atlanta.   When

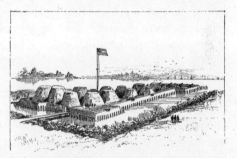

FORT McALLISTER.   FROM A WAR-TIME SKETCH.

the army had started from Atlanta, the right wing had moved direct toward Macon and the left toward Augusta.   Both cities were occupied by Confederate troops.   The movements of our army had caused the Confederate authorities at each of these important cities to demand not only the retention of the troops at each place, but had induced them to demand help

♱ At this time General Lee addressed the following letter to the Governor of South Carolina:

"HEADQUARTERS, ARMY N. VA., 27 January, '65. "HIS EXCELLENCY A. G. MAGRATH, Governor of South Carolina, Columbia. SIR: I received to-day your letter of the 16th inst., and regret exceedingly to learn the present condition of affairs in the South. I infer from your letter that you consider me able to send an army to arrest the march of General Sherman. If such was the case I should not have waited for your application, for I lament as much as you do his past success, and see the injury that may result from his further progress. I have no troops except those within this department, within which my operations are confined. According to your statement of General Sherman's force, it would require this whole army to oppose him. It is now confronted by General Grant with a far superior army. If it was transferred to South Carolina, I do not believe General Grant would remain idle on the James River. It would be as easy for him to move his army south as for General Sherman to advance north. You can judge whether the condition of affairs would be benefited by a concentration of the two large Federal armies in South Carolina, with the rest of the Confederacy stripped of defense. But should Charleston fall into the hands of the enemy, as grievous as would be the blow and as painful the result, I cannot concur in the opinion of your Excellency that our cause would necessarily be lost. Should our whole coast fall in the possession of our enemies, with our people true, firm, and united, the war could be continued and our purpose accomplished. As long as our armies are unsubdued and sustained, the Confederacy is safe. I therefore think it bad policy to shut our troops within intrenchments, where they can be besieged with superior forces, and prefer operating in the field. I recommend this course in South Carolina, and advise that every effort be made to prevent General Sherman reaching Charleston by contesting his advance. The last return made by General Hardee of his force which I have seen, gave his entire strength 20,500 of all arms; with 5000 South Carolina militia which he expected, and 1500 Georgia troops under General G. W. Smith, he would have 27,000. This is exclusive of Connor's brigade and Butler's division sent from this army, which ought to swell his force to 33,000. But I think it might be still further increased by a general turnout of all the men in Georgia and South Carolina, and that Sherman could be resisted until General Beauregard could arrive with reënforcements from the West. I see no cause for depression or despondency, but abundant reason for renewed exertion and unyielding resistance. With great respect, your Excellency's obedient servant, R. E. LEE, General." [Printed from the MS.]—EDITORS.

from every quarter.   Sherman had had no thought of attacking either place, and at the proper time the movements of both wings of the army were so directed as to unite them and leave both cities in our rear, with little or no force in our front.   On leaving Savannah our right wing threatened Charleston and the left again threatened Augusta, the two wings being again united in the interior of South Carolina, leaving the Confederate troops at Augusta with almost a certainty that Charleston must fall without a blow from Sherman.   On the arrival of the left wing at Sister's Ferry on the Savannah, instead of finding, as was anticipated, a river a few yards in width which could be easily crossed, they found a broad expanse of water which was utterly impassable.   The continuous rain-fall had caused the river to over-flow, so that the lowland on the South Carolina side was covered with water, extending nearly half a mile from the river.   We were delayed several days in vain efforts to effect a crossing, and were finally compelled to await the falling of the waters.   Our pontoon-bridge was finally constructed and the crossing commenced.   Each regiment as it entered South Carolina gave three cheers.   The men seemed to realize that at last they had set foot on the State which had done more than all others to bring upon the country the horrors of civil war.   In the narrow road leading from the ferry on the South Carolina side torpedoes had been planted, so that several of our men were killed or wounded by treading upon them.   This was unfortunate for that section of the State.   Planting torpedoes for the defense of a position is legitimate warfare, but our soldiers regarded the act of placing them in a highway where no contest was anticipated as something akin to poisoning a stream of water; it is not recognized as fair or legitimate warfare.   If that

RAILWAY DESTRUCTION AS A MILITARY ART.

SKIRMISHERS CROSSING THE NORTH EDISTO, S. C., ON A FLOATING FOOT-BRIDGE.
FROM A SKETCH MADE AT THE TIME.

section of South Carolina suffered more severely than any other, it was due in part to the blundering of people who were more zealous than wise.

About February 19th the two wings of the army were reunited in the vicinity of Branchville, a small village on the South Carolina Railroad at the point where the railroad from Charleston to Columbia branches off to Augusta. Here we resumed the work which had occupied so much of our time in Georgia, viz., the destruction of railroads. ↓

↓ A knowledge of the art of building railroads is certainly of more value to a country than that of the best means of destroying them; but at this particular time the destruction seemed necessary, and the time may again come when such work will have to be done. Lest the most effectual and expeditious method of destroying railroad tracks should become one of the lost arts, I will here give a few rules for the guidance of officers who may in future be charged with this important duty. It should be remembered that these rules are the result of long experience and close observation. A detail of men to do the work should be made on the evening before operations are to commence. The number to be detailed being, of course, dependent upon the amount of work to be done, I estimate that one thousand men can easily destroy about five miles of track per day, and do it thoroughly. Before going out in the morning the men should be supplied with a good breakfast, for it has been discovered that soldiers are more efficient at this work, as well as on the battle-field, when their stomachs are full than when they are empty. The question as to the food to be given the men for breakfast is not important, but I suggest roast turkeys, chickens, fresh eggs, and coffee, for the reason that in an enemy's country such a breakfast will cause no unpleasantness between the commissary and the soldiers, inasmuch as the commissary will only be required to provide the coffee. In fact it has been discovered that an army moving through a hostile but fertile country, having an efficient corps of foragers (vulgarly known in our army as "bummers"), requires but few articles of food, such as hard-tack, coffee, salt, pepper, and sugar. Your detail should be divided into three sections of about equal numbers. I will suppose the detail to consist of three thousand men. The first thing to be done is to reverse the relative positions of the ties and iron rails, placing the ties up and the rails under them. To do this, Section No. 1, consisting of one thousand men, is distributed along one side of the track, one man at the end of each tie. At a given signal each man seizes a tie, lifts it gently till it assumes a vertical position, and then at another signal pushes it forward so that when it falls the ties will be over the rails. Then each man loosens his tie from the rail. This done, Section No. 1 moves forward to another portion of the road, and Section No. 2 advances and is distributed along the portion of the road recently occupied by Section No. 1. The duty of the second section is to collect the ties, place them in piles of about thirty ties each — place the rails on the top of these piles, the center of each rail being over the center of the pile, and then set fire to the

THE RIGHT WING UNDER HOWARD CROSSING THE SALUDA RIVER.   FROM A WAR-TIME SKETCH.

Having effectually destroyed over sixty miles of railroads in this section, the army started for Columbia, the capital of South Carolina, each corps taking a separate road.   The left wing (Slocum) arrived at a point about three miles from Columbia on the 16th, and there received orders to cross the Saluda River, at Mount Zion's Church.   The Fourteenth Corps moved to the crossing, built a bridge during the night, crossed the river next day, and was followed by the Twentieth Corps and Kilpatrick's cavalry.   The right wing (Howard) moved direct to Columbia, the Fifteenth Corps moving through the city and camping outside on the Camden road.   The Seventeenth Corps did not enter Columbia.   During the night of February 17th the greater portion of the city of Columbia was burned.   The lurid flames could easily be seen from my camp, many miles distant.   Nearly all the public buildings, several churches, an orphan asylum, and many of the residences were destroyed. The city was filled with helpless women and children and invalids, many of whom were rendered houseless and homeless in a single night.   No sadder scene was presented during the war.   The suffering of so many helpless and innocent persons could not but move the hardest heart.   The question as to who was immediately responsible for this disaster has given rise to some controversy.   I do not believe that General Sherman countenanced or was in any degree responsible for it.   I believe the immediate cause of the disaster was a free use of whisky (which was supplied to the soldiers by citizens with great liberality).   A drunken soldier with a musket in one hand and a match in the other is not a pleasant visitor to have about the house on a dark, windy night, particularly when for a series of years you have urged him to come, so that you might have an opportunity of performing a surgical operation on him.

ties.   Section No. 2 then follows No. 1.   As soon as the rails are sufficiently heated Section No. 3 takes the place of No. 2; and upon this devolves the most important duty, viz., the effectual destruction of the rail.   This section should be in command of an efficient officer who will see that the work is not slighted.   Unless closely watched, soldiers will content themselves with simply bending the rails around trees.   This should never be permitted.   A rail which is simply bent can easily be restored to its original shape.   No rail should be regarded as properly treated till it has assumed the shape of a doughnut; it must not only be bent but twisted.   To do the twisting Poe's railroad hooks are necessary, for it has been found that the soldiers will not seize the hot iron bare-handed. This, however, is the only thing looking toward the destruction of property which I ever knew a man in Sherman's army to decline doing.   With Poe's hooks a double twist can be given to a rail, which precludes all hope of restoring it to its former shape except by re-rolling.— H. W. S.

From Columbia the army moved toward Fayetteville — the left wing crossing the Catawba River at Rocky Mount. While the rear of the Twentieth Corps was crossing, our pontoon-bridge was swept away by flood-wood brought down the river, leaving the Fourteenth Corps on the south side. This caused a delay of three days, and gave rise to some emphatic instructions from Sherman to the commander of the left wing —which instructions resulted in our damming the flood-wood to some extent, but not in materially expediting the march.

On the 3d of March we arrived at Cheraw, where we found a large supply of stores sent from Charleston for safe-keeping. Among the stores was a large quantity of very old wine of the

SHERMAN'S SOLDIERS GUARDING THE PALMETTO MONUMENT, COLUMBIA. FROM A SKETCH MADE AT THE TIME.

best quality, which had been kept in the cellars of Charleston many years, with no thought on the part of the owners that in its old age it would be drunk from tin cups by Yankee soldiers. Fortunately for the whole army the wine was discovered by the Seventeenth Corps and fell into the hands of the generous and chivalrous commander of that corps,—General Frank P. Blair,— who distributed it with the spirit of liberality and fairness characteristic of him. On the 6th we moved toward Fayetteville, where we arrived on the 10th. The march through South Carolina had been greatly delayed by the almost incessant rains and the swampy nature of the country. More than half the way we were compelled to corduroy the roads before our trains could be moved. To accomplish this work we had been supplied with axes, and the country was covered with saplings well suited to the purpose.

Three or four days prior to our arrival at Fayetteville General Sherman had received information that Wilmington was in possession of General Terry, and had sent two messengers with letters informing Terry when he would probably be at Fayetteville.♭

RAISING THE UNION FLAG OVER THE OLD STATE-HOUSE, COLUMBIA. FROM A SKETCH MADE AT THE TIME.

♭ After Hood had been driven from Tennessee, Schofield was ordered to bring the Twenty-third Corps, General Cox, to Washington, whence it was sent to Fort Fisher, N. C. Schofield assumed command of the combined forces, and captured Wilmington, February 22d, 1865. Thence Cox was sent to New Berne; there he organized a provisional corps and moved via Kinston to Goldsboro', while the greater part of Schofield's forces advanced directly to that place.— EDITORS.

CONTRABANDS IN THE WAKE OF SHERMAN'S ARMY.

Both messengers arrived safely at Wilmington, and on Sunday, the day after our arrival at Fayetteville, the shrill whistle of a steamboat floating the Stars and Stripes announced that we were once more in communication with our own friends. As she came up, the banks of the river were lined by our soldiers, who made the welkin ring with their cheers. The opening of communication with Wilmington not only brought us our mails and a supply of clothing, but enabled us to send to a place of safety thousands of refugees and contrabands who were following the army and seriously embarrassing it. We were dependent upon the country for our supplies of food and forage, and every one not connected with the army was a source of weakness to us. On several occasions on the march from Atlanta we had been compelled to drive thousands of colored people back, not from lack of sympathy with them, but simply as a matter of safety to the army. The refugee-train following in rear of the army was one of the most singular features of the march. Long before the war, the slaves of the South had a system of communication by which important information was transmitted from one section of the country to another. The advance of Sherman's army through a section never before visited by a Union soldier was known far and wide many miles in advance of us. It was natural that these poor creatures, seeking a place of safety, should flee to the army, and endeavor to keep in sight of it. Every day, as we marched on we could see, on each side of our line of march, crowds of these people coming to us through roads and across the fields, bringing with them all their earthly goods, and many goods which were not theirs. Horses, mules, cows, dogs, old family carriages, carts, and whatever they thought might be of use to them were seized upon and brought to us.

They were allowed to follow in rear of our column, and at times they were almost equal in numbers to the army they were following. As singular, comical, and pitiable a spectacle was never before presented. One day a large family of slaves came through the fields to join us. The head of the family, a venerable negro, was mounted on a mule, and safely stowed away behind him in pockets or bags attached to the blanket which covered

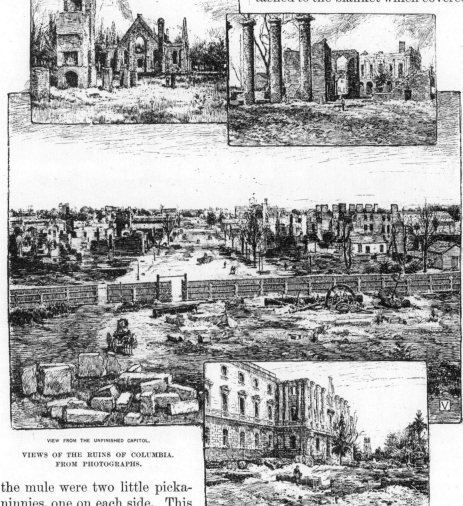

VIEW FROM THE UNFINISHED CAPITOL.

VIEWS OF THE RUINS OF COLUMBIA.
FROM PHOTOGRAPHS.

THE UNFINISHED CAPITOL, COLUMBIA.

the mule were two little pickaninnies, one on each side. This gave rise to a most important invention, *i. e.*, "the best way of transporting pickaninnies." On the next day a mule appeared in column, covered by a blanket with two pockets on each side, each containing a little negro. Very soon old tent-flies or strong canvas was used instead of the blanket, and often ten or fifteen pockets were attached to each side, so that nothing of the mule was visible except the head, tail, and feet, all else being covered by the black woolly heads and bright shining eyes of the little darkies. Occasionally a cow was made to

ARSENAL AT FAYETTEVILLE.

take the place of the mule; this was a decided improvement, as the cow furnished rations as well as transportation for the babies. Old stages,

SHERMAN'S MEN DRIVING THE ENEMY OUT OF FAYETTEVILLE. FROM A SKETCH MADE AT THE TIME.

family carriages, carts and lumber wagons filled with bedding, cooking-utensils and "traps" of all kinds, with men, women, and children loaded with bundles, made up the balance of the refugee-train which followed in our rear. As all the bridges were burned in front of us, our pontoon-trains were in constant use, and the bridges could be left but a short time for the use of the refugees. A scramble for precedence in crossing the bridge always occurred. The firing of a musket or pistol in rear would bring to the refugees visions of guerrillas, and then came a panic. As our bridges were not supplied with guard-rails, occasionally a mule would be crowded off, and with its precious load would float down the river.

Having thoroughly destroyed the arsenal buildings, machine-shops, and foundries at Fayetteville, we crossed the Cape Fear River on the 13th and 14th and resumed our march. We were now entering upon the last stage of the great march which was to unite the Army of the West with that of the East in front of Richmond. If this march could be successfully accomplished the Confederacy was doomed. General Sherman did not hope or expect to accomplish it without a struggle. He anticipated an attack and made provision for it. He ordered me to send my baggage-trains under a strong escort by an interior road on my right, and to keep at least four divisions with their artillery on my left, ready for an attack.

During the 15th of March Hardee was retreating before us, having for his rear-guard a brigade composed of the troops which had garrisoned Charleston, commanded by Colonel Alfred Rhett. Kilpatrick's cavalry was in advance of the left wing, and during the day some of the skirmishers had come suddenly upon Colonel Rhett, accompanied by a few of his men, and had captured him. Rhett before the war had been one of the editors of the Charleston "Mercury," one of the strongest secession papers of the South. He was sent by Kilpatrick to General Sherman. Sherman while stationed in Charleston before the war had been acquainted with Rhett, and not wishing to have him under his immediate charge, he sent him to me. Rhett spent that night in my tent, and as I had also been stationed at Fort Moultrie in 1854 and '55, and had often met him, we had a long chat over old times and about common acquaintances in Charleston. The following morning Rhett was sent to the rear in charge of the cavalry. He was handsomely dressed in the Confederate uniform, with a pair of high boots beautifully stitched. He was deeply mortified at having been "gobbled up" without a chance to fight. One of my staff told me that he saw Rhett a few days later, trudging along under guard, but the beautiful boots were missing,—a soldier had exchanged a very coarse pair of army shoes for them. Rhett said that in all his troubles he had one consolation, that of knowing that no one of Sherman's men could get on those boots.

On the following morning Kilpatrick came upon the enemy behind a line of intrenchments. He moved his cavalry to the right, and Jackson's and Ward's divisions of the Twentieth Corps were deployed in front of the enemy's line. General Sherman directed me to send a brigade to the left in order to get in rear of the intrenchments, which was done, and resulted in the retreat of the enemy and in the capture of Macbeth's Charleston Battery and 217 of Rhett's men. The Confederates were found behind another line of works a short distance in rear of the first, and we went into camp in their immediate front. During the night Hardee retreated, leaving 108 dead for us to bury, and 68 wounded. We lost 12 officers and 65 men killed and 477 men wounded. This action was known as the battle of Averysboro'.

THE FOURTEENTH CORPS ENTERING FAYETTEVILLE. FROM A SKETCH MADE AT THE TIME.

Our march to this point had been toward Raleigh. We now took the road leading to Goldsboro.' General Sherman rode with me on the 18th and left me at 6 A. M. on the 19th to join General Howard, who was marching on roads several miles to our right. On leaving me General Sherman expressed the opinion that Hardee had fallen back to Raleigh, and that I could easily reach the Neuse River on the following day. I felt confident I could accomplish the task. We moved forward at 6 A. M., and soon met the skirmishers of the enemy. The resistance to our advance became very stubborn. Carlin's division was deployed and ordered to advance. I believed that the force in my front consisted only of cavalry with a few pieces of artillery. Fearing that the firing would be heard by General Sherman and cause the other wing of the army to delay its march, I sent Major E. W. Guindon of my staff to General Sherman, to tell him that I had met a strong force of cavalry, but that I should not need assistance, and felt confident I should be at the Neuse at the appointed time. Soon after the bearer of the message to General Sherman had left me, word came from Carlin that he had developed a strong force of the enemy in an intrenched position. About the same time one of my officers brought to me an emaciated, sickly appearing young man about twenty-two or twenty-three years of age, dressed in the Confederate gray. He had expressed great anxiety to see the commanding officer at once. I asked him what he had to say. He said he had been in the Union army, had been taken prisoner, and while sick and in prison had been induced to enlist in the Confederate service. He said he had enlisted with the intention of deserting when a good opportunity presented itself, believing he should die if he remained in prison. In reply to my questions he informed me that he formerly resided at Syracuse, New York, and had entered the service at the commencement of the war, in a company raised by Captain Butler. I had been a resident of Syracuse, and knew the history of his company and regiment. While I was talking with him one of my aides, Major William G. Tracy, rode up and at once recognized the deserter as an old acquaintance whom he had known at Syracuse before the war. I asked how he knew General Johnston was in command and what he knew as to the strength of his force. He said General Johnston rode along the line early that morning, and that the officers had told all the men that "Old Joe" had caught one of Sherman's wings beyond the reach of support, that he intended to *smash* that wing and then go for the other. The man stated that he had had no chance of escaping till that morning, and had come to me to warn me of my danger. He said, "There is a very large force immediately in your front, all under command of General Joe Johnston." While he was making his statement General Carlin's division with four pieces of artillery became engaged with the enemy. A line for defense was at once selected, and as the troops came up they were placed in position and ordered to collect fence-rails and everything else available for barricades. The men used their tin cups and hands as shovels, and needed no urging to induce them to work. I regretted that I had sent the message to General Sherman assuring him I needed no help, and saw the necessity of giving him information at once as to the situation. This information was carried to General Sherman by a young man, not then twenty years of age, but who was full of energy and activity and was always reliable. He was then the youngest member of my staff. He is now [1888] Governor of Ohio — Joseph B. Foraker. His work on this day secured his promotion to the rank of captain. Some years after the close of the war Foraker wrote to me calling my attention to some errors in a published account of this battle of Bentonville, and saying:

" Firing between the men on the skirmish-line commenced before Sherman had left us on the morning of the 19th, but it was supposed there was nothing but cavalry in our front. It was kept up steadily, and constantly increased in volume. Finally there was a halt in the column. You expressed some anxiety, and Major W. G. Tracy and I rode to the front to see what was going on. At the edge of open fields next to the woods in which the barricades were we found our skirmish-line halted. . . . In a few minutes it moved forward again. The enemy partly reserved their fire until it got half-way or more across the field. This induced Tracy and me to think there was but little danger, and so we followed up closely, until suddenly they began again a very spirited firing, in the midst of which we were sorry to find ourselves. I remember we hardly knew what to do — we could do no good by going on and none by remaining. To be killed under such circumstances would look like a waste of raw material, we thought. But the trouble was to get out. We didn't want to turn back, as we thought that would not look well. While we were thus hesitating a spent ball struck Tracy on the leg, giving him a slight but painful wound. Almost at the same moment our skirmishers charged and drove the rebels. . . . I rode back with Tracy only a very short distance, when we met you hurrying to the front. I found you had already been informed of what had been discovered, and that you had already sent orders to everybody to hurry to the front. I remember, too, that a little later Major Mosely, I think, though it may have been some other member of your staff, suggested that you ought to have the advance division charge and drive them out of the way; that it could not be possible that there was much force ahead of us, and that if we waited for the others to come up we should lose a whole day, and if it should turn out that there was nothing to justify such caution it would look bad for the left wing; to which you replied in an earnest manner, ' I can afford to be charged with being dilatory or over-cautious, but I cannot afford the responsibility of another Ball's Bluff affair.' Do you remember it ? I presume not; but I was then quite young, and such remarks made a lasting impression. It excited my confidence and admiration, and was the first moment that I began to feel that there was really serious work before us. . . . You handed me a written message to take to General Sherman. The last words you spoke to me as I started were, ' Ride well to the right so as to keep clear of the enemy's left flank, and *don't spare horse-flesh.*' I reached General Sherman just about sundown. He was on the left side of the road on a sloping hillside, where, as I understood, he had halted only a few minutes before for the night. His staff were about him. I think General Howard was there, but I do not now remember seeing him,— but on the hillside twenty yards farther up Logan was lying on a blanket. Sherman saw me approaching and walked briskly toward me, took your message, tore it open, read it, and called out ' John Logan! where is Logan ?' Just then Logan jumped up and started toward us. He too walked briskly, but before he had reached us Sherman had informed him of the situation and ordered him to turn Hazen back and have him report to you. It was not yet dark when I rode away carrying an answer to your message. It was after midnight when I got back, the ride back being so much longer in point of time because the road was full of troops, it was dark, and my ' horse-flesh ' was used up."

General Carlin's division of the Fourteenth Corps had the advance, and as the enemy exhibited more than usual strength, he had deployed his division and advanced to develop the position of the enemy. Morgan's division of the same corps had been deployed on Carlin's right. Colonel H. G. Litchfield, inspector-general of the corps, had accompanied these troops. I was consulting with General Jeff. C. Davis, who commanded the Fourteenth Corps,

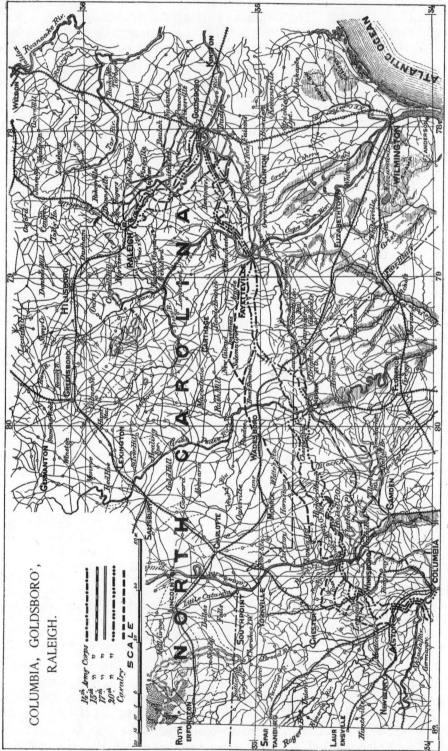

COLUMBIA, GOLDSBORO', RALEIGH.

14th Army Corps
15th   ,,   ,,
17th   ,,   ,,
20th   ,,   ,,
Cavalry

SCALE

REPRODUCED FROM THE " MEMOIRS OF GENERAL WILLIAM T. SHERMAN " (NEW YORK : D. APPLETON & CO.) BY PERM " OF AUTHOR AND PUBLISHERS.

when Colonel Litchfield rode up, and in reply to my inquiry as to what he had found in front he said, "Well, General, I have found something more than Dibrell's cavalry—I find infantry intrenched along our whole front, and enough of them to give us all the amusement we shall want for the rest of the day." [See map of the battle of Bentonville, p. 701.]

Foraker had not been gone half an hour when the enemy advanced in force, compelling Carlin's division to fall back. They were handled with skill and fell back without panic or demoralization, taking places in the line established. The Twentieth Corps held the left of our line, with orders to connect with the Fourteenth. A space between the two corps had been left uncovered, and Cogswell's brigade of the Twentieth Corps, ordered to report to General Davis, filled the gap just before the enemy reached our line.

The enemy fought bravely, but their line had become somewhat broken in advancing through the woods, and when they came up to our line, posted behind slight intrenchments, they received a fire which compelled them to fall back. The assaults were repeated over and over again until a late hour, each assault finding us better prepared for resistance. During the night Hazen reported to me, and was placed on the right of the Fourteenth Corps. Early on the next morning Generals Baird and Geary, each with two brigades, arrived on the field. Baird was placed in front of our works and moved out beyond the advanced position held by us on the preceding day. The 20th was spent in strengthening our position and developing the line of the enemy. On the morning of the 21st the right wing arrived. This wing had marched twenty miles over bad roads, skirmishing most of the way with the enemy. On the 21st General Johnston found Sherman's army united, and in position on three sides of him. On the other was Mill Creek. Our troops were pressed closely to the works of the enemy, and the entire day was spent in skirmishing. During the night of the 21st the enemy crossed Mill Creek and retreated toward Raleigh. The plans of the enemy to surprise us and destroy our army in detail were well formed and well executed, and would have been more successful had not the men of the Fourteenth and Twentieth corps been veterans, and the equals in courage and endurance of any soldiers of this or any other country.

BENTONVILLE THE MORNING AFTER THE BATTLE—THE SMOKE IS FROM RESIN THAT WAS FIRED BY THE CONFEDERATES. FROM A SKETCH MADE AT THE TIME.

THE OPPOSING FORCES IN THE CAMPAIGN OF THE CAROLINAS.

THE UNION ARMY.

Major-General William T. Sherman.

Headquarters' Guard: 7th Co. Ohio Sharp-shooters, Lieut. James Cox.

Engineers and Mechanics: 1st Mich., Maj. John B. Yates; 1st Mo. (5 co's), Lieut.-Col. William Tweeddale.

Artillery,⎟ Brig.-Gen. William F. Barry (chief-of-artillery).

RIGHT WING (Army of the Tennessee), Maj.-Gen. Oliver O. Howard.

Escort: K, 15th Ill. Cav., Capt. William Duncan; 4th Co. Ohio Cav., Capt. John L. King.

Pontoon Train Guard: E, 14th Wis., Capt. William I. Henry.

FIFTEENTH ARMY CORPS, Maj.-Gen. John A. Logan.

FIRST DIVISION, Brig.-Gen. Charles R. Woods.

First Brigade, Col. William B. Woods: 12th Ind., Col. Reuben Williams; 26th Iowa, Maj. John Lubbers; 27th Mo., Col. Thomas Curly; 31st and 32d Mo. (6 co's), Lieut.-Col. Abraham J. Seay; 76th Ohio, Lieut.-Col. Edward Briggs. *Second Brigade,* Col. Robert F. Catterson, Brig.-Gen. Charles C. Walcutt, Col. Robert F. Catterson: 26th Ill., Lieut.-Col. Ira J. Bloomfield; 40th Ill., Lieut.-Col. Hiram W. Hall; 103d Ill., Lieut.-Col. George W. Wright; 97th Ind., Capt. George Elliott, Lieut.-Col. Aden G. Cavins; 100th Ind., Maj. Ruel M. Johnson, Capt. John W. Headington; 6th Iowa, Lieut.-Col. William H. Clune; 46th Ohio, Lieut.-Col. Edward N. Upton. *Third Brigade,* Col. George A. Stone: 4th Iowa, Lieut.-Col. Samuel D. Nichols, Capt. Randolph Sry, Maj. Albert R. Anderson; 9th Iowa, Maj. Alonzo Abernethy; 25th Iowa, Lieut.-Col. David J. Palmer; 30th Iowa, Lieut.-Col. Aurelius Roberts; 31st Iowa, Lieut.-Col. Jeremiah W. Jenkins.

SECOND DIVISION, Maj.-Gen. William B. Hazen.

First Brigade, Col. Theodore Jones: 55th Ill., Capt. Charles A. Andress; 116th Ill., Lieut.-Col. John E. Maddux, Capt. Necolas Geschwind; 127th Ill., Capt. Charles Schryver, Lieut.-Col. Frank S. Curtiss; 6th Mo. (A and B, 8th Mo., attached), Lieut.-Col. Delos Van Deusen; 30th Ohio, Lieut.-Col. Emerson P. Brooks; 57th Ohio, Capt. John A. Smith, Lieut.-Col. Samuel R. Mott. *Second Brigade,* Col. Wells S. Jones: 111th Ill., Lieut.-Col. Joseph F. Black, Col. James S. Martin; 83d Ind., Capt. Charles W. White, Capt. William N. Craw; 37th Ohio, Lieut.-Col. Louis von Blessingh; 47th Ohio, Col. Augustus C. Parry; 53d Ohio, Capt. Robert Curren, Maj. Preston R. Galloway; 54th Ohio, Lieut.-Col. Israel T. Moore. *Third Brigade,* Brig.-Gen. John M. Oliver: 48th Ill., Lieut.-Col. Thomas L. B. Weems; 90th Ill., Lieut.-Col. Owen Stuart; 99th Ind., Capt. Josiah Farrar; 15th Mich., Lieut.-Col. Frederick S. Hutchinson; 70th Ohio, Lieut.-Col. Henry L. Philips.

THIRD DIVISION, Brig.-Gen. John E. Smith.

First Brigade, Brig.-Gen. William T. Clark: 63d Ill., Col. Joseph B. McCown, Capt. Joseph R. Stanford; 93d Ill., Lieut.-Col. Nicholas C. Buswell; 48th Ind., Capt. Newton Bingham; 59th Ind., Lieut.-Col. Jefferson K. Scott, Maj. Thomas A. McNaught; 4th Minn., Col. John E. Tourtellotte, Capt. Leverett R. Wellman; 18th Wis., Maj. James P. Millard. *Second Brigade,* Col. Clark R. Wever, Col. John E. Tourtellotte: 56th Ill., Lieut.-Col. John P. Hall; 10th Iowa, Capt. William H. Silsby; 17th Iowa (1 co.), Capt. William Horner; 26th Mo. (2 co's and detachment, 10th Mo.), Lieut. Theron M. Rice; 80th Ohio, Lieut.-Col. Pren Metham, Maj. Thomas C. Morris.

FOURTH DIVISION, Brig.-Gen. John M. Corse.

First Brigade, Col. Elliott W. Rice: 52d Ill., Lieut.-Col. Jerome D. Davis; 66th Ind., Lieut.-Col. Roger Martin; 2d Iowa, Col. Noel B. Howard; 7th Iowa, Lieut.-Col. James C. Parrott. *Second Brigade,* Col. Robert N.

Adams: 12th Ill., Lieut.-Col. Henry Van Sellar; 66th Ill., Capt. William S. Boyd, Lieut.-Col. Andrew K. Campbell; 81st Ohio, Maj. William C. Henry. *Third Brigade,* Col. Frederick J. Hurlbut: 7th Ill., Lieut.-Col. Hector Perrin; 50th Ill., Lieut.-Col. William Hanna; 57th Ill., Maj. Frederick A. Battey; 39th Iowa, Capt. Isaac D. Marsh, Lieut.-Col. Joseph M. Griffith. *Unassigned:* 110th U. S. C. T., Maj. William C. Hawley, Capt. Thomas Kennedy, Capt. Zac. C. Wilson, Capt. Jacob Kemnitzer.

ARTILLERY, Lieut.-Col. William H. Ross: H, 1st Ill., Capt. Francis DeGress, Lieut. Robert S. Gray; B, 1st Mich., Lieut. Edward B. Wright; H, 1st Mo., Capt. Charles M. Callahan; 12th Wis., Capt. William Zickerick.

UNASSIGNED: 29th Mo. (mounted), Maj. Christian Burkhardt, Col. Joseph S. Gage.

SEVENTEENTH ARMY CORPS, Maj.-Gen. Frank P. Blair, Jr.

Escort: G, 11th Ill. Cav., Capt. Stephen S. Tripp.

FIRST DIVISION, Maj.-Gen. Joseph A. Mower, Brig.-Gen. Manning F. Force.

First Brigade, Col. Charles S. Sheldon, Brig.-Gen. John W. Fuller: 64th Ill., Maj. Joseph S. Reynolds; 18th Mo., Lieut.-Col. William H. Minter, Col. Charles S. Sheldon, Lieut.-Col. William H. Minter, Maj. William M. Edgar; 27th Ohio, Maj. Isaac N. Gilruth; 39th Ohio, Capt. John W. Orr, Lieut.-Col. Daniel Weber. *Second Brigade,* Brig.-Gen. John W. Sprague, Col. Milton Montgomery, Brig.-Gen. John W. Sprague: 35th N. J., Col. John J. Cladek; 43d Ohio, Col. Wager Swayne, Maj. Horace Park; 63d Ohio, Maj. John W. Fouts, Capt. Otis W. Pollock, Maj. Oscar L. Jackson; 25th Wis., Lieut.-Col. Jeremiah M. Rusk, Col. Milton Montgomery, Lieut.-Col. J. M. Rusk. *Third Brigade,* Col. John Tillson, Col. Charles H. DeGroat, Lieut.-Col. James S. Wright, Col. John Tillson: 10th Ill., Lieut.-Col. M. F. Wood, Capt. David Gillespie; 25th Ind., Lieut.-Col. James S. Wright, Maj. William H. Crenshaw, Lieut.-Col. J. S. Wright; 32d Wis., Col. Charles H. DeGroat, Lieut.-Col. Joseph H. Carleton, Maj. William H. Burrows.

THIRD DIVISION, Brig.-Gen. Mortimer D. Leggett, Brig.-Gen. Manning F. Force, Brig.-Gen. Mortimer D. Leggett.

First Brigade, Brig.-Gen. Manning F. Force, Col. Cassius Fairchild, Brig.-Gen. Manning F. Force, Brig.-Gen., Charles Ewing: 20th Ill. (provost-guard of division to April 3d), Capt. Henry King; 30th Ill., Lieut.-Col. William C. Rhodes, Capt. John P. Davis; 31st Ill., Lieut.-Col. Robert N. Pearson; 45th Ill., Maj. John O. Duer; 12th Wis., Col. James K. Proudfit; 16th Wis., Capt. Joseph Craig, Col. Cassius Fairchild, Capt. Joseph Craig, Col. Cassius Fairchild. *Second Brigade,* Col. Greenberry F. Wiles, Brig.-Gen. Robert K. Scott: 20th Ohio, Lieut.-Col. Harrison Wilson; 68th Ohio, Lieut.-Col. George E. Welles; 78th Ohio, Capt. Israel C. Robinson, Col. G. F. Wiles, Lieut.-Col. Gilbert D. Munson; 17th Wis., Maj. Patrick H. McCauley, Lieut.-Col. Donald D. Scott, Col. Adam G. Malloy.

FOURTH DIVISION, Brig.-Gen. Giles A. Smith.

First Brigade, Brig.-Gen. Benjamin F. Potts: 14th and 15th Ill. (battalion), Capt. Alonzo J. Gillespie, Col. George C. Rogers; 53d Ill., Col. John W. McClanahan; 23d Ind., Lieut.-Col. George S. Babbitt, Capt. John W. Hammond; 53d Ind., Maj. Henry Duncan, Col. Warner L. Vestal; 32d Ohio, Lieut.-Col. Jefferson J. Hibbets. *Third Brigade,* Brig.-Gen. William W. Belknap: 32d Ill., Capt. John J. Rider; 11th Iowa, Lieut.-Col. Benjamin Beach; 13th Iowa, Lieut.-Col. Justin C. Kennedy; 15th Iowa, Maj. George Pomutz; 16th Iowa, Capt. Jesse H. Lucas, Capt. John F. Conyngham, Maj. J. Henry Smith.

⎟ See divisions and corps with which the batteries served.

ARTILLERY, Maj. Allen C. Waterhouse, Maj. Frederick Welker: C, 1st Mich., Lieut. William W. Hyzer; 1st Minn., Capt. William Z. Clayton; 15th Ohio, Lieut. Lyman Bailey, Capt. James Burdick. UNASSIGNED: 9th Ill. (mounted), Lieut.-Col. Samuel T. Hughes.

LEFT WING (Army of Georgia), Maj.-Gen. Henry W. Slocum.

Pontoniers: 58th Ind., Maj. William A. Downey.

FOURTEENTH ARMY CORPS, Brig.-Gen. Jefferson C. Davis.

FIRST DIVISION, Brig.-Gen. William P. Carlin, Col. George P. Buell, Brig.-Gen. Charles C. Walcutt.

First Brigade, Col. Harrison C. Hobart: 104th Ill., Maj. John H. Widmer; 42d Ind., Maj. Gideon R. Kellams; 88th Ind., Lieut.-Col. Cyrus E. Briant, Capt. William N. Voris, Maj. Lewis J. Blair; 33d Ohio, Capt. Joseph Hinson; 94th Ohio, Maj. William H. Snider; 21st Wis., Lieut.-Col. Michael H. Fitch, Maj Charles H. Walker, Lieut.-Col. Michael H. Fitch. *Second Brigade,* Col. George P. Buell, Lieut.-Col. Michael H. Fitch, Col. George P. Buell: 13th Mich., Col. Joshua B. Culver, Maj. Willard G. Eaton, Capt. Silas A. Yerkes; 21st Mich., Capt. Arthur C. Prince, Lieut.-Col. Loomis K. Bishop; 69th Ohio, Capt. Jacob J. Rarick, Lieut. Samuel P. Murray, Lieut.-Col. Joseph H. Brigham. *Third Brigade,* Lieut.-Col. David Miles, Lieut.-Col. Arnold McMahan, Col. Henry A. Hambright: 38th Ind., Capt. James H. Low, Capt. David H. Patton; 21st Ohio, Lieut.-Col. Arnold McMahan, Capt. Samuel F. Cheney, Lieut.-Col. Arnold McMahan; 74th Ohio, Maj. Robert P. Findley; 79th Pa., Maj. Michael H. Locker, Capt. John S. McBride.

SECOND DIVISION, Brig.-Gen. James D. Morgan.

Provost Guard: B, 110th Ill., Capt. William R. Hester.

First Brigade, Brig.-Gen. William Vandever: 16th Ill., Capt. Eben White, Capt. Herman Lund; 60th Ill., Lieut.-Col. George W. Evans, Maj. James H. McDonald; 10th Mich., Col. Charles M. Lum, Capt William H. Dunphy; 14th Mich., Lieut.-Col. George W. Grummond; 17th N. Y., Lieut.-Col. James Lake, Maj. Alexander S. Marshall. *Second Brigade,* Lieut.-Col. John S. Pearce, Brig.-Gen. John G. Mitchell: 34th Ill., Capt. Peter F. Walker, Lieut.-Col. Peter Ege; 78th Ill., Lieut.-Col. Maris R. Vernon; 98th Ohio, Capt. James R. McLaughlin, Lieut.-Col. John S. Pearce, Maj. David E. Roatch; 108th Ohio, Maj. Frederick Beck, Lieut.-Col. Joseph Good; 113th Ohio, Capt. Toland Jones, Capt. Otway Watson; 121st Ohio, Maj. Aaron B. Robinson. *Third Brigade,* Col. Benjamin D. Fearing, Lieut.-Col. James W. Langley: 85th Ill., Capt. James R. Griffith; 86th Ill., Lieut.-Col. Allen L. Fahnestock; 110th Ill. (A, 24th Ills., attached), Lieut.-Col. E. Hibbard Topping; 125th Ill., Lieut.-Col. James W. Langley, Capt. George W. Cook; 22d Ind., Capt. William H. Snodgrass; 37th Ind. (1 co.), Lieut. Socrates Carver; 52d Ohio, Lieut.-Col. Charles W. Clancy, Maj. James T. Holmes.

THIRD DIVISION, Brig.-Gen. Absalom Baird.

First Brigade, Col. Morton C. Hunter: 82d Ind., Lieut.-Col. John M. Matheny; 23d Mo. (4 co's), Maj. John H. Jolly; 11th Ohio (detachment), Capt. Francis H. Loring; 17th Ohio, Lieut.-Col. Benjamin H. Showers; 31st Ohio, Capt. Michael Stone, Capt. Eli Wilkin; 89th Ohio, Lieut.-Col. William H. Glenn; 92d Ohio, Lieut.-Col. John C. Morrow. *Second Brigade,* Lieut.-Col. Thomas Doan, Brig.-Gen. Newell Gleason: 75th Ind., Maj. Cyrus J. McCole, Lieut.-Col. William O'Brien; 87th Ind., Maj. Richard C. Sabin, Lieut.-Col. Edwin P. Hammond; 101st Ind., Maj. George W. Steele, Lieut.-Col. Thomas Doan; 2d Minn., Lieut.-Col. Judson W. Bishop; 105th Ohio, Lieut.-Col. George T. Perkins. *Third Brigade,* Col. George P. Este, Lieut.-Col. Hubbard K. Milward, Brig.-Gen. George S. Greene: 74th Ind., Lieut.-Col. Thomas Morgan; 18th Ky., Lieut.-Col. Hubbard K. Milward, Maj. John J. Hall, Lieut.-Col. H. K. Milward; 14th Ohio, Lieut.-Col. Albert Moore; 38th Ohio, Capt. Charles M. Gilbert.

ARTILLERY, Maj. Charles Houghtaling: C, 1st Ill., Lieut. Joseph R. Channel, Lieut. Palmer F. Scovel; I, 2d Ill., Lieut. Judson Rich; 19th Ind., Lieut. Samuel D. Webb, Lieut. Clinton Keeler; 5th Wis., Capt. John McKnight, Lieut. Elijah Booth, Jr.

TWENTIETH ARMY CORPS, Brig.-Gen. Alpheus S. Williams, Maj.-Gen. Joseph A. Mower.

FIRST DIVISION, Brig.-Gen. Nathaniel J. Jackson, Brig.-Gen. Alpheus S. Williams.

First Brigade, Col. James L. Selfridge: 5th Conn., Lieut.-Col. Henry W. Daboll; 123d N. Y., Col. James C. Rogers; 141st N. Y., Capt. William Merrell, Lieut.-Col. Andrew J. McNett; 46th Pa., Maj. Patrick Griffith. *Second Brigade,* Col. William Hawley: 2d Mass., Lieut.-Col. Charles F. Morse, Capt. Robert B. Brown, Capt. Edward A. Phalen; 13th N. J., Maj. Frederick H. Harris, Capt. John H. Arey; 107th N. Y., Col. Nirom M. Crane; 150th N. Y., Lieut.-Col. Alfred B. Smith; 3d Wis., Lieut.-Col. George W. Stevenson. *Third Brigade,* Brig.-Gen. James S. Robinson: 82d Ill., Maj. Ferdinand H. Rolshausen, Lieut.-Col. Edward S. Salomon; 101st Ill., Lieut.-Col. John B. Le Sage; 143d N. Y., Lieut.-Col. Hezekiah Watkins, Capt. Edward H. Pinny, Col. Horace Boughton; 61st Ohio, Capt. John Garrett; 82d Ohio, Lieut.-Col. David Thomson, Maj. James S. Crall; 31st Wis., Col. Francis H. West.

SECOND DIVISION, Brig.-Gen John W. Geary.

First Brigade, Col. Ario Pardee, Jr., Col. George W. Mindil: 5th Ohio, Lieut.-Col. Robert Kirkup; 29th Ohio, Lieut.-Col. Jonas Schoonover; 66th Ohio, Lieut.-Col. Eugene Powell, Capt. Theodoric G. Keller; 28th Pa., Col. John Flynn, Lieut.-Col. James Fitzpatrick; 147th Pa., Lieut.-Col. John Craig. *Second Brigade,* Col. George W. Mindil, Col. Patrick H. Jones: 33d N. J., Lieut.-Col. Enos Fourat, Col. George W. Mindil, Maj. Nathaniel K. Bray; 119th N. Y., Col. John T. Lockman; 134th N. Y., Capt. Perry E. McMaster, Lieut.-Col. Allan H. Jackson; 154th N. Y., Col. Patrick H. Jones, Lieut.-Col. Lewis D. Warner; 73d Pa., Capt. Samuel D. Miller, Maj. Christian H. Goebel; 109th Pa., Capt. William Geary. *Third Brigade,* Col. Henry A. Barnum: 60th N. Y., Capt. Abner B. Shipman, Lieut.-Col. Lester S. Willson; 102d N. Y., Lieut.-Col. Harvey S. Chatfield, Maj. Oscar J. Spaulding; 137th N. Y., Maj. Milo B. Eldridge, Lieut.-Col. Koert S. Van Voorhis; 149th N. Y., Capt. Henry N. Burhans, Lieut.-Col. Nicholas Grumbach; 29th Pa., Lieut.-Col. George E. Johnson, Col. Samuel M. Zulich; 111th Pa., Capt. William J. Alexander, Col. Thomas M. Walker.

THIRD DIVISION, Brig.-Gen. William T. Ward.

First Brigade, Col. Henry Case, Col. Benjamin Harrison: 102d Ill., Maj. Hiland H. Clay, Col. Franklin C. Smith; 105th Ill., Lieut.-Col. Everell F. Dutton; 129th Ill., Lieut.-Col. Thomas H. Flynn, Col. Henry Case; 70th Ind., Maj. Zachariah S. Ragan, Lieut.-Col. Samuel Merrill; 79th Ohio, Lieut.-Col. Azariah W. Doan. *Second Brigade,* Col. Daniel Dustin: 33d Ind., Lieut.-Col. James E. Burton; 85th Ind., Lieut.-Col. Alexander B. Crane; 19th Mich., Maj. David Anderson; 22d Wis., Capt. Darwin R. May, Capt. George H. Brown, Lieut.-Col. Edward Bloodgood. *Third Brigade,* Col. William Cogswell: 20th Conn., Lieut.-Col. Philo B. Buckingham; 33d Mass., Lieut.-Col. Elisha Doane; 136th N. Y., Maj. Henry L. Arnold, Capt. George H. Eldridge, Col. James Wood, Jr.; 55th Ohio, Lieut.-Col. Edwin H. Powers, Maj. Charles P. Wickham; 73d Ohio, Lieut.-Col. Samuel H. Hurst, Maj. Thomas W. Higgins; 26th Wis., Lieut.-Col. Frederick C. Winkler, Maj. Francis Lackner.

ARTILLERY, Maj. John A. Reynolds, Capt. Charles E. Winegar: I, 1st N. Y., Capt. Charles E. Winegar, Lieut. Warren L. Scott; M, 1st N. Y., Lieut. Edward P. Newkirk; C, 1st Ohio, Lieut. Jerome B. Stephens; E, Pa., Capt. Thomas S. Sloan.

CAVALRY.

THIRD DIVISION, Brig.-Gen. Judson Kilpatrick.

First Brigade, Col. Thomas J. Jordan: 3d Ind. (batt'n), Capt. Charles U. Patton; 8th Ind., Lieut.-Col. Fielder A. Jones; 2d Ky., Maj. Owen Star; 3d Ky., Lieut.-Col. Robert H. King; 9th Pa., Lieut.-Col. David H. Kimmel. *Second Brigade,* Col. Smith D. Atkins: 92d Ill. (mounted), Lieut.-Col. Mathew Van Buskirk; 9th Mich., Col. George S. Acker; 9th Ohio, Col. William D. Hamilton; 10th Ohio, Col. Thomas L. Sanderson; McLaughlin's Ohio Squadron, Capt. John Dalzell. *Third Brigade,* Col. George E. Spencer, Col. Michael Kerwin, Col. Thomas

T. Heath: 1st Ala., Maj. Francis L. Cramer, Capt. Jerome J. Hinds, Maj. Sanford Tramel; 5th Ky., Col. Oliver L. Baldwin, Maj. Christopher T. Cheek; 5th Ohio, Maj. George H. Rader; 13th Pa., Maj. George F. McCabe, Col. Michael Kerwin. *Fourth Brigade* (provisional organization of dismounted men), Maj. William B. Way: 1st Reg't, Maj. Charles A. Appel; 2d Reg't, Lieut.-Col. William Stough; 3d Reg't, Capt. John B. Riggs. *Artillery:* 23d N. Y. (assigned April 1st), Capt. Samuel Kittinger; 10th Wis. (relieved for muster-out April 8th), Capt. Yates V. Beebe.

CENTER ‡ (Army of the Ohio), Maj.-Gen. John M. Schofield.

Escort: G, 7th Ohio Cav., Capt. John A. Ashbury.

Engineers: 15th N. Y. (3 co's), Maj. Henry V. Slosson.

Artillery, Lieut.-Col. Terance J. Kennedy (chief of artillery).

TENTH ARMY CORPS, ↓ Maj.-Gen. Alfred H. Terry.

FIRST DIVISION ♭ (late Second Division, Nineteenth Corps), Brig.-Gen. Henry W. Birge.

Third Brigade, Col. Nicholas W. Day: 24th Iowa, Lieut.-Col. Edward Wright; 38th Mass., Lieut.-Col. James P. Richardson; 128th N. Y., Capt. Henry H. Sincerbos; 156th N. Y., Capt. Alfred Cooley; 175th N. Y. (5 co's), Capt. Chas. McCarthey; 176th N. Y., Maj. Chas. Lewis. *Artillery:* 22d Ind., Lieut. Geo. W. Alexander.

SECOND DIVISION (late Second Division, Twenty-fourth Corps), Brig.-Gen. Adelbert Ames.

First Brigade, Col. Rufus Daggett: 3d N. Y., Capt. George E. Fordham, Lieut.-Col. Alfred Dunham; 112th N. Y., Col. Ephraim A. Ludwick; 117th N. Y., Capt. Edward Downer; 142d N. Y., Lieut.-Col. William A. Jones, Col. Albert M. Barney. *Second Brigade,* Col. William B. Coan, Col. John S. Littell: 47th N. Y., Col. Christopher R. Macdonald; 48th N. Y., Capt. Van Renselaer K. Hilliard, Col. William B. Coan; 76th Pa., Maj. Charles Knerr; 97th Pa., Maj. William H. Martin, Lieut.-Col. John Wainwright; 203d Pa., Lieut.-Col. Amos W. Bachman. *Third Brigade,* Col. G. F. Granger: 13th Ind., Lieut.-Col. Samuel M. Zent; 9th Me., Lieut.-Col. Joseph Noble; 4th N. H., Capt. John H. Roberts; 115th N. Y., Lieut.-Col. Nathan J. Johnson; 169th N. Y., Lieut.-Col. Jas. A. Colvin. *Artillery:* 16th N.Y., Capt. Rich'd H. Lee.

THIRD DIVISION ↑ (late Third Division, Twenty-fifth Corps), Brig.-Gen. Charles J. Paine.

First Brigade, Col. Delavan Bates: 1st U. S., Lieut.-Col. Giles H. Rich; 30th U. S., Lieut.-Col. Hiram A. Oakman; 107th U. S., Col. William H. Revere, Jr. *Second Brigade,* Col. Samuel A. Duncan: 4th U. S., Lieut.-Col. George Rogers; 5th U. S., Col. Giles W. Shurtleff; 39th U. S., Col. Ozora P. Stearns. *Third Brigade,* Col. John H. Holman, Col. Albert M. Blackman: 6th U. S., Col. John W. Ames; 27th U. S., Lieut.-Col. John W. Donnellon; 37th U. S., Col. Nathan Goff, Jr. UNATTACHED: E, 3d U. S. Art'y, Lieut. John R. Myrick.

TWENTY-THIRD ARMY CORPS, Maj.-Gen. John M. Schofield; (after April 2d) Maj.-Gen. Jacob D. Cox. ☆

Engineer Battalion, Capt. Oliver S. McClure.

Provost Guard: H, 9th N. J., Capt. Edward S. Pullen.

Artillery, Lieut.-Col. George W. Schofield, Capt. Giles J. Cockerill.

FIRST DIVISION, Brig.-Gen. Thomas H. Ruger.

First Brigade, Col. Isaac N. Stiles: 120th Ind., Col. Allen W. Prather; 124th Ind., Col. John M. Orr; 128th Ind., Lieut.-Col. Jasper Packard; 180th Ohio, Col. Willard Warner. *Second Brigade,* Col. John C. McQuiston: 123d Ind., Lieut.-Col. Dewitt C. Walters; 129th Ind., Col. Charles A. Zollinger; 130th Ind., Col. Charles S. Parrish; 28th Mich., Col. William W. Wheeler. *Third Brigade,* Col. Minor T. Thomas: 25th Mass. (assigned April 2d), Lieut.-Col. James Tucker; 8th Minn., Maj. George A. Camp; 174th Ohio, Col. John S. Jones; 178th Ohio, Col. Joab A. Stafford. *Artillery:* 22d Ind. (transferred to First Division, Tenth Corps, April 5th), Lieut. George W. Alexander: F, 1st Mich. (ordered to New Berne April 6th), Capt. Byron D. Paddock; Elgin, Ill. (assigned April 8th), Capt. Andrew M. Wood.

SECOND DIVISION, Brig.-Gen. Nathaniel C. McLean, Col. Orlando H. Moore, Maj.-Gen. Darius N. Couch, Brig.-Gen. Joseph A. Cooper.

First Brigade, Col. Orlando H. Moore: 26th Ky., Col. Thomas B. Fairleigh; 25th Mich., Lieut.-Col. Benjamin F. Orcutt; 132d N. Y. (detachment 99th N. Y. attached), Col. Peter J. Claassen; 52d Pa., Lieut.-Col. John B. Conyngham; 6th Tenn. (relieved for muster-out March 31st), Lieut.-Col. Edward Maynard. *Second Brigade,* Col. John Mehringer: 107th Ill., Maj. Thomas J. Milholland; 80th Ind., Lieut.-Col. Alfred Dale Owen; 23d Mich., Col. Oliver L. Spaulding; 111th Ohio, Lieut.-Col. Isaac R. Sherwood; 118th Ohio, Lieut.-Col. Edgar Sowers. *Third Brigade,* Col. Silas A. Strickland: 91st Ind., Lieut.-Col. Charles H. Butterfield; 50th Ohio, Capt. John S. Conahan, Lieut.-Col. James A. Bope; 181st Ohio, Lieut.-Col. John E. Hudson, Col. John O'Dowd; 183d Ohio, Col. George W. Hoge. *Artillery:* 15th Ind. (detached at Wilmington April 5th), Capt. Alonzo D. Harvey; 19th Ohio, Capt. Frank Wilson.

THIRD DIVISION, Brig.-Gen. James W. Reilly, Brig.-Gen. Samuel P. Carter.

Provost Guard: F, 100th Ohio, Lieut. John P. Denney.

First Brigade, Col. Oscar W. Sterl: 12th Ky., Capt. John Travis, Lieut.-Col. Laurence H. Rousseau; 16th Ky., Lieut.-Col. John S. White; 100th Ohio, Capt. Frank Rundell; 104th Ohio, Lieut.-Col. William J. Jordan; 8th Tenn., Capt. James W. Berry. *Second Brigade,* Col. John S. Casement: 65th Ill., Maj. George H. Kennedy, Lieut.-Col. William S. Stewart; 65th Ind., Lieut.-Col. John W. Hammond; 9th N. J., Col. James Stewart, Jr.; 103d Ohio, Capt. Henry S. Pickands; 177th Ohio, Col. Arthur T. Wilcox, Lieut.-Col. William H. Zimmerman. *Third Brigade,* Col. Thomas J. Henderson: 112th Ill., Lieut.-Col. Emery S. Bond; 63d Ind., Lieut.-Col. Daniel Morris, Maj. Frank Wilcox; 140th Ind., Col. Thomas J. Brady; 17th Mass., Lieut.-Col. Henry Splaine. *Artillery:* 23d Ind. (detached at Wilmington April 6th), Capt. James H. Myers; D, 1st Ohio, Capt. Giles J. Cockerill, Lieut. Cecil C. Reed.

DIVISION FROM DISTRICT OF BEAUFORT (discontinued April 2d, and troops assigned to other commands), Brig.-Gen. Samuel P. Carter.

First Brigade, Col. Peter J. Claassen: 17th Mass., Lieut.-Col. Henry Splaine; 132d N. Y., Lieut.-Col. George H. Hitchcock. *Second Brigade,* Col. James Stewart, Jr.: 25th Mass., Capt. Samuel Harrington, Lieut.-Col. James Tucker; 9th N. J., Lieut.-Col. Samuel Hufty; 85th N. Y., Lieut.-Col. William W. Clarke. *Artillery,* Capt. William E. Mercer: C, 3d N. Y., Lieut. E. Barton Wood; I, 3d N. Y., Lieut. William Richardson.

CAVALRY: 12th N. Y., Col. James W. Savage; L, 1st N. C., Capt. George W. Graham.

RESERVE ARTILLERY (organized April 5th), Capt. William E. Mercer: C, 3d N. Y., Lieut. E. Barton Wood; D, 3d N. Y., Capt. Stephen Van Heusen; G, 3d N. Y., Capt. Wm. A. Kelsey; I, 3d N.Y., Lieut. Wm. Richardson.

The effective strength of General Sherman's army during the campaign is shown in the following table:

DATE.	Infantry.	Cavalry.	Artillery.	Total.
February 1	53,923	4438	1718	60,079
March 1	51,598	4401	1677	57,676
April 1	74,105	4781	2264	81,150
April 10	80,968	5537	2443	88,948

The losses of this army in the principal combats of the campaign were as follows:

PLACE.	Killed.	Wounded.	Captured or Missing.	Total.
Rivers's Bridge, S. C.	18	70	....	88
Near Kinston, N. C.	57	265	935	1257
Averysboro', N. C.	77	477	....	554
Bentonville, N. C.	191	1168	287	1646

‡ Joined the main army at Goldsboro' March 21st.   ↓ As organized April 2d; previously known as "Provisional Corps."
♭ The First Brigade at Morehead City and the Second Brigade at Wilmington.   ↑ Colored troops.
☆ From March 1st to 21st General Cox commanded "Provisional Corps" (Ruger's, Palmer's, and Carter's divisions).

THE CONFEDERATE ARMY. |

ARMY OF TENNESSEE.— General Joseph E. Johnston, General G. T. Beauregard (second in command).

Escort: Capt. E. M. Holloway.
HARDEE'S CORPS, ‡, Lieut.-Gen. William J. Hardee.
Escort and Scouts, Capts. W. C. Raum and J. B. L. Walpole. *Artillery,* Col. A. J. Gonzales.
BROWN'S (late Cleburne's) DIVISION, Maj.-Gen. John C. Brown.
Smith's Brigade, Brig.-Gen. James A. Smith: 1st Fla. (consolidated 1st, 3d, 4th, 6th, and 7th inf., and 1st cav.), Lieut.-Col. E. Marshburn; 1st Ga. (consolidated 1st, 57th, and 63d Ga.), Col. Charles H. Olmstead; 54th Ga. (consolidated 37th and 54th Ga., and 4th Batt'n Ga. Sharp-shooters), Col. T. D. Caswell. *Govan's Brigade,* Brig.-Gen. D. C. Govan: 1st Ark. (consolidated 1st, 2d, 5th, 6th, 7th, 8th, 13th, 15th, 19th, and 24th Ark., and 3d Confederate), Col. E. A. Howell; 1st Tex. (consolidated 6th, 7th, 10th, and 15th inf., and 17th, 18th, 24th, and 25th Tex., dismounted cavalry), Lieut.-Col. W. A. Ryan.
HOKE'S DIVISION, ↓ Maj.-Gen. R. F. Hoke.
Clingman's Brigade, Brig.-Gen. Thomas L. Clingman: 8th N. C., Lieut.-Col. R. A. Barrier; 31st N. C., Lieut.-Col. C. W. Knight; 36th and 40th N. C., Maj. W. A. Holland; 51st N. C., Capt. J. W. Lippitt; 61st N. C., Capt. S. W. Noble. *Colquitt's Brigade,* Brig.-Gen. A. H. Colquitt: 6th Ga., Maj. J. M. Culpepper; 19th Ga., Lieut.-Col. R. B. Hogan; 23d Ga., Col. M. R. Ballenger; 27th Ga., Lieut.-Col. H. Bussey; 28th Ga., Capt. G. W. Warthen. *Hagood's Brigade,* Brig.-Gen. Johnson Hagood: 11th S. C., Capt. B. F. Wyman; 21st S. C., Capt. J. A. W. Thomas, Col. R. F. Graham; 25th S. C., Capt. E. R. Lesesne; 27th S. C., Capt. Thomas Y. Simons; 7th S. C. Batt'n, Capt. William Clyburn, Lieut.-Col. James H. Rion. *Kirkland's Brigade,* Brig.-Gen. W. W. Kirkland: 17th N. C., Lieut.-Col. T. H. Sharp; 42d N. C., Col. John E. Brown; 50th N. C., Col. George Wortham; 66th N. C., Col. J. H. Nethercutt. *First Brigade Junior Reserves,* Brig.-Gen. L. S. Baker: 1st N. C., Lieut.-Col. C. W. Broadfoot; 2d N. C., Col. J. H. Anderson; 3d N. C., Col. J. W. Hinsdale; 1st N. C. Batt'n, Capt. C. M. Hall.
CHEATHAM'S DIVISION,) Maj.-Gen. B. F. Cheatham.
Palmer's Brigade, Brig.-Gen. Joseph B. Palmer: 1st Tenn. (consolidated 1st, 6th, 8th, 9th, 16th, 27th, 28th, and 34th Tenn., and 24th Tenn. Batt'n), Lieut.-Col. O. A. Bradshaw; 2d Tenn. (consolidated 11th, 12th, 13th, 29th, 47th, 50th, 51st, 52d, and 154th Tenn.), Lieut.-Col. George W. Pease; 3d Tenn. (consolidated 4th, 5th, 19th, 24th, 31st, 33d, 35th, 38th, and 41st Tenn.), Col. James D. Tillman; 4th Tenn. (consolidated 2d, 3d, 10th, 15th, 18th, 20th, 26th, 30th, 32d, 37th, and 45th Tenn., and 23d Tenn. Batt'n), Col. A. Searcy. *Gist's Brigade,* Col. W. G. Foster: 46th Ga., Lieut.-Col. A. Miles; 65th Ga. and 2d and 8th Ga. Batt'ns (consolidated), Lieut.-Col. Z. L. Walters; 16th and 24th S. C., Col. B. B. Smith.
ARTILLERY BATTALION, Maj. B. C. Manly: La. Battery, Capt. William M. Bridges; N. C. Battery, Capt. George B. Atkins; S. C. Battery, Capt. George H. Walter; S. C. Battery, Capt. W. E. Zimmerman; Va. Battery (Paris's), Lieut. Thomas Tucker.
STEWART'S CORPS, Lieut.-Gen. Alexander P. Stewart.
LORING'S DIVISION, Maj.-Gen. William W. Loring.
Featherston's Brigade, Brig.-Gen. W. S. Featherston: 1st Ark. (consolidated 1st and 2d Ark., M't'd Rifles, and 4th, 9th, and 25th Ark. Inf.), Col. H. G. Bunn; 3d Miss. (consolidated 3d, 31st, and 40th Miss.), Col. John M. Stigler; 22d Miss. (consolidated 1st, 22d, and 33d Miss., and 1st Miss. Batt'n), Col. M. A. Oatis; 37th Miss. Batt'n, Maj. Q. C. Heidelberg. *Lowry's Brigade,* Brig.-Gen. Robert Lowry: 29th Ala., Maj. H. B. Turner; 12th La., Capt. J. A. Dixon, Lieut.-Col. E. M. Graham; 14th Miss.

(consolidated 5th, 14th, and 43d Miss.), Col. R. J. Lawrence; 15th Miss. (consolidated 6th, 15th, 20th, and 23d Miss.), Lieut.-Col. T. B. Graham. *Shelley's Brigade,* Brig.-Gen. C. M. Shelley: 1st Ala. (consolidated 16th, 33d, and 45th Ala.), Col. Robert H. Abercrombie; 17th Ala., Col. E. P. Holcombe; 27th Ala. (consolidated 27th, 35th, 49th, 55th, and 57th Ala.), Col. Ed. McAlexander.
ANDERSON'S (late Taliaferro's) DIVISION, Maj.-Gen. Patton Anderson.
Elliott's Brigade, Brig.-Gen. Stephen Elliott, Jr., Lieut.-Col. J. Welsman Brown: 22d Ga. Batt'n Art'y, Maj. M. J. McMullan; 27th Ga. Batt'n, Maj. A. L. Hartridge; 2d S. C. Art'y, Lieut.-Col. J. W. Brown, Maj. F. F. Warley; Manigault's S. C. Batt'n, Lieut. H. Klatte, Capt. Thomas G. Boag. *Rhett's Brigade,* Col. William Butler: 1st S. C. (regulars), Maj. T. A. Huguenin, Lieut.-Col. Warren Adams; 1st S. C. Art'y, Lieut.-Col. Joseph A. Yates; Lucas's S. C. Batt'n, Maj. J. J. Lucas, Capt. T. B. Hayne.
WALTHALL'S (late McLaws's) DIVISION, Maj.-Gen. E. C. Walthall.
Harrison's Brigade, Col. George P. Harrison, Jr.: 1st Ga. (regulars), Col. R. A. Wayne; 5th Ga., Col. C. P. Daniel; 5th Ga. Reserves, Maj. C. E. McGregor; 32d Ga., Lieut.-Col. E. H. Bacon, Jr.; 47th Ga. and Bonaud's Battalion, ——. *Conner's Brigade,* Brig.-Gen. John D. Kennedy: 2d S. C. (consolidated 2d and 20th S. C., and Blanchard's Reserves), Col. William Wallace; 3d S. C. (consolidated 3d and 8th S. C., 3d S. C. Batt'n, and Blanchard's Reserves), Col. E. T. Stackhouse; 7th S. C. (consolidated 7th and 15th S. C., and Blanchard's Reserves), Col. John B. Davis.
ARTILLERY, Maj. A. Burnet Rhett: Ga. Battery, Capt. R. W. Anderson, Lieut. H. S. Greaves; Ga. Battery, Capt. John W. Brooks; La. Battery, Capt. G. Le Gardeur, Jr.; S. C. Battery, Capt. Ed. L. Parker; S. C. Battery, Capt. H. M. Stuart; Ga. Battery, Capt. J. F. Wheaton.
LEE'S CORPS, ⁊ Lieut.-Gen. S. D. Lee.
Escort, Capt. G. G. Ragland.
HILL'S DIVISION, Maj.-Gen. D. H. Hill.
Sharp's Brigade, Brig.-Gen. J. H. Sharp: 24th Ala. (consolidated 24th, 28th, and 34th Ala.), Col. John C. Carter; 8th Miss. Batt'n (consolidated 5th, 8th, and 32d Miss., and 3d Miss. Batt'n), Capt. J. Y. Carmack; 9th Miss. (consolidated 9th Batt'n Sharp-shooters and 7th, 9th, 10th, 41st, and 44th Miss.), Col. W. C. Richards; 19th S. C. (consolidated 10th and 19th S. C.), Maj. James O. Ferrell, Lieut.-Col. C. Irvine Walker. *Brantly's Brigade,* Brig.-Gen. W. F. Brantly: 22d Ala. (consolidated 22d, 25th, 39th, and 50th Ala.), Col. H. T. Toulmin; 37th Ala. (consolidated 37th, 42d, and 54th Ala.), Col. J. A. Minter; 24th Miss. (consolidated 24th, 27th, 29th, 30th, and 34th Miss.), Col. R. W. Williamson; 58th N. C. (consolidated 58th and 60th N. C.), Lieut.-Col. T. Coleman.
STEVENSON'S DIVISION, Maj.-Gen. Carter L. Stevenson.
Escort, Lieut. J. L. Johnston.
Henderson's Brigade, Brig.-Gen. R. J. Henderson: 1st Ga. Confed. Batt'n (consolidated 1st Ga. Confed., 1st Batt'n Ga. Sharp-shooters, 25th, 29th, 30th, and 66th Ga.), Capt. W. J. Whitsitt; 39th Ga. (consolidated 34th, 39th, and part of 56th Ga.), Lieut.-Col. W. P. Milton, Col. C. H. Phinizy; 40th Ga. Batt'n (consolidated 40th, 41st, and 43d Ga.), Lieut. W. H. Darnall, Capt. J. E. Stallings; 42d Ga. (consolidated 36th and 42d Ga., and parts of 34th and 56th Ga.), Lieut.-Col. L. P. Thomas. *Pettus's Brigade,* Brig.-Gen. E. W. Pettus: 19th Ala., Lieut.-Col. E. S. Gulley; 20th Ala., Lieut.-Col. J. R. Elliott; 23d Ala., Maj. J. T. Hester; 54th Va. Batt'n, Lieut.-Col. C. H. Lynch.

‖ As constituted after April 9th, upon which date it was partly reorganized.
‡ At Bentonville consisted of the divisions of Hoke, McLaws, and W. B. Taliaferro. Maj.-Gen. Lafayette McLaws was assigned April 10th to command the District of Georgia.
↓ From the Department of North Carolina, commanded by General Braxton Bragg.
) All the troops of Cheatham's old corps engaged at Bentonville were commanded by Maj.-Gen. W. B. Bate.
⁊ At Bentonville consisted of Stevenson's, Clayton's, and Hill's divisions, commanded by Maj.-Gen. D. H. Hill. Col. J. G. Coltart commanded Hill's division.

ARTILLERY: S. C. Battery, Capt. J. T. Kanapaux.

CAVALRY, Lieut.-Gen. Wade Hampton.

Consisted of Lieut.-Gen. Joseph Wheeler's corps and the division of Maj.-Gen. M. C. Butler, embracing, in part, the following-named organizations: 1st Ala., ——; 3d Ala., ——; 51st Ala., Col. M. L. Kirkpatrick; 1st Ga., ——; 2d Ga., ——; 3d Ga., ——; 4th Ga., ——; 5th Ga., Col. Edward Bird; 6th Ga., ——; 12th Ga., Capt. J. H. Graham; 1st Tenn., Col. James T. Wheeler; 2d Tenn., Col. H. M. Ashby; 4th Tenn., Col. Baxter Smith; 5th Tenn., Col. George W. McKenzie; 8th Tenn., ——; 9th Tenn. Battalion, Maj. James H. Akin; 3d Confederate, ——; 8th Confederate, Lieut.-Col. John S. Prather; 10th Confederate, ——; 1st Ky., ——; 3d Ky., ——; 9th Ky., ——; 3d Ark., Maj. W. H. Blackwell; 8th Tex., ——; 11th Tex., ——; Allison's Squadron, ——; S. C. Battery (Hart's), Capt. E. L. Halsey; S. C. Battery, Capt. William E. Earle.

Logan's Brigade, Brig.-Gen. T. M. Logan: 1st, 4th, 5th, and 6th S. C., and 19th S. C. Batt'n, ——; Phillips Ga. Legion, Maj. W. W. Thomas; Jeff. Davis Legion, Col. J. F. Waring; Cobb's Ga. Legion, Capt. R. B. Roberts; 10th Ga., Capt. E. W. Moise.

The division and brigade commanders mentioned in General Wheeler's official report of the campaign are W. Y. C. Humes, W. W. Allen, Robert H. Anderson, M. W. Hannon, James Hagan, George G. Dibrell, F. H. Robertson, Thomas Harrison, H. M. Ashby, and C. C. Crews.

UNATTACHED TROOPS.

Artillery Batt'n, Maj. Joseph Palmer; S. C. Batt'y, Capt. James I. Kelly; Miss. Batt'y (Swett's), Lieut. H. Shannon; Fla. Batt'y, Capt. Henry F. Abell; I, 10th N. C. Batt'n, Capt. Thomas I. Southerland; 3d N. C. Batt'n

Art'y, Maj. John W. Moore; 13th N. C. Batt'n Art'y, Lieut.-Col. Joseph B. Starr; Pioneer Reg't, Col. John G. Tucker; Naval Brigade, Rear-Admiral Raphael Semmes.

General Johnston reported his effective strength of infantry and artillery as follows: March 17th, 9513; March 23d, 15,027; March 27th, 14,678 (on this date the cavalry numbered 4093); March 31st, 16,014; April 7th, 18,182; April 17th, 14,770; April 24th, 15,188.

In his official report General Wheeler says that he had under his immediate command at the commencement of the campaign 4442 effectives; on February 16th, 5172, and on April 17th, 4965. The number of troops (combatants and non-combatants) paroled at Greensboro' was 30,045; at Salisbury, 2987, and at Charlotte, 4015, making a grand total of 37,047. General Johnston ("Narrative," p. 410) says: "The meeting between General Sherman and myself, and the armistice that followed, produced great uneasiness in the army. It was very commonly believed among the soldiers that there was to be a surrender, by which they would be prisoners of war, to which they were very averse. This apprehension caused a great number of desertions between the 19th and 24th of April—not less than 4000 in the infantry and artillery, and almost as many from the cavalry."

The Confederate loss in action at Rivers's Bridge, S. C., was 8 killed, 44 wounded, and 45 captured or missing = 97. Near Kinston, N. C., there were 11 killed, 107 wounded, and 16 captured or missing = 134. The loss at Averysboro' is estimated at about 700. At Bentonville it was 239 killed, 1694 wounded, and 673 captured or missing = 2606. With regard to the latter, however, General Sherman ("Personal Memoirs," Vol. II., p. 306) claims to have captured 1625 prisoners.

THE BATTLE OF BENTONVILLE.

BY WADE HAMPTON, LIEUTENANT-GENERAL, C. S. A.[†]

WHEN Sherman cut loose from Atlanta, after expelling the inhabitants and burning a part of the city, [‡] it was evident to every one who had given a thought to the subject that his objective point was a junction with General Grant's army. The Army of Tennessee, after its disastrous repulse before Franklin, was, with its shattered columns, in rear instead of in front of Sherman's advancing forces, and thus he was allowed to make his march to Savannah a mere holiday excursion. At this latter point there was no adequate force to oppose him, and when Hardee, who commanded there, withdrew, the city fell an easy prey. The situation then was as follows: Sherman had established a new base, where communication with the sea was open to him, while Hardee's line extended from the Savannah River to James Island, beyond Charleston, a distance of 115 miles. Outside of the garrison of Charleston he had but a handful of unorganized troops to hold this long line, and our true policy then would have been to abandon Charleston, to concentrate every available man in front of Sherman, and to dispute the passage of the rivers and swamps which were in his line of march, and which offered most admirable positions for an inferior force to strike a superior one. The garrison of Charleston consisted, I think, of about six-

teen thousand well-equipped, well-drilled infantry, fully supplied with excellent artillery. Stevenson's division, Army of Tennessee (Confederate), consisting of 2600 men, reached Columbia before the appearance of the enemy. In addition to the troops already mentioned, there were here Wheeler's and Butler's commands of cavalry, and several unattached bodies of State troops and reserves. A rapid concentration of these forces would have put from 25,000 to 30,000 men in front of Sherman, and an attack upon one wing of his army, when separated from the other, would either have resulted in a victory to our army or would have encumbered him with so many wounded men that he would have been forced to retreat to the sea, at Charleston. The views I have here expressed were entertained at the time spoken of, for as I happened to be in Columbia then,—not on duty, however,—I urged upon General Beauregard, who had assumed command about that time, the abandonment of Charleston and the concentration of his whole force at the first-named city. I pressed the same views on Governor Magrath, telling him that, important as Charleston was to us, Branchville, the junction of the railroads from Columbia, Augusta, and Charleston, was far more important. In these opinions, my

[†] On the 16th of January, 1865 (while on leave of absence), General Hampton, commander of the Cavalry Corps, Army of Northern Virginia, was assigned to the command of all the cavalry in the operations against Sherman.—EDITORS.

[‡] General Sherman ordered all railway tracks and buildings and all warehouses and public buildings that might be of military use to the Confederates to be destroyed, under the direction of Colonel O. M. Poe, Chief Engineer.—EDITORS.

recollection is that General Beauregard concurred, but why the movements suggested were not made I have never known. At all events Charleston was evacuated, February 17th, and its garrison was sent to Cheraw on the Pedee River, and thence by a long march to North Carolina. When the Federal army appeared before Columbia, the only troops in and around the city were Stevenson's division, Wheeler's cavalry, and a portion of Butler's division, in all about five thousand of all arms. Practically there was no force in the city, for the troops were on picket duty from a point three miles above Columbia to one twenty miles below. Of course no defense of the place was attempted, and it was surrendered by the mayor before the enemy entered it, with the hope that, as no resistance had been offered, it would be protected from pillage and destruction. Sherman, in his memoirs, tells its fate in these brief and suggestive words: "The army, having totally ruined Columbia, moved on toward Winnsboro'." [See p. 686.] Stevenson's division, which was above the city, was withdrawn, taking the road to Winnsboro', and I, having been assigned the night previous to the command of the cavalry, fell back in the same direction, covering the retreat of the infantry.

It would scarcely have been possible to disperse a force more effectually than was done in our case. Hardee was moving toward Fayetteville in North Carolina; Beauregard was directing Stevenson's march to Charlotte; Cheatham, with his division from the Army of Tennessee, had come from Augusta and was moving toward the same point as Stevenson, but on the west side of the Congaree and Broad rivers, while the cavalry kept in close observation of the enemy. Hardee's men, though good soldiers, had been kept so long on garrison duty that the long marches broke down many of them, and half of his command, or perhaps more, fell out of the ranks while going to the scene of action.

It was from these widely separated forces, these *disjecta membra*, that General Joseph E. Johnston, who was assigned to the command of this department, February 23d, had to form the army with which he fought the battle of Bentonville, and his first task was to bring together these detached bodies of troops. Hoke's fine division from the Army of Northern Virginia also joined him before the fight, and rendered gallant and efficient service. ‡ General Johnston had united all his available infantry at Smithfield, North Carolina; and Sherman, whose progress had been entirely unobstructed, except by a spirited fight made by Hardee at Averysboro' [see p. 691], and some affairs with our cavalry, was moving east from Fayetteville toward Goldsboro'. This being the condition of affairs, General Johnston realized that unless the advance of the enemy could be checked it would be only a question of time before Sherman would effect a

junction with Grant, when their united armies would overwhelm the depleted and exhausted Army of Northern Virginia. Under these circumstances, but two alternatives were presented to the Confederate general: one was to transport his infantry by rail rapidly to Virginia, where the reenforcements he could thus bring to General Lee might enable these two great soldiers to strike a decisive blow on Grant's left flank; the other was to throw his small force on the army confronting him, with the hope of crippling that army, if he could not defeat it. As we could hope for no reenforcements from Virginia, or indeed from any quarter, my judgment was that the first-named plan held out the best promise of success, and if my memory serves me right, I think that General Johnston mentions in his "Narrative" that he suggested it. Of this, however, I am not certain, and I cannot verify my impression, as his report is not within my reach. However the case may be, that plan was not adopted, and the general determined to resort to the other. His determination was a bold, I think a wise one; for, great as was the risk involved, it offered the only hope of success left to us.

The relative position of the opposing armies being then as has been described, the Confederate cavalry bivouacking about two miles south of the little hamlet of Bentonville, where the road from Smithfield intersected that from Fayetteville to Goldsboro', I received a dispatch from General Johnston about 12 o'clock on the night of March 17th. In this letter he asked if I could give him information as to the positions of the several corps of the Federal army; what I thought of the practicability of his attacking them; if advisable in my opinion to do so, when and where an attack could be made to most advantage; and requesting me to "give him my views." He was then, as I have said, at Smithfield, about sixteen miles from Bentonville, and I replied at once, telling him that the Fourteenth Corps [Davis's] was in my immediate front; the Twentieth Corps [Williams's] was on the same road, five or six miles in the rear; while the two other corps [Logan's and Blair's] were on a road some miles to the south, which ran parallel to the one on which we were. I suggested that the point at which I was encamped was an admirable one for the attack he contemplated, and that I would delay the enemy as much as possible, so as to enable us to concentrate there.

In a few hours a reply came from General Johnston saying that he would move at once to the position indicated, and directing me to hold it if possible. In obedience to these orders I moved out on the morning of the 18th to meet the enemy, with whom we skirmished until the afternoon, when I was pressed back by the force of numbers to the crest of a wooded hill which overlooked a very large field that I had selected as a proper place for the battle, which was to take place

‡ Hoke's division left the Army of Northern Virginia for Wilmington, North Carolina, December 20-22, 1864, and bore a part, under Bragg, in the defense of that city during the second attack on Fort Fisher, and subsequently at Fort Anderson. Wilmington was evacuated February 22, 1865, and the division, after an engagement with Cox's command near Kinston, March 8–10 [see General Slocum's article, p. 754], joined Johnston's army in time to participate in the battle of Bentonville.— EDITORS.

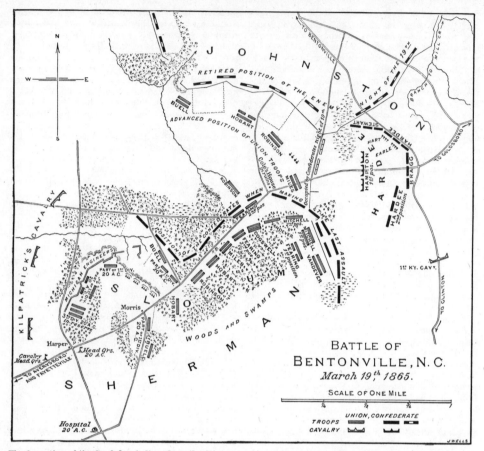

BATTLE OF
BENTONVILLE, N.C.
March 19th, 1865.

SCALE OF ONE MILE

The formation of the Confederate line along the Clinton road, near the crossing of the Goldsboro' road (as seen on the extreme right of the map), took place before the Union positions had been developed. Subsequently the Confederates deployed to the west and south to oppose the Union advance on both sides of the Goldsboro' road.

as soon as our infantry reached the ground. It was vitally important that this position should be held by us during the night, so I dismounted all my men, placing them along the edge of the woods, and at great risk of losing my guns I put my artillery some distance to the right of the road, where, though exposed, it had a commanding position. I knew that if a serious attack was made on me the guns would be lost, but I determined to run this risk in the hope of checking the Federal advance. As an illustration of the quick perception of our private soldiers, I recall an expression of one of them as I rode off after placing the guns in position. Turning to some of his comrades he said with a laugh, "Old Hampton is playing a bluff game, and if he don't mind Sherman will call him." He evidently understood the game of war as well as that of poker! It was near sunset when the enemy moved on this position, and recognizing its strength, not knowing also, I suppose, what number of troops held it, they withdrew after a rather feeble demonstration against us. We were thus left in possession of the ground chosen for the fight.

That night General Johnston reached Bentonville, as did a part of his command; but Hardee's troops had not been able to form a junction with the rest of our forces, as the distance they had to march was greater than had been anticipated. As soon as General Johnston had established his headquarters at Bentonville I reported to him, giving him all the information in my possession as to the position of the enemy and the character of the ground on which we had to operate. The following extracts from the report of the general will show the nature of our conference:

"Lieutenant-General Hampton . . . described the ground near the road abreast of us as favorable for our purpose. The Federal camp, however, was but five or six miles from that ground,—nearer, by several miles, than Hardee's bivouac,—and therefore we could not hope for the advantage of attacking the head of a deep column. . . . As soon as General Hardee's troops reached Bentonville next morning we moved by the left flank, Hoke's division leading, to the ground selected by General Hampton and adopted from his description."

As the general had not been able to examine the ground, I ventured to suggest such disposition of our forces as I thought would be most advantageous, and my suggestions were adopted. The plan proposed was that the cavalry should move out at daylight and occupy the position held by them on the previous evening. The infantry could then be deployed, with one corps across the main road and the other two obliquely in echelon to the right of the first. As soon as these positions were occupied I was to fall back with my command, through the first corps [Bragg's], and, passing to the rear of the infantry line, I was to take position on our extreme right. These movements were carried out successfully, except that Hardee had not reached his position in the center when the enemy who were following me struck Bragg's corps, which was in line of battle across the road. ♭ This absence of Hardee left a gap between Bragg and Stewart; and in order to hold this gap until the arrival of Hardee, I had two batteries of horse artillery—Captains Halsey's (Hart's) and Earle's—placed in the vacant space. The former of these batteries had constituted a part of the Hampton Legion; it had served with me during all the campaigns in Virginia, making an honorable and brilliant record, and had joined me at Bentonville just in time to render efficient service in the last battle in which we fought together. All the guns of both batteries were admirably served, and their fire held the enemy in their front until Hardee reached his allotted position. In the meantime Bragg's troops had repulsed the attack made on them, and the opportune moment had arrived when the other two corps, in accordance with the plan agreed on, should have been thrown on the flank of the retreating enemy. But unfortunately there occurred one of those incidents that so often change the fate of battles, and which broke in on the plan of this fight just at the crisis of the engagement. About the time the head of Hardee's column appeared a very heavy attack was made on Hoke's division, and Bragg, fearing he

could not maintain his ground, applied for reënforcements. General Johnston at once determined to comply with this request, and he directed Hardee to send a portion of his force to the support of Hoke. This movement was in my judgment the only mistake committed on our part during the fight, and when the general notified me of the intended change in the plans I advised that we should adhere to the one agreed on. It would

LIEUTENANT-GENERAL WADE HAMPTON, C. S. A. FROM A PHOTOGRAPH.

be great presumption in me to criticise any movement directed by General Johnston, in whose skill and generalship I have always entertained implicit confidence, and I should not now venture to express an opinion as to the propriety of the

♭ General Johnston, in his official report, gives the following general account of the battle of the 19th:

"General Bragg's were formed across it [the Goldsboro' road] at right angles, and the Army of Tennessee on their right, with its own strongly thrown forward. The ground in our front, north of the road, was open; that on the south of it, covered with thickets. We had but one road through dense black-jack for our movements, so that they consumed a weary time. While they were in progress a vigorous attack was made on General Bragg's left. Lieutenant-General Hardee was instructed to send one division to its support and the other to the extreme right, and with the latter and Stewart's troops to charge as they faced, which would bring them obliquely upon the enemy's left and center. General Bragg's troops were to join in the movement successively from right to left. In the meantime the attack upon General Bragg was repulsed with heavy loss, and another made on Stewart's corps, commanded by Major-General Loring, by whom the enemy was quickly driven back. These two affairs showed that the Fourteenth Corps was in our immediate front. It was near 3 o'clock before Hardee's troops were in position on the right. He then

made the charge with characteristic skill and vigor, well and gallantly seconded by Stewart, [D. H.] Hill, [W. W.] Loring, and the officers under him. Once, when he apprehended difficulty, Hardee literally led the advance. The Federals were routed in a few minutes, our brave fellows dashing successively over two lines of temporary breastworks, and following the enemy rapidly, but in good order. A mile in rear the Fourteenth rallied on the Twentieth Corps in a dense growth of young pines. In this position the Federal right rested on a swamp and was covered with intrenchments. Our troops continued to press the enemy back, except on the left, where we were held in check by the intrenchments just mentioned. Their progress was very slow, however, from the difficulty of penetrating thickets in line of battle. About 6 o'clock the Federal force was so greatly increased . . . that it seemed to attempt the offensive, but with little effect. They were able to hold their ground until night only by the dense thickets and breastworks. After burying our dead and bringing off our own and many of the Federal wounded, and three pieces of artillery (a fourth was left because we had not horses to draw it away) we returned to our first position." EDITORS.

order given to Hardee had not the general in his report stated that this movement was a mistake. He says in his "Narrative":

"The enemy attacked Hoke's division vigorously, especially its left — so vigorously that General Bragg apprehended that Hoke, although slightly intrenched, would be driven from his position. He therefore applied urgently for strong reënforcements. Lieutenant-General Hardee, the head of whose column was then near, was directed most injudiciously to send his leading division, McLaws's, to the assistance of the troops assailed."

Hoke repulsed the attack made on him fully and handsomely. Had Hardee been in the position originally assigned him at the time Hoke struck the enemy, and could his command and Stewart's have been thrown on the flanks of the retreating Federal forces, I think that the Fourteenth Corps would have been driven back in disorder on the Twentieth, which was moving up to its support. The fact that confronted General Johnston then was that much precious time had been lost by a delay in following up promptly the success gained by his troops in their first conflict with the enemy. His orders were that Bragg should change front to the left, which movement would have aligned him with the other corps and enabled him to attack on the flank.

For some reason not known to me these orders were not carried out promptly, or perhaps not at all, and hence delay occurred which, while hurtful to us, was of great value to the enemy, for time was given to him to bring up the Twentieth Corps to the support of the broken ranks of the Fourteenth. It thus happened that though the attack of the Fourteenth Corps was repulsed early in the morning, our counter-attack was delayed until quite late in the afternoon, when we encountered a force double that met in the morning, and found them behind breastworks. The fighting that evening was close and bloody. As General Johnston has described it far better than I could do, I quote his account :

"The Confederates passed over three hundred yards of the space between the two lines in quick time and in excellent order, and the remaining distance in double-quick, without pausing to fire until their near approach had driven the enemy from the shelter of their intrenchments, in full retreat, to their second line. After firing a few rounds the Confederates again pressed forward, and when they were near the second intrenchment, now manned by both lines of Federal troops, Lieutenant-General Hardee, after commanding the double-quick, led the charge, and with his knightly gallantry dashed over the enemy's breastworks on horseback in front of his men. Some distance in the rear there was a very thick wood of young pines, into which the Federal troops were pursued, and in which they rallied and renewed the fight. But the Confederates continued to advance, driving the enemy back slowly, notwithstanding the advantage given to the party on the defensive by the thicket, which made united action by the assailants impossible. On the extreme left, however, General Bragg's troops were held in check by the Federal right, which had the aid of breastworks and the thicket of black-jack. . . .

"The impossibility of concentrating the Confederate forces in time to attack the Federal left wing while in column on the march, made complete success also impossible, from the enemy's great numerical superiority."

Night closed upon a hard-fought field and a dearly won victory, for the losses in our handful of troops had been heavy. After dark General Johnston withdrew to the position from which he had moved to the attack, and our first line, with slight modifications, was resumed.

Early on the morning of the 20th, Brigadier-General Law, whom I had placed temporarily in command of Butler's division in the unavoidable absence of that officer, reported that the right wing of the Federal army, which had struck the road on which we were some miles to the east, was rapidly moving down on our rear and left flank. Hoke then held our left, and General Johnston directed him to refuse his left flank so that he could meet the attack of the approaching force. I prolonged the rear line taken by Hoke by placing Butler's and Wheeler's commands on his left, and while doing this we met and checked a sharp attack. Sherman thus had his whole army united in front of us, about 12 o'clock on the 20th, and he made repeated attacks during the day, mainly on Hoke's division. In all of them he was repulsed, and many of his wounded left in front of our lines were carried to our hospitals. Our line was a very weak one and our position was extremely perilous, for our small force was confronted, almost surrounded, by one nearly five times as large. Our flanks rested on no natural defenses, and behind us was a deep and rapid stream [Mill Creek] over which there was but one bridge, which gave the only means of withdrawal. Our left flank — far overlapped by the enemy — was held along a small stream which flowed into Mill Creek, and this was held only by cavalry videttes stationed at long intervals apart.

On the 21st there was active skirmishing on the left of our line, and my pickets reported that the enemy seemed to be moving in force to our left on the opposite side of the small stream, along which my videttes were stationed. I immediately rode down to report this fact to General Johnston, and I told him that there was no force present able to resist an attack, and that if the enemy broke through at that point, which was near the bridge, across the main stream, our only line of retreat would be cut off. The general directed me to return to the point indicated to ascertain the exact condition of affairs, and as I was riding back I met a courier, who informed me that the enemy in force had crossed the branch, had driven back the cavalry pickets, and were then very near the main road leading to the bridge. This attack rendered our position extremely dangerous, for if the attacking force had been able to attain possession of the road we could not have withdrawn without very heavy loss, if we could have done so at all.

Just before the courier who brought me the information of the advance of the army met me, I had passed a brigade, whose numbers were not more than sufficient to constitute a regiment, moving toward our left. This was Cumming's Georgia brigade, commanded then, I think, by Colonel Henderson, and I doubt if there were more than 200 to 250 in the command. Realizing the importance of prompt action, I ordered this command to move at once to the point threatened, and also ordered up a battery which I had passed. I then sent a courier to bring up all the mounted men he could find, and in a few minutes a portion of the 8th Texas Cavalry — sixty or eighty men — responded to my call. All of these troops were hurried up to meet the enemy, who were then within a few hundred yards of the road, and just as I had put them in position General Hardee arrived on the ground. Explaining the position to him and telling him of the dispositions I had made, he at once ordered a charge, and our small force was hurled against the advancing enemy. The attack was so sudden and so impetuous that it carried everything before it, and the enemy retreated hastily across the branch. This attack on our position was made by Mower's division, and it was repulsed by a force which certainly did not exceed, if it reached, three hundred men.‡ Sherman in his "Memoirs" says that he "ordered Mower back"; but if this statement is true, the order was obeyed with wonderful promptness and alacrity. General Hardee, who assumed command when he reached the field, led this charge with his usual conspicuous gallantry; and as he returned from it successful, his face bright with the light of battle, he turned to me and exclaimed: "That was Nip and Tuck, and for a time I thought Tuck had it." A sad incident marred his triumph, for his only son, a gallant boy of sixteen, who had joined the 8th Texas Cavalry two hours before, fell in the charge led by his father. This affair virtually ended the battle of Bentonville for that night. Johnston withdrew safely across Mill Creek, where he camped two miles beyond the bridge.

On the morning of the 22d there was a sharp skirmish at the bridge between some of Wheeler's cavalry and the advance-guard of the enemy, who tried to force a passage, but who were handsomely repulsed with some loss. I have not specified the services of the cavalry during the operations described, but they were important and were gallantly performed. The cavalry of

Butler and Wheeler numbered, I think, about three thousand men, and after the engagement became general nearly all this force fought alongside the infantry in their improvised breastworks. When Sherman moved up on our left flank they checked his advance until our main line could be refused on the left wing; and in Mower's subsequent repulse they bore an important part, for, in addition to the gallant charge of the 8th Texas made in conjunction with the infantry, other portions of my command struck his flank as he was retiring, and contributed largely to our success. The infantry forces of General Johnston amounted to about 14,100 men, and they were composed of three separate commands which had never acted together. These were Hardee's troops, brought from Savannah and Charleston; Stewart's, from the Army of Tennessee; and Hoke's division of veterans. Bragg, by reason of his rank, was in command of this division, but it was really Hoke's division, and Hoke directed the fighting. These troops, concentrated only recently for the first time, were stationed at and near Smithfield, eighteen miles from the field where the battle was fought, and it was from these points that General Johnston moved them to strike a veteran army numbering about 60,000 men. Of course General Johnston's only object in making this fight was to cripple the enemy and to impede his advance; and I think that if his original plan of battle could have been carried out, and if his orders had been executed promptly, he would have inflicted a very heavy, if not an irretrievable, disaster on the Fourteenth and the Twentieth corps. These two corps were opposed to him in the first day's fight, and in that of the last two days he was confronted by the whole of Sherman's army. It must be remembered, too, that General Schofield was in supporting distance of Sherman with 26,000 men. Few soldiers would have adopted the bold measure resorted to by General Johnston, and none could have carried it out more skillfully or more successfully than he did.

‡ Lieutenant George B. Guild, of Nashville, Tennessee, writes to the editors that he was acting adjutant-general of Harrison's brigade, and participated in this charge. The column that responded to General Hampton's call, he says, was composed of the 4th Tennessee and 8th Texas, and numbered about 200. Colonel Baxter Smith, of the 4th Tennessee, led, and Generals Hardee and Hampton were also in the charge.— EDITORS.

CLOSING OPERATIONS IN THE JAMES RIVER.

BY PROFESSOR JAMES RUSSELL SOLEY, U. S. N.

ON the 31st of August, 1862, the James River flotilla, under Captain Charles Wilkes, was disbanded, the withdrawal of McClellan from the Peninsula having rendered its further continuance unnecessary. For a long time thereafter the greater part of the river was left in the undisturbed possession of the Confederates, who took the opportunity to fit out a squadron of considerable strength. The nucleus of this squadron was found in the gun-boats which had assisted the *Merrimac* in Hampton Roads, viz., the *Patrick Henry*, *Beaufort*, *Raleigh*, and *Teazer*. The *Jamestown*, which had also been in Tattnall's squadron, was sunk as an obstruction at Drewry's Bluff.

Three other gun-boats, the *Hampton* and *Nansemond*, which had been built at Norfolk, and the *Drewry*, were added to the enemy's flotilla in the James. [See map, p. 494.]

Little of importance happened on the river in 1863. In the adjoining waters of Chesapeake Bay an active partisan warfare was carried on by various junior officers of the Confederate service, foremost among whom were Acting Master John Y. Beall and Lieutenant John Taylor Wood. Numerous conflicts occurred on the bay, but in November Beall was finally captured. The repression of this guerrilla warfare was chiefly intrusted to the Potomac flotilla, under Commander F. A.

Parker, while several raids were made upon Matthews county, the principal base of operations of the guerrillas, by gun-boats of the North Atlantic squadron. The most striking operation in the James River and adjacent waters in 1863 was the defense of the Nansemond, April 12–26. A sudden movement in force was made by the Confederates to cross the river and thereby reach Suffolk to attack General Peck. Admiral Lee hastily dispatched two flotillas to hold the line of the river: one composed of the *Stepping Stones* and seven other gun-boats under Lieutenant R. H. Lamson, in the upper Nansemond, and the other of four gun-boats under Lieutenant William B. Cushing, in the lower waters. Of special importance were the capture on the 19th of April of the battery at Hill's Point, by Lieutenant Lamson's flotilla, in conjunction with three hundred men under General Getty, and a landing expedition on the 22d to Chuckatuck, several miles inland, under Lieutenant Cushing.

After several months of inaction it was decided in August, 1863, to make a reconnoissance up the James River. The force consisted of the monitor *Sangamon*, the ferry-boat *Commodore Barney*, and the small steamer *Cohasset*, all under the command of Captain G. Gansevoort. General Foster accompanied the squadron in an army tug-boat, but afterward went on board the *Sangamon*. The expedition started on the 4th and proceeded without incident up the river to Dutch Gap, where the *Sangamon* came to anchor owing to the low stage of water. General Foster and his staff and Captain Gansevoort then went on board the *Commodore Barney*, and had gone only a few miles further, to Coxe's Landing, when two torpedoes exploded under the starboard bow of the *Barney*, producing a heavy concussion, lifting her bows, and tearing the planking. The wash from the torpedo carried twenty of the *Barney's* crew overboard, most of whom were rescued. The torpedoes consisted of five hundred pounds of powder, placed in tanks and fired by an electric connection on shore. They were in charge of Lieutenant Hunter Davidson. After the explosion the *Barney* was taken in tow by the *Cohasset*, and the two vessels dropped down to Dutch Gap. On the following day the *Sangamon*, with the two wooden boats, started down the river. Early in the morning, near Four Mile Creek, they had an engagement with a Confederate battery, hidden in thickets on the bank, and supported by infantry. The *Sangamon* and the *Barney* returned the fire, but the *Barney* was disabled by a shot through the boiler, and drifted ashore. The *Cohasset* got her off. A few hours later another engagement took place at Turkey Island Bend, but without any definite result. The wooden vessels were roughly handled; more than thirty round shot penetrated the *Barney*, and she was fairly peppered with musket-balls. The expedition arrived at Newport News on the morning of the 7th, having lost 3 killed and 3 wounded.

Meantime the Confederate Government had been constructing a powerful squadron for the defense of the river. Besides the *Patrick Henry*, which was used as a school-ship for midshipmen, there were the *Beaufort* and *Raleigh*, and the three later

gun-boats, of slight importance, the *Nansemond*, *Hampton*, and *Drewry*. The main force consisted of three new iron-clads. Of these, the *Fredericksburg* carried four 6-inch rifles with four inches of armor, the *Richmond* was still more powerful, and the *Virginia No. 2*, modeled after the first *Virginia* or *Merrimac*, was the most powerful of all, having a casemate with six inches of armor on the sides and eight on the ends. She carried two 8-inch and two 6-inch Brooke rifles, and was the strongest vessel at any time in the Confederate service.

The opening of the year 1864 found the North Atlantic squadron still in Hampton Roads, and without so much as a foothold in the James River. Early in the year two joint expeditions of the army and the navy were made into the country in the neighborhood of the Nansemond, then occupied by scattered forces of the enemy. The first of these, on February 1st, resulted in serious disaster, the principal army detachment and the army transport *Smith Briggs* being captured by the Confederates. The second expedition, on April 14th, composed of a larger force of troops, supported by the *Morris*, *Perry*, and *Barney*, failed of its main object, and retired without gaining any substantial advantage.

The James River campaign opened in May with the landing of the army at City Point and Bermuda Hundred. At daybreak on the 5th the fleet left Newport News. It was composed of five iron-clads, the monitors *Tecumseh*, *Canonicus*, and *Saugus*, the Quintard turret-ship *Onondaga*, and the casemated ram *Atlanta*, which Captain John Rodgers had captured the year before in Warsaw (Wassaw) Sound. The iron-clads were towed up the river by ten of the small steamers in the rear of the transports carrying the troops. The advance was composed of seven gun-boats, the *Osceola*, *Commodore Morris*, *Shokokon*, *Stepping Stones*, *Delaware*, *General Putnam*, and *Shawsheen*, which were to drag the river for torpedoes. Nothing occurred to impede the fleet, and on the evening of the same day the army was landed.

The gun-boats now proceeded to drag the river for torpedoes above City Point. On the 6th the *Commodore Jones*, while exploring near Four Mile Creek, was blown up by a torpedo fired by electricity from the shore; half her crew were killed or wounded. A boat from the *Mackinaw*, under Acting Master's Mate Blanchard, put out to search the banks, and captured the torpedo operators. One of the prisoners was then placed in the forward gun-boat employed in dragging for torpedoes, and was thus led to give much information in reference to their locality and the mode of operating them. On the 7th the gun-boat *Shawsheen* was destroyed by batteries from the shore, and most of her crew were captured.

During May the monitors remained between Trent's Reach and City Point, protecting the right flank of General Butler's army. [See map, p. 198.] The fighting was principally in Trent's Reach, where the Confederates were erecting batteries. They built a strong work at Howlett's, so placed that it could not be destroyed by the fire of the monitors.

This was the situation on the 14th of June, when General Grant arrived at the James. The advance division of the fleet, composed of the iron-clads, lay in or about Trent's Reach. The gun-boats searching for torpedoes occasionally went a little distance beyond, far enough even to draw the fire of Chaffin's Bluff, but Trent's Reach remained substantially the advance position of the fleet. The Confederate squadron, powerful as it was, was unequal to coping with the five Federal iron-clads. In view, however, of the overwhelming importance of the river as a base of operations and means of communication, General Grant had determined that he would not take the chances of a naval contest for its control, and he had previously ordered General Butler to procure and sink a number of hulks in the channel at Trent's Reach. The obstructions were put in position between the 15th and 18th of June, and the operations of the fleet for the remainder of the summer were confined to desultory engagements with batteries at various points along the base of the army. In July and August these engagements occurred with great frequency. Once on the 21st of June, soon after the sinking of the obstructions, the Confederate squadron came down below Dutch Gap, and in conjunction with the battery at Howlett's made an ineffectual demonstration—the only occasion during the year 1864 on which they were brought into action. During the summer and fall the iron-clads were gradually withdrawn, with the exception of the *Onondaga*, a double-turreted monitor carrying two 15-inch smooth-bores and two 150-pounder Parrott rifles.

Up to this time the Confederate squadron, under Commodore John K. Mitchell, had been clearly overmatched, and was therefore not in a position to take the offensive. When the last of the iron-clads had been taken off for the Fort Fisher expedition, however, leaving only the *Onondaga*, Mitchell determined to try conclusions and see if he could not open the river. After waiting for the river to rise, on the 22d of January a party was sent down to examine the obstructions, and found

that they could be passed without much difficulty. On the 23d the fleet, composed of the flag-ship *Virginia*, Lieutenant J. W. Dunnington, the *Richmond*, and the *Fredericksburg*, all iron-clads, the gun-boat *Drewry*, Davidson's torpedo boat, and three torpedo launches, proceeded down to Trent's Reach. The *Fredericksburg* passed safely through the obstructions, but the *Virginia* and *Richmond* ran aground. At daybreak they were discovered, and fire was opened on them from Fort Parsons, the Federal battery near by. The *Onondaga*, Captain William A. Parker, which, on the approach of the enemy, had retired down the river, according to the statement of Captain Parker, to obtain an advantageous position, now returned and joined in the attack. With the flood-tide the two iron-clads were floated off, and withdrew up the river. The *Drewry* and one of the torpedo launches were destroyed. The armor of the *Virginia* was penetrated. That night the Confederate squadron came down again with the intention of attacking the *Onondaga*, but retired after meeting with a warm reception from the batteries on the banks.↓

About the middle of February Commodore Mitchell was replaced in the command of the James River squadron by Admiral Semmes, lately the commander of the *Alabama*. During the six weeks that followed there was very little that the squadron could do. The obstructions at Trent's Reach had been strengthened, and additions had been made to the fleet below. Meantime the Union armies were closing in about Richmond, and at length the fall of the city was inevitable. On the 2d of April, in obedience to orders from Secretary Mallory, Semmes blew up his vessels, landed his men, and proceeded by rail to Danville, N. C., where he remained until Johnston's surrender. On the 3d of April Richmond was occupied, and on the following day the *Malvern*, Admiral Porter's flag-ship, carried President Lincoln up to the late capital of the Confederacy.

↓ From a brief narrative furnished to the editors by Chief Engineer Alexander Henderson, U. S. N., the following statement is condensed:

"At this time [January 23d, 1865] I was serving on board the *Onondaga*, which was lying at anchor some little distance below the obstructions in Trent's Reach. On the evening of the 23d I was preparing to lay torpedoes at the obstructions, in compliance with a suggestion made a short time before by General Grant. When the approach of the Confederate iron-clads was reported, I verified the report by going up in a picket launch, and signaled the fact to the *Onondaga* from the army signal tower on shore. During the remainder of the night, which was the darkest I ever saw, I was constantly moving back and forth between the obstructions and the signal station. My boat was so close to the *Fredericksburg* when she passed through that I could distinctly hear the closing of her furnace doors, the step of a man on some loose oars, and other sounds. I could also hear orders given, but in too low a tone to detect their import.

"What the Confederate vessels did is told in a letter written by Lieutenant E. T. Eggleston of the *Fredericksburg*, which I subsequently found in Richmond. He says:

"'We got under way at 6:30 P. M. Monday last [23d] and proceeded down the river, passing the upper end of Dutch Gap at 10:30 P. M., this vessel, with the *Hampton* in tow, leading, the *Virginia* and *Nansemond* next, followed by the *Richmond* and *Drewry* in the same order. It was a most complete surprise. The first picket that fired at us was at the foot of Signal Hill; the first heavy gun was opposite Dutch Gap. We had to anchor twice above the Yankee ob-

structions to wait for the other vessels, and having cut away some spars we passed safely through their obstructions at 1:15 A. M. and came to anchor some four hundred yards below to wait for the other vessels. . . . We waited for an hour and a half, when our captain (Sheppard) sent up and found the *Virginia*, *Richmond*, and *Drewry* hard aground, with the tide falling. . . . We came up and anchored above the *Virginia*. The enemy had opened on us from four mortar-batteries and several rifled guns, and were getting our range pretty well, but up to daylight no damage was done. About daylight a double-turreted monitor came up to within nine hundred yards of the *Virginia* and opened on her with 15 and 11 inch guns. Their land-batteries of 200 and 100 pounder Parrotts also opened with their mortars and 12 or 15 pieces of field-artillery (20 and 30 pounder Parrotts). She was struck between 125 and 150 times, but the only ones that did any damage were two 15-inch. One struck just above and to the right of the after-port on the port side, driving in the shield from the top of the port to the spar deck. The shield had six inches of iron and twenty-eight inches of old field pine. This shot killed one and wounded seven. Another struck amidships on the port side, driving in some two feet of the plating and the woodwork.

"'The *Richmond* sustained little or no damage. The greatest damage this vessel sustained was from a 200-pounder Parrott that struck on the fantail forward and cut our anchor chain, and the jar, it is supposed, started her leaking. We got under way Tuesday evening, but found the *Virginia's* exhaust-pipe and smoke-stack were so riddled as to fill the gun-deck with smoke and steam, which was the cause of our returning. The whole blame rests with the two pilots of the *Virginia*.'"   EDITORS.

MUSIC ON SHERIDAN'S LINE OF BATTLE.

FIVE FORKS AND THE PURSUIT OF LEE.

BY HORACE PORTER, BREVET BRIGADIER-GENERAL, U. S. A.

IT was 9 o'clock in the morning of the 29th of March, 1865. General Grant and the officers of his staff had bidden good-bye to President Lincoln and mounted the passenger car of the special train that was to carry them from City Point to the front, and the signal was given to start; the train moved off, Grant's last campaign had begun. Since 3 o'clock that morning the columns had been in motion and the Union Army and the Army of Northern Virginia were soon locked in a death-grapple. The President remained at City Point, where he could be promptly informed of the progress of the movement.

The military railroad connecting headquarters with the camps south of Petersburg was about thirteen miles long, or would have been if it had been constructed on a horizontal plane, but as the portion built by the army was a surface road, up hill and down dale, if the rise and fall had been counted in, its length would have defied all ordinary means of measurement. Its undulations were so striking that a train moving along it looked in the distance like a fly crawling over a corrugated washboard. The general sat down near the end of the car, drew from his pocket the flint and slow-match that he always carried, which, unlike a match, never missed fire in a gale of wind, and was soon wreathed in the smoke of the inevitable cigar. I took a seat near him with several other officers of the staff, and he at once began to talk over his plans in detail. They had been discussed in general terms before starting out from City Point. It was his custom, when commencing a movement in the field, to have his staff-officers understand fully the objects he wished to accomplish, and what each corps of the army was expected to do in different emergencies, so that these officers, when sent to distant points of the line, might have a full comprehension of the general's intentions, and so that, when communication with him was impossible or difficult, they might be able to instruct the subordinate commanders intelligently as to the intentions of the general-in-chief.

For a month or more General Grant's chief apprehension had been that the enemy might suddenly pull out from his intrenchments and fall back into the interior, where he might unite with General Joe Johnston against Sherman and force our army to follow Lee to a great distance from its base. General Grant had been sleeping with one eye open and one foot out of bed for many weeks, in the fear that Lee would thus give him the slip. He did not dare delay his movements against the enemy's right until the roads became dry enough to permit an army to move comfortably, for fear Lee would himself take advantage of the good roads to start first. Each army, in fact, was making preparations for either a fight or a foot-race — or both. Sheridan, with his cavalry command, had been ordered to move out in the direction of Dinwiddie Court House, and to be ready to strike the enemy's right and rear. It was the intention, as soon as he could take up a good position for this purpose, to reënforce him with a corps of infantry, and cut off Lee's retreat in the direction of Danville, in case we should break through his intrenched lines in front of Petersburg, and force him from his position there.

The weather had been fair for several days, and the roads were getting in good condition for the movement of troops; that is, as good as could be expected, through a section of country in which the dust in summer was generally so thick that the army could not see where to move, and the mud in winter was so deep that it could not move anywhere. The general, in speaking of what was expected of Sheridan, said: "I had a private talk with Sheridan after I gave him his written instructions at City Point. When he read that part of them which directed him, in certain contingencies, to proceed south along the Danville railroad and coöperate with Sherman by operating in Joe Johnston's rear, he looked so unhappy that I said to him, as I followed him out of the tent, that that part of the instructions was put in only as a blind, so that if he did not meet with entire success the people of the

North, who were then naturally restless and apt to become discouraged, might not look upon a temporary check as an entire defeat of a definite plan,—and that what I really expected was that he would remain with the armies operating against Lee, and end matters right here. This made him happy, and he has started out perfectly confident of the success of the present movement." Referring to Mr. Lincoln, he said: "The President is one of the few visitors I have had who has not attempted to extract from me a knowledge of my plans. He not

James, Parke and Wright holding our works in front of Petersburg, Ord extending to the intersection of Hatcher's Run and the Vaughan road, Humphreys stretching beyond Dabney's Mill, Warren on the extreme left reaching as far as the junction of the Vaughan road and the Boydton plank-road, and Sheridan at Dinwiddie Court House. The weather had become cloudy, and toward evening rain began to fall. It fell in torrents during the night and continued with but little interruption all the next day. The country was densely wooded, and the

UNION ARTILLERY AT PETERSBURG PROTECTED BY MANTELETS. FROM A WAR-TIME SKETCH.

only never asked them, but says it is better he should not know them, and then he can be certain to keep the secret. He will be the most anxious man in the country to hear the news from us, his heart is so wrapped up in our success, but I think we can send him some good news in a day or two." I never knew the general to be more sanguine of victory than in starting out on this campaign.

When we reached the end of the railroad we mounted our horses, which had been carried on the same train, started down the Vaughan road, and went into camp for the night in a field just south of that road, close to Gravelly Run. That night (March 29th) the army was disposed in the following order from right to left: Weitzel in front of Richmond, with a portion of the Army of the

ground swampy, and by evening of the 30th whole fields had become beds of quicksand in which horses sank to their bellies, wagons threatened to disappear altogether, and it seemed as if the bottom had fallen out of the roads. The men began to feel that if any one in after years should ask them whether they had been through Virginia, they could say, "Yes, in a number of places." The roads had become sheets of water; and it looked as if the saving of that army would require the services, not of a Grant, but of a Noah. Soldiers would call out to officers as they rode along: "I say, when are the gun-boats coming up?" The buoyancy of the day before was giving place to gloom, and some began to fear that the whole movement was premature. |

⌊ In his "Memoirs" (C. L. Webster & Co.) General Sheridan says that after the troops began to move he received the following letter from General Grant, whereupon he started at once for Grant's headquarters:

"'HEADQUARTERS, ARMIES OF THE UNITED STATES,
GRAVELLY RUN, March 30th, 1865.

"'MAJOR-GENERAL SHERIDAN: The heavy rain of to-day will make it impossible for us to do much until it dries up a little, or we get roads around our rear repaired. You may,

therefore, leave what cavalry you deem necessary to protect the left, and hold such positions as you deem necessary for that purpose, and send the remainder back to Humphreys's Station [on the military railroad], where they can get hay and grain. Fifty wagons loaded with forage will be sent you in the morning. Send an officer back to direct the wagons back to where you want them. Report to me the cavalry you will leave back, and the position you will occupy. Could not your cavalry go back by the way of Stoney Creek depot and destroy or capture the store of supplies there? — U. S. GRANT Lieutenant-General.'" EDITORS.

While standing in front of the general's tent on the morning of the 30th, discussing the situation with several others on the staff, I saw General Sheridan turning in from the Vaughan road with a staff-officer and an escort of about a dozen cavalry-men, and coming toward our headquarters camp. He was riding his white pacer, a horse which had been captured from General Breckinridge's adjutant-general at Missionary Ridge. But, instead of striking a pacing gait now, it was at every step driving its legs knee-deep into the quicksand with the regularity of a pile-driver. As soon as Sheridan dismounted, he was asked with much eagerness about the situation on the extreme left. He took a decidedly cheerful view of matters, and entered upon a very animated discussion of the coming movements. He said he could drive in the whole cavalry force of the enemy with ease, and if an infantry force were added to his command he would strike out for Lee's right and either crush it or force him so to weaken his intrenched lines that the troops in front of them could break through and march into Petersburg. He warmed up with the subject as he proceeded, threw the whole energy of his nature into the discussion, and his cheery voice, beaming countenance, and impassioned language showed the earnestness of his convictions.

"How do you propose to supply your command with forage if this weather lasts?" he was asked by one of the group.

"Forage?" said Sheridan; "I'll get all the forage I want. I'll haul it out if I have to set every man in the command to corduroying roads, and corduroy every mile of them from the railroad to Dinwiddie. I tell you I'm ready to strike out to-morrow and go to smashing things." And, pacing up and down, he chafed like a hound in the leash. We told him this was the kind of talk we liked to listen to at headquarters, and while General Grant fully coincided in these views it would still further confirm him in his judgment to hear such words as had just been spoken; we urged Sheridan to go and talk in the same strain to the general-in-chief, who was in his tent with General Rawlins. Sheridan, however, objected to obtruding himself unbidden upon his commander. Then we resorted to a bit of strategy. One of us went into the general's tent and told him Sheridan had just come in from the left and had been telling us some matters of much interest, and suggested that he be invited in and asked to state them. This was assented to, and Sheridan was told the general wanted to hear what he had to say. Sheridan then went in and began to speak to General Grant as he had been speaking to the staff. Several persons soon after came into the tent, and General Sheridan stepped out and accompanied General Ingalls to the latter's tent. A few minutes later General Grant went to this tent, General Ingalls came out, and Grant and Sheridan fully discussed the situation. In spite of the opposition which had arisen in some quarters to continuing offensive operations, owing to the state of the weather and the deplorable condition of the roads, General Grant decided to press the movement against the enemy with all vigor.

After his twenty-minutes talk with Grant, Sheridan mounted his horse, and, waving us a good-bye with his hand, rode off to Dinwiddie. The next morning, the 31st, he reported that the enemy had been hard at work intrenching at Five Forks and to a point about a mile west of there. Lee had been as prompt as Grant to recognize that Five Forks was a strategic point of great importance, and, to protect his right, had sent Pickett there with a large force of infantry and nearly all the cavalry. The rain continued during the night of the 30th, and on the morning of the 31st the weather was cloudy and dismal.

General Grant had expected that Warren would be attacked that morning, and had warned him to be on the alert. Warren advanced his corps to ascertain with what force the enemy held the White Oak road and to try to drive him from it; but before he had gone far he met with a vigorous assault. When news came of the attack General Grant directed me to go to the spot and look to the situation of affairs there. I found Ayres's division had been driven in, and both he and Crawford were falling back upon Griffin. Miles, of Humphreys's corps, was sent to reënforce Warren, and by noon the enemy was checked. As soon as General Grant was advised of the situation, he directed General Meade to take the offensive vigorously. Miles made a movement to the left and attacked in flank the troops in front of Warren, and the enemy soon fell back. General Grant had now ridden out to the front, and hearing that he was at Mrs. Butler's house near the Boydton plank-road, I joined him there. It was then a little after 1 o'clock. He had in the meantime ordered the headquarters camp to be moved to Dabney's Mill, on a cross-road running from the Boydton plank to the Vaughan road, and about two miles from Meade's headquarters, which were near the crossing of the Vaughan road and Hatcher's Run. The general was becoming apprehensive lest the infantry force that had moved against Warren might turn upon Sheridan, who had only cavalry with which to resist, as the weather had rendered it impracticable thus far to send him a corps of infantry as intended, and the general-in-chief was urgent that a strong forward movement should be made by the Fifth Corps for the purpose of deterring the enemy from detaching infantry from that portion of his line. This advance was made later in the afternoon, and with decided success. When this movement had been decided upon, General Grant directed me to go to Sheridan and explain what was taking place in Warren's and in Humphreys's front, and have a full understanding with him as to further operations in his vicinity. I rode rapidly down the Boydton plank-road, and soon came to Gravelly Run. Hearing heavy firing in the direction of the Five Forks road, I hurried on in that direction. Crossing by the Brooks road from the Boydton plank to the Five Forks road, which runs north from Dinwiddie, I saw a portion of our cavalry moving eastward, pressed by a heavy force of the enemy, and it was found that Devin and Davies, after holding on tooth and nail for hours, had been driven in by the force of superior numbers and were falling back toward the Boydton plank-road. The brigades of Gibbs and J. I. Gregg had rushed in on the right and rear of the enemy, and got in some very good work, but were soon after compelled to fall back toward Dinwiddie. I turned the corner of the Brooks cross-road and the Five Forks road just as the rear of our cavalry was passing it, and encountered one of Sheridan's bands,⚓ under a heavy fire, playing "Nellie Bly" as cheerily as if it were furnishing music for a country picnic.

I found Sheridan a little north of Dinwiddie Court House, and gave him an account of matters on the left of the Army of the Potomac. He said he had had one of the liveliest days in his experience, fighting infantry and cavalry with cavalry only, but that he was concentrating his command on the high ground just north of Dinwiddie, and would hold that position at all hazards. He did not stop here, but becoming more and more animated in describing the situation and stating his views and intentions, he declared his belief that with the corps of infantry he expected to be put under his command he could take the initiative the next morning and cut off the whole of the force that Lee had detached. He said: "This force is in more danger than I am — if I am cut off from the Army of the Potomac, it is cut off from Lee's army, and not a man in it should ever be allowed to get back to Lee. We at last have drawn the enemy's infantry out of its fortifications, and this is our chance to attack it." He begged me to go to General Grant at once and again urge him to send him the Sixth Corps, because it had been under him in the battles in the Valley of Virginia, and knew his way of fighting. I told him, as had been stated to him before, that the Sixth Corps was next to our extreme right, and that the only one which could reach him by daylight was the Fifth. I started out after for General Grant's headquarters at Dabney's Mill, a distance of about eight miles. I reached there at 7 o'clock P. M., and gave the general a full description of Sheridan's operations. He at once telegraphed the substance of my report to Meade, and preparations soon after began looking to the sending of the Fifth Corps to report to Sheridan. About 7:40 Captain M. V. Sheridan, of Sheridan's staff, brought still later news from Dinwiddie, saying that the cavalry had had more fighting but was holding its position.

It was finally decided that Warren should send Ayres down the Boydton plank and across by the Brooks road, and Griffin and Crawford by the Crump road, which runs from the White Oak road south to J. Boisseau's. [See map, p. 539.] Mackenzie's small division of cavalry was ordered to march to Dinwiddie and report to Sheridan. All haste was urged, in the hope that at daylight the enemy might be caught between Warren's two divisions of infantry on one side and Ayres's division and Sheridan's cavalry on the other, and be badly beaten. It was expected that the infantry

would reach its destination in ample time to take the offensive at break of day, but now one delay after another was met with, and Grant, Meade, and Sheridan spent a painfully anxious night in hurrying forward the movement. Ayres had to rebuild a bridge over Gravelly Run, which took till 2 A. M. Warren, with his other two divisions, did not get started from their position on the White Oak road till 5 A. M., and the hope of crushing the enemy was hourly growing less. This proved to be one of the busiest nights of the whole campaign. Generals were writing dispatches and telegraphing from dark till daylight. Staff-officers were rushing from one headquarters to another, wading through swamps, penetrating forests, and galloping over corduroy roads, engaged in carrying instructions, getting information, and making extraordinary efforts to hurry up the movement of the troops.

The next morning, April 1st, General Grant said to me: "I wish you would spend the day with Sheridan's command, and send me a bulletin every half-hour or so, advising me fully as to the progress of his movements. You know my views, and I want you to give them to Sheridan fully. Tell him the contemplated movement is left entirely in his hands, and he must be responsible for its execution. I have every confidence in his judgment and ability. I hope there may now be an opportunity of fighting the enemy's infantry outside of its fortifications."

I set out with half a dozen mounted orderlies to act as couriers in transmitting field bulletins. Captain Peter T. Hudson, of our staff, went with me. After traveling again by way of the Brooks road, I met Sheridan, about 10 A. M., on the Five Forks road not far from J. Boisseau's house. Ayres had his division on this road, having arrived about daylight, and Griffin had reached J. Boisseau's between 7 and 8 A. M. I had a full conference with Sheridan. He told me the force in front of him had fallen back early in the morning, that he had pursued with his cavalry and had had several brushes with the enemy, and was driving him steadily back; that he had his patience sorely tried by the delays that had occurred in getting the infantry to him, but he was going to make every effort to strike a heavy blow with all the infantry and cavalry, as soon as he could get them into position, provided the enemy should make a stand behind his intrenchments at Five Forks, which seemed likely. General Warren, who had accompanied Crawford's division, arrived at 11 o'clock and reported in person to Sheridan.

A few minutes before noon Colonel (afterward General) Babcock, of General Grant's staff, came over from headquarters and said to Sheridan: "General Grant directs me to say to you, that if in your judgment the Fifth Corps would do better under one of the division commanders, you are authorized to relieve General Warren, and order him to report to General Grant, at headquarters." General Sheridan replied, in effect, that

⚓ Sheridan's bands were generally mounted on gray horses, and instead of being relegated to the usual duty of carrying off the wounded and assisting the surgeons,

they were brought out to the front and made to play the liveliest airs in their repertory, with great effect on the spirits of the men.—H. P.

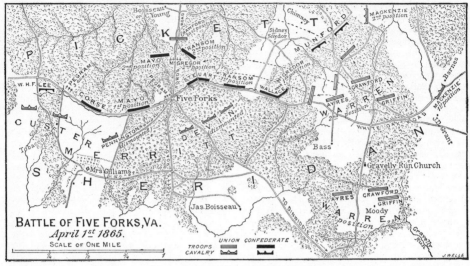

MAP OF THE BATTLE OF FIVE FORKS.

In his official report, General Fitzhugh Lee gives the following account of the battle of Five Forks from the Confederate point of view:

"Our position in the vicinity of Dinwiddie Court House [March 31st] brought us to the rear of the left of the infantry confronting the right of our line of battle at Burgess's Mills, and ascertaining during the night that that force, consisting of the Fifth Corps, had about-faced and was marching to the support of Sheridan and his discomfited cavalry, which would have brought them directly upon our left flank, at daylight on the 1st we commenced moving back to our former position at Five Forks, where Pickett placed his infantry in line of battle. W. H. F. Lee was on his right, one regiment of Munford's command on his left, uniting with the pickets of General Roberts's command, who filled the gap between our position and the right of our main army, then at Burgess's Mills. Rosser was placed just in rear of the center as a reserve, Hatcher's Run intervening between him and our line. Everything continued quiet until about 3 P. M., when reports reached me of a large body of infantry marching around and menacing our left flank. I ordered Munford to go in person, ascertain the exact condition of affairs, hold his command in readiness, and, if necessary, order it up at once. He soon sent for it, and it reached its position just in time to receive the attack. A division of two small brigades of cavalry was not able long to withstand the attack of a Federal corps of infantry, and that force soon crushed in Pickett's left flank, swept it away, and before Rosser could cross Hatcher's Run the position at the Forks was seized and held, and an advance toward the railroad made. It was repulsed by Rosser. Pickett was driven rapidly toward the prolongation of the right of his line of battle by the combined attack of this infantry corps and Sheridan's cavalry, making a total of over 26,000 men, to which he was opposed with 7000 men of all arms. Our forces were driven back some miles, the retreat degenerating into a rout, being followed up principally by the cavalry, whilst the infantry corps held the position our troops were first driven from, threatening an advance upon the railroad, and paralyzing the force of reserve cavalry by necessitating its being stationary in an interposing position to check or retard such an advance. . . . I remained in position on Hatcher's Run, near Five Forks, during the night, and was joined by the cavalry which was driven back the previous afternoon, and by Lieutenant-General [R. H.] Anderson with Wise's and Gracie's brigades, who, leaving the position at Burgess's Mills, had marched by a circuitous route to our relief. Had he advanced up the direct road it would have brought him on the flank and rear of the infantry forming the enemy's right, which attacked our left at Five Forks, and probably changed the result of the unequal contest. Whilst Anderson was marching, the Fifth Corps was marching back, and was enabled to participate in the attack upon our lines the next day, whilst the services of the three infantry brigades (which General Anderson reënforced us by, too late for use) and the five with Pickett, by their absence, increased the disparity between the contending forces upon the next day for the possession of the lines circumvallating Petersburg.   EDITORS.

he hoped such a step as that might not become necessary, and then went on to speak of his plan of battle. We all rode on farther to the front, and soon met General Devin, who was considerably elated by his successes of the morning, and was loudly demanding to be permitted to make a general charge on the enemy. Sheridan told him he didn't believe he had enough ammunition, to which Devin replied: "I guess I've got enough to give 'em one surge more."

General Babcock now left us to return to headquarters. About 1 o'clock it was reported by the cavalry that the enemy was retiring to his intrenched position at Five Forks, which was just north of the White Oak road, and parallel to it, his earth-works running from a point about three-quarters of a mile east of Five Forks to a point a mile west, with an angle or crotchet about one hundred yards long thrown back at right angles to his

left to protect that flank. Orders were at once given to the Fifth Corps to move up the Gravelly Run Church road to the open ground near the church, and form in order of battle, with Ayres on the left, Crawford on his right, and Griffin in rear as a reserve. The corps was to wheel to the left, and make its attack upon the "angle," and then, moving westward, sweep down in rear of the enemy's intrenched line. The cavalry, principally dismounted, was to deploy in front of the enemy's line and engage his attention, and, as soon as it heard the firing of our infantry, to make a vigorous assault upon his works.

The Fifth Corps had borne the brunt of the fighting ever since the army had moved out on the 29th, and the gallant men who composed it, and had performed a conspicuous part in nearly every battle in which the Army of the Potomac had been engaged, seemed eager once more to cross bayonets with their old antagonists. But the movement was slow, the required formation seemed to drag, and Sheridan, chafing with impatience and consumed with anxiety, became as restive as a racer when he nears the score and is struggling to make the start. He made every possible appeal for promptness, he dismounted from his horse, paced up and down, struck the clinched fist of one hand into the palm of the other, and fretted like a caged tiger. He said at one time: "This battle must be fought and won before the sun goes down. All the conditions may be changed in the morning; we have but a few hours of daylight left us. My cavalry are rapidly exhausting their ammunition, and if the attack is delayed much longer they may have none left." And then another batch of staff-officers were sent out to gallop through the mud and hurry up the columns.

At 4 o'clock the formation was completed, the order for the assault was given, and the struggle for Pickett's intrenched line began. The Confederate infantry brigades were posted from right to left as follows: Terry, Corse, Steuart, Ransom, and Wallace. General Fitzhugh Lee, commanding the cavalry, had placed W. H. F. Lee's two brigades on the right of the line, Munford's division on the left, and Rosser's in rear of Hatcher's Run to guard the trains. I rode to the front in company with Sheridan and Warren, with the head of Ayres's division, which was on the left. When this division became engaged, Warren took up a more central position with reference to his corps. Ayres threw out a skirmish-line and advanced across an open field, which sloped down gradually toward the dense woods, just north of the White Oak road. He soon met with a fire from the edge of this woods, a number of men fell, and the skirmish-line halted and seemed to waver. Sheridan now began to exhibit those traits that always made him such a tower of strength in the presence of an enemy. He put spurs to his horse and dashed along in front of the line of battle from left to right, shouting words of encouragement and having something cheery to say to every regiment. "Come on, men," he cried. "Go at 'em with a will. Move on at a clean jump or you'll not catch one of them. They're all getting ready to run now, and if you don't get on to them in five minutes, they'll every one get away from you! Now go for them." Just then a man on the skirmish-line was struck in the neck; the blood spurted as if the jugular vein had been cut. "I'm killed!" he cried, and dropped on the ground. "You're not hurt a bit," cried Sheridan; "pick up your gun, man, and move right on to the front." Such was the electric effect of his words that the poor fellow snatched up his musket and rushed forward a dozen paces before he fell never to rise again. The line of battle of weather-beaten veterans was now moving right along down the slope toward the woods with a steady swing that boded no good for Pickett's command, earth-works or no earth-works. Sheridan was mounted on his favorite black horse "Rienzi" that had carried him from Winchester to Cedar Creek, and which Buchanan Read made famous for all time by his poem of "Sheridan's

Ride." The roads were muddy, the fields swampy, the undergrowth dense, and "Rienzi," as he plunged and curveted, dashed the foam from his mouth and the mud from his heels. Had the Winchester pike been in a similar condition, he would not have made his famous twenty miles without breaking his own neck and Sheridan's too.

Mackenzie had been ordered up the Crump road with directions to turn east on the White Oak road and whip everything he met on that route. He met only a small cavalry command, and having whipped it according to orders, now came galloping back to join in the general scrimmage. He reported to Sheridan in person, and was ordered to strike out toward Hatcher's Run, then move west and get possession of the Ford road in the enemy's rear.

Soon Ayres's men met with a heavy fire on their left flank and had to change direction by facing more toward the west. As the troops entered the woods and moved forward over the boggy ground and struggled through the dense undergrowth, they were staggered by a heavy fire from the angle and fell back in some confusion. Sheridan now rushed into the midst of the broken lines, and cried out: "Where is my battle-flag?" As the sergeant who carried it rode up, Sheridan seized the crimson and white standard, waved it above his head, cheered on the men, and made heroic efforts to close up the ranks. Bullets were humming like a swarm of bees. One pierced the battle-flag, another killed the sergeant who had carried it, another wounded Captain A. J. McGonnigle in the side, others struck two or three of the staff-officers' horses. All this time Sheridan was dashing from one point of the line to another, waving his flag, shaking his fist, encouraging, threatening, praying, swearing, the very incarnation of battle. It would be a sorry soldier who could help following such a leader. Ayres and his officers were equally exposing themselves at all points in rallying the men, and soon the line was steadied, for such material could suffer but a momentary check. Ayres, with drawn saber, rushed forward once more with his veterans, who now behaved as if they had fallen back to get a "good-ready," and with fixed bayonets and a rousing cheer dashed over the earth-works, sweeping everything before them, and killing or capturing every man in their immediate front whose legs had not saved him.

Sheridan spurred "Rienzi" up to the angle, and with a bound the horse carried his rider over the earth-works, and landed in the midst of a line of prisoners who had thrown down their arms and were crouching close under their breastworks. Some of them called out, "Whar do you want us-all to go to?" Then Sheridan's rage turned to humor, and he had a running talk with the "Johnnies" as they filed past. "Go right over there," he said to them, pointing to the rear. "Get right along, now. Drop your guns; you'll never need them any more. You'll all be safe over there. Are there any more of you? We want every one of you fellows." Nearly 1500 were captured at the angle.

An orderly here came up to Sheridan and said: "Colonel Forsyth of your staff is killed, sir." "It's

VIEW ON THE CONFEDERATE LINES COVERING PETERSBURG. FROM A PHOTOGRAPH.

no such thing," cried Sheridan. "I don't believe a word of it. You'll find Forsyth's all right." Ten minutes after, Forsyth rode up. It was the gallant General Frederick Winthrop who had fallen in the assault and had been mistaken for him. Sheridan did not even seem surprised when he saw Forsyth, and only said: "There! I told you so." I mention this as an instance of a peculiar trait of Sheridan's character, which never allowed him to be discouraged by camp rumors, however disastrous.

The dismounted cavalry had assaulted as soon as they heard the infantry fire open. The natty cavalrymen, with tight-fitting uniforms, short jackets, and small carbines, swarmed through the pine thickets and dense undergrowth, looking as if they had been especially equipped for crawling through knot-holes. Those who had magazine guns created a racket in those pine woods that sounded as if a couple of army corps had opened fire.

The cavalry commanded by the gallant Merritt made a final dash, went over the earth-works with a hurrah, captured a battery of artillery, and scattered everything in front of them. Here Custer, Devin, Fitzhugh, and the other cavalry leaders were in their element, and vied with each other in deeds of valor. Crawford's division had advanced in a northerly direction, marching away from Ayres and leaving a gap between the two divisions. General Sheridan sent nearly all of his staff-officers to correct this movement, and to find General Warren, whom he was anxious to see.

After the capture of the angle I started off toward the right to see how matters were going there. I went in the direction of Crawford's divi-

sion, passed around the left of the enemy's works, then rode due west to a point beyond the Ford road. Here I met Sheridan again, just a little before dark. He was laboring with all the energy of his nature to complete the destruction of the enemy's forces, and to make preparation to protect his own detached command from an attack by Lee in the morning. He said he had relieved Warren, directed him to report in person to General Grant, and placed Griffin in command of the Fifth Corps. I had sent frequent bulletins during the day to the general-in-chief, and now dispatched a courier announcing the change of corps commanders and giving the general result of the round-up.

Sheridan had that day fought one of the most interesting technical battles of the war, almost perfect in conception, brilliant in execution, strikingly dramatic in its incidents, and productive of immensely important results.

About half-past seven o'clock I started for general headquarters. The roads in places were corduroyed with captured muskets. Ammunition trains and ambulances were still struggling forward for miles; teamsters, prisoners, stragglers, and wounded were choking the roadway. The coffee-boilers had kindled their fires. Cheers were resounding on all sides, and everybody was riotous over the victory. A horseman had to pick his way through this jubilant condition of things as best he could, as he did not have the right of way by any means. I traveled again by way of the Brooks road. As I galloped past a group of men on the Boydton plank, my orderly called out to them the news of the victory. The only response he got was from one of them who raised his open hand to his face, put his thumb to his nose, and yelled: "No, you don't — April fool!" I then realized that it was the 1st of April. I had ridden so rapidly that I reached headquarters at Dabney's Mill before the arrival of the last courier I had dispatched. General Grant was sitting with most of the staff about him before a blazing camp-fire. He

OUTER WORKS OF FORT SEDGWICK.

wore his blue cavalry overcoat, and the ever-present cigar was in his mouth. I began shouting the good news as soon as I got in sight, and in a moment all but the imperturbable general-in-chief were on their feet giving vent to wild demonstrations of joy. For some minutes there was a bewildering state of excitement, grasping of hands, tossing up of hats, and slapping of each other on the back. It meant the beginning of the end — the reaching of the "last ditch." It pointed to peace and home. Dignity was thrown to the winds. The general, as was expected, asked his usual question: "How many prisoners have been taken?" This was always his first inquiry when an engagement was reported. No man ever had such a fondness for taking prisoners. I think the gratification arose from the kindness of his heart, a feeling that it was much better to win in this way than by the destruction of human life. I was happy to report that the prisoners this time were estimated at over five thousand, and this was the

only part of my recital that seemed to call forth a responsive expression from his usually impassive features. After having listened to the description of Sheridan's day's work, the general, with scarcely a word, walked into his tent, and by the light of a flickering candle took up his "manifold writer," a small book which retained a copy of the matter written, and after finishing several dispatches handed them to an orderly to be sent over the field wires, came out and joined our group at the camp-fire, and said as coolly as if remarking upon the state of the weather: "I have ordered an immediate assault along the lines." This was about 9 o'clock.

General Grant was anxious to have the different

FORT SEDGWICK, KNOWN AS "FORT HELL," OPPOSITE THE CONFEDERATE FORT MAHONE. FROM PHOTOGRAPHS.

BOMB-PROOFS INSIDE FORT SEDGWICK.

commands move against the enemy's lines at once, to prevent Lee from withdrawing troops and sending them against Sheridan. General Meade was all activity and so alive to the situation, and so anxious to carry out the orders of the general-in-chief, that he sent word that he was going to have the troops make a dash at the works without waiting to form assaulting columns. General Grant, at 9:30 P. M., sent a message saying he did not mean to have the corps attack without assaulting columns, but to let the batteries open at once and to feel out with skirmishers; and if the enemy was

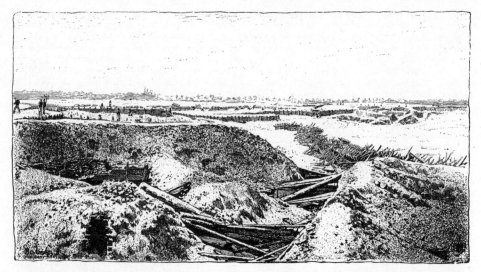

INTERIOR VIEW ON THE CONFEDERATE WORKS COVERING PETERSBURG. FROM A WAR-TIME PHOTOGRAPH.

found to be leaving, to let the troops attack in their own way. The corps commanders reported that it would be impracticable to make a successful assault till morning, but sent back replies full of enthusiasm.

The hour for the general assault was now fixed at 4 the next morning. Miles was ordered to march with his division at midnight to reënforce Sheridan and enable him to make a stand against Lee, in case he should move westward in the night. The general had not been unmindful of Mr. Lincoln's anxiety. Soon after my arrival he telegraphed him: "I have just heard from Sheridan. He has carried everything before him. He has captured three brigades of infantry and a train of wagons, and is now pushing up his success." He had this news also communicated to the several corps commanders, in accordance with his invariable custom to let the different commands feel that they were being kept informed of the general movements, and to encourage them and excite their emulation by notifying them of the success of other commanders. A little after midnight the general tucked himself into his camp-bed, and was soon sleeping as peacefully as if the next day were to be devoted to a picnic instead of a decisive battle.

About 3 A. M. Colonel F. C. Newhall, of Sheridan's staff, rode up bespattered with more than the usual amount of Virginia soil. He had the latest report from Sheridan, and as the general-in-chief would, no doubt, want to take this opportunity of sending further instructions as to the morning's operations on the extreme left, he was wakened, and listened to the report from Newhall, who stood by the bedside to deliver it. The general told him of the preparations being made by the Army of the Potomac, and the necessity of Sheridan's looking out for a push in his direction by Lee, and then began his sleep again where he had left off. Newhall then started to take another

fifteen-mile ride back to Sheridan. Every one at headquarters had caught as many cat-naps as he could, so as to be able to keep both eyes open the next day, in the hope of getting a sight of Petersburg, and possibly of Richmond. And now 4 o'clock came, but no assault. It was found that to remove abatis, climb over chevaux-de-frise, jump rifle-pits, and scale parapets, a little daylight would be of material assistance. At 4 : 45 there was a streak of gray in the heavens which soon revealed another streak of gray formed by Confederate uniforms in the works opposite, and the charge was ordered. The thunder of hundreds of guns shook the ground like an earthquake, and soon the troops were engaged all along the lines. The general awaited the result of the assault at headquarters, where he could be easily communicated with, and from which he could give general directions.

At a quarter past five a message came from Wright that he had carried the enemy's line and was pushing in. Next came news from Parke, that he had captured the outer works in his front, with 12 pieces of artillery and 800 prisoners. At 6:40 the general wrote a telegram with his own hand to Mr. Lincoln, as follows: "Both Wright and Parke got through the enemy's line. The battle now rages furiously. Sheridan with his cavalry, the Fifth Corps, and Miles's division of the Second Corps I sent to him since 1 this morning, is sweeping down from the west. All now looks highly favorable. Ord is engaged, but I have not yet heard the result on his part." A cheering dispatch was also sent to Sheridan, winding up with the words: "I think nothing is now wanting but the approach of your force from the west to finish up the job on this side."

Soon Ord was heard from, having broken through the intrenchments. Humphreys, too, had been doing gallant work; at half-past seven the line in his front was captured, and half an hour later

Hays's division of his corps had carried an important earth-work, with three guns and most of the garrison. At 8:25 A. M. the general sat down to write another telegram to the President, summing up the progress made. Before he had finished it a dispatch was brought in from Ord saying some of his troops had just captured the enemy's works south of Hatcher's Run, and this news was added to the tidings which the general was sending to Mr. Lincoln.

The general and staff now rode out to the front, as it was necessary to give immediate direction to the actual movements of the troops, and prevent confusion from the overlapping and intermingling of the several corps as they pushed forward. He urged his horse over the works that Wright's corps had captured, and suddenly came upon a body of three thousand prisoners marching to the rear. His whole attention was for some time riveted upon them, and we knew he was enjoying his usual satisfaction in seeing them. Some of the guards told the prisoners who the general was, and they became wild with curiosity to get a good look at him. Next he came up with a division of the Sixth Corps flushed with success, and rushing forward with a dash that was inspiriting beyond description. When they caught sight of the leader, whom they had patiently followed from the Rapidan to the Appomattox, their cheers broke forth with a will and their enthusiasm knew no bounds. The general galloped along toward the right, and soon met Meade, with whom he had been in constant communication, and who had been pushing forward the Army of the Potomac with all vigor. Congratulations were quickly exchanged, and both went to pushing forward the work. General Grant, after taking in the situation, directed both Meade and Ord to face their commands toward the east, and close up toward the inner lines which covered Petersburg. Lee had been pushed so vigorously that he seemed for a time to be making but little effort to recover any of his lost ground, but now he made a determined fight against Parke's corps, which was threatening his inner line on his extreme left and the bridge across the Appomattox. Repeated assaults were made, but Parke resisted them all successfully, and could not be moved from his position. Lee had ordered Longstreet from the north side of the James, and with these troops reënforced his extreme right. General Grant dismounted near a farm-house which stood on a knoll within a mile of the enemy's extreme line, and from which he could get a good view of the field of operations. He seated himself at the foot of a tree, and was soon busy receiving dispatches and writing orders to officers conducting the advance. The position was under fire, and as soon as the group of staff-officers was seen the enemy's guns began paying their respects. This lasted for nearly a quarter of an hour, and as the fire became hotter and hotter several of the officers, apprehensive of the general's safety, urged him to move to some less conspicuous position, but he kept on writing and talking without the least interruption from the shots falling around him, and apparently not noticing what a target

the place was becoming. After he had finished his dispatches, he got up, took a view of the situation, and as he started toward the other side of the farm-house said, with a quizzical look at the group around him: "Well, they do seem to have the range on us." The staff was now sent to various points of the advancing lines, and all was activity in pressing forward the good work. By

LIEUTENANT-GENERAL RICHARD H. ANDERSON, C. S. A.
FROM A PHOTOGRAPH.

noon, nearly all the outer line of works was in our possession, except two strong redoubts which occupied a commanding position, named respectively Fort Gregg and Fort Whitworth. The general decided that these should be stormed, and about 1 o'clock three of Ord's brigades swept down upon Fort Gregg. The garrison of 300 [under Lieutenant-Colonel J. H. Duncan] with two rifled cannon made a desperate defense, and a most gallant contest took place. For half an hour after our men had gained the parapet a bloody hand-to-hand struggle continued, but nothing could stand against the onslaught of Ord's troops, flushed with their morning's victory. By half-past two 57 of the brave garrison lay dead, and about 250 had surrendered. Fort Whitworth was at once abandoned, but the guns of Fort Gregg were opened upon the garrison as they marched out, and the commander [Colonel Joseph M. Jayne] and sixty men were surrendered.

About this time Miles had struck a force of the enemy at Sutherland's Station on Lee's extreme right, and had captured two pieces of artillery and nearly a thousand prisoners. At 4:40 the general, who had been keeping Mr. Lincoln fully advised of the history that was so rapidly being made that day, sent him a telegram inviting him to come out the next day and pay him a visit. A prompt reply came back from the President, saying: "Allow me to tender you and all with you the nation's grateful thanks for the additional and magnificent success. At your kind suggestion, I think I will meet you to-morrow."

Prominent officers now urged the general to make an assault on the inner lines and capture Petersburg that afternoon, but he was firm in his resolve not to sacrifice the lives necessary to accomplish such a result. He said the city would undoubtedly be evacuated during the night, and he would dispose the troops for a parallel march westward, and try to head off the escaping army. And thus ended the eventful Sunday.

The general was up at daylight the next morning, and the first report brought in was that Parke had gone through the lines at 4 A. M., capturing a few skirmishers, and that the city had surrendered at 4:28 to Colonel Ralph Ely. A second communication surrendering the place was sent in to Wright. The evacuation had begun about 10 the night before, and was completed before 3 on the morning of the 3d. Between 5 and 6 A. M. the general had a conference with Meade, and orders were given to push westward with all haste. About 9 A. M. the general rode into Petersburg. Many of the citizens, panic-stricken, had escaped with the army. Most of the whites who remained staid indoors, a few groups of negroes gave cheers, but the scene generally was one of complete desertion. Grant rode along quietly with his staff until he came to a comfortable-looking brick house, with a yard in front, situated on one of the principal streets, and here he and the officers accompanying him dismounted and took seats on the piazza. A number of the citizens soon gathered on the sidewalk and gazed with eager curiosity upon the commander of the Yankee armies.

Soon an officer came with a dispatch from Sheridan, who had been reënforced and ordered to strike out along the Danville railroad, saying he was already nine miles beyond Namozine Creek and pressing the enemy's trains. The general was anxious to move westward at once with the leading infantry columns, but Mr. Lincoln had telegraphed that he was on his way, and the general, though he had replied that he could not wait for his arrival, decided to prolong his stay until the President came up. Mr. Lincoln, accompanied by his little son "Tad," dismounted in the street and came in through the front gate with long and rapid strides, his face beaming with delight. He seized General Grant's hand as the general stepped forward to greet him, and stood shaking it for some time and pouring out his thanks and congratulations with all the fervor of a heart that seemed overflowing with its fullness of joy. I doubt whether Mr. Lincoln ever experienced a happier moment in his life. The scene was singularly affecting and one never to be forgotten. He then said:

"Do you know, General, I have had a sort of sneaking idea for some days that you intended to do something like this, though I thought some time ago that you would so manœuvre as to have Sherman come up and be near enough to coöperate with you."

"Yes," replied the general, "I thought at one time that Sherman's army might advance so far as to be in supporting distance of the Eastern armies when the spring campaign against Lee opened, but I have had a feeling that it is better to let Lee's old antagonists give his army the final blow and finish up the job. If the Western armies were even to put in an appearance against Lee's army, it might give some of our politicians a chance to stir up sectional feeling in claiming everything for the troops from their own section of country. The Western armies have been very successful in their campaigns, and it is due to the Eastern armies to let them vanquish their old enemy single-handed."

"I see, I see," said Mr. Lincoln, "but I never thought of it in that light. In fact, my anxiety has been so great that I didn't care where the help came from so the work was perfectly done."

"Oh," General Grant continued, "I do not suppose it would have given rise to much of the bickering I mentioned, and perhaps the idea would not have occurred to any one else. I feel sure there would have been no such feeling among the soldiers, but there might have been among our politicians. While I would not have risked the result of the campaign on account of any mere sentiment of this kind, I felt that our troops here are amply able to handle Lee."

Mr. Lincoln then began to talk about the civil complications that would follow the destruction of the Confederate armies in the field, and showed plainly the anxiety he felt regarding the great problems in statecraft that would soon be thrust upon him. He intimated very plainly, however, in a rambling talk of nearly half an hour, that thoughts of mercy and magnanimity were uppermost in his heart.

At 12:30 the general wrote a telegram to Weitzel at Richmond, asking news from him, and showed it to the President before sending it. The general hoped that he would hear before he parted with the President that Richmond was in our possession, but after the interview had lasted about an hour and a half, the general said he must ride on to the front and join Ord's column, and took leave of the President, who shook his hand cordially, and with great warmth of feeling wished him God-speed and every success.

The general and staff had ridden as far as Sutherland's Station, about nine miles, when a dispatch from Weitzel overtook him, which had come by a roundabout way. It read: "We took Richmond at 8:15 this morning. I captured many guns. Enemy left in great haste. The city is on fire in two places. Am making every effort to put it out." Although the news was expected, there were wild shouts of rejoicing from the group who heard it read. The general, who never manifested the slightest sign of emotion either in victories or defeats, merely said: "I am sorry I did not get this before we left the President. However, I suppose he has heard the news by this time," and then added: "Let the news be circulated among the troops as rapidly as possible."

Grant and Meade both went into camp at Sutherland's Station that evening, the 3d. The Army of

CAPTURE OF GUNS AND THE DESTRUCTION OF A CONFEDERATE WAGON-TRAIN AT PAINEVILLE, APRIL 5, BY
DAVIES'S CAVALRY BRIGADE OF CROOK'S DIVISION. FROM A SKETCH MADE AT THE TIME.

The wagon-train was escorted by Gary's cavalry with five guns. General Humphreys, in "The Virginia Campaign," says it is believed that "the papers of General Robert E. Lee's headquarters, containing many valuable reports, copies of but few of which are now to be found, were destroyed by the burning of these wagons."

the Potomac caught a few hours' sleep, and at 3 o'clock the next morning was again on the march. The pursuit had now become unflagging, relentless. Grant put a spur to the heel of every dispatch he sent. Sheridan "the inevitable," as the enemy had learned to call him, was in advance thundering along with his cavalry, followed by Griffin and the rest of the Army of the Potomac, while Ord was swinging along toward Burkeville to head off Lee from Danville, to which point it was naturally supposed he was pushing in order to unite with Joe Johnston's army. The 4th was another active day; the troops found that this campaign was to be won by legs, that the great walking-match had begun, and success would attend the army that should make the best distance record. General Grant marched this day with Ord's troops. Meade was sick, and had to take at times to an ambulance, but his loyal spirit never flagged, and his orders breathed the true spirit of the soldier. That night General Grant camped at Wilson's Station, on the South Side railroad, twenty-seven miles west of Petersburg. The next morning he sent a dispatch to Sherman in North Carolina, giving him an account of the situation and instructions as to his future movements, and winding up with the famous words, "Rebel armies are now the only strategic points to strike at." On the 5th he marched again with Ord's column, and at noon reached Nottoway Court House, about ten miles east of Burkeville, where he halted for a couple of hours. A young staff-officer here rode up to

General Ord, in a state of considerable excitement, and said to him: "Is that a way-station?" This grim old soldier, who was always jocular, replied with great deliberation: "This is Nott-o-way Station." The staff collected around General Grant on the front porch of the old town tavern, and while we were examining maps and discussing movements, a dispatch came from Sheridan, saying he had captured six guns and some wagons, and had intercepted Lee's advance toward Burkeville, that Lee was in person at Amelia Court House, etc. This news was given to the passing troops, and lusty cheers went up from every throat. They had marched about fifteen miles already that day, and now struck out as if they were good for fifteen more, and swore they were going to beat the record of the cavalry. We continued to move along the road which runs parallel to the South Side railroad till nearly dark, and had reached a point about half-way between Nottoway and Burkeville. The road was skirted by a dense woods on the north side, the side toward the enemy. There was a sudden commotion among the headquarters escort, and on looking around I saw some of our men dashing up to a horseman in full rebel uniform, who had suddenly appeared in the road, and they were in the act of seizing him as a prisoner. I recognized him at once as one of Sheridan's scouts, who had before brought us important dispatches; said to him: "How do you do, Campbell?" and told our men he was all right and was one of our own people. He told us he had

had a hard ride from Sheridan's camp, and had brought a dispatch for General Grant. By this time the general had recognized him, and had stopped in the road to see what he had brought. Campbell then took from his mouth a wad of tobacco, broke it open, and pulled out a little ball of tin-foil. Rolled up in this was a sheet of tissue paper on which was written the famous dispatch so widely published at the time, in which Sheridan

CAPTAIN JOHN R. TUCKER, C. S. N.
FROM A PHOTOGRAPH.

described the situation at Jetersville, and added: "I wish you were here yourself."

The general said he would go at once to Sheridan, and dismounted from his black pony "Jeff Davis," which he had been riding, and called for his big bay horse "Cincinnati." He stood in the road and wrote a dispatch, using the pony's back for a desk, and then, mounting the fresh horse, told Campbell to lead the way. It was found we would have to skirt the enemy's lines, and it was thought prudent to take some cavalry with us, but there was none near at hand, and the general said he would risk it with our mounted escort of fourteen men. Calling upon me and two or three other officers to accompany him, he started off. It was now after dark, but there was enough moonlight to enable us to see the way without difficulty. After riding nearly twenty miles, following crossroads through a wooded country, we struck Sheridan's pickets about half-past ten o'clock, and soon after reached his headquarters.

Sheridan was awaiting us, thinking the general would come after getting his dispatch. A good supper of coffee and cold chicken was spread out, and it was soon demonstrated that the night ride had not impaired any one's appetite.

When the general-in-chief had learned fully the

situation in Sheridan's front, he first sent a message to Ord to watch the roads running south from Burkeville and Farmville, and then rode over to Meade's camp near by. Meade was still suffering from illness. His views differed somewhat from General Grant's regarding the movements of the Army of the Potomac for the next day, and the latter changed the dispositions that were being made so as to have the army unite with Sheridan's troops in swinging round toward the south, and heading off Lee in that direction. The next day, the 6th, proved a decided field-day in the pursuit. It was found in the morning that Lee had retreated during the night from Amelia Court House, and from the direction he had taken, and the information received that he had ordered rations to meet him at Farmville, it was seen that he had abandoned all hope of reaching Burkeville and was probably heading for Lynchburg. Ord was to try to burn the High Bridge and push on to Farmville. Sheridan's cavalry was to work around on Lee's left flank, and the Army of the Potomac was to make another forced march and strike the enemy wherever it could reach him.

I spent a portion of the day with Humphreys's corps, which attacked the enemy near Deatonville and gave his rear-guard no rest. I joined General Grant later and with him rode to Burkeville, getting there some time after dark.

Ord had pushed out to Rice's Station, and Sheridan and Wright had gone in against the enemy and had fought the battle of Sailor's Creek, capturing six general officers and about seven thousand men, and "smashing things" generally.

Ord had sent Colonel Francis Washburn, of the 4th Massachusetts Cavalry, with two infantry regiments to destroy High Bridge and return to Burkeville Station, but becoming apprehensive for their safety, owing to the movements of the enemy, he sent Colonel Theodore Read of his staff with eighty cavalrymen to recall the command. Read advanced as far as Farmville, and on his return found Washburn's troops confronting Lee's advance. The enemy were now between Ord and this little command of less than six hundred infantry and cavalry. Finding himself thus cut off, the gallant Read resolved to sacrifice the command in a heroic effort to delay Lee's march, and repeatedly charged the advancing columns. He was soon mortally wounded and not long after Washburn fell. Most of the men were killed or wounded, and the rest finally surrendered. Their heroic act had delayed Lee's advance long enough to be of material service in aiding his pursuers to capture a large part of his wagon trains. The next day, the 7th, Lee crossed the Appomattox at High Bridge and fired the bridge after his passage, but Humphreys arrived in time to extinguish the fire before it had made much progress, and followed Lee to the north side of the river.

General Grant started from Burkeville early the next morning, the 7th, and took the direct road to Farmville. The columns were crowding the roads, and the men, aroused to still greater efforts by the inspiring news of the day before, were sweeping along, despite the rain that fell, like trained

THE CAPTURE OF EWELL'S CORPS, APRIL 6, 1865. FROM A SKETCH MADE AT THE TIME.

In his official report General Ewell gives the following account of the battle of Sailor's Creek and the capture of his corps:

" On crossing a little stream known as Sailor's Creek, I met General Fitzhugh Lee, who informed me that a large force of cavalry held the road just in front of General [R. H.] Anderson, and was so strongly posted that he had halted a short distance ahead. The trains were turned into the road nearer the river, while I hurried to General Anderson's aid. General [John B.] Gordon's corps turned off after the trains. General Anderson informed me that at least two divisions of cavalry were in his front, and suggested two modes of escape — either to unite our forces and break through, or to move to the right through the woods and try to strike a road which ran toward Farmville. I recommended the latter alternative, but as he knew the ground and I did not, and had no one who did, I left the dispositions to him. Before any were made the enemy appeared in rear of my column in large force preparing to attack. General Anderson informed me that he would make the attack in front, if I would hold in check those in the rear, which I did until his troops were broken and dispersed. I had no artillery, all being with the train. My line ran across a little ravine which leads nearly at right angles toward Sailor's Creek. General G. W. C. Lee was on the left with the Naval Battalion, under Commodore [John R.] Tucker, behind his right. Kershaw's division was on the right. All of Lee's and part of Kershaw's divisions were posted behind a rising ground that afforded some shelter from artillery. The creek was perhaps 300 yards in their front, with brush pines between and a cleared field beyond it. In this the enemy's artillery took a commanding position, and, finding we had none to reply, soon approached within 800 yards and opened a terrible fire. After nearly half an hour of this their infantry advanced, crossing the creek above and below us at the same time. Just as it attacked, General Anderson made his assault, which was repulsed in five minutes. I had ridden up near his lines with him to see the result, when a staff-officer, who had followed his troops in their charge, brought him word of its failure. General Anderson rode rapidly toward his command. I returned to mine to see if it were yet too late to try the other plan of escape. On riding past my left I came suddenly upon a strong line of the enemy's skirmishers advancing upon my left rear. This closed the only avenue of escape; as shells and even bullets were crossing each other from front and rear over my troops, and my right was completely enveloped, I surrendered myself and staff to a cavalry officer who came in by the same road General Anderson had gone out on. At my request he sent a messenger to General G. W. C. Lee, who was nearest, with a note from me telling him he was surrounded, General Anderson's attack had failed, I had surrendered, and he had better do so, too, to prevent useless loss of life, though I gave no orders, being a prisoner. Before the messenger reached him General [G. W. C.] Lee had been captured, as had General Kershaw, and the whole

of my command. My two divisions numbered about 3000 each at the time of the evacuation ; 2800 were taken prisoners, about 150 killed and wounded. The difference of over 3000 was caused mainly by the fatigue of four days' and nights' almost constant marching, the last two days with nothing to eat. Before our capture I saw men eating raw fresh meat as they marched in the ranks. I was informed at General Wright's headquarters, whither I was carried after my capture, that 30,000 men were engaged with us when we surrendered, namely, two infantry corps and Custer's and Merritt's divisions of cavalry."

General J. Warren Keifer, in a pamphlet on the battle of Sailor's Creek, says:

" General A. P. Hill, a corps commander in General Lee's army, was killed at Petersburg, April 2d, 1865, and this, or some other important reason, caused General Lee, while at Amelia Court House, to consolidate his army into two corps or wings, one commanded by Lieutenant-General Longstreet and the other by Lieutenant-General Ewell.

"The main body of the Confederate army had passed by toward Sailor's Creek. Pursuit with such troops as were up was promptly made by General Sheridan and conducted by General Horatio G. Wright, who commanded the Sixth Corps. The enemy's rear-guard fought stubbornly and fell back toward the stream. The Second Division of his corps, under General Frank Wheaton, arrived and joined the Third Division in the attack and pursuit. The main body of the cavalry, under General Merritt, was dispatched to intercept the Confederate retreat. General Merritt passed east and south of the enemy across Sailor's Creek, and again attacked him on the right rear. By about 5 P. M. the Confederate army was forced across the valley of Sailor's Creek, where it took up an unusually strong position on the heights immediately on the west bank of the stream. These heights, save on their face, were mainly covered with forests. There was a level bottom, wholly on the east bank of the creek, over which the Union forces would have to pass before reaching the stream, then swollen beyond its banks by recent rains, and which washed the foot of the heights on which General Ewell had rested the divisions of his army, ready for an attack if made, and with the hope that under cover of night the whole Confederate army might escape in safety to Danville.

"The pursuing troops were halted on the face of the hills skirting the valley, within the range of the enemy's guns, and lines were adjusted for an assault. Artillery was put in position on these hills, and a heavy fire was immediately opened. An effort was made to get up General G. W. Getty's division of the Sixth Corps, and a portion of the Second Brigade of the Third Division, which had been dispatched to attack a battery on the right, but the day was too far spent to await their arrival. After a few moments' delay, General Wright, as directed by General Sheridan, ordered an immediate assault to be made, by the infantry, under the cover of the artillery fire. Colonel Stagg's brigade of cavalry was, at the

pedestrians on a walking-track. As the general rode among them he was greeted with shouts and hurrahs, on all sides, and a string of sly remarks, which showed how familiar swords and bayonets become when victory furnishes the topic of their talk.

[For the continuation of this narrative see page 729.]

same time, ordered by General Sheridan to attack and, if possible, flank the extreme right of the enemy's position. General Merritt's cavalry divisions (First and Third) simultaneously attacked the Confederate army on its right and rear. Without waiting for reserves to arrive in sight, the two divisions of the Sixth Corps descended into the valley, and in single line of battle (First Division on the left and the Third on the right) moved steadily across the plain in the face of a destructive fire of the enemy, and, with shouldered guns and ammunition-boxes also, in most cases, over the shoulder, waded through the flooded stream. Though the water was from two to four feet deep, the stream was crossed without a halt or waver in the line. Many fell on the plain and in the water, and those who reached the west bank were in more or less disorder. The order to storm the heights was promptly given by the officers accompanying the troops, and it was at once obeyed. The infantry of the Sixth Corps began firing for the first time while ascending the heights, and when within only a few yards of the enemy. His advance line gave way, and an easy victory seemed about to be achieved by the Union forces. But before the crest of the heights was reached General Ewell's massed troops, in heavy column, made an impetuous charge upon and through the center of the assaulting line. The Union center was completely broken, and a disastrous defeat for the Union army was imminent. This large body of the Confederate infantry became, by reason of this success, exposed to the now renewed fire from General Wright's artillery remaining in position on the hills east of the stream.

"The right and left wings of the charging Union line met with better success, and each drove back all in its front, and, wholly disregarding the defeat of the center, persisted in advancing, each wheeling as upon a pivot, in the center of the line—then held by the Confederate masses. These masses were soon subjected to a terrible infantry fire upon both flanks as well as by the artillery in front. The swollen stream forbade a Confederate advance to attack the unguarded artillery. General Merritt and Colonel Stagg's cavalry, in a simultaneous attack, overthrew all before them on the right and rear. The Confederate officers gallantly struggled to avert disaster, and bravely tried to form lines to the right and left to repel the flank attacks. This latter proved impossible. The troops on the flanks were pushed up to within a few feet of the massed Confederates, which rendered any re-formation or change of direction by them out of the question, and speedily brought hopeless disorder. A few were bayoneted on each side. Flight was impossible, and nothing remained to put an end to the bloody slaughter but for them to throw down their arms and become captives. As the gloom of approaching night settled over the field, covered with dead and dying, the fire of artillery and musketry ceased, and General Ewell, together with eleven of his general officers [including Kershaw, G. W. C. Lee, Barton, Du Bose, Hunton, and Corse], and about all his gallant army that survived, were prisoners. Commodore Tucker and his Marine Brigade, numbering about 2000, surrendered to me a little later. They were under cover of a dense forest, and had been passed by in the first onset of the assault. Of the particular operations of the cavalry the writer of this, of his personal knowledge, knows little; but no less praise is due it than to the infantry. In this battle more men were captured in actual conflict without negotiation than on any other field in America."

CONFEDERATES DESTROYING THE RAILROAD FROM APPOMATTOX TOWARD LYNCHBURG, AND ARTILLERYMEN DESTROYING GUN-CARRIAGES, AT NIGHTFALL, SATURDAY, APRIL 8. FROM A SKETCH MADE AT THE TIME.

ON May 11th, 1865, General G. K. Warren, who was then in command of the Department of the Mississippi, addressed a letter to the "New York Times," in which he said:

"The operations of the enemy on the 31st of March made it necessary for me to send a portion of my corps during the night to support General Sheridan's cavalry, which had been forced back to near Dinwiddie Court House. One of my divisions was thus compelled to march all night, after having fought all day, and the rest of the corps moved toward the enemy that confronted the cavalry at daybreak.

"Our presence on the flank and rear of the enemy compelled him to fall back rapidly to the vicinity of the Five Forks, and General Sheridan, on advancing with the cavalry, found him slightly intrenched there. This force proved to be a complete division of the enemy's infantry, and all the cavalry of Lee's army.

"I received an order from General Meade, after joining General Sheridan, to report to him for duty, which I did, and the corps was halted by his direction at the point where we joined him, about 8 A. M. [April 1st]. At 1 P. M. I was directed to bring up the corps to Gravelly Run Church, a distance of about two and three-fourths miles from where they had been halted, and there form with two divisions in front and one in reserve, so as to move with the whole corps, and attack and turn the enemy's left flank on the White Oak road.

"My line was formed accordingly: Ayres on the left, in three lines of battle; Crawford on the right, in three lines of battle; and Griffin's division in reserve in masses. This occupied till 4 P. M. The forward movement then began. General Ayres's division became first engaged, wheeling to the left, from facing north to facing west, as it advanced. General Crawford's division also wheeled to the left on General Ayres's as on a pivot, but owing to the nature of the ground and forests, and the greater distance to gain, he lost his connection with General Ayres.

"Into the interval thus left General Griffin's division was placed. These two divisions steadily drove in the enemy's left flank. General Crawford's division moved on westward till it gained the road leading north from the center of the enemy's position, when it was wheeled to the south, and attacked the troops that were endeavoring to hold this road as an outlet for escape.

"All the divisions now closed in upon the enemy capturing the artillery that was attempting to move north, and nearly all the infantry, which their movements had thrown in the greatest confusion. I successively followed the operations of my divisions from left to right, being with General Crawford when the position was taken.

"While these movements above described were going on, the cavalry engaged the enemy along his whole front, which was facing south. The enemy still maintained the right of his line, confronting the cavalry, after we had swept away his left and center; but the Fifth Corps, crowding along the line, without waiting to re-form, captured all who remained, as it swept along. I was with the extreme advance in the last movement, and was relieved while there at 7 P. M., the battle being then over, and not even a fugitive enemy in sight. . . .

"I personally sought of General Sheridan a reason for his order; but he would not, or could not, give one, and

) General Warren resigned his volunteer commission May 27, 1865; he died Aug. 8, 1882, at Newport, R. I.

) In his "Memoirs" (C. L. Webster & Co., 1885), General Grant says:

"I was so much dissatisfied with Warren's dilatory movements in the battle of White Oak road, and in his failure to reach Sheridan in time, that I was very much afraid that at the last moment he would fail Sheridan. He was a man of fine intelligence, great earnestness, quick perception, and could make his dispositions as quickly as any officer, under difficulties where he was forced to act. But I had before discovered a defect which was beyond his control, that was very prejudicial to his usefulness in emergencies like the one just

declined to do so. I obeyed the order to report to General Grant that night, and was by him assigned to the command of the defenses at City Point and Bermuda Hundred. After the evacuation of Richmond and Petersburg I was given the command of the troops at the latter place and along the Southside Railroad, belonging to the Army of the Potomac. When these troops were relieved by troops from the Army of the James, I was left in Petersburg awaiting orders. I then addressed a letter, dated April 9th, to General Rawlins, chief-of-staff, soliciting an investigation. On the 22d of April I sent another, requesting permission to publish the first one, for the reasons set forth therein. On the 2d of May I telegraphed Colonel Bowers, adjutant-general, to ascertain if these had been received, and he answered, they 'were received, the latter during General Grant's absence. Orders have been sent you [me] to report here, when you can see the general.'

"On May 3d I received by telegraph an extract from General Orders No. 78, of May 1st, assigning me to the command of the Department of the Mississippi. I at once proceeded to Washington, and, after a personal interview with General Grant, received, on the 6th of May, an answer to my communications of the 9th and 22d of April, authorizing my publishing them, and stating the reasons for not granting me the investigation sought.")

A court of inquiry was finally granted to General Warren on the 9th of December, 1879, by President Hayes. As finally constituted, the court consisted of Brevet Major-Generals C. C. Augur and John Newton, and Brevet Lieutenant-Colonel Loomis L. Langdon, recorder. The inquiry related to four imputations contained in the final reports of Grant and Sheridan.

First. General Grant wrote:)

"On the morning of the 31st [of March] General Warren reported favorably to getting possession of the White Oak road, and was directed to do so. To accomplish this he moved with one division, instead of his whole corps, resulting in a repulse."

The court exonerated Warren, but held that he "should have been with his advanced divisions," and "should have started earlier to the front."

Second. General Sheridan says:

"Had Warren moved according to the expectations of the lieutenant-general there would appear to have been but little chance for the escape of the enemy's infantry in front of Dinwiddie Court House."

The court found that "it was not practicable for the Fifth Corps to have reached Sheridan at 12 o'clock on the night of March 31st," as Grant had expected; but that Warren should have moved Griffin and Crawford at once, as ordered.

Third. General Sheridan says:

"General Warren did not exert himself to get up his corps as rapidly as he might have done, and his manner gave me the impression that he wished the sun to go down before dispositions for the attack could be completed."

before us. He could see every danger at a glance before he had encountered it. He would not only make preparations to meet the danger which might occur, but he would inform his commanding officer what others should do while he was executing his move.

"I had sent a staff-officer to General Sheridan to call his attention to these defects, and to say that as much as I liked General Warren, now was not a time when we could let our personal feelings for any one stand in the way of success; and if his removal was necessary to success, not to hesitate. It was upon that authorization that Sheridan removed Warren. I was very sorry that it had been done, and regretted still more that I had not long before taken occasion to assign him to another field of duty."

The court found that there was no unnecessary delay in the march of the Fifth Corps, and that General Warren took the usual methods of a corps commander to prevent delay; and that "his actions do not appear to have corresponded with such [a] wish" as that imputed to him.

Fourth. Sheridan says:

"In the engagement portions of his line gave way, when not exposed to a heavy fire, and simply for want of confidence on the part of the troops, which General Warren did not exert himself to inspire."

The court found that Warren was exerting himself to remedy the divergence of Crawford and Griffin, after Ayres changed front to the left, and "thinks this was for him the essential point to be attended to, which also exacted his whole efforts to accomplish."

On the 21st of November, 1881, President Arthur directed "that the findings and opinion be published." No other action was taken.—EDITORS.

LEE'S REPORT OF THE SURRENDER AT APPOMATTOX.

On the 12th of April, 1865, from "Near Appomattox Court House," General R. E. Lee made the following report to Mr. Davis:

"MR. PRESIDENT: It is with pain that I announce to Your Excellency the surrender of the Army of Northern Virginia. The operations which preceded this result will be reported in full. I will therefore only now state that upon arriving at Amelia Court House on the morning of the 4th with the advance of the army, on the retreat from the lines in front of Richmond and Petersburg, and not finding the supplies ordered to be placed there, nearly twenty-four hours were lost in endeavoring to collect in the country subsistence for men and horses. This delay was fatal, and could not be retrieved. The troops, wearied by continual fighting and marching for several days and nights, obtained neither rest nor refreshment, and on moving on the 5th, on the Richmond and Danville railroad, I found at Jetersville the enemy's cavalry, and learned the approach of his infantry and the general advance of his army toward Burkeville. This deprived us of the use of the railroad, and rendered it impracticable to procure from Danville the supplies ordered to meet us at points of our march. Nothing could be obtained from the adjacent country. Our route to the Roanoke was therefore changed, and the march directed upon Farmville, where supplies were ordered from Lynchburg. The change of route threw the troops over the roads pursued by the artillery and wagon trains west of the railroad, which impeded our advance and embarrassed our movements. On the morning of the 6th General Longstreet's corps reached Rice's Station on the Lynchburg railroad. It was followed by the commands of Generals R. H. Anderson, Ewell, and Gordon, with orders to close upon it as fast as the progress of the trains would permit or as they could be directed on roads father west. General Anderson, commanding Pickett's and B. R. Johnson's divisions, became disconnected with Mahone's division, forming the rear of Longstreet. The enemy's cavalry penetrated the line of march through the interval thus left, and attacked the wagon-train moving toward Farmville. This caused serious delay in the march of the center and rear of the column, and enabled the enemy to mass upon their flank. After successive attacks Anderson's and Ewell's corps were captured or driven from their position. The latter general, with both of his division commanders, Kershaw and Custis Lee, and his brigadiers, were taken prisoners. Gordon, who all the morning, aided by General W. F. Lee's cavalry, had checked the advance of the enemy on the road from Amelia Springs and protected the trains, became exposed to his combined assaults, which he bravely resisted and twice repulsed; but the cavalry having been withdrawn to another part of the line of march, . . . the enemy, massing heavily on his [Gordon's] front and both flanks, renewed the attack about 6 P. M., and drove him from the field in much confusion. The army continued its march during the night, and every effort was made to reorganize the divisions which had been shattered by the day's operations; but, the men being depressed by fatigue and hunger, many threw away their arms, while others followed the wagon-trains and embarrassed their progress. On the morning of the 7th rations were issued to the troops as they passed Farmville, but the safety of the trains requiring their removal upon the approach of the enemy all could not be supplied. The army, reduced to two corps under Longstreet and Gordon, moved steadily on the road to Appomattox Court House; thence its march was ordered by Campbell Court House, through Pittsylvania, toward Danville. The roads were wretched and the progress slow. By great efforts the head of the column reached Appomattox Court House on the evening of the 8th, and the troops were halted for rest. The march was ordered to be resumed at 1 A. M. on the 9th. Fitz Lee, with the cavalry, supported by Gordon, was ordered to drive the enemy from his front, wheel to the left, and cover the passage of the trains, while Longstreet, who from Rice's Station had formed the rear-guard, should close up and hold the position. Two battalions of artillery and the ammunition wagons were directed to accompany the army, the rest of the artillery and wagons to move toward Lynchburg. In the early part of the night the enemy attacked Walker's artillery train near Appomattox Station on the Lynchburg railroad, and were repelled. Shortly afterward their cavalry dashed toward the Court House, till halted by our line. During the night there were indications of a large force massing on our left and front. Fitz Lee was directed to ascertain its strength, and to suspend his advance till daylight if necessary. About 5 A. M., on the 9th, with Gordon on his left, he moved forward and opened the way. A heavy force of the enemy was discovered opposite Gordon's right, which, moving in the direction of Appomattox Court House, drove back the left of the cavalry and threatened to cut off Gordon from Longstreet, his cavalry at the same time threatening to envelop his left flank. Gordon withdrew across the Appomattox River, and the cavalry advanced on the Lynchburg road and became separated from the army. Learning the condition of affairs on the lines, where I had gone under the expectation of meeting General Grant to learn definitely the terms he proposed in a communication received from him on the 8th, in the event of the surrender of the army, I requested a suspension of hostilities until these terms could be arranged. In the interview which occurred with General Grant in compliance with my request, terms having been agreed on, I surrendered that portion of the Army of Northern Virginia which was on the field, with its arms, artillery, and wagon-trains, the officers and men to be paroled, retaining their side-arms and private effects. I deemed this course the best under all the circumstances by which we were surrounded. On the morning of the 9th, according to the reports of the ordnance officers, there were 7892 organized infantry with arms, with an average of 75 rounds of ammunition per man; the artillery, though reduced to 63 pieces with 93 rounds of ammunition, was sufficient. These comprised all the supplies of ordnance that could be relied on in the State of Virginia. I have no accurate report of the cavalry, but believe it did not exceed 2100 effective men. The enemy was more than five times our numbers. If we could have forced our way one day longer it would have been at a great sacrifice of life, and at its end I did not see how a surrender could have been avoided. We had no subsistence for man or horse, and it could not be gathered in the country. The supplies ordered to Pamplin's Station from Lynchburg could not reach us, and the men, deprived of food and sleep for many days, were worn out and exhausted."

THE RUINS OF RICHMOND BETWEEN THE CANAL BASIN AND CAPITOL SQUARE. FROM A WAR-TIME PHOTOGRAPH.

THE FALL OF RICHMOND.

I. THE EVACUATION.—BY CLEMENT SULIVANE, CAPTAIN, C. S. A.

ABOUT 11:30 A. M. on Sunday, April 2d, [a strange agitation was perceptible on the streets of Richmond, and within half an hour it was known on all sides that Lee's lines had been broken below Petersburg; that he was in full retreat on Danville; that the troops covering the city at Chaffin's and Drewry's Bluffs were on the point of being withdrawn, and that the city was forthwith to be abandoned. A singular security had been felt by the citizens of Richmond, so the news fell like a bomb-shell in a peaceful camp, and dismay reigned supreme.

All that Sabbath day the trains came and went, wagons, vehicles, and horsemen rumbled and dashed to and fro, and, in the evening, ominous groups of ruffians—more or less in liquor—began to make their appearance on the principal thoroughfares of the city. As night came on pillage and rioting and robbing took place. The police and a few soldiers were at hand, and, after the arrest of a few ringleaders and the more riotous of their followers, a fair degree of order was restored. But Richmond saw few sleeping eyes during the pandemonium of that night.

The division of Major-General G. W. C. Lee, of Ewell's corps, at that time rested in the trenches eight miles below Richmond, with its right on the James River, covering Chaffin's Bluff. I was at the time its assistant adjutant-general, and was in the city on some detached duty connected with the "Local Brigade" belonging to the division,—a force composed of the soldiers of the army, detailed on account of their mechanical skill to work in the arsenals, etc., and of clerks and other employés of the War, Treasury, Quartermaster, and other departments.

Upon receipt of the news from Petersburg I reported to General Ewell (then in Richmond) for instructions, and was ordered to assemble and command the Local Brigade, cause it to be well supplied with ammunition and provisions, and await further orders. All that day and night I

was engaged in this duty, but with small result, as the battalions melted away as fast as they were formed, mainly under orders from the heads of departments who needed all their employés in the transportation and guarding of the archives, etc., but partly, no doubt, from desertions. When morning dawned fewer than 200 men remained, under command of Captain Edward Mayo.

Shortly before day General Ewell rode in person to my headquarters and informed me that General G. W. C. Lee was then crossing the pontoon at Drewry's; that he would destroy it and press on to join the main army; that all the bridges over the river had been destroyed, except Mayo's, between Richmond and Manchester, and that the wagon bridge over the canal in front of Mayo's had already been burned by Union emissaries. My command was to hasten to Mayo's bridge and protect it, and the one remaining foot-bridge over the canal leading to it, until General Gary, of South Carolina, should arrive. I hurried to my command, and fifteen minutes later occupied Mayo's bridge, at the foot of 14th street, and made military dispositions to protect it to the last extremity. This done, I had nothing to do but listen for sounds and gaze on the terrible splendor of the scene. And such a scene probably the world has seldom witnessed. Either incendiaries, or (more probably) fragments of bombs from the arsenals, had fired various buildings, and the two cities, Richmond and Manchester, were like a blaze of day amid the surrounding darkness. Three high arched bridges were in flames; beneath them the waters sparkled and dashed and rushed on by the burning city. Every now and then, as a magazine exploded, a column of white smoke rose up as high as the eye could reach, instantaneously followed by a deafening sound. The earth seemed to rock and tremble as with the shock of an earthquake, and immediately afterward hundreds of shells would explode in air and send their iron spray down far below the bridge. As the immense magazines of

[Mr Davis attended morning service at St. Paul's Church, where he received a dispatch, on reading which he left the church to prepare for the departure of the Government.— EDITORS.

cartridges ignited the rattle as of thousands of musketry would follow, and then all was still for the moment, except the dull roar and crackle of the fast-spreading fires. At dawn we heard terrific explosions about "The Rocketts," from the unfinished iron-clads down the river.

By daylight, on the 3d, a mob of men, women, and children, to the number of several thousands, had gathered at the corner of 14th and Cary streets and other outlets, in front of the bridge, attracted by the vast commissary depot at that point; for it must be remembered that in 1865 Richmond was a half-starved city, and the Confederate Government had that morning removed its guards and abandoned the removal of the provisions, which was impossible for the want of transportation. The depot doors were forced open and a demoniacal struggle for the countless barrels of hams, bacon, whisky, flour, sugar, coffee, etc., etc., raged about the buildings among the hungry mob. The gutters ran whisky, and it was lapped as it flowed down the streets, while all fought for a share of the plunder. The flames came nearer and nearer, and at last caught in the commissariat itself.

At daylight the approach of the Union forces could be plainly discerned. After a little came the clatter of horses' hoofs galloping up Main street. My infantry guard stood to arms, the picket across the canal was withdrawn, and the engineer officer lighted a torch of fat pine. By direction of the Engineer Department barrels of tar, surrounded by pine-knots, had been placed at intervals on the bridge, with kerosene at hand, and a lieutenant of engineers had reported for the duty of firing them at my order. The noisy train proved to be Gary's ambulances, sent forward preparatory to his final rush for the bridge. The muleteers galloped their animals about half-way down, when they were stopped by the dense mass of human beings. Rapidly communicating to Captain Mayo my instructions from General Ewell, I ordered that officer to stand firm at his post until

Gary got up. I rode forward into the mob and cleared a lane. The ambulances were galloped down to the bridge, I retired to my post, and the mob closed in after me and resumed its wild struggle for plunder. A few minutes later a long line of cavalry in gray turned into 14th street, and sword in hand galloped straight down to the river; Gary had come. The mob scattered right and left before the armed horsemen, who reined up at the canal. Presently a single company of cavalry appeared in sight, and rode at headlong speed to the bridge. "My rear-guard," explained Gary. Touching his hat to me he called out, "All over, good-bye; blow her to h—ll," and trotted over the bridge. That was the first and last I ever saw of General Gary, of South Carolina.

In less than sixty seconds Captain Mayo was in column of march, and as he reached the little island about half-way across the bridge, the single piece of artillery, loaded with grape-shot, that had occupied that spot, arrived on the Manchester side of the river. The engineer officer, Dr. Lyons, and I walked leisurely to the island, setting fire to the provided combustible matter as we passed along, and leaving the north section of Mayo's bridge wrapped in flame and smoke. At the island we stopped to take a view of the situation north of the river, and saw a line of blue-coated horsemen galloping in furious haste up Main street. Across 14th street they stopped, and then dashed down 14th street to the flaming bridge. They fired a few random shots at us three on the island, and we retreated to Manchester. I ordered my command forward, the lieutenant of engineers saluted and went about his business, and myself and my companion sat on our horses for nearly a half-hour, watching the occupation of Richmond. We saw another string of horsemen in blue pass up Main street, then we saw a dense column of infantry march by, seemingly without end; we heard the very welkin ring with cheers as the United States forces reached Capitol Square, and then we turned and slowly rode on our way.

II. THE OCCUPATION.— BY THOMAS THATCHER GRAVES, AIDE-DE-CAMP ON THE STAFF OF GEN. WEITZEL.

IN the spring of 1865 the total length of the lines of the Army of the James before Richmond (under General Godfrey Weitzel, commanding the Twenty-fifth Corps) was about eleven miles, not counting the cavalry front, and extended from the Appomattox River to the north side of the James. The Varina and New Market turnpikes passed directly through the lines into the city, which was the center of all our efforts.

About 2 o'clock on the morning of April 3d bright fires were seen in the direction of Richmond. Shortly after, while we were looking at these fires, we heard explosions, and soon a prisoner was sent in by General Kautz. The prisoner was a colored teamster, and he informed us that immediately after dark the enemy had begun making preparations to leave, and that they were sending all of the teams to the rear. A forward movement of our entire picket-line corroborated this report. As soon as it was light General Weitzel ordered

Colonel E. E. Graves, senior aide-de-camp, and Major Atherton H. Stevens, Jr., provost-marshal, to take a detachment of forty men from the two companies (E and H) of the 4th Massachusetts Cavalry, and make a reconnoissance. Slowly this little band of scouts picked their way in. Soon after we moved up the New Market road at a slow pace.

As we approached the inner line of defenses we saw in the distance divisions of our troops, many of them upon the double-quick, aiming to be the first in the city; a white and a colored division were having a regular race, the white troops on the turnpike and the colored in the fields. As we neared the city the fires seemed to increase in number and size, and at intervals loud explosions were heard.

On entering we found Capitol Square covered with people who had fled there to escape the fire and were utterly worn out with fatigue and fright.

Details were at once made to scour the city and press into service every able-bodied man, white or black, and make them assist in extinguishing the flames. General Devens's division marched into the city, stacked arms, and went to work. Parsons's engineer company assisted by blowing up houses to check its advance, as about every engine was destroyed or rendered useless by the mob. In this manner the fire was extinguished and perfect order restored in an incredibly short time after we occupied the city. ⚓ There was absolutely no plundering upon the part of our soldiers; orders were issued forbidding anything to be taken without remuneration, and no complaints were made of infringement of these orders. General G. F. Shepley was placed on duty as military governor. He had occupied a similar position in New Orleans after its capture in 1862, and was eminently fitted for it by education and experience. As we entered the suburbs the general ordered me to take half a dozen cavalry-

CITIZENS OF RICHMOND IN CAPITOL SQUARE DURING THE CONFLAGRATION.

men and go to Libby Prison, for our thoughts were upon the wretched men whom we supposed were still confined within its walls. It was very early in the morning, and we were the first Union troops to arrive before Libby. Not a guard, not an inmate remained; the doors were wide open, and only a few negroes greeted us with, "Dey's all gone, massa!"

The next day after our entry into the city, on passing out from Clay street, from Jefferson Davis's house, I saw a crowd coming, headed by President Lincoln, who was walking with his usual long, careless stride, and looking about with an inter-

ested air and taking in everything. Upon my saluting he said: "Is it far to President Davis's house?" I accompanied him to the house, which was occupied by General Weitzel as headquarters. The President had arrived about 9 o'clock, at the landing called Rocketts, upon Admiral Porter's flag-ship, the *Malvern*, and as soon as the boat was made fast, without ceremony, he walked on shore, and started off uptown. As soon as Admiral Porter was informed of it he ordered a guard of marines to follow as escort; but in the walk of about two miles they never saw him, and he was directed by negroes. At the Davis house, he was shown

⚓ As one of our aides was riding through the streets, engaged in gathering together the able-bodied men to assist in extinguishing the fire, he was hailed by a servant in front of a house, toward which the fire seemed to be moving. The servant told him that his mistress wished to speak to him. He dismounted and entered the house, and was met by a lady, who stated that her mother was an invalid, confined to her bed, and as the

fire seemed to be approaching she asked for assistance. The subsequent conversation developed the fact that the invalid was no other than the wife of General R. E. Lee, and the lady who addressed the aide was her daughter, Miss Lee. An ambulance was furnished by Colonel E. H. Ripley, of the 9th Vermont, and a corporal and two men guarded them until all danger was past.—T. T. G.

into the reception-room, with the remark that the housekeeper had said that that room was President Davis's office. As he seated himself he remarked, "This must have been President Davis's chair," and, crossing his legs, he looked far off with a serious, dreamy expression. At length he asked me if the housekeeper was in the house. Upon learning that she had left he jumped up and said, with a boyish manner, "Come, let's look at the house!" We went pretty much over it; I retailed all that the housekeeper had told me, and he seemed interested in everything. As we came down the staircase General Weitzel came, in breathless haste, and at once President Lincoln's face lost its boyish expression as he realized that *duty* must be resumed. Soon afterward Judge Campbell, General Anderson (Confederates), and others called and asked for an interview with the President. It was granted, and took place in the parlor with closed doors.

I accompanied President Lincoln and General Weitzel to Libby Prison and Castle Thunder, and heard General Weitzel ask President Lincoln what he (General Weitzel) should do in regard to the conquered people. President Lincoln replied that he did not wish to give any orders on that subject, but, as he expressed it, "If I were in your place I'd let 'em up easy, let 'em up easy."

A few days after our entry General R. E. Lee surrendered, and early one morning we learned that he had just arrived at his house in the city.

General Weitzel called me into a private room, and, taking out a large, well-filled pocket-book, said, "Go to General Lee's house, find Fitzhugh Lee, and say that his old West Point chum Godfrey Weitzel wishes to know if he needs anything, and urge him to take what he may need from that pocket-book." Upon reaching General Lee's house I knocked, and General Fitzhugh Lee came to the door. He was dressed in a Confederate uniform. Upon introducing myself he asked me in, showing me into a parlor with double or folding doors, explaining that the servants had not returned. He was so overcome by Weitzel's message that for a moment he was obliged to walk to the other end of the room. He excused himself, and passed into the inner room, where I noticed General R. E. Lee sitting, with a tired, worn expression upon his face. Fitzhugh Lee knelt beside his general, as he sat leaning over, and placed a hand upon his knee.

After a few moments he came back, and in a most dignified and courteous manner sent his love to Godfrey Weitzel, and assured him that he did not require any loan of money, but if it would be entirely proper for *Godfrey* Weitzel to issue a pass for some ladies of General Lee's household to return to the city it would be esteemed a favor; but he impressed me to state that if this would embarrass *General* Weitzel, on no account would they request the favor. It is needless to state that the ladies were back in the house as soon as possible.

PRESIDENT LINCOLN LEAVING THE DAVIS MANSION. FROM A SKETCH MADE AT THE TIME.

APPOMATTOX COURT HOUSE. FROM A WAR-TIME PHOTOGRAPH.

THE SURRENDER AT APPOMATTOX COURT HOUSE.

BY HORACE PORTER, BREVET BRIGADIER-GENERAL, U. S. A.

A LITTLE before noon on the 7th of April, 1865, General Grant, with his staff, rode into the little village of Farmville [see map, p. 569], on the south side of the Appomattox River, a town that will be memorable in history as the place where he opened the correspondence with Lee which led to the surrender of the Army of Northern Virginia. He drew up in front of the village hotel, dismounted, and established headquarters on its broad piazza. News came in that Crook was fighting large odds with his cavalry on the north side of the river, and I was directed to go to his front and see what was necessary to be done to assist him. I found that he was being driven back, the enemy (Munford's and Rosser's cavalry divisions under Fitzhugh Lee) having made a bold stand north of the river. Humphreys was also on the north side, isolated from the rest of our infantry, confronted by a large portion of Lee's army, and having some very heavy fighting. On my return to general headquarters that evening Wright's corps was ordered to cross the river and move rapidly to the support of our troops there. Notwithstanding their long march that day, the men sprang to their feet with a spirit that made every one marvel at their pluck, and came swinging through the main street of the village with a step that seemed as elastic as on the first day of their toilsome tramp. It was now dark, but they spied the general-in-chief watching them with evident pride from the piazza of the hotel.

Then was witnessed one of the most inspiring scenes of the campaign. Bonfires were lighted on the sides of the street, the men seized straw and pine knots, and improvised torches; cheers arose from throats already hoarse with shouts of victory, bands played, banners waved, arms were tossed high in air and caught again.   The night march had become a grand review, with Grant as the reviewing officer.

Ord and Gibbon had visited the general at the hotel, and he had spoken with them as well as with Wright about sending some communication to Lee that might pave the way to the stopping of further bloodshed.   Dr. Smith, formerly of the regular army, a native of Virginia and a relative of General Ewell, now one of our prisoners, had told General Grant the night before that Ewell had said in conversation that their cause was lost when they crossed the James River, and he considered that it was the duty of the authorities to negotiate for peace then, while they still had a right to claim concessions, adding that now they were not in condition to claim anything.   He said that for every man killed after this somebody would be responsible, and it would be little better than murder.   He could not tell what General Lee would do, but he hoped he would at once surrender his army.   This statement, together with the news that had been received from Sheridan saying that he had heard that General Lee's trains of provisions which had come by rail were at Appomattox, and that he expected to capture them before Lee could reach them, induced the general to write the following communication :

"HEADQUARTERS, ARMIES OF THE U. S.

"GENERAL R. E. LEE, Commanding C. S. A. :   5 P. M., April 7th, 1865.

" The results of the last week must convince you of the hopelessness of further resistance on the part of the Army of Northern Virginia in this struggle.   I feel that it is so, and regard it as my duty to shift from myself the responsibility of any further effusion of blood by asking of you the surrender of that portion of the Confederate States army known as the Army of Northern Virginia.   U. S. GRANT, Lieutenant-General."

This he intrusted to General Seth Williams, adjutant-general, with directions to take it to Humphreys's front, as his corps was close up to the enemy's rear-guard, and have it sent into Lee's lines.   The general decided to remain all night at Farmville and await the reply from Lee, and he was shown to a room in the hotel in which, he was told, Lee had slept the night before.   Lee wrote the following reply within an hour after he received General Grant's letter, but it was brought in by rather a circuitous route and did not reach its destination till after midnight :

"APRIL 7TH, 1865.

" GENERAL : I have received your note of this date.   Though not entertaining the opinion you express of the hopelessness of further resistance on the part of the Army of Northern Virginia, I reciprocate your desire to avoid useless effusion of blood, and therefore, before considering your proposition, ask the terms you will offer on condition of its surrender.

" R. E. LEE, General.

" LIEUTENANT-GENERAL U. S. GRANT, Commanding Armies of the U. S."

The next morning before leaving Farmville the following reply was given to General Williams, who again went to Humphreys's front to have it transmitted to Lee :

" APRIL 8TH, 1865.

" GENERAL R. E. LEE, Commanding C. S. A. :

" Your note of last evening in reply to mine of the same date, asking the conditions on which I will accept the surrender of the Army of Northern Virginia, is just received.   In reply I would say that, peace being my great desire, there is but one condition I would insist upon,—namely, that the men and officers surrendered shall be disqualified for taking up arms against the Government of the United States until properly exchanged. I will meet you, or will designate officers to meet any officers you may name for the same purpose, at any point agreeable to you, for the purpose of arranging definitely the terms upon which the surrender of the Army of Northern Virginia will be received.

"U. S. GRANT, Lieutenant-General."

There turned up at this time a rather hungry-looking gentleman in gray, in the uniform of a colonel, who proclaimed himself the proprietor of the hotel. He said his regiment had crumbled to pieces, he was the only man left in it, and he thought he might as well "stop off" at home. His story was significant as indicating the disintegrating process that was going on in the ranks of the enemy.

General Grant had been marching most of the way with the columns that were pushing along south of Lee's line of retreat; but expecting that a reply would be sent to his last letter and wanting to keep within easy communication with Lee, he decided to march this day with the portion of the Army of the Potomac that was pressing Lee's rear-guard. After issuing some further instructions to Ord and Sheridan, he started from Farmville, crossed to the north side of the Appomattox, conferred in person with Meade, and rode with his columns. Encouraging reports came in all day, and that night headquarters were established at Curdsville in a large white farm-house, a few hundred yards from Meade's camp. The general and several of the staff had cut loose from the headquarters trains the night he started to meet Sheridan at Jetersville, and had neither baggage nor camp-equipage. The general did not even have his sword with him. This was the most advanced effort yet made at moving in "light marching order," and we billeted ourselves at night in farm-houses, or bivouacked on porches, and picked up meals at any camp that seemed to have something to spare in the way of rations. This night we sampled the fare of Meade's hospitable mess and once more lay down with full stomachs.

General Grant had been suffering all the afternoon from a severe headache, the result of fatigue, anxiety, scant fare, and loss of sleep, and by night it was much worse. He

THE VILLAGE OF APPOMATTOX COURT HOUSE. THE McLEAN HOUSE ON THE RIGHT. FROM A WAR-TIME SKETCH.

had been induced to bathe his feet in hot water and mustard, and apply mustard plasters to his wrists and the back of his neck, but these remedies afforded little relief. The dwelling we occupied was a double house. The general threw himself upon a sofa in the sitting-room on the left side of the hall, while the staff-officers bunked on the floor of the room opposite to catch what sleep they could. About midnight we were aroused by Colonel Charles A. Whittier of Humphreys's staff, who brought another letter from Lee. Rawlins at once took it in to General Grant's room. It was as follows:

"APRIL 8TH, 1865.

"GENERAL: I received at a late hour your note of to-day. In mine of yesterday I did not intend to propose the surrender of the Army of Northern Virginia, but to ask the terms of your proposition. To be frank, I do not think the emergency has arisen to call for the surrender of this army, but, as the restoration of peace should be the sole object of all, I desired to know whether your proposals would lead to that end. I cannot, therefore, meet you with a view to surrender the Army of Northern Virginia; but as far as your proposal may affect the Confederate States forces under my command,⸗ and tend to the restoration of peace, I should be pleased to meet you at 10 A. M. to-morrow on the old stage road to Richmond, between the picket-lines of the two armies.   R. E. LEE, General.

"LIEUTENANT-GENERAL U. S. GRANT."

General Grant had been able to get but very little sleep. He now sat up and read the letter, and after making a few comments upon it to General Rawlins lay down again on the sofa.

About 4 o'clock on the morning of the 9th I rose and crossed the hall to ascertain how the general was feeling. I found his room empty, and upon going out of the front door saw him pacing up and down in the yard holding both hands to his head. Upon inquiring how he felt, he replied that he had had very little sleep, and was still suffering the most excruciating pain. I said: "Well, there is one consolation in all this, General: I never knew you to be ill that you did not receive some good news. I have become a little superstitious regarding these coincidences, and I should not be surprised if some good fortune overtook you before night." He smiled and said: "The best thing that can happen to me to-day is to get rid of the pain I am suffering." We were soon joined by some others of the staff, and the general was induced to go over to Meade's headquarters with us and get some coffee, in the hope that it would do him good. He seemed to feel a little better now, and after writing the following letter to Lee and dispatching it he prepared to move forward. The letter was as follows:

"APRIL 9TH, 1865.

"GENERAL: Your note of yesterday is received. I have no authority to treat on the subject of peace. The meeting proposed for 10 A. M. to-day could lead to no good. I will state, however, that I am equally desirous for peace with yourself, and the whole North entertains the same feeling. The terms upon which peace can be had are well understood. By the South laying down their arms, they would hasten that most desirable event, save thousands of human lives, and hundreds of millions of property not yet destroyed. Seriously hoping that all our difficulties may be settled without the loss of another life, I subscribe myself, etc.,

"U. S. GRANT, Lieutenant-General.

"GENERAL R. E. LEE."

It was proposed to him to ride during the day in a covered ambulance which was at hand, instead of on horseback, so as to avoid the intense heat of the sun, but this he declined to do, and soon after mounted "Cincinnati" and struck off toward New Store. From that point he went by way of a

---

⸗ Since February 9th, 1865, Lee had been general-in-chief of all the Confederate armies, and, evidently, was aiming here at a treaty of peace and general surrender.— EDITORS.

cross-road to the south side of the Appomattox with the intention of moving around to Sheridan's front. While riding along the wagon road that runs from Farmville to Appomattox Court House, at a point eight or nine miles east of the latter place, Lieutenant Charles E. Pease of Meade's staff overtook him with a dispatch. It was found to be a reply from Lee, which had been sent in to our lines on Humphreys's front. It read as follows:

"APRIL 9TH, 1865.

"GENERAL: I received your note of this morning on the picket-line, whither I had come to meet you and ascertain definitely what terms were embraced in your proposal of yesterday with reference to the surrender of this army. I now ask an interview, in accordance with the offer contained in your letter of yesterday, for that purpose.

"R. E. LEE, General.

"LIEUTENANT-GENERAL U. S. GRANT."

Pease also brought a note from Meade, saying that at Lee's request he had read the communication addressed to General Grant and in consequence of it had granted a short truce.

The general, as soon as he had read these letters, dismounted, sat down on the grassy bank by the roadside, and wrote the following reply to Lee:

"APRIL 9TH, 1865.

"GENERAL R. E. LEE, Commanding C. S. Army:

"Your note of this date is but this moment (11:50 A. M.) received, in consequence of my having passed from the Richmond and Lynchburg road to the Farmville and Lynchburg road. I am at this writing about four miles west of Walker's Church, and will push forward to the front for the purpose of meeting you. Notice sent to me on this road where you wish the interview to take place will meet me.

"U. S. GRANT, Lieutenant-General."

He handed this to Colonel Babcock of the staff, with directions to take it to General Lee by the most direct route. Mounting his horse again the general rode on at a trot toward Appomattox Court House. When five or six miles from the town, Colonel Newhall, Sheridan's adjutant-general, came riding up from the direction of Appomattox and handed the general a communication. This proved to be a duplicate of the letter from Lee that Lieutenant Pease had brought in from Meade's lines. Lee was so closely pressed that he was anxious to communicate with Grant by the most direct means, and as he could not tell with which column Grant was moving he sent in one copy of his letter on Meade's front and one on Sheridan's. Colonel Newhall joined our party, and after a few minutes' halt to read the letter we continued our ride toward Appomattox. On the march I had asked the general several times how he felt. To the same question now he said, "The pain in my head seemed to leave me the moment I got Lee's letter." The road was filled with men, animals, and wagons, and to avoid these and shorten the distance we turned slightly to the right and began to "cut across lots"; but before going far we spied men conspicuous in gray, and it was seen that we were moving toward the enemy's left flank, and that a short ride farther would take us into his lines. It looked for a moment as if a very awkward condition of things might possibly arise, and Grant become a prisoner in Lee's lines instead of Lee in his. Such a circumstance would have given rise to an important

McLEAN'S HOUSE, APPOMATTOX COURT HOUSE. FROM A PHOTOGRAPH.

cross-entry in the system of campaign book-keeping. There was only one remedy — to retrace our steps and strike the right road, which was done without serious discussion. About 1 o'clock the little village of Appomattox Court House, with its half-dozen houses, came in sight, and soon we were entering its single street. It is situated on some rising ground, and beyond the country slopes down into a broad valley. The enemy was seen with his columns and wagon trains covering the low ground. Our cavalry, the Fifth Corps, and part of Ord's command were occupying the high ground to the south and west of the enemy, heading him off completely. Generals Sheridan and Ord, with a group of officers around them, were seen in the road, and as our party came up General Grant said: "How are you, Sheridan?" "First-rate, thank you; how are you?" cried Sheridan, with a voice and look that seemed to indicate that on his part he was having things all his own way. "Is Lee over there?" asked General Grant, pointing up the street, having heard a rumor that Lee was in that vicinity. "Yes, he is in that brick house," answered Sheridan. "Well, then, we'll go over," said Grant.

The general-in-chief now rode on, accompanied by Sheridan, Ord, and some others, and soon Colonel Babcock's orderly was seen sitting on his horse in the street in front of a two-story brick house, better in appearance than the rest of the houses. He said General Lee and Colonel Babcock had gone into this house a short time before, and he was ordered to post himself in the street and keep a lookout for General Grant, so as to let him know where General Lee was. Babcock told me afterward that in carrying General Grant's last letter he passed through the enemy's lines and found General Lee a little more than half a mile beyond Appomattox Court House. He was lying down by the roadside on a blanket which had been spread over a few fence rails on the ground under an apple-tree, which was part of an orchard. This circumstance furnished the only ground for the widespread report that the surrender occurred under an apple-tree. Babcock dismounted upon coming near, and as he approached on foot, Lee sat up, with his feet hanging over the roadside embankment. The wheels of the wagons in passing along the road had cut away the earth of this embankment and left the roots of the tree projecting. Lee's feet were partly resting on these roots. One of his staff-officers came forward, took the dispatch which Babcock handed him and gave it to General Lee. After reading it, the general rose and said he would ride forward on the road on which Babcock had come, but was apprehensive that hostilities might begin in the meantime, upon the termination of the temporary truce, and asked Babcock to write a line to Meade informing him of the situation. Babcock wrote accordingly, requesting Meade to maintain the truce until positive orders from General Grant could be received. To save time it was arranged that a Union officer, accompanied by one of Lee's officers, should carry this letter through the enemy's lines. This route made the distance to Meade nearly ten miles shorter than by the round-about way of the Union lines. Lee now mounted his horse and directed Colonel Charles Marshall, his military secretary, to accompany him. They started for Appomattox Court House in company with Babcock and followed by a mounted orderly. When the party reached the village they met one of its residents, named Wilmer McLean, who was told that General Lee wanted to occupy a convenient room in some house in the town. McLean ushered them into the sitting-room of one of the first houses he came to, but upon looking about and finding it quite small and meagerly furnished, Lee proposed finding something more commodious and better fitted for the occasion. McLean then conducted the party to his own house, about the best one in the town, where they awaited General Grant's arrival.

The house had a comfortable wooden porch with seven steps leading up to it. A hall ran through the middle from front to back, and on each side was a room having two windows, one in front and one in rear. Each room had two doors opening into the hall. The building stood a little distance back from the street, with a yard in front, and to the left was a gate for carriages and a roadway running to a stable in rear. We entered the grounds by this gate and dismounted. In the yard were seen a fine large gray horse, which proved to be General Lee's, and a good-looking mare belonging to Colonel Marshall. An orderly in gray was in charge of them, and had taken off their bridles to let them nibble the grass.

General Grant mounted the steps and entered the house. As he stepped into the hall Colonel Babcock, who had seen his approach from the window, opened the door of the room on the left, in which he had been sitting with General Lee and Colonel Marshall awaiting General Grant's arrival. The general passed in, while the members of the staff, Generals Sheridan and Ord, and some general officers who had gathered in the front yard, remained outside, feeling that he would probably want his first interview with General Lee to be, in a measure, private. In a few minutes Colonel Babcock came to the front door and, making a motion with his hat toward the sitting-room, said: "The general says, come in." It was then about half-past one of Sunday, the 9th of April. We entered, and found General Grant sitting at a marble-topped table in the center of the room, and Lee sitting beside a small oval table near the front window, in the corner opposite to the door by which we entered, and facing General Grant. Colonel Marshall, his military secretary, was standing at his left. We walked in softly and ranged ourselves quietly about

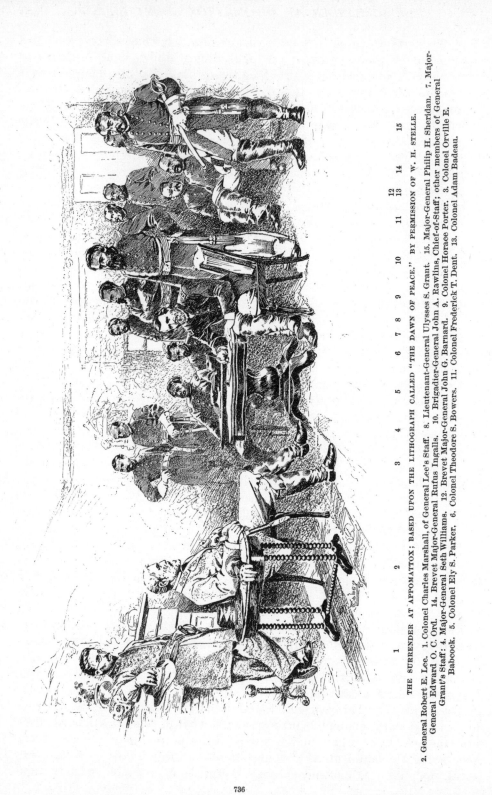

1 2 3 4 5 6 7 8 9 10 11 12 13 14 15

THE SURRENDER AT APPOMATTOX; BASED UPON THE LITHOGRAPH CALLED "THE DAWN OF PEACE," BY PERMISSION OF W. H. STELLE.

2. General Robert E. Lee. 1. Colonel Charles Marshall, of General Lee's Staff. 8. Lieutenant-General Ulysses S. Grant. 15. Major-General Philip H. Sheridan. 7. Major-General Edward O. C. Ord. 14. Brevet Major-General Rufus Ingalls. 10. Brigadier-General John A. Rawlins, Chief-of-Staff; other members of General Grant's Staff: 4. Major-General Seth Williams. 12. Brevet Major-General John G. Barnard. 9. Colonel Horace Porter. 3. Colonel Orville E. Babcock. 5. Colonel Ely S. Parker. 6. Colonel Theodore S. Bowers. 11. Colonel Frederick T. Dent. 13. Colonel Adam Badeau.

the sides of the room, very much as people enter a sick-chamber when they expect to find the patient dangerously ill. Some found seats on the sofa and the few chairs which constituted the furniture, but most of the party stood.

The contrast between the two commanders was striking, and could not fail to attract marked attention as they sat ten feet apart facing each other. General Grant, then nearly forty-three years of age, was five feet eight inches in height, with shoulders slightly stooped. His hair and full beard were a nut-brown, without a trace of gray in them. He had on a single-breasted blouse, made of dark-blue flannel, unbuttoned in front, and showing a waistcoat underneath. He wore an ordinary pair of top-boots, with his trousers inside, and was without spurs. The boots and portions of his clothes were spattered with mud. He had had on a pair of thread gloves, of a dark-yellow color, which he had taken off on entering the room. His felt "sugar-loaf" stiff-brimmed hat was thrown on the table beside him. He had no sword, and a pair of shoulder-straps was all there was about him to designate his rank. In fact, aside from these, his uniform was that of a private soldier.

Lee, on the other hand, was fully six feet in height, and quite erect for one of his age, for he was Grant's senior by sixteen years. His hair and full beard were a silver-gray, and quite thick, except that the hair had become a little thin in front. He wore a new uniform of Confederate gray, buttoned up to the throat, and at his side he carried a long sword of exceedingly fine workmanship, the hilt studded with jewels. It was said to be the sword that had been presented to him by the State of Virginia. His top-boots were comparatively new, and seemed to have on them some ornamental stitching of red silk. Like his uniform, they were singularly clean, and but little travel-stained. On the boots were handsome spurs, with large rowels. A felt hat, which in color matched pretty closely that of his uniform, and a pair of long buckskin gauntlets lay beside him on the table. We asked Colonel Marshall afterward how it was that both he and his chief wore such fine toggery, and looked so much as if they had turned out to go to church, while with us our outward garb scarcely rose to the dignity even of the "shabby-genteel." He enlightened us regarding the contrast, by explaining that when their headquarters wagons had been pressed so closely by our cavalry a few days before, and it was found they would have to destroy all their baggage, except the clothes they carried on their backs, each one, naturally, selected the newest suit he had, and sought to propitiate the god of destruction by a sacrifice of his second-best.

General Grant began the conversation by saying: "I met you once before, General Lee, while we were serving in Mexico, when you came over from General Scott's headquarters to visit Garland's brigade, to which I then belonged. I have always remembered your appearance, and I think I should have recognized you anywhere." "Yes," replied General Lee, "I know I met you on that occasion, and I have often thought of it and tried to recollect how you looked, but I have never been able to recall a single feature." After some further mention of Mexico, General Lee said: "I suppose, General Grant, that the object of our present meeting is fully understood. I asked to see you to ascertain upon what terms you would receive the surrender of my army." General Grant replied: "The terms I propose are those stated substantially in my letter of yesterday,— that is, the officers and men surrendered to be paroled and disqualified from taking up arms again until properly exchanged, and all arms, ammunition, and supplies to be delivered up as captured property." Lee nodded an assent, and said: "Those are about the conditions which I expected would be proposed." General Grant then continued: "Yes, I think our correspondence indicated pretty clearly the action that would be taken at our meeting; and I hope it may lead to a general suspension of hostilities and be the means of preventing any further loss of life."

Lee inclined his head as indicating his accord with this wish, and General Grant then went on to talk at some length in a very pleasant vein about the prospects of peace. Lee was evidently anxious to proceed to the formal work of the surrender, and he brought the subject up again by saying:

"I presume, General Grant, we have both carefully considered the proper steps to be taken, and I would suggest that you commit to writing the terms you have proposed, so that they may be formally acted upon."

"Very well," replied General Grant, "I will write them out." And calling for his manifold order-book, he opened it on the table before him and proceeded to write the terms. The leaves had been so prepared that three impressions of the writing were made. He wrote very rapidly, and did not pause until he had finished the sentence ending with "officers appointed by me to receive them." Then he looked toward Lee, and his eyes seemed to be resting on the handsome sword that hung at that officer's side. He said afterward that this set him to thinking that it would be an unnecessary humiliation to require the officers to surrender their swords, and a great hardship to deprive them of their personal baggage and horses, and after a short pause he wrote the sentence: "This will not embrace the side-arms of the officers, nor their private horses or baggage." When he had finished the letter he called Colonel (afterward General) Ely S. Parker, one of the military secretaries on the staff, to his side and looked it over with him and directed him as they went along to interline six or seven words and to strike out the word "their," which had been repeated. When this had been done, he handed the book to General Lee and asked him to read over the letter. It was as follows:

"GENERAL R. E. LEE, Commanding C. S. A.   "APPOMATTOX CT. H., VA., April 9, 1865.

"GENERAL: In accordance with the substance of my letter to you of the 8th inst., I propose to receive the surrender of the Army of Northern Virginia on the following terms, to wit: Rolls

There was no demand made for Gen. Lee's sword and no tender of it offered

U. S. Grant

of all the officers and men to be made in duplicate, one copy to be given to an officer to be designated by me, the other to be retained by such officer or officers as you may designate. The officers to give their individual paroles not to take up arms against the Government of the United States until properly [exchanged], and each company or regimental commander to sign a like parole for the men of their commands. The arms, artillery, and public property to be parked, and stacked, and turned over to the officers appointed by me to receive them. This will not embrace the side-arms of the officers, nor their private horses or baggage. This done, each officer and man will be allowed to return to his home, not to be disturbed by the United States authorities so long as they observe their paroles, and the laws in force where they may reside. Very respectfully,   U. S. GRANT, Lieutenant-General."

Lee took it and laid it on the table beside him, while he drew from his pocket a pair of steel-rimmed spectacles and wiped the glasses carefully with his handkerchief. Then he crossed his legs, adjusted the spectacles very slowly and deliberately, took up the draft of the letter, and proceeded to read it attentively. It consisted of two pages. When he reached the top line of the second page, he looked up, and said to General Grant: "After the words 'until properly,' the word 'exchanged' seems to be omitted. You doubtless intended to use that word."

"Why, yes," said Grant; "I thought I had put in the word 'exchanged.'"

"I presumed it had been omitted inadvertently," continued Lee, "and with your permission I will mark where it should be inserted."

"Certainly," Grant replied.

Lee felt in his pocket as if searching for a pencil, but did not seem to be able to find one. Seeing this and happening to be standing close to him, I handed him my pencil. He took it, and laying the paper on the table noted the interlineation. During the rest of the interview he kept twirling this pencil in his fingers and occasionally tapping the top of the table with it. When he handed it back it was carefully treasured by me as a memento of the occasion. When Lee came to the sentence about the officers' side-arms, private horses, and baggage, he showed for the first time during the reading of the letter a slight change of countenance, and was evidently touched by this act of generosity. It was doubtless the condition mentioned to which he particularly alluded when he looked toward General Grant as he finished reading and said with some degree of warmth in his manner: "This will have a very happy effect upon my army."

General Grant then said: "Unless you have some suggestions to make in regard to the form in which I have stated the terms, I will have a copy of the letter made in ink and sign it."

"There is one thing I would like to mention," Lee replied after a short pause. "The cavalrymen and artillerists own their own horses in our army. Its organization in this respect differs from that of the United States." This expression attracted the notice of our officers present, as showing how firmly the conviction was grounded in his mind that we were two distinct countries. He continued: "I would like to understand whether these men will be permitted to retain their horses?"

"You will find that the terms as written do not allow this," General Grant replied; "only the officers are permitted to take their private property."

Lee read over the second page of the letter again, and then said:

"No, I see the terms do not allow it; that is clear." His face showed plainly that he was quite anxious to have this concession made, and Grant said very promptly and without giving Lee time to make a direct request:

"Well, the subject is quite new to me. Of course I did not know that any private soldiers owned their animals, but I think this will be the last battle of the war — I sincerely hope so — and that the surrender of this army will be followed soon by that of all the others, and I take it that most of the men in the ranks are small farmers, and as the country has been so raided by the two armies, it is doubtful whether they will be able to put in a crop to carry themselves and their families through the next winter without the aid of the horses they are now riding, and I will arrange it in this way: I will not change the terms as now written, but I will instruct the officers I shall appoint to receive the paroles to let all the men who claim to own a horse or mule take the animals home with them to work their little farms." (This expression has been quoted in various forms and has been the subject of some dispute. I give the exact words used.)

Lee now looked greatly relieved, and though anything but a demonstrative man, he gave every evidence of his appreciation of this concession; and said, "This will have the best possible effect upon the men. It will be very gratifying and will do much toward conciliating our people." He handed the draft of the terms back to General Grant, who called Colonel T. S. Bowers of the staff to him and directed him to make a copy in ink. Bowers was a little nervous, and he turned the matter over to Colonel (afterward General) Parker, whose handwriting presented a better appearance than that of any one else on the staff. Parker sat down to write at the table which stood against the rear side of the room. Wilmer McLean's domestic resources in the way of ink now became the subject of a searching investigation, but it was found that the contents of the conical-shaped stoneware inkstand which he produced appeared to be participating in the general breaking up and had disappeared. Colonel Marshall now came to the rescue, and pulled out of his pocket a small box-wood inkstand, which was put at Parker's service, so that, after all, we had to fall back upon the resources of the enemy in furnishing the stage "properties" for the final scene in the memorable military drama.

Lee in the meantime had directed Colonel Marshall to draw up for his signature a letter of acceptance of the terms of surrender. Colonel Marshall wrote out a draft of such a letter, making it quite formal, beginning with "I have the honor to reply to your communication," etc. General Lee took it, and, after reading it over very carefully, directed that these formal expressions be stricken out and that the letter be otherwise shortened. He afterward went over it again and seemed to change some words, and then told the colonel to make a final copy in ink. When it came to providing the paper, it was found we had the only supply of that important ingredient in the recipe for surrendering an army, so we gave a few pages to the colonel. The letter when completed read as follows:

"HEADQUARTERS, ARMY OF NORTHERN VIRGINIA, April 9th, 1865.

"GENERAL: I received your letter of this date containing the terms of the surrender of the Army of Northern Virginia as proposed by you. As they are substantially the same as those expressed in your letter of the 8th inst., they are accepted. I will proceed to designate the proper officers to carry the stipulations into effect.

R. E. LEE, General.

"LIEUTENANT-GENERAL U. S. GRANT."

While the letters were being copied, General Grant introduced the general officers who had entered, and each member of the staff, to General Lee. The General shook hands with General Seth Williams, who had been his adjutant when Lee was superintendent at West Point, some years before the war, and gave his hand to some of the other officers who had extended theirs, but to most of those who were introduced he merely bowed in a dignified and formal manner. He did not exhibit the slightest change of features during this ceremony until Colonel Parker of our staff was presented to him. Parker was a full-blooded Indian, and the reigning Chief of the Six Nations. When Lee saw his swarthy features he looked at him with evident surprise, and his eyes rested on him for several seconds. What was passing in his mind probably no one ever knew, but the natural surmise was that he at first mistook Parker for a negro, and was struck with astonishment to find that the commander of the Union armies had one of that race on his personal staff.

Lee did not utter a word while the introductions were going on, except to Seth Williams, with whom he talked quite cordially. Williams at one time referred in rather jocose a manner to a circumstance which occurred during their former service together, as if he wanted to say something in a good-natured way to break up the frigidity of the conversation, but Lee was in no mood for pleasantries, and he did not unbend, or even relax the fixed sternness of his features. His only response to the allusion was a slight inclination of the head. General Lee now took the initiative again in leading the conversation back into business channels. He said:

"I have a thousand or more of your men as prisoners, General Grant, a number of them officers whom we have required to march along with us for several days. I shall be glad to send them into your lines as soon as it can be arranged, for I have no provisions for them. I have, indeed, nothing for my own men. They have been living for the last few days principally upon parched corn, and we are badly in need of both rations and forage. I telegraphed to Lynchburg, directing several train-loads of rations to be sent on by rail from there, and when they arrive I should be glad to have the present wants of my men supplied from them."

At this remark all eyes turned toward Sheridan, for he had captured these trains with his cavalry the night before, near Appomattox Station. General Grant replied: "I should like to have our men sent within our lines as soon as possible. I will take steps at once to have your army supplied with rations, but I am sorry we have no forage for the animals. We have had to depend upon the country for our supply of forage. Of about how many men does your present force consist?"

"Indeed, I am not able to say," Lee answered after a slight pause. "My losses in killed and wounded have been exceedingly heavy, and, besides, there have been many stragglers and some deserters. All my reports and public papers, and, indeed, my own private letters, had to be destroyed on the march, to prevent them from falling into the hands of your people. Many companies are entirely without officers, and I have not seen any returns for several days; so that I have no means of ascertaining our present strength."

General Grant had taken great pains to have a daily estimate made of the enemy's forces from all the data that could be obtained, and, judging it to be about 25,000 at this time, he said: "Suppose I send over 25,000 rations, do you think that will be a sufficient supply?" "I think it will be ample," remarked Lee, and added with considerable earnestness of manner, "and it will be a great relief, I assure you."

General Grant now turned to his chief commissary, Colonel (now General) M. R. Morgan, who was present, and directed him to arrange for issuing the rations. The number of officers and men surrendered was over 28,000. As to General Grant's supplies, he had ordered the army on starting out to carry twelve days' rations. This was the twelfth and last day of the campaign.

Grant's eye now fell upon Lee's sword again, and it seemed to remind him of the absence of his own, and by way of explanation he said to Lee:

"I started out from my camp several days ago without my sword, and as I have not seen my headquarters baggage since, I have been riding about without any side-arms. I have generally worn a sword, however, as little as possible, only during the actual operations of a campaign." "I am in the habit of wearing mine most of the time," remarked Lee; "I wear it invariably when I am among my troops, moving about through the army."

General Sheridan now stepped up to General Lee and said that when he discovered some of the Confederate troops in motion during the morning, which seemed to be a violation of the truce, he had sent him (Lee) a couple of notes protesting against this act, and as he had not had time to copy them he would like to have them long enough to make copies. Lee took the notes out of the breast-pocket of his coat and handed them to Sheridan with a few words expressive of regret that the circumstance had occurred, and intimating that it must have been the result of some misunderstanding.

After a little general conversation had been indulged in by those present, the two letters were signed and delivered, and the parties prepared to separate. Lee before parting asked Grant to notify Meade of the surrender, fearing that fighting might break out on that front and lives be uselessly lost. This request was complied with, and two Union officers were sent through the enemy's lines as the shortest route to Meade,—some of Lee's officers accompanying them to prevent their being interfered with. At a little before 4 o'clock General Lee shook hands with General Grant, bowed to the other officers, and with Colonel Marshall left the room. One after another we followed, and passed out to the porch. Lee signaled to his orderly to bring up his horse, and while the animal was being bridled the general stood on the lowest step and gazed sadly in the direction of the valley beyond where his army lay—now an army of prisoners. He smote his hands together a number of times in an absent sort of a way; seemed not to see the group of Union officers in the yard who rose respectfully at his approach, and appeared unconscious of everything about him. All appreciated the sadness that overwhelmed him, and he had the personal sympathy of every one who beheld him at this supreme moment of trial. The approach of his horse seemed to recall him from his reverie, and he at once mounted. General Grant now stepped down from the porch, and, moving toward him, saluted him by raising his hat. He was followed in this act of courtesy by all our officers present; Lee raised his hat respectfully, and rode off to break the sad news to the brave fellows whom he had so long commanded.

GENERAL LEE AND COLONEL MARSHALL LEAVING McLEAN'S HOUSE AFTER THE SURRENDER. FROM A SKETCH MADE AT THE TIME.

General Grant and his staff then mounted and started for the headquarters camp, which, in the meantime, had been pitched near by. The news of the surrender had reached the Union lines, and the firing of salutes began at several points, but the general sent orders at once to have them stopped, and used these words in referring to the occurrence: "The war is over, the rebels are our countrymen again, and the best sign of rejoicing after the victory will be to abstain from all demonstrations in the field."

Mr. McLean had been charging about in a manner which indicated that the excitement was shaking his system to its nervous center, but his real trials did not begin until the departure of the chief actors in the surrender. Then the relic-hunters charged down upon the manor-house and made various attempts to jump Mr. McLean's claims to his own furniture.⚓ Sheridan set a good example, however, by paying the proprietor twenty dollars in gold for the table at which Lee sat, for the purpose of presenting it to Mrs. Custer,

⚓ It is a singular historical coincidence that McLean's former home was upon a Virginia farm, near the battle-ground of the first Bull Run, and his house was used for a time as the headquarters of General Beauregard. [See Vol. I., p. 201.] To avoid the active theater of war he removed to the quiet village of Appomattox, only to find himself again surrounded by contending armies. Thus the first and last great scenes of the war in Virginia were enacted upon his property.—H. P.

and handed it over to her dashing husband, who started off for camp bearing it upon his shoulder. Ord paid forty dollars for the table at which Grant sat, and afterward presented it to Mrs. Grant, who modestly declined it, and insisted that Mrs. Ord should become its possessor. Bargains were at once struck for all the articles in the room, and it is even said that some mementos were carried off for which no coin of the realm was ever exchanged.

Before General Grant had proceeded far toward camp he was reminded that he had not yet announced the important event to the Government. He dismounted by the roadside, sat down on a large stone, and called for pencil and paper. Colonel (afterward General) Badeau handed his order-book to the general, who wrote on one of the leaves the following message, a copy of which was sent to the nearest telegraph station. It was dated 4:30 P. M.:

"Hon. E. M. Stanton, Secretary of War, Washington: General Lee surrendered the Army of Northern Virginia this afternoon on terms proposed by myself. The accompanying additional correspondence will show the conditions fully.   U. S. Grant, Lieut.-General."

Upon reaching camp he seated himself in front of his tent, and we all gathered around him, curious to hear what his first comments would be upon the crowning event of his life. But our expectations were doomed to disappointment, for he appeared to have already dismissed the whole subject from his mind, and turning to General Rufus Ingalls, his first words were: "Ingalls, do you remember that old white mule that so-and-so used to ride when we were in the city of Mexico?" "Why, perfectly," said Ingalls, who was just then in a mood to remember the exact number of hairs in the mule's tail if it would have helped to make matters agreeable. And then the general-in-chief went on to recall the antics played by that animal during an excursion to Popocatapetl. It was not until after supper that he said much about the surrender, when he talked freely of his entire belief that the rest of the rebel commanders would follow Lee's example, and that we would have but little more fighting, even of a partisan nature. He then surprised us by announcing his intention of starting to Washington early the next morning. We were disappointed at this, for we wanted to see something of the opposing army, now that it had become civil enough for the first time in its existence to let us get near it, and meet some of the officers who had been acquaintances in former years. The general, however, had no desire to look at the conquered, and but little curiosity in his nature, and he was anxious above all things to begin the reduction of the military establishment and diminish the enormous expense attending it, which at this time amounted to about four millions of dollars a day. When he considered, however, that the railroad was being rapidly put in condition and that he would lose no time by waiting till noon of the next day, he made up his mind to delay his departure.

That evening I made full notes of the occurrences which took place during the surrender, and from these the above account has been written.

There were present at McLean's house, besides Sheridan, Ord, Merritt, Custer, and the officers of Grant's staff, a number of other officers and one or two citizens who entered the room at different times during the interview.

UNION SOLDIERS SHARING THEIR RATIONS WITH THE CONFEDERATES. FROM A SKETCH MADE AT THE TIME.

About 9 o'clock on the morning of the 10th General Grant with his staff rode out toward the enemy's lines, but it was found upon attempting to pass through that the force of habit is hard to overcome, and that the practice which had so long been inculcated in Lee's army of keeping Grant out of his lines was not to be overturned in a day, and he was politely requested at the picket-lines to wait till a message could be sent to headquarters asking for instructions. As soon as Lee heard that his distinguished opponent was approaching, he was prompt to correct the misunderstanding at the picket-line, and rode out at a gallop to receive him. They met on a knoll that overlooked the lines of the two armies, and saluted respectfully, by each raising his hat. The officers present gave a similar salute, and then grouped themselves around the two chieftains in a semicircle, but withdrew out of ear-shot. General Grant repeated to us that evening the substance of the conversation, which was as follows:

Grant began by expressing a hope that the war would soon be over, and Lee replied by stating that he had for some time been anxious to stop the further effusion of blood, and he trusted that everything would now be done to restore harmony and conciliate the people of the South. He said the emancipation of the negroes would be no hindrance to the restoring of relations between the two sections of the country, as it would probably not be the desire of the majority of the Southern people to restore slavery then, even if the question were left open to them. He could not tell what the other armies would do or what course Mr. Davis would now take, but he believed it would be best for their other armies to follow his example, as nothing could be gained by further resistance in the field. Finding that he entertained these sentiments, General Grant told him that no one's influence in the South was so great as his, and suggested to him that he should advise the surrender of the remaining armies and thus exert his influence in favor of immediate peace.   Lee said he could not take such a course without consulting President Davis first.   Grant then proposed to Lee that he should do so, and urge the hastening of a result which was admitted to be inevitable.   Lee, however, was averse to stepping beyond his duties as a soldier, and said the authorities would doubtless soon arrive at the same conclusion without his interference.   There was a statement put forth that Grant asked Lee to see Mr. Lincoln and talk with him as to the terms of reconstruction, but this was erroneous.   I asked General Grant about it when he was on his death-bed, and his recollection was distinct that he had made no such suggestion. I am of opinion that the mistake arose from hearing that Lee had been requested to go and see the "President" regarding peace, and thinking that this expression referred to Mr. Lincoln, whereas it referred to Mr. Davis. After the conversation had lasted a little more than half an hour and Lee had requested that such instructions be given to the officers left in charge to carry out the details of the surrender, that there might be no misunderstanding as to the form of paroles, the manner of turning over the property, etc., the conference ended.   The two commanders lifted their hats and said good-bye.   Lee rode back to his camp to take a final farewell of his army, and Grant returned to McLean's house, where he seated himself on the porch until it was time to take his final departure.   During the conference Ingalls, Sheridan, and Williams had asked permission to visit the enemy's lines and renew their acquaintance with some old friends, classmates, and former comrades in arms who were serving in Lee's army.   They now returned, bringing with them Cadmus M. Wilcox, who had been General Grant's groomsman when he was married; Longstreet, who had also been at his wedding; Heth, who had been a subaltern with him in Mexico, besides Gordon, Pickett, and a number of others.   They all stepped up to pay their respects to General Grant, who received them very cordially and talked with them until it was time to leave.   The hour of noon had now arrived, and General Grant, after shaking hands with all present who were not to accompany him, mounted his horse, and started with his staff for Washington without having entered the enemy's lines.   Lee set out for Richmond, and it was felt by all that peace had at last dawned upon the land.   The charges were now withdrawn from the guns, the camp-fires were left to smolder in their ashes, the flags were tenderly furled,—those historic banners, battle-stained, bullet-riddled, many of them but remnants of their former selves, with scarcely enough left of them on which to imprint the names of the battles they had seen,—and the Army of the Union and the Army of Northern Virginia turned their backs upon each other for the first time in four long, bloody years.

GENERAL LEE'S RETURN TO HIS LINES AFTER THE SURRENDER. FROM A WAR-TIME SKETCH.

In his "Memoirs of Robert E. Lee" (J. M. Stoddart & Co.), General A. L. Long says of this scene: "When, after his interview with Grant, General Lee again appeared, a shout of welcome instinctively ran through the army. But instantly recollecting the sad occasion that brought him before them, their shouts sank into silence, every hat was raised, and the bronzed faces of the thousands of grim warriors were bathed with tears. As he rode slowly along the lines hundreds of his devoted veterans pressed around the noble chief, trying to take his hand, touch his person, or even lay a hand upon his horse, thus exhibiting for him their great affection. The general then, with head bare and tears flowing freely down his manly cheeks, bade adieu to the army. In a few words he told the brave men who had been so true in arms to return to their homes and become worthy citizens."

GENERAL LEE'S FAREWELL ADDRESS TO HIS ARMY. |

BY CHARLES MARSHALL, COLONEL, C. S. A.

GENERAL LEE's order to the Army of Northern Virginia at Appomattox Court House was written the day after the meeting at McLean's house, at which the terms of the surrender were agreed upon. That night the general sat with several of us at a fire in front of his tent, and after some conversation about the army, and the events of the day, in which his feelings toward his men were strongly expressed, he told me to prepare an order to the troops.

The next day it was raining, and many persons were coming and going, so that I was unable to write without interruption until about 10 o'clock, when General Lee, finding that the order had not been prepared, directed me to get into his ambulance, which stood near his tent, and placed an orderly to prevent any one from approaching me.

I sat in the ambulance until I had written the order, the first draft of which (in pencil) contained an entire paragraph that was omitted by General Lee's direction. He made one or two verbal changes, and I then made a copy of the order as corrected, and gave it to one of the clerks in the adjutant-general's office to write in ink. I took the copy, when made by the clerk, to the general, who signed it, and other copies were then made for transmission to the corps commanders and the staff

of the army. All these copies were signed by the general, and a good many persons sent other copies which they had made or procured, and obtained his signature. In this way many copies of the order had the general's name signed as if they were originals, some of which I have seen. The text of the order as issued was as follows:

"HEADQUARTERS, ARMY OF NORTHERN VIRGINIA, April 10th, 1865. After four years of arduous service, marked by unsurpassed courage and fortitude, the Army of Northern Virginia has been compelled to yield to overwhelming numbers and resources. I need not tell the survivors of so many hard-fought battles, who have remained steadfast to the last, that I have consented to this result from no distrust of them, but, feeling that valor and devotion could accomplish nothing that could compensate for the loss that would have attended the continuation of the contest, I have determined to avoid the useless sacrifice of those whose past services have endeared them to their countrymen.

"By the terms of the agreement, officers and men can return to their homes, and remain there until exchanged. You will take with you the satisfaction that proceeds from the consciousness of duty faithfully performed; and I earnestly pray that a merciful God will extend to you his blessing and protection.

"With an increasing admiration of your constancy and devotion to your country, and a grateful remembrance of your kind and generous consideration of myself, I bid you an affectionate farewell.

"R. E. LEE, General."

| From a letter dated September 27th, 1887, to General Bradley T. Johnson.

THE OPPOSING FORCES IN THE APPOMATTOX CAMPAIGN.

THE UNION ARMY.—Lieutenant-General Ulysses S. Grant.

Escort : B, F, and K, 5th U. S. Cav., Capt. Julius W. Mason.

Headquarters Guard : 4th U. S., Capt. Joseph B. Collins.

ARMY OF THE POTOMAC, Maj.-Gen. George G. Meade.

Provost Guard : Col. George N. Macy: K, 1st Ind. Cav., ——; C, 1st Mass. Cav., Capt. Edward A. Flint; D, 1st Mass. Cav., Capt. James J. Higginson; 3d Pa. Cav., Lieut.-Col. James W. Walsh; 1st Batt'n, 11th U. S., Capt. Alfred E. Latimer; 2d Batt'n, 14th U. S., Capt. William H. Brown.

Headquarters Guard : 3d U. S., Capt. Richard G. Lay.

Quartermaster's Guard : Oneida (N. Y.) Cav., Capt. James E. Jenkins.

Engineer Brigade : Brig.-Gen. Henry W. Benham: 15th N. Y. (9 co's), Col. Wesley Brainerd; 50th N. Y. Col. William H. Pettes.

Battalion U. S. Engineers, Capt. Franklin Harwood.

ARTILLERY, Brig.-Gen. Henry J. Hunt.

SIEGE TRAIN, Col. Henry L. Abbot: 1st Conn. Heavy, Maj. George Ager, Maj. George B. Cook; 3d Conn. Battery, Capt. Thomas S. Gilbert.

ARTILLERY RESERVE, Brig.-Gen. William Hays: 2d Me., Capt. Charles E. Stubbs; 3d Me., Capt. Ezekiel R. Mayo; 4th Me. (attached from Sixth Corps), Capt. Charles W. White; 6th Me. (attached from Second Corps), Capt. William H. Rogers; 5th Mass. (attached from Fifth Corps and detached with Ninth Corps), Capt Charles A. Phillips; 9th Mass. (detached from the Reserve with Ninth Corps), Capt. Richard S. Milton; 14th Mass. (attached to Ninth Corps), Capt. Joseph W. B. Wright; 3d N. J. (or C, 1st N. J.), Capt. Christian Woerner; C, 1st N. Y., Capt. David F. Ritchie; E, 1st N. Y. (attached from Fifth Corps and detached with Ninth Corps), Lieut. George H. Barse; G, 1st N. Y. (attached from Second Corps and detached with Ninth Corps), Capt. Samuel A. McClellan; L, 1st N. Y. (attached from Fifth Corps and detached with Ninth Corps), Lieut. De Witt M. Perine, Capt. George Breck; 12th N. Y. (attached from Second Corps), Capt. Charles A. Clark; H, 1st Ohio (attached from Sixth Corps), Capt. Stephen W. Dorsey; B, 1st Pa. (attached to Ninth Corps), Capt. William McClelland; F, 1st Pa. (attached from Second Corps), Lieut. John F. Campbell; E, 1st R. I. (attached from Sixth Corps), Lieut. Ezra K. Parker; 3d Vt. (attached from Sixth Corps), Capt. Romeo H. Start; C and I, 5th U. S. (attached from Second Corps and detached with Ninth Corps), Lieut. Valentine H. Stone.

SECOND ARMY CORPS, Maj.-Gen. Andrew A. Humphreys.

FIRST DIVISION, Brig.-Gen. Nelson A. Miles.

First Brigade, Col. George W. Scott: 26th Mich., Capt. Lucius H. Ives; 5th N. H. (batt'n), Lieut.-Col. Welcome A. Crafts; 2d N. Y. Heavy Art'y, Maj. Oscar F. Hulser; 61st N. Y., Maj. George W. Schaffer; 81st Pa., Lieut.-Col. William Wilson; 140th Pa., Capt. William A. F. Stockton. *Second Brigade,* Col. Robert Nugent: 28th Mass. (5 co's), Capt. Patrick H. Bird; 63d N. Y. (6 co's), Capt. William H. Terwilliger; 69th N. Y., Lieut.-Col. James J. Smith; 88th N. Y. (5 co's), Lieut.-Col. Denis F. Burke; 4th N. Y. Heavy Art'y, Maj. Seward F. Gould. *Third Brigade,* Col. Henry J. Madill, Col. Clinton D. MacDougall: 7th N. Y., Lieut.-Col. Anthony Pokorny; 39th N. Y., Col. Augustus Funk, Maj. John McE. Hyde; 52d N. Y., Lieut.-Col. Henry M. Karples; 111th N. Y., Col. C. D. MacDougall, Lieut.-Col. Lewis W. Husk; 125th N. Y., Lieut.-Col. Joseph Hyde; 126th N. Y. (batt'n), Capt. John B. Geddis, Capt. I. Hart Wilder. *Fourth Brigade,* Col. John Ramsey: 64th N. Y. (batt'n), Lieut.-Col. William Glenny; 66th N. Y., Capt. Nathaniel P. Lane; 53d Pa., Col. William M. Mintzer; 116th Pa., Maj. David W. Megraw, Capt. John R. Weltner; 145th Pa., Capt. James H. Hamlin; 148th Pa., Capt. A. A. Rhinehart, Capt. John F. Sutton; 183d Pa., Col. George T. Egbert.

SECOND DIVISION, Brig.-Gen. Wm. Hays (assigned to Artillery Reserve April 6th), Brig.-Gen. Francis C. Barlow.

First Brigade, Col. William A. Olmsted: 19th Me., Col. Isaac W. Starbird, Lieut.-Col. J. W. Spaulding; 19th Mass., Capt. Charles S. Palmer; 20th Mass., Lieut.-Col. Arthur R. Curtis; 7th Mich., Lieut.-Col. George W. La Point; 1st Minn. (2 co's), Capt. Frank Houston; 59th N. Y., Capt. William Ludgate; 152d N. Y., Maj. James E. Curtiss; 184th Pa., Col. John H. Stover; 36th Wis., Lieut.-Col. Clement E. Warner. *Second Brigade,* Col. James P. McIvor: 8th N. Y. Heavy Art'y, Col. Joel B. Baker; 155th N. Y., Capt. Michael Doheny; 164th N. Y., Capt. Timothy J. Burke; 170th N. Y., Capt. John Mitchell; 182d N. Y. (69th N. Y. N. G. Art'y), Capt. Robert Heggart. *Third Brigade,* Brig.-Gen. Thomas A. Smyth, Col. Daniel Woodall: 14th Conn., Capt. J. Frank Morgan; 1st Del., Col. Daniel Woodall, Maj. John T. Dent; 12th N. J., Maj. Henry F. Chew; 10th N. Y. (batt'n), Lieut.-Col. George F. Hopper; 108th N. Y., Lieut.-Col. Francis E. Pierce; 4th Ohio (4 co's), Lieut.-Col. Charles C. Calahan; 69th Pa., Capt. Charles McAnally; 106th Pa. (3 co's), Capt. John H. Gallager; 7th W. Va. (4 co's), Lieut.-Col. F. W. H. Baldwin. *Unattached :* 2d Co. Minn. Sharp-shooters, Lieut. Edward N. Schoff.

THIRD DIVISION, Brig.-Gen. Gershom Mott, Brig.-Gen. P. Regis de Trobriand.

First Brigade, Brig.-Gen. P. Regis de Trobriand, Col. Russell B. Shepherd: 20th Ind., Capt. John W. Shafer; 1st Me. Heavy Art'y, Col. Russell B. Shepherd, Lieut.-Col. Zemro A. Smith; 40th N. Y., Lieut.-Col. Madison M. Cannon; 73d N. Y., Lieut.-Col. Michael W. Burns; 86th N. Y., Lieut.-Col. Nathan H. Vincent; 124th N. Y., Lieut.-Col. Charles H. Weygant; 99th Pa., Capt. Jacob Giller; 110th Pa., Capt. Franklin B. Stewart. *Second Brigade,* Brig.-Gen. Byron R. Pierce: 17th Me., Lieut.-Col. William Hobson, Maj. Charles P. Mattocks; 1st Mass. Heavy Art'y, Maj. Nathaniel Shatswell; 5th Mich., Col. John Pulford; 93d N. Y., Lieut.-Col. Haviland Gifford; 57th Pa., Col. George Zinn; 105th Pa., Maj. James Miller; 141st Pa., Lieut.-Col. Joseph H. Horton. *Third Brigade,* Col. Robert McAllister: 11th Mass., Lieut.-Col. Charles C. Rivers; 7th N. J., Col. Francis Price, Jr.; 8th N. J., Maj. Henry Hartford; 11th N. J., Lieut.-Col. John Schoonover; 120th N. Y., Lieut.-Col. Abram L. Lockwood.

ARTILLERY BRIGADE, Maj. John G. Hazard: 10th Mass., Capt. J. Webb Adams; M, 1st N. H., Capt. George K. Dakin; 2d N. J. (or B, 1st N. J.), Capt. A. Judson Clark; 11th N. Y., Lieut. James A. Manning; C, 4th N. Y. Heavy, Capt. Richard Kennedy; L, 4th N. Y. Heavy, Lieut. Frank Seymour; B, 1st R. I., Lieut. William B. Wescott; K, 4th U. S., Capt. John W. Roder.

FIFTH ARMY CORPS, Maj.-Gen. Gouverneur K. Warren, Maj.-Gen. Charles Griffin.

Escort : C, 4th Pa. Cav., Capt. Napoleon J. Howell.

Provost Guard : 104th N. Y., Capt. William W. Graham.

FIRST DIVISION, Brig.-Gen. Charles Griffin, Brig.-Gen. Joseph J. Bartlett.

First Brigade, Brig.-Gen. Joshua L. Chamberlain: 185th N. Y., Col. Gustavus Sniper; 198th Pa., Col. Horatio G. Sickel, Maj. Edwin A. Glenn, Capt John Stanton. *Second Brigade,* Col. Edgar M. Gregory: 187th N. Y., Lieut.-Col. Daniel Myers; 188th N. Y., Lieut.-Col. Isaac Doolittle; 189th N. Y., Lieut.-Col. Joseph G. Townsend. *Third Brigade,* Brig.-Gen. Joseph J. Bartlett, Col. Alfred L. Pearson: 1st Me. Sharp-shooters, Capt. George R. Abbott; 20th Me., Lieut.-Col. Walter G. Morrill; 32d Mass., Lieut.-Col. James A. Cunningham; 1st Mich., Lieut.-Col. George Lockley; 16th Mich., Lieut.-Col. Benjamin F. Partridge; 83d Pa., Col. Chauncey P. Rogers; 91st Pa., Lieut.-Col. Eli G. Sellers; 118th Pa., Maj. Henry O'Neill; 155th Pa., Col. Alfred L. Pearson Maj. John A. Cline.

SECOND DIVISION, Brig.-Gen. Romeyn B. Ayres.

First Brigade, Col. Frederick Winthrop, Col. James Grindlay, Brig.-Gen. Joseph Hayes: 5th N. Y. (Veteran), Capt. Henry Schickhardt, Lieut.-Col. William F. Drum; 15th N. Y. Heavy Art'y, Lieut.-Col. Michael Wiedrich, Maj. Louis Eiche; 140th N. Y., Lieut.-Col. William S. Grantsynn; 146th N. Y., Col. James Grindlay, Lieut. Henry Loomis, Col. James Grindlay. *Second Brigade*, Col. Andrew W. Denison, Col. Richard N. Bowerman, Col. David L. Stanton: 1st Md., Col. David L. Stanton, Maj. Robert Neely; 4th Md., Col. Richard N. Bowerman, Maj. Harrison Adreon; 7th Md., Lieut.-Col. David T. Bennett, Maj. Edward M. Mobley; 8th Md., Lieut.-Col. E. F. M. Faehtz. *Third Brigade*, Col. James Gwyn: 3d Del., Capt. John H. Cade; 4th Del., Capt. W. H. Maclary, Maj. Moses B. Gist; 8th Del. (3 co's), Capt. John N. Richards; 157th (4 co's), 190th, and 191st Pa., Lieut.-Col. Joseph B. Pattee; 210th Pa., Col. William Sergeant, Lieut.-Col. Edward L. Witman.

THIRD DIVISION, Brig.-Gen. Samuel W. Crawford.

First Brigade, Col. John A. Kellogg: 91st N. Y., Col. Jonathan Tarbell; 6th Wis., Lieut.-Col. Thomas Kerr, Capt. Edward A. Whaley; 7th Wis., Lieut.-Col. Hollon Richardson. *Second Brigade*, Brig.-Gen. Henry Baxter: 16th Me., Col. Charles W. Tilden; 39th Mass., Lieut.-Col. Henry M. Tremlett, Capt. Joseph J. Cooper; 97th N. Y., Lieut.-Col. Rouse S. Egelston; 11th Pa., Maj. John B. Overmyer; 107th Pa., Col. Thomas F. McCoy. *Third Brigade*, Col. Richard Coulter: 94th N. Y., Maj. Henry H. Fish, Capt. Albert T. Morgan; 95th N. Y., Capt. George D. Knight; 147th N. Y., Maj. Dennis B. Dailey, Capt. James A. McKinley; 56th and 88th Pa., Maj. A. Laycock; 121st Pa., Maj. West Funk; 142d Pa., Lieut.-Col. Horatio N. Warren. *Unattached:* 1st Battalion N. Y. Sharp-shooters, Capt. Clinton Perry.

ARTILLERY BRIGADE, Col. Charles S. Wainwright: B, 1st N. Y., Capt. Robert E. Rogers; D, 1st N. Y., Lieut. Deloss M. Johnson; H, 1st N. Y., Capt. Charles E. Mink; M, 15th N. Y. Heavy, Capt. William D. Dickey; B, 4th U. S., Lieut. William P. Vose; D and G, 5th U. S., Lieut. Jacob B. Rawles.

SIXTH ARMY CORPS, Maj.-Gen. Horatio G. Wright.

Escort: E, 21st Pa. Cav., Capt. William H. Boyd, Jr.

FIRST DIVISION, Brig.-Gen. Frank Wheaton.

First Brigade, Col. William H. Penrose: 1st and 4th N. J. (batt'n), Lieut.-Col. Baldwin Hufty; 2d N. J. (2 co's), Capt. Adolphus Weiss; 3d N. J. (1 co.), Capt. James H. Comings; 10th N. J., Capt. James W. McNeely; 15th N. J., Maj. Ebenezer W. Davis; 40th N. J., Col. Stephen R. Gilkyson. *Second Brigade*, Col. Joseph E. Hamblin: 2d Conn. Heavy Art'y, Col. James Hubbard; 65th N. Y., Lieut.-Col. Henry C. Fisk; 121st N. Y., Lieut.-Col. Egbert Olcott; 95th Pa., Lieut.-Col. John Harper. *Third Brigade*, Col. Oliver Edwards: 37th Mass., Capt. Archibald Hopkins; 49th Pa., Lieut.-Col. Baynton J. Hickman; 82d Pa., Col. Isaac C. Bassett; 119th Pa., Lieut.-Col. Gideon Clark, Maj. William C. Gray; 2d R. I., Lieut.-Col. Elisha H. Rhodes; 5th Wis., Col. Thomas S. Allen.

SECOND DIVISION, Brig.-Gen. George W. Getty.

First Brigade, Col. James M. Warner: 62d N. Y., Lieut.-Col. Theodore B. Hamilton; 93d Pa., Col. Charles W. Eckman; 98th Pa., Lieut.-Col. Charles Reen, Capt. Bernhard Gessler; 102d Pa., Lieut.-Col. James Patchell; 139th Pa., Lieut.-Col. John G. Parr, Maj. James McGregor, Lieut.-Col. John G. Parr. *Second Brigade*, Brig.-Gen. Lewis A. Grant, Lieut.-Col. Amasa S. Tracy, Maj. Charles Mundee, Lieut.-Col. A. S. Tracy, Brig.-Gen. Lewis A. Grant: 2d Vt., Lieut.-Col. Amasa S. Tracy; 3d and 4th Vt., Lieut.-Col. Horace W. Floyd; 5th Vt., Lieut.-Col. Ronald A. Kennedy; 6th Vt., Capt. William J. Sperry, Lieut.-Col. Sumner H. Lincoln; 1st Vt. Heavy Art'y, Lieut.-Col. Charles Hunsdon. *Third Brigade*, Col. Thomas W. Hyde: 1st Me., Lieut.-Col. Stephen C. Fletcher; 43d N. Y. (5 co's), Lieut.-Col. Charles A Milliken; 49th N. Y. (5 co's), Lieut.-Col. Erastus D. Holt, Maj. G. H. Selkirk; 77th N. Y. (5 co's), Lieut.-Col. David J. Caw, Capt. Charles E. Stevens; 122d N. Y., Lieut.-Col. Horace H. Walpole; 61st Pa., Lieut.-Col. John W. Crosby, Col. George F. Smith.

THIRD DIVISION, Brig.-Gen. Truman Seymour.

First Brigade, Col. William S. Truex: 14th N. J., Lieut.-Col. Jacob J. Janeway; 106th N. Y., Col. Andrew N. McDonald; 151st N. Y. (5 co's), Lieut.-Col. Charles Bogardus; 87th Pa., Capt. James Tearney; 10th Vt., Lieut.-Col. George B. Damon. *Second Brigade*, Col. J. Warren Keifer: 6th Md., Maj. Clifton K. Prentiss, Lieut.-Col. Joseph C. Hill; 9th N. Y. Heavy Art'y, Lieut.-Col. James W. Snyder; 110th Ohio, Lieut.-Col. Otho H, Binkley; 122d Ohio, Lieut.-Col. Charles M. Cornyn; 126th Ohio, Col. Benjamin F. Smith; 67th Pa., Maj. William G. Williams; 138th Pa., Col. Matthew R. McClennan.

ARTILLERY BRIGADE, Capt. Andrew Cowan: 1st N. J. (or A, 1st N. J.), Capt. Augustin N. Parsons; 1st N. Y., Lieut. Orsamus R. Van Etten; 3d N. Y., Capt. William A. Harn; I, 9th N. Y. Heavy, Capt. S. Augustus Howe; G, 1st R. I., Capt. George W. Adams; H, 1st R. I., Capt. Crawford Allen, Jr.; E, 5th U. S., Lieut. John R. Brinckle; D, 1st Vt. Heavy, Capt. Charles J. Lewis.

NINTH ARMY CORPS, Maj.-Gen. John G. Parke.

Provost Guard: 79th N. Y., Maj. Andrew D. Baird.

FIRST DIVISION, Brig.-Gen. Orlando B. Willcox.

First Brigade, Col. Samuel Harriman: 8th Mich., Maj. Richard N. Doyle; 27th Mich., Lieut.-Col. Charles Waite; 109th N. Y., Lieut.-Col. Colwert K. Pier; 51st Pa., Col. William J. Bolton; 37th Wis., Lieut.-Col. John Green; 38th Wis., Col. James Bintliff, Maj. Robert N. Roberts. *Second Brigade*, Lieut.-Col. Ralph Ely: 1st Mich. Sharpshooters, Lieut.-Col. Asahel W. Nichols, Maj. Edwin J. Buckbee; 2d Mich., Capt. John C. Boughton; 20th Mich., Capt. Albert A. Day; 46th N. Y., Lieut.-Col. Adolph Becker; 60th Ohio, Lieut.-Col. Martin P. Avery; 50th Pa., Maj. Samuel K. Schwenk. *Third Brigade*, Lieut.-Col. Gilbert P. Robinson, Col. James Bintliff: 3d Md. Batt'n, Capt. Joseph F. Carter, Lieut.-Col. Gilbert P. Robinson; 29th Mass., Capt. John M. Deane; 57th Mass., Capt. Albert W. Cook; 59th Mass., Maj. Ezra P. Gould; 18th N. H., Lieut.-Col. Joseph M. Clough; 14th N. Y. Heavy Art'y, Maj. George M. Randall; 100th Pa., Maj. Norman J. Maxwell. *Acting Engineers:* 17th Mich., Lieut.-Col. Frederick W. Swift.

SECOND DIVISION, Brig.-Gen. Robert B. Potter, Brig.-Gen. Simon G. Griffin.

First Brigade, Col. John I. Curtin: 35th Mass., Col. Sumner Carruth; 36th Mass., Lieut.-Col. Thaddeus L. Barker; 58th Mass., Lieut.-Col. John C. Whiton; 39th N. J., Col. Abram C. Wildrick; 51st N. Y., Capt. Thomas B. Marsh; 45th Pa., Capt. Roland C. Cheeseman, Lieut.-Col. Theodore Gregg; 48th Pa., Col. George W. Gowan, Lieut.-Col. Isaac F. Brannon; 7th R. I., Lieut.-Col. Percy Daniels. *Second Brigade*, Brig.-Gen. Simon G. Griffin, Col. Walter Harriman: 31st Me., Lieut.-Col. Edward L. Getchell, Capt. Ebenezer S. Kyes; 2d Md., Lieut.-Col. Benjamin F. Taylor; 56th Mass., Maj. Zabdiel B. Adams, Col. Stephen M. Weld, Jr.; 6th N. H., Lieut.-Col. Phin. P. Bixby; 9th N. H., Capt. John B. Cooper; 11th N. H., Col. Walter Harriman, Capt. Hollis O. Dudley; 179th N. Y., Col. William M. Gregg, Maj. Albert A. Terrill; 186th N. Y., Col. Bradley Winslow, Lieut.-Col. E. Jay Marsh; 17th Vt., Maj. Lyman E. Knapp, Col. Francis V. Randall.

THIRD DIVISION, Brig.-Gen. John F. Hartranft.

First Brigade, Lieut.-Col. W. H. McCall, Col. Alfred B. McCalmont: 200th Pa., Maj. Jacob Rehrer, Lieut.-Col. W. H. H. McCall; 208th Pa., Lieut.-Col. Mish T. Heintzelman; 209th Pa., Lieut.-Col. George W. Frederick. *Second Brigade*, Col. Joseph A. Mathews: 205th Pa., Maj. B. Mortimer Morrow, Capt. Joseph G. Holmes; 207th Pa., Col. Robert C. Cox; 211th Pa., Col. Levi A. Dodd.

ARTILLERY BRIGADE, Col. John C. Tidball: 7th Me., Capt. Adelbert B. Twitchell; 11th Mass., Capt. Edward J. Jones; 19th N. Y., Capt. Edward W. Rogers; 27th N. Y., Capt. John B. Eaton; 34th N. Y., Capt. Jacob Roemer; D, Pa., Capt. Samuel H. Rhoads.

CAVALRY: 2d Pa., Col. William W. Sanders.

INDEPENDENT BRIGADE, Col. Charles H. T. Collis: 1st Mass. Cav., Maj. John Tewksbury; 61st Mass., Col. Charles F. Walcott; 80th N. Y. (20th Militia), Col. Jacob B. Hardenbergh; 68th Pa., Col. Andrew H. Tippin, Lieut.-Col. Robert E. Winslow; 114th Pa., Maj. Edward R. Bowen.

CAVALRY, Maj.-Gen. Philip H. Sheridan.
ARMY OF THE SHENANDOAH, Brig.-Gen. Wesley Merritt.
FIRST DIVISION, Brig.-Gen. Thomas C. Devin.
First Brigade, Col. Peter Stagg: 1st Mich., Lieut.-Col. George R. Maxwell, Capt. Edward L. Negus; 5th Mich., Lieut.-Col. Smith H. Hastings; 6th Mich., Lieut.-Col. Harvey H. Vinton; 7th Mich., Lieut.-Col. George G. Briggs. *Second Brigade,* Col. Charles L. Fitzhugh: 6th N. Y., Maj. Harrison White; 9th N. Y., Maj. James R. Dinnin; 19th N. Y. (1st N. Y. Dragoons), Maj. Howard M. Smith; 17th Pa., Lieut.-Col. Coe Durland; 20th Pa., Lieut.-Col. Gabriel Middleton. *Third (Reserve) Brigade,* Brig.-Gen. Alfred Gibbs: 2d Mass., Col. Casper Crowninshield; 6th Pa. (6 co's), Col. Charles L. Leiper; 1st U. S., Capt. Richard S. C. Lord; 5th U. S., Capt. Thomas Drummond, Lieut. Gustavus Urban; 6th U. S., Maj. Robert M. Morris. *Artillery:* C and E, 4th U. S., Capt. Marcus P. Miller.
THIRD DIVISION, Brig.-Gen. George A. Custer.
First Brigade, Col. Alexander C. M. Pennington: 1st Conn., Col. Brayton Ives; 3d N. J., Lieut.-Col. William P. Robeson, Jr.; 2d N. Y., Col. Alanson M. Randol; 2d Ohio, Lieut.-Col. A. Bayard Nettleton. *Second Brigade,* Col. William Wells: 8th N. Y., Maj. James Bliss; 15th N. Y., Col. John J. Coppinger; 1st Vt., Lieut.-Col. Josiah Hall. *Third Brigade,* Col. Henry Capehart: 1st N. Y., Lieut.-Col. Jenyns C. Battersby; 1st W. Va., Maj. Shesh B. Howe, Lieut.-Col. Charles E. Capehart; 2d W. Va., Lieut.-Col. James Allen; 3d W. Va., Maj. John S. Witcher.
SECOND DIVISION (Army of the Potomac), Maj.-Gen. George Crook.
First Brigade, Brig.-Gen. Henry E. Davies: 1st N. J., Col. Hugh H. Janeway, Maj. Walter R. Robbins; 10th N. Y., Col. M. Henry Avery; 24th N. Y., Col. Walter C. Newberry, Lieut.-Col. Melzer Richards, Maj. William A. Snyder; 1st Pa. (5 co's), Maj. Hampton S. Thomas; A, 2d U. S. Art'y, Lieut. James H. Lord. *Second Brigade,* Col. J. Irvin Gregg, Capt. Samuel B. M. Young: 4th Pa., Lieut.-Col. Alender P. Duncan; 8th Pa., Lieut.-Col. William A. Corrie; 16th Pa., Lieut.-Col. John K. Robison, Maj. William H. Fry; 21st Pa., Col. Oliver B. Knowles; H and I, 1st U. S. Art'y (detached with Art'y Brigade, 9th Corps), Lieut. Chandler P. Eakin. *Third Brigade,* Col. Charles H. Smith: 1st Me., Lieut.-Col. Jonathan P. Cilley; 2d N. Y., Mounted Rifles, Maj. Paul Chadbourne, Col. John Fisk; 6th Ohio, Capt. Matthew H. Cryer, Capt. Frank C. Loveland; 13th Ohio, Lieut.-Col. Stephen R. Clark.
ARMY OF THE JAMES, Maj.-Gen. Edward O. C. Ord.
Headquarters Guard: D, 3d Pa. Art'y, Capt. Edwin A. Evans; I, 3d Pa. Art'y, Capt. Osbourn Wattson.
Engineers: 1st N. Y., Col. James F. Hall. *Pontoniers:* I, 3d Mass. Art'y, Capt. John Pickering, Jr. *Unattached Cavalry:* I, L, and M, 4th Mass., Col. Francis Washburn; 5th Mass. (colored), Col. Charles F. Adams, Jr.; 7th N. Y. (1st Mounted Rifles), Col. Edwin V. Sumner.
DEFENSES OF BERMUDA HUNDRED, Maj.-Gen. George L. Hartsuff.
INFANTRY DIVISION, Brig.-Gen. Edward Ferrero.
First Brigade, Brevet Brig.-Gen. Gilbert H. McKibbin: 41st N. Y., Lieut.-Col. Detleo von Einsiedel; 103d N. Y., Capt. William Redlick; 2d Pa., H. Art'y, Maj. Benjamin F. Winger; 104th Pa., Lieut.-Col. Theophilus Kephart. *Second Brigade,* Col. George C. Kibbe: 6th N. Y. H. Art'y, Lieut.-Col. Stephen Baker; 10th N. Y. H. Art'y, Lieut.-Col. G. de Peyster Arden. *Artillery:* 33d N. Y., Capt. Alger M. Wheeler.
ARTILLERY: A and H, 13th N. Y. Heavy, Capt. Wm. Pendrell; 7th N. Y., Lieut. Martin V. McIntyre; E, 3d Pa. Heavy, Capt. Erskine M. Miles; M, 3d Pa. Heavy, Lieut. Sylvester W. Marshall.
SEPARATE BRIGADE, Brig.-Gen. Joseph B. Carr.
FORT POCAHONTAS, Lieut.-Col. Ashbel W. Angel: 38th N. J. (4 co's), Maj. William H. Tantum; 2d, 20th N. Y. Cav., Capt. Wayland F. Ford; E, 16th N. Y. H. Art'y, Capt. John W. Hees; H, 16th N. Y. H. Art'y, Capt. Henry C. Thompson; I, 184th N. Y., Capt. George Wetmore.

HARRISON'S LANDING, Col. Wardwell G. Robinson: 184th N. Y., Lieut.-Col. William P. McKinley; I, 1st U. S. Colored Cav., Lieut. Horace Hudson.
FORT POWHATAN, Col. William J. Sewell: 38th N. J. (6 co's), Col. William J. Sewell; F, 20th N. Y. Cav., Lieut. John C. Pollard; detachment 3d Pa. H. Art'y, Lieut. Frederick Grill; E, 1st U. S. Colored Cav., Capt. Charles W. Emerson.
TWENTY-FOURTH ARMY CORPS, Maj.-Gen. John Gibbon.
Headquarters Guard, Capt. Charles E. Thomas: F, 4th Mass. Cav., Capt. Joseph J. Baker; K, 4th Mass. Cav., Capt. Charles E. Thomas.
FIRST DIVISION, Brig.-Gen. Robert S. Foster.
First Brigade, Col. Thomas O. Osborn: 39th Ill., Capt. Homer A. Plimpton; 62d Ohio, Lieut.-Col. Henry R. West, Maj. Thomas J. Platt; 67th Ohio, Col. Alvin C. Voris; G, 85th Pa. (Provost Guard at division headquarters), Lieut. Absalom S. Dial; 199th Pa., Col. James C. Briscoe. *Third Brigade,* Col. George B. Dandy: 10th Conn., Lieut.-Col. Ellsworth D. S. Goodyear, Capt. Francis G. Hickerson; 11th Me., Lieut.-Col. Jonathan A. Hill, Maj. Charles P. Baldwin, Lieut.-Col. Jonathan A. Hill, Capt. Henry C. Adams; 24th Mass. (detached at Bermuda Hundred), Capt. Thomas F. Edmands; 100th N. Y., Maj. James H. Dandy, Capt. Edwin Nichols; 206th Pa., Col. Hugh J. Brady. *Fourth Brigade,* Col. Harrison S. Fairchild: 8th Me., Lieut.-Col. Edward A. True, Capt. Edward H. Reynolds; 89th N. Y., Maj. Frank W. Tremain, Capt. William Dobie; 148th N. Y., Col. John B. Murray; 158th N. Y., Lieut.-Col. William H. McNary. Maj. Hyron Kalt; 55th Pa., Capt. George H. Hill.
THIRD DIVISION, Brig.-Gen. Charles Devens, Jr.
First Brigade, Col. Edward H. Ripley: 11th Conn., Maj. Charles Warren; 13th N. H., Lieut.-Col. Normand Smith; 81st N. Y., Capt. Matthew T. Betton; 98th N. Y., Lieut.-Col. William Kreutzer; 139th N. Y., Maj. Theodore Miller; 19th Wis., Maj. Samuel K. Vaughan. *Second Brigade,* Col. Michael T. Donohoe: 8th Conn., Maj. William M. Pratt; 5th Md., Lieut.-Col. William W. Bamberger; 10th N. H., Capt. Warren M. Kelley; 12th N. H., Lieut.-Col. Thomas E. Barker; 96th N. Y., Capt. George W. Hindes; 118th N. Y., Lieut.-Col. Levi S. Dominy; 9th Vt., Lieut.-Col. Valentine G. Barney. *Third Brigade,* Col. Samuel H. Roberts: 21st Conn., Lieut.-Col. James F. Brown; 40th Mass., Lieut.-Col. John Pollack; 2d N. H., Lieut.-Col. Joab N. Patterson; 58th Pa., Lieut.-Col. Cecil Clay; 188th Pa., Lieut.-Col. George K. Bowen.
INDEPENDENT DIVISION, Brig.-Gen. John W. Turner.
First Brigade, Lieut.-Col. Andrew Potter: 34th Mass., Capt. Frank T. Leach; 116th Ohio, Lieut.-Col. Wilbert B. Teters; 123d Ohio, Lieut.-Col. Horace Kellogg. *Second Brigade,* Col. William B. Curtis: 23d Ill., Capt. Patrick M. Ryan; 54th Pa., Lieut.-Col. Albert P. Moulton; 12th W. Va., Capt. Erastus G. Bartlett. *Third Brigade,* Col. Thomas M. Harris: 10th W. Va., Capt. Marshal W. Coburn; 11th W. Va., Maj. Michael A. Ayers; 15th W. Va., Lieut.-Col. John W. Holliday.
ARTILLERY, Maj. Charles C. Abell: E, 3d N. Y., Capt. George E. Ashby; H, 3d N. Y., Capt. Enoch Jones; K, 3d N. Y., Capt. James R. Angel; M, 3d N. Y., Capt. John H. Howell; 17th N. Y., Capt. George T. Anthony; A, 1st Pa., Capt. William Stitt; F, 1st R. I., Lieut. Charles E. Guild; B, 1st U. S., Capt. Samuel S. Elder; L, 4th U. S., Lieut. Henry C. Hasbrouck; A, 5th U. S., Lieut. Charles P. Muhlenberg; F, 5th U. S., Lieut. Henry B. Beecher.
TWENTY-FIFTH ARMY CORPS,‡ Maj.-Gen. Godfrey Weitzel.
Provost Guard: E and H, 4th Mass. Cav., Maj. Atherton H. Stevens, Jr.
FIRST DIVISION, Brig.-Gen. August V. Kautz.
First Brigade, Col. Alonzo G. Draper: 22d U. S., Lieut.-Col. Ira C. Terry; 36th U. S., Lieut.-Col. Benjamin F. Pratt; 38th U. S., Col. Robert M. Hall; 118th U. S., Col. John C. Moon. *Second Brigade,* Brig.-Gen. Edward A. Wild: 29th Conn., Col. William B. Wooster; 9th U. S., Col. Thomas Bayley; 115th U. S. (detached from 1st Brigade, 2d Division), Col. Robert H. Earnest; 117th U. S., Col. Lewis G. Brown. *Third Brigade,* Brig.-Gen.

‡ The infantry was composed entirely of colored troops.

Henry G. Thomas: 19th U. S., Col. Joseph G. Perkins; 23d U. S., Lieut.-Col. Marshall L. Dempcy; 43d U. S., Col. S. B. Yeoman; 114th U. S., Lieut.-Col. Thomas D. Sedgewick. *Attached Brigade* (detached from 3d Brigade, 2d Division), Col. Charles S. Russell: 10th U. S., Lieut.-Col. Edward H. Powell; 28th U. S., Lieut.-Col. Thomas H. Logan.

Cavalry: 2d U. S. Colored, Lieut.-Col. George W. Cole.

SECOND DIVISION, Brig.-Gen. William Birney.

First Brigade, Col. James Shaw, Jr.: 7th U. S., Lieut.-Col. Oscar E. Pratt; 109th U. S., Col. Orion A. Bartholomew; 116th U. S., Lieut.-Col. George H. Laird. *Second Brigade*, Col. Ulysses Doubleday: 8th U. S., Col. Samuel C. Armstrong; 41st U. S., Col. Llewellyn F. Haskell; 45th U. S., Maj. Theodore C. Glazier; 127th U. S., Lieut.-Col. James Givin. *Third Brigade*, Col. William W. Woodward: 29th U. S., Col. Clark E. Royce; 31st U. S., Col. Henry C. Ward.

ARTILLERY BRIGADE, Capt. Loomis L. Langdon: 1st Conn., Capt. James B. Clinton; 4th N. J. (or D, 1st N. J.), Capt. Charles R. Doane; 5th N. J. (or E, 1st N. J.), Capt. Zenas C. Warren; E, 1st Pa., Capt. Henry Y. Wildey; C, 3d R. I., Capt. Martin S. James; D, 1st U. S., Lieut. Redmond Tully; M, 1st U. S., Lieut. Egbert W. Olcott; D, 4th U. S., Capt. Frederick M. Follett.

CAVALRY DIVISION, ⚓ Brig.-Gen. Ranald S. Mackenzie.

First Brigade, Col. Robert M. West: G, 20th N. Y.,

Capt. Thomas H. Butler; 5th Pa., Lieut.-Col. Christopher Kleinz. *Second Brigade*, Col. Samuel P. Spear: 1st D. C. (batt'n), Maj. J. Stannard Baker; 1st Md., Col. Andrew W. Evans; 11th Pa., Lieut.-Col. Franklin A. Stratton. *Artillery:* 4th Wis., Capt. Dorman L. Noggle.

The effective strength of the Union army at the beginning of the campaign approximated 120,000. The losses were as follows:

COMMAND.	*Killed.*	*Wounded.*	*Captured or Missing.*	*Total.*
Second Army Corps	203	1191	630	2,024
Fifth Army Corps	263	1656	546	2,465
Sixth Army Corps	203	1324	15	1,542
Ninth Army Corps...........	253	1305	161	1,719
Twenty-fourth Army Corps ...	119	807	20	946
Twenty-fifth Army Corps	10	40	40	90
Sheridan's Cavalry	190	961	339	1,490
Mackenzie's Cavalry..........	9	38	24	71
Provost Guard	2	1	....	3
Collis's Independent Brigade..	13	71	....	84
Abbot's Siege Batteries.......	6	8	53	67
Unattached Artillery	3	11	....	14
Aggregate...................	1274	7413	1828	10,515

⚓ Temporarily assigned April 1st, 1865, to Sheridan's cavalry command.

THE CONFEDERATE ARMY.

General Robert E. Lee.

Provost Guard: 1st Va. Batt'n, and B, 44th Va. Batt'n, Maj. D. B. Bridgford.

Escort: 39th Va. Batt'n, Capt. Samuel B. Brown.

Engineer Troops, Col. T. M. R. Talcott; 1st Reg't, ——; 2d Reg't, ——.

FIRST ARMY CORPS, Lieut.-Gen. James Longstreet.

PICKETT'S DIVISION, Maj.-Gen. George E. Pickett.

Steuart's Brigade, Brig.-Gen. George H. Steuart: 9th Va., Capt. John P. Wilson, Jr.; 14th Va., Maj. William D. Shelton; 38th Va., Col. George K. Griggs; 53d Va., Capt. Henry Edmunds; 57th Va., Lieut.-Col. William H. Ramsey. *Corse's Brigade*, Brig.-Gen. Montgomery D. Corse, Col. Arthur Herbert: 15th Va., Maj. Charles H. Clark; 17th Va., Col. Arthur Herbert; 29th Va., Lieut. John A. Coulson; 30th Va., Col. Robert S. Chew; 32d Va., Capt. Samuel W. Armistead. *Hunton's Brigade*, Brig.-Gen. Eppa Hunton, Maj. Michael P. Spessard: 8th Va., ——; 18th Va., Lieut. Charles H. Wilkinson; 19th Va., ——; 28th Va., Maj. Michael P. Spessard; 56th Va., Capt. John W. Jones. *Terry's Brigade*, Brig.-Gen. William R. Terry, Maj. William W. Bentley: 1st Va., ——; 3d Va., ——; 7th Va., ——; 11th Va., ——; 24th Va., Maj. William W. Bentley.

FIELD'S DIVISION, Maj.-Gen. Charles W. Field.

Perry's (late Law's) Brigade, Brig.-Gen. William F. Perry: 4th Ala., Lieut.-Col. L. H. Scruggs; 15th Ala., Col. A. A. Lowther; 44th Ala., Lieut.-Col. John A. Jones; 47th Ala., Capt. Eli D. Clower; 48th Ala., Maj. J. W. Wiggonton. *Anderson's Brigade*, Brig.-Gen. George T. Anderson: 7th Ga., Col. George H. Carmical; 8th Ga., Col. John R. Towers; 9th Ga., Maj. John W. Arnold; 11th Ga., Capt. W. H. Ramsey; 59th Ga., Col. Jack Brown. *Benning's Brigade*, Brig.-Gen. Henry L. Benning: 2d Ga., Capt. Thomas Chaffin, Jr.; 15th Ga., Maj. P. J. Shannon; 17th Ga., Maj. James B. Moore; 20th Ga., ——. *Gregg's Brigade*, Col. R. M. Powell: 3d Ark., Lieut.-Col. Robert S. Taylor; 1st Tex., Col. F. S. Bass; 4th Tex., Lieut.-Col. C. M. Winkler; 5th Tex., Capt. W. T. Hill. *Bratton's Brigade*, Brig.-Gen. John Bratton: 1st S. C., Col. James R. Hagood; 5th S. C., Col. A. Coward; 6th S. C., Col. John M. Steedman; 2d S. C. (Rifles), Col. Robert

E. Bowen; Palmetto (S. C.) Sharp-shooters, Capt. Alfred H. Foster.

KERSHAW'S DIVISION,⬥ Maj.-Gen. Joseph B. Kershaw.

Du Bose's Brigade, Brig.-Gen. Dudley M. Du Bosé, Capt. J. F. Espy: 16th Ga., Lieut. W. W. Montgomery; 18th Ga., Capt. J. F. Espy, Lieut. G. J. Lasseter; 24th Ga., Capt. J. A. Jarrard; 3d Ga. Batt'n Sharp-shooters, ——; Cobb's Ga. Legion, Lieut. W. G. Steed; Phillips Ga. Legion, Lieut. A. J. Reese. *Humphreys's Brigade*, Col. W. H. Fitzgerald, Capt. G. R. Cherry: 13th Miss., Lieut. W. H. Davis; 17th Miss., Capt. G. R. Cherry; 18th Miss., Lieut. John W. Gower; 21st Miss., Lieut. Benjamin George. *Simms's Brigade*, Brig.-Gen. James P. Simms, Capt. G. W. Waldron: 10th Ga., Lieut. J. B. Evans; 50th Ga., Capt. G. W. Waldron, Lieut. H. W. Cason; 51st Ga., Capt. H. R. Thomas; 53d Ga., Capt. R. H. Woods.

ARTILLERY, ⚐ Brig.-Gen. E. P. Alexander.

Haskell's Battalion, Lieut.-Col. John C. Haskell: N. C. Battery, Capt. Henry G. Flanner; N. C. Battery (Ramsey's), Lieut. Jesse F. Woodard; S. C. Battery, Capt. Hugh R. Garden; Va. Battery (Lamkin's), Lieut. Fletcher T. Massie. *Huger's Battalion*, Maj. Tyler C. Jordan: La. Battery (Moody's), Lieut. George Poindexter; S. C. Battery (Fickling's), Lieut. E. L. Purse; Va. Battery (Parker's), Lieut. E. S. Wooldridge; Va. Battery, Capt. J. Donnell Smith; Va. Battery (Taylor's), Lieut. John H. Weddel; Va. Battery, Lieut. James Woolfolk.

SECOND ARMY CORPS, Lieut.-Gen. John B. Gordon.

GRIMES'S (late Rodes's) DIVISION, Maj.-Gen. Bryan Grimes.

Battle's Brigade, Col. Edwin L. Hobson: 3d Ala., Capt. C. Robinson, Jr.; 5th Ala., Col. Edwin L. Hobson, Capt. Thomas L. Riley; 6th Ala., Maj. Isaac F. Culver; 12th Ala., Capt. Poleman D. Ross; 61st Ala., Capt. Augustus B. Fannin. *Grimes's Brigade*, Col. D. G. Cowand: 32d N. C., Capt. P. C. Shuford; 43d N. C., Capt. Wiley J. Cobb; 45th N. C., Col. John R. Winston; 53d N. C., Capt. Thomas E. Ashcraft; 2d N. C. Batt'n, ——. *Cox's Brigade*, Brig.-Gen. William R. Cox: 1st N. C., Maj. Louis

⬥ During the retreat Kershaw's and G. W. C. Lee's divisions, with other troops from the defenses of Richmond, were commanded by Lieut.-Gen. Richard S. Ewell.

⚐ The artillery of the army was commanded by Brig.-Gen. William N. Pendleton.

C. Latham; 2d N. C., Maj. James T. Scales; 3d N. C., Maj. William T. Ennett; 4th N. C., Capt. John B. Forcum; 14th N. C., Lieut.-Col. William A. Johnston; 30th N. C., Capt. David C. Allen. *Cook's Brigade*, Col. Edwin A. Nash: 4th Ga., Col. Edwin A. Nash, Capt. J. M. Shivers; 12th Ga., Capt. J. N. Beall; 21st Ga., Capt. Ed. Smith; 44th Ga., Capt. John A. Tucker; Ga. Battery (Patterson's), ——. *Archer's Battalion*, Lieut.-Col. F. H. Archer: 3d Battalion Va. Reserves, Capt. John A. Rogers; 44th Battalion Va. Reserves, Capt. A. B. Morrison.

EARLY'S DIVISION, Brig.-Gen. James A. Walker.

Johnston's Brigade, Col. John W. Lea: 5th N. C., Col. John W. Lea, Capt. J. M. Taylor; 12th N. C., Capt. P. Durham; 20th N. C., Lieut. Archibald F. Lawhon; 23d N. C., Capt. Abner D. Peace; 1st N. C. Batt'n, Lieut. R. W. Woodruff. *Lewis's Brigade*, Capt. John Beard: 6th N. C., Capt. Joseph H. Dickey; 21st N. C., Capt. John H. Miller; 54th N. C., ——; 57th N. C., Capt. John Beard. *Walker's (late Pegram's) Brigade*, Maj. Henry Kyd Douglas: 13th Va., Capt. George Cullen, Jr.; 31st Va., Maj. William P. Cooper; 49th Va., Capt. William D. Moffett; 52d Va., Capt. S. W. Paxton; 58th Va., Lieut. Robert L. Waldron.

GORDON'S DIVISION, Brig.-Gen. Clement A. Evans.

Evans's Brigade, Col. J. H. Lowe: 13th Ga., Lieut.-Col. Richard Maltbie; 26th Ga., Capt. James Knox; 31st Ga., Capt. E. C. Perry; 38th Ga., Lieut.-Col. P. E. Davant; 60th and 61st Ga., Col. Waters B. Jones; 9th Ga. Battalion Art'y, Serg't. H. L. Crawford; 12th Ga. Battalion Art'y, Capt. S. H. Crump; 18th Ga. Battalion Art'y, Capt. George W. Stiles. *Terry's Brigade*, Col. T. V. Williams: 2d Va., Capt. Joseph J. Jenkins; 4th Va., Capt. Hamilton D. Wade; 5th Va., Capt. Peter E. Wilson; 10th Va., Lieut.-Col. D. H. Lee Martz; 21st Va., Col. William A. Witcher; 23d Va., Lieut.-Col. John P. Fitzgerald; 25th Va., Maj. Wilson Harper; 27th Va., Capt. Franklin C. Wilson; 33d Va., Capt. Henry A. Herrell; 37th Va., Capt. John A. Preston; 42d Va., Lieut. James L. Tompkins; 44th Va., Maj. David W. Anderson; 48th Va., Col. Robert H. Dungan. *York's Brigade*, Col. Eugene Waggaman: 1st La., ——; 2d La., Capt. A. S. Blythe; 5th La., Lieut. H. Baxter; 6th La., Maj. W. H. Manning; 7th La., ——; 8th La., Capt. Louis Prados; 9th La., ——; 10th La., ——; 14th La., ——; 15th La., Col. Edmund Pendleton.

ARTILLERY, Brig.-Gen. Armistead L. Long.

Braxton's Battalion, Lieut.-Col. Carter M. Braxton: Va. Batt'y (Carpenter's), ——; Va. Batt'y (Cooper's), ——; Va. Batt'y, Capt. William W. Hardwicke. *Cutshaw's Battalion*, Capt. C. W. Fry: Ala. Batt'y (Reese's), ——; Va. Batt'y (Carter's), Lieut. L. D. Robinson; Va. Batt'y (Montgomery's), ——; Va. Batt'y (Fry's), Lieut. W. A. Deas; Va. Batt'y, Capt. Asher W. Garber; Va. Batt'y, Capt. Lorraine F. Jones. *Hardaway's Battalion*, Lieut.-Col. Robert A. Hardaway: Va. Batt'y (Dance's), Lieut. John R. Bagby; Va. Batt'y, Capt. Archibald Graham; Va. Batt'y, Capt. Charles B. Griffin; Va. Batt'y, Capt. Benjamin H. Smith, Jr. *Johnson's Battalion*, Lieut.-Col. Marmaduke Johnson: Va. Batt'y (Clutter's), Lieut. Lucas McIntosh; Va. Batt'y, Capt. John G. Pollock. *Lightfoot's Battalion*: Va. Batt'y (Caroline Art'y), ——; Va. Batt'y (Nelson Art'y), ——; Va. Batt'y (Surry Art'y), ——. *Stark's Battalion*, Lieut.-Col. Alexander W. Stark: La. Batt'y (Green's), ——; Va. Batt'y, Capt. David A. French; Va. Batt'y, Capt. A. D. Armistead.

THIRD ARMY CORPS, ☆ Lieut.-Gen. Ambrose P. Hill (k).

Provost Guard: 5th Ala. Batt'n, Capt. Wade Ritter.

HETH'S DIVISION, Maj.-Gen. Henry Heth.

Davis's Brigade, Brig.-Gen. Joseph R. Davis: 1st Confederate Batt'n, Capt. Anthony B. Bartlett; 2d Miss., ——; 11th Miss., ——; 26th Miss., ——; 42d Miss., ——. *Cooke's Brigade*, Brig.-Gen. John R. Cooke: 15th N. C., Col. William H. Yarborough; 27th N. C., Lieut.-Col. Joseph C. Webb; 46th N. C., Col. William L. Saunders; 48th N. C., Col. Samuel H. Walkup; 55th N. C., Capt. Walter A. Whitted. *MacRae's Brigade*, Brig.-Gen. William MacRae: 11th N. C., Col. William J. Martin;

26th N. C., Lieut.-Col. James T. Adams; 44th N. C., Maj. Charles M. Stedman; 47th N. C., ——; 52d N. C., Lieut.-Col. Eric Erson. *McComb's Brigade*, Brig.-Gen. William McComb: 2d Md. Batt'n, Capt. John W. Torsch; 1st Tenn. (Prov. Army), Maj. Felix G. Buchanan; 7th Tenn., Lieut.-Col. Samuel G. Shepard; 14th Tenn., Maj. James H. Johnson; 17th and 23d Tenn., Col. Horace Ready; 25th and 44th Tenn., ——; 63d Tenn., ——.

WILCOX'S DIVISION, Maj.-Gen. Cadmus M. Wilcox.

Thomas's Brigade, Brig.-Gen. Edward L. Thomas: 14th Ga., Col. Richard P. Lester; 35th Ga., Col. Bolling H. Holt; 45th Ga., Col. Thomas J. Simmons; 49th Ga., Maj. James B. Duggan. *Lane's Brigade*, Brig.-Gen. James H. Lane: 18th N. C., Maj. Thomas J. Wooten; 28th N. C., Capt. T. J. Linebarger; 33d N. C., Col. Robert V. Cowan; 37th N. C., Maj. Jackson L. Bost. *McGowan's Brigade*, Brig.-Gen. Samuel McGowan: 1st S. C. (Prov. Army), Lieut.-Col. Andrew P. Butler; 12th S. C., Capt. J. C. Bell; 13th S. C., Col. Isaac F. Hunt; 14th S. C., Lieut.-Col. Edward Croft; Orr's S. C. Rifles, Lieut.-Col. J. T. Robertson. *Scales's Brigade*, Col. Joseph H. Hyman: 13th N. C., Lieut.-Col. E. B. Withers; 16th N. C., Col. William A. Stowe; 22d N. C., Col. Thomas S. Gallaway; 34th N. C., Lieut.-Col. George M. Norment; 38th N. C., Col. John Ashford, Lieut.-Col. George W. Flowers.

MAHONE'S DIVISION, Maj.-Gen. William Mahone.

Forney's Brigade, Brig.-Gen. William H. Forney: 8th Ala., Lieut.-Col. John P. Emrich; 9th Ala., Maj. James M. Crow; 10th Ala., Maj. Louis W. Johnson; 11th Ala., Capt. Martin L. Stewart; 13th Ala., Capt. Samuel Sellers; 14th Ala., Capt. John A. Terrell. *Weisiger's Brigade*, Brig.-Gen. David A. Weisiger: 6th Va., Col. George T. Rogers; 12th Va., Maj. Richard W. Jones; 16th Va., Lieut.-Col. Richard O. Whitehead; 41st Va., Lieut.-Col. Joseph P. Minitree; 61st Va., Col. Virginius D. Groner. *Harris's Brigade*, Brig.-Gen. N. H. Harris: 12th Miss., Capt. A. K. Jones; 16th Miss., Capt. James H. Duncan; 19th Miss., Col. Richard W. Phipps; 48th Miss., Col. Joseph M. Jayne. *Sorrel's Brigade*, Col. George E. Tayloe: 3d Ga., Lieut.-Col. Claiborne Snead; 22d Ga., Capt. G. W. Thomas; 48th Ga., Capt. A. C. Flanders; 64th Ga., Capt. J. G. Brown; 2d Ga. Batt'n, Maj. Charles J. Moffett; 10th Ga. Batt'n, Capt. C. F. Hill. *Finegan's Brigade*, Col. David Lang: 2d Fla., Col. W. R. Moore; 5th Fla., ——; 8th Fla., Maj. Thomas E. Clarke; 9th Fla., ——; 10th Fla., Col. Charles F. Hopkins; 11th Fla., ——.

ARTILLERY, Brig.-Gen. R. L. Walker.

McIntosh's Battalion, Lieut.-Col. William M. Owen: Ala. Batt'y (Hurt's), Lieut. George A. Ferrell; La. Batt'y, Capt. Edward Owen; Md. Batt'y (Chew's), ——; Va. Batt'y (Chamberlayne's); Va. Batt'y, Capt. Berryman Z. Price; Va. Batt'y (Donald's), Lieut. William T. Wilson. *Poague's Battalion*, Lieut.-Col. William T. Poague: Miss. Batt'y (Richards's), Lieut. John W. Yeargain; N. C. Batt'y, Capt. Arthur B. Williams; Va. Batt'y, Capt. Charles F. Johnston; Va. Batt'y, Capt. Addison W. Utterback; Va. Batt'y, Capt. Nathan Perrick. *Thirteenth Virginia Battalion:* Otey Batt'y, Capt. David N. Walker; Ringgold Batt'y, Capt. Crispin Dickenson. *Richardson's Battalion*, Lieut.-Col. Charles Richardson; La. Batt'y, Capt. R. Prosper Landry; Va. Batt'y (Moore's), ——; Va. Batt'y (Grandy's), ——. *Pegram's Battalion*, Col. William J. Pegram, Lieut.-Col. Joseph McGraw: S. C. Batt'y, Capt. Thomas E. Gregg; Va. Batt'y, Capt. George M. Cayce; Va. Batt'y, Capt. Thomas Ellett; Va. Batt'y (Brander's), Lieut. James E. Tyler.

ANDERSON'S CORPS, Lieut.-Gen. Richard H. Anderson.

JOHNSON'S DIVISION, Maj.-Gen. Bushrod R. Johnson.

Wise's Brigade, Brig.-Gen. Henry A. Wise: 26th Va., Maj. William K. Perrin; 34th Va., Col. J. Thomas Goode; 46th Va., ——; 59th Va., Col. William B. Tabb. *Wallace's Brigade*, Brig.-Gen. W. H. Wallace: 17th S. C., Capt. E. A. Crawford; 18th S. C., Lieut.-Col. W. B. Allison; 22d S. C., Col. W. G. Burt; 23d S. C., Lieut.-Col. John M. Kinloch; 26th S. C., Maj. C. S. Land; Holcombe S. C. Legion, ——. *Moody's Brigade*, Brig.-Gen. Young M. Moody: 41st Ala., Col. Martin L. Stansel; 43d Ala., Maj. William J. Mims;

⚲ Temporarily attached during the retreat.   ☆ Attached to First Corps April 2d, after death of General Hill.

59th Ala., Maj. Lewis H. Crumpler; 60th Ala., Col. John W. A. Sanford; 23d Ala. Batt'n, Maj. N. Stallworth. *Ransom's Brigade,* Brig.-Gen. Matthew W. Ransom: 24th N. C., ——; 25th N. C., Col. Henry M. Rutledge; 35th N. C., Maj. R. E. Petty; 49th N. C., Maj. Charles Q. Petty; 56th N. C., Col. Paul F. Faison.

ARTILLERY, Col. H. P. Jones.

Blount's Battalion: Ga. Batt'y, Capt. C. W. Slaten; N. C. Batt'y (Cumming's), Lieut. Alexander D. Brown; Va. Batt'y (Miller's), ——; Va. Batt'y (Young's), ——. *Coit's Battalion:* Miss. Batt'y (Bradford's), ——; Va. Batt'y (R. G. Pegram's), ——; Va. Batt'y (Wright's), ——. *Stribling's Battalion:* Va. Batt'y (Dickerson's), ——; Va. Batt'y (Marshall's), Lieut. T. Marshall; Va. Batt'y (Macon's), ——; Va. Batt'y (Sullivan's), Lieut. William S. Archer. *Smith's Battalion,* Capt. William F. Dement: 1st Md. Batt'y, Lieut. John Gale; Va. Batt'y (Johnston's), Lieut. Thomas R. Adams; Va. Batt'y (Neblett's), Lieut. Robert J. Braswell; Va. Batt'y, Capt. John W. Drewry; Va. Batt'y, Capt. Thomas Kevill.

CAVALRY CORPS, Maj.-Gen. Fitzhugh Lee.

FITZHUGH LEE'S DIVISION, Brig.-Gen. Thos. T. Munford.

Munford's Brigade: 1st Va., Col. W. A. Morgan; 2d Va., Lieut.-Col. Cary Breckinridge; 3d Va., ——; 4th Va., Col. W. B. Wooldridge. *Payne's Brigade,* Brig.-Gen. William H. Payne, Col. R. B. Boston; 5th Va., Col. R. B. Boston; 6th Va., ——; 8th Va., ——; 36th Va. Batt'n, ——. *Gary's Brigade,* Brig.-Gen. Martin W. Gary: 7th Ga., Capt. W. H. Burroughs; 7th S. C., Col. Alexander C. Haskell; Hampton's S. C. Legion, Lieut.-Col. Robert B. Arnold; 24th Va., Col. William T. Robins.

W. H. F. LEE'S DIVISION, Maj.-Gen. W. H. F. Lee.

Barringer's Brigade, Brig.-Gen. Rufus Barringer: 1st N. C., ——; 2d N. C., ——; 3d N. C., ——; 5th N. C., ——. *Beale's Brigade,* Capt. S. H. Burt: 9th Va., ——; 10th Va., ——; 13th Va., ——; 14th Va., ——. *Roberts's Brigade,* Brig.-Gen. William P. Roberts: 4th N. C., ——; 16th N. C. Batt'n, ——.

ROSSER'S DIVISION, Maj.-Gen. Thomas L. Rosser.

Dearing's Brigade, Brig.-Gen. James Dearing, Col. A. W. Harman: 7th Va., ——; 11th Va., ——; 12th Va., Col. A. W. Harman; 35th Va. Batt'n, ——. *McCausland's Brigade:* 16th Va., ——; 17th Va., ——; 21st Va., ——; 22d Va., ——.

ARTILLERY, Lieut.-Col. R. B. Chew.

Chew's Battalion: Va. Batt'y (Graham's), ——; Va. Batt'y (McGregor's), ——. *Breathed's Battalion,* Maj. James Breathed: Va. Batt'y (P. P. Johnston's), ——; Va. Battery (Shoemaker's), ——; Va. Batt'y (Thomson's), ——.

G. W. C. LEE'S DIVISION, Maj.-Gen. G. W. Custis Lee. [Composed of Barton's and Crutchfield's brigades, with Tucker's naval battalion attached.]

The following battalions of artillery, borne on Lee's return for January 31st, 1865, are not enumerated in the parole list of April 9th, from which this roster of troops and commanders is mainly compiled, viz.: Cabell's of the First Corps, Nelson's of the Second Corps, Lane's and Eshleman's of the Third Corps, and Sturdivant's of Anderson's Corps. There were also some forces from the defenses of Richmond, known as Ewell's Reserve Corps, commanded by Lieut.-Col. Thomas J. Spencer, which are not embraced in the foregoing list.

The loss of Lee's army in killed and wounded is not known. The number paroled at Appomattox was, of infantry, 22,349; cavalry, 1559; artillery, 2576; and general headquarters and miscellaneous troops, 1747 = 28,231. In his official report of April 12th, 1865, General Lee says: "On the morning of the 9th, according to the reports of the ordnance officers, there were 7892 organized infantry with arms. . . . The artillery [was] reduced to 63 pieces. . . . I have no accurate report of the cavalry, but believe it did not exceed 2100 effective men."

Upon this subject General Grant ("Personal Memoirs," Vol. II., p. 500) remarks: "When Lee finally surrendered . . . there were only 28,356 officers and men left to be paroled, and many of these were without arms. It was probably this latter fact which gave rise to the statement sometimes made, North and South, that Lee surrendered a smaller number of men than what the official figures show. As a matter of official record, and in addition to the number paroled as given above, we captured between March 29th and the date of surrender 19,132 Confederates, to say nothing of Lee's other losses, killed, wounded, and missing, during the series of desperate conflicts which marked his headlong and determined flight." In regard to the statement that, of the troops surrendered, only about 8000 had arms, General Humphreys says: "If, indeed, that is correct, then the greater part of those men who had no arms must have thrown them away when they found that they must surrender. This was not difficult to do unobserved by their officers. The country was thickly wooded and open to them on the west and north-west. A walk of half an hour would bring them to ground that neither their officers nor ours would pass over during their brief stay in the vicinity."

At the end of February, 1865 (according to the inspection reports), the Army of Northern Virginia had 3005 officers and 43,052 men of infantry and cavalry "present effective for the field." The artillery at this time probably numbered 5000, Custis Lee's division in the defenses of Richmond 3000, and Rosser's cavalry (which joined in March) 2000. After making due allowance for losses at Fort Stedman and along the lines up to March 28th, the effective strength of Lee's army at the beginning of the campaign is estimated as follows: cavalry, 5000; artillery, 5000; infantry, 44,000 = 54,000. This does not include local troops and naval forces, of which no data are obtainable.

GRAVES OF UNION SOLDIERS AT CITY POINT. FROM A WAR-TIME PHOTOGRAPH.

FINAL OPERATIONS OF SHERMAN'S ARMY.

BY H. W. SLOCUM, MAJOR-GENERAL, U. S. V.

FROM Bentonville [March 22d, 1865] we marched to Goldsboro', and in two or three days were in camp, busily engaged in preparing for another campaign. We had made the march from Savannah to Goldsboro', a distance of 430 miles, in seven weeks. We had constructed bridges across the Edisto, Broad, Catawba, Pedee, and Cape Fear rivers, and had destroyed all the railroads to the interior of South Carolina. We had subsisted mainly upon the country, and our men and animals were in better condition than when we left Savannah. All this was done in the winter season.

We found Goldsboro' already occupied by our troops, the Twenty-third Corps, under General Schofield, and the Tenth Corps, under General Terry, having captured Wilmington and arrived at Goldsboro' a day or two in advance of us. ‡ The railroad to New Berne was soon put in running order, and supplies of all kinds were pouring in upon us. Soon after we were settled in the vicinity of Goldsboro' General Sherman went to City Point, where he met President Lincoln and Lieutenant-General Grant, and the situation of affairs was discussed by them while on board the *River Queen*, a small steamer lying near the wharf at City Point. Both Grant and Sherman expressed to Mr. Lincoln their firm conviction that the end was near at hand. During the conversation something was said about the disposition to be made of the rebel leaders, particularly Mr. Davis. Sherman made no secret of the fact that he wished to have Davis escape arrest, get out of the country, and thus save our Government all embarrassment as to his case. Mr. Lincoln said that, occupying the position he did, he could not say that he

hoped the leader of the great rebellion, which had brought so much misery upon the land, would escape, but that the situation reminded him of an anecdote. He said a man who had recently taken the temperance pledge was once invited to take a drink of spirits. He said, "No, I can't do it; I will take a glass of lemonade." When the lemonade was prepared, his friend suggested that its flavor would be improved by pouring in a little brandy. The man said, "If you could pour in a little of that stuff unbeknownst to me, I shouldn't get mad about it." If Mr. Davis had escaped from the country "unbeknownst" to Mr. Lincoln, he would not have grieved over it.

General Sherman soon returned, bringing with him an order constituting the left wing a distinct army under the title of the Army of Georgia, and assigning me to command. ↓ The Tenth and Twenty-third corps had already been constituted an army known as the Army of the Ohio, with Schofield as commander.

On April 5th General Sherman issued a confidential order to the army and corps commanders and the chiefs of the staff departments. It stated that the next grand objective was to place his armies north of the Roanoke River, facing west, and in full communication with the Army of the Potomac. Everything was to be in readiness on April 10th, and the movement was to commence on the morning of the 11th. The Army of Georgia was to have the left, the Army of the Ohio the center, and the Army of the Tennessee the right in the movement. The roads to be taken by each command were indicated in the order. We went to bed that night happy in the belief that we were soon to be

---

↕ See page 681 to page 705.—EDITORS.

‡ After the fall of Wilmington, Feb. 22d, 1865, General Schofield sent a column, under General J. D. Cox, to open the railway from New Berne to Goldsboro'. At Kinston (see map, p. 694) Cox encountered, March 8th, Bragg with Hoke's division and a portion of Hood's troops, under D. H. Hill. Fighting took place on the south side of the Neuse, March 8th to 10th. On the night of the 10th Bragg retreated toward Goldsboro', leaving a detachment at Kinston. Schofield occupied Kinston on the 14th, and reached Goldsboro' on the 21st.—EDITORS.

↓ On April 1st, 1865, General Sherman announced the organization of his army to be as follows: Right Wing (Army of the Tennessee), Maj.-Gen. O. O. Howard, commanding. Left Wing (Army of Georgia), Maj.-Gen. H. W. Slocum, commanding. Center (Army of the Ohio), Maj.-Gen. J. M. Schofield, commanding. Cavalry, Brevet Maj.-Gen. Judson Kilpatrick, commanding. Each of these commanders was authorized to exercise the powers prescribed by law for a general commanding a separate department or army in the field.—EDITORS.

in front of Richmond, with our right connecting with the Army of the Potomac, and after having marched through the entire South from Chattanooga, via Atlanta, Savannah, and Columbia, we were to have the honor of taking part in the capture of Lee's army and the capital of the Confederacy. The next day brought us news which dispelled this happy vision. Richmond had fallen, and Lee's army was marching to make a junction with Johnston. The news was received with great joy by the men of Sherman's army. Bonfires, rockets, and a general jubilee kept the inhabitants of Goldsboro' from sleep that night. This event, however, caused Sherman to change his plans. He decided to move direct to Raleigh, hoping to meet Johnston either there or at Smithfield. We commenced our march on the 10th, arrived at Smithfield on the 11th, only to find that General Johnston had retreated to Raleigh. On the 12th, while on the march to Raleigh, some person on horseback came riding up the road crying to the men as he passed, "Grant has captured Lee's army!" Soon after, Sherman's Special Field Orders, No. 54, dated Smithfield, North Carolina, April 12th, 1865, was brought to me and published to the troops. It read as follows:

"The general commanding announces to the army that he has official notice from General Grant that General Lee surrendered to him his entire army, on the 9th inst., at Appomattox Court House, Virginia. Glory to God and to our country, and all honor to our comrades in arms, toward whom we are marching! A little more labor, a little more toil on our part, and the great race is won, and our Government stands regenerated, after four long years of bloody war.

"W. T. SHERMAN, Major-General Commanding."

It is useless to attempt to describe the effect of this news upon the men of Sherman's army. Instead of looking forward to another long campaign through the South in pursuit of the united armies of Lee and Johnston, the vision of every man now turned homeward. Thoughts of meeting wives, children, and friends from whom they had been so long separated by the bloody struggle, occupied the minds of all. A happier body of men never before surrounded their camp-fires than were to be found along the roads leading to Raleigh.

On the 13th we passed through Raleigh and encamped within three or four miles of the city. Kilpatrick's cavalry followed the retreating enemy about twenty-five miles beyond Raleigh and went into camp at Durham Station, on the road toward Hillsboro'. On the 14th Sherman ordered

his army to move, with a view of preventing the retreat of Johnston in the direction of Salisbury and Charlotte. In this order, he said that in the hope of an early reconciliation no further destruction of railroads or private property would be permitted. We were authorized to take from the people forage and other necessary supplies, but were cautioned against stripping the poorer classes. On the morning of the day that this movement was to commence, General Sherman received from General Johnston a message requesting a cessation of hostilities with a view of negotiating terms of surrender. Sherman sent a reply at once, and arrangements were made for a personal interview on the 17th between the two commanders, at a point midway between our advance and the position held by the enemy.

As Sherman was entering a car on the morning of the 17th to attend this meeting, the telegraph operator stopped him and requested him to wait a few minutes, as he was just receiving an important dispatch, which he ought to see before he left. The dispatch was from Mr. Stanton announcing the assassination of Mr. Lincoln, and the attempt on the life of Mr. Seward and his son. ♭ General Sherman asked the operator if he had divulged the contents of the dispatch to any one, and being answered in the negative, he ordered him to keep it a secret until his return. Sherman and his staff met Johnston and Wade Hampton with a number of staff-officers at the house of Mrs. Bennett. None of the Confederate officers had heard of the assassination of Lincoln, and Sherman first made the fact known to them. They were much affected by the news, and apparently regretted it as much as did our own officers. In conversing as to the terms of surrender, Johnston suggested that they should be such as to embrace not only his army, but the armies under Dick Taylor and Kirby Smith in the Gulf States, and those under Maury, Forrest, and others. Sherman questioned Johnston's authority to negotiate the surrender of the other armies, and Johnston assured him that he could soon obtain the authority. A meeting was arranged for the following day.

Sherman returned to Raleigh and issued an order announcing the assassination of President Lincoln, which was published to the troops on the following morning. The men appreciated the generosity and nobleness of Mr. Lincoln's nature. The fact that he had carried us successfully through the great struggle caused them to feel toward him an attachment which the soldier always feels toward a great and successful leader. The startling

♭ On Sunday, April 9th, President Lincoln reached Washington on his return from his visit to the field of operations on the James, having left Richmond on the 6th. (See p. 727.) On the night of Friday, the 14th, the President visited Ford's Theatre, where he was shot by John Wilkes Booth. The next morning about 7 o'clock Mr. Lincoln died. Booth escaped from the city, and, guided by some confederates, crossed the Potomac near Port Tobacco, Maryland, to Mathias Point, Virginia (see map, p. 84), on Saturday night, April 22d. On Monday, the 24th, he crossed the Rappahannock from Port Conway to Port Royal and took refuge in a barn, where he was found on Wednesday, the 26th, by a detachment of Company L, 16th New York Cavalry, and killed. The

assassination of the President was the result of a conspiracy. Mr. Seward, the Secretary of State, was also attacked on the evening of April 14th by Lewis Payne, a fellow-conspirator, and was severely injured. The following persons were tried before a military commission convened at Washington, May 9th, 1865, on the charge of conspiracy to assassinate the President and other high officers of the Government: David E. Herold, G. A. Atzerodt, Lewis Payne, Michael O'Laughlin, Edward Spangler, Samuel Arnold, Mary E. Surratt, and Doctor Samuel A. Mudd. Herold, Atzerodt, Payne, and Mrs. Surratt were hanged; O'Laughlin, Arnold, and Mudd were imprisoned for life, and Spangler was imprisoned for six years.— EDITORS.

news of his death was received with gloom and sadness.

On the following day General Sherman met General Johnston and negotiated with him a conditional treaty for the surrender of all the Confederates then under arms. ⸙ The condition was that it should first be approved by the President. Pending these negotiations, and after the proposed terms had been made known to the leading officers of Sherman's army, I conversed with nearly all these officers, among them Logan, Howard, and Blair, and heard no word of dissent from any of them. I can now recall to mind but one general officer who, at the time, questioned the wisdom of General Sherman's action, and that was General Carl Schurz. General Schurz was then serving temporarily as my chief-of-staff, and when I returned from Sherman's headquarters about 12 o'clock on the night of the 18th I found General Schurz sitting up, waiting for me. He was eager to learn the terms, and when I stated them to him he expressed regret and predicted just what

⸙ Following is the text of the conditional treaty of April 18th:

"Memorandum, or Basis of Agreement, made this 18th day of April, A. D. 1865, near Durham's Station, in the State of North Carolina, by and between General Joseph E. Johnston, commanding the Confederate Army, and Major-General William T. Sherman, commanding the Army of the United States in North Carolina, both present:

"1. The contending armies now in the field to maintain the *status quo* until notice is given by the commanding general of any one to its opponent, and reasonable time—say forty-eight hours—allowed.

"2. The Confederate armies now in existence to be disbanded and conducted to their several State capitals, there to deposit their arms and public property in the State arsenal; and each officer and man to execute and file an agreement to cease from acts of war, and to abide the action of the State and Federal authority. The number of arms and munitions of war to be reported to the Chief of Ordnance at Washington City, subject to the future action of the Congress of the United States, and, in the meantime, to be used solely to maintain peace and order within the borders of the States respectively.

"3. The recognition by the Executive of the United States of the several State governments on their officers and legislatures taking the oaths prescribed by the Constitution of the United States, and where conflicting State governments have resulted from the war the legitimacy of all shall be submitted to the Supreme Court of the United States.

"4. The reëstablishment of all the Federal courts in the several States, with powers as defined by the Constitution of the United States and of the States respectively.

"5. The people and inhabitants of all the States to be guaranteed, so far as the Executive can, their political rights and franchises, as well as their rights of person and property, as defined by the Constitution of the United States and of the States respectively.

"6. The Executive authority of the Government of the United States not to disturb any of the people by reason of the late war, so long as they live in peace and quiet, abstain from acts of armed hostility, and obey the laws in existence at the place of their residence.

"7. In general terms—the war to cease; a general amnesty, so far as the Executive of the United States can command, on condition of the disbandment of the Confederate armies, the distribution of the arms, and the resumption of peaceful pursuits by the officers and men hitherto composing

⸙ On the 2d of March, 1865, General R. E. Lee addressed a letter to General Grant suggesting a meeting between them to arrange "to submit the subjects of controversy between the belligerents to a convention," etc. General Lee's letter was forwarded to the Secretary of War, and on the 4th of March the following was received in reply: "[Cipher.] OFFICE UNITED STATES MILITARY TELEGRAPH, HEADQUARTERS ARMIES OF THE UNITED STATES. Lieutenant-General GRANT: The President directs me to say to you that he

subsequently happened. He said the public mind of the North would be inflamed by the assassination of Lincoln, and now that the armies of the Confederacy were virtually crushed, anything looking toward leniency would not be well received. The terms were not approved by President Johnson, and General Grant came to Raleigh. ☆

His meeting with Sherman was a friendly one. He laid before Sherman a letter of instructions which he had received from Mr. Lincoln some time before the fall of Richmond, prohibiting him from embracing, in any negotiations he might have with General Lee, anything of a political nature. Had a copy of this letter been furnished General Sherman, his treaty with Johnston would not have been made. Sherman and all his officers were exceedingly anxious to prevent the Confederate armies from breaking up into guerrilla bands and roaming through the South, keeping the country in a disturbed condition for months, and perhaps for years. There never was the slightest justification for the criticisms that were showered upon him

said armies. Not being fully empowered by our respective principals to fulfill these terms, we individually and officially pledge ourselves to promptly obtain the necessary authority, and to carry out the above programme.

"W. T. SHERMAN, Major-General,
"Commanding Army of the United States
"in North Carolina.

"J. E. JOHNSTON, General,
"Commanding Confederate States Army
"in North Carolina."

☆ A copy of the memorandum of the 18th was sent to General Grant on the 20th. On the 24th Grant reached Sherman's headquarters, bringing the announcement of the Secretary of War that the negotiations were disapproved by President Johnson. Grant's own reply to Sherman was delivered at the same time as follows: "HEADQUARTERS, ARMIES OF THE UNITED STATES, WASHINGTON, D. C., April 21, 1865. Major-General W. T. SHERMAN, commanding Military Division of the Mississippi. GENERAL: The basis of agreement entered into between yourself and General J. E. Johnston, for the disbandment of the Southern army, and the extension of the authority of the General Government over all the territory belonging to it, sent for the approval of the President, is received. I read it carefully myself before submitting it to the President and Secretary of War, and felt satisfied that it could not possibly be approved. My reason for these views I will give you at another time, in a more extended letter.

"Your agreement touches upon questions of such vital importance that, as soon as read, I addressed a note to the Secretary of War, notifying him of their receipt, and the importance of immediate action by the President; and suggested, in view of their importance, that the entire Cabinet be called together, that all might give an expression of their opinions upon the matter. The result was a disapproval by the President of the basis laid down; a disapproval of the negotiations altogether—except for the surrender of the army commanded by General Johnston, and directions to me to notify you of this decision. I cannot do no better than by sending you the inclosed copy of a dispatch (penned by the late President, though signed by the Secretary of War) ⸾ in answer

wishes you to have no conference with General Lee, unless it be for the capitulation of Lee's army or on solely minor and purely military matters. He instructs me to say that you are not to decide, discuss, or confer upon any political question; such questions the President holds in his own hands, and will submit them to no military conferences or conventions. Meantime you are to press to the utmost your military advantages. EDWIN M. STANTON, Secretary of War."— EDITORS.

for his course in this matter. On the 26th of April General Johnston surrendered his army upon the same terms that General Lee had received. ⚓

During our stay in Raleigh I witnessed a scene which to me was one of the most impressive of the war. It was the review by General Sherman of a division of colored troops. These troops passed through the principal streets of the city. They were well drilled, dressed in new and handsome uniforms, and with their bright bayonets gleaming in the sun they made a splendid appearance. The sides of the streets were lined with residents of the city and the surrounding country,—many of them, I presume, the former owners of some of these soldiers.

Soon after the surrender, orders were issued for the right and left wings to march to Washington via Richmond. On the evening before we left Raleigh the mails from the North arrived, and with them a large number of New York papers. On the following day, when we were about five miles from the city, my attention was called to a group of soldiers standing around a cart under which they had built a fire. The cart and its contents were being burned, while a young man in citizen's dress, with the mule that had been taken from the cart, was looking on. I sent a staff-officer to learn the meaning of it. He soon returned to me and said that a soldier, who seemed to be the leader of the party, said, "Tell General Slocum that cart is loaded with New York papers for sale to the soldiers. These papers are filled with the vilest abuse of General Sherman. We have followed Sherman through a score of battles and through nearly two thousand miles of the enemy's country, and we do not intend to allow these vile slanders against him to be circulated among his men." This was the last property that I saw destroyed by the men of Sherman's army, and I witnessed the scene with keener satisfaction than I had felt over the destruction of any property since the day we left Atlanta.

A march of three or four days brought us in sight of Richmond. There were men in the Twentieth Corps who had been near enough to that city, on a former occasion, to enable them to see the spires of her churches. Some had been in the first Bull Run, many more in the Seven Days' battles about Richmond, nearly all of them had been at Chancellorsville, Antietam, and Gettysburg. After the repulse at Chickamauga they had been detached from the Army of the Potomac and sent by rail with all possible speed to Nashville. Thence they had marched via Chattanooga, Atlanta, Savannah, Columbia, and Raleigh to the point which, during the first two years of the war, they had struggled so hard to reach by approaching it from the north side. They had swung around the circle,—the largest circle ever swung around by an army corps.

After resting a few days near Richmond we

to me, on sending a letter received from General Lee, proposing to meet me for the purpose of submitting the question of peace to a convention of officers. Please notify General Johnston, immediately on receipt of this, of the termination of the truce, and resume hostilities against his army at the earliest moment you can, acting in good faith. Very respectfully, your obedient servant, U. S. GRANT, Lieutenant-General."

⚓ General Grant advised General Sherman to accept Johnston's surrender on the same terms as those made with Lee. The meeting of Johnston and Sherman took place on the 26th, and the following was agreed upon and approved by General Grant :

"Terms of a Military Convention, entered into this 26th day of April, 1865, at Bennett's House, near Durham's Station, North Carolina, between General Joseph E. Johnston, commanding the Confederate Army, and Major-General W. T. Sherman, commanding the United States Army in North Carolina :

"1. All acts of war on the part of the troops under General Johnston's command to cease from this date.

"2. All arms and public property to be deposited at Greensboro', and delivered to an ordnance officer of the United States Army.

"3. Rolls of all the officers and men to be made in duplicate ; one copy to be retained by the commander of the troops, and the other to be given to officer to officer to be designated by General Sherman. Each officer and man to give his individual obligation in writing not to take up arms against the Government of the United States until properly released from this obligation.

"4. The side-arms of officers, and their private horses and baggage, to be retained by them.

"5. This being done, all the officers and men will be permitted to return to their homes, not to be disturbed by the United States authorities, so long as they observe their obligation and the laws in force where they may reside.
 "W. T. SHERMAN, Major-General,
 "Commanding United States Forces in North Carolina.
 "J. E. JOHNSTON, General,
 "Commanding Confederate Forces in North Carolina.
 "Approved: U. S. GRANT, Lieutenant-General."

"SUPPLEMENTAL TERMS.

"1. The field transportation to be loaned to the troops for their march to their homes, and for subsequent use in their industrial pursuits. Artillery horses may be used in field transportation if necessary.

"2. Each brigade or separate body to retain a number of arms equal to one-seventh of its effective strength, which, when the troops reach the capitals of their States, will be disposed of as the general commanding the department may direct.

"3. Private horses, and other private property of both officers and men, to be retained by them.

"4. The commanding general of the Military Division of West Mississippi, Major-General Canby, will be requested to give transportation by water from Mobile or New Orleans to the troops from Arkansas and Texas.

"5. The obligations of officers and soldiers to be signed by their immediate commanders.

"6. Naval forces within the limits of General Johnston's command to be included in the terms of this convention.
 "J. M. SCHOFIELD, Major-General,
 "Commanding United States Forces in North Carolina.
 "J. E. JOHNSTON, General,
 "Commanding Confederate Forces in North Carolina."

On leaving his army, General Johnston issued the following farewell order :

"COMRADES : In terminating our official relations, I earnestly exhort you to observe faithfully the terms of pacification agreed upon, and to discharge the obligations of good and peaceful citizens as well as you have performed the duties of thorough soldiers in the field. By such a course you will best secure the comfort of your families and kindred, and restore tranquillity to our country.

"You will return to your homes with the admiration of our people, won by the courage and noble devotion you have displayed in this long war. I shall always remember with pride the loyal support and generous confidence you have given me.

"I now part with you with deep regret, and bid you farewell with feelings of cordial friendship, and with earnest wishes that you may have hereafter all the prosperity and happiness to be found in the world.
 "Official. J. E. JOHNSTON, General.
 "KINLOCH FALCONER, A. A.-G."

started for Washington over the battle-scarred route so familiar to the men who had fought under McDowell, McClellan, and subsequently under Grant, as well as to those who had served under Lee. The weather was pleasant and the march full of interest. On some of the fields where great battles had been fought we found the bodies of many Union soldiers lying unburied, apparently just as they had fallen on the field. Parties were detailed to bury the dead, and subsequently a party was sent from Washington to complete the work.

We went into camp in the vicinity of Alexandria, my own headquarters being very near the place I had occupied during the first winter of the war, when McClellan was organizing the Army of the Potomac. We were soon informed that the final scene of the war was to be a grand review of all the troops by the President and his Cabinet. All the foreign ministers resident in Washington, the governors of the States, and many other distinguished people had been invited to be present. The Eastern troops were to be reviewed on the 23d of May, and the Western on the day following. The leading officers of Sherman's command were invited to the stand to witness the review of the Army of the Potomac, and they gladly accepted the invitation. After the close of the review of that army, several of our officers assembled at Sherman's headquarters to discuss matters and prepare for the work to be done next day. In speaking of the review of the Army of the Potomac Sherman said : "It was magnificent. In dress, in soldierly appearance, in precision of alignment and marching we cannot beat those fellows." All present assented to this statement. Some one then suggested that we should not make the attempt, but should pass in review "as we went marching through Georgia"; that the for-

agers, familiarly known among us as "bummers," should form part of the column. This suggestion seemed to strike General Sherman favorably, and instructions were issued to carry it into effect. Early on the following morning the head of our column started up Pennsylvania Avenue and soon passed the reviewing stand, which was filled with distinguished people from all parts of the country. Sherman's men certainly presented a very soldierly appearance. They were proud of their achievements, and had the swing of men who had marched through half a dozen States. But the feature of the column which seemed to interest the spectators most was the attachments of foragers in rear of each brigade. At the review the men appeared "in their native ugliness" as they appeared on the march through Georgia and the Carolinas. Their pack-mules and horses, with rope bridles or halters, laden with supplies such as they had carried on the march, formed part of the column. It was a new feature in a grand review, but one which the who witnessed it will never forget.

Soon after the review the troops were ordered into various camps, where the paymaster paid them his last visit, and then they separated, never again to meet in large bodies, except on Memorial Day, the 30th of May, of each year, ↓ when they meet to honor the memory of comrades who gave their lives for their country, and at annual reunions of regimental associations, when they assemble to renew the ties of comradeship ♭ formed during the struggle of more than four years' duration, which cost us hundreds of thousands of lives and thousands of millions of treasure, but which has conferred, even upon the defeated South, blessings that more than compensate the country for all her losses.

↓ Confederate Memorial Services are usually held at different dates in April and May. In some localities veterans of both sides participate in all memorial ceremonies. Of late years reunions of Union and Confederate veterans on battle-fields have become frequent.— EDITORS.

♭ The Grand Army of the Republic, dating from 1866, numbering in 1888 over 350,000 members, is the largest veteran association in the country. Its membership is restricted to soldiers and sailors of the Union army and navy, who served during the Civil War, whether honorably discharged or still in service. The Military Order

of the Loyal Legion of the United States, numbering in 1888 about 6000 members (commissioned officers of the Union army and navy), was organized in 1865 to perpetuate the memories of the war. There are also numerous Union veteran associations, either fraternal or provident, or both; among them a national body of Naval Veterans, the societies of the Army of the Potomac, the Army of the Cumberland, the Army of the Tennessee, the Army of the Ohio, and societies of the several army corps, forming parts of the societies of the main armies.— EDITORS.

GRAND REVIEWING STAND IN FRONT OF THE WHITE HOUSE, WASHINGTON, MAY 23-24, 1865. FROM A PHOTOGRAPH.

THE UNION FORCES. *Cavalry Corps*, Military Division of the Mississippi.—Brevet Maj.-Gen. James H. Wilson.

Escort: 4th U. S., Lieut. William O'Connell.

FIRST DIVISION, Brig.-Gen. Edward M. McCook; (after April 20th) Brig.-Gen. John T. Croxton.

First Brigade, Brig.-Gen. John T. Croxton: 8th Iowa, Col. Joseph B. Dorr; 4th Ky. (M't'd Inf'y), Col. Robert M. Kelly; 6th Ky., Maj. William H. Fidler; 2d Mich., Lieut.-Col. Thomas W. Johnston. *Second Brigade*, Col. Oscar H. La Grange: 2d Ind. (battalion), Capt. Roswell S. Hill (w), Capt. Joseph B. Williams; 4th Ind., Lieut.-Col. Horace P. Lamson; 4th Ky., Col. Wickliffe Cooper; 7th Ky., Lieut.-Col. William W. Bradley (w), Maj. Andrew S. Bloom; 1st Wis., Lieut.-Col. Henry Harnden (w). *Artillery:* 18th Ind. Batt'y, Capt. Moses M. Beck.

SECOND DIVISION, Brig.-Gen. Eli Long (w), Col. Robert H. G. Minty.

First Brigade (mounted infantry), Col. Abram O. Miller (w), Col. Jacob G. Vail: 98th Ill., Lieut.-Col. Edward Kitchell; 123d Ill., Lieut.-Col. Jonathan Biggs (w), Capt.Owen Wiley; 17th Ind., Col. Jacob G. Vail, Lieut.-Col. Frank White; 72d Ind., Lieut.-Col. Chester G. Thomson. *Second Brigade*, Col. Robert H. G. Minty, Lieut.-Col. Horace N. Howland: 4th Mich., Lieut.-Col. Benjamin D. Pritchard; 3d Ohio, Lieut.-Col. Horace N. Howland, Maj. Darius E. Livermore; 4th Ohio, Lieut.-Col. George W. Dobb (k), Capt. William W. Shoemaker; 7th Pa., Col. Charles C. McCormick (w), Lieut.-Col. James F. Andress. *Artillery:*

Chicago Board of Trade Battery, Capt. George I. Robinson.

FOURTH DIVISION, Brig.-Gen. Emory Upton; (after April 20th) Brevet Brig.-Gen. Edward F. Winslow.

First Brigade, Col. Edward F. Winslow: 3d Iowa, Col. John W. Noble; 4th Iowa, Lieut.-Col. John H. Peters; 10th Mo., Lieut.-Col. Frederick W. Benteen. *Second Brigade*, Brevet Brig.-Gen. A. J. Alexander: 5th Iowa, Col. J. Morris Young; 1st Ohio, Col. Beroth B. Eggleston; 7th Ohio, Col. Israel Garrard. *Artillery:* I, 1st U. S., Lieut. George B. Rodney. The effective strength of the foregoing commands was about 13,000. The loss in action aggregated 99 killed, 598 wounded, and 28 missing = 725.

THE CONFEDERATE FORCES. *Cavalry Corps*, Department of Alabama, Mississippi, and East Louisiana.— Lieut.-Gen. N. B. Forrest.

CHALMERS'S DIVISION, Brig.-Gen. James R. Chalmers. (Composed of the brigades of Brig.-Gens. Frank C. Armstrong, Wirt Adams, and Peter B. Starke.)

JACKSON'S DIVISION, Brig.-Gen. William H. Jackson. (Composed of the brigades of Brig.-Gens. Tyree H. Bell and Lawrence W. Campbell.)

RODDEY'S BRIGADE, Brig.-Gen. Philip D. Roddey.

CROSSLAND'S BRIGADE, Col. Ed. Crossland.

There were also some militia and other forces under Major-Generals Howell Cobb and G. W. Smith, and Brigadier-Generals Felix H. Robertson, Daniel W. Adams, and R. C. Tyler and others.

WILSON'S RAID THROUGH ALABAMA AND GEORGIA. |

IN the spring of 1865 the cavalry corps commanded by General James H. Wilson was encamped at Gravelly Springs and Waterloo, Alabama [see map, p. 414], on the north bank of the Tennessee, with a base of supplies at Eastport, Mississippi. The following condensation of General Wilson's report of June 29th, 1865, summarizes the final operations of his corps:

"On the 23d of February [1865] General Thomas arrived at Eastport with instructions directing me to fit out an expedition of five or six thousand cavalry for the purpose of making a demonstration upon Tuscaloosa and Selma in favor of General Canby's operations against Mobile and Central Alabama. [See p. 411.] . . . The instructions of Lieutenant-General Grant, transmitted to me by General Thomas, allowed me the amplest discretion as an independent commander."

The movement was delayed nearly three weeks by heavy rains, and on the 18th of March the command crossed the Tennessee.

"At daylight on the 22d of March . . . the movement began. The entire valley of the Tennessee, having been devastated by two years of warfare, was quite as destitute of army supplies as the hill country south of it. It was therefore necessary to scatter the troops over a wide extent of country, and march as rapidly as circumstances would permit. This was rendered safe by the fact that Forrest's forces were at that time near West Point, Mississippi, 150 miles south-west of Eastport, while Roddey's occupied Montevallo, on the Alabama and Tennessee River railroad, nearly the same distance to the south-east. By starting on diverging roads the enemy was left in doubt as to our real object, and compelled to watch equally Columbus, Tuscaloosa, and Selma."

The command moved southward in three columns [see map, p. 414], General Emory Upton's division by Barton's Station, Russellville, and Mount Hope to Jasper, near the Black Warrior River; General Eli Long's, by Cherokee Station, Frankfort,

and Thorn Hill to the same point; while General Edward M. McCook's, following Long's route as far as Bear Creek, continued southward to Eldridge, thence moving east to Jasper. From Jasper the whole command moved across the two forks of the Black Warrior and were directed on Montevallo via Elyton.

"At Elyton, on the evening of the 30th, I directed General McCook to detach Croxton's brigade, with orders to move on Tuscaloosa as rapidly as possible, burn the public stores, military school, bridges, foundries, and factories at that place, return toward the main column by way of the Centreville road, and rejoin it at or in the vicinity of Selma. Besides covering our trains and inflicting a heavy blow upon the enemy, I hoped by this detachment to develop any movement on his part intended to intercept my main column."

While in the vicinity of Elyton, Upton's division destroyed the Cahawba Iron Works, including rolling-mills and collieries. After passing Montevallo, March 31st, Upton met a force under General P. D. Roddey disputing the road to Randolph. Two engagements ensued, and Roddey was driven back.

"At Randolph General Upton captured a rebel courier just from Centreville, and from his person took two dispatches, one from Brigadier-General W. H. Jackson, commanding one of Forrest's divisions, and the other from Major Anderson, Forrest's chief-of-staff. From the first I learned that Forrest with a part of his command was in my front (this had also been obtained from prisoners); that Jackson with his division and all the wagons and artillery of the rebel cavalry, marching from Tuscaloosa via Trion toward Centreville, had encamped the night before at Hill's plantation, three miles beyond Scottsboro'; that Croxton [Union], with the brigade detached at Elyton, had struck Jackson's rear-guard at Trion and interposed himself between it and the train; that Jackson had discovered this, and intended to attack Croxton at daylight of April 1st. I learned from the other dispatch that Chalmers had also arrived at Marion, Alabama, and had been ordered to cross to the east side

| See General James H. Wilson's article, "The Union Cavalry in the Hood Campaign," p. 465.— EDITORS.

of the Cahawba near that place for the purpose of joining Forrest in my front, or in the works at Selma. I also learned that a force of dismounted men was stationed at Centreville, with orders to hold the bridge over the Cahawba at that place as long as possible, and in no event to let it fall into our hands."

Wilson now pushed on toward Selma, encountering several detachments of Forrest's cavalry on the way. At Ebenezer Church, Forrest's right wing was found in position, covering the roads from Randolph and Old Maplesville, with a force estimated by General Wilson at five thousand. ⚓ Long's division advanced to the attack, and, reënforced by Alexander's brigade, of Upton's division, carried the position, the report says, "in less than an hour," the enemy retreating toward Selma.

"The whole corps bivouacked at sundown about Plantersville, nineteen miles from Selma. With almost constant fighting the enemy had been driven since morning twenty-four miles. At daylight of the 2d [of April] Long's division took the advance, closely followed by Upton's. Having obtained a well-drawn sketch and complete description of the defenses of Selma, I directed General Long, marching by the flanks of brigades, to approach the city and cross to the Summerville [Summerfield] road without exposing his men, and to develop his line as soon as he should arrive in front of the works. General Upton was directed to move on the Range Line road, sending a squadron on the Burnsville road. Lieutenant [Joseph] Rendlebrock, with a battalion of the 4th United States Cavalry, was instructed to move down the railroad, burning bridges, stations, and trestle-works as far as Burnsville. By rapid marching, without opposition, the troops were all in sight of the town, and mostly in position, by 4 P. M."

General McCook had been detached at Randolph to guard the right rear and, if possible, connect with Croxton, who was still west of the Cahawba. Long and Upton, with their men dismounted, carried the works at a single charge.

"The fortifications assaulted and carried consisted of a bastioned line, on a radius of nearly three miles, extending from the Alabama River below to the same above the city. The part west of the city is covered by a miry, deep, and almost impassable creek; that on the east side by a swamp extending from the river almost to the Summerfield road, and entirely impracticable for mounted men at all times. General Upton ascertained by a personal reconnoissance that dismounted men might with great difficulty work through it on the left of the Range Line road. The profile of that part of the line assaulted is as follows: Height of parapet, six to eight feet, thickness eight feet, depth of ditch five feet, width from ten to fifteen feet; height of stockade on the glacis, five feet, sunk into the earth four feet. The ground over which the troops advanced is an open field, generally level, sloping slightly toward the works, but intersected by one ravine and marshy soil, which both the right and left of Long's line experienced some difficulty in crossing. The distance which the troops charged, exposed to the enemy's fire of artillery and musketry, was six hundred yards. . . . General Long's report . . . states that the number actually engaged in the charge was 1550 officers and men. The portion of the line assaulted was manned by Armstrong's brigade, regarded as the best in Forrest's corps, and reported by him at more than 1500 men. The loss from Long's division was 40 killed, 260 wounded, and seven missing. General Long was wounded in the head, Colonels [A. O.] Miller and [C. C.] McCormick in the leg, and [Lieutenant] Colonel [Jonathan] Briggs in the breast. . . . The immediate fruits of our victory were 31 field-guns and one 30-pounder Parrott, which had been used against us; 2700 prisoners,

including 150 officers; a number of colors, and immense quantities of stores of every kind. Generals Forrest, Armstrong, Roddey, and Adams escaped, with a number of men, under cover of darkness, either by the Burnsville and River roads, or by swimming the Alabama River. A portion of Upton's division pursued on the Burnsville road until long after midnight, capturing four guns and many prisoners. I estimate the entire garrison, including the militia of the city and surrounding country, at 7000 men; the entire force under my command, engaged and in supporting distance, was 9000 men and eight guns."

General Upton's division was dispatched from Selma, on April 3d, to open communications with McCook and Croxton, west of the Cahawba. McCook had found the Confederate Jackson between him and Croxton, and had returned east of the Cahawba. He reached Selma in company with Upton on the 6th. Nothing was learned of Croxton.

"On the 6th of April, having ordered Major Hubbard to lay a bridge over the Alabama with the utmost dispatch, I went to Cahawba to see General Forrest, who had agreed to meet me there under a flag of truce for the purpose of arranging an exchange of prisoners. I was not long in discovering that I need not expect liberality in this matter, and that Forrest hoped to recapture the men of his command in my possession. During our conversation he informed me that Croxton had had an engagement with Wirt Adams near Bridgeville, 40 miles south-west of Tuscaloosa, two days before. Thus assured of Croxton's success and safety, I determined to lose no further time in crossing to the south side of the Alabama. I had also satisfied myself in the meantime that Canby had an ample force to take Mobile and march to central Alabama."

On the 8th and 9th the entire cavalry corps, excepting Croxton's brigade, crossed the Alabama, and General Wilson, believing that he had rendered Selma valueless by his thorough destruction of railroads and supplies, determined to march into Georgia by way of Montgomery. The mayor of Montgomery surrendered the city to Wilson's advance guard on the 12th of April. After destroying large quantities of stores, small-arms, and cotton, the command moved on the 14th, Upton in advance and striking for Columbus and West Point.

"About 2 P. M. of the 16th General Upton's advance, a part of Alexander's brigade, struck the enemy's pickets on the road and drove them rapidly through Girard to the lower bridge over the Chattahoochee at Columbus. The rebels hastily set fire to it, and thereby prevented its capture. After securing a position on the lower Montgomery road, General Upton detached a force to push around to the bridge at the Factory, three miles above the city. He then made a reconnoissance in person, and found the enemy strongly posted in a line of works covering all the bridges, with a large number of guns in position on both sides of the river. He had already determined to move Winslow's brigade to the Opelika or Summerville road, and assault the works on that side without waiting for the arrival of the Second Division. I reached the head of Winslow's brigade of the Fourth Division at 4 o'clock, and found the troops marching to the position assigned them by General Upton. Through an accident, Winslow did not arrive at his position till after dark; but General Upton proposed to make the assault in the night, and, coinciding with him in judgment, I ordered the attack. Three hundred men of the 3d Iowa Cavalry, Colonel Noble commanding, were dismounted, and after a slight skirmish moved forward and formed across the road under a heavy fire of artillery. The 4th Iowa and 10th Missouri were held in

⚓ General Thomas Jordan, in "Campaigns of Forrest's Cavalry," states that the Confederate force at Ebenezer Church numbered 1500.—EDITORS.

readiness to support the assaulting party. At half-past eight P. M., just as the troops were ready, the enemy, at a short distance, opened a heavy fire of musketry, and with a four gun battery began throwing canister and grape. Generals Upton and Winslow, in person, directed the movement; the troops dashed forward, opened a withering fire from their Spencers, pushed through a slashing abatis, pressed the rebel line back to their outworks, supposed at first to be the main line. During all this time the rebel guns threw out a perfect storm of canister and grape, but without avail. General Upton sent two companies of the 10th Missouri, Captain [R. B.] McGlasson commanding, to follow up the success of the dismounted men and get possession of the bridge. They passed through the inner line of works, and under cover of darkness, before the rebels knew it, had reached the bridge leading into Columbus. As soon as everything could be got up to the position occupied by the dismounted men, General Upton pressed forward again, swept away all opposition, took possession of the foot and railroad bridges, and stationed guards throughout the city. Twelve hundred prisoners, fifty-two field-guns, in position for use against us, large quantities of arms and stores, fell into our hands. . . . The splendid gallantry and steadiness of General Upton, Brevet Brigadier-General Winslow, and all the officers and men engaged in this night attack, is worthy of the highest commendation. The rebel force was over three thousand. They could not believe they had been dislodged from their strong fortifications by an attack of 300 men. General Winslow was assigned to the command of the city." ↓

The brigade of Colonel O. H. La Grange moved toward West Point.

"After much sharp skirmishing and hard marching, which resulted in the capture of fourteen wagons and a number of prisoners, La Grange's advance reached the vicinity of West Point at 10 A. M., April 16th. With [Captain M. M.] Beck's 18th Indiana Battery, the 2d and 4th Indiana cavalry, the enemy were kept occupied till the arrival of the balance of the brigade. Having thoroughly reconnoitered the ground, detachments of the 1st Wisconsin, 2d Indiana, and 7th Kentucky cavalry dismounted and prepared to assault Fort Tyler, covering the bridge. Colonel La Grange describes it as a remarkably strong bastioned earth-work, 35 yards square, surrounded by a ditch 12 feet wide and 10 feet deep, situated on a commanding eminence, protected by an imperfect abatis, and mounting two 32-pounders and two field-guns."

The fort was taken after a desperate fight, in which La Grange's men bridged the ditch, under fire. The Confederate commander, General R. C. Tyler, was killed. ♭ After destroying the bridges, railway equipment and stores, La Grange moved toward Macon.

"Before leaving Columbus General [Edward F.] Winslow destroyed the rebel ram *Jackson*, nearly ready for sea, mounting six 7-inch guns, burned 15 locomotives, 250 cars, the railroad bridge and foot bridges, 115,000 bales of cotton, four cotton factories, the navy yard, foundry, armory, sword and pistol factory, accouterment shops, three paper mills, over 100,000 rounds of artillery ammunition, besides immense stores of which no account could be taken. The rebels abandoned and burned the gun-boat *Chattahoochee* twelve miles below Columbus."

↓ At Columbus the Union loss was 6 killed and 24 wounded; the Confederate, 1200 captured.— EDITORS.

♭ The Union loss was 7 killed and 29 wounded; the Confederate, 19 killed, 28 wounded, and 218 missing.—EDITORS.

⚲ General Croxton says in his official report:

"During this time we marched 653 miles, most of the time through a mountainous country so destitute of supplies that the command could be subsisted and foraged only by the greatest efforts. Swimming four rivers, destroying five large

On the 18th the command was on the march to Macon, the Second Division, under General R. H. G. Minty, who had succeeded General Long (wounded at Selma), having the advance. On nearing Macon, April 20th, Wilson received a communication from General Beauregard, dated April 19th, informing him of the truce between Johnston and Sherman. [See p. 755.] The advance had already dashed into the city and received the surrender, and Generals Gustavus W. Smith, Howell Cobb, and W. W. Mackall, of the garrison, were held as prisoners of war. On the 21st a communication from General Sherman reached Wilson directing him to suspend hostilities until notified of the result of the negotiations then pending. General Croxton reported at Macon with his brigade, on May 1st. ⚲ His operations since his separation from the main column, at Elyton, March 30th, covered a skirmish at Trion, Alabama, April 2d; the capture of Tuscaloosa, April 5th, and the destruction of the Military School, together with military stores and public works, at that place. From Tuscaloosa he had returned northward as far as Jasper, recrossed the Black Warrior, and, after destroying the iron works and factories along the route, reached Carrollton, Georgia, on the 25th of April, and soon opened communications with Wilson.

"On the 13th of April I received notice of the final capitulation of the rebel forces east of the Chattahoochee, and the next day, by the hands of Colonel [F. B.] Woodall, the order of the Secretary of War annulling the first armistice, directing a resumption of hostilities and the capture of the rebel chiefs. I had been previously advised of [Jefferson] Davis's movements, and had given the necessary instructions to secure a clue to the route he intended following, with the hope of finally effecting his capture. I directed General Upton to proceed in person to Augusta, and ordered General Winslow, with the Fourth Division, to march to Atlanta for the purpose of carrying out the terms of the convention, as well as to make such a disposition of his forces, covering the country northward from Forsyth to Marietta, so as to secure the arrest of Jefferson Davis and party. I directed General Croxton, [then] commanding the First Division, to distribute it along the line of the Ocmulgee, connecting with the Fourth Division and extending southward to this place. Colonel Minty, commanding the Second Division, was directed to extend his troops along the line of the Ocmulgee and Altamaha rivers as far as Jacksonville. General McCook, with about five hundred men of his division, was sent to Tallahassee, Florida, with orders to receive the surrender of the rebels in that State and to watch the country to the north and eastward. In addition to this, troops from the First and Second divisions were directed to watch the Flint River crossings, and small parties were stationed at the principal railroad stations from Atlanta to Eufala, as well as at Columbus and West Point and Talladega. By these means I confidently expected to arrest all large parties of fugitives and soldiers, and by a thorough system of scouts hoped to obtain timely information of the movements of important personages." ☆

iron works,—the last in the cotton States,—three factories, numerous mills, immense quantities of supplies, capturing four pieces of artillery and several hundred small-arms, near 300 prisoners rejoining the corps; the men in fine spirits and the animals in good condition, having lost in all but four officers and 168 men, half of the latter having been captured at various points, while straggling from foraging parties and not in line of duty."

☆ For an account of the movements of Jefferson Davis and his cabinet, see notes pp. 763 and 766.

LAST DAYS OF THE CONFEDERACY.[)

BY BASIL W. DUKE, BRIGADIER-GENERAL, C. S. A.

WHEN General Lee began his retreat from Richmond and Petersburg Brigadier-General John Echols was in command of the Department of South-western Virginia. ⚓ Under him were General Wharton's division and the brigades of Colonels Trigg and Preston, between 4000 and 5000 infantry, and four brigades of cavalry, about 2200 men, commanded by Brigadier-Generals Vaughn and Cosby, Colonel Giltner, and myself. There was also attached to the departmental command Major Page's unusually well-equipped battalion of artillery. On the 2d day of April General Echols issued orders looking to a junction of his forces with those of General Lee. Marching almost constantly, by day and night, General Echols reached Christiansburg on the 10th, and concentrated his entire command there. He was confident that he would be able, within a few days, to join Lee somewhere to the south-west of Richmond, most probably in the vicinity of Danville. The command had halted for the night; General Echols and I were dismounted and standing upon the turnpike surrounded by the soldiers. Just then Lieutenant James B. Clay, who had been sent ahead three days before to gain information, galloped up and handed General Echols a dispatch. The latter's face flushed, and then grew deadly pale. The dispatch was from General Lomax, and in these words: "General Lee surrendered this morning at or near Appomattox Court House. I am trying with my own division and the remnants of Fitz Lee's and Rosser's divisions to arrange to make a junction with you."

After a brief conference we agreed that the news should be concealed from the men until the next day, if possible, and communicated that night only to the brigade and regimental commanders. We hoped that some plan might be devised which would enable us to hold the troops together until we could learn what policy would be pursued by Mr. Davis, and whether it would be our duty to endeavor to join General Johnston. But to conceal such a fact when even one man was aware of it was impossible. Before we had concluded our brief conversation, we knew from the hum and stir in the anxious, dark-browed crowds nearest us, from excitement which soon grew almost to tumult, that the terrible tidings had gotten abroad. That night no man slept. Strange as the declaration may sound now, there was not one of the six or seven thousand then gathered at Christiansburg who had entertained the slightest thought that such an event could happen, and doubtless that feeling pervaded the ranks of the Confederacy. We knew that the heroic army which had so long defended Richmond was in retreat. We knew that its operations could no longer be conducted upon the methods which support regular warfare, and that everything necessary to maintain its efficiency was lost. We could hazard no conjecture as to

what would be done; yet, that the Army of Northern Virginia, with Lee at its head, would ever surrender had never entered our minds. Therefore, the indescribable consternation and amazement which spread like a conflagration through the ranks when the thing was told can only be imagined by one who has had a similar experience.

During all that night officers and men were congregated in groups and crowds discussing the news, and it was curious to observe how the training and discipline of veteran soldiers were manifested even amid all this deep feeling and wild excitement. There was not one act of violence, not a harsh or insulting word spoken; the officers were treated with the same respect which they had previously received, and although many of the infantrymen who lived in that part of Virginia went off that night without leave and returned to their homes, none who remained were insubordinate or failed to obey orders with alacrity. Great fires were lighted. Every group had its orators, who, succeeding each other, spoke continuously. Every conceivable suggestion was offered. Some advocated a guerrilla warfare; some proposed marching to the trans-Mississippi, and thence to Mexico. The more practical and reasonable, of course, proposed that an effort to join General Johnston should immediately be made. Many, doubtless, thought of surrender, but I do not remember to have heard it mentioned.

On the next day General Echols convened a council of war composed of his brigade commanders. He proposed that the men of the infantry commands should be furloughed for sixty days, at the expiration of which time, if the Confederacy survived, they might possibly be returned to the service. The infantry commanders approved of this policy, and it was adopted. General Echols then requested the officers commanding the cavalry brigades to give expression to their views. General Cosby and Colonel Giltner frankly declared their conviction that further resistance was impossible, and that it was their duty to lose no time in making the best terms possible for their men. They expressed a determination to march to Kentucky and immediately surrender. General Vaughn and I believed that we were allowed no option in such a matter, but that, notwithstanding the great disaster of which we had just learned, we were not absolved from our military allegiance. We thought it clearly our duty to attempt to join General Johnston, and to put off surrender as long as the Confederate Government had an organized force in the field. We expressed ourselves ready to obey any order General Echols might issue. For my own part, I was convinced that all of the troops there would rather have their record protected than their safety consulted.

General Echols verbally notified each brigade commander of cavalry that he would be expected to take his brigade to General Johnston, and said

---

) Condensed from "The Southern Bivouac," for August, 1886.—EDITORS.
⚓ See p. 422. General Echols succeeded General Early in command of the department, March 30th, 1865.—EDITORS.

that a written order to march that evening would be delivered to each. I received such an order. The infantry ostensibly was furloughed, virtually it was disbanded, in accord with this programme. The guns of Page's batteries were spiked and the carriages burned. The artillery horses and several hundred mules taken from the large wagon-train, which was also abandoned, were turned over to my brigade that I might mount my men, for our horses had mostly been sent to North Carolina for the winter, and had not been brought back. I had been joined at Christiansburg by a detachment of paroled prisoners of John Morgan's old command. I permitted as many of them as I could mount to accompany me, and armed them with rifles left by the disbanded infantrymen. I was compelled peremptorily to order a very considerable number of these paroled men to remain in a camp established in the vicinity of Christiansburg. They were anxious to follow on foot. Late on the evening of the 11th General Echols, at the head of Vaughn's brigade and mine, the latter on mule-back, began the march toward North Carolina, which was to close with the final surrender of the last Confederate organization east of the Mississippi River. The rain was pouring in torrents. On the next day ninety men of Colonel Giltner's brigade, under Lieutenant-Colonel George Dimond, overtook us. They had learned, after our departure, of the result of the conference, and of General Echols's determination to join General Johnston.

As we approached the North Carolina border, we heard frequent rumors that a large force of Federal cavalry was in the vicinity, prepared to contest our progress. The point at which it was supposed we would encounter them, and where collision would be most dangerous to us, was "Fancy Gap," which, however, we passed in safety.

On the second day after entering North Carolina we crossed the Yadkin River, and on the evening of the next day thereafter reached Statesville. Here General Echols left us in order to proceed more promptly to General Johnston, who was supposed to be at Salisbury. Vaughn marched in the direction of Morganton, and I set out for Lincolnton, where I expected to find my horses and the detail, under Colonel Napier, which I had sent in charge of them to their winter quarters in that vicinity. Crossing the Catawba River on the top of the covered railroad bridge I pushed on rapidly.

I had obtained credible information that the Federal cavalry under Stoneman [see foot-note, p. 495] were now certainly very near, and also marching in the direction of Lincolnton. I was very anxious to get there first, for I feared that if the enemy anticipated me the horses and guard would either be captured or driven so far away as to be entirely out of my reach. Early in the afternoon I discovered unmistakable indications that the enemy was close at hand, and found that he was moving upon another main road to Lincolnton, nearly parallel with that which I was pursuing, and some three miles distant. My scouts began fighting with his upon every by-road which connected our respective routes; and I learned, to my great chagrin and discomfort, that my men were not meeting with the success in that sort of combat to which they were accustomed, and which an unusual amount of experience in it might entitle them to expect. They were constantly driven in upon the column, and showed a reluctance to fight amounting almost to demoralization. Every man whom I questioned laid the blame in the most emphatic manner on his "d—d mule." All declared that these animals were prejudiced against advancing or standing in any decent fashion.

I sent a party of some twenty-five or thirty, mounted on horses and better equipped than the others, with instructions to get into Lincolnton before the enemy and communicate with Colonel Napier. However, when I had come within three miles of the place, about sunset, I met this party retiring before a very much larger body of Federals. To countermarch would have destroyed the *morale* of the men; and if I had been attacked in rear my column would have dissolved in utter rout. Fortunately I had learned that a road, or rather trace, turned off to the left near this point, and led to other paths which conducted to the main road from Lincolnton to Charlotte. I turned into this road. Procuring guides, I marched some 15 miles and reached the Charlotte road late in the night.

At Charlotte, where we arrived the same day, we found General Ferguson's brigade of cavalry; the town was also crowded with paroled soldiers of Lee's army and refugee officials from Richmond. ⸸ On the next day Mr. Davis arrived, escorted by the cavalry brigades of General Dibrell, of Tennessee, and Colonel W. C. P. Breckinridge, of Kentucky.

In response to the greeting received from the citizens and soldiery, Mr. Davis made a speech which has been the subject of much comment, then and since. I heard it, and remember nothing said by him that could warrant much either of commendation or criticism. In the course of his remarks a dispatch was handed him by some gentleman in the crowd, who, I have been told since, was the mayor of Charlotte. It announced the assassination of Mr. Lincoln. Mr. Davis read it aloud, making scarcely any comment upon it at all. He certainly used no unkind language, nor did he display any feeling of exultation. The impression

⸸ On Sunday, April 2d, on receipt of dispatches from General Lee that the army was about to evacuate the Petersburg and Richmond lines, Mr. Davis assembled his cabinet and directed the removal of the public archives, treasure, and other property to Danville, Virginia. The members of the Government left Richmond during the night of the 2d, and on the 5th Mr. Davis issued a proclamation stating that Virginia would not be abandoned. Danville was placed in a state of defense, and Admiral Raphael Semmes was appointed a brigadier-general in command of the defenses, with a force consisting of a naval brigade and two battalions of infantry. Upon the surrender of Lee and his army (April 9th), the Confederate Government was removed to Greensboro', North Carolina. On the 18th Mr. Davis and part of his cabinet and his personal staff, accompanied by a wagon-train containing the personal property of the members of the Government and the most valuable archives, started for Charlotte, North Carolina. On the 24th the terms of the convention [see p. 755] between Generals Johnston and Sherman were approved by Mr. Davis as President of the Confederate States.— Editors.

produced on my mind by his manner and few words was that he did not credit the statement.

General John C. Breckinridge, who was then Secretary of War, had not accompanied Mr. Davis to Charlotte, but had gone to General Johnston's headquarters at Greensboro', and was assisting in the negotiations between Johnston and Sherman.

When General Breckinridge reached Charlotte, about two days after Mr. Davis's arrival, he was under the impression that the cartel he had helped to frame would be ratified by the Federal Government and carried into effect. I saw him and had a long conversation with him immediately upon his arrival. He was in cheerful spirits, and seemed to think the terms obtained some mitigation of the sting of defeat and submission.

In the afternoon of that day General Johnston telegraphed that the authorities at Washington refused to recognize the terms upon which he and Sherman had agreed, that the armistice had been broken off, and that he would surrender, virtually, upon any terms offered him. Upon the receipt of this intelligence Mr. Davis resolved at once to leave Charlotte and attempt to march, with all the troops willing to follow him, to Generals Taylor and Forrest, who were somewhere in Alabama. He was accompanied by the members of his cabinet and his staff, in which General Bragg was included.] The brigades of Ferguson, Dibrell, Breckinridge, and mine composed his escort, the whole force under the command of General Breckinridge. We made not more than twelve or fifteen miles daily. To the cavalry this slow progress was harassing, and a little demoralizing withal, as the men were inclined to construe such dilatoriness to mean irresolution and doubt on the part of their leaders. They were more especially of this opinion because a large body of Federal cavalry, the same which I had encountered at Lincolnton, were marching some ten or fifteen miles distant on our right flank, keeping pace with us, and evidently closely observing our movements. At Unionville I found Colonel Napier, with nearly all of the horses of my brigade and some seventy or eighty men.

Mr. Davis, General Breckinridge, Mr. Benjamin, and the other cabinet and staff officers mingled and talked freely with the men upon this march, and the effect was excellent. It was the general opinion that Mr. Davis could escape if he would, but that was largely induced by the knowledge that extraordinary efforts would be made to prevent his falling into the hands of the enemy. We all felt confident that General Breckinridge would not be made prisoner if duty permitted him to attempt escape. As Judge Reagan had been a frontiersman and, as we understood, a "Texas Ranger," the men thought his chances good; but all believed that Benjamin would surely be caught, and all deplored it, for he had made himself exceedingly popular. One morning he suddenly disappeared. When I next heard of him he was in England. ⸙

At Abbeville, South Carolina, Mr. Davis held a conference with the officers in command of the troops composing his escort, which he himself characterized as a council of war, and which I may be justified, therefore, in so designating. It was, perhaps, the last Confederate council of war held east of the Mississippi River, certainly the last in which Mr. Davis participated. We had gone into camp in the vicinity of the little town, and, although becoming quite anxious to understand what was going to be done, we were expecting no immediate solution of the problem. We were all convinced that the best we could hope to do was to get Mr. Davis safely out of the country, and then obtain such terms as had been given General Johnston's army, or, failing in that, make the best of our way to the trans-Mississippi. The five brigade commanders [S. W. Ferguson, George G. Dibrell, J. C. Vaughn, Basil W. Duke, and W. C. P. Breckinridge] each received an order notifying him to attend at the private residence in Abbeville, where Mr. Davis had made his headquarters, about 4 o'clock of that afternoon. We were shown into a room where we found Mr. Davis and Generals Breckinridge and Bragg. No one else was present. I had never seen Mr. Davis look better or show to better advantage. He seemed in excellent spirits and humor; and the union of dignity, graceful affability, and decision, which made his manner usually so striking, was very marked in his reception of us. After some conversation of a general nature, he said: "It is time, that we adopt some definite plan upon which the further prosecution of our struggle shall be conducted. I have summoned you for consultation. I feel that I ought to do nothing now without the advice of my military chiefs." He smiled rather archly as he used this expression, and we could not help thinking that such a term addressed to a handful of brigadiers, commanding altogether barely three thousand men, by one who so recently had been the master of legions was a pleasantry, yet he said it in a way that made it a compliment.

After we had each given, at his request, a statement of the equipment and condition of our respective commands, Mr. Davis proceeded to declare his conviction that the cause was not lost any more than hope of American liberty was gone amid the sorest trials and most disheartening reverses of the Revolutionary struggle; but that energy, courage, and constancy might yet save all. "Even," he said, "if the troops now with me be all that I can for the present rely on, three thousand brave men are enough for a nucleus around which the whole people will rally when the panic which now afflicts them has passed away." He then asked that we should make suggestions in regard to the future conduct of the war.

We looked at each other in amazement and with a feeling a little akin to trepidation, for we hardly knew how we should give expression to views

---

] In the party were General John C. Breckinridge, Secretary of War; Judah P. Benjamin, Secretary of State; S. R. Mallory, Secretary of the Navy; John H. Reagan, Postmaster General; General Samuel Cooper, Adjutant General; George Davis, Attorney General; Colonels

John Taylor Wood, William Preston Johnston, and Frank R. Lubbock, staff-officers, and Colonel Burton N. Harrison, private secretary to Mr. Davis.— EDITORS.

⸙ Mr. Benjamin escaped through Florida to the seacoast, thence to the Bahamas in an open boat.— EDITORS.

diametrically opposed to those he had uttered. Our respect for Mr. Davis approached veneration, and notwithstanding the total dissent we felt, and were obliged to announce, to the programme he had indicated, that respect was rather increased than diminished by what he had said.

I do not remember who spoke first, but we all expressed the same opinion. We told him frankly that the events of the last few days had removed from our minds all idea or hope that a prolongation of the contest was possible. The people were not panic-stricken, but broken down and worn out. We said that an attempt to continue the war, after all means of supporting warfare were gone, would be a cruel injustice to the people of the South. We would be compelled to live on a country already impoverished, and would invite its further devastation. We urged that we would be doing a wrong to our men if we persuaded them to such a course; for if they persisted in a conflict so hopeless they would be treated as brigands, and would forfeit all chance of returning to their homes.

He asked why then we were still in the field. We answered that we were desirous of affording him an opportunity of escaping the degradation of capture, and perhaps a fate which would be direr to the people than even to himself, in still more embittering the feeling between the North and South. We said that we would ask our men to follow us until his safety was assured, and would risk them in battle for that purpose, but would not fire another shot in an effort to continue hostilities.

He declared, abruptly, that he would listen to no suggestion which regarded only his own safety. He appealed eloquently to every sentiment and reminiscence that might be supposed to move a Southern soldier, and urged us to accept his views. We remained silent, for our convictions were unshaken; we felt responsible for the future welfare of the men who had so heroically followed us; and the painful point had been reached, when to speak again in opposition to all that he urged would have approached altercation. For some minutes not a word was spoken. Then Mr. Davis rose and ejaculated bitterly that all was indeed lost. He had become very pallid, and he walked so feebly as he proceeded to leave the room that General Breckinridge stepped hastily up and offered his arm.

I have undertaken to narrate very briefly what occurred in a conference which lasted for two or three hours. I believe that I have accurately given the substance of what was said; and that where I have put what was said by Mr. Davis in quotation marks, I have correctly reproduced it, or very nearly so.

Generals Breckinridge and Bragg took no part in the discussion. After Mr. Davis retired, both, however, assured us of their hearty approval of the position we had taken. They had forborne to say anything, because not immediately in command of the troops, and not supposed, therefore, to know their sentiments so well as we did. But they promised to urge upon Mr. Davis the necessity and propriety of endeavoring without further delay to get out of the country, and not permit other and serious complications to be produced by his capture and imprisonment, and perhaps execution.

It was determined that we should resume our march that night for Washington, Georgia, one or two days' march distant, and orders were issued by General Breckinridge to move at midnight. About 10 o'clock I received a message from General Breckinridge that he desired to see me immediately. I went to his quarters, and he informed me that the treasure which had been brought from Richmond was at the railroad station, and that it was necessary to provide for its removal and transportation. He instructed me to procure a sufficient number of wagons to remove it, and to detail a guard of fifty men under a field-officer for its protection. He further informed me that there was between five and six hundred thousand dollars in specie,—he did not know the exact amount,—the greater part gold. I must, he said, personally superintend its transfer from the cars to the wagons. This was not a very agreeable duty. I represented that if no one knew just what sum of money was there, it was rather an unpleasant responsibility to impose on the officer who was to take charge of it. I would have no opportunity to count it, nor any means of ascertaining whether the entire amount was turned over to me. He responded that all that had been considered, and bade me proceed to obey the order. I detailed fifty picked men as guard, and put them under command of Colonel Theophilus Steele and four of my best subalterns. I obtained six wagons, and began at once the task of removing the treasure. It was in charge of some of the former treasury clerks, and was packed in money-belts, shot-bags, a few small iron chests, and all sorts of boxes, some of them of the frailest description. In this shape I found it loaded in open box-cars. I stationed sentries at the doors, and rummaging through the cars by the faint light of a few tallow-candles gathered up all that was shown me, or that I could find. Rather more than an hour was consumed in making the transfer from the cars to the wagons, and after the latter had been started off and had gotten half a mile away, Lieutenant John B. Cole, one of the officers of the guard, rode up to me with a pine box, which may have held two or three thousand dollars in gold, on the pommel of his saddle. He had remained after the others had left, and ferreting about in a car which we thought we had thoroughly searched had discovered this box stuck in a corner and closely covered up with a piece of sacking. On the next day General Breckinridge directed me to increase the guard to two hundred men, and take charge of it in person. I suggested that instead of composing it entirely of men from my brigade, it should be constituted from details from all five. I thought this the best plan to allay any feeling of jealousy that might arise, and insure a more perfect vigilance, as I felt persuaded that these details would all carefully watch each other. My suggestion was adopted. Nearly the entire guard was kept constantly on duty, day and night, and a majority of the whole escort was usually about the wagons at every halt, closely inspecting the guard.

At the Savannah River, Mr. Davis ordered that the silver coin, amounting to one hundred and eight or ten thousand dollars, be paid to the troops in partial discharge of the arrears of pay due them. The quartermasters of the several brigades were engaged during the entire night in counting out the money, and until early dawn a throng of soldiers surrounded the little cabin where they were dividing "the pile" into their respective quotas. The sight of so much money seemed to banish sleep. My brigade received thirty-two dollars *per capita*, officers and men sharing alike. General Breckinridge was paid that sum, and, for the purpose, was borne on the roll of the brigade. On the next day, at Washington, Georgia, I turned over the residue of the treasure to Mr. M. H. Clarke, acting Treasurer of the Confederate States, and experienced a feeling of great relief. ☆

Mr. Davis, having apparently yielded to the advice pressed upon him, that he should endeavor to escape, started off with a select party of twenty, commanded by Captain Given Campbell, of Kentucky, one of the most gallant and intelligent officers in the service. I knew nearly all of these twenty personally. Among them were Lieutenants Lee Hathaway and Winder Monroe of my brigade. Escort and commander had been picked as men who could be relied on in any emergency, and there is no doubt in my mind that, if Mr. Davis had really attempted to get away or reach the trans-Mississippi, this escort would have exhausted every expedient their experience could have suggested, and, if necessary, fought to the death to accomplish his purpose. I have never believed, however, that Mr. Davis really meant or desired to escape after he became convinced that all was lost. I think that, wearied by the importunity with which the request was urged, he seemingly consented, intending to put himself in the way of being captured. I am convinced that he quitted the main body of the troops that they might have an opportunity to surrender before it was too late for surrender upon terms, and that he was resolved that the small escort sent with him should encounter no risk in his behalf. I can account for his conduct upon no other hypothesis. He well knew — and he was urgently advised — that his only chance of escape was in rapid and continuous movement. He and his party were admirably mounted, and could easily have outridden the pursuit of any party they were not strong enough to fight. Therefore, when he deliberately procrastinated as he did, when the fact

of his presence in that vicinity was so public, and in the face of the effort that would certainly be made by the Federal forces to secure his person, I can only believe that he had resolved not to escape.

Immediately after Mr. Davis's departure the greater portion of the troops were notified that their services would be no longer needed, and were given a formal discharge. Their officers made arrangements for their prompt surrender. General Breckinridge requested Colonel W. C. P. Breckinridge and myself to hold a body of our men together for two or three days, and, marching in a direction different from that Mr. Davis had taken, divert attention as much as possible from his movements. ǀ We accordingly marched with 350 men of our respective brigades toward Woodstock, or Woodville, — I do not certainly remember the name. I moved upon one road; Colonel Breckinridge, with whom the general was, upon another. We were to meet at the point I have mentioned. I arrived first, and halted to await the others. I found that a considerable force of Federal cavalry was just to the west of the place, and not more than three miles distant. The officer in command notified me in very courteous terms that he would not attack unless I proceeded toward the west, in which event he said he would, very much to his regret, be compelled "to use violence." He said that he hoped I would think proper to surrender, as further bloodshed was useless and wrong; but that he would not undertake to hasten the matter. I responded that I appreciated his sentiments and situation, and that I would give the matter of surrender immediate and careful consideration. That evening Colonel Breckinridge arrived. He had encountered a body of Federals, who had made to him almost the identical statement the officer in my front had addressed to me. He had parleyed with them long enough to enable General Breckinridge, with one or two officers who were to accompany him in his effort to escape, to get far enough away to elude pursuit, ⚓ and then, telling them where he wished to go, was allowed to march by upon the same road occupied by the Federal column. The men of the previously hostile hosts cheered each other as they passed, and the "Yanks" shouted, "You rebs better go home and stop this nonsense; we don't want to hurt each other!" The colonel brought an earnest injunction from General Breckinridge that we should both surrender without delay. We communicated his message to our comrades, and for us the long agony was over. ǀ

☆ The treasure brought from Richmond included about $275,000 belonging to some Richmond banks.— EDITORS.

ǀ Jefferson Davis was captured on the 10th of May near Irwinsville, Georgia, by a detachment of the 4th Michigan Cavalry (belonging to General R. H. G. Minty's division of General James H. Wilson's cavalry corps), under Lieutenant-Colonel Benjamin D. Pritchard. Pritchard left Macon, Georgia, on the 7th, and was moving south along the west bank of the Ocmulgee when he crossed the route on which Mr. Davis and his party were moving with about twenty-four hours' start of their pursuers. A detachment of the 1st Wisconsin Cavalry (belonging to General John T. Croxton's division), under Lieutenant-Colonel Henry Harnden, was following Mr. Davis in the direct road to Irwinsville, and Pritchard, making a swift march on another road, came upon the

fugitives in their camp, and arrested Mr. Davis just as the advance of Harnden's command reached the scene. — EDITORS.

⚓ Among those who surrendered at the time, besides Mr. Davis's family and the guard, were Mr. Reagan and Colonels Lubbock, Johnston, and Harrison. General Breckinridge and Colonel Wood escaped, and made their way to Florida, whence they sailed to Cuba in an open boat.— EDITORS.

ǀ On the 29th of May, 1865, President Johnson issued a proclamation of amnesty to all persons (with some notable exceptions) who had participated in the rebellion, and who should make oath to support the Constitution and the Union, and the proclamations and laws relating to emancipation. Among the exceptions, besides certain civil and diplomatic officers and agents, and others, were the officers of the Confederate service above the rank of colonel in the army and that of lieutenant in the navy, and those who had been educated at the United States Military and Naval Academies.

Amnesty was further extended by proclamations, on September 7th, 1867, and December 25th, 1868. In the first the military exceptions made in the amnesty of May 29th, 1865, were reduced to ex-Confederate officers above the rank of brigadier-general in the army, and of captain in the navy, and in the second all exceptions were re-moved and the pardon was unconditional and without the formality of any oath.

Mr. Davis was imprisoned at Fort Monroe immediately after his arrest, and was indicted on the charge of treason, by a Grand Jury in the United States Court for the District of Virginia, at Norfolk, May 8th, 1866. On May 13th, 1867, he was released on a bail-bond of $100,-000, signed by Cornelius Vanderbilt, Gerrit Smith, and Horace Greeley, and in December, 1868, a *nolle prosequi* was entered in the case.—EDITORS.

NOTES ON THE UNION AND CONFEDERATE ARMIES.

IN a statistical exhibit of deaths in the Union Army, compiled (1885), under the direction of Adjutant-General Drum, by Joseph W. Kirkley, the causes of death are given as follows: Killed in action, 4142 officers, 62,916 men; died of wounds received in action, 2223 officers, 40,789 men, of which number 99 officers and 1973 men were prisoners of war; died of disease, 2795 officers and 221,791 men, of which 83 officers and 24,783 men were prisoners; accidental deaths (except drowned), 142 officers and 3972 men, of which 2 officers and 5 men were prisoners; drowned, 106 officers and 4838 men, of which 1 officer and 6 men were prisoners; murdered, 37 officers and 483 men; killed after capture, 14 officers and 90 men; committed suicide, 26 officers and 365 men; executed by United States military authorities, 267 men; executed by the enemy, 4 officers and 60 men; died from sunstroke, 5 officers and 308 men, of which 20 men were prisoners; other known causes, 62 officers and 1972 men, of which 7 officers and 312 men were prisoners; causes not stated, 28 officers and 12,093 men, of which 9 officers and 2030 men were prisoners. Total, 9584 officers and 349,944 men, of which 219 officers and 29,279 men were prisoners. Grand aggregate, 359,528; aggregate deaths among prisoners, 29,498. Since 1885 the Adjutant-General has received evidence of the death in Southern prisons of 694 men not previously accounted for, which increases the number of deaths among prisoners to 30,192, and maks a grand aggregate of 360,222.

NOTES TO THE ADJOINING TABLE.

Figures in the column of deaths, opposite names of States, represent only such as occurred among *white troops* (losses among colored troops and Indians being given at the foot of the table). The table does not indicate losses among sailors and marines.

The colored soldiers organized under the authority of the General Government and not credited to any State were recruited as follows: In Alabama, 4969; Arkansas, 5526; Colorado, 95; Florida, 1044; Georgia, 3486; Louisiana, 24,052; Mississippi, 17,869; North Carolina, 5035; South Carolina, 5462; Tennessee, 20,133; Texas, 47; Virginia, 5723. There were also 5896 negro soldiers enlisted at large, or whose credits are not specifically expressed by the records.

The number of officers and men of the Regular Army among whom the casualties herein noted occurred is estimated at 67,000; the number in the Veteran Reserve Corps was 60,508; and in Hancock's Veteran Corps, 10,883.

The other organizations of white volunteers, organized directly by the U. S. authorities, numbered about 11,000.

In 82 national cemeteries (according to the report of June 30th, 1888) 325,230 men are buried: 176,397 known, and 148,833 unknown dead. These numbers include 1136 at Mexico City, most of whom lost their lives in the Mexican war; about 9500 Confederates; and about 8500 civilians.

COMPARATIVE STATEMENT OF THE NUMBER OF MEN FURNISHED THE UNITED STATES ARMY AND NAVY, AND OF THE DEATHS IN THE ARMY, 1861-5.

States, territories, etc.	Men furnished.				Aggregate of deaths.
	White troops.	Sailors & marines.	Colored troops.	Total.	
Alabama	2,576			2,576	345
Arkansas	8,289			8,289	1,713
California	15,725			15,725	573
Colorado	4,903			4,903	323
Connecticut	51,937	2,163	1,764	55,864	5,354
Dakota	206			206	6
Delaware	11,236	94	954	12,284	882
Dist. of Columbia	11,912	1,353	3,269	16,534	290
Florida	1,290			1,290	215
Georgia					15
Illinois	255,057	2,224	1,811	259,092	34,834
Indiana	193,748	1,078	1,537	196,363	26,672
Iowa	75,797	5	440	76,242	13,001
Kansas	18,069		2,080	20,149	2,630
Kentucky	51,743	314	23,703	75,760	10,774
Louisiana	5,224			5,224	945
Maine	64,973	5,030	104	70,107	9,398
Maryland	33,995	3,925	8,718	46,638	2,982
Massachusetts	122,781	19,983	3,966	146,730	13,942
Michigan	85,479	498	1,387	87,364	14,753
Minnesota	23,913	3	104	24,020	2,584
Mississippi	• 545			545	78
Missouri	100,616	151	8,344	109,111	13,885
Nebraska	3,157			3,157	239
Nevada	1,080			1,080	33
New Hampshire	32,930	882	125	33,937	4,882
New Jersey	67,500	8,129	1,185	76,814	5,754
New Mexico	6,561			6,561	277
New York	409,561	35,164	4,125	448,850	46,534
North Carolina	3,156			3,156	360
Ohio	304,814	3,274	5,092	313,180	35,475
Oregon	1,810			1,810	45
Pennsylvania	315,017	14,307	8,612	337,936	33,183
Rhode Island	19,521	1,878	1,837	23,236	1,321
Tennessee	31,092			31,092	6,777
Texas	1,965			1,965	141
Vermont	32,549	619	120	33,288	5,224
Virginia					42
Washington	964			964	22
West Virginia	31,872		196	32,068	4,017
Wisconsin	91,029	133	165	91,327	12,301
Indian Nations				*3,530	1,018
Colored Troops			99,337	†99,337	‡36,847
	2,494,592	101,207	178,975	2,778,304	
Veteran Reserve Corps					1,672
U. S. Veteran Volunteers (Hancock's Corps)					106
U. S. Volunteer Engineers and Sharp-shooters					552
U. S. Volunteer Infantry					243
General and general staff-officers, U. S. Volunt'rs					239
Miscellaneous U. S. Volunt'rs (brigade bands, etc.)					232
Regular Army					5,798
Grand aggregate					§359,528

* Indians.   † Number not credited to any State.
‡ Includes losses in all colored organizations excepting three regiments from Massachusetts whose deaths aggregated 574.
§ Increased by additional evidence since 1885 to 360,222.

On the 13th of April, 1865, the Secretary of War ordered the enrollment discontinued. The work of mustering out volunteers began April 29th, and up to August 7th 640,806 troops had been discharged; on September 14th the number had reached 741,107, and on November 15th 800,963.

On November 22d, 1865, the Secretary of War reported that Confederate troops surrendered and were released on parole, as follows:

Army of Northern Virginia, commanded by General R. E. Lee	27,805
Army of Tennessee and others, commanded by General Joseph E. Johnston	31,243
General Jeff. Thompson's Army of Missouri	7,978
Miscellaneous paroles, Department of Virginia.	9,072
Paroled at Cumberland, Maryland, and other stations	9,377
Paroled by General Edward M. McCook in Alabama and Florida	6,428
Army of the Department of Alabama, General Richard Taylor	42,293
Army of the Trans-Mississippi Department, General E. Kirby Smith	17,686
Paroled in the Department of Washington	3,390
Paroled in Virginia, Tennessee, Alabama, Louisiana, and Texas	13,922
Surrendered at Nashville and Chattanooga, Tennessee	5,029
	174,223

The following table, made from official returns, shows the whole number of men enrolled (present and absent) in the active armies of the Confederacy:

	Jan. 1, 1862.	Jan. 1, 1863.	Jan. 1, 1864.	Jan. 1, 1865.
Army of Northern Va..	84,225	144,605	92,0˜0	155,772
Dep't of Richmond.....	......	7,820	8,494	16,601
Dep't of Norfolk......	16,825	......	......	......
Dep't of the Peninsula	20,138	......	......	......
Dep't of Fredericksb'g.	10,645	......	......	......
Dep't of N. C..........	13,656	40,821	9,876	5,187
Dep't of Miss. and E. La.	4,390	73,114	46,906	32,148
Dep't of S. C. and Ga..	40,955	27,052	65,005	53,014
Dep't of Pensacola....	18,214	......	......	......
Dep't of N. Orleans ...	10,318	......	......	......
Dep't of the Gulf......	......	10,489	17,241	12,820
Western Dep't	24,784	......	......	......
Army of Tenn..........	......	82,799	88,457	86,995
Dep't of Ky	39,565	......	......	......
Dep't of East Tenn	......	18,768	52,821	......
Dep't of Northwest....	4,296	......	......	......
Dep't of Western Va...	......	10,116	18,642	7,138
Trans-Miss. Dep't.....	*30,000	*50,000	73,289	*70,000
Aggregate...........	318,011	465,584	472,781	439,675

* Estimated.

Very few, if any, of the local land forces, and none of the naval, are included in the tabular exhibit. If we take the 472,000 men in service at the beginning of 1864, and add thereto at least 250,000 deaths occurring prior to that date, it gives over 700,000. The discharges for disability and other causes and the desertions would probably increase the number (inclusive of the militia and naval forces) to over 1,000,000.

Northern writers have assumed that the Confederate losses equaled the Union losses; no data exist for a reasonably accurate estimate.

FORT SUMTER AT THE CLOSE OF THE WAR.   FROM A SKETCH MADE AT THE TIME.

THE END.

INDEX TO THE FOUR VOLUMES.

ALL names and military organizations mentioned in this work are indexed, except the lists of "Opposing Forces," or rosters, which, by their arrangement and classification with the principal battles and campaigns, are in a sense indices in themselves. The reader is also referred to the list of "Preliminary Events," Volume I., pp. 1–5.

Besides the usual abbreviations for titles and given names of persons, and for names of States, U stands for Union or Federals, C for Confederate or Confederates, por't for portrait, w for wounded, c for captured, m for missing, k for killed, inf. for infantry, cav. for cavalry, and art'y for artillery.

769

NOTE.—The reader is referred to the Index as the authority on names and titles, the few known errors of this sort that occur in the body of the work (some of them derived from errors in the Official Records) having been here corrected.